MODERN AUDITING

TO THE STUDENT: A Study Guide for the textbook is available through your college bookstore under the title Study Guide to accompany MODERN AUDITING 6th edition by *William C. Boynton* and *Walter G. Kell*. The Study Guide can help you with course material by acting as a tutorial, review, and study aid. If the Study Guide is not in stock, ask the bookstore manager to order a copy for you.

Modern Auditing

Sixth Edition

William C. Boynton
California Polytechnic State University at San Luis Obispo

Walter G. Kell
University of Michigan

John Wiley & Sons, Inc.
New York • Chichester • Brisbane • Toronto • Singapore

Cover Art by **Paul Schulenberg**

Acquisitions Editor **Mike Reynolds**
Production Manager **Linda Muriello**
Production Editor **Jeanine Furino**
Designer **Levavi & Levavi**
Manufacturing Manager **Susan Stetzer**
Illustration Coordinator **Rosa Bryant**

Recognizing the importance of preserving what has been written, it is a policy of John Wiley & Sons, Inc. to have books of enduring value published in the United States printed on acid-free paper, and we exert our best efforts to that end.

Library of Congress Cataloging in Publication Data:

Boynton, William C.
Modern auditing / William C. Boynton, Walter G. Kell.—6th ed.
p. cm
Rev. ed. of: Modern auditing / Walter G. Kell. 5th ed. 1992.
Includes bibliographical references and index.
ISBN 0-471-59687-6 (cloth)
1. Auditing. I. Kell, Walter Gerry, 1921– , II. Kell, Walter Gerry, 1921– Modern auditing. III. Title.
HF5667.K39 1995
867′.45—dc20 94-41807
CIP

Printed in the United States of America

10 9 8 7 6 5 4 3 2

Printed and bound by Courier Companies, Inc.

About the Authors

William C. Boynton, Ph.D., CPA, received his doctorate in accounting from Michigan State University. He is Dean of the College of Business, and professor of accounting at California Polytechnic State University at San Luis Obispo where he formerly served as head of the Accounting Department. He has served on the audit staffs of two international public accounting firms. He has also served as a regional chairperson of the Auditing Section of the American Accounting Association, and on a variety of committees for the American Accounting Association and the Federation of Schools of Accountancy. He is the author or coauthor of several articles and committee reports on accounting and auditing, and has served as codirector of the American Institute of Certified Public Accountants National Banking School. A member of the California Society of Certified Public Accountants, he has served on its Globalization Task Force and its Committees on Accounting Education, the 150-Hour Requirement, and Accounting Principles and Auditing Standards. In 1992, he received the California Society of Certified Public Accountants Faculty Excellence Award.

Walter G. Kell, Ph.D., CPA, received his doctorate in accounting from the University of Illinois. He is professor emeritus of accounting at the University of Michigan, where he has served as chairman of the Department of Accounting. He also has served as chairman of the Accounting Department of Syracuse University. He has been an active member of the American Institute of Certified Public Accountants and has served on its Committee on Auditing Procedure (predecessor to the Auditing Standards Board) and Auditing Standards Advisory Council. He is a past president of the American Accounting Association. Professor Kell has been a consulting editor and coeditor of the *Accountant's Handbook* and is the coauthor of an accounting principles textbook. He has also served as a member and chairman of the CPA Examination Review Board of the National Association of State Boards of Accountancy. A member of the Michigan Association of Certified Public Acountants, he has served on its Committee on Accounting and Auditing Procedures and its Board of Directors. Professor Kell is a recipient of the Association's Distinguished Service Award for his significant contributions to the public accounting profession.

PREFACE

Modern Auditing is designed primarily for the first course in auditing either at the undergraduate or graduate level. Materials in selected chapters and appendices, and cited in chapter bibliographies, may also serve as the core for a second or advanced course in auditing. Throughout the book, every effort has been made to integrate auditing theory and concepts with auditing methodology and practice. In addition, emphasis is given to the professional responsibilities of independent auditors, including the role of auditing in business, government, society, and the international arena.

Our goals in preparing this edition were to (1) make refinements in the style and clarity of presentation to maximize the effectiveness of the text as a learning resource for students, (2) make further refinements in the organization of the text to enhance its flexibility in accommodating different teaching schedules and preferences, and (3) provide comprehensive and integrated coverage of the latest developments in the environment, standards, and methodology of auditing.

HIGHLIGHTS OF CHANGES FROM THE PREVIOUS EDITION

In seeking the goals just enumerated, changes made in this edition include the following:

- A brief historical perspective on the auditing profession has been added to the first chapter.
- New material on general ethics and an ethical decision-making model precedes the completely updated presentation of the *Code of Professional Conduct*.
- The chapter on legal liability provides a perspective on the so-called litigation crisis, assesses the impact of important recent legal cases, and addresses the profession's call for additional legal reforms.
- All chapters containing material on internal controls have been updated to conform to the five-component framework adopted in the COSO report entitled *Internal Control—Integrated Framework*. (This framework is also being incorporated into the Auditing Standards Board's impending revision of *Statement on Auditing Standards No. 55*.)
- Specific transaction class and account balance audit objectives are more clearly defined and linked to tests of controls and substantive tests in each of the cycle chapters.
- The discussion of governmental auditing includes key elements of the 1994 revision of the GAO's *Yellow Book*.
- Increased attention is given to international auditing issues through "global boxes," selected comparisons of U.S. and international auditing practices, and citations to relevant international auditing standards in the chapter bibliographies.

- End-of-chapter materials now include research questions that require students to utilize a variety of professional publications, including the professional standards, professional journals, and SEC *Accounting and Auditing Enforcement Releases.* These can be assigned to individuals or groups, and can serve as a basis for individual or group class presentations by students to complement text coverage on a variety of topics.
- A new appendix to the text discusses the role of auditing research and provides guidance on research tools and their use.
- To assist students to make self-assessments of their understanding of key points, the 20 "review questions" formerly included in end-of-chapter materials are now interspersed throughout each chapter as "Learning Checks" following each major chapter section.

ORGANIZATION

The organization of the text continues to provide maximum flexibility in choosing the amount and order of material to be covered. For example, the entire-audit process is covered outside the cycle chapters. The chapters dealing with ethics, legal liability, and auditors' reports can be covered early or late in the course. The chapters on statistical sampling can be covered before the cycle chapters or be interspersed with the cycle chapters.

The Sixth Edition is organized into five parts as follows:

Part	Subject	Chapters
1	The Auditing Environment	1–4
2	Audit Planning	5–8
3	Audit Testing Methodology	9–13
4	Auditing the Transaction Cycles	14–18
5	Completing the Audit, Reporting, and Other Services	19–23

As shown in the foregoing tabulation, **Part 1, The Auditing Environment,** includes four chapters. Chapter 1, "Auditing and the Public Accounting Profession," provides an historical perspective on the auditing profession, differentiates the types of services performed by CPAs, explains the roles of the key private and public sector organizations that are associated with or influence the profession, and describes the elements of the multilevel regulatory framework that have as their objective enhancing the quality of services provided by the profession. Chapter 2, entitled "Financial Statement Audits and Auditors' Responsibilities," describes the role and limitations of financial statement audits, introduces auditing standards and the types of auditors' reports, and explains the expectation gap and related responsibilities regarding the detection of errors and irregularities, illegal client acts, and circumstances involving substantial doubt about the client's status as a going concern. Chapter 3, "Professional Ethics," begins with a discussion of ethics and morality from the perspective of both general and professional ethics, and provides in-depth discussions of the profession's *Code of Professional Conduct* and its enforcement. Chapter 4, "Auditor's Legal Liability," includes a thorough discussion of the legal environment and the auditor's exposure to liability under the common law and statutory law.

Part 2, Audit Planning, is also comprised of four chapters. Chapter 5, "Audit Objectives, Audit Evidence, and Working Papers," lays the foundation for audit planning through explanations of these three fundamentals of auditing. Coverage is given to the relationships among types of evidence, auditing procedures, classes of audit tests, and audit objectives, and to the importance of properly prepared working papers. Chapter 6, "Accepting the Engagement and Planning the Audit," begins with an overview of the four phases of a financial statement audit. Next, the factors that an auditor should evaluate before accepting an audit engagement are explained. The chapter then identifies the steps that should be performed in planning the audit, and concludes with coverage of the use of analytical procedures in audit planning. Chapter 7, "Materiality, Risk, and Preliminary Audit Strategies," provides a solid foundation in these three important auditing concepts. Part 2 concludes with Chapter 8, "Understanding the Internal Control Structure." Attention is focused on the definition, fundamental concepts, components, and limitations of internal control structures, and how the auditor obtains and documents an understanding of internal control structures. An appendix to Chapter 8 supplements the basic coverage of flowcharting that is provided within the body of the chapter.

Part 3, Audit Testing Methodology, includes five chapters. Chapter 9, "Assessing Control Risk/Tests of Controls," explains the auditor's methodology for meeting the second standard of field work under alternative audit strategies. Attention is given to the nature, timing, and extent of tests of controls and to documentating the assessed levels of control risk for assertions pertaining to transaction classes. Consideration is then given to combining control risk assessments for transaction class assertions to arrive at control risk assessments for account balance assertions. Chapter 10, "Detection Risk and the Design of Substantive Tests," explains the application of the audit risk model to determine the acceptable level of detection risk for account balance assertions. Consideration is then given to the effects of detection risk on the nature, timing, and extent of substantive tests. The chapter includes the development of a general framework that can be used in designing substantive tests for assertions in each of the transaction cycles.

The use of statistical and nonstatistical sampling in auditing is explained in Chapters 11 and 12. In Chapter 11, the focus is on tests of controls, whereas in Chapter 12 it is on substantive tests. The latter includes both probability-proportional-to-size, or dollar unit sampling, and classical variables sampling. Part 3 concludes with Chapter 13, "Auditing Electronic Data Processing Systems." Although EDP considerations are now integrated throughout the text, this chapter includes additional information on such topics as data organization and processing methods, EDP controls, and computer-assisted audit techniques including mainframe and microcomputer-based audit software.

Part 4, Auditing the Transaction Cycles, has five chapters. Chapters 14 and 15 deal with the revenue and expenditure cycles, respectively. Each chapter starts with an overview of the transaction classes, accounts, and activities associated with the cycle. The audit planning and testing methodologies developed in Parts 2 and 3 are then applied in (1) developing specific audit objectives for the cycle; (2) considering materiality, risk, and audit strategy; (3) obtaining an understanding of the internal control structure and assessing control risk; and (4) developing audit programs to meet the acceptable levels of detection risk for assertions pertaining to selected accounts. A similar pattern is followed in both Chapter 16, which covers the production and personnel services cycles that focus on inventory and payroll assertions, respectively, and Chapter 17, which covers the investing and financing cycles. Since transactions in five of the six cycles affect cash, the audit of cash balances is covered separately in Chapter 18.

The Sixth Edition concludes with **Part 5, Completing the Audit, Reporting, and Other Services.** Chapter 19 covers four topics: completing the field work, evaluating audit findings, communicating with the client, and fulfilling postaudit responsibilities. Chapter 20, "Reporting on Audited Financial Statements," provides in-depth explanations of the four reporting standards, the auditor's standard report, and circumstances requiring departures from the standard report. The chapter includes numerous illustrations of audit reports and a summary of the effects of circumstances on auditors' reports. Chapter 21, "Other Reports and Services," emphasizes the standards and reports associated with other attest and accounting services offered by CPAs. Chapter 22 is entitled "Internal, Operational, and Governmental Auditing." In addition to describing the standards applicable to each type of auditing, extensive consideration is given under governmental auditing to compliance auditing and the requirements of the Single Audit Act. Part 5 concludes with Chapter 23, "The Independent Accountant and the Securities and Exchange Commission." This chapter continues our coverage of the accountant's auditing and reporting responsibilities under the 1933 and 1934 securities acts. A final appendix to the text, which can be assigned at any point in the auditing course, deals with auditing research.

CONTINUING FEATURES

The following popular features of earlier editions are continued in this edition:

- Learning objectives for each chapter, now referenced in the text margins as well as being listed at the beginning of the chapter.
- Integration of material from authoritative auditing and professional literature throughout the text.
- Abundant illustrations of key concepts, flowcharts, and audit reports.
- Real-world vignettes illustrating contemporary applications of text materials interspersed throughout the text.
- Lists of key terms with page references, now located with the "Learning Checks" at the end of each major section of each chapter.
- Chapter bibliographies that include both relevant AICPA professional standards and selected readings from other official literature and accounting journals.

END-OF-CHAPTER MATERIALS

As in previous editions, there is an abundance of end-of-chapter materials, including numerous author-prepared questions, questions from professional examinations, and case studies drawn primarily from practice. In addition to the 20 review questions now interspersed throughout each chapter in the "Learning Checks," a typical chapter includes

- 6 to 15 multiple choice questions drawn from the Uniform CPA Examination unless stated otherwise.
- 10 to 15 comprehensive questions that include essay questions from professional examinations.
- 1 to 3 case studies that generally integrate several key concepts covered in the chapter.
- 1 or more research questions.

Comprehensive questions from professional examinations are designated as follows: AICPA (Uniform CPA Examination), ICMA (Certified Management Accountant Examination), IIA (Certified Internal Auditor Examination). In total, there are over 900 questions and cases that have been carefully edited to related chapter content.

SUPPLEMENTARY MATERIALS

The supplements to this edition of *Modern Auditing* consist of (1) an instructor's resource guide and solutions manual, (2) a test bank, (3) *Microtest* test-generating software, (4) a Lotus-based software package, and (5) a student study guide.

The *Instructor's Resource Guide and Solutions Manual* contains outlines of the text chapters; suggestions for lectures, classroom activities, and assignments; transparency masters; and references to videos and other supplementary aids the instructor may wish to use. As in previous editions, detailed solutions to the end-of-chapter questions and case studies are provided.

The *Test Bank* is available in hard copy and electronic format *(Microtest)* to facilitate test preparation on a personal computer. The test items are all original and include a large selection of multiple choice questions, correct/incorrect statements, matching questions, and short essay and analysis questions. Suggested solutions are included.

The Lotus-based software package, entitled *AUDSAMP: Statistical Sampling Templates for Lotus 1-2-3*, runs on IBM compatible personal computers. A master copy of a diskette and a brief accompanying manual are provided free of charge to adopters for local reproduction and distribution. The templates afford the student an opportunity to design and evaluate statistical samples and produce related working papers using a personal computer. Problems in several chapters of the text that can be solved with these templates have been marked with a disk icon.

The student *Study Guide* to accompany the Sixth Edition includes for each text chapter an expanded outline, 30 chapter highlights, 25 true/false statements, 15 completion questions, and 20 multiple choice questions. Solutions are included at the end of each chapter.

ACKNOWLEDGMENTS

We take this opportunity to express our sincere appreciation to individuals who have made significant contributions to the Sixth Edition of *Modern Auditing*.

First, we extend thanks to the many adopters of previous editions for their comments and suggestions.

Our sincere thanks are due to the following professors for comprehensive and constructive critiques of the Fifth Edition: Marvin Albin, University of Southern Mississippi; William Dilla, University of Illinois, Urbana-Champaign; and Mary Loyland, University of North Dakota. Special thanks are due to the following professors for comprehensive and constructive critiques of both the Fifth Edition and the manuscript for the Sixth Edition: Willard Galliart, Loyola University of Chicago, and T. Sterling Wetzel, Oklahoma State University.

We also gratefully acknowledge the permission given by the American Institute of Certified Public Accountants, the Institute of Management Accountants, and The Institute of Internal Auditors to use materials from their publications, including their professional examinations.

Last, but not least, we express our appreciation to our editor Mike Reynolds; Betty Pessagno, Copy Editor; Jeanine Furino, Production Editor; Linda Muriello, Production Manager; Rosa Bryant, Illustration Coordinator; Dawn Stanley, Designer; and Karen Allman, Marketing Manager; all of John Wiley & Sons.

William C. Boynton
Walter G. Kell
March, 1995

Contents in Brief

Part 1 The Auditing Environment

1 Auditing and the Public Accounting Profession
2 Financial Statement Audits and Auditors' Responsibilities
3 Professional Ethics
4 Auditor's Legal Liability

Part 2 Audit Planning

5 Audit Objectives, Evidence, and Working Papers
6 Accepting the Engagement and Planning the Audit
7 Materiality, Risk, and Preliminary Audit Strategies
8 Understanding the Internal Control Structure

Part 3 Audit Testing Methodology

9 Assessing Control Risk/Tests of Controls
10 Detection Risk and the Design of Substantive Tests
11 Audit Sampling in Tests of Controls
12 Audit Sampling in Substantive Tests
13 Auditing Electronic Data Processing Systems

Part 4 Auditing the Transaction Cycles

14 Auditing the Revenue Cycle
15 Auditing the Expenditure Cycle
16 Auditing the Production and Personnel Services Cycles
17 Auditing the Investing and Financing Cycles
18 Auditing Cash Balances

Part 5 Completing the Audit, Reporting, and Other Services

19 Completing the Audit/Postaudit Responsibilities
20 Reporting on Audited Financial Statements
21 Other Services and Reports
22 Internal, Operational, and Governmental Auditing
23 The Independent Accountant and the Securities and Exchange Commission

Appendix X: Auditing Research

Contents

Part I The Auditing Environment 1

1 Auditing and the Public Accounting Profession 2

Introduction to Contemporary Auditing 3
- Auditing Defined, 4
- Types of Audits, 4
- Types of Auditors, 5

The Public Accounting Profession: An Historical Perspective 8
- The Roots of Auditing, 8
- Rise of the U.S. Profession, 9

Services Performed by CPA Firms 10
- Attest Services, 10
- Nonattest Services, 12

Organizations Associated with the Public Accounting Profession 13
- Private Sector Organizations, 14
- Public Sector Organizations, 16

Regulatory Framework for Ensuring Quality Services 18
- Standard Setting, 19
- Firm Regulation, 20
- Self-Regulation, 21
- Government Regulation, 23

Summary 25
Bibliography 25
Objective Questions 26
Comprehensive Questions 27
Research Questions 30

2 Financial Statement Audits and Auditors' Responsibilities 32

Fundamentals Underlying Financial Statement Audits 33
- Relationship Between Accounting and Auditing, 33
- Verifiability of Financial Statement Data, 34
- Need for Financial Statement Audits, 35
- Economic Benefits of an Audit, 36
- Limitations of a Financial Statement Audit, 37

Independent Auditor Relationships 38
- Management, 38
- Board of Directors and Audit Committee, 38

Internal Auditors, 39
Stockholders, 39
AUDITING STANDARDS 40
Statements on Auditing Standards (SASs), 40
Generally Accepted Auditing Standards (GAAS), 41
Applicability of Auditing Standards, 44
Relationship of Auditing Standards to Auditing Procedures, 44
THE AUDITOR'S REPORT 45
The Standard Report, 45
Departures From the Standard Report, 49
Management Responsibility Report, 52
AUDITORS' RESPONSIBILITIES AND THE EXPECTATION GAP 53
Narrowing the Expectation Gap, 54
Errors and Irregularities, 54
Illegal Client Acts, 56
Reporting Doubts as to an Entity's Ability to Continue as a Going Concern, 58
SUMMARY 59
BIBLIOGRAPHY 60
OBJECTIVE QUESTIONS 60
COMPREHENSIVE QUESTIONS 63
CASES 66
RESEARCH QUESTIONS 68

3 PROFESSIONAL ETHICS **70**

ETHICS AND MORALITY 70
General Ethics, 71
Professional Ethics, 71
AICPA CODE OF PROFESSIONAL CONDUCT 72
AICPA Professional Ethics Division, 72
Composition of the AICPA Code, 73
Code Definitions, 73
Principles, 74
RULES OF CONDUCT 77
Rule 101-Independence, 78
Rule 102-Integrity and Objectivity, 84
Rule 201-General Standards, 86
Rule 202-Compliance with Standards, 86
Rule 203-Accounting Principles, 87
Rule 301-Confidential Client Information, 87
Rule 302-Contingent Fees, 88
Rule 501-Acts Discreditable, 89
Rule 502-Advertising and Other Forms of Solicitation, 89
Rule 503-Commissions and Referral Fees, 90
Rule 505-Form of Organization and Name, 91

ENFORCEMENT OF THE RULES 93
Joint Ethics Enforcement Procedures, 93
Joint Trial Board Procedures, 93
Automatic Disciplinary Provisions, 94
SUMMARY 95
BIBLIOGRAPHY 96
OBJECTIVE QUESTIONS 96
COMPREHENSIVE QUESTIONS 98
CASES 101
RESEARCH QUESTIONS 102

4 AUDITOR'S LEGAL LIABILITY 104
THE LEGAL ENVIRONMENT 104
The Litigation Crisis, 105
The Need for Legal Reform, 107
LIABILITY UNDER COMMON LAW 108
Liability to Clients, 108
Liability to Third Parties, 111
Common Law Defenses, 115
LIABILITY UNDER SECURITIES LAWS 118
Securities Act of 1933, 118
Securities Exchange Act of 1934, 122
OTHER CONSIDERATIONS 127
Liability Under Racketeer Influenced and Corrupt Organization Act, 127
Professional Standards and Legal Decisions, 128
Minimizing the Risk of Litigation, 129
SUMMARY 130
APPENDIX 4A: CHRONOLOGICAL SUMMARY OF ADDITIONAL SELECTED LEGAL CASES 131
BIBLIOGRAPHY 134
OBJECTIVE QUESTIONS 135
COMPREHENSIVE QUESTIONS 136
CASE 141
RESEARCH QUESTIONS 142

PART 2 AUDIT PLANNING 143

5 AUDIT OBJECTIVES, EVIDENCE, AND WORKING PAPERS 144
AUDIT OBJECTIVES 144
Management's Financial Statement Assertions, 145
Specific Audit Objectives, 148
AUDIT EVIDENCE 150
Statement and Purpose of the Third Standard of Field Work, 151

Types of Corroborating Information, 156
AUDIT PROCEDURES *161*
Types of Audit Procedures, 162
Relationships Among Audit Procedures, Types of Evidence, and Assertions, 165
Classification of Audit Procedures, 165
Evaluation of Evidence Obtained, 167
WORKING PAPERS *169*
Types of Working Papers, 169
Preparing Working Papers, 174
Reviewing Working Papers, 175
Working Paper Files, 175
Ownership and Custody of Working Papers, 175
SUMMARY *176*
BIBLIOGRAPHY *177*
OBJECTIVE QUESTIONS *177*
COMPREHENSIVE QUESTIONS *179*
CASES *183*
RESEARCH QUESTIONS *185*

6 ACCEPTING THE ENGAGEMENT AND PLANNING THE AUDIT ***188***
OVERVIEW OF A FINANCIAL STATEMENT AUDIT *188*
Accepting the Audit Engagement, 189
Planning the Audit, 189
Performing Audit Tests, 189
Reporting the Findings, 190
ACCEPTING THE ENGAGEMENT *191*
Evaluating the Integrity of Management, 192
Identifying Special Circumstances and Unusual Risks, 193
Assessing Competence to Perform the Audit, 194
Evaluating Independence, 196
Determining Ability to Use Due Care, 196
Preparing the Engagement Letter, 198
PLANNING THE AUDIT *201*
Steps in Planning the Audit, 202
Obtaining Understanding of Client's Business and Industry, 202
Performing Analytical Procedures, 206
SUMMARY *214*
APPENDIX 6A: KEY FINANCIAL RATIOS USED IN ANALYTICAL PROCEDURES *214*
BIBLIOGRAPHY *216*
OBJECTIVE QUESTIONS *217*
COMPREHENSIVE QUESTIONS *218*

CASE 222
RESEARCH QUESTIONS 222

7 **MATERIALITY, RISK, AND PRELIMINARY AUDIT STRATEGIES** **224**

MATERIALITY *224*
The Concept of Materiality, 225
Preliminary Judgments about Materiality, 225
Materiality at the Financial Statement Level, 226
Materiality at the Account Balance Level, 228
Allocating Financial Statement Materiality to Accounts, 229
Relationship Between Materiality and Audit Evidence, 230
AUDIT RISK *231*
Audit Risk Components, 231
Relationship Among Risk Components, 235
Audit Risk at the Financial Statement and Account Balance Levels, 237
Relationship Between Audit Risk and Audit Evidence, 237
Interrelationships Among Materiality, Audit Risk, and Audit Evidence, 238
Audit Risk Alerts, 238
PRELIMINARY AUDIT STRATEGIES *240*
Components of Preliminary Audit Strategies, 240
Primarily Substantive Approach, 241
Lower Assessed Level of Control Risk Approach, 242
Relationship Between Strategies and Transaction Cycles, 242
SUMMARY *244*
BIBLIOGRAPHY *244*
OBJECTIVE QUESTIONS *245*
COMPREHENSIVE QUESTIONS *246*
CASE *250*
RESEARCH QUESTIONS *251*

8 **UNDERSTANDING THE INTERNAL CONTROL STRUCTURE** **252**

INTRODUCTION TO INTERNAL CONTROL *253*
Importance of Internal Control, 253
Definition, Fundamental Concepts, and Components, 254
Entity Objectives and Related Internal Controls Relevant to an Audit, 255
Limitations of an Entity's Internal Control Structure, 256
Roles and Responsibilities, 257
COMPONENTS OF AN INTERNAL CONTROL STRUCTURE *259*
Control Environment, 259
Risk Assessment, 262

Information and Communication, 263
Control Activities, 264
Monitoring, 269
Application of Components to Small and Midsize Entities, 269
OBTAINING AN UNDERSTANDING OF INTERNAL CONTROL STRUCTURE COMPONENTS *272*
Effects of Preliminary Audit Strategies, 273
Understanding of Control Environment, 274
Understanding of Risk Assessment, 274
Understanding of Information and Communication, 275
Understanding of Control Activities, 275
Understanding of Monitoring, 276
Procedures to Obtain an Understanding, 276
DOCUMENTING THE UNDERSTANDING *277*
Questionnaires, 279
Flowcharts, 280
Narrative Memoranda, 282
SUMMARY *284*
APPENDIX 8A: COMPREHENSIVE FLOWCHARTING ILLUSTRATION *284*
BIBLIOGRAPHY *288*
OBJECTIVE QUESTIONS *288*
COMPREHENSIVE QUESTIONS *290*
CASES *294*
RESEARCH QUESTIONS *298*

PART 3 AUDIT TESTING METHODOLOGY *299*

9 ASSESSING CONTROL RISK/TESTS OF CONTROLS *300*

ASSESSING CONTROL RISK *301*
Consider Knowledge Acquired from Procedures to Obtain an Understanding, 301
Identify Potential Misstatements, 302
Identify Necessary Controls, 302
Perform Tests of Controls, 304
Evaluate Evidence and Make Assessment, 305
Effects of Preliminary Audit Strategies, 306
TESTS OF CONTROLS *309*
Concurrent Tests of Controls, 310
Additional or Planned Tests of Controls, 311
Designing Tests of Controls, 311
Audit Programs for Tests of Controls, 313
Using Internal Auditors in Tests of Controls, 315
Dual-Purpose Tests, 316

ADDITIONAL CONSIDERATIONS *317*
Assessing Control Risk for Account Balance Assertions Affected by a Single Transaction Class, 317
Assessing Control Risk for Account Balance Assertions Affected by Multiple Transaction Classes, 317
Combining Different Control Risk Assessments, 318
Documenting the Assessed Level of Control Risk, 319
Communication of Internal Control Structure Related Matters, 320
SUMMARY *322*
BIBLIOGRAPHY *322*
OBJECTIVE QUESTIONS *323*
COMPREHENSIVE QUESTIONS *324*
CASE *328*
RESEARCH QUESTIONS *329*

10 DETECTION RISK AND THE DESIGN OF SUBSTANTIVE TESTS ***330***
DETERMINING DETECTION RISK *331*
Evaluating the Planned Level of Substantive Tests, 331
Revising Planned Detection Risk, 332
Specifying Detection Risk for Different Substantive Tests of the Same Assertion, 332
DESIGNING SUBSTANTIVE TESTS *333*
Nature, 333
Timing, 338
Extent, 339
Summary of Relationships Among Audit Risk Components and the Nature, Timing, and Extent of Substantive Tests, 340
DEVELOPING AUDIT PROGRAMS FOR SUBSTANTIVE TESTS *341*
Relationships Among Assertions, Specific Audit Objectives, and Substantive Tests, 342
Illustrative Audit Program for Substantive Tests, 343
General Framework for Developing Audit Programs for Substantive Tests, 345
Audit Programs in Initial Engagements, 347
Audit Programs in Recurring Engagements, 347
SPECIAL CONSIDERATIONS IN DESIGNING SUBSTANTIVE TESTS *348*
Income Statement Accounts, 348
Accounts Involving Accounting Estimates, 350
Accounts Involving Related Party Transactions, 351
Comparison of Tests of Controls and Substantive Tests, 351
SUMMARY *353*
APPENDIX 10A: DETECTION RISK FOR ANALYTICAL PROCEDURES AND TESTS OF DETAILS *353*

BIBLIOGRAPHY *354*
OBJECTIVE QUESTIONS *355*
COMPREHENSIVE QUESTIONS *357*
CASE *361*
RESEARCH QUESTIONS *362*

11 AUDIT SAMPLING IN TESTS OF CONTROLS **364**
BASIC AUDIT SAMPLING CONCEPTS *364*
Nature and Purpose of Audit Sampling, 364
Uncertainty and Audit Sampling, 365
Sampling Risk and Nonsampling Risk, 365
Nonstatistical and Statistical Sampling, 367
Audit Sampling Techniques, 369
DESIGNING STATISTICAL ATTRIBUTE SAMPLES FOR TESTS OF CONTROLS *370*
Determine the Audit Objectives, 371
Define the Population and Sampling Unit, 371
Specify the Attributes of Interest, 372
Determine the Sample Size, 373
Determine the Sample Selection Method, 377
EXECUTING STATISTICAL ATTRIBUTE SAMPLES AND EVALUATING THE RESULTS *380*
Execute the Sampling Plan, 380
Evaluate the Sample Results, 380
Illustrative Case Study, 385
OTHER CONSIDERATIONS *387*
Discovery Sampling, 389
Nonstatistical Sampling, 389
SUMMARY *391*
BIBLIOGRAPHY *391*
OBJECTIVE QUESTIONS *391*
COMPREHENSIVE QUESTIONS *394*
CASES *399*
RESEARCH QUESTIONS *401*

12 AUDIT SAMPLING IN SUBSTANTIVE TESTS **402**
BASIC CONCEPTS *402*
Nature and Purpose, 402
Uncertainty, Sampling Risks, and Audit Risk, 403
Statistical Sampling Approaches, 403
PROBABILITY-PROPORTIONAL-TO-SIZE SAMPLING *405*
Sampling Plan, 405
Determine the Objectives of the Plan, 405
Define the Population and Sampling Unit, 406
Determine Sample Size, 407

Determine the Sample Selection Method, 409
Execute the Sampling Plan, 410
Evaluate the Sample Results, 411
Advantages and Disadvantages of PPS Sampling, 416
CLASSICAL VARIABLES SAMPLING *419*
Types of Classical Variables Sampling Techniques, 419
Mean-Per-Unit (MPU) Estimation, 420
Difference Estimation, 428
Ratio Estimation, 431
Advantages and Disadvantages of Classical Variables Sampling, 433
NONSTATISTICAL SAMPLING IN SUBSTANTIVE TESTING *435*
Determine the Sample Size, 435
Evaluate the Sample Results, 436
SUMMARY *437*
APPENDIX 12A: RELATING THE RISK OF INCORRECT ACCEPTANCE FOR A SUBSTANTIVE TEST OF DETAILS TO OTHER SOURCES OF AUDIT EVIDENCE *437*
BIBLIOGRAPHY *438*
OBJECTIVE QUESTIONS *439*
COMPREHENSIVE QUESTIONS *441*
CASE *446*
RESEARCH QUESTIONS *447*

13 AUDITING ELECTRONIC DATA PROCESSING SYSTEMS *448*
EDP SYSTEM COMPONENTS *449*
Computer Hardware, 449
Computer Software, 449
Data Organization and Processing Methods, 451
EFFECTS OF EDP ON THE INTERNAL CONTROL STRUCTURE *456*
Differences Between Computer and Manual Processing, 457
General Controls, 458
Application Controls, 464
METHODOLOGY FOR MEETING THE SECOND STANDARD OF FIELD WORK *467*
Obtaining an Understanding of the ICS, 467
Assessing Control Risk, 469
Tests of Controls Without the Computer, 471
Tests of Controls With the Computer, 472
Tests of Controls in On-line Entry/On-line Processing, 475
OTHER CONSIDERATIONS *476*
Generalized Audit Software, 476
Microcomputer-Based Audit Software, 478
Expert Systems, 478
Small Computer Systems, 479
Computer Service Organizations, 480

SUMMARY *482*
BIBLIOGRAPHY *483*
OBJECTIVE QUESTIONS *483*
COMPREHENSIVE QUESTIONS *485*
CASE *490*
RESEARCH QUESTIONS *492*

PART 4 AUDITING THE TRANSACTION CYCLES *493*

14 AUDITING THE REVENUE CYCLE *494*

NATURE OF THE REVENUE CYCLE *494*
- Audit Objectives, 495
- Materiality, Risk, and Audit Strategy, 496
- Consideration of Internal Control Structure Components, 498

CONTROL ACTIVITIES—CREDIT SALES TRANSACTIONS *503*
- Common Documents and Records, 504
- Functions, 504
- Obtaining the Understanding and Assessing Control Risk, 508

CONTROL ACTIVITIES—CASH RECEIPTS TRANSACTIONS *514*
- Common Documents and Records, 514
- Functions, 515
- Obtaining the Understanding and Assessing Control Risk, 517

CONTROL ACTIVITIES—SALES ADJUSTMENTS TRANSACTIONS *517*
SUBSTANTIVE TESTS OF ACCOUNTS RECEIVABLE *520*
- Determining Detection Risk, 520
- Designing Substantive Tests, 522
- Initial Procedures, 522
- Analytical Procedures, 524
- Tests of Details of Transactions, 526
- Tests of Details of Balances, 528
- Comparison of Statement Presentation with GAAP, 534

SUMMARY *535*
BIBLIOGRAPHY *536*
OBJECTIVE QUESTIONS *536*
COMPREHENSIVE QUESTIONS *539*
CASES *545*
RESEARCH QUESTIONS *547*

15 AUDITING THE EXPENDITURE CYCLE *550*

NATURE OF THE EXPENDITURE CYCLE *550*
- Audit Objectives, 551
- Materiality, Risk, and Audit Strategy, 551
- Consideration of Internal Control Structure Components, 554

CONTROL ACTIVITIES—PURCHASES TRANSACTIONS *557*
Common Documents and Records, 558
Functions, 558
Obtaining the Understanding and Assessing Control Risk, 563
CONTROL ACTIVITIES—CASH DISBURSEMENTS TRANSACTIONS *566*
Common Documents and Records, 566
Functions, 567
Obtaining the Understanding and Assessing Control Risk, 570
SUBSTANTIVE TESTS OF ACCOUNTS PAYABLE BALANCES *572*
Determining Detection Risk, 572
Designing Substantive Tests, 572
Initial Procedures, 573
Analytical Procedures, 573
Tests of Details of Transactions, 575
Tests of Details of Balances, 577
Comparison of Statement Presentation with GAAP, 578
SUBSTANTIVE TESTS OF PLANT ASSET BALANCES *579*
Determining Detection Risk, 579
Designing Substantive Tests, 580
Initial Procedures, 581
Analytical Procedures, 581
Tests of Details of Transactions, 584
Tests of Details of Balances, 585
Comparison of Statement Presentation with GAAP, 586
SUMMARY *587*
BIBLIOGRAPHY *587*
OBJECTIVE QUESTIONS *587*
COMPREHENSIVE QUESTIONS *589*
CASE *598*
RESEARCH QUESTIONS *599*

16 AUDITING THE PRODUCTION AND PERSONNEL SERVICES CYCLES *600*
THE PRODUCTION CYCLE *601*
Audit Objectives, 601
Materiality, Risk, and Audit Strategy, 601
Consideration of Internal Control Structure Components, 603
CONTROL ACTIVITIES—MANUFACTURING TRANSACTIONS *604*
Common Documents and Records, 605
Functions and Related Controls, 605
Obtaining the Understanding and Assessing Control Risk, 609
SUBSTANTIVE TESTS OF INVENTORY BALANCES *612*
Determining Detection Risk, 612
Designing Substantive Tests, 613
Initial Procedures, 613

Analytical Procedures, 613
Tests of Details of Transactions, 615
Tests of Details of Balances, 617
Comparison of Statement Presentation with GAAP, 624
THE PERSONNEL SERVICES CYCLE *624*
Audit Objectives, 625
Materiality, Risk, and Audit Strategy, 626
Consideration of Internal Control Structure Components, 626
CONTROL ACTIVITIES—PAYROLL TRANSACTIONS *627*
Common Documents and Records, 627
Functions and Related Controls, 628
Obtaining the Understanding and Assessing Control Risk, 632
SUBSTANTIVE TESTS OF PAYROLL BALANCES *634*
Determining Detection Risk, 635
Designing Substantive Tests, 635
SUMMARY *636*
BIBLIOGRAPHY *637*
OBJECTIVE QUESTIONS *637*
COMPREHENSIVE QUESTIONS *639*
CASE *647*
RESEARCH QUESTION *649*

17 AUDITING THE INVESTING AND FINANCING CYCLES 650

THE INVESTING CYCLE *651*
Audit Objectives, 652
Materiality, Risk, and Audit Strategy, 652
Consideration of Internal Control Structure Components, 653
SUBSTANTIVE TESTS OF INVESTMENT BALANCES *655*
Determining Detection Risk, 655
Designing Substantive Tests, 657
Initial Procedures, 657
Analytical Procedures, 657
Tests of Details of Transactions, 657
Tests of Details of Balances, 658
Comparison of Statement Presentation with GAAP, 661
THE FINANCING CYCLE *661*
Audit Objectives, 662
Materiality, Risk, and Audit Strategy, 662
Consideration of Internal Control Structure Components, 663
SUBSTANTIVE TESTS OF LONG-TERM DEBT BALANCES *665*
Determining Detection Risk, 665
Designing Substantive Tests, 665
Initial Procedures, 667
Analytical Procedures, 667

Tests of Details of Transactions, 667
Tests of Details of Balances, 669
Comparison of Statement Presentation with GAAP, 670
SUBSTANTIVE TESTS OF STOCKHOLDERS' EQUITY BALANCES *670*
Determining Detection Risk, 670
Designing Substantive Tests, 671
Initial Procedures, 671
Analytical Procedures, 671
Tests of Details of Transactions, 671
Tests of Details of Balances, 674
Comparison of Statement Presentation with GAAP, 676
SUMMARY *676*
BIBLIOGRAPHY *677*
OBJECTIVE QUESTIONS *677*
COMPREHENSIVE QUESTIONS *678*
CASE *683*
RESEARCH QUESTION *684*

18 AUDITING CASH BALANCES ***686***
GENERAL CONSIDERATIONS *686*
Relationship of Cash Balances to Transaction Cycles, 687
Audit Objectives, 687
Materiality, Risk, and Audit Strategy, 687
SUBSTANTIVE TESTS OF CASH BALANCES *689*
Determining Detection Risk, 689
Designing Substantive Tests, 690
Initial Procedures, 690
Analytical Procedures, 690
Tests of Details of Transactions, 692
Tests of Details of Balances, 696
Comparison of Statement Presentation with GAAP, 701
OTHER CONSIDERATIONS *702*
Tests to Detect Lapping, 702
Auditing Imprest Petty Cash Funds, 704
Auditing Imprest Payroll Bank Accounts, 705
SUMMARY *706*
BIBLIOGRAPHY *706*
OBJECTIVE QUESTIONS *706*
COMPREHENSIVE QUESTIONS *707*
CASE *713*
RESEARCH QUESTION *715*

PART 5 COMPLETING THE AUDIT, REPORTING, AND OTHER SERVICES 717

19 COMPLETING THE AUDIT/POSTAUDIT RESPONSIBILITIES 718

COMPLETING THE FIELD WORK 719
- Making Subsequent Events Review, 719
- Reading Minutes of Meetings, 722
- Obtaining Evidence Concerning Litigation, Claims, and Assessments, 722
- Obtaining Client Representation Letter, 724
- Performing Analytical Procedures, 725

EVALUATING THE FINDINGS 728
- Making Final Assessment of Materiality and Audit Risk, 728
- Making Technical Review of Financial Statements, 729
- Formulating Opinion and Drafting Audit Report, 729
- Making Final Review(s) of Working Papers, 731

COMMUNICATING WITH THE CLIENT 732
- Communicating Internal Control Structure Matters, 732
- Communicating Matters Pertaining to Conduct of Audit, 734
- Preparing Management Letter, 735

POSTAUDIT RESPONSIBILITIES 737
- Subsequent Events Between Date and Issuance of Report, 737
- Discovery of Facts Existing at Report Date, 737
- Discovery of Omitted Procedures, 738

SUMMARY 739

APPENDIX 19A: EXAMPLES OF REPORTABLE CONDITIONS 740

BIBLIOGRAPHY 741

OBJECTIVE QUESTIONS 741

COMPREHENSIVE QUESTIONS 743

CASES 748

RESEARCH QUESTIONS 751

20 REPORTING ON AUDITED FINANCIAL STATEMENTS 752

STANDARDS OF REPORTING 753
- First Standard of Reporting, 753
- Second Standard of Reporting, 755
- Third Standard of Reporting, 756
- Fourth Standard of Reporting, 756

THE AUDITOR'S REPORT 758
- Standard Report, 759
- Departures from Standard Report, 760

EFFECTS OF CIRCUMSTANCES CAUSING DEPARTURES FROM THE STANDARD REPORT 762

Scope Limitation, 762
Noncomformity with GAAP, 764
Inconsistency in Accounting Principles, 767
Inadequate Disclosure, 768
Uncertainty, 769
Substantial Doubt About Going Concern Status, 771
Emphasis of a Matter, 773
Opinion Based in Part on Report of Another Auditor, 773
Summary of Effects of Circumstances on Auditors' Reports, 776
OTHER REPORTING CONSIDERATIONS *779*
Reporting When the CPA Is Not Independent, 779
Circumstances Concerning Comparative Financial Statements, 779
Information Accompanying Audited Financial Statements, 782
Financial Statements Prepared for Use in Other Countries, 784
SUMMARY *785*
BIBLIOGRAPHY *785*
OBJECTIVE QUESTIONS *786*
COMPREHENSIVE QUESTIONS *788*
CASES *793*
RESEARCH QUESTIONS *795*

21 OTHER SERVICES AND REPORTS **796**
ACCEPTING AND PERFORMING ATTEST ENGAGEMENTS *797*
Attestation Standards, 797
Types of Attest Engagements, 799
Levels of Assurance and Attestation Risk, 799
Report Distribution, 800
SPECIAL REPORTS *801*
Other Comprehensive Bases of Accounting, 801
Specified Elements, Accounts, or Items of a Financial Statement, 802
Compliance Reports Related to Audited Financial Statements, 805
REVIEW SERVICES *806*
SAS 71 Review of Interim Financial Information, 807
SSARS Review of Financial Statements, 809
OTHER ATTEST SERVICES *811*
Reporting on Internal Control, 811
Reporting on Prospective Financial Information, 816
Compliance Attestation, 819
Summary of Attest Services, 820
NONATTEST ACCOUNTING SERVICES *821*
Unaudited Financial Statements of a Public Entity, 822
Compilation of Financial Statements of a Nonpublic Entity, 822
Compilation of Prospective Financial Statements, 824
Reporting on the Application of Accounting Principles, 825

Change of Engagement, 826
SUMMARY 827
BIBLIOGRAPHY 827
OBJECTIVE QUESTIONS 828
COMPREHENSIVE QUESTIONS 831
CASE 835
RESEARCH QUESTIONS 836

22 INTERNAL, OPERATIONAL, AND GOVERNMENTAL AUDITING 838
INTERNAL AUDITING 838
Internal Auditing Defined, 839
Evolution of Internal Auditing, 839
Objectives and Scope, 840
Practice Standards, 840
Relationship with External Auditors, 842
OPERATIONAL AUDITING 846
Operational Auditing Defined, 846
Phases of an Operational Audit, 847
Independent Public Accountant Involvement and Standards, 850
GOVERNMENTAL AUDITING 851
Types of Government Audits, 852
Generally Accepted Government Auditing Standards (GAGAS), 853
Reporting on Compliance with Laws and Regulations, 857
Reporting on Internal Control, 859
THE SINGLE AUDIT ACT 860
Objectives of the Act, 860
Applicability and Administration, 860.
Auditors' Responsibilities Under the Act, 861
SUMMARY 865
APPENDIX 22A: INTERNAL AUDITOR CODE OF ETHICS 865
BIBLIOGRAPHY 867
OBJECTIVE QUESTIONS 867
COMPREHENSIVE QUESTIONS 869
CASE 873
RESEARCH QUESTION 874

23 THE INDEPENDENT ACCOUNTANT AND THE SECURITIES AND EXCHANGE COMMISSION 876
SECURITIES AND EXCHANGE COMMISSION 877
Authority of the SEC, 877
Organization of the SEC, 878
REPORTING AND REGISTRATION REQUIREMENTS 880
Integrated Disclosure System, 881

Electronic Data Gathering, Analysis, and Retrieval System, 883
Types of Accounting Pronouncements, 883
Qualifications of Independent Accountants, 885
Requirements for Accountants' Reports, 886
Registration of Securities, 887
SECURITIES ACT OF 1933 *889*
Registration Under the 1933 Act, 890
Independent Accountant's Involvement in Registrations, 893
Accountant's Report, 896
SECURITIES EXCHANGE ACT OF 1934 *897*
Registration Under the 1934 Act, 898
Annual Reporting, 898
Quarterly Reporting, 900
Special Reporting, 901
ENFORCEMENT OF THE SECURITIES ACTS *902*
Injunctive Proceedings, 902
Administrative Proceedings, 903
The Securities Law Enforcement Remedies Act of 1990, 904
SUMMARY *905*
BIBLIOGRAPHY *905*
OBJECTIVE QUESTIONS *905*
COMPREHENSIVE QUESTIONS *907*
CASE *911*
RESEARCH QUESTIONS *911*

APPENDIX X: AUDITING RESEARCH ***912***

INDEX ***917***

PART

I

THE AUDITING ENVIRONMENT

CHAPTER 1

AUDITING AND THE PUBLIC ACCOUNTING PROFESSION

LEARNING OBJECTIVES

After studying this chapter, you should be able to

1. Explain the common attributes of activities defined as auditing.
2. Distinguish among the different types of audits and auditors.
3. Describe the historical roots of auditing.
4. Cite several milestones in the rise of the U.S. public accounting profession.
5. Explain the nature of attest services and describe several types performed by CPAs.
6. Explain the nature of nonattest services and describe several types performed by CPAs.
7. Identify several private sector organizations associated with the profession and explain their principal activities.

INTRODUCTION TO CONTEMPORARY AUDITING
- AUDITING DEFINED
- TYPES OF AUDITS
- TYPES OF AUDITORS

THE PUBLIC ACCOUNTING PROFESSION: AN HISTORICAL PERSPECTIVE
- THE ROOTS OF AUDITING
- RISE OF THE U.S. PROFESSION

SERVICES PERFORMED BY CPA FIRMS
- ATTEST SERVICES
- NONATTEST SERVICES

ORGANIZATIONS ASSOCIATED WITH THE PUBLIC ACCOUNTING PROFESSION
- PRIVATE SECTOR ORGANIZATIONS
- PUBLIC SECTOR ORGANIZATIONS

REGULATORY FRAMEWORK FOR ENSURING QUALITY SERVICES
- STANDARD SETTING
- FIRM REGULATION
- SELF-REGULATION
- GOVERNMENT REGULATION

SUMMARY

BIBLIOGRAPHY

OBJECTIVE QUESTIONS

COMPREHENSIVE QUESTIONS

RESEARCH QUESTIONS

Auditing plays a vital role in business, government, and our economy. Evidence of the importance of auditing is provided by the following:

- The financial statements of over 14,000 public companies are audited annually, including all companies whose securities are traded on the New York Stock Exchange.
- Each state and local government unit receiving $100,000 or more per year in financial assistance from the federal government must have an annual audit under the Single Audit Act.
- In 1993, the Internal Revenue Service audited nearly 1.2 million tax returns.

As a vocation, auditing offers the opportunity for challenging and rewarding careers in public accounting, industry, and government. Individuals choosing an auditing career in a public accounting firm will progress from a starting position of staff assistant, to senior auditor, to manager, and then to partner. Becoming a partner ordinarily takes from ten to twelve years. Auditing career paths in industry and government vary considerably. Some state and local government chief auditor positions are elective offices.

8. Identify several public sector organizations associated with the profession and explain their principal activities.
9. Describe the four components of the profession's multilevel regulatory framework.
10. State the nine elements of a system of quality control for a CPA firm.

CAREER PERSPECTIVES

The Jobs Rated Almanac ranks accounting sixth among 250 top occupations. The book rates jobs according to six factors: environment, outlook, stress, security, physical demands, and income. (*The Jobs Rated Almanac:* Pharos Books, 1992.)

The Bureau of Labor Statistics predicts positions for accountants and auditors will grow 25% to 34% between 1990 and 2005. The latest annual growth rates for professions finds accountants in the top 20 with 2.8%. (*Public Accounting Report:* June 30, 1993, p. 5.)

Of the 53,300 accounting graduates receiving bachelor's degrees and 7,070 receiving master's degrees in 1992, public accounting firms recruited 19,870 and 2,650, respectively, or approximately 37% of the graduates at each level. Of the new hires, 71% were assigned to accounting/auditing, 15% to management consulting services, and 14% to taxation. (*The Supply of Accounting Graduates and the Demand for Public Accounting Recruits—1993:* American Institute of Certified Public Accountants.)

1994 starting salaries for professional staff at public accounting firms were expected to fall in the following ranges for small to large firms: new staff assistant—$22,000 to $31,250; senior—$30,000 to $42,250; manager—$41,000 to $61,250. The starting compensation for newly admitted partners was expected to average $125,000. (*1994 Robert Half and Accountemps Salary Guide.*)

We begin this chapter with an introduction to contemporary auditing including discussions of several types of audits and auditors. Since this book deals primarily with audits of financial statements performed by independent auditors, we next provide a brief historical perspective of the public accounting profession, differentiate the types of services performed by CPA firms, and explain the roles of several important private and public sector organizations that are associated with, and directly influence, the profession. Finally, recognizing the important role the public accounting profession plays in today's society, attention is given to the multilevel regulatory framework that has evolved to help ensure that members of the profession render high quality professional services.

INTRODUCTION TO CONTEMPORARY AUDITING

The term *auditing* is used to describe a broad range of activities in our society. Before considering the different types of audits and auditors, we examine a broad definition of auditing that identifies a number of common attributes of most modern auditing activities.

AUDITING DEFINED

OBJECTIVE 1

Explain the common attributes of activities defined as auditing.

The Report of the Committee on Basic Auditing Concepts of the American Accounting Association (*Accounting Review*, vol. 47) defines **auditing** as

> a systematic process of objectively obtaining and evaluating evidence regarding assertions about economic actions and events to ascertain the degree of correspondence between those assertions and established criteria and communicating the results to interested users.

Several attributes of auditing contained in this definition merit special comment:

- A *systematic process* connotes a logical, structured, and organized series of steps or procedures.
- *Objectively obtaining and evaluating evidence* means examining the bases for the assertions and judiciously evaluating the results without bias or prejudice either for or against the individual (or entity) making the assertions.
- *Assertions about economic actions and events* are the representations made by the individual or entity. They comprise the subject matter of auditing. Assertions include information contained in financial statements, internal operating reports, and tax returns.
- *Degree of correspondence* refers to the closeness with which the assertions can be identified with established criteria. The expression of correspondence may be quantified, such as the amount of a shortage in a petty cash fund, or it may be qualitative, such as the fairness (or reasonableness) of financial statements.
- *Established criteria* are the standards against which the assertions or representations are judged. Criteria may be specific rules prescribed by a legislative body, budgets and other measures of performance set by management, or generally accepted accounting principles (GAAP) established by the Financial Accounting Standards Board (FASB) and other authoritative bodies.
- *Communicating the results* is achieved through a written report that indicates the degree of correspondence between the assertions and established criteria. The communication of results either enhances or weakens the credibility of the representations made by another party.
- *Interested users* are individuals who use (rely on) the auditor's findings. In a business environment, they include stockholders, management, creditors, governmental agencies, and the public.

TYPES OF AUDITS

OBJECTIVE 2

Distinguish among the different types of audits and auditors.

Audits are generally classified into three categories: financial statement, compliance, or operational. The basic nature of each type of audit is briefly described below.

Financial Statement Audit

A **financial statement audit** involves obtaining and evaluating evidence about an entity's statements for the purpose of expressing an opinion on whether they are presented fairly in conformity with established criteria—usually GAAP. This type of audit is made by *external auditors* appointed by the company whose statements are being audited. The results of financial statement audits are distributed to a wide spectrum of users such as stockholders, creditors, regulatory agencies, and the general public. Financial statement audits for major corporations are indispensable to the functioning of our national securities markets. Extensive consideration is given to financial statement audits in this text.

Compliance Audit

A **compliance audit** involves obtaining and evaluating evidence to determine whether certain financial or operating activities of an entity conform to specified conditions, rules, or regulations. The established criteria in this type of audit may come from a variety of sources. Management, for example, may prescribe policies (or rules) pertaining to overtime work, participation in a pension plan, and conflicts of interest. Compliance audits may also be based on criteria established by creditors. For instance, a bond contract may require the maintenance of a specified current ratio. Possibly the widest application of compliance audits relates to criteria based on government regulations. Corporations, for example, must comply with various labor-related laws such as the Equal Employment Opportunity Act and the Fair Labor Standards Act, and defense contractors must comply with the terms and conditions of government contracts. In addition, they are required to satisfy extensive income and other tax regulations.

Reports on compliance audits are generally directed to the authority that established the criteria and may include (1) a summary of findings or (2) an expression of assurance as to the degree of compliance with those criteria.

Operational Audit

An **operational audit** involves obtaining and evaluating evidence about the *efficiency* and *effectiveness* of an entity's operating activities in relation to specified objectives. This type of audit is sometimes referred to as a *performance audit* or *management audit.* In a business enterprise, the scope of the audit may encompass all the activities of (1) a department, branch, or division, or (2) a function that may cross business unit lines such as marketing or data processing. In the federal government, an operational audit might extend to all the activities of (1) an agency, such as the Federal Emergency Management Agency (FEMA), or (2) a particular program, such as the distribution of food stamps. The criteria or objectives against which efficiency and effectiveness are measured may be specified, for example, by management or enabling legislation. In other cases, the operational auditor may assist in specifying the criteria to be used. Reports on such audits typically include not only an assessment of efficiency and effectiveness, but also recommendations for improvement. When performed by CPA firms, such audits are as likely to involve personnel from the consulting department as the audit staff.

A comparative summary of the different types of audits is presented in Figure 1-1. Additional coverage of compliance and operational audits is provided in Chapter 22.

TYPES OF AUDITORS

Individuals who are engaged to audit economic actions and events for individuals and legal entities are generally classified into three groups: (1) independent

FIGURE 1-1 • COMPARATIVE SUMMARY OF TYPES OF AUDITS

Type of Audit	Nature of Assertions	Established Criteria	Nature of Auditor's Report
Financial statement	Financial statement data	Generally accepted accounting principles	Opinion on fairness of financial statements
Compliance	Claims or data pertaining to adherence to policies, laws, regulations, etc.	Management's policies, laws, regulations, or other third-party requirements	Summary of findings or assurance regarding degree of compliance
Operational	Operational or performance data	Objectives set, for example, by management or enabling legislation	Efficiency and effectiveness observed; recommendations for improvement.

auditors, (2) internal auditors, and (3) government auditors. Brief descriptions of each group and the type of auditing done by each are presented below.

Independent Auditors

Independent auditors are either individual practitioners or members of public accounting firms who render professional auditing services to clients. By virtue of their education, training, and experience, independent auditors are qualified to perform each of the types of audits described previously. The clients of independent auditors may include profit-making business enterprises, not-for-profit organizations, governmental agencies, and individuals.

Like members of the medical and legal professions, independent auditors work on a fee basis. There are similarities between the role of an independent auditor in a public accounting firm and an attorney who is a member of a law firm. However, there is also a major difference: The auditor is expected to be *independent* of the client in making an audit and in reporting the results, whereas the attorney is expected to be an *advocate* for the client in rendering legal services.

Audit independence involves both conceptual and technical considerations. It is enough to say at this point that to be independent, an auditor should be without bias with respect to the client under audit and should appear to be objective to

UNIFORM CPA EXAM

The Uniform CPA Examination is prepared by the Board of Examiners of the AICPA. It is used by the examining boards of all fifty states in the USA, the District of Columbia, Puerto Rico, Guam, and the Virgin Islands as a prerequisite for the issuance of CPA certificates. The exam consists of the following sections: Financial Accounting and Reporting—Business Enterprises; Accounting and Reporting—Taxation, Managerial, and Governmental and Not-for-Profit Organizations; Auditing; and Business Law and Professional Responsibilities (including ethics). The AICPA publishes the *CPA Examination Candidate Brochure* which contains content specifications for each section of the examination and describes the grading and other administrative aspects of the exam. The exam is given biannually. In 1993, 66,000 candidates took the exam in May and 74,000 took it in November.

those relying on the results of the audit. More attention will be given to independence in later chapters.

Most independent auditors are licensed to practice as CPAs. In general, licensing involves passing the uniform CPA examination and obtaining practical experience in auditing.

Internal Auditors

Internal auditors are employees of the companies they audit. This type of auditor is involved in an independent appraisal activity, called *internal auditing,* within an organization as a service to the organization. The objective of internal auditing is to assist the management of the organization in the effective discharge of its responsibilities.

The scope of the internal audit function extends to all phases of an organization's activities. Internal auditors are primarily involved with compliance and operational audits. However, as is explained later, the work of internal auditors may supplement the work of independent auditors in financial statement audits.

Many internal auditors are certified (CIAs) and some are also CPAs. The international association of internal auditors is the Institute of Internal Auditors (IIA), which prescribes certification criteria and administers the certified internal auditor examination. In addition, the IIA has established practice standards for internal auditing and a code of ethics.

Government Auditors

Government auditors are employed by various local, state, and federal governmental agencies. At the federal level, the three primary agencies are the General Accounting Office (GAO), the Internal Revenue Service (IRS), and the Defense Contract Audit Agency (DCAA).

In performing the audit function for Congress, GAO auditors engage in a wide range of audit activities, including financial statement audits, compliance audits, and operational audits. The results of these audits are reported to Congress and the public.

IRS auditors (or agents) audit the returns of taxpayers for compliance with applicable tax laws. Their findings are generally restricted to the agency and the taxpayer. The Defense Contract Audit Agency, as its name suggests, conducts audits of defense contractors and their operations, and reports to the Department of Defense.

The national organization for government accountants is the Association of Government Accountants (AGA). The AGA has not yet developed a certification program for government accountants. However, some government auditors hold CPA and/or CIA certificates.

As noted previously, this book deals primarily with financial statement audits performed by independent auditors practicing as members of the public accounting profession. We will learn more about financial statement audits in the next chapter. For now we turn our attention to some important background information about the public accounting profession.

LEARNING CHECK:

1-1 Explain the common attributes of activities defined as auditing.
1-2 Distinguish among the three principal types of audits and describe the nature of the auditor's report for each.
1-3 Distinguish among the three principal types of auditors and indicate the types of audits each may perform.

KEY TERMS:

Auditing, p. 4
Compliance audit, p. 5
Financial statements audit, p. 4
Government auditors, p. 7
Independent auditors, p. 6
Internal auditor, p. 7
Operational audit, p. 5

THE PUBLIC ACCOUNTING PROFESSION: AN HISTORICAL PERSPECTIVE

In contrast to the centuries-old preeminence of law and medicine as professions, public accounting gained prominence as a profession only during this century. In 1900, there were fewer than 250 CPAs in the United States and no more than 1,000 persons employed in all the nation's accounting firms.[1] Today there are nearly 500,000 licensed CPAs in the U.S.

THE ROOTS OF AUDITING

OBJECTIVE 3

Describe the historical roots of auditing

In the words of one accounting historian:

> The origin of auditing goes back to times scarcely less remote than that of accounting. . . . Whenever the advance of civilization brought about the necessity of one man being entrusted to some extent with the property of another the advisability of some kind of check upon the fidelity of the former would become apparent.[2]

Thus, in ancient Egypt authorities provided for independent checks on the recording of tax receipts, in early Greece inspections were made of the accounts of public officials, the Romans compared disbursements with payment authorizations, and the noblemen of medieval English manors appointed auditors to review the accounting records and reports prepared by their servants.

But the beginning of what we would recognize as a company audit can be linked to British legislation during the industrial revolution in the mid-1800s. Initially, company audits had to be performed by one or more stockholders, who were not company officers and who were designated by the other stockholders as their representatives. That legislation was soon revised to permit persons other

[1] T. A. Wise, "The Auditors Have Arrived," *Fortune* (November and December 1960).

[2] R. K. Mautz and Hussein A. Sharaf, *The Philosophy of Auditing* (Evanston, IL: American Accounting Association, 1961), p. 241, citing Richard Brown, *A History of Accounting and Accountants* (Edinburgh: T. C. And E. C. Jack, 1905), p. 74.

than stockholders to perform the audits, giving rise to the formation of auditing firms. Some of these early British firms, such as Deloitte & Co., Peat, Marwick, & Mitchell, and Price Waterhouse & Co., can be traced to firms still practicing in the U.S. or abroad.

The British influence migrated to the U.S. in the late 1800s as English and Scottish investors sent their own auditors to check on the condition of American companies in which they had heavily invested, particularly in brewery and railroad stocks. The focus of these early audits was on finding errors in the balance sheet accounts and stemming the growth of fraud associated with the increasing phenomenon of professional managers and absentee owners.

RISE OF THE U.S. PROFESSION

OBJECTIVE 4

Cite several milestones in the rise of the U.S. profession.

In 1896, New York became the first state to pass legislation providing for the licensing of CPAs. By 1921, all of the then forty-eight states had passed such legislation. In 1917, the American Institute of Accountants was established. Later renamed the American Institute of Certified Public Accountants (AICPA), it became, and remains, the leading voice of the profession.

During the early 1900s, the demand for audits expanded greatly due to rapid growth in the public ownership of corporate securities. Concurrently, the need for greater uniformity in financial reporting became apparent. In 1917, officials of the Federal Reserve Board, with help from members of the accounting profession, developed a proposal for uniform accounting. Published the next year, the booklet "Approved Methods for the Preparation of Balance Sheet Statements" was given considerable credit for advancing financial reporting and for making businessmen aware of the need to employ accountants who understood reporting requirements.

Nevertheless, a decade later following the stock market crash of 1929, significant deficiencies were recognized in financial reporting and the profession was challenged to provide stronger leadership in the further development of accounting and auditing. By then, the income statement had gained status, and attention had to be paid to measures of operating performance and concepts of income as well as financial condition.

In 1933, the New York Stock Exchange adopted a requirement that all listed corporations obtain an audit certificate from an independent CPA. The passage of the Securities Act of 1933 and the Securities Exchange Act of 1934 further added to the demand for audit services for publicly owned companies.

In response to these demands and growth in the size and complexity of businesses, by the 1940s three important changes in audit practice had evolved: (1) a shift from detailed verification of accounts to sampling or testing as the basis for rendering an opinion on the fairness of financial statements, (2) development of the practice of linking the testing to be done to the auditor's evaluation of a company's internal controls, and (3) deemphasis of the detection of fraud as an audit objective. The subject of controversy to this day, the latter change is still in the process of being reversed as the public's expectation that auditors will detect fraud persists. The auditor's evolving responsibility for detecting fraud is explained further in the next chapter.

But auditing is not solely responsible for the growth of the accounting profession in the U.S. The Revenue Act of 1913 was the first of many tax laws that have stimulated a strong demand for tax services by CPAs. And fairly early in this century, clients began to recognize that CPAs had a wealth of knowledge and skills to offer beyond audit and tax. This led to the emergence of consulting as a major activity of CPA firms as well as a variety of other services as explained in the next section.

GLOBAL PERSPECTIVE

In 1960, T. A. Wise wrote: "Accountants' numbers and influence are increasing in other countries as well as in the U.S.; but the scope and diversity of U.S. capitalism have made this country the modern center of the profession, and the American Institute of Certified Public Accountants is always playing host to droves of visitors from Italy, Japan, Israel, and many other nations who are eager to learn how auditing, and accounting in general, are practiced here." ("The Auditors Have Arrived," *Fortune* (November and December 1960).)

In contrast, upon the recent dissolution of the Soviet Union it was observed that since Soviet economic managers never needed profits or financing, the Soviet republics never developed a system of independent auditing or accounting for investment and returns. A recent study by a Russian, a Ukrainian, and an American expert on Soviet accounting refers to the current situation as a "crisis in accounting" and concludes that economic reforms in the former Soviet Union will fail unless a new accounting profession, including a whole new class of professional auditors, can be created in time. ("Help Wanted in Russia: Free Market Accountants," *Accounting Today*, November 9, 1992, p. 35.)

LEARNING CHECK:

1-4 a. What is the origin of what we would recognize as a company audit?
b. What led to the migration of the company audit to the U.S., when did the migration occur, and what was the focus of these early company audits?

1-5 Identify three important milestones in the rise of the U.S. public accounting profession.

1-6 a. Describe three important changes in audit practice that evolved by the 1940s.
b. Which of those changes has the profession come under pressure to reverse in recent years?

1-7 What besides auditing contributed to the growth of the public accounting profession in the U.S.?

SERVICES PERFORMED BY CPA FIRMS

OBJECTIVE 5

Explain the nature of attest services and describe several types performed by CPAs.

The professional staffs of CPA firms are qualified to render a variety of services. Each service may be classified as an attest service or a nonattest service.

ATTEST SERVICES

An **attest service** is one in which the CPA firm issues a written communication that expresses a conclusion about the reliability of a written assertion that is the responsibility of another party. In recent years, growing recognition of the skills and experience of CPAs has resulted in a demand from clients, regulating agencies, and others for a variety of attest services. These services may be further classified into four types.

Audit

The primary example of an **audit service** is the financial statement audit. This type of audit involves obtaining and evaluating evidence about an entity's historical financial statements which contain assertions made by the entity's management. Based on the audit, the CPA issues a "positive" expression of opinion on whether the statements are presented fairly in conformity with established criteria—usually generally accepted accounting principles. Note that the word "positive" means certain or confident, not necessarily favorable—that is, the evidence obtained in an audit may lead a CPA to a positive (certain) conclusion that the statements are not in conformity with GAAP.

Examination

The term **examination** is used to describe other services that culminate in the positive expression of an opinion as to whether or not another party's assertions conform to stated criteria. Examples include examinations of (1) prospective (rather than historical) financial statements, (2) management's assertions about the effectiveness of an entity's internal control structure, and (3) an entity's compliance with specified laws or regulations. The following examples of examinations made by major CPA firms of assertions made by other parties may be a bit more surprising: (1) the accuracy of the authors' presentation of material in an accounting textbook, (2) the ability of computer software to perform as claimed by the developer, (3) the average amount by which a manufacturer's particular brand of golf ball hit by amateurs outdistances its competitors, and (4) the appropriateness of the methodology used by a long-distance telephone carrier to compute cost savings claimed to accrue to its customers compared to a competitor's prices.

Review

A **review service** consists primarily of inquiries of an entity's management and comparative analyses of financial information. The scope of this service is significantly less than that of an audit or examination. The purpose is to give "negative assurance" as opposed to the positive expression of opinion given in an audit. Thus, instead of stating that financial statements are "presented fairly in conformity with GAAP," a report based on a review of financial statements states that the reviewer is "not aware of any material modifications that should be made to the statements in order for them to be in conformity with GAAP." This service is sometimes performed on the interim statements of public companies and the annual statements of nonpublic companies.

Agreed-upon Procedures

The scope of work in performing **agreed-upon procedures** is also less than that in an audit or examination. For example, the client and the CPA firm may agree that certain procedures will be performed on only specified elements or accounts in a financial statement as opposed to the financial statements as a whole. For this type of service, the CPA firm may issue a "summary of findings."

Professional standards covering the performance of all of the attest services just described are issued by the AICPA in the form of *Statements on Standards for Attestation Engagements (SSAEs).* These standards are developed jointly by three senior technical committees of the AICPA—the Auditing Standards Board, the Accounting and Review Services Committee, and the Management Consulting Services Executive Committee. In addition, the AICPA has issued more detailed standards pertaining to audit and review services in the form of *Statements on Auditing Standards (SASs)* (issued by the Auditing Standards Board) and *Statements on Standards for Accounting and Review Services (SSARs)* (issued by the Accounting and Review Services Committee). The *SASs* that pertain to audit services are covered at length in this book beginning in the next chapter. The *SSAEs* and *SSARs,* and expanded discussions of the attest services to which they apply, are presented in Chapter 21.

NONATTEST SERVICES

OBJECTIVE 6

Explain the nature of nonattest services and describe several types performed by CPAs.

The principal types of **nonattest services** rendered by CPA firms are accounting, tax, and consulting services. The common characteristic of these services is that they do not result in the expression of an opinion, negative assurance, summary of findings, or other form of assurance.

Accounting

A CPA firm may be engaged by a client to perform a variety of **accounting services.** These services include doing manual or automated bookkeeping, journalizing and posting adjusting entries, and preparing financial statements. The latter is also referred to as a **compilation service.** In performing one of these services, the firm serves as a substitute for, or a supplement to, the accounting personnel of the client. Accounting services are a major activity for some individual practitioners and local firms. Standards for certain accounting services are included in the AICPA's *Statements on Standards for Accounting and Review Services* issued by the Accounting and Review Services Committee.

Tax

Individuals and business enterprises are required to file and pay a variety of taxes. Most CPA firms have tax specialists, and many have separate tax departments. **Tax services** include assistance in filing tax returns, tax planning, estate planning, and representation of clients before governmental agencies in tax matters. Tax services constitute a very significant part of the practice of most CPA firms. The AICPA's Federal Taxation Executive Committee issues *Statements on Responsibilities in Tax Practice (SRTPs),* which provide guidance for CPAs who perform tax services.

Consulting

In performing **consulting services,** practitioners utilize their technical skills, education, observations, and experiences to provide advice and technical assistance to

FIGURE 1-2 • SUMMARY OF SERVICES PERFORMED BY CPA FIRMS

Type of Service	Applicable Standards	Nature of Attestation Report
Attest Services		
Audit	SSAEs and SASs	Positive expression of opinion
Examination	SSAEs	Positive expression of opinion
Review	SSAEs and SSARs	Negative assurance
Agreed-upon procedure	SSAEs	Summary of findings
Nonattest Services		
Accounting	SSARs	Not applicable
Tax	SRTPs	Not applicable
Consulting	SSCSs	Not applicable

clients. These services help clients to improve the use of their capabilities and resources in achieving their objectives. The consulting process includes defining problems or opportunities, fact-finding, evaluating alternatives, formulating proposed actions, communicating results, implementing actions plans, and follow-up. But the CPA consultant should stop short of making management decisions. Most larger CPA firms have separate consulting departments. Today, consulting services represent a significant and growing proportion of the total billings of CPA firms. The AICPA, through its Management Consulting Services Executive Committee, issues *Statements on Standards for Consulting Services (SSCSs).*

A summary of the types of attest and nonattest services performed by CPA firms, applicable standards, and attestation report forms is presented in Figure 1-2.

LEARNING CHECK:

1-8 Explain the nature of attest services and identify several types performed by CPA firms.

1-9 Explain the nature of nonattest services and identify several types performed by CPA firms.

1-10 Identify three sets of professional standards that pertain at least in part to attest services and three sets that pertain in part to nonattest services.

1-11 Name three types of attestation reports and the type(s) of attest services to which each pertains.

KEY TERMS:

Accounting service, p. 12
Agreed-upon procedures, p. 11
Attest service, p. 10
Audit service, p. 11
Compilation, p. 12
Consulting service, p. 12
Examination, p. 11
Nonattest service, p. 12
Review service, p. 11
Tax service, p. 12

ORGANIZATIONS ASSOCIATED WITH THE PUBLIC ACCOUNTING PROFESSION

The modern profession of public accounting is influenced by a number of professional and regulatory organizations that either function within the profession

FIGURE 1-3 • ORGANIZATIONS ASSOCIATED WITH THE PUBLIC ACCOUNTING PROFESSION

Private Sector Organizations	Public Sector Organizations
American Institute of Certified Public Accountants	State Boards of Accountancy
State Societies of Certified Public Accountants	Securities and Exchange Commission
Practice Units (CPA Firms)	U.S. General Accounting Office
Accounting Standard Setting Bodies: FASB and GASB	Internal Revenue Service
	State and Federal Courts
	U.S. Congress

itself or directly influence the profession through their standard-setting and regulatory activities. These organizations, representing both the private and public sectors, are identified in Figure 1-3.

PRIVATE SECTOR ORGANIZATIONS

An explanation of the nature and principal activities of each of the organizations in this group follows.

American Institute of Certified Public Accountants

OBJECTIVE 7

Identify several private sector organizations associated with the profession and explain their principal activities.

The public accounting profession's national professional organization is the AICPA. As stated in its annual report, the mission of the AICPA is to act on behalf of its members and provide necessary support to assure that CPAs serve the public interest in performing quality professional services.

Membership in the AICPA is voluntary. Currently, there are over 300,000 members of which 45% are in public accounting, 40% are in business and industry, and the remainder are in education or government or are retired.

The AICPA provides a broad range of services to its members. Through its senior technical committees, members participate in the establishment of standards to guide the performance of professional services, as well as standards dealing with quality control, quality review, and ethical conduct. In addition, the AICPA develops and distributes continuing professional education (CPE) materials and courses, provides technical accounting and auditing assistance through a technical information hotline and an extensive library of technical references, and publishes a variety of books, studies, and surveys, as well as three periodicals—the *Journal of Accountancy, The Tax Advisor,* and *The CPA Letter.*

The AICPA operates through a number of divisions. Four of those divisions have a direct impact on auditing. Two, the Division for CPA Firms and the Quality Review Division, are discussed further in this chapter. A third, the Auditing Standards Division, is discussed further in Chapter 2, and the fourth, the Professional Ethics Division, is discussed further in Chapter 3.

State Societies of Certified Public Accountants

CPAs within each state have formed a state society (or association) of CPAs. Like the national organization, membership in a state society is voluntary. Many CPAs are members of both the AICPA and a state society. State societies function through small full-time staffs and committees composed of their members. State associations have their own codes of professional ethics that closely parallel the AICPA Code of Professional Conduct. Although they are autonomous, state societies usually cooperate with both each other and the AICPA in areas of mutual interest, such as continuing professional education and ethics.

Practice Units (CPA Firms)

A CPA may practice as a sole practitioner or as a member of a firm. A CPA firm may be organized as a proprietorship, partnership, professional corporation, or any other form of organization permitted by state law or regulation. There are approximately 45,000 practice units in the United States. These firms are often classified into four groups—the Big Six, second-tier, regional, and local firms.

The six largest firms in the United States are referred to as the *Big Six.* Together, their clients include over 95 percent of the "Fortune 500" companies and thousands of smaller clients. The combined U.S. revenues of the Big Six exceeded $12 billion in 1993, or about one quarter of the total revenues of the U.S. profession. Two of these firms had worldwide revenues exceeding $6 billion each. With offices in the principal cities of the United States as well as major cities throughout the world, these are truly international firms. For example, one has 135 offices in the U.S. and, with its overseas affiliates, 1,100 offices worldwide. Selected additional data for these and several other practice units are presented in Figure 1-4.

As the figure shows, distinct gaps in the size of revenues separate the *second-tier* firms from both the Big Six and smaller firms. Though the international reach of these firms is significantly less than that of the Big Six, the domestic practice of each is national in scope. Thus, these firms provide competition for the Big Six in serving large, publicly held as well as other clients of all sizes.

Figure 1-4 also includes two examples of *regional firms.* The offices of these firms tend to be concentrated in a more limited geographical area such as the East or Midwest. While these firms serve some publicly owned companies, their clients tend to be smaller than those of the Big Six and second-tier firms.

Local firms may have one or several offices within a state. The local firm is by far the most common form of practice unit. While some local firms serve public companies, their clients are primarily smaller businesses and individuals. Some of the smallest local firms decline to perform audit services because of the high cost of maintaining competence and the increased exposure to legal liability.

To remain competitive, many smaller and mid-sized firms join an association of CPA firms. There are more than two dozen associations in the U.S. with as few as 6 and as many as 60 practice unit members. Associations vary widely in the services provided to members, but most offer staff training programs, a directory of experts in member firms available for consultation with other member firms about their areas of expertise, assistance in recruiting personnel, and client referral services.

FIGURE 1-4 • SELECTED PRACTICE UNIT DATA

Rank by Rev.	Firm	U.S. Rev. ($mil)	No. of U.S. Offices	No. of Partners	No. of Prof. Staff	Revenue Source (%) Actg/Aud	Revenue Source (%) Tax	Revenue Source (%) MCS/Other
Big Six								
1	Arthur Andersen & Co.	$2,922	91	1,435	20,140	35	19	46
2	Ernst & Young	2,400	109	1,870	12,350	52	22	26
3	Deloitte & Touche	2,055	113	1,426	10,774	54	23	23
4	KPMG Peat Marwick	1,822	135	1,493	11,486	55	30	15
5	Coopers & Lybrand	1,642	122	1,199	11,240	56	19	25
6	Price Waterhouse	1,430	106	928	8,708	44	26	30
Second Tier								
7	Grant Thornton	$ 224	48	282	1,540	53	31	16
8	McGladrey & Pullen	197	69	375	1,428	49	35	16
9	Kenneth Leventhal & Co.	193	13	71	789	56	12	32
10	BDO Seidman	182	40	234	1,300	57	33	10
Regional								
11	Baird Kurtz & Dobson	$ 62	19	112	442	49	33	18
12	Crowe, Chizek & Co.	58	8	70	465	42	21	37
Local								
50	Rubin, Brown, Gornstein	$ 12	1	16	126	50	36	14

SOURCE: *Accounting Today Special Report: Top 60 1993.*

Accounting Standard Setting Bodies

The Financial Accounting Standards Board (FASB) and Governmental Accounting Standards Board (GASB) are independent private sector standard-setting bodies whose primary functions are the development of generally accepted accounting principles for business and not-for-profit entities, and state and local governmental entities, respectively. The statements and interpretations issued by both boards have been officially recognized by the AICPA as constituting GAAP.

The FASB consists of seven full-time members who are assisted by a research staff and an advisory council. Before its *Statements of Financial Accounting Standards (SFASs)* are issued, a due process is followed including issuing exposure drafts for public comment and, in some cases, the holding of public hearings. The GASB follows a similar process in issuing its *Statements of Governmental Accounting Standards (SGASs).*

PUBLIC SECTOR ORGANIZATIONS

OBJECTIVE 8

Identify several public sector organizations associated with the profession and explain their principal activities.

Several public sector organizations, both at the state and federal levels, directly influence the public accounting profession. The nature and activities of these organizations are explained in the following sections.

State Boards of Accountancy

There are 54 boards of accountancy: one in each state, one in the District of Columbia, and one in each U.S. territory. State boards usually consist of five to seven

CPAs and at least one public member, who are generally appointed by the governor. A full-time executive secretary and a small (three- to five-member) administrative staff are common. Each board administers its state accountancy laws, which set forth the conditions for licensing of CPAs, codes of professional ethics, and in most cases mandatory continuing professional education requirements. State boards are also becoming more active in positive enforcement programs aimed at maintaining high quality in audit practice. The primary functions of the boards are issuing licenses to practice as a CPA, renewing licenses, and suspending or revoking licenses to practice. State boards work independently of the AICPA and state societies.

Securities and Exchange Commission

The SEC is a federal government agency that was created under the 1934 Securities Exchange Act to regulate the distribution of securities offered for public sale and subsequent trading of securities on stock exchanges and over-the-counter markets. Under the provisions of this act, the SEC has the authority to establish GAAP for companies under its jurisdiction. Throughout its history, the SEC has, with few exceptions, delegated this authority to the private sector, and it currently recognizes the pronouncements of the FASB as constituting GAAP in the filing of financial statements with the agency. In some instances, however, the SEC's disclosure requirements exceed GAAP.

The SEC also exerts considerable influence over auditing and the public accounting profession. Its regulations contain qualifications for determining the independence of the accountant, as well as standards of reporting. These requirements are basically the same as the standards prescribed by the AICPA. The SEC has the authority to take punitive action against independent accountants who do not comply with its regulations. Over the years, the SEC has not been reluctant to use this authority. Further consideration is given to the independent auditor's responsibilities in filings with the SEC in Chapters 4 and 23.

U.S. General Accounting Office

The GAO is the nonpartisan, federal audit agency of the U.S. Congress. Headed by the Comptroller General of the United States, the GAO has the authority to issue standards pertaining to the audit of governmental organizations, programs, activities, and functions. Its standards have been published in a booklet called *Government Auditing Standards,* also known as the "yellow book" after the color of its cover. These standards apply not only to government auditors, but to CPAs who perform audits of federal agencies and other entities that receive federal financial assistance including state and local governments, institutions of higher education, and certain nonprofit organizations and contractors.

Internal Revenue Service

The IRS is the division of the U.S. Treasury Department responsible for administration and enforcement of the federal tax laws. A publication that has a major influence on CPAs who perform tax services is the IRS's *Circular 230, Rules Governing the Practice of Attorneys and Agents Before the Internal Revenue Service.* CPAs who depart from these rules are subject to fines and other penalties that can be imposed by the IRS.

State and Federal Courts

Occasionally, CPA firms are sued for alleged substandard work in performing audits or other services. In reaching a judgment in a particular case, generally the courts have looked to the standards of performance established by the profession itself. But occasionally, the courts have ruled that the profession's standards were not adequate for the protection of the public. Following a number of such court decisions, the profession has responded by clarifying existing practice standards or issuing new standards. Examples include mandating the use of particular auditing procedures pertaining to accounts receivable, inventories, related-party transactions, and the discovery of significant events occurring between a client's balance sheet date and the issuance of the auditor's report.

U.S. Congress

The fact that the AICPA maintains an office and staff in Washington, D.C., is evidence of its concern about the impact of congressional actions on the profession. Of course, pending tax legislation is one area the profession monitors and attempts to influence. But following a number of widely publicized audit failures, several investigations of the accounting profession have been undertaken by congressional committees over the past two decades. The investigations have focused on such matters as the independence of CPA firms, their effectiveness in auditing publicly held companies, their responsibilities for detecting and reporting fraud and illegal client acts (whistle blowing), and whether the profession's regulatory system is adequate to protect the public. With each investigation, the specter of greater government regulation of the accounting profession is raised. But this outcome has been largely avoided through swift responses on the part of the profession in the form of upgrading professional standards and strengthening the profession's self-regulatory efforts. The profession's present regulatory framework is the subject of the final part of this chapter.

LEARNING CHECK:

1-12 Identify four private sector organizations associated with the public accounting profession and briefly describe their principal activities.

1-13 Name four divisions of the AICPA that have a direct impact on auditing.

1-14 a. In what forms may a CPA firm be organized?
b. In what four groups are CPA firms often classified?

1-15 Identify six public sector organizations associated with the public accounting profession and briefly describe one or two principal activities of each.

REGULATORY FRAMEWORK FOR ENSURING QUALITY SERVICES

Every profession is concerned about the quality of its services, and the public accounting profession is no exception. Quality services are essential to ensure that the profession meets its responsibilities to clients, the general public, and regulators.

To help assure quality in the performance of audits and other professional services, the profession has developed a multilevel regulatory framework. This framework encompasses many of the activities of the private and public sector organizations associated with the profession that were described in previous sections of this chapter. For purposes of describing the multilevel framework, these activities may be organized into four components as follows:

OBJECTIVE 9

Describe the four components of the profession's multilevel regulatory framework.

- **Standard setting.** The private sector establishes standards for accounting, professional services, ethics, and quality control to govern the conduct of CPAs and CPA firms.
- **Firm regulation.** Each CPA firm adopts policies and procedures to assure that practicing accountants adhere to professional standards.
- **Self- or peer regulation.** The AICPA has implemented a comprehensive program of self-regulation including mandatory continuing professional education, peer review, audit failure inquiries, and public oversight.
- **Government regulation.** Only qualified professionals are licensed to practice, and auditor conduct is monitored and regulated by state boards of accountancy, the SEC, and the courts.

Each component is discussed further in the following sections.

STANDARD SETTING

The private sector role of the FASB and GASB in setting accounting standards, and of the AICPA in setting standards for the various types of attest and nonattest services, has been noted in previous sections. It was also noted that the AICPA has a Professional Ethics Division through which it establishes standards of professional conduct for CPAs as discussed more fully in Chapter 3. All of these standards provide guidance to *individual* practitioners who aspire to do high quality work.

But the pursuit of quality practice must occur at the *firm* level as well as at the individual level. To assist firms in this goal, in 1979, the AICPA established **quality control standards** for CPA firms.

Quality Control Standards

Statement on Quality Control Standards No. 1, "System of Quality Control for A CPA Firm," mandates that a CPA firm shall have a system of quality control. The *Statement* identifies nine **quality control elements** that should be considered by a firm in adopting quality control policies and procedures to provide reasonable assurance of conforming with professional standards in performing auditing and accounting and review services. Their application to other services such as tax and consulting is voluntary. The nine elements, their purpose, and examples of related policies and procedures are shown in Figure 1-5.

OBJECTIVE 10

State the nine elements of a system of quality control for a CPA firm.

The first element, independence, pertains to the performance of attest services only. The rationale for, and rules pertaining to, independence are discussed at length in the next two chapters. The next seven elements are simply common sense elements of assuring quality in rendering professional services. The ninth element requires a periodic internal review to determine that the system of quality control is functioning as intended.

FIGURE 1-5 • QUALITY CONTROL ELEMENTS

Elements	Purpose	Policies & Procedures
Independence	All professionals should be independent of clients when performing attest services.	Communicate rules on independence to professional staff. Monitor compliance with independence rules.
Assigning personnel to engagements	Personnel should have the technical training and proficiency required by the engagement.	Designate an appropriate person to assign personnel to engagements. Permit partner in charge of engagement to approve assignments.
Consultation	Personnel should seek assistance, when necessary, from persons having appropriate expertise, judgment, and authority.	Designate individuals as experts. Identify areas and specialized situations for which consultation is required.
Supervision	Work at all levels should be supervised to assure that it meets the firm's standards of quality.	Establish procedures for reviewing work papers and reports. Provide for ongoing supervision of work.
Hiring	New employees should possess the appropriate characteristics to perform competently.	Maintain a recruiting program to obtain new employees at entry level. Establish qualifications for evaluating potential hirees at each professional level.
Professional development	Personnel should have the knowledge required to fulfill assigned responsibilities.	Provide programs to develop expertise in specialized areas. Make available to personnel information about new professional pronouncements.
Advancement	Personnel should have the qualifications fo fulfill responsibilities they may be called on to assume in the future.	Establish qualifications necessary for each level of responsibility in the firm. Make periodic evaluations of personnel.
Acceptance and continuance of clients	The firm should minimize the likelihood of being associated with a client whose management lacks integrity.	Establish criteria for evaluating new clients. Establish review procedures for continuing a client.
Inspection	The firm should determine that procedures relating to the other elements are being effectively applied.	Define scope and content of inspection program. Provide for reporting inspection results to appropriate management levels in the firm.

FIRM REGULATION

Firm regulation occurs within a CPA firm. A prime example is implementing a system of quality control as mandated by the quality control standards discussed in the preceding section. This means that the firm's day-to-day actions will comply with the policies and procedures pertaining to the quality control elements. For example, to assist staff in meeting professional standards, firms provide on-the-job training and require their professionals to participate in continuing professional education courses. Personnel who adhere to standards for professional services will receive pay raises and promotions. Personnel whose work is identified as substandard should be terminated if rapid improvement is not forthcoming.

For a CPA firm, there are numerous incentives to do good work. These include pride, professionalism, and a desire to be competitive with other firms. Additional motivation results from the desire to avoid the expense and damage to the firm's reputation that accompanies litigation and other actions brought against the firm for alleged noncompliance with professional standards.

SELF-REGULATION

Self-regulation, also called peer regulation, relates to the activities of professional entities outside the firm to enhance the quality of practice. The AICPA's Division for CPA Firms and its Quality Review Division play key roles in this component of the regulatory framework. Since 1988, CPAs in public practice have been able to retain membership in the AICPA only if they practice in a firm that participates in one of the practice monitoring programs of these two divisions.

Division for CPA firms

The **Division for CPA Firms** consists of two sections: the SEC Practice Section and the Private Companies Practice Section. The AICPA cannot force a firm to enroll in either section. However, a bylaw change approved by the AICPA membership in 1990 provides that Institute members associated with firms that audit SEC clients cannot retain membership in the AICPA unless their firms enroll in the SEC Practice Section. Thus, virtually all firms that audit SEC clients have joined this section.

Each section has its own objectives, membership and peer review requirements, and governing body (executive committee). In general, the objectives and requirements of the SEC Practice Section are more extensive than those of the Private Companies Practice Section. The objectives and membership requirements common to both sections are as follows:

Objectives

- Improve the quality of services by CPA firms through the establishment of practice requirements for member firms.
- Establish and maintain an effective system of self-regulation of member firms by means of mandatory peer reviews, required maintenance of appropriate quality controls, and the imposition of sanctions for failure to meet membership requirements.

Membership Requirements

- Adhere to quality control standards established by the AICPA.
- Submit to a **peer review** of the firm's accounting and auditing practice every three years or at such additional times as designated by the executive committee, the reviews to be conducted in accordance with review standards established by the section's peer review committee.
- Ensure that all professionals in the firm residing in the United States, including CPAs and non-CPAs, participate in at least 20 hours of continuing professional education every year and in at least 120 hours every three years.

Additional requirements for membership in the SEC Practice Section include (1) rotating audit partners on SEC engagements periodically, (2) having an audit partner, other than the partner in charge of the SEC engagement, review and concur in the audit report before it is issued, and (3) refraining from performing certain proscribed management consulting services for SEC audit clients as explained in Chapter 3. There are no additional requirements for membership in the Private Companies Practice Section.

The quality control standards for peer reviews are based on the nine elements of quality control discussed earlier in this chapter. Peer reviews are conducted by review teams (1) appointed by the peer review committee of the section, (2) formed by a member firm engaged by the firm under review (currently, for example, every Big Six firm is reviewed by another Big Six firm), or (3) formed by an authorized entity engaged by the firm under review such as a state CPA society or an association of CPA firms. Each review team is required to report its findings to the section, and these reports are included in the public files of the section. A peer review letter is illustrated in Figure 1-6.

The primary goal of the peer review process is to improve future practice. However, when a firm fails to take the corrective action considered necessary by the section, the section may impose such sanctions as (1) additional continuing professional education requirements; (2) accelerated or special peer reviews; (3) admonishments, censures, or reprimands; (4) monetary fines; (5) suspension from membership; or (6) expulsion from membership in the section.

FIGURE 1-6 • PEER REVIEW LETTER

Deloitte & Touche

Ten Westport Road
P.O. Box 820
Wilton, Connecticut 06897-0820
Telephone: (203) 761-3000

ITT Telex: 66262
Facsimile: (203) 834-2200

To the Partners of
Price Waterhouse

November 1, 1990

We have reviewed the system of quality control for the accounting and auditing practice of Price Waterhouse (the Firm) in effect for the year ended June 30, 1990. Our review was conducted in conformity with standards for peer reviews promulgated by the peer review committee of the SEC Practice Section of the AICPA Division for CPA Firms (the Section). We tested compliance with the Firm's quality control policies and procedures at the Firm's National Office and at selected practice offices in the United States and with the membership requirements of the Section to the extent we considered appropriate. These tests included the application of the Firm's policies and procedures on selected accounting and auditing engagements. We tested the supervision and control of portions of engagements performed outside the United States.

In performing our review, we have given consideration to the general characteristics of a system of quality control as described in quality control standards issued by the AICPA. Such a system should be appropriately comprehensive and suitably designed in relation to a firm's organizational structure, its policies and the nature of its practice. Variance in individual performance can affect the degree of compliance with a firm's prescribed quality control policies and procedures. Therefore, adherence to all policies and procedures in every case may not be possible.

In our opinion, the system of quality control for the accounting and auditing practice of Price Waterhouse in effect for the year ended June 30, 1990, met the objectives of quality control standards established by the AICPA and was being complied with during the year then ended to provide the Firm with reasonable assurance of conforming with professional standards. Also, in our opinion the Firm was in conformity with the membership requirements of the Section in all material respects.

Deloitte & Touche

AUDIT FAILURE INQUIRIES. In spite of the measures the profession takes to ensure quality audits, lawsuits alleging audit deficiencies are often filed against auditors. Firms enrolled in the SEC Practice Section must report to the Section's **Quality Control Inquiry Committee (QCIC)** all litigation or regulatory proceedings involving audits of public companies within 30 days of receiving a complaint.

It is then the QCIC's responsibility to determine whether the allegations in a case suggest (1) an aberrational error that no system can totally eliminate, (2) a shortcoming in the charged firm's quality controls or its compliance with them, or (3) a shortcoming in professional standards. When the QCIC concludes the second or third situation pertains, the case is not closed until the Committee is satisfied the firm has properly addressed any weaknesses in its quality controls, or that shortcomings in standards have been reported to the appropriate accounting or auditing standard-setting body for their consideration.

PUBLIC OVERSIGHT. To enhance the effectiveness and credibility of the SEC Practice Section's self-regulatory activities, a five-member, autonomous **Public Oversight Board** closely monitors the work of the Section. To ensure its independence, the Board appoints its own members who have extensive experience in business, professional, regulatory, and legislative matters. The Board's staff directly oversees each peer review conducted by the Section and all QCIC inquiries into alleged audit failures. The Board distributes an annual report on its activities to all interested parties and recommends improvements when it sees an opportunity for the SEC Practice Section to strengthen its self-regulatory activities.

Quality Review Division

In 1988, the AICPA established a **Quality Review Division.** The primary activities of this Division are to establish and conduct, in cooperation with state CPA societies, a quality review program for local firms engaged in the practice of public accounting that are not enrolled in one of the Sections of the Division for CPA firms.[3] The executive committee of the Division issues *Standards for Performing and Reporting on Quality Reviews* that apply to reviews conducted by individuals and firms who perform quality review services for a fee, or by review teams established by the Division itself, state societies, or associations of CPA firms.

The program provides for variations in the nature of the review based on the types of services rendered by a firm. For example, firms that perform audits of financial statements must have on-site quality reviews, while firms that do not perform audits may undergo a more limited off-site review. Participating firms submit to review every three years. The purposes of the program are educational, rehabilitative, and corrective in nature—not punitive.

GOVERNMENT REGULATION

Government regulation of the profession occurs primarily through the activities of state boards of accountancy, the SEC, and state and federal courts as discussed

[3] In February 1994, the Board of Directors of the AICPA approved a request of the Private Companies Practice Section to proceed with development of a plan to combine its peer review program with the quality review program of the Quality Review Division. Implementation is targeted for 1995. The Division for CPA Firms will continue to oversee the peer review program for SEC Practice Section members.

in previous sections. There is also the possibility that the U.S. Congress will enact additional regulatory legislation to be administered by the SEC or some other body if it is not convinced that the existing regulatory framework is adequate to deal with any perceived deficiencies in services rendered by the profession.

The SEC also plays an important role in linking self-regulation and government regulation. It does this by performing its own independent evaluation of the effectiveness of the practice-monitoring program of the SEC Practice Section of the AICPA's Division for Firms. This includes review of work performed by peer review teams, the Public Oversight Board, and the Quality Control Inquiry Committee. Based on these evaluations, the SEC has concluded that the "peer review process contributes significantly to improving the quality control systems of member firms and, therefore, should enhance the consistency and quality of practice before the Commission."

FIGURE 1-7 • COMPONENTS OF THE REGULATORY FRAMEWORK

Component	Regulatory Organization	Primary Activities
Standard-Setting	FASB and GASB	Promulgate generally accepted accounting principles.
	AICPA Senior Technical Committees and Divisions	Establish standards for rendering professional services.
		Establish and enforce rules of professional conduct.
		Establish quality control and quality review standards.
Firm Regulation	CPA Firms	Establish and maintain a system of quality control.
		Supervise and review work done on each audit.
		Provide and encourage continuing education for individual CPAs.
Self-Regulation	AICPA Division for Firms	Administer peer review program.
	AICPA Quality Review Division	Establish quality review programs and conduct quality reviews.
	State Societies of CPAs	Cooperate in quality review programs and establish and enforce rules of professional conduct.
Government Regulation	State Boards of Accountancy	Establish qualifications for taking the CPA examination and issue, suspend, and revoke licenses to practice public accounting.
		Establish and enforce code of ethics.
	Securities and Exchange Commission	Establish qualifications for accountants to practice before the SEC and punish violators of securities acts. Monitor profession's self-regulatory efforts.
	State and Federal Courts	Resolve litigation against CPAs pertaining to substandard work and impose monetary damages for violations of the law.

Continued vigilance on the part of the profession and responsiveness to congressional concerns should prove helpful in maintaining an appropriate balance between government regulation and the other components of the regulatory framework. A summary of the profession's current multilevel regulatory framework is presented in Figure 1-7.

LEARNING CHECK:

1-16 What is the purpose of the profession's multilevel regulatory framework?
1-17 Describe the four components of the multilevel regulatory framework.
1-18 State the nine elements of a system of quality control for a CPA firm.
1-19 a. What are the two sections of the AICPA's Division for CPA firms?
b. What are the unique membership requirements of the SEC practice section?
1-20 What are the roles of the Quality Control Inquiry Committee and the Public Oversight Board?

KEY TERMS:

Division for CPA Firms, p. 21
Firm regulation, p. 20
Government regulation, p. 23
Peer review, p. 21
Public Oversight Board, p. 23
Quality control elements, p. 19
Quality Control Inquiry Committee, p. 23
Quality control standards, p. 19
Quality Review Division, p. 23
Self-regulation, p. 21

SUMMARY

Auditing offers a variety of career opportunities in public accounting, industry, and government. Over the past century, auditing services provided by the public accounting profession have emerged as a vital component of the U.S. free market economy. The U.S. profession's role in financial reporting continues to serve as a model for the developing profession in countries spanning the globe. Public recognition of the wealth of knowledge and skills of CPAs has led the profession to respond to strong demand for a variety of other attest and nonattest services. The modern profession is influenced by a number of professional and regulatory organizations from both the private and public sectors. The collective standard-setting and regulatory activities of these organizations comprise a multilevel regulatory framework that helps to ensure that the profession provides quality services in meeting its responsibilities to clients, the general public, and regulators.

BIBLIOGRAPHY

AICPA Professional Standards:
Section QC—Quality Control.
Section QR—Quality Review.

SSAE 1 (AT 100), Attestation Standards.

IAU[4] 7 (AU 8007), Control of the Quality of Audit Work.

Carey, J. L. *The Rise of the Accounting Profession from Technician to Professional.* New York: American Institute of Certified Public Accountants, 1969.

Committee on Basic Auditing Concepts. *A Statement of Basic Auditing Concepts.* Sarasota, FL.: American Accounting Association, 1973.

Deis, D. R., Jr., and Giroux, G. A. "Determinants of Audit Quality in the Public Sector," *The Accounting Review* (July 1992), pp. 462–479.

Felix, William L., Jr., and Prawitt, Douglas F. "Self-Regulation: An Assessment by SECPS Members," *Journal of Accountancy* (News Report) (July 1993), pp. 20–21.

Hall, William D. "What Does it Take to Be an Auditor?" *Journal of Accountancy* (January 1989), pp. 72–80.

Huff, Bruce N., and Kelley, Thomas B. "Quality Review and You," *Journal of Accountancy* (February 1989), pp. 34–40.

Jeffords, Raymond, and Thibadoux, Greg M. "TQM and CPA Firms," *Journal of Accountancy* (July 1993), pp. 59–63.

Mednick, Robert, and Previts, Gary John. "The Scope of CPA Services: A View of the Future from the Perspective of a Century of Progress," *Journal of Accountancy* (May 1987), pp. 220–238.

Roy, R. H., and MacNeil, J. H. *Horizons for a Profession.* New York: American Institute of Certified Public Accountants, 1967.

Zeff, Steven A. "Does the CPA Belong to a Profession?" *Accounting Horizons* (June 1987), pp. 65–68.

OBJECTIVE QUESTIONS

Indicate the *best* answer for each of the following multiple choice questions.

1-21 These questions pertain to types of audits and other services performed by CPA firms.

1. A governmental audit may extend beyond an audit leading to the expression of an opinion on the fairness of financial presentation to include

	Program Results	Compliance	Economy & Efficiency
a.	Yes	Yes	No
b.	Yes	Yes	Yes
c.	No	Yes	Yes
d.	Yes	No	Yes

2. Operational audits generally have been conducted by internal auditors and governmental audit agencies, but may be performed by certified public accountants. A primary purpose of an operational audit is to provide
   a. A means of assurance that internal controls are functioning as planned.
   b. Aid to the independent auditor, who is conducting the audit of the financial statements.
   c. The results of internal examinations of financial and accounting matters to a company's top-level management.
   d. A measure of management performance in meeting organizational goals.

3. An attestation engagement is one in which a CPA is engaged to
   a. Issue a written communication expressing a conclusion about the reliability of a written assertion that is the responsibility of another party.

[4] International Auditing Standard.

b. Provide tax advice or prepare a tax return based on financial information the CPA has **not** audited or reviewed.
c. Testify as an expert witness in accounting, auditing, or tax matters, given certain stipulated facts.
d. Assemble prospective financial statements based on the assumptions of the entity's management without expressing any assurance.

1-22 These questions relate to quality control standards.

1. Which of the following are elements of a CPA firm's quality control that should be considered in establishing its quality control policies and procedures?

	Advancement	Inspection	Consultation
a.	Yes	Yes	No
b.	Yes	Yes	Yes
c.	No	Yes	Yes
d.	Yes	No	Yes

2. A CPA firm studies its personnel advancement experience to ascertain whether individuals meeting stated criteria are assigned increased degrees of responsibility. This is evidence of the firm's adherence to prescribed standards of
   a. Supervision and review.
   b. Continuing professional education.
   c. Professional development.
   d. Quality control.

3. A CPA firm would be reasonably assured of meeting its responsibility to provide services that conform with professional standards by
   a. Adhering to generally accepted auditing standards.
   b. Having an appropriate system of quality control.
   c. Joining professional societies that enforce ethical conduct.
   d. Maintaining an attitude of independence in its engagements.

Comprehensive Questions

1-23 **(Types of audits and auditors)** J. Cowan, an engineer, is the president of Arco Engineering. At a meeting of the board of directors, Cowan was asked to explain why audits of the company are made by (1) internal auditors, (2) independent auditors, and (3) government auditors. One board member suggested that the company's total audit expense might be less if all auditing was done by internal auditors. J. Cowan was unable to distinguish between the three types of auditors or to satisfactorily respond to the board member's suggestion.

Required

a. Explain the different kinds of audits made by each type of auditor.
b. Identify the sources of practice standards applicable to each type of auditor.
c. Comment on the board member's suggestion to have all auditing done by internal auditors.

1-24 **(Types of audits and auditors)** After performing an audit, the auditor determines that

1. The financial statements of a corporation are presented fairly.
2. A company's receiving department is inefficient.
3. A company's tax return does not conform with IRS regulations.
4. A government supply depot is not meeting planned program objectives.

5. The financial statements of a physician are properly prepared on a cash basis.
6. A foreman is not carrying out his assigned responsibilities.
7. The IRS is in violation of an established government employment practice.
8. A company is meeting the terms of a government contract.
9. A municipality's financial statements correctly show actual cash receipts and disbursements.
10. The postal service in midtown is inefficient.
11. A company is meeting the terms of a bond contract.
12. A department is not meeting the company's prescribed policies concerning overtime work.

REQUIRED

a. Indicate the type of audit that is involved: (1) financial, (2) compliance, or (3) operational.
b. Identify the type of auditor that is involved: (1) independent, (2) internal, (3) government-GAO, or (4) government-IRS.
c. Identify the primary recipient(s) of the audit report: stockholders, management, Congress, and so on. Use the following format for your answers:

Type of Audit	Type of Auditor(s)	Primary Recipient(s)

1-25 **(Accounting profession)** The public accounting profession has achieved remarkable growth and stature in the United States since the beginning of this century, to the point that by the 1960s, some claimed the U.S. was the international center of the modern profession.

a. What factors contributed to the growth of the U.S. accounting profession during the first half of this century?
b. What evidence exists that supports the contention that the U.S. represented the modern center of the profession by the 1960s.
c. Contrast the role and state of development of the accounting professions in the Western world and countries comprising the former Soviet bloc.

1-26 **(Organizations associated with profession)** Several private and public sector organizations are associated with the public accounting profession. Listed below are activities pertaining to these organizations.

1. License individuals to practice as CPAs.
2. Promulgate GAAP.
3. Issue *Statements on Auditing Standards.*
4. Regulate the distribution and trading of securities offered for public sale.
5. Establish its own code of professional ethics.
6. Issue *Statements of Financial Accounting Standards.*
7. Impose mandatory continuing education as a requirement for renewal of license to practice as a CPA.
8. Issue disclosure requirements for companies under its jurisdiction that may exceed GAAP.
9. Issue auditing interpretations.
10. Cooperate with the AICPA in areas of mutual interest such as continuing professional education and ethics enforcement.
11. Take punitive action against an independent auditor.

12. Establish accounting principles for state and local governmental entities.
13. Establish GAAS.
14. Suspend or revoke a CPA's license to practice.
15. Establish quality control standards.
16. Operate as proprietorships, partnerships, or professional corporations.
17. Issue government auditing standards.
18. Administer federal tax laws.

REQUIRED

Indicate the organization or organizations associated with each activity.

1-27 **(Regulatory framework)** The accounting profession's commitment to achieving high quality in rendering professional services is demonstrated by the breadth and effectiveness of its multilevel regulatory framework.

REQUIRED

a. One component of this framework is standard-setting which occurs primarily in the private sector. Identify four types of standards included in this component and the private sector bodies which establish them.
b. Identify and briefly describe the other three components of the regulatory framework.

1-28 **(Quality control elements)** The AICPA has established nine elements of quality control. Listed below are specific policies and procedures adopted by the CPA firm of Baily, Brown & Co.:

1. Periodic evaluations are made of personnel.
2. Ongoing supervision is given to less experienced personnel.
3. An experienced CPA is designated as a public utility industry expert.
4. Rules on independence are communicated to the professional staff.
5. The scope and content of the firm's inspection program are defined.
6. All new employees must be college graduates.
7. Copies of *Statements on Auditing Standards* are provided for all professional staff.
8. A partner assigns personnel to engagements.
9. All new clients must be solvent at the time the engagement is accepted.

REQUIRED

a. Identify the quality control element that applies to each of the foregoing items.
b. For each element of quality control identified in (a), state the purpose of the element.
c. Indicate another policy or procedure that applies to the element. Use the following format for your answers:

Policy/ Procedure No.	Element (a)	Purpose (b)	Additional Procedure (c)

1-29 **(Self-regulation)** The AICPA's Division for CPA Firms and Quality Review Division play important roles in the profession's self-regulation activities.

REQUIRED

a. The activities of these two divisions are directed toward CPA firms. How, if at all, do these divisions have a direct impact on individual members?
b. The Division for CPA Firms has two sections. Identify the sections and discuss the similarities in their objectives and membership requirements.
c. Identify the similarities in peer review objectives of the two sections and the common responsibilities and functions of the peer review teams used by each.
d. What are the responsibilities of the Quality Control Inquiry Committee and the Public Oversight Board, and with which section are they involved?
e. What are the primary activities of the Quality Review Division?

1-30 **(Government regulation)** Government regulation is one component of the profession's regulatory framework.

REQUIRED

a. Identify the regulatory organizations involved in government regulation and indicate the primary activities of each.
b. What link exists between the profession's self-regulation activities and the SEC?
c. What impact has the U.S. Congress had on the self-regulation and government regulation components of the profession's regulatory framework?

RESEARCH QUESTIONS

1-31 **(Local accountancy laws)** Boards of accountancy administer accountancy laws in the fifty states, the District of Columbia, and each U.S. territory. For your jurisdiction (e.g., your state or the jurisdiction in which you intend to seek employment), determine the following:

a. A citation (chapter, title number, etc.) of the statutes and rules and regulations pertaining to the board of accountancy.
b. The name of the governmental department, division, or agency of which the board of accountancy is a part.
c. The qualifications to be a board member, how they are appointed, the number of board members, the length of their terms, and (optional) the names and affiliations of the current board members.
d. Whether there is provision for more than one class of licensed accountants and if so what their designations are.
e. The requirements to sit for the CPA examination and other qualifications for certification as a CPA.
f. Whether the board mandates continuing professional education and, if so, the nature of the requirements.
g. A brief description of board-mandated practice-monitoring or quality review activities, if any, for practice units.

1-32 **(Local accounting profession)** Prepare a brief profile of the public accounting profession in your state or other jurisdiction. You might include information such as the number of licensed practice units, the number of licensed CPAs, the extent to which the Big Six and second-tier firms are present, the identity of two or three regional and local firms, which firms recruit graduates of your accounting program, and the name, location, and size of the state professional organization of CPAs (not the board of accountancy) and local chapter of that organization, if applicable.

CHAPTER

2

FINANCIAL STATEMENT AUDITS AND AUDITORS' RESPONSIBILITIES

LEARNING OBJECTIVES

After studying this chapter, you should be able to

1. Explain the relationship between accounting and auditing.
2. Cite the conditions that create a demand for, and the benefits and limitations of, financial statement audits.
3. Describe the auditor's relationship with the board of directors and audit committee and other important groups.
4. State who issues auditing standards and the forms in which they are published.
5. Enumerate the ten generally accepted auditing standards.
6. Prepare the auditor's standard report and explain its basic elements.
7. Indicate the types of departures from the standard report and the circumstances when each is appropriate.

FUNDAMENTALS UNDERLYING FINANCIAL STATEMENT AUDITS
- RELATIONSHIP BETWEEN ACCOUNTING AND AUDITING
- VERIFIABILITY OF FINANCIAL STATEMENT DATA
- NEED FOR FINANCIAL STATEMENT AUDITS
- ECONOMIC BENEFITS OF AN AUDIT
- LIMITATIONS OF A FINANCIAL STATEMENT AUDIT

INDEPENDENT AUDITOR RELATIONSHIPS
- MANAGEMENT
- BOARD OF DIRECTORS AND AUDIT COMMITTEE
- INTERNAL AUDITORS
- STOCKHOLDERS

AUDITING STANDARDS
- STATEMENTS ON AUDITING STANDARDS (SASs)
- GENERALLY ACCEPTED AUDITING STANDARDS (GAAS)
- APPLICABILITY OF AUDITING STANDARDS
- RELATIONSHIP OF AUDITING STANDARDS TO AUDITING PROCEDURES

THE AUDITOR'S REPORT
- THE STANDARD REPORT
- DEPARTURES FROM THE STANDARD REPORT
- MANAGEMENT RESPONSIBILITY REPORT

AUDITORS' RESPONSIBILITIES AND THE EXPECTATION GAP
- NARROWING THE EXPECTATION GAP
- ERRORS AND IRREGULARITIES
- ILLEGAL CLIENT ACTS
- REPORTING DOUBTS AS TO AN ENTITY'S ABILITY TO CONTINUE AS A GOING CONCERN

SUMMARY

BIBLIOGRAPHY

OBJECTIVE QUESTIONS

COMPREHENSIVE QUESTIONS

CASES

RESEARCH QUESTIONS

As noted in the previous chapter, financial statement audits play an indispensable role in our free market economy. We begin this chapter by examining several fundamentals and important auditor relationships that underlie financial statement audits. Next, we identify the source and form of the *generally accepted auditing standards* (GAAS) that guide the performance of audits. Then, we introduce the *auditor's standard report* on financial statements together with several alternative types of reports and the circumstances when each is appropriate. Finally, we examine the "expectation gap" that currently exists between what the public expects of auditors and what the profession believes its responsibilities should be in three troublesome areas—detecting and reporting errors and irregu-

8. Understand the nature of the *expectation gap* and the profession's response.
9. Explain the auditor's responsibilities for detecting and reporting errors and irregularities and illegal client acts.
10. State the effect on the auditor's report of uncertainty about an entity's ability to continue as a going concern.

larities which include fraud, detecting and reporting illegal client acts, and reporting when there is uncertainty about the ability of an entity to continue as a going concern.

FUNDAMENTALS UNDERLYING FINANCIAL STATEMENT AUDITS

In this section, we examine the relationship between accounting and auditing, identify an important assumption on which auditing is based, and consider the conditions that have created a demand for auditing, as well as the economic benefits and limitations of financial statement audits.

RELATIONSHIP BETWEEN ACCOUNTING AND AUDITING

OBJECTIVE 1

Explain the relationship between accounting and auditing.

There are significant differences in the methods, objectives, and parties responsible for the accounting process by which the financial statements are prepared and the audit of the statements.

Accounting methods involve identifying the events and transactions that effect the entity. Once identified, these items are measured, recorded, classified, and summarized in the accounting records. The result of this process is the preparation and distribution of financial statements that are in conformity with generally accepted accounting principles (GAAP). The ultimate objective of accounting is the communication of relevant and reliable financial data that will be useful for decision making. Thus, accounting is a creative process. An entity's employees are involved in the accounting process, and ultimate responsibility for the financial statements lies with the entity's management.

The typical audit of financial statements involves obtaining and evaluating evidence concerning management's financial statements to enable the auditor to verify whether the statements do in fact present fairly the entity's financial position, results of operations, and cash flows in conformity with GAAP. The auditor is responsible for adhering to generally accepted auditing standards in gathering and evaluating the evidence, and in issuing an audit report that contains the auditor's conclusion expressed in the form of an *opinion* on the financial statements. Rather than creating new information, the primary objective of auditing is to add credibility to the financial statements prepared by management.

The relationship between accounting and auditing in the financial reporting process is illustrated in Figure 2-1.

FIGURE 2-1 • RELATIONSHIP BETWEEN ACCOUNTING AND AUDITING

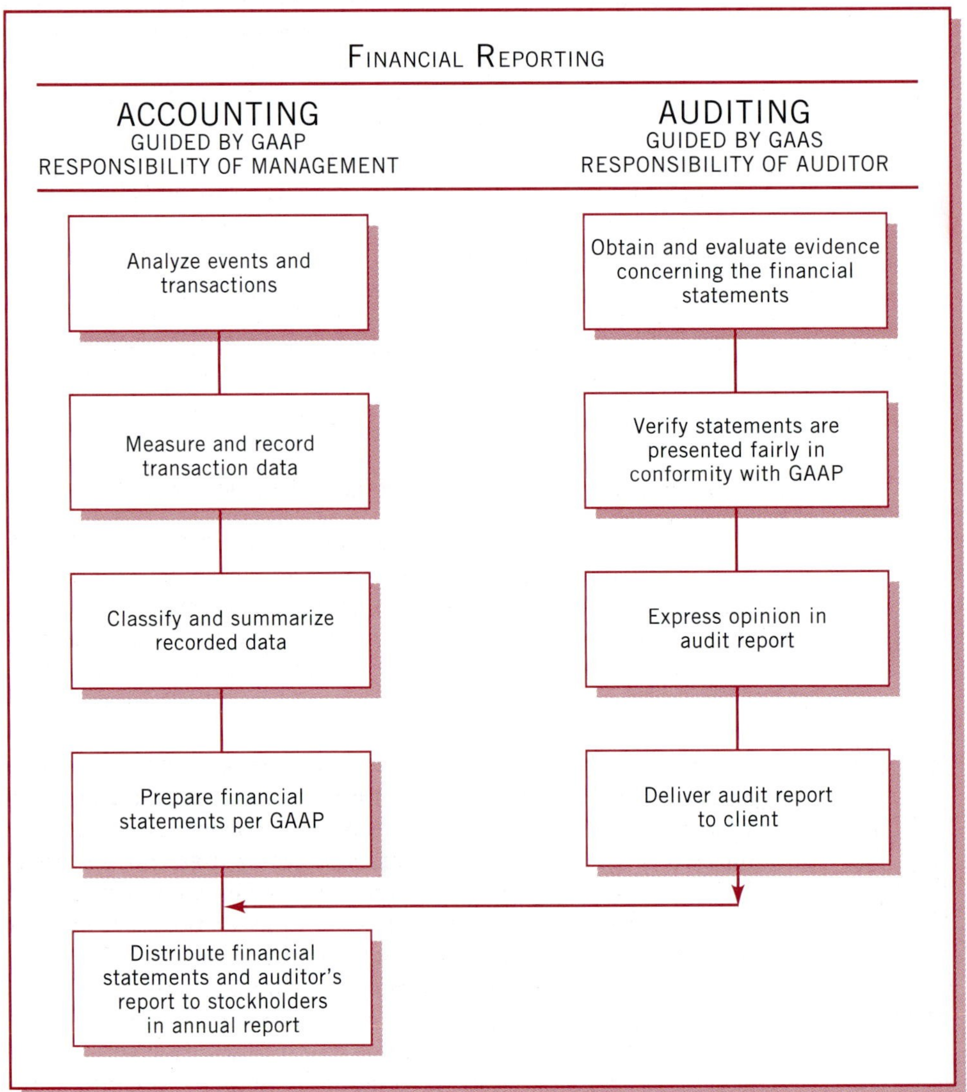
FINANCIAL REPORTING
ACCOUNTING
GUIDED BY GAAP
RESPONSIBILITY OF MANAGEMENT
AUDITING
GUIDED BY GAAS
RESPONSIBILITY OF AUDITOR
Analyze events and transactions
Measure and record transaction data
Classify and summarize recorded data
Prepare financial statements per GAAP
Distribute financial statements and auditor's report to stockholders in annual report
Obtain and evaluate evidence concerning the financial statements
Verify statements are presented fairly in conformity with GAAP
Express opinion in audit report
Deliver audit report to client

VERIFIABILITY OF FINANCIAL STATEMENT DATA

Auditing is based on the assumption that financial statement data are verifiable. Data are **verifiable** when two or more qualified individuals, working independently of one another, reach essentially similar conclusions from an examination of the data. *Verifiability* is primarily concerned with the availability of evidence attesting to the validity of the data being considered.

In some disciplines, data are considered verifiable only if the examiners can prove beyond all doubt that the data are either true or false, or right or wrong, but this is not the case in accounting and auditing. The auditor seeks only a reasonable basis for the expression of an opinion on the *fairness* of the financial statements. In making the examination, the auditor obtains evidence to ascertain the validity and propriety of the accounting treatment of transactions and balances. In this context, **validity** means authentic, true, sound, or well-grounded, and **propriety** means conforming to established accounting rules and customs.

Financial statements contain many specific assertions about individual items. With respect to inventories, for example, management asserts that the inventory is in existence, owned by the reporting entity, and properly valued at the lower of cost or market. In auditing the statements, the auditor believes the individual assertions are verifiable (or auditable) and that it is possible to reach a conclusion about the fairness of the statements taken as a whole by verifying the accounts that comprise the statements. The use and importance of audited financial statements provide proof that the assumption of verifiability is well founded.

NEED FOR FINANCIAL STATEMENT AUDITS

The FASB, in *Statement of Financial Accounting Concepts No. 2,* states that *relevance* and *reliability* are the two primary qualities that make accounting information useful for decision making. Users of financial statements look to the independent auditor's report for assurance that these two qualities have been met.

The need for independent audits of financial statements can further be attributed to four conditions as follows:

OBJECTIVE 2

Cite the conditions that create a demand for, and the benefits and limitations of, financial statement audits.

- **Conflict of Interest.** Many users of financial statements are concerned about an actual or potential conflict of interest between themselves and the management of the reporting entity. This apprehension extends to a fear that the financial statements and accompanying data prepared by management may be intentionally biased in management's favor. Conflicts of interest may also exist among the different classes of users of financial statements such as creditors and stockholders. Thus, users seek assurance from outside independent auditors that the information is both (1) free from management bias and (2) neutral with respect to the various user groups (i.e., the information is not presented in a way that favors one user group over another).
- **Consequence.** Published financial statements represent an important and, in some cases, the only source of information used in making significant investment, lending, and other decisions. Thus, users want the financial statements to contain as much relevant data as possible. This need is recognized by the extensive disclosure requirements imposed by the SEC on companies under its jurisdiction. Because of the significant economic, social, and other consequences of their decisions, statement users look to the independent auditor for assurance that the financial statements have been prepared in conformity with GAAP, including all the appropriate disclosures.
- **Complexity.** Both the subject matter of accounting and the process of preparing financial statements have become increasingly complex. Accounting and reporting standards for leases, pensions, income taxes, and earnings per share are examples of this fact. As the level of complexity increases, so does

the risk of misinterpretations and unintentional errors. Finding it more difficult, or even impossible, to evaluate the quality of the financial statements themselves, users rely on independent auditors to assess the quality of the information contained therein.

- **Remoteness.** Distance, time, and cost make it impractical even for the most knowledgeable users of financial statements to seek direct access to the underlying accounting records to perform their own verifications of the financial statement assertions. Rather than accept the quality of the financial data on faith, once again users rely on the independent auditor's report to meet their needs.

These four conditions collectively contribute to **information risk,** which is the risk that the financial statements may be incorrect, incomplete, or biased. Thus, it can be said that financial statement audits enhance the credibility of financial statements by reducing information risk.

ECONOMIC BENEFITS OF AN AUDIT

The annual audit fee for a large company like General Electric or IBM, or a large governmental entity like New York City, can approach or even exceed $10 million. Clearly, economic benefits must accrue from audits to justify such costs. Among the economic benefits of financial statement audits are the following:

- **Access to Capital Markets.** As noted previously, public companies must satisfy statutory audit requirements under the federal securities acts in order to register securities and have them traded in the securities markets. Additionally, stock markets may impose their own requirements for listing securities. Without audits companies would be denied access to these capital markets.
- **Lower Cost of Capital.** Small companies often have financial statement audits to obtain bank loans or more favorable borrowing terms. Because of the reduced information risk associated with audited financial statements, creditors may offer lower interest rates, and investors may be willing to accept a lower rate of return on their investment.
- **Deterrent to Inefficiency and Fraud.** Research has demonstrated that when *employees* know that an independent audit is to be made, they take care to make fewer errors in performing the accounting function and are less likely to misappropriate company assets. Thus, the data in company records will be more reliable and losses from embezzlements, etc., will be reduced. In addition, the fact that their financial statement assertions are to be verified reduces the likelihood that *management* will engage in fraudulent financial reporting.
- **Control and Operational Improvements.** Based on observations made during a financial statement audit, the independent auditor can often make suggestions to improve controls and and achieve greater operating efficiencies within the client's organization. This economic benefit is especially valuable to small and medium-size companies.

It has been observed that the release of audited financial statements generally has little or no direct effect on the market price of a company's securities. This is because financial results and audit findings are often made available by management to the financial press before the formal issuance of the audited statements. However, such statements help to assure the efficiency of the financial markets by deterring the prior dissemination of inaccurate information or limiting its life.

THE VALUE OF AUDITS

A research study published by the Graduate School of Business of the University of Texas at Austin reports that "audits detected overstatement bias in about 60 percent of the financial statements," and asserts that the number "would be even greater if those companies had not anticipated being audited." The findings further disclose that adjustments to statements as the result of audits are, on average, two to eight times the minimum amount of what would constitute a material misstatement of financial results, and that sales and receivables tend to be overstated while cost of sales and payables tend to be understated.

The study's conclusions are based on an analysis of nine separate research projects covering some 1,500 audits over a 15-year period, with similar results being found for companies in the United States, Canada, the United Kingdom, and South America.

SOURCE: *Accounting Today*, October 18, 1993, pp. 10–11.

LIMITATIONS OF A FINANCIAL STATEMENT AUDIT

A financial statement audit made in accordance with GAAS is subject to a number of inherent limitations. One constraint is that the auditor works within fairly restrictive economic limits. To be useful, the audit must be made at a reasonable cost and within a reasonable length of time. The limitation on cost results in selective testing, or sampling, of the accounting records and supporting data.

The auditor's report on the financial statements is usually issued within three months of the balance sheet date. This time constraint may affect the amount of evidence that can be obtained concerning events and transactions after the balance sheet date that may have an effect on the financial statements. Moreover, there is a relatively short time period available for the resolution of uncertainties existing at the statement date.

Another significant limitation is the established accounting framework for the preparation of financial statements. Alternative principles are often permitted under GAAP, estimates are an inherent part of the accounting process, and no one, including auditors, can foresee the outcome of uncertainties. An audit cannot add exactness and certainty to the financial statements when these factors do not exist. Despite these limitations, a financial statement audit adds credibility to the financial statements.

LEARNING CHECK:

2-1 a. Contrast accounting and auditing as to objectives, methodology, applicable standards, and responsible parties.
b. What assumption underlies financial statement audits?

2-2 Cite four factors that contribute to the need for financial statement audits?
2-3 Explain the economic benefits of a financial statement audit.
2-4 Describe the limitations of a financial statement audit.

KEY TERMS:

Complexity, p. 35
Conflict of interest, p. 35
Consequence, p. 35
Information risk, p. 36
Propriety, p. 35
Remoteness, p. 36
Validity, p. 35
Verifiable, p. 34

INDEPENDENT AUDITOR RELATIONSHIPS

In a financial statement audit, the auditor maintains professional relationships with four important groups: (1) management, (2) the board of directors and audit committee, (3) internal auditors, and (4) stockholders.

MANAGEMENT

The term **management** refers collectively to individuals who actively plan, coordinate, and control the operations and transactions of the client. In an auditing context, management refers to the company officers, controller, and key supervisory personnel.

OBJECTIVE 3

Describe the auditor's relationship with the board of directors and audit committee and other important groups.

During the course of an audit, there is extensive interaction between the auditor and management. To obtain the evidence needed in an audit, the auditor often requires confidential data about the entity. It is imperative, therefore, to have a relationship based on mutual trust and respect. An adversary relationship will not work. The typical approach the auditor should take towards management's assertions may be characterized as one of **professional skepticism.** This means that the auditor should neither disbelieve management's assertions nor glibly accept them without concern for their truthfulness. Rather, the auditor recognizes the need to objectively evaluate conditions observed and evidence obtained during the audit.

BOARD OF DIRECTORS AND AUDIT COMMITTEE

The **board of directors** of a corporation is responsible for seeing that the corporation is operated in the best interests of the stockholders. The auditor's relationship with the directors depends largely on the composition of the board. When the board consists primarily of company officers, the auditor's relationship with the board and management is essentially one and the same.

However, when the board has a number of outside members, a different relationship is possible. Outside members are not officers or employees of the company. In such cases, the board, or a designated **audit committee** composed exclusively or primarily of outside members of the board, can serve as an intermediary between the auditor and management.

In the past decade, there has been a marked increase in the use of audit committees as a means of strengthening the independence of auditors. The functions of an audit committee that directly affect the independent auditor are

- Nominating the public accounting firm to conduct the annual audit.
- Discussing the scope of the audit with the auditor.
- Inviting direct auditor communication on major problems encountered during the course of the audit.
- Reviewing the financial statements and the auditor's report with the auditor on completion of the engagement.

Audit committees have been endorsed by the AICPA, the American Stock Exchange, and the SEC, and they are required for companies listed on the New York Stock Exchange.

INTERNAL AUDITORS

An independent auditor ordinarily has a close working relationship with the client's internal auditors. Management, for example, may ask the independent auditor to review the internal auditors' planned activities for the year and report on the quality of their work. The independent auditor also has a direct interest in the work of internal auditors that pertains to the client's internal control structure. Moreover, it is permissible for the internal auditor to provide *direct assistance* to the independent auditor in performing a financial statement audit.

The *internal auditor's* work cannot be used as a *substitute* for the independent auditor's work. However, it can be an important *complement.* In determining the effect of such work on the audit, the independent auditor should (1) consider the competence and objectivity of the internal auditor and (2) evaluate the quality of the internal auditor's work. More is explained about this in a later chapter.

STOCKHOLDERS

Stockholders rely on audited financial statements for assurance that management has properly discharged its stewardship responsibility. The auditor therefore has an important responsibility to stockholders as the primary users of the audit report. During the course of an engagement, the auditor is not likely to have direct personal contact with stockholders who are not officers, key employees, or directors of the client. Auditors may, however, attend the annual stockholders' meeting and respond to stockholders' questions.

LEARNING CHECK:

2-5 Identify four important groups related to a client with whom the auditor may maintain professional relationships.

2-6 How may the typical approach the auditor should take toward management's assertions be characterized? Explain.

2-7 a. What is an audit committee, what is its ideal composition, and why has there been a marked increase in their use?

b. What are the functions of audit committees?

2-8 Explain how the work of a client's internal auditors might affect the work of the independent auditor and state the determining factors that should be considered.

KEY TERMS:

Audit committee, p. 38
Board of directors, p. 38
Management, p. 38
Professional skepticism, p. 38

AUDITING STANDARDS

As indicated in the previous chapter, three organizations establish auditing standards in the United States: the AICPA, the IIA, and the GAO. Our concern in this chapter is with the auditing standards promulgated by the AICPA for financial statement audits. Standards for internal audits and governmental audits are considered in Chapter 22.

OBJECTIVE 4

State who issues auditing standards and the forms in which they are published.

The Auditing Standards Division of the AICPA is responsible for establishing auditing standards for the public accounting profession. One arm of this Division is the **Auditing Standards Board (ASB),** which has been designated as the senior technical body of the AICPA to issue pronouncements on auditing standards. The ASB also is responsible for providing auditors with guidance for implementing its pronouncements by approving interpretations and audit guides prepared by the staff of the Auditing Standards Division. The ASB's 15 members are all members of the AICPA.

The ASB's Planning Committee consists of six members whose primary responsibility is to establish the ASB's agenda and monitor the progress of ASB projects. In fulfilling its responsibilities, the committee determines whether the ASB is responding to auditing issues identified by both the profession and the public that the profession serves.

STATEMENTS ON AUDITING STANDARDS (SASs)

The pronouncements of the ASB are called ***Statements on Auditing Standards.*** Before an SAS is issued, an exposure draft of the proposed statement is widely circulated for comment to CPA firms, regulatory agencies such as the SEC, accounting educators, and others. The proposed statement and comments received on it are then further deliberated by the Board in open meetings prior to adoption. The approval of two-thirds of the ASB members is required for issuance of an SAS. SASs explain the nature and extent of an auditor's responsibility and offer guidance to an auditor in performing the audit. Compliance with SASs is mandatory for AICPA members who must be prepared to justify any departures from such statements.

When issued, SASs and all related auditing interpretations are codified by auditing section (AU) number. They are then incorporated into the AICPA's looseleaf service entitled *Professional Standards, Volume 1.* Once a year, the AICPA publishes a bound copy of the standards for its members. In addition, a commercial company publishes similar volumes annually, and they are available in electronic format on disk and on-line as part of the *Professional Literature* file of the *National Automated Accounting Research System* (NAARS).

A list of all SASs in effect when this text went to press, together with the corresponding AU section numbers, is provided on the inside front cover of this text. Also, references to applicable SASs and AU section numbers are provided in the bibliographies at the end of each chapter of this text.

GENERALLY ACCEPTED AUDITING STANDARDS (GAAS)

OBJECTIVE 5

Enumerate the ten generally accepted auditing standards.

The most widely recognized auditing standards associated with the public accounting profession are known as the ten **generally accepted auditing standards.** These standards were originally approved by the members of the AICPA in the late 1940s. They have since been incorporated into the *Statements on Auditing Standards.* All of the other standards contained in the SASs are sometimes referred to as interpretations or extensions of the ten GAAS.

The ten GAAS are presented in Figure 2-2 which also identifies the three categories into which they have been grouped. Together they establish the quality of performance and the overall objectives to be achieved in a financial statement

FIGURE 2-2 • GENERALLY ACCEPTED AUDITING STANDARDS

General Standards

- The audit is to be performed by a person or persons having adequate technical training and proficiency as an auditor.
- In all matters relating to the assignment, an independence in mental attitude is to be maintained by the auditor or auditors.
- Due professional care is to be exercised in the performance of the audit and the preparation of the report.

Standards of Field Work

- The work is to be adequately planned, and assistants, if any, are to be properly supervised.
- A sufficient understanding of the internal control structure is to be obtained to plan the audit and to determine the nature, timing, and extent of tests to be performed.
- Sufficient competent evidential matter is to be obtained through inspection, observation, inquiries, and confirmations to afford a reasonable basis for an opinion regarding the financial statements under audit.

Standards of Reporting

- The report shall state whether the financial statements are presented in accordance with generally accepted accounting principles.
- The report shall identify those circumstances in which such principles have not been consistently observed in the current period in relation to the preceding period.
- Informative disclosures in the financial statements are to be regarded as reasonably adequate unless otherwise stated in the report.
- The report shall either contain an expression of opinion regarding the financial statements, taken as a whole, or an assertion to the effect that an opinion cannot be expressed. When an overall opinion cannot be expressed, the reasons therefor should be stated. In all cases where an auditor's name is associated with financial statements, the report should contain a clear-cut indication of the character of the auditor's work, if any, and the degree of responsibility the auditor is taking.

SOURCE: AICPA Professional Standards, AU 150.02, hereinafter referred to only by auditing section number.

audit. Accordingly, they are used by peers, regulatory agencies such as the SEC, and courts of law in evaluating the auditor's work.

General Standards

The general standards relate to the qualifications of the auditor and to the quality of the auditor's work. As indicated in Figure 2-2, there are three general standards.

ADEQUATE TECHNICAL TRAINING AND PROFICIENCY. In every profession, there is a premium on technical competence. The competency of the auditor is determined by three factors: (1) formal university education for entry into the profession, (2) practical training and experience in auditing, and (3) continuing professional education during the auditor's professional career. The importance of the first factor is highlighted by the AICPA's requirement that effective in the year 2000 all new members must have earned the equivalent of 150 semester units of college credit. Similar requirements have been adopted by more than 30 state boards of accountancy as a condition for granting the CPA license. Continuing professional education requirements mandated by the AICPA, state societies, and many state boards of accountancy were discussed in Chapter 1.

INDEPENDENCE IN MENTAL ATTITUDE. Competency alone is not sufficient. The auditor must also be free of client influence in performing the audit and in reporting the findings. The second general standard likens the auditor's role in an audit to the role of an arbitrator in a labor dispute or a judge in a legal case. The auditor must also meet the independence requirements in the AICPA's *Code of Professional Conduct* as discussed in the next chapter.

DUE PROFESSIONAL CARE. Just as the physician is expected to be prudent and thorough in performing a physical examination and making a diagnosis, the auditor is expected to be diligent and careful in performing an audit and issuing a report on the findings. In meeting this standard, the experienced auditor should critically review the work done and the judgments exercised by less experienced personnel that participate in the audit. The standard of due care requires the auditor to act in good faith and not to be negligent in an audit.

Standards of Field Work

The field work standards are so named because they pertain primarily to the conduct of the audit at the client's place of business; that is, in the field. A major portion of this text, Chapters 5 through 19, deals extensively with meeting the three standards of field work.

ADEQUATE PLANNING AND PROPER SUPERVISION. For the audit to be both effective and efficient, it must be adequately planned. Planning includes the development of audit strategies and the design of audit programs for the conduct of the audit. Proper supervision is essential in an audit because major portions of the audit programs are often executed by staff assistants with limited experience.

UNDERSTANDING THE INTERNAL CONTROL STRUCTURE. The client's internal control structure is an important factor in an audit. For example, a well-designed and effective internal control structure will safeguard the client's assets and produce reliable financial data. Conversely, ineffective controls may permit misappropriation of assets and result in unreliable financial information. It is essential, therefore, for the auditor to have an understanding of the internal control structure to plan an effective and efficient audit.

OBTAINING SUFFICIENT COMPETENT EVIDENTIAL MATTER. The ultimate objective of this field work standard is to require the auditor to have a *reasonable basis* for expressing an opinion on the client's financial statements. Meeting this standard requires the exercise of professional judgment in determining both the amount (sufficiency) and the quality (competence) of evidence needed to support the auditor's opinion.

Standards of Reporting

In reporting the results of the audit, the auditor must meet four reporting standards. Many SASs have been issued to assist auditors in meeting these standards.

FINANCIAL STATEMENTS PRESENTED IN ACCORDANCE WITH GAAP. The first reporting standard requires the auditor to identify GAAP as the established criteria used to evaluate management's financial statement assertions. As indicated earlier, generally accepted accounting principles include the pronouncements of authoritative bodies such as the FASB and the GASB. Special provisions for meeting this standard when a company uses a comprehensive basis of accounting other than GAAP are discussed in Chapter 21.

CONSISTENCY IN THE APPLICATION OF GAAP. Meeting this standard requires the auditor to explicitly refer in the auditor's report to any circumstance where GAAP have *not* been consistently followed in the current period in relation to the preceding period. This standard is designed to enhance the comparability of financial statements from period to period. Under this standard, when GAAP have been consistently applied there is no reference to consistency in the auditor's report.

ADEQUACY OF INFORMATIVE DISCLOSURES. This standard relates to the adequacy of the notes to the financial statements and other supplemental forms of disclosure. The standard has an impact on the auditor's report only when management's disclosures are inadequate. In most such cases, the auditor is required to include the necessary disclosures in the auditor's report.

EXPRESSION OF OPINION. The final reporting standard requires the auditor to either express an opinion on the financial statements taken as a whole, or state that an opinion cannot be expressed. In most audits, it is possible for the auditor to express one of several types of opinions. The different types of opinion that may be expressed are briefly explained later in this chapter.

The four reporting standards are discussed in greater depth in Chapters 20 and 21 of this text.

APPLICABILITY OF AUDITING STANDARDS

Auditing standards are applicable in each financial statement audit made by an independent auditor regardless of the size of the client, the form of business organization, the type of industry, or whether the entity is for profit or not-for-profit. Thus, the standards apply equally to the audit of the financial statements of an unincorporated corner grocery store, a school district, and a large corporation such as Exxon or General Motors.

The concepts of *materiality* and *risk* affect the application of all the standards. This is particularly true of the field work and reporting standards. Materiality pertains to the relative importance of an item. For example, inventories in a manufacturing company are more important to the auditor than prepaid insurance because of the possible magnitude of the effects of misstatements in inventories on the financial statements. Risk relates to the likelihood that an item is incorrect. For example, accounts receivable may be more susceptible to misstatements than plant assets. These relationships are explored in greater depth in later chapters.

RELATIONSHIP OF AUDITING STANDARDS TO AUDITING PROCEDURES

Auditing procedures are the methods used and the acts performed by the auditor during an audit. Auditing procedures include such steps as counting petty cash, examining a client-prepared bank reconciliation, observing an inventory count,

INTERNATIONAL STANDARDS ON AUDITING

In 1977, 63 accountancy bodies (including the AICPA) representing 49 countries signed an agreement creating the International Federation of Accountants (IFAC). The broad objective of IFAC is "the development of a world-wide coordinated accountancy profession with harmonized standards." Toward this end, IFAC established, as a standing subcommittee, the International Auditing Practices Committee (IAPC) with the responsibility and authority to issue International Standards on Auditing. Compliance with the international standards is voluntary and they do not override local standards (e.g., the SASs in the United States). Where differences exist between the international standards and local standards, the local member body (e.g., the AICPA's Auditing Standards Board) is expected to give prompt consideration to such differences with a view to achieving harmonization.

The international auditing standards are included in the AICPA's *Professional Standards, Volume 2,* together with a direct comparison with corresponding SASs where applicable. Several instances of these differences will be pointed out in appropriate sections of this text. References to applicable international standards are also included in the bibliographies at the end of each chapter.

The recent endorsement of the international auditing standards by the International Organization of Securities Commissions representing 60 countries is expected to boost the acceptance of the standards in international securities offerings and in reporting by multinational issuers. To date, the SEC has not indicated it will accept financial statements audited in accordance with the international standards in lieu of U.S. GAAS.

and inspecting legal title to a motor vehicle purchased by a company. In contrast to auditing standards that are applicable in every financial statement audit, auditing procedures may vary from client to client because of differences in an entity's size, ownership characteristics, and the nature and complexity of its operations.

LEARNING CHECK:

2-9 What is the ASB, with what organization is it affiliated, and what is its composition?

2-10 What are SASs, what is the process for their issuance, and in what forms are they accessible?

2-11 a. Identify the three categories of the ten generally accepted auditing standards.
b. Briefly indicate the subject matter of each of the ten standards.

2-12 Who issues *International Standards on Auditing* and what is their standing relative to local national standards such as the AICPA's SASs?

KEY TERMS:

Auditing procedures, p. 44
Auditing Standards Board, p. 40
Generally accepted auditing standards, p. 41
Statements on Auditing Standards, p. 40

THE AUDITOR'S REPORT

The audit report is the auditor's formal means of communicating to interested parties a conclusion about the audited financial statements. In issuing an audit report, the auditor must meet the four generally accepted auditing standards of reporting.

THE STANDARD REPORT

Know

A *standard report* is the most common report issued. It contains an **unqualified opinion** stating that the financial statements present fairly, in all material respects, the financial position, results of operations, and cash flows of the entity in conformity with generally accepted accounting principles. This conclusion may be expressed only when the auditor has formed such an opinion on the basis of an audit performed in accordance with GAAS.

OBJECTIVE 6

Prepare the auditor's standard report and explain its basic elements.

Because of its importance in a financial statement audit, a basic understanding of the form and content of the standard report is essential. In 1988, the ASB changed the form and content of the standard report by issuing SAS No. 58, *Reports on Audited Financial Statements* (AU 508). The new report was designed to better communicate to users of audited financial statements the work done by the auditor and the character and limitations of an audit. A second objective was to clearly differentiate between the responsibilities of management and the independent auditor in the financial statement audit.

FIGURE 2-3 • AUDITOR'S STANDARD REPORT

Sample Auditor's Standard Report		Basic Elements of Auditor's Standard Report
Report of Independent Public Accountants	Title	Includes the word independent
To the Stockholders and the Board of Directors of Delta Air Lines, Inc.:	Addressee	Board of Directors and/or Stockholders of Entity
We have audited the accompanying consolidated balance sheets of DELTA AIR LINES, INC. (a Delaware corporation) and subsidiaries as of June 30, 1992 and 1991, and the related consolidated statements of operations, cash flows and common stockholders' equity for each of the three years in the period ended June 30, 1992. These financial statements are the responsibility of the Company's management. Our responsibility is to express an opinion on these financial statements based on our audits.	Introductory Paragraph	Identifies: • type of service performed ("We have audited") • financial statements audited • entity audited • dates of statements • management's responsibility for statements • auditor's responsibility for opinion
We conducted our audits in accordance with generally accepted auditing standards. Those standards require that we plan and perform the audit to obtain reasonable assurance about whether the financial statements are free of material misstatement. An audit includes examining, on a test basis, evidence supporting the amounts and disclosures in the financial statements. An audit also includes assessing the accounting principles used and significant estimates made by management, as well as evaluating the overall financial statement presentation. We believe that our audits provide a reasonable basis for our opinion.	Scope Paragraph	States: • audit conducted in accordance with GAAS, which requires: o planning and performing audit to obtain reasonable assurance that statements are free of material misstatement o examining evidence on a test basis o assessing accounting principles used and significant estimates made by management o evaluating overall financial statement presentation • auditor's belief that audit provides reasonable basis for opinion
In our opinion, the financial statements referred to above present fairly, in all material respects, the financial position of Delta Air Lines, Inc. and subsidiaries as of June 30, 1992, and 1991, and the results of their operations and their cash flows for the periods stated, in conformity with generally accepted accounting principles.	Opinion Paragraph	Expresses: • auditor's opinion as to whether financial statements: o present fairly, in all material respects, o the company's financial position at balance sheet date o the results of operations and cash flows for period o in conformity with GAAP
Arthur Andersen & Co.	Firm's signature	Manual or printed
August 14, 1992	Date	Last day of field work

An example of a standard report on comparative financial statements is presented in Figure 2-3. To the right of the sample report is a listing of the basic elements of the report. Each of these elements is prescribed in AU 508. It should be noted that the standard report has three paragraphs, which are referred to as the introductory, scope, and opinion paragraphs. Each of these paragraphs is explained in the following sections.

Introductory Paragraph

The **introductory paragraph** of the report contains three factual statements. A primary objective of this paragraph is to clearly distinguish between the responsibility of management and the auditor. The wording of this paragraph is presented below:

We have audited the . . . balance sheets . . . of the X Company . . . for the years then ended.

This sentence states that the auditor has audited specific financial statements of a designated company. Each of the financial statements is identified together with the dates appropriate to each statement.

These financial statements are the responsibility of management.

This wording acknowledges that responsibility for the financial statements rests with management. Conversely, this sentence is intended to refute the notion that the auditor develops the representations underlying the financial statements.

Our responsibility is to express . . . based on our audits.

This sentence specifically indicates the auditor's responsibility. The auditor's role is to make an audit and to express an opinion based on the findings. When read in conjunction with the second sentence, there is a clear differentiation between the responsibility of management and the responsibility of the auditor.

Scope Paragraph

As its name suggests, the **scope paragraph** describes the nature and scope of the audit. It satisfies the portion of the fourth reporting standard that requires the auditor to give a clear-cut indication of the character of the audit. The scope paragraph also identifies several limitations of an audit. The wording of this paragraph is:

We conducted our audits in accordance with generally accepted auditing standards.

In this context, generally accepted auditing standards includes both the ten GAAS and all applicable SASs. This sentence asserts that the auditor has met these standards. The inference is that these standards are professional standards. However, neither the source of the standards (the AICPA) nor the specific standards are identified.

These standards require that we . . . audit to obtain reasonable assurance . . . financial statements are free of material misstatements.

This sentence identifies two significant limitations of an audit. First is the acknowledgment that the auditor seeks only reasonable, rather than absolute, assurance. Thus, the reader is informed that there is some risk in an audit. Second, the concept of materiality is introduced. An audit is planned and performed to discover material, but not all, misstatements in the financial statements.

An audit includes examining, on a test basis, evidence supporting . . . the financial statements.

This wording further explains the nature of the audit. The words *test basis* indicate that less than 100% of the evidence was examined. Furthermore, a test basis implies that there is a risk that evidence not examined may be important in assessing the fairness of the overall financial statement presentation and disclosures.

> *An audit also includes assessing the accounting principles . . . significant estimates . . . evaluating the overall financial statement presentation.*

This sentence provides further insight into the character of the audit. It states that the auditor exercises judgment in assessing and evaluating management's financial statement representations. Reference to significant estimates by management means that the financial statements are not based entirely on fact.

> *We believe that our audits provide a reasonable basis for our opinion.*

This sentence identifies another limitation of an audit by stating that only a reasonable basis is needed for an opinion. The concept of a reasonable, rather than a conclusive or absolute, basis is consistent with the concepts of test basis and reasonable assurance stated earlier in the paragraph. This sentence also contains an assertion that the auditor has formed a positive conclusion about the scope of the audit work performed.

Opinion Paragraph

The **opinion paragraph** satisfies the four reporting standards. The wording of the opinion paragraph is explained below.

> *In our opinion, the financial statements referred to above . . .*

In interpreting the meaning and significance of this clause, it is proper to conclude that the opinion is being expressed by a *professional, experienced,* and *expert* person or persons. It is incorrect, however, to conclude that this phrase says, *We certify, We guarantee,* or *We are certain (or positive).* The second part of this clause makes reference to the financial statements identified in the introductory paragraph; the titles of the individual statements are not repeated. The expression of an opinion satisfies the fourth standard of reporting.

> *. . . present fairly, in all material respects . . . financial position . . . results of its operations and its cash flows . . .*

The intended connotation of the words *present fairly* is that the financial statements are presented reasonably and without bias or distortion. An auditor does not use the words *accurately, truly, factually, correctly,* or *exactly* because of the existence of estimates in the financial statements. The auditor's opinion on fairness pertains to each financial statement taken as a whole. It does not apply to the accuracy or correctness of individual accounts or components of each financial statement. An unqualified opinion expresses the auditor's belief that the financial statements accomplish their stated purpose by presenting fairly financial position (balance sheet), results of operations (income and retained earnings statements), and cash flows (statement of cash flows). An unqualified opinion also means that any differences between management and the auditor on accounting matters have been resolved to the auditor's satisfaction.

The phrase *in all material respects* informs users that the auditor's opinion does not attest to the absolute accuracy of the financial statements. This limitation is stated because of the test basis of an audit and the inclusion of significant estimates in the financial statements.

. . . *in conformity with generally accepted accounting principles* . . .

This clause satisfies the first standard of reporting that states the report shall indicate whether the financial statements are prepared in accordance with GAAP. The term *generally accepted accounting principles* provides the criteria for the auditor's judgment as to the fairness of the financial statements. Independent auditors agree on the existence of a body of U.S. GAAP. The sources of GAAP are detailed in SAS 69, *The Meaning of Present Fairly in Conformity with Generally Accepted Accounting Principles in the Independent Auditor's Report* (AU 411.05). These sources are listed and discussed in Chapter 20 of this text.

As stated earlier, the second and third standards of reporting require comment in the auditor's report only when there has been an inconsistency in applying GAAP or management has failed to make all required disclosures. Thus, in the absence of any comments on these matters in the auditor's report, the appropriate conclusion is that these two reporting standards have been met.

DEPARTURES FROM THE STANDARD REPORT

OBJECTIVE 7

Indicate the types of departures from the standard report and the circumstances when each is appropriate.

Circumstances may arise when it is inappropriate for the auditor to issue a standard report. Departures from the standard report fall into one of two categories:

- Standard report with explanatory language.
- Other types of opinions.

Standard Report with Explanatory Language

The distinguishing characteristic of this category of reports is that the opinion paragraph continues to express an unqualified opinion because the financial statements are in conformity with GAAP. However, some circumstance exists that requires the auditor to add an **explanatory paragraph** or other explanatory language to the standard report. For example, when an entity elects to make a change in accounting principles, such as changing depreciation methods, it should follow the guidance in APB Opinion No. 20, which requires the entity to justify the change, apply the appropriate method of accounting for the particular type of change, and make appropriate disclosures in the footnotes. If the entity does all this, the auditor is nonetheless required to add a fourth (explanatory) paragraph to the standard report to call the reader's attention to this circumstance.

AU 508 provides guidance as to other circumstances that require this type of departure from the standard report. While the explanatory information is usually provided in an explanatory paragraph *following* the opinion paragraph, in some cases it merely involves the addition of explanatory wording within the three standard paragraphs, and in other cases an explanatory paragraph is added before the opinion paragraph.

Other Types of Opinions

The second category of departures results when either of the following circumstances occurs:

- The financial statements contain a material departure from GAAP.
- The auditor has been unable to obtain sufficient competent evidence regarding one or more of management's assertions, and as a result does not have a reasonable basis for an unqualified opinion on the financial statements as a whole.

In these cases, the auditor will express one of the following types of opinions:

- A **qualified opinion** which states that except for the effects of the matter(s) to which the qualification relates, the financial statements present fairly . . . in conformity with GAAP.
- An **adverse opinion** which states that the financial statements do *not* present fairly . . . in conformity with GAAP.
- A **disclaimer of opinion** which states that the auditor does not express an opinion on the financial statements.

Departures from GAAP include using accounting principles that are not generally accepted, misapplying GAAP, and failing to make disclosures required by GAAP. For example, if an entity's financial statements reflect a change in accounting principles that was not made in accordance with APB Opinion No. 20, or if the statements were prepared on a current cost basis rather than the historical cost basis, the statements contain a departure from GAAP. In these circumstances, the auditor will express either a *qualified opinion* or an *adverse opinion,* the latter being used only for departures that have an extremely material effect on the financial statements.

Circumstances in which the auditor has been unable to obtain sufficient competent evidence to verify whether one or more assertions are in conformity with GAAP are known as **scope limitations.** In these cases, the auditor will issue either a *qualified opinion* or a *disclaimer of opinion,* the latter being used only for scope limitations that pertain to matters that could have an extremely material effect on the statements.

Whenever one of these other types of opinions is expressed, the reason(s) for the opinion should be explained in one or more explanatory paragraphs immediately *before* the opinion paragraph. The opinion paragraph then begins with a reference to the explanatory paragraph(s), followed by wording appropriate to the type of opinion being expressed as indicated in the three bullets above.

A summary of the types of auditors' reports discussed in this chapter, the circumstances when each is appropriate, and a typical profile for each type of report is presented in Figure 2-4. It should be noted that this summary does not cover all variations of audit reports. The page numbers in Figure 2-4 refer to illustrations of the indicated types of reports in Chapter 20 where much more extensive coverage of reports on audited financial statements is provided.

FIGURE 2-4 • TYPES OF AUDITORS' REPORTS AND CIRCUMSTANCES

		Departures from Standard Report			
	Standard Report	Standard Report with Explanatory Language	Other Types of Opinions		
Circumstance	**Unqualified Opinion**	**Unqualified Opinion**	**Qualified**	**Adverse**	**Disclaimer**
Financial statements conform to GAAP, audit completed in accordance with GAAS, and: • Circumstances requiring explanatory language do not exist.	√ p.759[a]				
• Circumstances requiring explanatory language do not exist.		√ pp.768,771, 772,775			
Financial statements contain a **departure from GAAP>**			√ Material pp.767,768, 769	√ Extremely material p.766	
Auditor unable to obtain sufficient competent evidence (**scope limitation**)			√ Material p.764		√ Extremely material p.766

Typical Report Profiles

Standard Report (Unqualified Opinion):
- TITLE
- Addressee
- Introductory paragraph
- Scope paragraph
- Unqualified opinion paragraph
- Signature
- Date

Standard Report with Explanatory Language (Unqualified Opinion):
- TITLE
- Addressee
- Introductory paragraph
- Scope paragraph
- Unqualified opinion paragraph
- Explanatory paragraph[c]
- Signature
- Date

Other Types of Opinions:
- TITLE
- Addressee
- Introductory paragraph
- Scope paragraph[b]
- Explanatory paragraph
- Qual. adverse, or disclaimer of op.
- Signature
- Date

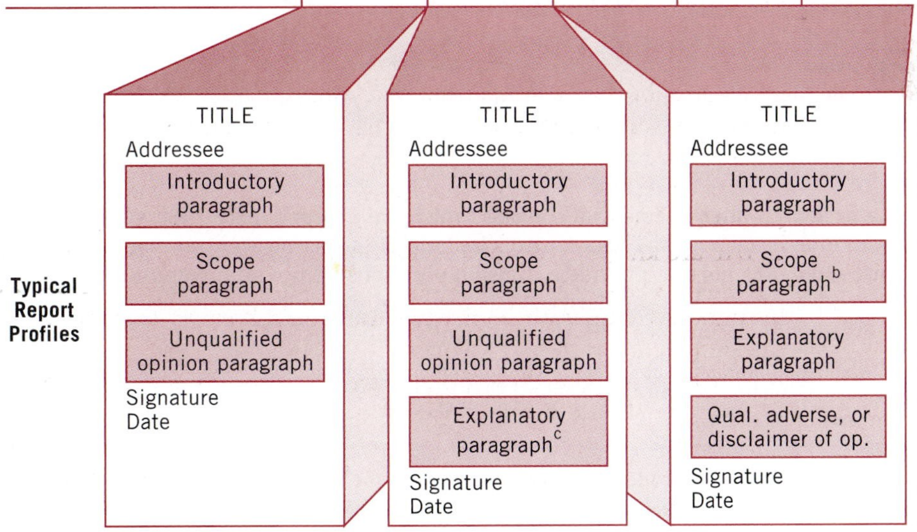

[a] Indicates page for illustration of this type report in Chapter 20.

[b] Scope paragraph omitted for disclaimer of opinion.

[c] Explanatory paragraph located before opinion paragraph in some cases.

MANAGEMENT RESPONSIBILITY REPORT

In the first section of this chapter, it was noted that management is responsible for preparing the financial statements and the auditor is responsible for expressing an opinion on them. Recall that the auditor emphasizes this division of responsibility in the introductory paragraph of the auditor's standard report.

The auditor may, nonetheless, assist in the preparation of financial statements. For example, he or she may counsel management as to the applicability of a new accounting standard, or propose adjustments to the client's statements based on audit findings. However, management's acceptance of this advice and the inclusion of the suggested adjustments in the financial statements do not alter the basic separation of responsibilities. Ultimately, management is responsible for all decisions concerning the form and content of the statements.

To further highlight the division of responsibilities between management and the independent auditor, many companies include a **management responsibility report** in their annual reports to stockholders. A sample report for Delta Air Lines, Inc. is shown in Figure 2-5. Note the report also includes comments pertaining to internal control, internal auditing, and the independent auditor's access to the board of directors and audit committee. The management report is often presented on the same page as the auditor's report, as noted in the illustration.

Recently, the AICPA recommended that the SEC require audit committees of public companies to include a statement in the annual report describing their responsibilities and how those responsibilities were discharged. Few audit committees have elected to do this in the absence of an SEC requirement.

FIGURE 2-5 • MANAGEMENT RESPONSIBILITY REPORT

Report of Management

The integrity and objectivity of the information presented in this Annual Report are the responsibility of Delta management. The financial statements contained in this report have been audited by Arthur Andersen & Co., independent public accountants whose report appears on this page.

Delta maintains a system of internal financial controls which are independently assessed on an ongoing basis through a program of internal audits. These controls include the selection and training of the Company's managers, organizational arrangements that provide a division of reponsibilities, and communication programs explaining the Company's policies and standards. We believe that this system provides reasonable assurance that transactions are executed in accordance with management's authorization; that transactions are appropriately recorded to permit preparation of financial statements that, in all material respects, are presented in conformity with generally accepted accounting principles; and that assets are properly accounted for and safeguarded against loss from unauthorized use.

The Board of Directors pursues its responsibilities for these financial statements through its Audit Committee, which consists solely of directors who are neither officers nor employees of the Company. The Audit Committee meets periodically with the independent public accountants, the internal auditors and representatives of management to discuss internal accounting control, auditing and financial reporting matters.

Tom Roeck	Ronald W. Allen
THOMAS J. ROECK, JR.	RONALD W. ALLEN
Senior Vice President–Finance and	Chairman of the Board
Chief Financial Officer	and Chief Executive Officer

LEARNING CHECK:

2-13 a. What are the seven basic elements of the auditor's standard report?
b. What is the significance of the date of the auditor's standard report?

2-14 How is compliance with the four standards of reporting of GAAS indicated in the auditor's standard report?

2-15 a. Identify two categories of departures from the auditor's standard report.
b. Identify three types of circumstances that require a departure from the auditor's standard report and indicate the type or types of opinion appropriate for each.

2-16 State the wording in the opinion paragraph that differentiates each of the four types of opinions that may be expressed.

KEY TERMS:

Adverse opinion, p. 50
Departure from GAAP, p. 50
Disclaimer of opinion, p. 50
Explanatory paragraph, p. 49
Introductory paragraph, p. 46
Management responsibility report, p. 52
Opinion paragraph, p. 48
Qualified opinion, p. 50
Scope limitation, p. 50
Scope paragraph, p. 47
Unqualified opinion, p. 45

AUDITORS' RESPONSIBILITIES AND THE EXPECTATION GAP

OBJECTIVE 8

Understand the nature of the expectation gap and the profession's response.

Users of audited financial statements expect auditors to

- Perform the audit with technical competence, integrity, independence, and objectivity.
- Search for and detect material misstatements, whether intentional or unintentional.
- Prevent the issuance of misleading financial statements.[1]

Some users have concluded that these expectations are not being met, leading to what has become known as the **expectation gap.** They cite incidences of business failures and investment losses related to entities whose financial statements were audited, and which had received unqualified opinions from the auditors. They equate these business failures and investment losses with audit failures. In most such cases, the auditors claim to have met their responsibilities by having performed the audits in accordance with GAAS.

The expectation gap relates largely to three troublesome areas: (1) detecting and reporting on errors and irregularities, especially fraud, (2) detecting and reporting on illegal client acts, and (3) reporting when there is uncertainty about the ability of an entity to continue as a going concern. We deal with each of these after first considering the profession's recent efforts to address the expectation gap.

[1] Report of the National Commission on Fraudulent Financial Reporting, 1987, p. 49.

NARROWING THE EXPECTATION GAP

In 1985, a blue-ribbon commission was formed through the cooperative efforts of five national accounting organizations, including the AICPA, to study ways to eliminate the issuance of fraudulent financial reports by publicly held companies. After an extensive two-year investigation, the commission, known as the National Commission on Fraudulent Financial Reporting (also called the Treadway Commission after the name of its chairman), issued its final report in October 1987. The Commission's conclusions were made in the form of recommendations to (1) public companies, (2) independent public accountants, (3) the SEC and others to improve the regulatory and legal environment, and (4) education.

The Commission concluded that the primary responsibility for fraudulent reporting rests with the management and board of directors of the company that issues the report. However, the Commission found that while the independent public accountant's role was secondary to management and the board of directors, it was crucial in detecting and preventing fraudulent financial reporting.

Accordingly, it recommended to independent public accountants that (1) auditing standards be changed to better recognize the auditor's responsibility for detecting fraudulent financial reporting and (2) the auditor's standard report be improved to better communicate the work done by the auditor. In response, the ASB issued nine new SASs as shown in Figure 2-6.

Seven of the SASs either superseded or expanded existing standards. SAS 58 is discussed in this chapter and is discussed further in later chapters. SASs 53, 54, and 59 are discussed in the remaining sections of this chapter. The remaining SASs are explained in subsequent chapters.

ERRORS AND IRREGULARITIES

SAS 53, *The Auditor's Responsibility to Detect and Report Errors and Irregularities* (AU 316.02 and .03), defines these terms as follows: The term **errors** refers to *unintentional* misstatements or omissions in financial statements. Errors may involve

FIGURE 2-6 • THE EXPECTATION GAP STATEMENTS ON AUDITING STANDARDS

More detection of material misstatements
- SAS No. 53, The Auditor's Responsibility to Detect and Report Errors and Irregularities
- SAS No. 54, Illegal Acts by Clients

Performance of more effective audits
- SAS No. 55, Consideration of the Internal Control Structure in a Financial Statement Audit
- SAS No. 56, Analytical Procedures
- SAS No. 57, Auditing Accounting Estimates

Better communication with users
- SAS No. 58, Reports on Audited Financial Statements
- SAS No. 59, The Auditor's Consideration of an Entity's Ability to Continue as a Going Concern

Improved communication with management and directors
- SAS No. 60, Communication of Internal Control Structure Related Matters Noted in an Audit
- SAS No. 61, Communication with Audit Committees

SOURCE: Dan M. Guy and Jerry D. Sullivan, "The Expectation Gap SASs," *Journal of Accountancy* (April 1989), p. 37 (adapted).

OBJECTIVE 9

Explain the auditor's responsibilities for detecting and reporting errors and irregularities and illegal client acts.

- Mistakes in gathering or processing accounting data from which financial statements are prepared.
- Incorrect accounting estimates arising from oversight or misinterpretations of facts.
- Mistakes in the application of accounting principles relating to amount, classification, manner of presentation, or disclosure.

The term **irregularities** refers to *intentional* misstatements or omissions in financial statements. Irregularities include **fraudulent financial reporting** undertaken to render financial statements misleading, sometimes called **management fraud,** and misappropriation of assets, sometimes called *defalcations, embezzlements, or* **employee fraud.** Irregularities may involve the following:

- Manipulation, falsification, or alteration of accounting records or supporting documents from which financial statements are prepared.
- Misrepresentation or intentional omission of events, transactions, or other significant information.
- Intentional misapplication of accounting principles relating to amounts, classification, manner of presentation, or disclosure.

The primary factor that distinguishes errors from irregularities is whether the underlying cause of a misstatement is intentional or unintentional.

Responsibility to Detect Errors and Irregularities

Prior to the issuance of SAS 53, the auditor's responsibility was stated as simply to plan the audit to *search* for errors and irregularities that would have a material effect on the financial statements. SAS 53 (AU 316.05) extends the auditor's responsibility to include all of the following:

- Specifically assess the risk that errors and irregularities may cause the financial statements to contain a material misstatement.
- Based on that assessment, design the audit to provide reasonable assurance of *detecting* such errors and irregularities.
- Exercise due care and a proper degree of professional skepticism in performing the audit and evaluating the findings.

There was a presumption when these requirements were adopted that they would lead to the detection of most material misstatements. However, AU 316.08 acknowledges that, because the auditor's opinion on the financial statements is based on the concept of *reasonable assurance,* the auditor's report is not a guarantee. Thus, the profession has taken the position that failing to detect a material misstatement in the financial statements does not, in and of itself, indicate that the audit was not made in accordance with GAAS. In particular, it is claimed that even the most carefully planned and executed audit may not lead to the detection of fraud when management, employees, and third parties conspire to mislead the auditor by providing cleverly falsified documents and records.

Nevertheless, because of continuing incidences of undetected high profile fraudulent financial reporting, the profession is under pressure to improve its performance in this area. In particular, the profession has been encouraged to conduct a more careful analysis of audit failures with a view toward (1) developing more comprehensive guidelines for identifying factors that point toward a heightened likelihood of management fraud, and (2) prescribing additional audit procedures to be performed when such factors are present. Assessing risk factors and designing audit procedures are discussed further in subsequent chapters.

Responsibility to Report Errors and Irregularities

When the auditor concludes that the financial statements are materially misstated due to an error or irregularity, the financial statements are not prepared in conformity with GAAP. Accordingly, the auditor should insist that the financial statements be revised by management. When this is done, the auditor can issue a standard audit report and express an unqualified opinion. However, if the financial statements are not revised, the auditor should express a qualified opinion or an adverse opinion because of the departure from GAAP and disclose all substantive reasons therefor in the audit report.

In either case, the auditor is also required to communicate to the audit committee any material irregularities detected during the audit. The auditor ordinarily has no responsibility to disclose material irregularities to parties outside the client. Rule 301 of the AICPA's *Code of Professional Conduct* requires the auditor to maintain a confidential relationship with the client. Normally, the auditor can disclose the irregularities only when they affect his or her opinion on the financial statements. Disclosure to outsiders, however, may be required in extenuating circumstances. For example, the auditor must inform (1) the court in response to a subpoena and (2) the SEC when the auditor has withdrawn or been dismissed from the engagement.

In some cases, the auditor may be unable to obtain sufficient evidence as to whether the financial statements are materially misstated because of an irregularity. This circumstance represents a scope limitation, and the auditor should express either a qualified opinion or a disclaimer of opinion. In addition, the auditor should report the findings in writing to the audit committee or board of directors. In lieu of the foregoing, the auditor has the option to withdraw from the engagement and to communicate the reasons to the audit committee.

ILLEGAL CLIENT ACTS

An **illegal act** refers to such acts as the payment of bribes, the making of illegal political contributions, and the violation of other specific laws and governmental regulations. All U.S. companies are subject to the illegal payments provisions of the Foreign Corrupt Practices Act, which prohibits payments to foreign government officials for the purpose of obtaining or retaining business in a foreign country.

Responsibility to Detect Illegal Client Acts

Two characteristics of illegal acts influence the auditor's responsibility for detection.

- The determination of whether an act is illegal is dependent on legal judgment that normally is beyond the auditor's professional competence.
- Illegal acts vary considerably in their relation to financial statements. Some laws and regulations such as income tax laws have a direct and material effect on the financial statements. However, other laws such as those pertaining to occupational safety and health and to environmental protection have only an indirect effect on the financial statements.

SAS 54, *Illegal Acts by Clients* (AU 317.05), indicates that the auditor's responsibility for misstatements resulting from illegal acts having a direct and material effect on the determination of financial statement amounts is the same as for errors and irregularities. That is, the auditor should design the audit to *detect* such illegal acts. Prior to the issuance of SAS 54, the auditor was only required to be aware of the possibility of these illegal acts. For these acts, the auditor should apply auditing procedures to ascertain whether any have occurred. In contrast, the auditor's responsibility for all other illegal acts is restricted to information that comes to his or her attention. Because of the foregoing characteristics of illegal acts, an audit made in accordance with GAAS provides no assurance that all illegal acts will be detected.

AU 317.09 states that, during the course of the audit, the following information may provide evidence concerning possible illegal acts: (1) unauthorized transactions, (2) investigations by governmental agencies, and (3) failures to file tax returns. When the auditor suspects that an illegal act has been committed, he or she should discuss the matter with an appropriate level of management and consult with the client's legal counsel. If necessary, the auditor should also apply additional procedures to obtain an understanding of the act and its effects on the financial statements.

Responsibility to Report Illegal Client Acts

The effects on the audit report of an illegal act are the same as for irregularities. When an illegal act having a material effect on the financial statements is not properly accounted for or disclosed, the auditor should express a qualified opinion or an adverse opinion because the financial statements are not in conformity with GAAP. If the auditor is unable to obtain sufficient evidence about an illegal

WHISTLE BLOWING

Many members of the U.S. Congress and others believe that auditors should be held responsible for **whistle blowing,** i.e., informing appropriate authorities including the SEC, when suspected fraud and other illegalities are discovered in the course of an audit. After years of resisting proposed legislation requiring such action, the profession has been encouraged, and now appears willing, to accept this responsibility when the client's management or board of directors fails to take necessary action with respect to suspected illegalities brought to their attention. Several bills containing such provisions have made it out of congressional committees in recent years but have died when not making it through both the House and Senate before adjournment. Similar legislation was pending at the time this text went to press in 1994.

act, there is a scope limitation and the auditor should express a qualified opinion or disclaim an opinion on the financial statements. If the client refuses to accept the auditor's report, the auditor should withdraw from the engagement and indicate the reasons to the audit committee in writing.

The auditor should communicate any illegal acts that come to his or her attention to the audit committee. The auditor's responsibilities to disclose illegal client acts to outside parties is the same as for material irregularities.

REPORTING DOUBTS AS TO AN ENTITY'S ABILITY TO CONTINUE AS A GOING CONCERN

OBJECTIVE 10

State the effect on the auditor's report of uncertainty about an entity's ability to continue as a going concern.

An auditor is not responsible for predicting future conditions or events. Under GAAS, the auditor is required to state in his report whether the financial statements are presented fairly in conformity with GAAP. Fair presentation is not a guarantee of the continuation of an entity as a going concern. Thus, the fact that an entity becomes bankrupt subsequent to the issuance of a standard audit report does not, in itself, indicate a substandard performance or audit failure by the auditor. However, SAS 59, *The Auditor's Consideration of an Entity's Ability to Continue as a Going Concern* (AU 341), provides that the auditor has a responsibility to evaluate whether there is substantial doubt about the entity's ability to continue as a going concern for a reasonable period of time, not to exceed one year beyond the date of the financial statements being audited.

Doubt as to the entity's ability to continue as a going concern may result from evidence obtained in the audit that the entity has suffered recurring net losses, defaulted on loan contracts, or is attempting to restructure debt. In such circumstances, AU 341.07 indicates that the auditor should (1) obtain information about management's plans to mitigate the conditions or events, and (2) assess the likelihood that such plans can be effectively implemented.

When the auditor concludes that there is substantial doubt about the entity's ability to continue as a going concern during this time period, the auditor should state this conclusion in the audit report:

- If management's disclosures in the financial statements concerning the entity's ability to continue as a going concern are considered adequate by the auditor, an unqualified opinion should be expressed and an explanatory paragraph should be added following the opinion paragraph describing the uncertainty with reference to management's disclosures.
- If management's disclosures in the financial statements are considered inadequate by the auditor, there is a departure from GAAP and the auditor should express either a qualified opinion or an adverse opinion and explain the reasons therefor in an explanatory paragraph preceding the opinion paragraph.

From one of the foregoing auditor disclosures, users of audited financial statements should be forewarned about the possible discontinuance of the entity as a going concern. Further consideration is given to SAS 59 in Chapter 20.

LEARNING CHECK:

2-17 To what does the term *expectation gap* refer and how has the Auditing Standards Board responded to it?

2-18 a. Distinguish between the terms *errors* and *irregularities.*
b. How did the auditor's responsibility for detecting errors and irregularities change upon the issuance of SAS 53?

2-19 a. Explain the auditor's responsibility for detecting illegal client acts.
b. Explain the auditor's reporting responsibilities for (1) errors and irregularities and (2) illegal client acts.

2-20 Indicate the alternative circumstances and effects on the auditor's report when the auditor concludes there is substantial doubt about the entity's ability to continue as a going concern for a reasonable period of time beyond the date of the financial statements.

KEY TERMS:

Employee fraud, p. 55
Errors, p. 54
Expectation gap, p. 53
Fraudulent financial reporting, p. 55
Illegal act, p. 56
Irregularities, p. 55
Management fraud, p. 55
Whistle blowing, p. 57

SUMMARY

The relationship between accounting and auditing in the financial reporting process involves a basic division of responsibilities between the management of an entity and its independent auditors. Management is responsible for preparing the statements in conformity with GAAP, and the auditor is responsible for expressing an opinion on the statements based on an audit performed in accordance with GAAS. GAAS are issued by the AICPA's Auditing Standards Board. Users of financial statements look to auditors for assurance that the financial information in the statements meets the qualitative characteristics of relevance and reliability, and that the statements taken as a whole are presented fairly in conformity with GAAP. The auditor's standard report on audited financial statements clearly distinguishes the responsibilities of management and the auditor, explains the character and limitations of an audit, and expresses the auditor's opinion as to whether the statements are presented fairly. Variations of the standard report are used when there are circumstances requiring the addition of explanatory language, or there is a departure from GAAP or a scope limitation. The auditing profession continues to face an expectation gap related to the difference between what users of audited financial statements expect of auditors and the responsibility auditors have been willing or capable of assuming in three areas—detecting and reporting errors and irregularities including fraud, detecting and reporting illegal client acts, and reporting when there is uncertainty about the ability of an entity to continue as a going concern.

BIBLIOGRAPHY

AICPA Professional Standards:

SAS 1 (AU 110), Responsibilities and Functions of the Independent Auditor.

SAS 1 (AU 150), Generally Accepted Auditing Standards.

SAS 53 (AU 316), The Auditor's Responsibility to Detect and Report Errors and Irregularities.

SAS 54 (AU 317), Illegal Acts by Clients.

SAS 58 (AU 508), Reports on Audited Financial Statements.

SAS 59 (AU 341), The Auditor's Consideration of an Entity's Ability to Continue as a Going Concern.

IAU 1 (AU 8001), Objective and Basic Principles Governing an Audit.

IAU 11 (AU 8011), Fraud and Error.

IAU 13 (AU 8013), The Auditor's Report on Financial Statements.

IAU 23 (AU 8023), Going Concern.

IAU 31 (AU 8031), Consideration of Laws and Regulations in an Audit of Financial Statements.

Bowes, Albert J. "The Role of Corporate Audit Committees," *Journal of Accountancy* (October 1987), pp. 151–56.

Carmichael, D. R. "The Auditor's New Guide to Errors, Irregularities, and Illegal Acts," *Journal of Accountancy* (September 1988), pp. 40–48.

Epstein, Marc J., and Geiger, Marshall A. "Recent Evidence of the Expectation Gap," *Journal of Accountancy* (January 1994), pp. 60–66.

Goldstein, J. I., and Dixon, C. "New Teeth for the Public's Watchdog: Expanding the Role of the Independent Accountant in Detecting, Preventing, and Reporting Fraud," *The Business Lawyer* (February 1989), pp. 439–502.

Guy, Dan M., and Sullivan, Gerry D. "The Expectation Gap Auditing Standards," *Journal of Accountancy* (April 1989), pp. 36–46.

Mautz, R. K., and Scharaf, Hussein A. *The Philosophy of Auditing.* Monograph No. 6. Sarasota, FL.: American Accounting Association, 1961. Chapter 3: "The Postulates of Auditing," pp. 37–52.

Neebes, Donald L., Guy, Dan M., and Whittington, O. Ray. "Illegal Acts: What Are the Auditor's Responsibilities?" *Journal of Accountancy* (January 1991), pp. 82–93.

Report of the National Commission on Fraudulent Financial Reporting. Washington, D.C., National Commission on Fraudulent Financial Reporting, 1987.

Vershoor, Curtis C. "Benchmarking the Audit Committee," *Journal of Accountancy* (September 1993), pp. 59–64.

Wallace, Wanda A. *The Economic Role of the Audit in Free and Regulated Markets.* Auditing Monographs. New York: Macmillan, 1985.

OBJECTIVE QUESTIONS

Indicate the *best* answer for each of the following multiple choice questions.

2-21 These questions pertain to basic considerations in financial statement audits.

1. One of the following is not a proper condition that supports the need for an independent audit of financial statements.
   a. Conflict of interest between management and the CPA.
   b. Complexity of the financial statements.
   c. Remoteness of users from the accounting records.
   d. Consequence of the financial statements in the user's decision process.

2. An independent audit aids in the communication of economic data because the audit
   a. Confirms the accuracy of management's financial representations.
   b. Lends credibility to the financial statements.
   c. Guarantees that financial data are fairly presented.
   d. Assures the readers of financial statements that any fraudulent activity has been corrected.

3. To emphasize auditor independence from management, many corporations follow the practice of
   a. Appointing a partner of the CPA firm conducting the examination to the corporation's audit committee.
   b. Establishing a policy of discouraging social contact between employees of the corporation and the staff of the independent auditor.
   c. Requesting that a representative of the independent auditor be on hand at the annual stockholders' meeting.
   d. Having the independent auditor report to an audit committee of outside members of the board of directors.

2-22 These questions involve AICPA auditing standards.

1. Which of the following statements best describes the phrase "generally accepted auditing standards"?
   a. They identify the policies and procedures for the conduct of the audit.
   b. They define the nature and extent of the auditor's responsibilities.
   c. They provide guidance to the auditor with respect to planning the audit and writing the audit report.
   d. They set forth a measure of the quality of the performance of audit procedures.

2. The general group of the generally accepted auditing standards includes a requirement that
   a. The auditor's report state whether or not the financial statements conform to generally accepted accounting principles.
   b. The field work be adequately planned and supervised.
   c. Due professional care be exercised by the auditor.
   d. Informative disclosures in the financial statements be reasonably adequate.

3. Auditing standards differ from auditing procedures in that procedures relate to
   a. Measures of performance.
   b. Audit principles.
   c. Acts to be performed.
   d. Audit judgments.

2-23 These questions relate to the auditor's report.

1. Which of the following representations does an auditor make explicitly and which implicitly when issuing an unqualified opinion?

	Conformity with GAAP	Adequacy of Disclosure
a.	Explicitly	Explicitly
b.	Implicitly	Implicitly
c.	Implicitly	Explicitly
d.	Explicitly	Implicitly

2. When financial statements are presented that are *not* in conformity with generally accepted accounting principles, an auditor may issue a (an)

	Qualified Opinion	Disclaimer of an Opinion
a.	Yes	No
b.	Yes	Yes
c.	No	Yes
d.	No	No

3. How are management's responsibility and the auditor's responsibility represented in the standard auditor's report?

	Management's Responsibility	Auditor's Responsibility
a.	Explicitly	Explicitly
b.	Implicitly	Implicitly
c.	Implicitly	Explicitly
d.	Explicitly	Implicitly

4. The existence of audit risk is recognized by the statement in the auditor's standard report that the auditor
   a. Obtains reasonable assurance about whether the financial statements are free of material misstatement.
   b. Assesses the accounting principles used and also evaluates the overall financial statement presentation.
   c. Realizes some matters, either individually or in the aggregate, are important while other matters are **not** important.
   d. Is responsible for expressing an opinion on the financial statements, which are the responsibility of management.

5. The following explanatory paragraph was included in an auditor's report to indicate a lack of consistency:

   "As discussed in note T to the financial statements, the company changed its method of computing depreciation in 1990."

   How should the auditor report on this matter if the auditor concurred with the change?

Type of Opinion	Location of Explanatory Paragraph
a. Unqualified	Before opinion paragraph
b. Unqualified	After opinion paragraph
c. Qualified	Before opinion paragraph
d. Qualified	After opinion paragraph

2-24 These questions involve the auditor's responsibilities for errors, irregularities, and illegal acts.

1. Which of the following statements concerning illegal acts by clients is correct?
   a. An auditor's responsibility to detect illegal acts that have a direct and material effect on the financial statements is the same as that for errors and irregularities.
   b. An audit in accordance with generally accepted auditing standards normally includes audit procedures specifically designed to detect illegal acts that have an indirect but material effect on the financial statements.
   c. An auditor considers illegal acts from the perspective of the reliability of management's representations rather than their relation to audit objectives derived from financial statement assertions.
   d. An auditor has no responsibility to detect illegal acts by clients that have an indirect effect on the financial statements.

2. Under Statements on Auditing Standards, which of the following would be classified as an error?
   a. Misappropriation of assets for the benefit of management.
   b. Misinterpretation by management of facts that existed when the financial statements were prepared.
   c. Preparation of records by employees to cover a fraudulent scheme.
   d. Intentional omission of the recording of a transaction to benefit a third party.

3. With respect to errors and irregularities, the auditor should plan to
   a. Detect errors that would have a material effect and irregularities that would have either a material or immaterial effect on the financial statements.
   b. Discover irregularities that would have a material effect and errors that would have either a material or immaterial effect on the financial statements.
   c. Detect errors or irregularities that would have a material effect on the financial statements.
   d. Discover errors or irregularities that have either a material or immaterial effect on the financial statements.

4. Which of the following statements describes why a properly designed and executed audit may **not** detect a material irregularity?
   a. Audit procedures that are effective for detecting an unintentional misstatement may be ineffective for an intentional misstatement that is concealed through collusion.
   b. An audit is designed to provide reasonable assurance of detecting material errors, but there is **no** similar responsibility concerning material irregularities.
   c. The factors considered in assessing control risk indicated an increased risk of intentional misstatements, but only a low risk of unintentional errors in the financial statements.
   d. The auditor did **not** consider factors influencing audit risk for account balances that have effects pervasive to the financial statements taken as a whole.

COMPREHENSIVE QUESTIONS

2-25 **(Relationship between accounting and auditing)** Listed below in alphabetical order are the steps that are included in preparing, auditing, and distributing financial statements.

1. Analyze events and transactions.
2. Classify and summarize recorded data.
3. Deliver audit report to client.
4. Distribute financial statements and auditor's report to stockholders in annual report.
5. Express opinion in audit report.
6. Measure and record transaction data.
7. Obtain and evaluate evidence concerning the financial statements.
8. Prepare financial statements per GAAP.
9. Verify statements are presented fairly in conformity with GAAP.

REQUIRED

a. Prepare a diagram of the relationship between accounting and auditing in the preparation and audit of financial statements. Show each of the steps in the proper sequence.
b. Management and the independent auditor share the responsibility for the assertions contained in financial statements. Evaluate and discuss the accuracy of this statement.

2-26 **(Financial statement audits)** The following two statements are representative of attitudes and opinions sometimes encountered by CPAs in their professional practices:

1. Today's audit consists of test checking. This is dangerous because test checking depends on the auditor's judgment, which may be defective. An audit can be relied on only if every transaction is verified.

2. An audit by a CPA is essentially negative and contributes to neither the gross national product nor the general well-being of society. The auditor does not create; he merely checks what someone else has done.

REQUIRED

Evaluate each of the above statements and indicate

a. Areas of agreement with the statement, if any.
b. Areas of misconception, incompleteness, or fallacious reasoning included in the statement, if any.
   Complete your discussion of each statement (both parts a and b) before going on to the next statement.

AICPA *(adapted)*

2-27 **(Management and auditor responsibilities)** Footnotes are important in determining whether the financial statements are presented fairly in accordance with generally accepted accounting principles. Following are two sets of statements concerning footnotes.

1. Student A says that the primary responsibility for the adequacy of disclosure in the financial statements and footnotes rests with the auditor in charge of the audit field work. Student B says that the partner in charge of the engagement has the primary responsibility. Student C says that the staff person who drafts the statements and footnotes has the primary responsibility. Student D contends that it is the client's responsibility.

REQUIRED

Which student is correct?

2. It is important to read the footnotes to financial statements, even though they often are presented in technical language and are incomprehensible. The auditor may reduce his exposure to third-party liability by stating something in the footnotes that contradicts completely what he has presented in the balance sheet or income statement.

REQUIRED

Evaluate the above statement and indicate:

a. Areas of agreement with the statement, if any.
b. Areas of misconception, incompleteness, or fallacious reasoning included in the statements, if any.

AICPA *(adapted)*

2-28 **(Audit committees)** For many years, the financial and accounting community has recognized the importance of the use of audit committees and has endorsed their formation. At this time, the use of audit committees has become widespread. Independent auditors have become increasingly involved with audit committees and consequently have become familiar with their nature and function.

REQUIRED

a. Describe what an audit committee is.
b. Identify the reasons why audit committees have been formed and are currently in operation.
c. What are the functions of an audit committee?

AICPA

2-29 **(Generally accepted auditing standards)** There are ten GAAS. Listed below are statements that relate to these standards.

1. The auditor is careful in doing the audit and writing the audit report.
2. A more experienced auditor supervises the work of an inexperienced auditor.
3. The auditor investigates and reaches conclusions about the client's internal controls.
4. A predesigned schedule is followed during the audit.
5. The auditor is an accounting graduate with several years of experience in auditing.
6. In the auditor's judgment, the financial statements conform to all FASB statements.
7. The auditor is objective and unbiased in performing the audit.
8. The client used the same accounting principles this year as last year.
9. The audit produced all the evidence needed to reach a conclusion about the client's financial statements.
10. The client's notes to the financial statements contain all essential data.
11. The auditor expresses an opinion on the financial statements.

REQUIRED

a. Identify by category and number within each category the GAAS to which each statement relates (i.e., general standard no. 1, field work standard no. 2, etc.).
b. For each answer in (a) above, provide the full statement of the standard. Use the following format for your answers:

Identification of Standard	Statement of Standard

2-30 **(GAAP vs. GAAS)** The auditor's standard report contains the terms *generally accepted auditing standards* and *generally accepted accounting principles.*

REQUIRED

a. Indicate the paragraph(s) of the standard report in which each term appears.
b. Distinguish between the terms.
c. Why is it important that the auditor state that the audited financial statements are in conformity with GAAP?
d. What is the relationship, if any, between *Statements on Auditing Standards* and GAAS?

2-31 **(Auditor's standard report)** The auditor's standard report contains standardized wording. Listed below are the sentences in the standard report.

1. We conducted our audit in accordance with generally accepted auditing standards.
2. We believe that our audit provides a reasonable basis for our opinion.
3. In our opinion, the financial statements referred to above present fairly, in all material respects, the financial position of X Company as of December 31, 19X2 and 19X1, and the results of its operations and its cash flows for the years then ended in conformity with generally accepted accounting principles.
4. We have audited the accompanying balance sheets of X Company as of December 31, 19X2 and 19X1, and the related statements of income, retained earnings, and cash flows for the years then ended.
5. An audit includes examining, on a test basis, evidence supporting the amounts and disclosures in the financial statements.
6. Our responsibility is to express an opinion on these financial statements based on our audits.

7. Those standards require that we plan and perform the audit to obtain reasonable assurance about whether the financial statements are free of material misstatement.
8. An audit also includes assessing the accounting principles used and significant estimates made by management, as well as evaluating the overall financial statement presentation.
9. These financial statements are the responsibility of the Company's management.

REQUIRED

a. Identify the paragraph in which each sentence appears. If there is more than one sentence in the paragraph indicate the sequence of the sentence in the paragraph.
b. State the primary purpose of each of the paragraphs in the standard report.

2-32 **(Departures from standard report)** Circumstances may necessitate a departure from the auditor's standard report.

REQUIRED

a. Indicate the two types of departures from the auditor's standard report.
b. Indicate the effects on the auditor's report when a company makes a change in an accounting principle in conformity with GAAP.
c. State the other types of opinions an auditor may express.
d. Indicate the effects on the auditor's report when the auditor wishes to express a qualified opinion because of nonconformity with GAAP.

2-33 **(Errors and irregularities)** Reed, CPA, accepted an engagement to audit the financial statements of Smith Company. Reed's discussions with Smith's new management and the predecessor auditor indicated the possibility that Smith's financial statements may be misstated due to the possible occurrence of errors, irregularities, and illegal acts.

REQUIRED

a. Identify and describe Reed's responsibilities to detect Smith's errors and irregularities. Do **not** identify specific audit procedures.
b. Identify and describe Reed's responsibilities to report Smith's errors and irregularities.

AICPA (adapted)

2-34 **(Illegal client acts)** During the year under audit, a client may have committed an illegal act.

a. Define the term *illegal act.*
b. What characteristics of illegal acts influence the auditor's responsibilities?
c. The auditor's responsibility for illegal client acts is the same regardless of their effects on the financial statements. Do you agree? Explain.
d. What information during the course of an audit may be indicative of possible illegal acts? How should the auditor respond to this evidence?
e. What are the possible effects of illegal acts on the auditor's report? What other responsibilities does the auditor have to communicate illegal acts to others?

CASES

2-35 **(Generally accepted auditing standards)** Ray, the owner of a small company, asked Holmes, CPA, to conduct an audit of the company's records. Ray told Holmes that an audit is to be completed in time to submit audited financial statements to a bank as a part of a loan application. Holmes immediately accepted the engagement and agreed to provide an auditor's report within three weeks. Ray agreed to pay Holmes a fixed fee plus a bonus if the loan was granted.

Holmes hired two accounting students to conduct the audit and spent several hours telling them exactly what to do. Holmes told the students not to spend time reviewing the controls, but instead to concentrate on proving the mathematical accuracy of the ledger accounts and summarizing the data in the accounting records that support Ray's financial statements. The students followed Holmes's instructions and after two weeks gave Holmes the financial statements that did not include footnotes. Holmes reviewed the statements and prepared an unqualified auditor's report. The report, however, did not refer to generally accepted accounting principles nor to the year-to-year application of such principles.

REQUIRED

Briefly describe each of the generally accepted auditing standards and indicate how the action(s) of Holmes resulted in a failure to comply with *each* standard. Organize your answer as follows:

Brief Description of Generally Accepted Auditing Standards	Holmes's Actions Resulting in Failure to Comply with Generally Accepted Auditing Standards

AICPA

2-36 **(Detection of fraud)** Several years ago, Dale Holden organized Holden Family Restaurants. Holden started with one restaurant that catered to the family trade. Holden's first restaurant became very popular because the quality of the food and service was excellent, the restaurant was attractive yet modest, and the prices were reasonable.

The success with his first restaurant encouraged Dale Holden to expand by opening additional Holden Family Restaurants in other metropolitan locations throughout the state. Holden has opened at least one new restaurant each year for the last five years, and there are now a total of eight restaurants. All of the restaurants are successful because Holden has been able to maintain the same high standards that were achieved with the original restaurant.

With the rapid expansion of business, Holden has hired a controller and supporting staff. The financial operations of the restaurants are managed by the controller and his department. This allows Holden to focus his attention on the restaurant operations and plan for future locations.

Holden has applied to the bank for additional financing to open another restaurant this year. For the first time ever, the bank asked him to provide financial statements audited by a CPA. The bank assured Holden that the certified statements were not being required because it doubted his integrity or thought him to be a poor credit risk. The loan officer explained that bank policy required all businesses over a certain size to supply audited statements with loan applications, and Holden's business had reached that size.

Holden was not surprised by the bank's requirement. He had ruled out an audit previously because he has great respect for his controller's ability, and he wanted to avoid the fee associated with the first audit as long as possible. However, the growth of his business and the increased number of restaurant locations make an audit a sound business requirement. He also believes that an additional benefit of the independent audit will be the probable detection of any fraud which may be occurring at his restaurants.

To fulfill the bank request for audited statements, Dale Holden has hired Hill & Associates, CPAs.

REQUIRED

a. Hill & Associates has been hired to perform an audit leading to the expression of an opinion on Holden Family Restaurant's financial statements. Discuss Hill & Associates' responsibility for the detection of fraud in a general-purpose audit.

b. What effect, if any, would the detection of fraud during the audit of Holden Family Restaurants by Hill & Associates have on their expression of an opinion on the financial statements? Give the reasons for your answer.

CMA (adapted)

RESEARCH QUESTIONS

2-37 **(Professional standards)** In this chapter you were introduced to the *Statements on Auditing Standards* that are issued by the AICPA's Auditing Standards Board. Using your school's library or computer lab, obtain access to the SASs through one of the printed or electronic media described in the chapter. Acquaint yourself with the body of standards by scanning the table of contents and browsing through a part of the full text of the standards. Then, using the table of contents, topical index, or electronic search facility, locate the relevant section of the professional standards for each of the following items. For each item, briefly summarize the pertinent information from the professional standards and give an appropriate citation of the source. For example, the citation for the illustrated form of the auditor's standard report on financial statements may be given as either SAS No. 58, paragraph .08 (SAS 58.08) or AU Section No. 508, paragraph .08 (AU 508.08). If you are using an electronic version of the standards and your facility permits printing selected text, you may elect to print pertinent sections (usually not more than one or two paragraphs) rather than summarizing them. However, be sure to add a proper citation if it is not included on your printout.

a. The chapter emphasized that there is a distinction between the responsibilities of management and the independent auditor in financial reporting, and noted that this distinction is explicitly stated in the introductory paragraph to the auditor's standard report. Where else is this distinction officially recognized in the auditing standards?

b. In this chapter, you were introduced to the generally accepted auditing standards. In Chapter 1, you were informed about quality control standards. How does the Auditing Standards Board view the relationship between GAAS and the quality control standards?

c. A change in accounting principle made in accordance with GAAP is one example of a circumstance when explanatory language should be added to the auditor's standard report. The Auditing Standards Board identified a number of other circumstances when this type of reporting is appropriate. What are they?

d. The concept of *professional skepticism* was introduced in this chapter and is identified in the professional literature as bearing directly on the auditor's responsibility for detecting errors and irregularities. What guidance has the Auditing Standards Board provided to auditors about management's selection of accounting policies when circumstances suggest there is a significant risk of management intentionally distorting financial statements?

e. When conditions and events cause the auditor to have substantial doubt as to an entity's ability to continue as a going concern, the auditor should inquire about any plans management may have to mitigate the conditions or events. Such plans may in turn alleviate the doubt about the entity's going concern status. Name four types of management plans that may be relevant to the auditor's consideration of this matter.

f. The auditor's standard report varies from country to country. In fact, the unqualified report form recommended in the international auditing standards is quite different from the auditor's standard report under U.S. GAAS. Summarize the differences between the two recommended unqualified report forms.

2-38 **(Whistleblowing legislation)** It was noted in the chapter that in recent years several "whistleblowing" bills had been introduced in the U.S. Congress that would require the auditor to report actual or suspected fraud and other illegal activities by clients. Determine whether any such bills were passed subsequent to January 1, 1994, or are currently pending. Give a proper citation for any such bill and a description of the precise responsibilities specified for the auditor.

2-39 **(AAER)** The SEC's *Accounting and Auditing Enforcement Releases (AAERs)* describe cases of fraudulent financial reporting. In some of these cases, the SEC takes enforcement action against the auditors upon finding they failed to meet professional standards. One such case is described in *AAER No.* 274.

a. Who were the parties involved in this case, what was the major accounting problem, and how, in the SEC's view, did the auditors fail to meet professional standards?
b. What might have alerted the auditor to the problem that subsequently came to light?
c. What action was taken against the auditor?

CHAPTER

3

PROFESSIONAL ETHICS

ETHICS AND MORALITY
- General Ethics
- Professional Ethics

AICPA CODE OF PROFESSIONAL CONDUCT
- AICPA Professional Ethics Division
- Composition of the AICPA Code
- Code Definitions
- Principles

RULES OF CONDUCT
- Rule 101—Independence
- Rule 102—Integrity and Objectivity
- Rule 201—General Standards
- Rule 202—Compliance with Standards
- Rule 203—Accounting Principles
- Rule 301—Confidential Client Information
- Rule 302—Contingent Fees
- Rule 501—Acts Discreditable
- Rule 502—Advertising and Other Forms of Solicitation
- Rule 503—Commissions and Referral Fees
- Rule 505—Form of Organization and Name

ENFORCEMENT OF THE RULES
- Joint Ethics Enforcement Procedures
- Joint Trial Board Procedures
- Automatic Disciplinary Provisions

SUMMARY

BIBLIOGRAPHY

OBJECTIVE QUESTIONS

COMPREHENSIVE QUESTIONS

CASES

RESEARCH QUESTIONS

LEARNING OBJECTIVES

After studying this chapter, you should be able to

1. Explain the nature of general ethics.
2. State the purpose of professional ethics.
3. Describe the components of the AICPA's *Code of Professional Conduct* and related pronouncements.
4. Define terms essential to understanding the applicability of the Code.
5. Identify and state the essence of the Code's six ethical principles.
6. Identify and state the essence of the Code's eleven rules of conduct.
7. State the organizations and procedures involved in enforcing the rules of conduct.

One of the distinguishing characteristics of any profession is the existence of a code of professional conduct or ethics for its members. In Chapter 1, we noted that the AICPA, state societies of CPAs, and state boards of accountancy are all involved in establishing and enforcing codes of ethics. It was also noted that these activities constitute an important part of the profession's multilevel regulatory framework.

But ethical behavior requires consideration of more than a few rules of conduct and regulatory activities. No professional code of ethics or regulatory framework can anticipate all the situations that might arise requiring personal judgments about ethical behavior. Accordingly, we begin this chapter with a brief discussion of general ethics before moving on to the subject of professional ethics. We then examine the AICPA's *Code of Professional Conduct* in considerable detail. The chapter concludes with a discussion of the ethics enforcement procedures used by the AICPA and state societies of CPAs.

ETHICS AND MORALITY

Ethics is derived from the Greek word *ethos,* meaning "character." Another name for ethics is **morality** which comes from the Latin *mores,* meaning "custom." Morality focuses on the "right" and "wrong" of human behavior. Thus, ethics deals with questions about how people act towards one another. Philosophers and ethicists have developed numerous theories of ethical conduct.

GENERAL ETHICS

OBJECTIVE 1

Explain the nature of general ethics.

People are constantly confronted with the need to make choices that have consequences both for themselves and others. Too often, an **ethical dilemma** arises wherein what is good for one party affected by the choice is not good for another party affected by the choice. It has been said that in such situations, individuals should ask two questions: "What good do I seek?" and "What is my obligation in this circumstance?"

General ethics attempts to deal with these questions by defining what is good for the individual and society, and by trying to establish the nature of obligations or duties that individuals owe themselves and each other. But inability to agree on what "good" and "obligation" are has led philosophers to divide into two groups. One group, the *ethical absolutists,* says there are universal standards that do not change over time that apply to everyone. The other group, the *ethical relativists,* says that people's ethical judgments are determined by the changing customs and traditions of the society in which they live. Some argue that both are right—that every individual makes numerous life choices that must be guided by unchanging universal standards, and many other choices that are subject to the changing mores of society.

Because no universal set of standards or changing code of ethics can clearly point to the correct choice of behavior in all situations, some ethicists have worked on developing frameworks for general ethical decision making. Following is one such six-step framework:

- Obtain the facts relevant to the decision.
- Identify the ethical issues from the facts.
- Determine who will be affected by the decision and how.
- Identify the decision maker's alternatives.
- Identify the consequences of each alternative.
- Make the ethical choice.

PROFESSIONAL ETHICS

OBJECTIVE 2

State the purpose of professional ethics.

Professional ethics must extend beyond moral principles. They include standards of behavior for a professional person that are designed for both practical and idealistic purposes. While professional codes of ethics may be designed in part to encourage ideal behavior, they must be both realistic and enforceable. To be meaningful, they should be above the law but below the ideal.

Professional ethics are imposed by a profession on its members who voluntarily accept standards of professional behavior more rigorous than those required by law. A code of ethics significantly affects the reputation of a profession and the confidence in which it is held. Professional ethics evolve over time and continue to be in the process of change as the practice of public accounting changes.

The following preamble in the AICPA's Code of Professional Conduct emphasizes the importance of ethical standards for CPAs.

Membership in the American Institute of Certified Public Accountants is voluntary. By accepting membership, a certified public accountant assumes an obligation of self-discipline above and beyond the requirements of laws and regulations.

The Principles of the Code of Professional Conduct of the American Institute of Certified Public Accountants express the profession's recognition of its responsibilities to the public, to clients, and to colleagues. They guide members in the performance of their professional responsibilities and express the basic tenets of ethical and professional conduct. The Principles call for an unswerving commitment to honorable behavior, even at the sacrifice of personal advantage.

LEARNING CHECK:

3-1 How does general ethics guide human behavior?
3-2 What is the difference between the ethical absolutists and ethical relativists schools of thought?
3-3 What are the six steps in a general framework for ethical decision making?
3-4 a. What is the purpose of professional ethics?
b. How are professional ethics imposed?

KEY TERMS:

Ethical dilemma, p. 71
Ethics, p. 70
General ethics, p. 71
Morality, p. 70
Professional ethics, p. 71

AICPA CODE OF PROFESSIONAL CONDUCT

We now turn our attention to the AICPA's *Code of Professional Conduct* which is administered by the Institute's Professional Ethics Division.

AICPA PROFESSIONAL ETHICS DIVISION

The bylaws of the AICPA provide that there shall be a Professional Ethics Division. This division is headed by a director, who is responsible to the vice president of regulation and review of the AICPA. The division consists of a relatively small full-time staff, active volunteer members, and ad hoc investigatory volunteers, as needed. The division functions through an executive committee, which also serves as the Professional Ethics Committee of the AICPA, and three subcommittees. The executive committee is responsible for

- Planning the programs of the division's subcommittees and supervising their implementation.
- Issuing formal policy statements and pronouncements.
- Establishing *prima facie* violations of the Code or bylaws for possible disciplinary action.
- Proposing changes in the Code.

FIGURE 3-1 • CODE SECTIONS AND RELATED PRONOUNCEMENTS Test

	Component	Nature	Enforceable?
Code Section:	Principles	Express the basic tenets of ethical conduct and provide the framework for the Rules.	No
	Rules of Conduct	Establish minimum standards of acceptable conduct in the performance of professional services.	Yes
Related Pronouncement:	Interpretations of Rules of Conduct	Provide guidelines about the scope and applicability of specific rules.	No, but the CPA must justify any departures.
	Ethics Rulings	Indicate the applicability of the Rules and Interpretations to particular factual circumstances.	No, but the CPA must justify any departures.

COMPOSITION OF THE AICPA CODE

OBJECTIVE 3

Describe the components of the AICPA's Code of Professional Conduct and related pronouncements.

There are two sections in the AICPA's **Code of Professional Conduct** as revised and adopted by the membership of 1988:

- **Principles** that express the basic tenets of ethical conduct and provide the framework for the Rules.
- **Rules of Conduct** that establish minimum standards of acceptable conduct in the performance of professional services.

As expressions of ideals of professional conduct, the Principles are not set forth as enforceable standards. In contrast, the Rules of Conduct establish minimum standards of acceptable conduct and are enforceable.

In addition to these two sections of the Code, the Professional Ethics Division's Executive Committee issues the following pronouncements:

- **Interpretations of the Rules of Conduct** that provide guidelines about the scope and applicability of specific rules.
- **Ethics Rulings** that indicate the applicability of the Rules of Conduct and Interpretations to a particular set of factual circumstances.

Members who depart from the Interpretations or Ethics Rulings must justify such departures in disciplinary hearings. A summary of the Code sections and related pronouncements is shown in Figure 3-1.

CODE DEFINITIONS

OBJECTIVE 4

Define terms essential to understanding the applicability of the Code.

The Code is written in technical language. Knowledge of the following **code definitions** is essential to understanding the applicability of the Code's Principles and Rules:

Client. Any person or entity, other than the member's employer, that engages a member or a member's firm to perform professional services or a person or entity with respect to which professional services are performed.

Council. The Council of the AICPA.

Enterprise. Synonymous with the term "client."

Firm. A form of organization permitted by state law or regulation whose characteristics conform to resolutions of Council that is engaged in the practice of public accounting, including the individual owners thereof.

Institute. The AICPA.

Member. A member, associate member, or international associate of the AICPA.

Practice of public accounting. Performance for a client, by a member or a member's firm, while holding out as CPA(s), of the professional services of accounting, tax, personal financial planning, litigation support services, and those professional services for which standards are promulgated by bodies designated by Council. However, a member or a member's firm, while holding out as CPA(s), is not considered to be in the practice of public accounting if the member or the member's firm does not perform, for any client, any of the professional services described above.

Professional services. All services performed by a CPA while holding out as a CPA.

Holding out. Any action initiated by a member that informs others of his or her status as a CPA or AICPA accredited specialist.

PRINCIPLES

OBJECTIVE 5

Identify and state the essence of the Code's six ethical principles.

In the Code, the six principles are identified as follows:

- Responsibilities
- The public interest.
- Integrity
- Objectivity and independence.
- Due care.
- Scope and nature of services.

The statement of each principle and a brief explanation are given below.

Responsibilities

In carrying out their responsibilities as professionals, members should exercise sensitive professional and moral judgments in all their activities.[1]

CPAs render important and essential services in our free enterprise system. All members have responsibilities to those who use their professional services. In addition, members have an ongoing responsibility to cooperate with other members to (1) improve the art of accounting, (2) maintain the public's confidence in the profession, and (3) carry out the self-regulatory activities described in this chapter. The overall objective in meeting this principle is to maintain and enhance the stature of the public accounting profession.

---

[1] All definitions of principles and rules are from applicable ethics sections of *AICPA Professional Standards,* Volume 2 (New York: AICPA, 1993).

The Public Interest

> Members should accept the obligation to act in a way that will serve the public interest, honor the public trust, and demonstrate commitment to professionalism.

The public interest is defined as the collective well-being of the community of people and institutions that CPAs serve. The CPA's public interest includes clients, credit grantors, governmental agencies, employees, stockholders, and the general public. A distinguishing mark of a profession is acceptance of its responsibility to the public.

CPAs are expected to meet both quality and professional standards in all engagements. In serving the public interest, members should conduct themselves in a manner that clearly shows a level of professionalism consistent with the principles of the Code.

Integrity

> To maintain and broaden public confidence, members should perform all professional responsibilities with the highest sense of integrity.

Integrity is a personal characteristic that is indispensable in a CPA. This element is the benchmark by which members must ultimately judge all decisions made in an engagement. Integrity is also the quality on which public trust is based.

In meeting this principle, members must be honest and candid. Integrity can allow an inadvertent error and genuine differences of opinion. However, it cannot tolerate intentional distortion of facts or subordination of judgment.

Objectivity and Independence

> A member should maintain objectivity and be free of conflicts of interest in discharging professional responsibilities. A member in public practice should be independent in fact and appearance when providing auditing and other attestation services.

Objectivity is a state of mind. Although this principle is not precisely measurable, it nevertheless is held up to members as an imperative. Objectivity means being impartial and unbiased in all matters pertaining to an engagement. Adherence to this principle is enhanced when members avoid circumstances that involve conflicts of interest. For example, having an ownership interest in a client might impair a member's objectivity in auditing the client.

Independence is the cornerstone of the profession's philosophical structure. No matter how competent CPAs may be in performing auditing and other attestation services, their opinions will be of little value to those who rely on their reports unless they are independent. In rendering these services, members must be independent in fact. This means members should act with integrity and objectivity. Members must also be independent in appearance. To meet this test, members should not have a financial interest or a key business relationship with the client. For example, CPAs should not be part of management or serve on the board of directors. Members in public practice should continuously assess their relationships with clients to avoid situations that may impair their independence.

Due Care

A member should observe the profession's technical and ethical standards, strive continually to improve competence and the quality of services, and discharge professional responsibility to the best of the member's ability.

The principle of due care is at the center of the profession's ongoing quest for excellence in the performance of professional services. Due care requires each member to discharge his or her professional responsibilities with competence and diligence.

Competence is the product of education and experience. Education begins with preparation for entry into the profession. It extends to continuing professional education throughout a member's career. Experience involves on-the-job training and acceptance of increased responsibilities during a member's professional life.

Diligence involves steady, earnest, and energetic application and effort in performing professional services. Moreover, it means that a member should (1) be thorough in his or her work, (2) observe applicable technical and ethical standards, and (3) complete the service promptly.

Due care extends to the planning and supervision of engagements for which a member is responsible. For example, each member is expected to properly supervise any assistants participating in the engagement.

Scope and Nature of Services

A member in public practice should observe the Principles of the Code of Professional Conduct in determining the scope and nature of services to be provided.

This principle applies only to a member who renders services to the public. In deciding whether to provide specific services in a given situation, a member should consider all of the preceding principles. If any principle cannot be met, the engagement should be declined.

In addition, a member should

- Practice only in a firm that has implemented internal quality control procedures.
- Determine whether the scope and nature of other services requested by an audit client would create a conflict of interest in providing auditing services for that client.
- Assess whether the requested service is consistent with the role of a professional.

LEARNING CHECK:

3-5 What are the responsibilities of the AICPA's Professional Ethics Division?

3-6 a. Identify the two sections of the AICPA's Code of Professional Conduct and the two types of pronouncements related to them.
b. Explain the enforceability of each of the sections and related pronouncements.

3-7 a. What is the meaning of the term "practice of public accounting?"
b. What is the meaning of the term "holding out?"

3-8 a. What is the significance of the Principles of the AICPA's Code?
b. State the essence of the six principles in the Code.

KEY TERMS:

Code definitions, p. 73
Code of Professional Conduct, p. 73
Ethics rulings, p. 73
Interpretations of the Rules of Conduct, p. 73
Principles, p. 73
Rules of Conduct, p. 73

RULES OF CONDUCT

OBJECTIVE 6

Identify and state the essence of the Code's eleven rules of conduct.

The second section of the AICPA's *Code of Professional Conduct* consists of 11 enforceable rules, as categorized and listed in Figure 3-2. In formulating the rules, the AICPA strives to serve the best interests of its members, the profession, and the public. The rules are modified from time to time to recognize evolving norms of ethical conduct and other influences such as changes mandated by government agencies. For example, the gap in the numbering system for the rules resulted from the elimination of several rules in the 400s that dealt with responsibilities to colleagues. These rules were dropped because ultimately they were thought to be too self-serving and in some cases had been challenged by the federal government as an unwarranted restraint on competition. Several instances of additional changes mandated by the government to eliminate practices deemed to restrain trade are explained below.

The bylaws of the AICPA require that members adhere to the Rules of Conduct. The Rules are applicable to all members and to all professional services performed except when (1) the wording of the rule indicates otherwise (e.g., several rules indicate they pertain only to members in public practice), and (2) a member is practicing outside the United States and conforms to the rules of the organized accounting profession of the host country.

FIGURE 3-2 • RULES OF CONDUCT

Section/Rule	Applicability: All Members	Applicability: Members in Public Practice
Section 100. Independence, Integrity, and Objectivity		
101 Independence		✓
102 Integrity and Objectivity	✓	
Section 200. General Standards and Accounting Principles		
201 General Standards	✓	
202 Compliance with Standards	✓	
203 Accounting Principles	✓	
Section 300. Responsibilities to Clients		
301 Confidential Client Information		✓
302 Contingent Fees		✓
Section 400. Responsibilities to Colleagues (No currently effective rules in this section.)		
Section 500. Other Responsibilities and Practices		
501 Acts Discreditable	✓	
502 Advertising and Other Forms of Solicitation		✓
503 Commissions and Referral Fees		✓
505 Form of Organization and Name		✓

A member in public practice may be held responsible for compliance with the rules of all persons under the member's supervision or who are the member's partners or shareholders in the practice. In addition, a member cannot permit others to carry out acts in his or her behalf that, if carried out by the member, would violate the rules.

The statement of each rule and an explanation of its essential features are given in the following sections.

RULE 101—INDEPENDENCE

> A member in public practice shall be independent in the performance of professional services as required by standards promulgated by bodies designated by Council.

This rule incorporates into the Code, by reference, the independence requirements in technical standards issued by the AICPA. The bodies which have issued standards that include a requirement that the CPA be independent are the Auditing Standards Board and the Accounting and Review Services Committee. For example, a member must be independent in performing attest services such as a financial statement audit (as per SAS 1), an examination of prospective financial statements (as per SSAE 1), and a review of the financial statements of a nonpublic entity (as per SSARS 1). A member is not required to be independent in rendering nonattest services such as accounting, tax, and management consulting services.

There are currently eleven published interpretations pertaining to Rule 101. In issuing interpretations on independence, the AICPA uses the criterion of whether reasonable persons, having knowledge of all the facts and taking into consideration normal strength of character and behavior under the circumstances, would conclude that a specified relationship between a CPA and a client is an unacceptable threat to the CPA's independence.

Interpretation 101-1

When Rule 101 was adopted, it was issued with the following initial interpretation (as revised). Note that the interpretation has two major parts—Part A which deals with prohibited *financial interests* related to a client, and Part B which deals with *other business relationships* with a client that are prohibited.

> Interpretation 101-1. Independence shall be considered to be impaired if, for example, a member had any of the following transactions, interests, or relationships:
>
> A. During the period of a professional engagement or at the time of expressing an opinion, a member or a member's firm
>   1. Had or was committed to acquire any direct or material indirect financial interest in the enterprise.
>   2. Was a trustee of any trust or executor or administrator of any estate if such trust or estate had or was committed to acquire any direct or material indirect financial interest in the enterprise.
>   3. Had any joint, closely held business investment with the enterprise or with any officer, director, or principal stockholders thereof that was material in relation to the member's net worth or to the net worth of the member's firm.
>   4. Had any loan to or from the enterprise or any officer, director, or principal stockholder of the enterprise except as specifically permitted in interpretation 101-5.
>
> B. During the period covered by the financial statements, during the period of the professional engagement, or at the time of expressing an opinion, a member or a member's firm
>   1. Was connected with the enterprise as a promoter, underwriter, or voting trustee, as a director or officer, or in any capacity equivalent to that of a member of management or of an employee.
>   2. Was a trustee for any pension or profit-sharing trust of the enterprise.
>
> The above examples are not intended to be all-inclusive.

PART A—FINANCIAL INTERESTS. The prohibitions on financial interest are very explicit. First, under A(1), the member or member's firm cannot have (or be committed to have) any *direct financial interest* in the client. The prohibition against a direct financial interest is absolute. Thus, a member may not directly own or have an option to buy even one share of stock in the client. For purposes of this interpretation, ownership of stock in a client through an investment club is considered to be a direct financial interest. An *indirect financial interest* exists, for example, when (1) a member or the member's firm owns stock in a mutual fund that, in turn, owns stock in the client or (2) a member's nondependent close relative has a financial interest in the client. The restriction against indirect financial interest is based on materiality. Independence is impaired in the foregoing examples only if the mutual fund's holdings in the client are extensive, or the relative's financial interest is material to his or her own net worth, *and the member has knowl-*

edge of the interest. Further consideration of the effects of financial interests held by other family members is presented in a later section.

Second, under A(3), a member is not allowed to have a joint, closely held business investment with a client company or officers, directors, or principal stockholders of such enterprise that is material to either the member's or the firm's net assets. Such a situation would exist when the CPA and an officer of the client each contributed a third of the capital needed to finance a joint investment, if the amounts were material.

Third, under A(4), a member is not permitted to have any loan to or from a client, or its officers, directors, or principal stockholders except as specifically permitted under *Interpretation 101-5.* The latter permits exceptions for two categories of loans when such loans (1) have been obtained from a financial institution client for whom services are performed requiring independence, (2) are obtained under normal lending procedures, terms, and requirements, and (3) are kept current as to all terms at all times. The two exception categories are:

- **Grandfathered loans** that were permitted and obtained under rules in effect before January 1, 1992, for
  - Home mortgages.
  - Other secured loans for which the value of collateral equals or exceeds the balance of the loan at all times.
  - Loans not material to the member's net worth.
- **Personal loans** as follows:
  - Automobile loans and leases collateralized by the automobile.
  - Loans of the surrender value under terms of an insurance policy.
  - Borrowings fully collaterized by cash deposits at the same financial institution (e.g., passbook loans).
  - Credit cards and cash advances on checking accounts with an aggregate balance not paid currently of $5,000 or less.

PART B—OTHER BUSINESS RELATIONSHIPS. Note that among the other business relationships prohibited in this part of *Interpretation 101-1,* a member may not serve in any capacity as a member of management or as an employee of the client without impairing independence. Applying this part of the interpretation is more complex when the CPA has a family member who has an *other business relationship* with the client as discussed further in a later section.

TIME PERIODS. It should be noted that the time periods to which the Part A and Part B prohibitions apply are not identical. Three time periods are identified in the interpretation:

- The period of the professional engagement, which starts when the member begins to perform professional services requiring independence for a client, and ends with the member's or client's notification of the termination of that relationship.
- The time of expressing an opinion (or other form of assurance), which is the date of the member's report.
- The period covered by the financial statements, which is usually the client's fiscal year.

Note that the prohibitions pertaining to financial interests (Part A) relate to just the first two time periods identified above. In contrast, the prohibitions pertaining to other business relationships (Part B) relate to all three time periods. Thus, the following circumstances might apply to a prospective new client who approaches a member in June about doing the audit for the year ending the following December 31. If the member owned stock in the prospective client for all or any part of the current fiscal year prior to beginning work on the engagement, independence would not be impaired provided the stock were sold prior to beginning work on the audit. This is because disposal of the financial interest prior to beginning the audit would eliminate any bias or impairment of objectivity related to the financial interest. However, if the auditor served, for example, as a director, member of management, or employee of the client during any part of the period covered by the financial statements to be audited, independence would be impaired, and the impairment would not be resolved by terminating the relationship prior to beginning work on the audit. The reason for this is that even if the relationship is terminated, the member would still be auditing and reporting on the results of decisions he or she participated in during part of the year while serving in one of those capacities. In such case, it is unlikely that the member would be unbiased, and in any case, would not appear to be independent to others.

MEANING OF PHRASE "MEMBER OR MEMBER'S FIRM." Both Parts A and B of *Interpretation 101-1* use the phrase *member or member's firm* in identifying whose financial and business relationships are prohibited. According to *Interpretation 101-9*, the expression **member or member's firm** includes all of the following:

- All individuals (of any rank) participating in the engagement, except those who perform only routine clerical functions, such as typing and photocopying.
- All individuals with a managerial position located in an office participating in a significant portion of the engagement (e.g., the director of human resources).
- All proprietors, partners, or shareholders of the member's firm, whether or not participating in the engagement.
- Any entity (for example, a partnership, corporation, trust, joint venture, or pool) whose operating, financial, or accounting policies can be controlled by one or more of the persons described above or by two or more such persons if they choose to act together.

For all purposes of complying with Rule 101, the phrase *member or member's firm* includes not only the individuals named in the above groups, but also their spouses (whether or not dependent) and all of their dependents (whether or not related). Thus, for example, just as a member participating in an engagement requiring independence cannot have a direct or material indirect financial interest in the client, neither can that member's spouse or dependent have such an interest. The effects of a client's employment of spouses and dependents is explained further below.

According to *Interpretation 101-9*, the phrase *member or member's firm* does not include *nondependent* close relatives such as children, siblings, grandparents, parents, or parents-in-law. Nevertheless, the interpretation states that the independence of a member or a member's firm can be impaired because of the financial and business relationships of such relatives. For example, this would be the case if during the time periods specified in Part A of *Interpretation 101-1,* a close relative held a financial interest in a client that was both material to the relative and known to the member.

Interpretation 101-9 indicates that employment of a member's relatives by a client during the time periods specified in Part B of *Interpretation 101-1* impairs independence only in the following circumstances:

- **AUDIT-SENSITIVE POSITION.** A spouse, dependent, or nondependent close relative has a position with the client involving activities that are audit-sensitive (i.e., a position that is subject to, or an element of, significant internal accounting controls, such as cashier, internal auditor, accounting supervisor, purchasing agent, or inventory warehouse supervisor). This prohibition pertains only to said relatives of members participating in the engagement.
- **SIGNIFICANT INFLUENCE.** A spouse, dependent, or nondependent close relative has a position with the client that allows significant influence over the client's operating, financial, or accounting policies (e.g., qualifying positions include director, or chief executive, operating, financial, or accounting officer). This prohibition pertains to said relatives of (1) any member participating in the engagement, and (2) any proprietor, partner, or shareholder who is located in an office participating in a significant portion of the engagement. With respect to spouses and dependents only, the prohibition extends to any proprietor, partner or shareholder in any office who has the ability to exercise influence over the engagement, or has any other involvement with the engagement (for example, consultation on accounting or auditing issues).

Clearly, these interpretations indicate the profession goes to great lengths to ensure the independence of members who perform attest services. A summary of important considerations in complying with *Interpretation 101-1,* including family relationships, is presented in Figure 3-3.

Other Independence Matters

Several other important matters that bear on a member's independence are not specifically covered in Rule 101. These include the effects of (1) performing accounting services for attest clients, (2) management consulting services, (3) litigation, and (4) unpaid fees due from clients.

ACCOUNTING SERVICES. A CPA who performs manual or automated bookkeeping services for an attest client must meet the following requirements to retain the appearance that he or she is not an employee, and therefore lacking in independence, in the eyes of a reasonable observer:

- The CPA must not have any other relationships, such as a financial interest, which would impair his or her integrity and objectivity.
- The client must accept full responsibility for its financial statements.
- The CPA must not assume the role either of an employee or management in the client's operations (e.g., the CPA should not initiate transactions or sign checks).
- The CPA must conform to GAAS in performing the audit.

FIGURE 3-3 • APPLICATION OF INTERPRETATION 101-1 (INCLUDING FAMILY RELATIONSHIPS)

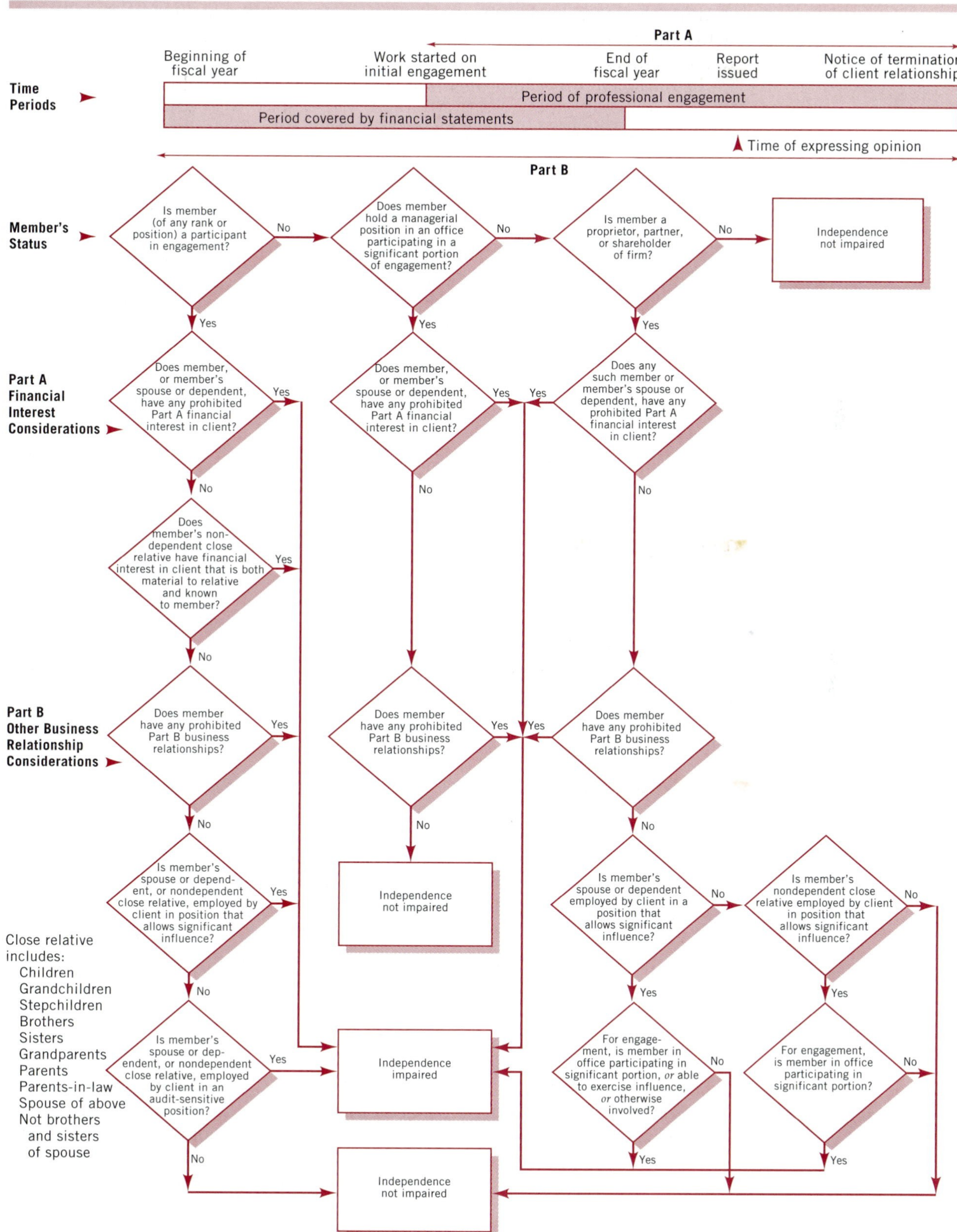

Although meeting the above requirements will avoid violating the AICPA's Rule 101, a CPA is precluded by SEC regulations from performing any accounting services for clients for whom attest services are provided in connection with SEC filings.

MANAGEMENT CONSULTING SERVICES (MCS). Concern has been expressed in some segments of government and academia that the rendering of MCS to an audit client by the client's auditor impairs the auditor's independence. This position is based on the belief that the auditor would be reviewing his or her own work and might be biased in doing so.

The AICPA has consistently maintained that MCS are entirely compatible with independence as long as the CPA serves only as an adviser to management in making the business decision. If the auditor is the decision maker, audit independence is impaired because the auditor would then be acting in "a capacity equivalent to that of a member of management."

To date, there have been no known instances when MCS have compromised independence. However, a CPA firm is required to refrain from performing the following MCS for its SEC audit clients:

- Psychological testing.
- Public opinion polls.
- Merger and acquisition assistance for a finder's fee.
- Executive recruitment.
- Actuarial services to insurance companies.

LITIGATION. Litigation involving CPAs and their clients raises questions about a member's independence. In general, independence is impaired whenever the existence or expressed threat of litigation has significantly altered, or is expected to materially change, the normal relationship between a client and a CPA. Litigation that results in an adversary position between a client and a CPA, or which links management and the CPA as co-conspirators in withholding information from stockholders, would impair the CPA's independence. In contrast, litigation brought by stockholders against a CPA would not necessarily affect independence.

UNPAID FEES. The existence of unpaid fees for professional services has been deemed to assume the characteristics of a loan from the member to the client within the meaning of Rule 101 and its interpretations. Therefore, independence of the member's firm is considered to be impaired if, when the CPA's report on the client's current year is issued, fees remain unpaid, whether billed or unbilled, for professional services provided more than one year prior to the date of the report. This ruling does not apply to fees outstanding from a client in bankruptcy.

Examples of additional circumstances dealt with in other interpretations and ethics rulings on independence are presented in Figure 3-4.

RULE 102—INTEGRITY AND OBJECTIVITY

> In the performance of any professional service, a member shall maintain objectivity and integrity, shall be free of conflicts of interest, and shall not knowingly misrepresent facts or subordinate his or her judgment to others.

FIGURE 3-4 • ILLUSTRATIVE INTERPRETATIONS AND ETHICS RULINGS ON INDEPENDENCE

FINANCIAL INTERESTS OR ASSOCIATIONS OF A MEMBER OR A MEMBER'S FIRM DEEMED TO RESULT IN INDEPENDENCE BEING

Impaired	Not Impaired
Direct financial interest in a partnership that invests in member's client [Interpretation 101-8 (ET 101.10)]	Purely honorary position held as director or trustee of not-for-profit client when clearly so indicated in entity's literature and member does not vote or participate in management functions [Interpretation 101-1 (ET 101.03)]
Acceptance of more than a token gift from a client [Ethics Ruling 1 (ET 191.002)]	Transactions, interests, or relationships of former practitioners (1) to whom any continuing payments by the firm are fixed as to amount and date and (2) who do not participate in the firm's business or professional activities [Interpretation 101-2 (ET 104.04)]
Stock owned in client public corporation and put in trust created as an education fund for member's minor son [Ethics Ruling 26 (ET 191.052)]	Membership held in a trade association which is a client but member does not serve in a management capacity.
Membership held in investment club which holds shares in a client company [Ethics Ruling 36 (ET 191.072)]	Immaterial stock ownership in a bank from which a client has borrowings [Ethics Ruling 13 (ET 191.026)]
Attorney/CPA providing legal services as general counsel for auditing client [Ethics Ruling 51 (ET 191.102)]	Service as director or treasurer of a local United Fund that distributes funds to, but does not exercise management control over, a client entity [Ethics Ruling 14 (ET 191.028)]
Direct financial interest in a client organization held in a blind trust [Ethics Ruling 68 (ET 191.137)]	Membership in client country club in which membership requirements involve ownership of a pro rata share of the club's equity or debt securities [Ethics Ruling 17 (ET 191.034)]

This rule extends to all professional services and to all members. For example, in dealing with his or her employer's external accountant, a member in industry must be candid and not knowingly misrepresent facts or knowingly fail to disclose material facts. Furthermore, if a member in industry or in public practice has a disagreement or dispute with a supervisor relating to an accounting or auditing issue that is of significance to the financial statements or auditor's report, the member should take steps to ensure that the situation does not constitute a subordination of judgment. Such steps should include determining whether the supervisor's position represents an acceptable alternative under GAAP or GAAS, as appropriate. If so, the member need do nothing further; but, if not, the member should bring the matter to the attention of someone at a higher level in the organization, such as the supervisor's superior. Ultimately, if the disagreement is not resolved satisfactorily to the member, he or she should consider (1) documenting the situation, and (2) whether to continue his or her relationship with the employer. In addition, a member in public practice should not subordinate his or her judgments concerning the application of technical standards to the directives of clients. Finally, a member performing a professional service for a client or employer should not have a significant relationship with another person, entity, product, or service that could be viewed as impairing the member's objectivity.

RULE 201—GENERAL STANDARDS

A member shall comply with the following standards and with any interpretations thereof by bodies designated by Council.

A. *Professional Competence.* Undertake only those professional services that the member or the member's firm can reasonably expect to be completed with professional competence.
B. *Due Professional Care.* Exercise due professional care in the performance of professional services.
C. *Planning and Supervision.* Adequately plan and supervise the performance of professional services.
D. *Sufficient Relevant Data.* Obtain sufficient relevant data to afford a reasonable basis for conclusions or recommendations in relation to any professional services performed.

These general standards should not be confused with the three general standards of GAAS introduced in the last chapter. The four general standards in Rule 201 apply to all members, including those not in public practice, and to all types of professional services, not just to audits.

Rule 201A, *Professional competence,* involves not only the technical qualifications of the member and the member's staff, but also the CPA's ability to supervise and evaluate the quality of the work performed by others. This part of Rule 201 is specifically directed at the member's decision-making process when the CPA is deciding whether to accept or decline an engagement. If, on the basis of facts known at the time, the CPA believes he or she has the capability to complete the assignment in accordance with professional standards, it is ethically permissible to accept the engagement. However, if, for example, neither the CPA nor the firm has the computer expertise required to audit a client with a sophisticated electronic data processing system, and cannot acquire the necessary knowledge, it is not ethically proper to accept the engagement.

Due professional care, planning and supervision, and sufficient relevant data codify practices that must be followed in performing any service. Adherence to these requirements contributes to the quality of performance of professional engagements for the benefit of the public and the profession.

RULE 202—COMPLIANCE WITH STANDARDS

A member who performs auditing, review, compilation, management consulting, tax, or other professional services shall comply with standards promulgated by bodies designated by Council.

Currently, the technical standards that fall under this rule are those issued by the Auditing Standards Board, the Accounting and Review Services Committee, and the Management Consulting Services Executive Committee. In addition, for purposes of this rule, Council has designated two bodies to promulgate standards of disclosure for financial information outside the basic financial statements in published financial reports containing financial statements. They are the FASB and the GASB.

RULE 203—ACCOUNTING PRINCIPLES

A member shall not (1) express an opinion or state affirmatively that the financial statements or other financial data of any entity are presented in conformity with generally accepted accounting principles or (2) state that he or she is not aware of any material modifications that should be made to such statements or data in order for them to be in conformity with generally accepted accounting principles, if such statements or data contain any departure from an accounting principle promulgated by bodies designated by Council to establish such principles that has a material effect on the statements or data taken as a whole. If, however, the statements or data contain such a departure and the member can demonstrate that due to unusual circumstances the financial statements or data would otherwise have been misleading, the member can comply with the rule by describing the departure, its approximate effects, if practicable, and the reasons why compliance with the principle would result in a misleading statement.

Rule 203 applies to all members, whether or not in public practice, who perform the acts described. Such acts will occur, for example, in (1) making a financial statement audit, (2) performing an examination of prospective financial statements, and (3) reviewing interim financial information. The rule covers all services for which standards have been promulgated regarding GAAP, including engagements to report on a comprehensive basis other than GAAP. Council has designated two groups to promulgate accounting principles: (1) the GASB for state and local government entities and (2) the FASB for all other entities.

RULE 301—CONFIDENTIAL CLIENT INFORMATION

A member in public practice shall not disclose any confidential client information without the specific consent of the client.

This rule shall not be construed (1) to relieve a member of his or her professional obligations under rules 202 and 203, (2) to affect in any way the member's obligation to comply with a validly issued and enforceable subpoena or summons, or to prohibit a member's compliance with applicable laws and government regulations, (3) to prohibit review of a member's professional practice under AICPA or state CPA society or Board of Accountancy authorization, or (4) to preclude a member from initiating a complaint with, or responding to any inquiry made by, the professional ethics division or trial board of the Institute or a duly constituted investigative or disciplinary body of a state CPA society or Board of Accountancy.

Members of any of the bodies identified in (4) above and members involved with professional practice reviews identified in (3) above shall not use to their own advantage or disclose any member's confidential client information that comes to their attention in carrying out those activities. This prohibition shall not restrict members' exchange of information in connection with the investigative or disciplinary proceedings described in (4) above or the professional practice reviews described in (3) above.

It is fundamental that a CPA in public practice hold in strict confidence all information about a client's business affairs. Confidentiality is indispensable in establishing a basis of mutual trust between CPA and client.

Rule 301 requires the member to obtain the specific consent of the client before disclosing confidential client information. Preferably, the consent should be in writing. Consent is not required when any of the four exceptions stated in the rule are applicable.

The exceptions to Rule 301 enable the member to fulfill both professional and legal responsibilities. For example, in issuing an audit report, the member may disclose information required under GAAP that is not included in the financial statements.

The Rule 301 requirement to maintain confidentiality should be distinguished from the legal concept of **privileged communication.** Federal and state statutes grant privileged communication in certain relationships such as those between attorney and client, doctor and patient, and priest and parishioner. In these cases, communications between the professional and the client cannot be revealed even to a court unless the client waives privilege. No federal statute extends privileged communication status to CPA-client relationships. However, state statutes do exist in eighteen states.[2]

Rule 301 is the source of a number of ethical dilemmas for CPAs. For example, suppose an auditor has a Client A with a material receivable that A believes to be collectible from the auditor's Client B. But in auditing Client B, the auditor acquires confidential information casting serious doubt on B's ability to pay the balance owed to A. Or, suppose in auditing Client A, an auditor discovers A is overcharging Client B for inventory purchases.[3] In addition, in the absence of a legislative or regulatory mandate, whistleblowing by auditors in cases involving illegal client acts runs counter to Rule 301.

RULE 302—CONTINGENT FEES

A member in public practice shall not:

(1) Perform for a contingent fee any professional services for, or receive such a fee from, a client for whom the member or member's firm performs:
   (a) an audit or review of a financial statement; or
   (b) a compilation of a financial statement when the member expects, or reasonably might expect, that a third party will use the financial statement and the member's compilation report does not disclose a lack of independence; or
   (c) an examination of prospective financial information;

   or,

(2) Prepare an original or amended tax return or claim for a tax refund for a contingent fee for any client.

The prohibition in (1) above applies during the period in which the member or the member's firm is engaged to perform any of the services listed above and the period covered by any historical financial statements involved in any such listed services.

---

[2] The states with CPA-client privileged communication statutes are Arizona, Colorado, Florida, Georgia, Illinois, Indiana, Iowa, Kentucky, Louisiana, Maryland, Michigan, Missouri, Montana, Nevada, New Mexico, Pennsylvania, Tennessee, and Texas. Puerto Rico also has such a statute.

[3] For an actual case of this type, see writeup of *Fund of Funds, Ltd.* v. *Arthur Andersen & Co.* in Chapter 4, p. 125.

Except as stated in the next sentence, a **contingent fee** is a fee established for the performance of any service pursuant to an arrangement in which no fee will be charged unless a specified finding or result is attained, or in which the amount of the fee is otherwise dependent upon the finding or result of such service. Solely for purposes of this rule, fees are not regarded as being contingent if fixed by courts or other public authorities, or, in tax matters, if determined based on the results of judicial proceedings or the findings of governmental agencies.

A member's fees may vary depending, for example, on the complexity of services rendered.

Prior to being amended in 1990, this rule contained a general prohibition against members accepting contingent fees in connection with any service for any client. In 1990, the AICPA changed the rule to comply with an order from the U.S. Federal Trade Commission (FTC), which deemed the former rule to be in restraint of trade. In its current form, the rule represents a compromise between the AICPA, which wanted to retain the general prohibition, and the FTC, which wanted the rule eliminated in its entirety.

The rule does not prohibit a member from charging a fee based on the complexity or number of hours or days needed to complete the service. A member may also elect to lower per diem billing rates for a financially troubled client or perform services without charge for a charitable organization.

RULE 501—ACTS DISCREDITABLE

A member shall not commit an act discreditable to the profession.

Under Rule 501, **acts discreditable** are actions by a member that may damage or otherwise impinge on the reputation and integrity of the profession. This rule enables disciplinary action to be taken against a member for unethical acts not specifically covered by other rules. Discreditable acts include the actions discussed later that result in automatic disciplinary provisions, and they also include failing to comply with continuing professional education requirements.

In interpretations, the following acts are designated as discreditable: (1) retention of client records and auditor working papers, such as adjusting entries, necessary to complete the client's records; (2) discrimination in employment; (3) failure to follow standards and/or other procedures or other requirements in governmental audits; and (4) negligence in the preparation of financial statements. A member who commits a discreditable act usually is suspended or expelled from the AICPA.

RULE 502—ADVERTISING AND OTHER FORMS OF SOLICITATION

A member in public practice shall not seek to obtain clients by advertising or other forms of solicitation in a manner that is false, misleading, or deceptive. Solicitation by the use of coercion, overreaching, or harassing conduct is prohibited.

This rule also reflects a compromise. Some members of the AICPA believe all advertising and solicitation should be banned because it is unprofessional. However, the AICPA must comply with other provisions contained in the FTC's 1990 Order to the AICPA that pertain to Rule 502.

Under the agreement with the FTC, this rule can be enforced to prevent members from engaging in falsehood or deception. However, the rule can no longer be used to prevent or discourage members from (1) soliciting potential clients by any means, including direct solicitation, and (2) using advertising that includes self-laudatory or comparative claims, testimonials, or endorsements, or material not considered by the AICPA to be professionally dignified or in good taste.

Some state boards of accountancy have rules against direct solicitation of clients and some forms of advertising.

RULE 503—COMMISSIONS AND REFERRAL FEES

A. Prohibited commissions.
A member in public practice shall not for a **commission** recommend or refer to a client any product or service, or for a commission recommend or refer any product or service to be supplied by a client, or receive a commission, when the member or the member's firm also performs for that client:
(a) an audit or review of a financial statement; or
(b) a compilation of a financial statement when the member expects, or reasonably might expect, that a third party will use the financial statement and the member's compilation report does not disclose a lack of independence; or
(c) an examination of prospective financial information.
This prohibition applies during the period in which the member is engaged to perform any of the services listed above and the period covered by any historical financial statements involved in such listed services.

B. Disclosure of permitted commissions.
A member in public practice who is not prohibited by this rule from performing services for or receiving a commission and who is paid or expects to be paid a commission shall disclose that fact to any person or entity to whom the member recommends or refers a product or service to which the commission relates.

C. Referral fees.
Any member who accepts a **referral fee** for recommending or referring any service of a CPA to any person or entity or who pays a referral fee to obtain a client shall disclose such acceptance or payment to the client.

This rule was also modified significantly in 1990 to comply with the FTC Order to the AICPA. The former rule contained a general prohibition against members accepting any commission, even when disclosed to, and approved by, the client. Again, the FTC deemed the rule to be in restraint of trade.

Under the current rule, a CPA may accept a disclosed commission, for example, from a computer manufacturer based on equipment purchased by a client on the CPA's recommendation, except when the CPA performs any of the services described in the rule for the same client. Payments by a CPA to obtain a client, barred under the old rule, are now permitted provided disclosure is made to the client.

STATE LIMITS ON CONTINGENT FEES AND COMMISSIONS

When the FTC Order leading to the amendment of Rules 302 and 503 was imposed in 1990, CPAs in fifty of the fifty-four jurisdictions nonetheless remained subject to state statutes or state board of accountancy regulations that barred them from accepting contingent fees and commissions. By the end of 1993, ten states had eliminated or reduced limits on these arrangements for nonattest services, namely, Colorado, Illinois, Kansas, North Carolina, Ohio, Oklahoma, Texas, Utah, Vermont, and Wisconsin. A majority of the remaining states barred contingent fees and commissions through state board regulations, while the following eleven states did so through statutes—Arkansas, California, Connecticut, Florida, Idaho, Iowa, Nevada, New Mexico, Oregon, Rhode Island, and Tennessee. Some states permit contingent fees but not commissions. One permits CPAs to accept, but not pay, commissions and referral fees.

SOURCE: *Public Accounting Report,* November 30, 1993, p. 3.

RULE 505—FORM OF ORGANIZATION AND NAME

A member may practice public accounting only in a form of organization permitted by state law or regulation whose characteristics conform to resolutions of Council.

A member shall not practice public accounting under a firm name that is misleading. Names of one or more past owners may be included in the firm name of a successor organization. Also, an owner surviving the death or withdrawal of all other owners may continue to practice under a name which includes the name of past owners for up to two years after becoming a sole practitioner.

A firm may not designate itself as "Members of the American Institute of Certified Public Accountants" unless all of its owners are members of the Institute.

Prior to being amended in 1992, Rule 505 mandated that members practice public accounting only in the form of a proprietorship, partnership, or professional corporation. The rule was changed to permit members to take advantage of changes in state laws. For example, by early 1994, forty-two states had adopted legislation permitting CPA firms to organize as limited liability corporations (LLCs) or limited liability partnerships (LLPs). Rule 505 was further amended in 1994 to eliminate a former restriction on ownership of CPA firms to licensed CPAs. As noted in Rule 505, however, whatever form of organization is chosen, a CPA firm's characteristics must conform to certain **resolutions of Council** of the AICPA, chief among which are the following:

- A super majority (66 2/3%) of the ownership of a firm must belong to CPAs. Non-CPA owners must be actively engaged in providing services to the firm's clients as their principal occupation. Ownership by others is considered against the public interest and continues to be prohibited.
- A CPA must have ultimate responsibility for all services provided by the firm that are governed by *Statements on Auditing Standards* or *Statements on Standards for Accounting and Review Services.*

- Non-CPA owners must abide by the AICPA Code of Professional Conduct, meet certain education requirements, and complete the same work-related continuing professional education requirements as CPAs.

Under Rule 505, the name of the firm cannot be misleading. This prohibition is consistent with the rule on advertising, which prohibits statements that are false or misleading. A member may use a fictitious or trade name such as "Suburban Tax Services," or indicate a specialization such as "Tax Accountants," as long as the name is not deceptive.

LEARNING CHECK:

3-9 a. What authority underlies the Rules of the Code?
b. To whom and in what circumstances do the Rules apply?

3-10 a. State Rule 101—Independence.
b. Indicate the bodies who have issued technical standards that include a requirement that a CPA be independent.

3-11 For Interpretation 101—1 pertaining to independence, explain:
a. The meaning of the expression "a member or a member's firm."
b. The time periods identified and the prohibitions to which they are applicable.

3-12 a. Distinguish between direct and indirect financial interest in Interpretation 101—1.
b. Indicate the types of business relationships that are prohibited by this interpretation.

3-13 a. State the Rule 201—General Standards.
b. Enumerate the four subcategories of this rule.

3-14 a. What is the essence of Rule 301—Confidential Client Information?
b. Explain the circumstances in which contingent fee arrangements are prohibited under Rule 302.

3-15 Explain the acts that are prohibited under:
a. Rule 501—Acts Discreditable.
b. Rule 502—Advertising and Other Forms of Solicitation.
c. Rule 503—Commissions and Referral Fees.

3-16 a. Identify the forms of organization of practice units permitted under Rule 505.
b. What requirements must be met for a CPA to practice in any of these forms?

KEY TERMS:

Audit-sensitive position, p. 82
Acts discreditable, p. 89
Commission, p. 90
Contingent fee, p. 89
Member or member's firm, p. 81
Privileged communication, p. 88
Referral fee, p. 90
Resolutions of Council, p. 91
Significant influence, p. 82

ENFORCEMENT OF THE RULES

A member can only be charged with a violation of the Rules of the Code of Professional Conduct. However, in the event of an alleged violation of a rule, a member may have to justify any departures from applicable Interpretations of the Rules of Conduct and Ethics Rulings. Enforcement actions may be initiated as a result of (1) complaints by members and nonmembers, (2) review of newspapers and publications, such as the SEC *Docket* and the IRS *Bulletin,* by personnel in the Professional Ethics Division, and (3) transmittal of possible violations to the AICPA by state and federal agencies.

OBJECTIVE 7

State the organizations and procedures involved in enforcing the rules of conduct.

Enforcement of the Rules rests with two groups: the AICPA and state societies of CPAs. Both have the authority to make investigations of complaints, conduct hearings, and impose sanctions on those who have violated the Rules.

The AICPA's enforcement machinery resides in its Professional Ethics Division and a **joint trial board.** The maximum sanction that the AICPA can impose is to expel the member from the Institute.

State society enforcement is achieved through each state's ethics committee and the joint trial board. As in the case of the AICPA, the most severe sanction to be imposed by a state society is loss of membership in the society.

JOINT ETHICS ENFORCEMENT PROCEDURES

In an effort to make enforcement of the Rules of Conduct more effective and disciplinary action more uniform, the AICPA has developed a **Joint Ethics Enforcement Program (JEEP).** Under JEEP, complaints against a member may be filed with either the AICPA or the state society. Normally, the AICPA has jurisdiction over cases involving (1) more than one state, (2) litigation, and (3) issues of broad national concern. The jurisdictional groups may act independently or jointly.

JEEP also provides for increased liaison between the AICPA and state society ethics committees. The Professional Ethics Division holds frequent meetings with state societies in an effort to improve the overall handling of ethics matters and to consult with the states on ways to increase the amount of resources devoted to ethics enforcement. The Professional Ethics Division reports semiannually to the membership of the AICPA on ethics cases processed under JEEP.

JOINT TRIAL BOARD PROCEDURES

There is a single joint trial board consisting of at least 36 AICPA members elected by Council from present or former Council members. The trial board becomes involved only when earlier enforcement procedures have found the complaint to be serious or the member involved has refused to cooperate. Trial board hearings are generally held by subboards comprised of at least five board members appointed to maximize representation from the general area in which the member resides. A member may request the full trial board to review the subboard's decision.

The joint trial board may take one of the following **disciplinary actions:**

- Admonish the member.
- Suspend the member for a period of no more than two years.
- Expel the member.

When the deficiency is attributable to a departure from the profession's technical standards, the trial board has the authority to impose additional requirements. For example, the board may require the member to complete specified professional development courses and report to the trial board upon their completion. The joint trial board must notify the Professional Ethics Division of its decision in each case.

AUTOMATIC DISCIPLINARY PROVISIONS

The bylaws (BL 7.3.1) of the AICPA include **automatic disciplinary provisions** that mandate suspension or termination of membership without a hearing in certain situations. Suspension results when the Secretary of the Institute is notified that a judgment or conviction has been imposed on a member for

- A crime punishable by imprisonment for more than one year.
- Willful failure to file any income tax return that the member, as an individual taxpayer, is required by law to file.
- The filing of a false or fraudulent income tax return on the member's or a client's behalf.
- Willful aiding in the preparation and presentation of a false and fraudulent income tax return of a client.

Termination of membership occurs when the member has exhausted all legal appeals on the judgment or conviction.

Under the automatic disciplinary provisions of the bylaws, membership in the AICPA shall be terminated without a hearing should a member's certificate as a CPA be revoked, withdrawn, or canceled as a disciplinary measure by any governmental agency. This provision also applies when a member's last or only certificate is revoked by a state board of accountancy for failing to meet continuing professional education requirements, unless the member is retired or disabled.

LEARNING CHECK:

3-17 Identify the two groups responsible for enforcement of the Rules of Conduct and indicate the maximum sanction that can be imposed by each.

3-18 What is the purpose of the Joint Ethics Enforcement Program (JEEP) and how does it operate?

3-19 What is the composition of the joint trial board, when does it become involved, and what disciplinary actions can it take?

3-20 Explain the automatic disciplinary provisions of the AICPA and the actions by members that result in application of the provisions.

ETHICS DIVISION INVESTIGATION ACTIVITY

The following is a statistical report from the Professional Ethics Division of investigation activity for the year ended December 31, 1993. The AICPA and the state CPA societies participate in the Joint Ethics Enforcement Program. This report includes investigations conducted by state societies resulting in findings of ethics code violations.

Activities:		**Disposition of Closed Cases***	
Investigations open at start of period:		Trial board / settlement	68
Active	446	Letter of required corrective action	121
Deferred-Litigation	235	No violation	92
Subtotal	681	Complaint dismissed	115
Add investigations opened during period	424	Complied with follow-up	39
Less investigations closed during period	(471)	No jurisdiction	4
Investigations open at end of period:		Transfer / return to state society	10
Active	413	Automatic termination or suspension	8
Deferred-Litigation	221	Complaint withdrawn	2
		Other	12
Total	634	Total	471

* Letters of required corrective action and trial board decisions usually require respondents to attend certain CPE courses and thereafter submit examples of their workproducts for ethics division review. As of December 31, 1993, there were 176 case investigations being monitored for CPE attendance and follow-up review.

SOURCE: *The CPA Letter* (May 1994), p. 5.

KEY TERMS:

Automatic disciplinary provisions, p. 94
Disciplinary actions, p. 94
Joint Ethics Enforcement Program (JEEP), p. 93
Joint trial board, p. 93

SUMMARY

Ethics deals with how people act towards one another. General ethicists differ as to whether all behavior should be based on unchanging universal standards or be governed by changing customs and traditions. In either case, a general framework for ethical decision making can be applied. Professional ethics include standards of conduct for a professional person that are designed for both idealistic and practical purposes. The AICPA's *Code of Professional Conduct* addresses lasting ideals through its Principles, and it addresses practical and enforceable standards through its Rules of Conduct which evolve over time to reflect changes in the profession and in society. The willingness of CPAs to voluntarily subscribe to the

Code has contributed significantly to the stature and reputation of the profession. The AICPA and state societies of CPAs cooperate in a Joint Ethics Enforcement Program that provides mechanisms for investigating complaints of unethical conduct, and imposing sanctions on members who violate the Rules of Conduct.

BIBLIOGRAPHY

AICPA Professional Standards:
Section ET—Code of Professional Conduct.

Albrecht, W. Steve. *Ethical Issues in The Practice of Accounting.* Cincinnati, OH: South-Western Publishing Co., 1992.

Code of Ethics for Professional Accountants. New York: International Federation of Accountants, 1992.

Elliot, Robert K., and Jacobson, Peter D. "Auditor Independence: Concept and Application," *The CPA Journal* (March 1992), pp. 26–32.

Mautz, R. K., and Sharaf, H. A. *The Philosophy of Auditing.* Sarasota, FL: American Accounting Association, 1961, Chapter 9: "Ethical Conduct," pp. 232–239.

Mednick, Robert. "Independence: Let's Get Back to Basics," *Journal of Accountancy* (January 1990), pp. 68–93.

Pany, Kurt, and Reckers, Philip M. J. "Auditor Performance of MAS: A Study of Its Effects on Decisions and Perceptions," *Accounting Horizons* (June 1988), pp. 31–38.

Magill, Harry T., and Previts, Gary John. *Professional Responsibilities: An Introduction.* Cincinnati, OH: South-Western Publishing Co., 1991.

Shaub, Michael K. "Restructuring the Code of Professional Ethics: A Review of the Anderson Committee Report and Its Implications," *Accounting Horizons* (December 1988), pp. 89–97.

Tidrick, Donald E. "Enforcement of the AICPA's Code of Ethics During the 1980s," *The CPA Journal* (October 1990), pp. 11, 105–106.

OBJECTIVE QUESTIONS

Indicate the *best* answer choice for each of the following multiple choice questions.

3-21 These questions relate to the nature and purpose of the AICPA Code of Professional Conduct.

1. Which of the following statements best describes why the CPA profession has deemed it essential to promulgate ethical standards and to establish means for ensuring their observance?
   a. A requirement for a profession is the establishment of ethical standards that stress primarily a responsibility to clients and colleagues.
   b. A requirement of most state laws calls for the profession to establish a code of ethics.
   c. An essential means of self-protection for the profession is the establishment of flexible ethical standards by the profession.
   d. A distinguishing mark of a profession is its acceptance of responsibility to the public.

2. The AICPA Code of Professional Conduct contains both principles that are aspirational in character and also a
   a. List of violations that would cause the automatic suspension of the CPA's license.
   b. Set of specific, mandatory rules describing minimum levels of conduct the CPA must maintain.
   c. Description of the CPA's procedures for responding to an inquiry from a trial board.
   d. List of specific crimes that would be considered as acts discreditable to the profession.

3. Pursuant to the AICPA Code of Professional Conduct, the auditor's responsibility to the profession is defined by
   a. The AICPA Code of Professional Conduct.
   b. Federal laws governing licensed professionals who are involved in interstate commerce.
   c. Statements on Auditing Standards.
   d. The Bylaws of the AICPA.

3-22 These questions pertain to the CPA's independence.

1. According to the profession's ethical standards, an auditor would be considered independent in which of the following instances?
   a. The auditor's checking account, which is fully insured by a federal agency, is held at a client financial institution.
   b. The auditor is also an attorney who advises the client as its general counsel.
   c. An employee of the auditor donates service as treasurer of a charitable organization that is a client.
   d. The client owes the auditor fees for two consecutive annual audits.

2. A CPA purchased stock in a client corporation and placed it in a trust as an educational fund for the CPA's minor child. The trust securities were not material to the CPA but were material to the child's personal net worth. Would the independence of the CPA be considered impaired with respect to the client?
   a. Yes, because the stock would be considered a direct financial interest and, consequently, materiality is *not* a factor.
   b. Yes, because the stock would be considered an indirect financial interest that is material to the CPA's child.
   c. No, because the CPA would *not* be considered to have a direct financial interest in the client.
   d. No, because the CPA would *not* be considered to have a material indirect financial interest in the client.

3. Which of the following legal situations would be considered to impair the auditor's independence?
   a. An expressed intention by the present management to commence litigation against the auditor alleging deficiencies in audit work for the client, although the auditor considers that there is only a remote possibility that such a claim will be filed.
   b. Actual litigation by the auditor against the client for an amount *not* material to the auditor or to the financial statements of the client arising out of disputes as to billings for management advisory services.
   c. Actual litigation by the auditor against the present management alleging management fraud or deceit.
   d. Actual litigation by the client against the auditor for an amount *not* material to the auditor or to the financial statements of the client arising out of disputes as to billings for tax services.

3-23 These questions involve other rules in the Code of Professional Conduct.

1. Without the consent of the client, a CPA should *not* disclose confidential client information contained in working papers to a
   a. Voluntary quality control review board.
   b. CPA firm that has purchased the CPA's accounting practice.
   c. Federal court that has issued a valid subpoena.
   d. Disciplinary body created under state statute.

2. The profession's ethical standards would most likely be considered to have been violated when the CPA represents that specific consulting services will be performed for a stated fee and it is apparent at the time of the representation that the

a. CPA would *not* be independent.
b. Fee was a competitive bid.
c. Actual fee would be substantially higher.
d. Actual fee would be substantially lower than the fees charged by other CPAs for comparable services.

3. On completing an audit, Larkin, CPA, was asked by the client to provide technical assistance in the implementation of a new EDP system. The set of pronouncements designed to guide Larkin in this engagement is the Statements on
a. Auditing Standards.
b. Standards for Management Advisory Services.
c. Quality Control Standards.
d. Standards for Accountants' EDP Services.

COMPREHENSIVE QUESTIONS

3-24 **(General and professional ethics)** The membership of the AICPA has adopted the *Code of Professional Conduct* that is administered by the Institute's Professional Ethics Division.

a. With the many general theories of ethics developed by philosophers and ethicists, why is it necessary or desirable for the profession to adopt such a Code?

b. In what respects, if any, does the AICPA's Code reflect the ethical absolutists and the ethical relativists schools of thought?

c. Identify an ethical dilemma that an auditor might face where answers to the questions "What good do I seek?" and "What is my obligation in this circumstance?" would be relevant.

d. According to the Preamble to the AICPA's Code, to what three groups does the CPA have obligations or responsibilities?

3-25 **(Framework for ethical decision making)** Assume that you are the audit partner on an engagement for a client that has had a string of operating losses. The company still has a positive net worth, but you are worried that the company could have to close down within the next year or so. When you tell the client's management that it should make full disclosure in the footnotes concerning substantial doubt about the entity's ability to continue as a going concern, management says "Hogwash! There's no substantial doubt. The probability of our having to close down is remote. We'll make no such disclosure. To do so would only make our customers and creditors nervous, possibly making such a disclosure a self-fulfilling prophecy. Our competitors are as bad off as we are, and their auditors aren't making them send out a distress signal." You agree that the determination of "substantial doubt" is a judgment call.

REQUIRED

Apply the six-step general framework for ethical decision making to this dilemma.

3-26 **(Sections of the Code)** Ethical standards for the profession have been published in the form of the AICPA's *Code of Professional Conduct.*

REQUIRED

a. Identify and distinguish between the two sections of the Code.
b. Are both sections enforceable? Explain.
c. State each of the principles of the Code.

d. For each principle, identify two courses of action that will enable the member to meet the principle.
e. Explain the applicability of the Rules to the members of the AICPA.

3-27 **(Independence)** An auditor must not only appear to be independent; he or she must also be independent in fact.

REQUIRED

a. Explain the concept of an "auditor's independence" as it applies to third-party reliance on financial statements.
b. 1. What determines whether or not an auditor is independent in fact?
   2. What determines whether or not an auditor appears to be independent?
c. Explain how an auditor may be independent in fact but not appear to be independent.
d. Would a CPA be considered independent for an audit of the financial statements of a
   1. Church for which he or she is serving as treasurer without compensation? Explain.
   2. Country club for which his or her spouse is serving as treasurer-bookkeeper if he or she is not to receive a fee for the audit? Explain.

AICPA (adapted)

3-28 **(Independence)** The attribute of independence has been traditionally associated with the CPA's function of auditing and expressing opinions on financial statements.

REQUIRED

a. What is meant by "independence" as applied to the CPA's function of auditing and expressing opinions on financial statements? Discuss.
b. CPAs have imposed on themselves certain rules of professional conduct that induce their members to remain independent and to strengthen public confidence in their independence. Which of the Rules of Conduct are concerned with the CPA's independence? Discuss.
c. The Wallydrug Company is indebted to a CPA for unpaid fees and has offered to issue to the CPA unsecured interest-bearing notes. Would acceptance of these notes have any bearing on the CPA's independence with respect to Wallydrug Company? Discuss.
d. The Rocky Hill Corporation was formed on October 1, 19X0, and its fiscal year will end on September 30, 19X1. You audited the corporation's opening balance sheet and rendered an unqualified opinion on it. A month after rendering your report, you are offered the position of secretary of the company because of the need for a complete set of officers and for convenience in signing various documents. You will have no financial interest in the company through stock ownership or otherwise, will receive no salary, will not keep the books, and will not have any influence on its financial matters other than occasional advice on income tax matters and similar advice normally given a client by a CPA.
   1. Assume that you accept the offer but plan to resign the position prior to conducting your annual audit with the intention of again assuming the office after rendering an opinion on the statements. Can you render an independent opinion on the financial statements? Discuss.
   2. Assume that you accept the offer on a temporary basis until the corporation has gotten under way and can employ a secretary. In any event, you would permanently resign the position before conducting your annual audit. Can you render an independent opinion on the financial statements? Discuss.

AICPA

3-29 **(Independence/commissions) PART I:** During 19X0, your client, Nuesel Corporation, requested that you conduct a feasibility study to advise management of the best way the corporation can utilize electronic data processing equipment and which computer, if any, best meets the corporation's requirements. You are technically competent in this area and accept the engagement. On completion of your study, the corporation accepts your suggestions and installs the computer and related equipment that you recommended.

REQUIRED

a. Discuss the effect the acceptance of this management advisory services engagement would have on your independence in expressing an opinion on the financial statements of the Nuesel Corporation.
b. A local printer of data processing forms customarily offers a commission for recommending him as supplier. The client is aware of the commission offer and suggests that you accept it. Would it be proper for you to accept the commission with the client's approval? Discuss.

PART II: Alex Pratt, a retired partner of your CPA firm, has just been appointed to the board of directors of Palmer Corporation, your firm's client. Pratt is also a member of your firm's income tax committee that meets monthly to discuss income tax problems of the partnership's clients. The partnership pays Pratt $100 for each committee meeting he attends and a monthly retirement benefit of $1,000.

REQUIRED

Discuss the effect of Pratt's appointment to the board of directors of Palmer Corporation on your partnership's independence in expressing an opinion on the Palmer Corporation's financial statements.

AICPA (adapted)

3-30 **(Rules of conduct)** There currently are 11 rules in the *Code of Professional Conduct.* Listed below are circumstances pertaining to these rules.

1. A member shall not express an opinion that the financial statements are presented in conformity with GAAP unless the pronouncements of the FASB have been followed.
2. A member shall not discriminate in employment of assistants.
3. A member shall not include self-laudatory statements that are not based on verifiable facts in advertisements.
4. A member shall not accept a commission for a referral to a client of products or services of others.
5. A member's fees may vary depending on the complexity of the service rendered.
6. A member is not precluded from responding to an inquiry by a Trial Board of the AICPA.
7. A member may not serve as a trustee for any pension trust of the client during the period covered by the financial statements.
8. A member shall adequately plan and supervise an engagement.
9. A member may not have or be committed to acquire any direct financial interest in the client.
10. A member shall not practice under a misleading firm name.
11. A member shall not knowingly subordinate his or her judgment to others.
12. A member shall follow the technical standards of the Auditing Standards Board in an audit engagement.
13. A member bases the fee on the findings determined by the IRS in a tax audit case.
14. A member discloses confidential information in a peer review of the firm's practice.
15. A member issues an unqualified opinion when a client departs from GAAP because of a conceptual disagreement with the FASB.

REQUIRED

a. Identify the rule to which each circumstance relates.
b. Indicate one other circumstance that pertains to each rule identified in (a) above.

3-31 **(Rules of conduct)** In the practice of public accounting, an auditor who is a member of the AICPA is expected to comply with the rules of the Code of Professional Conduct. Listed below are circumstances that raise a question about an auditor's ethical conduct.

1. The auditor has a bank loan with a bank that is an audit client.
2. An unqualified opinion is expressed when the financial statements of a county are prepared in conformity with principles established by the Governmental Accounting Standards Board.
3. An auditor retains client's records as a means of enforcing payment of an overdue audit fee.
4. The auditor makes retirement payments to individuals who formerly were members of his firm.
5. An auditor sells her shares of stock in a client company in April prior to beginning work on the audit for the year ending December 31.
6. An auditor accepts an engagement knowing that he does not have the expertise to do the audit.
7. The auditor quotes a client an audit fee but also states that the actual fee will be contingent on the amount of work done.
8. The auditor's firm states in a newspaper advertisement that it has had fewer lawsuits than its principal competitors.
9. The auditor resigns her position as treasurer of the client on May 1, prior to beginning the audit for the year ending December 31.
10. The auditor discloses confidential information about a client to a successor auditor.
11. The auditor accepts an audit engagement when he has a conflict of interest.
12. An auditor prepares a small brochure containing testimonials from existing clients that he mails to prospective clients.
13. An auditor complies with the technical standards of the Accounting and Review Services Committee in reviewing the financial statements of a nonpublic entity.
14. An auditor examines the financial statements of a local bank and also serves on the bank's committee that approves loans.
15. An auditor pays a commission to an attorney to obtain a client.

REQUIRED

a. Identify the rule of the *Code of Professional Conduct* that applies to each circumstance.
b. Indicate for each circumstance whether the effect on the rule is (1) a violation, (2) not a violation, or (3) indeterminate. Give the reason(s) for your answer.

CASES

3-32 **(Ethical issues)** Gilbert and Bradley formed a corporation called Financial Services, Inc., each taking 50% of the authorized common stock. Gilbert is a CPA and a member of the American Institute of CPAs. Bradley is a CPCU (Chartered Property Casualty Underwriter). The corporation performs auditing and tax services under Gilbert's direction and insurance services under Bradley's supervision. The opening of the corporation's office was announced by a three-inch, two-column ad in the local newspaper.

One of the corporation's first audit clients was the Grandtime Company. Grandtime had total assets of $600,000 and total liabilities of $270,000. In the course of the audit, Gilbert found that Grandtime's building with a book value of $240,000 was pledged as security for a 10-year term note in the amount of $200,000. The client's statements did not mention that the building was pledged as a security for the note. However, as the failure to disclose the lien did not affect either the value of the assets or the amount of the liabilities and the audit was satisfactory in all other respects, Gilbert rendered an unqualified opinion on Grandtime's financial statements. About two months after the date of the opinion, Gilbert learned that an insurance company was planning a loan to Grandtime of $150,000 in the form of a first-mortgage note on the building. Realizing that the insurance company was unaware of the existing lien on the building, Gilbert had Bradley notify the insurance company of the fact that Grandtime's building was pledged as security for the term note.

Shortly after the events described above, Gilbert was charged with a violation of professional ethics.

REQUIRED

Identify and discuss the ethical implication of those acts by Gilbert that were in violation of the AICPA Code of Professional Conduct.

AICPA

3-33 **(Ethical issues)** The following situations involve Herb Standard, staff accountant with the regional CPA firm of Cash & Green:

1. The bookkeeper of Ethical Manufacturing Company resigned two months ago and has not yet been replaced. As a result, Ethical's transactions have not been recorded and the books are not up to date. To comply with terms of a loan agreement, Ethical needs to prepare interim financial statements but cannot do so until the books are posted. Ethical looks to Cash & Green, their independent auditors, for help and wants to borrow Herb Standard to perform the work. They want Herb because he did their audit last year.
2. Herb Standard discovered that his client, Ethical Manufacturing Company, materially understated net income on last year's tax return. Herb informs his supervisor about this and the client is asked to prepare an amended return. The client is unwilling to take corrective measures. Herb informs the Internal Revenue Service.
3. While observing the year-end inventory of Ethical Manufacturing Company, the plant manager offers Herb Standard a fishing rod, which Ethical manufactures, in appreciation for a job well done.
4. Herb Standard's acquaintance, Joe Lender, is chief loan officer at Local Bank, an audit client of Cash & Green. Herb approaches Joe for an unsecured loan from Local Bank and Joe approves the loan.
5. Herb Standard is a member of a local investment club composed of college fraternity brothers. The club invests in listed stocks and is fairly active in trading. Last week the club purchased the stock of Leverage Corp., a client of another Cash & Green office. Herb has no contact with the members of this office.

REQUIRED

For each situation, (a) identify the ethical issues that are involved and (b) discuss whether there has or has not been any violation of ethical conduct. Support your answers by reference to the rules of the Code of Professional Conduct.

RESEARCH QUESTIONS

3-34 **(State codes of ethics)** Obtain a copy of any code of ethics issued by your state society of CPAs or board of accountancy. Prepare a summary comparison of it with the AICPA's *Code of Professional Conduct* in terms of structure and the specifics of the rules of conduct.

3-35 **(State regulations and laws regarding areas of the code)** For your state, determine whether there are any laws or board of accountancy rules or regulations, other than those in a code of ethics, that deal with the matters listed below. If so, determine whether they differ from the related AICPA rules of conduct and summarize any differences.

a. Contingent fees.
b. Commissions and referral fees.
c. Form of organization for practice units.

3-36 **(SEC rules on independence)** The SEC has at times taken the lead in requiring auditors to observe strict rules pertaining to independence. Determine (1) what each of the following SEC documents has to say about independence, (2) whether the documents are still in effect, and (3) the extent to which current SEC independence requirements exceed those of the AICPA's *Code of Professional Conduct.*

a. Regulation S-X.
b. Accounting Series Release No. 250.
c. Financial Reporting Release No. 10.

3-37 **(AAERs dealing with ethics)** Lack of independence on the part of the auditor has been a factor in several of the SEC's *Accounting and Auditing Enforcement Releases.* Choose one of the following *AAERs* (Nos. 2, 57, 68, 192, or 244) and determine (1) how the auditor's independence was impaired and (2) what sanctions the SEC imposed on the auditor.

CHAPTER

4

AUDITOR'S LEGAL LIABILITY

LEARNING OBJECTIVES

After studying this chapter, you should be able to

1. Comprehend the impact of the changing legal environment on the profession.
2. Describe the auditor's legal liability to clients and third parties under common law.
3. Identify important cases that have defined auditor's liability to third parties under common law.
4. State the common law defenses available to auditors.
5. Explain and distinguish the auditor's liability under the securities acts of 1933 and 1934.
6. Indicate the auditor's liability under the Racketeer Influenced and Corrupt Organization Act.
7. Discuss alternative views of the relative importance of professional standards on legal decisions.
8. Enumerate precautions a CPA can take to minimize the risk of litigation.

THE LEGAL ENVIRONMENT
- THE LITIGATION CRISIS
- THE NEED FOR LEGAL REFORM

LIABILITY UNDER COMMON LAW
- LIABILITY TO CLIENTS
- LIABILITY TO THIRD PARTIES
- COMMON LAW DEFENSES

LIABILITY UNDER SECURITIES LAWS
- SECURITIES ACT OF 1933
- SECURITIES EXCHANGE ACT OF 1934

OTHER CONSIDERATIONS
- LIABILITY UNDER RACKETEER INFLUENCED AND CORRUPT ORGANIZATION ACT
- PROFESSIONAL STANDARDS AND LEGAL DECISIONS
- MINIMIZING THE RISK OF LITIGATION

SUMMARY

APPENDIX 4A: CHRONOLOGICAL SUMMARY OF ADDITIONAL SELECTED LEGAL CASES

BIBLIOGRAPHY

OBJECTIVE QUESTIONS

COMPREHENSIVE QUESTIONS

CASE

RESEARCH QUESTIONS

Legal liability may be incurred by an accountant in rendering any professional service. Consideration in this chapter, however, is limited primarily to the CPA's legal liability in connection with performing audits of financial statements. We begin by assessing the impact of the current legal environment on the profession and the need for legal reform. We then consider separately the auditor's exposure to liability under the common law and the securities laws, and a number of precedent-setting cases related to each. Other topics include the auditor's liability under the Racketeer Influenced and Corrupt Organization Act, the impact of professional auditing standards on legal decisions, and precautions CPAs can take to minimize the risk of litigation.

THE LEGAL ENVIRONMENT

As a matter of perspective, we should note that throughout its history the public accounting profession has had an extremely low percentage of alleged audit failures to the total number of audits conducted. But in recent years, both the volume and cost of litigation related to alleged audit deficiencies has reached alarming proportions. This can be attributed in part to some widely reported business failures that resulted in significant losses to investors and taxpayers, such as the savings and loan association debacle of the late 1980s and early 1990s. But not all

OBJECTIVE 1

Comprehend the impact of the changing legal environment on the profession.

business failures can be equated with audit failures. There is a growing consensus that too often following a business failure and alleged fraudulent financial reporting, plaintiffs and their attorneys prey on auditors regardless of their degree of fault simply because the auditors may be the only party left with sufficient financial resources to indemnify the plaintiffs' losses (the so-called **deep pockets** theory). Moreover, there is evidence that the high costs of litigation together with the perception that jurors are often ill qualified to render fair and unbiased verdicts in such cases, has led to a tendency for auditors to reach out-of-court settlements with plaintiffs even when the auditors had fully complied with GAAS in performing the audit.

THE LITIGATION CRISIS

The seriousness of the current legal environment is conveyed by the following:[1]

- By the end of 1992, the accounting profession faced more than 4,000 liability suits with unsettled claims estimated to exceed a staggering $30 *billion*.
- In 1992, for the Big Six accounting firms "net protection costs" (judgments and settlements paid, plus legal fees, plus liability insurance premiums, less insurance recoveries) exceeded $598 million, or 11% of the firms' accounting and auditing revenues. This made practice protection costs the second highest cost of doing business, exceeded only by salaries.
- In 1992, 1993, and 1994, three of the Big Six firms agreed to pay federal regulators $400 million, $82 million, and $312 million, respectively, to settle government claims related to audits of failed banks and savings and loan associations.
- Since 1985, liability insurance costs for Big Six firms have increased tenfold to more than $5,000 per Big Six accountant, while deductibles have jumped from $2 million to within the range of $25 to $50 million and coverage limits per firm have dropped from $200 million to $100 million or less. For small and medium-sized firms, premiums have increased 200 to 300%, with the median deductible increasing nearly six times from $42,000 to $240,000. Moreover, there has been a sharp decline in the number of insurance companies offering liability policies for CPA firms.
- Firms of all sizes have retreated from serving high-risk audit clients, and many smaller firms have ceased performing audits altogether, a trend that may be counter to the public interest. For example, a survey of 1,500 California firms revealed the proportion performing audits dropped from 61% in 1988 to 53% in 1992.
- In 1992, the nation's seventh largest accounting firm, Laventhol & Horwath, declared bankruptcy, largely as a result of its liability burden.
- There is evidence that the litigation crisis may be causing young people to avoid the profession, staff to choose not to become partners, and partners to question staying with the firms.

---

[1]Statistical data from various sources including: *Big Six Report to SEC*, June 1993; *The Liability Crisis in the United States: Impact on the Accounting Profession*—A Statement of Position by the Big Six accounting firms; and Report of the Professional Accountability Task Force of the California Society of CPAs.

Nor is the crisis limited to the accounting profession. A 1993 study by the Law and Economics Consulting Group found that securities fraud class action suits, many unwarranted, have been brought against 1 of every 8 companies on the New York Stock Exchange, 1 of every 18 companies on the American Exchange, and 1 of every 20 companies on the NASDAQ.[2] It has been shown that emerging high-technology companies are sued disproportionately, often based solely on a downward movement in their stock prices. These companies and their accountants are often coerced into settling with plaintiffs, even when a suit is meritless, because of the high costs of mounting a defense and the risk that juries will be biased, particularly against "deep pocket" defendants like accountants. As evidence, the Big Six firms have reported that for a major class of securities lawsuits brought against them in a recent year, the average claim was for $85 million, the average settlement was for $2.7 million ("suggesting there might have been little or no merit to the original claim"), and the average legal cost per claim was $3.5 million.[3] This result has caused some to claim that attorneys are using the legal system as a tool whereby speculators can recoup losses from risky investments, or in effect, it is being used as a risk transfer mechanism by transferring the risk of loss to other parties such as the auditors. This has led to a growing recognition among executives, members of Congress, and senators, as well as accountants, that an epidemic of litigation threatens not only the independent audit function and the financial reporting system, but also the strength of the U.S. capital markets and the competitiveness of the U.S. economy.

How could a profession with a multilevel regulatory framework, including technical, ethical, and quality control standards, and a system of quality or peer reviews, find itself in such a predicament? To be sure, there have been some audits that did not measure up to existing standards. And some litigation can be attributed to the expectation gap discussed in Chapter 2. Still other cases can be attributed to ambiguous accounting standards. For example, Walter Schuetze, chief accountant of the Securities and Exchange Commission, has expressed the view that "ambiguous accounting principles, not auditing failure, are to blame for the litigation and resultant auditor liability arising out of the S&L catastrophe."[4] But most knowledgeable observers agree that a major part of the litigation epidemic can be attributed to a judicial system that has run amuck. In 1992 Congressman Tauzin introduced one legal reform bill before the House of Representatives with the following words:

> The judicial system, no longer able to distinguish between meritorious and meritless claims, is standing on its head, and the fraud really is being perpetrated by a small number of predatory attorneys and plaintiffs. The defendants are the victims, along with their employees, shareholders, and the U.S. economy.[5]

---

[2] Gilbert Simonetti, Jr., and Andrea R. Andrews, "A Profession at Risk / A System in Jeopardy," *Journal of Accountancy* (April 1994), p. 50.

[3] "The Liability Crisis in the United States: Impact on the Accounting Profession," A Statement of Position by the Six Largest Public Accounting Firms (August 6, 1992), p. 2.

[4] Walter P. Schuetze, "The Liability Crisis in the U.S. and Its Impact on Accounting," *Accounting Horizons* (June 1993), p. 89.

[5] Hon. W. J. Tauzin, "Introduction of the Securities Litigation and Civil Justice Preservation Act of 1992 (H.R.5828), August 11, 1992, p. 1.

THE NEED FOR LEGAL REFORM

Growing awareness of a problem with the judicial system led to the formation in 1992 of the Coalition to Eliminate Abusive Securities Suits (CEASS). Joined by the AICPA, the Big Six accounting firms, insurance underwriters, and over 300 manufacturers, retailers, and trade associations, the coalition set out to win legal reforms that will curb unwarranted litigation. Among the reforms proposed by this and other groups are the following.

- **Proportionate Liability.** A principal cause of unwarranted litigation against the accounting profession is **joint and several liability.** Under this doctrine, a single defendant (e.g., the auditors) can be held liable for the entire loss caused by all defendants in a case (e.g., management, promoters, underwriters, etc.). For example, often in cases where the client has gone bankrupt, and management has no assets, plaintiff's attorneys seek full recovery of losses from the auditors even when the auditors were not at fault or were only minimally at fault. Under **proportionate liability,** damages are assessed against each defendant based only on that defendant's degree of fault.
- **Transfer of Fees.** Under the so-called **American rule,** successful defendants have no effective means of recovering legal costs. Thus, the system encourages plaintiffs to bring frivolous and unwarranted litigation that "coerces" defendants to settle to avoid higher defense costs. Adoption of the so-called **English rule** would discourage meritless suits because plaintiffs would know that failure to win their cases would make them liable for the out-of-pocket defense costs of defendants.
- **Limitations on Punitive Damages.** Relaxation of judicial restrictions on the types of cases in which punitive damages, as opposed to mere recovery of losses, may be awarded made accountants prime targets under certain state and federal statutes. For example, in the late 1980s and early 1990s, many suits were brought against accountants under the federal statute known as RICO which provides for treble damages. As discussed later in the chapter, a recent Supreme Court case is expected to provide some relief in this area.
- **Limitations on Rights of Third Parties to Sue.** After years of expanding exposure to third party litigation, several recent state and federal court decisions limiting the rights of third parties to sue appear to provide some relief to auditors. In addition, several states have adopted new *privity legislation* limiting liability to third parties. These matters are discussed later in the chapter.
- **Level of Ownership.** By requiring plaintiffs to hold a certain amount of a company's stock, a reform of this nature seeks to eliminate the attorneys' practice of recruiting "professional plaintiffs" to join in on class action suits.
- **Form of Organization.** As noted in Chapter 3, some states have adopted limited liability partnership and limited liability corporation statutes. Eventually, all states are expected to adopt some form of similar legislation that would *not* place limits on liability resulting from an individual's own substandard work. However, it would limit an individual's liability arising from the substandard work of other partners or shareholders in the professional organization (CPA firm) to the individual's capital investment in the organization. Thus, a partner or shareholder in a CPA firm would not need to fear losing his or her home and other personal assets as a result of shortcomings in another's work.

It should be noted that in seeking these reforms, the profession is not asking to be held harmless when at fault. Rather, it is asking that it be granted equity in the judicial process and that it not be blocked by unwarranted liability from providing a service essential to the functioning of our free market economy.

LEARNING CHECK:

4-1 Why are auditors targeted in lawsuits out of proportion to their degree of wrongdoing?
4-2 Explain what is meant by "coerced out-of-court settlements."
4-3 Why should the litigation crisis facing auditors be of concern to other businesspeople, professionals, senators, or others?
4-4 Identify several proposed legal reforms and state how they would contribute to resolving the litigation crisis.

KEY TERMS:

American rule, p. 107
Deep pockets, p. 105
English rule, p. 107
Joint and several liability, p. 107
Proportionate liability, p. 107

LIABILITY UNDER COMMON LAW

OBJECTIVE 2

Describe the auditor's legal liability to clients and third parties under common law.

Common law is frequently referred to as unwritten law. It is based on judicial precedent rather than legislative enactment. Common law is derived from principles based on justice, reason, and common sense rather than absolute, fixed, or inflexible rules. The principles of common law are determined by the social needs of the community. Hence, common law changes in response to society's needs. In a specific case, the accountant's liability is determined by a state or federal court that attempts to apply case law precedents that it feels are controlling. Because there are 51 such independent jurisdictions in the United States, different decisions may result with respect to relatively similar factual circumstances.[6] In a common law case, the judge has the flexibility to consider social, economic, and political factors as well as prior case law doctrines (precedents). Under common law, a CPA's legal liability extends principally to two classes of parties: clients and third parties.

LIABILITY TO CLIENTS

A CPA is in a direct contractual relationship with clients. In agreeing to perform services for clients, the CPA assumes the role of an independent contractor. The specific service(s) to be rendered should preferably be set forth in an engagement letter, as described in Chapter 6. The term **privity of contract** refers to the contractual relationship that exists between two or more contracting parties. In the typical

[6] The 50 states and the District of Columbia constitute the 51 jurisdictions.

auditing engagement, it is assumed that the audit is to be made in accordance with professional standards (i.e., generally accepted auditing standards) unless the contract contains specific wording to the contrary. An accountant may be held liable to a client under either contract law or tort law.

Contract Law

An auditor may be liable to a client for **breach of contract** when he or she

- Issues a standard audit report when he or she has not made an audit in accordance with GAAS.
- Does not deliver the audit report by the agreed-upon date.
- Violates the client's confidential relationship.

A CPA's liability for breach of contract extends to subrogees. A **subrogee** is a party who has acquired the rights of another by substitution. For example, the bonding of employees is considered an important part of a company's internal control environment. When an embezzlement occurs, the bonding company reimburses the insured for its losses. Then, under the right of subrogation to the insured's contractual claim, it can bring suit against the CPA for failing to discover the defalcation.

When a breach of contract occurs, the plaintiff usually seeks one or more of the following remedies: (1) specific performance of the contract by the defendant, (2) direct monetary damages for losses incurred due to the breach, or (3) incidental and consequential damages that are an indirect result of nonperformance.

Tort Law

A CPA may also be liable to a client under tort law. A **tort** is a wrongful act that injures another person's property, body, or reputation. A tort action may be based on any one of the following causes:

- **Ordinary Negligence.** Failure to exercise that degree of care a person of ordinary prudence (a reasonable person) would exercise under the same circumstances.
- **Gross Negligence.** Failure to use even slight care in the circumstances.
- **Fraud.** Intentional deception, such as the misrepresentation, concealment, or nondisclosure of a material fact, that results in injury to another.[7]

Under tort law, the injured party normally seeks monetary damages. The auditor's working papers are vital in refuting charges for breach of contract and breach of duty in a tort action.

In many cases, the plaintiff has the option to sue under either contract or tort law. The best course of action in a given case involves legal technicalities that are beyond the scope of this book.

---

[7] In some cases, a distinction is made between fraud and **constructive fraud.** The latter may be inferred from gross negligence or reckless disregard for the truth.

Cases Illustrating Liability to Clients

Two cases pertaining to liability to clients are considered below. The first case involves negligence and the second relates to breach of contract.

1136 TENANTS' CORP. V. MAX ROTHENBERG & CO. (1971) LIABILITY TO CLIENT FOR NEGLIGENCE[8]

The plaintiff, a corporation owning a cooperative apartment house, sued the defendant, a CPA firm, for damages resulting from the failure of the defendant to discover the embezzlement of over $110,000 by the plaintiff's managing agent, Riker. Riker had orally engaged Rothenberg at an annual fee of $600.

The plaintiff maintained that Rothenberg had been engaged to perform all necessary accounting and auditing services. The defendant claimed he was only engaged to do write-up work and prepare financial statements and related tax returns. As evidence of their respective contentions, the plaintiff booked the accountant's fee as auditing expenses and the defendant marked each page of the financial statements as unaudited. In addition, the accountant in a letter of transmittal to the financial statements stated that (1) the statements were prepared from the books and records of the corporation and (2) no independent verifications were undertaken thereon. The trial court found that the defendant was engaged to perform an audit because Rothenberg admitted that he had performed some limited auditing procedures such as examining bank statements, invoices, and bills. In fact, the CPA's working papers included one entitled "Missing Invoices," which showed over $40,000 of disbursements that did not have supporting documentation. The CPA did not inform the plaintiff of these invoices and no effort was made to find them. The trial court also found the CPA negligent in the performance of the service and awarded damages totaling $237,000. The appellate court affirmed saying

- Regardless of whether the CPA was making an audit or performing write-up work, there was a duty to inform the client of known wrongdoing or other suspicious actions by the client's employees.
- Defendant's work sheets indicate that defendant did perform some audit procedures.
- The record shows that the defendant was engaged to audit the books and records and the procedures performed by the defendant were "incomplete, inadequate, and improperly performed."

The *1136 Tenants'* case has frequently been used to demonstrate the importance of having a written contract (engagement letter) for each professional engagement. A written contract is important, but it was not an issue in this case. The critical issue was the CPA's failure to inform the client of employee wrongdoings, *regardless of the type of service rendered.*

The second case is *Fund of Funds, Ltd.* v. *Arthur Andersen & Co.*[9] In this case, the plaintiff sued the auditors for breach of contract because the auditors failed to disclose irregularities to the client when the auditors' engagement letter contained a specific representation that any irregularities would be revealed. The irregularities, totaling over $120 million, resulted from overcharges on a contract between the plaintiff and King Resources, both audited by Andersen. Andersen admitted

[8] *1136 Tenants' Corp.* v. *Max Rothenberg & Co.* (36 A2d 30 NY2d 804), 319 NYS2d 1007 (1971).

[9] *Fund of Funds, Ltd.* v. *Arthur Andersen & Co.*, 545 F Supp. 1314 (S.D.N.Y. 1982).

discovery of the violation of the contract in auditing King but declined to disclose the irregularities to Fund of Funds because of the AICPA's Ethics Rule 301 that prohibits disclosure of confidential information. The court ruled for the plaintiff on the grounds that the defendants failed to comply with the terms of their engagement letter. Further consideration is given to other issues in this case later in the chapter.

LIABILITY TO THIRD PARTIES

The common law liability of the auditor to third parties is important in any discussion of the auditor's legal liability. A **third party** may be defined as an individual who is not in privity with the parties to a contract. From a legal standpoint, there are two classes of third parties: (1) a primary beneficiary and (2) other beneficiaries. A **primary beneficiary** is anyone identified to the auditor by name prior to the audit who is to be the primary recipient of the auditor's report. For example, if at the time the engagement letter is signed, the client informs the auditor that the report is to be used to obtain a loan at the City National Bank, the bank becomes a primary beneficiary. In contrast, **other beneficiaries** are unnamed third parties, such as creditors, stockholders, and potential investors.

The auditor is liable to *all* third parties for gross negligence and fraud under tort law. In contrast, the auditor's liability for ordinary negligence has traditionally been different between the two classes of third parties.

Liability to Primary Beneficiaries

The privity of contract doctrine extends to the primary beneficiary of the auditor's work. The landmark case, *Ultramares Corp.* v. *Touche,* and its major findings are as follows.

***ULTRAMARES CORP. V. TOUCHE* (1931) LIABILITY FOR NEGLIGENCE[10]**

The defendant auditors, Touche, failed to discover fictitious transactions that overstated assets and stockholders equity by $700,000 in the audit of Fred Stern & Co. On receiving the audited financial statements, Ultramares loaned Stern large sums of money that Stern was unable to repay because it was actually insolvent. Ultramares sued the CPA firm for negligence and fraud.

The court found the auditors guilty of negligence but ruled that accountants should not be liable to any third party for negligence *except to a primary beneficiary*. Judge Cardozo said

> If liability for negligence exists, a thoughtless slip or blunder, the failure to detect a theft or forgery beneath the cover of deceptive entries may expose accountants to a liability in indeterminate amounts, for an indeterminate time, to an indeterminate class. The hazards of a business conducted on these terms are so extreme as to enkindle doubt whether a flaw may not exist in the implication of a duty that exposes to these consequences.

The court also ruled that the finding on negligence does not emancipate accountants from the consequences of fraud. It concluded that gross negligence may constitute fraud.

[10] *Ultramares Corp.* v. *Touche,* 255 N.Y. 170, 174 N.E. 441 (1931).

In essence, *Ultramares* upheld the privity of contract doctrine under which third parties cannot sue auditors for ordinary negligence. However, Judge Cardozo's decision extended to primary beneficiaries the rights of one in privity of contract. Hence, Ultramares as a primary beneficiary could sue and recover for losses suffered because of the auditor's ordinary negligence.

An analysis of the decision reveals several significant environmental factors that are particularly interesting in view of the current legal environment described earlier in this chapter. First, the judge recognized that extending liability for ordinary negligence to any third party might discourage individuals from entering the accounting profession, thus depriving society of a valuable service. Second, he feared the impact that a broader encroachment on the privity doctrine might have on other professionals such as lawyers and doctors. Third, the decision reaffirmed the auditor's liability to any third party for gross negligence or fraud.

Liability to Other Beneficiaries

The *Ultramares* decision remained virtually unchallenged for 37 years, and it still is followed today in many jurisdictions. However, since 1968, several court decisions have served to extend the auditor's liability for ordinary negligence beyond the privity of contract doctrine. The following environmental factors contributed to this development:

- The concept of liability evolved significantly to include consumer protection from the wrongdoing of both manufacturers (product-liability) and professionals (service-liability).
- Businesses and accounting firms grew in size, making them better able to shoulder the new threshold of responsibility.
- The number of individuals and groups relying on audited financial statements grew steadily.

Court decisions have recognized two categories of other third-party beneficiaries as follows: (1) foreseen class and (2) foreseeable parties.

A Foreseen Class. The first shift away from *Ultramares* occurred in the form of judicial acceptance of the specifically **foreseen class** concept. This concept is explained in *Restatement (Second) of Torts* § 552 as follows.[11]

(1) One who, in the course of his (her) business, profession, or employment, or in any other transaction in which he (she) has a pecuniary interest, supplies false information for the guidance of others in their business transactions, is subject to liability for pecuniary loss caused to them by their justifiable reliance upon the information, if he (she) fails to exercise reasonable care or competence in obtaining or communicating the information.

(2) Except as stated in Subsection(3), the liability stated in Subsection(1) is limited to loss suffered
  (a) by a person or one of a limited group of persons for whose benefit and guidance he (she) intends to supply the information or knows that the recipient intends to supply it; and
  (b) through reliance upon it in a transaction that he (she) intends the information to influence or knows that the recipient so intends or in a substantially similar transaction.

(3) The liability of one who is under a public duty to give the information extends to loss suffered by any of the class of persons for whose benefit the duty is created, in any of the transactions in which it is intended to protect them.

---

[11] *Restatement (Second) of Torts* § 552 (1977).

Subsection (2) extends the auditor's liability to "*a limited group of persons* for whose benefit the CPA intends to supply the information." Thus, if the client informs the CPA that the audit report is to be used to obtain a bank loan, all banks are foreseen parties, but trade creditors and potential stockholders would not be part of the foreseen class. The liability is limited to losses suffered through reliance on the information in a transaction known by the auditor or a similar transaction. In the above instance, this means that the accountant would not be liable if the audit report was used by a bank to invest capital in the client's business in exchange for common stock instead of granting a loan.

The foreseen class concept does not extend to all present and future investors, stockholders, or creditors. Court decisions have not required that the injured party be specifically identified, but the *class* of persons to which the party belonged had to be limited and known at the time the auditor provided the information.

FORESEEABLE PARTIES. Individuals or entities whom the auditor either knew or should have known would rely on the audit report in making business and investment decisions are **foreseeable parties.** This concept extends the auditor's duty of due care to any foreseeable party who suffers a pecuniary loss from relying on the auditor's representation. Foreseeable parties include all creditors, stockholders, and present and future investors. Foreseeability is used extensively by the courts in cases involving physical injury. For example, foreseeability is almost universally used in product liability cases when the manufacturer's negligence causes the physical injury. This concept was first applied in an audit negligence case in the early 1980s.

OBJECTIVE 3

Identify important cases that have defined auditor's liability to third parties under common law.

Cases Illustrating Liability to Other Beneficiaries

The leading cases that extended the accountant's liability for ordinary negligence to foreseen parties and to foreseeable parties are as follows.

RUSCH FACTORS INC. V. LEVIN (1968) LIABILITY TO FORESEEN PARTIES[12]

The plaintiff had asked the defendant accountant to audit the financial statements of a corporation seeking a loan. The certified statements indicated that the potential borrower was solvent when, in fact, it was insolvent. Rusch Factors sued the auditor for damages resulting from its reliance on negligent and fraudulent misrepresentations in the financial statements. The defendant asked for dismissal on the basis of lack of privity of contract.

The court ruled in favor of the plaintiff. While the decision could have been decided on the basis of the primary benefit rule set forth in *Ultramares,* the court instead said

> . . . The accountant should be liable in negligence for careless financial misrepresentation relied upon by *actually foreseen and limited classes of persons.* In this case, the defendant knew that his certification was to be used for *potential financiers of the . . . corporation* (emphasis added).

[12] *Rusch Factors, Inc.* v. *Levin,* 284 F. Supp. 85 (D.C.R.I 1968).

The finding in *Rusch Factors Inc.*, which provides the same liability exposure as the *Restatement (second) of Torts* adopted in 1977, was the prevailing rule of law in most jurisdictions until 1983, when *Rosenblum* v. *Adler* occurred.

ROSENBLUM V. ADLER (1983) LIABILITY TO FORESEEABLE PARTIES[13]

The plaintiffs, Harry and Barry Rosenblum, acquired common stock of Giant Stores Corporation, a publicly traded corporation, in conjunction with the sale of their business to Giant. The stock subsequently proved to be worthless after Giant's audited financial statements were found to be fraudulent. The defendant, Adler, was a partner in Touche Ross & Co. that audited the Giant financial statements.

Plaintiffs claimed negligence in the conduct of the audit and that the auditor's negligence was a proximate cause of their loss. Defendants argued for dismissal of the suit because plaintiffs were not in privity with the auditors and they were not a foreseen party.

The Supreme Court of New Jersey denied dismissal, stating

- When the independent auditor furnishes an opinion with no limitation in the certificate regarding to whom the company (audited) may disseminate the financial statements, he has a duty to all those whom that auditor should reasonably foresee as recipients from the company of the statements for its proper business purposes, provided that the recipients rely on the statements pursuant to those business purposes.
- Certified financial statements have become the benchmark for various reasonably foreseeable business purposes, and accountants have been engaged to satisfy these ends. In such circumstances, accounting firms should no longer be permitted to hide within the citadel of privity and avoid liability for their malpractice. The public interest will be served by the rule we promulgate this day.
- Irrespective of whether the defendants had actual knowledge of Giant's proposed use of the audited financial statements in connection with the merger, it was reasonably foreseeable that Giant would use the statements in connection with the merger and its consummation.

In reaching its decision in *Rosenblum*, the New Jersey Supreme Court cited the following public policy factors that appear, in part, aimed at countering Judge Cardozo's arguments in upholding the privity doctrine in *Ultramares:* (1) insurance is available to accountants to cover these risks, (2) the CPA has a moral responsibility to anyone relying on his or her opinion, and (3) more rigid standards will cause accountants to do better work.

The foreseeability standard was subsequently embraced by similar rulings in Wisconsin, California, and Mississippi. Fortunately, several recent developments have begun to reverse the trend toward unlimited liability exposure for accountants under the common law.

---

[13] *H. Rosenblum Inc.* v. *Adler,* 461A 2d 138 (N.J. 1983).

Thus, if a plaintiff has contributed to his or her own injury (loss) by his or her own negligence, the law considers him or her to be as responsible as the defendant for the injury. In such a case, there is no basis for recovery because the negligence of one party nullifies the negligence of the other party. For example, the plaintiff may have withheld vital information from the CPA during the audit or in the preparation of the tax return.

In most states, contributory negligence is a defense for the auditor only when the negligence directly contributes to the auditor's failure to perform. In a leading case, the fact that the client's internal control structure did not prevent an accounting problem from arising was not sufficient to insulate the auditor from liability.[15]

LEARNING CHECK:

4-5 Under common law, a CPA may be liable to a client.
   a. Explain the meaning and importance of the term *privity of contract.*
   b. How may an auditor breach a contract?
   c. What causes ordinarily underlie a tort action?

4-6 a. Who are the classes of third parties that may sustain suits against auditors under common law?
   b. Under what circumstances may an auditor be held liable to third parties?

4-7 Distinguish between foreseen and foreseeable parties. Give examples of each.

4-8 Indicate the significance of the *Ultramares, Rusch Factors, Rosenblum, Credit Alliance,* and *Bily* cases on the auditor's liability for negligence.

4-9 a. What are the accountant's primary defenses in tort actions?
   b. Define contributory negligence.
   c. When does contributory negligence ordinarily represent a valid defense?

KEY TERMS:

Breach of contract, p. 109
Common law, p. 108
Constructive fraud, p. 109
Contributory negligence, p. 116
Due care defense, p. 116
Foreseeable parties, p. 113
Foreseen class, p. 112
Fraud, p. 109
Gross negligence, p. 109
Ordinary negligence, p. 109
Other beneficiaries, p. 111
Primary beneficiary, p. 111
Privity of contract, p. 108
Subrogee, p. 109
Third party, p. 111
Tort, p. 109

[15] *National Surety Corp.* v. *Lybrand,* 256 AD226, 9 NYS 2d 554 (1939).

LIABILITY UNDER SECURITIES LAWS

OBJECTIVE 5

Explain and distinguish the auditor's liability under the securities acts of 1933 and 1934.

Securities laws fall under **statutory law** which is established by state and federal legislative bodies. Most states have **blue sky laws** for the purpose of regulating the issuing and trading of securities within a state. Usually, these statutes require that audited financial statements be filed with a designated regulatory agency. The two most important federal statutes affecting auditors are the Securities Act of 1933 and the Securities Exchange Act of 1934, which are administered by the Securities and Exchange Commission (SEC). The 1933 Act requires audited financial statements to be included in registration statements filed with the SEC when nonexempt entities initially offer securities for sale to the public. The 1934 Act requires public companies with assets in excess of $5 million and more than 500 stockholders to file *annual* reports with the SEC, including audited financial statements.

Two factors contribute to a broader exposure to legal liability under the securities laws than under common law: (1) the 1933 Act grants certain unnamed third parties rights against auditors for ordinary negligence, and (2) criminal indictments may be brought against auditors under both the 1933 and 1934 Acts. In the following sections, in-depth consideration is given to the auditor's legal liability under federal securities laws.

SECURITIES ACT OF 1933

The 1933 Act is known as the *Truth in Securities Act*. It is designed to regulate security offerings to the public through the mails or in interstate commerce. Suits against auditors under this act are usually based on Section 11, Civil Liabilities on Account of False Registration Statement, which states, in part:

> In case any part of the registration statement, when such part became effective, contained an untrue statement of a material fact or omitted to state a material fact required to be stated therein or necessary to make the statements therein not misleading, any person acquiring such security (unless it is proved that at the time of such acquisition he knew of such untruth or omission) may . . . sue. . . .

It should be noted that "any person" purchasing or otherwise acquiring the securities may sue. This includes unnamed third parties. The act makes the auditor liable for losses to third parties resulting from ordinary negligence, as well as from fraud and gross negligence, to the effective date of the registration statement, which may be 20 working days after the statement is filed with the agency.

Section 11 includes two key terms: a **material fact** and **misleading financial statement.** These terms are defined by the SEC as follows:

> The term "material," when used to qualify a requirement for the furnishing of information as to any subject, limits the information required to those matters about which an average prudent investor ought reasonably to be informed.[16]
>
> Financial statements are presumed to be misleading or inaccurate when a material matter is presented in a financial statement in accordance with an accounting principle that has no authoritative support, or has authoritative support but where the SEC has ruled against its use.[17]

Under the civil provisions of the 1933 Act, monetary damages recoverable by a plaintiff are limited to the difference between (1) the amount the investor paid for the security and (2) the market or sales price at the time of the suit. If the security has been sold, the amount recoverable is the difference between the amount paid and the sales price. Criminal penalties are provided under Sections 17 and 24. For example, Section 24 provides for penalties on conviction of no more than $10,000 in fines or imprisonment of not more than five years, or both, for *willfully* making an untrue statement or omitting a material fact in a registration statement.

Bringing Suit Under the 1933 Act

The principal effects of this Act on the parties involved in a suit may be summarized as follows:

Plaintiff

- May be any person acquiring securities described in the registration statement, whether or not he or she is a client of the auditor.
- Must base the claim on an alleged material false or misleading financial statement contained in the registration statement.
- Does not have to prove reliance on the false or misleading statement or that the loss suffered was the proximate result of the statement if purchase was made before the issuance of an income statement covering a period of at least 12 months following the effective date of the registration statement.
- Does not have to prove that the auditors were negligent or fraudulent in certifying the financial statements involved.

Defendant

- Has the burden of establishing freedom from negligence by proving that he (or she) had made a reasonable investigation and accordingly had reasonable ground to believe, and did believe, that the statements certified were true at the date of the statements and as of the time the registration statement became effective, or
- Must establish, by way of defense, that the plaintiff's loss resulted in whole or in part from causes other than the false or misleading statements.

The reasonable investigation concept is often referred to as the **due diligence defense.** Section 11(c) states that the standard of reasonableness is the care required of a prudent person in the management of his (or her) own property. For an

[16] SEC, Rule 1-102, regulation S–X.

[17] SEC, Financial Reporting Release No. 1, Section 101 (1982).

auditor, the basis for a reasonable investigation of audited financial statements is GAAS.

Cases Brought Under the 1933 Act

A major civil case under the Securities Act of 1933 is the *BarChris* case. The auditing issues in this case are described below.

ESCOTT V. BARCHRIS CONSTRUCTION CORP. (1968) CIVIL LIABILITY UNDER SECURITIES ACT OF 1933[13]

BarChris was a company that was in constant need of cash. Purchasers of debentures filed suit under Section 11 when the company filed for bankruptcy, alleging that the registration statement pertaining to the sale of the bonds contained material false statements and material omissions. One of the defendants was a national public accounting firm, Peat, Marwick, Mitchell & Co., which pleaded the due diligence defense.

In certifying the registration statement that preceded the bankruptcy by 17 months, the accounting firm performed a subsequent events review, called an S–1 review by the SEC. The purpose of the review was to ascertain whether, subsequent to the certified balance sheet, any material changes had occurred that needed to be disclosed to prevent the balance sheet from being misleading.

The court concluded that Peat Marwick's written audit program for the review was in conformity with generally accepted auditing standards. However, it also found that the work done by a senior who was performing his first S–1 review was unsatisfactory. In ruling that the accounting firm had not established a due diligence defense, the court said

- The senior's review was useless because it failed to discover a material change for the worse in BarChris's financial position that required disclosure to prevent the balance sheet from being misleading.
- The senior did not meet the standards of the profession because he did not take some of the steps prescribed in the written program.
- The senior did not spend an adequate amount of time on a task of this magnitude and, most important of all, he was too easily satisfied with glib answers.
- There were enough danger signals in the materials examined to require some further investigation.

As a result of this case, an SAS was issued on subsequent events that includes specific review procedures, as is explained in Chapter 19.

A major criminal case brought under Section 24 of the 1933 Act is described next.

UNITED STATES V. SIMON (1969) CRIMINAL LIABILITY[19]

This case, also called the *Continental Vending* case, involved loans made by Continental Vending to its affiliated company, Valley Commercial Corporation, which subsequently lent the money to the president of Continental (Roth). The loans to Roth were secured primarily by the pledging of Continental common stock owned by Roth. Valley, in turn, pledged this stock as collateral against the loans from Continental. The auditor for Continental did not audit Valley. The defendants (a senior partner, a junior partner, and an audit senior of an international accounting firm) approved the following note:

---

[18] *Escott* v. *BarChris Construction Corp.,* 283 F Supp 643 (S.D.N.Y. 1968).

[19] *United States* v. *Simon* [425 F 2d 796 (2d Cir. 1969)].

> The amount receivable from Valley Commercial Corp. (an affiliated company of which Mr. Harold Roth is an officer, director, and stockholder) bears interest at 12% a year. Such amount, less the balance of the notes payable to that company, is secured by the assignment to the Company of Valley's equity in certain marketable securities. As of February 15, 1963, the amount of such equity at current market quotations exceeded the net amount receivable.

The government argued that the note should have said

> The amount receivable from Valley Commercial Corp. (an affiliated company of which Mr. Harold Roth is an officer, director, and stockholder), which bears interest at 12% a year, was uncollectible at September 30, 1962, since Valley had loaned approximately the same amount to Mr. Roth, who was unable to pay. Since that date, Mr. Roth and others have pledged as security for the repayment of his obligation to Valley and its obligation to Continental (now $3,900,000 against which Continental's liability to Valley cannot be offset) securities which, as of February 14, 1963, had a market value of $2,978,000. Approximately 80% of such securities are stock and convertible debentures of the Company.

Specifically, the government charged that the defendant's note was false and misleading because

- Continental's footnote did not show that Roth obtained the money.
- The nature of the collateral was not disclosed even though 80% of it consisted of unregistered securities issued by Continental.
- The net amount of the Valley receivables was improper because the Valley payable that had been offset represented notes discounted with outsiders.
- Reference to the secured position in February did not disclose the significant increase in the Valley receivables at that date.

The defendants, supported by the testimony of eight leaders in the accounting profession, contended that their note was in conformity with GAAP and that such compliance was a conclusive defense against criminal charges of misrepresentation. However, the trial judge rejected this argument and instructed the jury that the "critical test" was whether the balance sheet fairly presented financial position without reference to generally accepted accounting principles. The jury concluded that the balance sheet did not present fairly, and the three defendants were convicted of the criminal charges. The U.S. court of appeals refused to reverse the decision and held that

> We do not think the jury was . . . required to accept the accountants' evaluation whether a given fact was material to overall fair presentation, at least not when the accountant's testimony was not based on specific rules and prohibitions to which they could point, but only on the need for the auditor to make an honest judgment and their conclusion that nothing in the financial statements themselves negated the conclusion that an honest judgment had been made. Such evidence may be highly persuasive, but it is not conclusive, and so the trial judge correctly charged.

The defendants were found guilty. They were fined $17,000 and their licenses to practice as CPAs were revoked.

As a result of this case, an SAS was issued on the meaning of "present fairly." A major conclusion of this SAS was that the auditor's judgment on fairness should be applied within the framework of GAAP. In addition, an SAS was published on the auditor's responsibilities for related party transactions. These SASs are discussed in later chapters.

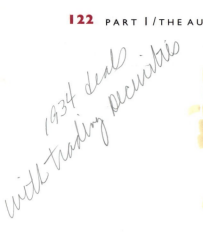

SECURITIES EXCHANGE ACT OF 1934

This Act was passed by Congress to regulate the public trading of securities. The 1934 Act requires companies included under the Act to (1) file a registration statement when the securities are publicly traded on a national exchange or over the counter for the first time and (2) keep the registration statement current through the filing of annual reports, quarterly reports, and other information with the SEC. Certain financial information, including the financial statements, must be audited by independent public accountants. Because of the recurring reporting requirements with the SEC, the Act is often referred to as the *Continuous Disclosure Act*. The principal liability provisions of the 1934 Act are set forth in Sections 18, 10, and 32.

Section 18 Liability

Under Section 18(a)

> Any person who shall make or cause to be made any statement in any application, report, or document filed pursuant to this title . . . which . . . was made false or misleading with respect to any material fact, shall be liable to any person (not knowing that such statement was false or misleading) who, in reliance upon such statement, shall have purchased or sold a security at a price which was affected by such statement, for damages caused by such reliance, unless the person sued shall prove that he acted in good faith and had no knowledge that such statement was false or misleading.

Section 18 liability is relatively narrow in scope because it relates only to a false or misleading statement in documents "filed" with the SEC under the Act.

Section 10 Liability

Section 10(b) provides that

> It shall be unlawful for any person, directly or indirectly, by the use of any means or instrumentality of interstate commerce or of the mails, or of any facility of any national securities exchange to use or employ, in connection with the purchase or sale of any security registered on a national securities exchange or any security not so registered, any manipulative or deceptive device or contrivance in contravention of such rules and regulations as the Commission may prescribe as necessary or appropriate in the public interest or for the protection of investors.

Under this section, the SEC promulgated Rule 10b-5, which states that it is unlawful for any person, directly or indirectly, to

- Employ any device, scheme, or artifice to *defraud.*
- Make *any untrue statement* of a material fact or *omit* to state a material fact necessary to make the statements made, in the light of the circumstances under which they were made, not misleading.

- Engage in any act, practice, or course of business that operates, or would operate, as a *fraud* or *deceit* on any person in connection with the purchase or sale of any security.

Section 10(b) and Rule 10b-5 are often referred to as the antifraud provisions of the 1934 Act. Section 10 is broad in scope because it applies both to the public and private trading of securities.

Section 32 Liability

Section 32(a) establishes criminal liability for "willfully" and "knowingly" making false or misleading statements in reports filed under the 1934 Act. This section also provides for criminal penalties for violating the antifraud provisions of Section 10(b) consisting of fines of not more than $100,000 or imprisonment for not more than five years, or both.

Bringing Suit Under the 1934 Act

There are similarities and differences in the effects of Sections 10 and 18 on the parties involved. Under both sections, the plaintiff (1) may be any person buying or selling the securities, (2) must prove the existence of a material false or misleading statement, and (3) must prove reliance on such statement and damage resulting from such reliance. However, the responsibility of the plaintiff differs under the two sections in terms of proof of auditor fraud. Under Section 18, the plaintiff does not have to prove that the auditor acted fraudulently, but in a Section 10, Rule 10b-5 action, such proof is required.

The defendant in a Section 18 suit must prove that he or she (1) acted in good faith and (2) had no knowledge of the false or misleading statement. This means that the minimum basis for liability is gross negligence. Accordingly, the auditor's position under Section 18 is the same as under the common law doctrine of *Ultramares* in which he or she may also be held liable to third parties for gross negligence. An injured plaintiff in a Section 18 action is allowed to recover "out-of-pocket" losses, which are determined by the difference between the contract price and the real or actual value on the transaction date. The latter is generally established by the market price when the misrepresentation or omission occurred.

Differences Between the 1933 and 1934 Acts

The securities acts apply to different situations. The 1933 Act applies to the initial distribution of securities (capital stock and bonds) to the public by the issuing corporation, whereas the 1934 Act applies to the initial sale and trading of securities for national security markets. Differences between Section 11 of the 1933 Act and Sections 10 and 18 of the 1934 Act exist as to (1) the plaintiff, (2) proof of reliance on the false or misleading financial statements, and (3) the auditor's liability for ordinary negligence. These differences are summarized in Figure 4-2. Many more cases have been brought against auditors under the 1934 Act than the 1933 Act because the former applies to annual filings as well as certain registration statements.

FIGURE 4-2 • SUMMARY OF DIFFERENCES IN KEY SECTIONS OF 1933 AND 1934 ACTS

Item	1933 Act	1934 Act
Plaintiff	Any person acquiring the security	Either the buyer or seller of the security
Plaintiff must prove reliance	No	Yes
Defendant liable for ordinary negligence	Yes	No

Cases Brought Under the 1934 Act

Lawsuits against auditors under the 1934 Act are usually based on Section 10(b) and Rule 10b-5. During the decade of the mid-1960s to the mid-1970s, plaintiffs were able to obtain a number of judgments against CPA firms for ordinary negligence under these provision. A 1976 decision by the U.S. Supreme Court in *Ernst & Ernst* (now Ernst & Young) v. *Hochfelder* marked the end of the accountant's liability for ordinary negligence under Section 10 of the 1934 Act. This landmark case is explained below.

ERNST & ERNST V. HOCHFELDER (1976) CIVIL LIABILITY FOR NEGLIGENCE UNDER RULE 10B-5 OF 1934 ACT[20]

The plaintiffs (Hochfelder) were investors in an escrow account allegedly kept by the president (Lester K. Nay) of First Securities Co., a small brokerage firm, audited by the defendant CPA firm (now Ernst & Young).

The escrow account, in which a high rate of return was promised, was a ruse perpetrated by Nay. To prevent detection, all investors were instructed to make their checks payable to Nay and to mail them directly to him at First Securities. Within the brokerage house, Nay imposed a "mail rule" that such mail was to be opened only by himself. The escrow account was not recorded on First Securities' books. The fraud was uncovered in Nay's suicide note.

Plaintiffs sued Ernst for damages under Rule 10b-5 for aiding and abetting the embezzlement. They based their claim entirely on the premise that the accountants were negligent in their audit because they had not challenged or investigated the "mail rule."

Following conflicting lower court decisions, the U.S. Supreme Court ruled in favor of the defendants, saying

> When a statute speaks so specifically in terms of manipulation and deception, and of implementing devices and contrivances—the commonly understood terminology of intentional wrongdoing—and when its history reflects no more expansive intent, we are quite unwilling to extend the scope of the statute to negligent conduct.

The Supreme Court failed to rule on whether reckless behavior is sufficient for liability under Rule 10b-5.

---

[20] *Ernst & Ernst* v. *Hochfelder,* 425 US 185, 96 S Ct 1375, 47 L Ed 2d 668 (1976).

Based on this decision, an auditor is no longer liable to third parties under Section 10(b) and Rule 10b-5 of the 1934 Act for ordinary negligence. That is, the auditor has no liability in the absence of any intent to deceive or defraud (legally called **scienter**).[21]

The following case dealt with several legal issues and elaborated on the requisite scienter under Rule 10b-5.

THE FUND OF FUNDS LIMITED V. ARTHUR ANDERSEN & CO. (1982) CIVIL LIABILITY UNDER 1934 ACT, COMMON LAW FRAUD, AND BREACH OF CONTRACT[22]

The Fund of Funds Limited (FOF), a mutual investment fund, entered into an oral contract as part of a diversification program to purchase oil and gas properties from King Resources Corporation (KRC) at prices no *less favorable* than the seller received from other customers.

Arthur Andersen & Co. (AA) was the auditor for both companies, and the same key audit personnel participated in both engagements. In its engagement letter to FOF, AA made the *specific representation* that any irregularities discovered by the accounting firm would be revealed to the client. In auditing KRC, AA discovered that FOF was being billed at prices that were significantly higher than other customers. AA, however, failed to inform FOF because it did not wish to breach the rule of confidential client information. Plaintiff claimed that AA was required to disclose the overcharge or to resign at least one of the two accounts.

As an open-ended mutual fund, FOF was required to value its investment portfolio, which included its investments in natural resources, on a daily basis. The daily share value was used for redeeming investor shares. In its December 31, 1969, financial statements, FOF booked a significant upward revaluation in certain natural resource interests. Their evaluation was based in part on non-arm's length non-bona fide sales of small portions of the same interests by KRC. These sales did not satisfy the guidelines established by AA for issuing an unqualified opinion on KRC's financials, but such an opinion was nevertheless issued. AA claimed that their report on KRC was not the cause of FOF's revaluation and that they had no knowledge of the non-bona fide sales prior to issuing their report.

The jury found AA liable for aiding and abetting violations of securities laws (Rule 10b-5) and common law fraud because of their failure to disclose their knowledge of KRC's wrongdoings to FOF. In addition, the jury found the accounting firm guilty of breach of contract because they did not comply with the specific representation in their engagement letter. Plaintiff was awarded damages of $81 million. The judge in the case subsequently reduced the damages to an undisclosed amount.

The decision also included a finding on reckless behavior. The jury found that the requisite of scienter was met through the accountant's recklessness. It said

- A reckless misrepresentation, or reckless omission to state information necessary to make that which is stated not misleading, is one that disregards the truth or falsity of the information disclosed in light of a known danger or patently obvious danger.

---

[21] Scienter may be established by proof of either (1) actual knowledge of the falsity of the representation or (2) a reckless disregard for the truth or falsity of the representation.

[22] *Fund of Funds, Ltd.* v. *Arthur Andersen & Co., op. cit.*

- The accountants acted with requisite scienter in disregarding known and obvious risks to FOF in issuing its unqualified opinion.
- We also find support for a finding of gross recklessness as the auditors conspicuously failed to test the arm's length nature of the transactions.

Following is an example of a criminal case brought under Section 32 of the 1934 Act.

UNITED STATES V. _NATELLI_ (1975) CRIMINAL LIABILITY[23]

In this case, commonly known as the *National Student Marketing Corporation* case, two auditors were convicted of criminal liability for failing to properly disclose the writeoff of uncollectible accounts. In the financial statements of the current year (1969), uncollectible accounts pertaining to 1968 regular sales on advertising contracts, which had only been verified by telephone, were reported in part as a retroactive adjustment against sales acquired by pooling in 1968. The accompanying footnote failed to state that regular sales for 1968 were overstated 20% and that actual net earnings were only 46% of reported earnings. The court concluded that

- The treatment of the retroactive adjustment was done intentionally to conceal errors in the 1968 statements.
- A professional cannot escape criminal liability on a plea of ignorance when they have shut their eyes to what was plainly to be seen.

Recent Developments

Many of the growing body of abusive securities suits mentioned at the beginning of this chapter have been brought under Section 10(b) of the 1934 Act. Accountants and other professionals such as attorneys and underwriters have frequently been cited under this section for aiding-and-abetting securities fraud. **Aiding-and-abetting** means an indirect involvement or tangential role in purported wrongdoing. In a 1994 decision in the case of *Central Bank of Denver N. A.* v. *First Interstate Bank of Denver N.A.,* the U.S. Supreme Court ruled that professionals cannot be sued under that section for mere aiding-and-abetting.[24] The decision, which directly involved private suits, did not clarify whether the SEC can continue to bring aiding-and-abetting actions under Section 10(b).

LEARNING CHECK:

4-10 a. Who may bring suit under the 1933 Securities Act?
b. What is the basis for such action?

4-11 What are the responsibilities of the plaintiff and the defendant in a 1933 Act suit?

4-12 State the issues and the court's conclusions in the *BarChris* case.

---

[23] *United States* v. *Natelli,* 527 F.2d 311 (1975).

[24] "Justices Deal Investors a Blow in Certain Suits," *The Wall Street Journal,* April 20, 1994, p. A3.

4-13 a. Who may bring suit under the 1934 Securities Exchange Act?
b. Is the basis for action the same as in a 1933 Act suit? Explain.

4-14 Explain the conditions associated with liability under Rule 10b-5 of the 1934 Act.

4-15 What are the responsibilities of the plaintiff and the defendant in a 1934 Act suit?

4-16 a. What was the basis for the *Hochfelder* case?
b. What is the significance of the decision in the case?

4-17 a. Indicate the jury's findings in the *Fund of Funds* case.
b. State the accounting issue and the jury's findings in the *Continental Vending* case.

KEY TERMS:

Aiding-and-abetting, p. 126
Blue sky laws, p. 118
Due diligence defense, p. 119
Material fact, p. 118
Misleading financial statement, p. 118
Scienter, p. 125
Statutory law, p. 118

OTHER CONSIDERATIONS

Although the majority of suits against auditors under statutory law cite violations of the securities laws discussed in the preceding sections, the 1980s and early 1990s saw a groundswell of activity under RICO, another fraud statute.

LIABILITY UNDER RACKETEER INFLUENCED AND CORRUPT ORGANIZATION ACT

OBJECTIVE 6

Indicate the auditor's liability under the Racketeer Influenced and Corrupt Organization Act.

RICO was originally drafted as part of the 1970 Organized Crime Control Act to curtail the inroads of organized crime into legitimate business. RICO contains civil provisions that permit all private persons victimized by a "pattern of racketeering activity" to sue for treble damages and attorneys' fees. Despite its focus on organized crime, the provisions of RICO have been extended to losses suffered from fraudulent securities offerings and failures of legitimate businesses. CPAs have often been named as codefendants on the theory that their involvement with the issuance of materially false financial statements for a minimum of two years out of a ten-year period constitutes a pattern of racketeering activity. The possibility of treble damages and the transfer of plaintiff's attorneys' fees to losing defendants served as powerful incentives for plaintiffs to bring actions against auditors under RICO whenever possible and for auditors to feel coerced to settle out of court.

The extension of the scope of RICO to cover cases involving legitimate business enterprises and individuals affiliated with those enterprises, such as directors, officers, and professional accountants, has been challenged in court on several occasions. But the U.S. Supreme Court in *Sedima* v. *Imrex* (1985), a case that did not involve auditors, approved the expansive scope to which RICO was being applied. In rendering its decision, the Court conceded that RICO may have evolved into something quite different from the original conception of its enactors, but concluded that "this defect—if defect it is—is inherent in the statute as written, and its correction must lie with Congress."

Nearly a decade later in 1993, with no intervening action by Congress to correct the statute, the U.S. Supreme Court heard another case known as *Reves* v. *Ernst & Young*. In this case, which involved investor losses related to a farmers' cooperative that went bankrupt, the Court ruled that RICO "requires some participation in the operation or management of the enterprise itself."[25] It further concluded that the auditor's provision of unqualified audit reports for two consecutive years on the co-op's alleged misleading financial statements did not meet the participation test. Many observers hope this decision will mark an end to a majority of RICO actions against auditors. It should be noted, however, that auditors may remain culpable under RICO if a court concludes the auditor's relationship with a client went beyond the traditional role of auditing. Two earlier cases under RICO with less favorable outcomes are summarized in the appendix to this chapter.

PROFESSIONAL STANDARDS AND LEGAL DECISIONS

A difference of opinion exists among the AICPA, the SEC, and the courts about the relative importance of professional standards in legal decisions. An awareness of these differences may be useful in understanding the present legal climate.

OBJECTIVE 7

Discuss alternative views of the relative importance of professional standards on legal decisions.

The AICPA has made the following statements concerning the importance of professional standards and the conclusiveness of expert testimony concerning the standards:

- The standard of communication required is measured by specific generally accepted accounting principles (GAAP) and GAAS, and, in the absence of specific rules or customs, by the views of experts (professional CPAs).
- The jury (or court in a case of trial without jury) is never authorized to question the wisdom of the professional standard.[26]

In contrast, the SEC has taken the following positions on professional standards and expert testimony of auditors:

- The auditor has an obligation that goes beyond specific GAAP and GAAS or professional custom to effectively communicate material information.
- If GAAP and GAAS are found lacking, the SEC will not hesitate to invoke its authority to establish meaningful standards of performance regardless of expert testimony as to professional standards.[27]

The SEC position requires *effective* communication of material information to fairly and meaningfully inform the layperson investor.

---

[25] Richard J. Bergstrom and Jeanne Lunsford Morrison, "RICO: Has the "Ultimate Weapon" Been Crushed?" *Journal of Accountancy* (News—Special Report) (June 1993), p. 17.

[26] "AICPA Amicus Brief, Continental Vending Case," *Journal of Accountancy* (May 1970), pp. 69–73.

[27] Denzil Y. Causey, Jr., *Duties and Liabilities of the Public Accountant, Revised Edition* (Homewood, IL: Dow-Jones Irwin, 1982), p. 10.

An indication of the courts' position on these two matters is as follows:

- Where the profession has established specific GAAS for reasonably dealing with a perceived problem, the professional duty will be limited to conformance with the standard if resulting financial statements fairly and meaningfully inform the investor. Even if the auditor fails to follow professional standards, liability is imposed only when the resulting financials actually cause damage to plaintiffs. However, when misleading financials cause losses, the courts will not hesitate to penalize the auditor despite strong evidence of conformity with GAAP and GAAS.
- Where application of auditing standards requires expertise in evaluating and testing internal controls, statistical sampling of transactions, and obtaining competent evidential matter, expert testimony will be conclusive. However, where communication of findings is involved, expert testimony as to compliance with GAAP will be persuasive but not conclusive.[28]

MINIMIZING THE RISK OF LITIGATION

OBJECTIVE 8

Enumerate precautions a CPA can take to minimize the risk of litigation.

CPAs, like other professionals such as doctors and lawyers, are currently practicing in a climate where national public policy is emphasizing protection for the consumer (general public) from substandard work by professionals. An analysis of court cases involving CPAs reveals the following precautions that a CPA may take to minimize the risk of becoming involved in litigation.

- *Use Engagement Letters for All Professional Services.* Such letters provide the basis for the contractual arrangements and minimize the risk of misunderstanding about the services that have been agreed on.
- *Make a Thorough Investigation of Prospective Clients.* As is explained in Chapter 6, investigation is necessary to minimize the likelihood that the CPA will be associated with a client whose management lacks integrity.
- *Emphasize Quality of Service Rather Than Growth.* The ability of a firm to properly staff an engagement is vital to the quality of the work that will result. Acceptance of new business that will likely lead to excessive overtime, abnormally heavy workloads, and limited supervision by experienced professionals should be resisted.
- *Comply Fully with Professional Pronouncements.* Strict adherence to *Statements on Auditing Standards* is essential. An auditor must be able to justify any material departures from established guidelines.
- *Recognize the Limitations of Professional Pronouncements.* Professional guidelines are not all-encompassing. In addition, it should be recognized that subjective tests of reasonableness and fairness will be used by judges, juries, and regulatory agencies in judging the auditor's work. The auditor must use sound professional judgment during the audit and in the issuance of the audit report.
- *Establish and Maintain High Standards of Quality Control.* As suggested in Chapter 1, both the CPA firm and individual auditors have clearly established responsibilities for quality control. Outside peer reviews provide important independent assurance of the quality and the continued effectiveness of prescribed procedures.

---

[28] *Ibid.* p. 10.

- *Exercise Caution in Engagements Involving Clients in Financial Difficulty.* The impending threat of insolvency or bankruptcy may lead to intentional misrepresentations in the financial statements. Many lawsuits against auditors have resulted from the bankruptcies of companies following the issuance of the auditor's report. The auditor should carefully weigh the sufficiency and competency of the evidence obtained in audits of such companies.

LEARNING CHECK:

4-18 a. Contrast the original intent of the Racketeer Influenced and Corrupt Organization Act (RICO) with the courts' interpretations of its provisions.
b. What advantages does a plaintiff have in a RICO suit compared with a suit brought under the federal securities acts?
c. How may accountants be involved in a RICO suit?

4-19 Contrast the positions of the AICPA, the SEC, and the courts on the relative importance of professional standards in legal cases.

4-20 Identify actions the auditor may take to minimize the risk of litigation.

KEY TERMS:

RICO, p. 127

SUMMARY

Although the proportion of audit failures to all audits is very low, the consequences of even a few large audit failures can be significant for investors, creditors, and other market participants, as well as for auditors. Litigation has had a significant impact on the public accounting profession in the past 30 years, incrementally clarifying auditors' responsibilities and serving as a catalyst to the further development and refinement of auditing standards. However, by the early 1990s, concerned individuals both within and outside the accounting profession viewed the explosion in abusive securities suits and coerced out-of-court settlements as approaching crisis proportions, threatening the accounting profession itself and the role it plays in our free market economy. Accordingly, the profession has called for legal reforms at both the state and federal levels that would impact the auditor's exposure under the common law, the securities laws, and other statutory laws. Although a number of recent court decisions appear to provide some relief for accountants, even a short history of audit-related litigation shows that the courts can do quick turnabouts on important legal issues surrounding ambiguous standards and laws. Moreover, attorneys and others can and do pursue legislative initiatives to suit their own interests. Thus, it is important for the profession to continue to seek legislative reforms. In the meantime, to minimize the risk of litigation, auditors should adhere to high standards of professional practice.

APPENDIX 4A CHRONOLOGICAL SUMMARY OF ADDITIONAL SELECTED LEGAL CASES

Following are summaries of a number of important case supplementing those summarized in the chapter. They have been classified as follows: (1) cases under the common law, (2) cases under the securities laws, and (3) RICO cases.

Cases Under the Common Law

RHODE ISLAND HOSPITAL TRUST NATIONAL BANK V. SWARTZ, BRESENHOFF, YAVNER & JACOBS (1972). The defendant auditors issued a disclaimer of opinion on audited financial statements. The plaintiff bank was a foreseen (but unnamed) party. The suit charged that the auditors were guilty of ordinary negligence because the reasons for the disclaimer in the auditors' report contained wording that was misleading. The reasons stated that

> Additions to fixed assets were found to include principally warehouse improvements. . . . Practically all of this work was done by company employees. . . . Unfortunately, complete detailed cost records were not kept and no exact determination could be made as to the actual cost of said improvements.

The court found no cost records, and the capital expenditures were fictitious. Because the disclaimer referred to only valuation and not existence, the court ruled for the plaintiff saying that a general disclaimer cannot relieve the auditor of liability stemming from the impression conveyed by other statements in his report.

CREDIT ALLIANCE CORPORATION ET AL. V. ARTHUR ANDERSEN & CO. (1985). The plaintiffs were major financial service companies engaged primarily in financing the purchase of capital equipment through installment sales or leasing agreements. Plaintiff granted additional credit to L. B. Smith Inc., based on Andersen's unqualified annual audit reports of Smith for the three years ending February 28, 1979. In 1980, Smith filed a petition for bankruptcy after defaulting on several millions of dollars of obligations to plaintiffs. Plaintiffs argued that Smith's statements, on which they relied, overstated Smith's assets, net worth, and general financial health because the auditors failed to meet proper auditing standards, thereby failing to discover Smith's precarious financial condition and the serious possibility that Smith would be unable to survive as a going concern. They charged Andersen with both negligence and fraud, claiming that the defendants (1) knew or should have known and were on notice the financial statements were to be utilized by Smith to obtain additional credit, (2) knew that the certified statements were being shown to plaintiffs for this purpose, and (3) knew or recklessly disregarded facts that indicated the 1977 and 1979 statements were misleading. The Supreme Court of New York dismissed the charge of negligence. In essence, the Court found that there was neither a relationship of contractual privity between the plaintiff and defendants or a relationship sufficiently intimate to be equated with privity. The Court also dismissed the charge of fraud, saying that the single allegation of scienter, reckless disregard for the facts, was insufficient cause for judgment against defendants.

***Bily v. Arthur Young & Co.* (1992).** This case relates to a suit brought by investors in the Osborne Computer Corporation which introduced the first portable personal computer in 1981. Within two years, its sales had reached $10 million per month. Venture capitalists eagerly invested in a private offering, and other investors acquired shares held by existing shareholders. Within a few short months, however, following manufacturing problems and new competition from IBM-compatible computers, Osborne declared bankruptcy. The investors subsequently asserted that Arthur Young was negligent in conducting its audit of Osborne's 1982 financial statements and that the audit report contained errors.

In reversing a Court of Appeal's decision, the California Supreme Court distinguished three types of wrongful acts: negligence, negligent misrepresentation, and intentional fraud. In ruling that the auditor owes no general duty of care regarding the conduct of an audit to persons other than the client, the Supreme Court showed a detailed understanding of the nature of the audit function and its economic implications. The Court cited an "uncertain connection between investment and credit losses and the auditor's report," and noted the ease with which remote parties can assert that they relied on audit reports. It also noted that investors and lenders should be encouraged to rely on their own prudence, diligence, and other informational tools, not just an auditor's report. Finally, it countered the argument made by other courts that allowing unrestricted third-party negligence lawsuits against auditors would result in more accurate auditing and efficient loss spreading. Instead, it acknowledged that, at least as likely, would be an increase in the costs and a decrease in the availability of audits with no compensating increase in audit quality. Regarding negligent misrepresentation through the audit report, the Court concurred with the standing given to third parties in the rule adopted in the Restatement (Second) of Torts. The Court also reaffirmed that an auditor can be held liable to any third party for fraud.

Cases Under the Securities Laws

***McKesson & Robbins* (1940).** The SEC found that the auditors failed to employ a necessary degree of diligence and inquisitiveness that resulted in their failure to discover an overstatement of assets that management had created through recording and manipulation of fictitious inventories. The SEC noted that

- Numerous auditing procedures require strengthening (e.g., inventory, accounts receivable, accounts payable, investigation of new clients, audit committee reviews).
- Auditors should be responsible for detecting gross misstatements whether resulting from collusion or otherwise.
- Auditors must recognize their responsibility to the public investor by including management activities in their review.

***United States v. White* (1941).** The auditor was convicted of criminal fraud under Section 17 of the Securities Act of 1933 for his failure to disclose several instances of questionable accounting practices in connection with a registration statement. The Court expressed the following thought with respect to the sufficiency of evidence in a criminal case:

> Items of questionable accounting, which taken individually do not demonstrate knowledge of falsity, may acquire greater significance as proof when considered together.

UNITED STATES V. BENJAMIN (1964). The auditor was convicted in a criminal action under Section 24 of the 1933 Act for his failure to exercise due diligence that would have revealed misrepresentations in pro forma financial statements used in conjunction with sales of unregistered securities. The Court stated:

> In our complex society, the accountant's certificate and the lawyer's opinion can be instruments for inflicting pecuniary loss more potent than the chisel or the crowbar. Of course, Congress did not mean that any mistake of law or misstatement of fact should subject an attorney or an accountant to criminal liability simply because more skilled practitioners would not have made them. But Congress equally could not have intended that men holding themselves out as members of these ancient professions should be able to escape criminal liability on a plea of ignorance when they have shut their eyes to what was plainly to be seen or have represented a knowledge they knew they did not possess.

FISCHER V. KLETZ (1967). In this case, commonly known as *Yale Express,* the auditor did not disclose errors in a previously issued audit report that were discovered three months later during a management services engagement. In ruling on the case that involved actions under common law and Section 10(b), Rule 10b-5, and Section 18 of the 1934 Act, the court noted that

> An auditor has a duty to anyone still relying on his report to disclose subsequently discovered errors in the report. This duty exists regardless of the auditor's lack of financial interest in any transactions to which the information relates. The obligation arises because of the auditor's special relationship that provides access to the information.

UNITED STATES V. WEINER (1975). In this case, three auditors of Equity Funding Corp. of America were convicted after a jury trial of multiple counts of securities fraud and filing false statements with the SEC. The case involved the auditors' failure to detect that $2.1 billion of the company's $3.2 billion of assets were fraudulently obtained through computer-produced, bogus insurance policies. The fraud covered several years. In addition to criminal convictions against the three auditors, five accounting firms paid $44 million in damages.

CENCO INCORPORATED V. SEIDMAN & SEIDMAN (1982). In this case, the U.S. Court of Appeals for the Seventh Circuit in Chicago, Illinois, in a three-judge decision, upheld an earlier jury verdict in favor of the auditors, Seidman & Seidman. The defendants were charged with violating various federal securities laws and SEC rules, notably Rule 10b-5. The case pertained to the auditors' failure to detect a $25 million inventory fraud perpetrated by top management. In the decision, the judges distinguished between management fraud and employee fraud and said

- Auditors are not detectives hired to ferret out fraud.
- Auditors must investigate if they suspect fraud; but in this case, the former management made fraud difficult to detect because top executives turned the company "into an engine of theft against outsiders."

The court also gave the auditors permission to sue Cenco for the amount paid ($3.5 million) as damages to Cenco stockholders in a 1980 class action suit settlement pertaining to the fraud.

RICO Cases

***SCHACHT V. BROWN* (1983).** This was the first audit failure case brought under RICO. Three separate auditing firms were found to be liable for alleged damages of $100 million (before RICO-trebling) for "fraudulent prolongation of the corporation's life beyond solvency." Plaintiff claimed that each CPA firm knew of the subsidiary company's insolvency. However, each firm still issued unqualified opinions on the company's consolidated financial statements for the years 1974–77.

***ESM GOVERNMENT SECURITIES LITIGATION V. ALEXANDER GRANT & CO.* (NOW GRANT THORNTON & CO.) (1986).** In this RICO case, the management of ESM devised a scheme of fictitious transactions to conceal operating losses from 1977 through 1984. The defendant's partner in charge of the audits beginning with the 1978 audit was advised by management subsequent to the 1978–79 audits that the Grant audit team had failed to detect the fraud. Faced with potential damage to his career, the partner agreed to forgo disclosure of the fraud to give management one year to make up the losses. Management failed to do so, but the partner continued to cover up the scheme until the company collapsed in 1985. Defendant is reported to have reached out-of-court settlements approaching $50 million.

BIBLIOGRAPHY

AICPA Professional Standards:

SAS 53 (AU 316), The Auditor's Responsibility to Detect and Report Errors and Irregularities.

IAU 11 (AU 8011), Fraud and Error.

Brecht, D. "Accountants' Duty to the Public for Audit Negligence: Self Regulation and Legal Liability," *Business and Professional Ethics Journal* (Spring 1991), pp. 85–100.

Lochner, Philip R., Jr. "Accountant's Legal Liability: A Crisis That Must be Addressed," *Accounting Horizons* (June 1993), pp. 92–96.

McCarroll, Thomas. "Who's Counting?" *Time* (April 13, 1992), pp. 48–50.

O'Malley, Shaun F. "Legal Liability Is Having a Chilling Effect on the Auditor's Role," *Accounting Horizons* (June 1993), pp. 82–87.

Paetzold, R. A., and Huss, H. F., "The Standard of Care for Independent Public Accountants: Insights for Self-Regulation and Standard Setting," *Research in Accounting Regulation* (Vol. 7, 1993), pp. 61–80.

Palmrose, Zoe-Vonna. "An Analysis of Auditor Litigation and Audit Service Quality," *Accounting Review* (January 1988), pp. 55–73.

Report of the National Commission on Fraudulent Financial Reporting. Washington, D.C., National Commission on Fraudulent Financial Reporting, 1987.

Schuetze, Walter P. "The Liability Crisis in the U.S. and Its Impact on Accounting," *Accounting Horizons* (June 1993), pp. 88–91.

Simonetti, Gilbert, Jr., and Andrews, Andrea R. "A Profession at Risk/A System in Jeopardy," *Journal of Accountancy* (April 1994), pp. 45–54.

Wilburn, Kay O., and Broom, Lowsell S. "Alternative Strategies for Litigation Battles," *Journal of Accountancy* (Liability Issues) (March 1994), pp. 77–80.

OBJECTIVE QUESTIONS

4-21 These questions pertain to the auditor's liability under common law.

1. If a stockholder sues a CPA for common law fraud based on false statements contained in the financial statements audited by the CPA, which of the following is the CPA's best defense?
   a. The CPA did *not* financially benefit from the alleged fraud.
   b. There was contributory negligence of the client.
   c. The stockholder lacks privity to sue.
   d. The false statements were immaterial.
2. In a common law action against an accountant, the lack of privity is a viable defense if the plaintiff
   a. Is a creditor of the client who sues the accountant for negligence.
   b. Can prove the presence of gross negligence, which amounts to a reckless disregard for the truth.
   c. Is the accountant's client.
   d. Bases his action on fraud.
3. Starr Corp. approved a plan of merger with Silo Corp. One of the determining factors in approving the merger was the strong financial statements of Silo, which were audited by Cox & Co., CPAs. Starr had engaged Cox to audit Silo's financial statements. While performing the audit, Cox failed to discover certain irregularities, which have subsequently caused Starr to suffer substantial losses. For Cox to be liable under common law, Starr at a minimum must prove that Cox
   a. Acted recklessly or with a lack of reasonable grounds for belief.
   b. Knew of the irregularities.
   c. Failed to exercise due care.
   d. Was grossly negligent.

4-22 These questions relate to the auditor's liability under statutory law.

1. One of the elements necessary to recover damages if there has been a material misstatement in a registration statement filed pursuant to the Securities Act of 1933 is that the
   a. Plaintiff suffered a loss.
   b. Plaintiff gave value for the security.
   c. Issuer and plaintiff were in privity of contract with each other.
   d. Issuer failed to exercise due care in connection with the sale of the securities.
2. To be successful in a civil action under Section 11 of the Securities Act of 1933 concerning liability for a misleading registration statement, the plaintiff must prove

	Defendant's Intent to Deceive	Plaintiff's Reliance on the Registration Statement
a.	Yes	Yes
b.	Yes	No
c.	No	Yes
d.	No	No

3. In which of the following statements concerning a CPA firm's action is scienter or its equivalent absent?
   a. Actual knowledge of fraud.
   b. Performance of substandard auditing procedures.
   c. Reckless disregard for the truth.
   d. Intent to gain monetarily by concealing fraud.

4. Sharp & Co., CPAs, was engaged by Radar Corp. to audit its financial statements. Sharp issued an unqualified opinion on Radar's financial statements. Radar has been accused of making negligent misrepresentations in the financial statements that Wisk relied on when purchasing Radar stock. Sharp was not aware of the misrepresentations nor was it negligent in performing the audit. If Wisk sues Sharp for damages based on Section 10(b) and Rule 10b-5 of the Securities Exchange Act of 1934, Sharp will
   a. Lose because the statements contained negligent misrepresentations.
   b. Lose because Wisk relied on the financial statements.
   c. Prevail because some element of scienter must be proved.
   d. Prevail because Wisk was *not* in privity of contract with Sharp.

5. How does the Securities Act of 1933, which imposes civil liability on auditors for misrepresentations or omissions of material facts in a registration statement, expand auditors' liability to purchasers of securities beyond that of common law?
   a. Purchasers only have to prove loss caused by reliance on audited financial statements.
   b. Privity with purchasers is **not** a necessary element of proof.
   c. Purchasers have to prove either fraud or gross negligence as a basis for recovery.
   d. Auditors are held to a standard of care described as "professional skepticism."

Comprehensive Questions

4-23 **(Common law—constructive fraud, negligence)** Astor Inc. purchased the assets of Bell Corp. A condition of the purchase agreement required Bell to retain a CPA to audit Bell's financial statements. The purpose of the audit was to determine whether the unaudited financial statements furnished to Astor fairly presented Bell's financial position. Bell retained Salam & Co., CPAs, to perform the audit.

While performing the audit, Salam discovered that Bell's bookkeeper had embezzled $500. Salam had some evidence of other embezzlements by the bookkeeper. However, Salam decided that the $500 was immaterial and that the other suspected embezzlements did not require further investigation. Salam did not discuss the matter with Bell's management. Unknown to Salam, the bookkeeper had, in fact, embezzled large sums of cash from Bell. In addition, the accounts receivable were significantly overstated. Salam did not detect the overstatement because of Salam's inadvertent failure to follow its audit program.

Despite the foregoing, Salam issued an unqualified opinion on Bell's financial statements and furnished a copy of the audited financial statements to Astor. Unknown to Salam, Astor required financing to purchase Bell's assets and furnished a copy of Bell's audited financial statements to City Bank to obtain approval of the loan. Based on Bell's audited financial statements. City loaned Astor $600,000.

Astor paid Bell $750,000 to purchase Bell's assets. Within six months, Astor began experiencing financial difficulties resulting from the undiscovered embezzlements and overstated accounts receivable. Astor later defaulted on the City loan.

City has commenced a lawsuit against Salam based on the following causes of action:

- Constructive fraud
- Negligence

REQUIRED

In separate paragraphs, discuss whether City is likely to prevail on the causes of action it has raised, setting forth reasons for each conclusion.

AICPA

4-24 **(Common law—negligence, fraud)** Tyler Corp. is insolvent. It has defaulted on the payment of its debts and does not have assets sufficient to satisfy its unsecured creditors. Slade, a supplier of raw materials, is Tyler's largest unsecured creditor and is suing Tyler's auditors, Field & Co., CPAs. Slade had extended $2 million of credit to Tyler based on the strength of Tyler's audited financial statements. Slade's complaint alleges that the auditors were either (1) negligent in failing to discover and disclose fictitious accounts receivable created by management or (2) committed fraud in connection therewith. Field believes that the financial statements of Tyler were prepared in accordance with GAAP and, therefore, its opinion was proper. Slade has established that:

- The accounts receivable were overstated by $10 million.
- Total assets were reported as $24 million of which accounts receivable were $16 million.
- The auditors did not follow their own audit program, which required that confirmation requests be sent to an audit sample representing 80% of the total dollar amount of outstanding receivables. Confirmation requests were sent to only 45%.
- The responses that were received represented only 20% of the total dollar amount of outstanding receivables. This was the poorest response in the history of the firm, the next lowest being 60%. The manager in charge of the engagement concluded that further inquiry was necessary. This recommendation was rejected by the partner in charge.
- Field had determined that a $300,000 account receivable from Dion Corp. was nonexistent. Tyler's explanation was that Dion had reneged on a purchase contract before any products had been shipped. At Field's request, Tyler made a reversing entry to eliminate this overstatement. However, Field accepted Tyler's explanation as to this and several similar discrepancies without further inquiry.

Slade asserts that Field is liable:

- As a result of negligence in conducting the audit.
- As a result of fraud in conducting the audit.

REQUIRED

Answer the following, setting forth reasons for any conclusions stated.

Discuss Slade's assertions and the defenses that might be raised by Field.

AICPA

4-25 **(Common law—privity defense)** Perfect Products Co. applied for a substantial bank loan from Capitol City Bank. In connection with its application, Perfect engaged William & Co., CPAs, to audit its financial statements. William completed the audit and rendered an unqualified opinion. On the basis of the financial statements and William's opinion, Capitol granted Perfect a loan of $500,000.

Within three months after the loan was granted, Perfect filed for bankruptcy. Capitol promptly brought suit against William for damages, claiming that it had relied to its detriment on misleading financial statements and the unqualified opinion of William.

William's audit workpapers reveal negligence and possible other misconduct in the performance of the audit. Nevertheless, William believes it can defend against liability to Capitol based on the privity defense.

REQUIRED

Answer the following, setting forth reasons for any conclusions stated.

a. Explain the privity defense and evaluate its application to William.
b. What exceptions to the privity defense might Capitol argue?

AICPA

4-26 **(Common law—review service)** Mason & Dilworth, CPAs, were the accountants for Monrad Corporation, a closely held corporation. Mason & Dilworth had been previously engaged by Monrad to perform certain compilation and tax return work. Crass, Monrad's president, indicated he needed something more than the previous type of services rendered. He advised Walker, the partner in charge, that the financial statements would be used internally, primarily for management purposes, and also to obtain short-term loans from financial institutions. Walker recommended that a review of the financial statements be performed. Walker did not prepare an engagement letter.

In the course of the review, Walker indicated some reservations about the financial statements. Walker indicated at various stages that "he was uneasy about certain figures and conclusions" but that "he would take the client's word about the validity of certain entries since the review was primarily for internal use in any event and was not an audit."

Mason & Dilworth did not discover a material act of fraud committed by management. The fraud would have been detected had Walker not relied wholly on the representations of management concerning the validity of certain entries about which he had felt uneasy.

REQUIRED

Answer the following, setting forth reasons for any conclusions stated.

a. What is the role of the engagement letter when a CPA has agreed to perform a review of a closely held company? What points should be covered in a typical engagement letter that would be relevant to the parties under the facts set forth above?
b. What is the duty of the CPA in the event suspicious circumstances are revealed as a result of the review?
c. What potential liability does Mason & Dilworth face and who may assert claims against the firm?

AICPA

4-27 **(Statutory law—1933 Act)** The Dandy Container Corporation engaged the accounting firm of Adams and Adams to audit financial statements to be used in connection with a public offering of securities. The audit was completed and an unqualified opinion was expressed on the financial statements that were submitted to the Securities and Exchange Commission along with the registration statement. Two hundred thousand shares of Dandy Container common stock were offered to the public at $11 a share. Eight months later, the stock fell to $2 a share when it was disclosed that several large loans to two "paper" corporations owned by one of the directors were worthless. The loans were secured by the stock of the borrowing corporation that was owned by the director. These facts were not disclosed in the financial report. The director involved and the two corporations are insolvent.

1. The Securities Act of 1933 applies to the above-described public offering of securities in interstate commerce.
2. The accounting firm has potential liability to any person who acquired the stock in reliance on the registration statement.
3. An investor who bought shares in Dandy Container would make a prima facie case if he alleges that the failure to explain the nature of the loans in question constituted a false statement or misleading omission in the financial statements.

4. The accountants could avoid liability if they could show they were neither negligent nor fraudulent.
5. The accountants could avoid or reduce the damages asserted against them if they could establish that the drop in price was due in whole or in part to other causes.
6. The Dandy investors would have to institute suit within one year after discovery of the alleged untrue statements or omissions.
7. The SEC would defend any action brought against the accountants in that the SEC examined and approved the registration statement.

REQUIRED

Indicate whether each of the above statements is true or false under statutory law. Give the reason(s) for your answer.

AICPA

4-28 **(Statutory law—1934 Act; common law—negligence)** To expand its operations, Dark Corp. raised $4 million by making a private interstate offering of $2 million in common stock and negotiating a $2 million loan from Safe Bank. The common stock was properly offered pursuant to the Securities Act of 1933.

In connection with this financing, Dark engaged Crea & Co., CPAs, to audit Dark's financial statements. Crea knew that the sole purpose for the audit was so that Dark would have audited financial statements to provide to Safe and the purchasers of the common stock. Although Crea conducted the audit in conformity with its audit program, Crea failed to detect material acts of embezzlement committed by Dark's president. Crea did not detect the embezzlement because of its inadvertent failure to exercise due care in designing its audit program for this engagement.

After completing the audit, Crea rendered an unqualified opinion on Dark's financial statements. The financial statements were relied on by the purchasers of the common stock in deciding to purchase the shares. In addition, Safe approved the loan to Dark based on the audited financial statements.

Within 60 days after the sale of the common stock and the making of the loan by Safe, Dark was involuntarily petitioned into bankruptcy. Because of the president's embezzlement, Dark became insolvent and defaulted on its loan to Safe. Its common stock became virtually worthless. Actions have been commenced against Crea by:

- The purchasers of the common stock who have asserted that Crea is liable for damages under Section 10(b) and Rule 10b-5 of the Securities Exchange Act of 1934.
- Safe, based on Crea's negligence.

REQUIRED

In separate paragraphs, discuss the merits of the actions commenced against Crea, indicating the likely outcomes and the reasons therefor.

AICPA (adapted)

4-29 **(Statutory law—1934 Act; common law—negligence)** Astor Electronics, Inc. is engaged in the business of marketing a wide variety of computer-related products throughout the United States. Astor's officers decided to raise $1,000,000 by selling shares of Astor's common stock in an exempt offering under the Securities Act of 1933. In connection with the offering, Astor engaged Apple & Co., CPAs, to audit Astor's 19X9 financial statements. The audited financial statements, including Apple's unqualified opinion, were included in the offering memorandum given to prospective purchasers of Astor's stock. Apple was aware that Astor intended to include the statements in the offering materials.

On Astor's financial statements, certain inventory items were reported at a cost of $930,000 when, in fact, they had a fair market value of less than $100,000 because of technological obsolescence. Apple accepted the assurances of Astor's controller that cost was the appropriate valuation, despite the fact that Apple was aware of ongoing sales of the products at prices substantially less than cost. All of this was thoroughly documented in Apple's working papers.

Musk purchased 10,000 shares of Astor's common stock in the offering at a total price of \$300,000. In deciding to make the purchase, Musk had reviewed the audited financial statements of Astor that accompanied the other offering materials and Musk was impressed by Astor's apparent financial strength.

Shortly after the stock offering was completed, Astor's management discovered that the audited financial statements reflected the materially overstated valuation of the company's inventory. Astor advised its shareholders of the problem.

Musk, on receiving notice from Astor of the overstated inventory amount, became very upset because the stock value was now substantially less than what it would have been had the financial statements been accurate. In fact, the stock is worth only about \$200,000.

Musk has commenced an action against Apple, alleging that Apple is liable to Musk based on the following causes of action:

- Common law fraud.
- Negligence.
- A violation of Section 10(b) and Rule 10b-5 of the Securities Exchange Act of 1934.

During the course of the litigation, Apple has refused to give to Musk its working papers pertaining to the Astor audit, claiming that these constituted privileged communications. The state in which the actions have been commenced has no accountants' privileged communication statute.

The state law applicable to this action follows the *Ultramares* decision with respect to accountants' liability to third parties for negligence or fraud.

Apple has also asserted that the actions should be dismissed because of the absence of any contractual relationship between Apple and Musk, i.e., a lack of privity.

REQUIRED

Answer the following, setting forth reasons for any conclusions stated:

a. What elements must be established by Musk to support his cause of action based on negligence?
b. What elements must be established by Musk to support his cause of action based on a Rule 10b-5 violation?
c. Is Apple's assertion regarding lack of privity correct with regard to Musk's causes of action for negligence and fraud?

AICPA (adapted)

4-30 **(Statutory law—1934 Act; common law)** The following information applies to both Parts I and II:

James Danforth, CPA, audited the financial statements of the Blair Corporation for the year ended December 31, 19X1. Danforth rendered an unqualified opinion on February 6, 19X2. The financial statements were incorporated into Form 10-K and filed with the Securities and Exchange Commission. Blair's financial statements included as an asset a previously sold certificate of deposit (CD) in the amount of \$250,000. Blair had purchased the CD on December 29, 19X1, and sold it on December 30, 19X1, to a third party, who paid Blair that day. Blair did not deliver the CD to the buyer until January 8, 19X2. Blair deliberately recorded the sale as an increase in cash and other revenue, thereby significantly overstating working capital, stockholders' equity, and net income. Danforth confirmed Blair's purchase of the CD with the seller and physically observed the CD on January 5, 19X2.

PART I: Assume that on January 18, 19X2, while auditing other revenue, Danforth discovered that the CD had been sold. Further assume that Danforth agreed that in exchange for an additional audit fee of \$20,000, he would render an unqualified opinion on Blair's financial statements (including the previously sold CD).

REQUIRED

Answer the following, setting forth reasons for any conclusions stated:

a. The SEC charges Danforth with criminal violations of the Securities Exchange Act of 1934. Will the SEC prevail? Include in your discussion what the SEC must establish in this action.
b. Assume the SEC discovers and makes immediate public disclosure of Blair's action with the result that no one relies to his detriment on the audit report and financial statements. Under these circumstances, will the SEC prevail in its criminal action against Danforth?

PART II: Assume that Danforth performed his audit in accordance with generally accepted auditing standards (GAAS) and exercised due professional care, but did not discover Blair's sale of the CD. Two weeks after issuing the unqualified opinion, Danforth discovered that the CD had been sold. The day following this discovery, at Blair's request, Danforth delivered a copy of the audit report, along with the financial statements, to a bank that in reliance thereon made a loan to Blair that ultimately proved uncollectible. Danforth did not advise the bank of his discovery.

REQUIRED

Answer the following, setting forth reasons for any conclusions stated:

If the bank sues Danforth for the losses it sustains in connection with the loan, will it prevail?

AICPA

CASE 4-31 **(Statutory law; common law)**

PART I: The common stock of Wilson, Inc. is owned by 20 stockholders who live in several states. Wilson's financial statements as of December 31, 19X5, were audited by Doe & Co., CPAs, who rendered an unqualified opinion on the financial statements. In reliance on Wilson's financial statements, which showed net income for 19X5 of $1,500,000, Peters, on April 10, 19X6, purchased 10,000 shares of Wilson stock for $200,000. The purchase was from a shareholder who lived in another state. Wilson's financial statements contained material misstatements. Because Doe did not carefully follow GAAS, it did not discover that the statements failed to reflect unrecorded expenses that reduced Wilson's actual net income to $800,000. After disclosure of the corrected financial statements, Peters sold his shares for $100,000, which was the highest price he could obtain.

Peters has brought an action against Doe under federal securities law and state common law.

REQUIRED

Answer the following, setting forth reasons for any conclusions stated:

a. Will Peters prevail on his federal securities law claims?
b. Will Peters prevail on his state common law claims?

PART II: Able Corporation decided to make a public offering of bonds to raise needed capital. On June 30, 19X6, it publicly sold $2,500,000 of 12% debentures in accordance with the registration requirements of the Securities Act of 1933.

The financial statements filed with the registration statement contained the unqualified opinion of Baker & Co., CPAs. The statements overstated Able's net income and net worth. Through negligence Baker did not detect the overstatements. As a result, the bonds, which originally sold for $1,000 per bond, have dropped in value to $700.

Ira is an investor who purchased $10,000 of the bonds. He promptly brought an action against Baker under the Securities Act of 1933.

REQUIRED

Answer the following, setting forth reasons for any conclusions stated:

Will Ira prevail on his claim under the Securities Act of 1933?

AICPA

RESEARCH QUESTIONS

4-32 **(State common law liability for ordinary negligence)** As noted in the chapter, the courts in different states follow different precedents in deciding on third-party ordinary negligence actions, ranging from the *Ultramares* precedent, to *Rusch Factors, Rosenblum,* and *Credit Alliance.* In addition, several states have recently enacted privity legislation. For your state, (1) determine what the auditor's common law exposure for ordinary negligence is currently, and (2) prepare a brief summary of a recently decided court case, citing the nature of the alleged negligence and the court's findings.

4-33 **(AAERs dealing with legal liability)** Several of the SEC's *Accounting and Auditing Enforcement Releases* pertain to incidences of auditors being involved in fraudulent financial reporting. For any one such *AAER,* (1) prepare a brief description of the fraudulent activity in which the auditor was found to have participated, and (2) indicate the nature of the disciplinary actions taken by the SEC against the auditor.

PART

2

AUDIT PLANNING

CHAPTER

5

AUDIT OBJECTIVES, EVIDENCE, AND WORKING PAPERS

LEARNING OBJECTIVES

When you have completed the study of this chapter, you should be able to

1. State the five categories of management's financial statement assertions.
2. Derive specific audit objectives from the categories of assertions.
3. Indicate the factors that affect the sufficiency and competency of evidential matter.
4. Identify the types of corroborating information available to the auditor.
5. Enumerate and describe the types of audit procedures that may be used in an audit.
6. Describe the three classifications of audit procedures and the purpose of each.
7. Explain the nature and purpose of audit working papers.
8. Apply the essential techniques of good working paper preparation.

AUDIT OBJECTIVES
- MANAGEMENT'S FINANCIAL STATEMENT ASSERTIONS
- SPECIFIC AUDIT OBJECTIVES

AUDIT EVIDENCE
- STATEMENT AND PURPOSE OF THE THIRD STANDARD OF FIELD WORK
- TYPES OF CORROBORATING INFORMATION

AUDIT PROCEDURES
- TYPES OF AUDIT PROCEDURES
- RELATIONSHIPS AMONG AUDIT PROCEDURES, TYPES OF EVIDENCE, AND ASSERTIONS
- CLASSIFICATION OF AUDIT PROCEDURES
- EVALUATION OF EVIDENCE OBTAINED

WORKING PAPERS
- TYPES OF WORKING PAPERS
- PREPARING WORKING PAPERS
- REVIEWING WORKING PAPERS
- WORKING PAPER FILES
- OWNERSHIP AND CUSTODY OF WORKING PAPERS

SUMMARY

BIBLIOGRAPHY

OBJECTIVE QUESTIONS

COMPREHENSIVE QUESTIONS

CASES

RESEARCH QUESTIONS

Now that consideration of the environmental factors pertaining to auditing has been completed, it is time to begin explaining the components and specifics of a financial statement audit. We start with a discussion of the following four fundamentals of auditing: (1) audit objectives, (2) audit evidence, (3) audit procedures, and (4) the documentation of audit evidence in working papers.

AUDIT OBJECTIVES

As indicated in Chapter 2, the **overall objective** of a financial statement audit is the expression of an opinion on whether the client's financial statements are presented fairly, in all material respects, in conformity with GAAP. To meet this objective, it is customary in the audit to identify numerous **specific audit objectives** for each account reported in the financial statements. These specific objectives are derived from the assertions made by management that are contained in the financial statements.

MANAGEMENT'S FINANCIAL STATEMENT ASSERTIONS

Financial statements include both explicit and implicit management assertions. For example, consider the following balance sheet component:

Current Assets:	
Cash	*$252,900*

In reporting this item in the balance sheet, management makes the following two explicit assertions: (1) cash exists and (2) the correct amount of cash is $252,900. Management also makes the following three implicit assertions: (1) all cash that should be reported has been included, (2) all the reported cash is owned by the entity, and (3) there are no restrictions on the use of cash. The latter assertion follows from the presentation of cash in current assets and the absence of any reference to footnote disclosures. If any of these assertions is a misrepresentation, the financial statements could be materially misstated.

Similar assertions underlie all of the asset, liability, revenue, and expense components of financial statements. Accordingly, the Auditing Standards Board in SAS 31, *Evidential Matter* (AU 326.03), has recognized the following five broad categories of **financial statement assertions:**

OBJECTIVE 1

State the five categories of management's financial statement assertions.

- Existence or occurrence
- Completeness
- Rights and obligations
- Valuation or allocation
- Presentation and disclosure

In the sections below, we first present the descriptions provided for each category of assertions in AU 326 followed by examples of each. We then illustrate a set of specific audit objectives for cash derived from the categories of assertions.

Existence or Occurrence

Assertions about **existence or occurrence** deal with whether assets or liabilities of the entity exist at a given date and whether recorded transactions have occurred during a given period.

Management's assertions about *existence* extend to assets with physical substance, such as cash and inventories, as well as to accounts without physical substance, such as accounts receivable and accounts payable. In the example cited above, the existence assertion pertains to whether items included in cash, such as petty cash funds, undeposited receipts, and checking accounts, exist. This assertion does not extend to whether $252,900 is the correct amount for these items. The latter relates to the valuation or allocation assertion as explained further later.

Under this assertion, management also asserts that the revenues and expenses shown in the income statement are the results of transactions and events that *occurred during the reporting period.* Again, this assertion extends only to whether transactions and events occurred, not to whether the amounts reported are correct. A misrepresentation of this assertion would result if fictitious sales were included in reporting sales, or if reported sales included transactions that should have been reported in another period.

The auditor's concern about this category of assertions relates primarily to the *overstatement* of financial statement components through the inclusion of items that do not exist or the effects of transactions that did not occur. It does not extend to whether items that do exist, and the effects of transactions that did occur, have been included at the correct dollar amounts.

Completeness

Assertions about **completeness** deal with whether all transactions and accounts that should be presented in the financial statements are so included.

For each financial statement account presented in the financial statements, management implicitly asserts that all related transactions and events have been included. For example, management asserts that the cash balance of $252,900 includes the effects of all cash transactions and all of the cash funds mentioned above. A misrepresentation of the completeness assertion for cash would result if the effects of some cash receipts transactions were omitted.

The auditor's concern about completeness assertions relates primarily to the possible *understatement* of financial statement components through the omission of items that exist, or omission of the effects of transactions that occurred. If omissions are identified, the issue of the correct dollar amounts at which they should be included relates to the valuation or allocation assertion.

Rights and Obligations

Assertions about **rights and obligations** deal with whether assets are the rights of the entity and liabilities are the obligations of the entity at a given date.

Note that this assertion, because it deals only with assets and liabilities, pertains only to the balance sheet, while each of the other assertions pertains to all of the statements. This assertion normally refers to ownership rights and legal obligations. For example, management implicitly asserts that it owns the cash, inventory, and other assets reported in the balance sheet, and that accounts payable and other liabilities are the legal obligations of the reporting entity. The rights and obligations assertion also extends to rights to the use of property and to certain liabilities that are not legal obligations. For example, property owned by a lessor is properly included as an asset in the lessee's balance sheet when rights to use the property have been acquired under a capital lease. And unfunded pension costs may properly be included as a liability even though the reporting entity may not be legally obligated for them.

Valuation or Allocation

Assertions about **valuation or allocation** deal with whether asset, liability, revenue, and expense components have been included in the financial statements at appropriate amounts.

The reporting of a financial statement component at an appropriate amount means that the amount (1) has been determined in conformity with GAAP and (2) is clerically and mathematically accurate.[1]

CONFORMITY WITH GAAP. Determining amounts in conformity with GAAP includes the proper measurement of assets, liabilities, revenues, and expenses which includes all of the following:

- Proper application of valuation principles such as cost, net realizable value, market value, and present value.
- Proper application of the matching principle.
- The reasonableness of management's accounting estimates.
- Consistency in the application of accounting principles.

Thus, for example, current receivables are reported at net realizable value; inventories at the lower of cost or market; investments, depending on their characteristics, at cost, amortized cost, market value, or an amount determined by the equity method; fixed assets at historical cost less accumulated depreciation; and noncurrent receivables and payables generally at present values. Period costs are matched against revenues of the period, and the costs of noncurrent tangible and intangible assets are allocated to expense and matched against revenues as the revenues are earned. Accounting estimates such as salvage values, uncollectible accounts, and warranty liabilities should be reasonable. And the accounting principles should be consistently applied across periods except when a change is justified.

CLERICAL AND MATHEMATICAL ACCURACY. Clerical accuracy refers to such matters as accuracy in entering details on source documents, in recording journal entries, in posting to ledgers, and in maintaining agreement between control accounts and subsidiary ledgers. Mathematical accuracy refers to such matters as determining arithmetically correct totals for invoices, journals, and account balances, as well as to the correctness of computations for such items as accruals and depreciation. Continuing our previous cash illustration, a misstatement in the valuation or allocation assertion for cash would result from clerical errors in recording cash receipts or disbursements or in posting the cash receipts or disbursements journals to the general ledger cash account, or from

[1] In practice, some auditors limit the valuation or allocation assertion to GAAP and recognize clerical and mathematical accuracy as a separate category of assertions.

mathematical errors in summing the cash receipts or disbursements journals or the cash account itself.

VALUATION IS NOT EXISTENCE

Auditors disclaimed an opinion on a client's financial statements citing the following reason:

> Additions to fixed assets were found to include principally warehouse improvements. . . . Unfortunately, complete detailed cost records were not kept and no exact determination could be made as to the actual cost of said improvements.

In reality there were no warehouse improvements. The courts concluded that the disclaimer was misleading because it referred only to the valuation assertion and not to the existence assertion. Thus, the auditors were found guilty of negligence in doing the audit.

SOURCE: *Rhode Island Hospital Trust National Bank v. Swartz, Bresenhoff, Yavner & Jacobs*, 482 F.2nd 1000 (4th Cir. 1973).

Presentation and Disclosure

Assertions about **presentation and disclosure** deal with whether particular components of the financial statements are properly classified, described, and disclosed.

In the financial statements, management implicitly asserts that the components are properly presented and accompanying disclosures are adequate. In the cash example, it would be a misrepresentation of this assertion if there were restrictions on the use of cash and the notes to the financial statements did not indicate this fact. Similarly, there would be a misrepresentation of this assertion if unrestricted cash were classified as a noncurrent asset.

A summary of the five management assertions is presented in Figure 5-1.

SPECIFIC AUDIT OBJECTIVES

In obtaining evidence to support an opinion on the financial statements, the auditor develops **specific audit objectives** for each account in the financial statements.

FIGURE 5-1 • CATEGORIES OF MANAGEMENT'S FINANCIAL STATEMENT ASSERTIONS

Assertion Category	Nature
Existence or occurrence	Assets and liabilities of the entity exist at a given date, and revenue and expense transactions occurred during a given period.
Completeness	All transactions and accounts that should be included in the financial statements are so included.
Rights and obligations	Assets are the rights of the entity and liabilities are the obligations of the entity at a given date.
Valuation or allocation	Asset, liability, revenue, and expense components have been included in the financial statements at appropriate amounts.
Presentation and disclosure	Particular components of the financial statements are properly classified, described, and disclosed.

OBJECTIVE 2

Derive specific audit objectives from management's assertions.

The categories of management's financial statement assertions described above are a useful starting point in developing the specific objectives. The following tabulation illustrates the derivation of specific audit objectives for cash based on the discussions of the categories of assertions above:

Assertion Category	Specific Audit Objective
Existence or occurrence	The petty cash funds, undeposited receipts, checking accounts, and any other items reported as cash exist at the balance sheet date.
Completeness	Reported cash includes all petty cash funds, undeposited receipts, and other cash on hand. Reported cash includes all unrestricted bank balances.
Rights and obligations	All items included in cash are owned by the entity at the balance sheet date.
Valuation or allocation	The items comprising cash have been correctly totaled. Cash receipts and disbursements journals are mathematically correct and have been properly posted to the general ledger. Cash on hand has been correctly counted. Checking account balances have been properly reconciled.
Presentation and disclosure	All items included in cash are unrestricted and the cash is available for operations. Required disclosures such as compensating balance agreements have been made.

It is important to recognize that specific audit objectives are tailored to fit each client. AU 326.09 indicates that the auditor should consider the circumstances in which the client operates, the nature of its economic activity, and the accounting practices unique to its industry. For example, additional specific objectives would be required when part of an entity's cash is in a foreign currency. Also, the number of specific objectives for each category of assertions may vary as indicated in the foregoing listing.

In performing the audit, the auditor obtains evidence concerning each of the specific objectives. From the evidence accumulated, the auditor reaches a conclusion as to whether any of management's assertions are misrepresentations. Subsequently, conclusions about the individual assertions are combined to reach an opinion on the fairness of the financial statements as a whole.

LEARNING CHECK:

5-1 a. What is the overall objective of a financial statement audit?
b. How does the auditor customarily meet this overall objective?

5-2 State the five categories of management's financial statement assertions and briefly explain each.

5-3 What is the difference in the nature of a misstatement resulting from a misrepresentation of the existence or occurrence assertion versus a misrepresentation of the completeness assertion?

5-4 a. What two aspects of reporting a financial statement component at an appropriate amount are encompassed in the valuation or allocation assertion?
b. Identify four aspects of proper measurement that should be considered in determining whether an amount is in conformity with GAAP.

5-5 a. To what should specific audit objectives relate?
b. What constitutes a useful starting point for deriving such objectives?
c. Identify three factors the auditor should consider in tailoring specific audit objectives to each client.

KEY TERMS:

Financial statement assertions, p. 145
  Existence or occurrence, p. 145
  Completeness, p. 146
  Rights and obligations, p. 146
  Valuation or allocation, p. 147
  Presentation and disclosure, p. 148
Overall objective, p. 144
Specific audit objectives, p. 148

AUDIT EVIDENCE

Audit evidence is a fundamental concept in auditing. In SASs, audit evidence is referred to as **evidential matter.** AU 326.14 states that evidential matter consists of **underlying accounting data** (e.g., the underlying accounting or financial records) and all **corroborating information** available to the auditor. Examples of types of evidence in each category and the relationship of the categories to the third standard of field work are shown in Figure 5-2. In an electronic data processing (EDP)

FIGURE 5-2 • CATEGORIES AND TYPES OF EVIDENTIAL MATTER

Nature of Evidential Matter	Third Standard of Field Work
UNDERLYING ACCOUNTING DATA • Books of original entry. • General and subsidiary ledgers. • Related accounting manuals. • Informal and memorandum records, such as work sheets, computations, and reconciliations. CORROBORATING INFORMATION • Documents such as checks, invoices, contracts, and minutes of meetings. • Confirmations and other written representations. • Information from inquiry, observation, inspection, and physical examination. • Other information obtained or developed by the auditor.	SUFFICIENT COMPETENT EVIDENTIAL MATTER

SOURCE: AU 326.14-.16.

system, the underlying accounting data and some of the corroborating information may exist in the form of electronic media such as magnetic tapes and disks, and may also be available in hard copy or printed form.

Both categories of evidential matter are required in making an audit in accordance with GAAS. It should be obvious that underlying accounting data are indispensable, for they provide the basis for the client's financial statements. However, these records may not be reliable. Thus, it is imperative that the auditor obtain supportive evidence of the reliability of the financial records. Much of this evidence is available within the client organization, but recourse to knowledgeable persons outside the company is also necessary.

The process of identifying specific sources of evidence to meet specific audit objectives for individual account balances is covered extensively in Parts III and IV of this book. This chapter establishes a general framework for identifying the types of evidence and the financial statement assertions to which they relate.

STATEMENT AND PURPOSE OF THE THIRD STANDARD OF FIELD WORK

The third standard of field work states

> Sufficient competent evidential matter is to be obtained through inspection, observation, inquiries, and confirmations to afford a reasonable basis for an opinion regarding the financial statements under audit.

OBJECTIVE 3

Indicate the factors that affect the sufficiency and competency of evidential matter.

Four sources of evidential matter are identified in the foregoing standard—inspection, observation, inquiries, and confirmations. These sources relate to the four *auditing procedures* of inspecting, observing, inquiring, and confirming. At this point, it should be recognized that there are more than four auditing procedures available to the auditor. These and other procedures are explained later in the chapter.

The standard also specifies that *sufficient* (i.e., enough) *competent* (i.e., reliable) evidential matter should be obtained to provide a *reasonable* (i.e., rational) basis for an opinion. AU 326.20 states that "the amount and kinds of evidential matter required to support an informed opinion are matters for the auditor to determine in the exercise of his professional judgment after a careful study of the circumstances in the particular case."

Sufficiency of Evidential Matter

This element of the third standard of field work pertains to the quantity of evidential matter. Factors that may affect the auditor's judgment as to sufficiency include

- Materiality and risk.
- Economic factors.
- Size and characteristics of the population.

MATERIALITY AND RISK. In general, more evidence is needed for accounts that are material to the financial statements than for accounts that are immaterial. Thus, in the audit of a manufacturing company, the quantity of evidence in support of the audit objectives for inventories will be greater than the quantity needed for the audit objectives pertaining to prepaid expenses.

Similarly, more evidence is normally required for accounts that are likely to be misstated than for accounts that are likely to be correct. For example, normally there is a higher risk of error in the valuation of inventory than there is in the valuation of land used as a plant site. Additional consideration is given to the effects of materiality and risk in Chapter 7.

ECONOMIC FACTORS. An auditor works within economic limits that dictate that sufficient evidence must be obtained within a reasonable time and at reasonable cost. Thus, the auditor is frequently faced with a decision as to whether the additional time and cost will produce commensurate benefits in terms of the persuasiveness of the evidence obtained. For example, to verify the existence of a client's 25 petty cash funds, the auditor could personally count each fund. A less costly alternative is to personally count five of the funds and, upon finding the funds to agree with the recorded amounts, to rely on the reports of the client's internal auditors for the other 20. While economic factors are a valid consideration in making decisions at the margin about gathering additional evidence, cost alone is never a valid basis for not obtaining sufficient evidence to support the auditor's opinion.

POPULATION SIZE AND CHARACTERISTICS. The size of a population refers to the number of items contained in the population, such as, for example, the number of sales transactions in the sales journal, the number of customer accounts in the accounts receivable ledger, or the number of dollars in an account balance. The size of the accounting populations underlying many financial statement items makes sampling a practical necessity in gathering evidence. Generally, the larger the population, the larger the quantity of evidence required to obtain a reasonable basis for reaching a conclusion about it. But the exact relationship between population and sample size depends on the purpose and nature of the sampling plan being used, as explained in later chapters.

The characteristics of a population include the homogeneity or variability of the individual items that comprise the population. In the case of accounts receivable, one such factor is the range of the dollar amount of individual customer balances comprising the total. A larger sample yielding more corroborating information is generally required to reach a conclusion about a highly variable population than for a uniform population. The effect of variability on sample size can often be mitigated to some extent by stratifying the population into several more homogeneous strata or groups before sampling. For example, when a few large customer accounts comprise a large percentage of the total receivables balance, the auditor might decide to obtain evidence about all the accounts with balances in excess of a specified dollar amount and a sample of the remaining accounts. This strategy might well yield more evidence about the total receivables balance than would be obtained from a larger sample of customer accounts taken without first stratifying the population based on the size of the individual customer account balances. Again, the specifics of sampling on both statistical and nonstatistical bases are explained further in later chapters.

Competency of Evidential Matter

The competency (or reliability) of both underlying accounting data and corroborating information is involved in this aspect of the third standard of field work. The reliability of the accounting records is directly related to the effectiveness of the client's internal controls. Strong internal controls enhance the accuracy and reliability of the financial records, whereas weak internal controls often do not prevent or detect errors and irregularities in the accounting process.

The competency of corroborating information depends on many factors. The considerations that have the widest applicability in auditing are

- Relevance
- Source
- Timeliness
- Objectivity

RELEVANCE. This factor means that the evidence must be pertinent to the auditor's objective. Thus, if the auditor's objective is to determine the existence of inventory, the auditor can obtain evidence by observing the client's inventory-taking. However, such evidence might not be as relevant in determining whether the goods are owned by the client (rights and obligations assertion) or their cost (valuation or allocation assertion).

The auditor should be fully aware of the importance of this factor. Unnecessary cost and time result when the auditor obtains irrelevant evidence. Moreover, such evidence may also lead to erroneous conclusions in forming an opinion of the client's financial statements.

SOURCE. Several circumstances related to the source of evidence affect its competence. The importance of this criterion can be illustrated by some examples. Suppose that as an auditor you seek evidence concerning the amount owed by customer X. The customer can be asked to communicate directly to you the balance owed, or you can examine evidence developed within the client's organization such as the shipping orders and duplicate sales invoices for the transactions comprising the balance. In this case, the former evidence is considered more competent because it is obtained from a third party who is independent of the client.

As another example, assume you are reviewing bank reconciliations prepared by two different clients. For client A, the reconciliation is prepared by an internal auditor who is not otherwise involved in the processing of cash transactions. For client B, it is prepared by the cashier who records cash receipts, posts them to the accounts receivable subsidiary ledger, and makes the daily bank deposit. The reconciliation prepared by client A would be more competent because it was generated under better internal control.

For a third example, suppose you need evidence as to the amount of cash on hand. You could count the cash yourself or you could ask the client to count the cash on hand for you. If you make the count, you have direct personal knowledge of the amount, whereas if the client makes the count and reports it to you, you have indirect knowledge of the amount. Clearly, the former provides more competent evidence.

Consistent with these examples, AU 326.19 recognizes the following presumptions about the effects of the source of the information on the competence or reliability of evidential matter:

- When evidential matter can be obtained from independent sources outside an entity, it provides greater assurance of reliability than that secured solely within the entity.
- The more effective the internal control structure, the more assurance it provides about the reliability of the accounting data and financial statements.
- The independent auditor's direct personal knowledge, obtained through physical examination, observation, computation, and inspection, is more persuasive than information obtained indirectly.

TIMELINESS. This criterion relates to the date to which the evidence is applicable. The timeliness of the evidence is especially important in verifying current asset, current liability, and related income statement balances. For these accounts, the auditor seeks evidence that the client has made a proper cutoff of cash, sales, and purchase transactions at the statement date. This task is facilitated when appropriate auditing procedures are applied at or near that date. Similarly, evidence obtained from physical counts at the balance sheet date provides better evidence of quantities on hand at that date than counts made at other times.

OBJECTIVITY. Evidence that is objective in nature is generally considered more reliable than evidence that is subjective. For example, evidence of the existence of tangible resources can be ascertained with a substantial degree of conclusiveness through physical inspection. Furthermore, evidence obtained from outside independent sources is considered more objective than evidence provided solely by the client.

In contrast, evidence in support of management's estimates of inventory obsolescence and product warranties may be largely subjective. In such a case, the auditor should (1) consider the qualifications and integrity of the individual making the estimate and (2) assess the appropriateness of the decision-making processes followed by the client in making the judgments.

Figure 5-3 summarizes the effects of the foregoing considerations on the competency of evidential matter.

Reasonable Basis

The auditor is not expected, or required, by the third standard of field work to have an absolute, certain, or guaranteed basis for an opinion. The requirement of a reasonable basis pertains to the overall level of assurance the auditor needs at the conclusion of the audit to express an opinion on the financial statements.

In executing an audit program, the auditor may quantify statistically the levels of assurance for some individual items in the statements. It is not possible, however, to combine statistically the individual levels of assurance into an objective evaluation of the overall reasonableness of the financial statements taken as a whole. The latter requires the exercise of professional judgment.

Because professional judgment is involved, different auditors will not always reach identical conclusions about the quantity and quality of evidence needed to reach an opinion on a given set of financial statements. However, several factors contribute to achieving a fairly uniform application of the reasonable basis requirement. First, the SASs contain many specific requirements about evidential matter, and they provide guidance about ways to meet these requirements. Auditors are required to justify any departures from SASs.

FIGURE 5-3 • COMPETENCY OF EVIDENTIAL MATTER

LESS COMPETENT EVIDENCE	COMPETENCY FACTORS	MORE COMPETENT EVIDENCE
Indirectly relevant	RELEVANCE	Directly relevant
Solely within the enterprise Unsatisfactory internal control Indirect knowledge	SOURCE	Independent outside source Satisfactory internal control Direct personal knowledge
Evidence applicable to date other than balance sheet date	TIMELINESS	Evidence applicable to balance sheet date
Subjective	OBJECTIVITY	Objective

Second, in the practice of public accounting, there are two counterbalancing forces. On one hand, competition among firms tends to make the individual firm cost and fee conscious. Accordingly, the firm is restrained from obtaining an inordinately high degree of assurance in a specific engagement because the client may be attracted to another firm, which, while complying with the reasonable basis requirement, will perform the audit at a lower cost. On the other hand, the auditing firm is well aware that an inadequate basis for an opinion may result in sanctions by peer review committees and government regulators, and lawsuits by those harmed by reliance on an incorrect auditor's report.

TYPES OF CORROBORATING INFORMATION

As noted previously, evidential matter consists of underlying accounting data and corroborating information. The auditing student should already be familiar with the basic components of underlying accounting data identified in Figure 5-2, i.e., journals, ledgers, worksheets, reconciliations, etc. In this section, we identify and elaborate upon eight principal types of corroborating information as follows:

OBJECTIVE 4

Identify the types of corroborating information available to the auditor.

- Analytical evidence
- Documentary evidence
- Confirmations
- Written representations
- Mathematical evidence
- Oral evidence
- Physical evidence
- Electronic evidence

For each type, consideration is given to its nature, reliability, and the categories of assertions to which it is most relevant. Selected observations are also made regarding relative cost and frequency of use.

Analytical Evidence

Analytical evidence involves comparisons of current-period client data, such as total revenues or return on assets, with expected values for the data based on (1) historical or budgeted amounts for the client or (2) industry data. The comparisons are then used to draw inferences about the fairness of financial statement assertions.

The reliability of analytical evidence is dependent on the relevance of the comparable data. For example, if there have been no significant changes in the nature and size of the client's operations, customer base, and other factors from the previous year or several years, a comparison of the historical pattern of monthly sales with the monthly sales data for the current period should provide reliable analytical evidence about the fairness of total revenues reported for the current period. Similarly, if it is reasonable to expect that a company's operations and results will mirror those of the industry in which it operates, comparison of client and industry data can provide useful analytical evidence.

When several related financial variables all conform to expectations, the reliability of the analytical evidence may be further enhanced. For example, when recorded sales and cost of sales, gross margin, and the accounts receivable and inventory turnover ratios all conform to expectations, the analytical evidence may be viewed as supporting the existence or occurrence, completeness, and valuation or allocation assertions for sales and cost of sales.

Documentary Evidence

Documentary evidence includes a wide variety of source documents as well as such items as minutes of board of director or executive committee meetings, lease agreements, various other contracts, and bank statements. Ordinarily, these documents, which may be generated externally or internally, are contained in client files and are available for the auditor's inspection upon request.

Examples of externally generated documents include customer order forms, suppliers' invoices, tax bills, and bank statements. Externally generated documents are generally considered to be more reliable than internally generated documents. The reliability of externally generated documents is further enhanced when they are sent directly from the external party to the auditor, thus eliminating the opportunity for the client to alter the documents before the auditor sees them. Thus, while bank statements are normally sent from banks directly to clients throughout the year, the auditor may request the client to have the bank send a regular or special (cutoff) bank statement as of a particular date directly to the auditor for use in verifying cash balances.

Examples of internally generated documents include sales order forms, shipping documents, sales invoices, purchase requisitions, purchase orders, receiving reports, time cards, and paid (canceled) checks. Since it is possible for internal documents to be created by client employees merely to support journal entries for fictitious transactions, the reliability of internally generated documents is enhanced when they bear evidence of having been circulated to external parties before being placed in the client's files. For example, a shipping document prepared by the client, but signed or stamped by the shipping company acknowledging acceptance of the shipment for delivery to the customer, provides strong evidence that the transaction occurred. Similarly, a check issued to pay a supplier or employee, bearing the payee's endorsement as well as the stamps of the banks that processed the check for payment before it was returned with the client's bank statement, provides strong evidence that the payment actually occurred. And a receipted deposit slip provides strong evidence that a bank deposit actually was made. In contrast, duplicate file copies of sales invoices and purchase requisitions that bear no evidence of external circulation may be less reliable.

The physical characteristics of documents may also affect their reliability. For example, the use of special papers and inks, prenumbering, and machine-imprinted data are all designed to make it more difficult to alter documents or to create phony documentation.

DOCUMENT FRAUD ON THE RISE

"Many financial institutions these days are finding that counterfeiting is far more than a nuisance. Whether it's fraudulent money orders, corporate checks, traveler's checks, or fake securities posted as collateral for loans, document fraud is on the rise. According to the Secret Service's Financial Crimes Division, losses to banks from fraud cases under investigation doubled in 1993, to $1.4 billion."

> "The boom in document fraud stems from the ready availability of computers, laser printers, and color copiers. With these machines, even relative novices can produce replicas of currency and other similar instruments that are often just as hard to detect as documents created by skilled counterfeiters . . .Estimates of losses from check fraud alone, by far the most costly and widespread form of document fraud, run as high as $10 billion annually. . . .

SOURCE: "The (Funny) Money Supply is Soaring," *Business Week,* May 23, 1994, p. 109.

Documentary evidence is used extensively in auditing, and depending on the circumstances it may pertain to any of the five categories of management assertions. Two special classes of documentary evidence, confirmations and written representations, are discussed separately in the next two sections. The effects of circulation on the reliability of documentary evidence are summarized in Figure 5-4.

FIGURE 5-4 • EFFECTS OF CIRCULATION ON RELIABILITY OF DOCUMENTARY EVIDENCE

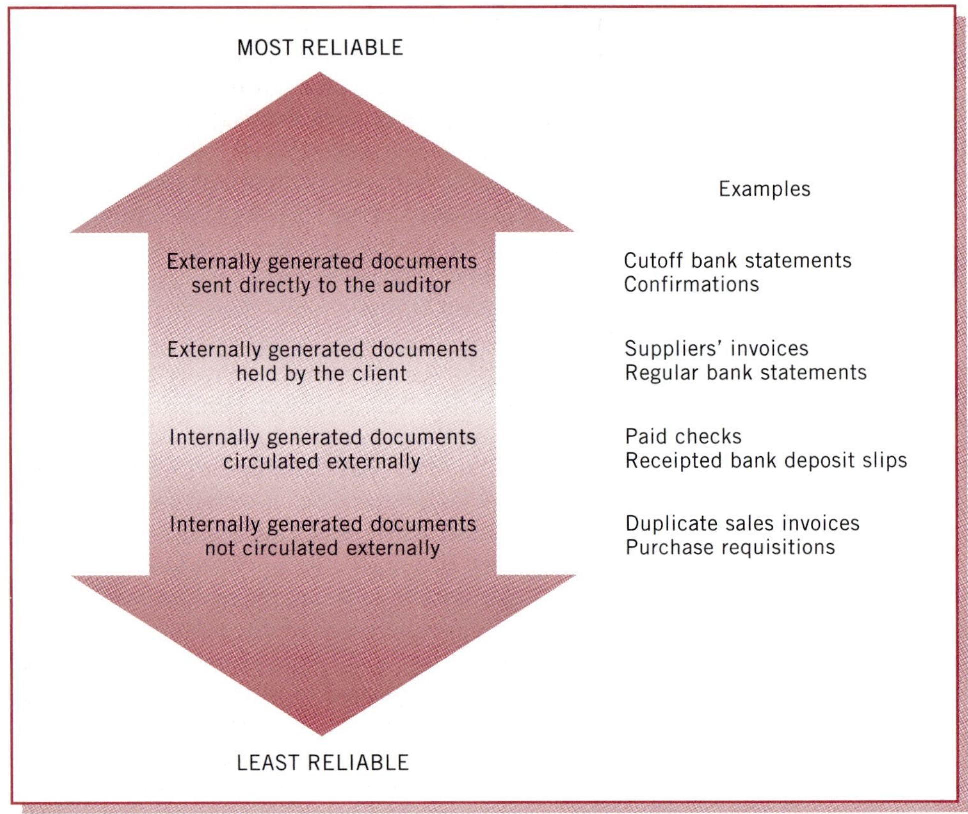

Confirmations

Confirmations constitute a special class of documentary evidence involving direct written responses by knowledgeable third parties to specific requests for factual information. The following are illustrative of items that are frequently confirmed:

Item	Knowledgeable Respondent
Cash in bank	Bank
Accounts receivable	Individual customers
Inventory stored in public warehouse	Warehouse custodian
Inventory out on consignment	Consignee
Accounts, notes, and mortgages payable	Creditors/lenders
Bonds payable	Bond trustee
Lease terms	Lessor
Shares of common stock	Stock registrar
Insurance coverage	Insurance company

Auditing standards require the auditor to obtain confirmation evidence for accounts receivable whenever it is practical and reasonable to do so, and it is standard practice to obtain confirmations for bank balances. Their use in other applications depends on the relative cost and reliability of alternative forms of evidence that may be available to the auditor. The effort involved in preparing and sending confirmation requests and in analyzing the responses can be quite time consuming, often making this a costly form of evidence.

When confirmations are obtained directly by the auditor from third parties, they are generally considered to have a high degree of reliability. Although confirmations may be designed to obtain evidence in support of any of the five categories of assertions, they are most often used in connection with existence or occurrence assertions.

Written Representations

Another special class of documentary evidence, **written representations** are signed statements by responsible and knowledgeable individuals that bear on one or more of management's assertions. Written representations may be differentiated from confirmations in two ways: (1) they may originate either from within the client's organization or from external sources, and (2) they may contain subjective information or an individual's opinion about a matter rather than factual information.

The auditor is required by GAAS to obtain certain written representations from management in meeting the third standard of field work. Commonly presented in the form of a *rep letter,* such representations are designed to document management's replies to inquiries made by the auditor during the audit. These representations may reveal information that is not shown in the accounting records, such as the existence of contingencies that may require further investigation. The reliability of a rep letter depends on the auditor's ability to corroborate the representations by other evidence. An example of a rep letter is presented in Chapter 19 under "Completing the Field Work."

During the course of the audit, the auditor may also request written representations from outside experts. The auditor is not expected to possess the expertise of a lawyer in evaluating litigation pending against the client, a geologist in estimating the quantity of ore in a mine, or an appraiser in valuing a fine arts collection. When such evidence is needed, SAS 73, *Using the Work of a Specialist* (AU 336), states that the auditor may use the work of a specialist to obtain competent evidential matter. The specialist's written representations may be received in the form of a letter, report, or other written communication. A relatively high degree of reliance may be placed on this type of evidence when the auditor is satisfied as to the professional qualifications and reputation of the specialist.

Written representations may pertain to any of the assertion categories.

Mathematical Evidence

Mathematical evidence results from recomputations by the auditor and comparison of those results with the client's computations. This may involve the results of (1) routine recalculations such as verifying the totals of journals, ledgers, and supporting schedules, or (2) complicated recalculations of such items as the present value of minimum lease payments, pension fund obligations, and earnings per share data. Mathematical evidence generated by the auditor is reliable, has a relatively low cost, and contributes to the basis for the auditor's conclusions about valuation or allocation assertions.

Oral Evidence

During an audit, an auditor receives oral responses to numerous inquiries directed to officers and employees of the client and others. This **oral evidence** is not regarded as highly reliable by itself. Its primary value lies in directing the auditor to other sources of evidence, corroborating other evidential matter, and disclosing matters that may merit further investigation and documentation. Oral evidence may cover a broad range of topics such as an interpretation of a board of directors' resolution, an explanation of the accounting treatment of a merger, an evaluation of the collectibility of a customer's account, and the assumptions underlying various other accounting estimates made by management.

When oral evidence plays a key role in an audit decision, the source, nature, and date of the evidence should be documented in the working papers. When obtained from management, the auditor may request that key oral evidence be reaffirmed in writing in management's rep letter, as described in the previous section on written representations. Oral evidence may pertain to any of the categories of financial statement assertions.

Physical Evidence

Physical evidence is obtained from the physical examination or inspection of tangible assets. For example, the auditor will acquire direct personal knowledge of the existence of undeposited cash receipts, inventories, and plant and equipment items by examining or inspecting them. Physical evidence may also be helpful in determining the quality or condition of assets that may relate to valuation or allocation assertions. In some cases, the auditor may not be qualified to determine quality, condition, or value based on the physical evidence, and may instead engage an expert or specialist to examine the physical evidence. The auditor would then rely on the expert's written representation together with the physical evidence.

Electronic Evidence

The term **electronic evidence** refers to any information produced or maintained by electronic means that is used by an auditor to form an opinion about an assertion. The term *electronic means* includes the use of computers, scanners, sensors, magnetic media, and other electronic devices associated with the creation, manipulation, transmission, and reception of electronic data.

Although electronic data processing systems have been widely used in accounting for several decades, auditors have continued to rely in large part on the systems' ability to generate evidence in traditional formats such as printouts of documents, journals, ledgers, and other reports produced by the computer. Although it hasn't occurred at the pace or to the extent once predicted, the promise of the paperless office is nevertheless becoming a reality. For example, it is no longer uncommon for a client's computer to (1) determine when an inventory item needs to be reordered, (2) generate and electronically transmit the order to a supplier's computer, (3) receive shipping and billing information directly from the supplier's computer, and (4) initiate the electronic transfer of funds from the client's bank account to the supplier's bank account to pay for the order, all without the production of any traditional transaction documents by either the client or the supplier.

In such cases, the auditor must use the electronic evidence of the transactions. The reliability of such evidence is a function of the controls over the creation, alteration, and completeness of such data, as well as the auditor's understanding of the client's system and controls, and the competence of the tools (audit software) used by the auditor to access the electronic evidence.

New opportunities and challenges are also posed by the impact of technology on other traditional forms of evidence, such as the faxing of confirmations. Again, controls related to the origination, transmission, and receipt of faxed information must be considered in assessing the reliability of the evidence.

The AICPA currently has a task force working on a variety of issues related to the use of electronic evidence. Since such evidence may substitute for several of the traditional types of evidence discussed previously, it may pertain to any of the categories of assertions.

LEARNING CHECK:

5-6 Identify the two categories of evidential matter recognized in SASs.

5-7 Indicate the factors that affect the sufficiency and competency of evidential matter.

5-8 An auditor is expected to have a conclusive basis for expressing an opinion on financial statements. Do you agree or disagree? Explain.

5-9 List the types of corroborating information that may be obtained in an audit and indicate the categories of management assertions to which each type relates.

5-10 Indicate the effects of circulation on the reliability of documentary evidence.

KEY TERMS:

Corroborating information, p. 150
- Analytical evidence, p. 156
- Confirmations, p. 158
- Documentary evidence, p. 156
- Electronic evidence, p. 160
- Mathematical evidence, p. 159
- Oral evidence, p. 160
- Physical evidence, p. 160
- Written representations, p. 159

Evidential matter, p. 150

Underlying accounting data, p. 150

AUDIT PROCEDURES

Audit procedures are the acts performed or the methods and techniques used by the auditor to gather and evaluate audit evidence. They may be applied to the underlying accounting data or to the process of obtaining and evaluating corroborating information.

TYPES OF AUDIT PROCEDURES

OBJECTIVE 5

Enumerate and describe the types of audit procedures that may be used in an audit.

The following ten types of audit procedures are discussed below:

- Analytical procedures
- Inspecting
- Confirming
- Inquiring
- Counting
- Tracing
- Vouching
- Observing
- Reperforming
- Computer-assisted audit techniques

The selection of procedures to be used to audit a particular account or assertion occurs in planning the audit. Both the potential effectiveness of procedures in meeting specific audit objectives, and the cost of performing the procedures should be considered.

Analytical Procedures

Analytical procedures consist of the study and comparison of relationships among data. These procedures include the calculation and use of simple ratios, vertical analysis or common size statements, comparisons of actual amounts with historical data or budget expectations, and the use of mathematical and statistical models such as regression analysis. The latter may involve the use of nonfinancial data (e.g., number of employees) as well as financial data. Analytical procedures produce analytical evidence.

Inspecting

Inspecting involves careful scrutiny or detailed examination of documents and records, and physical examination of tangible resources. This procedure is used extensively in auditing.

Inspecting documents provides a means for evaluating documentary evidence. Thus, through inspection the auditor can assess the authenticity of documents, or perhaps detect the existence of alterations or questionable items. Inspection of documents also permits determination of the precise terms of invoices, contracts, etc. Terms such as reviewing, reading, and examining are synonymous with inspecting documents and records. A derivation of inspecting is scanning, which involves less careful scrutiny of documents and records.

Inspecting tangible resources provides the auditor with direct personal knowledge of their existence and physical condition. Thus, inspecting also provides a means for evaluating physical evidence.

Confirming

Confirming is a form of inquiry that enables the auditor to obtain information directly from an independent source outside the client organization. In the usual case, the client makes the request of the outside party in writing, but the auditor controls the mailing of the inquiry. The request should include instructions requiring the recipient to send the response directly to the auditor. This auditing procedure produces confirmation evidence. It is used extensively in auditing.

Inquiring

Inquiring involves either oral or written inquiry by the auditor. Such inquiries may be made internally to management or employees, as in the case of questions pertaining to the obsolescence of inventory or collectibility of receivables, or externally, as in inquiries to lawyers concerning the probable outcome of litigation. Inquiry produces either oral evidence or evidence in the form of written representations.

Counting

The two most common applications of **counting** are (1) the physical counting of tangible resources such as the amount of cash or inventory on hand, and (2) accounting for all prenumbered documents. The first provides a means for evaluating the physical evidence of the quantity on hand. The second may be viewed as providing a means for evaluating documentary evidence of the completeness of accounting records.

Tracing

In **tracing** (sometimes also called retracing), the auditor (1) selects documents created when transactions are executed and (2) determines that information from the documents is properly recorded in the accounting records (journals and ledgers). The direction of testing is from the documents to the accounting records, thus, retracing the original flow of the data through the accounting system. Because this procedure provides assurance that data from source documents were ultimately included in the accounts, it is especially useful for detecting understatements in the accounting records. Thus, it is an important procedure in obtaining evidence pertaining to completeness assertions. The effectiveness of the procedure is enhanced when serially prenumbered documents are used by the client. Tracing pertains primarily to documentary evidence.

Vouching

Vouching involves (1) selecting entries in the accounting records and (2) obtaining and inspecting the documentation that served as the basis for the entries to determine the validity and accuracy of the recorded transactions. In vouching, the direction of testing is opposite to that used in tracing. Vouching is used extensively to detect overstatements in the accounting records. Thus, it is an important procedure in obtaining evidence pertaining to existence or occurrence assertions. Vouching pertains to documentary evidence. Figure 5-5 shows the principal differences between vouching and tracing.

Observing

Observing pertains to watching or witnessing the performance of some activity or process. The activity may be the routine processing of a particular type of transaction such as cash receipts to see that employees are performing their assigned duties in accordance with company policies and procedures. Or the auditor might observe the care being taken by client employees in conducting the annual physi-

FIGURE 5-5 • DIRECTIONAL TESTING—VOUCHING AND TRACING

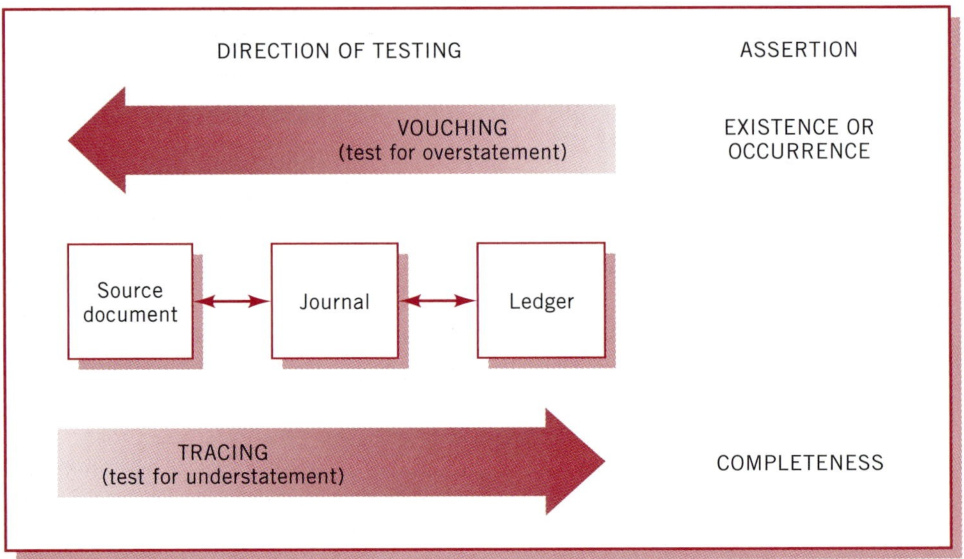

cal inventory. The latter provides an opportunity to distinguish between observing and inspecting. That is, on one hand the auditor may *observe the process of client employees taking the physical inventory*. On the other hand, the auditor may also *inspect or examine certain inventory items* to make her or his own assessment of their condition. Thus, the subject matter of observing is personnel, procedures, and processes. From these observations, the auditor obtains direct personal knowledge of the activities in the form of physical evidence.

Reperforming

A major application of this procedure is **reperforming** calculations and reconciliations made by the client. Examples include recalculating journal totals, depreciation expense, accrued interest, and quantity times unit price extensions on inventory summary sheets, as well as the totals on supporting schedules and reconciliations. Mathematical evidence is produced by this procedure. The auditor may also reperform selected aspects of the processing of selected transactions to determine that the original processing conformed to prescribed control policies and procedures. For example, the auditor may reperform the customer credit check for a sales transaction to determine that the customer did indeed have sufficient credit available at the time the transaction was processed.

Computer-Assisted Audit Techniques

When the client's accounting records are maintained on electronic media, the auditor may use **computer-assisted audit techniques** to assist in performing several of the procedures described in the preceding sections. For example, the auditor can use computer audit software to perform the calculations and comparisons used in analytical procedures, select a sample of accounts receivable for confirmation, scan a file to determine that all documents in a series have been accounted for, compare data elements in different files for agreement (such as the prices on sales invoices with a master file containing authorized prices), and reperform a variety of calculations such as totaling the accounts receivable subsidiary ledger or inventory file. Computer-assisted audit techniques are explained in greater detail in Chapter 13 of this text.

RELATIONSHIPS AMONG AUDIT PROCEDURES, TYPES OF EVIDENCE, AND ASSERTIONS

During the course of an audit, in meeting the numerous specific audit objectives derived from management's financial statement assertions, the auditor will use many, if not all, of the audit procedures and types of evidence described in this chapter. Some examples of the relationships among audit procedures, types of evidence, and assertions are depicted in Figure 5-6.

From the figure, we can see that the three procedures of tracing, vouching, and inspecting involve the use of documentary evidence. The procedure of inspecting alternatively may involve the use of physical evidence, as do the procedures of counting and observing. Also, note that inquiring may produce either written representations or oral evidence, depending on the nature of the inquiry and the response.

The captions above the lines connecting the procedure and evidence boxes describe illustrative applications. The captions below the lines indicate the assertions to which the indicated combinations of procedures and types of evidence pertain. It should be kept in mind that these are illustrative only. In a given situation, the manner in which the procedure is performed may affect the number of assertions to which the evidence pertains. For example, the casual inspection of physical assets may be done only to obtain evidence as to their existence. Alternatively, a more thorough inspection may indicate damage or obsolescence, and, thus, the evidence would pertain to valuation as well.

CLASSIFICATION OF AUDIT PROCEDURES

OBJECTIVE 6

Describe the three classifications of audit procedures and the purpose of each.

Auditing procedures are usually classified by purpose into the following categories: (1) **procedures to obtain an understanding** of the internal control structure, (2) **tests of controls,** and (3) **substantive tests.**

Procedures to Obtain an Understanding

The second standard of field work requires the auditor to obtain an understanding of the client's internal control structure sufficient to plan the audit. In meeting this standard, the auditor may inquire of management about internal control policies and procedures and inspect accounting manuals and flowcharts of the accounting system. In addition, the auditor may obtain knowledge about the internal control structure by observing the entity's activities and operations. In performing these procedures, the auditor is concerned primarily with the *design* of the client's internal control structure, that is, how it is supposed to work. Procedures to obtain an understanding of the internal control structure are required in every financial statement audit.

FIGURE 5-6 • RELATIONSHIPS AMONG AUDIT PROCEDURES, TYPES OF EVIDENCE, AND ASSERTIONS

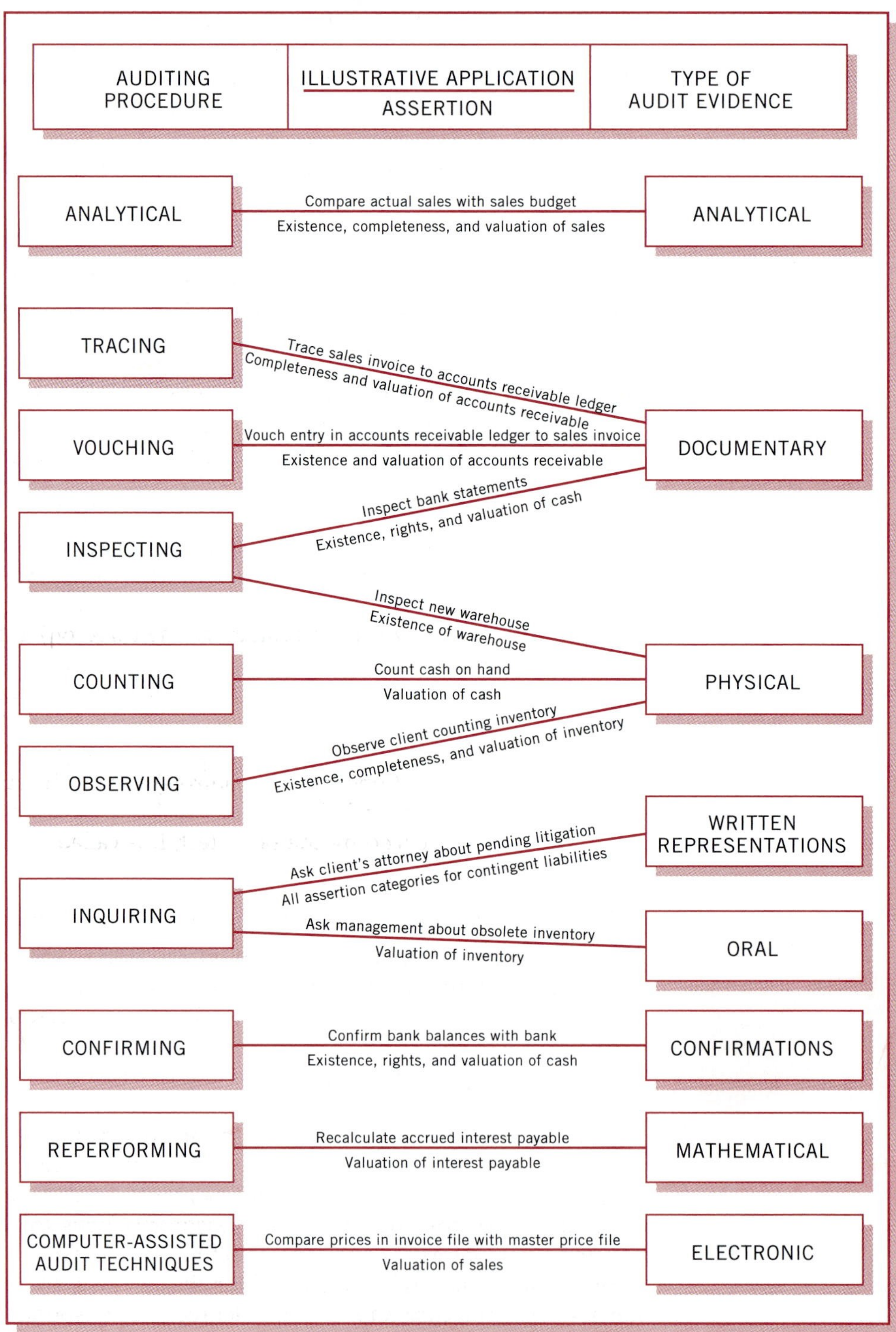

Tests of Controls

Tests of controls are made to provide evidence about the *effectiveness* of the design and operation of internal control structure policies and procedures. Assume, for example, that the control procedure provides for depositing cash in the bank daily. The auditor can test the effectiveness of the control by observing actual deposits or by examining duplicate deposit slips. Tests of controls also include inquiry of employees as to their performance of control procedures and reperforming control procedures by the auditor. The performance of tests of controls is not required in a financial statement audit. However, they are performed in most audits.

Substantive Tests

Substantive tests consist of (1) **analytical procedures,** (2) **tests of details of transactions,** and (3) **tests of details of balances.** This category of auditing procedures provides evidence as to the fairness of management's financial statement assertions. As explained earlier in the chapter, analytical procedures involve the use of comparisons to assess fairness as, for example, comparing an account balance with the prior year balance or a budgeted amount. Tests of details of transactions involve examining support for the individual debits and credits posted to an account as, for example, vouching the debits in accounts receivable to entries in the sales journal and supporting sales invoices. Similarly, tracing the details from source documents to journals and the affected ledger accounts constitutes a test of details of transactions. Tests of details of balances involve examining support for the ending balance directly as, for example, confirming an ending account receivable balance directly with the customer. The three types of substantive tests are complementary. The extent to which each type is used on a given account can vary based on such factors as its relative effectiveness for that account and cost.

In some cases, the auditor may perform tests of transactions to determine that both (1) all applicable company control policies and procedures were followed in processing the transactions (tests of controls) and (2) the substantive details of the transactions were accurately journalized and posted to the ledger accounts. When both purposes are served by the same test, it is called a **dual-purpose test.**

EVALUATION OF EVIDENCE OBTAINED

In combination, the three classes of audit procedures should enable the auditor to obtain the evidence needed to satisfy the third standard of field work. To ensure that this is the case, the evaluation of evidence occurs throughout the audit as each financial statement assertion is verified, and at the end of the audit when the auditor must decide on the type of opinion that should be expressed in the audit report.

To have a reasonable basis for an opinion on the financial statements, the auditor needs a preponderance (i.e., a consensus or majority) of persuasive evidence for each financial statement assertion that is material. You may recall from Chapter 2 that when the auditor lacks a reasonable basis for an opinion, a qualified opinion or disclaimer of opinion should be issued. When a reasonable basis for an opinion has been obtained, the auditor should issue an unqualified, qualified, or adverse opinion, depending on the degree of correspondence between the assertions in the financial statements and GAAP as established by the evidence obtained.

FIGURE 5-7 • OBTAINING AND EVALUATING AUDIT EVIDENCE

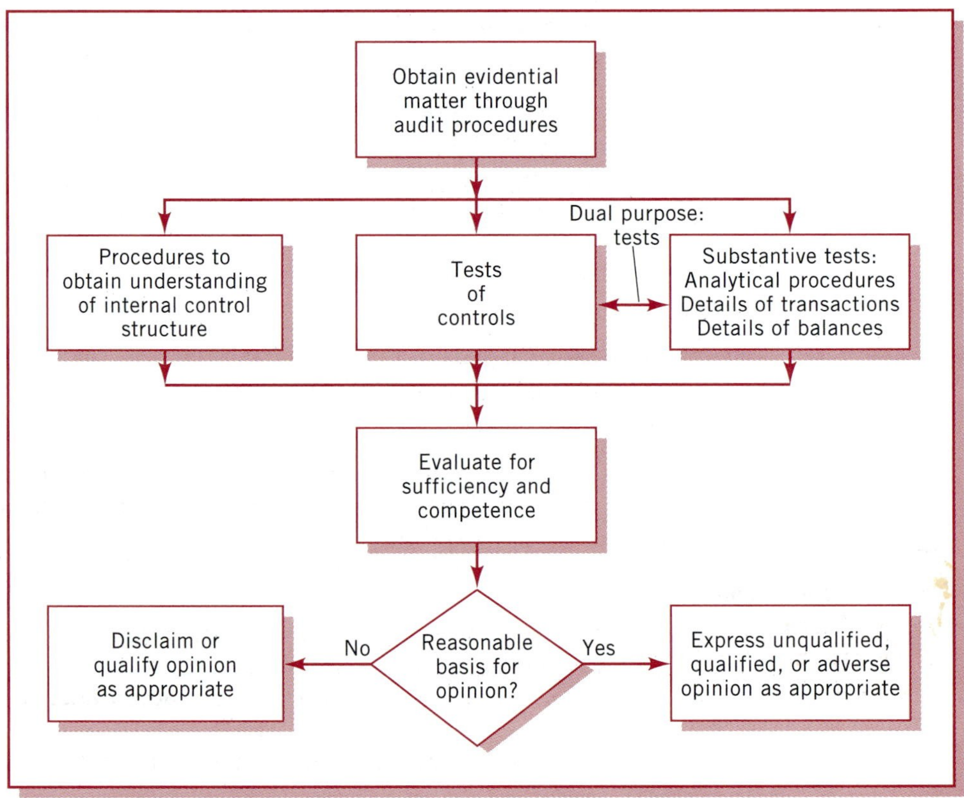

The process of obtaining and evaluating audit evidence and determining the effects on the auditor's report is summarized in Figure 5-7.

LEARNING CHECK:

5-11 a. Identify the types of audit procedures that may be used to obtain and evaluate evidence.
b. State two factors that should be considered in selecting the procedures to be used to obtain evidence about a particular account or assertion.

5-12 What are the principal differences between tracing and vouching?

5-13 Identify three classifications of audit procedures and describe the purpose of each.

5-14 a. Identify three types of substantive tests and indicate how they relate to one another.
b. What is a dual-purpose test?

5-15 When does the evaluation of evidence obtained from audit procedures occur and what effects can it have on the auditor's report?

KEY TERMS:

Audit procedures, p. 161, 167
- Analytical procedures, p. 162
- Computer-assisted audit techniques, p. 164
- Confirming, p. 162
- Counting, p. 163
- Inquiring, p. 163
- Inspecting, p. 162
- Observing, p. 163
- Reperforming, p. 164
- Tracing, p. 163
- Vouching, p. 163

Dual-purpose test, p. 167
Procedures to obtain an understanding, p. 165
Substantive tests, p. 165
Tests of controls, p. 165
Tests of details of transactions, p. 167
Tests of details of balances, p. 167

WORKING PAPERS

OBJECTIVE 7

Explain the nature and purpose of audit working papers.

The documentation of audit evidence is provided in working papers. SAS 41, *Working Papers* (AU 339.03), describes **working papers** as the records kept by the auditor of the procedures applied, the tests performed, the information obtained, and the pertinent conclusions reached in the audit. Working papers provide

- The principal support for the auditor's report. → opinion
- A means for coordinating and supervising the audit.
- Evidence that the audit was made in accordance with GAAS.

Working papers should be tailored to meet the needs of the specific engagement.

TYPES OF WORKING PAPERS

Many types of working papers are prepared in an audit. These include (1) a working trial balance, (2) schedules and analyses, (3) audit memoranda and documentation of corroborating information, and (4) adjusting and reclassifying entries.

Working papers may be prepared manually or through software developed for microcomputers. Figure 5-8 is an example of a microcomputer-generated working paper.

Working Trial Balance

A partial **working trial balance** is illustrated in Figure 5-8. Note that columns are provided for the current year's ledger balances (before audit adjustments and reclassifications), adjustments, adjusted balances, reclassifications, and final (audited) balances. Inclusion of the final (audited) balances for the prior year facilitates the performance of certain analytical procedures.

A working trial balance is of paramount importance in an audit because it

- Serves as the connecting link between the client's general ledger accounts and the items reported in the financial statements.
- Provides a basis for controlling all the individual working papers.

FIGURE 5-8 • PARTIAL WORKING TRIAL BALANCE WORKING PAPER

W/P Ref: AA-1

Omni, Inc.
Working Trial Balance—Balance Sheet
December 31, 19X1

Prepared By: JBC Date: 2/20/x2
Reviewed By: ARE Date: 2/15/x2

W/P REF	Acct. No.	Description	Final Balance 12/31/x0	Ledger Balance 12/31/x1	Adjustments AJE REF	Adjustments Debit (Credit)	Adjusted Balance 12/31/x1	Reclassifications RJE REF	Reclassifications Debit (Credit)	Final Balance 12/31/x1
		Current Assets								
A		Cash	392,000	427,000	(1)	50,000	477,000			477,000
B	150	Marketable Securities	52,200	62,200			62,000			62,200
C		Receivables (net)	1,601,400	1,715,000	(1)	(50,000)	1,665,000	(A)	10,000	1,675,000
D	170	Inventories	2,542,500	2,810,200	(2)	133,000	2,943,200			2,943,200
E		Prepaid Expenses	24,900	19,500			19,500			19,500
		Total Current	4,613,000	5,033,900		133,000	5,166,900		10,000	5,176,900
F	240	Long-term Investments		190,000			190,000			190,000
G		Property, Plant & Equipment (NET)	3,146,500	3,310,900			3,310,900			3,310,900
		Total	7,759,500	8,534,800		133,000	8,667,800		10,000	8,677,800
		Liabilities and Stockholders' Equity								
		Current Liabilities								
M	400	Notes Payable	750,000	825,000			825,000			825,000
N	410	Accounts Payable	2,150,400	2,340,300	(2)	(133,000)	2,473,300	(A)	(10,000)	2,483,300
O	420	Accrued Payables	210,600	189,000			189,000			189,000
P	430	Income Taxes Payable	150,000	170,000			170,000			170,000
		Total Current	3,261,000	3,524,300		(133,000)	3,657,300		(10,000)	3,667,300
R	500	Bonds Payable	1,000,000	1,200,000			1,200,000			1,200,000
S	600	Common Stock	2,400,000	2,400,000			2,400,000			2,400,000
T	700	Retained Earnings	1,098,500	1,410,500			1,410,500			1,410,500
		Total	7,759,500	8,534,800		(133,000)	8,667,800		(10,000)	8,677,800

- Identifies the specific working papers containing the audit evidence for each financial statement item.

For example, Figure 5-8 indicates that the amount reported in the financial statements for marketable securities is based on general ledger account 150 and that the evidence used by the auditor to evaluate management's assertions about marketable securities can be found in a section of the working papers with a reference or index of B. The absence of an account number for Cash in Figure 5-8, indicates that this financial statement item is the aggregate of several general ledger cash accounts. In such cases, the initial working paper of the section referenced on the working trial balance (A in this case) should contain a group schedule showing what general ledger accounts have been combined for this financial statement item as explained further in the next section. The link between the cash line in the working trial balance for Omni, Inc. (working paper AA-1) and Omni's balance sheet presentation of cash is illustrated in the bottom portion of Figure 5-9.

Schedules and Analyses

The terms **working paper schedule** and **working paper analysis** are used interchangeably to describe the individual working papers that contain the evidence supporting the items in the working trial balance. As noted in the previous paragraph, when several general ledger accounts are combined for reporting purposes, a **group schedule** (also called a **lead schedule**) should be prepared. In addition to showing the individual ledger accounts comprising the group, the lead schedule identifies the individual working paper schedules or analyses that contain the audit evidence obtained for each account comprising the group. The middle portion of Figure 5-9 illustrates the use of a cash lead schedule for Omni, Inc. (working paper A) and how it is linked both to the cash line of the working trial balance (working paper AA-1) and the supporting working papers for the two general ledger cash accounts listed on the lead schedule (i.e., working paper A-1 for A/C 100—Petty Cash and working paper A-2 for A/C 101—Cash in Bank).

Individual schedules or analyses often show the composition of an account balance at a particular date as in working paper A-1 of Figure 5-9. Other examples would include a list of customer balances comprising the accounts receivable control account balance and a list of investments comprising the marketable securities account balance. Working paper schedules may also show the changes in one or more related account balances during the period covered by the financial statements as illustrated in Figure 5-10. In some cases, the auditor has the client prepare the schedule which may be indicated by the letters "PBC" for "prepared by client." The auditor then performs the work indicated by the tickmarks and related explanations on the working paper as also illustrated in Figure 5-10.

Audit Memoranda and Corroborating Information

Audit memoranda refer to written data prepared by the auditor in narrative form. Memoranda may include comments on the performance of auditing procedures and conclusion reached. Documentation of corroborating information includes such items as (1) extracts of minutes of board of director meeting, (2) confirmation

FIGURE 5-9 • INTEGRATED WORKING PAPERS FOR CASH

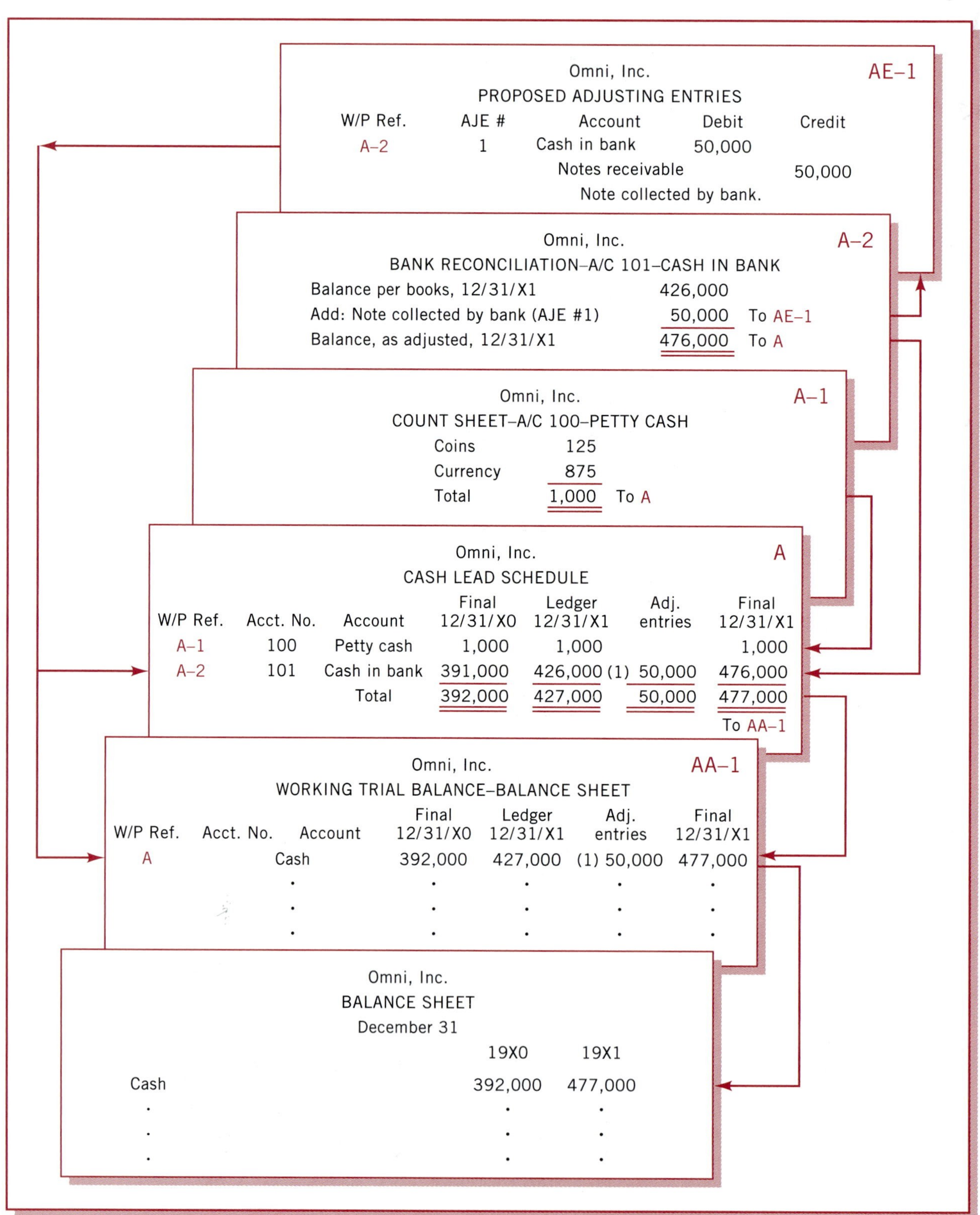

Omni, Inc. AE–1
PROPOSED ADJUSTING ENTRIES

W/P Ref.	AJE #	Account	Debit	Credit
A–2	1	Cash in bank	50,000	
		Notes receivable		50,000
		Note collected by bank.		

Omni, Inc. A–2
BANK RECONCILIATION–A/C 101–CASH IN BANK

Balance per books, 12/31/X1	426,000	
Add: Note collected by bank (AJE #1)	50,000	To AE–1
Balance, as adjusted, 12/31/X1	476,000	To A

Omni, Inc. A–1
COUNT SHEET–A/C 100–PETTY CASH

Coins	125	
Currency	875	
Total	1,000	To A

Omni, Inc. A
CASH LEAD SCHEDULE

W/P Ref.	Acct. No.	Account	Final 12/31/X0	Ledger 12/31/X1	Adj. entries	Final 12/31/X1
A–1	100	Petty cash	1,000	1,000		1,000
A–2	101	Cash in bank	391,000	426,000	(1) 50,000	476,000
		Total	392,000	427,000	50,000	477,000
						To AA–1

Omni, Inc. AA–1
WORKING TRIAL BALANCE–BALANCE SHEET

W/P Ref.	Acct. No.	Account	Final 12/31/X0	Ledger 12/31/X1	Adj. entries	Final 12/31/X1
A		Cash	392,000	427,000	(1) 50,000	477,000
		.	.	.	.	.
		.	.	.	.	.
		.	.	.	.	.

Omni, Inc.
BALANCE SHEET
December 31

	19X0	19X1
Cash	392,000	477,000
.	.	.
.	.	.
.	.	.

FIGURE 5-10 • NOTES RECEIVABLE AND INTEREST WORKING PAPER

Omni, Inc.
Notes Receivable and Interest
December 31, 19X1

PBC

Accts. 160,161,450

Prepared By: ACE W/P Ref: C-4
Date: 1/20/x2
Reviewed By: PAR Date: 2/4/x2

Maker	Date Made	Date Due	Interest Rate	Face Amount	Notes Receivable: Balance 12/31/x0	Debits	Credits	Balance 12/31/x1	Interest: Accrued 12/31/x0	Earned 19x1	Collected 19x1	Accrued 12/31/x1
Coffman, Inc.	7/1/X0	6/30/X1	10%	25,000	25,000 ✓		25,000	—	1,250 ✓	1,250 ∜	2,500 CR	—
Morrison Bros.	11/1/X0	10/31/X1	10%	30,000	30,000 ✓		30,000	—	500 ✓	2,500 ∜	3,000 CR	—
Shirley and Son	4/1/X1	3/31/X2	12%	40,000 ✓	—	40,000		40,000 ν	—	3,600 ∜	—	3,600
Warner Corporation	10/1/X1	9/30/X2	12%	20,000 ✓	—	20,000		20,000 ν	—	600 ∜	—	600
					55,000	60,000	55,000	60,000 ^	1,750	7,950	5,500	4,200^
					F	F	F	FF To C	F	F	F	FF To C

✓ Agreed to 12/31/x0 working papers
ν Confirmed with maker - no exceptions
✓ Examined note during cash count
F Footed
FF Footed and crossfooted
^ Traced to ledger balance
CR Traced collections to cash receipts and deposit slips
∜ Verified computations

responses, (3) written representations from management and outside experts, and (4) copies of important contracts.

Adjusting and Reclassifying Entries

It is important to distinguish between adjusting entries and reclassifying entries. Audit **adjusting entries** are corrections of client errors of omission or misapplications of GAAP. Thus, adjusting entries ultimately deemed to be material, individually or in the aggregate, are expected to be recorded by the client. In contrast, **reclassifying entries** pertain to the proper financial statement presentation of correct account balances. For example, assume that the accounts receivable balance includes some customer accounts with credit balances pertaining to customer advances. Although it is not necessary for the client to record the reclassifying entry on its books, for reporting purposes an entry should be made on the working trial balance in which accounts receivable is debited to offset the customer advances and advances from customers (a liability account) is credited. This is illustrated in Figure 5-8 and will result in the reclassification being reflected in the financial statements. As with adjusting entries, only reclassifications that have a material effect need be made.

In the working papers, each proposed entry should be shown on (1) the schedule or analysis of each account it affects, (2) any lead schedules affected, (3) separate summaries of proposed adjusting and reclassifying entries, and (4) the working trial balance. This is illustrated in Figure 5-9 on working papers A-2, A, AE-1, and AA-1.

The summaries of adjusting and reclassifying entries are initially designated as "proposed" entries because the auditor's final judgment as to which entries must be made may not occur until the end of the audit, and because the client must approve them. The disposition of each proposed entry should ultimately be recorded on the working papers. Of course, if the client declines to make adjusting or reclassifying entries that the auditor feels are necessary, the auditor's report must be appropriately modified.

PREPARING WORKING PAPERS

OBJECTIVE 8

Know the essential techniques of good working paper preparation.

A number of basic techniques or mechanics are widely used in preparing working papers. The following essential techniques of good working paper preparation should always be observed:

- **Heading.** Each working paper should contain the name of the client, a descriptive title identifying the content of the working paper, such as *Bank Reconciliation—City National Bank,* and the balance sheet date or the period covered by the audit.
- **Index Number.** Each working paper is given an index or reference number, such as A-1, B-2, and so forth, for identification and filing purposes.
- **Cross-referencing.** Data on a working paper that is taken from another working paper or that is carried forward to another working paper should be cross-referenced with the index numbers of those working papers as illustrated in Figure 5-9.
- **Tick Marks.** Tick marks are symbols, such as check marks, that are used on working papers to indicate that the auditor has performed some procedure

on the item to which the tick mark is affixed, or that additional information about the item is available elsewhere on the working paper. A *legend* on the working paper should explain the nature and extent of the work represented by each tick mark or provide the additional information applicable to the items so marked.

- **Signatures and Dates.** Upon completing their respective tasks, both the preparer and reviewer of a working paper should initial and date it. This establishes responsibility for the work performed and the review.

The astute student may observe that the partial working papers in Figure 5-9 do not show all of these essential points. This is because not all of the information could be fit onto the multiple working papers in that figure, which was designed primarily to illustrate indexing and cross-referencing. However, Figure 5-10 does illustrate all of the essential points described above.

REVIEWING WORKING PAPERS

There are several levels in the review of working papers within a CPA firm. The first-level review is made by the preparer's supervisor, such as a senior or manager. This review occurs when the work on a specific segment of the audit has been completed. The reviewer is primarily interested in the work done, the evidence obtained, the judgment exercised, and the conclusions reached by the preparer of the working paper.

Other reviews are made of the working papers when all the field work has been completed. These reviews are explained in Chapter 19 under "Evaluating the Findings."

WORKING PAPER FILES

Working papers are generally filed under the following two categories: (1) a permanent file and (2) a current file. The **permanent file** contains data that are expected to be useful to the auditor on many future engagements with the client. In contrast, the **current file** contains corroborating information pertaining to the execution of the current year's audit program.

Items typically found in the permanent file are

- Copies of the articles of incorporation and bylaws.
- Chart of accounts and procedure manuals.
- Organization charts.
- Plant layout, manufacturing processes, and principal products.
- Terms of capital stock and bond issues.
- Copies of long-term contracts, such as leases, pension plans, and profit-sharing and bonus agreements.
- Schedules for amortization of long-term debt and depreciation of plant assets.
- Summary of accounting principles used by the client.

OWNERSHIP AND CUSTODY OF WORKING PAPERS

Working papers belong to the auditor. The auditor's ownership rights, however, are subject to constraints imposed by the auditor's own profession. Rule 301 of the

AICPA's *Code of Professional Conduct* stipulates that a CPA shall not disclose any confidential information obtained during the course of a professional engagement, without the consent of the client, except for certain circumstances as stated in the rule.

Custody of the working papers rests with the auditor, and he or she is responsible for their safekeeping. Working papers included in the permanent file are retained indefinitely. Current working papers should be retained for as long as they are useful to the auditor in servicing a client or are needed to satisfy legal requirements for record retention. The statute of limitations rarely extends beyond six years.

ARE WORKING PAPERS REALLY CONFIDENTIAL?

After nine years of judicial proceedings, the U.S. Supreme Court ruled that an auditor's working papers used to determine a client's income tax liability are relevant to an Internal Revenue Service tax audit. The Court concluded that the audit working papers are not protected from disclosure in response to an IRS summons issued under the Internal Revenue Code even though they were not used in preparing the tax returns. Thus, in preparing working papers, an auditor should realize that they may be subjected to public scrutiny through courts of law even in situations when the auditor is not a litigant.

SOURCE: *United States v. Arthur Young & Co., et al.*, U.S. Supreme Court, No. 82-687 (March 1984).

LEARNING CHECK:

5-16 Explain the nature and purpose of audit working papers.

5-17 Identify four major types of working papers.

5-18 Describe five essential techniques of good working paper preparation.

5-19 Identify two categories of working paper files and differentiate the contents of each.

5-20 a. Who owns and maintains custody of the working papers?
b. Is it ever appropriate for the auditor to disclose the contents of working papers to anyone other than the client?

KEY TERMS:

Adjusting entries, p. 174
Audit memoranda, p. 171
Current file, p. 175
Group schedule, p. 171
Lead schedule, p. 171
Permanent file, p. 175
Reclassifying entries, p. 174
Working paper analysis, p. 171
Working papers, p. 169
Working paper schedule, p. 171
Working trial balance, p. 169

SUMMARY

The auditor's overall objective of rendering an opinion on the financial statements is achieved by collecting and evaluating evidence pertaining to numerous specific audit objectives. These objectives are derived from the management assertions contained in the components of financial statements. Five categories of management assertions are recognized—existence or occurrence, completeness, rights and obligations, valuation or allocation, and presentation and disclosure.

In performing the audit, the auditor exercises professional judgment in selecting from a variety of auditing procedures and types of evidence to meet the numerous specific audit objectives. Judgment is also exercised at the conclusion of the audit in evaluating whether sufficient competent evidence has been obtained to afford a reasonable basis for the opinion on the overall statements. The procedures performed, the evidence obtained, and the auditor's evaluation thereof should be fully documented in working papers that should provide the support for the auditor's report and evidence of the auditor's compliance with GAAS.

BIBLIOGRAPHY

AICPA Professional Standards:

SAS 31 (AU 326), Evidential Matter.
SAS 41 (AU 339), Working Papers.
SAS 73 (AU 336), Using the Work of a Specialist.
IAU 8 (AU 8008), Audit Evidence.
IAU 9 (AU 8009), Documentation.
IAU 18 (AU 8018), Using the Work of an Expert.

Buchholz, David L., and Moraglio, Joseph F. "IRS Access to Auditors' Work Papers: The Supreme Court Decision," *Journal of Accountancy* (September 1984), pp. 91–100.

Hadnot, B. L. "Audit Evidence—What Kind and How Much?" *The CPA Journal* (October 1979), pp. 23–29.

Holstrum, Gary L., and Mock, Theodore J. "Audit Judgment and Evidence Evaluation," *Auditing: A Journal of Practice and Theory* (Fall 1985), pp. 101–108.

Marchant, Garry. "Analogical Reasoning and Hypothesis Generation in Auditing," *The Accounting Review* (July 1989), pp. 500–513.

Mautz, R. K., and Sharaf, Hussein A. *The Philosophy of Auditing*, Sarasota, FL: American Accounting Association, 1961. Chapter 5: "Evidence," pp. 68–110.

Moeckel, Cindy L., and Plumlee, R. David. "Auditors' Confidence in Recognition of Audit Evidence," *The Accounting Review* (October 1989), pp. 653–666.

Whittington, Ray, Zulinski, Marilyn, and Ledwith, James W. "Completeness—The Elusive Assertion," *Journal of Accountancy* (August 1983), pp. 89–92.

OBJECTIVE QUESTIONS

Indicate the *best* answer choice for each of the following multiple choice questions.

5-21 These questions pertain to financial statement assertions.

1. Inquiries of warehouse personnel concerning possible obsolete or slow-moving inventory items provide assurance about management's assertion of
   a. Completeness.
   b. Existence.
   c. Presentation.
   d. Valuation.

2. An auditor most likely would inspect loan agreements under which an entity's inventories are pledged to support management's financial statement assertion of
   a. Existence or occurrence.

b. Completeness.
c. Presentation and disclosure.
d. Valuation or allocation.

3. Which of the following procedures would an auditor most likely perform to verify management's assertion of completeness?
   a. Compare a sample of shipping documents to related sales invoices.
   b. Observe the client's distribution of payroll checks.
   c. Confirm a sample of recorded receivables by direct communication with the debtors.
   d. Review standard bank confirmations for indications of kiting.

5-22 These questions relate to evidential matter.

1. Two assertions for which confirmation of accounts receivable balances provides primary evidence are
   a. Completeness and valuation.
   b. Valuation and rights and obligations.
   c. Rights and obligations and existence.
   d. Existence and completeness.

2. Which of the following statements relating to the competence of evidential matter is always true?
   a. Evidential matter gathered by an auditor from outside an enterprise is reliable.
   b. Accounting data developed under satisfactory conditions of internal control are more relevant than data developed under unsatisfactory internal control conditions.
   c. Oral representations made by management are not valid evidence.
   d. Evidence gathered by auditors must be both valid and relevant to be considered competent.

3. Audit evidence can come in different forms with different degrees of persuasiveness. Which of the following is the *least* persuasive type of evidence?
   a. Bank statement obtained from the client.
   b. Computations made by the auditor.
   c. Prenumbered client sales invoices.
   d. Vendor's invoice.

4. Which of the following statements is generally correct about the competence of evidential matter?
   a. The auditor's direct personal knowledge, obtained through observation and inspection, is more persuasive than information obtained indirectly from independent outside sources.
   b. To be competent, evidential matter must be either valid or relevant, but need *not* be both.
   c. Accounting data alone may be considered sufficient competent evidential matter to issue an unqualified opinion on financial statements.
   d. Competence of evidential matter refers to the amount of corroborative evidence to be obtained.

5-23 These questions pertain to audit procedures.

1. A basic premise underlying analytical review procedures is that
   a. These procedures **cannot** replace tests of balances and transactions.
   b. Statistical tests of financial information may lead to the discovery of material errors in the financial statements.
   c. The study of financial ratios is an acceptable alternative to the investigation of unusual fluctuations.
   d. Relationships among data may reasonably be expected to exist and continue in the absence of known conditions to the contrary.

2. Which of the following ultimately determines the specific audit procedures necessary to provide an independent auditor with a reasonable basis for the expression of an opinion?
   a. The audit program.
   b. The auditor's judgment.
   c. Generally accepted auditing standards.
   d. The auditor's working papers.

3. In the context of an audit of financial statements, substantive tests are audit procedures that
   a. May be eliminated under certain conditions.
   b. Are designed to discover significant subsequent events.
   c. May be either tests of transactions, tests of balances, or analytical tests.
   d. Will increase proportionately with the auditor's detection risk.

5-24 These questions apply to working papers.

1. An auditor's working papers should
   a. Not be permitted to serve as a reference source for the client.
   b. Not contain critical comments concerning management.
   c. Show that the accounting records agree or reconcile with the financial statements.
   d. Be considered the primary support for the financial statements being audited.

2. Which of the following statements concerning working papers is incorrect?
   a. An auditor may support an opinion by other means in addition to working papers.
   b. The form of working papers should be designed to meet the circumstances of a particular engagement.
   c. An auditor's working papers may **not** serve as a reference source for the client.
   d. Working papers should show that the internal control structure has been studied and evaluated to the degree necessary.

3. The current file of the auditor's working papers generally should include
   a. A flowchart of the internal accounting controls.
   b. Organization charts.
   c. A copy of the financial statements.
   d. Copies of bond and note indentures.

4. The audit working paper that reflects the major components of an amount reported in the financial statements is the
   a. Interbank transfer schedule.
   b. Carryforward schedule.
   c. Supporting schedule.
   d. Lead schedule.

COMPREHENSIVE QUESTIONS

5-25 **(Assertions)** In planning the audit of a client's inventory, an auditor derived the following specific audit objectives from the five categories of management's financial statement assertions:

1. Inventories are properly stated at the lower of cost or market.
2. Inventories included in the balance sheet are present in the warehouse on the balance sheet date.
3. Inventory quantities include all products, materials, and supplies on hand.
4. Liens on the inventories are properly disclosed in notes to the financial statements.
5. The client has legal title to the inventories.

6. Inventories include all items purchased by the company that are in transit at the balance sheet date and that have been shipped to customers on consignment.
7. Inventories received on consignment from suppliers have been excluded from inventory.
8. Quantities times prices have been properly extended on the inventory listing, the listing is properly totaled, and the total agrees with the general ledger balance for inventories.
9. Slow-moving items included in inventory have been properly identified and priced
10. Inventories are properly classified in the balance sheet as current assets.

REQUIRED

a. Identify and briefly explain the five categories of management's financial statement assertions.
b. Identify the category of assertions from which each of the specific audit objectives in items 1 through 10 above was derived.

5-26 **(Evidential matter)** The third GAAS of field work requires that the auditor obtain sufficient competent evidential matter to afford a reasonable basis for an opinion regarding the financial statements under audit. In considering what constitutes sufficient competent evidential matter, a distinction should be made between underlying accounting data and all corroborating information available to the auditor.

REQUIRED

a. Discuss the nature of evidential matter to be considered by the auditor in terms of the underlying accounting data, all corroborating information available to the auditor, and the methods by which the auditor tests or gathers competent evidential matter.
b. State the presumptions that can be made about the validity of the evidential matter with respect to (1) corroborating information and (2) underlying accounting data.

AICPA (adapted)

5-27 **(Audit evidence)** In an audit of financial statements, an auditor must judge the validity of the audit evidence obtained.

REQUIRED

a. In the course of an audit, the auditor asks many questions of client officers and employees.
   1. Describe the factors that the auditor should consider in evaluating oral evidence provided by client officers and employees.
   2. Discuss the validity and limitations of oral evidence.
b. An audit may include computation of various balance sheet and operating ratios for comparison to prior years and industry averages. Discuss the validity and limitations of ratio analysis in an audit.
c. In connection with his audit of the financial statements of a manufacturing company, an auditor is observing the physical inventory of finished goods, which consists of expensive, highly complex electronic equipment. Discuss the validity and limitations of the audit evidence provided by the procedure.

AICPA

5-28 **(Objectives and audit evidence)** In the audit of financial statements, the CPA is concerned with the examination and accumulation of audit evidence.

REQUIRED

a. What is the objective of the CPA's examination and accumulation of audit evidence during the course of an audit?

b. The source of the audit evidence is of primary importance in the CPA's evaluation of its quality. Audit evidence may be classified according to source. For example, one class originates within the client's organization, passes through the hands of third parties, and returns to the client where it may be examined by the auditor. List the classifications of audit evidence according to source, briefly discussing the effect of the source on the reliability of the evidence.

c. In evaluating the quality of the audit evidence, the CPA also considers factors other than the sources of the evidence. Briefly discuss these other factors.

AICPA (adapted)

5-29 **(Audit evidence)** During the course of an audit, the auditor examines a wide variety of documentation. Listed below are some forms of documentary evidence and the sources from which they are obtained.

1. Bank statement sent directly to the auditor by the bank.
2. Creditor monthly statement obtained from client's files.
3. Vouchers in client's unpaid voucher file.
4. Duplicate sales invoices in filled order file.
5. Time tickets filed in payroll department.
6. Credit memo in customer's file.
7. Material requisitions filed in storeroom.
8. Bank statement in client's files.
9. Management working papers in making accounting estimates.
10. Paid checks returned with bank statement in (1) above.
11. Letter in customer file from collection agency on collectibility of balance.
12. Memo in customer file from treasurer authorizing the writeoff of the account.

REQUIRED

a. Classify the evidence by source into one of four categories: (1) directly from outsiders, (2) indirectly from outsiders, (3) internal but validated externally, and (4) entirely internal.

b. Comment on the reliability of the four sources of documentary evidence.

5-30 **(Audit procedures and evidence)** A variety of specific audit procedures for obtaining audit evidence are listed below.

1. Inspect and count securities on hand.
2. Confirm inventories stored in public warehouses.
3. Obtain written report from a chemical engineer on grades of gasoline held as inventory by an oil company.
4. Recompute depreciation charges.
5. Learn about possible lawsuit in conversation with client's legal counsel during luncheon.
6. Compute and compare gross profit rates for the current and preceding years.
7. Examine certificates of title to delivery trucks purchased during the year.
8. Obtain letter from management on pledging of assets under loan agreements.
9. Vouch sales journal entries to sales invoices.
10. Observe the client's count of cash on hand.
11. Trace "paid" checks to check register entries.
12. Use computer to scan file to determine that all documents in a numbered series have been accounted for.

REQUIRED

a. Indicate (1) the type of evidence obtained by each procedure and (2) the assertion or assertions to which it pertains.

b. List by number the types of evidence that are (1) obtained directly from the independent sources outside the enterprise and (2) obtained by the auditor's direct personal knowledge.

5-31 **(Substantive tests and audit evidence)** In meeting the third standard of field work, the auditor may perform the following types of substantive tests: (a) tests of details of transactions, (b) tests of details of balances, and (c) analytical procedures. Below are listed specific audit procedures that fall within one of these categories.

1. Compare actual results with budget expectations.
2. Vouch entries in check register to "paid" checks.
3. Recalculate accrued interest payable.
4. Confirm customer balances.
5. Calculate inventory turnover ratios and compare with industry data.
6. Reconcile bank accounts at year-end.
7. Vouch sales journal entries to sales invoices.
8. Count office supplies on hand at year-end.
9. Examine deeds of ownership for land purchased during year.
10. Obtain representation letter from management.
11. Scan postings to repair expense for evidence of charges that should be capitalized.
12. Ask storeroom supervisor about obsolete items.

REQUIRED

List the numbers of the foregoing procedures. For each procedure, indicate the type of substantive test and the type of corroborating information obtained. Use the following format for your answers:

Procedure No.	Type of Substantive Test	Type of Corroborating Information

5-32 **(Audit procedures)** Auditors frequently refer to the terms "standards" and "procedures." Standards deal with measures of the quality of the auditor's performance. Standards specifically refer to the ten GAAS. Procedures relate to those acts that are performed by the auditor while trying to gather evidence. Procedures specifically refer to the methods or techniques used by the auditor in the conduct of the examination.

REQUIRED

List the different types of procedures that an auditor would use during an audit of financial statements. For example, a type of procedure that an auditor would frequently use is the observation of activities and conditions. Do not discuss specific accounts.

AICPA (adapted)

5-33 **(Working papers)** The preparation of working papers is an integral part of a CPA's audit of financial statements. On a recurring engagement, a CPA reviews his audit programs and working papers from his prior audit while planning his current audit to determine their usefulness for the current engagement.

REQUIRED

a. 1. What are the purposes or functions of working papers?
   2. What records may be included in working papers?

b. What factors affect the CPA's judgment of the type and content of the working papers for a particular engagement?
c. To comply with GAAS, a CPA includes certain evidence in his working papers—for example, "evidence that the engagement was planned and work of assistants was supervised and reviewed." What other evidence would a CPA include in audit working papers to comply with generally accepted auditing standards?

AICPA (adapted)

5-34 **(Working papers)** Smith is the partner in charge of the audit of Blue Distributing Corporation, a wholesaler that owns one warehouse containing 80% of its inventory. Smith is reviewing the working papers that were prepared to support the firm's opinion on Blue's financial statements and Smith wants to be certain essential audit records are well documented.

REQUIRED

What evidence should Smith find in the working papers to support the fact that the audit was adequately planned and the assistants were properly supervised?

AICPA (adapted

5-35 **(Adjusting and reclassifying entries)** The accountant for the Brian Co. is preparing financial statements for the year-ended December 31. Your review of the accounting records discloses the need for the following adjusting and reclassifying entries:

1. Office Supplies has a balance of $2,400. An inventory at December 31 shows $1,700 of supplies on hand.
2. There are two insurance accounts in the trial balance, Prepaid Insurance—$9,200 and Insurance Expense—$2,800. Unexpired insurance at the statement date is $3,000.
3. All rent receipts ($25,000) were credited to rent income. At the end of the year, $5,000 of rentals are unearned.
4. The allowance for uncollectibles has a credit balance of $6,000. An aging schedule shows estimated uncollectibles of $14,000.
5. The balance in accounts payable is $122,400. Included in this amount is $10,400 of advance deposits made by Brian Co. on future purchases.
6. The ledger shows interest receivable of $3,200 at the beginning of the year. All interest collections have been credited to interest revenue. At December 31 of the current year, accrued interest receivable totals $3,800.
7. A capital expenditure of $6,000 was debited to repairs expense on October 1. The annual rate of depreciation on the machinery is 10%.
8. Freight-in of $5,000 was debited to Freight-out.
9. Accounts receivable has a balance of $118,400. This balance is net of customers with credit balances of $15,000.
10. Bonds payable has a balance of $550,000. Bonds maturing within the next year total $50,000.

REQUIRED

Journalize the adjusting and reclassifying entries. Identify the adjustments by number and the reclassifications by letter.

CASES

5-36 **(Working papers)** The following schedule was prepared by staff accountant C. B. Sure on completing the verification of a December 31 client-prepared reconciliation of the City Bank General Account in the audit of Bold, Inc.

Bold, Inc. **#102 City Bank—Reconciliation**			**A-1** **Prepared by: Client** **Reviewed by: C. B. Sure**
Per Bank			$62,765.18 ✓
Deposit in transit			1,452.20 ✓
Outstanding checks			
	87.10 ✓	619.75 ✓	
	232.90 ✓	1,100.00 ✓	
	17.20 ✓	472.19 ✓	(2,529.14)
Other (see AJEs 12 and 13 on cash lead Schedule A)			510.55
Reconciled balance			$62,198.79
✓ Verified			✓

As a senior on the job, you discuss the work done with Sure and determine

1. The balance per bank agreed with the amount shown on the bank confirmation received directly from the bank.
2. The deposit in transit was traced to the January bank statement.
3. All outstanding checks were traced to the December check register.
4. Adjusting entry 12 was for the collection of a $515 noninterest bearing note by the bank; entry 13 was for December bank charges of $4.45.
5. The recorded balance per books at December 31, is $61,267.69.
6. In comparing "paid" checks with the check register, an error was discovered. Check number 2640 for $980 to a creditor was recorded by Bold, Inc., as $890. The bank paid the correct amount.
7. The final step, done on January 7, was to check the mathematical accuracy of the schedule.

REQUIRED

a. Prepare the bank reconciliation working paper in good form, showing adjusted balances per bank and per books.
b. Prepare the adjusting entries that presumably were made.
c. Prepare a cash lead schedule assuming (1) account number 101, Petty Cash $5,000 (working paper A-2, no adjustments) and (2) account number 103, City Bank—Payroll $20,000 (working paper A-3, no adjustment).
d. Show how cash will appear in the working trial balance.

5-37 **(Working papers)** The long-term debt working paper on pages 186 and 187 was prepared by client personnel and audited by AA, an audit assistant during the calendar year 1988 audit of American Widgets, Inc., a continuing audit client. The engagement supervisor is reviewing the working papers thoroughly.

REQUIRED

Identify the deficiencies in the working paper that the engagement supervisor should discover.

(AICPA)

RESEARCH QUESTIONS

5-38 **(Professional standards)** In obtaining evidence about existence or occurrence, rights and obligations, valuation or allocation, and presentation and disclosure assertions, the auditor considers transactions and accounts that are included in the financial statements. That is, the assertions deal with transactions or accounts that are a matter of record. In contrast, in obtaining evidence about completeness assertions the auditor considers whether transactions and accounts have been improperly excluded from the financial statements. Thus, obtaining evidence about completeness assertions may be more difficult because there may be no record of the transaction or account from which to start. Because of this, the Auditing Standards Board has provided additional guidance pertaining to the auditor's consideration of the completeness assertion.

a. In what form was this guidance issued? Give an appropriate citation from the professional standards.
b. One source of evidence about completeness is oral evidence and written representations obtained from management. Is this sufficient? If not, what else should the auditor do when he or she has concluded there is a risk of material omissions?

5-39 **(AAER)** The SEC's *Accounting and Auditing Enforcement Release No. 69* illustrates an action taken against an auditor for failing to obtain sufficient competent evidence. Who were the parties in this case? For what assertions was the evidence deficient, and how was the evidence deficient? What action was taken against the auditor?

Index	K-1	
	Initials	Date
Prepared By	AA	3/22/89
Approved By		

American Widgets, Inc.
WORKING PAPERS
December 31, 1988

Lender	Interest Rate	Payment Terms	Collateral	Balance 12/31/87	1988 Borrowings	1988 Reductions	Balance 12/31/88	Interest Paid to	Accrued Interest Payable 12/31/88	Comments
Φ First Commercial Bank	12%	Interest only on 25th of month, principal due in full 1/1/92; no prepayment penalty	Inventories	$ 50,000 √	$300,000 A 1/31/88	$100,000 ⊕ 6/30/88	$ 250,000 CX	12/25/88	$2,500 NR	Dividend of $80,000 paid 9/2/88 (W/P N-3) violates a provision of the debt agreement, which thereby permits lender to demand immediate payment; lender has refused to waive this violation.
Φ Lender's Capital Corp.	Prime plus 1%	Interest only on last day of month, principal due in full 3/5/90	2nd Mortgage on Park St. Building	100,000 √	50,000 A 2/29/88	—	200,000 C	12/31/88	—	Prime rate was 8% to 9% during the year.

Φ Gigantic Building & Loan Assoc.	12%	$5,000 principal plus interest due on 5th of month, due in full 12/31/99	1st Mortgage on Park St. Building	720,000 √	—	60,000 ○	660,000 C	12/5/88	5,642 R	Reclassification entry for current portion proposed (See RJE-3).
Φ J. Lott, majority stockholder	0%	Due in full 12/31/91	Unsecured	300,000 √	—	100,000 N 12/31/88	200,000 C	—	—	Borrowed additional $100,000 from J. Lott on 1/7/89.
				$1,170,000 √	$350,000	$260,000	$1,310,000 T/B		$8,142 T/B	
				F	F	F	F		F	

Tickmark Legend

F	Readded, foots correctly
C	Confirmed without exception, W/P K-2
CX	Confirmed with exception W/P K-3
NR	Does not recompute correctly
A	Agreed to loan agreement, validated bank deposit ticket, and board of directors authorization, W/P W-7
○	Agreed to canceled checks and lender's monthly statements
N	Agreed to cash disbursements journal and canceled check dated 12/31/88, clearing 1/8/89
T/B	Traced to working trial balance
√	Agreed to 12/31/87 working papers
Φ	Agreed interest rate, term, and collateral to copy of note and loan agreement
⊕	Agreed to canceled check and board of directors' authorization, W/P W-7

Overall conclusions

Long-term debt, accrued interest payable, and interest expense are correct and complete at 12/31/88.

Interest costs from long-term debt

Interest expense for year	$ 281,333 T/B
Average loan balance outstanding	$1,406,667 R

Five year maturities (for disclosure purposes)

Year-end	12/31/89	$ 60,000
	12/31/90	260,000
	12/31/91	260,000
	12/31/92	310,000
	12/31/93	60,000
	Thereafter	360,000
		$1,310,000
		F

CHAPTER

6

ACCEPTING THE ENGAGEMENT AND PLANNING THE AUDIT

LEARNING OBJECTIVES

After you have completed your study of this chapter, you should be able to

1. Identify the phases of a financial statement audit.
2. State the steps involved in accepting an audit engagement.
3. Indicate the purpose and content of an engagement letter.
4. Enumerate the components of audit planning.
5. Describe the procedures used in obtaining an understanding of the client's business and industry.
6. Explain the role of analytical procedures in audit planning.

OVERVIEW OF A FINANCIAL STATEMENT AUDIT
- ACCEPTING THE AUDIT ENGAGEMENT
- PLANNING THE AUDIT
- PERFORMING AUDIT TESTS
- REPORTING THE FINDINGS

ACCEPTING THE ENGAGEMENT
- EVALUATING THE INTEGRITY OF MANAGEMENT
- IDENTIFYING SPECIAL CIRCUMSTANCES AND UNUSUAL RISKS
- ASSESSING COMPETENCE TO PERFORM THE AUDIT
- EVALUATING INDEPENDENCE
- DETERMINING ABILITY TO USE DUE CARE
- PREPARING THE ENGAGEMENT LETTER

PLANNING THE AUDIT
- STEPS IN PLANNING THE AUDIT
- OBTAINING UNDERSTANDING OF CLIENT'S BUSINESS AND INDUSTRY
- PERFORMING ANALYTICAL PROCEDURES

SUMMARY

APPENDIX 6A: KEY FINANCIAL RATIOS USED IN ANALYTICAL PROCEDURES

BIBLIOGRAPHY

OBJECTIVE QUESTIONS

COMPREHENSIVE QUESTIONS

CASE

RESEARCH QUESTIONS

This chapter has three major parts. First, the phases of a financial statement audit are identified and briefly explained. Second, the steps involved in completing the initial phase of an audit—accepting the engagement—are discussed. Third, the steps involved in the planning phase of the audit are identified, followed by in-depth coverage of the first two components—obtaining an understanding of the client's business and industry, and performing analytical procedures.

OVERVIEW OF A FINANCIAL STATEMENT AUDIT

The audit of a small unincorporated company may involve one or two auditors, less than 100 hours of work, and an audit fee of less than $5,000. In contrast, the audit of a Fortune 500 corporation may require scores of auditors, thousands of hours of work, and an audit fee in the millions of dollars.

The following four **phases of an audit** can be identified:

- Accepting the audit engagement.
- Planning the audit.
- Performing audit tests.
- Reporting the findings.

OBJECTIVE 1

Identify the phases of a financial statement audit.

In each phase, the auditor should be mindful of the environment in which audits are performed as described in the preceding chapters. Environmental factors include the impact of regulation, the public's expectations, exposure to litigation, and the need to comply with professional standards. Figure 6-1 depicts a model of the environmental factors with particular emphasis on the relationship of GAAS to the four phases of the audit. Note that the general standards apply to each phase and, except for accepting the engagement, two categories of standards apply to each of the other phases.

ACCEPTING THE AUDIT ENGAGEMENT

The initial phase of a financial statement audit involves a decision to accept (or decline) the opportunity to become the auditor for a new client or to continue as auditor for an existing client. As shown in Figure 6-1, only the general standards of GAAS apply to this phase. In most cases, the decision to accept (or decline) is made six to nine months before the client's fiscal year-end. An explanation of the factors to be considered in accepting the audit engagement is given in this chapter.

PLANNING THE AUDIT

The second phase of the audit requires the development of an audit strategy for the conduct and scope of the audit. Planning is crucial to a successful audit engagement. From Figure 6-1, it can be seen that both the general and field work standards apply to this phase of an audit. Audit planning is usually done from three to six months prior to the end of the client's fiscal year. Explanations of the components involved in audit planning are considered in this and the next two chapters.

PERFORMING AUDIT TESTS

The third phase of the audit is performing audit tests. This phase is also referred to as performing the **field work** because the tests are usually done on the client's premises. The primary purpose of this phase is to obtain audit evidence about the effectiveness of the client's internal control structure and the fairness of its financial statements. As illustrated in Figure 6-1, both the general and field work standards apply to this phase, which constitutes the major portion of an audit. Audit tests are typically performed from three to four months before to one to three months after the end of the client's fiscal year. Audit tests are explained in Chapters 9 through 18 of this text.

FIGURE 6-1 • PHASES OF THE AUDIT AND THE AUDITING ENVIRONMENT

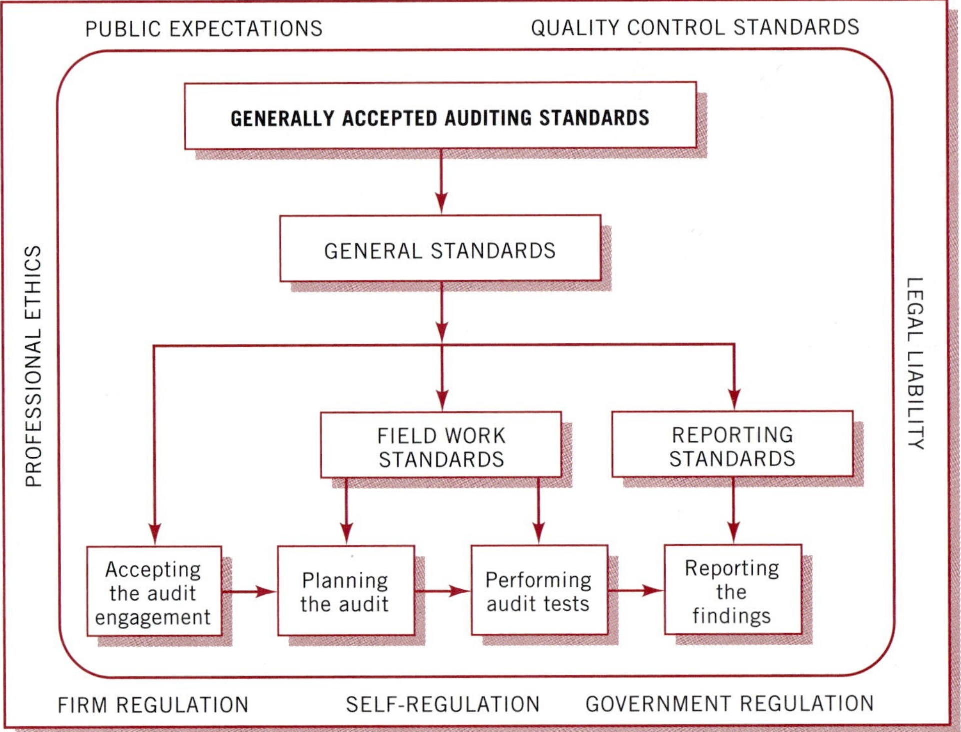

REPORTING THE FINDINGS

The fourth and final phase of an audit is reporting the findings. As indicated in Chapter 2, the audit report may be standard or there may be a departure from the standard report. As shown in Figure 6-1, the general and reporting standards must be met in reporting the findings. The audit report is generally issued within one to three weeks of completing the field work. Further consideration to this phase of an audit is given in Chapters 20 and 21.

LEARNING CHECK:

6-1 a. Identify the four phases of a financial statement audit.
b. State the typical time frame in which each of the four phases occurs.

6-2 a. Indicate which categories of the generally accepted auditing standards apply to each phase of the audit.
b. Identify other environmental factors that have an impact on the phases of an audit.

KEY TERMS:

Field work, p. 189

Phases of an audit, p. 189

ACCEPTING THE ENGAGEMENT

OBJECTIVE 2

State the steps involved in accepting an audit engagement.

Within the public accounting profession, there is considerable competition among firms for clients. This includes clients seeking an audit for the first time and clients seeking a change in auditors. Companies recently changing auditors include Continental Airlines, Toys "R" Us, Fisher-Price, and Six Flags Theme Parks. Auditor changes result from a variety of factors including (1) mergers between corporations with different independent auditors, (2) the need for expanded professional services, (3) dissatisfaction with a firm, (4) a desire to reduce the audit fee, and (5) mergers between CPA firms.

An auditor is not obligated to perform a financial statement audit for any entity that requests it. In accepting an engagement, an auditor takes on professional responsibilities to the public, the client, and other members of the public accounting profession. The auditor must sustain the public's confidence in the profession by maintaining independence, integrity, and objectivity. The client's best interests must be served with competence and professional concern. And to other members of the profession, the auditor has a responsibility to enhance the stature of the profession and its ability to serve the public. Thus, a decision to accept a new audit client or continue a relationship with an existing client should not be taken lightly.

COLA WARS HIT CPAS

How could accountants become pawns in the cola wars between Pepsi and Coke? When the CPA firms of Ernst & Ernst and Arthur Young merged to form Ernst & Young, the firm became the auditors for both cola giants. However, Ernst & Young was told by the Coca Cola Company that it could not stand for re-election as the auditor for both companies. Subsequently, Ernst & Young reluctantly informed Pepsi officials that they must withdraw as auditors for Pepsi. The Pepsi account, with an estimated audit fee of $9 million, was won by KPMG Peat Marwick.

SOURCE: *Accounting Today*, March 19, 1990.

FIGURE 6-2 • STEPS IN ACCEPTING AN AUDIT ENGAGEMENT

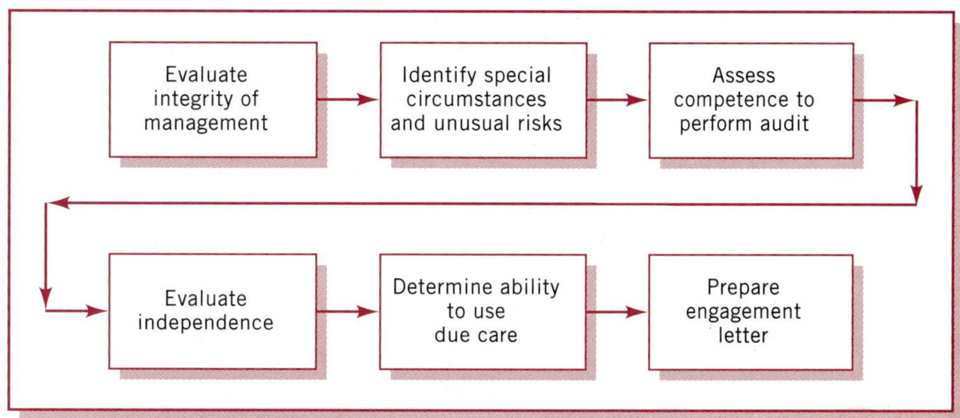

The importance of this decision is reflected in the inclusion of *acceptance and continuation of clients* as one of the nine quality control elements for CPA firms as discussed previously in Chapter 1 of this text. Considerations relevant to the acceptance decision also relate directly to the auditor's ability to comply with specific requirements of GAAS and of the Code of Professional Conduct. Figure 6-2 identifies a number of steps that can be taken by CPA firms to ensure acceptance of only those audit engagements that can be completed in accordance with all applicable professional standards. Each step is discussed below.

EVALUATING THE INTEGRITY OF MANAGEMENT

The primary purpose of a financial statement audit is to express an opinion on management's financial statements. Accordingly, it is important that an auditor accept an audit engagement only when reasonable assurance exists that the client's management can be trusted. When management lacks integrity, there is a greater likelihood that material errors and irregularities may occur in the accounting process from which the financial statements are developed. This, in turn, increases the risk that an unqualified opinion will be expressed when the financial statements are materially misstated. For a new client, the auditor may obtain information about the integrity of management by communicating with the predecessor auditor, if applicable, and making inquiries of other third parties. For an existing client, the auditor's previous experience with the client's management should be considered.

Communicate with the Predecessor Auditor

For a client who has been audited, the knowledge of the client's management acquired by the **predecessor auditor** is considered essential information for a **successor auditor.** Before accepting the engagement, SAS 7, *Communication Between Predecessor and Successor Auditors* (AU 315.02), requires the successor auditor to take the initiative to communicate, either orally or in writing, with the predecessor auditor. The communication should be made with the client's permission, and the client should be requested to authorize the predecessor to respond fully to the successor's inquiries. Authorization is required because the profession's code of ethics prohibits an auditor from disclosing confidential information obtained in an audit without the client's permission.

In the communication, the successor auditor should make specific and reasonable inquiries regarding matters that may affect the decision to accept an engagement, such as

- The integrity of management.
- Disagreements with management about accounting principles and auditing procedures.
- The predecessor's understanding of the reasons for a change in auditors.

The predecessor auditor is expected to respond promptly and fully, assuming the client gives consent. If the client's consent is not given or the predecessor auditor does not respond fully, the successor auditor should consider the implications in deciding whether to accept the engagement.

Make Inquiries of Other Third Parties

Information about management's integrity may also be obtained from knowledgeable persons such as attorneys, bankers, and others in the financial and business community who have had business relationships with the prospective client. In some cases, making an inquiry of the local chamber of commerce and the better business bureau may also be helpful.

Other potential sources of information include (1) reviewing news items on top management changes in the financial press, and (2) in the case of prospective SEC clients who have been audited previously, reviewing a report filed with the SEC concerning a change in auditors.

Review Previous Experience with Existing Clients

Before making a decision to continue an engagement with an audit client, the auditor should carefully consider prior experiences with the client's management. For example, the auditor should consider any material errors or irregularities and illegal acts discovered in prior audits. During an audit, the auditor makes inquiries of management about such matters as the existence of contingencies, the completeness of all minutes of board of director meetings, and compliance with regulatory requirements. The truthfulness of management's responses to such inquiries in prior audits should be carefully considered in evaluating the integrity of management.

IDENTIFYING SPECIAL CIRCUMSTANCES AND UNUSUAL RISKS

Matters pertaining to this step in accepting an engagement include identifying the intended users of the audited financial statements, making a preliminary assessment of the prospective client's legal and financial stability, and evaluating the entity's auditability.

Identify Intended Users of Audited Statements

Chapter 4 points out that the auditor's legal responsibilities in an audit may vary based on the intended users of the statements. Thus, the auditor should consider the prospective client's status as a private or public company, any named beneficiaries or foreseen or foreseeable third parties to whom the potential for liability exists under the common law, and what, if any, statutes apply in the circumstances. The auditor should also consider whether a common set of audited statements will meet the needs of all intended users or whether any special reports will be required. For example, regulated companies may be required to furnish certain audited information not required by GAAP. Added reporting requirements may mean additional competency requirements, add to audit costs, and broaden the auditor's legal liability exposure.

Assess Prospective Client's Legal and Financial Stability

If an entity experiences legal difficulties, and if plaintiffs can find any pretext for claiming reliance on the financial statements, it is widely recognized that such litigation will likely involve the auditors who are often thought to have "deep pockets." Thus, auditors may incur the financial and other costs of defending themselves no matter how professionally they perform their services.

For this reason, auditors should attempt to identify and reject prospective clients that pose a high risk of litigation. This might include companies whose operations or principal products are the subject of investigations by authorities or are the subject of material lawsuits, the outcome of which could adversely impact the viability of the business. It might also include companies already known to be experiencing financial instability such as inability to meet debt payments or raise needed capital. Even when there are no signs of current difficulties, consideration should be given to the likelihood of such matters as future write-downs associated with evolving business conditions. Procedures the auditor can use to identify such matters are inquiries of management, reviews of credit bureau reports, analysis of previously issued audited or unaudited financial statements, and, if applicable, previous filings with regulatory agencies.

Evaluate Entity's Auditability

Before accepting an engagement, the auditor should evaluate whether other conditions exist that raise questions as to the prospective client's auditability. Such conditions might include the absence, or poor condition, of important accounting records, management's disregard of its responsibility to maintain other elements of an adequate internal control structure, or restrictions imposed by the prospective client on the conduct of the audit. In such cases, the engagement should be declined or there should be a clear understanding with the client of the possible effects of such conditions on the auditor's report.

ASSESSING COMPETENCE TO PERFORM THE AUDIT

The first general standard of GAAS states:

> The audit is to be performed by a person or persons having adequate technical training and proficiency as an auditor.

Thus, before accepting an audit engagement, auditors should determine whether they have the professional competence to complete the engagement in accordance with GAAS. This generally involves identifying the key members of the audit team and considering the need to seek assistance from consultants and specialists during the course of the audit.

Identify the Audit Team

It may be recalled that *assigning personnel to engagements* is one of the nine quality control elements. The objective of this element is to see that the technical expertise and experience levels of the audit team match the professional staffing needs of the engagement. In making assignments, the nature and extent of supervision to be provided should also be taken into account. Generally, the more able and experienced the personnel assigned to a particular engagement, the less is the need for direct supervision.

The typical **audit team** consists of

- A partner, who has both overall and final responsibility for the engagement.
- One or more managers, who coordinate and supervise the execution of the audit program.
- One or more seniors, who may have responsibility for parts of the audit program and who supervise and review the work of staff assistants.
- Staff assistants, who perform many of the required procedures.

The key members of the audit team are generally identified prior to acceptance of the engagement to ensure their availability. In addition, when a prospective client has invited a firm to submit a proposal to obtain the engagement, it is common practice to include the resumes of the key members of the proposed audit team. This allows the prospective client to assess the credentials of the individuals who will be assigned to the engagement.

Consider Need for Consultation and the Use of Specialists

In determining whether to accept an engagement, it is appropriate for an auditor to consider using consultants and specialists to assist the audit team in performing the audit. In fact, the quality control element of *consultation* states that firms should adopt policies and procedures to provide reasonable assurance that personnel will seek assistance, to the extent required, from persons having appropriate levels of knowledge, competence, judgment, and authority. Thus, for example, it may be anticipated that an audit team in a practice office may need to consult with a computer or industry expert in the firm's national office to deal with complex client issues that arise in the course of the audit.

Similarly, certain matters may require the use of a **specialist** outside the auditor's firm. An auditor is not expected to have the expertise of a person trained for, or qualified to engage in, the practice of another profession or occupation. SAS 73, *Using the Work of a Specialist* (AU 336), recognizes that the auditor may use the work of specialists to obtain competent evidential matter. Examples include the use of

- Appraisers to provide evidence about the valuation of assets such as art.
- Engineers to determine the quantities of mineral reserves on hand.
- Actuaries to determine amounts used in accounting for a pension plan.
- Attorneys to assess the probable outcome of pending litigation.
- Environmental consultants to determine the impact of environmental laws and regulations.

Before using a specialist, the auditor is expected to become satisfied as to the professional qualifications, reputation, and objectivity of the specialist. For example, the auditor should consider whether the specialist has acquired the professional certification, license, or other recognition of competence appropriate in the specialist's field, make inquiries of the specialist's peers and others familiar with his or her reputation and professional standing, and determine whether the specialist has any relationship with the client that might impair his or her objectivity.

EVALUATING INDEPENDENCE

The second general standard of GAAS states:

> In all matters relating to the assignment, an independence in mental attitude is to be maintained by the auditor or auditors.

In addition, independence on audit engagements is required by Rule 101 of the AICPA's *Code of Professional Conduct* and is one of the quality control elements. Furthermore, if the prospective client is required to file audited financial statements with the SEC, the auditor must comply with the Commission's requirements pertaining to independence.

Thus, before accepting a new audit client, the auditing firm must evaluate whether there are any circumstances that would impair its independence with respect to the client. One procedure is to circulate the name of a prospective client to all professional staff to identify any prohibited financial or business relationships. If it is concluded that the independence requirements cannot be met, the engagement should be declined or the potential client should be informed that the firm will be required to issue a disclaimer of opinion on the financial statements. In addition, the firm should determine that acceptance of the client would not result in any conflicts of interest with other clients.

DETERMINING ABILITY TO USE DUE CARE

The third general standard of GAAS states:

> Due professional care is to be exercised in the performance of the audit and the preparation of the report.

Due care in the performance of all professional services is also required by Rule 201 of the AICPA's *Code of Professional Conduct.* Thus, an engagement should be declined if due professional care cannot be exercised throughout the audit. This includes provision for the critical review at every level of supervision of both the work done and the judgments exercised by those assisting in the audit. Two important factors in determining the ability to use due care are the timing of the appointment and the scheduling of field work.

Assess Timing of Appointment

Earlier in this chapter, it was noted that the first phase of the audit (accepting the engagement) ideally occurs six to nine months prior to the client's year-end. However, in some cases, acceptance may occur just before, or even after, the close of the client's fiscal year.

Early appointment by the client and acceptance by the auditor facilitate audit planning. For example, acceptance of the engagement early in the client's fiscal year gives the auditor much greater flexibility in scheduling field work.

In contrast, acceptance near or after the close of the fiscal year may impose severe constraints on planning the audit and performing the field work, including possibly having to forego procedures often performed as of the balance sheet date, such as the observation of the physical inventory. The latter might be remedied by postponing the physical inventory or taking another one that the auditor can observe. If the auditor is uncertain as to whether the circumstances will permit an audit in accordance with GAAS, the prospective client should be informed of the possibility that an unqualified opinion on the financial statements may not be possible because of the limitations on the timing and scope of the audit.

Consider the Scheduling of Field Work

It is customary to classify the timing of field work into the following two categories:

- **Interim work** that is typically performed within the three-to four-month period immediately prior to the balance sheet date.
- **Year-end work** that is typically performed within a period extending from shortly before the balance sheet date to as long as three months following the balance sheet date.

The performance of field work at interim dates helps to compensate for the fact that many clients will have a common fiscal year-end, and it permits the auditing firm to spread its workload more evenly throughout the year.

The detailed schedule for completing an engagement may not be finalized until after acceptance and after several steps in the audit planning phase have been completed. Nonetheless, the probable impact of accepting a new client on the firm's overall work schedule and ability to service existing clients must be considered prior to acceptance.

TIME BUDGETS. Preliminary work on a **time budget** for the audit is often done, in accepting the engagement, as part of the scheduling considerations. The development of a time budget involves estimating the hours expected to be required at each staff level (partner, manager, senior, and so on) to complete each part of the audit with due care. These time estimates may then be multiplied by the per diem rates for each staff level and combined with estimated travel and other out-of-pocket costs to arrive at an estimate of total costs for the engagement. These estimates may in turn be used as the basis for discussions with the prospective client about fee arrangements. Although some audits are done on a fixed-fee basis, the use of per diem rates plus reimbursement of out-of-pocket costs is the more typical arrangement.

If the engagement is accepted, details of the time budget and scheduling of field work will be further developed as additional steps in the planning phase are performed. The engagement partner should approve the initial time budget and any modifications to it. Then, as work on each area of the audit progresses, actual hours can be monitored and compared with the budget as an aid in controlling overall audit costs.

AUDIT COSTS

How much does an audit cost? The *MAPI Survey on Outside Audit Fees: 1993* found U.S. audit fees averaged 0.029% of sales ($0.00029 per sales dollar). This average is based on survey responses from 208 members of the Manufacturers' Alliance for Productivity and Innovation (MAPI). Most of the respondents employed Big Six firms. Their sales volumes ranged from less than $15 million to more than $50 billion. Although audit costs can vary significantly from one company to another, they tended to be lower per sales dollar for larger companies and higher for smaller companies. The 1993 average shows a marked decline in audit costs from the first MAPI survey taken in 1976 when audit fees were found to average 0.1% of sales ($0.001 per sales dollar). As to fee arrangements, 57% of the respondents in the 1993 survey said their company had an open-ended fee arrangement, 36% had a fixed-fee arrangement, and 7% reported a capped-fee arrangement subject to override with mutual consent.

SOURCE: "Audit Fees Remain Steady," *Public Accounting Report*, October 15, 1993, p. 5.

CLIENT PERSONNEL. The use of client personnel can also have a significant impact on staffing and scheduling, and thus on audit cost. As explained in Chapter 2, the work of internal auditors can have an effect on the independent auditor's work. This effect can extend to all three categories of auditing procedures—procedures to obtain an understanding of the internal control structure, tests of controls, and substantive tests. In addition, other client personnel can be used to perform tasks such as

- Preparing the working trial balance of the general ledger.
- Reconciling control and subsidiary accounts.
- Aging accounts receivable.
- Preparing schedules of insurance policies in force, notes receivable, and plant asset additions and disposals.

To meet the due care standard, the auditor must, of course, plan to review and test all such work.

PREPARING THE ENGAGEMENT LETTER

As the final step in the acceptance phase, it is good professional practice to confirm the terms of each engagement in an **engagement letter** as illustrated in Figure 6-3. The form and content of engagement letters may vary for different clients, but they should generally include the following:

FIGURE 6-3 • ENGAGEMENT LETTER

REDDY & ABEL CERTIFIED PUBLIC ACCOUNTANTS

March 15, 19X1

Mr. Thomas Thorp, President
Melville Co., Inc.
Route 32
Midtown, New York 11746

Dear Mr. Thorp:

This will confirm our understanding of the arrangements for our audit of the financial statements of Melville Co., Inc., for the year ending December 31, 19X1.

We will audit the Company's balance sheet at December 31, 19X1, and the related statements of income, retained earnings, and cash flows for the year then ended, for the purpose of expressing an opinion on them. Our audit will be in accordance with generally accepted auditing standards, which require that we plan and perform the audit to obtain reasonable assurance that the financial statements are not materially misstated.

Our audit will include examining, on a test basis, evidence supporting the amounts and disclosures in the financial statements. We will also assess the accounting principles used and significant estimates made by management, and evaluate the overall financial statement presentation.

Because of the characteristics of irregularities, a properly designed and executed audit may not detect all material irregularities. We will, of course, report to you anything that appears to us during our audit to be unusual or abnormal.

We remind you that the preparation of the Company's financial statements, including adequate disclosure, is the responsibility of the Company's management. This includes the selection and application of accounting policies, and the maintenance of an internal control structure that provides reasonable assurance of achieving Company objectives regarding the effectiveness and efficiency of operations, the safeguarding of assets, the reliability of financial reporting, and compliance with applicable laws and regulations. As part of our audit process, we will request from management certain written representations concerning information provided to us in connection with the audit.

We will review the Company's Federal and State [identify states] income tax returns for the year ended December 31, 19X1. These returns, we understand, will be prepared by you. Further, we will be available during the year to consult with you on the tax effects of transactions or contemplated changes in business policies.

Our fee for this audit will be at our regular per diem rates, plus travel and other costs. Invoices will be rendered every two weeks and are payable on presentation.

We are pleased to have this opportunity to serve you. If this letter correctly expresses your understanding, please sign the enclosed copy and return it to us.

Very truly yours,
REDDY & ABEL
Ivan M. Reddy
Partner

APPROVED:

By: ______________________________

Date: ______________________________

OBJECTIVE 3

Indicate the purpose and content of an engagement letter.

- Clear identification of the entity and the financial statements to be audited.
- The objective or purpose of the audit.
- Reference to the professional standards (e.g., GAAS) to which the auditor will adhere (and, if applicable, to governing legislation or regulations, as when performing certain government required audits).
- An explanation of the nature and scope of the audit and the auditor's responsibilities.

- A statement to the effect that a properly designed and executed audit may not detect all material irregularities.
- A reminder to management that it is responsible for the preparation of the financial statements and for the maintenance of an adequate internal control structure.
- An indication that management will be asked to provide certain written representations to the auditor.
- A description of any auxillary services to be provided by the auditor such as the preparation or review of tax returns.
- The basis on which fees will be computed and any billing arrangements.
- A request for the client to confirm the terms of the engagement by signing and returning a copy of the letter to the auditor.

To eliminate the need to prepare a new letter each year on recurring audits, a statement may be added to the initial letter to the effect that it will be effective for future years unless it is terminated, amended or superseded. Of course, if there are any significant future changes in the terms of the engagement, the nature or size of the client's business, its management, or legal requirements, a revised letter should be prepared.

U.S. auditing standards neither require engagement letters nor provide guidance as to their preparation. *International Standard on Auditing No. 2,* though not explicitly requiring engagement letters, provides guidance in a manner that presumes their use. The guidelines and sample letter included in IAU 2 (AU 8002) are similar to those presented in this text.

An engagement letter constitutes a legal contract between the auditor and the client and should be renewed each year. By clearly stating the nature of services to be performed and the responsibilities of the auditor, as noted in Chapter 4, such letters may help the auditor to avoid becoming involved in litigation.

LEARNING CHECK:

6-3 a. State the steps involved in accepting an audit engagement.
b. Contrast the manner in which the auditor can evaluate the integrity of management between a new and a recurring audit engagement.

6-4 a. Why is it considered necessary for a successor auditor to communicate with a predecessor auditor?
b. Identify three matters about which the successor auditor should direct inquiries to the predecessor auditor.

6-5 Before accepting an audit engagement, the auditor should identify special circumstances and unusual risks.
a. Why is it important to identify the intended users of financial statements?

b. Why should a prospective client's legal and financial stability be evaluated?

c. Identify three conditions that raise questions as to a prospective client's auditability.

6-6 a. Why is it essential for auditors to determine whether they have the competence to complete an engagement before accepting it?

b. What is involved in making this determination?

6-7 a. What is the composition of a typical audit team?

b. Is it ever appropriate to accept an engagement in which the members of the proposed audit team do not possess all the expertise needed to complete the audit? Explain.

6-8 a. State four examples of situations in which an auditor might want to use the services of a specialist outside the auditor's firm.

b. What should an auditor do before relying on the work of a specialist?

c. Is it ever appropriate to use a specialist that has a relationship with the client? Explain.

6-9 a. Why is it important for an auditor to evaluate independence in deciding whether to accept a new client?

b. What should an auditor do if he or she concludes that independence requirements cannot be met?

6-10 a. State two critical factors in determining the ability to use due care in completing an audit.

b. Why is it advisable to accept a new audit engagement early in the client's fiscal year?

6-11 a. Distinguish the time frames in which interim and year-end work are typically performed.

b. Why do auditors prefer to perform part of the field work at an interim date?

6-12 a. What are the purposes of an engagement letter?

b. Who prepares the engagement letter, to whom is it sent, and what is its disposition?

KEY TERMS:

Audit team, p. 195
Engagement letter, p. 198
Interim work, p. 197
Predecessor auditor, p. 192
Specialist, p. 195
Successor auditor, p. 192
Time budget, p. 197
Year-end work, p. 197

PLANNING THE AUDIT

A vital phase of every audit engagement is planning. Planning serves much the same purpose in auditing that it does in personal planning for college or a ski trip to Aspen, and in business planning for the development of a new product like a fax machine. In each instance, planning results in an orderly arrangement of the parts or steps to achieve the desired objective. The first GAAS of field work states:

The work is to be adequately planned, and assistants, if any, are to be properly supervised.

OBJECTIVE 4

Enumerate the components of audit planning.

Audit planning involves the development of an overall strategy or game plan for the expected conduct and scope of the audit. The auditor should plan the audit with an attitude of professional skepticism about such matters as the integrity of management, errors and irregularities, and illegal acts. The amount of planning required in an engagement will vary with the size and complexity of the client, and the auditor's knowledge of and experience with the client. As to be expected, considerably more effort is needed to adequately plan an initial audit than a recurring audit.

Supervision involves directing the assistants on the audit team who participate in accomplishing the objectives of the audit, and determining that the objectives have been achieved. The extent of supervision required on an engagement depends on, among other factors, the qualifications of the persons performing the work. Thus, in planning the audit, provision should be made for more supervision when several members of the audit team are inexperienced than when they are all experienced.

STEPS IN PLANNING THE AUDIT

The steps in planning the audit are shown in Figure 6-4. The first two steps are discussed in the remainder of this chapter. Steps 3, 4, and 5 are discussed in Chapter 7, and step 6 is discussed in Chapter 8.

OBTAINING UNDERSTANDING OF CLIENT'S BUSINESS AND INDUSTRY

To adequately plan an audit, the auditor should obtain sufficient knowledge of the client's business to understand events, transactions, and practices that may have a

FIGURE 6-4 • STEPS IN PLANNING THE AUDIT

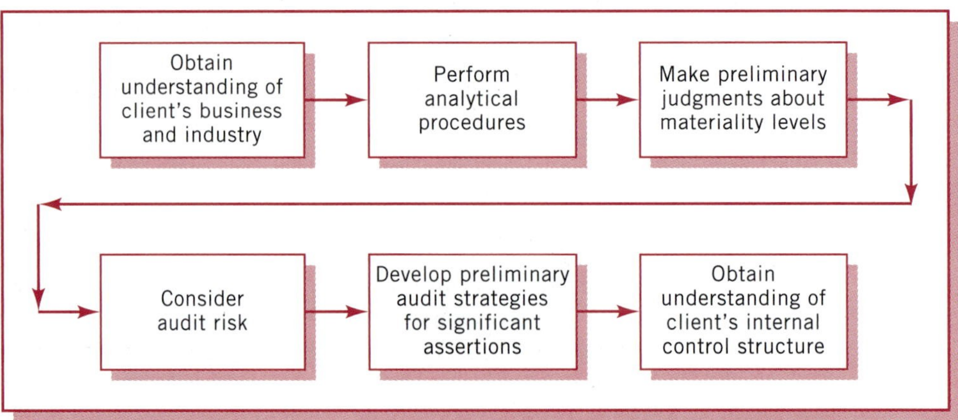

OBJECTIVE 5

Describe the procedures used in obtaining an understanding of the client's business and industry.

significant effect on the financial statements. The auditor needs knowledge about the

- Type of business, types of products and services, company locations, and operating characteristics of the entity, such as its production and marketing methods.
- Type of industry, vulnerability of industry to changing economic conditions, and major industry policies and practices.
- Existence of related party transactions.
- Government regulations that affect the entity and its industry.
- Entity's internal control structure.
- Nature of reports to be filed with regulatory agencies such as the SEC.

A variety of procedures may be used to acquire this knowledge. Those with the widest application are discussed in the following sections.

Review Prior Years' Working Papers

In a recurring audit engagement, the auditor can review the firm's prior years' working papers for knowledge about the client. In addition, the working papers may indicate problem areas that have occurred in prior audits that may be expected to continue in the future. For instance, the client may have ongoing internal control weaknesses and complicated pension and profit-sharing bonus plans.

For a new client, the predecessor auditor's working papers may be helpful. The client must consent to the successor's review of the working papers and the predecessor auditor is then expected to cooperate. The review is normally limited to matters of continuing audit significance, such as analyses of balance sheet accounts and contingencies. During the review, the predecessor auditor should be available for consultation. At such time, the successor auditor can make inquiries concerning matters that may affect the current audit.

Review Industry and Business Data

Information about the industry in which the client operates may be obtained from reading industry data accumulated by the auditing firm and industry publications. The auditor may also obtain useful information from the many industry audit and accounting guides published by the AICPA.

To obtain knowledge about the client's business, the auditor may

- Review the articles of incorporation and bylaws.
- Read the minutes of directors' and stockholders' meetings to obtain information about such events as dividend declarations and stockholder approval of business combinations.
- Analyze recent annual and interim financial statements, tax returns, and reports to regulatory agencies.
- Become familiar with applicable government regulations.
- Read important continuing contracts such as loan agreements, leases, and labor contracts.

- Read trade and industry publications concerning current business and industry developments.

The information obtained should be documented by the auditor and retained in a permanent file for use in subsequent audits.

Tour Client Operations

A tour of the operating facilities and offices is a significant help to an auditor in obtaining knowledge about a new client's operating characteristics. From a tour of the plant, an auditor should become familiar with the layout of the plant, the operating (manufacturing) process, storage facilities, and potential trouble spots such as unlocked storerooms, obsolete materials, and excessive scrap.

During a tour of the office, an auditor should become knowledgeable about the types and locations of the accounting records and EDP facilities, and the work habits of personnel. An important by-product of both tours is the opportunity to meet personnel who occupy key positions within the client's organization. The auditor should document the information obtained from the plant and office tours.

In a recurring engagement, the tour of client operations is often limited to major changes that have occurred since the completion of last year's audit. For a multidivisional company, tours of divisions may be done on a rotating basis.

Make Inquiries of Audit Committee

The audit committee of the board of directors may provide the auditor with special insights into the client's business and industry. For example, the committee may have information about strengths or weaknesses in the company's internal controls in a specific division, a recently acquired subsidiary, or a newly implemented EDP systems application. The committee may also be able to inform the auditor of significant changes in the company's management and organizational structure.

As previously explained, one of the primary functions of an audit committee is to discuss the scope of the audit with the auditor. In some cases, the audit committee may request additions or modifications to the auditor's planned audit.

Make Inquiries of Management

For both new and recurring clients, discussions with management may reveal current business developments affecting the entity that may have audit significance. In addition, management should be knowledgeable about new industry and governmental regulations that affect the company. In some cases, areas of particular audit interest to management may be discussed such as a new division or subsidiary.

Inquiries may also be made of management concerning the extent and timing of involvement of client personnel in preparing schedules and analyses for the auditor.

Determine Existence of Related Parties

GAAP include special disclosure requirements, and in some cases prescribe special accounting treatment, for transactions with **related parties.** The concern about related party transactions results from the realization that one of the participants may be in a position to significantly influence the other participant to the extent that "arm's length" bargaining of terms and conditions is not possible. Alternatively, related parties might conspire to enter a transaction motivated by a desire to obscure financial or other business problems that would otherwise manifest themselves in the financial statements. Hence, the auditor will ordinarily require more competent evidence for related party transactions than for transactions between unrelated parties. To ensure that such evidence is obtained, the auditor must take steps in the planning phase to determine the existence of related parties.

Certain relationships may be clearly evident, such as transactions between a parent company and subsidiary, between or among subsidiaries of a common parent, or between a company and its executive officers. SAS 45, *Omnibus Statement on Auditing Standards—1983, Related Parties* (AU 334.07), indicates that specific auditing procedures, including the following, should be used to determine the existence of other related parties:

- Evaluating the company's procedures for identifying and properly accounting for related party transactions, such as conflict of interest statements obtained from management.
- Reviewing filings with the SEC and other regulatory agencies that include related party disclosures.
- Reviewing prior years' working papers for the names of known related parties.
- Reviewing material investment transactions during the period under audit to determine whether their nature and extent created new related parties.

Identified related parties should be made known to all members of the audit team so that they can be alert to evidence of transactions with these parties.

Consider Impact of Applicable Accounting and Auditing Pronouncements

Although all auditors are knowledgeable of GAAP and GAAS, special accounting principles and auditing procedures may apply in certain industries or to certain types of business activities. For example, the AICPA has issued 27 audit and accounting guides, each of which describes distinctive characteristics of the industry or activity covered, alerts the auditor to unusual problems, and explains regulations and other special factors to take into account. The guides also illustrate financial statement treatment, and the form and wording of auditors' reports whenever applicable. Updates to the guides are issued as needed in the form of *AICPA Statements of Position.*

The impact of applicable pronouncements of regulatory agencies such as the SEC should also be considered. Finally, special consideration should be made in the planning phase of the audit for the impact of any newly effective SFASs and SASs.

AICPA AUDIT AND ACCOUNTING GUIDES:

INDUSTRY GUIDES
Agricultural Producers
Airlines
Banks
Brokers and Dealers in Securities
Casinos
Certain Nonprofit Organizations
Colleges and Universities
Common Interest Realty Associations
Construction Contractors
Credit Unions *(As of 12/1/92)*
Employee Benefit Plans
Entities with Oil and Gas Producing Activities
Federal Government Contractors
Finance Companies
Investment Companies
Property & Liability Insurance Companies
Providers of Health Care Services
Savings Institutions
State and Local Governmental Units
Stock Life Insurance Companies
Voluntary Health & Welfare Organizations

GENERAL AUDIT GUIDES
Audit Sampling
Computer-Assisted Audit Techniques
Consideration of the Internal Control Structure in a Financial Statement Audit
Personal Financial Statements
Prospective Financial Information
Real Estate Appraisal Information

PERFORMING ANALYTICAL PROCEDURES

OBJECTIVE 6

Explain the role of analytical procedures in audit planning.

SAS 56, *Analytical Procedures* (AU 329.02), defines **analytical procedures** as "evaluations of financial information made by a study of plausible relationships among both financial and nonfinancial data." Such procedures range from simple comparisons to the use of complex mathematical and statistical models involving many relationships and data elements.

Analytical procedures are used in auditing for the following purposes:

- In the planning phase of the audit, to assist the auditor in planning the nature, timing, and extent of other auditing procedures.
- In the testing phase, as a substantive test to obtain evidential matter about particular assertions related to account balances or classes of transactions.
- At the conclusion of the audit, in a final review of the overall reasonableness of the audited financial statements.

The first and third uses are required on all financial statement audits. The second use is optional. The remainder of this chapter focuses on the first use only.

Analytical procedures can assist the auditor in planning by (1) enhancing the auditor's understanding of the client's business, and (2) identifying unusual relationships and unexpected fluctuations in data that may indicate areas of greater risk of misstatement. The latter is often described as the *attention directing objective* of analytical procedures.

The effective use of analytical procedures in the planning phase involves the systematic completion of the following steps:

- Identify the calculations/comparisons to be made.
- Develop expectations (estimated probable outcomes).
- Perform the calculations/comparisons.
- Analyze data and identify significant differences.
- Investigate significant unexpected differences.
- Determine effects on audit planning.

Each step is discussed below. A comprehensive case study is then presented to illustrate the performance of each of the steps.

Identify Calculations/Comparisons to Be Made

The sophistication and extent of analytical procedures used in planning vary based on the size and complexity of the client, the availability of data, and the auditor's judgment. The types of calculations and comparisons commonly used include the following:

- **Absolute data comparisons.** This procedure involves simply comparing a current amount, such as an account balance, with an expected or predicted amount.
- **Common-size financial statements.** Also known as **vertical analysis,** this technique involves calculating the percentage of a related total that a financial statement component represents (e.g., cash as a percentage of total assets, or gross margin as a percentage of sales). The percentage is then compared with an expected amount.
- **Ratio analysis.** Numerous ratios frequently used by management or financial analysts can be calculated and compared with expected values for the ratios. The calculated amounts can be analyzed individually or in related groups such as solvency, efficiency, and profitability ratios. (Appendix 6A explains the purpose, calculation, and interpretation of ten common financial ratios used in analytical procedures).
- **Trend analysis.** Trend analysis involves comparing certain data (absolute, common-size, or ratio) for more than two accounting periods to identify important changes that may not be obvious from comparisons limited to just the current and prior period.

Generally, analytical procedures performed in the planning phase use highly aggregated, company-wide data based on year-to-date or projected annual data. However, for companies with diverse operations, some disaggregation by product line or division may be necessary for the procedures to be effective. In other cases, such as when the company's business is seasonal, it may be desirable to perform the analysis on monthly or quarterly data rather than year-to-date or annual data.

Develop Expectations

A basic premise underlying the use of analytical procedures in auditing is that relationships among data may be expected to continue in the absence of known conditions to the contrary. This premise is used in developing expectations from a variety of sources. These sources include both historical and future-oriented internal (client) data and external (industry) data. Also, both financial and nonfinancial data may be used in developing the expectations. Examples include the following:

- **Client financial information for comparable prior period(s) giving consideration to known changes.** Under this approach, in the absence of known conditions to the contrary, it is simply assumed that a current account balance, common-size percentage, or ratio should approximate the prior period amount. An example of giving consideration to a known change is expecting that total payroll costs will equal last year's amount adjusted for a predictable increase resulting from higher wage rates under a new union contract and/or higher payroll taxes.
- **Anticipated results based on formal budgets or forecasts.** This approach includes the use of client prepared budgets and forecasts for the current period as well as auditor prepared forecasts. The latter may include extrapolations from prior interim or annual data.
- **Relationships among elements of financial information within the period.** This includes considering how changes in one account would be expected to affect other accounts. For example, an increase in the average amount of debt outstanding would lead to an expected increase in interest expense. Similarly, an increase in credit sales might lead to an expected increase in bad debts expense.
- **Industry data.** Common-size percentages, ratios, and trend data typical of companies within an industry are available for comparison purposes from sources such as Dun & Bradstreet, Robert Morris Associates, and Standard & Poor's. In some cases, only a broad industry average is published for a given data element. In other cases, three values are published for a data element, representing the upper quartile, median, and lower quartile values of the reporting companies.
- **Relationships of financial information with relevant nonfinancial information.** Nonfinancial data such as the number of employees, square footage of selling space, and volume of goods produced may be used in estimating related account balances such as payroll expense, sales, and cost of goods manufactured.

In all cases, the reliability and suitability of the data used in developing expectations need to be considered. For example, audited prior year client data are considered more reliable than unaudited prior year data. The reliability of budget data depends on the continuing validity of the assumptions used in their preparation and the care used in compiling the budgeted amounts. The usefulness of industry data depends on the degree of similarity between a company's operations and accounting methods and those of the industry. Thus, industry comparisons may be of limited value when, for example, client data reflect the effects of operating in multiple industries, or when inventory or depreciation methods used by the client differ from those typically used in an industry.

Because the process of developing expectations generally requires considerable audit judgment and business expertise, this step is usually performed by the senior or manager on the audit team.

Perform the Calculations/Comparisons

This step includes accumulating the data to be used in calculating the absolute amount and percentage differences between current and prior year amounts, calculating the common-size and ratio data, and so on. Because planning occurs several months before current year-end account balances are available, this step involves the use of actual year-to-date data and/or projected year-end data. It also includes gathering the industry data for comparison purposes. Computer software is commonly used in making the calculations and comparisons, and may also be used in extracting information from company and industry databases.

When tend analysis is performed, it is common practice to use carry forward schedules. A part of the permanent working paper file, these schedules are designed to permit the addition of a column each year for current period data while avoiding having to recopy the prior year data for comparison purposes.

Analyze Data and Identify Significant Differences

Analysis of the calculations and comparisons should further the auditor's understanding of the client's business. For example, analysis of appropriate ratio data facilitates the ongoing assessment of the company's solvency, efficiency, and profitability relative to prior years and other companies in the industry. Similarly, comparison of the company's prior and current year data may help the auditor to understand the effects of significant events or decisions on the company's financial statements.

A key part of the analysis is identifying fluctuations in the data that are unexpected or the absence of expected fluctuations that may signal an increased risk of misstatements. A critical element in this process is specifying the magnitude of difference or fluctuation that should trigger a decision to investigate.

Some firms use statistical models as a decision aid in determining when a difference is large enough to warrant investigation. However, most firms continue to use simple rules of thumb such as investigating differences in excess of (1) a predetermined dollar amount, (2) a percentage difference, or (3) a combination of both. The auditor should be aware that even a small percentage change between the prior year and current year amount of an account with a large balance such as sales could result in a much larger percentage change in net income. Also, even a large percentage change in an expense account with a small balance might involve an absolute difference so small as to have little impact on net income. Ultimately, the process of determining when a difference is significant involves the exercise of judgment and the concept of materiality, which is discussed in the next chapter.

Investigate Significant Unexpected Differences

Significant unexpected differences should be investigated. This usually involves reconsidering the methods and factors used in developing the expectations and making inquiries of management. Sometimes new information will support revising the expectation, which in turn eliminates the significant difference. Before such action is taken based on management's responses to inquiries, the responses should ordinarily be corroborated with other evidential matter. When an explanation for the difference cannot be obtained, the auditor must determine the impact on the audit plan.

Determine Effects on Audit Planning

Unexplained significant differences are ordinarily viewed as indicating an increased risk of misstatement in the account or accounts involved in the calculation or comparison. In such case, the auditor will usually plan to perform more detailed tests of the account or accounts. By directing the auditor's attention to areas of greater risk, the analytical procedures may contribute to performing a more effective and efficient audit.

Illustrative Case Study

We now illustrate each of the steps described above using hypothetical data for Example Company, a continuing client.

IDENTIFY CALCULATIONS/COMPARISONS TO BE MADE. This illustration is limited to the use of absolute data comparisons and ratio analysis. The procedures utilize current and prior year data only. We further assume the company operates in a single industry, eliminating the need to consider disaggregation of the data.

DEVELOP EXPECTATIONS. Expectations for the Example Company reflect the following assumptions:

- The company has experienced no unusual events during the current year. Thus, current period account balances and ratios are expected to differ little from the prior period except for the effects of the following:
  - In spite of a no-growth year for the industry, the company's sales are expected to increase by 4 to 5 percent because of a continuing aggressive advertising campaign begun in the previous year to increase market share.
  - The scheduled retirement of $500,000 (one-ninth) of its long-term debt occurred at the beginning of the year.
- The company's operations and accounting policies are typical of those of the industry in which it operates. The industry has been stable for the past several years with no significant changes in key financial ratios. Thus, except for the effects of the debt retirement, the relationships between the company's ratio data for the current and prior periods relative to the industry averages are expected to be about the same.

PERFORM CALCULATIONS/COMPARISONS. Figures 6-5 and 6-6 present the calculations and comparisons for Example Company. It is assumed that year-to-date unaudited ledger balances as of the date the procedures are performed are extrapolated to arrive at the estimated current year-end amounts shown in column 1 of Figure 6-5. The amounts in column 2 are taken from the prior year's working papers. Differences expressed as absolute amounts and percentage changes are then calculated on each line as shown in columns 3 and 4. These data, and data extracted from the most up-to-date industry source available, are then used to arrive at the ratio data shown in Figure 6-6.

FIGURE 6-5 • EXAMPLE COMPANY—ABSOLUTE DATA COMPARISONS

(000s Omitted)

	(1) Current Year (Unaudited)	(2) Prior Year (Audited)	(3) Difference Amount	(4) Difference Percent
Assets				
Cash	584	564	20	3.5
Accounts Receivable	4,411	4,313	98	2.3
Allowance for Uncollectible Accounts	(78)	(76)	(2)	2.6
Inventories	8,047	7,160	887	12.4
Prepaid Expenses	175	134	41	30.6
Total Current Assets	13,139	12,095	1,044	8.6
Property, Plant, and Equipment	9,636	9,436	200	2.1
Accumulated Depreciation	(1,244)	(1,139)	(105)	9.2
Total Assets	21,531	20,392	1,139	5.6
Liabilities and Equity				
Accounts Payable	5,146	4,759	387	8.1
Accrued Liabilities	353	371	(18)	(4.9)
Current Portion of Long-term Debt	500	500	0	0.0
Total Current Liabilities	5,999	5,630	369	6.6
Long-term Debt	4,000	4,500	(500)	(11.1)
Total Liabilities	9,999	10,130	(131)	(1.3)
Capital Stock	5,300	5,300	0	0.0
Retained Earnings	6,232	4,962	1,270	25.6
Total Equity	11,532	10,262	1,270	12.4
Total Liabilities and Equity	21,531	20,392	1,139	5.6
Revenues and Expenses				
Sales	30,160	28,876	1,284	4.4
Cost of Sales	(15,043)	(14,932)	(111)	0.7
Gross Margin	15,117	13,944	1,173	8.4
Selling, General, and Administrative	(10,684)	(10,547)	(137)	1.3
Interest	(480)	(540)	60	(11.1)
Income before Income Taxes	3,953	2,857	1,096	38.4
Income Taxes	(550)	(524)	(26)	5.0
Net Income	3,403	2,333	1,070	45.9

FIGURE 6-6 • EXAMPLE COMPANY—RATIO ANALYSIS

Ratio*	(1) Current Year (Unaudited)	(2) Prior Year (Audited)	(3) Percent Difference	(4) Industry Average
Solvency Ratios				
Quick Ratio (times)	0.82	0.85	−3.53	0.96
Current Ratio (times)	2.19	2.15	1.86	2.43
Debt to Equity (%)	87.00	99.00	−12.12	77.30
Times Interest Earned	9.24	6.29	46.90	14.73
Efficiency				
Accounts Receivable Turnover (times)	6.84	6.70	2.09	5.21
Inventory Turnover (times)	1.87	2.09	−10.53	1.97
Asset Turnover (times)	1.40	1.42	−1.41	1.20
Profitability (%)				
Return on Sales	11.28	8.08	39.60	10.00
Return on Assets	15.81	11.44	38.20	12.00
Return on Stockholders' Equity	29.51	22.73	29.83	21.27

* An explanation of the calculation, purpose, and interpretation of these ratios is provided in Appendix 6A.

ANALYZE DATA AND IDENTIFY SIGNIFICANT DIFFERENCES. For Example Company, recall that current data are expected to remain about the same as the prior year, except for the effects of an increase in sales of 4 to 5 percent and the retirement of one-ninth of the long-term debt. Accordingly, the auditor proceeds to analyze the data and identify significant differences as follows:

Analytical Procedure	Result
From absolute data comparisons, identify financial statement totals and accounts with differences greater than 10 percent.	12.4% increase in inventories—could indicate overstatement of inventories and understatement of cost of sales. 30.6% increase in prepaid expenses—could indicate overstatement of prepaid expenses and understatement of selling, general, and administrative (SG&A) expenses. 11.1% decrease in long-term debt—difference expected due to retirement of one-ninth of long-term debt. 11.1% decrease in interest expense—difference expected due to debt retirement. Significant increases in net income, income before taxes, and retained earnings reflect the differences noted above.
Examine absolute data comparisons for other unusual relationships among the data.	Sales increased by 4.4% whereas cost of sales increased by only 0.7%—could indicate understatement of cost of sales consistent with possible overstatement of inventories noted above. Sales increase accompanied by increase in SG&A expenses of only 1.3%—could indicate understatement of SG&A consistent with possible overstatement of prepaid expenses noted above. Income before taxes increased by 38.4%, while income tax expense increased by only 5%—could indicate understatement of income tax expense and liability.

Analytical Procedure	Result
Examine ratio data for unusual relationships.	Significant drop in debt to equity ratio and increase in times interest earned expected due to debt retirement, causing these ratios to move in direction of industry averages. Decline in inventory turnover ratio could reflect possible overstatement of inventory and understatement of cost of sales noted above. Significant increases in all three profitability ratios could also reflect the possible understatements of cost of sales, SG&A expenses, and income taxes noted above.

INVESTIGATE SIGNIFICANT UNEXPECTED DIFFERENCES. The foregoing analysis reveals the presence of *expected* fluctuations in long-term debt, sales, and interest expense, and in the debt to equity and times interest earned ratios. These differences do not require investigation. However, the significant increases in inventories and prepaid expenses were *unexpected.* Furthermore, increases in cost of sales and SG&A expenses fall short of what would be expected based on the increase in sales, and the small increase in income taxes appears unusual in relation to the large increase in income before taxes. Thus, the auditor decides to investigate these items by reviewing the processes used to develop the expectations and making inquiries of management.

It is quickly realized that in projecting the year-to-date prepaid expense balance to December 31, additional amortization of prepaid expenses amounting to $40,000 was overlooked. No explanations for the other differences are obtained.

DETERMINE EFFECTS ON AUDIT PLANNING. In the Example Company, the analytical procedures have directed the auditor's attention to the possible overstatement of inventories and understatement of cost of sales, SG&A expenses, and the income tax expense and liability. Concluding that these accounts have a greater risk of material misstatement, the auditor decides to expand planned auditing procedures related to the existence and valuation assertions for inventories (risk of overstatement), and the completeness and valuation assertions for the other accounts (risk of understatement).

LEARNING CHECK:

6-13 a. State the first standard of field work.
b. Identify the components of audit planning.

6-14 a. What information about a client is essential in audit planning?
b. What procedures may be used by the auditor to acquire the information?

6-15 a. What specific information should an auditor seek to obtain from taking a tour of the client's operations?
b. What is the purpose of having the auditor communicate with the audit committee in the planning phase of the audit?

6-16 a. Why is it important for the auditor to identify related parties in the planning phase of the audit?
b. Give three examples of transactions involving related parties.

c. What specific auditing procedures can be used to determine the existence of related parties?

6-17 In addition to currently effective SFASs and SASs, what other types of pronouncements should be considered for their potential impact on an audit engagement?

6-18 a. State three uses of analytical procedures in an audit engagement.
b. Which uses are required on all audits?

6-19 a. How can analytical procedures assist the auditor in audit planning?
b. List the steps involved in the effective use of analytical procedures in the planning phase.

6-20 a. Describe the types of calculations and comparisons commonly used in analytical procedures.
b. What premise underlies the use of analytical procedures in auditing?
c. Identify five sources of information that may be used by the auditor in developing expectations.

KEY TERMS:

Absolute data comparison, p. 207
Analytical procedures, p. 206
Audit planning, p. 202
Common-size financial statements, p. 207
Ratio analysis, p. 207
Related parties, p. 205
Trend analysis, p. 207
Vertical analysis, p. 207

SUMMARY

Prior to accepting an audit engagement, the auditor should ascertain that it can be completed in accordance with all applicable professional standards including GAAS, the *Code of Professional Conduct,* and the quality control standards. Important steps in accepting the engagement include evaluating the integrity of management, identifying any special circumstances and unusual risks, assessing competence, evaluating independence, determining that the engagement can be completed with due care, and issuing an engagement letter.

Proper planning is crucial in performing an audit that is both efficient and effective. Planning steps include obtaining an understanding of the client's business and industry, performing analytical procedures, making preliminary judgments about materiality levels, considering audit risks, developing preliminary audit strategies for significant assertions, and obtaining an understanding of the client's internal control structure. The first two steps were discussed in this chapter. The remaining steps are discussed in the next two chapters.

APPENDIX 6A KEY FINANCIAL RATIOS USED IN ANALYTICAL PROCEDURES

Users of financial statements can obtain valuable insights into a company's financial condition and performance through analysis of key financial ratios. The same analysis performed by auditors provides them with a better understanding of a client's business. Further, when ratios calculated on current data are compared with expectations developed from previous years' data, budgeted amounts, or industry norms, insights can be gained into areas with a high risk of misstatement. For example, when comparisons reveal unexpected fluctuations, or when expected fluctuations do not occur, the auditor will generally want to investigate whether the aberration is due to the misstatement of one or more variables used in calculating the ratio.

This appendix explains the calculation of the ten ratios used in Figure 6-6 in the chapter. In addition, comments are provided on the purpose of each ratio and how it is interpreted. The comments on interpretation are general in nature and would be tailored according to a particular client's circumstances such as its recent experience and the industry in which it operates.

Ratio	Calculation	Purpose and Interpretation
Solvency Ratios:		
Quick Ratio	(Cash + Accounts Receivable + Temporary Investments) / Total Current Liabilities	To reveal protection afforded by cash or near-cash assets to short-term creditors. The larger the ratio, the greater the liquidity.
Current Ratio	Total Current Assets / Total Current Liabilities	To measure the degree to which current liabilities are covered by current assets. The higher the ratio, the greater the assurance that current liabilities can be paid in a timely manner.
Debt to Equity	Total Liabilities / Stockholders' Equity	To measure extent to which a company is using its debt financing capacity. In general, this ratio should not exceed 100% because in such cases creditors will have more at stake than owners.
Times Interest Earned	Income Before Interest and Income Taxes / Interest Expense	To measure the number of times a company can meet its fixed interest charges with earnings. This ratio can also be calculated on an after-tax basis.
Efficiency Ratios:		
Accounts Receivable Turnover	Net Sales / Accounts Receivable	To measure the number of times receivables are collected during the period. When used in analytical procedures, some auditors prefer to use the ending receivables balance rather than average receivables which would make a misstatement more difficult to detect. A variation, *the collection period,* is found by dividing the turnover ratio into 365. This ratio may be useful in evaluating the adequacy of the allowance for uncollectible accounts.
Inventory Turnover	Cost of Sales / Inventory	To indicate how rapidly inventory turns over. When used in analytical procedures, some auditors prefer to use the ending inventory balance rather than average inventories which would make a misstatement more difficult to detect. Although the ratio varies widely among

Ratio	Calculation	Purpose and Interpretation
		industries, low values may indicate excessively high inventories and slow-moving items. Conversely, extremely high values might reflect insufficient merchandise to meet customer demand resulting in lost sales.
Asset Turnover	$\frac{\text{Net Sales}}{\text{Total Assets}}$	To measure the efficiency with which a company uses its assets to generate sales. For the reasons noted above, ending rather than average assets may be preferred in the calculation of this ratio.
Profitability Ratios:		
Return on Net Sales	$\frac{\text{Net Income}}{\text{Net Sales}}$	To reveal profits earned per dollar of sales. Indicates ability to earn satisfactory profits for owners. Also ability to withstand adverse conditions such as falling prices, rising costs, and declining sales.
Return on Total Assets	$\frac{\text{Net Income}}{\text{Total Assets}}$	To indicate profitability based on total assets available. Companies efficiently using assets will have a high ratio; less efficient companies, a low ratio.
Return on Net Worth	$\frac{\text{Net Income}}{\text{Net Worth}}$	To reveal management's ability to earn an adequate return on capital invested by owners. Generally, a minimum of 10% is considered desirable to provide funds for dividends and growth.

BIBLIOGRAPHY

AICPA Professional Standards:

- SAS 1 (AU 310), Relationship Between the Auditor's Appointment and Planning.
- SAS 7 (AU 315), Communication Between Predecessor and Successor Auditors.
- SAS 22 (AU 311), Planning and Supervision.
- SAS 45 (AU 334), Omnibus Statement on Auditing Standards—1983, Related Parties.
- SAS 56 (AU 329), Analytical Procedures.
- SAS 61 (AU 380), Communication with Audit Committees.
- SAS 73 (AU 336), Using the Work of a Specialist.
- IAU 2 (AU 8002), Audit Engagement Letters.
- IAU 4 (AU 8004), Planning.
- IAU 12 (AU 8012), Analytical Procedures.
- IAU 17 (AU 8017), Related Parties.
- IAU 18 (AU 8018), Using the Work of an Expert.
- IAU 30 (AU 8030), Knowledge of the Business.

Blocker, Edward J., and Cooper, Jean C. "A Study of Auditors' Analytical Review Performance," *Auditing: A Journal of Practice and Theory* (Spring 1988), pp. 1–28.

Callahan, Patrick S., Jaenicke, Henry R., and Neebes, Donald L. "SASs Nos. 56 and 57: Increasing Audit Effectiveness," *Journal of Accountancy* (October 1988), pp. 56–68.

Godwin, Larry. "Enhanced Engagement Letters," *Journal of Accountancy* (June 1993), pp. 53–58.

Harper, Robert M., Strawser, Jerry R., and Twang, Kwei. "Establishing Investigation Thresholds for Preliminary Analytical Procedures," *Auditing: A Journal of Practice & Theory* (Fall 1990), pp. 115–133.

Holder, W. W. "Analytical Review Procedures in Planning the Audit: An Application Study," *Auditing: A Journal of Practice & Theory* (Spring 1983), pp. 100–107.

Hull, Rita P., and Mitchem, Cheryl. "Practitioners' Views on Communications Between Predecessor and Successor Auditors and Accountants." *Accounting Horizons* (June 1987), pp. 61–69.

McAllister, John P., and Dirsmith, Mark W. "How the Client's Business Environment Affects the Audit," *Journal of Accountancy* (February 1982), pp. 68–74.

Van Son, W. Peter, and Winters, Alan J. "The Preaudit Conference: A Communication Tool," *Journal of Accountancy* (November 1982), pp. 86–93.

Wright, Arnold, and Ashton, Robert H. "Identifying Audit Adjustments with Attention-Directing Procedures," *Accounting Review* (October 1989), pp. 710–728.

OBJECTIVE QUESTIONS

Indicate the *best* answer for each of the following multiple choice questions:

6-21 These questions involve accepting an audit engagement.

1. Before accepting an audit engagement, a successor auditor should make specific inquiries of the predecessor auditor regarding the predecessor's
   a. Awareness of the consistency in the application of GAAP between periods.
   b. Evaluation of all matters of continuing accounting significance.
   c. Opinion of any subsequent events occurring since the predecessor's audit report was issued.
   d. Understanding as to the reasons for the change of auditors.

2. A CPA is most likely to refer to one or more of the three general auditing standards in determining
   a. The nature of the CPA's report qualification.
   b. The scope of the CPA's auditing procedures.
   c. Requirements for the review of the internal control structure.
   d. Whether the CPA should undertake an audit engagement.

3. Engagement letters are widely used in practice for professional engagements of all types. The primary purpose of the engagement letter is to
   a. Remind management that the primary responsibility for the financial statements rests with management.
   b. Satisfy the requirements of the CPA's liability insurance policy.
   c. Provide a starting point for the auditor's preparation of the preliminary audit program.
   d. Provide a written record of the agreement with the client as to the services to be provided.

4. The exercise of due professional care requires that an auditor
   a. Examine all available corroborating evidence.
   b. Critically review the judgment exercised at every level of supervision.
   c. Reduce control risk below the maximum.
   d. Attain the proper balance of professional experience and formal education.

6-22 These questions relate to planning the engagement.

1. The element of the audit planning process most likely to be agreed on with the client before implementation of the audit strategy is the determination of the

a. Methods of statistical sampling to be used in confirming accounts receivable.
b. Pending legal matters to be included in the inquiry of the client's attorney.
c. Evidence to be gathered to provide a sufficient basis for the auditor's opinion.
d. Schedules and analyses to be prepared by the client's staff.

2. An abnormal fluctuation in gross profit that might suggest the need for extended audit procedures for sales and inventories would most likely be identified in the planning phase of the audit by the use of
   a. A review of prior years' working papers.
   b. An evaluation of the entity's internal control structure.
   c. Specialized audit programs.
   d. Analytical procedures.

3. Analytical procedures used in planning an audit should focus on identifying
   a. Material weakness in the internal control structure.
   b. The predictability of financial data from individual transactions.
   c. The various assertions that are embodied in the financial statements.
   d. Areas that may represent specific risks relevant to the audit.

4. For all audits of financial statements made in accordance with GAAS, the use of analytical procedures is required to some extent

	In the Planning Stage	As a Substantive Test	In the Review Stage
a.	Yes	No	Yes
b.	No	Yes	No
c.	No	Yes	Yes
d.	Yes	No	No

COMPREHENSIVE QUESTIONS

6-23 **(Accepting the engagement)** Sunny Energy Applications Co. sells solar-powered swimming pool heaters. Sunny contracts 100% of the work to other companies. As Sunny is a new company, its balance sheet has total assets of $78,000, including $24,000 of "stock subscriptions receivable." The largest asset is $42,000 worth of "unrecovered development costs." The equity side of the balance sheet is made up of $78,000 of "Common Stock Subscribed."

The company is contemplating a public offering to raise $1 million. The shares to be sold to the public for the $1 million will represent 40% of the then issued and outstanding stock. There are two officer-employees of the company, Mike Whale and Willie Float. Whale and Float are former officers of Canadian Brass Co. Float is being sued by the SEC for misusing funds raised by Canadian Brass in a public offering. The funds were used as compensatory balances for loans to a Physics Inc. Physics Inc. was controlled by Float and is the predecessor for Sunny Energy Applications.

Canadian Brass is being sued by the SEC for reporting improper (exaggerated) income. Float was chief executive at the time. There are many organizations engaged in researching the feasibility of using solar energy. Most of the organizations are considerably larger and financially stronger than Sunny Energy. The company has not been granted any patents that would serve to protect it from competitors.

REQUIRED

a. What potential risks may be present in this engagement?
b. What specific auditing and accounting problems appear to exist?

c. What additional information do you feel you need to know about the company?
d. Do you believe the engagement should be accepted or rejected? Why?

6-24 **(Communication with predecessor/engagement letter)** The audit committee of the Board of Directors of Unicorn Corp. asked Tish & Field, CPAs, to audit Unicorn's financial statements for the year ended December 31, 19X3. Tish & Field explained the need to make an inquiry of the predecessor auditor and requested permission to do so. Unicorn's management agreed and authorized the predecessor auditor to respond fully to Tish & Field's inquiries.

After a satisfactory communication with the predecessor auditor, Tish & Field drafted an engagement letter that was mailed to the audit committee of the Board of Directors of Unicorn Corp. The engagement letter clearly set forth arrangements concerning the involvement of the predecessor auditor and other matters.

REQUIRED

a. What information should Tish & Field have obtained during their inquiry of the predecessor auditor prior to acceptance of the engagement?
b. Describe what other matters Tish & Field would generally have included in the engagement letter.

AICPA

6-25 **(Using work of a specialist)** Kent, CPA, is engaged in the audit of Davidson Corp.'s financial statements for the year ended December 31, 19X9. Kent is about to commence auditing Davidson's employee pension expense, but Kent's preliminary inquiries concerning Davidson's defined benefit pension plan lead Kent to believe that some of the actuarial computations and assumptions are so complex that they are beyond the competence ordinarily required of an auditor. Kent is considering engaging Park, an actuary, to assist with this portion of the audit.

REQUIRED

a. What are the factors Kent should consider in the process of selecting Park?
b. What are the matters that should be understood among Kent, Park, and Davison's management as to the nature of the work to be performed by Park?

AICPA (adapted)

6-26 **(Engagement letter)** A CPA has been asked to audit the financial statements of a company for the first time. All preliminary verbal discussions and inquiries have been completed between the CPA, the company, the predecessor auditor, and all other necessary parties. The CPA is now preparing an engagement letter.

REQUIRED

a. List the items that should be included in the typical engagement letter.
b. Describe the benefits derived from preparing an engagement letter.
c. Who should prepare and sign the engagement letter?
d. When should the engagement letter be sent?
e. Why should the engagement letter be renewed periodically?

AICPA (adapted)

6-27 **(Engagement letter)** The CPA firm of Test & Check has been appointed auditors for the XYZ Corporation by the company's audit committee. The engagement is limited to making an audit of the company's financial statements. The audit fee is to be at the firm's regular per diem rates plus travel costs. To confirm the arrangements, Test & Check sends the following engagement letter:

March 10, 19X1

Mr. D. R. Rand, Controller
XYZ Corporation
Maintown, ME. 03491

Dear Mr. Rand:

This will confirm our understanding of the arrangements for our examination of the financial statements of XYZ Corporation for the year ending December 31, 19X1.

We will examine the Company's balance sheet at December 31, 19X1, and the related statements of income, retained earnings, and cash flows for the year then ended, for the purpose of auditing them. Our audit will be in accordance with generally accepted auditing standards, which require that we plan and perform the audit to assure that the financial statements are correct.

Our audit will include examining, on a test basis, evidence supporting the financial statements. We will also assess the accounting methods used and significant estimates made by management.

Because of the characteristics of irregularities, our audit cannot detect all material irregularities. We will, of course, report to you anything that appears to us during our audit that looks suspicious.

Our fee for this audit will be on a cost-plus basis, including travel costs. Invoices will be rendered every two weeks and are payable on presentation.

We are pleased to have this opportunity to serve you. If this letter correctly expresses your understanding, please sign the enclosed copy and return it to us.

Very truly yours,
Test & Check, CPAs

M. E. Test

Partner

Approved:
By: ______________________
Date: ______________________

REQUIRED

List the deficiencies in the engagement letter. For each deficiency, indicate the proper wording. Use the following format for your answers—do not write a proper engagement letter:

Deficiency	Proper Wording

6-28 **(Accepting the engagement)** Dodd, CPA, audited Adams Company's financial statements for the year ended December 31, 19X8. On November 1, 19X9, Adams notified Dodd that it was changing auditors and that Dodd's services were being terminated. On November 5, 19X9, Adams invited Hall, CPA, to make a proposal for an engagement to audit its financial statements for the year ended December 31, 19X9.

REQUIRED

a. What procedures concerning Dodd should Hall perform before accepting the engagement?

b. What additional procedures should Hall consider performing during the planning phase of this audit (after acceptance of the engagement) that would **not** be performed during the audit of a continuing client?

AICPA

6-29 **(Audit planning)** The first standard of field work includes adequate planning of the work.

REQUIRED

a. What is the objective of audit planning?
b. What information about the client is essential in planning?
c. Identify the principal procedures used by the auditor to obtain the essential information.
d. Explain two specific types of information that can be obtained from each of the procedures identified in (c) above.

AICPA (adapted)

6-30 **(Audit planning)** In late spring of 19X4, you are advised of a new assignment as in-charge accountant of your CPA firm's recurring annual audit of a major client, the Lancer Company. You are given the engagement letter for the audit covering the calendar year December 31, 19X4, and a list of personnel assigned to this engagement. It is your responsibility to plan and supervise the field work for the engagement.

REQUIRED

Discuss the necessary preparation and planning for the Lancer Company annual audit prior to the beginning field work at the client's office. In your discussion, include the sources you should consult, the type of information you should seek, the preliminary plans and preparation you should make for the field work, and any actions you should take relative to the staff assigned to the engagement. Do not write an audit program.

AICPA

6-31 **(Related parties)** Temple, CPA, is auditing the financial statements of Ford Lumber Yards, Inc., a privately held corporation with 300 employees and five stockholders, three of whom are active in management. Ford has been in business for many years, but has never had its financial statements audited. Temple suspects that the substance of some of Ford's business transactions differs from their form because of the pervasiveness of related party relationships and transactions in the local building supplies industry.

REQUIRED

Describe the audit procedures Temple should apply to identify related party relationships and transactions.

AICPA

6-32 **(Analytical procedures)** Analytical procedures consist of evaluations of financial information made by a study of plausible relationships among both financial and nonfinancial data. They range from simple comparisons to the use of complex models involving many relationships and elements of data. They involve comparisons of recorded amounts, or ratios developed from recorded amounts, to expectations developed by the auditors.

REQUIRED

a. Describe the broad purposes of analytical procedures.
b. Identify the sources of information from which an auditor develops expectations.
c. Describe the factors that influence an auditor's consideration of the reliability of data for purposes of achieving audit objectives.

6-33 **(Analytical procedures)** Over the past two decades, increasing recognition has been given to the importance of analytical procedures in performing financial statement audits. Their use has been required since SAS 56 became effective in 1989.

REQUIRED

a. What are analytical procedures?
b. Where in the audit process can analytical procedures be performed? Which uses of analytical procedures are required by SAS 56 and which are optional?
c. What are the steps involved in performing analytical procedures?
d. What are some of the types of calculations and comparisons commonly used in applying analytical procedures?
e. What sources of data may be used in developing expectations?
f. In analyzing the results of analytical procedures, what factors should be considered in deciding whether a difference or fluctuation in data requires investigation?
g. What steps are taken in investigating unexpected differences?
h. What effect do unexplained significant differences have on audit planning?
i. In comparing the following ratios calculated on current year unaudited data with prior year ratios based on audited data, you discover the following differences. Give the possible reasons for the changes.
   1. The rate of inventory turnover has decreased from the prior year's rate.
   2. The collection period for accounts receivable has increased from the prior year.

CASE

6-34 **(Analytical procedures)** Pro-Tex Company is a wholesale distributor of professional equipment and supplies. The company's sales have averaged about $900,000 annually for the three-year period 19X3–19X5. The firm's total assets at the end of 19X5 amounted to $850,000. Pro-Tex is a new audit client. At your request, the controller and his staff accumulate the following ratios for the three-year period ending December 31, 19X5:

	19X3	19X4	19X5
Current ratio	1.80	1.92	1.96
Acid-test (quick) ratio	1.08	0.99	0.87
Accounts receivable turnover	8.75	7.71	6.42
Inventory turnover	4.73	4.32	3.42
Percent of total debt to total assets	48.0	45.0	42.0
Percent of long-term debt to total assets	28.0	24.0	21.0
Sales to fixed assets (fixed asset turnover)	1.58	1.69	1.79
Sales as a percent of 19X1 sales	1.00	1.03	1.05
Gross margin percentage	36.0	34.7	34.6
Net income to sales (%)	7.0	7.0	7.2
Return on total assets (%)	7.7	7.7	7.8
Return on stockholders' equity (%)	13.6	13.1	12.7

REQUIRED

a. Identify any unusual relationships in individual ratios that you believe may have audit significance for your 19X6 audit.
b. From the data, identify significant trends in the company's financial position and operating results.
c. Identify any unusual fluctuations in the trend results that you believe may have audit significance for your 19X6 audit.

RESEARCH QUESTIONS

6-35 **(AICPA Audit and Accounting Guides)** Obtain access to the printed or electronic version of any one of the industry guides listed in the box on page 206. For the chosen guide, scan through the table of contents to view the scope of topical coverage. Then:

a. Select a section that deals with some unique aspect of accounting in that industry, read the section, and prepare a brief summary of the unique accounting.
b. Select a section that deals with some unique aspect of auditing in that industry, read the section, and prepare a brief summary of the unique auditing aspect.

6-36 **(Industry conditions and risks)** Choose an industry of interest to you. Assume that you have just received your first audit assignment as a staff assistant on an audit engagement for a client in this industry. Eager to show your boss that you know something about this industry, you decide to read up on the current state of the industry before the first planning meeting. Obtain access to a printed or electronic source of current information about conditions, developments, trends, risks, etc. in this industry and prepare a brief outline of points that you think might be relevant to bring up in the planning meeting.

6-37 **(AAER on audit planning)** The SEC's *Accounting and Auditing Enforcement Release No. 200* addresses a number of issues pertaining to audit planning. Summarize the facts and conclusions of the SEC on these matters as set forth in the AAER.

6-38 **(AAER on identifying related parties)** The SEC's *Accounting and Auditing Enforcement Release No. 150* pertains to a situation involving the auditor's identification of related parties in audit planning. Summarize the facts and conclusions of the SEC on this matter as set forth in the AAER.

6-39 **(AAER on the use of analytical procedures in audit planning)** The SEC's *Accounting and Auditing Enforcement Release No. 109A* describes a situation involving increased risks of misstatements signaled by analytical procedures. Summarize the facts and conclusions of the SEC pertaining to this matter as set forth in the AAER.

CHAPTER

7

MATERIALITY, RISK, AND PRELIMINARY AUDIT STRATEGIES

LEARNING OBJECTIVES

After studying this chapter, you should be able to

1. Define the concept of materiality used in auditing.
2. State how the auditor arrives at preliminary judgments about materiality at the financial statement and account balance levels.
3. Describe the relationship between materiality and audit evidence.
4. Explain the importance of the concept of audit risk and its three components.
5. Describe the relationship between audit risk and audit evidence.
6. State the interrelationships among materiality, audit risk, and audit evidence.
7. Differentiate between alternative preliminary audit strategies that may be used in audit planning.

MATERIALITY
- The Concept of Materiality
- Preliminary Judgments about Materiality
- Materiality at the Financial Statement Level
- Materiality at the Account Balance Level
- Allocating Financial Statement Materiality to Accounts
- Relationship Between Materiality and Audit Evidence

AUDIT RISK
- Audit Risk Components
- Relationship Among Risk Components
- Audit Risk at the Financial Statement and Account Balance Levels
- Relationship Between Audit Risk and Audit Evidence
- Interrelationships Among Materiality, Audit Risk, and Audit Evidence
- Audit Risk Alerts

PRELIMINARY AUDIT STRATEGIES
- Components of Preliminary Audit Strategies
- Primarily Substantive Approach
- Lower Assessed Level of Control Risk Approach
- Relationship Between Strategies and Transaction Cycles

SUMMARY

BIBLIOGRAPHY

OBJECTIVE QUESTIONS

COMPREHENSIVE QUESTIONS

CASE

RESEARCH QUESTIONS

In this chapter, three additional steps in audit planning are explained. First, we define the concept of materiality used in auditing and discuss factors considered by the auditor in making preliminary judgments about this important variable. Second, we explore the concept of audit risk, and identify and explain its three components. Finally, we consider alternative preliminary audit strategies that may be used in planning the audit of specific financial statement assertions.

MATERIALITY

Materiality underlies the application of generally accepted auditing standards, particularly the standards of field work and reporting. Materiality thus has a pervasive effect in a financial statement audit. SAS 47, *Audit Risk and Materiality in Conducting an Audit* (AU 312.08), requires the auditor to consider materiality in (1) planning the audit and (2) evaluating whether the financial statements taken as a whole are presented fairly in conformity with generally accepted accounting principles. The meaning of this concept and its relevance to audit planning are explained below.

THE CONCEPT OF MATERIALITY

The Financial Accounting Standards Board defines **materiality** as

> The magnitude of an omission or misstatement of accounting information that, in the light of surrounding circumstances, makes it probable that the judgment of a reasonable person relying on the information would have been changed or influenced by the omission or misstatement.[1]

This definition requires the auditor to consider both (1) the circumstances pertaining to the entity and (2) the information needs of those who will rely on the audited financial statements. For example, an amount that is material to the financial statements of one entity may not be material to the financial statements of another entity of a different size or nature. Also, what is material to the financial statements of a particular entity might change from one period to another. Thus, the auditor may conclude that the materiality levels for working capital accounts should be lower for a company on the brink of bankruptcy than for a company with a 4 : 1 current ratio. In considering the information needs of users, it might be appropriate to assume, for example, that the users will be reasonably informed investors.

OBJECTIVE 1

Define the concept of materiality used in auditing.

PRELIMINARY JUDGMENTS ABOUT MATERIALITY

The auditor makes preliminary judgments about materiality levels in planning the audit. This assessment, often referred to as **planning materiality** may ultimately differ from the materiality levels used at the conclusion of the audit in evaluating the audit findings because (1) the surrounding circumstances may change and (2) additional information about the client will have been obtained during the course of the audit. For example, the client may have obtained the financing needed to continue as a going concern that was in doubt when the audit was planned, and the audit may affirm that the company's short-term solvency has significantly improved during the year. In such cases, the materiality level used in evaluating the audit findings might be higher than planning materiality.

In planning an audit, the auditor should assess materiality at the following two levels:

OBJECTIVE 2

State how the auditor arrives at preliminary judgments about materiality at the financial statement and account balance levels.

- The *financial statement level* because the auditor's opinion on fairness extends to the financial statements taken as a whole.

[1] "Qualitative Characteristics of Accounting," *Statement of Financial Accounting Concepts No. 2.* Stamford, Conn.: Financial Accounting Standards Board, 1980, p. xv.

- The *account balance level* because the auditor verifies account balances in reaching an overall conclusion on the fairness of the financial statements.[2]

Factors that should be considered in making preliminary judgments of materiality at each level are explained in the following sections.

MATERIALITY AT THE FINANCIAL STATEMENT LEVEL

Financial statement materiality is the minimum aggregate misstatement in a financial statement that is important enough to prevent the statement from being presented fairly in conformity with GAAP. In this context, misstatements may result from misapplication of GAAP, departures from fact, or omissions of necessary information.

In audit planning, the auditor should recognize that there may be more than one level of materiality relating to the financial statements. Each statement, in fact, could have several levels. For the income statement, materiality could be related to total revenues, operating income, income before taxes, or net income. For the balance sheet, materiality could be based on total assets, current assets, working capital, or stockholders' equity.

In making a preliminary judgment about materiality, the auditor initially determines the aggregate (overall) level of materiality for each statement. For example, it may be estimated that errors totaling $100,000 for the income statement and $200,000 for the balance sheet would be material. It would be inappropriate in this case for the auditor to use balance sheet materiality in planning the audit because if balance sheet misstatements amounting to $200,000 also affect the income statement, the income statement would be materially misstated. For planning purposes, the auditor should use the *smallest aggregate level of misstatements considered to be material to any one of the financial statements.* This decision rule is appropriate because (1) the financial statements are interrelated and (2) many auditing procedures pertain to more than one statement. For instance, the auditing procedure to determine whether year-end credit sales are recorded in the proper period provides evidence about both accounts receivable (balance sheet) and sales (income statement).

The auditor's preliminary judgments about materiality are often made six to nine months before the balance sheet date. Thus, the judgments may be based on annualized interim financial statement data. Alternatively, they may be premised on one or more prior years' financial results adjusted for current changes, such as the general condition of the economy and industry trends.

Materiality judgments involve both quantitative and qualitative considerations.

Quantitative Guidelines

Currently, neither accounting nor auditing standards contain official guidelines on quantitative measures of materiality. The following are illustrative of some guidelines used in practice:

- 5% to 10% of net income before taxes (10% for smaller incomes, 5% for larger ones).

[2] This level also may be identified with *classes of transactions,* such as sales, purchases, and so on.

- ½% to 1% of total assets.
- 1% of equity.
- ½% to 1% of gross revenue.
- A variable percentage based on the greater of total assets or revenue.

An example of the last guideline is presented in Figure 7-1, which shows a table used by a Big Six accounting firm to calculate planning materiality. Applying this approach to Delta Airlines' 1990 financial statements, which showed total assets of $7.227 billion and revenue of $8.582 billion, results in planning materiality of $7.56 million (i.e., $3,830,000 + (.00067 × ($8.582 billion − $3 billion))). Similarly, the table indicates that planning materiality would be $18,450 when the greater of total assets or gross revenue is $1 million and $85,200 when the base is $10 million.

EMPIRICAL DATA ON MATERIALITY RULES OF THUMB

In a comparative study of materiality rules of thumb, researchers calculated five materiality measures for three companies considered representative of manufacturing, retail, and financial audit clients. Among the reported results are the following, which are based on ten-year averages (1977 to 1986) of actual financial data for the three companies:

ABSOLUTE SIZE OF MATERIALITY MEASURES AND RATIOS (000s OMITTED)

	Concord Fabrics Inc.	Mott's Supermarkets	Golden West Financial
Materiality measures			
1. 5% of average of income	$150	$240	$3,560
2. Variable % of gross profit	180	510	N/A
3. ½% of total assets	200	220	35,760
4. 1% of equity	210	240	2,680
5. ½% of revenues	470	1,310	3,730
Ratios			
Largest to smallest	3.1	6.0	13.3

The researchers observed, "The results of this 'small sample' study provide empirical evidence that among five commonly employed 'rules of thumb' definitions for materiality, sizable differences can occur depending on the industry of the client and the definition chosen. For example, for the financial company examined, the largest of the materiality measures was, on average, over 13 times bigger than the smallest measures. . . . Such large differences in materiality definitions would presumably lead to correspondingly large differences in audit scope decisions depending on which definition is chosen to quantify "planning materiality." They further conclude, "While more evidence is needed, it appears that additional authoritative guidance would be helpful."

SOURCE: Kurt Pany and Stephen Wheeler, "A Comparison of Various Materiality Rules of Thumb," *The CPA Journal* (June 1989), pp. 62–63.

FIGURE 7-1 • MATERIALITY LEVELS BASED ON A VARIABLE PERCENTAGE OF TOTAL ASSETS OR REVENUE

If the Greater of Total Assets or Revenue is			
Over	**But Not Over**	**Materiality is**	**Of Excess Over**
$0	$30 thousand	$0 + .059	$0
30 thousand	100 thousand	1,780 + .031	30 thousand
100 thousand	300 thousand	3,970 + .0214	100 thousand
300 thousand	1 million	8,300 + .0145	300 thousand
1 million	3 million	18,400 + .0100	1 million
3 million	10 million	38,300 + .0067	3 million
10 million	30 million	85,500 + .0046	10 million
30 million	100 million	178,000 + .00313	30 million
100 million	300 million	397,000 + .00214	100 million
300 million	1 billion	856,000 + .00145	300 million
1 billion	3 billion	1,840,000 + .00100	1 billion
3 billion	10 billion	3,830,000 + .00067	3 billion
10 billion	30 billion	8,550,000 + .00046	10 billion
30 billion	100 billion	17,800,000 + .00031	30 billion
100 billion	300 billion	39,700,000 + .00021	100 billion
300 billion	. . .	82,600,000 + .00015	300 billion

Qualitative Considerations

Qualitative considerations relate to the causes of misstatements. A misstatement that is quantitatively immaterial may be qualitatively material. This may occur, for instance, when the misstatement is attributable to an irregularity or an illegal act by the client. Discovery of either occurrence might cause the auditor to conclude there is a significant risk of additional similar misstatements. AU 312.13 states that although the auditor should be alert for misstatements that could be qualitatively material, it ordinarily is not practical to design procedures to detect them.

MATERIALITY AT THE ACCOUNT BALANCE LEVEL

Account balance materiality is the minimum misstatement that can exist in an account balance for it to be considered materially misstated. Misstatement up to that level is known as **tolerable misstatement.** The concept of materiality at the account balance level should not be confused with the term *material account balance*. The latter term refers to the *size of a recorded account balance*, whereas the concept of materiality pertains to the *amount of misstatement* that could affect a user's decision. The recorded balance of an account generally represents the upper limit on the amount by which an account can be overstated. Thus, accounts with balances much smaller than materiality are sometimes said to be immaterial in terms of the risk of overstatement. However, there is no limit on the amount by which an account with a very small recorded balance might be understated. Thus, it should be realized that accounts with seemingly immaterial balances may contain understatements that exceed materiality.

In making judgments about materiality at the account balance level, the auditor must consider the relationship between it and financial statement materiality. This consideration should lead the auditor to plan the audit to detect misstatements that may be immaterial individually, but that, when aggregated with misstatements in other account balances, may be material to the financial statements taken as a whole.

ALLOCATING FINANCIAL STATEMENT MATERIALITY TO ACCOUNTS

When the auditor's preliminary judgments about *financial statement materiality* are quantified, a preliminary estimate of materiality for each account may be obtained by allocating financial statement materiality to the individual accounts. The allocation may be made to both balance sheet and income statement accounts. However, because most income statement misstatements also affect the balance sheet and because there are fewer balance sheet accounts, many auditors make the allocation on the basis of the balance sheet accounts.

In making the allocation, the auditor should consider (1) the likelihood of misstatements in the account and (2) the probable cost of verifying the account. For example, misstatements are more likely to exist in inventories than in plant assets, and it usually is more costly to audit inventories than plant assets.

To illustrate the allocation, assume that the total assets of Hart Company consist of the following:

	Balance	**%**
Cash	$ 500,000	5
Accounts receivable	1,500,000	15
Inventories	3,000,000	30
Plant assets	5,000,000	50
	$10,000,000	100

The auditor anticipates few misstatements in cash and plant assets and some misstatements in accounts receivable and inventories. Based on prior experience with the client, the auditor expects the cash and plant asset accounts will be significantly less costly to audit than the other accounts. Assuming the preliminary estimate of financial statement materiality is 1% of total assets, or $100,000, consider the following alternative allocation plans:

	Materiality Allocation			
Account	**Plan A**	**%**	**Plan B**	**%**
Cash	$ 5,000	5	$ 2,000	2
Accounts receivable	15,000	15	18,000	18
Inventories	30,000	30	50,000	50
Plant assets	50,000	50	30,000	30
Total	$100,000	100	$100,000	100

In plan A, materiality has been allocated proportionately to each account without regard to expected monetary misstatements or audit costs. In plan B, larger materiality allocations are made to receivables and inventories for which more misstatements are expected and the costs of detection are higher. Thus, the amount of evidence needed on these accounts is reduced, compared to plan A, because of the inverse relationship between account balance materiality and evidence. *In effect, the auditor is simply allowing for a greater proportion of the total allowable misstatements to remain in those accounts where it would be most expensive to detect the misstatements.* Although the smaller materiality allocations for cash and plant assets increase the amount of evidence needed for those accounts, compared to plan A, the fact that they are less costly to audit should result in an overall savings.

The allocation of the preliminary estimate of materiality may be revised as the field work is performed. For example, under plan B, if after auditing accounts receivable the maximum misstatement in that account is estimated to be $8,000, the $10,000 unused portion of materiality for that account can be reallocated to inventories.

Although the foregoing illustration suggests a certain degree of precision in allocating financial statement materiality to accounts, in the final analysis the process is heavily dependent on the subjective judgment of the auditor.

RELATIONSHIP BETWEEN MATERIALITY AND AUDIT EVIDENCE

OBJECTIVE 3

Describe the relationship between materiality and audit evidence.

As noted in Chapter 5, materiality is one of the factors that affects the auditor's judgment about the sufficiency (quantity needed) of evidential matter. In making generalizations about this relationship, the distinction between the terms *materiality* and *material account balance* mentioned previously must be kept in mind. For example, it is generally correct to say that the lower the materiality level, the greater the amount of evidence needed (inverse relationship). This is the same as saying that it takes more evidence to obtain reasonable assurance that any misstatement in the recorded inventory balance does not exceed $100,000 than it does to be assured the misstatement does not exceed $200,000. It is also generally correct to say that the larger or more significant an account balance is, the greater the amount of evidence needed (direct relationship). This is the same as saying that more evidence is needed for inventory when it represents 30% of total assets than when it represents 10%.

LEARNING CHECK:

7-1 a. Define materiality.
 b. What requirements are imposed on the auditor by this definition?

7-2 State the two levels at which preliminary judgments of materiality should be made in the planning phase and state the reason for each.

7-3 Why might planning materiality differ from the materiality level used in evaluating audit findings?

7-4 a. In audit planning, the auditor should recognize that there may be more than one level of materiality relating to the financial statements. Explain.
 b. What decision rule should be used when different materiality levels are identified for the balance sheet and income statement? Why?

7-5 a. What official quantitative guidelines exist for financial statement materiality?
 b. State five quantitative guidelines commonly used in practice.

7-6 a. How do qualitative considerations relate to making materiality judgments?

b. A misstatement that is quantitatively immaterial may be qualitatively material. Explain.

7-7 a. Define materiality at the account-balance level.
b. What is another name for materiality at this level?
c. Distinguish between the terms *material account balance* and *materiality.*

7-8 a. Identify two factors the auditor should consider in allocating financial statement materiality to accounts.
b. If the amount of error found in an account is less than its materiality allocation, what effect might this have on the audit of other accounts?
c. How are materiality and audit evidence related? Explain.

KEY TERMS:

Account balance materiality, p. 228
Financial statement materiality, p. 226
Materiality, p. 225
Planning materiality, p. 225
Tolerable misstatement, p. 228

AUDIT RISK

In planning the audit, the auditor should also consider audit risk. AU 312.02 defines audit risk as follows:

> **Audit risk** is the risk that the auditor may unknowingly fail to appropriately modify his or her opinion on financial statements that are materially misstated.

OBJECTIVE 4

Explain the importance of the concept of audit risk and its three components.

The more certain the auditor wants to be of expressing the correct opinion, the lower will be the audit risk he or she is willing to accept. If 99% certainty is desired, audit risk is 1%, whereas if 95% certainty is considered satisfactory, audit risk is 5%. The auditor might elect to specify audit risk at a lower level when auditing the financial statements of a public company, for which there are many users of the statements and audit report, than for a private company where there would be fewer users. Similarly, the auditor might specify audit risk at a lower level when the client has a greater likelihood of financial failure than when the client is financially sound.

The auditor formulates an opinion on the financial statements taken as a whole on the basis of evidence obtained through the verification of assertions related to individual account balances or transaction classes. The objective is to restrict audit risk at the account balance level so that at the conclusion of the audit, the audit risk in expressing an opinion on the financial statements as a whole will be at an appropriately low level.

AUDIT RISK COMPONENTS

There are three components of audit risk as follows: inherent risk, control risk, and detection risk. Each is discussed in a following section.

Inherent Risk

Inherent risk is the susceptibility of an assertion to a material misstatement, assuming that there are no related internal control structure policies or procedures.

The assessment of inherent risk requires consideration of matters that may have a pervasive effect on assertions for all or many accounts and matters that may pertain only to assertions for specific accounts.

Examples of matters that may have pervasive effects include

- Profitability of the entity relative to the industry.
- Sensitivity of operating results to economic factors.
- Going concern problems such as lack of sufficient working capital.
- Nature, cause, and amount of known and likely misstatements detected in the prior audit.
- Management turnover, reputation, and accounting skills.
- The impact of technological developments on the company's operations and competitiveness.

Matters that may pertain only to specific accounts include

- Difficult-to-audit accounts or transactions.
- Contentious or difficult accounting issues.
- Susceptibility to misappropriation.
- Complexity of calculations.
- Extent of judgment related to assertions.
- Sensitivity of valuations to economic factors.
- Nature cause, and amount of known and likely misstatements detected in the prior audit.[3]

Inherent risk may be greater for some assertions than for others. For example, the existence or occurrence assertion for cash is more susceptible to misstatement through misappropriation than is the same assertion for plant assets. Similarly, the valuation or allocation assertion for leased assets is more susceptible to misstatement due to the complex nature of capital lease calculations than is the same assertion for accumulated depreciation based on simple straight-line computations.

Inherent risk exists independently of the audit of financial statements. Thus, the auditor cannot change the *actual level* of inherent risk. However, the auditor can change the *assessed level* of inherent risk. For example, the auditor can forego attempting to assess inherent risk at an appropriate level and simply assess it at the maximum. The auditor might choose this option when he or she concludes that the effort required to evaluate inherent risk for an assertion would exceed the potential reduction in the extent of auditing procedures derived from using a lower assessment.

---

[3] AICPA, Audit Guide, *Consideration of the Internal Control Structure in a Financial Statement Audit* (1990), p. 210.

The auditor's assessments of inherent risk are made primarily in the planning phase of the audit.

Control Risk

Control risk is the risk that a material misstatement that could occur in an assertion will not be prevented or detected on a timely basis by the entity's internal control structure policies or procedures.

Control risk is a function of the effectiveness of the client's internal control structure policies and procedures. Effective internal controls over an assertion reduce control risk, whereas ineffective internal controls increase control risk. Control risk can never be zero because internal controls cannot provide complete assurance that all material misstatements will be prevented or detected. For instance, controls may be ineffective on occasion because of human failures due to carelessness or fatigue.

Like inherent risk, the *actual level* of control risk for an assertion cannot be changed by the auditor. The auditor can, however, vary his or her *assessed level* of control risk by modifying (1) the procedures used to obtain an understanding of the internal control structure related to the assertion, and (2) the procedures used to perform tests of controls. These procedures are explained in detail in Chapters 8 and 9 of this text. Generally, more extensive use of both of these classes of procedures is required when the auditor wishes to support a lower assessed level of control risk.

Normally, auditors determine a **planned assessed level of control risk** for each significant financial statement assertion in the planning phase of the audit. Planned assessed levels are based on *assumptions* about the effectiveness of the design and operation of relevant portions of the client's internal control structure. In repeat engagements, the planned assessed levels are often based on information in the prior year's working papers. An **actual assessed level of control risk** is subsequently determined for each assertion based on evidence obtained from the study and evaluation of the client's internal control structure during interim work in the testing phase of the current audit.[4]

Detection Risk

Detection risk is the risk that the auditor will not detect a material misstatement that exists in an assertion.

Detection risk is a function of the effectiveness of auditing procedures and of their application by the auditor. Unlike inherent and control risk, the *actual level* of detection risk can be changed by the auditor by varying the nature, timing, and

[4] Some auditors do not attempt to make separate assessments of inherent and control risk. Instead they make a combined assessment that represents the risk that an assertion is materially misstated.

FIGURE 7-2 • SUMMARY OF RISK COMPONENTS

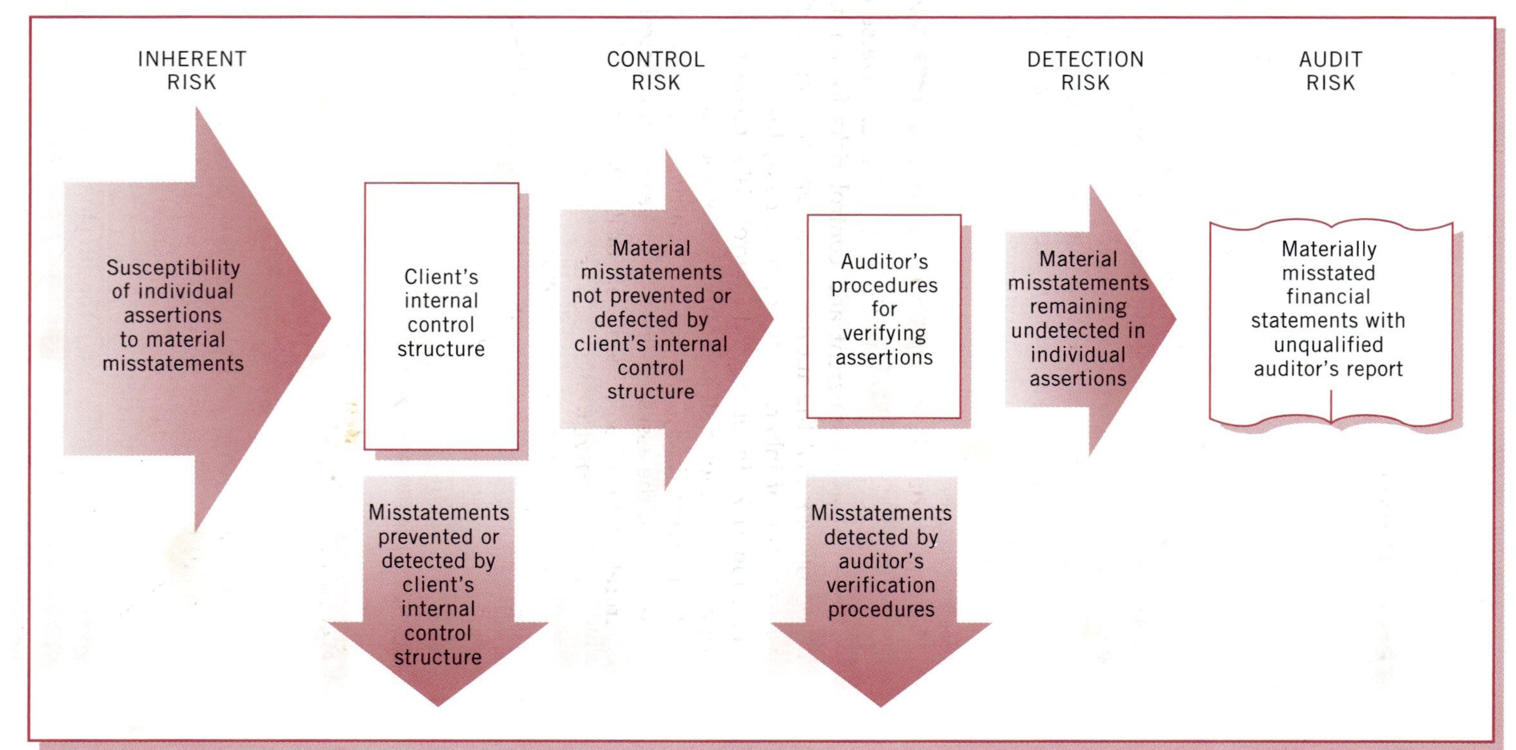

extent of substantive tests performed on an assertion. For example, the use of more effective procedures results in a lower level of detection risk than the use of less effective procedures. Similarly, substantive tests performed at or near the balance sheet date rather than at an interim date, and the use of larger rather than smaller samples, result in lower levels of detection risk.

In determining detection risk, the auditor should also consider the likelihood that he or she will make an error, such as misapplying an auditing procedure or misinterpreting the evidence obtained. These aspects of detection risk can be reduced through adequate planning and proper supervision and adherence to quality control standards.

In the planning phase of the audit, a **planned acceptable level of detection risk** is determined for each significant assertion by applying an audit risk model which relates the components of audit risk as explained in the next section. The planned levels of detection risk are subsequently revised, when necessary, based on evidence obtained about the effectiveness of internal controls.

A summary of the components of audit risk is presented in Figure 7-2.

RELATIONSHIP AMONG RISK COMPONENTS

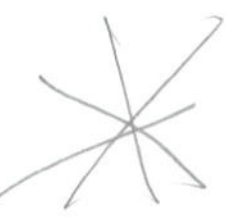

For a specified level of audit risk, there is an inverse relationship between the assessed levels of inherent and control risks for an assertion and the level of detection risk that the auditor can accept for that assertion. Thus, the lower the assessments of inherent and control risks, the higher is the acceptable level of detection risk. Inherent and control risks relate to the client's circumstances, whereas detection risk is controllable by the auditor as explained in the preceding section. Accordingly, the auditor controls audit risk by adjusting detection risk according to the assessed levels of inherent and control risks.

In relating the components of audit risk, the auditor may express each component in quantitative terms, such as percentages, or nonquantitative terms, such as very low, low, moderate, high, and maximum. In either case, an understanding of the relationships expressed in the audit risk model is essential in determining the planned acceptable level of detection risk.

Audit Risk Model

The **audit risk model** expresses the relationship among the audit risk components as follows:

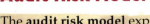

$$AR = IR \times CR \times DR$$

The symbols represent audit, inherent, control, and detection risk, respectively.

To illustrate the use of the model, assume the auditor has made the following risk assessments for a particular assertion, such as the valuation or allocation assertion for inventories:

$$IR = 50\%$$
$$CR = 50\%$$

Further, assume the auditor has specified an overall AR of 5%. Detection risk can be determined by solving the model for DR as follows:

$$DR = \frac{AR}{IR \times CR}$$
$$= \frac{0.05}{0.5 \times 0.5}$$
$$= 20\%$$

If the auditor decides that *IR* cannot be quantified, or that the effort to do so will exceed the benefits of a lower assessment, he or she can take the conservative approach of assessing *IR* at the maximum (100%). In this case, holding the other factors in the preceding example constant, the model yields a *DR* of 10% (i.e., $0.05/(1.0 \times 0.5)$). If the auditor also assesses *CR* at the maximum level, *DR* becomes 5% (i.e., $0.05/(1.0 \times 1.0)$).

When the audit risk model is used in the planning phase to determine the planned detection risk for an assertion, *CR* is based on the auditor's planned assessed level of control risk. If it is subsequently determined that the actual assessed level of control risk for an assertion differs from the planned level, the model can be reapplied using the actual assessed level for *CR*. The revised detection risk is then used in finalizing the design of substantive tests.

In practice, many auditors do not attempt to quantify each of the risk components, making it impossible to mathematically solve the risk model. However, even when not solved mathematically, familiarity with the model makes the following relationship clear: to hold audit risk to a specified level, the higher the assessed levels of inherent and control risks, the lower will be the acceptable level of detection risk.

Risk Components Matrix

Some auditors who use nonquantitative expressions for risk use a **risk components matrix** like the one shown in Figure 7-3 to relate the risk components. Study of the matrix indicates that it is consistent with the audit risk model in that the acceptable levels of detection risk are inversely related to the inherent and control

FIGURE 7-3 • RISK COMPONENTS MATRIX

Inherent Risk Assessment	Control Risk Assessment			
	Maximum	**High**	**Moderate**	**Low**
	Acceptable Level of Detection Risk to Achieve Low Audit Risk			
Maximum	Very low	Very low	Low	Low
High	Very low	Low	Low	Moderate
Moderate	Low	Low	Moderate	High
Low	Low	Moderate	High	*

* Substantive tests may not be necessary for a particular assertion.

risk assessments. The matrix indicates, for example, that if inherent risk is assessed as high and control risk as moderate, the acceptable level of detection risk is low.

This matrix assumes audit risk is restricted to a *low* level. Additional matrices could be developed to determine the detection risk consistent with other levels of audit risk.

AUDIT RISK AT THE FINANCIAL STATEMENT AND ACCOUNT BALANCE LEVELS

The auditor specifies an overall audit risk level to be achieved for the financial statements taken as a whole. Generally, that same level applies to each account balance and all related assertions. Currently, if an auditor were to use different audit risk levels for different accounts and assertions, there would be no generally accepted way of combining the results to determine the achieved overall audit risk level for the financial statements as a whole.

In contrast, the assessed levels of inherent and control risk, and the acceptable level of detection risk, can vary for each account and assertion. As noted previously, the auditor does not control the levels of inherent and control risk, and intentionally varies the acceptable level of detection risk inversely with the assessed levels of the other risk components to hold audit risk constant. Thus, expressions of the levels of inherent, control, and detection risk pertain to individual assertions at the account balance level, not to the financial statements taken as a whole.

RELATIONSHIP BETWEEN AUDIT RISK AND AUDIT EVIDENCE

OBJECTIVE 5

Describe the relationship between audit risk and audit evidence.

Like materiality, risk is also mentioned in Chapter 5 as one of the factors that affects the auditor's judgment about the sufficiency of evidential matter. In making generalizations about this relationship, care must be taken in specifying the risk term about which a generalization is being made.

There is an inverse relationship between *audit risk* and the amount of evidence needed to support the auditor's opinion on the financial statements. That is, for a particular client, the lower the level of audit risk to be achieved, the greater the amount of evidence needed. This inverse relationship also holds true for *detection risk*. For a particular assertion, the lower the acceptable level of detection risk determined by the auditor, the greater the amount of evidence needed to restrict detection risk to that level. Conversely, *inherent and control risks* are directly related to the amount of evidence needed. Less evidence is needed when these risks are low because in such case detection risk can be high.

It should be recognized, however, that it is not appropriate under GAAS for the auditor to conclude that inherent and control risks are so low that it is not necessary to perform any substantive tests for *all* of the assertions pertaining to an account. Some evidence must always be obtained from substantive tests for each significant account balance, though not necessarily for *each assertion* related to the account.

INTERRELATIONSHIPS AMONG MATERIALITY, AUDIT RISK, AND AUDIT EVIDENCE

OBJECTIVE 6

State the interrelationships among materiality, audit risk, and audit evidence.

In separate sections, we previously explained that there is an inverse relationship between materiality and audit evidence, and an inverse relationship between audit risk and audit evidence. Figure 7-4 illustrates these relationships, as well as the interrelationships among all three concepts. For example, if in Figure 7-4, we hold audit risk constant and reduce the materiality level, audit evidence must increase to complete the circle. Similarly, if we hold the materiality level constant and reduce audit evidence, audit risk must increase to complete the circle. Or, if we wish to reduce audit risk, we can do any one of the following: (1) increase the materiality level while holding audit evidence constant, (2) increase audit evidence while holding the materiality level constant, or (3) make smaller increases in both the amount of audit evidence and the materiality level.

AUDIT RISK ALERTS

Periodically, the AICPA staff, in consultation with the Auditing Standards Board, issues **audit risk alerts.** They are intended to provide auditors with an overview of recent economic, professional, and regulatory developments that may affect audits for clients in many industries. In addition to the general audit risk alerts, updates are issued covering developments related to specific industries.

AUDIT RISK ALERT—1993

Following are three examples of subjects discussed in the AICPA's *Audit Risk Alert—1993:*

- **Implications of the current economic environment.** Explains why obtaining management's representations about its plans is not enough to allay doubts about going concern and discusses why an explanatory paragraph in the auditor's report is not a substitute for loss recognition. Also covers how the availability of alternatives increases the importance of disclosure of the accounting policies for goodwill, how corporate downsizing can create the need to recognize a variety of costs, and how the decline in interest rates can affect the measurement of pension and post-retirement benefit obligations.
- **Regulatory developments.** SEC literature on environmental contingencies and liabilities has been added, various "red flags" that may indicate an increased risk of exposure to environmental liabilities are described, and guidelines on providing access to or photocopies of workpapers to regulators are explained.
- **New auditing and attestation pronouncements.** Lists an overview of recent pronouncements including reports on service organizations and reporting on internal control; a summary of key points in SSAE No. 3 on compliance attestation; and an alert about an auditing procedures study regarding computer environments involving microcomputers, LANs and other technologies.

SOURCE: *The CPA Letter,* November 1993, p. 3.

FIGURE 7-4 • INTERRELATIONSHIPS AMONG MATERIALITY, AUDIT RISK, AND AUDIT EVIDENCE

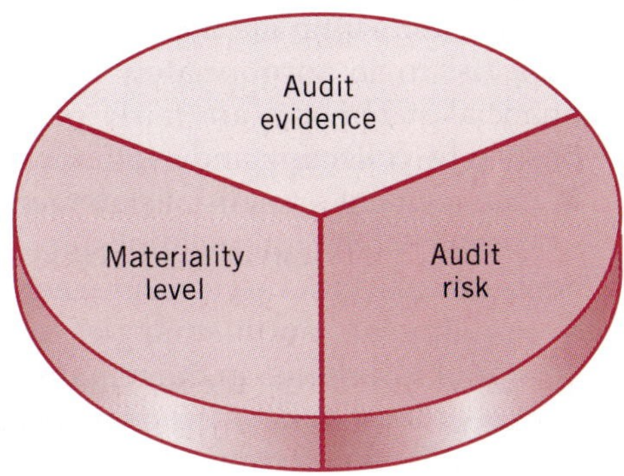

LEARNING CHECK:

7-9 a. What is audit risk?
  b. Name the three components of audit risk.

7-10 a. Define inherent risk.
  b. When might an auditor choose to forego assessing inherent risk for an assertion?

7-11 a. Define control risk.
  b. Can control risk be zero? Explain.
  c. What must the auditor do to support a lower assessed level of control risk?

7-12 a. Define detection risk.
  b. What influences the actual level of detection risk for an assertion?

7-13 What is the relationship among the audit risk components?

7-14 a. What is the audit risk model and when is it used?
  b. What is a risk components matrix and when is it used?

7-15 Generally, the auditor specifies an overall audit risk level for the financial statements as a whole and then uses that same level for each assertion. However, the levels of inherent, control, and detection risk can vary by assertion. Explain.

7-16 Is it ever appropriate under GAAS for the auditor to conclude that inherent and control risks are so low that it is unnecessary to verify any assertions for a material account balance? Explain.

KEY TERMS:

Actual assessed level of control risk, p. 233
Audit risk, p. 231
Audit risk alerts, p. 238
Audit risk model, p. 235
Control risk, p. 233
Detection risk, p. 233
Inherent risk, p. 232
Planned acceptable level of detection risk, p. 235
Planned assessed level of control risk, p. 233
Risk components matrix, p. 236

PRELIMINARY AUDIT STRATEGIES

OBJECTIVE 7

Differentiate between alternative preliminary audit strategies that may be used in audit planning.

The auditor's ultimate objective in planning and performing the audit is to reduce *audit risk* to an appropriately low level to support an opinion as to whether the financial statements are fairly presented in all *material* respects. This is accomplished by collecting and evaluating evidence concerning the assertions contained in management's financial statements.

Because of the interrelationships among evidence, materiality, and the components of audit risk discussed earlier, the auditor may choose from among alternative preliminary audit strategies in planning the audit of individual assertions or groups of assertions. In the remainder of this chapter, we identify the components of preliminary audit strategies, describe two alternative strategies, and explain their application to transaction classes and cycles.

COMPONENTS OF PRELIMINARY AUDIT STRATEGIES

In developing preliminary audit strategies for assertions, the auditor specifies four components as follows:

- The planned assessed level of control risk.
- The extent of understanding of the internal control structure to be obtained.
- Tests of controls to be performed in assessing control risk.
- The planned level of substantive tests to be performed to reduce audit risk to an appropriately low level.

A **preliminary audit strategy** is not a detailed specification of auditing procedures to be performed in completing the audit. Instead, it represents the auditor's preliminary judgments about an *audit approach* and is based on certain assumptions about the conduct of the audit. In an initial audit for example, the third and fourth strategy components would typically not include a listing of the specific tests of controls and substantive tests to be performed, but rather simply a tentative conclusion about the *relative emphasis* to be given to the two classes of tests. In a repeat engagement, the specification of these components *might* include a presumption by the auditor that the tests of controls and substantive tests used in the prior year will be appropriate for use in the current year as well. Final decisions on these matters are made as the audit progresses.

The manner in which the auditor specifies the four components of an audit strategy is explained in the following sections for two alternative strategies. The two strategies are the **primarily substantive approach** and the **lower assessed level of control risk approach.** These strategies represent the opposite ends of a continuum of possible strategies involving different specifications for each of the components identified above. Figure 7-5 provides a graphic overview of the different specifications for the first component and the varying degrees of emphasis given to the last three components under alternative strategies. The bottom segment of the figure indicates the *potential* for cost savings under the lower assessed level of control risk approach.

FIGURE 7-5 • PRELIMINARY AUDIT STRATEGIES FOR MATERIAL FINANCIAL STATEMENT ASSERTIONS

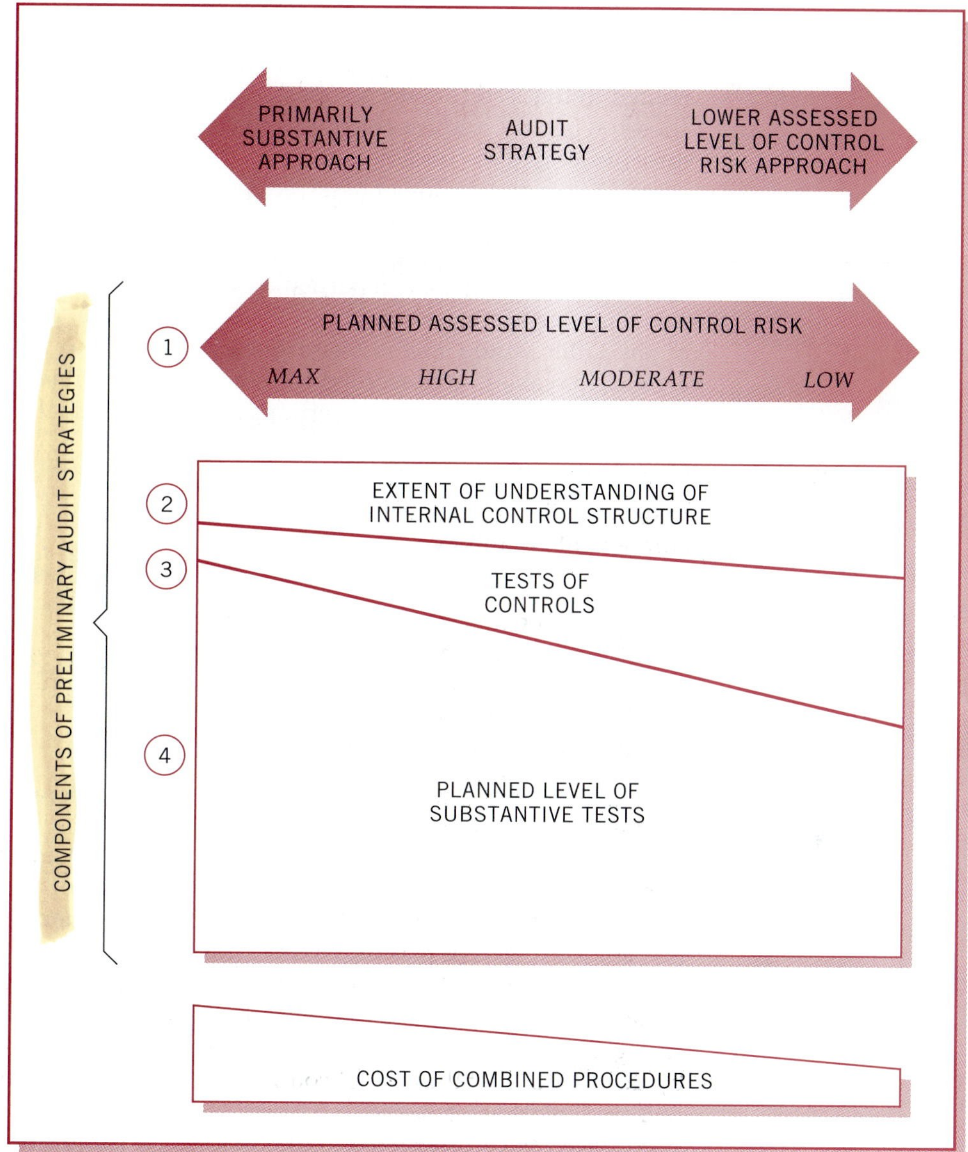

PRIMARILY SUBSTANTIVE APPROACH

Under this approach, the auditor specifies the components of the audit strategy as follows:

- Use a planned assessed level of control risk of *maximum* (or *slightly below the maximum*).
- Plan to obtain a minimum understanding of relevant portions of the internal control structure.

- Plan few, if any, tests of controls.
- Plan extensive substantive tests based on a low planned acceptable level of detection risk.

The auditor might choose this approach when he or she knows in advance, perhaps from prior experience with the client or earlier planning steps, that controls related to the assertion do not exist or are ineffective. This strategy might also be chosen when the auditor concludes that the costs of performing additional procedures to obtain an understanding of the internal control structure and tests of controls to support a lower assessed level of control risk would exceed the cost of performing more extensive substantive tests. These circumstances might pertain to assertions for accounts that are affected primarily by (1) infrequent transactions or (2) adjusting entries. In a particular audit, examples of the former might include assertions pertaining to plant assets, bonds payable, and capital stock. Examples of the latter would include assertions pertaining to accumulated depreciation, accrued payables, and accrued receivables. The primarily substantive approach may also be used for more assertions in initial audits than in recurring audits.

LOWER ASSESSED LEVEL OF CONTROL RISK APPROACH

Under this approach, the auditor specifies the components of the audit strategy as follows:

- Use a planned assessed level of control risk of *moderate* or *low.*
- Plan to obtain an extensive understanding of relevant portions of the internal control structure.
- Plan extensive tests of controls.
- Plan restricted substantive tests based on a moderate or high planned acceptable level of detection risk.

The auditor might choose this strategy when he or she believes that controls related to an assertion are well designed and highly effective. In addition, the auditor must believe that the cost of performing the more extensive procedures to obtain the understanding of the internal control structure and to test the controls will be more than offset by cost savings from performing less extensive substantive tests. This will often be the case for assertions pertaining to accounts that are affected by a high volume of routine transactions such as sales, accounts receivable, inventory, and payroll expenses. This approach is also likely to be used for more assertions in recurring audits than in initial audits.

RELATIONSHIP BETWEEN STRATEGIES AND TRANSACTION CYCLES

The strategies described in the preceding sections are not intended to characterize the approach to an entire audit. Rather, they represent alternative approaches to auditing individual assertions. In most audits, each approach is used for numerous assertions.

Frequently, however, a common strategy is applied to groups of assertions affected by a **transaction class** within a **transaction cycle.** The rationale is that many internal controls focus on the processing of a single type of transaction within one of the cycles. Although CPA firms use different names for the transaction classes and cycles, and in some cases even differ in specifying which transaction classes belong to which cycles, the following framework used in this text is representative of practice:

Cycle	Major Classes of Transactions
Revenue	Sales, cash receipts, and sales adjustments
Expenditure	Purchases and cash disbursements
Personnel services	Payroll
Production	Manufacturing
Investing	Temporary and long-term investments
Financing	Long-term debt and capital stock

The following example illustrates how this framework is used in planning and organizing the audit. Two accounts that nearly always have a significant effect on the financial statements are sales in the income statement and accounts receivable in the balance sheet. These are among a group of accounts usually identified with the revenue cycle. The account balances for sales and accounts receivable are increased by sales transactions that are often voluminous. Thus, the existence or occurrence assertion for both accounts is affected by the existence or occurrence assertion for the transaction class, sales. Accordingly, the auditor's expectations about the effectiveness of internal controls related to the processing of sales transactions are considered in specifying the planned assessed level of control risk component of the preliminary audit strategies for the account balance assertions for sales. Because the accounts receivable balance is also affected by cash receipts and sales adjustments transactions as well as sales transactions, the auditor's expectations about the effectiveness of controls of all three transaction classes are considered in developing the preliminary audit strategies for accounts receivable assertions.

In the next three chapters, we explain in greater detail how the auditor applies the primarily substantive and lower assessed level of control risk approaches for planning and organizing the audit within the transaction cycle framework. Chapter 8 focuses on obtaining the understanding of the internal control structure required under each approach. Chapter 9 explains the methodology for testing controls and assessing control risk under each approach. In both of these chapters, the emphasis is on gathering information and assessing control risk for transaction classes. Chapter 9 also explains how the information obtained on transaction classes is used in determining control risk assessments for account balance assertions. Chapter 10 explains how those assessments in turn affect the determination of detection risk and the design of substantive tests. The general framework developed in these chapters is then applied to each of the cycles and transaction classes in the chapters comprising Part IV of this text.

LEARNING CHECK:

7-17 What is the auditor's ultimate objective in planning and performing the audit?

7-18 a. What is a preliminary audit strategy?
b. Name two alternative audit strategies.

7-19 a. Identify four components of audit strategies.
b Contrast the four components of audit strategies under the primarily substantive approach versus the lower assessed level of control risk approach.

7-20 a. Discuss the relative costs of the two alternative preliminary audit strategies.
b. Why may a common strategy be used for a group of assertions affected by the same class of transactions?

KEY TERMS:

Lower assessed level of control risk approach, p. 240
Preliminary audit strategy, p. 240
Primarily substantive approach, p. 240
Transaction class, p. 242
Transaction cycle, p. 242

SUMMARY

Three important components of audit planning are making preliminary judgments about materiality levels, considering audit risk, and developing preliminary audit strategies. Materiality is considered at both the financial statement and account balance levels and may be expressed in either quantitative or nonquantitative terms. There is an inverse relationship between materiality levels and the amount of evidence needed.

Audit risk consists of three components. The inherent and control risk components are beyond the auditor's control and are merely assessed by the auditor. Detection risk is inversely related to the other components. The auditor keeps audit risk to an appropriately low level by controlling detection risk. Like materiality, audit risk may be expressed in either quantitative or nonquantitative terms, and it has an inverse effect on the amount of evidence needed.

Different preliminary audit strategies can be adopted for significant financial statement assertions. Two alternative strategies identified in the auditing literature are the primarily substantive approach and the lower assessed level of control risk approach.

BIBLIOGRAPHY

AICPA Professional Standards:

SAS 47 (AU 312), Audit Risk and Materiality in Conducting an Audit.

IAU 25 (AU 8025), Materiality and Audit Risk.

Alderman, C. Wayne, and Tabor, Richard H. "The Case for Risk-Driven Audits," *Journal of Accountancy* (March 1989), pp. 55–61.

Control Risk Audit Guide Task Force. *Audit Guide: Consideration of the Internal Control Structure in a Financial Statement Audit.* New York: AICPA, 1990.

Holt, D. L., and Morrow, P. C. "Risk Assessment Judgments of Auditors and Bank Lenders: A Comparative Analysis of Conformance to Bayes' Theorem," *Accounting, Organizations and Society* (Vol. 17, No. 6, 1992), pp. 549–559.

Jennings, Marianne, Kneer, Dan C., and Reckers, Philip M. J. "A Reexamination of the Concept of Materiality: Views of Auditors, Users, and Officers of the Court," *Auditing: A Journal of Practice and Theory* (Spring 1987), pp. 104–115.

Leslie, Donald A. *Materiality, the Concept and Its Application to Auditing*. Toronto: Canadian Institute of Chartered Accountants, 1985.

Pany, Kurt, and Wheeler, Stephen. "A Comparison of Various Materiality Rules of Thumb," *The CPA Journal* (June 1989), pp. 62–63.

Yardley, J. "Explaining the Conditional Nature of the Audit Risk Model," *Journal of Accounting Education* (Vol. 7, 1989), pp. 107–114.

OBJECTIVE QUESTIONS

Indicate the best answer for each of the following multiple choice questions.

7-21 The following questions pertain to materiality.

1. Which of the following underlies the application of generally accepted auditing standards, particularly the standards of field work and reporting?
   a. Internal control structure.
   b. Corroborating evidence.
   c. Materiality and relative risk.
   d. Reasonable assurance.

2. Which one of the following statements is correct concerning the concept of materiality?
   a. Materiality is determined by reference to guidelines established by the AICPA.
   b. Materiality depends only on the dollar amount of an item relative to other items in the financial statements.
   c. Materiality depends on the nature of an item rather than the dollar amount.
   d. Materiality is a matter of professional judgment.

3. The concept of materiality would be least important to an auditor in determining the
   a. Transactions that should be reviewed.
   b. Need for disclosure of a particular fact or transaction.
   c. Scope of the CPA's audit program relating to various accounts.
   d. Effects of direct financial interest in the client upon the CPA's independence.

7-22 These questions pertain to audit risk and its components.

1. In planning an audit, the auditor considers audit risk, which is the
   a. Susceptibility of an account balance to material error assuming the client does not have any related internal controls.
   b. Risk that a material error in an account will not be prevented or detected on a timely basis by the client's internal control structure.
   c. Risk that the auditor's procedures for verifying account balances will not detect a material error when in fact such error exists.
   d. Risk that the auditor may unknowingly fail to appropriately modify the opinion on financial statements that are materially misstated.

2. The risk that an auditor's procedures will lead to the conclusion that a material misstatement does *not* exist in an assertion when, in fact, such misstatement does exist is referred to as
   a. Audit risk.
   b. Inherent risk.
   c. Control risk.
   d. Detection risk.

3. Which of the following audit risk components may be assessed in nonquantitative terms?

	Inherent Risk	Control Risk	Detection Risk
a.	Yes	Yes	No
b.	Yes	No	Yes
c.	No	Yes	Yes
d.	Yes	Yes	Yes

7-23 The following questions deal with preliminary audit strategies (these questions were written by the authors).

1. Which of the following best describes the nature of a preliminary audit strategy?
   a. It is a detailed specification of auditing procedures to be performed.
   b. It represents the auditor's plan for meeting the general standards of GAAS.
   c. It represents the auditor's preliminary judgments about an audit approach and reflects certain assumptions about the conduct of the audit.
   d. It is the auditor's plan for meeting the second standard of field work.
2. In developing a preliminary audit strategy, the auditor specifies each of the following components except
   a. The extent of understanding of the internal control structure to be obtained.
   b. The tests of details of transactions and balances to be performed.
   c. The planned assessed level of control risk.
   d. The extent of tests of controls to be performed.
3. Use of the lower assessed level of control risk approach is least likely when
   a. The auditor expects that controls related to an assertion are well designed and highly effective.
   b. An assertion is affected by a high volume of routine transactions that are subject to processing controls.
   c. The account to which an assertion pertains is affected primarily by infrequent transactions or adjusting entries.
   d. The cost of performing more extensive procedures to obtain the understanding of the internal control structure and test controls will be more than offset by cost savings from performing less extensive substantive tests.

COMPREHENSIVE QUESTIONS

7-24 **(Audit risk and materiality concepts)** Audit risk and materiality should be considered when planning and performing an audit of financial statements in accordance with generally accepted auditing standards. Audit risk and materiality should also be considered together in determining the nature, timing, and extent of auditing procedures and in evaluating the results of those procedures.

REQUIRED

a. 1. Define audit risk.
   2. Describe its components of inherent risk, control risk, and detection risk.
   3. Explain how these components are interrelated.

b. 1. Define materiality.
   2. Discuss the factors affecting its determination.
   3. Describe the relationship between materiality for planning purposes and materiality for evaluation purposes.

AICPA

7-25 **(Planning materiality)** Figure 6-5 on page 211 presents balance sheet and income statement data for Example Company.

REQUIRED

a. A number of guidelines, or rules of thumb, are used in practice for determining planning materiality. Using the current year (unaudited) data in Figure 6-5, calculate several alternative quantitative measures of planning materiality at the financial statement level as follows:
   1. Two alternative measures for the balance sheet.
   2. Two alternative measures for the income statement.

b. How would an auditor choose from among these alternative measures of materiality?

c. Suppose the auditor decides to use $200,000 as the aggregate level of planning materiality for the balance sheet. Prepare two plans for allocating this amount to the asset accounts shown in Figure 6-5 and state the rationale for each plan.

7-26 **(Materiality concepts)** Financial statements are materially misstated when they contain errors or irregularities whose effect, individually or in the aggregate, is important enough to prevent the statements from being presented fairly in conformity with GAAP.

REQUIRED

a. Financial statements may be misstated when they contain departures from facts. Identify two other types of circumstances that may cause the statements to be misstated.

b. In planning the audit, materiality should be assessed at two levels. Identify the two levels and state the reason for each.

c. Audit planning may occur in July for a client with a December 31 year-end. If data are available for the first six months of the year only, how can the auditor determine planning materiality for the annual audit?

d. The size of an account balance sets an upper limit on the amount of misstatement in the account. Is this statement correct? Explain.

e. Distinguish between the terms *material account balance* and *materiality* and state how each relates to the amount of evidence needed for an assertion.

7-27 **(Detection risk and audit evidence)** Shown below are four situations in which the auditor wishes to determine planned acceptable levels of detection risk and the planned levels of evidence needed for specific financial statement assertions. The auditor has used judgment in arriving at the nonquantitative expressions for audit, inherent, and control risk.

	Situation			
	A	**B**	**C**	**D**
Desired audit risk	Low	Low	Low	Low
Assessed inherent risk	Moderate	High	Low	Low
Planned assessed level of control risk	Low	Maximum	High	Low
Planned detection risk	________	________	________	________
Planned evidence	________	________	________	________

REQUIRED

a. Using the risk components matrix in Figure 7-3, determine the acceptable level of detection risk for each situation.

b. Rank the four situations from most evidence required (1) to least evidence required (4). Explain your ranking of Situation D.

7-28 **(Risk components and relationships)** Shown below are seven situations in which the auditor wishes to use the audit risk model to determine planned acceptable levels of detection risk and the planned levels of evidence needed for specific financial statement assertions. The auditor has used judgment in arriving at the quantitative expressions for audit, inherent, and control risk.

	Situation						
	A	**B**	**C**	**D**	**E**	**F**	**G**
Desired audit risk	1%	1%	5%	5%	5%	5%	10%
Assessed inherent risk	20%	50%	20%	50%	20%	50%	50%
Planned assessed level of control risk	50%	50%	50%	40%	20%	25%	20%
Planned detection risk	___	___	___	___	___	___	___
Planned evidence	___	___	___	___	___	___	___

REQUIRED

a. Define the four types of risk listed above.
b. Using the audit risk model, calculate the planned detection risk for each of the situations above.
c. Rank the seven situations from most evidence required (1) to least evidence required (7).
d. What do the results obtained for situations (E) and (G) mean with respect to procedures to obtain evidence to achieve planned detection risk?
e. State how your answers to part (b) would be affected by a change in only one of the following factors while the other two factors are held constant at the levels indicated in the table:
   1. Increase in desired audit risk.
   2. Decrease in assessed inherent risk.
   3. Increase in planned assessed level of control risk.

7-29 **(Inherent risk)** Following are ten pairs of assertions:

1. a. Existence or occurrence of inventory. higher risk
   b. Existence or occurrence of building.
2. a. Valuation or allocation of cash.
   b. Valuation or allocation of deferred income taxes.
3. a. Existence or occurrence of accounts payable.
   b. Completeness of accounts payable.
4. a. Rights and obligations of accrued wages payable.
   b. Rights and obligations of liability under warranties. higher risk
5. a. Presentation and disclosure of repairs and maintenance expense.
   b. Presentation and disclosure of telephone expense.
6. a. Valuation or allocation of long-term investments.
   b. Valuation or allocation of land.
7. a. Existence or occurrence of accounts receivable.
   b. Completeness of accounts receivable.
8. a. Existence or occurrence of cash.
   b. Valuation or allocation of cash.
9. a. Valuation or allocation of bad debts expense. higher risk
   b. Valuation or allocation of depreciation expense.
10. a. Valuation or allocation of receivable due from affiliate.
    b. Valuation or allocation of note payable to bank.

REQUIRED

a. For each pair of assertions, indicate whether (a) or (b) would typically have the higher inherent risk and state why.
b. In addition to factors that affect individual assertions, the assessment of inherent risk requires consideration of matters that may have a pervasive effect on many or all accounts or assertions in an entity's financial statements. State five examples of matters that may have such pervasive effects.

7-30 **(Risk components)** Following are a number of factors recognized by the auditor as having an effect on one or another of the components of audit risk for one or more of management's financial statement assertions:

1. Manufactured equipment is leased to customers under a variety of lease terms tailored to the customers' needs.
2. The company's control policies and procedures over receiving and depositing cash are ineffective.
3. The company's management is under intense pressure to meet projected annual growth in revenues of 20%.
4. The availability of external nonfinancial data that are highly correlated with the company's sales causes the auditor to believe that analytical procedures will be effective in determining whether revenue is misstated.
5. The company has experienced high turnover in key management positions.
6. The auditor decides to confirm accounts receivable at the balance sheet date rather than at an interim date.
7. The company suffers from inadequate working capital.
8. High levels of overtime experienced by clerical employees have resulted in numerous errors in processing accounting information due to fatigue and carelessness.
9. To ensure that audit risk is kept to an acceptably low level, the auditor plans to make extensive use of tests of details of balances.
10. The company's primary activities are in the field of genetic engineering.

REQUIRED

Using the following codes, identify the risk component that is directly affected by each of the foregoing factors:

IR = Assessed level of inherent risk
CR = Planned assessed level of control risk
DR = Planned detection risk

7-31 **(Preliminary audit strategies)** A major part of audit planning is selecting an appropriate audit strategy for obtaining sufficient competent evidence for each significant financial statement assertion. These strategies are based on the interrelationships among evidence, materiality, and the components of audit risk.

REQUIRED

a. Define the term *preliminary audit strategy.*
b. What components should be specified in developing a preliminary audit strategy?
c. Identify two alternative strategies. Contrast the specification of the four strategy components under the two strategies.
d. State the circumstances that favor the use of each strategy including how cost considerations affect the choice of a strategy.

7-32 **(Preliminary audit strategies)** Several significant financial statement assertions and related circumstances (not necessarily for a single client) are listed below:

1. Existence or occurrence of sales revenue—the client operates a chain of music video stores.

2. Valuation or allocation of property, plant, and equipment—the client had only two acquisitions and two disposals during the year.
3. Valuation or allocation of depreciation—the company uses straight-line depreciation for all depreciable assets.
4. Valuation or allocation of sales revenue—all the client's revenues are based on per diem rates used in monthly billings to a government agency under one large contract.
5. Completeness of cash disbursements—the company processes approximately 2,000 checks per month for payments to vendors based on approved vouchers.
6. Existence or occurrence of long-term investments—for the past eight years, the company has owned a 30% interest in two subsidiary companies.
7. Valuation or allocation of liability under warranties—all of the company's products are warranted for 12 months.
8. Existence or occurrence of salaries and wages expense—the company has 600 employees who are paid biweekly.
9. Valuation or allocation of deferred income taxes—timing differences relate primarily to differences in depreciation and inventory costing methods used for book and tax purposes.
10. Valuation or allocation of common stock—the company had a significant number of stock transactions, but the auditor believes it will not be cost effective to perform tests of controls.

REQUIRED

Based on the limited information given, indicate the preliminary audit strategy that the auditor would likely choose for each of the foregoing assertions.

CASE

7-33 **(Risk analysis)** Green, CPA is considering audit risk at the financial statement level in planning the audit of the National Federal Bank (NFB) Company's financial statements for the year ended December 31, 1990. Audit risk at the financial statement level is influenced by a combination of factors related to management, the industry, and the entity. In assessing such factors, Green has gathered the following information concerning NFB's environment.

NFB is a federally insured bank that has been consistently more profitable than the industry average by marketing mortgages on properties in a prosperous rural area, which has experienced considerable growth in recent years. NFB packages its mortgages and sells them to large investment trusts. Despite recent volatility of interest rates, NFB has been able to continue selling its mortgages as a source of new lendable funds.

NFB's board of directors is controlled by Smith, the majority stockholder, who also acts as the chief executive officer. Management at the bank's branch offices has authority for directing and controlling NFB's operations and is compensated based on branch profitability. The internal auditor reports directly to Harris, a minority shareholder, who is chairman of the audit committee.

The accounting department has experienced little turnover in personnel during the five years Green has audited NFB. NFB's formula consistently underestimates the allowance for loan losses, but its controller has always been receptive to Green's suggestions to increase the allowance.

During 1990, NFB opened a branch office in a suburban town 30 miles from its principal place of business. Although this branch is not yet profitable due to competition from several well-established regional banks, management believes that the branch will be profitable by 1992.

Also, during 1990, NFB increased the efficiency of its accounting operations by installing a new sophisticated computer system.

REQUIRED

Based only on the information above, indicate the factors that most likely would (a) increase and (b) decrease the risk of material misstatements.

AICPA (adapted)

RESEARCH QUESTIONS

7-34 **(Audit Risk Alerts)** Each year, the AICPA issues a general audit risk alert document and a number of industry audit risk alerts. If you can obtain access to a current copy of either the general alert or one of the industry alerts, prepare a summary of the major points covered.

7-35 **(AAER on Materiality)** The SEC's *Accounting and Auditing Enforcement Release No. 111* deals with the issue of materiality. Summarize the facts and conclusions of the SEC set forth in this AAER.

7-36 **(AAER on Risk and Materiality)** The SEC's *Accounting and Auditing Enforcement Release No. 129* deals with risk and materiality issues. Summarize the facts and conclusions of the SEC set forth in this AAER.

CHAPTER

8

Understanding the Internal Control Structure

Learning Objectives

When you have completed your study of this chapter, you should be able to

1. Appreciate the importance of internal control to an entity, its external auditors, and others.
2. Define internal control and explain four underlying fundamental concepts.
3. State the inherent limitations of internal control structures.
4. Explain the roles and responsibilities of various parties for an entity's internal control structure.
5. Describe the five components of an internal control structure.
6. Explain the understanding of the internal control structure components needed to plan an audit and how the understanding is used.
7. Indicate the audit procedures used to obtain the understanding.
8. State the requirements, and alternate methods, for documenting the understanding.

Introduction to Internal Control
- Importance of Internal Control
- Definition, Fundamental Concepts, and Components
- Entity Objectives and Related Internal Controls Relevant to an Audit
- Limitations of an Entity's Internal Control Structure
- Roles and Responsibilities

Components of an Internal Control Structure
- Control Environment
- Risk Assessment
- Information and Communication
- Control Activities
- Monitoring
- Application of Components to Small and Midsize Entities

Obtaining an Understanding of Internal Control Structure Components
- Effects of Preliminary Audit Strategies
- Understanding of Control Environment
- Understanding of Risk Assessment
- Understanding of Information and Communication
- Understanding of Control Activities
- Understanding of Monitoring
- Procedures to Obtain an Understanding

Documenting the Understanding
- Questionnaires
- Flowcharts
- Narrative Memoranda

Summary

Appendix 8A-Comprehensive Flowcharting Illustration

Bibliography

Objective Questions

Comprehensive Questions

Cases

Research Questions

The second generally accepted auditing standard of field work states that

> A sufficient understanding of the internal control structure is to be obtained to plan the audit and to determine the nature, timing, and extent of tests to be performed.

This chapter begins with an introduction to internal control and an explanation of the components of an entity's internal control structure (hereinafter, alternately referred to as the *ICS*). Consideration is then given to obtaining an understanding of the internal control structure sufficient to plan the audit, and to documenting the understanding in audit working papers.

INTRODUCTION TO INTERNAL CONTROL

In this section, we first chronicle the expanding importance of internal control to management, independent auditors, and external parties. We then examine a contemporary definition of internal control and several fundamental concepts embodied in that definition. In addition, we consider which entity objectives addressed by internal controls are relevant to a financial statement audit, describe the components of an internal control structure, acknowledge certain inherent limitations of internal control structures, and specify the roles and responsibilities of various parties for an entity's ICS.

IMPORTANCE OF INTERNAL CONTROL

The importance of internal control to management and independent auditors has been recognized in the professional literature for many years. A 1947 publication by the AICPA entitled *Internal Control* cited the following factors as contributing to the expanding recognition of the significance of internal control:

OBJECTIVE 1

Appreciate the importance of internal control to an entity, its external auditors, and others.

- The scope and size of the business entity has become so complex and widespread that management must rely on numerous reports and analyses to effectively control operations.
- The check and review inherent in a good system of internal control afford protection against human weaknesses and reduce the possibility that errors or irregularities will occur.
- It is impracticable for auditors to make audits of most companies within economic fee limitations without relying on the client's system of internal control.

During the five decades following this publication, even greater importance has been placed on internal control by management, independent auditors, and increasingly, external parties, such as regulators.

In 1977, a new dimension was imposed with the passage of the **Foreign Corrupt Practices Act (FCPA).** Under this Act, management and directors of companies subject to the reporting requirements of the Securities Exchange Act of 1934, whether or not they operate outside the United States, are required to comply with antibribery and accounting standards provisions. The latter requires the maintenance of a satisfactory system of internal control. The FCPA is administered by the Securities and Exchange Commission (SEC), and management and directors who do not comply with the provisions are subject to fines, penalties, and/or imprisonment.

Ten years later, the **National Commission on Fraudulent Financial Reporting** (Treadway Commission) reemphasized the importance of internal control in reducing the incidence of fraudulent financial reporting. The Commission's final report, issued in October 1987, included the following on page 11:

- Of overriding importance in preventing fraudulent financial reporting is the "tone set by top management" that influences the corporate environment within which financial reporting occurs.
- All public companies should maintain internal controls that will provide reasonable assurance that fraudulent financial reporting will be prevented or subject to early detection.
- The organizations sponsoring the Commission (including the Auditing Standards Board [ASB]) should cooperate in developing additional guidance on internal control systems.

Subsequent to the release of the Commission's report, in 1988 the ASB issued SAS 55, *Consideration of the Internal Control Structure in a Financial Statement Audit* (AU 319). The SAS significantly expanded both the meaning of internal control and the auditor's responsibilities in meeting the second standard of field work. In 1990, the AICPA issued a 262-page audit guide with the same title as the SAS (hereafter referred to as the *Internal Control Audit Guide*) to assist auditors in applying SAS 55.

Finally, following up on the last recommendation of the Treadway Commission referred to previously, in 1992 the **Committee of Sponsoring Organizations (COSO)** of the Treadway Commission issued a report entitled *Internal Control—Integrated Framework.* COSO included representatives from the AICPA, the American Accounting Association, The Institute of Internal Auditors, the Institute of Management Accountants, and the Financial Executives Institute. Its report includes four volumes as follows: (1) *Executive Summary,* (2) *Framework,* (3) *Evaluation Tools,* and (4) *Reporting to External Parties.* According to COSO, the two principal purposes of its efforts were to

- Establish a common definition of internal control serving the needs of different parties, and
- Provide a standard against which business and other entities can assess their control systems and determine how to improve them.

At the time this text went to press, the ASB was in the process of revising SAS 55 to conform to the framework and language used in the COSO report. The revised SAS was expected to be published in 1995. Accordingly, portions of this chapter are based on the COSO report, while other portions are based on sections of SAS 55 and sections of the related 1990 *Internal Control Audit Guide* that were not slated for revision.

DEFINITION, FUNDAMENTAL CONCEPTS, AND COMPONENTS

The COSO report defines internal control as follows:

OBJECTIVE 2

Define internal control and explain four underlying fundamental concepts.

> **Internal control** is a process, effected by an entity's board of directors, management, and other personnel, designed to provide reasonable assurance regarding the achievement of objectives in the following categories:
>
> - Reliability of financial reporting.
> - Compliance with applicable laws and regulations.
> - Effectiveness and efficiency of operations.

The COSO report places special emphasis on the following **fundamental concepts** that are embodied in the foregoing definition:

- Internal control is *a process.* It is a means to an end, not an end in itself. It consists of a series of actions that are pervasive and integrated with, not added onto, an entity's infrastructure.
- Internal control is effected by *people.* It is not merely policy manuals and forms, but people at every level of an organization, including the board of directors, management, and other personnel.
- Internal control can be expected to provide only *reasonable assurance,* not absolute assurance, to an entity's management and board because of limitations inherent in all internal control systems and the need to consider the relative costs and benefits of establishing controls.
- Internal control is geared to the achievement of *objectives* in the overlapping categories of financial reporting, compliance, and operations.[1]

Implicit in the last fundamental concept is the assumption that management and the board do in fact formulate and periodically update entity objectives in each of the three categories.

To provide a further framework or structure for considering the many possible internal controls related to the achievement of an entity's objectives, the COSO report identifies five interrelated **components of internal control** as follows: (1) control environment, (2) risk assessment, (3) information and communication, (4) control activities, and (5) monitoring. These five components are described in detail in later sections of this chapter.

ENTITY OBJECTIVES AND RELATED INTERNAL CONTROLS RELEVANT TO AN AUDIT

As noted previously, management adopts internal controls to provide reasonable assurance of achieving three categories of objectives: (1) reliability of financial information, (2) compliance with applicable laws and regulations, and (3) effectiveness and efficiency of operations. Because not all of those objectives and related controls are relevant to an audit of financial statements, one of the auditor's first tasks in meeting the second standard of field work is to identify those objectives and controls that are relevant. Generally, this includes those that pertain directly to the first category—reliability of financial reporting. Thus, of particular significance are controls that are intended to provide reasonable assurance that financial statements prepared by management for external users are fairly presented in conformity with generally accepted accounting principles.[2]

Other objectives and related controls may also be relevant if they pertain to data the auditor uses in applying audit procedures. Examples include objectives and related controls that pertain to

---

[1] Committee of Sponsoring Organizations of the Treadway Commission, *Internal Control—Integrated Framework* (Jersey City, NJ: American Institute of Certified Public Accountants, 1992), pp. 9–12.

[2] An entity may also adopt objectives and controls pertaining to the preparation of financial statements on an "other comprehensive basis of accounting" (other than GAAP). Such reporting is explained in Chapter 21.

- Nonfinancial data used in analytical procedures such as the number of employees, volume of goods manufactured, and other production and marketing statistics.
- Certain financial data developed primarily for internal purposes, such as budgets and performance data, used by the auditor to obtain evidence about the amounts reported in the financial statements.

Chapter 2 of this text explained the auditor's responsibilities for detecting errors and irregularities, including management and employee fraud, and for detecting certain illegal acts. Thus, an entity's objectives and controls related to these matters are also relevant to the auditor. In particular, objectives and controls in the category compliance with applicable laws and regulations are relevant when noncompliance could have a direct and material effect on the financial statements.

Many objectives and related controls pertaining to the third category—effectiveness and efficiency of operations—although important to the entity are not relevant to the audit. However, the COSO report includes in this category controls relating to the *safeguarding of assets* against unauthorized acquisition, use, and disposition. These controls are relevant to an audit when they play a role in ensuring that related losses, such as from theft, are properly reflected in the entity's financial statements. Controls designed solely to reduce the risk of bad operating decisions, such as selling a product at too low a price or incurring expenditures for unproductive research and development or ineffective advertising, are not ordinarily considered relevant to a financial statement audit.

LIMITATIONS OF AN ENTITY'S INTERNAL CONTROL STRUCTURE

OBJECTIVE 3

State the inherent limitations of internal control structures.

One of the fundamental concepts identified earlier in the chapter is that internal control can provide only reasonable assurance to management and the board of directors regarding the achievement of an entity's objectives. Reasons for this include the following **inherent limitations** in any entity's internal control structure:

- **Mistakes in Judgment.** Occasionally, management and other personnel may exercise poor judgment in making business decisions or in performing routine duties because of inadequate information, time constraints, or other pressures.
- **Breakdowns.** Breakdowns in established controls may occur because personnel may misunderstand instructions or make errors due to carelessness, distractions, or fatigue. Temporary or permanent changes in personnel or in systems or procedures may also contribute to breakdowns.
- **Collusion.** Individuals acting together, such as an employee who performs an important control acting with another employee, customer, or supplier, may be able to perpetrate and conceal an irregularity so as to prevent its detection by the internal control structure (e.g., collusion among three employees from the personnel, manufacturing, and payroll departments to initiate payments to fictitious employees, or kickback schemes between an employee in the purchasing department and a supplier or between an employee in the sales department and a customer).

- **Management Override.** Management can overrule prescribed policies or procedures for illegitimate purposes such as personal gain or enhanced presentation of an entity's financial condition or compliance status (e.g., inflating reported earnings to increase a bonus pay-out or the market value of the entity's stock, or to hide violations of debt covenant agreements or noncompliance with laws or regulations). Override practices include making deliberate misrepresentations to auditors and others such as by issuing false documents to support the recording of fictitious sales transactions.

- **Costs Versus Benefits.** The cost of an entity's internal control structure should not exceed the benefits that are expected to ensue. Because precise measurement of both costs and benefits usually is not possible, management must make both quantitative and qualitative estimates and judgments in evaluating the cost-benefit relationship.

As an example of the cost-benefit tradeoff, an entity could eliminate losses from bad checks by accepting only certified or cashiers' checks from customers. However, because of the possible adverse effects of such a policy on sales, most companies believe that requiring identification from the check writer offers reasonable assurance against this type of loss.

ROLES AND RESPONSIBILITIES

OBJECTIVE 4

Explain the roles and responsibilities of various parties for an entity's internal control structure.

The COSO report concludes that everyone in an organization has some responsibility for, and is actually a part of, the organization's internal control structure. In addition, several external parties, such as independent auditors and regulators, may contribute information useful to an organization in effecting control, but they are not responsible for the effectiveness of, nor a part of, the ICS. Several key responsible parties and their roles are as follows:

- **Management.** It is management's responsibility to establish and maintain an effective internal control structure. In particular, the chief executive officer should set the "tone at the top" for control consciousness throughout the organization, and see that all the components of internal control are in place as discussed further in the next section. Senior managers in charge of organizational units (divisions, etc.) should be accountable for controlling the activities of their units. Financial and accounting officers play a central role in designing, implementing, and monitoring an entity's financial reporting system, developing entitywide budgets and plans, tracking and analyzing performance, and preventing and detecting fraudulent financial reporting, all of which constitute a part of the ICS.
- **Board of Directors and Audit Committee.** Board members, as part of their general governance and oversight responsibilities, should determine that management meets its responsibilities for establishing and maintaining the internal control structure. The audit committee (or in its absence, the board itself) should be vigilant to identify instances of management override of controls or fraudulent financial reporting and to take appropriate action in such cases.
- **Internal Auditors.** Internal auditors should periodically examine and evaluate the adequacy of an entity's internal control structure and make recom-

mendations for improvements, but they do not have primary responsibility for establishing and maintaining the ICS.

- **Other Entity Personnel.** The roles and responsibilities of all other personnel who provide information to, or use information provided by, the internal control structure should be well defined and communicated. For example, all personnel should understand they have a responsibility to communicate any problems with noncompliance with the ICS or illegal acts of which they become aware to a higher level in the organization.
- **Independent Auditors.** As a result of procedures performed in an audit of financial statements, an external auditor may discover deficiencies in internal control that he or she communicates to management, the audit committee, or the board, together with recommendations for improvements. This applies primarily to financial reporting controls and to a lesser extent to compliance and operations controls. But because the auditor's study of a client's internal control structure in a financial statement audit is performed primarily to enable the auditor to properly plan the audit, it neither results in the expression of an opinion on the effectiveness of the internal control structure itself, nor can it be relied upon to identify all or necessarily even most significant weaknesses in the ICS. This is especially the case for areas of the audit where the auditor has adopted the primarily substantive approach as the preliminary audit strategy as discussed in Chapter 7. A CPA may undertake a separate attest engagement to examine and report to external parties on separate management assertions about an entity's internal control structure. Such an engagement, which is explained in Chapter 21, involves a more in-depth study of the ICS than is done in a financial statement audit.
- **Other External Parties.** Legislators and regulators establish minimum statutory and regulatory requirements for the establishment of internal controls by certain entities. The Foreign Corrupt Practices Act of 1977 mentioned earlier in this chapter is an example. Another example is the Federal Deposit Insurance Corporation Improvement Act of 1991 which requires that certain banks report on the effectiveness of their internal controls over financial reporting and that such reports be accompanied by an independent accountant's attestation report on management's assertions about effectiveness.

In the next section, we examine in detail the five components of an internal control structure.

LEARNING CHECK:

8-1 a. Who administers the Foreign Corrupt Practices Act of 1977 and to whom does it pertain?
    b. What provisions of the Act relate to internal control and how?

8-2 a. What recommendations regarding internal control were made by the National Commission on Fraudulent Financial Reporting?
    b. What is COSO, what were the two principal purposes of its efforts regarding internal control, and why did it undertake these efforts?

8-3 a. State the COSO definition of internal control.
    b. Identify four fundamental concepts reflected in the definition.

c. Which entity objectives and related internal controls are of primary relevance in a financial statement audit?

8-4 Identify and briefly describe several inherent limitations of internal control structures.

8-5 Identify several parties that have roles and responsibilities related to an entity's internal control structure and briefly describe their roles and responsibilities.

KEY TERMS:

Committee of Sponsoring Organizations (COSO), p. 254
Components of internal control, p. 255
Foreign Corrupt Practices Act of 1977 (FCPA), p. 253
Fundamental concepts, p. 255
Inherent limitations, p. 256
Internal control, p. 254
National Commission on Fraudulent Financial Reporting, p. 253

COMPONENTS OF AN INTERNAL CONTROL STRUCTURE

OBJECTIVE 5

Describe the five components of an internal control structure.

As noted previously, the COSO report identifies five interrelated **internal control structure components** as follows:

- Control environment.
- Risk assessment.
- Information and communication.
- Control activities.
- Monitoring.

Each of the five components includes numerous control policies and procedures that are needed to achieve entity objectives in each of the three categories of objectives identified previously—financial reporting, compliance, and operations.

Each internal control structure component is explained in turn in a following section. These explanations focus on the relationship of each component to those entity objectives and related internal controls in each category that are of greatest relevance to a financial statement audit—namely, those that are designed to prevent or detect material misstatements in the financial statements.

CONTROL ENVIRONMENT

The **control environment** sets the tone of an organization, influencing the control consciousness of its people. It is the foundation for all other components of internal control, providing discipline and structure.[3]

[3] This definition and those of the other four internal control structure components presented later in this chapter are based on a draft of the proposed revision of SAS 55 expected to be approved in 1995. The proposed SAS definitions, which focus on the relationship of the components to financial reporting, were extracted by the ASB from the broader definitions of the components presented in the COSO report.

Numerous factors comprise the control environment in an entity. Among these are the following:

- Integrity and ethical values.
- Commitment to competence.
- Board of directors and audit committee.
- Management's philosophy and operating style.
- Organizational structure.
- Assignment of authority and responsibility.
- Human resource policies and practices.

The extent to which each factor is formally addressed by an entity will vary based on such considerations as its size and maturity. These factors constitute a major part of an entity's culture. Brief discussions of each of these control environment factors follow.

Integrity and Ethical Values

Chapter 3 of this text explains the importance of professional ethics to the public accounting profession. Increasingly, constituents of businesses such as employees, customers, and suppliers, and the public at large, are demanding high standards of **integrity and ethical values** on the part of business managers as well. The COSO report notes that managers of well-run entities have in turn increasingly accepted the view that "ethics pays—that ethical behavior is good business."

In order to emphasize the importance of integrity and ethical values among all personnel of an organization, the CEO and other members of top management should

- *Set the tone by example,* by themselves consistently demonstrating integrity and practicing high standards of ethical behavior.
- *Communicate* to all employees, verbally and through written policy statements and codes of conduct, that the same is expected of them, that each employee has a responsibility to report known or suspected violations to a higher level in the organization, and that violations will result in penalties.
- *Provide moral guidance* to any employees whose poor moral backgrounds have made them ignorant regarding what is right and wrong.
- *Reduce or eliminate incentives and temptations* that might lead individuals to engage in dishonest, illegal, or unethical acts. Examples of incentives for negative behavior include placing undue emphasis on short-term results or meeting unrealistic performance targets, and bonus and profit-sharing plans with terms that in the absence of necessary controls might elicit fraudulent financial reporting practices. Examples of temptations include the absence of other essential factors in a good control environment such as an ineffective board of directors and lack of clarity in the assignment of authority and responsibility.

Commitment to Competence

To achieve entity objectives, personnel at every level in the organization must possess the requisite knowledge and skills needed to perform their jobs effectively. **Commitment to competence** includes management's consideration of the knowledge and skills needed, and the mix of intelligence, training, and experience required to develop that competence. For example, meeting financial reporting objectives in a large publicly held company generally requires higher levels of competence on the part of chief financial officers and accounting personnel than would be the case for a small privately held company.

Board of Directors and Audit Committee

The composition of the **board of directors and audit committee** and the manner in which they exercise their governance and oversight responsibilities have a major impact on the control environment. Factors that affect the effectiveness of the board and audit committee include their independence from management which relates to the proportion of outside directors, the experience and stature of their members, the extent of their involvement and scrutiny of management's activities, the appropriateness of their actions, the degree to which they raise and pursue difficult questions with management, and the nature and extent of their interaction with internal and external auditors. As noted previously, an audit committee comprised solely of outside directors can contribute significantly to an entity's meeting its financial reporting objectives by exercising oversight over financial reporting and by enhancing the independence of the external auditors.

Management's Philosophy and Operating Style

Many characteristics may form a part of **management's philosophy and operating style** and have an impact on the control environment. These characteristics include management's

- Approach to taking and monitoring business risks.
- Reliance on informal face-to-face contacts with key managers versus a formal system of written policies, performance indicators, and exception reports.
- Attitudes and actions toward financial reporting.
- Conservative or aggressive selection from available alternative accounting principles.
- Conscientiousness and conservatism in developing accounting estimates.
- Attitudes toward information processing and accounting functions and personnel.

The last four characteristics are of particular significance in assessing the control environment over financial reporting.

Organizational Structure

An **organizational structure** contributes to an entity's ability to meet its objectives by providing an overall framework for planning, executing, controlling, and monitoring the entity's activities. Developing an organizational structure for an entity involves determining the key areas of authority and responsibility and appropriate lines of reporting. These will depend in part on the entity's size and the nature of its activities. An entity's organizational structure is usually depicted in an organization chart that should accurately reflect lines of authority and reporting relationships. An auditor needs to understand these relationships to properly assess the control environment and how it may impact the effectiveness of particular control policies and procedures.

Assignment of Authority and Responsibility

The **assignment of authority and responsibility** is an extension of the development of an organizational structure. It includes the particulars of how and to whom authority and responsibility for all entity activities are assigned, and should enable each individual to know (1) how his or her actions interrelate with those of others in contributing to the achievement of the entity's objectives and (2) for what each individual will be held accountable. Written job descriptions should delineate specific duties and reporting relationships. This factor also includes policies dealing with appropriate business practices, knowledge and experience of key personnel, and resources provided for carrying out duties.

Human Resource Policies and Practices

A fundamental concept of internal control stated previously is that it is effected or implemented by people. Thus, for the internal control structure to be effective, it is critical that **human resource policies and practices** be employed that will ensure the entity's personnel possess the expected levels of integrity, ethical values, and competence. Such practices include well-developed recruiting policies and screening processes in hiring; orientation of new personnel to the entity's culture and operating style; training policies that communicate prospective roles and responsibilities; disciplinary actions for violations of expected behavior; evaluating, counseling, and promoting people based on periodic performance appraisals; and compensation programs that motivate and reward superior performance while avoiding disincentives to ethical behavior.

This concludes the description of control environment factors, any one of which may affect the effectiveness of each of the remaining four components of an internal control structure that are discussed next.

RISK ASSESSMENT

Risk assessment for financial reporting purposes is an entity's identification, analysis, and management of risks relevant to the preparation of financial statements that are fairly presented in conformity with generally accepted accounting principles.

Management's risk assessment for financial reporting purposes is similar to the external auditor's concern with inherent risks as explained in Chapter 7. Both are concerned with the relationship of the risks to specific financial statement assertions and the related activities of recording, processing, summarizing, and reporting financial data. However, whereas management's purpose is to determine how to manage identified risks, the auditor's purpose is to evaluate the likelihood that material misstatements exist in the financial statements. To the extent that management appropriately identifies risks *and* successfully initiates control activities to address those risks, the auditor's combined assessment of inherent and control risks for related assertions will be lower. In some cases, however, management may simply decide to accept a risk without imposing controls because of cost or other considerations.

Management's risk assessment should include special consideration of the risks that can arise from changed circumstances, such as new areas of business or transactions that require unfamiliar accounting procedures, changes in accounting standards, new laws or regulations, changes associated with revisions to systems or new technologies used in information processing, rapid growth of the entity that puts a strain on the information processing and reporting functions, and changes in personnel involved in the information processing and reporting functions.

INFORMATION AND COMMUNICATION

The **information system** relevant to financial reporting objectives, which includes the **accounting system,** consists of the methods and records established to identify, assemble, analyze, classify, record, and report entity transactions (as well as events and conditions) and to maintain accountability for the related assets and liabilities. **Communication** involves providing a clear understanding of individual roles and responsibilities pertaining to the internal control structure over financial reporting.

As noted in the foregoing, a major focus of the accounting system is on transactions. **Transactions** consist of exchanges of assets and services between an entity and outside parties, as well as the transfer or use of assets and services within an entity. It follows that a major focus of control policies and procedures related to the accounting system is that transactions be handled in a way that prevents misstatements in management's financial statement assertions. Thus, an effective accounting system should

- Identify and record *only the valid* transactions of the entity that occurred in the current period (existence or occurrence assertion).
- Identify and record *all* valid transactions of the entity that occurred in the current period (completeness assertion).
- Ensure that recorded assets and liabilities are the result of transactions that produced entity rights to, or obligations for, those items (rights and obligations assertion).
- Measure the value of transactions in a manner that permits recording their proper monetary value in the financial statements (valuation or allocation assertion).
- Capture sufficient detail of all transactions to permit their proper presentation in the financial statements, including proper classification and required disclosures (presentation and disclosure assertion).

It may be noted that consistent with the introduction to the five categories of financial statement assertions provided in Chapter 5, the first two requirements above include determining the time period in which transactions occurred to permit their recording in the proper accounting period. Thus, controls related to establishing a proper cutoff are included here as part of the existence or occurrence and completeness assertions consistent with AU 326. Some auditors associate controls related to recording transactions in the correct accounting period with a separate objective or assertion identified as proper cutoff.

An entity's accounting system should provide a complete **audit trail** or **transaction trail** for each transaction. A transaction trail is a chain of evidence provided by coding, cross references, and documentation connecting account balances and other summary results with original transaction data. Transaction trails are essential both to management and auditors. For example, management uses the trail in responding to inquiries from customers or suppliers concerning account balances. Auditors use the trail in tracing and vouching transactions as explained in Chapter 5.

Communication includes making sure that personnel involved in the financial reporting system understand how their activities relate to the work of others both inside and outside the organization. This includes the role of the system in reporting exceptions to higher levels within the entity. Policy manuals, accounting and financial reporting manuals, a chart of accounts, and memoranda also constitute part of the **information and communication component** of the internal control structure.

CONTROL ACTIVITIES

Control activities are those policies and procedures that help ensure that management directives are carried out. They help ensure that necessary actions are taken to address risks to achievement of the entity's objectives. Control activities have various objectives and are applied at various organizational and functional levels.

Control activities that are relevant to a financial statement audit may be categorized in many different ways. One way is as follows:

- Information processing controls.
  - General controls.
  - Application controls.
    - Proper authorization
    - Documents and records.
    - Independent checks.
- Segregation of duties.
- Physical controls.
- Performance reviews.

These categories are explained in the following sections.

Information Processing Controls

Of particular relevance to an audit are **information processing controls** that address risks related to the authorization, completeness, and accuracy of transactions. Most entities, regardless of size, now use computers for information processing in general and for accounting systems in particular. In such cases, information processing controls are often further categorized as follows:

- **General controls** that pertain to data center operations as a whole and include controls related to such matters as data center organization, hardware and systems software acquisition and maintenance, and backup and recovery procedures.
- **Application controls** that pertain to the processing of specific types of transactions such as billing customers, paying suppliers, and preparing payroll.

Controls related to the processing of specific types of transactions, whether in a computerized or manual environment, may also be grouped as follows: (1) proper authorization, (2) documents and records, and (3) independent checks. Each of these types of application controls is discussed next. General controls and additional types of computerized application controls are explained further in Chapter 13.

PROPER AUTHORIZATION. A major purpose of **proper authorization** procedures is to assure that transactions are authorized by management personnel acting within the scope of their authority. Authorizations may be general or specific. The former relates to the general conditions under which transactions are authorized such as standard price lists for products and credit policies for charge sales. The latter relates to the granting of the authorization on a case-by-case basis. This may occur, for example, in nonroutine transactions, such as major capital expenditures and capital stock issues. Specific authorization may also apply to routine transactions that exceed the limits prescribed in the general authorization such as granting credit to a customer who does not meet specified credit conditions because of extenuating circumstances.

In modern accounting systems, transactions are sometimes initiated by the computer. For example, some inventory programs generate purchase orders automatically when stock levels reach a predetermined reorder level, and transmit the orders electronically to suppliers' computers without human intervention. In such cases, management's authorization is encoded in the computer program.

There is a difference between management authorization and employee approval. For instance, acting within the scope of credit policies authorized by management, credit department personnel can approve credit to individual customers. Authorization procedures are also important in limiting access to assets, documents and records, and computer equipment, programs, and files as explained later in the section on Physical Controls.

Proper authorization procedures often have a direct effect on control risk for existence or occurrence assertions and, in some cases, valuation or allocation assertions. Authorization of transactions is usually followed by the execution of the transactions, thus relating to the existence or occurrence assertion. In addition, transactions are sometimes executed at an authorized price. For example, the board of directors may authorize the purchase of a subsidiary at a designated amount. In such case, the authorization relates to the valuation or allocation assertion for the acquisition.

DOCUMENTS AND RECORDS. **Documents** provide evidence of the occurrence of transactions and the price, nature, and terms of the transactions. Invoices, checks, contracts, and time tickets are illustrative of common types of documents. When duly signed or stamped, documents also provide a basis for establishing responsibility for the executing and recording of transactions. Prenumbered documents are useful in maintaining control and accountability. Prenumbering helps to assure (1) that all transactions are recorded and (2) that no transactions are recorded more than once. When prenumbering exists, all voided documents should be retained.

Documentation procedures should provide for the timely preparation of documents by operating personnel as transactions are executed. The recording of transactions is facilitated when documents are promptly forwarded to accounting. Documents should subsequently be filed in an orderly manner.

Records include employee earnings records, which show cumulative payroll data for each employee, and perpetual inventory records. Another type of record is daily summaries of documents issued, such as sales invoices and checks. The summaries are then independently compared with the sum of corresponding daily entries to determine whether all transactions have been recorded.

In some systems, documents and records may exist only in electronic format. Examples of documents and records control procedures and their relationship to control risk assessments for financial statement assertions include the following:

- Properly maintained records such as perpetual inventory records, accounts receivable master files, and employee earnings files relate to existence or occurrence assertions.
- The use of, and accounting for the sequence of, prenumbered documents relate to completeness assertions.
- Source documents such as sales invoices and checks provide the amounts to be used in recording transactions which relates directly to valuation or allocation assertions.

INDEPENDENT CHECKS. **Independent checks** involve the verification of (1) work previously performed by other individuals or departments or (2) the proper valuation of recorded amounts. Examples of independent checks and the assertions to which they relate are as follows:

- A shipping clerk verifies the agreement of goods received from the warehouse with the details on a duplicate copy of the approved sales order before shipping the goods (existence or occurrence and completeness assertions).
- A sales supervisor checks prices on invoices prepared by billing clerks to an authorized price list before mailing them (valuation or allocation assertion).
- A treasurer compares the amounts on checks prepared by accounts payable personnel with amounts on supporting documentation before signing the checks (valuation or allocation assertion).
- An accounting supervisor verifies the agreement of the amount shown on a receipted bank deposit slip received from the cashier with a computer printout of the totals posted to accounts receivable and cash for the day's cash remittances from customers (existence or occurrence, completeness, and valuation or allocation assertions).

- A routine in a computer program compares a computer-generated total of credits posted to accounts receivable with a manually prepared batch total keyed in at the beginning of the computer run and prints the result (existence or occurrence, completeness, and valuation or allocation assertions).

Independent checks may be made with varying degrees of frequency. Manual clerical checks may be made daily on all or selected transactions. Computer-programmed controls may be applied to batches of transactions processed together or to individual transaction entries.

Segregation of Duties

Segregation of duties involves ensuring that individuals do not perform incompatible duties. Duties are considered incompatible from a control standpoint when it is possible for an individual to commit an error or irregularity and then be in a position to conceal it in the normal course of his or her duties. For example, an individual who processes cash remittances from customers should not also have authority to approve and record credits to customers' accounts for sales returns and allowances or write-offs of bad debts. In such a case, the individual could steal a cash remittance and cover the theft by recording a sales return or allowance or bad-debt write-off.

This type of reasoning supports segregation of duties in the following four types of situations:

- **Responsibility for executing a transaction, recording the transaction, and maintaining custody of the assets resulting from the transaction should be assigned to different individuals or departments.** For example, purchasing department personnel should initiate purchase orders, accounting department personnel should record the goods received, and storeroom personnel should assume custody of the goods. Before recording the purchase, accounting personnel should ascertain that the purchase was authorized and that the goods ordered were received. The accounting entry, in turn, provides a basis of accountability for the goods in the storeroom.
- **The various steps involved in executing a transaction should be assigned to different individuals or departments.** Thus, in executing a sales transaction in a manufacturing company, responsibility for authorizing the sale, filling the order, shipping the goods, and billing the customer may be assigned to different individuals.
- **Responsibility for certain accounting operations should be segregated.** For example, in a manual accounting system, different personnel should maintain the general ledger and the accounts receivable subsidiary ledger, and personnel involved in recording cash receipts and disbursements should not reconcile the bank accounts.
- **There should be proper segregation of duties within the electronic data processing (EDP) department and between EDP and user departments.** Several functions within EDP such as systems analysis, programming, computer operations, and data control should be segregated. In addition, EDP should not correct data submitted by user departments, and should be organizationally independent of user departments. Organization and operation controls for EDP departments are explained further in Chapter 13.

When duties are segregated in a way that the work of one individual automatically provides a cross-check on the work of another individual, the added benefit of an independent check results. In this connection, it may be observed that an independent check always involves segregating duties, but segregating duties does not always involve an independent check.

Following are examples of how segregation of duties affects control risk for three assertions:

- Separating custody of assets from maintaining the accounting record of the assets reduces the risk of theft because the perpetrator will not have an opportunity to cover up the theft by eliminating the record of the assets (existence or occurrence assertion).
- Segregation of duties for processing cash disbursements transactions and reconciling the bank accounts reduces the risk of unrecorded payments by check because they would be detected in the reconciliation process (completeness assertion).
- Segregating responsibility for approving credit from initiating sales orders reduces the risk of uncollectible accounts that might result from sales made to bad credit risks to achieve sales targets or boost commissions (valuation or allocation assertion).

Physical Controls

Physical controls are concerned with limiting the following two types of access to assets and important records: (1) direct physical access and (2) indirect access through the preparation or processing of documents such as sales orders and disbursement vouchers that authorize the use or disposition of assets. Thus, these controls pertain primarily to security devices and measures for the safekeeping of assets, documents, records, and computer programs and files. Security devices include on-site safeguards such as fireproof safes and locked storerooms, and off-site safeguards such as bank deposit vaults and certified public warehouses. Security measures include limiting access to storage areas to authorized personnel. Such controls reduce the risk of theft and are thus relevant in assessing control risk for existence or occurrence assertions.

Physical controls also involve the use of mechanical and electronic equipment in executing transactions. For example, cash registers help to assure that all cash receipts transactions are rung up, and they provide locked-in summaries of daily receipts. Such controls are relevant in assessing control risk for completeness assertions.

When EDP equipment is used, access to the computer, computer records, data files, and programs should be restricted to authorized personnel. The use of passwords, keys, and identification badges provide means of controlling access. When such safeguards are in place, control risk may be reduced for various existence or occurrence, completeness, and valuation or allocation assertions related to transaction classes and accounts processed in EDP.

Finally, physical control activities include periodic counts of assets and comparison with amounts shown on control records. Examples include petty cash counts and physical inventories. These activities may be relevant in assessing existence or occurrence, completeness, and valuation or allocation assertions as discussed further in subsequent chapters.

Performance Reviews

Examples of **performance reviews** include management review and analysis of

- Reports that summarize the detail of account balances such as an aged trial balance of accounts receivable or reports of sales activity by region, division, salesperson, or product line.
- Actual performance versus budgets, forecasts, or prior period amounts.
- The relationship of different sets of data such as nonfinancial operating data and financial data (for example, comparison of hotel occupancy statistics with revenue data).

Although management's use of these types of reviews may primarily be to assess performance, they may serve another purpose similar to the auditor's use of analytical procedures in audit planning. That is, by relating the reported data to its own expectations, management may be able to detect instances where there is a higher risk of a misstatement having occurred. Such misstatements might involve existence or occurrence, completeness, valuation or allocation, or presentation and disclosure assertions.

This concludes the discussion of the control activities component of an internal control structure. We now consider the final component, monitoring.

MONITORING

Monitoring is a process that assesses the quality of the internal control structure's performance over time. It involves assessment by appropriate personnel of the design and operation of controls on a suitably timely basis to determine that the ICS is operating as intended and that it is modified as appropriate for changes in conditions.

Monitoring can occur through *ongoing activities.* For example, problems with the internal control structure may come to management's attention through complaints received from customers about billing errors or from suppliers about payment problems, or from alert managers who receive reports with information that differs significantly from their first-hand knowledge of operations. Monitoring can also occur through *separate periodic evaluations.* For example, internal auditors generally assess different parts of an entity's ICS at various intervals and report weaknesses to management or the audit committee with recommendations for improvements where appropriate. Finally, management may receive information from regulators, such as bank examiners, and external auditors about weaknesses and recommended improvements.

APPLICATION OF COMPONENTS TO SMALL AND MIDSIZE ENTITIES

All five internal control structure components are applicable to entities of all sizes. However, the degree of formality and the specifics of how the components are implemented may vary considerably for practical and sound reasons. AU 319 identifies the following factors to be considered in deciding on how to implement each of the five components:

- The entity's size.
- Its organization and ownership characteristics.
- The nature of its business.
- The diversity and complexity of its operations.
- Its methods of processing data.
- Its applicable legal and regulatory requirements.

Following are some of the differences typical of smaller versus larger entities: Smaller entities are less likely to have written codes of conduct, outside directors, formal policy manuals, sufficient personnel to provide for optimal segregation of duties, or internal auditors. However, they can mitigate these conditions by nonetheless developing a culture that places an emphasis on integrity, ethical values, and competence. In addition, owner-managers can assume responsibility for certain critical tasks such as approving credit, signing checks, reviewing bank reconciliations, and monitoring customer balances and approving the write-off of uncollectible accounts. Moreover, the familiarity that managers of smaller entities can have with all critical areas of operations, and the simpler and shorter lines of communication, can obviate the need for numerous other formalized control activities that are essential in larger entities.

This concludes the discussion of the components of an internal control structure. A summary of the components is presented in Figure 8-1.

LEARNING CHECK:

8-6 a. Name the five components of an internal control structure.
 b. In a financial statement audit, the auditor focuses on each component's relationship to entity objectives and related controls that are designed to do what?

8-7 a. List the factors that comprise the control environment.
 b. State four things the CEO and other members of top management should do to emphasize the importance of integrity and ethical values among all entity personnel.

8-8 How is management's risk assessment for financial reporting purposes similar to and different from the auditor's risk assessment?

8-9 a. In addition to its being a part of the information and communication component, how would you describe the *accounting system?*
 b. What are the attributes of an effective accounting system?
 c. Relate each of the attributes identified in (b) above with one or more of the five categories of financial statement assertions.

8-10 a. Information and processing controls is one category of control activities. What risks are addressed by these controls?
 b. Name two major subcategories of information processing controls in a computerized system.
 c. Name three subcategories of application controls that apply to both manual and computerized systems.

FIGURE 8-1 • COMPONENTS OF AN INTERNAL CONTROL STRUCTURE

Component	Description Relative to Financial Reporting	Key Factors
Control environment	Sets the tone for an organization; influences control consciousness of its people; is the foundation for all other components of the ICS.	Control environment factors: • Integrity and ethical values. • Commitment to competence. • Board of directors and audit committee. • Management's philosophy and operating style. • Organizational structure. • Assignment of authority and responsibility. • Human resource policies and practices.
Risk assessment	Entity's identification, analysis, and management of risks relevant to the preparation of financial statements that are fairly presented in conformity with GAAP.	Process should consider: • Relationship of risks to specific financial statement assertions and the related activities of recording, processing, summarizing, and reporting financial data. • Internal and external events and circumstances. • Special consideration of changed circumstances. Similar to auditor's assessment of inherent risk.
Information and communication	The information system includes the *accounting system* and consists of the methods and records established to identify, assemble, analyze, classify, record, and report entity transactions and maintain accountability for related assets and liabilities; *communication* involves providing a clear understanding of individual roles and responsibilities pertaining to the ICS over financial reporting.	Focus of accounting system is on transactions: • Effective accounting system should result in handling of transactions in a way that prevents misstatements in management's financial statement assertions. • System should provide a complete *audit* or *transaction trail*. Includes policy manuals, chart of accounts, and memoranda.
Control activities	Policies and procedures that help ensure that management directives are carried out and that necessary actions are taken to address risks to achievement of entity objectives; have various objectives and are applied at various organizational and functional levels.	Categories: • Information processing controls. ◦ General controls. ◦ Application controls. ▪ Proper authorization. ▪ Documents and records. ▪ Independent checks. • Segregation of duties. • Physical controls. • Performance reviews.
Monitoring	Process by appropriate personnel that assesses the quality of the ICS's performance over time; includes assessment of design, whether operating as intended, and whether modified as appropriate for changed conditions.	Can occur through: • Ongoing activities. • Separate periodic evaluations. May include input from: • Internal sources such as management and internal auditors. • External sources such as customers, suppliers, regulators, and external auditors.

8-11 a. What is the objective of segregation of duties? Explain.
b. Identify four types of situations in which appropriate segregation of duties may be important.

8-12 Differentiate between (a) independent checks, (b) performance reviews, and (c) monitoring.

KEY TERMS:

Accounting system, p. 263
Application controls, p. 265
Assignment of authority and responsibility, p. 262
Audit trail, p. 264
Board of directors and audit committee, p. 261
Commitment to competence, p. 261
Control activities, p. 264
Control environment, p. 259
Documents and records, p. 266
General controls, p. 265
Human resource policies and practices, p. 262
Independent checks, p. 266
Information and communication component, p. 264
Information processing controls, p. 264
Information system, p. 263
Integrity and ethical values, p. 260
Internal control structure components, p. 259
Management's philosophy and operating style, p. 261
Monitoring, p. 269
Organizational structure, p. 261
Performance reviews, p. 269
Physical controls, p. 268
Proper authorization, p. 265
Risk assessment, p. 262
Segregation of duties, p. 267
Transaction trail, p. 264
Transactions, p. 263

OBTAINING AN UNDERSTANDING OF INTERNAL CONTROL STRUCTURE COMPONENTS

OBJECTIVE 6

Explain the understanding of the internal control structure components needed to plan an audit and how the understanding is used.

The auditor's methodology for meeting the second standard of field work involves three major activities:

- Obtaining a sufficient understanding of the components of the internal control structure to plan the audit.
- Assessing control risk for each significant assertion contained in the account balance, transaction class, and disclosure components of the financial statements.
- Designing substantive tests for each significant financial statement assertion.

The first of these activities is the subject of the remainder of this chapter. The second and third activities are addressed in Chapters 9 and 10, respectively.

Obtaining an understanding involves performing procedures to

- Understand the design of policies and procedures pertaining to each ICS component.
- Determine whether the policies and procedures have been placed in operation.

The latter extends only to whether the control policies and procedures are being used, not to their *effectiveness* which is part of assessing control risk.

AU 319 indicates that the understanding of the ICS components should be used by the auditor to

- Identify types of potential misstatements.
- Consider factors that affect the risk of material misstatements.
- Design substantive tests to provide reasonable assurance of detecting the misstatements related to specific assertions.

Following is an example of the application of this approach:

Based on the understanding of an entity's internal control structure, the auditor identifies overstatement of sales and accounts receivable through the recording of fictitious sales transactions (existence or occurrence assertion) as a potential misstatement. A factor that affects this risk, learned while obtaining an understanding of the control environment, is that because of the desire to show favorable results before a public stock offering scheduled for the next year, top management is exerting heavy pressure on division managers to show significant growth in sales in spite of a sluggish economy. Moreover, knowledge obtained from the understanding of control activities in each division reveals that sales are recorded based only on sales invoices, which could be fictitious because there is no requirement for matching approved sales order forms and shipping documents that would help to establish the validity of the transactions. Accordingly, the auditor decides to include the following substantive tests to obtain evidence concerning the existence or occurrence assertion for sales and accounts receivable: (1) vouch a sample of recorded sales transactions to supporting sales invoices *and* corresponding entries in perpetual inventory records; (2) perform analytical procedures to relate sales volume data to purchases and inventory data, (3) confirm a sample of accounts receivable balances to obtain evidence of the validity of billed sales that have not yet been collected; and (4) examine the volume of sales returns recorded early in the following year to determine the possibility of unauthorized shipments to customers before year end.

In summary, effective audit planning requires the auditor to know what misstatements can occur in an entity's financial statements and the likelihood of their occurrence in order to properly design substantive tests.

EFFECTS OF PRELIMINARY AUDIT STRATEGIES

In Chapter 7, two alternative preliminary audit strategies for planning the audit of significant financial statement assertions are identified and explained—(1) the primarily substantive approach and (2) the lower assessed level of control risk approach. An understanding of the ICS is needed regardless of which strategy is chosen. But the level of understanding of ICS components sufficient to plan different parts of the audit under each audit strategy is a matter of professional judgment. Normally, a greater understanding of ICS policies and procedures is needed under the lower assessed level of control risk approach than under the primarily substantive approach. This is particularly true of the control activities component as explained further in a subsequent section.

AU 319 suggests several other factors that should be considered in reaching a judgment about the required level of understanding as follows:

- Knowledge of the client from previous audits.
- Preliminary assessments of inherent risk and materiality (as explained in Chapter 7).
- An understanding of the industry in which the entity operates.
- The complexity and sophistication of the entity's operations and accounting system.

Some specific examples of differences in the required level of understanding needed under each audit strategy are indicated in the following discussions of each component.

UNDERSTANDING OF CONTROL ENVIRONMENT

The auditor should obtain sufficient knowledge of this internal control structure component to understand (1) the attitude, awareness, and actions of management and the board of directors concerning the control environment and (2) the pervasive and specific effects these factors may have on the effectiveness of the other control structure components. The auditor should understand the substance, not just the form, of management's policies and procedures for this component. For example, management's establishment of a formal written code of conduct for entity personnel will mean little if management itself violates the code or acts in a manner that condones violations by others.

The required level of understanding of several of the control environment factors, such as management's philosophy and operating style, organizational structure, and board of directors or audit committee, will ordinarily be the same for each audit strategy. For some factors, however, additional knowledge may be necessary for the lower assessed level of control risk approach. Thus, in contrast to a basic understanding of the entity's human resource policies and practices that would be obtained under the primarily substantive approach, the auditor may want specific knowledge about the hiring, experience, and training of computer personnel and others who have important control responsibilities, such as cashiers, warehouse custodians, and payroll supervisors. For example, knowledge that the entity employs trustworthy and competent warehouse custodians may be useful in assessing control risk for the existence or occurrence assertion for inventories.

UNDERSTANDING OF RISK ASSESSMENT

The auditor should determine how management identifies risks relevant to the fair presentation of financial statements, the care with which it assesses the significance of those risks, and how it decides on control activities or other actions to address those risks. Also of importance is an understanding of how management identifies and reacts to changes in both external and internal circumstances that might affect risks related to financial reporting. A more extensive understanding of this component is ordinarily required under the lower assessed level of control risk strategy than under the primarily substantive approach.

UNDERSTANDING OF INFORMATION AND COMMUNICATION

An entity's information system significantly affects the risk of material misstatements in the financial statements. In particular, a well-designed and effectively operating accounting system should provide reliable accounting data, whereas a poorly designed system will have contrary results.

AU 319 indicates that the auditor should obtain sufficient knowledge of the *information system relevant to financial reporting* to understand

- The classes of transactions in the entity's operations that are significant to the financial statements.
- How those transactions are initiated.
- The accounting records, supporting documents, and specific accounts in the financial statements involved in the processing and reporting of transactions.
- The accounting processing involved from the initiation of a transaction to its inclusion in the financial statements, including how the computer is used to process data.
- The financial reporting process used to prepare the entity's financial statements, including significant accounting estimates and disclosures.

Classes of transactions that generally have a significant effect on the financial statements include sales, purchases, cash receipts, cash disbursements, payroll, and, if applicable, manufacturing. There is often a high volume of these transactions which require extensive accounting processing and involve a higher risk of misstatements, necessitating a greater understanding by the auditor. Conversely, in a given period for a given entity, investing and financing transactions may be minimal, requiring less of an understanding. The auditor should also obtain an understanding of how the entity *communicates* roles and responsibilities and other significant matters related to financial reporting.

Generally, greater levels of understanding of the information and communication component are required for the more sophisticated and complex parts of information systems that affect assertions for which the auditor elects to use the lower assessed level of control risk approach.

UNDERSTANDING OF CONTROL ACTIVITIES

In obtaining an understanding of the control environment, risk assessment, information and communication, and monitoring components of the internal control structure, the auditor will invariably obtain knowledge about some control activities. This level of understanding may suffice for purposes of audit planning for areas of the audit for which the auditor has decided to use a primarily substantive approach. Because in such cases the auditor assesses control risk as high or maximum and plans extensive substantive tests, it generally is neither efficient nor necessary to acquire an understanding of additional control activities pertaining to the related financial statement assertions. However, for areas of the audit for which the auditor hopes to use the lower assessed level of control risk approach, he or she will likely want to obtain an understanding of additional control activities relevant to specific assertions. Procedures for obtaining the required levels of understanding are explained in a later section.

UNDERSTANDING OF MONITORING

It is important to understand the types of activities used by the entity to monitor the effectiveness of the internal control structure components in meeting financial reporting objectives. Knowledge should also be obtained as to how corrective actions are initiated based on information gleaned from the monitoring activities.

Information obtained from monitoring procedures performed by internal auditors may be especially useful to external auditors. For example, the external auditor might obtain an understanding of the design of a new computerized sales and accounts receivable system by reviewing the internal auditors' flowcharts of the system. Similarly, a review of internal auditors' reports may reveal that specific ICS policies and procedures have been placed in operation.

The external auditor is not required to test the work of internal auditors that pertains to obtaining an understanding, but he or she may elect to do so. Obtaining an understanding, however, should include making inquiries of appropriate management and internal audit personnel concerning such matters as (1) the internal audit staff's standing within the entity, (2) its activities, (3) its adherence to internal auditing professional standards, and (4) the nature, timing, and extent of its work.

PROCEDURES TO OBTAIN AN UNDERSTANDING

In Chapter 5, three classes of audit procedures were introduced, one of which was labeled *Procedures to Obtain Understanding of Internal Control Structure.* The **procedures to obtain an understanding** consist of

OBJECTIVE 7

Indicate the audit procedures used to obtain the understanding.

- Reviewing previous experience with the client.
- Inquiring of appropriate management and supervisory and staff personnel.
- Inspecting documents and records.
- Observing entity activities and operations.

When the auditor has previous experience with the client, the previous year's working papers should contain a great deal of information relevant to the current year's audit. For example, the previous year's conclusions about strengths and weaknesses in the internal control structure can be used as the starting point, with the auditor making inquiries about changes that may have occurred in the current year that would affect the previous conclusions. The working papers should also contain information about the types of misstatements found in prior audits and their causes. For example, the working papers should show whether misstatements resulted from (1) lack of adequate controls, (2) deliberate circumvention of prescribed controls, or (3) unintentional noncompliance with prescribed controls by inexperienced personnel. The auditor can follow up on this information to determine whether corrective actions have been taken.

Relevant documents and records of the entity should be inspected. Examples include organization charts, policy manuals, the chart of accounts, accounting ledgers, journals, and source documents, transaction flowcharts, and reports used by management in performance reviews such as comparative reports showing actual and budgeted data and variances. These inspections will inevitably lead to additional inquiries about specific controls and changes in conditions. Observation of the performance of some controls will be needed to determine that they have been placed in operation.

To reinforce the understanding of some aspects of the accounting system and certain control activities, some auditors perform a **transaction walk-through review.** To perform the review, one or a few transactions within each major class of transactions is traced through the transaction trail, and the related control policies and procedures are identified and observed.

LEARNING CHECK:

8-13 a. Identify two matters that should be covered in obtaining an understanding of the internal control structure.
b. How should knowledge of the ICS components be used by the auditor?

8-14 a. What effect does the auditor's choice of a preliminary audit strategy for a portion of the audit have on the level of understanding needed for related internal control structure policies and procedures?
b. What other factors affect the auditor's judgment about the required level of understanding?

8-15 a. What should the auditor understand based on obtaining sufficient knowledge of the factors comprising the control environment component of the ICS?
b. What aspects of the information system relevant to financial reporting should be included in the auditor's understanding?

8-16 a. What procedures can be used in obtaining an understanding of the ICS?
b. What is a *transaction walk-through review*?

KEY TERMS:

Obtaining an understanding, p. 272
Procedures to obtain an understanding, p. 276
Transaction walk-through review, p. 277

DOCUMENTING THE UNDERSTANDING

OBJECTIVE 8

State the requirements, and alternate methods, for documenting the understanding.

Documenting the understanding of the internal control structure components is required in all audits. Documentation in the working papers may take the form of completed questionnaires, flowcharts, decision tables (in a computerized accounting system), and narrative memoranda. In an audit of a large entity involving a combination of audit strategies, all four types of documentation may be used for different parts of the understanding. In an audit of a small entity where the primarily substantive approach predominates, a single memorandum may suffice to document the understanding of all the components.

The auditor may document the understanding concurrent with obtaining it. For example, auditors frequently record clients' responses to inquiries in preprinted questionnaires that become part of the working papers. Auditors can also document the understanding of parts of the entity's accounting system and certain control activities by preparing flowcharts or including in the working papers flowcharts provided by the client for the auditor's use. In a repeat engagement, it may only be necessary to update questionnaires, flowcharts, or narrative memoranda carried forward from the prior year's working papers. Documentation should pertain only to portions of the internal control structure components that are relevant to the audit.

FIGURE 8-2 • EXCERPTS FROM INTERNAL CONTROL QUESTIONNAIRE —CONTROL ENVIRONMENT

Client Amalgamated Products, Inc. **Balance Sheet Date** 12/31/x1

Completed by RSC **Date** 9/12/x1 **Reviewed by** JEG **Date** 9/29/x1

Internal Control Questionnaire
Component: Control Environment

Question	Yes, No, N/A	Comments
Integrity and ethical values: 1. Does management set the "tone at the top" by demonstrating a commitment to integrity and ethics through both its words and deeds? 2. Have appropriate entity policies regarding acceptable business practices, conflicts of interest, and codes of conduct been established and adequately communicated? 3. Have incentives and temptations that might lead to unethical behavior been reduced or eliminated?	Yes Yes Yes	Management is conscious of setting an example. Entity does not have a formal code of conduct; expectations of employees included in a policy manual distributed to all employees. Profit sharing plan monitored by audit committee.
Board of directors and audit committee: 1. Are there regular meetings of the board and are minutes prepared on a timely basis? 2. Do board members have sufficient knowledge, experience, and time to serve effectively? 3. Is there an audit committee composed of outside directors?	Yes Yes No	Board consists of nine inside members, three of whom currently serve on audit committee. Consideration is being given to adding three outside members to board who would comprise the audit committee.
Management's philosophy and operating style: 1. Are business risks carefully considered and adequately monitored? 2. Is management's selection of accounting principles and development of accounting estimates consistent with objective and fair reporting? 3. Has management demonstrated a willingness to adjust the financial statements for material misstatements?	Yes Yes Yes	Management is conservative about business risks. Management has readily accepted all proposed adjustments in prior audits.
Human resource policies and practices: 1. Do existing personnel policies and procedures result in recruiting or developing competent and trustworthy people necessary to support an effective internal control structure? 2. Do personnel understand the duties and procedures applicable to their jobs? 3. Is the turnover of personnel in key positions at an acceptable level?	Yes Yes Yes	Formal job descriptions are provided for all positions. Normal turnover.

QUESTIONNAIRES

A **questionnaire** consists of a series of questions about ICS policies and procedures that the auditor considers necessary to prevent material misstatements in the financial statements. The questions are usually phrased so that either a Yes, No, or N/A (not applicable) answer results, with a Yes answer indicating a favorable condition. Space is also provided for comments such as who performs a control procedure and how often.

Standardized questionnaires are used on a majority of audits. In some cases, questionnaires developed for a particular industry or even a particular client are used. Some firms use different questionnaires for large versus small clients. A single questionnaire may be developed to cover all five ICS components, or there may be separate questionnaires for each component. In the case of the accounting system and related control activities, there may be separate questionnaires dealing with different classes of transactions such as sales or cash disbursements. Combined, these questionnaires may be many pages long.

Excerpts from two questionnaires are illustrated in Figures 8-2 and 8-3. These illustrations pertain to parts of the control environment and control activities

FIGURE 8-3 • EXCERPTS FROM INTERNAL CONTROL QUESTIONNAIRE—CONTROL ACTIVITIES

Client Amalgamated Products, Inc. **Balance Sheet Date** 12/31/x1
Completed by RSC **Date** 10/12/x1 **Reviewed by** JEG **Date** 10/29/x1

Internal Control Questionnaire
Component: Control Activities

Question	Yes, No, N/A	Comments
Cash disbursements transactions:		
1. Is there an approved payment voucher with supporting documents for each check prepared?	Yes	
2. Are prenumbered checks used and accounted for?	Yes	
3. Are unused checks stored in a secure area?	Yes	Safe in treasurer's office.
4. Are only authorized personnel permitted to sign checks?	Yes	Only the treasurer and assistant treasurer can sign checks.
5. Do check signers verify agreement of details of check and payment voucher before signing?	Yes	
6. Are vouchers and supporting documents cancelled after payment?	Yes	Vouchers and all supporting documents are stamped "Paid."
7. Is there segregation of duties for:		
a. Approving payment vouchers and signing checks?	Yes	
b. Signing checks and recording checks?	Yes	
8. Is there an independent check of agreement of daily summary of checks issued with entry to cash disbursements?	No	Comparison currently made by assistant treasurer; will recommend comparison be performed by asst. controller.
9. Are there periodic independent reconciliations of checking accounts?	Yes	Performed by assistant controller.

components of an internal control structure. In Figure 8-3, it may be observed that there are questions related to several possible categories of control activities. For example, questions 1 and 4 pertain to authorization procedures, 2 and 6 to documents and records, 5, 8, and 9 to independent checks, 3 to physical controls, and 7a and b to segregation of duties. More importantly, the questions may also be linked to financial statement assertions. For example, 'No' answers to the questions listed below could signal the potential for misstatements in the indicated related assertions for cash disbursements:

- Questions 1, 4, 6, or 7a — Existence or occurrence
- Question 2, 3, 7b, 8, or 9 — Completeness
- Questions 5, 8, 9 — Valuation or allocation

Note that some questions pertain to more than one assertion.

Some auditing firms have automated their internal control questionnaires. That is, the staff auditor enters the Yes, No, and N/A responses into a notebook computer as the information is being obtained from the client. The auditor's software then analyzes the pattern of responses across related questions and guides the auditor through subsequent steps in assessing control risk and designing substantive tests for specific financial statement assertions.

Some auditing firms also provide special training for staff in interviewing skills used in administering questionnaires. For example, by being alert to nonverbal signals given by interviewees, such as a hesitancy to respond, apparent lack of familiarity with controls, or undue nervousness during interviews, the auditor's understanding can be significantly enhanced.

As a means of documenting the understanding, questionnaires offer a number of advantages. They are usually developed by very experienced professionals and provide excellent guidance to the less experienced staff who may be obtaining understanding of a particular audit. They are relatively easy to use, and they significantly reduce the possibility of overlooking important internal control structure matters.

FLOWCHARTS

A **flowchart** is a schematic diagram using standardized symbols, interconnecting flow lines, and annotations that portray the steps involved in processing information through the accounting system. Flowcharts vary in the extent of detail shown. A broad overview flowchart containing just a few symbols can be prepared for the accounting system as a whole or for a particular transaction cycle such as the revenue cycle. In addition, very detailed flowcharts can be prepared depicting the processing of individual classes of transactions such as sales, cash receipts, purchases, cash disbursements, payroll, and manufacturing.

Detailed flowcharts should adequately display the following essential components:

- All significant operations performed in processing the class of transactions.
- The methods of processing (manual or computerized).
- The extent of segregation of duties by identifying each operation with a functional area, department, or individual.

FIGURE 8-4 • ILLUSTRATIVE PARTIAL FLOWCHART FOR PROCESSING OF MAIL RECEIPTS TRANSACTIONS

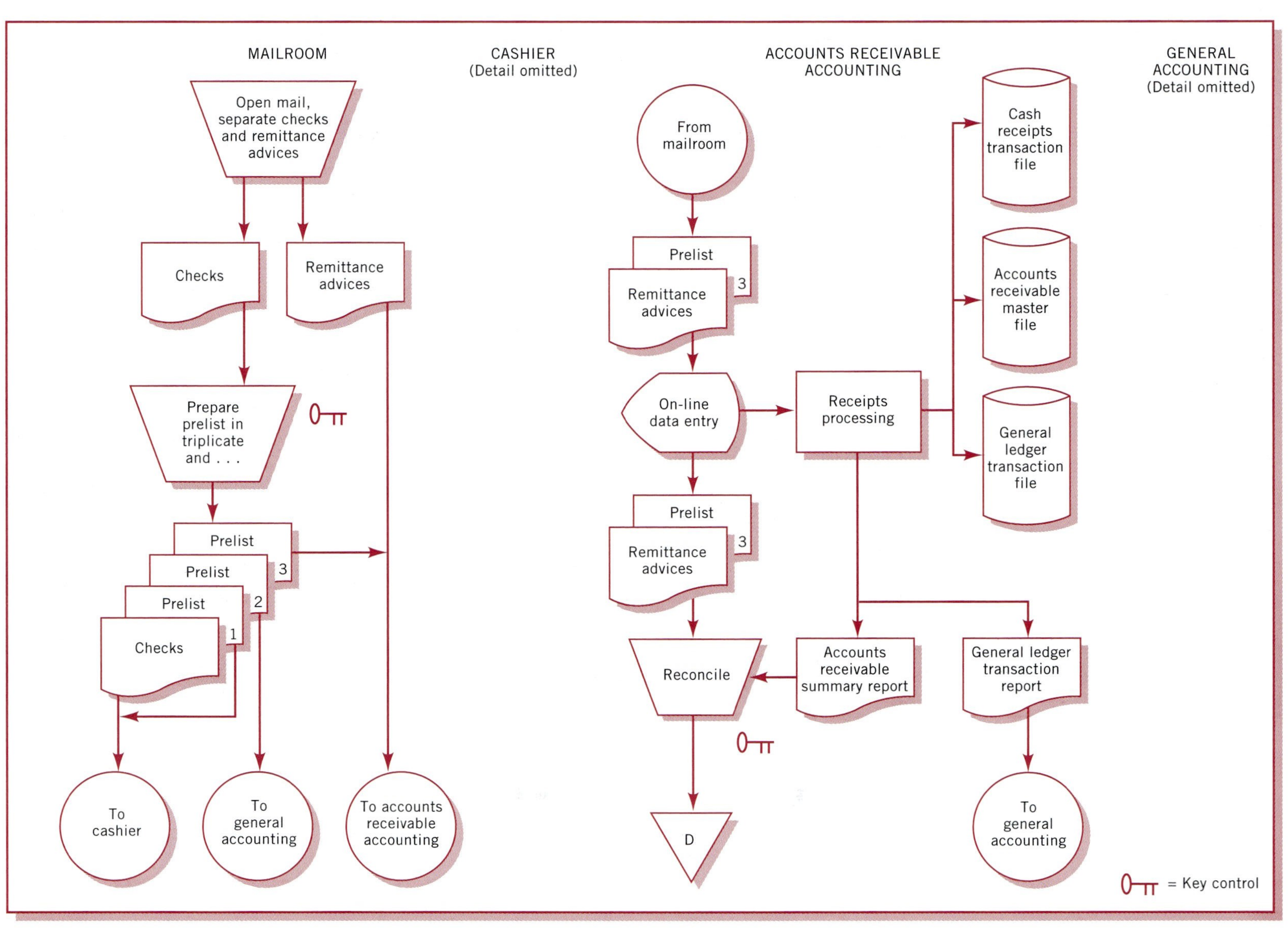

- The source, flow, and disposition of relevant copies of the documents, records, and reports involved in processing.

These essential components are illustrated in Figure 8-4 which is a *partial* flowchart of a system for processing cash (checks) and remittance advices received in the mail from customers. (An example of a remittance advice is the portion of a telephone bill or credit card statement that the customer returns with the payment.) A reading of the descriptions on selected flowchart symbols reveals the following four displayed operations: in the Mailroom—(1) opening the mail and separating the checks and remittance advices; (2) preparing a *prelist* (in triplicate) of the checks (this would show the amount of each remittance and the grand total); in Accounts Receivable Accounting—(3) entering the remittance data into the computer for processing; and (4) reconciling a computer-generated summary with the input documents. The first, second, and fourth operations involve manual processing which is indicated by the use of the trapeziodal-shaped symbols. The third operation is represented by the symbol labeled *On-line Data Entry* and the rectangular symbol labeled *Receipts Processing,* which indicate computer processes. The segregation of duties is indicated in this illustration by dividing the flowchart into four vertical partitions representing the four departments involved with the cash receipts processing (the details of only two of which are shown here to keep the illustration simple). Finally, the illustration shows the source, flow, and disposition of the following documents and records: (1) the remittance advices and checks received in the mail; (2) the three copies of the prelist of checks prepared in the mailroom, and (3) the two computer-generated reports that are produced as a result of entering the remittance data into the computer in Accounts Receivable Accounting. It may also be observed that the flowchart indicates the computerized receipts processing results in the updating of three computer files maintained on disk (the symbols in the Accounts Receivable Accounting partition that look like cans).

Once a flowchart is obtained from the client or prepared by the auditor, many auditors perform a transaction walk-through as described previously to test its accuracy and completeness. The flowchart should then be studied to identify strengths and weaknesses. For example, *key* symbols are used in Figure 8-4 to indicate the following strengths: (1) the preparation of a *Prelist* of cash remittances to establish immediate accountability for the total remittances received; (2) reconcilation of the computer-generated *Accounts Receivable Summary Report* with the *Prelist* which affords an opportunity to detect errors in entering the data into the computer. Any observed weaknesses could be annotated on the flowchart or written up in a memorandum.

A more complete illustration of flowcharting is presented in Appendix A to this chapter. In addition to extending the illustration of the system partially represented in Figure 8-4, the Appendix includes an explanation of additional standardized flowcharting symbols and some helpful guidelines for preparing flowcharts.

NARRATIVE MEMORANDA

A **narrative memorandum** consists of written comments concerning the auditor's consideration of the ICS. A memorandum may be used to supplement the other forms of documentation by summarizing the auditor's overall understanding of

FIGURE 8-5 • NARRATIVE MEMORANDUM DOCUMENTING UNDERSTANDING OF CONTROL ENVIRONMENT

CLIENT	Owmco, Inc.			**BALANCE SHEET DATE**	12/31		
Completed by:	m/w	**Date:**	9/30/X5	**Reviewed by:**	jp	**Date:**	11/02/X5
Updated by:	m/w	**Date:**	9/15/X6	**Reviewed by:**	jp	**Date:**	10/29/X6

Understanding of the Control Environment

The Company manufactures plastic fishing worms at one location and is managed by its sole owner, Ed Jones. Management of the company is dominated by Jones, who is responsible for marketing, purchasing, hiring, and approving major transactions. He has a good understanding of the business and the industry in which it operates. Jones believes that hiring experienced personnel is particularly important because there are no layers of supervisory personnel and thus, because of limited segregation of duties, few independent checks of employees' work. Jones has a moderate-to-conservative attitude toward business risks. The business has demonstrated consistent profitability and, because Jones considers lower taxes to be as important as financial results, he has a conservative attitude toward accounting estimates.

Jones and Pat Willis, the bookkeeper, readily consult with our firm on routine accounting questions, including the preparation of accounting estimates (tax accrual, inventory obsolescence, or bad debts). Our firm also assists in assembling the financial statements.

The Company's board of directors is composed of family members. The board is not expected to monitor the business or the owner-manager's activities.

Most of the significant accounting functions are performed by Willis, the bookkeeper, and Jones's secretary, Chris Ross. Willis was hired by the company in 19X0, has a working knowledge of accounting fundamentals, and we have no reason to question her competence. Willis regularly consults with our firm on unusual transactions, and past history indicates that it is rare for adjustments to arise from errors in the processing of routine transactions.

Jones made the decision to purchase a microcomputer and a turnkey accounting software package. The source code is not available for this software. Access to the computer and computer files is limited to Willis, Ross, and Jones, who effectively have access to all computer files.

The owner-manager carefully reviews computer generated financial reports, such as reports on receivable aging, and compares revenues and expenses with prior years' performance. He also monitors the terms of the long-term debt agreement that requires certain ratios and compensating balances.

SOURCE: AICPA Audit Guide, *Consideration of the Internal Control Structure in a Financial Statement Audit* (1990), p. 117–118.

the control structure, individual components of the control structure, or specific control policies or procedures. In audits of small entities, a narrative memorandum may serve as the only documentation of the auditor's understanding. Figure 8-5 illustrates this type of documentation for a small owner-managed company.

LEARNING CHECK:

8-17 a. What methods can be used to document the auditor's understanding of ICS components?

b. Can documentation occur concurrently with obtaining an understanding? Explain.

8-18 a. What is the general nature of the questions included in internal control questionnaires?

b. Identify several advantages of using questionnaires to document the auditor's understanding of relevant parts of an ICS.

8-19 a. What is a flowchart?

b. What essential components of a system should be displayed in a flowchart?

8-20 a. How may narrative memoranda supplement other forms of documentation?
b. Would a narrative memorandum ever be appropriate as the sole documentation of the auditor's understanding of the ICS?

KEY TERMS:

Documenting the understanding, p. 277
Flowchart, p. 280
Narrative memorandum, p. 282
Questionnaire, p. 279

SUMMARY

Increasing recognition is being given to the importance of internal control by management, independent auditors, and other external parties such as regulators. The second standard of field work requires the auditor to obtain a sufficient understanding of an entity's ICS components to plan the audit. This includes understanding the design of ICS policies and procedures and determining whether they have been placed in operation, but it does not include determining their effectiveness. The auditor uses the understanding to identify types of potential misstatements that could affect management's financial statement assertions, to consider factors that affect the risk of such misstatements, and to design substantive tests to provide reasonable assurance of detecting the misstatements. The nature and extent of procedures used in obtaining an understanding are affected by such factors as the audit strategy (primarily substantive or lower assessed level of control risk approach), previous experience with the client, and the size and complexity of the client's operation. The auditor's understanding should be documented in the working papers through completed questionnaires, flowcharts, and/or narrative memoranda. The auditor's additional responsibilities in meeting the second standard of field work are considered in the next two chapters.

APPENDIX 8A: COMPREHENSIVE FLOWCHARTING ILLUSTRATION

Flowcharting is a creative task, making it unlikely that any two people would draw flowcharts exactly alike for a given system. The more commonly used flowcharting symbols are shown in Figure 8-6. Some firms supplement these basic symbols with more extensive sets of special purpose symbols.

In addition to the four essential components of flowcharts listed on pages 280 and 282, the following guidelines are helpful in preparing useful flowcharts:

- Identify the class(es) of transactions to be included in a flowchart.
- Collect the necessary information through interviews, observations, and review of documents.

FIGURE 8-6 • FLOWCHARTING SYMBOLS

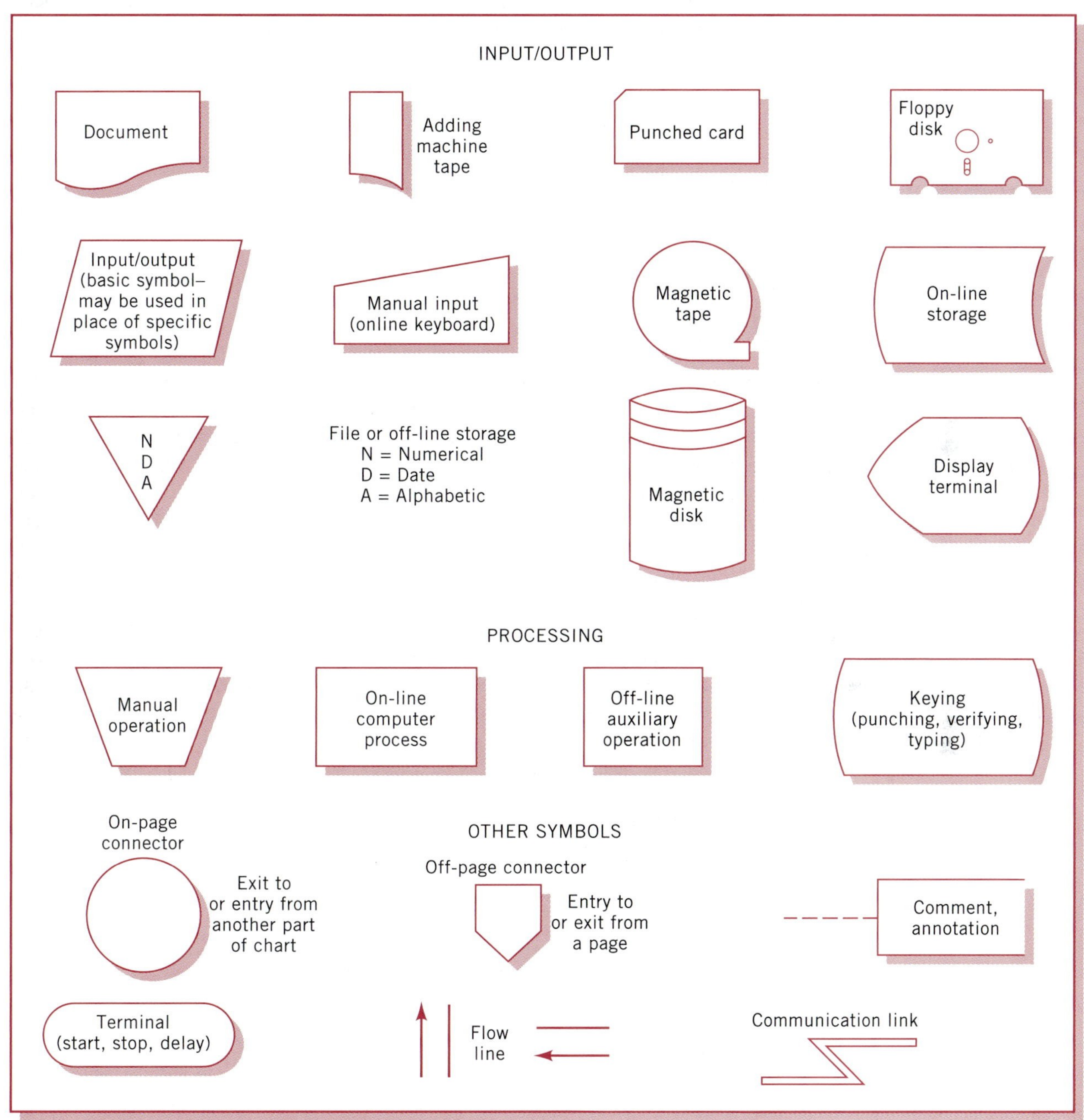

- Visualize an organizational format for the flowchart (e.g., the number and order of columns needed to represent departments, functions, or individuals) and prepare a rough sketch.
- Prepare the flowchart in good form.
- Test the completeness and accuracy of the flowchart by tracing a hypothetical transaction through the flowchart.

To illustrate, assume the auditor wishes to prepare a flowchart depicting the Hayes Company's processing of mail cash receipts. The following description of the processing system is based on information obtained through inquiries of client personnel, observations, and review of documents (note—this is an extension of the system illustrated previously in Figure 8-4):

All receipts from customers are received by mail and are accompanied by a preprinted remittance advice (bottom portion of the billing originally sent to the customer). In the Mailroom, the checks and remittance advices are separated. The checks are restrictively endorsed (For Deposit Only) and a listing (prelist) of the checks is prepared in triplicate and totaled. The checks and one copy of the prelist are then forwarded to the Cashier. The remittance advices and a copy of the prelist are sent to Accounts Receivable Accounting, and another copy of the prelist is sent to General Accounting.

The Cashier prepares a bank deposit slip in duplicate and makes the daily bank deposit. The Cashier forwards the validated copy of the bank deposit slip (stamped and dated by bank) to General Accounting and files the prelist by date.

In Accounts Receivable Accounting, the remittances are processed on a computer. The accounts receivable clerk keys the remittance data into a cash receipts transaction file via an on-line terminal. This file is then processed to (1) update the accounts receivable master file and (2) generate an entry in the general ledger transaction file, which is subsequently used to update the general ledger. This processing routine also generates two printed reports. An Accounts Receivable Summary Report shows the total credits posted to the accounts receivable master file and is reconciled to the total on the prelist received from the Mailroom. The remittance advices, prelist, and summary report are then filed by date. The General Ledger Transaction Report shows the daily totals for cash, discounts, and accounts receivable and is forwarded to General Accounting.

General Accounting compares the totals from the prelist received from the Mailroom, the validated deposit slip received from the Cashier, and the General Ledger Transaction Report received from Accounts Receivable Accounting and resolves any discrepancies. The documents are then collated and filed by date.

After considering the above information, the auditor envisions a flowchart with four columns for the Mailroom, Cashier, Accounts Receivable Accounting, and General Accounting. After first preparing a rough sketch, the flowchart depicted in Figure 8-7 is prepared.

It should be emphasized that a flowchart is a means to an end, not an end in itself. A flowchart should enable an auditor to see the relationships that exist between controls, and facilitate the identification of key controls related to specific financial statement assertions. For example, from studying the flowchart in Figure 8-7, the following controls, among others, can be observed:

- Documents and records
  - Use of preprinted *remittance advices* returned by customers with payments.
  - Preparation of *prelist* of cash receipts in triplicate for use in subsequent control.
  - Retention of *validated (receipted) deposit slip* for use in subsequent control.
  - Generation of *Accounts Receivable Summary Report* and *General Ledger Transaction Report* for use in subsequent controls.

FIGURE 8-7 • ILLUSTRATIVE FLOWCHART FOR PROCESSING OF MAIL RECEIPTS TRANSACTIONS

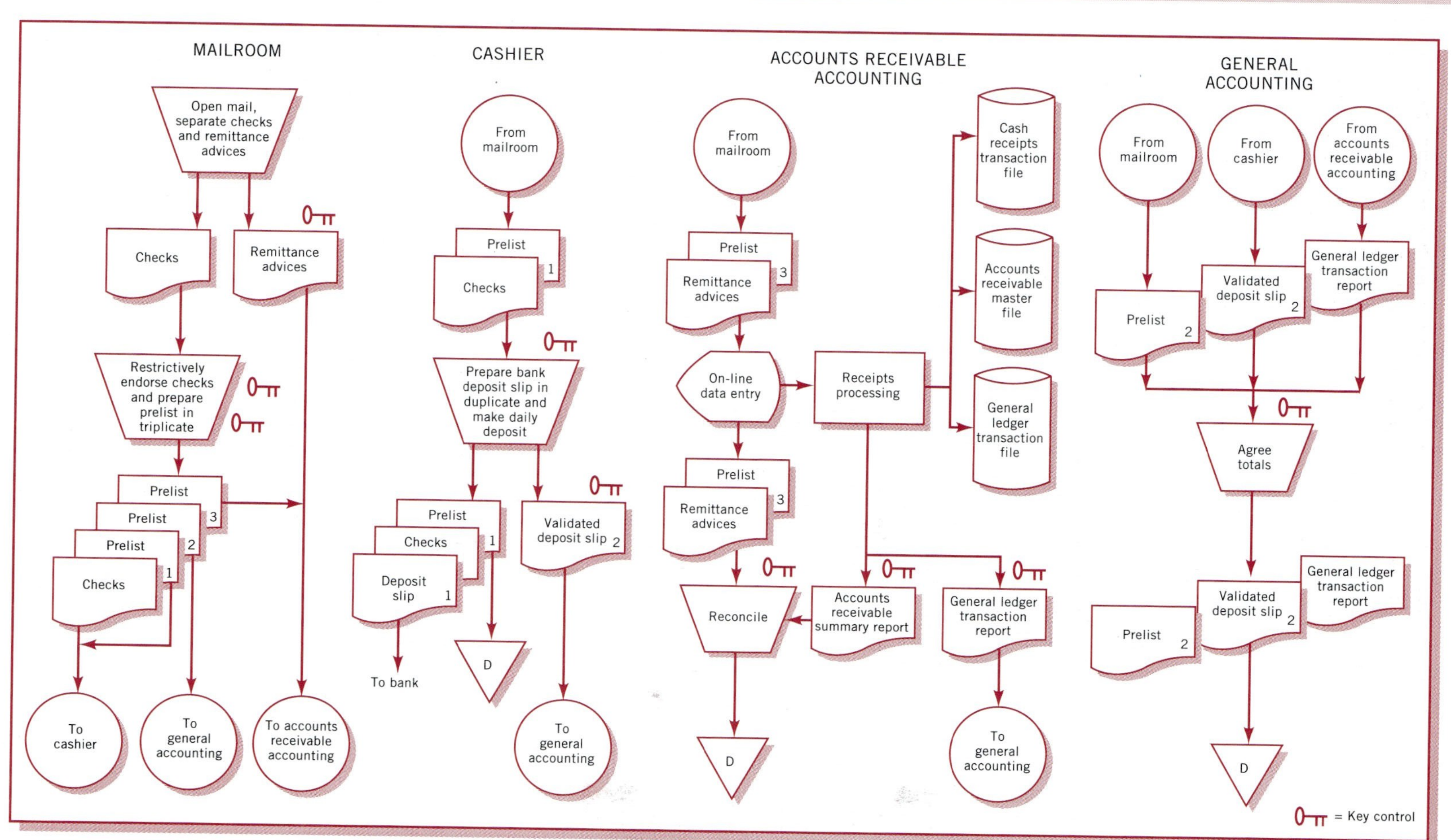

- Segregation of handling cash (Mailroom and Cashier) from accounting for cash and receivables (General Accounting and Accounts Receivable Accounting).
- Independent checks
  - Reconciliation of *Accounts Receivable Summary Report* in Accounts Receivable Accounting with total on *prelist* received from Mailroom.
  - Reconciliation by General Accounting of amounts reported on *prelist* received from Mailroom, *validated deposit slip* received from cashier, and *General Ledger Transaction Report* received from Accounts Receivable Accounting.
- Other control activities
  - Restrictive endorsement of checks immediately upon receipt.
  - Deposit of receipts intact daily.

Additional controls may be documented by making written notes on a flowchart. For example, in this illustration a note might be added to indicate that an independent monthly reconciliation is made of the bank account. Similarly, annotations about any observed weaknesses could be added to the flowchart.

BIBLIOGRAPHY

AICPA Professional Standards:

AU 319, Consideration of the Internal Control Structure in a Financial Statement Audit.

SAS 65 (AU 322), The Auditor's Consideration of the Internal Audit Function in an Audit of Financial Statements.

IAU 6 (AU 8006), Risk Assessment and Internal Control.

IAU 10 (AU 8010), Using the Work of an Internal Auditor.

International Statement on Auditing (AU 10050), Particular Considerations in the Audit of Small Businesses.

AICPA, Audit Guide: *Consideration of the Internal Control Structure in a Financial Statement Audit,* New York, 1990.

Committee of Sponsoring Organizations of the Treadway Commission, *Internal Control—Integrated Framework,* Jersey City, NJ: American Institute of Certified Public Accountants, 1992.

Kelley, Thomas P. "The COSO Report: Challenge and Counterchallenge," *Journal of Accountancy* (February 1993), pp. 10–18.

Libby, Robert, Artman, James T., and Willingham, John J. "Process Susceptibility, Control Risk, and Audit Planning," *The Accounting Review* (April 1985), pp. 212–228.

National Commission on Fradulent Financial Reporting, *Report of the National Commission on Fraudulent Financial Reporting,* Washington, DC, 1987.

Willingham, John J., and Wright, William F. "Financial Statement Errors and Internal Control Judgments," *Auditing: A Journal of Practice and Theory* (Fall 1985), pp. 57–70.

OBJECTIVE QUESTIONS

Indicate the *best* answer for each of the following multiple choice questions.

8-21 These questions relate to internal control structure components.

1. Which of the following is not a component of an entity's internal control structure?
   a. Audit risk.
   b. Control activities.

c. Information and communication.
d. Control environment.

2. Which of the following components of an entity's internal control structure includes the development of employee promotion and training policies?
   a. Control activities.
   b. Control environment.
   c. Information and communication.
   d. Quality control system.

3. An auditor's primary consideration regarding an entity's internal control structure policies and procedures is whether they
   a. Prevent management override.
   b. Relate to the control environment.
   c. Reflect management's philosophy and operating style.
   d. Affect the financial statement assertions.

4. Which of the following is not a reason an auditor should obtain an understanding of the components of an entity's internal control structure in planning an audit?
   a. To identify the types of potential misstatements that can occur.
   b. To design substantive tests.
   c. To consider the operating effectiveness of the internal control structure.
   d. To consider factors that affect the risk of material misstatements.

8-22 These questions pertain to obtaining an understanding of the internal control structure.

1. The primary objective of procedures performed to obtain an understanding of the internal control structure is to provide an auditor with
   a. Evidential matter to use in reducing detection risk.
   b. Knowledge necessary to plan the audit.
   c. A basis from which to modify tests of controls.
   d. Information necessary to prepare flowcharts.

2. During consideration of the internal control structure in a financial statement audit, an auditor is **not** obligated to
   a. Search for significant deficiencies in the operation of the internal control structure.
   b. Understand the internal control environment and the accounting system.
   c. Determine whether the control procedures relevant to audit planning have been placed in operation.
   d. Perform procedures to understand the design of the internal control structure policies.

3. When obtaining an understanding of an entity's control environment, an auditor should concentrate on the substance of management's policies and procedures rather than their form because
   a. The auditor may believe that the policies and procedures are inappropriate for that particular entity.
   b. The board of directors may **not** be aware of management's attitude toward the control environment.
   c. Management may establish appropriate policies and procedures but **not** act on them.
   d. The policies and procedures may be so weak that **no** reliance is contemplated by the auditor.

8-23 These questions involve documenting the auditor's understanding of the internal control structure.

1. An auditor's flowchart of a client's accounting system is a diagrammatic representation that depicts the auditor's
   a. Program for tests of controls.

b. Understanding of the system.
c. Understanding of the types of irregularities that are probable, given the present system.
d. Documentation of the study and evaluation of the system.

2. The auditor's understanding of the internal control structure is documented to substantiate
   a. Conformity of the accounting records with GAAP.
   b. Compliance with GAAS.
   c. Adherence to requirements of management.
   d. The fairness of the financial statement presentation.

3. Which of the following statements regarding auditor documentation of the client's internal control structure is correct?
   a. Documentation must include flowcharts.
   b. Documentation must include procedural write-ups.
   c. No documentation is necessary, although it is desirable.
   d. No one particular form of documentation is necessary, and the extent of documentation may vary.

COMPREHENSIVE QUESTIONS

8-24 **(Internal control fundamentals)** The importance of internal control has gained increasing recognition among management, external auditors, regulators, and others.

REQUIRED

a. What is internal control and what is it intended to provide to an entity?
b. What fundamental concepts are embodied in the definition of internal control?
c. List the five components of an internal control structure.
d. When considering the effectiveness of an internal control structure, what are the inherent limitations that should be considered.
e. Identify six parties who have a role or responsibility regarding an entity's ICS and briefly state the role or responsibility of each.

8-25 **(Obtaining an understanding)** In meeting the second generally accepted auditing standard of field work, the auditor is required to obtain a sufficient understanding of each of the components of an entity's internal control structure to plan the audit of the entity's financial statements.

REQUIRED

a. What knowledge should be obtained about the control structure components in obtaining an understanding?
b. How does the auditor obtain the understanding?
c. Is it necessary in all cases to document the understanding?
d. Briefly discuss the alternative methods available for documenting the understanding and comment on the relative advantages or disadvantages of each.

8-26 **(Control environment)** Peterson, CPA, is auditing the financial statements of publicly held manufacturing company, Amalgamated Products, Inc. In complying with the second standard of field work, Peterson seeks to obtain an understanding of Amalgamated's control environment.

REQUIRED

a. Identify the control environment factors that can affect the effectiveness of specific policies and procedures related to the other components of an internal control structure.
b. What should the auditor understand about the control environment and the factors that comprise it to have a sufficient knowledge of this component?
c. What effect may the preliminary audit strategy have on the required level of understanding of the control environment factors?

8-27 **(Components of an ICS)** Five components of an internal control structure are identified in the chapter. Listed below are specific control policies or procedures prescribed by Suntron Company.

1. Management gives careful consideration to the requisite knowledge and skills needed by personnel at all levels of the organization.
2. General controls and application controls are established in the electronic data processing department.
3. Management acts to reduce or eliminate incentives and temptations that might lead individuals to engage in dishonest or illegal acts.
4. Management is alert to complaints received from customers about billing errors.
5. Management gives special consideration to the risks that can arise from changed circumstances such as new lines of business.
6. Employees' responsibilities are assigned in a way so as to avoid any individual's being in a position to both commit an error or irregularity and then conceal it.
7. The accounting system includes provision for properly measuring the value of transactions in a manner that permits recording their proper monetary value in the financial statements.
8. Management identifies and analyzes risks relevant to the preparation of fairly presented financial statements.
9. Amalgamated's internal audit staff periodically assesses the effectiveness of various ICS components.
10. Policy manuals, accounting and financial reporting manuals, and a chart of accounts have been developed and implemented.

REQUIRED

a. Identify the ICS component to which each policy or procedure relates.
b. For each of the five ICS components, identify one additional policy or procedure not included in the preceding list.

8-28 **(Components of an ICS in small and midsize entities)** Although all five components of an ICS are applicable to entities of all sizes, the degree of formality and specifics of how the components are implemented may vary considerably for practical and sound reasons.

REQUIRED

a. What factors should be considered in deciding how the components should be implemented in a particular entity?
b. Identify several differences that can be expected in how smaller versus larger entities implement the ICS components. Include comments on (1) how some of the problems associated with limited personnel in a small business can be mitigated, and (2) what characteristics of smaller entities may obviate the need for more numerous and formal controls.

8-29 **(Segregation of duties)** The Richmond Company, a client of your firm, has come to you with the following problem. It has three clerical employees who must perform the following functions:

1. Maintain general ledger.
2. Maintain accounts payable ledger.
3. Maintain accounts receivable ledger.
4. Prepare checks for signature.
5. Maintain disbursements journal.
6. Issue credits on returns and allowances.
7. Reconcile the bank account.
8. Handle and deposit cash receipts.

Required

Assuming there is no problem as to the ability of any of the employees, the company requests your advice on assigning the above functions to the three employees in such a manner as to achieve the highest degree of internal control. It may be assumed that these employees will perform no other accounting functions than the ones listed.

a. State how you would recommend distributing the above functions among the three employees. Assume that, with the exception of the nominal jobs of the bank reconciliation and the issuance of credits on returns and allowances, all functions require an equal amount of time. (*Hint:* Give each employee a job title.)
b. List four possible unsatisfactory combinations of the above-listed functions.

AICPA (adapted)

8-30 **(Control activities)** Several categories of control activities are identified in the chapter using the following framework:

A. Information processing controls:
   1. General controls.
   2. Application controls:
      a. Proper authorization.
      b. Documents and records.
      c. Independent checks.
B. Segregation of duties.
C. Physical controls.
D. Performance reviews.

Listed below are specific control procedures prescribed by Landry Company.

1. Material requisition forms are required to withdraw raw materials from the storeroom.
2. Cash registers are used for over-the-counter cash receipts.
3. Different individuals approve the payroll, write the payroll checks, and distribute the checks.
4. Checks are prenumbered.
5. Credit is approved by the credit department prior to sale.
6. Inventory is stored in locked warehouses.
7. Shipping clerks verify agreement of goods received from the warehouse with a duplicate copy of the sales order before releasing the goods for shipment.
8. Perpetual inventory records are periodically adjusted based on physical inventory counts.
9. Off-site storage facilities are used for backup computer files and arrangements for backup facilities have been made in case of a disaster.
10. Management carefully reviews monthly operating reports showing variances from budgeted revenues and expenses and follows up on unexpected variances.

Required

a. Using the letters and numbers in the framework at the beginning of the question, identify the category of control activity to which each control applies. The first two items are answered below as examples.

1. A(2)(b).
2. C.

b. Differentiate *management authorization* from *employee approval.*

c. State two types of access to assets and records that should be limited by physical controls.

d. How may the preliminary audit strategy affect the required level of understanding of the control activities component of the ICS?

8-31 **(Control activities and related assertions)** The ICS of the Trusty Company includes the following control procedures:

1. A voucher package including a vendor's invoice, receiving report, and purchase order is required for each check issued.
2. Two authorized signatures are required on every check.
3. Each month management carefully reviews the aged trial balance of accounts receivable to identify old balances that should be written off.
4. Overtime work must be approved by a supervisor.
5. Prenumbered sales invoices are used in billing.
6. A second clerk is required to verify the mathematical accuracy of each voucher.
7. Employee payroll records are kept in a locked file cabinet.
8. An accounting supervisor reviews journal entries periodically for reasonableness of account classifications.
9. Checks received from customers and related remittance advices are separated in the mailroom and subsequently processed by different individuals.
10. All vouchers must be stamped *paid* on payment.
11. Only EDP equipment operators are allowed in the computer room.
12. A supervisor reconciles accounts receivable control with the customer ledger monthly.

REQUIRED

a. Indicate the category of control activities applicable to each procedure. (You may use the framework shown at the beginning of Question 8-30.)

b. Identify an assertion to which each procedure pertains.

8-32 **(Control procedures for cash receipts)** At the Main Street Theater, the cashier, located in a box office at the entrance, receives cash from customers and operates a machine that ejects serially numbered tickets. To gain admission to the theater, a customer hands the ticket to a doorperson stationed some 50 feet from the box office at the entrance to the theater lobby. The doorperson tears the ticket in half, opens the door, and returns the stub to the customer. The other half of the ticket is dropped by the doorperson into a locked box.

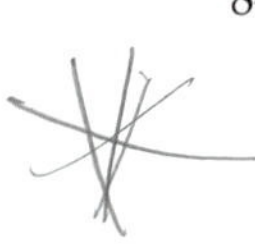

REQUIRED

a. What internal controls are present in this phase of handling cash receipts?

b. What steps should be taken regularly by the manager or other supervisor to give maximum effectiveness to these controls?

c. Assume that the cashier and doorperson decided to collaborate in an effort to abstract cash receipts. What action might they take?

d. Continuing the assumption made in (c) above of collusion between the cashier and doorperson, what features of the control procedures would be likely to disclose the embezzlement?

AICPA

8-33 **(Flowchart for cash receipts/key controls)** PML Manufacturing, Inc., a privately held corporation, manufactures office equipment. The cash receipts portion of the revenue cycle is described below.

1. Mail is opened in the Mailroom. Remittances (a check and a copy of the invoice) are separated.
2. A control list of checks is prepared and sent to the controller.
3. Checks are sent to the cashier and the remittance advices (copies of the invoices) to the accounts receivable department for posting.
4. Cashier 1 endorses the checks and prepares a duplicate deposit slip.
5. Cashier 2 compares the checks and deposit slips. He investigates any discrepancies, and a messenger deposits the cash daily.
6. A messenger takes the deposit to the bank.
7. The messenger returns the validated duplicate deposit slip directly to the controller.
8. The controller reconciles the control list of checks and duplicate deposit slip and resolves any differences.
9. The controller files the reconciliation, duplicate deposit slip, and control list of checks received chronologically.

REQUIRED

a. Prepare a flowchart of the cash receipts procedures.
b. Identify the key controls in your flowchart.

CASES

8-34 **(Identifying control strengths and weaknesses)** Brown Company provides office services for more than 100 small clients. These services consist of

1. Supplying temporary personnel.
2. Providing monthly bookkeeping services.
3. Designing and printing small brochures.
4. Copying and reproduction services.
5. Preparing tax reports.

Some clients pay for these services on a cash basis; some use 30-day charge accounts; and some operate on a contractual basis with quarterly payments. Brown's new office manager was concerned about the effectiveness of controls over sales and cash flow. At the manager's request, the process was reviewed and disclosed the following:

1. Contracts were written by account executives and then passed to the accounts receivable department where they were filed. Contracts had a limitation (ceiling) as to the types of services and the amount of work covered. Contracts were payable quarterly, in advance.
2. Client periodic payments on contracts were identified to the contract, and a payment receipt was placed in the contract file. Accounting records showed Credit Revenue; Debit Cash.
3. Periodically, a clerk reviewed the contract files to determine their status.
4. Work orders relating to contract services were placed in the contract file. Accounting records showed Debit Cost of Services; Credit Cash or Accounts Payable or Accrued Payroll.
5. Monthly bookkeeping services were usually paid for when the work was complete. If not paid in cash, a copy of the financial statement marked "Unpaid $_____" was put into a cash pending file. It was removed when cash was received, and accounting records showed Debit Cash; Credit Revenue.
6. Design and printing work was handled like bookkeeping. However, a design and printing order form was used to accumulate costs and to compute the charge to be made to the client. A copy of the order form served as a billing to the client and when cash was received as a remittance advice.

7. Reproduction (copy) work was generally a cash transaction that was rung up on a cash register and balanced at the end of the day. Some reproduction work was charged to open accounts. A billing form was given to the client with the work and a copy was put in an open file. It was removed when paid. In both cases, when cash was received, the accounting entry was Debit Cash; Credit Revenue.
8. Tax work was handled like the bookkeeping services.
9. Cash from cash sales was deposited daily. Cash from receipts on account or quarterly payments on contracts was deposited after being matched with evidence of the receivable.
10. Bank reconciliations were performed using the deposit slips as original data for the deposits on the bank statements.
11. A cash log was maintained of all cash received in the mail. This log was retained and used for reference purposes when a payment was disputed.
12. Monthly comparisons were made of the costs and revenues of printing, design, bookkeeping, and tax service. Unusual variations between revenues and costs were investigated. However, the handling of deferred payments made this analysis difficult.

REQUIRED

a. List eight examples of poor internal control that are evident.
b. List six examples of good internal control that are in effect.

IIA

8-35 **(Flowcharting; key controls)** Charting, Inc., a new audit client of yours, processes its sales and cash receipts documents in the following manner:

1. *Payment on Account.* The mail is opened each morning by a mail clerk in the sales department. The mail clerk prepares a remittance advice (showing customer and amount paid) if one is not received. The checks and remittance advices are then forwarded to the sales department supervisor, who reviews each check and forwards the checks and remittance advices to the accounting department supervisor.

   The accounting department supervisor, who also functions as credit manager in approving new credit and all credit limits, reviews all checks for payments on past due accounts and then forwards the checks and remittance advices to the accounts receivable clerk, who arranges the advices in alphabetical order. The remittance advices are posted directly to the accounts receivable ledger cards. The checks are endorsed by stamp and totaled. The total is posted to the cash receipts journal. The remittance advices are filed chronologically.

   After receiving the cash from the previous day's cash sales, the accounts receivable clerk prepares the daily deposit slip in triplicate. The third copy of the deposit slip is filed by date, and the second copy and the original accompany the bank deposit.
2. *Sales.* Sales clerks prepare sales invoices in triplicate. The original and second copy are presented to the cashier. The third copy is retained by the sales clerk in the sales book. When the sale is for cash, the customer pays the sales clerk, who presents the money to the cashier with the invoice copies.

   A credit sale is approved by the cashier from an approved credit list after the sales clerk prepares the three-part invoice. After receiving the cash or approving the invoice, the cashier validates the original copy of the sales invoice and gives it to the customer. At the end of each day, the cashier recaps the sales and cash received and forwards the cash and the second copy of all sales invoices to the accounts receivable clerk.

   The accounts receivable clerk balances the cash received with cash sales invoices and prepares a daily sales summary. The credit sales invoices are posted to the accounts receivable ledger, and then all invoices are sent to the inventory control clerk in the

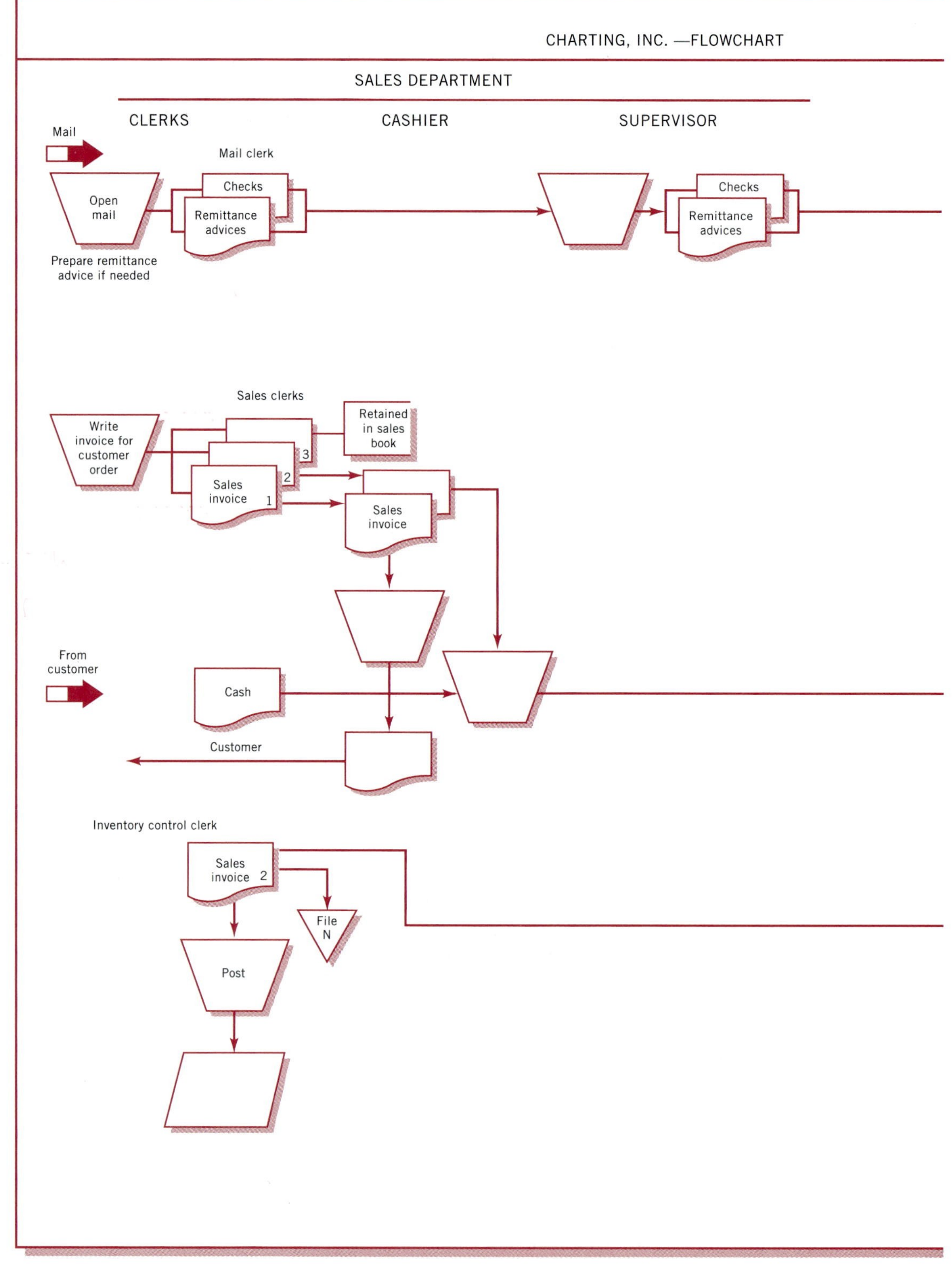
CHARTING, INC. —FLOWCHART
SALES DEPARTMENT
CLERKS
CASHIER
SUPERVISOR
Mail
Mail clerk
Open mail
Checks
Remittance advices
Prepare remittance advice if needed
Checks
Remittance advices
Sales clerks
Write invoice for customer order
Retained in sales book
3
2
Sales invoice 1
Sales invoice
From customer
Cash
Customer
Inventory control clerk
Sales invoice 2
File N
Post

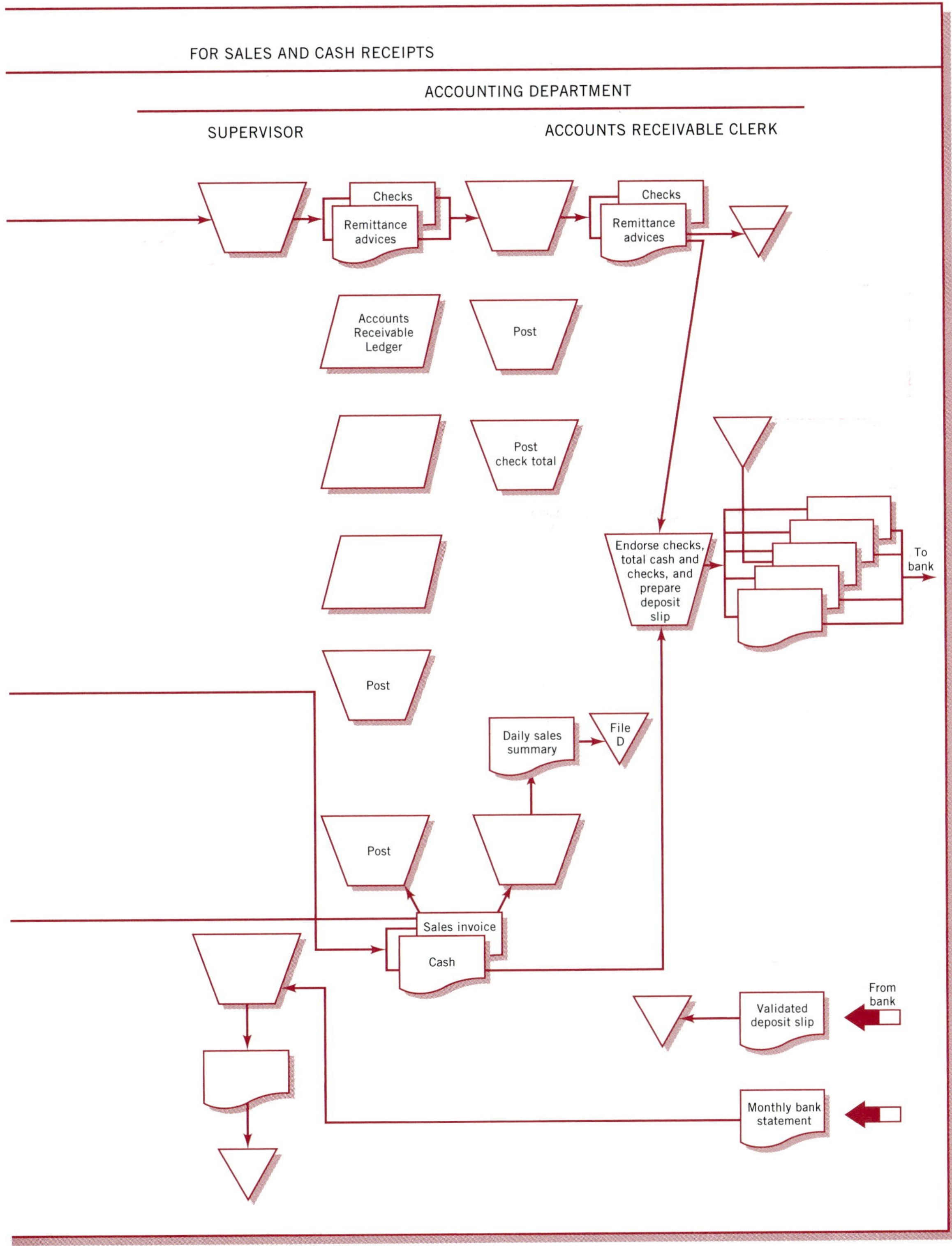
FOR SALES AND CASH RECEIPTS
ACCOUNTING DEPARTMENT
SUPERVISOR
ACCOUNTS RECEIVABLE CLERK
Checks
Remittance advices
Checks
Remittance advices
Accounts Receivable Ledger
Post
Post check total
Endorse checks, total cash and checks, and prepare deposit slip
To bank
Post
Daily sales summary
File D
Post
Sales invoice
Cash
Validated deposit slip
From bank
Monthly bank statement

sales department for posting to the inventory control cards. After posting, the inventory control clerk files all invoices numerically. The accounts receivable clerk posts the daily sales summary to the cash receipts journal and sales journal and files the sales summaries by date.

The cash from sales is combined with the cash received on account to comprise the daily bank deposit.

3. *Bank Deposits.* The bank validates the deposit slip and returns the second copy to the accounting department, where it is filed by date by the accounts receivable clerk.

   Monthly bank statements are reconciled promptly by the accounting department supervisor and filed by date.

Required

a. You recognize that there are weaknesses in the existing system and believe a chart of information and document flows would be beneficial in evaluating this client's internal control in preparing for your examination of the financial statements. Complete the flowchart for sales and cash receipts of Charting, Inc., by labeling the appropriate symbols and indicating information flows on pages 296 and 297. The chart is complete as to symbols and document flows.
b. List the key controls in the flowchart.

AICPA

Research Questions

8-36 **(Revision of SAS 55 and related audit guide)** As noted at the beginning of this chapter, at the time this text went to press the Auditing Standards Board was working on revisions to SAS 55 (AU 319) and its related audit guide, *Consideration of the Internal Control Structure in a Financial Statement Audit.* Determine whether the revision of either has been published as of the time you complete this assignment. If so, depending on availability, read or scan the revised SAS or AU section, related audit guide, or any journal article(s) written about either document. In doing so, (1) determine the effective date of the AICPA document(s) and (2) attempt to determine whether there are any differences between the revised AICPA document(s) and the presentations in this chapter pertaining to (a) the components of an internal control structure and their descriptions, (b) obtaining an understanding of the components, and (c) documenting the understanding. Hopefully, there will be few, if any, differences, but if any are found briefly describe them.

8-37 **(SEC actions regarding control environment)** Like a number of other regulatory agencies, the SEC has shown considerable interest in the control environment component of an internal control structure.

a. Identify an SEC *Accounting and Auditing Enforcement Release* in which the control environment was raised as an issue by the SEC. Identify the parties involved and briefly summarize the issue(s) raised and the conclusions reached.
b. Cite any other (non-AAER) SEC publication addressing the control environment. Note the date of the document. Read or scan the document. You need not prepare a written summary.

PART

3

Audit Testing Methodology

CHAPTER

9

ASSESSING CONTROL RISK/ TESTS OF CONTROLS

LEARNING OBJECTIVES

After studying this chapter, you should be able to

1. Enumerate the steps in assessing control risk for transaction class assertions.
2. Explain the differences in assessing control risk under the two major preliminary audit strategies.
3. State the purpose of tests of controls and distinguish between concurrent and additional or planned tests of controls.
4. Indicate the considerations that affect the nature, timing, and extent of planned tests of controls.
5. Describe how internal auditors may be used in tests of controls.
6. Explain the process of assessing control risk for account balance assertions affected by single and multiple transaction classes.
7. State the requirements for documenting the control risk assessment.
8. Indicate the auditor's requirements for communicating internal control structure related matters.

ASSESSING CONTROL RISK
- CONSIDER KNOWLEDGE ACQUIRED FROM PROCEDURES TO OBTAIN AN UNDERSTANDING
- IDENTIFY POTENTIAL MISSTATEMENTS
- IDENTIFY NECESSARY CONTROLS
- PERFORM TESTS OF CONTROLS
- EVALUATE EVIDENCE AND MAKE ASSESSMENT
- EFFECTS OF PRELIMINARY AUDIT STRATEGIES

TESTS OF CONTROLS
- CONCURRENT TESTS OF CONTROLS
- ADDITIONAL OR PLANNED TESTS OF CONTROLS
- DESIGNING TESTS OF CONTROLS
- AUDIT PROGRAMS FOR TESTS OF CONTROLS
- USING INTERNAL AUDITORS IN TESTS OF CONTROLS
- DUAL-PURPOSE TESTS

ADDITIONAL CONSIDERATIONS
- ASSESSING CONTROL RISK FOR ACCOUNT BALANCE ASSERTIONS AFFECTED BY A SINGLE TRANSACTION CLASS
- ASSESSING CONTROL RISK FOR ACCOUNT BALANCE ASSERTIONS AFFECTED BY MULTIPLE TRANSACTION CLASSES
- COMBINING DIFFERENT CONTROL RISK ASSESSMENTS
- DOCUMENTING THE ASSESSED LEVEL OF CONTROL RISK
- COMMUNICATION OF INTERNAL CONTROL STRUCTURE RELATED MATTERS

SUMMARY

BIBLIOGRAPHY

OBJECTIVE QUESTIONS

COMPREHENSIVE QUESTIONS

CASE

RESEARCH QUESTION

As noted in the previous chapter, the auditor's methodology for meeting the second standard of field work involves three major activities: (1) obtaining a sufficient understanding of the components of the internal control structure (ICS) to plan the audit, (2) assessing control risk for each significant assertion contained in the account balance, transaction class, and disclosure components of the financial statements, and (3) designing substantive tests for each significant financial statement assertion. The first activity was explained in Chapter 8. The second activity is the subject of this chapter. The final activity is the subject of the next chapter.

This chapter begins with an overview of the methodology for assessing control risk for transaction class assertions. Consideration is given to differences in the methodology for each of the two preliminary audit strategies that may be used for different parts of the audit. We then examine in depth the category of audit procedures known as tests of controls. We conclude with explanations of some special considerations in assessing control risk, including assessing control risk for account balance assertions affected by single and multiple transaction classes, the requirements for documenting control risk assessments, and auditor communications concerning internal control structure related matters.

ASSESSING CONTROL RISK

OBJECTIVE 1

Enumerate the steps in assessing control risk for transaction class assertions.

Assessing control risk is the process of evaluating the effectiveness of the design and operation of an entity's internal control structure policies and procedures in preventing or detecting material misstatements in the financial statements. Control risk is assessed in terms of individual financial statement assertions. But because the accounting system focuses on the processing of transactions, and because many control activities pertain to the processing of a particular type of transaction, it is common to begin by assessing control risk for transaction class assertions such as the existence or occurrence, completeness, and valuation or allocation assertions for cash receipts and cash disbursements transactions. These assessments are then combined as appropriate in assessing control risk for the related account balance assertions that are affected by the transaction classes. Thus, for example, relevant control risk assessments for cash receipts and cash disbursements transactions are combined to arrive at assessments for the related assertions for the cash account balance. It is important to keep in mind that control risk assessments are made for individual assertions, not for the internal control structure as a whole, individual control structure components, or individual policies or procedures.

In making an assessment of control risk for an assertion, it is necessary for the auditor to

- Consider knowledge acquired from *procedures to obtain an understanding* about whether controls pertaining to the assertion have been *designed and placed in operation* by the entity's management.
- Identify *potential misstatements* that could occur in the entity's assertion.
- Identify the *necessary controls* that would likely prevent or detect the misstatements.
- Perform *tests of controls* on the necessary controls to determine the *effectiveness of their design and operation.*
- Evaluate the evidence and *make the assessment.*

The next to last step, performing tests of controls, is not required when control risk is assessed at the maximum. Each of these steps in the assessment process is discussed in a following section.

CONSIDER KNOWLEDGE ACQUIRED FROM PROCEDURES TO OBTAIN AN UNDERSTANDING

As described in Chapter 8, the auditor performs **procedures to obtain an understanding** of relevant ICS policies and procedures for significant financial statement assertions. He or she documents the understanding in the form of completed internal control questionnaires, flowcharts, and/or narrative memoranda. Analysis of this documentation is the starting point for assessing control risk. In particular, AU 319 states the understanding is to be used by the auditor to (1) identify types of potential misstatements and (2) consider factors that affect the risk of material misstatements, such as whether controls necessary to prevent or detect the misstatements have been designed and placed in operation. Thus, for policies and procedures relevant to particular assertions, the auditor carefully considers the Yes, No, and N/A responses and written comments in the questionnaires and the strengths and weaknesses noted in flowcharts and narrative memoranda.

IDENTIFY POTENTIAL MISSTATEMENTS

As mentioned in Chapter 8, some auditing firms now use computer software that links responses to specific questions in computerized questionnaires to potential misstatements for particular assertions. Alternatively, most auditing firms have developed checklists that enumerate the types of **potential misstatements** that could occur in specific assertions. Using either the computer software aid or checklists and his or her understanding of the entity's ICS, the auditor identifies the potential misstatements applicable to specific assertions given the entity's circumstances.

Potential misstatements may be identified for assertions pertaining to each major class of transactions and for assertions pertaining to each significant account balance. For example, potential misstatements may be identified for cash disbursements assertions and for the two primary account balances affected by cash disbursements—cash and accounts payable. The manner in which misstatements in transaction class assertions can affect account balance assertions is explained in a later section. Examples of potential misstatements for several assertions pertaining to cash disbursements transactions are shown in the first column of Figure 9-1.

IDENTIFY NECESSARY CONTROLS

Whether by using computer software that processes internal control questionnaire responses or manually by using checklists, auditors can identify **necessary controls** that could likely prevent or detect specific potential misstatements. The second column in Figure 9-1 illustrates such a list. Note that in some cases, several controls may pertain to a given potential misstatement. In other cases, a single control may apply. In addition, a single control may pertain to more than one type of potential misstatement. For example, the control *periodic independent bank reconciliations* shown at the bottom of the second column may detect unrecorded checks (completeness assertion) or checks made out for the right amount but recorded in the cash disbursements journal at an incorrect amount (valuation or allocation assertion).

At this point, it is recommended that the reader compare the information in the first and second columns of Figure 9-1 with the questions presented in Figure 8-3 on page 279. This illustrates how a questionnaire that a new staff auditor might be asked to administer can be developed by more experienced staff in a manner that facilitates the subsequent analysis of potential misstatements and necessary controls. Note that the questions in Figure 8-3 don't necessarily appear in the same order as the necessary controls in Figure 9-1 because some controls pertain to more

FIGURE 9-1 • POTENTIAL MISSTATEMENTS, NECESSARY CONTROLS, AND TESTS OF CONTROLS—CASH DISBURSEMENTS TRANSACTIONS

Potential Misstatement/ Assertion	Necessary Control	Test of Control
A cash disbursement may be made for an unauthorized purpose (existence or occurrence of valid transaction).	Approved payment voucher with matching supporting documents (vendor's invoice, receiving report, and approved purchase order) for each disbursement transaction.	For sample of cash disbursement transactions, determine existence of approved payment voucher and matching supporting documents for each disbursement.
	Only authorized personnel permitted to sign checks.	Observe individuals signing checks and / or compare signatures on cancelled (paid) checks with list of authorized signers.
	Segregation of duties for approving payment vouchers and signing checks.	Observe segregation of duties.
A voucher may be paid twice (existence or occurrence of valid transaction).	Stamp payment voucher and supporting documents "Paid" when check is issued.	Observe documents being stamped and / or inspect sample of paid documents for presence of "Paid" stamp.
A check may be issued for the wrong amount (valuation or allocation).	Check signers verify agreement of details of check and payment voucher before signing.	Observe check signers performing independent check of agreement and / or reperform independent check.
A cash disbursement transaction may not be recorded (completeness) or it may be recorded for the wrong amount (valuation or allocation).	All disbursement transactions made by check.	Inquire about methods of making cash disbursements and / or inspect paid checks for sample of disbursement transactions.
	All checks prenumbered and accounted for.	Examine evidence of use of and accounting for prenumbered checks and / or scan sequence of check numbers in check register or cash disbursements journal.
	Unused checks stored in a secure area.	Observe handling and storage of unused checks.
	Independent check of agreement of daily summary of checks issued with entry to cash disbursements.	Observe performance of independent check and / or reperform independent check.
	Periodic independent bank reconciliations.	Observe performance of bank reconciliations and / or inspect bank reconciliations.

than one assertion. Consideration of potential misstatements and necessary controls like those shown in Figure 9-1 is also useful in analyzing flowcharts to identify strengths and weaknesses.

Specifying necessary controls also requires consideration of circumstances and judgment. For example, where there is a very high volume of cash disbursements transactions, an independent check of the agreement of a daily summary of checks issued with the entry in the cash disbursements journal, thus permitting timely detection of errors, may be critical. When the volume of cash disbursements is light and timely detection of errors is not as essential, periodic independent bank reconciliations may adequately compensate for the lack of a daily independent check. In such a circumstance, the bank reconciliation might be referred to as a **compensating control.**

The necessary controls shown in Figure 9-1 may all be classified as belonging to the control activities component of an internal control structure. The auditor should be aware that certain control policies and procedures pertaining to the other ICS components may simultaneously affect the risk of potential misstatements in assertions pertaining to several transaction classes or account balances. For example, the competency and trustworthiness of certain managers, as well as employees involved in the processing of cash disbursement transactions, can affect any of the assertions for that transaction class. In fact, a lack of competence and trustworthiness in key managers or employees can negate the effectiveness of other control activities. Thus, the auditor must assimilate information about a wide variety of possible control policies and procedures related to any of the ICS components in considering the risk of potential misstatements in particular assertions. This concept may be represented graphically as follows:

Relevant Control Policies and Procedures	Assessment of Control Risk
Control environment Risk assessment Information and communication Control activities Monitoring	Each assertion

From the knowledge acquired from procedures to obtain an understanding and the identification of potential misstatements and the necessary controls to prevent or detect those misstatements, the auditor can make an *initial assessment* of control risk. However, even a thorough understanding of the *design of controls and whether they have been placed in operation* will only permit the auditor to assess control risk for an assertion at the *maximum.* To arrive at an assessment of control risk below the maximum, either concurrent with obtaining the understanding or subsequent thereto evidence must be obtained from *tests of controls* about the *effectiveness of the design and operation* of the necessary controls.

PERFORM TESTS OF CONTROLS

Column 3 of Figure 9-1 lists a possible test of control for each of the necessary controls specified in column 2. The tests described include selecting a sample and inspecting related documents, inquiring of client personnel, observing client personnel performing control procedures, and the auditor's reperformance of certain controls. The results of each **test of controls** should provide evidence about the *effectiveness of the design and/or operation* of the related necessary control. For example, by comparing the signatures on a sample of paid checks with the list of authorized check signers and noting any exceptions, the auditor obtains evidence about the effectiveness of the *proper authorization* control which is intended to limit check signers to authorized personnel.

In determining the tests to be performed, the auditor considers the type of evidence that will be provided and the cost of performing the test. Once the tests to be performed have been selected, it is customary for the auditor to prepare a formal written audit program for the planned tests of controls. Additional information on planning and performing tests of controls, and preparing audit programs for tests of controls, is provided in a later section of this chapter.

EVALUATE EVIDENCE AND MAKE ASSESSMENT

The final assessment of control risk for a financial statement assertion is based on evaluating the evidence gained from (1) procedures to obtain an understanding of relevant ICS policies and procedures and (2) related tests of controls. Based on the nature of the procedures performed, the information obtained might be in the form of any combination of documentary, electronic, mathematical, oral, or physical evidence. When different types of evidence support the same conclusion about the effectiveness of a control, the degree of assurance increases. Conversely, when they support different conclusions, the degree of assurance decreases. For example, the initials of an employee may be consistently present on documents indicating performance of a control procedure, but the auditor's inquiries of the person initialing the documents might reveal the employee's lack of understanding of the control procedure being applied. The latter oral evidence would reduce the assurance obtained from the inspection of initials on the documents.

The evaluation of evidence involves both quantitative and qualitative considerations. In forming a conclusion about the effectiveness of a control policy or procedure, the auditor often uses guidelines concerning the tolerable frequency of deviations (usually expressed as a percentage) from the proper performance of a control. If the test results lead the auditor to conclude that the frequency of deviations is less than or equal to the tolerable level, the operation of the control is considered effective. When it is concluded that the frequency of deviations exceeds the tolerable level, the control is considered ineffective. Before finalizing this conclusion, the auditor should also consider the causes of the deviations. For example, the auditor may attach different significance to excessive deviations caused solely by a vacation replacement rather than by an experienced employee. It is also essential in reaching a conclusion about effectiveness to determine whether a deviation is attributable to unintentional errors or to deliberate misrepresentations (irregularities). Evidence of one deviation due to an irregularity may be more important to the auditor than more frequent deviations caused by errors.

Finally, as noted in Chapter 7, control risk assessments may be expressed in quantitative terms (such as there is a 40% risk that relevant controls will not prevent or detect a particular type of misstatement) or qualitative terms (such as there is a low, moderate, high, or maximum risk that relevant controls will not prevent or detect the particular type of misstatement). It should also be recalled that assessing control risk for an assertion is a critical factor in determining the acceptable level of detection risk for that assertion, which in turn affects the planned level of substantive tests including the nature, timing, and extent of such tests to be performed in completing the audit. If control risk is assessed too low, detection risk may be set too high and the auditor may not perform sufficient substantive tests resulting in an ineffective audit. Conversely, if control risk is assessed too high, more substantive testing may be done than necessary, resulting in an inefficient audit.

EFFECTS OF PRELIMINARY AUDIT STRATEGIES

Regardless of the preliminary audit strategy chosen for a particular part of the audit, the auditor is required to identify types of potential misstatements in the assertions. However, the manner in which the auditor considers factors that affect the risk of misstatements and assesses that risk can vary in several respects based on the audit strategy chosen. Figure 9-2 highlights the differences in the two approaches to meeting the second standard of field work.

Primarily Substantive Approach

OBJECTIVE 2

Explain the differences in assessing control risk under the two major preliminary audit strategies.

It may be recalled from the discussions in Chapters 7 and 8 that the procedures to obtain the understanding of relevant internal control structure policies and procedures and the documentation of the understanding may be less extensive when the primarily substantive approach is chosen. In particular, under this approach, it may not be necessary to extend the procedures to the control activities component of the ICS. The level of understanding and documentation of each of the other four components of the ICS may be less extensive as well.

A number of differences may be noted in the portion of Figure 9-2 labeled *Assess Control Risk.* First, as discussed in Chapter 7, one of the components of the primarily substantive approach strategy for an assertion is a planned assessed level of control risk of maximum or high. This is based on the assumption that one of the following pertains:

- There are no significant control policies or procedures that pertain to the assertion.
- Any relevant control policies or procedures are unlikely to be effective.
- It would not be efficient to obtain evidence to evaluate the effectiveness of relevant control policies or procedures.

The decision paths in the primarily substantive approach column in Figure 9-2 allow for affirmation of, or changes to, these assumptions. Note that the first decision symbol (diamond shape) raises the question as to whether any tests of controls were performed concurrent with the procedures used to obtain the understanding. An example of a concurrent test of controls is the *transaction walk-through review* described in Chapter 8 in which the auditor traces a representative transaction from a class of transactions through all processing steps as a way of confirming the understanding obtained through questionnaires or flowcharts. Additional examples of concurrent tests of controls are explained in a later section.

If no concurrent tests of controls were performed, the auditor must assess control risk at the maximum and document that conclusion in the working papers, because only through tests of controls can evidence be obtained that controls are sufficiently effective to reduce control risk below the maximum level. If, however, one or more concurrent tests of controls provide some limited evidence about the effectiveness of controls, the auditor may make an **initial assessment of control risk** of slightly below the maximum or high. In such case, the auditor may be

FIGURE 9-2 • METHODOLOGIES FOR MEETING THE SECOND STANDARD OF FIELD WORK

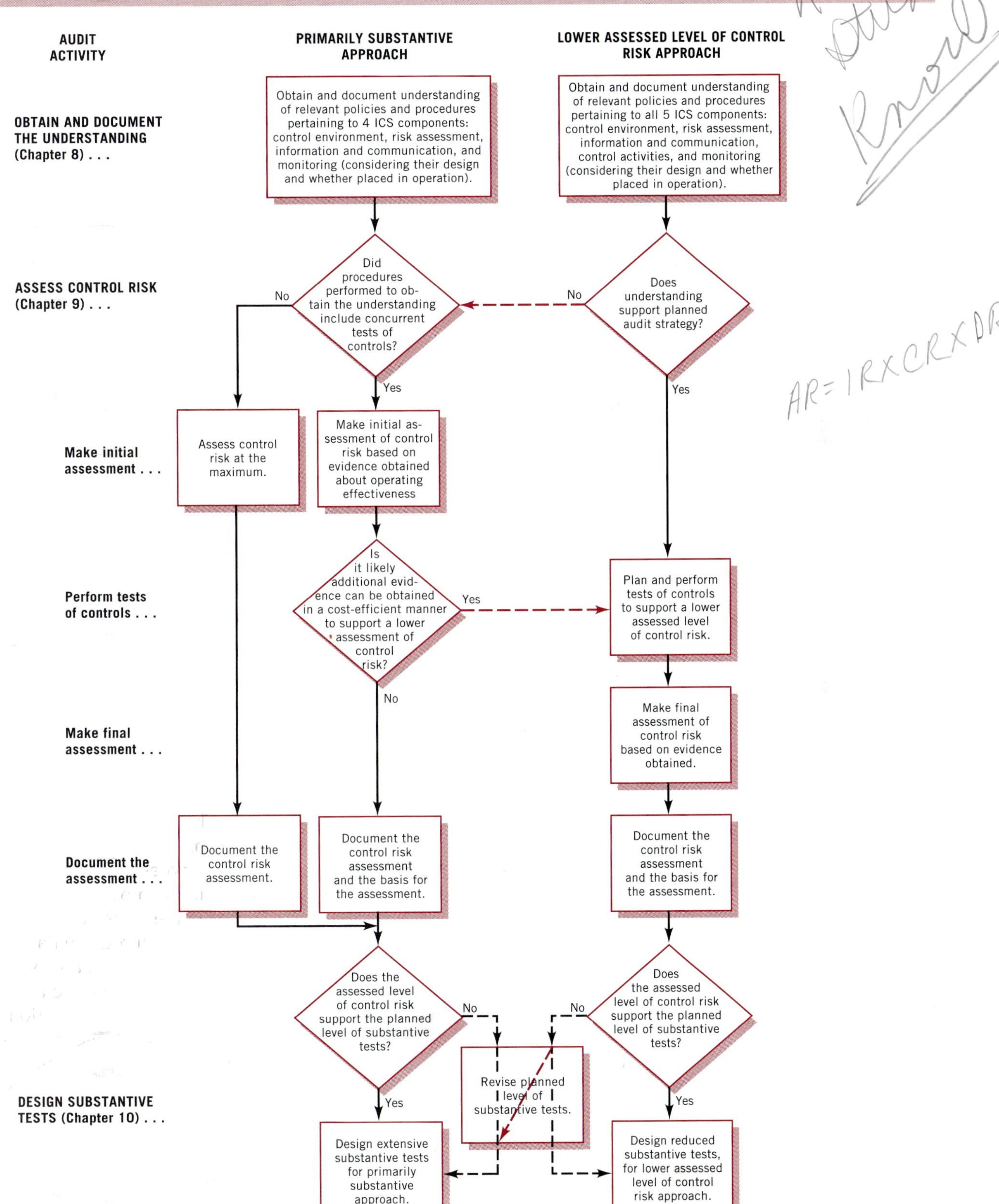

sufficiently encouraged to consider changing the audit strategy to the lower assessed level of control risk approach.

In making the decision of whether to change strategies, consideration should be given to the likelihood that evidence can be obtained in a cost-efficient manner to support a lower assessment of control risk such as moderate or low. To be **cost-efficient,** the combined costs of performing (1) additional tests of controls and (2) the reduced substantive tests that would be appropriate assuming a lower control risk assessment is supported should be less than the costs of performing the higher level of substantive testing required by the primarily substantive approach. This decision is reflected in the second decision symbol in the primarily substantive approach column where the *Yes* branch (dotted line extending to the right from that symbol) represents a change in strategy to the lower assessed level of control risk approach. If the decision is made not to change strategies, the assessment of control risk at slightly below the maximum or high, and the basis for that assessment, should be documented.

The final decision symbol in the primarily substantive approach column requires the auditor to consider whether the actual assessed level of control risk supports the planned level of substantive tests, and if not, to revise the planned level of substantive tests. For example, the auditor might have originally specified a planned assessed level of control risk at the maximum, resulting in the highest planned level of substantive tests. But, if evidence from concurrent tests of controls supports an actual assessment of control risk of slightly below the maximum or high, revision of the planned level of substantive tests to a slightly lower level would be appropriate. The auditor then proceeds with the detailed design of the appropriate level of substantive tests.

Lower Assessed Level of Control Risk Approach

It will be recalled that under this approach, a more extensive understanding and documentation of relevant control policies and procedures for all five components of the ICS is ordinarily appropriate in order to support the auditor's planned assessed level of control risk of moderate or low for an assertion. Conceivably, based on evidence from the procedures to obtain the understanding, the auditor might find that contrary to expectations one or more of the three conditions (bullets) listed on page 306 pertains. In such case, it may be appropriate to change strategies to the primarily substantive approach. In Figure 9-2, this is reflected in the *No* branch extending to the left from the first decision symbol in the lower assessed level of control risk approach column.

If the auditor continues with the lower assessed level of control risk approach, he or she plans and performs the additional tests of controls required to obtain the evidence needed to support the planned assessed level of control risk of moderate or low. The evidence obtained from the tests of controls is then evaluated to make the **final or actual assessment of control risk.** Both the final assessment and the basis for that assessment are then documented in the working papers.

The final decision symbol in the lower assessed level of control risk approach column in Figure 9-2 requires the auditor to consider whether the actual assessed level of control risk supports the planned level of substantive tests, and if not, to revise the planned level of substantive tests. For example, the auditor might have originally specified a planned assessed level of control risk of low, resulting in the lowest planned level of substantive tests. But, if evidence from the tests of controls leads to an actual assessed level of control risk of moderate, revision of the planned level of substantive tests to a higher level would be appropriate. Or, if contrary to expectations the controls are found to be highly ineffective resulting in a final assessment of control risk of high or maximum, the auditor would need to revise the planned level of substantive tests to reflect a change to the primarily substantive approach. This is represented by the dotted line slanting downward to the left in the *revise planned level of substantive tests* block near the bottom of Figure 9-2. In either case, the final step involves designing the detailed substantive tests appropriate for the circumstances.

LEARNING CHECK:

9-1 a. What is meant by the term *assessing control risk?*
 b. Control risk is assessed in terms of what?

9-2 Enumerate five steps involved in the process of assessing control risk.

9-3 How are potential misstatements and necessary controls identified in a typical audit?

9-4 a. Explain the role of evidence obtained from *procedures to obtain an understanding* in assessing control risk.
 b. Explain the role of evidence obtained from *tests of controls* in assessing control risk.

9-5 How are guidelines concerning the *tolerable frequency of deviations* from controls used in assessing control risk?

9-6 What qualitative factors should be considered in forming a conclusion about the effectiveness of a control policy or procedure?

9-7 Explain several differences in the methodologies for meeting the second standard of field work under the primarily substantive approach versus the lower assessed level of control risk approach.

KEY TERMS:

Assessing control risk, p. 301
Compensating control, p. 304
Cost-efficient, p. 308
Final or actual assessment of control risk, p. 308
Initial assessment of control risk, p. 306
Necessary controls, p. 302
Potential misstatements, p. 302
Procedures to obtain an understanding, p. 301
Tests of controls, p. 304

TESTS OF CONTROLS

As explained previously, **tests of controls** are auditing procedures performed to determine the effectiveness of the design and/or the operation of control structure policies and procedures. Tests of controls pertaining to design are concerned with

OBJECTIVE 3

State the purpose of tests of controls and distinguish between concurrent and additional or planned tests of controls.

whether the policy or procedure is suitably designed to prevent or detect material misstatements in a specific financial statement assertion. For example, the auditor may conclude that management's plan to store inventory in locked warehouses should prevent or significantly reduce the risk of misstatements in the existence or occurrence assertion for inventories.

Tests of controls pertaining to effectiveness of operation are concerned with whether control policies and procedures are actually working. In the inventory example, observing whether inventory is actually stored in locked warehouses would provide a test of the effectiveness of operation. Tests of controls pertaining to effectiveness of operation focus on three questions.

- How was the control applied?
- Was it applied consistently during the year?
- By whom was it applied?

A control policy or procedure is operating effectively when it has been properly and consistently applied during the year by the employee(s) authorized to apply it. In contrast, the failure to properly and consistently apply a control, or application by an unauthorized employee, indicates ineffective operation. Such failures are referred to as **deviations, occurrences,** or **exceptions.** This terminology is preferable to the term *error* because a failure in performance indicates only that there *may* be an error in the accounting records. For instance, the failure of a second employee to independently verify the accuracy of a sales invoice is a deviation, but the document could still be correct if the first employee correctly prepared it.

Tests of controls may be performed on controls that pertain to a major class of transaction and/or an account balance. The tests should only be performed on controls that are considered relevant by the auditor in preventing or detecting a material misstatement in a financial statement assertion.

Tests of controls may be performed during audit planning and during interim work. As explained previously, tests of controls may also be performed under either audit strategy.

CONCURRENT TESTS OF CONTROLS

Concurrent tests of controls are performed in conjunction with obtaining an understanding. These tests are performed at the option of the auditor under either audit strategy. Concurrent tests of controls consist of procedures for obtaining an understanding that also provide evidence about the effectiveness of a control policy or procedure. For instance, the auditor may make inquiries about the existence of a budgetary system in obtaining an understanding. At the same time, inquiries regarding the frequency of budget reports and the nature of management's follow-up action on budget variances may enable the auditor to determine the operating effectiveness of the budgeting system. Concurrent tests of controls are usually very cost efficient, and they may reduce the extent of additional tests of controls to be performed later in the audit.

Concurrent tests of controls may occur as a by-product of obtaining an understanding, or they may be planned. Evidence from concurrent tests of controls normally will only support an assessed level of control risk in the range *slightly below the maximum* to *high*. For instance, because a concurrent test of controls is performed during audit planning, it will not, in itself, provide evidence of the proper and consistent application of a control policy or procedure by an authorized employee during the entire year under audit.

ADDITIONAL OR PLANNED TESTS OF CONTROLS

These tests of controls are performed during field work and should provide evidence of the proper and consistent application of a control policy or procedure throughout the entire year under audit. They are not ordinarily performed under the primarily substantive approach. However, such tests are performed when, based on favorable results from concurrent tests of controls, the auditor decides to switch from the primarily substantive to the lower assessed level of control risk approach. In this circumstance, the tests are sometimes called **additional tests of controls.** They are performed only when it is likely that additional evidence will be obtained to lower the initial assessment of control risk and it is cost-efficient to do so.

When these tests are performed as part of an initial lower assessed level of control risk strategy for specific assertions, they are sometimes called **planned tests of controls.** They are performed to support the initial planned assessed level of control risk of moderate or low and the corresponding planned level of substantive tests.

DESIGNING TESTS OF CONTROLS

Besides choosing between concurrent and additional or planned tests of controls for certain assertions, the auditor has additional choices to make about the nature of audit procedures to be used in performing the tests, and the timing and extent of the tests.

Nature of Tests

OBJECTIVE 4

Indicate the considerations that affect the nature, extent, and timing of planned tests of controls.

The auditor's choices as to the **nature of tests of controls** are

- *Inquiring* of personnel concerning the performance of their duties.
- *Observing* personnel in the performance of their duties.
- *Inspecting* documents and reports indicating performance of controls.
- *Reperforming* the control by the auditor.

It will be recalled that the first three procedures are also used by the auditor in obtaining an understanding of the ICS. The fourth procedure, reperformance, is not used in obtaining an understanding.

In performing the tests, the auditor selects the procedure that will provide the most reliable evidence about the effectiveness of the control policy or procedure. No one test of controls is always applicable or equally effective in providing evidence.

Inquiring is designed to determine (1) an employee's understanding of his or her duties, (2) the individual's performance of those duties, and (3) the frequency, causes, and disposition of deviations. Unsatisfactory answers from an employee may indicate improper application of a control. Observing the employee's performance provides similar evidence. Ideally, this procedure should be performed without the employee's knowledge or on a surprise basis. Inquiring and observing are especially useful in obtaining evidence about the control procedure of segregation of duties.

Inspecting documents and records is applicable when there is a transaction trail of performance in the form of signatures and validation stamps that indicate whether the control was performed and the individual who performed it. Any document or record that fails to have evidence of performance is a deviation, regardless of whether the document itself is correct.

Some auditors maintain that reperformance of a control by the auditor provides the best evidence of its effectiveness. To illustrate, assume the control procedure of independent checks requires a second clerk in the billing department to independently verify the correctness of unit selling prices on all sales invoices by comparing them to an authorized price list. On doing so, the employee initials a copy of the invoice to indicate performance. In testing this control procedure by reperformance, the auditor compares selling prices on invoices to the authorized price list. Thus, in this example, there would be the following two possible deviations from the control: (1) initialed invoices for which selling prices do not agree with the authorized price list, and (2) invoices that do not have the employee's initials. From the foregoing, it can be seen that manual reperformance is a more costly auditing procedure than inspecting the invoices for evidence of performance by client personnel. However, the use of computer-assisted audit techniques to reperform a control can be very cost-efficient.

The auditor may use tests of controls in combination. For example, inspection of documents provides evidence that the control was performed and the identity of the person who performed it. By reperforming the control, the auditor can determine how well it was performed. The auditor can also ascertain how well a control was performed through observation and inquiry.

Timing of Tests

The **timing of tests of controls** refers to when they are performed and the part of the accounting period to which they relate. Additional tests of controls are performed during interim work, which may be several months before the end of the year under audit. These tests, therefore, only provide evidence of the effectiveness of controls from the beginning of the year to the date of the tests. However, the auditor is required by GAAS to have evidence about effectiveness for the entire year covered by the financial statements. Thus, from the standpoint of audit efficiency, the tests of controls should be performed as late in the interim period as possible.

The need to perform additional tests of controls later in the year depends on essentially the same factors mentioned above for using evidence from prior audits. In this case, the length of the remaining period and any significant changes in controls subsequent to interim testing should also be considered. When significant changes have occurred, the auditor should revise his or her understanding of the internal control structure and consider (1) performing tests of controls on the changed policies or procedures, or (2) performing more substantive tests for the remaining period.

Extent of Tests

More extensive tests of controls will ordinarily provide more evidence of the operating effectiveness of a control policy or procedure than less extensive tests. For example, in the case of inquiry, asking more than one individual about the same control procedure will provide more evidence than a single inquiry. Similarly, observing all credit department employees in approving credit provides more assurance of the performance of necessary control procedures than observing only one employee.

The following two limitations should be recognized about evidence obtained from observation: (1) the employee may perform the control differently when not being observed, and (2) the evidence applies only to the time when the observation occurs. The effects of the latter are reduced by observing personnel at different points in time. As to be expected, more extensive inspection of documents for initials or signatures indicating performance of a control procedure provides more evidence than when fewer documents are examined. The same is true of the auditor's reperformance of control procedures.

The **extent of tests of controls** is directly affected by the auditor's planned assessed level of control risk. More extensive testing will be needed for a low assessed level of control risk than for a moderate assessed level of control risk. The extent of additional testing will also be affected by the intended use of evidence about effectiveness from prior audits. To evaluate the relevance of such evidence for the current audit, the auditor should consider

- The significance of the assertion involved.
- The specific ICS policies and procedures evaluated during the prior audits.
- The degree to which the effective design and operation of those policies and procedures were evaluated.
- The results of the tests of controls used to make the evaluations.

In considering such evidence, the auditor should recognize that the longer the time interval since the performance of tests of controls, the less assurance they provide. Moreover, before using evidence from prior audits, the auditor should ascertain whether there have been any significant changes in the design or operation of the control policies and procedures since the prior tests. For example, there may have been turnover of key personnel or important changes in computer programs used to process a major class of transactions. When significant changes have occurred, evidence from prior audits will provide little, if any, assurance for the current audit. Consideration of the foregoing factors may result in either increasing or decreasing the amount of testing in the current audit.

AUDIT PROGRAMS FOR TESTS OF CONTROLS

The auditor's decisions regarding the nature, extent, and timing of tests of controls should be documented in an audit program and related working papers. A sample audit program for tests of controls of cash disbursements transactions is illustrated in Figure 9-3. Note that the program lists the procedures to be used in performing

FIGURE 9-3 • ILLUSTRATIVE PARTIAL AUDIT PROGRAM FOR TESTS OF CONTROLS

Prepared by:_________ Date:_________
Reviewed by:_________ Date:_________

Amalgamated Products, Inc.
Planned Tests of Controls—Cash Disbursements Transactions
Year Ending December 31, 19X1

Working Paper Reference	Assertion/ Test of Control	Auditor	Date
	Existence or occurrence: 1. Select a sample of cash disbursement transactions from the cash disbursements journal and determine existence of a. Matching canceled (paid) checks. b. Matching approved payment vouchers and supporting documents. 2. Compare signatures on checks from (1) above to list of authorized check signers. 3. Inspect payment vouchers and supporting documents from (1) above for presence of "Paid" stamp. 4. Observe segregation of duties for approving payment vouchers and signing checks. *Completeness:* 5. Examine evidence of use of and accounting for prenumbered checks and scan sequence of check numbers in cash disbursements journal. 6. Observe handling and storage of unused checks. *Valuation or allocation:* 7. For transactions selected in (1) above, examine evidence of independent verification of agreement of details of checks with supporting payment vouchers and test by reperformance. 8. Select a sample of dates and examine evidence of independent check of agreement of daily summary of checks issued with entry to cash disbursements and test by reperformance. 9. Inspect independent bank reconciliations. (Note: Steps 8 and 9 also provide evidence of control over completeness.)		

the tests pertaining to the indicated assertions, and provides columns to indicate (1) cross-references to the working papers where the results of the tests are documented, (2) who performed the tests, and (3) the date the tests were completed. Details concerning the extent and timing of the tests may be indicated in the audit program or in the cross-referenced working papers as assumed in this illustration. The preparation of working papers showing the details of samples and the results of tests of controls is explained and illustrated in Chapter 11 of this text, which covers attribute sampling in tests of controls.

It may be noted that the tests listed in the formal audit program in Figure 9-3 are derived from the possible tests of controls listed in column 3 of Figure 9-1 on page 303. Some of the tests have been rearranged and combined, however, to make their performance more efficient.

USING INTERNAL AUDITORS IN TESTS OF CONTROLS

OBJECTIVE 5

Describe how internal auditors may be used in tests of controls.

Companies with many divisions, such as IBM and General Electric, or many branches, such as Chase Manhattan Bank and Sears Roebuck, usually employ internal auditors. Whenever a client has an internal audit function, the auditor may (1) coordinate his or her audit work with the internal auditors, and/or (2) use the internal auditors to provide direct assistance in the audit.[1]

Coordination of Audit with Internal Auditors

In the circumstances mentioned above, internal auditors will usually monitor ICS policies and procedures in each division or branch as part of their regular duties. The monitoring may include periodic reviews. In such case, the auditor may coordinate work with the internal auditors and reduce the number of entity locations at which the auditor would otherwise perform tests of controls. In coordinating work with internal auditors, it may be efficient for the auditor to (1) have periodic meetings with the internal auditors, (2) review their work schedules, (3) obtain access to their working papers, and (4) review internal audit reports.

When there is coordination of the work, the auditor should evaluate the quality and effectiveness of the internal auditors' work. In making the evaluation, the auditor should test the internal auditors' work and determine whether the

- Scope of work is appropriate to meet the objectives.
- Audit programs are adequate.
- Working papers adequately document work performed, including evidence of supervision and review.
- Conclusions are appropriate in the circumstances.
- Reports are consistent with the work performed.

Direct Assistance

The auditor may request internal auditors to provide direct assistance in performing tests of controls. When this occurs, SAS 65, *The Auditor's Consideration of the Internal Audit Function in a Financial Statement Audit* (AU 322.27), indicates that the auditor should

- Consider the internal auditors' competence and objectivity, and supervise, review, evaluate, and test the work performed.
- Inform the internal auditors of their responsibilities, the objectives of the procedures they are to perform, and matters that may affect the nature, timing, and extent of the tests.
- Inform the internal auditors that all significant accounting and auditing issues identified during their work should be brought to the external auditor's attention.

[1] In this section, the word *auditor* refers to the independent auditor.

DUAL-PURPOSE TESTS

In most audits, additional tests of controls are performed primarily during interim work, and substantive tests are performed primarily during year-end work. However, it is permissible under GAAS to perform substantive tests of details of transactions to detect monetary errors in the accounts during interim work. When this occurs, the auditor may simultaneously perform tests of controls on the same transactions. For instance, the auditor may examine sales invoices for the signature of employees authorized to independently verify the accuracy of the documents. At the same time, the auditor may tabulate the monetary errors in the invoices.

This type of testing is referred to as **dual-purpose testing.** When this type of testing is done, the auditor should exercise care in designing the tests to ensure that evidence is obtained as to both the effectiveness of controls and monetary errors in the accounts. In addition, the auditor should be careful in evaluating the evidence obtained. Dual-purpose testing is used by some firms because it may be more cost-efficient to perform the tests simultaneously than separately.

LEARNING CHECK:

9-8 a. Tests of controls only relate to the effectiveness of the operation of a control. Do you agree? Explain.
b. On what three questions do tests of controls of effectiveness of operation focus?

9-9 a. Distinguish between (1) concurrent and (2) additional or planned tests of controls.
b. Indicate the range of assessed levels of control risk that evidence from each type of test of controls may support.

9-10 a. Which audit procedures are commonly used in tests of controls?
b. Which procedure provides the best evidence of the operating effectiveness of a control? Why?

9-11 a. What effect will the auditor's planned assessed level of control risk have on the extent of tests of controls?
b. What factors should be considered by the auditor in using evidence of effectiveness from prior audits?

9-12 a. Is it necessary for the auditor to obtain evidence of effectiveness for the entire year covered by the financial statements?
b. What actions should be taken by the auditor when significant changes in the ICS have occurred since the interim tests of controls were performed?

9-13 What factors should be considered by the auditor in evaluating the work done by internal auditors under a
a. Coordination of work arrangement?
b. Direct assistance arrangement?

9-14 What are dual-purpose tests?

KEY TERMS:

Additional tests of controls, p. 311
Concurrent tests of controls, p. 310
Deviations, p. 310
Dual-purpose testing, p. 316
Exceptions, p. 310
Extent of tests of controls, p. 313
Nature of tests of controls, p. 311
Occurrences, p. 310
Planned tests of controls, p. 311
Tests of controls, p. 309
Timing of tests of controls, p. 312

ADDITIONAL CONSIDERATIONS

OBJECTIVE 6

Explain the process for assessing control risk for account balance assertions affected by single and multiple transaction classes.

As illustrated earlier in the chapter, the auditor typically first assesses control risk for assertions pertaining to transaction classes such as cash receipts and cash disbursements. These assessments are then used in assessing control risk for significant account balance assertions so that the appropriateness of the planned level of substantive tests for the account balances can be determined and specific substantive tests can be designed. This process is considered next, first for accounts affected by a single transaction class and then for accounts affected by multiple transaction classes.

ASSESSING CONTROL RISK FOR ACCOUNT BALANCE ASSERTIONS AFFECTED BY A SINGLE TRANSACTION CLASS

The process of assessing control risk for account balance assertions is straightforward for accounts that are affected by a single transaction class. This is the case for most income statement accounts. For example, sales is increased by credits for sales transactions in the revenue cycle, and many expense accounts are increased by debits for purchases transactions in the expenditure cycle. In these cases, the auditor's control risk assessment for each account balance assertion is the same as the control risk assessment for the same transaction class assertion. For example, the control risk assessment for the existence or occurrence assertion for the sales account balance should be the same as the control risk assessment for the existence or occurrence assertion for sales transactions. Similarly, the control risk assessment for the valuation or allocation assertion for many expenses should be the same as for the valuation or allocation assertion for purchases transactions.

ASSESSING CONTROL RISK FOR ACCOUNT BALANCE ASSERTIONS AFFECTED BY MULTIPLE TRANSACTION CLASSES

Many balance sheet accounts are significantly affected by more than one transaction class. For example, the cash balance is increased by cash receipts transactions in the revenue cycle and decreased by cash disbursements transactions in the expenditure cycle. In these cases, assessing control risk for an account balance assertion requires consideration of the relevant control risk assessments for each transaction class that significantly affects the balance. Thus, the control risk assessment for the valuation or allocation assertion for the cash balance is based on the control risk assessments for the valuation or allocation assertions for both cash receipts and cash disbursements transactions.

For an account affected by more than one transaction class, the control risk assessment for a particular account balance assertion is based on the control risk assessment for the same assertion pertaining to each transaction class that affects the account balance, *with one major exception.* The control risk assessments for the existence or occurrence and completeness assertions for a transaction class that *decreases* an account balance relate to the opposite assertion for the account balance affected. This perhaps unexpected relationship is illustrated in the following tabulation, which shows the relevant control risk assessments for transaction class assertions that are used to assess control risk for the existence or occurrence and completeness assertions for the cash balance:

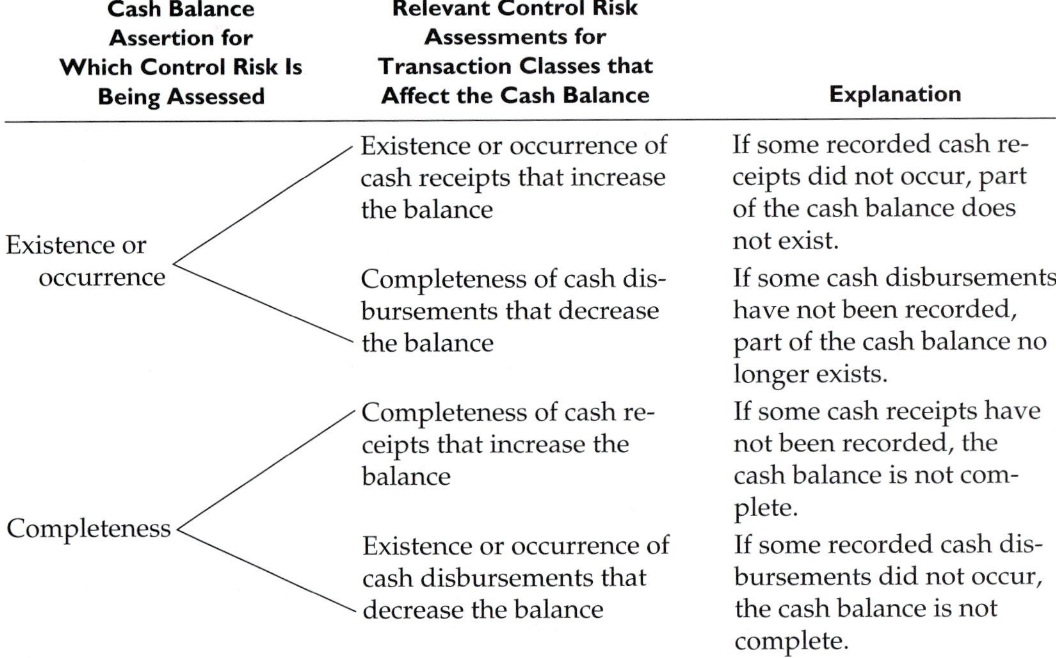

Cash Balance Assertion for Which Control Risk Is Being Assessed	Relevant Control Risk Assessments for Transaction Classes that Affect the Cash Balance	Explanation
Existence or occurrence	Existence or occurrence of cash receipts that increase the balance	If some recorded cash receipts did not occur, part of the cash balance does not exist.
	Completeness of cash disbursements that decrease the balance	If some cash disbursements have not been recorded, part of the cash balance no longer exists.
Completeness	Completeness of cash receipts that increase the balance	If some cash receipts have not been recorded, the cash balance is not complete.
	Existence or occurrence of cash disbursements that decrease the balance	If some recorded cash disbursements did not occur, the cash balance is not complete.

A summary of the relationships between account balance assertions and transaction class assertions is presented in Figure 9-4.

COMBINING DIFFERENT CONTROL RISK ASSESSMENTS

Referring to the previous example, suppose in assessing control risk for the existence or occurrence assertion for the cash balance, the auditor obtained the following control risk assessments from the working papers based on his or her understanding of relevant portions of the internal control structure and the results of tests of controls:

FIGURE 9-4 • SUMMARY OF RELATIONSHIPS BETWEEN ACCOUNT BALANCE ASSERTIONS AND TRANSACTION CLASS ASSERTIONS

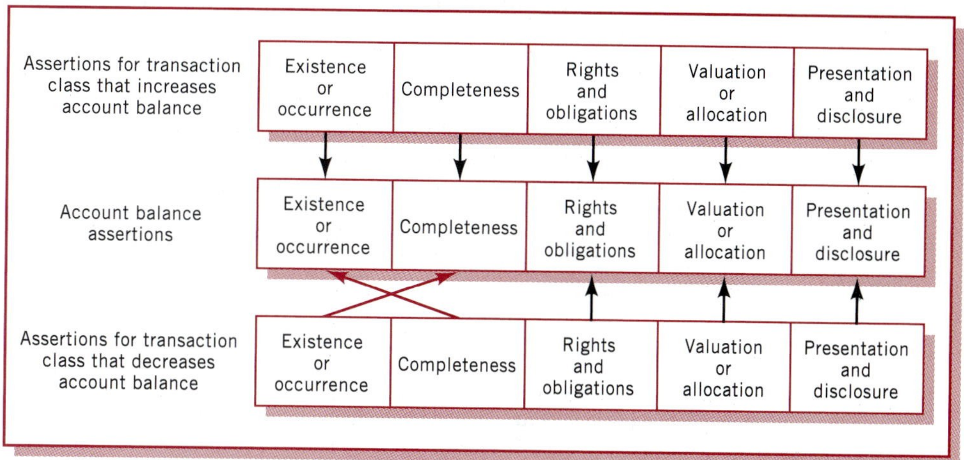

Assertion	Control Risk Assessment
Existence or occurrence of cash receipts	Low
Completeness of cash disbursements	Moderate

When the control risk assessments for the relevant transaction class assertions differ, the auditor may judgmentally weigh the significance of each assessment in arriving at a combined assessment. Alternatively, some firms elect to use the most conservative (highest) of the relevant assessments. If that approach were applied to this example, the auditor would assess control risk for the existence or occurrence assertion for the cash balance as moderate. Similarly, if the auditor's control risk assessments for the valuation or allocation assertions for cash receipts and cash disbursements transactions were moderate and high, respectively, control risk for the valuation or allocation assertion for the cash balance would be high.

Once control risk for the account balance assertion has been determined, it should be compared with the planned assessed level of control risk. When the planned level is supported, the auditor can proceed to design substantive tests based on the planned level of substantive tests. If the planned assessed level of control risk is not supported, the planned level of substantive tests must be revised before designing substantive tests.

DOCUMENTING THE ASSESSED LEVEL OF CONTROL RISK

OBJECTIVE 7

State the requirements for documenting control risk assessments.

The auditor's working papers should include **documentation of the control risk assessment.** The requirements are

Control Risk at Maximum— Only this conclusion needs to be documented.

Control Risk below Maximum— The basis for the assessment must be documented.

FIGURE 9-5 • PARTIAL DOCUMENTATION OF CONTROL RISK ASSESSMENTS

CLIENT Young Fashions, Inc. **BALANCE SHEET DATE** 09/30/X5
Completed by: CRS **Date** 05/19/X5 **Reviewed by:** EMT **Date** 05/28/X5
Control risk assessment for: Sales Transactions

COMPLETENESS

Client internal control structure policies and procedures relevant to completeness relate primarily to the computer listing of unmatched sales orders, bills of lading, packing slips, and sales invoices. Based on discussions with accounts receivable personnel on 5/11/X5 and with selected shipping personnel at Texas and California locations on 4/18/X5 and 5/8/X5, respectively, it normally can take up to two weeks between the placing of a sales order and shipment. It is rare, however, for an unmatched bill of lading or packing slip to remain on the unmatched documents report for more than two days. This was corroborated by examining the unmatched documents report for selected days (see W/P XX-4-2 [not illustrated here]) where the longest period a bill of lading or packing slip was outstanding was two days. Selected transactions on these reports were traced to underlying documents with no exceptions.

Based on this examination of evidential matter, combined with the results of inquiry of accounts receivable and shipping personnel and corroborating observations, control risk is assessed as slightly below the maximum.

RIGHTS AND OBLIGATIONS

Control risk is assessed at the maximum.

SOURCE: AICPA Audit Guide: *Consideration of the Internal Control Structure in a Financial Statement Audit* (1990), p. 145. (Adapted)

AU 319 does not illustrate or offer guidance on the form of the documentation. In practice, a common approach is to use narrative memoranda organized by financial statement assertions. This approach is illustrated in Figure 9-5, which documents the control risk assessments for selected sales transaction assertions.

Note that the *basis for the assessment* below the maximum for the completeness assertion, is given whereas *only the conclusion* is stated when the assessment is at the maximum, as indicated for the rights and obligations assertion.

OBJECTIVE 8

Indicate the auditor's requirements for communicating internal control structure related matters.

COMMUNICATION OF INTERNAL CONTROL STRUCTURE RELATED MATTERS

The auditor is required to identify and report to the audit committee, or other entity personnel with equivalent authority and responsibility, certain conditions that relate to an entity's internal control structure observed during an audit of financial statements. SAS 60, *Communication of Internal Control Structure Related Matters Noted in an Audit* (AU 325.02), defines a **reportable condition** as a

> significant deficiency in the design or operation of the internal control structure, which could adversely affect the organization's ability to record, process, summarize, and report financial data consistent with the assertions of management in the financial statements.

A reportable condition may be of such magnitude as to constitute a material weakness in internal control. AU 325.15 defines a **material weakness** as a reportable condition in which the design or operation of the specific internal control structure components do not reduce to a relatively low level the risk that misstatements in amounts that would be material in relation to the financial statements being audited may occur and not be detected within a timely period by employees in the normal course of performing their assigned functions.

An auditor may, but is not required to, separately identify in his or her communication with the audit committee those reportable conditions that are material weaknesses. Additional information about the **communication of internal control structure matters** is presented in the portion of Chapter 19 dealing with completing the audit.

REPORTED INTERNAL CONTROL DEFICIENCIES

Grant Thornton was dismissed as independent accountant for CAI Wireless Systems after informing management of a series of deficiencies in the Albany, N.Y. company's internal control structure.

Among other things, the auditors voiced concerns about the "absence of appropriate segregation of duties" among CAI's financial personnel, as well as an "understaffed accounting department" which Grant Thornton said may prevent the company from preparing reliable financial statements on a timely basis.

The outside accountants also raised eyebrows over the client's "failure to properly safeguard blank checks," or to adequately prevent unauthorized access to the company's electronic data processing system.

For their part, officials at CAI told the SEC that the problems cited by Grant Thornton date back to a period when the company was privately owned and had "no operations and very little activity, such as supervising investments and related matters for its shareholders."

Once the company acquired assets last August, CAI "had adequate control procedures in place that included heavy owner-management review of the detailed internal financial statements," chief executive Jared E. Abbruzzese maintained.

"A number of Grant Thornton's recommendations—including tighter security for CAI's computer systems—have now been implemented," he added.

However, officials at the company balked at the accountants' suggestion that they increase CAI's fidelity insurance coverage from the current $100,000 level.

Coopers & Lybrand was named as the company's new certifying accountant.

SOURCE: *Accounting Today*, June 6, 1994, p. 10.

LEARNING CHECK:

9-15 Explain the process for assessing control risk for
   a. Account balance assertions affected by a single transaction class.
   b. Account balance assertions affected by multiple transaction classes.

9-16 How may the auditor assess the level of control risk for an account balance assertion when the assessed levels of control risk for multiple related transaction class assertions are not all the same?

9-17 What are the requirements for documenting the assessed level of control risk for an assertion?

9-18 What form does the documentation often take in practice?

9-19 What responsibility does the auditor have for communicating internal control structure related matters?

9-20 Differentiate the terms *reportable condition* and *material weakness.*

KEY TERMS:

Communication of internal control structure matters, p. 321
Documentation of the control risk assessment, p. 319
Material weakness, p. 320
Reportable condition, p. 320

SUMMARY

The methodology for assessing control risk for specific transaction class and account balance assertions is an important part of a financial statement audit. The methodology includes identifying potential misstatements and necessary controls, evaluating evidence from procedures to obtain an understanding of relevant control policies and procedures and from tests of controls, making and documenting the assessment, and comparing the actual assessed level of control risk with the planned assessed level to determine whether the planned level of substantive tests must be revised before designing specific substantive tests of the related assertions. The process varies slightly depending on whether the primarily substantive or lower assessed level of control risk approach is being used for particular assertions. A correct control risk assessment is vital to an effective and efficient audit. Certain reportable conditions discovered in the process of assessing control risk must be reported to the audit committee or other entity personnel with equivalent authority and responsibilities.

BIBLIOGRAPHY

AICPA Professional Standards:

AU 319, Consideration of the Internal Control Structure in a Financial Statement Audit.

SAS 60 (AU 325), Communication of Internal Control Structure Related Matters Noted in an Audit.

SAS 65 (AU 322), The Auditor's Consideration of the Internal Audit Function in an Audit of Financial Statements.

IAU 6 (AU 8006), Risk Assessment and Internal Control.

IAU 10 (AU 8010), Using the Work of an Internal Auditor.

International Statement on Auditing (AU 10050), Particular Considerations in the Audit of Small Businesses.

AICPA, Audit Guide: *Consideration of the Internal Control Structure in a Financial Statement Audit,* New York, 1990.

AICPA, Auditing Procedure Study: *The Independent Auditor's Use of the Work of Internal Auditors,* New York, 1989.

Brown, Clifton E., and Solomon, Ira. "Auditor Configural Information Processing in Control Risk Assessment," *Auditing: A Journal of Practice and Theory* (Fall 1990), pp. 17–38.

Committee of Sponsoring Organizations of the Treadway Commission, *Internal Control—Integrated Framework,* Jersey City, NJ: American Institute of Certified Public Accountants, 1992.

Reimers, Jane, Wheeler, Stephen, and Dusenbury, Richard. "The Effect of Response Mode on Auditors' Control Risk Assessments," *Auditing: A Journal of Practice and Theory* (Fall 1993), pp. 62–78.

Spires, Eric E. "Auditors' Evaluation of Test-of-Control Strength," *Accounting Review* (April 1991), pp. 259–276.

OBJECTIVE QUESTIONS

Indicate the *best* answer for each of the following multiple choice questions.

9-21 These questions pertain to assessing control risk.

1. After obtaining an understanding of the internal control structure and assessing control risk, an auditor decided not to perform additional tests of controls. The auditor most likely concluded that the
   a. Additional evidence to support a further reduction in control risk was *not* cost-beneficial to obtain.
   b. Assessed level of inherent risk exceeded the assessed level of control risk.
   c. Internal control structure was properly designed and justifiably may be relied on.
   d. Evidence obtainable through tests of controls would *not* support an increased level of control risk.

2. When an auditor increases the assessed level of control risk because certain control procedures were determined to be ineffective, the auditor would most likely increase the
   a. Extent of tests of controls.
   b. Planned level of detection risk.
   c. Planned level of substantive tests.
   d. Level of inherent risk.

3. Which of the following is *not* a step in an auditor's decision to assess control risk at below the maximum?
   a. Evaluate the effectiveness of the internal control procedures with tests of controls.
   b. Obtain an understanding of the entity's accounting system and control environment.
   c. Perform tests of details of transactions to detect material misstatements in the financial statements.
   d. Consider whether control procedures can have a pervasive effect on financial statement assertions.

4. The ultimate purpose of assessing control risk is to contribute to the auditor's evaluation of the risk that
   a. Specified controls requiring segregation of duties may be circumvented by collusion.
   b. Entity policies may be overridden by senior management.
   c. Tests of controls may fail to identify procedures relevant to assertions.
   d. Material misstatements may exist in the financial statements.

9-22 These questions relate to tests of controls.

1. A procedure that would most likely be used by an auditor in performing tests of control procedures that involve segregation of functions and that leave no transaction trail is
   a. Inspection.
   b. Observation.
   c. Reperformance.
   d. Reconciliation.

2. To obtain evidential matter about control risk, an auditor ordinarily selects tests from a variety of techniques, including
   a. Analysis.
   b. Confirmation.
   c. Reperformance.
   d. Comparison.

3. The objective of tests of details of transactions performed as tests of controls is to
   a. Detect material misstatements in the account balances of the financial statements.
   b. Evaluate whether an internal control structure policy of procedure operated effectively.
   c. Determine the nature, timing, and extent of substantive tests for financial statement assertions.
   d. Reduce control risk, inherent risk, and detection risk to an acceptably low level.

4. An auditor wishes to perform tests of controls on a client's cash disbursements procedures. If the control procedures leave *no* audit trail of documentary evidence, the auditor most likely will test the procedures by
   a. Confirmation and observation.
   b. Observation and inquiry.
   c. Analytical procedures and confirmation.
   d. Inquiry and analytical procedures.

9-23 The following questions relate to documenting control risk assessments.

1. When control risk is assessed at the maximum level for all financial statement assertions, an auditor should document the auditor's

	Understanding of the entity's internal control structure components	**Conclusion that control risk is at the maximum level**	**Basis for concluding that control risk is at the maximum level**
a.	Yes	No	No
b.	Yes	Yes	No
c.	No	Yes	Yes
d.	Yes	Yes	Yes

2. When an auditor assesses control risk below the maximum level, the auditor is required to document the auditor's

	Basis for concluding that control risk is below the maximum level	**Understanding of the entity's internal control structure components**
a.	No	No
b.	Yes	Yes
c.	Yes	No
d.	No	Yes

COMPREHENSIVE QUESTIONS

9-24 **(Assessing control risk)** An auditor is required to obtain a sufficient understanding of each of the components of an entity's internal control structure to plan the audit of the entity's financial statements and to assess control risk for the assertions embodied in the account balance, transaction class, and disclosure components of the financial statements.

REQUIRED

a. Explain the reasons why an auditor may assess control risk at the maximum level for one or more assertions embodied in an account balance.
b. What must an auditor do to support assessing control risk at less than the maximum level when the auditor has determined that controls have been placed in operation?
c. What should an auditor consider when seeking a further reduction in the planned assessed level of control risk?
d. What are an auditor's documentation requirements concerning an entity's internal control structure and the assessed level of control risk?

AICPA (adapted)

9-25 **(Effects of audit strategies on assessing control risk)** As an audit manager at Gung & Ho, CPAs, you have been scheduled to serve as the discussion leader for an in-office training session on *consideration of the internal control structure in a financial statement audit.*

REQUIRED

Prepare an outline of comments you plan to make to indicate similarities and differences in how each of the following items is handled under the primarily substantive approach versus the lower assessed level of control risk approach:

a. Obtaining and documenting the understanding.
b. Performing concurrent tests of controls.
c. Making an initial assessment of control risk.
d. Performing additional or planned tests of controls.
e. Making a final assessment of control risk.
f. Documenting the control risk assessment.
g. Designing substantive tests.

9-26 **(Tests of controls)** Jane Byrd is participating in her first audit, the audit of the Marion Company's financial statements for 19X7. Jane seeks your help in answering the following questions she has about tests of controls.

1. What is the overall purpose of tests of controls?
2. When are tests of controls normally performed?
3. What auditing procedures may be used in performing tests of controls?
4. Is there any difference in the quality of evidence provided by each auditing procedure? Explain.
5. What questions, if any, need to be answered by tests of controls?
6. What responsibility, if any, does the auditor have to perform tests of controls after interim work has been completed?
7. What are dual-purpose tests and is it true that such tests may be used as a substitute for tests of controls?
8. How, if at all, may Marion's internal auditors be used in performing tests of controls?

REQUIRED

a. Answer Jane's questions.
b. Explain to Jane the content of an audit program for tests of controls.
c. Describe for Jane the circumstances that represent a *deviation* when the test of controls involves inspecting documents. What is the significance of a deviation on the remainder of the audit?

9-27 **(Potential misstatements and tests of controls)** Your firm has been engaged to audit the financial statements of the Haven Company. In obtaining an understanding of internal controls pertaining to cash disbursements transactions, the following questionnaire is used:

1. Are there periodic independent reconciliations of bank accounts?
2. Is a daily summary of checks prepared and agreed to checks issued?
3. Are supporting documents stamped *paid* after payment?
4. Are unused checks stored in a secure area with access limited to authorized personnel?
5. Are checks prenumbered and accounted for?
6. Is there supervisory approval of account classifications in journalizing?
7. Is a check protection device used to imprint check amounts?
8. Are there periodic comparisons of the petty cash account with cash on hand?
9. Is there segregation of duties between journalizing and posting?
10. Is there independent check of daily check summary with check register entries?
11. Is there independent check of agreement of entry dates with dates on checks?

REQUIRED

a. Identify a potential misstatement that could occur, assuming a *No* answer to each question.
b. Identify a possible test of controls for the control procedure, assuming a *Yes* answer to each question. (Present your answers in tabular form with separate columns for each part.)

9-28 **(Necessary controls and tests of controls)** In your audit of the Megan Company, you identify the following potential misstatements that could occur for financial statement assertions in accounts affected by cash disbursements transactions:

1. An issued check may not be accounted for.
2. A check may be issued to an unauthorized payee.
3. Unused printed checks may be stolen from the unlocked supply closet.
4. An issued check may not be listed on the daily check summary.
5. The bank balance per books may not reconcile to balance per the bank.
6. Approved supporting documentation may be paid twice.
7. The check signer also journalizes and posts cash disbursements transactions.
8. An issued check is improperly classified in journalizing.
9. A check may be signed by an unauthorized signer.
10. An issued check may not be journalized.

REQUIRED

a. Identify necessary control procedures that could prevent or detect each misstatement.
b. Identify a possible test of controls for each control procedure in (a) above. (Present your answers in tabular form using one column for each part.)

9-29 **(Potential misstatements and necessary controls)** Nancy Neuman, the manager on the audit of the DeVieu Company, decides that additional tests of controls should be performed on controls pertaining to cash disbursements transactions in an effort to further reduce the control risk assessments. Nancy gives you the following audit program for the tests of controls.

1. Review evidence of monthly bank reconciliations.
2. Inquire about access to vault where unused checks are stored.
3. Observe segregation of duties between approving checks for payment and the signing of checks.
4. Examine evidence of internal verification of daily check summary with checks recorded.
5. Examine evidence of internal verification of agreement of daily check summary with checks issued.
6. Inquire of accounting supervisor about misclassifications in journalizing.

7. Examine supporting documentation for issuance of checks.
8. Examine signatures of check signers on canceled checks.
9. Compare name of payee on checks with payee on supporting documentation.
10. Observe cancellation of documents on payment.
11. Scan check register for sequential journalizing of checks.
12. Inspect checks for prenumbering.
13. Observe access controls over check writing equipment.

REQUIRED

a. Identify a control procedure to which each test pertains.
b. Identify a misstatement that may be prevented or detected by each control procedure in (a) above.

9-30 **(Using the work of internal auditors)** North, CPA, is planning an audit of the financial statements of General Company. In planning the study and evaluation of General Company's internal control structure, North is considering General's internal audit function, which is staffed by Tyler.

REQUIRED

a. In what ways may Tyler's work be relevant to North, the independent auditor?
b. What factors should North consider and what inquiries should North make in deciding whether to use Tyler's work?

9-31 **(Assessing control risk for account balance assertions)** After completion of interim work, Jan Jackson, manager of the Melville Company audit, makes the following control risk assessments for transaction classes:

	Assertion		
	Existence or Occurrence	**Completeness**	**Valuation or Allocation**
Revenue cycle			
Credit sales	Low	Moderate	High
Collections from customers (cash receipts)	Moderate	Moderate	Moderate
Expenditure cycle			
Purchases	Low	High	Moderate
Cash disbursements	Low	Low	Low
Personnel services cycle			
Payroll	Low	Low	Moderate

All sales and purchase transactions of the Melville Company are made on account.

Jan takes a conservative approach to risk assessments. Before finalizing the design of substantive tests, Jan realizes that she must determine control risk assessments for the existence or occurrence, completeness, and valuation or allocation account balance assertions for the following accounts:

Cash	Accounts Payable
Accounts Receivable	Sales
Inventory	Salaries and Wages Expense

She assesses control risk at the maximum for the rights and obligations and presentation and disclosure account balance assertions for each account where applicable.

REQUIRED

Identify the transaction class or classes that affect each account balance. Then determine the appropriate control risk assessment for the indicated account balance assertions. Use the following format for your solution:

	Transaction Class That		Account Balance Control Risk Assessment		
Account	Increases Account	Decreases Account	Existence or Occurrence	Completeness	Valuation or Allocation

CASE

9-32 **(Evaluation of internal control structure)** Harlan, Inc., is a large, highly diversified organization engaged in feed and flour milling, the manufacture of plastic products, the manufacture of highly specialized machinery, and the operation of poultry hatcheries, farms, and processing plants. The company's facilities are located throughout the United States.

During the past several years, the company has been expanding the business through acquisitions, mergers, and natural growth of the original operations.

The company finances poultry growing operations of feed customers until the flocks are marketed. Poultry prices have been depressed for the past several years, and as a result, large loan losses have been sustained. Many accounts are secured by collateral other than poultry and are not considered current assets.

In obtaining an understanding of the current internal control structure, you discover the following changes from prior years:

1. The company organized an internal audit staff during the year.
2. The internal audit staff is reconciling all bank accounts.
3. The company has instituted a procedure whereby divisions send the Home Office an "invoice apron" that lists the information required for payment of the invoices and the due date. The other invoices and other supporting data (e.g., receiving reports, purchase orders) remain at the receiving location.
4. Excess funds are now invested in short-term securities. The treasurer has sole authority for purchase and sale of the investments. Securities purchases are credited to a company account at a local brokerage house. The securities are held in the treasurer's name. All correspondence relating to the investments is sent directly to the treasurer. He, in turn, forwards brokerage advices to the controller's office for recording in the accounts.
5. A physical inventory of office furniture and fixtures has been taken at the home office.

Discussions with company personnel and tests of controls disclosed the following information:

1. The company plans to discontinue extending credit to certain customers whose poultry-raising operations have deteriorated to the point that their ability to repay the company is doubtful. It is anticipated that a large provision for doubtful accounts may be necessary to reduce these accounts to estimated realizable value on a forced-realization basis (the company has second mortgages as collateral on many of the farms).
2. The tool crib inventory consists of a conglomeration of miscellaneous items, most of which are small quantities with very minor unit prices. This inventory totals $42,395.89, which is an insignificant portion of the total inventories.
3. The purchased parts stockroom at another plant is segregated from the production areas by a wire fence. While visiting this plant, you noted that the gate was left open

all day and access to the stockroom (which contains many valuable and easily concealed items) was available to any employee. The stockroom's perpetual inventory records were formerly checked by an employee who made periodic test counts. This employee has retired and not been replaced. As a result, such counting has ceased. You expanded your tests in view of these situations and are satisfied that the perpetual records reasonably reflect the quantities on hand.

REQUIRED

a. Identify the control environment factors that impact on the company's internal control structure.
b. List the strengths and weaknesses in Harlan's controls.
c. Indicate your suggestions for improving the weaknesses identified in (b) above.
d. For the accounts marketable securities, accounts receivable, and purchased parts inventory identify one assertion for which you would assess control risk at the maximum or slightly below the maximum.

RESEARCH QUESTIONS

9-33 **(Using the work of internal auditors)** Page 315 of this chapter presents a discussion of the external auditor's use of internal auditors in tests of controls, including a citation to SAS 65 (AU 322), *The Auditor's Consideration of the Internal Audit Function in a Financial Statement Audit.* The AICPA has provided additional guidance on this matter in its *Auditing Procedure Study: The Independent Auditor's Use of the Work of Internal Auditors,* published in 1989. If you can obtain access to a copy of this study, scan the table of contents and browse through the entire document. Then prepare a brief summary of areas covered by the *Auditing Procedures Study* and indicate how it expands on the guidance provided on page 315 of this chapter.

9-34 **(Reportable conditions/material weaknesses)** The chapter provides a brief summary of the auditor's responsibilities regarding the communication of internal control structure related matters to the audit committee or other personnel of the audited entity. From time to time, auditors' findings of reportable conditions or material weaknesses in clients' internal control structures find their way into the financial press as illustrated in the box on page 321. Sometimes the information is released as a result of information included in a required SEC filing following a change of auditors. Locate information about any such occurrence described in the financial press or other source and prepare a brief report identifying the client entity, the auditing firm, the reported deficiencies in internal control, and the outcome of the situation.

CHAPTER

10

DETECTION RISK AND THE DESIGN OF SUBSTANTIVE TESTS

LEARNING OBJECTIVES

After studying this chapter, you should be able to

1. Explain the process for evaluating the planned level of substantive tests as specified in the preliminary audit strategy.
2. Determine a revised acceptable level of detection risk when appropriate.
3. Indicate how the nature, timing, and extent of substantive tests are varied to achieve an acceptable level of detection risk.
4. Discuss the relationships among assertions, specific audit objectives, and substantive tests.
5. State the nature and uses of audit programs for substantive tests.
6. Describe and apply a general framework for developing audit programs for substantive tests.
7. Indicate special considerations in designing substantive tests for selected types of accounts.
8. Contrast tests of controls and substantive tests.

DETERMINING DETECTION RISK
- EVALUATING THE PLANNED LEVEL OF SUBSTANTIVE TESTS
- REVISING PLANNED DETECTION RISK
- SPECIFYING DETECTION RISK FOR DIFFERENT SUBSTANTIVE TESTS OF THE SAME ASSERTION

DESIGNING SUBSTANTIVE TESTS
- NATURE
- TIMING
- EXTENT
- SUMMARY OF RELATIONSHIPS AMONG AUDIT RISK COMPONENTS AND THE NATURE, TIMING, AND EXTENT OF SUBSTANTIVE TESTS

DEVELOPING AUDIT PROGRAMS FOR SUBSTANTIVE TESTS
- RELATIONSHIPS AMONG ASSERTIONS, SPECIFIC AUDIT OBJECTIVES, AND SUBSTANTIVE TESTS
- ILLUSTRATIVE AUDIT PROGRAM FOR SUBSTANTIVE TESTS
- GENERAL FRAMEWORK FOR DEVELOPING AUDIT PROGRAMS FOR SUBSTANTIVE TESTS
- AUDIT PROGRAMS IN INITIAL ENGAGEMENTS
- AUDIT PROGRAMS IN RECURRING ENGAGEMENTS

SPECIAL CONSIDERATIONS IN DESIGNING SUBSTANTIVE TESTS
- INCOME STATEMENT ACCOUNTS
- ACCOUNTS INVOLVING ACCOUNTING ESTIMATES
- ACCOUNTS INVOLVING RELATED PARTY TRANSACTIONS
- COMPARISON OF TESTS OF CONTROLS AND SUBSTANTIVE TESTS

SUMMARY

APPENDIX 10A: DETECTION RISK FOR ANALYTICAL PROCEDURES AND TESTS OF DETAILS

BIBLIOGRAPHY

OBJECTIVE QUESTIONS

COMPREHENSIVE QUESTIONS

CASE

RESEARCH QUESTIONS

In Chapter 8, we considered how the auditor obtains and documents an understanding of the internal control structure consistent with the preliminary audit strategy chosen for each significant financial statement assertion. In Chapter 9, for each strategy we considered how the auditor assesses control risk for significant transaction class and account balance assertions based on the understanding of the ICS and the results of tests of controls. In this chapter, we explain how this information is used in completing the third major audit activity required in meeting the second standard of field work—designing substantive tests, which involves determining the nature, timing, and extent of the tests to be performed.

Topics in this chapter include the following: (1) determining detection risk, (2) general considerations in designing substantive tests, (3) the nature, use, and development of audit programs, and (4) special considerations in designing substantive tests for different types of accounts.

DETERMINING DETECTION RISK

Recall that **detection risk** is the risk that the auditor will not detect a material misstatement that exists in an assertion. As explained in Chapter 7, a **planned acceptable level of detection risk** is specified for each significant financial statement assertion. Furthermore, recall that regardless of whether the auditor chooses to use quantitative or nonquantitative expressions of the risk levels, planned detection risk is determined based on the relationships expressed in the following model:

$$DR = \frac{AR}{IR \times CR}$$

The model shows that for a given level of audit risk (*AR*) specified by the auditor, detection risk (*DR*) is inversely related to the assessed levels of inherent risk (*IR*) and control risk (*CR*). When used in the planning phase to determine planned detection risk, *CR* represents the planned assessed level of control risk specified as the first component of the preliminary audit strategy.[1]

Planned detection risk is the basis for the **planned level of substantive tests** that is specified as the fourth and final component of the auditor's preliminary audit strategy for an assertion. The relationships among preliminary audit strategies, planned detection risk, and planned levels of substantive tests that were explained in Chapter 7 may be summarized as follows:

Preliminary Audit Strategy	Planned Detection Risk	Planned Level of Substantive Tests
Primarily substantive approach	Low or very low	Higher level
Lower assessed level of control risk approach	Moderate or high	Lower level

Before designing substantive tests, the auditor must determine whether the planned level of substantive tests and associated planned detection risk need to be revised.

OBJECTIVE 1

Explain the process for evaluating the planned level of substantive tests as specified in the preliminary audit strategy.

EVALUATING THE PLANNED LEVEL OF SUBSTANTIVE TESTS

After obtaining an understanding of relevant internal control structure policies and procedures and assessing control risk for a financial statement assertion, the auditor should compare the *actual* or *final* assessed level of control risk with the

[1] At this point, it is suggested that the student review Figure 7-5 on page 241, which depicts the interrelationships among the four components of audit strategies under the primarily substantive and lower assessed level of control risk approaches.

planned assessed level of control risk for that assertion. If the final assessed level is the same as the planned assessed level of control risk, the auditor may proceed to design specific substantive tests based on the planned level of substantive tests specified as the fourth component of the preliminary audit strategy. Otherwise the level of substantive tests must be revised before designing specific substantive tests to accommodate a revised acceptable level of detection risk.[2]

For example, assume the preliminary audit strategy was based on the lower assessed level of control risk approach and included a planned assessed level of control risk of low and a minimal planned level of substantive tests associated with a planned detection risk of high. If the final assessed level of control risk was moderate or high, the auditor would need to increase the level of substantive tests in order to accommodate a lower acceptable level of detection risk.

REVISING PLANNED DETECTION RISK

OBJECTIVE 2

Determine a revised acceptable level of detection risk when appropriate.

When appropriate, a **revised or final acceptable level of detection risk** is determined for each assertion in the same manner as the planned detection risk except that it will be based on the *actual* or *final* assessment of control risk rather than the *planned* assessed level of control risk for the assertion. If the auditor chooses to quantify the risk assessments, the revised detection risk level can be determined by solving the audit risk model for *DR*. If the risk assessments are not quantified, the revised detection risk is determined judgmentally or with the aid of a risk matrix like the one shown in Figure 7-3 on page 236.

SPECIFYING DETECTION RISK FOR DIFFERENT SUBSTANTIVE TESTS OF THE SAME ASSERTION

The term *detection risk* as used in the preceding sections refers to the risk that all the substantive tests used to obtain evidence about an assertion will collectively fail to detect a material misstatment. In designing substantive tests, the auditor may want to specify different detection risk levels to be used with different substantive tests of the same assertion. For example, based on the assumption that evidence obtained from one test or group of tests will reduce the risk of a material misstatement remaining undetected after the test or tests have been performed, it may be appropriate to use a higher level of detection risk for the remaining tests.

Appendix A to this chapter illustrates an expanded risk components matrix that can be used to determine a detection risk level for all substantive tests of details to be applied to an assertion, given an assumption about the level of risk that analytical procedures applied first will not detect material misstatements. As would be expected, the lower the risk that analytical procedures will not detect material misstatements, the higher the detection risk can be for the tests of details which

[2] For a reminder of where these steps fit graphically into the overall methodology for meeting the second standard of field work, it is suggested the student review Figure 9-2 on page 307.

follow. A quantitative model for determining the acceptable level of detection risk for an *individual* test of details is described in Appendix 12A.

LEARNING CHECK:

10-1 For each of the two preliminary audit strategies, state the appropriate *levels* of (1) planned detection risk and (2) substantive tests.

10-2 When and how does the auditor evaluate the planned level of substantive tests that was specified as the fourth component of the audit strategy for an assertion?

10-3 When and how does an auditor determine a revised or final acceptable level of detection risk for an assertion?

10-4 When more than one substantive test is performed to obtain evidence about a particular assertion, should the same acceptable level of detection risk be specified for each test? Explain.

KEY TERMS:

Detection risk, p. 331
Planned acceptable level of detection risk, p. 331
Planned level of substantive tests, p. 331
Revised or final acceptable level of detection risk, p. 332

DESIGNING SUBSTANTIVE TESTS

OBJECTIVE 3

Indicate how the nature, timing, and extent of substantive tests are varied to achieve an acceptable level of detection risk.

To have a reasonable basis for an opinion on the client's financial statements, the auditor must obtain sufficient competent evidential matter as required by the third standard of field work. Substantive tests provide evidence about the fairness of each significant financial statement assertion. Conversely, substantive tests may reveal monetary errors or misstatements in the recording or reporting of transactions and balances. Designing substantive tests involves determining the nature, timing, and extent of the tests necessary to meet the acceptable level of detection risk for each assertion.

NATURE

The **nature of substantive tests** refers to the type and effectiveness of the auditing procedures to be performed. When the acceptable level of detection risk is low, the auditor must use more effective, and usually more costly, procedures. When the acceptable level of detection risk is high, less effective and less costly procedures can be used. As explained in Chapter 5, the following are the three types of substantive tests: analytical procedures, tests of details of transactions, and tests of details of balances. The types of tests and their relative effectiveness and cost are discussed in the following sections.

Analytical Procedures

The use of **analytical procedures** in audit planning to identify areas of greater risk of misstatement is explained in Chapter 6. Analytical procedures may also be used in the testing phase of the audit as a substantive test to obtain evidence about a particular assertion. In some cases, they are used as a supplement to tests of details. In other cases, they may be used as the primary substantive test.

For many assertions, analytical procedures are considered less effective than tests of details. In some cases, however, the opposite is true. For example, comparisons of aggregate payments to suppliers with goods received may indicate excessive payments that may be more difficult to detect by testing individual transactions. Similarly, comparisons of aggregate salaries with the number of personnel employed may indicate unauthorized payments more readily than tests of transactions.

In some cases where analytical procedures are effective, they may also add to the efficiency of the audit. For example, for public utilities, such as electric, gas, and cable companies, relatively small amounts of revenue are billed to and collected from many thousands of customers each month. Tests of details of these high-volume, low-value revenue transactions would be very tedious and costly. On the other hand, revenues in such cases can often be estimated with a fair degree of precision using independent variables such as number of subscribers, billing rates for various types of services, temperature data (for electric and gas utilities), and so on. For example, for a cable company client, the auditor could multiply data about the average number of subscribers for each type of service offered by the monthly fee for that service times 12 to estimate total revenues for the year. The auditor's estimated balance for revenues can then be compared with the reported balance as part of the evidence used in determining whether revenues are fairly stated. In other cases, the expected relationship of one account balance to another might be used. For example, total sales commissions expense could normally be estimated from total sales revenues rather than examining the details of entries to sales commissions.

SAS 56, *Analytical Procedures* (AU 329.11), indicates that the expected effectiveness and efficiency of analytical procedures depends on the

- Nature of the assertion.
- Plausibility and predictability of the relationship.
- Availability and reliability of the data used to develop the expectation.
- Precision of the expectation.

When the results of the analytical procedures conform to expectations, and the acceptable level of detection risk for the assertion is high, it may not be necessary to perform tests of details.

Analytical procedures are generally the least costly tests to perform. Thus, consideration should be given to the extent to which these procedures can contribute to achieving the acceptable level of detection risk before selecting tests of details.

EFFICACY OF ANALYTICAL PROCEDURES

How effective are analytical procedures in detecting misstatements? In a study of 281 misstatements requiring financial statement adjustments in 152 audits, researchers found the following: Auditors' expectations of errors based on prior audits of the client and their discussions with client personnel led to the detection of 19 percent of all errors, 24 percent of the 82 largest errors, and 27 percent of the 26 extremely large errors. After analytical procedures were applied, 45.6 percent of all errors, 54.9 percent of the 82 largest errors, and 69 percent of the extremely large errors were signaled. The authors concluded that increased utilization of these procedures "might improve the auditor's effectiveness and/or efficiency in detecting errors, and also allow a 'fine tuning' of substantive tests of details."

SOURCE: : R. E. Hylas and R. H. Ashton, "Audit Detection of Financial Statement Errors," *Accounting Review* (October 1982), pp. 751–765.

Tests of Details of Transactions

Tests of details of transactions primarily involve tracing and vouching. For example, the details of transactions may be traced from source documents such as sales invoices and vouchers to entries in accounting records such as the sales journal and voucher register. Or the details of entries in accounting records such as the cash disbursements journal and perpetual inventory records can be vouched to supporting documents such as canceled checks and vendors' invoices. The auditor's focus in performing these tests is on finding monetary errors rather than deviations from controls. As noted in Chapter 5, tracing is useful in testing for understatements, and vouching is useful in testing for overstatements. Other procedures may also be involved, such as inquiring and reperforming calculations.

In these tests, the auditor uses evidence obtained about some (a sample) or all of the individual debits and credits in an account to reach a conclusion about the account balance. These tests generally use documents available in client files. The effectiveness of the tests depends on the particular procedure and documents used. For example, it will be recalled that externally generated documents, and internally generated documents that are circulated externally, are more reliable than internally generated documents that have not been circulated externally.

Tests of details of transactions are typically more time consuming and thus more costly to perform than analytical procedures, but less costly than tests of details of balances. Their cost-efficiency is enhanced when performed concurrent with tests of controls as **dual-purpose tests**.

Tests of Details of Balances

Tests of details of balances focus on obtaining evidence directly about an account balance rather than the individual debits and credits comprising the balance. For example, the auditor may request banks to confirm cash balances and customers to confirm accounts receivable balances. The auditor may also inspect plant assets, and observe the client's inventory taking and perform pricing tests of the ending inventory.

The effectiveness of these tests also depends on the particular procedure performed and the type of evidence obtained. The following illustrates how the effectiveness of tests of balances can be tailored to meet different detection risk levels for the valuation or allocation assertion for cash in bank:

Detection Risk	Test of Details of Balances
High	Scan client-prepared bank reconciliation and verify mathematical accuracy of reconciliation.
Moderate	Review client-prepared bank reconciliation and verify major reconciling items and mathematical accuracy of reconciliation.
Low	Prepare bank reconciliation using bank statement obtained from client and verify major reconciling items and mathematical accuracy.
Very low	Obtain bank statement directly from bank, prepare bank reconciliation, and verify all reconciling items and mathematical accuracy.

Note in this illustration that when detection risk is high, the auditor uses internally prepared documentation and performs limited auditing procedures. In contrast, when detection risk is very low, the auditor uses documentation obtained directly from the bank and performs extensive auditing procedures.

Tests of details of balances often involve the use of external documentation and/or the direct personal knowledge of the auditor. Therefore, they can be very effective. They also tend to be the most time consuming and costly to perform.

Illustration of Nature of Substantive Tests

The application of the three types of substantive tests discussed in the preceding sections may be illustrated in the context of the following accounts:

Accounts Receivable

Beg. Bal.	xx		
Credit sales transactions	xx	Collections from customers	xx
	xx		xx
	xx	Write-offs	xx
	xx		xx
	xx	Returns & allowances	xx
			xx
End. Bal.	xx		

Sales Revenue

		Credit sales transactions	xx
			xx
			xx
			xx
			xx
			xx
			xx
			xx
		End. Bal.	xx

Commissions Expense

Commission accrual	xx		
	xx		
	xx		
	xx		
	xx		
	xx		
	xx		
	xx		
End. Bal.	xx		

To simplify the illustration, only one *Accounts Receivable* account is shown. In practice, of course, there would typically be a control account backed up by a subsidiary ledger of customer accounts containing the individual debits and credits for transactions affecting each customer's account. We will assume the beginning balance of accounts receivable is fairly stated based on the prior year's audit. To determine that the ending balance of accounts receivable is fairly stated, the auditor might consider obtaining evidence from any of the following substantive tests:

- *Analytical procedures.* Possibilities include:
  - Comparing the absolute value of this year's ending balance in the control account with the prior year's balance, a budgeted amount, or other expected value.
  - Using the ending balance to determine the percentage of accounts receivable to current assets for comparison with the prior year, industry data, or other expected value.
  - Using the ending balance to calculate the accounts receivable turnover ratio for comparison with the prior year, industry data, or other expected value.
- *Tests of details of transactions.* Possibilities include:
  - Vouching a sample of the individual debits and credits in customer accounts for the transaction classes indicated to the offsetting entries (for example, vouching the debits to the offsetting credits in sales revenue) and supporting documentation (such as sales invoices, bad-debt write-off authorizations, and credit memos for authorized sales returns and allowances).
  - Tracing transactions data from source documents and journals (such as the sales journal) to the corresponding entries in the customer accounts for the transaction classes indicated.
- *Tests of details of balances.* Possibilities include:
  - Determining that the ending balances in the individual customer accounts add up to the control account balance.
  - Confirming the ending balances for a sample of customer accounts directly with the customers.

In the case of accounts receivable, it is common to apply each of the three types of substantive tests to some extent. For other accounts, only one or two of the types of tests might be performed in obtaining sufficient evidence to meet the acceptable level of detection risk.

For simplicity, the *Sales Revenue* account shown in the illustration shows the credits representing the individual sales transactions. In practice, the sales revenue account might show only daily, weekly, or monthly totals posted from the sales journal. In either case, to determine that sales revenue is fairly stated, the auditor might obtain evidence from any of the following:

- *Analytical procedures.* Possibilities include:
  - Comparing the absolute value of the ending balance with the prior year's balance, a budgeted amount, or other expected value.
  - Comparing the ending balance with an independent estimate of the ending balance (as illustrated previously for a cable company's revenues).
- *Tests of details of transactions.* Possibilities include:
  - Vouching the individual credits to the offsetting debits in accounts receivable and to supporting documentation such as sales invoices, shipping documents, and sales orders.

  - Tracing transactions data from source documents. If applicable, this may involve tracing transactions data to the sales journal and then tracing postings from the sales journal to the sales account.
- *Tests of details of balances.* This type of test is less likely to be applicable unless separate accounts are used to record revenues earned under contract with a few major customers. In such cases, revenues under the contracts might be recomputed and/or confirmed. In other cases, because of the direct relationship between accounts receivable and sales, some evidence may be obtained by extending an inference to the sales revenue account from evidence obtained from tests of details of balances performed on accounts receivable.

In many cases, both analytical procedures and tests of details are applied to the sales revenue account to achieve the acceptable level of detection risk. In some cases, analytical procedures alone may suffice, as discussed further in a later section.

The *Commissions Expense* account shown in the illustration is a good example of where just one of the three types of substantive tests may be all that is needed to achieve the acceptable level of detection risk. The details of the individual debits to the account could be tested by examining source documents and recalculating the individual commissions. However, for this type of account, obtaining evidence by calculating an independent estimate of the total for commissions expense using an expected relationship with the sales revenue account balance (such as 3 percent) and then comparing the estimate with the recorded balance for commissions expense may suffice.

TIMING

The acceptable level of detection risk may affect the **timing of substantive tests.** If detection risk is high, the tests may be performed several months before the end of the year. In contrast, when detection risk for an assertion is low, the substantive tests will ordinarily be performed at or near the balance sheet date.

Substantive Tests Prior to Balance Sheet Date

An auditor may apply substantive tests to the details of an account at an interim date. The decision to perform the tests prior to the balance sheet date should be based on whether the auditor can

- Control the added audit risk that material misstatements existing in the account at the balance sheet date will not be detected by the auditor. This risk becomes greater as the time period remaining between the date of the interim tests and the balance sheet date is lengthened.
- Reduce the cost of substantive tests necessary at the balance sheet date to meet planned audit objectives so that testing prior to the balance sheet date will be cost effective.

The potential added audit risk can be controlled if substantive tests for the remaining period can provide a reasonable basis for extending the audit conclusions from the tests performed at the interim date to the balance sheet date. SAS 45,

Omnibus Statement on Auditing Standards—1983 (AU 313.05), states that conditions contributing to the control of this risk are (1) the internal control structure during the remaining period is effective, (2) there are no conditions or circumstances that might predispose management to misstate the financial statements in the remaining period, (3) the year-end balances of the accounts examined at the interim date are reasonably predictable as to amount, relative significance, and composition, and (4) the client's accounting system will provide information concerning significant unusual transactions and significant fluctuations that may occur in the remaining period. If these conditions do not exist, the account should be examined at the balance sheet date.

In practice, early substantive testing of account balances is not done unless tests of controls have provided convincing evidence that internal control structure policies and procedures are operating effectively. Moreover, it is unlikely that the auditor will perform substantive tests prior to the balance sheet date on all assertions pertaining to an account. For example, the auditor might observe the client's inventory taking on an early date in meeting the existence or occurrence and completeness assertions. However, he or she would obtain market value quotations at the balance sheet date in meeting the valuation or allocation assertion.

Substantive tests prior to the balance sheet date do not eliminate the need for substantive tests at the balance sheet date. Such tests for the remaining period ordinarily should include

- Comparison of the account balances at the two dates to identify amounts that appear to be unusual and investigation of such amounts.
- Other analytical procedures or other substantive tests of details to provide a reasonable basis for extending the interim audit conclusions to the balance sheet date.

When properly planned and executed, the combination of substantive tests prior to the balance sheet date and substantive tests for the remaining period should provide the auditor with sufficient competent evidential matter to have a reasonable basis for an opinion on the client's financial statements.

EXTENT

More evidence is needed to achieve a low acceptable level of detection risk than a high detection risk. The auditor can vary the amount of evidence obtained by changing the **extent of substantive tests** performed. Extent is used in practice to mean the number of items or sample size to which a particular test or procedure is applied. Thus, more extensive substantive tests are being performed when the auditor confirms 200 accounts receivable rather than 100 accounts, or vouches 100 sales journal entries to supporting documents rather than 50 entries. The sample size to which a particular test is applied is a matter of professional judgment. Statistical sampling for substantive tests may be used to assist the auditor in determining the sample size needed to achieve a specified level of detection risk. This topic is discussed in Chapter 12.

SUMMARY OF RELATIONSHIPS AMONG AUDIT RISK COMPONENTS AND THE NATURE, TIMING, AND EXTENT OF SUBSTANTIVE TESTS

A graphic summary of several important relationships among the audit risk components and the nature, timing, and extent of substantive tests is presented in Figure 10-1.

As noted at the beginning of this part of the chapter, designing substantive tests involves determining the nature, timing, and extent of substantive tests for each significant financial statement assertion. In the next section, we consider how the auditor relates assertions, specific audit objectives, and substantive tests in developing written audit programs for substantive tests.

FIGURE 10-1 • RELATIONSHIPS AMONG AUDIT RISK COMPONENTS AND THE NATURE, TIMING, AND EXTENT OF SUBSTANTIVE TESTS

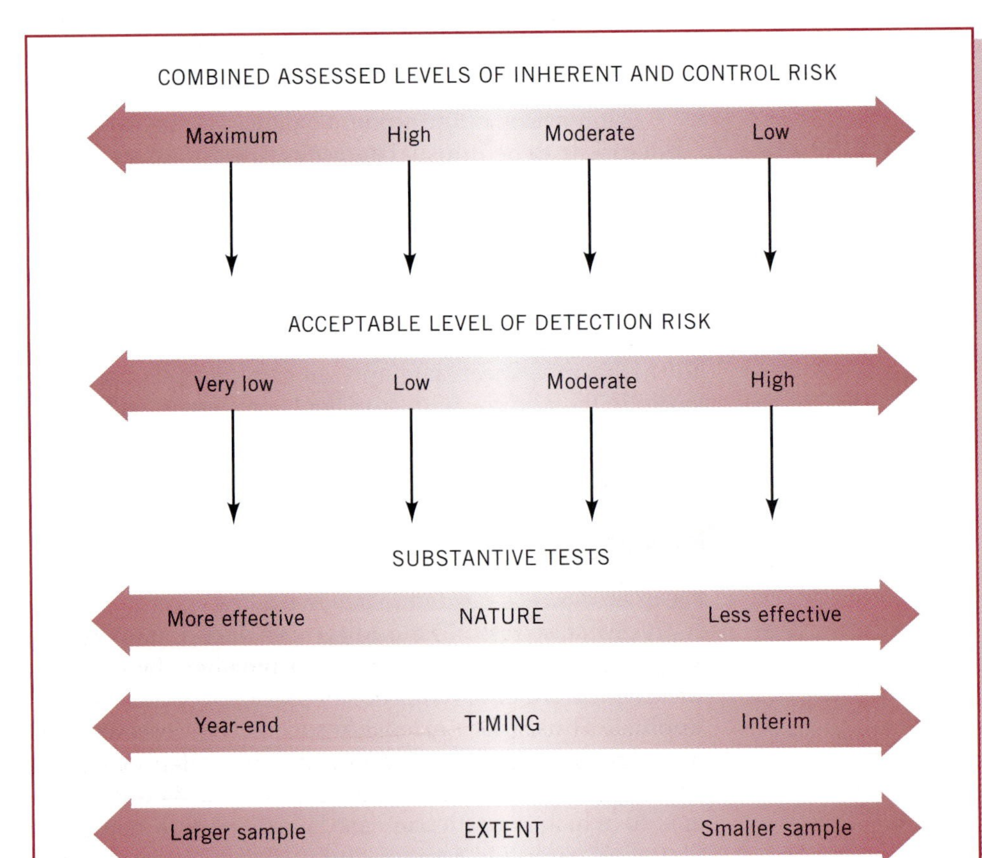

LEARNING CHECK:

10-5 a. What is the purpose of substantive tests?
b. What is involved in designing substantive tests?

10-6 a. What are the advantages and disadvantages of using analytical procedures as substantive tests?
b. What factors affect the expected effectiveness and efficiency of analytical procedures as substantive tests?

10-7 a. What are the primary audit procedures used in performing tests of details of transactions?
b. How does the cost of tests of details of transactions compare with the cost of the other two types of substantive tests? How might they be made more cost efficient?

10-8 a. Contrast the focus of tests of details of balances versus tests of details of transactions.
b. What is the relative effectiveness and costliness of tests of details of balances?

10-9 a. What factors should be considered by the auditor in deciding whether to perform substantive tests prior to the balance sheet date?
b. How may the auditor control the potential added audit risk for the period from the date of testing to the balance sheet date?

10-10 What is the relationship between the acceptable level of detection risk and the extent of substantive tests?

KEY TERMS:

Analytical procedures, p. 334
Dual-purpose tests, p. 335
Extent of substantive tests, p. 339
Nature of substantive tests, p. 333
Tests of details of balances, p. 335
Tests of details of transactions, p. 335
Timing of substantive tests, p. 338

DEVELOPING AUDIT PROGRAMS FOR SUBSTANTIVE TESTS

As previously stated in this text, the overall objective of a financial statement audit is the expression of an opinion on whether the client's financial statements are presented fairly, in all material respects, in conformity with GAAP. Furthermore, as noted in Chapter 5, it is customary to develop numerous specific audit objectives for each account based on the five categories of financial statement assertions. In designing substantive tests, the auditor should determine that appropriate tests have been identified to achieve each of the specific audit objectives pertaining to each assertion. If this is done for each account, the overall objective will be met.

RELATIONSHIPS AMONG ASSERTIONS, SPECIFIC AUDIT OBJECTIVES, AND SUBSTANTIVE TESTS

OBJECTIVE 4

Discuss the relationships among assertions, specific audit objectives, and substantive tests.

Figure 10-2 illustrates the relationships among assertions, specific audit objectives, and substantive tests for the inventories of a manufacturing company. Study of the tests shown in the third column indicates that a mix of analytical procedures and tests of details of both transactions and balances is included. In some cases, a test is listed more than once because the evidence from the test relates to more than one specific audit objective or assertion. The illustration is not intended to include a listing of all possible substantive tests that might be used in auditing inventory, nor should it be inferred that all the listed tests would be performed in every audit.

FIGURE 10-2 • ILLUSTRATION OF ASSERTIONS, SPECIFIC AUDIT OBJECTIVES, AND SUBSTANTIVE TESTS

Assertion	Specific Audit Objective	Examples of Substantive Tests
Existence or occurrence	Inventories included in the balance sheet physically exist.	Observe physical inventory counts. Obtain confirmation of inventories at locations outside the entity.
	Additions to inventories represent transactions that occurred in the current period.	Test cutoff procedures for purchases, movement of goods through manufacturing, and sales.
	Inventories represent items held for sale or used in the normal course of business.	Review perpetual inventory records, production records, and purchasing records for indications of current activity. Compare inventories with a current sales catalog and subsequent sales and delivery reports.
Completeness	Inventory quantities include all products, materials, and supplies on hand.	Observe physical inventory counts. Account for all inventory tags and count sheets used in making the physical inventory counts. Analytically review the relationship of inventory balances to recent purchasing, production, and sales activities. Test cutoff procedures for purchases, movement of goods through manufacturing, and sales.
	Inventory quantities include all products, materials, and supplies owned by the company that are in transit or stored at outside locations.	Obtain confirmation of inventories at locations outside the entity. Analytically review the relationship of inventory balances to recent purchasing, production, and sales activities. Test cutoff procedures for purchases, movement of goods through manufacturing, and sales.
Rights and obligations	The entity has legal title or similar rights of ownership to the inventories.	Observe physical inventory counts. Obtain confirmation of inventories at locations outside the entity. Examine paid vendors' invoices, consignment agreements, and contracts.
	Inventories exclude items billed to customers or owned by others.	Examine paid vendors' invoices, consignment agreements, and contracts. Test cutoff procedures for purchases, movement of goods through manufacturing, and sales.

FIGURE 10-2 *Continued)*

	Specific Audit Objective	Examples of Substantive Tests
Valuation or allocation	Inventory records are accurately compiled and the totals are properly included in the inventory accounts.	Review activity in general ledger accounts for inventories and investigate unusual items. Verify extensions of quantities times unit prices and totals of inventory records, and agreement with general ledger. Trace test counts recorded during physical inventory observation to inventory records. Reconcile physical counts to perpetual records and general ledger balances and investigate significant fluctuations.
	Inventories are properly stated at cost (except when market is lower).	Examine paid vendors' invoices. Review direct labor rates. Test computation of standard overhead rates and standard costs, if applicable. Examine analyses of purchasing and manufacturing standard cost variances, if applicable.
	Slow-moving, excess, defective, and obsolete items included in inventories are properly identified.	Inquire of production and sales personnel concerning possible excess or obsolete inventory items. Examine an analysis of inventory turnover. Review industry experience and trends. Analytically review the relationship of inventory balances to anticipated sales volume.
	Inventories are reduced, when appropriate, to replacement cost or net realizable value.	Obtain current market value quotations.
Presentation and disclosure	Inventories are properly classified in the balance sheet as current assets.	Review drafts of the financial statements.
	The basis of valuation is adequately disclosed in the financial statements.	Compare the disclosures made in the financial statements to the requirements of generally accepted accounting principles.
	The pledge or assignment of any inventories is appropriately disclosed.	Obtain confirmation of inventories assigned or pledged under loan agreements.

SOURCE: AU 326.24 (ADAPTED).

ILLUSTRATIVE AUDIT PROGRAM FOR SUBSTANTIVE TESTS

OBJECTIVE 5

State the nature and uses of audit programs for substantive tests.

The auditor's decisions regarding the design of substantive tests are required to be documented in the working papers in the form of written audit programs (AU 311.09). An **audit program** is a list of audit procedures to be performed. Unlike Figure 10-2, the procedures are generally not listed by assertion or specific audit objective in order to avoid the multiple listing of procedures that apply to more than one assertion or objective.

In addition to listing audit procedures, each audit program should have columns for (1) a cross-reference to other working papers containing the evidence obtained from each procedure (when applicable), (2) the initials of the auditor who performed each procedure, and (3) the date performance of the procedure was completed. Figure 10-3 shows an audit program in this format. The tests in the program are based on the ones shown in Figure 10-2 except that each test is listed only once, and they are listed in a sequence that is logical for the development of the program and/or performance of the procedures.

FIGURE 10-3 • ILLUSTRATIVE AUDIT PROGRAM FOR SUBSTANTIVE TESTS OF INVENTORIES

Prepared by:______ Date:______
Reviewed by:______ Date:______

XYZ Manufacturing Company, Inc.
Audit Program for Substantive Tests of Inventories
December 31, 19X1

Substantive Test	W/P Ref.	Auditor	Date
1. Verify totals and agreement of inventory balances and records that will be subjected to further testing: a. Trace beginning inventory balances to prior year's working papers. b. Review activity in inventory accounts and investigate unusual items. c. Verify totals of perpetual records and other inventory schedules and their agreement with ending general ledger balances.			
2. Perform analytical procedures: a. Review industry experience and trends. b. Examine an analysis of inventory turnover. c. Review relationship of inventory balances to recent purchasing, production, and sales activities. d. Compare inventory balances to anticipated sales volume.			
3. Test details of inventory transactions: a. Vouch additions to inventory records to vendor's invoices (raw materials), manufacturing cost records (work-in process), and completed production reports (finished goods). b. Trace data from purchases, manufacturing, and completed production records to inventory records. c. Test cutoff of purchases (receiving), movement of goods through manufacturing, and sales (shipping).			
4. Observe client's physical inventory count: a. Make test counts. b. Look for indications of slow-moving, damaged, or obsolete inventory. c. Account for all inventory tags and count sheets used in physical count.			
5. Test clerical accuracy of inventory records: a. Recalculate extensions of quantities times unit prices. b. Trace test counts to records. c. Vouch items on inventory listings to inventory tags and count sheets. d. Reconcile physical counts to perpetual records and general ledger balances.			
6. Test inventory pricing: a. Examine vendor's paid invoices for purchased inventory. b. Examine propriety of direct labor and overhead rates, standard costs, and variances pertaining to manufactured inventories. c. Obtain market quotations and perform lower-of-cost-or-market test. d. Review perpetual inventory records, production records, and purchasing records for indications of current activity. e. Compare inventories with current sales catalog and sales reports. f. Inquire about slow-moving, excess, or obsolete inventories and determine need for write-downs.			
7. Confirm inventories at locations outside the entity.			
8. Examine consignment agreements and contracts.			
9. Confirm agreements for assignment and pledging of inventories.			
10. Review presentation and disclosures for inventories in drafts of financial statements and determine conformity with GAAP.			

In practice, auditors hold different views on the extent of detail to be shown in an audit program. For example, certain details of the sample design, including sample size, for the various tests can be shown on the audit program itself or, as presumed in Figure 10-3, in the supporting working papers that are cross-referenced on the audit program. In any case, audit programs should be sufficiently detailed to provide

- An outline of the work to be done.
- A basis for coordinating, supervising, and controlling the audit.
- A record of the work performed.

The audit program in Figure 10-3 is presented at this time solely to illustrate the format of audit programs for substantive tests and how they can be developed. The application of the substantive tests shown in the figure is explained further in Chapter 16, which includes coverage of inventories as part of the audit of an entity's production cycle.

GENERAL FRAMEWORK FOR DEVELOPING AUDIT PROGRAMS FOR SUBSTANTIVE TESTS

OBJECTIVE 6

Describe and apply a general framework for developing audit programs for substantive tests.

Referring again to Figure 10-3 and to the previous discussion of designing substantive tests, we can construct a general framework for developing audit programs for substantive tests. Such an approach is described in Figure 10-4, which should be read in its entirety at this time.

The steps listed in the upper portion of Figure 10-4 summarize the application of several important concepts and procedures explained in Chapters 5 through 9. Note that the first step listed in the lower portion of the figure corresponds to the first step in Figure 10-3. Because subsequent substantive tests are often performed on the subsidiary records or supporting schedules, or samples drawn therefrom, it is logical to start by ascertaining that the supporting records do in fact tie in with the general ledger. When applicable, it is also logical to establish the agreement of beginning balances with audited amounts in the prior year's working papers so that tests performed in the current audit can be focused on the effects of transactions that occurred in the current period and the ending balance. Two additional examples of analogous steps in other areas of the audit are as follows: (1) verifying the totals and determining the agreement of the general ledger accounts receivable control account and the accounts receivable subsidiary ledger and (2) verifying the totals and determining the agreement of a general ledger investment portfolio account and a spreadsheet listing the details of the related investments.

The specification of analytical procedures is considered next because if effective procedures are available, they may reduce or eliminate the need for more expensive tests of details. Note that even though there are several analytical procedures listed in item 2 of Figure 10-3, in the case of inventories tests of details cannot be eliminated entirely because of the requirement to observe the physical inventory-taking and make test counts among other factors.

Tests of details of transactions are ordinarily considered next because in some cases they will be cheaper to perform than tests of details of balances. Note that the specification of these tests, as illustrated in item (3) of Figure 10-3, generally includes references to specific documents and portions of the audit trail applicable to processing the transactions. Recall that some of these tests may be performed concurrently with tests of controls during interim work as dual-purpose tests.

Finally, the program should specify tests of details of balances, special requirements not previously addressed, and procedures to determine that the presentation and disclosures pertaining to the assertions covered by the program are in conformity with GAAP. In specifying the latter procedures, the auditor uses his or her knowledge of relevant business practices and financial reporting disclosure requirements such as, in the case of inventories, those pertaining to the method of valuation and the consignment, assignment, and pledging of inventories.

FIGURE 10-4 • GENERAL FRAMEWORK FOR DEVELOPING AUDIT PROGRAMS FOR SUBSTANTIVE TESTS

Complete Preliminary Planning

1. Identify the financial statement assertions to be covered by the audit program (for example, existence or occurrence, completeness, rights and obligations, valuation or allocation, and presentation and disclosure assertions pertaining to ending inventory balances).
2. Develop specific audit objectives for each category of assertions (as illustrated in Figure 10-2).
3. Assess inherent and control risk and determine the final acceptable level of detection risk for each assertion consistent with the overall level of audit risk and applicable materiality level.
4. From knowledge acquired from procedures to obtain an understanding of relevant internal control structure policies and procedures, envision the accounting records, supporting documents, accounting process (including the audit trail), and financial reporting process pertaining to the assertions.
5. Consider options regarding the design of substantive tests:
   - Alternatives for accommodating varying acceptable levels of detection risk:
     - *Nature—Analytical procedures*
       Tests of details of transactions
       Tests of details of balances.
     - *Timing—Interim versus yearend.*
     - *Extent— Sample size.*
   - Possible types of corroborating evidence available:

Analytical	*Documentary*	*Mathematical*	*Physical*
Confirmations	*Electronic*	*Oral*	*Written representations*

   - Possible types of audit procedures available:

Analytical procedures	*Confirming*	*Observing*
Computer-assisted	*Counting*	*Reperforming*
audit tech-	*Inquiring*	*Tracing*
niques	*Inspecting*	*Vouching*

Specify Substantive Tests to Be Included in Audit Program

1. Specify initial procedures to
   a. Trace beginning balances to prior year's working papers (if applicable).
   b. Review activity in applicable general ledger accounts and investigate unusual items.
   c. Verify totals of supporting records or schedules to be used in subsequent tests and determine their agreement with general ledger balances, when applicable, to establish tie-in of detail with control accounts.
2. Specify analytical procedures to be performed.
3. Specify tests of details of transactions to be performed.
4. Specify tests of details of balances (in addition to 1a, b, and c above) to be performed.
5. Consider whether there are any special requirements or procedures applicable to assertions being tested in the circumstances such as procedures required by SASs (for example, observation of inventories) or by regulatory agencies that have not been included in (3) and (4) above.
6. Specify procedures to determine conformity of presentation and disclosure with GAAP.

The general framework for developing audit programs described in Figure 10-4 underlies the numerous illustrations of audit programs for substantive tests presented in subsequent chapters of this text.

AUDIT PROGRAMS IN INITIAL ENGAGEMENTS

In an **initial engagement,** the detailed specification of substantive tests in audit programs is generally not completed until after the study and evaluation of the internal control structure has been completed and the acceptable level of detection risk has been determined for each significant assertion as explained earlier in this chapter. Two matters requiring special consideration in designing audit programs for initial audits are (1) determining the propriety of the account balances at the beginning of the period being audited, and (2) ascertaining the accounting principles used in the preceding period as a basis for determining the consistency of application of such principles in the current period.

AUDIT PROGRAMS IN RECURRING ENGAGEMENTS

In a **recurring engagement,** the auditor has access to audit programs used in the preceding period(s) and the working papers pertaining to those programs. In such cases, the auditor's preliminary audit strategies are often based on a presumption that the risk levels and audit programs for substantive tests used in the previous period will be appropriate for the current period. Thus, the audit programs for the current engagement are often prepared before the auditor completes the study and evaluation of the internal control structure. If information obtained in the current period indicates the presumed risk levels and prepared programs are no longer appropriate, the programs will need to be modified.

LEARNING CHECK:

10-11 a. What is the overall objective of a financial statement audit?
b. What steps does the auditor take in relation to each account to ensure that the overall objective of the audit is met?

10-12 How should the auditor's decisions regarding the design of substantive tests to be performed be documented in the working papers?

10-13 a. What is an *audit program*?
b. What essential information about procedures performed should be documented on an audit program?
c. Audit programs should be sufficiently detailed to fulfill three functions. What are they?

10-14 a. List five steps in completing preliminary planning before specifying the substantive tests to be included in an audit program.
b. List six steps in the general framework for specifying substantive tests to be included in an audit program.

10-15 Identify several differences in preparing audit programs for initial engagements versus recurring engagements.

KEY TERMS:

Audit program, p. 343
Initial engagement, p. 347
Recurring engagement, p. 347

SPECIAL CONSIDERATIONS IN DESIGNING SUBSTANTIVE TESTS

OBJECTIVE 7

Indicate special considerations in designing substantive tests for selected types of accounts.

The foregoing discussions of detection risk, designing substantive tests, and developing audit programs pertain in general to all accounts. In this section, we explain some special considerations relevant to designing substantive tests for selected types of accounts. The section concludes with a summary that highlights the differences between tests of controls as presented in Chapter 9 and substantive tests as presented in this chapter.

INCOME STATEMENT ACCOUNTS

Traditionally, tests of details of balances have focused more on financial statement assertions that pertain to balance sheet accounts than on income statement accounts. This approach is both efficient and logical because each income statement account is inextricably linked to one or more balance sheet accounts. Examples include the following:

Balance Sheet Account	Related Income Statement Account
Accounts receivable	Sales
Inventories	Cost of sales
Prepaid expenses	Various related expenses
Investments	Investment income
Plant assets	Depreciation expense
Intangible assets	Amortization expense
Accrued payables	Various related expenses
Interest-bearing liabilities	Interest expense

The assertions for the accounts are linked as well. For example, evidence that accounts receivable do not exist may indicate that sales did not occur. (Note this is not necessarily the case because a once valid receivable may no longer exist owing to failure of the entity to record a payment remitted by the customer.) Similarly, if interest-bearing liabilities are not complete, interest expense may not be complete, and so on. Recall that all the categories of assertions pertain to income statement accounts except the rights and obligations assertion.

Because of these relationships, as compared with substantive tests of balance sheet accounts, tests of income statement accounts rely more heavily on analytical procedures and less on tests of details.

Analytical Procedures for Income Statement Accounts

Analytical procedures can be a powerful audit tool in obtaining audit evidence about income statement balances. This type of substantive testing may be used directly or indirectly. Direct tests occur when a revenue or an expense account is compared with other relevant data to determine the reasonableness of its balance. For example, the ratio of sales commissions to sales can be compared with the results of prior years and budget data for the current year. Additional examples involving comparisons with nonfinancial information are illustrated in the following table.

Account	Analytical Procedure
Hotel room revenue	Number of rooms × Occupancy rate × Average room rate.
Tuition revenue	Number of equivalent fulltime students × Tuition rate for a fulltime student.
Wages expense	Average number of employees per pay period × Average pay per period × Number of pay periods.
Gasoline expense	Number of miles driven ÷ Average miles per gallon × Average per gallon cost.

Indirect tests occur when evidence concerning income statement balances can be derived from analytical procedures applied to related balance sheet accounts. For example, accounts receivable turnover may be used in verifying accounts receivable, and the findings may impact on whether bad-debts expense and sales are fairly stated.

In some cases, the auditor may elect to use analytical procedures as the only direct test of some income statement balances. For example, if the acceptable level of detection risk is high because inherent and control risks for purchases transactions are low, expenses such as those for repairs, gasoline, and advertising may only be audited through analytical procedures. Similarly, if controls over sales adjustments transactions are reliable, only analytical procedures may be applied to the sales returns and allowance account.

Tests of Details for Income Statement Accounts

When the evidence obtained from analytical procedures and from tests of details of related balance sheet accounts does not reduce detection risk to an acceptably low level, direct tests of details of assertions pertaining to income statement accounts are necessary. This may be the case when

- *Inherent risk is high.* This may occur in the case of assertions affected by nonroutine transactions and management's judgments and estimates.
- *Control risk is high.* This situation may occur when (1) related internal controls for nonroutine and routine transactions are ineffective or (2) the auditor elects not to test the internal controls.
- *Analytical procedures reveal unusual relationships and unexpected fluctuations.* These circumstances are explained in a preceding section.

- *The account requires analysis.* Analysis is usually required for accounts that (1) require special disclosure in the income statement, (2) contain information needed in preparing tax returns and reports for regulatory agencies such as the SEC, and (3) have general account titles that suggest the likelihood of misclassifications and errors.

Accounts requiring separate analysis generally include

Legal expense and professional fees	Taxes, licenses, and fees
Maintenance and repairs	Rents and royalties
Travel and entertainment	Contributions
Officers' salaries and expenses	Advertising

ACCOUNTS INVOLVING ACCOUNTING ESTIMATES

An **accounting estimate** is an approximation of a financial statement element, item, or account in the absence of exact measurement. Examples of accounting estimates include periodic depreciation, the provision for bad debts, and warranty expense. Management is responsible for establishing the process and controls for preparing accounting estimates. Judgment is required in making an accounting estimate. Accounting estimates may have a significant effect on a company's financial statements.

SAS 57, *Auditing Accounting Estimates* (AU 342.07), states that the auditor's objective in evaluating accounting estimates is to obtain sufficient competent evidential matter to provide reasonable assurance that

- All accounting estimates that could be material to the financial statements have been developed.
- The accounting estimates are reasonable in the circumstances.
- The accounting estimates are presented in conformity with applicable accounting principles and are properly disclosed.

In determining whether all necessary estimates have been made, the auditor should consider the industry in which the entity operates, its methods of conducting business, and new accounting pronouncements.

An entity's internal control structure may reduce the likelihood of material misstatements of accounting estimates and thereby reduce the extent of substantive tests. To evaluate the reasonableness of an estimate, AU 342.09 explains that the auditor should normally concentrate on the key factors and assumptions used by management including those that are (1) significant to the accounting estimate, (2) sensitive to variations, (3) deviations from historical patterns, and (4) subjective and susceptible to misstatement and bias.

Evidence of the reasonableness of an estimate may be obtained by the auditor from one or a combination of the following approaches:

- Perform procedures to review and test management's process in making the estimate.
- Prepare an independent expectation of the estimate.
- Review subsequent transactions and events occurring prior to completing the audit that pertain to the estimate.

The procedures to be performed include (1) considering the relevance, reliability, and sufficiency of the data and other factors used by management, (2) evaluating the reasonableness and consistency of the assumptions, and (3) reperforming the calculations made by management. In some cases, it may be useful to obtain the opinion of a specialist regarding the assumptions.

ACCOUNTS INVOLVING RELATED PARTY TRANSACTIONS

As explained in Chapter 6, the auditor should identify **related party transactions** in audit planning.[3] These types of transactions are a concern to the auditor because they may not be executed on an arm's-length basis. The auditor's objective in auditing related party transactions is to obtain evidential matter as to the purpose, nature, and extent of these transactions and their effect on the financial statements. The evidence should extend beyond inquiry of management. SAS 1, *Related Parties* (AU 334.09), indicates that substantive tests should include the following:

- Obtain an understanding of the business purpose of the transaction.
- Examine invoices, executed copies of agreements, contracts, and other pertinent documents, such as receiving reports and shipping documents.
- Determine whether the transaction has been approved by the board of directors or other appropriate officials.
- Test for reasonableness the compilation of amounts to be disclosed, or considered for disclosure, in the financial statements.
- Arrange for the audits of intercompany account balances to be performed as of concurrent dates, even if the fiscal years differ, and for the examination of specified, important, and representative related party transactions by the auditors for each of the parties, with appropriate exchange of relevant information.
- Inspect or confirm and obtain satisfaction concerning the transferability and value of collateral.

In auditing identified related party transactions, the auditor is not expected to determine whether a particular transaction would have occurred if the parties had not been related or what the exchange price and terms would have been. The auditor is required, however, to determine the substance of the related party transactions and their effects on the financial statements.

COMPARISON OF TESTS OF CONTROLS AND SUBSTANTIVE TESTS

OBJECTIVE 8

Contrast tests of controls and substantive tests.

As indicated in Chapter 6, the third phase of an audit is performing audit tests. These tests consist of tests of controls and substantive tests. Figure 10-5 presents a comparison of the two classes of tests, including the types of tests in each class, their purpose, and the risk component to which each class relates, among other factors.

[3] Examples of related parties are presented in Chapter 6 on page 205.

FIGURE 10-5 • SUMMARY OF AUDIT TESTS

	Tests of Controls	Substantive Tests
Types	Concurrent. Additional.	Analytical procedures. Tests of details of transactions. Tests of details of balances.
Purpose	Determine effectiveness of design and operation of internal control structure policies and procedures.	Determine fairness of significant financial statement assertions.
Nature of test measurement	Frequency of deviations from control structure policies and procedures.	Monetary errors in transactions and balances.
Applicable audit procedures	Inquiring, observing, inspecting, reperforming, and computer-assisted audit techniques.	Same as tests of controls, plus analytical procedures, counting, confirming, tracing, and vouching.
Timing	Primarily interim work.[1]	Primarily at or near balance sheet date.[2]
Audit risk component	Control risk.	Detection risk.
Primary field work standard	Second.	Third.
Required by GAAS	No.	Yes.

[1] Concurrent tests of controls are performed in audit planning with procedures to obtain an understanding of the internal control structure. Additional tests of controls are performed during interim field work.

[2] Tests of details of transactions may also be performed with tests of controls as *dual-purpose tests* during interim field work.

We continue the study of audit tests in the next three chapters. In these chapters, consideration is given to the use of audit sampling (statistical and nonstatistical) in performing tests of controls and substantive tests, and to the impact of electronic data processing on audit tests.

LEARNING CHECK:

10-16 The role of analytical procedures relative to tests of details may be greater for income statement accounts than balance sheet accounts. Why?

10-17 What circumstances may result in applying tests of details directly to income statement accounts?

10-18 a. What is the auditor's objective in auditing accounting estimates?
b. Indicate the factors to be considered in evaluating the reasonableness of accounting estimates.

10-19 a. What are the auditor's objectives in auditing related party transactions?
b. Identify the substantive tests that may be used in auditing related party transactions.

10-20 Contrast tests of controls and substantive tests as to (a) types, (b) purpose, (c) nature of test measurement, (d) applicable audit procedures, (e) timing, (f) audit risk component, (g) primary field work standard, and (h) whether required by GAAS.

KEY TERMS:

Accounting estimate, p. 350

Related party transactions, p. 351

SUMMARY

After obtaining an understanding of the internal control structure policies and procedures relevant to an assertion and assessing control risk, the auditor evaluates the planned level of substantive tests and associated planned detection risk that were specified in the preliminary audit strategy. When necessary, the audit risk model is used to determine a revised acceptable level of detection risk as the basis for determining a revised level of substantive tests. The auditor then designs specific substantive tests to achieve the acceptable level of detection risk by exercising judgments about the nature, timing and extent of such tests. The auditor also relates the tests to specific audit objectives for each category of assertions to ensure that the overall objective of rendering an opinion on the financial statements as a whole will be met. The auditor's decisions about the design of substantive tests are documented in the form of written audit programs, which provide an outline of the work to be done and a means for controlling the audit and recording the work performed. A general framework may be used in developing effective and efficient audit programs for substantive tests tailored to the client's circumstances. Special considerations are appropriate for selected types of accounts.

APPENDIX 10A DETECTION RISK FOR ANALYTICAL PROCEDURES AND TESTS OF DETAILS

On determining the acceptable level of detection risk for a financial statement assertion, the auditor must decide the level of detection risk to be used in designing each substantive test related to the assertion. One approach to this task is first to assess the risk that analytical procedures will not detect material misstatements in the assertion, and then determine the acceptable level of detection risk for all tests of details related to the assertion. A risk matrix like the following may be used for this purpose:

Inherent Risk Assessment	Control Risk Assessment	Risk That Analytical Procedures Will Not Detect Material Misstatements: High	Moderate	Low	Very Low
		Detection Risk for Tests of Details			
Maximum	Maximum	Very low	Very low	Very low	Low
	High	Very low	Very low	Low	Moderate
	Moderate	Very low	Low	Moderate	*
	Low	Low	Moderate	High	*
High	Maximum	Very low	Very low	Low	Moderate
	High	Very low	Low	Moderate	*
	Moderate	Moderate	Moderate	High	*
	Low	Moderate	High	*	*
Moderate	Maximum	Very low	Low	Moderate	High
	High	Low	Moderate	High	*
	Moderate	Moderate	High	*	*
	Low	High	*	*	*
Low	Maximum	Low	Moderate	High	*
	High	Moderate	High	*	*
	Moderate	High	*	*	*
	Low	*	*	*	*

* Substantive tests of details may not be necessary.

To illustrate the use of this matrix, assume the following:

Inherent risk assessment	Moderate
Control risk assessment	Low
Risk that analytical procedures will not detect material misstatements	High

Based on these assessments, the matrix indicates that the acceptable detection risk for tests of details is high. The auditor then proceeds to make choices regarding the nature, timing, and extent of tests of details. The matrix further indicates that if the risk that analytical procedures will not detect material misstatement is moderate or lower, tests of details for the assertion might not be necessary because the acceptable detection risk level will be achieved by the analytical procedures alone.

BIBLIOGRAPHY

AICPA Professional Standards:

SAS 45 (AU 313), Omnibus Statement on Auditing Standards—1983, Substantive Tests Prior to the Balance-Sheet Date.

SAS 46 (AU 334), Omnibus Statement on Auditing Standards—1983, Related Parties.

SAS 47 (AU 312), Materiality and Audit Risk.

SAS 56 (AU 329), Analytical Procedures.

SAS 57 (AU 342), Auditing Accounting Estimates.

IAU 12 (AU 8012), Analytical Procedures.

IAU 17 (AU 8017), Related Parties.

IAU 25 (AU 8025), Materiality and Audit Risk.
IAU 26 (AU 8026), Audit of Accounting Estimates.
IAU 28 (AU 8028), First Year Audit Engagements—Opening Balances.

Biggs, Stanley F., Mock, Theodore J., and Watkins, Paul R. "Auditor's Use of Analytical Review in Audit Program Design" (A Small Sample Study), *The Accounting Review* (January 1988), pp. 148–161.

Blocher, Edward J., and Cooper, Jean C. "A Study of Auditors' Analytical Review Performance," *Auditing: A Journal of Practice and Theory* (Spring 1988), pp. 1–28.

Coglitore, Frank, and Berryman, R. Glen. "Analytical Procedures: A Defensive Necessity," *Auditing: A Journal of Practice and Theory* (Spring 1988), pp. 150–163.

Gillett, Peter. "Automated Dynamic Audit Programme Tailoring: An Expert System Approach," *Auditing: A Journal of Practice and Theory* (Supplement 1993), pp. 173–189.

Hylas, R. E., and Ashton, R. H. "Audit Detection of Financial Statement Errors," *The Accounting Review* (October 1982), pp. 751–765.

Loebbecke, J. K., and Steinbart, P. J. "An Investigation of the Use of Preliminary Analytical Review to Provide Substantive Evidence," *Auditing: A Journal of Practice and Theory* (Spring 1987), pp. 74–89.

Mock, Theodore, J., and Wright, Arnold. "An Exploratory Study of Auditors' Evidential Planning Judgments," *Auditing: A Journal of Practice and Theory* (Fall 1993), pp. 39–61.

Scott, Richard A., and Dale, Donald M. "Interim Testing of Assets and Liabilities," *The CPA Journal* (November 1984), pp. 22–32.

Srinidhi, B. N., and Vasarhelyi, M. A. "Auditor Judgment Concerning Establishment of Substantive Tests Based on Internal Control Reliability," *Auditing: A Journal of Practice and Theory* (Spring 1986), pp. 64–76.

OBJECTIVE QUESTIONS

Indicate the *best* answer for each of the following multiple choice questions.

10-21 These questions relate to detection risk.

1. The risk that an auditor's procedures will lead to the conclusion that a material misstatement does not exist in an account balance when, in fact, such misstatement does exist is referred to as
   a. Audit risk.
   b. Inherent risk.
   c. Control risk.
   d. Detection risk.
2. As the acceptable level of detection risk decreases, the assurance directly provided from
   a. Substantive tests should increase.
   b. Substantive tests should decrease.
   c. Tests of controls should increase.
   d. Tests of controls should decrease.
3. An auditor assesses control risk because it
   a. Indicates where inherent risk may be the greatest.
   b. Affects the level of detection risk the auditor may accept.
   c. Determines whether sampling risk is sufficiently low.
   d. Includes the aspects of nonsampling risk that are controllable.

10-22 These questions relate to the nature, timing and extent of substantive tests.

1. As the acceptable level of detection risk decreases, an auditor may change the
   a. Timing of substantive tests by performing them at an interim date rather than at year end.

b. Nature of substantive tests from a less effective to a more effective procedure.
c. Timing of tests of controls by performing them at several dates rather than at one time.
d. Assessed level of inherent risk to a higher amount.

2. Before applying principal substantive tests to the details of asset and liability accounts at an interim date, the auditor should
   a. Assess the difficulty in controlling incremental audit risk.
   b. Investigate significant fluctuations that have occurred in the asset and liability accounts since the previous balance sheet date.
   c. Select only those accounts that can effectively be sampled during year-end audit work.
   d. Consider the tests of controls that must be applied at the balance sheet date to extend the audit conclusions reached at an interim date.

3. An auditor uses the knowledge provided by the understanding of the internal control structure and the final assessed level of control risk primarily to determine the nature, timing, and extent of the
   a. Attribute tests.
   b. Concurrent tests of controls.
   c. Additional tests of controls.
   d. Substantive tests.

4. An auditor's decision either to apply analytical procedures as substantive tests or to perform tests of transactions and account balances usually is determined by the
   a. Availability of data aggregated at a high level.
   b. Relative effectiveness and efficiency of the tests.
   c. Timing of tests performed after the balance sheet date.
   d. Auditor's familiarity with industry trends.

5. Auditors try to identify predictable relationships when using analytical procedures. Relationships involving transactions from which of the following accounts most likely would yield the highest level of evidence?
   a. Accounts receivable.
   b. Interest expense.
   c. Accounts payable.
   d. Travel and entertainment expense.

10-23 These questions apply to special considerations in designing substantive tests and audit programs.

1. After identifying related party transactions, an auditor most likely would
   a. Substantiate that the transactions were consummated on terms equivalent to those prevailing in arms-length transactions.
   b. Discuss the implications of the transactions with third parties, such as the entity's attorneys and bankers.
   c. Determine whether the transactions were approved by the board of directors or other appropriate officials.
   d. Ascertain whether the transactions would have occurred if the parties had not been related.

2. In designing written audit programs, an auditor should establish specific audit objectives that relate primarily to the
   a. Timing of audit procedures.
   b. Cost-benefit of gathering evidence.
   c. Selected audit techniques.
   d. Financial statement assertions.

3. The procedures specifically outlined in an audit program are primarily designed to
   a. Protect the auditor in the event of litigation.
   b. Detect errors or irregularities.
   c. Test internal control structures.
   d. Gather evidence.

4. Which of the following is required documentation in an audit in accordance with generally accepted auditing standards?
   a. A flowchart or narrative of the accounting system describing the recording and classification of transactions for financial reporting.
   b. An audit program setting forth in detail the procedures necessary to accomplish the engagement's objectives.
   c. A planning memorandum establishing the timing of the audit procedures and coordinating the assistance of entity personnel.
   d. An internal control questionnaire identifying policies and procedures that assure specific objectives will be achieved.

5. In evaluating an entity's accounting estimates, one of an auditor's objectives is to determine whether the estimates are
   a. Not subject to bias.
   b. Consistent with industry guidelines.
   c. Based on objective assumptions.
   d. Reasonable in the circumstances.

COMPREHENSIVE QUESTIONS

10-24 **(Determining detection risk)** All of the internal control work in the audit of the Hurst Corporation has been completed, and the final assessed levels of control risk have been compared with the planned assessed levels of control risk for specified assertions. The auditor's preliminary audit strategy for these assertions was the lower assessed level of control risk approach.

REQUIRED

a. What should the auditor do next before designing specific substantive tests?
b. If it is necessary to determine a revised acceptable level of detection risk for some assertions, how can that be done?
c. When multiple substantive tests are designed for the same assertion, must the same acceptable level of detection risk be specified for each test? Explain.

10-25 **(Designing substantive tests)** Final acceptable levels of detection risk have been determined for several assertions. The auditor is prepared to proceed with designing specific substantive tests.

REQUIRED

a. What is the purpose of substantive tests?
b. What factors pertaining to substantive tests can be varied to accommodate different acceptable levels of detection risk? Explain how each factor is varied to accommodate a low versus a high acceptable level of detection risk.
c. Indicate the three types of substantive tests and the relative effectiveness and cost of each.

10-26 **(Audit programs)** After determining the acceptable level of detection risk for specified assertions for a new audit client and completing all other preliminary planning steps, the auditor develops an audit program for substantive tests.

REQUIRED

a. Describe the basic features and purposes of audit programs for substantive tests.
b. Describe a general framework for developing an audit program for substantive tests for a group of assertions assuming all preliminary planning steps have been completed.
c. Contrast the preparation of audit programs for an initial versus a recurring audit engagement.

10-27 **(Audit objectives/financial statement assertions)** In designing the audit program for substantive tests of accounts receivable and plant assets in the Abbott Company, the auditor identified the following audit objectives:

1. Accounts receivable include all claims on customers at the balance sheet date.
2. Recorded plant assets represent assets that are in use at the balance sheet date.
3. Accounts receivable are properly identified and classified in the balance sheet.
4. Plant assets are stated at cost less accumulated depreciation.
5. The allowance for uncollectible accounts is a reasonable estimate of future bad debts.
6. The entity has ownership rights to all plant assets at the balance sheet date.
7. Accounts receivable represent legal claims on customers for payment.
8. Plant asset balances include the effects of all transactions and events that occurred during the period.
9. Accounts receivable represent claims on customers at the balance sheet date.
10. Depreciation methods used by the client are adequately disclosed in the notes to the financial statements.
11. The accounts receivable balance represents gross claims on customers and agrees with the sum of the accounts receivable subsidiary ledger.
12. Capital lease agreements are disclosed in accordance with GAAP.
13. Appropriate disclosures are made of accounts receivable that are assigned or pledged at the balance sheet date.
14. Plant assets are properly identified and classified in the balance sheet.

REQUIRED

Identify the financial statement assertion to which each objective relates. Use the following format for your answers:

Objective	Assertion				
(Use number)	EO	C	RO	VA	PD

10-28 **(Audit procedures/assertions)** The purpose of all audit procedures is to gather sufficient competent evidence for an auditor to form an opinion regarding the financial statements taken as a whole.

REQUIRED

a. In addition to the example below, identify and describe five audit procedures for gathering audit evidence used to evaluate a client's inventory balance.

Procedure	Description
Observation	An auditor watches the performance of some function, such as a client's annual inventory count.

b. Identify the five general assertions regarding a client's inventory balance and describe one different substantive test for each assertion. Use the format illustrated below.

Assertion	Substantive Test

AICPA

10-29 **(Types of substantive tests, types of evidence, and assertions)** Audit procedures used in performing substantive tests during the audit of the Harris Company are as follows:

1. Count cash on hand.
2. Confirm accounts receivable.
3. Vouch plant asset additions to purchase documents.
4. Recalculate accrued interest on notes payable.
5. Inquire of management about pledging of plant assets as security for long-term debt.
6. Compute inventory turnover ratio.
7. Vouch ending inventory pricing to purchase invoices.
8. Review client-prepared bank reconciliation.
9. Verify accuracy of accounts receivable balance and agreement with subsidiary ledger.
10. Obtain written representation from geologist concerning probable tons of ore in mine.
11. Compare statement disclosures for leases with GAAP.
12. Review adequacy of client's provision for uncollectible accounts.
13. Examine certificates of title for delivery equipment.
14. Compare cash balances with budget expectations.
15. Trace bad-debt write-off authorizations to accounts receivable.
16. Observe client's inventory taking.
17. Trace unpaid vendors' invoices to accounts payable at year end.
18. Compute number of times bond interest is earned.

REQUIRED

For each of the audit procedures, identify (a) the type of substantive test (1—analytical procedure, 2—test of details of transactions, or 3—test of details of balances), (b) the type of evidence obtained (documentary, confirmation, physical, etc.), and (c) one assertion to which the test relates. Present your answer in columnar form using the following headings:

Audit Procedure	Type of Test	Type of Evidence	Assertion

You may identify the audit procedure by number.

10-30 **(Misstatements/assertions/substantive tests)** The following misstatements were detected by the auditor in performing substantive tests of inventories during the audit of Wixon Company.

1. Slow-moving, defective, and obsolete items are included in the inventory but not properly identified.
2. Inventory quantities do not include all goods on hand.
3. Some items are not held for sale or used in the normal course of business.
4. Inventories are stated at cost even when market value is lower.
5. The major categories of inventories are not disclosed in the balance sheet.
6. All inventories included in the balance sheet do not physically exist.
7. The entity does not have legal title to all inventories.
8. Inventories pledged as collateral are not disclosed in the financial statements.
9. Inventory quantities do not include all items stored at outside locations.
10. Inventories include items billed to customers and owned by others.
11. Inventory listings of quantities do not include all tag numbers.
12. The bases of inventory valuation are not disclosed in the financial statements.
13. Goods in transit at the balance sheet date shipped F.O.B. shipping point are not included in inventories.
14. Some manufacturing inventories are classified in the balance sheet as a noncurrent asset.
15. Inventories are stated at the higher of cost or current replacement cost.

The following substantive tests were used by the auditor:

a. Observe physical inventory counts.
b. Confirm inventories at locations outside the entity.
c. Review perpetual inventory records for current activity.
d. Compare inventories with current sales catalog.
e. Test shipping and receiving cutoff procedures.
f. Account for all inventory tags.
g. Test clerical accuracy of inventory listings.
h. Examine consignment agreements and contracts.
i. Examine paid vendors' invoices.
j. Compute inventory turnover.
k. Obtain current market value quotations.
l. Review drafts of the financial statements.
m. Inquire about inventories pledged under loan contracts.

REQUIRED

For each misstatement, indicate (a) the financial statement assertion that is relevant and (b) the substantive test(s) that was (were) used for the discovery. Present your answer in tabular form with the following column headings: Misstatement, Assertion, and Substantive Test. Misstatements may be identified by number and substantive tests by letter.

Note: A substantive test may apply to more than one misstatement, and more than one test may have been used.

10-31 **(Substantive tests prior to the balance sheet date)** Cook, CPA, has been engaged to audit the financial statements of General Department Stores, Inc., a continuing audit client, which is a chain of medium-sized retail stores. General's fiscal year will end on June 30, 19X6, and General's management has asked Cook to issue the auditor's report by August 1, 19X6. Cook will not have sufficient time to perform all of the necessary field work in July, 19X6, but will have time to perform most of the field work as of an interim date, April 30, 19X6.

For the accounts to be tested at the interim date, Cook will also perform substantive tests covering the transactions of the final two months of the year. This will be necessary to extend Cook's conclusions to the balance sheet date.

REQUIRED

a. Describe the factors Cook should consider before applying principal substantive tests to General's balance sheet accounts at April 30, 19X6.
b. For accounts tested at April 30, 19X6, describe how Cook should design the substantive tests covering the balances as of June 30, 19X6, and the transactions of the final two months of the year.

(AICPA adapted)

10-32 **(Nature and timing of substantive tests)** Tina Thomas is participating in her first audit engagement. As a manager on the audit, you have the responsibility of briefing Tina on the firm's policies about substantive tests.

REQUIRED

Explain to Tina

a. The circumstances that may permit substantive tests prior to the balance sheet date.
b. How the auditor may control the potential audit risk from such testing for the remainder of the year under audit.
c. The nature of substantive testing for the remainder of the year.
d. How substantive tests are typically applied to income statement account balances.
e. How analytical procedures may be applied to income statement accounts.
f. The circumstances that may necessitate performing tests of details to income statement accounts.

10-33 **(Related party transactions/accounting estimates)** Don Drake has had limited auditing experience. Prior to beginning a new audit engagement, Don asks you, as audit manager, questions about auditing related party transactions and accounting estimates.

REQUIRED

Answer the following questions:

a. What are the audit objectives for these two types of special accounts?
b. What audit procedures may be used to obtain evidence for each type of account?
c. Are there any restrictions or constraints in auditing related party transactions?
d. How do the responsibilities of management and the auditor differ for accounting estimates?
e. What are the key factors that should be considered in evaluating the reasonableness of accounting estimates?
f. What are the principal sources of evidence concerning the reasonableness of accounting estimates?

CASE

10-34 **(General framework for developing audit program for substantive tests)** Apex Manufacturing Company was formed ten years ago. At that time it took out a 30-year mortgage to purchase land and a factory building that continues to house all of its manufacturing, warehousing, and office facilities. It also owns various manufacturing and office equipment acquired at various dates. It is in the process of self-constructing an addition to the factory building to provide more warehouse space. The addition is approximately 50% complete and should be completed during the next fiscal year. The general ledger for Apex includes the following accounts for plant assets: Land, Factory Building, Manufacturing Equipment,

Office Equipment, and related accumulated depreciation control accounts for each of the last three accounts. The details of the cost and accumulated depreciation for each item of manufacturing and office equipment are maintained in separate sections of a plant ledger. There is also a Construction-in-Progress account for the accumulated costs of the warehouse addition.

Apex is a new audit client that has never been audited before. You have completed the preliminary planning for the audit of plant assets and are about to design substantive tests. Under the circumstances, you have assessed both inherent and control risk as high for all plant asset assertions.

REQUIRED

a. Using only your general knowledge of accounting for plant assets and the general framework for developing an audit program for substantive tests described in the chapter, develop an audit program for your first audit of the plant asset accounts of Apex Manufacturing Company.
b. Following each procedure in your audit program, indicate the assertion or assertions to which it applies by using the letters EO, C, RO, VA, and PD for the existence of occurrence, completeness, rights and obligations, valuation or allocation, and presentation and disclosure assertions, respectively.

RESEARCH QUESTIONS

10-35 **(Analytical procedures)** The bibliography for this chapter contains several references to articles on the use of analytical procedures in an audit. Select any one of these articles, or any more recent article that you may locate on analytical procedures, and prepare a brief review of the article. Include comments as to areas of agreement or disagreement with the presentation of analytical procedures in this chapter of the text, particularly with respect to the use of analytical procedures as primary substantive tests as opposed to their use in the preliminary planning and final review phases of the audit.

10-36 **(Auditing accounting estimates)** In 1994, the AICPA's Accounting Standards Executive Committee approved a *Statement of Position* (SOP) titled *Disclosure of Certain Significant Risk and Uncertainties,* subject to being "cleared" by the Financial Accounting Standards Board prior to implementation. The SOP requires management to make disclosures about the use of estimates in the preparation of financial statements. First, determine whether the FASB cleared the SOP. If so, obtain a copy of the SOP, or if unavailable, copies of any journal or newspaper articles on the SOP published after March 1994. Review the SOP or related articles and prepare a brief report giving your assessment of the SOP's potential effect on the audit of accounting estimates relative to the discussion of this topic presented in the chapter on page 350.

10-37 **(Auditing "soft" accounting information)** The AICPA has appointed a task force on *Auditing "Soft" Accounting Information.* Examples of "soft" accounting information are the estimates contained in financial statements. From documents issued by the AICPA or the task force, journal or newspaper articles, or other sources, prepare a brief report summarizing the purposes of the task force and any activities it has completed or undertaken to date. To the extent possible, assess whether the activities of the task force have had, or are expected to have, an impact on the audit of accounting estimates as discussed in the chapter on page 350.

10-38 **(AAERs on audit programs)** The SEC's *Accounting and Auditing Enforcement Release Nos. 39* and *115* involve situations pertaining to audit programs. Summarize the facts and conclusions of the SEC relative to audit programs as set forth in these AAERs.

CHAPTER

11

AUDIT SAMPLING IN TESTS OF CONTROLS

LEARNING OBJECTIVES

After studying this chapter, you should be able to

1. Define audit sampling and discuss its applicability.
2. State the relationship of generally accepted auditing standards to audit sampling.
3. Differentiate sampling and nonsampling risk and explain the four types of sampling risk.
4. Explain the steps in designing a statistical attribute sample for tests of controls.
5. Indicate the factors that affect sample size and how.
6. Explain the steps in executing a statistical attribute sample and evaluating the results.
7. Prepare working papers for a statistical attribute sampling plan.
8. Identify circumstances when discovery sampling is appropriate.
9. Describe the differences between nonstatistical and statistical sampling in tests of controls.

BASIC AUDIT SAMPLING CONCEPTS
- NATURE AND PURPOSE OF AUDIT SAMPLING
- UNCERTAINTY AND AUDIT SAMPLING
- SAMPLING RISK AND NONSAMPLING RISK
- NONSTATISTICAL AND STATISTICAL SAMPLING
- AUDIT SAMPLING TECHNIQUES

DESIGNING STATISTICAL ATTRIBUTE SAMPLES FOR TESTS OF CONTROLS
- DETERMINE THE AUDIT OBJECTIVES
- DEFINE THE POPULATION AND SAMPLING UNIT
- SPECIFY THE ATTRIBUTES OF INTEREST
- DETERMINE THE SAMPLE SIZE
- DETERMINE THE SAMPLE SELECTION METHOD

EXECUTING STATISTICAL ATTRIBUTE SAMPLES AND EVALUATING THE RESULTS
- EXECUTE THE SAMPLING PLAN
- EVALUATE THE SAMPLE RESULTS
- ILLUSTRATIVE CASE STUDY

OTHER CONSIDERATIONS
- DISCOVERY SAMPLING
- NONSTATISTICAL SAMPLING

SUMMARY

BIBLIOGRAPHY

OBJECTIVE QUESTIONS

COMPREHENSIVE QUESTIONS

CASES

RESEARCH QUESTIONS

In contemporary auditing, sampling is well established. The importance of audit sampling in current practice is underscored by the issuance of SAS 39, *Audit Sampling* (AU 350). In addition, the AICPA has published a comprehensive audit and accounting guide entitled *Audit Sampling* (hereinafter referred to as the *Audit Sampling Guide*) to assist auditors in implementing the SAS.

This chapter explains the basic concepts of audit sampling and emphasizes the application of statistical sampling in tests of controls. The chapter is divided into four sections: (1) basic audit sampling concepts, (2) designing statistical attribute samples for tests of controls, (3) executing statistical attribute samples and evaluating the results, and (4) other considerations, including discovery sampling and nonstatistical sampling in tests of controls.

BASIC AUDIT SAMPLING CONCEPTS

NATURE AND PURPOSE OF AUDIT SAMPLING

AU 350.01 defines **audit sampling** as the application of an audit procedure to less than 100% of the items within an account balance or class of transactions for the purpose of evaluating some characteristics of the balance or class.

OBJECTIVE 1

Define audit sampling and discuss its applicability.

Audit sampling is applicable to both tests of controls and substantive tests. However, it is not equally applicable to all the auditing procedures that may be used in performing these tests. For example, audit sampling is widely used in vouching, confirming, and tracing, but it is ordinarily not used in inquiring, observing, and analytical procedures.

UNCERTAINTY AND AUDIT SAMPLING

OBJECTIVE 2

State the relationship of generally accepted auditing standards to audit sampling.

Both the second and third standards of field work contain an element of uncertainty. For example, the auditor's assessment of control risk affects the *nature, timing,* and *extent of* other auditing procedures to be performed. In meeting the evidential matter standard, the auditor is required only to have a *reasonable basis* for an opinion.

The auditor is justified in accepting some uncertainty when the cost and time required to make a 100% examination of the data are, in his judgment, greater than the adverse consequences of possibly expressing an erroneous opinion from examining only a sample of the data. Because this is normally the case, sampling is widely used in auditing.

The uncertainties inherent in auditing are collectively referred to as audit risk. Audit sampling applies to two components of audit risk: (1) control risk and (2) detection risk. As explained in earlier chapters, control risk is the risk that internal controls will not detect or prevent material misstatements in financial statement assertions, and detection risk is the risk that the material misstatements will not be discovered by the auditor. Audit sampling in tests of controls provides information that is directly related to the auditor's assessment of control risk, and audit sampling in substantive tests assists the auditor in quantifying and controlling detection risk.

SAMPLING RISK AND NONSAMPLING RISK

OBJECTIVE 3

Differentiate sampling and nonsampling risk and explain the four types of sampling risk.

When sampling is used in meeting the second and third standards of field work, it should be recognized that uncertainties may result from factors (1) associated directly with the use of sampling (sampling risk) and (2) unrelated to sampling (nonsampling risk).

Sampling Risk

Sampling risk relates to the possibility that a properly drawn sample may not be representative of the population. Thus, the auditor's conclusion about internal controls or the details of transactions and balances based on the sample may be different from the conclusion that would result from the examination of the entire population. In performing tests of controls and substantive tests, the following types of sampling risk may occur

Tests of Controls

The **risk of assessing control risk too low** is the risk that the assessed level of control risk based on the sample supports the planned assessed level of control risk when the true operating effectiveness of the control structure policy or procedure, if known, would not be considered adequate to support the planned assessed level. (This risk is also called the **risk of overreliance**.)

The **risk of assessing control risk too high** is the risk that the assessed level of control risk based on the sample does not support the planned assessed level of control risk when the true operating effectiveness of the control structure policy or procedure, if known, would be considered adequate to support the planned assessed level. (This risk is also called the **risk of underreliance**.)

Substantive Tests

The **risk of incorrect acceptance** is the risk that the sample supports the conclusion that the recorded account balance is not materially misstated when it is materially misstated.

The **risk of incorrect rejection** is the risk that the sample supports the conclusion that the recorded account balance is materially misstated when it is not materially misstated.

These risks have a significant impact on both the effectiveness and efficiency of the audit. The risk of assessing control risk too low and the risk of incorrect acceptance, each of which may be described as the *beta risk* in general statistical terminology, relate to audit effectiveness. When the auditor reaches either of these erroneous conclusions, the auditor's combined procedures may not be sufficient to detect material misstatements, and he or she may not have a reasonable basis for an opinion. In contrast, the risk of assessing control risk too high and the risk of incorrect rejection, each of which may be described as *alpha risk* in general statistical terminology, relate to the efficiency of the audit. When either of these erroneous conclusions are reached, the auditor will increase substantive tests unnecessarily. However, such effort will ordinarily lead ultimately to a correct conclusion, and the audit will nevertheless be effective.

The types of sampling risks for tests of controls and substantive tests and their effects on the audit are summarized in Figure 11-1.

Nonsampling Risk

Nonsampling risk refers to the portion of audit risk that is not due to examining only a portion of the data. Sources of nonsampling risk include (1) human mistakes, such as failing to recognize errors in documents, (2) applying auditing procedures inappropriate to the audit objective, (3) misinterpreting the results of a sample, and (4) relying on erroneous information received from another party, such as an erroneous confirmation response. Nonsampling risk can never be

FIGURE 11-1 • SAMPLING RISKS FOR TESTS OF CONTROLS AND SUBSTANTIVE TESTS

TYPES OF SAMPLING RISKS FOR TESTS OF CONTROLS:

		True Operating Effectiveness of Client's Control Structure Policy or Procedure	
		Adequate for Planned Assessed Level of Control Risk	*Inadequate for Planned Assessed Level of Control Risk*
Assessed Level of Control Risk Based on Sample	▶ *Supports Planned Assessed Level of Control Risk*	Correct Decision	**Risk of Assessing Control Risk Too Low** (*Audit ineffective*)
	▶ *Does* **NOT** *Support Planned Assessed Level of Control Risk*	**Risk of Assessing Control Risk Too High** (*Audit inefficient*)	Correct Decision

TYPES OF SAMPLING RISK FOR SUBSTANTIVE TESTS:

		True State of Client's Recorded Account Balance	
		Not Materially Misstated	*Materially Misstated*
Sample Estimate of Account Balance or Error in Account Balance	▶ *Supports Conclusion Recorded Account Balance Is* **NOT** *Materially Misstated*	Correct Decision	**Risk of Incorrect Acceptance** (*Audit ineffective*)
	▶ *Supports Conclusion Recorded Account Balance* **IS** *Materially Misstated*	**Risk of Incorrect Rejection** (*Audit inefficient*)	Correct Decision

mathematically measured. However, by proper planning and supervision and adherence to the quality control standards described in Chapter 1, nonsampling risk can be held to a negligible level.

NONSTATISTICAL AND STATISTICAL SAMPLING

In performing audit tests in accordance with GAAS, the auditor may use either **nonstatistical sampling** or **statistical sampling** or both. Both types of sampling require the exercise of judgment in planning and executing the sampling plan and evaluating the results. Moreover, both types of sampling can provide sufficient

FIGURE 11-2 • AUDIT SAMPLING: STATISTICAL AND NONSTATISTICAL

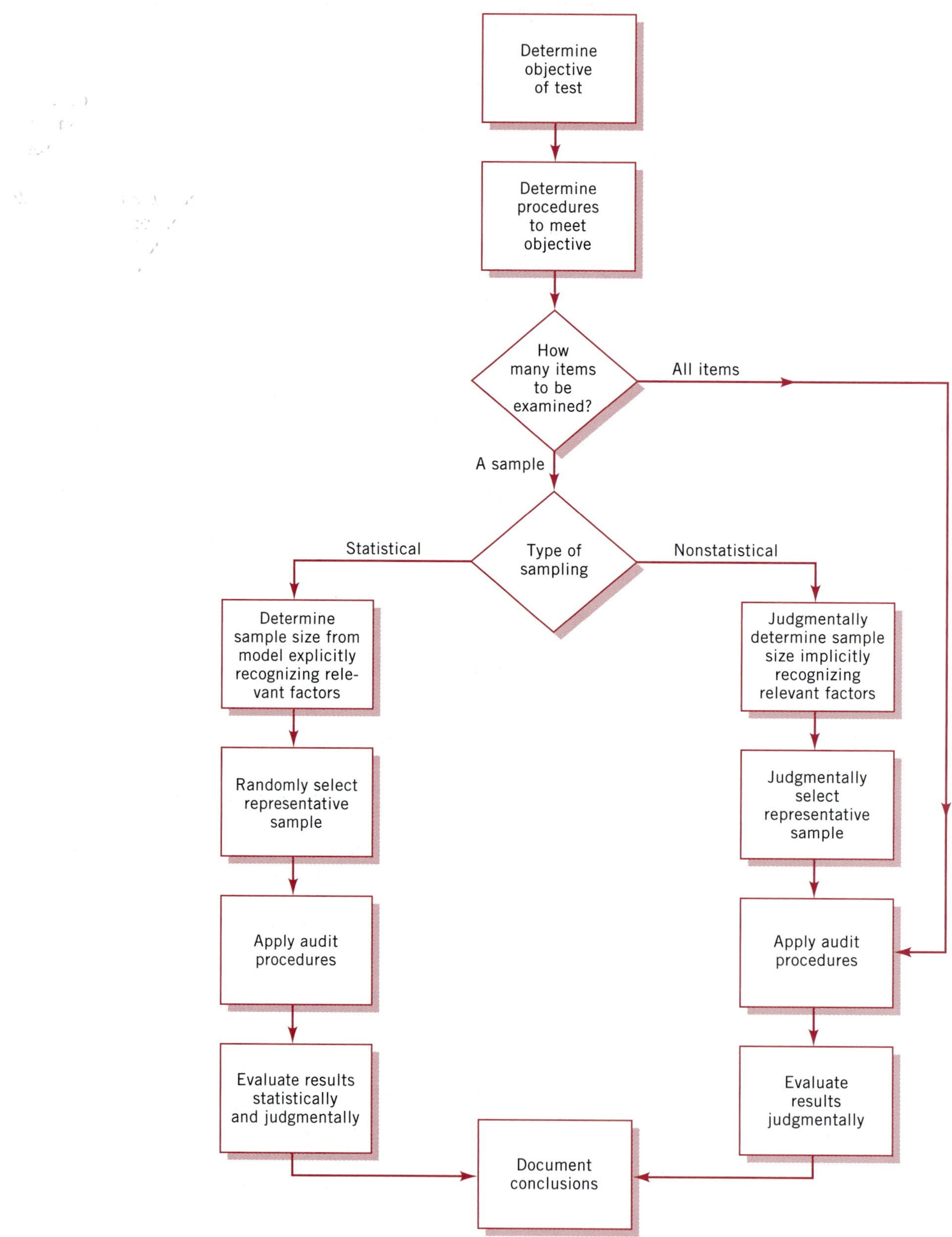

evidential matter as required by the third standard of field work. Both types of audit sampling are also subject to some sampling and nonsampling risk. The critical difference between the two types of sampling is that the laws of probability are used to control sampling risk in statistical sampling.

The choice between the two types of sampling is based primarily on cost/benefit considerations. Nonstatistical sampling may be less costly than statistical sampling, but the benefits from statistical sampling may be significantly greater than from nonstatistical sampling.

In nonstatistical sampling, the auditor determines sample size and evaluates sample results entirely on the basis of subjective criteria and his or her own experience. Thus, he or she may unknowingly use too large a sample in one area and too small a sample in another. To the extent that the sufficiency of audit evidence is based on a sample, the auditor may, in turn, obtain more (or less) evidence than is actually needed to have a reasonable basis for expressing an opinion. However, a properly designed nonstatistical sample may be just as effective as a statistical sample.

In statistical sampling, substantial costs may be required to train auditors in the use of statistics and the design and implementation of the sampling plan. However, statistical sampling should benefit the auditor in (1) designing an efficient sample, (2) measuring the sufficiency of the evidence obtained, and (3) evaluating sample results. Most important, statistical sampling enables the auditor to quantify and control sampling risk.

The choice of nonstatistical or statistical sampling does not affect the selection of auditing procedures to be applied to a sample. Moreover, it does not affect the competence of evidence obtained about individual sample items or the appropriate response by the auditor to errors found in sample items. These matters require the exercise of professional judgment. The relationship between nonstatistical and statistical sampling is graphically shown in Figure 11-2.

AUDIT SAMPLING TECHNIQUES

An auditor may use sampling to obtain information about many different characteristics of a population. However, most audit samples lead either to an estimate of (1) a deviation rate or (2) a dollar amount. When statistical sampling is used, these sampling techniques are identified as **attribute sampling** and **variables sampling,** respectively. The essential differences between these techniques are summarized in Figure 11-3.

In the remaining pages of this chapter, consideration is given to audit sampling in tests of controls. Variables sampling techniques for substantive tests are explained in Chapter 12.

FIGURE 11-3 • ATTRIBUTE AND VARIABLES SAMPLING TECHNIQUES

Sampling Technique	Type of Test	Purpose
Attribute sampling	Test of controls	To estimate the rate of deviations from prescribed controls in a population
Variables sampling	Substantive test	To estimate the total dollar amount of a population or the dollar amount of error in a population

LEARNING CHECK:

11-1 Warren Boyd, a beginning staff accountant, believes that audit sampling applies only to tests of controls, but may be used with all auditing procedures relating to tests of controls. Is Warren correct? Explain.

11-2 Mary Todd is uncertain about several relationships pertaining to audit sampling. As Mary's supervisor, explain the application of audit sampling to (1) GAAS and (2) the components of audit risk.

11-3 a. Distinguish between sampling risk and nonsampling risk.
b. Explain the types of sampling risk that may occur in auditing and their potential effects on the audit.

11-4 a. What are the basic similarities and differences between statistical and nonstatistical sampling?
b. Identify the benefits to the auditor in using statistical sampling.

11-5 a. Indicate the types of statistical sampling techniques that may be used in auditing.
b. Explain the essential differences between the techniques.

KEY TERMS:

Attribute sampling, p. 369
Audit sampling, p. 364
Nonsampling risk, p. 366
Nonstatistical sampling, p. 367
Risk of assessing control risk too low, p. 366
Risk of assessing control risk too high, p 366
Risk of incorrect acceptance, p. 366
Risk of incorrect rejection, p. 366
Risk of overreliance, p. 366
Risk of underreliance, p. 366
Sampling risk, p. 365
Statistical sampling, p. 367
Variables sampling, p. 369

DESIGNING STATISTICAL ATTRIBUTE SAMPLES FOR TESTS OF CONTROLS

OBJECTIVE 4

Explain the steps in designing a statistical attribute sample for tests of controls.

Attribute sampling in tests of controls is used only when there is a trail of documentary evidence of the performance of control procedures. Such control procedures normally fall into the categories of authorization procedures, documents and records, and independent checks. Audit sampling is generally used only when additional tests of controls are performed to obtain support for a lower assessed level of control risk.

The steps in a statistical sampling plan for tests of controls are

1. Determine the audit objectives.
2. Define the population and sampling unit.
3. Specify the attributes of interest.
4. Determine the sample size.
5. Determine the sample section method.
6. Execute the sampling plan.
7. Evaluate the sample results.

Steps 1–5 involve designing the sample and are completed during audit planning. The remaining steps are performed during field work. Each of the steps should be documented in the working papers.

DETERMINE THE AUDIT OBJECTIVES

The overall purpose of tests of controls is to evaluate the effectiveness of the design and operation of internal controls. One or more attribute sampling plans may be designed to evaluate the effectiveness of controls related to a specific class of transactions. For instance, for sales transactions, one sampling plan may be used for tests of controls that affect control risk for the existence or occurrence assertion, and another sampling plan for tests of controls that affect control risk for the completeness assertion. The results of the tests of controls included in an attribute sampling plan are then used to assess control risk for the related account balance assertions affected by that class of transactions.

DEFINE THE POPULATION AND SAMPLING UNIT

In a test of controls, the **population** is the class of transactions being tested. The auditor should determine that the physical representation of the population is appropriate for the objective(s) of the plan. For example, if the objective is to test the effectiveness of controls related to the completeness assertion for purchases transactions, evidence should be obtained that all approved vouchers have been recorded. The appropriate physical representation of the population of purchases transactions from which the sample should be drawn is all approved vouchers, not all entries in the voucher register. If entries in the voucher register were used as the population, unrecorded vouchers would not be included in the sample.

The identification of the population also includes a consideration of the population's homogeneity with respect to the controls to be tested. Accordingly, cash disbursements may be stratified as to amount when there are significant differences in prescribed controls for disbursements over a specified dollar amount.

When there are multiple client locations, such as branches and divisions, the auditor may elect to regard each segment as a separate population. This choice would clearly be warranted when there are significantly different controls at each location. However, when the controls are similar throughout the organization and consolidated statements are prepared, one population for all locations may suffice.

The auditor is faced with a similar choice when the client has made a change in a control during the year. If the auditor wishes to rely on both controls, the population should include transactions processed both before and after the change. In contrast, if reliance is to be placed only on the new control, the population may be defined solely for transactions processed after the change.

It is not necessary in attribute sampling to know the exact size of the population, although a reasonable approximation of population size may be needed when the population is relatively small (i.e., 5,000 or less). As will be shown later, population size has little or no effect on sample size.

The **sampling unit** is an individual element in the population. A sampling unit may be a document, a line item of a document, an entry in a journal or register or a record in a computer file. For the completeness assertion above, the sampling unit should be the voucher. In contrast, if the objective is to determine the existence or occurrence of fictitious transactions in the voucher register, the sampling unit should be an entry in the register.

The sampling unit may have significant impact on audit efficiency. Assume, for instance, that sales invoices average four line items per invoice. If in testing a control over the accuracy of pricing the sampling unit is defined as the invoice, and sample size is 150 invoices, the auditor would have to test 600 prices. In contrast, if the line item is the sampling unit, only 150 prices would be tested.

Efficiency will be further enhanced when the sample item can be used to evaluate the effectiveness of controls for multiple assertions. For example, a sample in which the sampling unit is line items selected from the sales journal might be used to test controls related to both the existence or occurrence and valuation or allocation assertions for sales transactions.

SPECIFY THE ATTRIBUTES OF INTEREST

On the basis of knowledge of the internal control structure, the auditor should be able to identify attributes that relate to the effectiveness of the control being tested. An **attribute** should be identified for each control necessary to reduce control risk for an assertion. If the control requires credit department approval of credit prior to shipment, the attribute may be stated as: "Approval of credit by authorized credit department personnel." When the control requires action by a specified individual, the attribute of interest is "approval of voucher by Jones." Care should be exercised in specifying the attributes because they provide the basis for the subsequent determination of the number of deviations from controls.

Figure 11-4 illustrates the attributes that may be specified in an attribute sampling plan to test controls related to the existence or occurrence and valuation or allocation assertions for sales transactions. It is assumed in this illustration that the company prepares a sales order on receipt of the customer order.

Each attribute should relate to a control for which the auditor seeks an assessed level of control risk below the maximum. However, each attribute may not be of equal importance. In a given case, the auditor may consider credit approval to be

FIGURE 11-4 • ATTRIBUTES OF INTEREST FOR TESTS OF CONTROLS RELATED TO THE EXISTENCE OR OCCURRENCE AND VALUATION OR ALLOCATION ASSERTIONS FOR SALES TRANSACTIONS

Attribute	Description of Attribute
1.	Existence of sales invoice copy with supporting shipping document, sales order, and customer order.
2.	Authorization of sale by appropriate sales order department personnel.
3.	Sales order department verification of agreement of sales order with customer order as to quantities, descriptions, and prices.
4.	Approval of credit by authorized credit department personnel.
5.	Shipping department verification of goods shipped with sales order.
6.	Billing department verification of agreement of sales invoice with shipping document and sales order.
7.	Billing department verification of pricing and mathematical accuracy of sales invoice.
8.	Agreement of details of sales journal and subsidiary ledger entry with sales invoice.

more important than the verification of mathematical accuracy. The relative importance of each attribute should be considered in setting the statistical parameters that must be specified to determine sample size and to evaluate sample results. Ordinarily, more stringent statistical parameters are set for the more critical attributes.

The attributes in Figure 11-4 relate to control procedures that leave a trail of documentary evidence of performance. In each case, the auditor can determine that a required document or entry exists, or that a document is properly initialed, signed, or stamped to indicate performance of the control by an employee. In addition, the auditor may reperform certain controls such as checking the mathematical accuracy of a sales invoice.

DETERMINE THE SAMPLE SIZE

In order to determine a sample size for each attribute or control to be tested, the auditor must specify a numerical value for each of the following factors:

OBJECTIVE 5

Indicate the factors that affect sample size and how.

- Risk of assessing control risk too low.
- Tolerable deviation rate.
- Expected population deviation rate.

In addition, when sampling from a small population (fewer than 5,000 units), the population size must be approximated as explained further in a later section.

We will first examine the mechanical process of using tables to determine sample size based on the three factors listed above. We will then consider how the auditor determines a value for each of the factors, and explore how a change in the value of each factor affects sample size when the other factors are held constant.

Sample Size Tables

Figure 11-5 illustrates one type of table the auditor can use to determine sample size. Notice that the figure contains two tables: Table 1 for a 5% risk of assessing control risk too low, and Table 2 for a 10% risk of assessing control risk too low. To use the tables, it is necessary to

- Select the table that corresponds to the specified risk of assessing control risk too low.
- Locate the column that pertains to the specified tolerable deviation rate.
- Locate the row that contains the expected population deviation rate.
- Read the sample size from the intersection of the column and row determined in steps two and three.

For practice in using the tables, the student should verify the sample sizes shown in column 4 of the following tabulation by looking up the values of the factors specified in columns 1 to 3:

Risk of Assessing Control Risk Too Low (%)	Tolerable Deviation Rate (%)	Expected Population Deviation Rate (%)	Sample Size
5	4	1.0	156
5	6	2.0	127
10	5	1.0	77
10	6	2.0	88

FIGURE 11-5 • SAMPLE SIZE TABLES

Statistical Sample Sizes for Tests of Controls
(for populations ≥ 5000 units)

Table 1. 5% Risk of Assessing Control Risk Too Low

Expected Population Deviation Rate (%)	Tolerable Deviation Rate								
	2%	**3%**	**4%**	**5%**	**6%**	**7%**	**8%**	**9%**	**10%**
0.00	149	99	74	59	49	42	36	32	29
0.50	*	157	117	93	78	66	58	51	46
1.00	*	*	156	93	78	66	58	51	46
1.50	*	*	192	124	103	66	58	51	46
2.00	*	*	*	181	127	88	77	68	46
2.50	*	*	*	*	150	109	77	68	61
3.00	*	*	*	*	195	129	95	84	61
4.00	*	*	*	*	*	*	146	100	89
5.00	*	*	*	*	*	*	*	158	116
6.00	*	*	*	*	*	*	*	*	179

Table 2. 10% Risk of Assessing Control Risk Too Low

Expected Population Deviation Rate (%)	Tolerable Deviation Rate								
	2%	**3%**	**4%**	**5%**	**6%**	**7%**	**8%**	**9%**	**10%**
0.00	114	76	57	45	38	32	28	25	22
0.50	194	129	96	77	64	55	48	42	38
1.00	*	176	96	77	64	55	48	42	38
1.50	*	*	132	105	64	55	48	42	38
2.00	*	*	198	132	88	75	48	42	38
2.50	*	*	*	158	110	75	65	58	38
3.00	*	*	*	*	132	94	65	58	52
4.00	*	*	*	*	*	149	98	73	65
5.00	*	*	*	*	*	*	160	115	78
6.00	*	*	*	*	*	*	*	182	116

* Sample size is too large to be cost/effective for most audit applications.
SOURCE: AICPA, *Audit and Accounting Guide: Audit Sampling,* pp. 106–107 (adapted).

Tables for additional values of the risk of assessing control risk too low are available. Many auditors now enter the values in columns 1 to 3 on the previous page into personal computer software to determine the appropriate sample size instead of using printed tables.

We will now consider how the auditor specifies a value for each of the factors that determine sample size.

Risk of Assessing Control Risk Too Low

As explained earlier, two types of sampling risk are associated with tests of controls: (1) the risk of assessing control risk too high, which relates to the efficiency of the audit, and (2) the risk of assessing control risk too low, which relates to the effectiveness of the audit. Due to the potentially serious consequences associated with an ineffective audit, and because tests of controls may be the primary source of evidence regarding deviations, the auditor desires to keep the risk of assessing control risk too low at a low level.

In attribute sampling, the risk of assessing control risk too low must be stated explicitly.[1] Some auditors specify one level of this risk, such as 5%, for all tests of controls. Alternatively, other auditors vary the risk level directly with planned control risk as illustrated below.

Planned Control Risk	Risk of Assessing Control Risk Too Low (%)
Low	5
Moderate	10
High	15

The risk of assessing control risk too low has an inverse effect on sample size; at a 5% risk, sample size will be larger than at a 10% risk. Thus, varying the risk level directly with planned control risk has the desired effect of providing more evidence to support a low planned control risk and less evidence to support a moderate planned control risk.

The effect of varying the level of this risk on sample size can be seen by holding the other sample size factors constant. Assuming a tolerable deviation rate of 5% and an expected population deviation rate of 1%, the following sample sizes are given in Figure 11-5 when the risk of assessing control risk too low is changed as indicated:

Risk of Assessing Control Risk Too Low (%)	Sample Size
10	77
5	93

Tolerable Deviation Rate

The **tolerable deviation rate** is the maximum rate of deviations from a control that an auditor is willing to accept and still use the planned control risk. In deciding on the tolerable rate, the auditor should consider the relationship of each deviation to

- The accounting records being tested.
- Any related internal controls.
- The purpose of the auditor's evaluation.

The auditor should recognize that deviations from controls increase the *risk*, but not necessarily the number, of errors in the accounting records. For example, the lack of approval on a voucher is a deviation, but the voucher may nevertheless pertain to a valid transaction that should be recorded.

[1] The factor *reliability* or *confidence level* is sometimes used in attribute sampling. This factor is the complement of the risk of assessing control risk too low. Thus, specifying 95% reliability is the equivalent of a 5% risk of assessing control risk too low.

Related controls exist when there are compensating or auxiliary controls to a specified control. The significance of a deviation from the specified control, such as the approval of a voucher, is affected by the potential effectiveness of related controls, such as the review of supporting documentation by one or more authorized signers of company checks.

Tolerable deviation rates vary directly with the auditor's planned control risk for a control procedure—the lower the planned level, the lower the tolerable rate and vice versa. The *Audit Sampling Guide* (p. 32, adapted) includes the following guidelines for quantifying an acceptable range for the tolerable deviation rate:

Planned Control Risk	Tolerable Deviation Rate Range (%)
Low	2–7
Moderate	6–12
High	11–20

Tolerable deviation rate has an inverse effect on sample size. Figure 11-5 indicates the sample sizes shown below for the varying levels of the tolerable deviation rate shown, when the risk of assessing control risk too low and the expected population deviation rate are held constant at 5% and 0%, respectively:

Tolerable Deviation Rate (%)	Sample Size	Tolerable Deviation Rate (%)	Sample Size
2	149	6	49
4	74	8	36

Expected Population Deviation Rate

The auditor uses one or more of the following to estimate the **expected population deviation rate** for each control:

- Last year's sample deviation rate, adjusted judgmentally for current year changes in the effectiveness of the control. actual rates
- An estimate based on the current year's initial assessment of the control.
- The rate found in a preliminary sample of approximately 50 items. use (w) new client

If the expected rate is equal to or greater than the tolerable rate, the auditor cannot reasonably expect to obtain support for a lower assessed level of control risk and the test of controls should not be performed.

The expected population deviation rate has a significant and direct effect on sample size. When the risk of assessing control risk too low and the tolerable deviation rate are held constant, increases and decreases from a given expected population deviation rate will result in larger and smaller sample sizes, respectively. Figure 11-5 shows the effect of this factor on sample size as follows, assuming a 5% risk of assessing control risk too low and a 5% tolerable deviation rate:

Expected Population Deviation Rate (%)	Sample Size	Expected Population Deviation Rate (%)	Sample Size
0.0	59	1.5	124
1.0	93	2.0	181

These effects recognize that as the expected population deviation rate approaches the tolerable rate, more precise information is needed and a larger sample size results.

Population Size

As previously explained, population size has little or no effect on sample size. The *Audit Sampling Guide* (p. 35) illustrates the following effects of changes in population size on sample size, assuming 5% risk of assessing control risk too low, a 5% tolerable deviation rate, and a 1% expected population deviation rate:

Population Size	Sample Size	Population Size	Sample Size
100	64	2,000	92
500	87	5,000	93
1,000	90	100,000	93

As the tabulation shows, there is little difference in the sample size needed from a population of 500 units versus 5,000 units, and no difference between 5,000 units and 100,000 units.

When the population is over 5,000 units, it is appropriate in statistical sampling to consider the population as infinite. The sample size tables in Figure 11-5 are for use when the population consists of 5,000 or more units. In that case, it is not necessary to state more precisely what the population size is. For populations smaller than 5,000 units, a close estimate of the population size must be made, and then either a formula or multiple tables for different population sizes should be used to determine sample size. In all remaining examples in this chapter, and in all of the end-of-chapter problems, it is assumed that the population consists of 5,000 or more units, making the use of the tables in Figure 11-5 appropriate.

A summary of the factors that affect attribute sample size, and how, is presented in Figure 11-6.

DETERMINE THE SAMPLE SELECTION METHOD

Once sample size has been determined, a method of selecting sampling units from the population must be chosen. Sample items should be selected in a manner that results in a sample that is representative of the population. Thus, all items in the population should have a chance of being selected. To accomplish this, statistical sampling plans require the use of *random* selection methods. The principal random selection methods used in attribute sampling are random number sampling and systematic sampling.

FIGURE 11-6 • FACTORS THAT AFFECT ATTRIBUTE SAMPLE SIZE

Factor	Relationship to Sample Size
Risk of assessing control risk too low	Inverse
Tolerable deviation rate	Inverse
Expected population deviation rate	Direct
Population size	
Increases above 5,000 units	No effect
Fewer than 5,000 units	Direct

Random Number Sampling

To use **random number sampling** (sometimes called *simple random sampling*), the auditor must have a basis for relating a unique number to each item in the population. Then, either by reference to a table of random numbers or a computer program that generates random numbers, a selection of numbers can be made to choose the individual items that will make up the sample.

The use of random number tables is facilitated when the items in a population are consecutively numbered. In using tables, the auditor must (1) pick a starting point in the tables by making a "blind stab" or arbitrarily choosing a starting point, and (2) determine the direction or route (top to bottom, left to right, etc.) to be used in reading the tables. The route must be followed consistently.

A random number table is shown in Figure 11-7. To illustrate its use, assume that a sample is desired from a population of sales invoices numbered 0001 to 4000. Assume further that the auditor elects to use the first 4 digits, of each 5-digit number, start with row 6 of column 1, and read from top to bottom. In such a case, the first 10 invoices in the sample would be those indicated in the shaded boxes. Note that the starting number, 9287, is rejected because it falls outside the range of sales invoice numbers in the population (0001 to 4000). Similarly, the numbers 7748 and 4837 are rejected, and so on.

In using a random number table, it is possible that the same number may be drawn more than once. When the duplicate number is ignored (i.e., skipped), the auditor is said to be **sampling without replacement.** Statistical tables used by auditors to determine sample size, like those illustrated earlier in this chapter, are often based on **sampling with replacement.** As a practical matter, however, the auditor usually samples without replacement because no new information would be obtained from examining the same item twice. The use of tables based on sampling with replacement results in larger sample sizes and is therefore considered by auditors to be a conservative approach.

Many computer software packages offer a standard program that includes a random number generator. Such a program can provide a list of random numbers to fit any size sample. In addition, the software can be instructed to produce numbers that correspond solely to numbers appearing in the population (that is,

FIGURE 11-7 • PARTIAL RANDOM NUMBER TABLE

	Columns				
Row	(1)	(2)	(3)	(4)	(5)
1	04734	4 39426	91035	54839	76873
2	10417	5 19688	83404	42038	48226
3	07514	48374	10 35658	38971	53779
4	52305	86925	16223	25946	90222
5	96357	6 11486	30102	82679	57983
6	Start → 92870	7 05921	65698	27993	86406
7	1 00500	75924	38803	05386	10072
8	2 34862	93784	52709	15370	96727
9	3 25809	8 21860	36790	76883	20435
10	77487	9 38419	20631	48694	12638

numbers in the range 0001 to 4000 for the preceding illustration). Random number generators greatly expedite the process of obtaining the list of sample items.

Systematic Sampling

Systematic sampling consists of selecting every *n*th item in the population from one or more random starts. The interval between items is usually referred to as the **skip interval.** When a single random start is used, the interval can be computed by dividing the population size by the sample size. Therefore, when a sample of 40 is to be obtained from a population of 2,000, the skip interval is 50 (i.e., 2,000 ÷ 40). The starting point in this method of selection should be a number from a random number table that falls within the interval from 1 to 50.

A major advantage of systematic selection is that it may take less time than other selection methods. Once the interval and starting point are determined, selection of the sample can be started immediately. In addition, it is unnecessary to number the items in the population to use this method. The auditor (or the computer) simply counts every *n*th item.

When using systematic selection, the auditor must be alert to the possibility of any cyclical pattern within the population coinciding with the skip interval. In that event, systematic selection could produce a nonrandom sample, and another selection method should be considered. Alternatively, the auditor can minimize the chance of bias by picking multiple starting points for the selection process. When multiple random starting points are used, the skip interval, as determined earlier in this section, is multiplied by the number of random starts, thus keeping total sample size the same.

LEARNING CHECK:

11-6 a. State the steps in a sampling plan for tests of controls.
b. Identify the phases of an audit to which each step applies.

11-7 a. Define an *attribute of interest*.
b. What evidence should exist for attributes?

11-8 Identify four factors that may affect the auditor's identification of the population to be sampled.

11-9 a. Define the sampling unit.
b. Identify the different kinds of sampling units that may be selected.

11-10 a. Why does the auditor normally specify a low level for the risk of assessing control risk too low?
b. What effect does the risk of assessing control risk too low have on sample size?

11-11 a. Define the term *tolerable deviation rate* and indicate the factors that should be considered in deciding on the tolerable rate.
b. What effect does this rate have on sample size?

11-12 a. Indicate the information that may be used by the auditor to estimate the expected population deviation rate.
b. What effect does this factor have on sample size?

11-13 a. Identify and briefly explain the sample selection methods that may be used in statistical sampling.

b. Using Figure 11-7, select the first five vouchers from a population of 8,000 vouchers prenumbered consecutively from number 2,001. Use the last 4 digits in each 5-digit block, starting with column 2, row 3, and moving from top to bottom and left to right.

KEY TERMS:

Attribute, p. 372
Expected population deviation rate, p. 376
Population, p. 371
Random number sampling, p. 378
Sampling unit, p. 371
Sampling with replacement, p. 378
Sampling without replacement, p. 378
Skip interval, p. 379
Systematic sampling, p. 379
Tolerable deviation rate, p. 375

EXECUTING STATISTICAL ATTRIBUTE SAMPLES AND EVALUATING THE RESULTS

OBJECTIVE 6

Explain the steps in executing a statistical attribute sample and evaluating the results.

Executing the sample involves retrieving the items selected for the sample and performing the tests of controls on those items. Evaluating the results involves determining whether or not the sample supports the planned control risk based on the frequency of deviations from controls observed in the sample.

EXECUTE THE SAMPLING PLAN

After the sampling plan has been designed, sample items are selected and examined to determine the nature and frequency of deviations from prescribed controls. Deviations include missing documents, absence of initials indicating performance of a control, discrepancies in the details of related documents and records, and unauthorized prices and mathematical errors found through reperformance of controls by the auditor.

When the sampling unit is a document, the auditor may select a quantity that is slightly larger than the required amount. The "extras" are used as replacements when voided, or nonapplicable items are selected in the required sample. A nonapplicable item occurs when a control or attribute does not pertain to the item selected. For instance, if the attribute being examined is "existence of receiving report to support voucher," a voucher for the payment of a monthly bill from a public utility would not be applicable because receiving reports are not prepared for such services. Thus, this voucher would be replaced by an extra in executing the sample plan.

EVALUATE THE SAMPLE RESULTS

Deviations found in the sample must be tabulated, summarized, and evaluated. Professional judgment is required in the evaluation of the following factors leading to an overall conclusion.

Calculate the Sample Deviation Rate

A **sample deviation rate** for each control tested is calculated by dividing the number of deviations found by the sample size examined. This rate is the auditor's best estimate of the true deviation rate in the population.

Determine the Upper Deviation Limit

The **upper deviation limit** indicates the maximum deviation rate in the population based on the *number* of deviations discovered in the sample. The upper limit is expressed as a percentage, which is sometimes alternately referred to as the *achieved upper precision limit* or *maximum population deviation rate.*

The upper deviation limit is determined from evaluation tables like those shown in Figure 11-8. To use the tables, it is necessary for the auditor to

- Select the table that corresponds to the risk of assessing control risk too low.
- Locate the column that contains the actual *number* of deviations (not the deviation rate) found in the sample.
- Locate the row that contains the sample size used.
- Read the upper deviation limit from the intersection of the column and row determined in steps two and three.[2]

Illustrative upper deviation limits are as follows:

Risk of Assessing Control Risk Too Low (%)	Number of Deviations	Sample Size	Upper Deviation Limit
5	1	100	4.7
5	2	150	4.1
10	3	120	5.5
10	4	200	4.0

When the sample size used does not appear in the evaluation tables, the auditor may (1) use the largest sample size in the table, not exceeding the actual sample size used, (2) interpolate, (3) obtain more extensive tables, or (4) use a computer program that will produce an upper limit for any sample size. The upper deviation limit determined from tables implicitly includes an allowance for sampling risk. Thus, the upper deviation limit can be used to determine whether a sample supports planned control risk. If the upper deviation limit is less than or equal to the tolerable deviation rate specified in designing the sample, the results support planned control risk; otherwise, the results do not support planned control risk.

Determine the Allowance for Sampling Risk

It will be recalled that sampling risk relates to the possibility that a properly drawn sample may nonetheless not be representative of the population. As indicated

---

[2] It may be observed that both the evaluation tables in Figure 11-8 and the sample size tables in Figure 11-5 are based on a one-tailed rather than a two-tailed statistical test. This is because the auditor is not concerned with a lower bound on the population deviation rate. Instead, the auditor is only concerned that the actual population deviation rate does not exceed an upper bound defined as the tolerable deviation rate.

FIGURE 11-8 • STATISTICAL SAMPLE EVALUATION TABLES

Statistical Sample Results Evaluation Table for Tests of Controls Upper Deviation Limit (for populations ≥ 5,000 units)

Table 3. 5% Risk of Assessing Control Risk Too Low

Sample Size	Actual Number of Deviations Found								
	0	1	2	3	4	5	6	7	8
25	11.3	17.6	*	*	*	*	*	*	*
30	9.5	14.9	19.5	*	*	*	*	*	*
35	8.2	12.9	16.9	*	*	*	*	*	*
40	7.2	11.3	14.9	18.3	*	*	*	*	*
45	6.4	10.1	13.3	16.3	19.2	*	*	*	*
50	5.8	9.1	12.1	14.8	17.4	19.9	*	*	*
55	5.3	8.3	11.0	13.5	15.9	18.1	*	*	*
60	4.9	7.7	10.1	12.4	14.6	16.7	18.8	*	*
65	4.5	7.1	9.4	11.5	13.5	15.5	17.4	19.3	*
70	4.2	6.6	8.7	10.7	12.6	14.4	16.2	18.0	19.7
75	3.9	6.2	8.2	10.0	11.8	13.5	15.2	16.9	18.4
80	3.7	5.8	7.7	9.4	11.1	12.7	14.3	15.8	17.3
90	3.3	5.2	6.8	8.4	9.9	11.3	12.7	14.1	15.5
100	3.0	4.7	6.2	7.6	8.9	10.2	11.5	12.7	14.0
125	2.4	3.7	4.9	6.1	7.2	8.2	9.3	10.3	11.3
150	2.0	3.1	4.1	5.1	6.0	6.9	7.7	8.6	9.4
200	1.5	2.3	3.1	3.8	4.5	5.2	5.8	6.5	7.1

Table 4. 10% Risk of Assessing Control Risk Too Low

Sample Size	Actual Number of Deviations Found								
	0	1	2	3	4	5	6	7	8
20	10.9	18.1	*	*	*	*	*	*	*
25	8.8	14.7	19.9	*	*	*	*	*	*
30	7.4	12.4	16.8	*	*	*	*	*	*
35	6.4	10.7	14.5	18.1	*	*	*	*	*
40	5.6	9.4	12.8	15.9	19.0	*	*	*	*
45	5.0	8.4	11.4	14.2	17.0	19.6	*	*	*
50	4.5	7.6	10.3	12.9	15.4	17.8	*	*	*
55	4.1	6.9	9.4	11.7	14.0	16.2	18.4	*	*
60	3.8	6.3	8.6	10.8	12.9	14.9	16.9	18.8	*
70	3.2	5.4	7.4	9.3	11.1	12.8	14.6	16.2	17.9
80	2.8	4.8	6.5	8.3	9.7	11.3	12.8	14.3	15.7
90	2.5	4.3	5.8	7.3	8.7	10.1	11.4	12.7	14.0
100	2.3	3.8	5.2	6.6	7.8	9.1	10.3	11.5	12.7
120	1.9	3.2	4.4	5.5	6.6	7.6	8.6	9.6	10.6
160	1.4	2.4	3.3	4.1	4.9	5.7	6.5	7.2	8.0
200	1.1	1.9	2.6	3.3	4.0	4.6	5.2	5.8	6.4

* Over 20%.

SOURCE: AICPA, *Audit and Accounting Guide: Audit Sampling*, pp. 108–109 (adapted).

above, the evaluation of a sample can be made without explicitly calculating the allowance for sampling risk. However, knowing how the allowance can be determined and its effects is helpful in the evaluation process. The allowance for sampling risk is added to the sample deviation rate to produce an upper deviation limit that will exceed the true population deviation rate a known proportion of the time. When evaluation tables are used, the **allowance for sampling risk** is determined by subtracting the sample deviation rate from the upper deviation limit. Thus, in the first case on page 381, the sample deviation rate is 1% (1⁄100) and the allowance is 3.7% (4.7%−1.0%).[3] If three deviations had been found in the sample of 100, the upper deviation limit would be 7.6%, the sample deviation rate would be 3% (3⁄100), and the allowance for sampling risk would be 4.6% (7.6%−3.0%).

The allowance for sampling risk is directly related to the number of deviations found in the sample as illustrated by the increase from 3.7 to 4.6% in this example. It follows, in statistical sampling, that when the sample deviation rate exceeds the expected population deviation rate, the allowance for sampling risk will be large enough to cause the upper deviation limit to exceed the tolerable deviation rate specified in designing the sample. Thus, the following generalizations can be stated:

- Whenever the sample deviation rate exceeds the expected population deviation rate used to determine sample size, the upper deviation limit will exceed the tolerable deviation rate at the specified risk of assessing control risk too low and the sample results will not support planned control risk.
- Conversely, whenever the sample deviation rate is less than or equal to the expected population deviation rate, the upper deviation limit will be less than or equal to the tolerable deviation rate at the specified risk of assessing control risk too low and the sample results will support planned control risk.

From the above, it can be seen that it is not always necessary to compare the upper deviation limit with the tolerable deviation rate in evaluating sample results. The basis for the auditor's evaluation should be documented in the working papers. The working paper in Figure 11-9 permits an evaluation using either the upper deviation limit or the sample deviation rate. The sample design and evaluation of results shown in this microcomputer-generated working paper were developed using the ATTRB template in the software package called *AUDSAMP,* which is available as a supplement to this text.

Consider the Qualitative Aspects of Deviations

It would be a mistake to conclude that the auditor is interested only in the frequency of the deviations. Each deviation from a prescribed control should be analyzed to determine its nature and a cause. Deviations may result from such factors as a new employee, an inexperienced replacement, an employee on vacation or sick leave, misunderstanding of instructions, incompetence, carelessness, and deliberate violation.

The auditor should also consider whether the deviation may have a direct effect on the financial statements. For instance, the failure of unit prices on a sales invoice to agree with authorized prices has an impact on the statements. In contrast, the absence of verification of the mathematical accuracy of an invoice that is mathematically correct does not indicate a misstatement in the financial state-

---

[3] The allowance for sampling risk can also be computed directly using binomial probability distribution theory.

FIGURE 11-9 • ATTRIBUTE SAMPLING PLAN WORKING PAPER

DEXTER COMPANY
ATTRIBUTE SAMPLE -- SALES TRANSACTIONS
12/31/X1

W/P REF: *H-2*
PREPARED BY: *C.J.G.* DATE: *10/6/X1*
REVIEWED BY: *R.C.P.* DATE: *10/10/X1*

SAMPLE DESIGN — SAMPLE RESULTS

OBJECTIVE: TO TEST EFFECTIVENESS OF CONTROLS RELATED TO THE EXISTENCE OR OCCURRENCE AND VALUATION OR ALLOCATION ASSERTIONS FOR SALES TRANSACTIONS

SAMPLING UNIT AND POPULATION: LINE ITEMS IN SALES JOURNAL REPRESENTING 5000 SALES INVOICES NUMBERED A76500-A81499 JOURNALIZED IN SEQUENCE

SELECTION METHOD: SIMPLE RANDOM; COMPUTER GENERATED LIST

(1) ATTRIBUTES NO.	DESCRIPTION	(2) RISK OF ASSESSING CONTROL RISK TOO LOW	(3) TOLERABLE DEVIATION RATE	(4) EXPTD. POP. DEVIATION RATE	(5) SAMPLE SIZE PER TABLE	(6) SAMPLE SIZE USED	(7) NUMBER OF DEVIATIONS	(8) SAMPLE DEVIATION RATE	(9) UPPER DEVIATION LIMIT	(10) ALLOWANCE FOR SAMPLING RISK	(11) TEST UDL <= TDR
1	EXISTENCE OF SALES INVOICE COPY WITH SUPPORTING SHIPPING DOCUMENT, SALES ORDER, AND CUSTOMER ORDER	5	3	0.5	157	160	0	0.0	2	2.0	YES
2	AUTHORIZATION OF SALE BY APPROPRIATE SALES ORDER DEPT. PERSONNEL	5	3	0.5	157	160	0	0.0	2	2.0	YES
3	ORDER DEPT. VERIF. OF AGREEMENT OF SALES ORDER WITH CUSTOMER ORDER	10	6	2	88	90	1	1.1	4.3	3.2	YES
4	APPROVAL OF CREDIT BY AUTHORIZED CREDIT DEPT. PERSONNEL	5	3	0.5	157	160	5	3.1	6.9	3.8	NO
5	SHIPPING DEPT. VERIF. OF GOODS SHIPPED WITH SALES ORDER	10	5	1.5	105	105	0	0.0	2.3	2.3	YES
6	BILLING DEPT. VERIF. OF AGREEMENT OF SALES INVOICE WITH SHIPPING DOCUMENT AND SALES ORDER	5	4	1	156	160	1	0.6	3.1	2.5	YES
7	BILLING DEPT. VERIF. OF PRICING AND MATH ACCURACY OF SALES INVOICE	5	4	1	156	160	1	0.6	3.1	2.5	YES
8	AGREEMENT OF DETAILS OF SALES JOURNAL AND SUBSIDIARY LEDGER ENTRY WITH SALES INVOICE	5	3	0.5	157	160	0	0.0	2	2.0	YES

CONCLUSION: *Planned control risk is supported for all controls except approval of credit (attribute #4). Effect on planned control risk, detection risk, and substantive tests documented on w/p H-4.*

MANAGEMENT COMMUNICATION: *Deviations from attribute 4 represent a reportable condition to be communicated to management and the audit committee.*

ments. A further consideration is whether the deviation constitutes an irregularity. Nonsystematic deviations are generally accidental and unintentional. However, a systematic pattern of deviations may be indicative of a serious breakdown in a control leading to numerous unintentional errors or deliberate efforts to misrepresent facts or conceal misappropriations. Obviously, deviations that directly affect the financial statements or appear to be irregularities have greater audit significance.

Reach an Overall Conclusion

The auditor uses the results of the sample, knowledge about the control environment and accounting system, and professional judgment to make a final assessment of control risk for the controls represented by the attributes included in the sampling plan. This assessment is then used to assess control risk for the relevant financial statement assertions affected by the class of transactions tested.

When the final assessment of control risk for an assertion does not support the planned level of control risk specified in the auditor's preliminary audit strategy, the strategy must be revised. This involves increasing control risk and lowering the acceptable level of detection risk. To achieve the latter, the auditor ordinarily needs to modify the planned level of substantive tests, which affects the auditor's choices regarding nature, timing, and extent in designing such tests. Before revising strategy, the auditor should consider whether any compensating controls exist that if tested and found effective would support the original strategy. Deviations from control structure policies and procedures that are considered reportable conditions, as defined in Chapter 9, should be communicated to management and the audit committee.

ILLUSTRATIVE CASE STUDY

In the audit of Dexter Company, a continuing client, the auditor decides to use attribute sampling in tests of controls related to the existence or occurrence and valuation or allocation assertions for sales transactions. The evidence obtained about the effectiveness of these controls will be used to make a final assessment of control risk for related financial statement assertions for sales and accounts receivable. The auditor plans to obtain support for a low planned control risk assessment so that detection risk can be set high and restricted substantive tests can be performed. The case study is divided into the following three parts: (1) the design of the sampling plan, (2) executing the plan, and (3) evaluating the results.

OBJECTIVE 7

Prepare working papers for a statistical attribute sampling plan.

The *design of the sampling plan* involves the first five steps of the sampling plan. These are presented in the sample design section of the working paper in Figure 11-9. The objective of the plan, the sampling unit and population, and the sample selection method are identified at the top of the working paper. Then, the attributes of interest are listed in column 1, and the factors used to determine sample size are specified in columns 2–4. In this plan, attributes 3 and 5 are considered less critical than the others; hence, the statistical parameters for these attributes are less stringent than for the more critical conditions. Sample sizes are next determined from the tables shown in Figure 11-5 and are entered in column 5. In the Dexter Company, the auditor decides to round up sample sizes to provide extra units. These amounts are entered in column 6. For purposes of this illustration, assume that these are the actual numbers of items examined for each attribute.

In *executing the plan,* the sample items are randomly selected and the transactions are examined for each attribute. As deviations are found, they are recorded and summarized on a worksheet as shown in Figure 11-10.

In *evaluating the results,* the number of deviations from each attribute is entered in column 7 of Figure 11-9. Then, the deviation rates are computed and entered in column 8 and may be compared with the corresponding expected population deviation rates in column 4. In this case study, the sample rate for attribute 4 exceeds the expected rate. Thus, it can be foreseen that the upper deviation limit

FIGURE 11-10 • DEVIATIONS LISTING WORKING PAPER

W/P: H-3

Prepared by: CJH Date: 10/6/X1
Reviewed by: RCP Date: 10/9/X1

Dexter Company
Sales Transactions Attribute Sample
Deviations Listing
12/31/X1

Invoice Number	Attribute 1	2	3	4	5	6	7	8
A76504			√					
A76550				√				
A76720				√				
A76745						√		
A77001				√				
A77022							√	
A79268				√				
A80743				√				
Total No. of Deviations	0	0	1	5	0	1	1	0
Sample Size	160	160	90	160	105	160	160	160
Sample Deviation Rate	0	0	1.1	3.1	0	0.6	0.6	0

will exceed the tolerable rate for this attribute. Next, the auditor uses the evaluation tables in Figure 11-8, to determine the upper deviation limit for each attribute. These results are entered in column 9. The upper deviation limit is then compared with the tolerable rate for each attribute. When the upper deviation limit exceeds the tolerable rate, the sample results do not support the auditor's planned control risk. In the Dexter Company, as foreseen, this occurs only for attribute 4. Finally, for illustrative purposes, the allowance for sampling risk (column 9—column 8) is entered in column 10.

To form an overall conclusion about each control, the auditor makes a qualitative assessment of the deviations to determine their nature, cause, and significance. This analysis is documented in a working paper as shown in Figure 11-11. Observe that this working paper also indicates the effects of the deviations on substantive tests and whether any matters should be reported to management.

In this case, the auditor concludes that both the statistical evaluation and the qualitative assessment support the planned control risk for all of the controls except the one related to attribute 4. The deviations from attribute 4 are considered to be a reportable condition that must be communicated to management and the audit committee. These conclusions are documented on the bottom of the working paper in Figure 11-9.

LEARNING CHECK:

11-14 a. What is involved in executing a sampling plan?
b. Give several examples of deviations from prescribed controls.

11-15 a. Why might the auditor select some *extra* sample items when sampling from a population of documents?
b. State what is meant by a *nonapplicable item* and give an example.

11-16 a. Identify the three steps involved in quantitatively evaluating sample results.
b. Indicate the steps involved in using sample evaluation tables.

11-17 a. What factors should be considered in qualitatively evaluating sample results?
b. What alternative courses of action should be considered when sample results do not support the auditor's planned control risk?

KEY TERMS:

Allowance for sampling risk, p. 383
Sample deviation rate, p. 381
Upper deviation limit, p. 381

OTHER CONSIDERATIONS

This final section of the chapter deals with (1) discovery sampling and (2) nonstatistical sampling in tests of controls.

FIGURE 11-11 • ANALYSIS OF SAMPLE DEVIATIONS WORKING PAPER

W/P: H-4
Prepared by: CJH Date: 10/6/X1
Reviewed by: RLP Date: 10/9/X1

Dexter Company
Sales Transactions Attribute Sample
Analysis of Sample Deviations
12/31/X1

Attribute	Number of Deviations	Explanation of Deviations	Final Assessment of Control Risk	Effects on Detection Risk and Substantive Tests	Matters to be Communicated
3	1	Verification of agreement of sales order and customer order not indicated, but they did in fact agree.	Low	As planned	None
4	5	Authorized credit approval not evident on five invoices. No explanation offered by credit dept. personnel. Planned control risk not supported.	High	Detection risk for valuation assertion for accounts receivable must be restricted by expanding audit procedures for confirming accounts and reviewing adequacy of allowance for uncollectible accounts.	Deviations represent a reportable condition to be communicated to management and the audit committee
6	1	Verification not indicated on one invoice involving a back order. Processing of backorders otherwise appropriate.	Low	As planned	None
7	1	Evidence of verification not indicated on one invoice; however invoice price agreed with authorized price list and invoice was mathematically accurate	Low	As planned	None

DISCOVERY SAMPLING

OBJECTIVE 8

Identify circumstances when discovery sampling is appropriate.

Discovery sampling is a form of attribute sampling that is designed to locate at least one exception if the rate of deviations in the population is at or above a specified rate. This method of sampling is used to search for critical deviations that may indicate the existence of an irregularity such as the issuance of payroll checks to fictitious employees. Discovery sampling is appropriate when the expected deviation rate is very low and the auditor wants a sample that will provide a specified probability of observing one occurrence.

Discovery sampling may be useful when the auditor

- Is examining a large population composed of items that contain a very high proportion of control risk.
- Suspects that irregularities have occurred.
- Seeks additional evidence in a given case to determine whether a known irregularity is an isolated occurrence or part of a recurring pattern.

Discovery sampling generally is not used to find a "needle in the haystack" or a "once in a lifetime occurrence." Because of the limited applicability of this method, it will not be illustrated in this chapter.

NONSTATISTICAL SAMPLING

OBJECTIVE 9

Describe the differences between nonstatistical and statistical sampling in tests of controls.

As explained earlier, the auditor may use nonstatistical sampling in tests of controls. The steps involved in the design and execution of the sampling plan are similar regardless of the type of sampling. Moreover, the factors to be considered in determining sample size and evaluating sample results are identical, although they may not be quantified and explicitly stated in nonstatistical applications. The major differences between nonstatistical and statistical sampling in performing the steps are summarized below.

Determine the Sample Size

As in statistical sampling applications, the major determinants of sample size in nonstatistical sampling are (1) the risk of assessing control risk too low, (2) the tolerable deviation rate, and (3) the expected population deviation rate for each attribute. In nonstatistical sampling, it is not necessary for the auditor to quantify these factors explicitly in determining sample size. However, the auditor must subjectively recognize the following effects on sample size of a change in one factor when other factors are held constant:

Factor	Effect on Sample Size
Risk of assessing control risk too low	Inverse
Tolerable deviation rate	Inverse
Expected population deviation rate	Direct

The auditor may, but is not required to, use the information from statistical tables as a guide in determining sample size in a nonstatistical sample.

Determine the Sample Selection Method

In addition to random number and systematic sampling described earlier, the auditor may use block or haphazard sampling in selecting items in nonstatistical sampling.

BLOCK SAMPLING. At one time, block sampling was the most common selection method. The method consists of selecting similar transactions occurring within a specified time period. For example, the sample may consist of all vouchers processed during a two-week period. If *enough* blocks are selected, this method of selection may be suitable in nonstatistical sampling. However, selection of a single block from a whole year's transactions is no longer considered appropriate in most circumstances.

HAPHAZARD SAMPLING. This method involves selecting items at will, without regard to document number, amount, or other feature. Thus, the auditor may haphazardly select a sample of 50 invoices from a file. If bias is avoided in making the selection, the sample may be representative of the population.

Evaluate the Sample Results

In nonstatistical samples, it is not possible to determine (1) an upper deviation limit or (2) a statistically derived allowance for sampling risk associated with a sample result and a specified risk of assessing control risk too low. However, the auditor should relate the deviation rate found in a sample to the corresponding tolerable rate specified in determining sample size. The difference may be viewed as an allowance for sampling risk.[4]

To illustrate, if a sample deviation rate of 1% is found for an attribute for which the tolerable rate was 7%, the auditor may view the difference of 6% as an adequate allowance for sampling risk and conclude the sample provides an acceptably low level of risk of assessing control risk too low. In doing so, the auditor is relying on experience and professional judgment that the sample deviation rate is sufficiently small relative to the tolerable deviation rate (the allowance for sampling risk is sufficiently large) to ensure that the true population deviation rate does not exceed the tolerable deviation rate. On the other hand, if a sample deviation rate of 5% is found for an attribute for which a tolerable rate of 6% was specified, the difference of 1% may be viewed as an inadequate allowance for sampling risk, resulting in an unacceptably high risk of assessing control risk too low. That is, the auditor is concerned that even though the sample deviation rate is less than the specified tolerable rate, the actual population deviation rate may nonetheless exceed the tolerable rate.

In evaluating the results of nonstatistical samples, as is the case in evaluating statistical samples, the auditor should consider the qualitative aspects of deviations found in a sample, as well as the frequency of the deviations.

---

[4] It should be recognized that this determination of sampling risk differs significantly from the allowance for sampling risk in statistical sampling.

LEARNING CHECK:

11-18 Describe the circumstances in which discovery sampling may be useful in auditing.

11-19 Contrast the method of (a) determining sample size and (b) evaluating sample results between a nonstatistical and a statistical sampling plan.

11-20 Distinguish between block and haphazard sampling selection and identify the circumstances under which each method may produce a representative sample.

KEY TERMS:

Discovery sampling, p. 389

SUMMARY

Both statistical and nonstatistical sampling may be used in performing tests of controls. The critical difference between the two types of sampling is that the laws of probability are used to control sampling risk in statistical sampling. Under either type of sampling, the auditor is primarily concerned about obtaining sufficient evidence to support the planned level of control risk specified in the auditor's preliminary audit strategy. When the planned level of control risk for an assertion is not supported, a higher control risk must be specified together with a lower acceptable level of detection risk. Substantive tests appropriate to the acceptable level of detection risk are then designed.

BIBLIOGRAPHY

AICPA Professional Standards:
SAS 39 (AU 350), Audit Sampling
IAU 19 (AU 8019), Audit Sampling

AICPA, *Audit and Accounting Guide: Audit Sampling.* New York: AICPA, 1983

Akresh, Abraham D., and Tatum, Kay W. "Audit Sampling—Dealing with the Problems," *Journal of Accountancy* (December 1988), pp. 58–64.

Epstein, B. J. "Attributes Sampling: A Local Firm's Experience," *Journal of Accountancy* (January 1986), pp. 130–135.

Guy, Dan M., Carmichael, Douglas, and Whittington, O. Ray. *Audit Sampling: An Introduction,* Third Edition. New York: John Wiley & Sons, Inc., 1994.

OBJECTIVE QUESTIONS

Indicate the *best* answer for each of the following multiple choice questions.

11-21 These questions pertain to the use of sampling in auditing.

1. An advantage to using statistical over nonstatistical sampling methods in tests of controls is that the statistical methods
   a. Afford greater assurance than a nonstatistical sample of equal size.
   b. Provide an objective basis for quantitatively evaluating sample risks.

c. Can more easily convert the sample into a dual purpose test useful for substantive testing.
d. Eliminate the need to use judgment in determining appropriate sample sizes.

2. The risk of incorrect acceptance and the likelihood of assessing control risk too low relate to the
   a. Effectiveness of the audit.
   b. Efficiency of the audit.
   c. Preliminary estimates of materiality levels.
   d. Allowable risk of tolerable error.

3. If fraud or gross error is suspected in the population, the auditor would most likely use
   a. Variables sampling.
   b. Attribute sampling.
   c. Discovery sampling.
   d. Dollar-unit sampling.

4. The diagram below depicts the auditor's estimated maximum deviation rate compared with the tolerable rate, and also depicts the true population deviation rate compared with the tolerable rate.

Auditor's estimate based on sample results \ *True state of population*	Deviation rate is less than tolerable rate	Deviation rate exceeds tolerable rate
Maximum deviation rate is less than tolerable rate	I.	III.
Maximum deviation rate exceeds tolerable rate	II.	IV.

   As a result of tests of controls, the auditor assesses control risk higher than necessary and thereby increases substantive testing. This is illustrated by situation
   a. I.
   b. II.
   c. III.
   d. IV.

11-22 These questions pertain to determining sample size in an attribute sampling plan.

1. To determine the sample size for a test of controls, an auditor should consider the tolerable deviation rate, the allowable risk of assessing control risk too low, and the
   a. Expected deviation rate.
   b. Upper precision limit.
   c. Risk of incorrect acceptance.
   d. Risk of incorrect rejection.

2. Which of the following combinations results in a decrease in sample size in a sample for attributes?

	Risk of Assessing Control Risk Too Low	Tolerable Rate	Expected Population Deviation Rate
a.	Increase	Decrease	Increase
b.	Decrease	Increase	Decrease
c.	Increase	Increase	Decrease
d.	Increase	Increase	Increase

3. Which of the following statements is correct concerning statistical sampling in tests of controls?
   a. The population size has little or *no* effect on determining sample size except for very small populations.
   b. The expected population deviation rate has little or *no* effect on determining sample size except for very small populations.
   c. As the population size doubles, the sample size also should double.
   d. For a given tolerable rate, a larger sample size should be selected as the expected population deviation rate decreases.

4. In planning a statistical sample for a test of controls, an auditor increased the expected population deviation rate from the prior year's rate because of the results of the prior year's tests of controls and the overall control environment. If other factors remain constant, compared to last year this will cause an increase in
   a. Tolerable rate.
   b. Allowance for sampling risk.
   c. Risk of assessing control risk too low.
   d. Sample size.

11-23 These questions pertain to the selection of items for a statistical sample.

1. An underlying feature of random-based selection of items is that each
   a. Stratum of the accounting population be given equal representation in the sample.
   b. Item in the accounting population be randomly ordered.
   c. Item in the accounting population should have an opportunity to be selected.
   d. Item must be systematically selected using replacement.

2. When performing tests of controls over cash disbursements, a CPA may use a systematic sampling technique with a start at any randomly selected item. The biggest disadvantage of this type of sampling is that the items in the population
   a. Must be recorded in a systematic pattern before the sample can be drawn.
   b. May occur in a systematic pattern, thus destroying the sample randomness.
   c. May systematically occur more than once in the sample.
   d. Must be systematically replaced in the population after sampling.

3. An auditor plans to examine a sample of 20 checks for countersignatures as prescribed by the client's internal control procedures. One of the checks in the chosen sample of 20 cannot be found. The auditor should consider the reasons for this limitation and
   a. Evaluate the results as if the sample size had been 19.
   b. Treat the missing check as a deviation for the purpose of evaluating the sample.
   c. Treat the missing check in the same manner as the majority of the other 19 checks, that is, countersigned or not.
   d. Choose another check to replace the missing check in the sample.

11-24 These questions pertain to evaluating the results of an attribute sampling plan.

1. In the audit of the financial statements of Delta Company, the auditor determines that in performing a test of controls, the deviation rate in the sample does not support the

planned control risk when, in fact, the true deviation rate in the population does support the planned control risk. This situation illustrates the risk of

a. Assessing control risk too high.
b. Assessing control risk too low.
c. Incorrect rejection.
d. Incorrect acceptance.

Items 2 and 3 are based on the following:

An auditor desired to test credit approval on 10,000 sales invoices processed during the year. The auditor designed a statistical sample that would provide 1% risk of assessing control risk too low (99% confidence) that not more than 7% of the sales invoices lacked approval. The auditor estimated from previous experience that about 2½% of the sales invoices lacked approval. A sample of 200 invoices was examined and 7 of them were lacking approval. The auditor then determined the achieved upper precision limit to be 8%.

2. In the evaluation of this sample, the auditor decided to increase the level of the preliminary assessment of control risk because the
   a. Tolerable deviation rate (7%) was less than the achieved upper precision limit (8%).
   b. Expected deviation rate (7%) was more than the percentage of errors in the sample (3½%).
   c. Achieved upper precision limit (8%) was more than the percentage of errors in the sample (3½%).
   d. Expected deviation rate (2½%) was less than the tolerable rate (7%).

3. The allowance for sampling risk was
   a. 5½%
   b. 4½%
   c. 3½%
   d. 1%

4. What is an auditor's evaluation of a statistical sample for attributes when a test of 50 documents results in 3 deviations if the tolerable rate is 7%, the expected population deviation rate is 5%, and the allowance for sampling risk is 2%.
   a. Modify the planned assessed level of control risk because the tolerable rate plus the allowance for sampling risk exceeds the expected population deviation rate.
   b. Accept the sample results as support for the planned assessed level of control risk because the sample deviation rate plus the allowance for sampling risk exceeds the tolerable rate.
   c. Accept the sample results as support for the planned assessed level of control risk because the tolerable rate less the allowance for sampling risk equals the expected population deviation rate.
   d. Modify the planned assessed level of control risk because the sample deviation rate plus the allowance for sampling risk exceeds the tolerable rate.

COMPREHENSIVE QUESTIONS

11-25 **(Sampling for attributes—statistical and nonstatistical)** Sampling for attributes is often used to allow an auditor to reach a conclusion concerning a rate of occurrence in a population. A common use in auditing is to test the rate of deviation from a prescribed internal control procedure to obtain support for a planned level of control risk.

REQUIRED

a. When an auditor samples for attributes, identify the factors that should influence the auditor's judgment concerning the determination of
   1. Acceptable level of risk of assessing control risk too low,
   2. Tolerable deviation rate, and
   3. Expected population deviation rate.
b. State the effect on sample size of an increase in each of the following factors, assuming all other factors are held constant:
   1. Acceptable level of risk of assessing control risk too low.
   2. Tolerable deviation rate, and
   3. Expected population deviation rate.
c. Assuming nonstatistical sampling is used, evaluate the sample results of a test for attributes if authorizations are found missing on 7 check requests out of a sample of 100 tested. The population consists of 2,500 check requests, the tolerable deviation rate is 8%, and the risk of assessing control risk too low should be held to a low level.
d. How may the use of statistical sampling assist the auditor in evaluating the sample results described in c, above?

AICPA (adapted)

11-26 **(Uncertainties in audit sampling)** One of the generally accepted auditing standards states that sufficient competent evidential matter is to be obtained through inspection, observation, inquiries, and confirmation to afford a reasonable basis for an opinion regarding the financial statements under examination. Some degree of uncertainty is implicit in the concept of "a reasonable basis for an opinion," because the concept of sampling is well established in auditing practice.

REQUIRED

a. Explain the auditor's justification for accepting the uncertainties that are inherent in the sampling process.
b. Discuss the uncertainties that collectively embody the concept of audit risk.
c. Discuss the nature of sampling risk and nonsampling risk. Include the effect of sampling risk on tests of controls in the auditor's study and evaluation of the internal control structure.

AICPA (adapted)

11-27 **(Steps in attribute sampling)** Jiblum, CPA, is planning to use attribute sampling to determine the effectiveness of internal controls over sales transactions. Jiblum has begun to develop an outline of the main steps in the sampling plan as follows:

1. State the objective(s) of the plan (e.g., to test the effectiveness of controls related to the existence or occurrence and valuation or allocation assertions for sales transactions).
2. Define the population (define the period covered by the test and the completeness of the population).
3. Define the sampling unit (e.g., client copies of sales invoices).

REQUIRED

a. What are the remaining steps in the above outline that Jiblum should include in the statistical test of sales invoices? *Do not present a detailed analysis of tasks that must be performed to carry out the objectives of each step. Parenthetical examples need not be provided.*
b. How does statistical methodology help the auditor to develop a satisfactory sampling plan?

AICPA (adapted)

11-28 **(Determining sample size)** This problem focuses on the determination of sample sizes.

REQUIRED

a. Given the constraints of an 8% tolerable deviation rate and an expected population deviation rate from 1% to 5%, indicate the specific combinations of these factors at both 5% and 10% levels of risk of assessing control risk too low that will result in sample sizes that will not be less than 125 or more than 200.

b. At a 5% risk of assessing control risk too low, a 5% tolerable deviation rate, and a 2% expected population deviation rate, sample size is 181. Compute the new sample size for each of the following changes, assuming other factors are held constant at the amounts stated above:
   1. Increase tolerable deviation rate to 7%.
   2. Decrease tolerable deviation rate to 4%.
   3. Decrease expected population deviation rate to 1%.
   4. Increase expected population deviation rate to 3%.
   5. Increase risk of assessing control risk too low to 10%.

11-29 **(Judgment in statistical sampling)** The use of statistical sampling techniques in an audit of financial statements does not eliminate judgmental decisions.

REQUIRED

a. Identify and explain four areas in which judgment may be exercised by a CPA in planning a statistical sampling test.
b. Assume that a CPA's sample shows an unacceptable deviation rate. Describe the various actions that he or she may take based on this finding.
c. A nonstratified sample of 80 accounts payable vouchers is to be selected from a population of 3,200. The vouchers are numbered consecutively from 1 to 3,200 and are listed, 40 to a page, in the voucher register. Describe two different techniques for selecting a sample of vouchers for tests of controls.

AICPA (adapted)

11-30 **(Designing and evaluating an attribute sample)** In the audit of the Joan Company, the auditor specifies 10 attributes of interest. The statistical parameters for each condition and the number of deviations found in the sample are as follows:

Attribute	Tolerable Deviation Rate (%)	Risk of Assessing Control Risk Too Low	Expected Population Deviation Rate (%)	Number of Sample Deviations
1	4	5	1.5	1
2	3	5	0.5	0
3	6	5	2.0	4
4	6	5	2.5	5
5	8	5	3.0	2
6	3	10	1.0	0
7	4	10	1.5	2
8	5	10	2.0	4
9	6	10	2.0	1
10	7	10	3.0	4

REQUIRED

a. Assuming a large population, determine the sample size for each attribute.
b. Rounding sample size down to the nearest sample size in the tables in Figure 11-8, determine the upper deviation limit for each attribute.
c. Determine the allowance for sampling risk for each attribute.
d. Identify the controls that support the auditor's planned control risk.
e. Identify the controls that do not support the auditor's planned control risk.

11-31 **(Defining the population and determining sample size)** Mavis Stores had two billing clerks during the year. Snow worked three months and White worked nine months. As the auditor for Mavis Stores, Jones, CPA, uses attribute sampling to test clerical accuracy for the entire year, but due to the lack of internal verification, the system depends heavily on the competence of the billing clerks. The quantity of bills per month is constant.

REQUIRED

a. Jones decided to treat the billing by Snow and White as two separate populations. Discuss the advisability of this approach, considering the circumstances.
b. Jones decided to use the same risk of assessing control risk too low, deviation rate, and tolerable deviation rate for each population. If we assume he decided to select a sample of 200 to test Snow's work, approximately how large a sample is necessary to test White's?

AICPA (adapted)

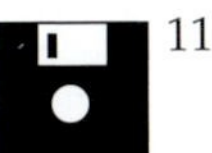

11-32 **(Designing and evaluating an attribute sample)** In your audit of the December 31, 19X0, financial statements for the Harns Company, you elect to use statistical sampling in tests of controls for sales transactions. You decide to use shipping documents for the purpose of testing whether all shipments have been billed. The shipping document is selected as the sampling unit. There are 5,000 shipping documents in the population and you elect to use random sampling in drawing your sample. Pertinent data concerning attributes of interest are as follows:

Attribute	Tolerable Deviation Rate (%)	Risk of Assessing Control Risk Too Low (%)	Expected Population Deviation Rate (%)
1. Prenumbered sales order for each shipping document	6	5	1.0
2. Prenumbered sales invoice for each shipping document	6	5	1.0
3. Agreement of details of shipping document with details of sales order	6	10	1.0
4. Agreement of details of shipping document with details of sales invoice	5	5	1.0
5. Signature of shipping clerk on shipping document	7	10	2.0
6. Receipt from carrier attached to shipping document	7	10	0.5

Assume that the results of the sample reveal the following number of deviations for each attribute: (1) 2, (2) 0, (3) 2, (4) 2, (5) 1, (6) 0.

REQUIRED

a. Prepare a sampling plan worksheet like Figure 11-9 (assume auditor rounded sample size per table up to next number ending in zero for sample actually used; e.g., 78 to 80).
b. Statistically interpret the results of the sample.
c. Explain the alternative courses of action that are available to the auditor when the sample deviation rate plus the allowance for sampling risk exceeds the tolerable deviation rate.

11-33 **(Designing and evaluating an attribute sample)** You have obtained an understanding of the Morgan Company's internal control structure. Based on this understanding, you have designed a tentative audit program for the December 31, 19X1, audit. Your next step is to perform tests of controls to confirm or challenge your planned control risk assessments for specific financial statement assertions.

A major area of tests of controls is cash disbursements. Monthly, the company processes an average of 420 vouchers, paying 600 invoices. Each voucher contains a copy of the check along with supporting documentation, such as vendor's invoices, purchase orders, and receiving reports.

You intend to examine a sample of vouchers listed in the voucher register using attribute sampling to evaluate the effectiveness of several controls. The attributes for testing the controls are set forth in your audit program as

1. Approval of account distribution.
2. Invoice and purchase order agreement.
3. Purchase order approval.
4. Purchase order and requisition agreement.
5. Invoice and receiving report agreement.
6. Discounts taken.
7. Invoice canceled after approval.
8. Approval of check request.

From experience, you expect a deviation rate of about 2% for attributes, 1, 2, 5, and 6, and 1% for all others.

After consideration of a number of related audit steps, you decide on a tolerable deviation rate of 7% for controls 1 through 6 and 6% for attributes 7 and 8. A 5% risk of assessing control risk too low is elected because you want to obtain sufficient evidence to support a low planned control risk for the assertions affected by these controls.

REQUIRED

a. Document the sample design by completing the appropriate sections of a sampling plan worksheet like the one in Figure 11-9.
b. Assume that on examining each sample item, given the sample sizes determined in (a), you find the following deviations:

   - Seven occurrences of inappropriate account distributions.
   - Three occurrences of invoices being paid after the discount date.
   - Two cases of invoices not being canceled after approval for payment.

   The remaining attributes had no deviations. Complete the sample results section of the sampling plan worksheet.
c. State your conclusions and any matters to be communicated to management and the audit committee on the bottom of the worksheet.
d. State what impact these findings would have on the execution of the remainder of your audit program.

11-34 **(Designing and evaluating an attribute sample)** The manager of the engagement team performing the December 31, 19X1, audit of the Milan Company asks you to design and execute an attribute sampling plan pertaining to controls over the processing of sales returns and allowances. The population consists of 5,200 recorded credit memos issued throughout the year and numbered consecutively beginning with 3,801. The attributes of interest are as follows:

1. Supporting request for credit (letter from customer).
2. Supporting receiving report for goods returned for credit.
3. Initials on credit memo indicating supervisor's approval.

REQUIRED

a. Prepare a sampling plan worksheet like the one in Figure 11-9 to document the sample design. Assume the following:

- You are willing to accept a 10% risk of assessing control risk too low for each attribute.
- You are willing to accept the maximum tolerable deviation rate for each attribute compatible with a low planned level of control risk.
- You expect a deviation rate of 2% for the first two attributes listed above, and a rate of 3% for the third attribute.

b. Using the random number generator in the *AUDSAMP* supplement to this text, or the table of random numbers in Figure 11-7 on page 378, determine the numbers of the first 10 credit memos to be included in your sample. (If you use the table in Figure 11-7, start with the first number in column two and move down each column and then to the right using the first four digits of each number.)

c. Assume that the sample size used and the number of deviations found for each attribute were as follows:

Attribute	Sample Size Used	Number of Deviations
1	75	1
2	75	0
3	100	5

Complete the sample results and conclusions sections of the sampling plan worksheet.

CASES

11-35 **(Designing and evaluating an attribute sample)** The audit team has obtained an understanding of the internal control structure of Yates Company and has determined that it is cost beneficial to perform tests of controls related to the *expenditure cycle.* The tests will be restricted to inventory purchases. The results will affect the nature, timing, and extent of the substantive test work related to the valuation or allocation assertion for inventory.

The audit team has determined that they are willing to accept a 5% risk of assessing control risk too low.

The audit team has had favorable results in performing this test in prior years, but the client has experienced a significant number of personnel changes this past year.

The audit team has asked you to provide them with a number of alternative sampling plans from which they could make a selection.

REQUIRED

a. Assuming that the number of deviations expected is 2%, what is (1) the minimum sample size based on a low planned control risk and (2) the maximum sample size based on moderate planned control risk.

b. Based on the assumptions stated in (1) above, what conclusions can the auditor make if the sample results show (1) one deviation, and (2) three deviations?

c. One of the attributes tested is "evidence of management approval of vendor's invoice." In your testing, you discover the following:

1. The manager's initials are not present, although you observed the manager reviewing the documentation. There were no errors in information contained on the documents or in the invoice extensions.
2. Management reviewed and approved the invoice and initialed the documents. However, the supporting documentation shows a difference in quantities received compared with the invoice, and no correction has been made.
3. The invoice was reviewed and approved by management prior to payment. The manager's initials are present, and the auditor reviewed the steps performed and found no exceptions.

Which of the foregoing, if any, represent a deviation from the control procedure?

11-36 **(Critique of attribute sample application)** Baker, CPA, was engaged to audit Mill Company's financial statements for the year ended September 30, 1991. After obtaining an understanding of Mill's internal control structure, Baker decided to obtain evidential matter about the effectiveness of both the design and operation of the policies and procedures that may support a low assessed level of control risk concerning Mill's shipping and billing functions. During the prior years' audits Baker used nonstatistical sampling, but for the current year Baker used a statistical sample in the tests of controls to eliminate the need for judgment.

Baker wanted to assess control risk at a low level, so a tolerable rate of deviation or acceptable upper precision limit (UPL) of 20% was established. To estimate the population deviation rate and the achieved UPL, Baker decided to apply a discovery sampling technique of attribute sampling that would use a population expected error rate of 3% for the 8,000 shipping documents, and decided to defer consideration of allowable risk of assessing control risk too low (risk of overreliance) until evaluating the sample results. Baker used the tolerable rate, the population size, and the expected population error rate to determine that a sample size of 80 would be sufficient. When it was subsequently determined that the actual population was about 10,000 shipping documents, Baker increased the sample size to 100.

Baker's objective was to ascertain whether Mill's shipments had been properly billed. Baker took a sample of 100 invoices by selecting the first 25 invoices from the first month of each quarter. Baker then compared the invoices to the corresponding prenumbered shipping documents.

When Baker tested the sample, eight errors were discovered. In addition, one shipment that should have been billed at $10,443 was actually billed at $10,434. Baker considered this $9 to be immaterial and did not count it as an error.

In evaluating the sample results, Baker made the initial determination that a reliability level of 95% (risk of assessing control risk too low 5%) was desired and, using the appropriate statistical sampling table, determined that for eight observed deviations from a sample size of 100, the achieved UPL was 14%. Baker then calculated the allowance for sampling risk to be 5%, the difference between the actual sample deviation rate (8%) and the expected error rate (3%). Baker reasoned that the actual sample deviation rate (8%) plus the allowance for sampling risk (5%) was less than the achieved UPL (14%); therefore, the sample supported a low level of control risk.

REQUIRED

Describe each incorrect assumption, statement, and inappropriate application of attribute sampling in Baker's procedures.

(AICPA)

RESEARCH QUESTIONS

11-37 **(Practical issues in audit sampling)** The articles by Akresh and Epstein listed in the bibliography of this chapter address some of the practical issues related to audit sampling. Select one of these articles, obtain access to it through your college library, read it, and prepare a brief summary of the key points covered in the article.

11-38 **(Sequential or stop-and-go sampling)** The bibliography of this chapter lists the AICPA's *Audit and Accounting Guide: Audit Sampling,* and a book by Guy, Carmichael, and Whittington called *Audit Sampling: An Introduction.* Each of these references contains a section on *sequential sampling* or *stop-and-go sampling.* Obtain access to one of these references through your college library. Read the section on sequential or stop-and-go sampling and prepare a brief written summary describing the technique and explaining why an auditor might elect to use this technique.

CHAPTER 12

AUDIT SAMPLING IN SUBSTANTIVE TESTS

LEARNING OBJECTIVES

After studying this chapter, you should be able to

1. Explain the applicability of audit sampling to substantive tests.
2. Recognize and define the components of audit risk associated with audit sampling in substantive tests.
3. Determine which sampling approach is most appropriate for various sampling application circumstances.
4. Explain and apply the essential steps in designing, executing, and evaluating a probability-proportional-to-size sampling plan.
5. Enumerate and apply the essential steps for each of the three techniques in classical variables sampling plans.
6. Describe the differences between nonstatistical and statistical sampling plans for substantive tests.

BASIC CONCEPTS
- NATURE AND PURPOSE
- UNCERTAINTY, SAMPLING RISKS, AND AUDIT RISK
- STATISTICAL SAMPLING APPROACHES

PROBABILITY-PROPORTIONAL-TO-SIZE SAMPLING
- SAMPLING PLAN
- DETERMINE THE OBJECTIVES OF THE PLAN
- DEFINE THE POPULATION AND SAMPLING UNIT
- DETERMINE SAMPLE SIZE
- DETERMINE THE SAMPLE SELECTION METHOD
- EXECUTE THE SAMPLING PLAN
- EVALUATE THE SAMPLE RESULTS
- ADVANTAGES AND DISADVANTAGES OF PPS SAMPLING

CLASSICAL VARIABLES SAMPLING
- TYPES OF CLASSICAL VARIABLES SAMPLING TECHNIQUES
- MEAN-PER-UNIT (MPU) ESTIMATION
- DIFFERENCE ESTIMATION
- RATIO ESTIMATION
- ADVANTAGES AND DISADVANTAGES OF CLASSICAL VARIABLES SAMPLING

NONSTATISTICAL SAMPLING IN SUBSTANTIVE TESTING
- DETERMINE THE SAMPLE SIZE
- EVALUATE THE SAMPLE RESULTS

SUMMARY

APPENDIX 12A: RELATING THE RISK OF INCORRECT ACCEPTANCE FOR A SUBSTANTIVE TEST OF DETAILS TO OTHER SOURCES OF AUDIT EVIDENCE

BIBLIOGRAPHY

OBJECTIVE QUESTIONS

COMPREHENSIVE QUESTIONS

CASE

RESEARCH QUESTIONS

The basic concepts of audit sampling and the application of sampling in tests of controls were explained in the preceding chapter. This chapter considers the use of audit sampling in substantive tests. The chapter is divided into the following four sections: (1) basic concepts, (2) probability-proportional-to-size sampling, (3) classical variables sampling, and (4) nonstatistical sampling in substantive testing.

BASIC CONCEPTS

NATURE AND PURPOSE

As explained in Chapter 11, audit sampling is the application of auditing procedures to fewer than 100% of the items within a population, such as an account balance or class of transactions, for the purpose of evaluating some characteristic of the population. Whereas attribute sampling is used to obtain information about the rate of occurrence of deviations from prescribed controls, the audit sampling

OBJECTIVE 1

Explain the applicability of audit sampling to substantive tests.

methods described in this chapter are used to obtain information about monetary amounts. Thus, they serve the purpose of substantive tests, which is to obtain evidence as to the fairness of management's financial statement assertions.

Sampling plans for substantive tests may be designed to (1) obtain evidence that an account balance is not materially misstated (for example, the book value of accounts receivable) or (2) make an independent estimate of some amount (for example, to value an inventory for which no recorded book value exists). The emphasis in this chapter is on the first objective.

UNCERTAINTY, SAMPLING RISKS, AND AUDIT RISK

OBJECTIVE 2

Recognize and define the components of audit risk and sampling risks associated with audit sampling in substantive tests.

The auditor is justified in accepting some uncertainty in substantive tests when the cost and time required to make a 100% examination of items in a population are, in his or her judgment, greater than the consequences of possibly expressing an erroneous opinion from examining only a sample of the data.

Audit sampling in substantive tests is subject to both sampling risk and nonsampling risk. As explained in Chapter 11, the sampling risks associated with substantive tests are

- **Risk of incorrect acceptance** (sometimes referred to as the beta risk)—the risk that the sample supports the conclusion that the recorded account balance is not materially misstated when it is materially misstated.
- **Risk of incorrect rejection** (sometimes referred to as the alpha risk)—the risk that the sample supports the conclusion that the recorded account balance is materially misstated when it is not materially misstated.

It will be recalled that the risk of incorrect acceptance relates to the effectiveness of the audit, whereas the risk of incorrect rejection relates to audit efficiency. For a graphical summary of these relationships, it is suggested that the student review the lower half of Figure 11-1 on page 367 at this time.

The risk of incorrect acceptance in audit sampling relates to the detection risk associated with the *specific substantive test of details* that is to be applied to the sample items selected. This risk, therefore, does not refer to the likelihood that *all* substantive tests that may be applied to the account being examined will fail to detect any material misstatements.

STATISTICAL SAMPLING APPROACHES

OBJECTIVE 3

Determine which sampling approach is most appropriate for various sampling application circumstances.

The following two statistical sampling approaches may be used by the auditor in substantive tests: (1) probability-proportional-to-size (PPS) sampling and (2) classical variables sampling.

The fundamental difference between the two approaches is that PPS sampling is based on *attribute sampling theory,* whereas classical variables sampling is based on *normal distribution theory.* Each approach can contribute to obtaining sufficient evidence under the third standard of field work. However, in certain circumstances, as described in this chapter, one approach may be more practical and appropriate in meeting the auditor's objective than the other.

The principal circumstances affecting the choice between the two approaches are tabulated in Figure 12-1. It may be observed, for example, that PPS sampling

FIGURE 12-1 • CIRCUMSTANCES AFFECTING SELECTION OF SAMPLING APPROACH FOR SUBSTANTIVE TESTS

Sampling Application Circumstances	Appropriate Sampling Approach: PPS	Appropriate Sampling Approach: Classical Variables
AVAILABILITY OF INFORMATION		
Book values for sampling units not available		X
Number of units in population unknown at start of sampling	X	
Variability of population unknown	X	
CHARACTERISTICS OF POPULATION UNITS		
Existence of zero or credit balances		X
EXPECTATIONS REGARDING MISSTATEMENTS		
Expect no misstatements or only a few overstatements	X	
Expect many misstatements or both under- and overstatements		X

may be more appropriate when (1) the number of units in and the variability of the population are unknown, (2) the population contains only debit balances, and (3) no misstatements or only a few overstatements are expected in the population.

LEARNING CHECK:

12-1 a. When is the auditor justified in accepting some uncertainty in performing substantive tests?
b. Jane Boyd contends that audit sampling in substantive tests is subject to both sampling and nonsampling risk. Is Jane correct? Explain.

12-2 a. Gary Kerr, a beginning staff accountant, believes that the sampling risks for substantive tests are the same as the sampling risks for tests of controls. Is Gary correct? Explain.
b. How are the components of sampling risk in substantive tests related to detection risk?

12-3 a. Identify the two statistical approaches that may be used in substantive tests.
b. What is the fundamental difference between the two approaches?
c. Will both approaches satisfy the third standard of field work?

12-4 a. For each of the following, indicate its effect on the selection of the most appropriate sampling approach: (1) book values for population items, (2) number of units in the population, and (3) variability of the population items.
b. What effect does the auditor's expectations about misstatements have on the selection of a sampling approach?

KEY TERMS:

Risk of incorrect acceptance, p. 403
Risk of incorrect rejection, p. 403

PROBABILITY-PROPORTIONAL-TO-SIZE SAMPLING

OBJECTIVE 4

Explain and apply the essential steps in designing, executing, and evaluating a probability-proportional-to-size sampling plan.

PPS sampling is an approach that uses attribute sampling theory to express a conclusion in dollar amounts rather than as a rate of deviations.[1] This form of sampling may be used in substantive tests of both transactions and balances.

The PPS sampling approach illustrated in this chapter is based on the PPS sampling model described in the AICPA's *Audit and Accounting Guide: Audit Sampling* (hereinafter referred to as the *Audit Sampling Guide*). The model in the *Audit-Sampling Guide* is primarily applicable in testing transactions and balances for overstatement. It may be especially useful in tests of

- Receivables when unapplied credits to customer accounts are insignificant.
- Investment securities.
- Inventory price tests when few differences are anticipated.
- Plant asset additions.

PPS sampling may not be the most cost-effective approach for receivables and inventories when the foregoing conditions are not met and where the primary objective is to independently estimate the value of a class of transactions or balances.

SAMPLING PLAN

The steps in a PPS sampling plan are similar but not identical to those used in attribute sampling. The steps are

- Determine the objectives of the plan.
- Define the population and sampling unit.
- Determine the sample size.
- Determine the sample selection method.
- Execute the sampling plan.
- Evaluate the sample results.

The considerations involved in executing these steps are explained in the following sections, and a case study is used to illustrate each step. The auditor should document each step in the working papers.

DETERMINE THE OBJECTIVES OF THE PLAN

The most common objective of PPS sampling plans is to obtain evidence that a recorded account balance is not materially misstated. The specific financial state-

[1] Three variations of PPS sampling are (1) dollar unit sampling (DUS), (2) cumulative monetary amount (CMA) sampling, and (3) combined attribute variables (CAV) sampling. The distinctions among these variations are beyond the scope of this text.

ment assertions to which the sample evidence pertains depend on the auditing procedures applied to the sample items. To illustrate this application, it is assumed that the auditor's objective is to obtain evidence from applying confirmation procedures to a sample of Harris Company's accounts receivable. This substantive test of details is a source of evidence about several assertions including existence and rights. It may be necessary for the auditor to apply other tests to the sample or other items in the population before concluding that all the assertions related to the account are free of material misstatements. Thus, the evidence from the sample will represent only one of several sources of support the auditor will seek before reaching a conclusion that the account is not materially misstated.

DEFINE THE POPULATION AND SAMPLING UNIT

The **population** consists of the class of transactions or the account balance to be tested. For each population, the auditor should decide whether all the items should be included. For example, four populations are possible when the population is based on account balances in the accounts receivable ledger; that is, all balances, debit balances, credit balances, and zero balances.

The **sampling unit** in PPS sampling is the individual dollar, and the population is considered a *number* of dollars equal to the total dollar amount of the population. Each dollar in the population is given an equal chance of being selected in the sample. Although individual dollars are the basis for sample selection, the auditor does not actually examine individual dollars in the population. Rather, he or she examines the account, transaction, document, or line item associated with the dollar selected. Individual dollars selected for a sample are sometimes thought of as hooks that, on selection, snag or bring in the entire item with which they are associated. The item snagged (account, document, etc.) is known as a **logical sampling unit.**

It is this feature that gives PPS sampling its name. The more dollars associated with a logical unit, the greater its chance of being snagged. Thus, the likelihood of selection is proportional to its size. This feature is also responsible for two limitations of PPS sampling. In testing assets, zero and negative balances should be excluded from the population because such balances have no chance of being selected in the sample. Similarly, PPS sampling is not suitable in testing liabilities for understatement because the more an item is understated, the less is its chance of being included in the sample.

The auditor chooses a logical sampling unit compatible with the nature of the auditing procedures to be performed. Accordingly, if the auditor intends to seek confirmation of customer account balances, he or she would ordinarily choose the customer account as the logical unit. Alternatively, the auditor might choose to seek confirmation of specific transactions with customers. In that case, the auditor might choose sales invoices as the logical unit. The auditor then selects the sample items from a physical representation of the population, such as a computer printout of customer balances, or computer audit software may be used to select the sample items directly from a machine-readable form of the physical representation. Before selecting the sample, the auditor should determine that the physical representation is complete. This may be done by manually reconciling the printout to a control account balance, or by using the computer to reconcile a machine-readable file to a control total.

For the Harris Company, (1) the population is defined as customer accounts with debit balances, (2) the aggregate book value of these accounts is $600,000, (3) the customer account is defined as the logical sampling unit, and (4) the printout from which the accounts are to be selected has been reconciled to the control account balance of $600,000 referred to above.

DETERMINE SAMPLE SIZE

The formula for determining sample size in PPS sampling is

$$n = \frac{BV \times RF}{TM - (AM \times EF)}$$

where

BV = book value of population tested
RF = reliability factor for the specified risk of incorrect acceptance
TM = tolerable misstatement
AM = anticipated misstatement
EF = expansion factor for anticipated misstatement

Each of these factors is explained below.

Book Value of Population Tested

The book value specified in determining sample size must relate precisely to the definition of the population as described in the preceding section. The amount of the book value has a direct effect on sample size—the larger the book value being tested, the larger the sample size.

Reliability Factor for Specified Risk of Incorrect Acceptance

In specifying an acceptable level of risk of incorrect acceptance, the auditor should consider (1) the level of audit risk that he or she is willing to take that a material misstatement in the account will go undetected, (2) the assessed level of control risk, and (3) the results of tests of details and analytical procedures. For example, if the auditor concludes that control risk is low, and if other auditing procedures provide some assurance that the book value being tested is not materially misstated, he or she will be willing to accept a higher risk of incorrect acceptance for the PPS sample, perhaps up to 30%. If control risk is high, and if other substantive procedures provide little assurance about the account being tested, then greater assurance must be obtained from the test and the auditor will specify a low risk of incorrect acceptance, perhaps as low as 5%. Experience and professional judgment must be used in making these determinations.[2] The risk of incorrect acceptance has an inverse effect on sample size—the lower the specified risk, the larger the sample size.

---

[2] A model for relating the risk for a substantive test of details to other sources of audit assurance is presented in Appendix 12A of this chapter.

FIGURE 12-2 • RELIABILITY FACTORS FOR DETERMINING PPS SAMPLE SIZES

RELIABILITY FACTORS FOR ZERO OVERSTATEMENTS

	Risk of Incorrect Acceptance								
	1%	5%	10%	15%	20%	25%	30%	37%	50%
Reliability Factor	4.61	3.00	2.31	1.90	1.61	1.39	1.21	1.00	0.70

SOURCE: AICPA, *Audit and Accounting Guide: Audit Sampling,* p. 117 (adapted).

The **reliability factor *(RF)*** for this risk is obtained from Figure 12-2. It is based on the risk of incorrect acceptance specified by the auditor and *zero number of misstatements,* regardless of the number of misstatements anticipated. In the Harris Company, the auditor specifies a 5% risk of incorrect acceptance. Thus, the reliability factor is 3.0.

Tolerable Misstatement

Tolerable misstatement *(TM)* is the maximum misstatement that can exist in an account before it is considered materially misstated. Some auditors use the term *materiality* (or material amount) as an alternative to *TM*. In specifying this factor, the auditor should realize that misstatements in individual accounts, when aggregated with misstatements in other accounts, may cause the financial statements as a whole to be materially misstated.

TM has an inverse effect on sample size—the smaller the *TM,* the larger the sample size. For the Harris Company, the auditor specifies a *TM* equal to 5% of book value, or $30,000.

Anticipated Misstatement and Expansion Factor

In PPS sampling, the auditor does not quantify the risk of incorrect rejection. This risk is controlled indirectly, however, by specifying the **anticipated misstatement *(AM)*** that is inversely related to the risk of incorrect rejection and directly related to sample size.

The auditor uses prior experience and knowledge of the client and professional judgment in determining an amount for *AM*. The auditor must bear in mind that an excessively high amount will unnecessarily increase sample size, whereas too low an estimate will result in a high risk of incorrect rejection. For the Harris Company, the auditor specifies *AM* of $6,000.

The **expansion factor *(EF)*** is required only when misstatements are anticipated. It is obtained from Figure 12-3, using the auditor's specified risk of incorrect acceptance. The smaller the specified risk of incorrect acceptance, the larger the *EF*. Like anticipated misstatement, the *EF* has a direct effect on sample size. In the Harris case study, the *EF* for anticipated misstatement is 1.6. The combined effect of anticipated misstatement and *EF* is then subtracted from tolerable misstatement in determining sample size.

FIGURE 12-3 • EXPANSION FACTORS FOR PPS SAMPLING

EXPANSION FACTORS FOR ANTICIPATED MISSTATEMENTS

	Risk of Incorrect Acceptance								
	1%	5%	10%	15%	20%	25%	30%	37%	50%
Expansion Factor	1.9	1.6	1.5	1.4	1.3	1.25	1.2	1.15	1.0

SOURCE: AICPA, *Audit and Accounting Guide: Audit Sampling*, p. 118 (adapted).

Calculation of Sample Size

The factors for determining sample size in the Harris Company are BV = \$600,000; RF = 3.0; TM = \$30,000; AM = \$6,000; and EF = 1.6. Thus, sample size is 88, computed as follows:

$$n = \frac{\$600{,}000 \times 3.0}{\$30{,}000 - (\$6{,}000 \times 1.6)} = 88$$

The effect on sample size of a change in the value of one factor, while holding the other factors constant, may be summarized as follows:

Factor	Relationship to Sample Size
Book value	Direct
Risk of incorrect acceptance	Inverse
Tolerable misstatement	Inverse
Anticipated misstatement	Direct
Expansion factor for anticipated misstatement	Direct

It may be noted that specifying a low risk of incorrect acceptance makes sample size larger in the following two ways: (1) by increasing the value of the numerator in the formula through the RF factor, and (2) by decreasing the value of the denominator through the EF. Also, whereas the relationship between AM and n is direct, the relationship between the risk of incorrect rejection (which is controlled through the AM factor) and n is inverse.

DETERMINE THE SAMPLE SELECTION METHOD

The most common selection method used in PPS sampling is systematic selection. This method divides the total population of dollars into equal intervals of dollars. A logical unit is then systematically selected from each interval. Thus, a **sampling interval** ***(SI)*** must be calculated as follows:

know

$$SI = \frac{BV}{n}$$

In the Harris Company, the sampling interval is \$6,818 (\$600,000 ÷ 88).

FIGURE 12-4 • SYSTEMATIC SELECTION PROCESS

Logical Unit (Customer Number)	Book Value	Cumulative Balance	Dollar Unit Selected	Book Value of "Hooked" Sample Item
			Random start ↓	
01001	$1,200	$1,200		
01025	6,043	7,243	5,000	$6,043
01075	2,190	9,433	+ 6,818	
01140	3,275	12,708	11,818	3,275
01219	980	13,688	+ 6,818	
01365	1,647	15,335		
01431	4,260	19,595	18,636	4,260
01592	480	20,075	+ 6,818	
01667	7,150	27,225	25,454	7,150
	•	•	•	
	•	•	•	•
	•	•	•	•
Total	$600,000			

The initial step in the selection process is to pick a starting random number between 1 and 6,818. The sample will then include each logical unit that contains every 6,818th dollar thereafter in the population. In the selection process, it is necessary to determine the cumulative balance of the book values of the logical units to determine which logical units are "hooked" or "snagged" by the individual dollar units selected. The process is illustrated for the Harris Company in Figure 12-4, where (1) the customer account number is used to identify the logical units and (2) the starting random number is 5,000. Note that the amounts in the dollar unit selected column represent every 6,818th dollar after 5,000. The dollar unit selected causes the entire book value of the related logical sampling unit to be included in the sample. It may be observed that the selection process will result in the selection of *all* logical units with book values equal to or greater than the sampling interval. The use of a computer program facilitates the selection process. However, it is also possible to select the logical sampling units with the aid of an adding machine.

EXECUTE THE SAMPLING PLAN

In this phase of the plan, the auditor applies appropriate auditing procedures to determine an audit value for each logical unit included in the sample. In the Harris sample, this includes obtaining confirmations for as many sample units as possible and applying alternative procedures when no response is received to the confirmation request.

When differences occur, the auditor records both the book and audit values in the working papers. This information is then used to project the total misstatement in the population as explained in the next section.

EVALUATE THE SAMPLE RESULTS

material

In evaluating the results of the sample, the auditor calculates an **upper misstatement limit (*UML*)** from the sample data and compares it with the tolerable misstatement specified in designing the sample. If *UML* is less than or equal to tolerable misstatement, the sample results support the conclusion that the population book value is not misstated by more than *TM* at the specified risk of incorrect acceptance.

The *UML* is calculated as follows:

$$UML = PM + ASR$$

where

PM = total projected misstatement in the population
ASR = allowance for sampling risk

The *UML, PM,* and *ASR* factors, respectively, are analogous to the upper deviation limit, sample deviation rate, and allowance for sampling risk used in evaluating the results of an attribute sampling plan as discussed in Chapter 11. However, in PPS sampling, each factor is expressed as a dollar amount rather than as a percentage. The evaluation differs in PPS sampling, depending on whether any misstatements are found in the sample.

No Misstatements

The results of the sample are used to estimate the total **projected misstatement (*PM*)** in the population. When no misstatements are discovered in the sample, the *PM* factor in the formula above is zero dollars.

In the case of no misstatements, the **allowance for sampling risk (*ASR*)** factor consists of one component sometimes referred to as **basic precision (*BP*)**. The amount is obtained by multiplying the reliability factor (*RF*) for zero misstatements at the specified risk of incorrect acceptance times the sampling interval (*SI*). Ordinarily, the auditor uses the same risk of incorrect acceptance in this calculation that was specified in determining sample size. Thus, in the Harris Company, basic precision is \$20,454, computed as follows:

$$\begin{aligned} BP &= RF \times SI \\ &= 3.0 \times \$6{,}818 \\ &= \$20{,}454 \end{aligned}$$

Because *PM* is zero, *UML* is equal to *ASR* of \$20,454, which is less than the \$30,000 *TM* specified in the sample design. When no misstatements are found in the sample and anticipated misstatement was specified as zero, the allowance for sampling risk and the upper misstatement limit will always equal tolerable misstatement. If anticipated misstatement was greater than zero (as was the case for Harris Company), the allowance for sampling risk and the upper misstatement limit will be less than tolerable misstatement. Thus, when no misstatements are found but some were anticipated, the auditor can conclude, without making additional computations, that the book value of the population is not overstated by more than *TM*. If the auditor chooses to make the above calculation, he or she may state the more precise conclusion that the book value of the population is not overstated by more than \$20,454 at a 5% risk of incorrect acceptance.

Some Misstatements

If misstatements are found in the sample, the auditor must calculate both the total projected misstatements in the population and the allowance for sampling risk to determine the upper misstatement limit for overstatements. The *UML* is then compared with *TM*.

PROJECTED POPULATION MISSTATEMENT. A projected misstatement amount is calculated for each logical unit containing a misstatement. These amounts are then summed to arrive at *PM* for the entire population. The projected misstatement is calculated differently for (1) logical units with book values less than the sampling interval and (2) logical units with book values equal to or greater than the sampling interval.

For *each* logical unit with a book value less than the sampling interval that contains a misstatement, a **tainting percentage *(TP)*** and projected misstatement are calculated as follows:

Tainting percentage = (book value − audit value) ÷ book value
Projected misstatement = tainting percentage × sampling interval

The calculations recognize that each logical unit included in the sample represents one sampling interval of the dollars in the population book value. Thus, the degree to which a logical unit is "tainted" with misstatement is projected to all of the dollars in the sampling interval it represents.

For each logical unit for which the book value is equal to or greater than the sampling interval, the projected misstatement is the amount of misstatement found in the unit (book value − audit value). Because the logical unit itself is equal to or greater than the sampling interval, a tainting percentage to project the misstatement to the interval is unnecessary. Rather, the actual amounts of such misstatements are used in arriving at *PM* for the population as a whole.

To illustrate, assume the PPS sample of the Harris Company's accounts receivable reveals the following misstatements:

Book Value (BV)	Audit Value (AV)	Tainting Percentage [TP = (BV − AV)/BV]	Sampling Interval (SI)	Projected Misstatement (TP × SI) or (BV − AV)
$ 950	$ 855	10	$6,818	$ 682
2,500	1,250	50	6,818	3,409
7,650	6,885	N/A*	N/A*	765
5,300	5,035	5	6,818	341
8,000	—0—	N/A*	N/A*	8,000
$24,400	$14,025			$13,197

* Logical unit is greater than sampling interval; therefore, projected misstatement equals actual misstatement (*BV* − *AV*).

Note that the first, second, and fourth logical units containing misstatements have book values less than the sampling interval. Accordingly, *TP*s have been calculated and used to determine the projected misstatements. The third and fifth units have book values greater than the sampling interval. Therefore, the projected misstatement for each is the difference between the book value and the audit value. The total misstatement in the sample is $10,375 ($24,400 − $14,025), and the total *PM* in the population is $13,197.

ALLOWANCE FOR SAMPLING RISK. The *ASR* for samples containing misstatements has two components as indicated in the following formula:

$$ASR = BP + IA$$

where

BP = basic precision
IA = incremental allowance resulting from the misstatements

The calculation of *BP* is the same whether or not there are misstatements found in the sample. Thus, in the Harris Company, this component is again $20,454, based on the *RF* of 3.0 (for zero errors and a 5% risk of incorrect acceptance) times the *SI* of $6,818.

To calculate the **incremental allowance for sampling risk *(IA)***, the auditor must consider separately the logical units with book values less than the sampling interval and those with book values equal to or greater than the sampling interval. Because all logical units equal to or greater than the sampling interval will have been examined, there is no sampling risk associated with them. Consequently, the calculation of *IA* involves only misstatements related to logical units with book values less than the sampling interval.

The calculation of *IA* involves the following steps

- Determine the appropriate incremental change in reliability factors.
- Rank the projected misstatements for logical units less than the sampling interval from highest to lowest.
- Multiply the ranked projected misstatements by the appropriate factor and sum the products.

The following tabulation illustrates the first step:

5% Risk of Incorrect Acceptance

Number of Overstatements	Reliability Factor	Incremental Change in Reliability Factor	Incremental Change in Reliability Factor Minus One
0	3.00	—	—
1	4.75	1.75	0.75
2	6.30	1.55	0.55
3	7.76	1.46	0.46
4	9.16	1.40	0.40

The data in the first two columns above are taken from Figure 12-5 for the specified risk of incorrect acceptance (5% in this illustration). Each entry in the third

FIGURE 12-5 • RELIABILITY FACTORS FOR EVALUATING PPS SAMPLE RESULTS

RELIABILITY FACTORS FOR OVERSTATEMENTS

Number of Overstatements	Risk of Incorrect Acceptance								
	1%	5%	10%	15%	20%	25%	30%	37%	50%
0	4.61	3.00	2.31	1.90	1.61	1.39	1.21	1.00	0.70
1	6.64	4.75	3.89	3.38	3.00	2.70	2.44	2.14	1.68
2	8.41	6.30	5.33	4.72	4.28	3.93	3.62	3.25	2.68
3	10.05	7.76	6.69	6.02	5.52	5.11	4.77	4.34	3.68
4	11.61	9.16	8.00	7.27	6.73	6.28	5.90	5.43	4.68
5	13.11	10.52	9.28	8.50	7.91	7.43	7.01	6.49	5.68
6	14.57	11.85	10.54	9.71	9.08	8.56	8.12	7.56	6.67
7	16.00	13.15	11.78	10.90	10.24	9.69	9.21	8.63	7.67
8	17.41	14.44	13.00	12.08	11.38	10.81	10.31	9.68	8.67
9	18.79	15.71	14.21	13.25	12.52	11.92	11.39	10.74	9.67
10	20.15	16.97	15.41	14.42	13.66	13.02	12.47	11.79	10.67

SOURCE: AICPA, *Audit and Accounting Guide: Audit Sampling*, p. 117 (adapted).

column is the reliability factor on the same line less the reliability factor on the previous line. The column 4 factors are obtained by subtracting one from each of the column 3 factors.

The second and third steps are illustrated below.

Ranked Projected Misstatements	Incremental Change in Reliability Factor Minus One	Incremental Allowance
$3,409	0.75	$2,557
682	0.55	375
341	0.46	157
		$3,089

Observe that (1) only the projected misstatements from the tabulation on page 412 for logical units with book values less than the sampling interval are ranked and (2) the appropriate reliability factor is obtained from column 4 of the tabulation on page 413.[3] The incremental allowances for the projected misstatements are then added to determine the total incremental allowance of $3,089. Thus, the total allowance for sampling risk in the Harris Company is $23,543, computed as follows:

[3] Alternatively, the ranked projected misstatements can be multiplied by the incremental change in reliability factors shown in column 3 on page 413 to obtain an upper misstatement limit for *each* ranked projected misstatement. The projected misstatement for each item is then subtracted from the upper misstatement limit to get the related incremental allowance. Thus, for the first ranked projected misstatement in the tabulation, the calculation would be

$$\$3,409 \times 1.75 = \$5,966 - \$3,409 = \$2,557$$

Yet another alternative is to sum the upper misstatement limits calculated for the ranked projected misstatements and then subtract the sum of the ranked projected misstatements to get the total incremental allowance. Subtracting one from each incremental change in reliability factor, as illustrated in the tabulation above, provides the simpler and more direct way of calculating the incremental allowance.

BP	$20,454
IA	3,089
ASR	$23,543

UPPER MISSTATEMENT LIMIT FOR OVERSTATEMENTS. The *UML* equals the sum of *PM* and *ASR*. For the Harris sample, the *UML* is

PM	$13,197
ASR	23,543
UML	$36,740

Thus, the auditor may conclude that the book value is not overstated by more than $36,740 at a 5% risk of incorrect acceptance.

In the Harris sample, the *UML* exceeds the *TM* of $30,000 specified in designing the sample. When this occurs, the auditor should consider several possible reasons and alternative courses of action. These matters are discussed below in the section on Reaching an Overall Conclusion. However, whether *UML* is less than, equal to, or greater than *TM*, certain qualitative considerations should be made prior to reaching an overall conclusion.

QUALITATIVE CONSIDERATIONS. As in attribute sampling, the auditor should consider the qualitative aspects of the monetary misstatements. Misstatements may be due to (1) differences in principle or application or (2) errors or irregularities. Consideration should also be given to the relationship of the misstatements to other phases of the audit. For example, if misstatements are discovered in substantive tests in amounts or frequency greater than implied by the assessed level of control risk used in arriving at the risk of incorrect acceptance specified for the sample, the auditor should consider whether that assessment is still appropriate. If it is not appropriate, the auditor should redesign the sampling plan.

REACHING AN OVERALL CONCLUSION. The auditor uses professional judgment in combining evidence from several sources to reach an overall conclusion about whether an account balance is free from material misstatement. When (1) the results of a PPS sample reveal the *UML* to be less than or equal to *TM*, (2) the results of other substantive tests do not contradict this finding, and (3) analysis of the qualitative considerations reveals no evidence of irregularities, the auditor can generally conclude that the population is not materially misstated. When any of these conditions do not hold, further evaluation of the circumstances is necessary.

For example, if the *UML* is greater than *TM*, the auditor should consider the following possible reasons and actions:

- The sample is not representative of the population. The auditor might suspect this is the case when all other related evidence suggests the population is not materially misstated. In this case, the auditor might examine additional sampling units or perform alternative procedures to determine whether the population is misstated.[4]

- The amount of anticipated misstatement specified in designing the sample may not have been large enough relative to tolerable misstatement to adequately limit the allowance for sampling risk. That is, the population may not be misstated by more than *TM*, but because the amount of misstatement in the population is greater than anticipated, more precise information is needed from the sample. In this situation the auditor may examine additional sampling units and reevaluate or perform alternative auditing procedures to determine whether the population is misstated by more than *TM*.
- The population may be misstated by more than *TM*. The auditor may request the client investigate the misstatements and, if appropriate, adjust the book value.

As a result of any of these courses of action, the client's book value might be adjusted. If the *UML* after adjustment is less than *TM*, the sample results would support the conclusion that the population, as adjusted, is not misstated by more than *TM* at the specified risk of incorrect acceptance. For example, in the Harris sample, one receivable with a book value of $8,000 was found to have an audit value of zero. If this account were written off, the *PM* for the population would be reduced by $8,000 to $5,197. The allowance for sampling risk would remain the same at $23,543, and *UML* would become $28,740 ($36,740 − $8,000), which is less than the $30,000 *TM* specified in designing the sample.

Figure 12-6 illustrates how the application of PPS sampling in the audit of Harris Company's receivables may be documented. The sample design and evaluation of results shown in this microcomputer-generated working paper were developed using the PPS template in the software package called *AUDSAMP*, which is available as a supplement to this test.

ADVANTAGES AND DISADVANTAGES OF PPS SAMPLING

The AICPA's *Audit Sampling Guide* (pp. 68–69) identifies several advantages and disadvantages of PPS sampling. The advantages of PPS sampling are

- It is generally easier to use than classical variables sampling because the auditor can calculate sample sizes and evaluate sample results by hand or with the assistance of tables.
- The size of a PPS sample is not based on any measure of the estimated variation of audit values.
- PPS sampling automatically results in a stratified sample because items are selected in proportion to their dollar values.
- PPS systematic sample selection automatically identifies any item that is individually significant if its value exceeds an upper monetary cutoff.
- If the auditor expects no misstatements, PPS sampling will usually result in a smaller sample size than under classical variables sampling.

---

[4] A simple method of expanding the sample is to divide the sampling interval in half. This will produce a sample containing all the units in the original sample plus an equal number of additional units. Other methods of expanding the sample size are beyond the scope of this text.

FIGURE 12-6 • PPS SAMPLING PLAN WORKING PAPER

HARRIS COMPANY
PPS SAMPLE - ACCOUNTS RECEIVABLE
DECEMBER 31, 19X1

W/P REF: B-2
PREPARED BY: W.C.B DATE: 1/22/X2
REVIEWED BY: R.E.J DATE: 1/25/X2

OBJECTIVE: TO OBTAIN EVIDENCE THAT THE AGGREGATE BOOK VALUE OF CUSTOMER ACCOUNTS WITH DEBIT BALANCES AS OF 12/31/X1 IS NOT MATERIALLY MISSTATED.

POPULATION AND SAMPLING UNIT: TOTAL BOOK VALUE OF ACCOUNTS WITH DEBIT BALANCES PER MASTER FILE PRINTOUT. LOGICAL SAMPLING UNIT = CUSTOMER ACCOUNT.

SAMPLE SIZE:

BOOK VALUE OF POPULATION	600,000 (BV)	
RISK OF INCORRECT ACCEPTANCE	5 %	RF = 3.00
TOLERABLE MISSTATEMENT	30,000 (TM)	
ANTICIPATED MISSTATEMENT	6,000 (AM)	EF = 1.60
SAMPLE SIZE = n = (BV * RF)/(TM - (AM * EF))	88 (n)	

SAMPLE SELECTION:

SAMPLING INTERVAL = BV/n	6,818 (SI)
RANDOM START	5,000
LOGICAL SAMPLING UNITS SELECTED LISTED ON W/P	B-3

EXECUTION OF SAMPLING PLAN:

AUDIT PROCEDURES APPLIED LISTED ON W/P	B-1
BOOK AND AUDIT VALUES FOR SAMPLE ITEMS WITH MISSTATEMENTS LISTED BELOW	

EVALUATION OF SAMPLE RESULTS:

PROJECTED MISSTATEMENT:

	BOOK VALUE (BV)	AUDIT VALUE (AV)	TAINTING % (TP) = ((BV-AV)/BV)	SAMPLING INTERVAL (SI)	PROJECTED MISSTATEMENT (TP * SI) OR (BV-AV)
1	950	855	10.00	6,818	682
2	2,500	1,250	50.00	6,818	3,409
3	7,650	6,885	NA	NA	765
4	5,300	5,035	5.00	6,818	341
5	8,000	0	NA	NA	8,000
	24,400	14,025		TOTAL	13,197 (PM)

ALLOWANCE FOR SAMPLING RISK:
BASIC PRECISION = RF * SI — 20,454 (BP)
INCREMENTAL ALLOWANCE:

	RANKED PROJECTED MISSTATEMENT	INCREMENTAL CHANGE IN RELIABILITY FACTOR MINUS ONE	INCREMENTAL ALLOWANCE FOR SAMPLING RISK
1	3,409	0.75	2,557
2	682	0.55	375
3	341	0.46	157
4	0	0.40	0
5	0	0.36	0
		TOTAL	3,089 (IA)

ASR = BP + IA — 23,543 (ASR)

UPPER MISSTATEMENT LIMIT:
UML = PM + ASR — 36,740 (UML > TM)

CONCLUSION: *UML of $36,740 exceeds TM of $30,000. Client subsequently agreed to write off one account with a book value of $8,000 and audit value of zero. This reduces both PM and UML by $8,000, making UML $28,740 which is less than TM. See adjusting entry on WP AE-1. Results support conclusion that the aggregate book value of customer accounts with debit balances, as adjusted, is not materially misstated.*

- A PPS sample can be designed more easily, and sample selection may begin before the complete population is available.

In contrast, PPS sampling has the following disadvantages:

- It includes an assumption that the audit value of a sampling unit should not be less than zero or greater than book value. When understatements or audit values of less than zero are anticipated, special design considerations may be required.
- If understatements are identified in the sample, the evaluation of the sample may require special considerations.
- The selection of zero balances or balances of a different sign requires special consideration.
- PPS evaluation may overstate the *ASR* when misstatements are found in the sample. As a result, the auditor may be more likely to reject an acceptable book value for the population.
- As the expected number of misstatements increases, the appropriate sample size increases. Thus, a larger sample size may result than under classical variables sampling.

Professional judgment should be exercised by the auditor in determining the appropriateness of this approach in a given audit circumstance.

LEARNING CHECK:

12-5 a. Indicate the steps in a PPS sampling plan.
b. What is the most common objective of a PPS sampling plan?

12-6 a. Distinguish between the sampling unit and the logical sampling unit in a PPS sample.
b. Why do units with zero and credit balances require special consideration in a PPS sampling plan?

12-7 a. Give the formula for calculating sample size in PPS sampling.
b. Explain what each element in the formula represents and how a change in that element, other things constant, affects sample size.

12-8 What role does the specification of anticipated misstatement play in designing a PPS sample?

12-9 What three factors are considered in evaluating a PPS sample?

12-10 What are the two components of the allowance for sampling risk for PPS samples?

12-11 Explain the terms *tainting percentage* and *projected misstatement* as they pertain to individual items in a PPS sample.

KEY TERMS:

Allowance for sampling risk (ASR), p. 411
Anticipated misstatement (AM), p. 408
Basic precision (BP), p. 411
Expansion factor (EF), p. 408
Incremental allowance for sampling risk (IA), p. 413
Logical sampling unit, p. 406
Population, p. 406

PPS sampling, p. 405
Projected misstatement (PM), p. 411
Reliability factor (RF), p. 408
Sampling interval (SI), p. 409
Sampling unit, p. 406
Tainting percentage (TP), p. 412
Tolerable misstatement (TM), p. 408
Upper misstatement limit (UML), p. 411

CLASSICAL VARIABLES SAMPLING

As explained earlier, the auditor may use a **classical variables sampling** approach in substantive testing. Under this approach, normal distribution theory is used in evaluating the characteristics of a population based on the results of a sample drawn from the population.

Classical variables sampling may be useful to the auditor when the audit objective relates to either the possible under- or overstatement of an account balance and other circumstances when PPS sampling is not appropriate or cost effective.

TYPES OF CLASSICAL VARIABLES SAMPLING TECHNIQUES

OBJECTIVE 5

Enumerate and apply the essential steps for each of the three techniques in classical variables sampling plans.

The following three techniques (or methods) may be used in classical variables sampling: (1) mean-per-unit (MPU), (2) difference, and (3) ratio. All three techniques require the determination of the total number of units in the population and an audit value for each item in the sample. The *Audit Sampling Guide* (pp. 90–91) identifies the following constraints that should be considered in selecting the technique that is most appropriate in the circumstances:

- *The ability to design a stratified sample.* Stratification may significantly reduce sample size under the MPU method but may not materially affect sample size under the difference or ratio techniques.
- *The expected number of differences between audit and book values.* A minimum number of differences must exist between these values in the sample to use either the difference or ratio techniques.
- *The available information.* Book values must be available for each sampling unit in ratio and difference estimation. Book values are not required with the MPU technique.

When all the constraints can be satisfied by any of the methods, the auditor ordinarily will prefer either difference or ratio estimation because these methods generally require a smaller sample size than the MPU method. Thus, they are more cost efficient in meeting the auditor's objectives.

The sampling plan for each technique involves the same steps required in PPS sampling. However, as explained below, there is some variation in the way some of the steps are performed among the three techniques.

MEAN-PER-UNIT (MPU) ESTIMATION[5]

MPU estimation sampling involves determining an audit value for each item in the sample. An average of these audit values is then calculated and multiplied by the number of units in the population to obtain an estimate of the total population value. An allowance for sampling risk associated with this estimate is also calculated for use in evaluating the sample results.

Determine the Objectives of the Plan

The objective of an MPU sampling plan may be to (1) obtain evidence that a recorded account balance is not materially misstated or (2) develop an independent estimate of an amount when no recorded book value is available. For illustrative purposes, it is assumed that the auditor seeks to achieve the first objective for the book value of loans receivable in the Ace Finance Company. As in the case of a PPS sample, the specific assertions to which the evidence pertains depends on the auditing procedures applied to the sample items.

Define the Population and Sampling Unit

In defining the **population,** the auditor should consider the nature of the items comprising the population and whether all items should be eligible for inclusion in the sample. It is not necessary, however, to verify that the book values for the individual items sum to the total recorded book value of the population because the individual book values are not a variable in MPU calculations.

The **sampling unit** should be compatible with the audit objective and the auditing procedures to be performed. For example, if the objective is to determine that the recorded balance for accounts receivable is not materially misstated, and evidence is to be obtained by seeking confirmation of account balances from customers, the *customer account* should be the sampling unit. Alternatively, if the objective is to determine that the sales account is not materially misstated, and evidence is to be obtained by examining documents supporting recorded sales transactions, then *line entries* in the sales journal would be an appropriate sampling unit. A physical representation of all units comprising the population, such as a list of customer accounts, facilitates the process of selecting units for the sample.

For the Ace Finance Company, (1) the population is defined as 3,000 small loans receivable, (2) the recorded book value of these receivables is $1,340,000, (3) individual loans are defined as the sampling unit, and (4) the physical representation from which sample items are selected is a computer printout listing all loans receivable.

Determine the Sample Size

The following factors determine sample size in an MPU estimation sample:

- Population size (number of units).
- Estimated population standard deviation.

---

[5] This technique is sometimes referred to as the *simple extension* method.

- Tolerable misstatement.
- Risk of incorrect rejection.
- Risk of incorrect acceptance.
- Planned allowance for sampling risk.

POPULATION SIZE. It is critical to have accurate knowledge of the number of units in the population because this factor enters into the calculation of both the sample size and sample results. Population size directly affects sample size—that is, the larger the population, the larger the sample size. As noted above, the population for the Ace Finance Company consists of 3,000 loans receivable.

ESTIMATED POPULATION STANDARD DEVIATION. In MPU estimation, the sample size required to achieve specified statistical objectives is related directly to the variability of the values of the population items. The measure of variability used is the **standard deviation.** Because an audit value is not obtained for every population item, the standard deviation of the audit values for the items in the sample is used as an estimate of the population standard deviation. But because the sample standard deviation is not known before the sample is selected, it also must be estimated.

There are three ways of estimating this factor. First, in a recurring engagement, the standard deviation found in the preceding audit may be used to estimate the standard deviation for the current year. Second, the standard deviation can be estimated from available book values. Third, the auditor can take a small presample of 30 to 50 items and base the estimate of the current year's population standard deviation on the audit values of these sample items. When this is done, the presample may be made a part of the final sample. Computer programs for MPU estimation sampling include a routine to calculate the estimated standard deviation.

The formula for calculating the standard deviation is

$$S_{x_j} = \sqrt{\sum_{j=1}^{n} \frac{(x_j - \bar{x})^2}{n - 1}}$$

where

$\sum_{j=1}^{n}$ = *sum of sample values;* $j = 1$ means the summary should begin with the first item and n means that the summary should end with the last item in the sample

x_j = audit values of individual sample items

$\bar{x}$ = mean of the audit values of sample items

n = number of items audited

A primary concern of the auditor in MPU sampling is whether the population should be stratified. **Stratified sampling** involves dividing the population into relatively homogeneous groups or strata. A homogeneous group in this context is one that has little variability in the values of the items comprising the group or stratum. Sampling is performed separately on each stratum, and sample results for each stratum are subsequently combined to evaluate the total sample.

Stratification may be advantageous because the combined sample size often will be significantly less than a single sample size based on an unstratified population. This follows from the fact that sample size decreases as the variability of the population decreases. In fact, a change in the variability of a population affects sample size by the square of the relative change. Consequently, when the variation in the population changes from 200 to 100 (i.e., halved), the sample size required to meet the same statistical objectives is decreased by a factor of 4 (one-half squared equals one-fourth).

The optimal number of strata depends on the pattern of variation in the population values and the additional costs associated with designing, executing, and evaluating each stratified sample. Because of the complexity of the procedure, stratification is generally used only when appropriate computer software is available. To simplify subsequent illustrations in this chapter, unstratified samples are used. In practice, when population values are highly variable and stratification is not feasible, the auditor may be able to use either difference or ratio estimation to achieve a reduction from the sample size that MPU sampling would require.

The Ace Finance Company limits loans to a maximum of $500 per customer. Thus, variability is low and the auditor concludes there is no need to stratify the population. Based on last year's audit, the auditor estimates a standard deviation of $100.

TOLERABLE MISSTATEMENT. The considerations applicable to *TM* are the same in MPU sampling as in PPS sampling. *TM* has an inverse effect on sample size. For the Ace Finance Company, the auditor specifies a *TM* of $60,000.

RISK OF INCORRECT REJECTION. This factor permits the auditor to control the risk that the sample results will support the conclusion that the recorded account balance is materially misstated when it is not. The principal consequence of this risk is the potential incurrence of additional costs associated with expanded audit procedures following the initial rejection. However, the additional auditing procedures should ultimately result in the conclusion that the balance is not materially misstated.

In contrast to PPS sampling, the auditor must quantify the risk of incorrect rejection in MPU sampling as well as the risk of incorrect acceptance. The risk of incorrect rejection has an inverse effect on sample size. If the auditor specifies a very low risk of incorrect rejection, the size and cost of performing the initial sample will be larger. Therefore, the auditor's experience and knowledge of the client should be used to specify an appropriate risk of incorrect rejection to balance the costs associated with the initial sample and the potential costs of later expanding the sample.

In some computer software programs, the auditor inputs the risk of incorrect rejection directly as a percentage figure. Other programs require the auditor to input a *confidence* or *reliability* level, which is the complement of the risk of incorrect rejection. In either case, the computer then converts the percentage into an appropriate standard normal deviate or **U_R factor** for use in calculating the sample size. If the sample size is being calculated manually, a U_R factor for the specified risk of incorrect rejection is obtained from a table like the one illustrated in Figure 12-7.

The auditor decides to specify a 5% risk of incorrect rejection in the Ace Finance Company. Thus, the U_R factor is 1.96.

RISK OF INCORRECT ACCEPTANCE. The factors to be considered in specifying this risk are the same as in PPS sampling. The risk of incorrect accept-

FIGURE 12-7 • SELECTED RISK OF INCORRECT REJECTION PERCENTAGES AND CORRESPONDING STANDARD NORMAL DEVIATES OR U_R FACTORS

Risk of Incorrect Rejection	Standard Normal Deviate (U_R Factor)	Corresponding Confidence or Reliability Level*
0.30	±1.04	0.70
0.25	±1.15	0.75
0.20	±1.28	0.80
0.15	±1.44	0.85
0.10	±1.64	0.90
0.05	±1.96	0.95
0.01	±2.58	0.99

* For information purposes only.

ance of a materially misstated balance is ordinarily specified in the range from 5 to 30%, depending on the auditor's assessed level of control risk and the results of other substantive tests. The risk of incorrect acceptance has an inverse effect on sample size—the lower the specified risk, the larger the sample size. In Ace Finance, the auditor specifies a 20% risk of incorrect acceptance.

PLANNED ALLOWANCE FOR SAMPLING RISK. The **planned allowance for sampling risk** (sometimes referred to as "desired precision") is derived from the following formula:

$$A = R \times TM$$

where

A = desired or planned allowance for sampling risk
R = ratio of desired allowance for sampling risk to tolerable misstatement
TM = tolerable misstatement

The ratio for the R factor is based on the specified risks of incorrect acceptance and incorrect rejection. The amount of the ratio is obtained from the table shown in Figure 12-8. For example, if the aforementioned risks are set at 20 and 10%, respectively, the R factor is 0.661. In the Ace Finance Company, the foregoing risks have been specified at 20 and 5%. Thus, the R factor is 0.70. This factor is then multiplied by the TM of $60,000 to produce an allowance for sampling risk of $42,000.

SAMPLE SIZE FORMULA. The following formula is used to determine sample size for an MPU estimation sample:

$$n = \left(\frac{N \cdot U_R \cdot S_{x_j}}{A}\right)^2$$

where

N = population size
U_R = the standard normal deviate for the desired risk of incorrect rejection

FIGURE 12-8 • RATIO OF DESIRED ALLOWANCE FOR SAMPLING RISK TO TOLERABLE MISSTATEMENT

Risk of Incorrect Acceptance	Risk of Incorrect Rejection 0.20	0.10	0.05	0.01
0.01	0.355	0.413	0.457	0.525
0.025	0.395	0.456	0.500	0.568
0.05	0.437	0.500	0.543	0.609
0.075	0.471	0.532	0.576	0.641
0.10	0.500	0.561	0.605	0.668
0.15	0.511	0.612	0.653	0.712
0.20	0.603	0.661	0.700	0.753
0.25	0.653	0.708	0.742	0.791
0.30	0.707	0.756	0.787	0.829
0.35	0.766	0.808	0.834	0.868
0.40	0.831	0.863	0.883	0.908
0.45	0.907	0.926	0.937	0.952
0.50	1.000	1.000	1.000	1.000

SOURCE: AICPA, *Audit and Accounting Guide: Audit Sampling,* p. 115 (adapted).

S_{x_j} = estimated population standard deviation
A = desired or planned allowance for sampling risk

In the Ace Finance Company, these four factors are 3,000, 1.96, $100, and $42,000, respectively. Thus, the sample size is 196, computed as follows:

$$n = \left(\frac{3{,}000 \times 1.96 \times \$100}{\$42{,}000}\right)^2 = 196$$

This formula assumes sampling with replacement (i.e., an item once selected is put back into the population and is eligible for selection again). When sampling without replacement, a **finite correction factor** is recommended when the relationship between n (sample size) and N (population size) is greater than 0.05. The adjusted sample size (n') is determined as follows:

$$n' = \frac{n}{1 + \dfrac{n}{N}}$$

Because n/N is greater than 0.05 ($196 \div 3{,}000 = 0.065$) in Ace Finance, the adjusted sample size is

$$n' = \frac{196}{1 + \dfrac{196}{3{,}000}} = 184$$

The effect on sample size of a change in the value of one factor, while holding the other factors constant, may be summarized as follows:

Factor	Relationship to Sample Size
Population size	Direct
Variation in the population (standard deviation)	Direct
Risk of incorrect rejection	Inverse
Planned allowance for sampling risk	Inverse
Risk of incorrect acceptance	Inverse
Tolerable misstatement	Inverse

Although the last two factors listed above do not appear in the sample size formula, they affect sample size in the manner indicated through their effect on the calculation of the planned allowance for sampling risk.

Determine the Sample Selection Method

Either the simple random number selection method or the systematic selection method discussed in Chapter 11 may be used in selecting the sample under the MPU technique. In the Ace Finance Company, the auditor decides to use a computer random number generator to identify the 184 loans receivable to be examined.

Execute the Sampling Plan

The execution phase of an MPU estimation sampling plan includes the following steps:

- Perform appropriate auditing procedures to determine an audit value for each sample item.
- Calculate the following statistics based on the sample data:
  - the average of the sample audit values ($\bar{x}$)
  - the standard deviation of the sample audit values (S_{x_j}).

The average and standard deviation statistics for the sample may be computed manually or by a computer.

For the Ace Finance sample, the sum of the audit values is assumed to be \$81,328, resulting in an average audit value of \$442 (\$81,328 ÷ 184). The standard deviation of the audit values is assumed to be \$90.

Evaluate the Sample Results

In this, the final step of the sampling plan, the auditor makes both a quantitative and a qualitative assessment of the results and then reaches an overall conclusion.

QUANTITATIVE ASSESSMENT. In making this evaluation in an MPU sampling plan, the auditor calculates

- The estimated total population value.
- The achieved allowance for sampling risk, sometimes referred to as *achieved precision*.
- A range for the estimated total population value, sometimes referred to as the *precision interval*.

The **estimated total population value ($\hat{X}$)** is calculated as follows:

$$\hat{X} = N \cdot \bar{x}$$

Thus, the estimated total population value for Ace Finance Company's 3,000 loans receivable is

$$\hat{X} = 3{,}000 \times \$442 = \$1{,}326{,}000$$

The basic formula for calculating the **achieved allowance for sampling risk (A′)** is

$$A' = N \cdot U_R \cdot \frac{S_{x_j}}{\sqrt{n}}$$

where S_{x_j} is the *standard deviation of the sample audit values.* Note that the value for S_{x_j} is not the value for S_{x_j} used in determining sample size.

When the finite correction factor has been used in determining sample size, the formula is modified as follows:

$$A' = N \cdot U_R \cdot \frac{S_{x_j} \cdot \sqrt{1 - \dfrac{n'}{N}}}{\sqrt{n'}}$$

Therefore, the achieved allowance for sampling risk for Ace Finance is

$$A' = 3{,}000 \times 1.96 \times \frac{\$90\sqrt{1 - \dfrac{184}{3{,}000}}}{\sqrt{184}} = \$37{,}798$$

The **range for the estimated total population value** is derived from the estimated total population value and the achieved allowance for sampling risk. The range is

$$\hat{X} \pm A'$$

In Ace Finance Company, the calculation is as follows:

$$\begin{aligned} \hat{X} \pm A' &= \$1{,}326{,}000 \pm \$37{,}798 \\ &= \$1{,}288{,}202 \text{ to } \$1{,}363{,}798 \end{aligned}$$

If the book value falls within this range, the sample results support the conclusion that the book value is not materially misstated. This conclusion is valid in the case study as the book value of $1,340,000 falls within the range.

It should be recognized that the sample results may support the conclusion that the book value is not materially misstated, but not within the level of risk of incorrect acceptance specified by the auditor. To stay within the desired risk, achieved allowance for sampling risk *(A′)* must be equal to or less than planned allowance for sampling risk *(A)*. *A′* will be greater than *A* whenever the standard deviation of audit values is greater than the estimated population standard deviation used in determining sample size. For example, if the standard deviation of audit values in the Harris Company had been \$110, A' would have been \$46,197, which is greater than the \$42,000 specified for A. In such a case, the auditor computes the **adjusted achieved allowance for sampling risk (A'')** by the following formula where TM is the tolerable misstatement specified in the sampling plan:

$$A'' = A' + TM\left(1 - \frac{A'}{A}\right)$$

A'' is \$40,197, computed as follows:

$$A'' = \$46{,}197 + \$60{,}000\left(1 - \frac{\$46{,}197}{\$42{,}000}\right)$$
$$= \$40{,}197$$

Note that A'', \$40,197, is less than A, \$42,000. A'' is then substituted for A' in the formula used to calculate the range for the estimated population value. Using A'', the estimated population range is \$1,326,000 ± \$40,197 or \$1,285,803 to \$1,366,197. Because the book value of \$1,340,000 falls within the range, the sample results indicate that the book value is not materially misstated at the planned risk of incorrect acceptance.

The book value may fall outside the range because the achieved allowance for sampling risk is significantly smaller than the planned allowance. When this occurs, the auditor (1) calculates the difference between the book value and the far end of the range and (2) compares the difference to TM. If the difference is equal to or less than TM, the sample results indicate that the book value is not materially misstated. For example, if the achieved allowance in Ace Finance Company is \$12,000, the range becomes \$1,314,000 to \$1,338,000 and the book value (\$1,340,000) falls outside the precision interval. The difference between the book value and the far end of the range is \$26,000 (\$1,340,000 − \$1,314,000). Because this is less than the TM of \$60,000, the book value is supported.

QUALITATIVE ASSESSMENT. Prior to reaching an overall conclusion, the auditor should consider the qualitative aspects of the sample results. These considerations are the same in MPU sampling as in PPS sampling.

REACHING AN OVERALL CONCLUSION. When either the auditor's quantitative (statistical) or qualitative assessments of sample results support the conclusion that the population is materially misstated, professional judgment should be used in deciding on an appropriate course of action. The possible causes and actions are as follows:

Causes	Actions
1. The sample is not representative of the population.	Expand the sample and reevaluate the results.
2. The achieved allowance for sampling risk may be larger than the desired allowance because the sample size was too small.	Same as above.
3. The population book value may be misstated by more than tolerable misstatement.	Have client investigate and, if warranted, adjust the book value and reevaluate the sample results.

Figure 12-9 summarizes the steps performed in designing, executing, and evaluating the MPU sampling plan to test the book value of Ace Finance Company's loans receivable and illustrates how these steps can be documented in a working paper. This working paper was generated with the MPU template of the *AUDSAMP* software package.

DIFFERENCE ESTIMATION

In **difference estimation sampling,** a difference is calculated for each sample item equal to the item's audit value minus its book value. The average of the differences is then used to obtain an estimate of the total population value, and the variability of the differences is used in determining the achieved allowance for sampling risk. The following three conditions are indispensable in using this technique:

- The book value of each population item must be known.
- The total book value of the population must be known and correspond to the sum of the book values of the individual items.
- More than a few differences between audit and book values must be expected.

As explained below, the calculation of the allowance for sampling risk in difference estimation is based on the *variability of the differences* in the sample. Without a sufficient number of differences, the variability measure is unreliable. Among statisticians, the minimum number of differences required to ensure reliability varies considerably, ranging from 20 to 50.

The steps in performing difference estimation are explained in the following sections. The Ace Finance Company loans receivable case study is used again to highlight the similarities and differences between the MPU and difference estimation techniques.

Determine the Objectives and Define the Population and Sampling Unit

Because book values must be known in difference estimation, this method can be used only to obtain evidence that a recorded balance is not materially misstated. Other considerations relevant to these steps are the same as in MPU sampling. Accordingly, the following assumptions for the Ace Finance Company in the MPU illustration are continued: (1) population = 3,000 loans receivable, (2) book value of population = $1,340,000, and (3) sampling unit = the individual loan.

Determine the Sample Size

The same factors are required in determining sample size for MPU and difference estimation samples, with one exception. In difference estimation, the estimated standard deviation of the differences between the audit and book values is used rather than the estimated standard deviation of the audit values themselves. The auditor may base this estimate on the results of the prior year's sample or on the differences found in a presample in the current audit. As stated earlier, the estimate may be unreliable if it is based on too few differences.

FIGURE 12-9 • MEAN-PER-UNIT SAMPLING PLAN WORKING PAPER

ACE FINANCE COMPANY
MPU SAMPLE - LOANS RECEIVABLE
DECEMBER 31, 19X1

W/P REF: B-4
PREPARED BY: W.C.B DATE: 1/22/X2
REVIEWED BY: R.E.J DATE: 2/5/X2

OBJECTIVE:	TO OBTAIN EVIDENCE THAT THE BOOK VALUE FOR LOANS RECEIVABLE AS OF 12/31/X1 IS NOT MATERIALLY MISSTATED.		
POPULATION AND SAMPLING UNIT:	3000 LOANS RECEIVABLE ON COMPUTER LISTING PREPARED FROM MASTER FILE. SAMPLING UNIT = INDIVIDUAL LOAN RECEIVABLE.		
SAMPLE SIZE:	POPULATION SIZE	3,000 (N)	
	ESTIMATED STANDARD DEVIATION	100 (Sxj)	
	TOLERABLE MISSTATEMENT	60,000 (TM)	
	RISK OF INCORRECT REJECTION	5 %	Ur = 1.96
	RISK OF INCORRECT ACCEPTANCE	20 %	
	RATIO OF DESIRED ALLOWANCE FOR SAMPLING RISK (A) TO TM	0.700 (R)	
	DESIRED ALLOWANCE FOR SAMPLING RISK = R * TM	42,000 (A)	
	n = ((N * Ur * Sxj)/A)^2	196 (n)	
	n' = n/(1 + (n/N))	184 (n')	
SAMPLE SELECTION:	SIMPLE RANDOM USING COMPUTER GENERATED RANDOM NUMBER LIST TO CORRESPOND TO LOAN NUMBERS.		
	SAMPLING UNITS SELECTED LISTED ON W/P	B-5	
EXECUTION OF SAMPLING PLAN:	AUDIT PROCEDURES APPLIED LISTED ON W/P	B-1	
	AUDIT VALUES OF SAMPLE ITEMS SHOWN ON W/P	B-5	
	SUM OF SAMPLE AUDIT VALUES	81,328	
	AVERAGE OF SAMPLE AUDIT VALUES	442.00 ($\bar{x}$)	
	STANDARD DEVIATION OF SAMPLE AUDIT VALUES	90.00 (Sxj)	
EVALUATION OF SAMPLE RESULTS:	ESTIMATED TOTAL POPULATION VALUE:		
	$x\text{^} = N * \bar{x}$	1,326,000 (x^)	
	ACHIEVED ALLOWANCE FOR SAMPLING RISK:		
	$A' = N * Ur * (Sxj * \sqrt{1-(n'/N)}/\sqrt{n'})$	37,798 (A')	
	RANGE:		
	X^ +- A' = 1,288,202 TO 1,363,798		

CONCLUSION Total book value of $1,340,000 falls within calculated range for the estimated total population value. Sample results support conclusion that loans receivable are not misstated by more than tolerable misstatement.

Changes are required in the formulas used earlier in MPU estimation for computing the standard deviation and sample size. In the **standard deviation** formula (p. 421), the following substitutions in symbols are required:

- S_{d_j} (estimated standard deviation of population differences) for S_{x_j}.
- d_j (differences between audit and book values of individual sample items) for x_j.
- $\bar{d}$ (mean of the differences between audit and book values for the sample items) for $\bar{x}$.

In the sample size formula (p. 423), S_{d_j} is substituted for S_{x_j}.

For the Ace Finance Company, the auditor estimates that S_{d_j} is $70. Other assumptions continued from the MPU illustrations are N = 3,000, TM = $60,000, risk of incorrect rejection = 0.05 (U_R = 1.96), risk of incorrect acceptance = 0.20, and A = $42,000. Therefore, sample size is 96 items, computed as follows:

$$n = \left(\frac{N \cdot U_R \cdot S_{d_j}}{A}\right)^2 = \left(\frac{3{,}000 \times 1.96 \times \$70}{\$42{,}000}\right)^2 = 96$$

Observe that the sample size is considerably smaller than the sample size of 196 in the MPU example. This is due to the fact that the estimated standard deviation of the differences between audit and book values ($70) is smaller than the estimated standard deviation of the audit values used in the MPU illustration ($100). In this example, an adjustment of the sample size by a finite correction factor is unnecessary because n/N is less than 0.05 (96 ÷ 3,000 = 0.032).

Determine the Sample Selection Method

The performance of this step is the same in both MPU and difference estimation.

Execute the Sampling Plan

The initial step in executing the sampling plan is to determine the audit value for each sample item. Thus, this is the same as in MPU sampling. However, then the following steps occur:

- Calculate a difference for each sample item equal to the item's audit value minus its book value. The difference may be positive (audit value exceeds book value), negative (audit value is less than book value), or zero (audit value equals book value). Note that a positive difference indicates understatement of the book value and a negative difference means the book value is overstated.
- Sum the differences of the individual sample items (Σd_j).
- Divide the sum of the differences by the number of items in the sample to obtain the average (or mean) difference ($\bar{d}$).
- Compute the standard deviation of the sample differences (S_{d_j}).

In our case study, the following sample results are assumed:

$$\sum d_j = \$-480$$
$$\bar{d} = \$-5$$
$$S_{d_j} = \$68$$

As in MPU sampling, both quantitative and qualitative assessments are made in reaching an overall conclusion based on the sample results.

In making the quantitative assessment, in difference estimation the **estimated total projected difference ($\hat{D}$)** in the population is first determined as follows:

$$\hat{D} = N \times \bar{d}$$

Therefore, in the Ace Finance Company, $\hat{D}$ is

$$\hat{D} = 3{,}000 \times (\$ - 5) = \$ - 15{,}000$$

The negative sign indicates the projected error is an overstatement (audit value is less than book value).

The **estimated total population value** is then determined as follows:

$$\hat{X} = BV + \hat{D}$$

Thus, the estimated total population value is

$$\hat{X} = \$1{,}340{,}000 + (\$ - 15{,}000) = \$1{,}325{,}000$$

The second step in making the quantitative assessment is computing the **achieved allowance for sampling risk.** In making this calculation, it is necessary to substitute the standard deviation of the sample differences (S_{d_j}) for the standard deviation of the sample audit values (S_{x_j}). Because the finite correction factor was not used in determining sample size in this case study, the formula is

$$A' = N \cdot U_R \cdot \frac{S_{d_j}}{\sqrt{n}}$$

The achieved allowance is $40,808, computed as follows:

$$A' = 3{,}000 \times 1.96 \times \frac{\$68}{\sqrt{96}} = \$40{,}808$$

Because A' ($40,808) is less than A ($42,000), it is not necessary to calculate A''.

The final step in the quantitative assessment is to calculate the **range for the estimated total population value** and determine whether the book value falls within the range. As in the case of MPU sampling, the range is equal to $\hat{X} \pm A'$. The range, therefore, is $1,284,192 to $1,365,808. Because the book value falls within the range, the quantitative assessment supports the conclusion that the book value is not materially misstated. This is the same conclusion that was supported by the MPU technique.

Finally, the same *qualitative considerations* that were explained previously for MPU sample results should be made prior to reaching an overall conclusion. Figure 12-10 shows a difference estimation sampling plan working paper produced with the DIFF template of the *AUDSAMP* software.

RATIO ESTIMATION

In **ratio estimation sampling,** the auditor determines an audit value for each item in the sample. A ratio is calculated next by dividing the sum of the audit values by the sum of the book values for the sample items. This ratio is multiplied by the total book value to arrive at an estimate of the total population value. An allow-

FIGURE 12-10 • DIFFERENCE ESTIMATION SAMPLING PLAN WORKING PAPER

ACE FINANCE COMPANY
DIFFERENCE ESTIMATION SAMPLE - LOANS RECEIVABLE
DECEMBER 31, 19X1

W/P REF: *B-4*
PREPARED BY: *W.C.B* DATE: *1/23/X2*
REVIEWED BY: *R.E.Z* DATE: *2/5/X2*

OBJECTIVE:	TO OBTAIN EVIDENCE THAT THE BOOK VALUE FOR LOANS RECEIVABLE AS OF 12/31/X1 IS NOT MATERIALLY MISSTATED.		
POPULATION AND SAMPLING UNIT:	3000 LOANS RECEIVABLE ON COMPUTER LISTING PREPARED FROM MASTER FILE.		
	SAMPLING UNIT = INDIVIDUAL LOAN RECEIVABLE.		
	TOTAL BOOK VALUE OF POPULATION	1,340,000 (BV)	
SAMPLE SIZE:	POPULATION SIZE	3,000 (N)	
	ESTIMATED STANDARD DEVIATION OF DIFFERENCES	70 (Sdj)	
	TOLERABLE MISSTATEMENT	60,000 (TM)	
	RISK OF INCORRECT REJECTION	5 %	Ur = 1.96
	RISK OF INCORRECT ACCEPTANCE	20 %	
	RATIO OF DESIRED ALLOWANCE FOR SAMPLING RISK (A) TO TM	0.70 (R)	
	DESIRED ALLOWANCE FOR SAMPLING RISK = R * TM	42,000 (A)	
	n = ((N * Sdj * Ur)/A) ^2	96 (n)	
SAMPLE SELECTION:	SIMPLE RANDOM USING COMPUTER GENERATED RANDOM NUMBER LIST TO CORRESPOND TO LOAN NUMBERS.		
	SAMPLING UNITS SELECTED LISTED ON W/P	*B-5*	
EXECUTION OF SAMPLING PLAN:	AUDIT PROCEDURES APPLIED LISTED ON W/P	*B-3*	
	BOOK AND AUDIT VALUES OF SAMPLE ITEMS SHOWN ON W/P	*B-5*	
	SUM OF DIFFERENCES OF SAMPLE ITEMS	-480.00	
	AVERAGE OF DIFFERENCES	-5.00 ($\bar{d}$)	
	STANDARD DEVIATION OF SAMPLE DIFFERENCES	68.00 (Sdj)	
EVALUATION OF SAMPLE RESULTS:	ESTIMATED TOTAL PROJECTED DIFFERENCE		
	$D\text{\^{}} = N * \bar{d}$	(15,000)(D^)	
	ESTIMATED TOTAL POPULATION VALUE:		
	X^ = BV + D^	1,325,000 (X^)	
	ACHIEVED ALLOWANCE FOR SAMPLING RISK:		
	$A' = N * Ur * (Sdj/\sqrt{n})$	40,808 (A')	
	RANGE:		
	X^ +- A' = 1,284,192 TO 1,365,808		
CONCLUSION:	*Total book value of $1,340,000 falls within calculated range for the estimated total population value. Sample results support conclusion that loans receivable are not misstated by more than tolerable misstatement.*		

ance for sampling risk is then calculated based on the variability of the ratios of the audit and book values for the individual sample items.

The conditions for using ratio estimation are the same as those for difference estimation. The choice between ratio and difference estimation depends primarily on whether there is any correlation between the amount of the individual differences and their book values. When the differences are closely proportional to book value (i.e., the amount of the differences tend to increase as book values increase), ratio estimation will require a smaller sample size and therefore be more efficient. Computer programs are available that permit the auditor to input book and audit values for a presample to determine the sample size under both difference and ratio estimation. The auditor can then choose the technique that appears most efficient in the circumstances.

The steps in ratio estimation are the same as in difference estimation except as explained in the following sections.

Execute the Sampling Plan

After an audit value for each sample item has been determined, it is necessary in ratio estimation to

- Calculate the ratio of the sums of the audit and book values for the sample items (R).
- Calculate the ratio of the audit and book values for each item.
- Compute the standard deviation of the individual ratios of the sample items (S_{r_j}).

Evaluate the Sample Results

In ratio estimation, the **estimated total population value** is derived from the following formula:

$$\hat{X} = BV \times R$$

Consequently, if the sums of the audit and book values of the sample items in the Ace Finance Company are \$196,000 and \$200,000, respectively, the R factor is 98%, and the estimated value of the population is \$1,313,200 (\$1,340,000 × 98%).

The formula for determining the **achieved allowance for sampling risk** is the same as in difference estimation, except the standard deviation of the individual ratios in the sample is substituted for the standard deviation of the differences. The standard deviation of ratios is an extremely cumbersome calculation, and it is rarely done in practice without the assistance of a computer. Accordingly, manual calculation of this factor is not illustrated.

Once the estimated total population value and achieved allowance for sampling risk are computed, the **range for the estimated total population value** is determined. The sample results are then assessed quantitatively and qualitatively in the same manner as for MPU or difference estimation.

ADVANTAGES AND DISADVANTAGES OF CLASSICAL VARIABLES SAMPLING

Now that the three techniques of classical variables sampling have been explained, it is possible to evaluate this statistical approach. The *Audit Sampling Guide* (p. 87) identifies several advantages and disadvantages of classical variables sampling. The principal advantages are

- The samples may be easier to expand than PPS samples, if that becomes necessary.
- Zero balances and different sign balances do not require special design considerations.
- If there is a large number of differences between book and audit values, the auditor's objectives may be met with a smaller sample size than in PPS sampling.

The disadvantages consist primarily of the following:

- Classical variables sampling is more complex than PPS sampling; generally, an auditor needs the assistance of computer programs to design an efficient sample and evaluate sample results.
- To determine sample size, the auditor must have an estimate of the standard deviation of the characteristic of interest in the population.

The auditor should use professional judgment in selecting the approach that is most appropriate in the circumstances.

LEARNING CHECK:

12-12 Identify three classical sampling techniques used in substantive testing.

12-13 a. Give the formula for determining sample size in a mean-per-unit sampling plan.
b. Explain what each element in the formula represents.
c. How does the formula differ for (1) difference estimation and (2) ratio estimation?

12-14 a. How is the risk of incorrect acceptance controlled in classical variables sampling plans?
b. Explain three ways of estimating the standard deviation for a mean-per-unit sampling plan.

12-15 Explain the role of each of the following in a classical variables sampling plan:
a. Planned allowance for sampling risk.
b. Achieved allowance for sampling risk.
c. Adjusted achieved allowance for sampling risk.

12.16 What alternatives exist when sample results do not support the book value?

12-17 a. Why do the difference and ratio estimation techniques generally produce more efficient samples than mean-per-unit estimation?
b. Describe briefly the technique by which the estimated total population value is determined under (1) mean-per-unit, (2) difference, and (3) ratio estimation sampling.

KEY TERMS:

Achieved allowance for sampling risk (A′), pp. 426, 431, 433
Adjusted achieved allowance for sampling risk (A″), p. 427
Classical variables sampling, p. 419
Difference estimation sampling, p. 428
Estimated total population value ($\hat{X}$), pp. 426, 431, 433
Estimated total projected difference ($\hat{D}$), p. 431
Finite correction factor, p. 424
MPU estimation sample, p. 420
Planned allowance for sampling risk (A), p. 423
Population, p. 420
Range for the estimated total population value, pp. 426, 431, 433
Ratio estimation sampling, p. 431
Sampling unit, p. 420
Standard deviation, pp. 421, 430
Stratified sampling, p. 421
U_R factor, p. 422

NONSTATISTICAL SAMPLING IN SUBSTANTIVE TESTING

OBJECTIVE 6

Describe the differences between nonstatistical and statistical sampling plans for substantive tests.

As explained earlier, the auditor may choose to use **nonstatistical sampling** in certain substantive testing applications. The major differences between statistical and nonstatistical sampling are in the steps for determining sample size and evaluating sample results. These steps are often perceived as being more objective or rigorous in statistical sampling and more subjective and judgmental in nonstatistical samples. However, judgment is also required in statistical applications, and certain relationships considered explicitly in statistical samples may be helpful in designing and evaluating nonstatistical samples.

DETERMINE THE SAMPLE SIZE

Careful consideration of sample design must be made to achieve efficient and effective samples. This is accomplished in statistical samples through explicit specification of key factors and relating them through mathematical models. Consideration of the same factors in nonstatistical samples may help to produce more efficient and effective samples, even if the factors are not explicitly quantified. For example, the auditor should consider the following relationships:

Factor	Effect on Sample Size
Population size	Direct
Variation in the population	Direct
Tolerable misstatement	Inverse
Expected misstatement	Direct
Risk of incorrect acceptance	Inverse
Risk of incorrect rejection	Inverse

Careful subjective analysis of these factors in a particular circumstance, combined with the auditor's experience and judgment, should result in a sample size that is more appropriate than an arbitrarily determined sample size. The auditor may, but is not required to, consult statistical tables or models in evaluating the appropriateness of judgmentally determined sample sizes.

EVALUATE THE SAMPLE RESULTS

In nonstatistical as well as statistical sampling, the auditor should (1) project misstatements found in the sample to the population and (2) consider the sampling risk in evaluating sample results.

Two acceptable methods of projecting misstatements in nonstatistical samples are

- Divide the total dollar amount of misstatement in the sample by the fraction of total dollars from the population included in the sample.
- Multiply the average difference between audit and book values for sample items by the number of units in the population.

To illustrate, assume the following data for the Norris Company:

Number of items in population	2,500
Total book value of population	$800,000
Number of items in sample	100
Total book value of sample items	$32,000
Total audit value of sample items	$33,600

Under the first method described above, **projected misstatement** is determined as follows:

$$\frac{\$33{,}600 - \$32{,}000}{\$32{,}000 \div \$800{,}000} = \frac{\$1{,}600}{0.04} = \$40{,}000$$

The second method results in the following calculation:

$$\frac{\$33{,}600 - \$32{,}000}{100} \times 2{,}500 = \$40{,}000$$

Thus, both methods yield total projected misstatement of $40,000. Because the total audit value of the sample items exceeds their total book value, the projected misstatement represents an understatement of the true value of the population.

In nonstatistical samples, the auditor cannot calculate an **allowance for sampling risk** for specific, measurable levels of risk of incorrect acceptance and rejection. However, the difference between projected and tolerable misstatement may be viewed as an allowance for sampling risk. If tolerable misstatement exceeds projected misstatement by a large amount, the auditor may be reasonably assured that there is an acceptably low sampling risk that the actual misstatement exceeds tolerable misstatement. For example, if tolerable misstatement is $80,000 in the Norris Company, actual misstatement in the population would have to exceed twice the $40,000 projected misstatement from the sample before exceeding tolerable misstatement. On the other hand, if tolerable misstatement is $42,000, there is only a $2,000 difference between tolerable and projected misstatement. In such case, the auditor may conclude that there is an unacceptably high sampling risk that the actual misstatement exceeds tolerable misstatement.

The number and size of misstatements found in the sample relative to expected misstatements are also helpful in assessing sampling risk. When the sample has been carefully designed and the number and size of misstatements found do not exceed the auditor's expectations, he or she can generally conclude that there is an acceptably low risk that actual misstatement exceeds tolerable misstatement.

When the results of a nonstatistical sample do not appear to support the book value, the auditor may (1) examine additional sample units and reevaluate, (2) apply alternative auditing procedures and reevaluate, or (3) ask the client to investigate and, if appropriate, make an adjustment. As in statistical sampling, prior to reaching an overall conclusion, consideration should be given to the qualitative characteristics of the misstatements.

LEARNING CHECK:

12-18 How does the process of determining sample size differ in a statistical versus a nonstatistical sampling plan for a substantive test?

12-19 Describe two acceptable methods for projecting misstatements found in nonstatistical samples.

12-20 What may be viewed as the allowance for sampling risk in nonstatistical samples? Explain.

KEY TERMS:

Allowance for sampling risk, p. 436
Projected misstatement, p. 436
Nonstatistical sampling, p. 435

SUMMARY

Audit sampling is widely used in substantive tests. Both statistical and nonstatistical audit sampling can contribute to the evidence needed by the auditor to have a reasonable basis for an opinion. The use of statistical sampling, especially the PPS model, has increased significantly in practice in recent years, and this trend can be expected to continue in the future.

APPENDIX 12A RELATING THE RISK OF INCORRECT ACCEPTANCE FOR A SUBSTANTIVE TEST OF DETAILS TO OTHER SOURCES OF AUDIT EVIDENCE

The appendix to AU 350 contains the following expanded audit risk model:

$$AR = IR \times CR \times AP \times TD$$

It will be recalled that the basic audit risk model presented in Chapter 7 is $AR = IR \times CR \times DR$, where the terms represent overall audit risk, inherent risk, control risk, and detection risk, respectively. Thus, the difference between the basic and expanded models is the substitution of AP and TD for DR. The new terms are defined in AU 350 as follows:

AP = the auditor's assessment of the risk that analytical procedures and other relevant substantive tests would fail to detect misstatements that could occur in an assertion equal to tolerable misstatement, given that such misstatements occur and are not detected by the internal control structure.

TD = the allowable risk of incorrect acceptance for the substantive test of details, given that misstatements equal to tolerable misstatement occur in an assertion and are not detected by the internal control structure or analytical procedures and other relevant substantive tests.

By splitting the detection risk term of the basic model into two components, the expanded model may be helpful to the auditor in specifying an appropriate risk of incorrect acceptance for a planned substantive test of details. Solving the expanded model for *TD* yields the following:

$$TD = \frac{AR}{IR \times CR \times AP}$$

The assessment of the risk for each factor involves a considerable amount of subjectivity and the exercise of professional judgment. For purposes of illustration, we will assume that, prior to performing a particular test of details for an assertion, the auditor has

- Specified an overall audit risk *(AR)* of 5%.
- Subjectively assessed inherent risk *(IR)* as 100%.
- Subjectively assessed control risk *(CR)* as 30%.
- Subjectively assessed the risk that analytical procedures and other relevant substantive tests might fail to detect misstatements equal to tolerable misstatement *(AP)* as 50%.

TD in the expanded model is computed as follows:

$$TD = \frac{0.05}{1.0 \times 0.30 \times 0.50} = 33\%$$

In analyzing this result, the auditor may decide that the performance of another relevant substantive test may lower the risk for *AP* to 30%. In such a case, the risk of incorrect acceptance for the tests of details becomes 55% [i.e., $0.05/(1.0 \times 0.30 \times 0.30) = 55\%$]. The auditor must then decide whether the cost of performing the additional relevant auditing procedure is warranted by the cost savings that will result from the reduction in sample size due to the higher *TD* for the planned test of details.

Though many auditors are reluctant to quantify the subjective risk assessments required to solve the model for *TD*, a basic understanding of the relationships expressed in the model may be helpful to auditors in subjectively deciding on an acceptable risk of incorrect acceptance for a test of details.

BIBLIOGRAPHY

AICPA Professional Standards:
SAS 39 (AU 350), Audit Sampling
IAU 19 (AU 8019), Audit Sampling

AICPA, *Audit and Accounting Guide: Audit Sampling*. New York: AICPA, 1983.

Akresh, Abraham D., and Tatum, Kay W. "Audit Sampling—Dealing with the Problems," *Journal of Accountancy* (December 1988), pp. 58–64.

Felix, William L., Grimlund, Richard A., Koster, Frank J., and Roussey, Robert S. "Arthur Andersen's New Monetary Unit Sampling Approach," *Auditing: A Journal of Practice and Theory* (Fall 1990), pp. 1–16.

Guy, Dan M., Carmichael, Douglas, and Whittington, O. Ray. *Audit Sampling: An Introduction*, Third Edition. New York: John Wiley & Sons, Inc., 1994.

Kachelmeier, Steven J., and Messier, William F., Jr. "Nonstatistical Sample Sizes: The Effect of the Audit Guide Decision Aid," *The CPA Journal* (March 1991), pp. 55–57.

Neter, John, and Loebbecke, James K. *Behavior of Major Statistical Estimators in Sampling Accounting Populations.* Auditing Research Monograph No. 2. New York: AICPA, 1975.

Robertson, Jack C., and Rouse, Robert. "Substantive Audit Sampling—The Challenge of Achieving Efficiency Along with Effectiveness," *Accounting Horizons* (Spring 1994), pp. 35–44.

Tatum, Kay W. "Solving Audit Sampling Problems," *The CPA Journal* (August 1987), pp. 91–97.

OBJECTIVE QUESTIONS

Indicate the *best* answer for each multiple choice question.

12-21 The following questions relate to a variety of issues concerning audit sampling in substantive testing.

1. An auditor may use either of two statistical sampling approaches in substantive testing, probability-proportional-to-size (PPS) sampling and classical variables sampling. PPS sampling is primarily applicable in testing for
   a. The number of errors in year-end sales cutoff.
   b. An overstatement of accounts receivable.
   c. An understatement of accounts payable.
   d. Proper segregation of duties in accounts receivable collections.

2. Which of the following would be designed to estimate a numerical measurement of a population, such as a dollar value?
   a. Sampling for variables.
   b. Sampling for attributes.
   c. Discovery sampling.
   d. Numerical sampling.

3. In a probability-proportional-to-size sample with a sampling interval of $10,000, an auditor discovered that a selected account receivable with a recorded amount of $5,000 had an audit amount of $2,000. The projected error of this sample was
   a. $3,000
   b. $4,000
   c. $6,000
   d. $8,000

4. What is the primary objective of using stratification as a sampling method in auditing?
   a. To increase the risk of incorrect acceptance at which a decision will be reached from the results of the sample selected.
   b. To determine the deviation rate for a given characteristic in the population being studied.
   c. To decrease the effect of variance in the total population.
   d. To determine the precision interval of the sample selected.

5. Which of the following most likely would be an advantage in using classical variables sampling rather than probability-proportional-to-size (PPS) sampling?
   a. An estimate of the standard deviation of the population's recorded amounts is not required.
   b. The auditor rarely needs the assistance of a computer program to design an efficient sample.
   c. Inclusion of zero and negative balances generally does not require special design considerations.
   d. Any amount that is individually significant is automatically identified and selected.

12-22 The following questions relate to the relationship between risk and audit sampling.

1. While performing a substantive test of details during an audit, the auditor determined that the sample results supported the conclusion that the recorded account balance was materially misstated. It was, in fact, not materially misstated. This situation illustrates the risk of
   a. Incorrect rejection.
   b. Incorrect acceptance.
   c. Assessing control risk too low.
   d. Assessing control risk too high.

2. If the achieved allowance for sampling risk of a statistical sample at a given risk level is greater than the desired allowance, this is an indication that the
   a. Standard deviation was larger than expected.
   b. Standard deviation was smaller than expected.
   c. Population was larger than expected.
   d. Population was smaller than expected.

3. An advantage of using statistical sampling techniques is that such techniques
   a. Mathematically measure risk.
   b. Eliminate the need for judgmental decisions.
   c. Define the values of tolerable error and risk of incorrect acceptance required to provide audit satisfaction.
   d. Have been established in the courts to be superior to judgment sampling.

4. The risk that an auditor will conclude, based on substantive tests, that a material error does not exist in an account balance when, in fact, such error does exist is referred to as
   a. Sampling risk.
   b. Detection risk.
   c. Nonsampling risk.
   d. Inherent risk.

5. An auditor may decide to increase the risk of incorrect rejection when
   a. Increased reliability from the sample is desired.
   b. Many differences (audit value minus recorded value) are expected.
   c. Initial sample results do not support the planned level of control risk.
   d. The cost and effort of selecting additional sample items are low.

12-23 The following questions relate to the difference and ratio estimation techniques of variables sampling.

1. An auditor is performing substantive tests of pricing and extensions of perpetual inventory balances consisting of a large number of items. Past experience indicates numerous pricing and extension errors. Which of the following statistical sampling approaches is most appropriate?
   a. Unstratified mean-per-unit.
   b. Probability-proportional-to-size.
   c. Stop or go.
   d. Ratio estimation.

2. The major reason that the difference and ratio estimation methods would be expected to produce audit efficiency is that the
   a. Number of members of the population of differences of ratios is smaller than the number of members of the population of book values.
   b. Beta risk may be completely ignored.
   c. Calculations required in using difference or ratio estimation are less arduous and fewer than those required when using MPU estimation.
   d. Variability of the populations of differences or ratios is less than that of the populations of book values or audit values.

3. Using statistical sampling to assist in verifying the year-end accounts payable balance, an auditor has accumulated the following data:

	Number of Accounts	Book Balance	Balance Determined by the Auditor
Population	4,100	$5,000,000	?
Sample	200	$ 250,000	$300,000

   With the ratio estimation technique, the auditor's estimate of the year-end accounts payable balance would be
   a. $6,150,000
   b. $6,000,000
   c. $5,125,000
   d. $5,050,000

COMPREHENSIVE QUESTIONS

12-24 **(PPS sampling)** Edwards has decided to use probability-proportional-to-size (PPS) sampling, sometimes called dollar-unit sampling, in the audit of a client's accounts receivable balance. Few, if any, errors of overstatement are expected.

Edwards plans to use the following PPS sampling table:

5% Reliability Factors for Overstatements

Number of Overstatements	Risk of Incorrect Acceptance				
	1%	5%	10%	15%	20%
0	4.61	3.00	2.31	1.90	1.61
1	6.64	4.75	3.89	3.38	3.00
2	8.41	6.30	5.33	4.72	4.28
3	10.05	7.76	6.69	6.02	5.52
4	11.61	9.16	8.00	7.27	6.73

REQUIRED

a. Identify the advantages of using PPS sampling over classical variables sampling.
Note: Requirements (b) and (c) are *not* related.
b. Calculate the sampling interval and the sample size Edwards should use, given the following information:

Tolerable misstatement $15,000
Risk of incorrect acceptance 5%
Number of misstatements allowed 0
Recorded amount of accounts receivable $300,000

c. Calculate total projected misstatement if the following three misstatements were discovered in a PPS sample:

	Recorded Amount	Audit Amount	Sampling Interval
1st misstatement	$ 400	$ 320	$1,000
2nd misstatement	500	0	1,000
3rd misstatement	3,000	2,500	1,000

AICPA

12-25 **(PPS sampling)** In the December 31, 19X1, audit of Lark Corporation, an auditor employs monetary-unit (probability-proportional-to-size) sampling in testing the valuation of physical inventory. The book value of inventory is $500,000 and represents the cumulative value of 2,000 vouchers. The maximum tolerable misstatement (or level of materiality) is determined to be $25,000 and the auditor decides on a 10% risk of incorrect acceptance. This completes the auditor's design specifications for the sample.

The test revealed one voucher that was on the books at $500 but had an audit value of $400. No other misstatements were found.

REQUIRED

a. What sample size and sampling interval were used by the auditor?
b. Under the assumption that the auditor wrote a conclusion based on the data presented, what would the conclusion state?
c. Critique the auditor's sampling plan and describe what actions the auditor might take given the sample results.
d. What are the advantages of using monetary-unit (probability-proportional-to-size) sampling as an audit tool?

IIA (adapted)

12-26 **(PPS sampling)** You have completed a pricing test of the Grapefruit Computer Company's December 31, 19X1, inventory using a PPS sampling plan. The sample design for your test of the $4,000,000 inventory (book value) specified a risk of incorrect acceptance of 15% and tolerable misstatement of $300,000. You anticipated not more than $40,000 of misstatement in the inventory due to excellent internal controls.

REQUIRED

a. What size sample should you have examined?
b. What was your sampling interval?
c. If you assume no misstatements were found in the sample, what is your conclusion (state as precisely as possible)?
d. If you assume the sample yielded a projected misstatement of $39,800 and an incremental allowance for sampling risk of $19,500, what conclusion might you draw from the sample?

12-27 **(Evaluating a PPS sample)** Assume the following misstatements were found in a PPS sample:

Sample Item	Book Value	Audit Value
1	$ 650	$ 585
2	540	0
3	1,900	0
4	2,200	1,650
5	2,800	2,660

REQUIRED

a. Calculate the projected misstatement assuming
   1. The sampling interval was $1,800.
   2. The sampling interval was $2,000.
b. If a risk of incorrect acceptance of 15% was specified in the sample design, the sampling interval was $2,000, and five misstatements were found as enumerated above, calculate
   1. Basic precision.
   2. The incremental allowance for sampling risk.
   3. The upper misstatement limit.
c. If tolerable misstatement was $50,000 and anticipated misstatement was $10,000, what conclusion would you reach based on your results in (b) above?

12-28 **(PPS sampling)** You decide to use statistical sampling to test the reasonableness of the recorded book value of the Key West Company's accounts receivable. Because the company's internal control procedures over accounts receivable have been evaluated by you as excellent and you believe few misstatements will be found, you decide to use probability-proportional-to-size sampling. The company has 4,000 customer accounts with a total book value of $3,000,000. You decide $150,000 is the maximum tolerable misstatement and anticipate that there may be $30,000 of misstatement in the population. You wish to limit the risk of incorrect acceptance to 10%. It is your intention to seek positive confirmation of accounts included in your sample and to apply alternative procedures to accounts for which no reply is received.

REQUIRED

a. Compute the sample size.
b. Compute the sampling interval.
c. Assume the following misstatements were found in the sample:

Sample Item	Book Value	Audit Value
1	$ 800	$ 0
2	1,500	1,350
3	13,000	0
4	15,000	14,250

   Calculate
   1. Projected misstatement.
   2. Allowance for sampling risk.
   3. Upper misstatement limit.
d. State your conclusion based on the results in (c).

12-29 **(Mean-per-unit sampling)** A contractor has 1,520 homes in various states of construction. From a random presample of 50 homes, you determine that the estimated population standard deviation is $2,000. On the basis of audit risk and other factors, you set desired allowance for sampling risk at $250,000 and desired risk of incorrect rejection at 10%.

REQUIRED

a. Determine sample size, assuming mean-per-unit sampling with replacement.
b. What would sample size be if the standard deviation was increased to $2,500?
c. Assume the auditor elects to limit sample size to 325 in the interest of cost efficiencies. What risk of incorrect rejection can be achieved if desired allowance for sampling risk remains at $250,000 and the standard deviation remains at $2,000?
d. What allowance for sampling risk results if the risk of incorrect rejection is held at 10% and sample size is 325?
e. Redo part (a) above assuming sampling without replacement.

12-30 **(Sampling risk in classical sampling plans)** This question is designed to test your knowledge of sampling risks in classical variables sampling plans.

REQUIRED

a. Will your resulting sample size be larger or smaller if control risk is 50% rather than 10%, when all other factors are equal?
b. Will your sample be larger or smaller if you specify a risk of incorrect acceptance of 15% for a test of details rather than 20%?
c. If you desire risk of incorrect rejection of 10% and risk of incorrect acceptance of 20%, what amount should your planned allowance for sampling risk be when tolerable misstatement is $100,000?
d. If the achieved allowance for sampling risk is greater than the planned allowance, then the actual risk of incorrect acceptance is (greater/less) than the planned risk?
e. Assuming tolerable misstatement is $200,000, the planned risks of incorrect rejection and acceptance are 10% and 20%, respectively, and the achieved allowance for sampling risk if $160,000, calculate the adjusted achieved allowance for sampling risk.

12-31 **(Mean-per-unit sampling)** Data relative to three MPU sampling plans are presented below.

	1	2	3
Tolerable misstatement	$110,000	$140,000	$170,000
Size of population	5,000	6,000	8,000
Risk of incorrect rejection	10%	5%	10%
Estimated population standard deviation	$ 80	$ 105	$ 125
Risks that misstatements accumulating to greater than tolerable misstatements will not be detected by:			
Internal control	50%	40%	40%
Analytical and other substantive procedures (excluding this test of details)	25%	50%	85%
Desired overall audit risk	5%	5%	5%
Inherent risk	100%	100%	100%

REQUIRED

a. Using the model in Appendix 12A, determine an appropriate risk of incorrect acceptance for each population.
b. Calculate sample size in each of the plans. Show computations.

12-32 **(Mean-per-unit sampling)** Data relevant to the December 31, 19X1, audit of accounts receivable in two of your clients is presented in the tabulation below.

	Company X	Company Y
Client's book value	$90,000	$200,000
Population size	1,000	2,000
Desired risk of incorrect acceptance	20%	30%
Desired risk of incorrect rejection	10%	5%
Tolerable misstatement	$9,000	$10,000
Estimated standard deviation	$50	$25

REQUIRED

a. Determine sample size for each company using MPU estimation sampling.
b. Assume the total audited value of the Company X sample is $13,600 and the standard deviation is $52. Evaluate the sample results.

c. Assume the average of the sample audit values in the Company Y sample is $90 and the standard deviation is $30. Evaluate the sample results.

12-33 **(Difference estimation sampling)** The following facts pertain to a difference estimation sampling plan for Kay Corp.:

1. Objective is to determine whether book value is fairly stated.
2. Population consists of 4,000 customer accounts.
3. Book value of accounts receivable is $2.75 million at December 31, 19X1.
4. The preliminary estimated standard deviation of the differences used to determine sample size is $150.
5. Tolerable misstatement is $150,000.
6. Overall audit risk is 5%.
7. Risk of incorrect rejection is 5%.
8. Risk of incorrect acceptance is 25%.
9. Sample size is 112.
10. Audit value of the sample items is $76,440 and book value is $77,000.
11. The standard deviation of the sample differences is $160.

REQUIRED

a. Verify the sample size indicated above in item 9.
b. Compute achieved allowance for sampling risk. Is this consistent with the planned risk of incorrect acceptance? Why or why not? If not, compute the adjusted allowance.
c. Is book value fairly stated? Explain.

12-34 **(Classical variables sampling)** The Hard Finance Company has 2,500 loans outstanding at a recorded book value of $975,000. As the auditor on this engagement, Mary Jones selects a sample of 250 loans for vouching. These loans have a reported book value of $97,500 and an audit value of $95,000.

REQUIRED

Compute the estimated total value of the loans by (a) mean-per-unit estimation, (b) difference estimation, and (c) ratio estimation.

12-35 **(Nonstatistical sampling)** Wheeler and Jones, CPAs, are examining the December 31, 19X1, inventory of Better Parts, Inc., a distributor of electronic parts. They have already performed procedures to satisfy themselves that (1) a computer printout listing inventory at year end in ascending sequence by stock number and lot number is complete, (2) the quantities shown thereon are correct, (3) the extensions of quantity times price are accurate, (4) the listing is properly footed, and (5) the total agrees to the general ledger ending inventory account balance.

As the next step, Wheeler and Jones decide to use a nonstatistical sample to test the pricing of the inventory. They plan to perform this test by checking prices to (1) vendor's invoices and (2) current price lists provided by vendors. The ending inventory consists of 3,000 stock items with a total recorded value of $1,900,000. A perpetual inventory record is maintained for each stock item. Additionally, an inventory tag showing the quantity on hand at year end is on file for each item.

Wheeler and Jones agree that a misstatement of $85,000 or more in the inventory balance, when combined with misstatements in other accounts, might result in material misstatement of the financial statements.

REQUIRED

a. To what component of audit risk does the inventory pricing test relate?
b. What factors should influence Wheeler and Jones's determination of sample size?
c. What should the sampling unit be and how should the sample items be selected?

d. Assume that a sample of the pricing of 100 stock items was examined. The total recorded value for these items was $75,000. Eight of the items in the sample had pricing errors resulting in those items being overstated by $4,800. How should Wheeler and Jones interpret the sample results?

CASE

12-36 **(Variables sampling)** Fairview Publishing Company, incorporated in 19X4, is a small, closely held publisher of high school textbooks. A local accounting firm has reviewed the preparation of the financial statements, performed certain auditing procedures, and prepared the tax returns for many years. The accountants' report has always contained a disclaimer of opinion, because the stockholders would not permit confirmation of receivables or observation of inventories.

The company plans to "go public" in about three years. In anticipation of this, they engaged you in May to perform an audit for the year ended June 30.

The company's first fiscal quarter is usually the most profitable; the last quarter is usually a break-even situation.

The company has a job order cost system for determining its unit cost prices for each textbook. If a book has not been ordered by any customer for 12 months, it is "no valued," scrapped, and discounted. Only a minimal quantity is maintained of each title until a firm order is received. The company expects that it has no more than a $3,000 inventory of any one title.

You have completed your year-end inventory work and found the client's perpetual records were remarkably accurate with respect to quantities, unit prices, and extensions. No misstatements were located, and it was concluded that the perpetual records can be relied on for beginning inventory quantities.

However, as to the beginning inventory amount, the client is not able to produce a listing with detail sufficient to provide a transaction trail. They can find only an adding machine tape to support the recorded amount, $1,405,165. The tape is in no particular order.

At June 30 of the prior year, the company had exactly 1,000 different titles in inventory. This agrees with the number of entries on the tape and the number of perpetual records having a quantity at the beginning of the current year.

In this case, $140,000 is considered the maximum tolerable misstatement.

The risks that misstatements accumulating to greater than tolerable misstatement will not be detected by (1) internal controls and (2) by analytical procedures and substantive tests other than this test of details are 40% and 50%, respectively. The overall audit risk is 5%. Inherent risk is 100%.

A 5% risk of incorrect rejection is also viewed as acceptable. Based on this year's inventory, the standard deviation should approximate $525 and you have decided to use one stratum.

REQUIRED

a. What is the nature and objective of the test?
b. Compute the risk of incorrect acceptance.
c. What planned allowance for sampling risk should be used in determining sample size?
d. Calculate sample size (without replacement) using the estimated standard deviation of $525 and the planned allowance determined in (c) above.

e. Assuming the sample produces an audit value of sample items of $130,000 and a standard deviation of $550, calculate (1) the estimated total population value and (2) the achieved allowance for sampling risk.
f. Compute the adjusted achieved allowance.
g. Interpret the results of the sample.

RESEARCH QUESTIONS

12-37 **(PPS sampling and understatements)** The coverage of PPS sampling in this chapter dealt only with situations involving overstatements. Refer to one of the general references on audit sampling in the bibliography for this chapter and prepare a brief paper on the issues related to dealing with understatements in PPS sampling, including how the sample design and evaluation of sample results are affected by understatements.

12-38 **(Stratified mean-per-unit estimation sampling)** One approach to making mean-per-unit estimation sampling more efficient is to stratify the population to be sampled. Refer to one of the general references on audit sampling in the bibliography for this chapter and prepare a brief paper on the issues related to stratifying mean-per-unit estimation samples, including how the sample design and evaluation of sample results are affected by stratification.

12-39 **(Behavior of statistical estimators)** A problem associated with the use of the difference and ratio estimation sampling techniques is that these models are based on certain assumptions about the underlying populations being sampled that are often not valid in accounting populations. If available in your college library, consult the Neter and Loebbecke work, *Auditing Research Monograph No. 2,* cited in the bibliography of this chapter and prepare a brief paper on the issues addressed in the *Monograph* about the behavior of the statistical estimators used in difference and ratio estimation.

CHAPTER 13

AUDITING ELECTRONIC DATA PROCESSING SYSTEMS

LEARNING OBJECTIVES

When you have finished your study of this chapter, you should be able to

1. Describe the basic hardware and software components of an EDP system.
2. Distinguish the principal data organization and processing methods used in EDP systems.
3. Understand some of the major differences between computer and manual processing that affect internal control.
4. Explain the types of general and application controls used in EDP systems.
5. Indicate the level of understanding of the internal control structure needed in an EDP system.
6. State the types of computer-assisted audit techniques used in performing tests of controls.
7. Explain the nature and uses of generalized audit software.
8. Explain the auditing implications of microcomputer-based audit software, expert systems, small computer systems, and computer service organizations.

EDP SYSTEM COMPONENTS
- COMPUTER HARDWARE
- COMPUTER SOFTWARE
- DATA ORGANIZATION AND PROCESSING METHODS

EFFECTS OF EDP ON THE INTERNAL CONTROL STRUCTURE
- DIFFERENCES BETWEEN COMPUTER AND MANUAL PROCESSING
- GENERAL CONTROLS
- APPLICATION CONTROLS

METHODOLOGY FOR MEETING THE SECOND STANDARD OF FIELD WORK
- OBTAINING AN UNDERSTANDING OF THE ICS
- ASSESSING CONTROL RISK
- TESTS OF CONTROLS WITHOUT THE COMPUTER
- TESTS OF CONTROLS WITH THE COMPUTER
- TESTS OF CONTROLS IN ON-LINE ENTRY/ON-LINE PROCESSING

OTHER CONSIDERATIONS
- GENERALIZED AUDIT SOFTWARE
- MICROCOMPUTER-BASED AUDIT SOFTWARE
- EXPERT SYSTEMS
- SMALL COMPUTER SYSTEMS
- COMPUTER SERVICE ORGANIZATIONS

SUMMARY

BIBLIOGRAPHY

OBJECTIVE QUESTIONS

COMPREHENSIVE QUESTIONS

CASE

RESEARCH QUESTIONS

Electronic data processing (EDP) has been one of the most important technological developments in the latter half of the twentieth century. Computer installations now range in size from microcomputers to minicomputers to large mainframe computers linked together in complex international communication networks. A company may elect to lease or own its computer system or to use outside, independent computer service organizations to process accounting data. Thus, even a very small audit client will likely have some data processed electronically. Coupled with the greater use of computers in business has been a corresponding increase in computer-related frauds.

The primary objective of this chapter is to explain and illustrate the auditor's responsibilities in meeting the second standard of field work when EDP is used in significant accounting applications. To provide a basis for this discussion, the chapter begins with a consideration of the basic components of EDP systems. The chapter also includes an explanation of audit software and the auditing effects of microcomputers and computer service organizations.

EDP SYSTEM COMPONENTS

The auditor should be familiar with the following components of an EDP system:

- Hardware.
- Software.
- Data organization and processing methods.

COMPUTER HARDWARE

OBJECTIVE 1

Describe the basic hardware and software components of an EDP system.

Hardware is the physical equipment associated with the system. The basic hardware configuration consists of the central processing unit (CPU) and peripheral input and output devices. The principal hardware component is the CPU. It is composed of a control unit, an internal storage unit, and an arithmetic-logic unit. The control unit directs and coordinates the entire system, including the entry and removal of information from storage, and the routing of the data between storage and the arithmetic-logic unit. The internal storage unit, or computer "memory," stores the program instructions and the data to be processed. The arithmetic-logic unit is so named because it is capable of performing mathematical computations and certain logical operations. Peripheral to the CPU are input devices, output devices, and auxiliary storage devices. Peripheral equipment in direct communication with the CPU is considered to be on-line. Figure 13-1 illustrates common types of computer hardware.

COMPUTER SOFTWARE

This component consists of the programs and routines that facilitate the programming and operation of a computer. There are several kinds of computer software. Of particular interest to auditors are systems programs and application programs.

Systems Programs

Systems programs, sometimes called *supervisory programs,* perform general functions required for the operation of the computer as it executes specific tasks. Systems programs include the following

- *Operating systems* direct the operation of the computer, including input and output devices, main storage, execution of programs, and management of files.
- *Utility programs* perform common data processing tasks, such as copying, reorganizing data in a file, sorting, merging, and printing. Other kinds of utility programs may be used to gather information about the use of the hardware and software, aid in the detection of unauthorized use or changes to programs and data, provide documentation of program logic, and facilitate testing of new systems.

FIGURE 13-1 • COMPUTER HARDWARE

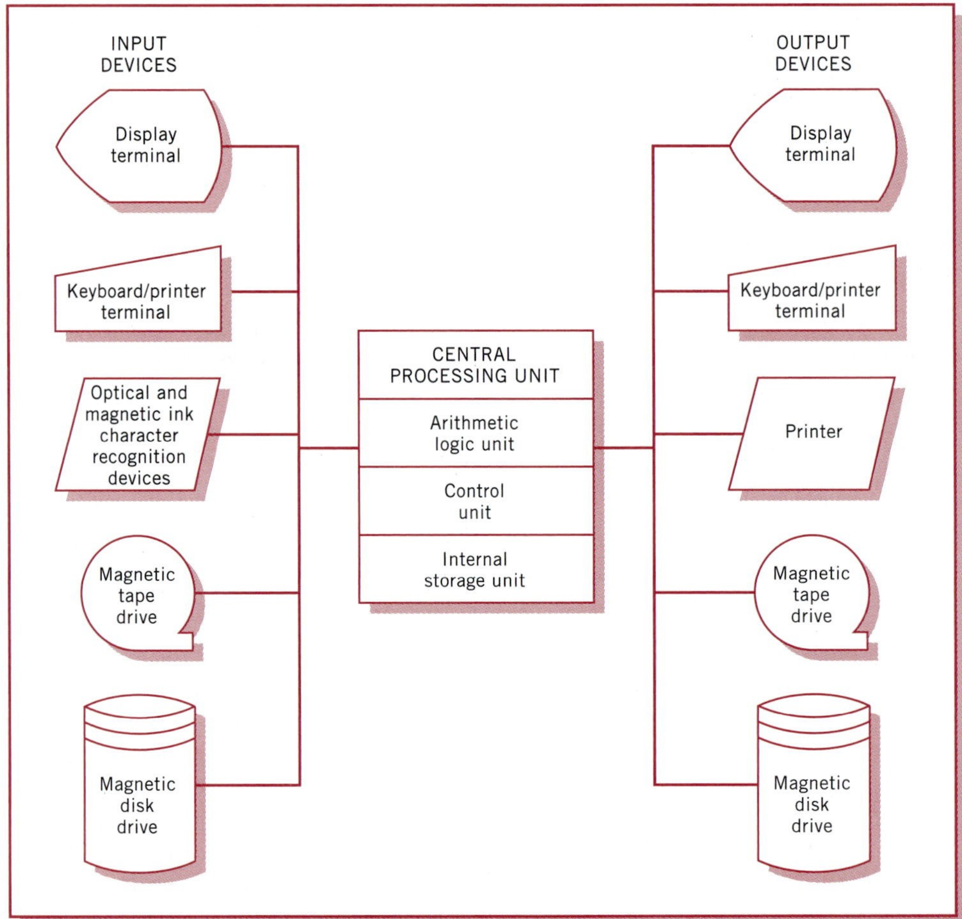

- *Compilers and assemblers* translate specific programming languages into instructions in a language that can be understood by the computer. Each computer has a specific machine language determined by the engineers who designed it.
- *Database management systems* are utilized by companies employing a computerized database. These programs control the data records and files independently of the application programs that allow changes in or use of the data.

Systems programs generally are purchased from hardware suppliers and software companies. They are then adapted, as necessary, by each user to suit individual needs.

Application Programs

Application programs contain instructions that enable the computer to perform specific data processing tasks for the user. These tasks include financial accounting, budgeting, engineering design, quality control, and so on. Within financial accounting, specific applications include general ledger accounting; sales order, shipping, billing, and accounts receivable; purchasing, receiving, vouchers payable, and cash disbursements; inventory; and payroll, among others. In some cases, the programs operate as stand-alone applications. Increasingly, in modern systems, they are designed to operate as parts of integrated systems. Application programs may be developed by the user or purchased from software vendors.

DATA ORGANIZATION AND PROCESSING METHODS

OBJECTIVE 2

Distinguish the principal data organization and processing methods used in EDP systems.

The accounting function often involves recording, updating, retrieving, and reporting on large volumes of transaction data and related information. To understand how all this information is handled in an EDP environment, the auditor must be familiar with the principal methods of data organization and data processing as explained in the following sections.

Data Organization Methods

The term **data organization methods** refers to the way data are organized within a computer file. The two principal methods of data organization are the traditional file method and the database method.

TRADITIONAL FILE METHOD. The **traditional file method** of data organization predominates in accounting applications. Under this method, the following two types of files are maintained: (1) *master files* that contain up-to-date information about a given class of data such as the current balances of customers' accounts or the current quantities of inventory items and (2) *transaction files* that contain the details of individual transactions of the same class such as a day's credit sales or a day's cash disbursements.

These files may be organized for *sequential* or *direct access* processing. In sequential files, information is maintained in a particular sequence or order. When a master file is organized sequentially, related transaction file data must be sorted into the same order before they can be used to update the master file. For example, if an accounts receivable master file is organized by customer number, the daily credit sales transaction file must be sorted into the same sequence before updating occurs. Sequential files are usually kept on magnetic tape.

In direct access files, neither the master nor related transaction file data needs to be maintained in any particular order. Thus, the transaction file need not be sorted prior to processing.

Under the traditional file method, separate master and transaction files are maintained for each application such as accounts receivable, inventory, payroll, and sales. Typically, the data in these files are accessible only by the single application program for which the files were created. Because of this, redundancy of data across files is common. For instance, a payroll file generally includes the following data elements among others: employee name, social security number, address, and pay rate. All these same data elements are likely to be repeated in a separate personnel file. The creation and maintenance of the same data elements in several files is costly. The single program access and redundancy drawbacks of the traditional file method are overcome in the database method as explained in the following paragraphs.

DATABASE METHOD. The **database method** of data organization is the principal alternative to the traditional file method. This method is based on the creation and maintenance of a single common direct access file for all applications using common data. Thus, each data element is stored only once, but is accessible by all authorized application programs. In the case of the payroll and personnel applications mentioned earlier, the employee name, social security number, address, and pay rate data would be included in the file just once, but would be usable in both application programs. Sophisticated *database management system software* is designed to provide control over which users and applications can access and change specific data elements.

Once used only in very large systems, the database method is gaining popularity in medium and smaller systems as well. Audit approaches to EDP systems that utilize the database method are more complex than those based on the traditional file method. Specialized knowledge and the use of sophisticated software are often required.

Data Processing Methods

The term **data processing methods** refers to the way data are entered into and processed by the computer. The following sections explain these three widely used methods: (1) batch entry / batch processing, (2) on-line entry / batch processing, and (3) on line entry / on-line processing.

BATCH ENTRY/BATCH PROCESSING. Under **batch entry/batch processing,** data are accumulated by classes of transactions such as sales or cash disbursements, and are both entered and processed in batches. The processing of similar transactions together generally makes this an efficient method. Other advantages include the ability to generate batch or control totals prior to processing and the use of batch numbers as transaction trail or processing references. One disadvantage of this type of processing is that the master file cannot be updated until the batch data are accumulated. In addition, there are usually delays in correcting processing errors identified by edit routines because errors in source documents or in converting data into machine-readable form must be completely recycled.

In EDP systems using batch processing, the traditional audit trail is most likely to exist. In relatively small systems with frequent printouts, the audit trail may exist in printed form. In other cases, the audit trail may exist only in machine-readable form. An illustration of batch entry / batch processing is provided in Figure 13-2.

ON-LINE ENTRY/BATCH PROCESSING. Under the **on-line entry/ batch processing** method of processing, individual transactions are entered directly into the computer via a terminal as they occur. A machine-readable validated transaction file is accumulated as the transactions are entered. This file is subsequently processed to update the master file. An advantage of this method is that the data are subjected to certain edit or validation checks by the computer program at the time of entry and error messages are communicated immediately to the terminal operator. For example, the programmed edit routine may detect missing, incomplete, or invalid data such as a nonexistent customer number. This permits immediate detection and correction of most data entry errors. The method

FIGURE 13-2 • BATCH ENTRY/BATCH PROCESSING

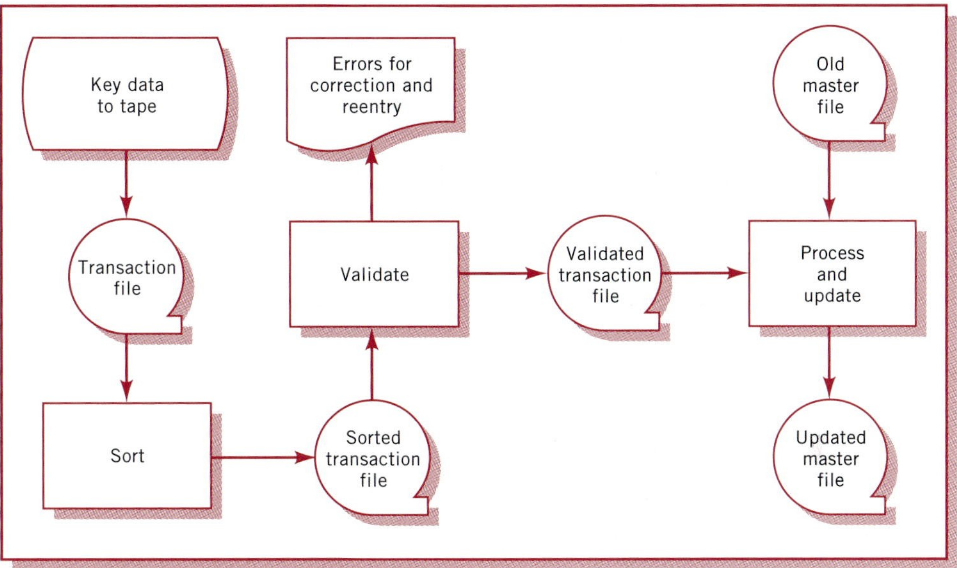

also retains the control advantages of batch entry/batch processing—namely, batch control totals and batch reference numbers.

On-line entry/batch processing may be used either with reference access to the related master file or with no access. In reference access, the file may be read but not updated from the terminal. Reference access is necessary in cash receipts processing in which payments received from customers must be matched with open invoices in the customer's file. In contrast with no access, the related master file cannot be read when the transaction data are entered. Figure 13-3 illustrates on-line entry/batch processing both with and without access.

ON-LINE ENTRY/ON-LINE PROCESSING. The **on-line entry/on-line processing** method differs from on-line entry/batch processing in the following two respects: (1) master files are updated concurrently with data entry, and (2) a transaction log is produced that consists of a chronological record of all transactions. To provide a transaction trail, each transaction is assigned a unique identifying number by the computer program.

On-line entry/on-line processing is used in airline and hotel reservations systems. A common accounting application is found in many retail stores where electronic cash registers immediately update inventory records when the sale is rung up.

The major disadvantages of this type of processing are the risk of errors in the master file from concurrent updating and the possible loss of part or all of the master files in case of hardware failure. To minimize these risks, some companies use memo updating of the master file at the time of data entry. This involves the use of a copy of the master file. The transaction log is then used to update the actual master file periodically. Figure 13-4 illustrates both immediate processing and memo updating of the master file under on-line entry/on-line processing.

FIGURE 13-3 • ON-LINE ENTRY/BATCH PROCESSING

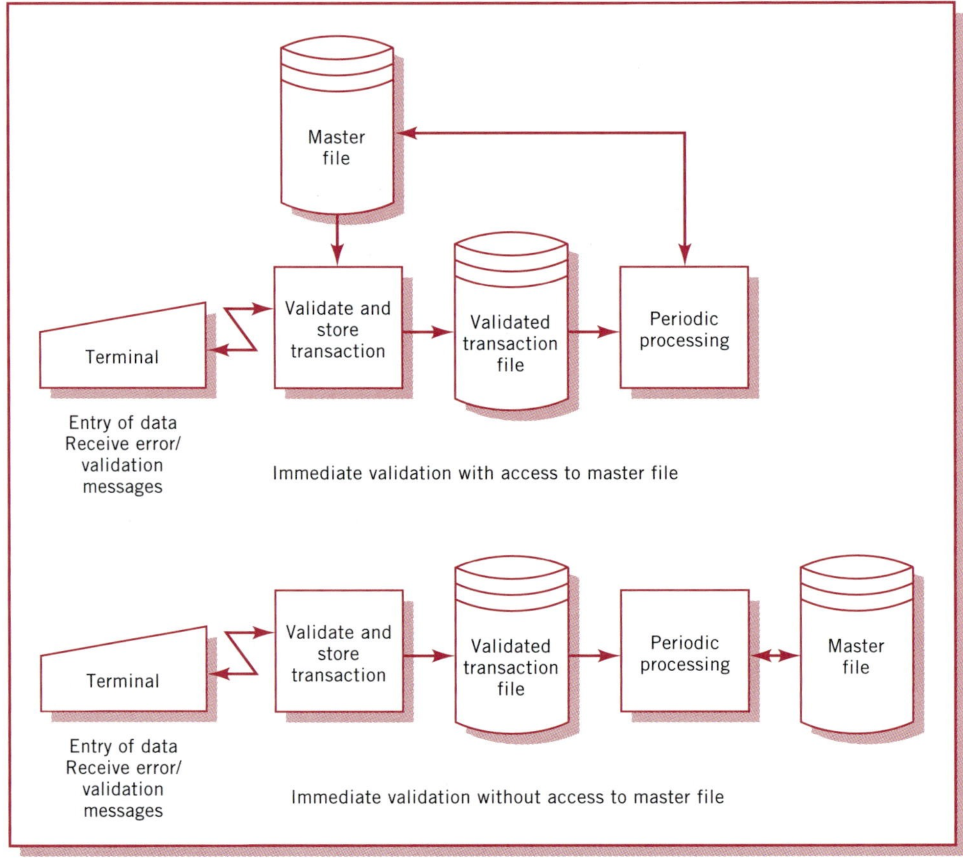

SOURCE: Gordon B. Davis, Donald L. Adams, and Carol A. Schaller, *Auditing and EDP,* Second Edition. New York: American Institute of Certified Public Accountants, 1983, pp. 147–148.

LEARNING CHECK:

13-1 a. What is the principal hardware component in an EDP system?
b. What hardware components are peripheral to the principal hardware component?

13-2 a. Explain the nature and functions of computer software.
b. Distinguish between systems programs and application programs.

13-3 a. Distinguish between the traditional file and database methods of organizing data.
b. Distinguish between sequential and direct access processing.

13-4 For each of the three methods of data processing, indicate (a) their essential characteristics and (b) an advantage and a disadvantage.

FIGURE 13-4 • ON-LINE ENTRY/ON-LINE PROCESSING

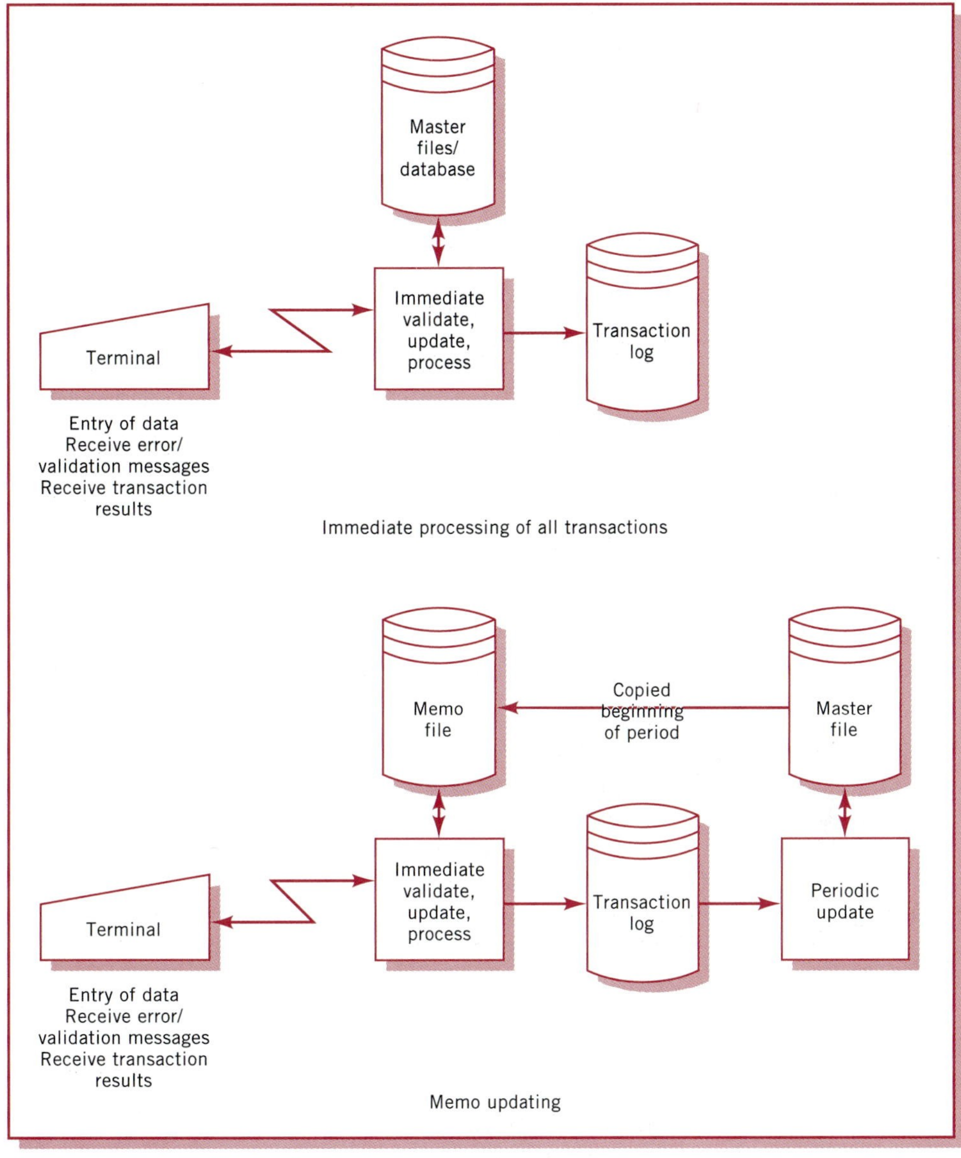

SOURCE: *Auditing and EDP,* p. 145.

KEY TERMS:

Application programs, p. 450
Batch entry/batch processing, p. 452
Database method, p. 452
Data organization methods, p. 451
Data processing methods, p. 452
On-line entry/batch processing, p. 452
On-line entry/on-line processing, p. 453
Systems programs, p. 449
Traditional file method, p. 451

EFFECTS OF EDP ON THE INTERNAL CONTROL STRUCTURE

Nearly all companies now use computers to some extent in their accounting systems. The extent of usage varies from one or two stand-alone applications, such as billing and payroll, to numerous applications fully integrated with the general ledger. The latter includes the capability to produce completely up-to-date, computer-generated financial statements on demand. In complex EDP systems, the computer may also initiate transactions. For example, the computer may automatically generate purchase orders when inventory quantities fall to preestablished reorder points. Moreover, using electronic data interchange (EDI) systems, a company's computer can use dial-up communications lines to electronically transmit purchase orders to suppliers' computers, eliminating the preparation and mailing of printed purchase orders. These systems can also electronically invoice customers' computers when goods are shipped.

ACCOUNTING IN CYBERSPACE

By the early 1990s, electronic data interchange (EDI) had made significant inroads into corporate accounting, being used to varying extents by about 75% of the Fortune 100 companies and 39% of the Fortune 500. The following examples were reported in the September 12, 1990 issue of the *Los Angeles Times:*

- Computers at over 3,000 suppliers to Chrysler accept purchase orders transmitted by computers at Chrysler assembly plants, and in turn electronically invoice Chrysler's computers for parts shipped.
- Texas Instruments electronically trades about 30 types of documents with more than 1,000 customers, suppliers, banks, and other entities.
- Wal-Mart, which operates the largest EDI program in the retail industry, processes about 75% of its payments to suppliers with EDI.

It was also reported that proponents claimed that EDI could cut in half the then estimated 7% of corporate spending absorbed by processing orders, sending invoices, and other administrative costs.

More recently, *The Wall Street Journal,* in its April 8, 1994 issue, reported that a consortium of 50 major players including Hewlett-Packard Co., Apple Computer Inc., Sun Microsystems Inc., Lockheed Corp., and BankAmerica Corp. were expected to launch what was believed to be the first large-scale effort to transact business on the Internet via a utility called CommerceNet. With over 25 million users on the Internet, the new service was designed to use encryption software to protect sensitive information such as credit card numbers and to allow for *authentication* of transacting parties.

Regardless of the extent of computerization or the methods of data processing being used, management is responsible for establishing and maintaining an appropriate internal control structure (ICS). Similarly, the auditor has the responsibility to obtain an understanding of the ICS for the EDP system sufficient to plan the audit and to determine the effects of the ICS on the nature, timing, and extent of tests to be performed. To meet this responsibility, and also be in compliance with the first general standard of the generally accepted auditing standards, the auditor must have adequate technical training and proficiency in EDP systems and computer auditing techniques. Such expertise may reside in the general audit staff member or one or more computer specialists assigned to an audit team. Moreover, in planning an audit for clients who use computer processing, SAS 22, *Planning and Supervision* (AU 311.09), states that the auditor should consider matters such as

- The extent to which the computer is used in each significant accounting application.
- The complexity of the client's computer operations, including the use of an outside service organization.
- The organizational structure of the computer processing activities.
- The availability of data in hard copy and computer-readable forms.
- The use of computer-assisted audit techniques to increase the efficiency of performing auditing procedures.

In the remainder of this section of the chapter, we first consider some of the differences between computer and manual processing that affect the ICS. We then examine the information processing controls used in an EDP system and how those controls relate to several of the ICS components studied in Chapter 8.

DIFFERENCES BETWEEN COMPUTER AND MANUAL PROCESSING

OBJECTIVE 3

Understand some of the major differences between computer and manual processing that affect internal control.

Following are some of the major differences between computer and manual processing that have an effect on the ICS:

- The EDP system may produce a transaction trail that is available for audit purposes for only a short period of time.
- There is often less documentary evidence of the performance of control procedures in computer systems than in manual systems.
- Information in manual systems is visible. In contrast, files and records in EDP systems are usually in machine-sensible form and cannot be read without a computer.
- The decrease of human involvement in EDP processing can obscure errors that might be observed in manual systems.
- Information in EDP systems may be more vulnerable to physical disaster, unauthorized manipulation, and mechanical malfunction than information in manual systems.
- Various functions may be concentrated in EDP systems, with a corresponding reduction in the traditional segregation of duties followed in manual systems.
- Changes in the system are often more difficult to implement and control in EDP systems than in manual systems.
- EDP systems can provide greater consistency in processing than manual systems because they uniformly subject all transactions to the same controls.

- More timely computer-generated accounting reports may provide management with more effective means of supervising and reviewing the operations of the company.

Although the last two items above are advantages of computer processing, the first seven items represent problems or risks that must be addressed by the ICS.

Traditionally, controls in an EDP system have been classified as *general controls* or *application controls.* These controls and their relationship to several of the ICS components identified in Chapter 8 are explained next.

GENERAL CONTROLS

OBJECTIVE 4

Explain the types of general and application controls used in EDP systems.

The following five types of **general controls** are widely recognized:

- Organization and operation controls.
- Systems development and documentation controls.
- Hardware and systems software controls.
- Access controls.
- Data and procedural controls.[1]

The common attribute of these controls is that they pertain to the EDP environment and all EDP activities as opposed to a single EDP application. Thus, these controls are pervasive in their effect. Each of the general controls is explained in a following section.[2]

Organization and Operation Controls

Organization and operation controls relate to the *management philosophy and operating style* and *organizational structure* control environment factors. In addition, these general controls pertain to the segregation of duties within the EDP department and between EDP and user departments. Weaknesses in these controls usually affect all EDP applications.

[1] Computer Services Executive Committee, Audit and Accounting Guide, *The Auditor's Study and Evaluation of Internal Control in EDP Systems.* New York: American Institute of Certified Public Accountants, 1977, p. 25.

[2] In Chapter 8, based on the proposed revision of SAS 55 (AU 319) general controls were identified as one category of information and processing controls in the control activities component of an ICS. However, the components of an ICS are not mutually exclusive. Some of these general controls relate closely to several of the factors identified with the control environment component or the information and communication component of an ICS. The Auditing Standards Board has noted that dividing the internal control structure into the five components facilitates discussion of its nature and how the auditor considers it in an audit. But it has further noted that the auditor's primary consideration is whether a specific aspect of the internal control structure affects financial statement assertions rather than its classification into any particular component.

FIGURE 13-5 • ORGANIZATION CHART OF AN EDP DEPARTMENT IN A LARGE COMPANY

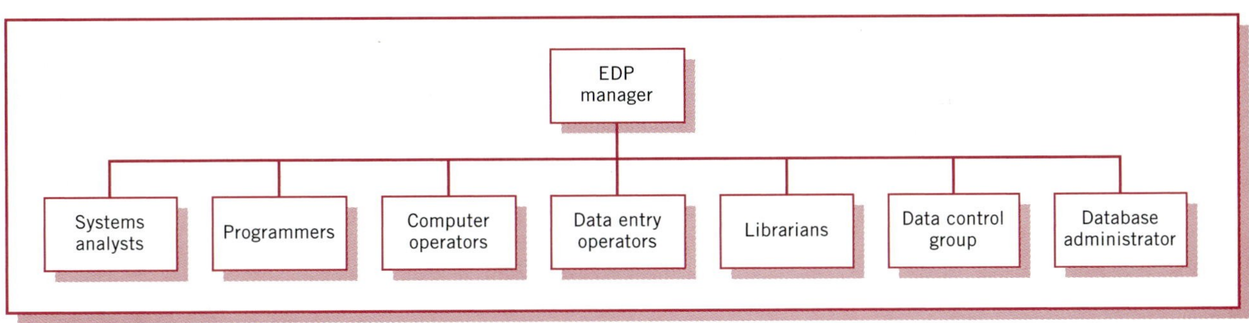

The organization structure shown in Figure 13-5 illustrates an arrangement that provides for clear-cut lines of authority and responsibility within the EDP department. The primary responsibilities for each position are as follows:

Position	Primary Responsibilities
EDP manager	Exercises overall control, develops short- and long-range plans, and approves systems.
Systems analyst	Evaluates existing systems, designs new systems, outlines the systems, and prepares specifications for programmers.
Programmer	Flowcharts logic of computer programs, develops and documents programs, and debugs programs.
Computer operator	Operates the computer hardware and executes the program according to operating instructions.
Data entry operator	Prepares data for processing by recording it on machine-readable media, e.g., by keying data onto magnetic tape. (Alternatively, data entry may be performed directly by individual user departments.)
Librarian	Maintains custody of systems documentation, programs, and files.
Data control group	Acts as liaison with user departments and monitors input, processing, and output.
Database administrator	Designs content and organization of the database and controls access to and use of the database.

In small installations, the positions of systems analysts and programmers may be combined. However, the combining of these two duties with the duties of the computer operator generally results in incompatible duties. When these three duties are performed by one individual, that person is in a position to both commit and conceal errors. A number of computer frauds have resulted when these duties were combined.

The EDP department should be organizationally independent of user departments. Thus, the EDP manager should report to an executive, such as the chief financial officer, who is not regularly involved in authorizing transactions for computer processing. In addition, EDP personnel should not correct errors unless they originate within EDP. For example, EDP should return a sales order with an invalid code number to sales for correction. Furthermore, EDP personnel should not authorize or initiate transactions or have custody of resulting assets. When the organizational plan does not provide for appropriate segregation of duties, the auditor may have serious doubts about the reliability of the results produced by the system.

Systems Development and Documentation Controls

Systems development and documentation controls are an integral part of the information and communication component of the ICS. Systems development controls relate to (1) review, testing, and approval of new systems; (2) control of program changes; and (3) documentation procedures. The following procedures are helpful in providing the necessary controls:

- Systems design should include representatives of user departments and, as appropriate, the accounting department and internal auditors.
- Each system should have written specifications that are reviewed and approved by management and the user department.
- Systems testing should be a cooperative effort of users and EDP personnel.
- The EDP manager, the database administrator, user personnel, and the appropriate level of management should give final approval to a new system before it is placed in normal operation.
- Program changes should be approved before implementation to determine whether they have been authorized, tested, and documented.[3]

Documentation controls pertain to the documents and records maintained by a company to describe computer processing activities. Adequate documentation is important to both management and the auditor. For management, documentation provides a basis for (1) reviewing the system, (2) training new personnel, and (3) maintaining and revising existing systems and programs. For the auditor, documentation provides the primary source of information about the flow of transactions through the system and the related accounting controls. Documentation includes

- Descriptions and flowcharts of the systems and programs.
- Operating instructions for computer operators.
- Control procedures to be followed by operators and users.
- Descriptions and samples of required inputs and outputs.

In database management systems, an important documentation control is the *data dictionary/directory*. The directory is software that keeps track of the definitions and locations of data elements in the database.

---

[3] Computer Services Executive Committee, *op. cit.*, pp. 30–34.

Hardware and Systems Software Controls

Modern computer technology has achieved a high degree of reliability in computer equipment. Contributing factors are the existence of **hardware and systems software controls** that are designed to detect any malfunctioning of the equipment. This category of controls includes the following:

- *Dual Read.* Input data are read twice, and the two readings are compared.
- *Parity Check.* Data are processed by the computer in arrays of bits (binary digits of 0 or 1). In addition to bits necessary to represent the numeric or alphabetic characters, a parity bit is added, when necessary, to make the sum of all the "1" bits always odd or even. As data are entered and ultimately transferred within the computer, the parity check is applied by the computer to assure that bits are not lost during the process.
- *Echo Check.* The echo check involves transmitting data received by an output device back to the source unit for comparison with the original data.
- *Read after Write.* The computer reads back the data after they have been recorded, either in storage or on the output device, and verifies the data by comparison with their original source.

To achieve maximum benefit from these controls, (1) there should be a program of preventive maintenance on all hardware and (2) controls over changes in systems software should parallel the systems development and documentation controls described above.

Access Controls

Access controls should prevent unauthorized use of EDP equipment, data files, and computer programs. The specific controls include both physical and procedural safeguards.

Access to computer hardware should be limited to authorized individuals, such as computer operators. Physical safeguards include the housing of the equipment in an area that is separate from user departments. Access to the area should be restricted by security guards, door locks, or special keys. Procedural safeguards involve management review of computer utilization reports.

Access to data files and programs should be designed to prevent unauthorized use of such data. Physical controls exist in the form of a library and a librarian. Access to program documentation and data files should be limited to individuals authorized to process, maintain, or modify particular systems. Ordinarily, the librarian keeps a log of the use of files and programs. Alternatively, under the database method of filing, the data dictionary software provides an automated log of access to programs and data elements.

In systems with on-line entry of data, many users have direct access to the CPU through remote input devices. Access often extends beyond company employees to outside agents and even to customers who have special keys, such as magnetic cards issued by banks, that activate the computer. To provide the necessary control, each user of a remote input device is given a key, code, or card that identifies the holder as an authorized user. Other access controls are (1) computer call-back procedures when the telephone is used to dial the computer and (2) passwords that are checked by the computer before a person can enter a transaction.

Data and Procedural Controls

Data and procedural controls provide a framework for controlling daily computer operations, minimizing the likelihood of processing errors, and assuring the continuity of operations in the event of a physical disaster or computer failure. These controls may be considered to be a part of the control activities component of the ICS.

The first two objectives are achieved through a control function performed by individuals or departments that are organizationally independent of computer operations. This responsibility is often assumed by the data control group within EDP. The control function involves

- Receiving and screening all data to be processed.
- Accounting for all input data.
- Following up on processing errors.
- Verifying the proper distribution of output.

The ability to maintain the continuity of computer operations involves (1) the use of off-premises storage for important files, programs, and documentation; (2) physical protection against environmental hazards; (3) formal record retention and recovery plans for data; and (4) arrangements for use of backup facilities at another location in the event of a disaster.

CPA Firm's Disaster Plan Saves Day

When a fire gutted the Philadelphia offices of Deloitte & Touche in February 1991, the office's minicomputer burned. Two weeks worth of internal accounting and time and billing data on the computer's disk drive were also lost. Fortunately, as part of D&T's disaster plan, every data file stored on the firm's forty-plus minicomputers is backed up on a daily basis and saved at the firm's national data center in Tennessee. Within 72 hours after the fire, a duplicate of the Philadelphia computer system was created by simply copying the backup files onto a new minicomputer. Officials estimated that good disaster planning probably saved the firm two weeks of recovery time.

Source: *Accounting Today*, April 8, 1991.

The ability to reconstruct data files is equally important. When sequential processing is used, a common method of records reconstruction is the **grandfather-father-son concept** illustrated in the top panel of Figure 13-6. Under this concept, the new updated master file is the son. The master file utilized in the updating run that produced the son is the father, and the previous master file is the grandfather. To update these earlier master files, records of transactions for the current and prior periods also must be retained. In the event that the current computer master file is destroyed, the system then has the capability to replace it. Ideally, the three generations of master files and the transaction files should be stored in separate locations to minimize the risk of losing all the files at one time. When direct access processing is used, the master file and transaction logs should be dumped, or copied, periodically to tape. In the event the on-line files are destroyed or damaged, these tapes may be used with a special recovery program to reconstruct the master file as illustrated in the lower panel of Figure 13-6.

FIGURE 13-6 • BACKUP AND RECOVERY FOR MAGNETIC TAPE AND DISK FILES

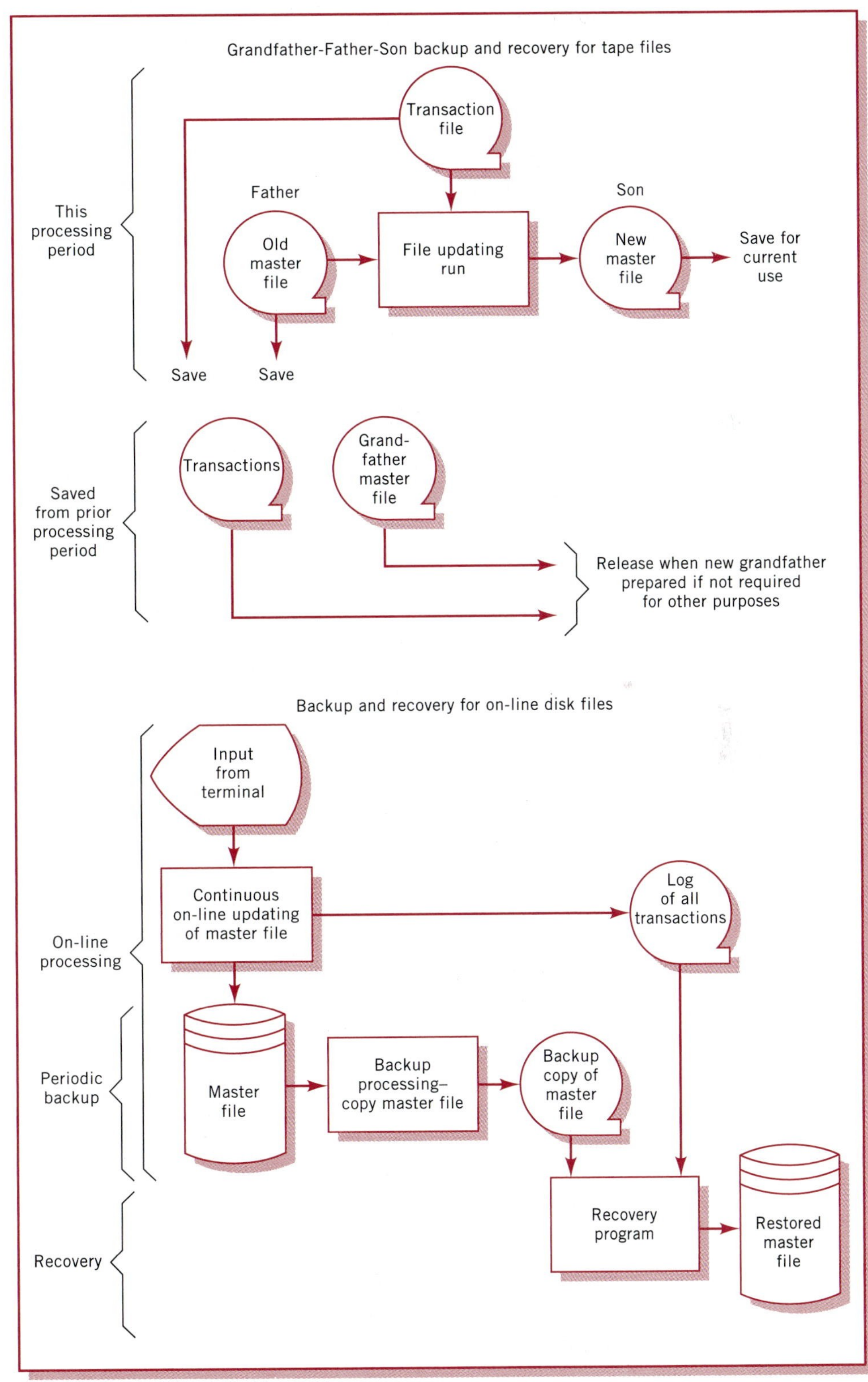

APPLICATION CONTROLS

The following three groups of **application controls** are widely recognized:

- Input controls.
- Processing controls.
- Output controls.

These controls are designed to provide reasonable assurance that the recording, processing, and reporting of data by EDP are properly performed for specific applications. Thus, the auditor must consider these controls separately for each significant accounting application such as billing customers and preparing payroll checks. These controls form part of the control activities component of an ICS.

Input Controls

Input controls are of vital importance in an EDP system because most of the errors occur at this point. Input controls are designed to provide reasonable assurance that data received for processing have been properly authorized and converted into machine-sensible form. These controls also include the rejection, correction, and resubmission of data that were initially incorrect.

AUTHORIZATION. Each transaction entry should be properly authorized and approved in accordance with management's general or specific authorization. When documents are individually processed, authorization is usually provided in the form of a signature or stamp on the source document; in contrast, when input data are assembled in batches, there ordinarily is user department approval of each batch of documents. In some cases, the computer performs the authorization function. For instance, a purchase requisition is automatically initiated when inventory quantities are reduced to a specified reorder level. Control here occurs after the fact by review of the output by the data control group or the user department.

CONVERSION OF INPUT DATA. Controls over the conversion of data into machine-sensible form are intended to ensure that the data are correctly entered and converted data are valid. Specific controls include

- *Verification Controls.* These include rekeying of all or a selected portion of the input data from the source document by a second person, with a comparison of the results.
- *Computer Editing.* These are computer routines that are intended to detect incomplete, incorrect, or unreasonable data. They include
  - *Missing data check* to assure that all required data fields have been completed and no blanks are present.
  - *Valid character check* to verify that only alphabetical, numerical, or other special characters appear as required in data fields.
  - *Limit (reasonableness) check* to determine that only data falling within predetermined limits are entered (e.g., time cards exceeding a designated number of hours per week may be rejected).
  - *Valid sign check* to determine that the sign of the data, if applicable, is correct.

  - *Valid code check* to match a classification (i.e., expense account number) or transaction code (i.e., cash receipts entry) against a master list of codes permitted for the type of transaction to be processed.
  - *Check digit* to determine that an account, employee, or other identification number has been correctly entered by applying a specific arithmetic operation to the identification number and comparing the result with the check digit.
- *Control Totals.* Also known as batch totals, these controls include
  - *Document or record counts,* which are the number of documents or records to be processed.
  - *Financial totals,* which are computed from source documents containing financial information.
  - *Hash totals,* which are computed by adding values that would not usually be added together (e.g., employee or product numbers, which sums have no meaning other than as a control device).

ERROR CORRECTION. The correction and resubmission of incorrect data are vital to the accuracy of the accounting records. For example, if processing of a valid sales invoice is stopped because of an error, accounts receivable and sales will both be understated until the error is eliminated and the processing completed. Errors should be corrected by those responsible for the mistake. Thus, errors in source documents should be corrected by user departments, whereas errors in conversion or movement of input data should be corrected by the EDP department. For control purposes, errors should be logged and their disposition should be periodically reviewed by the data control group.

Processing Controls

Processing controls are designed to provide reasonable assurance that the computer processing has been performed as intended for the particular application. Thus, these controls should preclude data from being lost, added, duplicated, or altered during processing.

Processing controls take many forms, but the most common are programmed controls incorporated into the individual applications software. They include the following:

- *Control Totals.* Provision for accumulating control totals is written into the computer program to facilitate the balancing of input totals with processing totals for each run. Similarly, run-to-run totals are accumulated to verify processing performed in stages.
- *File Identification Labels.* External labels are physically attached to magnetic tape or disks to permit visual identification of a file. Internal file labels are in machine-readable form and are matched electronically with specified operator instructions (or commands) incorporated into the computer program before processing can begin or be successfully completed.
- *Limit and Reasonableness Checks.* This control is the same as described earlier under computer editing.
- *Before-and-After Report.* This report shows a summary of the contents of a master file before and after each update.

- *Sequence Tests.* If transactions are given identification numbers (as in some direct-entry systems) or if records should be processed in a specific order, the transaction file can be tested for sequence, as well as for duplicate or missing items.
- *Process Tracing Data.* This control involves a printout of specific data for visual inspection to determine if the processing is correct. For evaluating changes in critical data items, tracing data may include the contents before and after the processing.

Output Controls

Output controls are designed to ensure that the processing result is correct and that only authorized personnel receive the output. The accuracy of the processing result includes both updated machine-sensible files and printed output. This objective is met by the following:

- *Reconciliation of Totals.* Output totals that are generated by the computer programs are reconciled to input and processing totals by the data control group and user departments.
- *Comparison to Source Documents.* Output data are subject to detailed comparison with source documents.
- *Visual Scanning.* The output is reviewed for completeness and apparent reasonableness. Actual results may be compared with estimated results.

Control over the distribution of output is usually maintained by the data control group. Special care should be exercised by this group over the distribution of confidential output. To facilitate control over the disposition of output, systems documentation should include a report distribution sheet.

LEARNING CHECK:

13-5 Indicate five characteristics that distinguish computer processing from manual processing.

13-6 a. Identify five types of general controls and state their common attribute.
b. Identify the customary positions in an EDP department and the primary applications of segregation of duties in EDP.

13-7 a. What are documentation controls in an EDP department?
b. Why is documentation important to management and the auditor?
c. What items should be included in documentation for an EDP department?

13-8 a. Explain the purposes and nature of access controls.
b. Enumerate the access controls that may be used in an on-line entry system.

13-9 a. Indicate the scope of data and procedural controls.
b. Describe the activities of a data control group.

13-10 a. Indicate the purpose of each of the three types of application controls.
b. Identify the categories of controls pertaining to the conversion of data.

KEY TERMS:

Access controls, p. 461
Application controls, p. 464
Data and procedural controls, p. 462
General controls, p. 458
Grandfather-father-son concept, p. 462
Hardware and systems software controls, p. 461
Input controls, p. 464
Organization and operation controls, p. 458
Output controls, p. 466
Processing controls, p. 465
Systems development and documentation controls, p. 460

METHODOLOGY FOR MEETING THE SECOND STANDARD OF FIELD WORK

The methodology for meeting the second standard of field work in an EDP system is conceptually the same as in a manual system. The effects of an EDP system on the steps in obtaining an understanding of the ICS and assessing control risk are explained in the following sections.

OBTAINING AN UNDERSTANDING OF THE ICS

OBJECTIVE 5

Indicate the level of understanding of the internal control structure needed in an EDP system.

When EDP is used in significant accounting applications, the auditor should obtain an understanding of the EDP control structure sufficient to plan the audit. The understanding should extend to all five control structure components and include both general controls and application controls. As in a manual system, the auditor is concerned with both the design of the EDP controls and whether they have been placed in operation.

The nature and extent of the procedures to be performed to obtain an understanding of EDP controls varies with the size and complexity of the EDP system, and with the preliminary audit strategy adopted for specific assertions affected by an EDP application. Procedures will be more extensive when the auditor has adopted the lower assessed level of control risk strategy than under the primarily substantive approach.

In microcomputer applications, the auditor may obtain the understanding by inquiry of personnel, observation of computer operations, and inspection of the output produced by the computer. In mainframe applications, it is usually necessary for the auditor also to review documentation, including flowcharts and manuals. In advanced EDP systems, the auditor may need the assistance of an EDP specialist. The inspection of exception reports, or *error listings,* generated by the computer as a result of control procedures enables the auditor to determine whether the controls have been placed in operation.

The auditor should obtain sufficient knowledge of the EDP system to understand

- The classes of transactions in the entity's operations that are processed by the EDP system and that are significant to the financial statements.

- The accounting records, supporting documents, machine-readable information, and specific accounts in the financial statements involved in the EDP processing and reporting of these significant classes of transactions.
- How the computer is used to process data, from the initiation of the transaction to its final inclusion in the financial statements.
- The types of potential misstatements that could occur.

FIGURE 13-7 • INTERNAL CONTROL QUESTIONNAIRE—EDP GENERAL CONTROLS

Internal Control Questionnaire

Question	Yes, No, N/A	Comments
ORGANIZATION AND OPERATION CONTROLS		
1. Are the following duties segregated within the EDP department:		
a. Systems design?		
b. Computer programming?		
c. Computer operations?		
d. Data entry?		
e. Custody of systems documentation, programs, and files?		
f. Data control?		
2. Are the following duties performed only outside the EDP department:		
a. Initiation and authorization of transactions?		
b. Authorization of changes in systems, programs, and master files?		
c. Preparation of source documents?		
d. Correction of errors in source documents?		
e. Custody of assets?		
SYSTEMS DEVELOPMENT AND DOCUMENTATION CONTROLS		
1. Is there adequate participation by users and internal auditors in new systems development?		
2. Is proper authorization, testing, and documentation required for systems and program changes?		
HARDWARE AND SYSTEMS SOFTWARE CONTROLS		
1. Are built-in hardware and systems software controls adequate to detect equipment malfunctions?		
2. Are systems software changes properly authorized, tested, and documented?		
ACCESS CONTROLS		
1. Is access to computer facilities restricted to authorized personnel?		
2. Is access to data files and programs restricted to authorized personnel by librarian?		
DATA AND PROCEDURAL CONTROLS		
1. Is there a data control function that controls data input, processing, and output?		
2. Is there a disaster contingency plan to ensure continuity of operations?		
3. Is there off-premises storage of backup files and programs?		

The auditor's understanding of the EDP control structure should be documented in the working papers. Generally, the extent of the documentation will vary directly with the size and complexity of the control structure. As in a manual control structure, documentation may be in the form of completed questionnaires. Representative lists of questions for general controls and application controls are illustrated in Figures 13-7 and 13-8.

ASSESSING CONTROL RISK

The process of assessing control risk is the same in an EDP control structure as in a manual structure. Thus, it is necessary in an EDP structure to (1) consider the knowledge acquired from procedures to obtain an understanding, (2) identify

FIGURE 13-8 • INTERNAL CONTROL QUESTIONNAIRE—APPLICATION CONTROLS

Internal Control Questionnaire

Question	Yes, No, N/A	Comments
INPUT CONTROLS		
1. Are input data:		
a. Initiated and authorized in user departments?		
b. Screened by the data control group?		
2. Is the accuracy of data conversion ensured by the use of:		
a. Verification controls?		
b. Computer editing?		
c. Control totals?		
3. Do error correction procedures include:		
a. Maintenance of error logs?		
b. Returning erroneous source documents to user departments for correction?		
c. Follow-up by the data control group?		
PROCESSING CONTROLS		
1. Is assurance that appropriate files are processed and updated obtained by:		
a. External file labels?		
b. Internal file labels?		
2. Is reasonable assurance that data are not lost, added, duplicated, or altered during processing provided by:		
a. Control tools?		
b. Limit and reasonableness checks?		
c. Sequence tests?		
OUTPUT CONTROLS		
1. Is the accuracy of output checked by reconciliation of control totals by:		
a. The data control group?		
b. User departments?		
2. Is the distribution of output to only authorized users assured by:		
a. Report distribution control sheets?		
b. Data control group monitoring?		

potential misstatements that may occur in assertions, (3) identify control procedures necessary to prevent or detect such misstatements, (4) perform tests of controls, and (5) evaluate the evidence and make the assessment.

Figures 13-9 and 13-10 show representative listings of potential misstatements and necessary controls for general controls and application controls, respectively. It will be recalled that these data are developed from the auditor's knowledge of the client acquired from procedures to obtain an understanding and computer aids or checklists provided by the auditing firm, adapted to the client.

FIGURE 13-9 • CONTROL RISK ASSESSMENT CONSIDERATIONS FOR EDP GENERAL CONTROLS

Potential Misstatements	Necessary Controls	Possible Tests of Controls
ORGANIZATION AND OPERATION CONTROLS		
Computer operators may modify programs to bypass programmed controls.	Segregation of duties within EDP for computer programming and computer operations.	Observe segregation of duties within EDP.
EDP personnel may initiate and process unauthorized transactions.	Segregation of duties between user departments and EDP for initiating and processing transactions.	Observe segregation of duties between user departments and EDP.
SYSTEMS DEVELOPMENT AND DOCUMENTATION CONTROLS		
Systems designs may not meet the needs of user departments or auditors.	Participation of personnel from user departments and internal audit in designing and approving new systems.	Inquire about participants in designing new systems; examine evidence for approval of new systems.
Unauthorized program changes may result in unanticipated processing errors.	Internal verification of proper authorization, testing, and documentation of program changes before implementation.	Examine evidence of internal verification; trace selected program changes to supporting documentation.
HARDWARE AND SYSTEMS SOFTWARE CONTROLS		
Equipment malfunctions may result in processing errors.	Built-in hardware and systems software controls to detect malfunctions.	Examine hardware and systems software specifications.
Unauthorized changes in system software may result in processing errors.	Approval and documentation of all systems software changes.	Examine evidence of approval and documentation of changes.
ACCESS CONTROLS		
Unauthorized users may gain access to EDP equipment.	Physical security of EDP facilities; management review of utilization reports.	Inspect security arrangements and utilization reports.
Data files and programs may be processed or altered by unauthorized users.	Use of a library, librarian, and logs to restrict access and monitor usage.	Inspect facilities and logs.
DATA AND PROCEDURAL CONTROLS		
Errors may be made in inputting or processing data or distributing output.	Use of a data control group responsible for maintaining control over data input, processing, and output.	Observe operation of data control group.
Continuity of operations may be disrupted by a disaster such as a fire or flood.	Contingency plan including arrangements for use of off-premises backup facilities.	Examine contingency plan.
Data files and programs may be damaged or lost.	Storage of backup files and programs off premises; provision for reconstruction of data files.	Examine storage facilities; evaluate file reconstruction capability.

FIGURE 13-10 • CONTROL RISK ASSESSMENT CONSIDERATIONS FOR EDP APPLICATION CONTROLS

Potential Misstatements	Necessary Controls	Possible Tests of Controls
INPUT CONTROLS		
Data for unauthorized transactions may be submitted for processing.	Authorization and approval of data in user departments; screening of data by data control group.	Examine source documents and batch transmittals for evidence of approval; observe data control group.
Valid data may be incorrectly converted to machine-sensible form.	Verification (rekeying); computer editing; control totals.	Observe data verification procedures; use test data to test edit routines; examine control total reconciliations.
Errors on source documents may not be corrected and resubmitted.	Maintenance of error logs; return to user department for correction; follow-up by data control group.	Inspect logs and evidence of follow-up by data control group.
PROCESSING CONTROLS		
Wrong files may be processed and updated.	Use of external and internal file labels.	Observe use of external file labels; examine documentation for internal file labels.
Data may be lost, added, duplicated, or altered during processing.	Use of control totals; limit and reasonableness checks; sequence tests.	Examine evidence of control total reconciliations; use test data.
OUTPUT CONTROLS		
Output may be incorrect.	Reconciliation of totals by data control group and user departments.	Examine evidence of reconciliations.
Output may be distributed to unauthorized users.	Use of report distribution control sheets; data control group monitoring.	Inspect report distribution control sheets; observe data control group monitoring.

It will be recalled that tests of controls are performed to obtain evidence as to the effectiveness of the design or operation of a control. The auditor performs such tests when there is reason to believe the evidence obtained will permit a further reduction in the assessed level of control risk, and when the evidence can be obtained in a cost-efficient manner. Column 3 of Figures 13-9 and 13-10 shows possible tests of controls. The auditor will know whether the necessary controls have been designed and placed in operation from the understanding of the EDP control structure.

In a computerized system, some control procedures may be performed by the computer. When the computer produces visible evidence to verify that the procedures were in operation and to evaluate the propriety of performance, tests of EDP controls may pertain to the inspection of documentation as in a manual system. However, if such evidence is not generated by the computer, the tests of the controls must be done by computer-assisted audit techniques.

TESTS OF CONTROLS WITHOUT THE COMPUTER

Testing controls without the computer, also known as **auditing around the computer,** is similar to testing controls in a manual control structure. This type of testing occurs when the processing applications are well documented and sufficient printed output exists, or can be generated by the client. Auditing without the computer offers the following advantages:

- The auditor can use familiar auditing procedures in performing the tests.
- Recourse to the complexities of computer programs is unnecessary.

The principal disadvantages of auditing around the computer are not utilizing the capabilities of the computer in gathering audit evidence, and not realizing possible cost savings in audit time and effort.

Because general controls are pervasive in their effect, these controls should be tested before application controls are tested. Most general controls can be tested for effectiveness without using the computer. For example, all of the possible tests of controls shown in Figure 13-9 can be done manually.

Similarly, all the possible tests of input and output controls shown in Figure 13-10, except those pertaining to computer editing, are performed without the computer. However, auditing by testing input and output instead of the computer processing itself does not enable the auditor to detect program errors that do not show up in the output reports. Although error listings provide evidence that some controls are functioning, they do not reveal missing controls. The auditor must rely on user department and output controls to compensate for any missing processing controls.

TESTS OF CONTROLS WITH THE COMPUTER

OBJECTIVE 6

State the types of computer-assisted audit techniques used in performing tests of controls.

Testing controls with the computer, also known as **auditing through the computer,** involves the use of computer-assisted audit techniques. These tests are used extensively in testing input validation routines (computer editing) and programmed processing controls. The auditor may find that using the computer in tests of controls is advantageous when

- A significant part of the internal controls is embodied in a computer program.
- There are significant gaps in the visible transaction trail.
- There are large volumes of records to be tested.

The major disadvantages of testing with the computer are the special knowledge and skills required, and the possible disruption of the client's EDP operations while the auditor uses the EDP equipment, programs, and files.

Three computer-assisted audit techniques widely used to test the operation of specific programmed application controls are parallel simulation, test data, and integrated test facility.

Parallel Simulation

In **parallel simulation,** actual company data are reprocessed using an auditor-controlled software program. This method is so named because the software is designed to reproduce or simulate the client's processing of real data. A graphic portrayal of this approach is shown in the left half of Figure 13-11.

Parallel simulation may be performed at different times during the year under audit, and it may also be applied to the reprocessing of historical data. This approach does not contaminate client files, and it may be conducted at an independent computer facility.

This approach has the following advantages:

- Because real data are used, the auditor can verify the transactions by tracing them to source documents and approvals.
- The size of the sample can be greatly expanded at relatively little additional cost.
- The auditor can independently run the test.

If the auditor decides to use parallel simulation, care must be taken to determine that the data selected for simulation are representative of actual client transactions. It is also possible that the client's system may perform operations that are beyond the capacity of the auditor's software.

Test Data

Under the **test data approach,** dummy transactions are prepared by the auditor and processed under auditor control by the client's computer program. The test data consist of one transaction for each valid or invalid condition the auditor wishes to test. For example, payroll test data may include both a valid and an invalid overtime pay condition. The output from processing the test data is then compared with the auditor's expected output to determine whether the controls

FIGURE 13-11 • PARALLEL SIMULATION VERSUS TEST DATA APPROACH

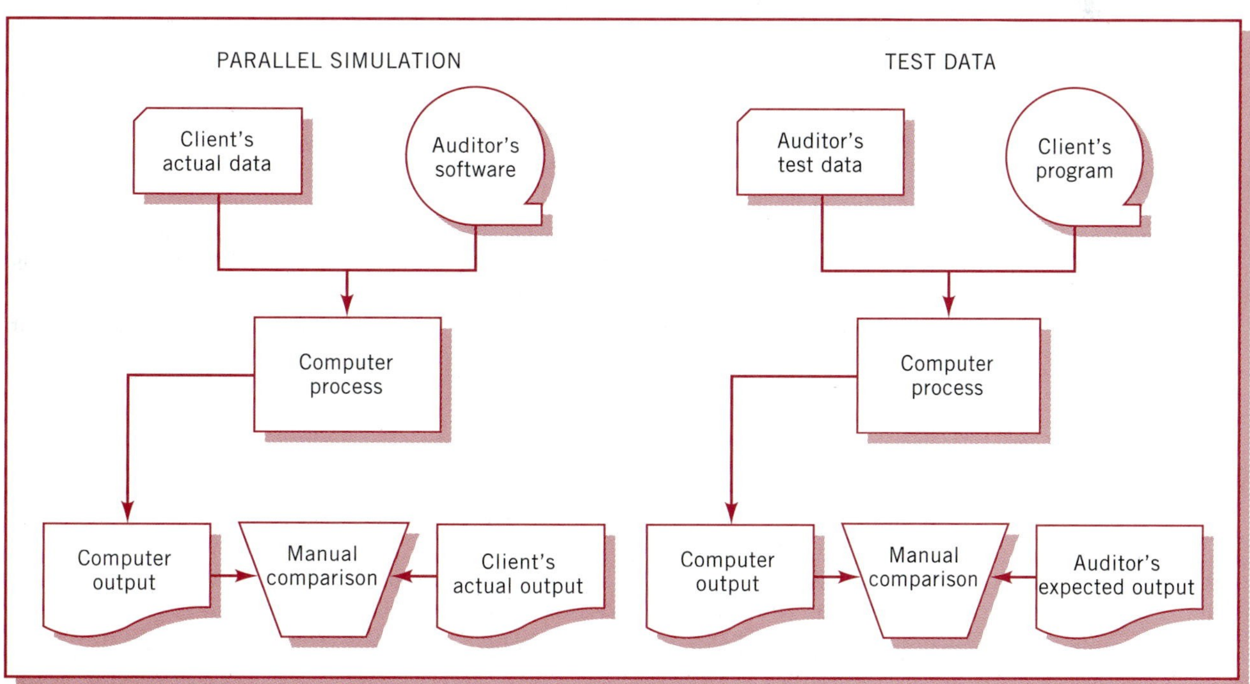

are operating effectively. This approach to testing is relatively simple, quick, and inexpensive. However, the method has the following major audit deficiencies:

- The client's program is tested only at a specific point in time rather than throughout the audit period.
- The method is a test of only the presence and functioning of controls in the program tested.
- There is no examination of documentation actually processed by the system.
- Computer operators know that test data are being run, which could reduce the validity of the output.
- The scope of the test is limited by the auditor's imagination and knowledge of the controls within the application.

A graphic portrayal of the test data approach is shown in the right half of Figure 13-11.

Integrated Test Facility

The **integrated test facility (ITF) approach** requires the creation of a small subsystem (a minicompany) within the regular EDP system. This may be accomplished by creating dummy master files or appending dummy master records to existing client files. Test data, specially coded to correspond to the dummy master files, are introduced into the system together with actual transactions. The test data should include all kinds of transaction errors and exceptions that may be encountered. In this manner, the test data are subjected to the same programmed controls as the actual data. For the subsystem, or dummy files, a separate set of outputs is produced. The results can be compared with those expected by the auditor.

The ITF method has as a disadvantage the risk of potentially creating errors in client data. In addition, modification may be necessary to the client's programs to accommodate the dummy data.

Comparison of Approaches

The primary differences between the parallel simulation and test data approaches are shown in Figure 13-11. The comparison of the output under each approach is done manually by the auditor. The integrated test facility technique combines features of each of these methods as both test data and actual transactions are processed simultaneously.

Irrespective of the choice among these three methods of testing the effectiveness of programmed controls, the procedures performed are analogous to the manual procedure of tracing transactions through all or selected components of the client's control structure to determine the existence and effectiveness of selected internal controls. Unlike the manual case, however, the procedures are performed by the computer and leave no visible trail. Only in the case of a transaction that does not satisfy a specific control incorporated into the program will an error message be generated.

TESTS OF CONTROLS IN ON-LINE ENTRY/ON-LINE PROCESSING

It is possible to use test data to test controls in an on-line entry/on-line processing system (also known as an on-line real-time [OLRT] system). However, this approach is not widely used by auditors because of the contamination of file data and the difficulty of reversing the hypothetical data. Parallel simulation may also be used, but the availability of generalized audit software that can be used to simulate an OLRT processing system is very limited.

In lieu of traditional testing, the auditor often arranges for **continuous monitoring** of the system. Under this technique, an audit routine is added to the client's processing programs. Transactions entering the system are sampled at random intervals, and the output from the routine is used in testing the controls.

To provide for the integration of audit software into an OLRT processing system, **audit hook** capabilities must be built into the client's computer programs—both the operating and application programs—at the time they are created. Audit hooks are points in a program that allow *audit modules,* or programs, to be integrated into the system's normal processing activities. These audit modules provide the auditor with a means of selecting transactions possessing characteristics of interest to the auditor, such as a transaction of a certain kind, or an amount greater or lesser than a given value. Once a particular transaction has been identified as being of interest, a record of it can be retained by one of several methods. Two of these methods are tagging transactions and audit logs.

Tagging Transactions

Tagging transactions involves placing an indicator, or tag, on selected transactions. The presence of this tag enables a transaction to be traced through the system as it is being processed. The system must be programmed to provide for the creation of hard-copy printout of all paths followed by the transaction. Data with which the tagged transaction interacts at designated steps in the processing can be captured as well.

Audit Log

An **audit log,** sometimes called a **systems control audit review file (SCARF),** is a record of certain processing activities. The log is used to record events that meet auditor specified criteria as they occur at designated points in the system. Identified transactions or events are written onto a file available only to the auditor. The auditor can later print or use other techniques to analyze the file and make further tests as appropriate.

LEARNING CHECK:

13-11 What knowledge of the EDP system should the auditor acquire in obtaining an understanding?

13-12 a. Under what circumstances can tests of controls be performed without the use of the computer?

b. What are the advantages and disadvantages of auditing around the computer?

13-13 a. Under what circumstances may it be advantageous to test controls with the computer?

b. What are the disadvantages of auditing through the computer?

13-14 What are the advantages and disadvantages of the computer-assisted audit technique known as parallel simulation?

13-15 a. What is the difference between the conventional test data approach and the integrated test facility approach?

b. In lieu of traditional testing, what approaches can be used in on-line entry/on-line processing systems?

KEY TERMS:

Auditing around the computer, p. 471
Auditing through the computer, p. 472
Audit hook, p. 475
Audit log, p. 475
Continuous monitoring, p. 475
Integrated test facility (ITF) approach, p. 474
Parallel simulation, p. 472
Systems control audit review file (SCARF), p. 475
Tagging transactions, p. 475
Test data approach, p. 473

OTHER CONSIDERATIONS

When EDP is used for significant accounting transactions, the auditor has an opportunity to use audit software packages in the audit. Audit software has been developed for a wide variety of applications including both tests of controls and substantive tests. It may also be necessary for the auditor to consider the effects on the examination of microcomputer systems and computer service centers.

GENERALIZED AUDIT SOFTWARE

OBJECTIVE 7

Explain the nature and uses of generalized audit software.

One common type of audit software in use today is known as **generalized audit software.** This software is adaptable for use by auditors with client EDP files produced under a variety of data organization and processing methods. Thus, it is transportable from one client to another. Until recently, these packages were very costly to develop and maintain. However, they are now available at moderate cost from software vendors, the AICPA, and CPA firms who market their own internally developed packages. Depending on the application, one or more of the following distinct phases may be involved in using audit software packages:

- Identifying the audit objective and the tests to be performed.
- Determining the feasibility of using a software package with the client's system.
- Designing the application, which may include the logic, calculations, and form of the output.
- Coding and testing the application, including preparation of standard forms and keying the information.

- Processing of the application on actual client file data and reviewing the results.

The use of generalized audit software enables the auditor to deal effectively with large quantities of data. This may permit the accumulation of either the same quantity of evidence at less cost compared with performing an examination without the computer, or more evidence at an economical cost. Its use also permits the auditor to place less reliance on the client's EDP personnel. The use of generalized audit software in auditing is limited only by the availability of client data files and the auditor's ingenuity. The software may be designed to perform nearly any of the auditing procedures that an auditor might perform manually.

Generalized audit software can be used in both tests of controls and substantive tests. Examples of the former include a comparison of prices on a computerized file of sales invoices to a master file of authorized prices to determine the frequency of use of unauthorized prices, and a comparison of the detail of charges to customer accounts with authorized credit file data to determine the frequency with which credit was granted in excess of authorized limits. In both cases, the software would be used to produce exception reports. Some examples of substantive testing applications are explained in the following sections.

Selecting and Printing Audit Samples

The computer can be programmed to select audit samples according to whatever criteria are specified by the auditor. These samples can be used for a variety of purposes. Individual customer accounts receivable accounts may be selected for confirmation, or the auditor may be interested in obtaining a listing of all items over a certain dollar amount. The samples selected may be based on multiple criteria. In the case of confirmation requests, the computer may also be used to print the confirmation letter as well as the envelope. A more comprehensive discussion of the use of confirmations in performing substantive tests of accounts receivable is presented in Chapter 14.

Testing Calculations and Making Computations

Another common use of the computer is to test the accuracy of computations in machine-readable data files. Tests of extensions, footings, or other computations may be performed. Inventory quantities may be extended by a unit cost and the amount of the inventory recalculated; individual customer accounts receivable records may be individually footed and a total of all accounts prepared. If client files contain sufficient information, the recalculation of certain year-end adjusting entries also may be possible. Because of the speed with which computer processing is performed, recomputations can be performed on a more extensive basis than is practicable in a manual system.

Summarizing Data and Performing Analyses

The auditor frequently desires to have the client data reorganized in a manner that will suit a special purpose. For instance, the auditor may want to determine slow-moving inventory items, debit balances in accounts payable, or past-due accounts receivable. Similarly, in performing analytical procedures, the auditor may utilize the computer to compute desired ratios and other comparative data.

Comparing Audit Data with Computer Records

Audited data resulting from work performed by the auditor may be compared with information in the computer records. The audited data must, of course, first be converted into machine-readable form. Test counts made by the auditor of inventory quantities on hand may be compared with the quantity shown on the perpetual inventory record or the quantity determined by the company as the result of a physical inventory count.

MICROCOMPUTER-BASED AUDIT SOFTWARE

OBJECTIVE 8

Explain the auditing implications of microcomputer-based audit software, expert systems, small computer systems, and computer service organizations.

The increasing power and portability of the microcomputer is revolutionizing how audits are being performed. Many software packages, with a variety of capabilities, are available. Unlike the *generalized audit software* described before, these microcomputer-based packages are user friendly and menu driven, with capabilities useful in both the execution and administration of the audit. If the audit client utilizes a microcomputer system, the microcomputer-based audit software may provide the auditor with the ability to read and analyze client data files.

Examples of common applications of **microcomputer-based audit software** packages include

- Preparation of a trial balance and financial statements.
- Preparation of lead schedules and working papers.
- Generation of audit programs for tests of controls and substantive tests.
- Performance of analytical procedures.
- Preparation of standardized audit correspondence such as engagement letters, confirmations, and audit reports.
- Performance of engagement administrative tasks such as preparation of the time budget, recording time worked, and tabulating observance of audit deadlines.

These applications offer the potential for reducing clerical time in an engagement and increasing the productivity of the audit staff.

Increasingly, auditors are using portable microcomputers to perform the same tasks as formerly done with generalized audit software operating on mainframe computers. With the increased memory, processing speeds, and disk-drive capacity available on today's microcomputers, the auditor can download substantial amounts of file data from the client's mainframe to the microcomputer. Proprietary software or purchased utility software can then be used to perform each of the tasks described in the previous sections on generalized audit software.

EXPERT SYSTEMS

An **expert system** is a computer model that incorporates the knowledge of human experts to assist others in performing functions or making decisions. The models are developed by carefully studying and modeling the decision processes used by experts in arriving at a decision or judgment. Once developed, the expert system software uses prompts to elicit data from users, and processes the data according to patterns used by the experts. Such models are emerging in audit practice to assist auditors in making higher quality, more uniform judgments in such difficult areas as

- Determining planning materiality.
- Assessing inherent and control risks including identifying potential misstatements, necessary controls, and possible tests of controls.
- Developing audit programs for tests of controls and substantive tests tailored to the auditor's risk specifications.

Many professionals believe the further development of these systems holds considerable potential for improving the quality of audit practice.

SMALL COMPUTER SYSTEMS

The decade of the 1980s witnessed the widespread proliferation of **small computer systems.** These systems may be used as stand-alone computers, or they may be linked in networks. The distinction once made between two classes of these computers, minicomputers and microcomputers, is no longer precise. Some of today's "supermicros" with high-speed processing chips, large hard disk storage capacity, and data communications abilities rival minicomputers in their serviceability.

Minicomputers may be used to process a particular accounting application such as inventories or several applications comprising an integrated general ledger package in large- and medium-sized businesses. In these businesses, microcomputers are often used as personal productivity tools to prepare special analyses rather than to process routine accounting applications. Accounting applications, or even an integrated general ledger package, however, may be maintained on a microcomputer in a small business. The audit considerations when mini- and microcomputers are used to process accounting data are similar.

Internal Control Structure Considerations

Both of the two categories of EDP controls discussed earlier in the chapter are relevant to small computer systems. However, the characteristics of these systems may limit the applicability of specific controls.

General controls may be weak because of

- *Lack of Segregation of Duties between the EDP Department and Users.* In many cases, the user can initiate and authorize transactions and control both the processing and distribution of the output.
- *Location of the Computer.* In many systems, the computer is located in the user department. As a result, there may be weaknesses in access controls that may result in improper use or manipulation of data files and unauthorized modifications of computer programs.

- *Lack of Segregation of Duties within the EDP Department.* Because of the limited number of personnel in the EDP department, the functions of programming and operations may not be separated.
- *Limited Knowledge of EDP.* Personnel in the EDP department may have limited experience and knowledge of computers. Thus, systems may not meet management's objectives, and the review and approval of new programs by such individuals may be ineffective.[4]

The application controls described earlier for large systems are equally important in small systems. Areas that may require special consideration in small computer systems are as follows:

- *Data Entry.* Because data are entered directly into the system through terminals, more importance is attached to controls over original source data and the detection of errors at the time of entry.
- *Data Processing.* Controls to prevent the processing of wrong files may not exist. To compensate for this weakness, greater emphasis must be placed on external file labels.
- *Absence of Limit and Reasonableness Tests.* Most systems use purchased software packages that may not contain these tests, or the tests provided may not be useful to the user. More emphasis on controls over original source documents may help to compensate for this weakness.[5]

Meeting the Second Standard of Field Work

The auditor's responsibility for meeting the second standard of field work is not affected by the size of the computer system. When EDP is used in significant accounting applications, the auditor must consider the EDP controls. As explained above, general controls are often weak in a small computer environment. Thus, the auditor may find it more cost effective to concentrate on application controls. With due recognition of weaknesses in general controls, the auditor should be able to anticipate errors and irregularities that could occur in specific EDP applications. In some cases, EDP application controls and manual controls may be sufficient to provide a basis for assessing control risk below the maximum. When this does not occur, the auditor will be required to assess control risk at the maximum level and design expanded substantive tests in completing the audit.

The testing of controls involves the same techniques described earlier for large computer systems. Special considerations, however, may be required in planning the tests due to the number of data records that can be retained on magnetic media in small systems, and the limited time period the audit trail can be retained.

COMPUTER SERVICE ORGANIZATIONS

A **computer service organization** is an entity that provides EDP services for other entities referred to as user organizations. Computer service organizations include,

---

[4] Computer Services Guidelines, *Audit and Control Considerations in a Minicomputer or Small Business Computer Environment.* New York: American Institute of Certified Public Accountants, 1981, pp. 3–5 (adapted).

[5] Gordon B. Davis, Donald L. Adams, and Carol A. Schaller, *Auditing and EDP,* Second Edition. New York: American Institute of Certified Public Accountants, 1983, p. 299 (adapted).

for example, *EDP service centers* that process transactions and related data for others, *bank trust departments* that invest and hold assets for employee benefit plans, and *mortgage bankers* that service mortgages for others. When a service organization is used, it affects the independent auditor's consideration of the user organization's internal control structure because the user organization's financial statements are subjected to policies and procedures of the service organization that are, at least in part, physically and operationally separate from the user organization. In such cases, the user organization's auditors (hereafter, user auditors) should consider the significance of the involvement of the service organization based on such factors as the nature and materiality of the transactions processed by the service organization and the degree of interaction between the user and service organizations' control policies and procedures.

The use of a service organization may affect the availability of evidence to the auditor of the user organization for obtaining an understanding of the internal control structure, assessing control risk, and determining substantive tests. SAS 70, *Reports on the Processing of Transactions by Service Organizations* (AU 324) makes the following observations concerning evidence:

- **Obtaining an Understanding.** In obtaining an understanding, the user auditor may consider all of the following sources of evidence:
  - Information in the user organization's possession about the service organization's policies and procedures such as system overviews and manuals and related reports by the service organization's external or internal auditors, the user organization's internal auditors, or regulatory authorities. For example, the service organization's external auditors (hereafter, service auditors) may issue a *report on policies and procedures placed in operation* intended to meet the needs of the user auditors of all the service organization's customers (AU 324.09).
  - Information acquired from (1) the service organization by special request, (2) procedures performed by the service auditors at the user auditor's request, or (3) procedures performed at the service organization by the user auditor (AU 324.10).
- **Assessing Control Risk.** When the user auditor seeks support for an assessed level of control risk below the maximum, evidence about the effectiveness of relevant controls should be obtained from one or more of the following (AU 324.12):
  - Tests of the *user organization's controls* over the activities of the service organization (for example, the user auditor may test the user organization's independent reperformance of selected items processed by an EDP service center or test the user organization's reconciliation of output reports with source documents).
  - A service auditor's report on (1) *policies and procedures placed in operation and tests of operating effectiveness* or (2) the application of agreed-upon procedures that describes relevant tests of controls.
  - Appropriate tests of controls performed by the user auditor at the service organization.
- **Performing Substantive Tests.** The results of substantive tests performed by service auditors either (1) as agreed upon by the user organization and its auditor and the service organization and its auditor or (2) pursuant to requirements imposed by governmental authorities may be used by user auditors as part of the evidence necessary to support their opinions (AU 324.17).

Before relying on a service auditor's report, the user auditor should make inquiries of appropriate sources, such as the AICPA, state society of CPAs, and other professionals, concerning the service auditor's professional reputation. Additional information on the responsibilities of service auditors and on the types of reports they render to meet the needs of user auditors is presented in Chapter 21.

LEARNING CHECK:

13-16 a. What is generalized audit software?
b. Explain how generalized audit software can be used in (1) tests of controls and (2) substantive tests.

13-17 a. What is microcomputer-based audit software?
b. Identify several common applications of this software.

13-18 a. What is an expert system?
b. Indicate several areas in which expert systems may be used in auditing.

13-19 a. Identify four circumstances that may cause weaknesses in general controls in small computer systems.
b. Indicate three areas pertaining to application controls that may require special consideration by the auditor in small computer systems.
c. What approach may be followed in the study and evaluation of internal control in a small computer system?

13-20 a. Describe the types of computer service organizations that may be used by an entity.
b. Indicate the effects of service organizations on the auditor's consideration of the ICS.

KEY TERMS:

Computer service organization, p. 480
Expert system, p. 478
Generalized audit software, p. 476
Microcomputer-based audit software, p. 478
Small computer systems, p. 479

SUMMARY

EDP systems usually have a significant effect on an entity's ICS. In such cases, the auditor must have adequate technical training and proficiency in EDP systems, including a knowledge of EDP system components and relevant general and application controls. The methodology in meeting the second standard of field work is conceptually the same as in a manual system. However, in performing tests of controls and substantive tests, the auditor may use computer-assisted audit techniques using either mainframe or microcomputer-based audit software. The further development of expert systems by auditors holds considerable potential for improving the quality of audit practice. The auditor should be aware of the characteristics of small computer systems that may limit the applicability of specific controls. An entity's use of a computer service organization to process transactions and related data requires the user auditor to consider the significance of the involvement of the service organization, and the effects on evidence available for obtaining an understanding of the ICS, assessing control risk, and performing substantive tests.

BIBLIOGRAPHY

AICPA Professional Standards:

AU 319, Consideration of the Internal Control Structure in a Financial Statement Audit.

SAS 70 (AU 324), Reports on the Processing of Transactions by Service Organizations.

IAU 6 (AU8006A), Risk Assessment and Internal Control—EDP Characteristics and Considerations.

IAU 6 (AU8006B), Audit Considerations Relating to Entities Using Service Organizations.

IAU 15 (AU 8015), Auditing in an EDP Environment.

IAU 16 (AU 8016), Computer-Assisted Audit Techniques.

International Statements on Auditing:

(AU 10,010), EDP Environments—Stand-Alone Microcomputers.

(AU 10,020), EDP Environments—On-Line Computer Systems.

(AU 10,030), EDP Environments—Database Systems.

Computer Auditing Subcommittee, *Auditing Procedure Study: Auditing With Computers.* New York: American Institute of Certified Public Accountants, 1994.

Computer Auditing Subcommittee, *Auditing Procedure Study: Consideration of the Internal Control Structure in a Computer Environment: A Case Study.* New York: American Institute of Certified Public Accountants, 1991.

Computer Services Guidelines, *Audit and Control Considerations in a Minicomputer or Small Business Computer Environment.* New York: American Institute of Certified Public Accountants, 1981.

Davis, Gordon, B., Adams, Donald L., and Schaller, Carol A. *Auditing and EDP,* Second Edition. New York: American Institute of Certified Public Accountants, 1983.

Essinger, J. "Fraud Prevention Is the Priority," *Accountancy* (September 1991), pp. 64–66.

Ewer, Sid R., Willis, Harold E., and Nichols, Richard L. "How Safe Are Your Data Transmissions?" *Journal of Accountancy* (September 1993), pp. 66–70.

Gillett, Peter. "Automated Dynamic Audit Programme Tailoring: An Expert System Approach," *Auditing: A Journal of Practice and Theory* (Supplement 1993), pp. 173–189.

Houle, Y. "Why Client's Computers Are an Ongoing Concern," *CA Magazine* (July 1989), pp. 50–52.

IT Section, *Audit and Security Issues with Expert Systems.* Jersey City, NJ: American Institute of Certified Public Accountants, 1992.

Jacobson, Scott D., and Wolfe, Christopher. "Auditing with Your Microcomputer," *Journal of Accountancy* (February 1990), pp. 70–78.

Sadgwani, A., Kim, I., and Helmerci, J. "EDI's Effects on Internal Controls," *EDPACS* (July 1989), pp. 1–11.

Vahtera, P. "Electronic Data Interchange: The Auditor's Slant," *EDPACS* (November 1991), pp. 1–14.

OBJECTIVE QUESTIONS

Indicate the *best* answer for each of the following multiple choice questions.

13-21 These questions pertain to the ICS in an EDP system.

1. Internal control is ineffective when computer department personnel
   a. Participate in computer software acquisition decisions.
   b. Design documentation for computerized systems.
   c. Originate changes in master files.
   d. Provide physical security for program files.

2. Which of the following computer documentation would an auditor most likely utilize in obtaining an understanding of the ICS?
   a. Systems flowcharts.
   b. Record counts.
   c. Program listings.
   d. Record layouts.

3. Which of the following most likely constitutes a weakness in the ICS of an EDP system?
   a. The control clerk establishes control over data received by the EDP department and reconciles control totals after processing.
   b. The application programmer identifies programs required by the systems design and flowcharts the logic of these programs.
   c. The systems analyst reviews output and controls the distribution of output from the EDP department.
   d. The accounts payable clerk prepares data for computer processing and enters the data into the computer.

4. One of the steps in assessing control risk in an EDP control system is identifying necessary controls to prevent data from being lost, added, duplicated, or altered during processing. An example of this type of control is the
   a. Authorization and approval of the data in user departments and screening of data by data control groups.
   b. Review of data output by data control groups.
   c. Use of external and internal file labels.
   d. Use of control totals, limit and reasonableness checks, and sequence tests.

5. Which of the following is *not* a major reason why an accounting audit trail should be maintained for a computer system?
   a. Query answering.
   b. Deterrent to irregularities.
   c. Monitoring purposes.
   d. Analytical procedures.

13-22 These questions relate to tests of EDP controls.

1. Which of the following computer-assisted auditing techniques allows fictitious and real transactions to be processed together without client operating personnel being aware of the testing process?
   a. Parallel simulation.
   b. Generalized audit software programming.
   c. Integrated test facility.
   d. Test data approach.

2. An auditor may decide not to perform tests of controls related to the control procedures within the EDP portion of the client's ICS. Which of the following would *not* be a valid reason for choosing to omit tests of controls?
   a. The controls duplicate operative controls existing elsewhere in the structure.
   b. There appear to be major weaknesses that would preclude the control from preventing errors or irregularities.
   c. The time and dollar costs of testing exceed the time and dollar savings in substantive testing if the tests show the controls to be effective.
   d. The controls appear adequate.

3. When an auditor tests a computerized accounting system, which of the following is true of the test data approach?
   a. Test data must consist of all possible valid and invalid conditions.
   b. The program tested is different from the program used throughout the year by the client.
   c. Several transactions of each type must be tested.
   d. Test data are processed by the client's computer programs under the auditor's control.

4. A primary advantage of using generalized audit software packages to audit the financial statements of a client that uses an EDP system is that the auditor may
   a. Consider increasing the use of substantive tests of transactions in place of analytical procedures.
   b. Substantiate the accuracy of data through self-checking digits and hash totals.
   c. Reduce the level of required tests of controls to a relatively small amount.
   d. Access information stored on computer files while having a limited understanding of the client's hardware and software features.

COMPREHENSIVE QUESTIONS

13-23 **(Organization of EDP department)** The plan of organization is an important aspect of an EDP activity.

REQUIRED

a. Diagram an appropriate structure for an EDP department.
b. Briefly describe the primary responsibilities of each individual or group identified in the diagram.
c. Indicate the conditions in an EDP structure that would result in incompatible functions.

13-24 **(General and application controls)** Two categories and eight types of EDP controls are identified in the chapter. Listed below are a number of specific control procedures.

1. EDP manager reports to chief financial officer.
2. Backup files.
3. Written approval of all program changes.
4. Physical controls for data files and programs.
5. Batch controls.
6. Reconciliation of output totals.
7. File identification labels.
8. Echo checks.
9. Limit and reasonableness checks.
10. Record counts.

REQUIRED

a. Indicate the category and type of control to which each procedure pertains.
b. Identify and explain one other control procedure for each of the eight types.

13-25 **(General and application controls)** When auditing an EDP system, the independent auditor should have a general familiarity with the effects of the use of EDP on the various characteristics of internal control and on the auditor's consideration of such controls. The independent auditor must be aware of those control procedures that are commonly referred to as "general" controls and those that are commonly referred to as "application" controls. General controls relate to all EDP activities, and application controls relate to specific accounting tasks.

REQUIRED

a. What are the general controls that should exist in an EDP internal control structure?
b. What are the purposes of each of the following categories of application controls?
   1. Input controls.
   2. Processing controls.
   3. Output controls.

AICPA

13-26 **(Application controls)** In the design and operation of an information system, three types of controls must be addressed—managerial controls, internal controls, and data or application controls. Managerial controls and internal controls are not unique to computer-based information systems. However, data or application controls are more specific to computer-based systems. Although many controls can be useful at more than one stage, specific data controls are usually categorized as input, processing, or output controls.

REQUIRED

a. Explain the general purpose of
   1. Input controls.
   2. Processing controls.
   3. Output controls.
b. Define and identify the objective of each of the following input controls:
   1. Hash totals.
   2. Limit checks.
   3. Check digits.
c. Define and identify the objective of each of the following processing controls:
   1. Sequence checks.
   2. File identification.
   3. Operating logs.
d. Define and identify the objective of the following output control:
   1. Review by knowledgeable parties.

ICMA (adapted)

13-27 **(Application controls)** A well-designed management information system using EDP equipment will include methods of assuring that the data are appropriate to the situation and are accurate.

REQUIRED

a. Describe procedures that should exist to assure that the input data are accurate and appropriate.
b. Describe procedures that would assure that all data were processed and processed properly.
c. Describe procedures that would assure that the output data are accurate and appropriate.

ICMA

13-28 **(Input validation or edit checks)** Talbert Corporation hired an independent computer programmer to develop a simplified payroll application for its newly purchased computer. The programmer developed an on-line, databased microcomputer system that minimized the level of knowledge required by the operator. It was based on typing answers to input cues that appeared on the terminal's viewing screen, examples of which follow:

a. Access routine:
   1. Operator access number to payroll file?
   2. Are there new employees?

b. New employees routine:
   1. Employee name?
   2. Employee number?
   3. Social security number?
   4. Rate per hour?
   5. Single or married?
   6. Number of dependents?
   7. Account distribution?
c. Current payroll routine:
   1. Employee number?
   2. Regular hours worked?
   3. Overtime hours worked?
   4. Total employees this payroll period?

The independent auditor is attempting to verify that certain input validation (edit) checks exist to ensure that misstatements resulting from omissions, invalid entries, or other inaccuracies will be detected during the typing of answers to the input cues.

REQUIRED

Identify the various types of input validation (edit) checks the independent auditor would expect to find in the EDP system. Describe the assurances provided by each identified validation check. Do not discuss the review and evaluation of these controls.

AICPA

13-29 **(General controls)** You are performing an audit of the EDP function of a chemical company with about $150 million in annual sales. In obtaining an understanding of the ICS, you discover the following points:

1. The EDP manager reports to the director of accounting, who in turn reports to the controller. The controller reports to the treasurer, who is one of several vice presidents in the company. The EDP manager has made several unsuccessful requests to the director of accounting for another printer.
2. There is no written charter for the EDP function, but the EDP manager tells you that the primary objective is to get the accounting reports out on time.
3. Transaction tapes are used daily to update the master file and are then retired to the scratch tape area.
4. A third-generation computer with large disk capacity was installed three years ago. The EDP activity previously used a second-generation computer, and many of the programs written for that computer are used on the present equipment by means of an emulator.
5. You observe that the output from the computer runs is written on tape for printing at a later time. Some output tapes from several days' runs are waiting to be printed.
6. The EDP manager states that the CPU could handle at least twice the work currently being processed.

REQUIRED

a. Identify the defect inherent in each of the six conditions shown above.
b. Briefly describe the probable effect if the condition continues.
   Note: On your answer sheet, show the defect, followed immediately by the probable effect, for each condition.

IIA (adapted)

13-30 **(General controls, potential misstatements, and tests of controls)** In considering the ICS for the Aliva Company, Joan Davies, CPA, develops an internal control questionnaire for EDP general controls that includes the following questions:

1. Is there adequate segregation of duties between programmers and computer operators?
2. Is access to computer facilities restricted to authorized personnel?
3. Are systems software changes properly authorized, tested, and documented?
4. Is there a disaster contingency plan?
5. Is there a data control function to control input and output processing?
6. Is the initiation and authorization of transactions done outside the EDP department?
7. Is there proper authorization, testing, and documentation for systems and program changes?
8. Is access to data files and programs restricted to authorized users?
9. Are hardware and systems software controls adequate to detect equipment malfunctions?
10. Is there adequate participation by users and internal auditors in new systems development?
11. Is the correction of source documents done by user departments?
12. Is there off-premises storage of backup files and programs?

Required

a. Identify the category of general controls to which each question pertains.
b. Indicate a possible misstatement that could occur, assuming a No answer to each question.
c. Identify a possible test of controls, assuming a Yes answer to each question. (Present your answers in tabular form using a separate column for each part.)

13-31 **(Necessary application controls/tests of controls)** In auditing the financial statements of the Marshall Company, you discover the following misstatements in the application controls of the company's EDP system:

1. Valid data were incorrectly converted to machine-sensible form.
2. Output data did not agree with original source documents.
3. Processing errors were made on valid input data.
4. The wrong file was processed and updated.
5. Output was distributed to unauthorized users.
6. Erroneous input data from a user department was corrected and processed by the EDP department.
7. Input data were processed twice during handling.
8. Unauthorized input data were processed.
9. Erroneous input data from a user department were returned for correction but were not resubmitted for processing.

Required

a. Identify the application control function (input, processing, or output) that is relevant to each error or irregularity.
b. Identify a control that could have prevented each misstatement.
c. Identify a possible test of controls for each necessary control identified in part (b). (Present your answers in tabular form using separate columns for each part.)

13-32 **(Auditing around versus through the computer)** CPAs may audit "around" or "through" computers in examining financial statements of clients who use computers to process accounting data.

Required

a. Describe the auditing approach referred to as auditing "around" the computer.
b. Under what conditions does the CPA decide to audit "through" the computer instead of "around" the computer?
c. In auditing "through" the computer, the CPA may use test data.

1. What are test data?
2. Why does the CPA use test data?

d. How can the CPA become satisfied that the computer program tapes presented by the client are actually being used to process its accounting data?

AICPA

13-33 **(Controls in an on-line real-time system)** You have been engaged by Central Savings and Loan Association to audit its financial statements for the year ended December 31, 19X1. The CPA who audited the financial statements at December 31, 19X0, rendered an unqualified opinion.

In January 19X1, the Association installed an on-line real-time computer system. Each teller in the association's main office and seven branch offices has an on-line input-output terminal. Customer's mortgage payments and savings account deposits and withdrawals are recorded in the accounts by the computer from data input by the teller at the time of the transaction. The teller keys the proper account by account number and enters the information in the terminal keyboard to record the transaction. The accounting department at the main office also has direct access to the computer via on-line terminals. The computer is housed at the main office.

In addition to servicing its own mortgage loans, the association acts as a mortgage servicing agency for three life insurance companies. In this latter activity, the association maintains mortgage records and serves as the collection and escrow agent for the mortgagees (the insurance companies), who pay a fee to the Association for these services.

REQUIRED

You would expect the association to have certain internal controls in effect because an on-line real-time computer system is employed. List the internal controls that should be in effect solely because this EDP system is employed, classifying them as

a. Those controls pertaining to input of information.
b. All other types of computer controls.

AICPA (adapted)

13-34 **(Evaluation of general and application controls)** George Beemster, CPA, is auditing the financial statements of the Louisville Sales Corporation, which recently installed a new mainframe computer. The following comments have been extracted from Mr. Beemster's notes on computer operations and the processing and control of shipping notices and customer invoices:

1. To minimize inconvenience, Louisville converted without change its existing data processing system, which utilized obsolete equipment. The computer company supervised the conversion and has provided training to all computer department employees (except data entry operators) in systems design, operations, and programming.
2. Each computer run is assigned to a specific employee, who is responsible for making program changes, running the program, and answering questions. This procedure has the advantage of eliminating the need for records of computer operations because each employee is responsible for his own computer runs.
3. At least one computer department employee remains in the computer room during office hours, and only computer department employees have keys to the computer room.
4. System documentation consists of those materials furnished by the computer company—a set of record formats and program listings. These and the tape library are kept in a corner of the computer department.
5. The corporation considered the desirability of programmed controls but decided to retain the manual controls from its existing system.

6. Corporation products are shipped directly from public warehouses, which forward shipping notices to general accounting. There, a billing clerk enters the price of the item and accounts for the numerical sequence of shipping notices from each warehouse. The billing clerk also prepares daily adding machine tapes ("control tapes") of the units shipped and the unit prices.
7. Shipping notices and control tapes are forwarded to the computer department for data entry and processing. Extensions are made on the computer. Output consists of invoices (in six copies) and a daily sales register. The daily sales register shows the aggregate totals of units shipped and unit prices, which the computer operator compares with the control tapes.
8. All copies of the invoice are returned to the billing clerk. The clerk mails three copies to the customer, forwards one copy to the warehouse, maintains one copy in a numerical file, and retains one copy in an open invoice file that serves as a detailed accounts receivable record.

REQUIRED

a. Describe weaknesses in internal control over information and data flows and the procedures for processing shipping notices and customer invoices, and recommend improvements in these controls and processing procedures. Organize your answer sheets as follows:

Weakness	Recommended Improvement

b. Indicate which of the five categories of general controls or three categories of application controls is applicable to each weakness.

AICPA (adapted)

13-35 **(Use of microcomputer-based audit software)** Microcomputer software has been developed to improve the efficiency and effectiveness of the audit. Electronic spreadsheets and other software packages are available to aid in the performance of auditing procedures otherwise performed manually.

REQUIRED

Describe the potential benefits to an auditor of using microcomputer software in an audit compared with performing an audit without the use of a computer.

AICPA

CASE

13-36 **(Evaluation of EDP controls)** You have been assigned to the annual audit of Explosives, Inc. You contact the senior, Bob Good, as instructed and arrange a date to discuss the client and the current year's audit.

At your meeting with Good, the company and the current year's audit were discussed. During the discussion, Good emphasized that he wanted to take a good look at the data processing (DP) department. He had attended the firm's one-week course on computer auditing and felt strongly about the need for such review.

On the eighth day of the job, Bob received word that his immediate attention was needed on another job. He had performed most of the work on the DP department and wants you to complete it. Good left the following working papers to help you:

General Background

The DP department has evolved from a strictly batch entry/batch processing operation and currently uses a mix of tape and on-line disk processing methods. The department is under the supervision of Gus Sampson, who has worked in it since its inception. He reports to the controller.

The department is located on the third floor of the east office wing. It shares office space with the research department and the general accounting department. The machines, however, are physically separated from the other departments by glass doors. The chemical mixing department is located just below on the second floor. The first floor houses the plant personnel department, various conference rooms, and other administrative offices.

The DP department services corporate accounting, the local plant, and three other plant locations elsewhere in the country. The department recently upgraded its computer.

Within the DP department, there are three groups each with specific duties:

1. Data entry.
2. Systems analysis.
3. Programming and operations.

Each group has its own supervisor who reports to the DP manager.

Computer Room Operations

All the machine operators know the jobs they run quite well and have the knowledge to make changes in the operating procedures and programs when they encounter difficulties. This has greatly increased efficiency as less time is lost due to machine halts caused by program interruptions. Gus stated that because of the operators' familiarity with the various jobs, he does not have to devote much time to supervising them.

When asked about operating manuals for the operators, Gus replied it would be a waste of time to prepare them because the operators are so familiar with the programs and jobs. If a problem develops, an operator can simply look at a source program listing and make the necessary correction. Gus said he seldom reviewed any console sheets because of the confidence he had in his operators. He complained, however, about the accounting people always giving him bad data and then complaining about the output. "GIGO is the rule," he said.

During my tour of the computer room with Gus, I noticed that reels of tape, some with labels and some without, were in file racks, on tables, on top of equipment, and in the corner of the floor. In another corner, I noticed open boxes of various forms and payroll checks. I had expected to see only two or three operators in the computer room, but there were five or six people in it. When I asked Gus about these conditions, he said he had read all the books and publications on controlling the computer room and felt most of the alleged dangers were exaggerated. He trusted his employees and felt his shop was one of the best in the area. As for the additional people, he felt that too many people are mystified by the computer. Consequently, he maintains an open door policy so people can come in and see "what the monster is all about."

Programming Group

Information about this group was obtained from Betty James, the head programmer, who reports to Gus Sampson. The members of this group mainly write new programs and maintain current programs, about 75% of which were written years ago using an earlier generation programming language. These programs are currently being rewritten in a more modern and efficient language for use on the upgraded computer.

Documentation for the old programs and some of the new ones consists of source listings. The old programs were written by Gus, Betty, and a fellow who has left the company.

Because Gus and Betty are still around, there has not been any need to prepare additional documentation. Betty said, however, that Gus has been thinking about developing documentation standards for all programs.

Betty mentioned numerous problems have arisen lately due to an operator or programmer making an undocumented "patch" in a program so the job can be run. Sometimes, the change causes other errors to occur. Gus has attempted to stop the operators from making changes, but with the programs being accessible to everyone, it has been impossible to enforce.

REQUIRED

a. Draw an organization chart of the EDP department.
b. For each of the eight EDP controls mentioned in the chapter, discuss (1) the weaknesses in the ICS of Explosives, Inc., and (2) your recommendations for improvement.

RESEARCH QUESTIONS

13-37 **(Computer fraud)** Through the years there have been a number of widely publicized audit failures involving computer fraud. Perform a search of an electronic database or printed media to identify any one case of computer fraud and read the related articles or other sources found in your search. Prepare a brief report (3–5 pages) on the issues involved in the case. Include any particulars relative to the alleged deficiencies in the audit or audits involved.

13-38 **(Auditing Procedures Study)** After this chapter went to press in 1994, the AICPA issued a new *Auditing Procedures Study (APS)* titled *Auditing with Computers.* If you can obtain access to this document, scan the contents and compare it with the contents of this chapter. Identify any areas covered in the *APS* either not covered in the chapter or covered significantly more extensively in the *APS.* Prepare a brief report (3–5) pages summarizing the material found in the *APS* but not in the chapter.

PART

4

AUDITING THE TRANSACTION CYCLES

CHAPTER

14

AUDITING THE REVENUE CYCLE

LEARNING OBJECTIVES

After studying this chapter, you should be able to

1. Describe the nature of the revenue cycle and the transaction classes and accounts involved.
2. Identify transaction class and account balance audit objectives for the revenue cycle.
3. Apply the concepts of materiality, risk, and audit strategy to the revenue cycle.
4. Explain the applicability of relevant aspects of the internal control structure components to the revenue cycle.
5. Discuss considerations applicable to assessing control risk for credit sales transactions.
6. Discuss considerations applicable to assessing control risk for cash receipts and sales adjustments transactions.
7. Indicate the factors involved in determining the acceptable level of detection risk for accounts receivable assertions.

NATURE OF THE REVENUE CYCLE
- AUDIT OBJECTIVES
- MATERIALITY, RISK, AND AUDIT STRATEGY
- CONSIDERATION OF INTERNAL CONTROL STRUCTURE COMPONENTS

CONTROL ACTIVITIES—CREDIT SALES TRANSACTIONS
- COMMON DOCUMENTS AND RECORDS
- FUNCTIONS
- OBTAINING THE UNDERSTANDING AND ASSESSING CONTROL RISK

CONTROL ACTIVITIES—CASH RECEIPTS TRANSACTIONS
- COMMON DOCUMENTS AND RECORDS
- FUNCTIONS
- OBTAINING THE UNDERSTANDING AND ASSESSING CONTROL RISK

CONTROL ACTIVITIES—SALES ADJUSTMENTS TRANSACTIONS

SUBSTANTIVE TESTS OF ACCOUNTS RECEIVABLE
- DETERMINING DETECTION RISK
- DESIGNING SUBSTANTIVE TESTS
- INITIAL PROCEDURES
- ANALYTICAL PROCEDURES
- TESTS OF DETAILS OF TRANSACTIONS
- TESTS OF DETAILS OF BALANCES
- COMPARISON OF STATEMENT PRESENTATION WITH GAAP

SUMMARY

BIBLIOGRAPHY

OBJECTIVE QUESTIONS

COMPREHENSIVE QUESTIONS

CASES

RESEARCH QUESTIONS

This is the first of five chapters pertaining to auditing the transaction cycles. This chapter begins with an explanation of the nature and importance of the revenue cycle. Then attention is given to internal control matters pertaining to the major classes of transactions within the cycle. The chapter concludes with a discussion of substantive tests of accounts receivable balances.

NATURE OF THE REVENUE CYCLE

An entity's **revenue cycle** consists of the activities relating to the exchange of goods and services with customers and to the collection of the revenue in cash. Different entities have different sources of revenue. For example, merchandising

8. Design and execute an audit program for substantive tests to achieve specific audit objectives for accounts receivable.
9. Explain the use of confirmation procedures in auditing accounts receivable.

OBJECTIVE 1

Describe the nature of the revenue cycle and the transaction classes and accounts involved.

and manufacturing companies have sales; doctors, attorneys, and CPAs have fees; theaters, sports arenas, and amusement parks have admissions; banks and financial institutions have interest and dividends; and mass transit companies have fares. The discussions and illustrations in this chapter are based on a merchandising company. However, much of the commentary can easily be adapted to other types of entities.

For a merchandising company, the classes of transactions in the revenue cycle include (1) credit sales, (2) cash receipts (collections on account and cash sales), and (3) sales adjustments (discounts, returns and allowances, and uncollectible accounts [provisions and write-offs]). These transactions affect the following accounts:

- Sales
- Accounts receivable
- Cost of sales
- Inventory
- Cash
- Sales discounts
- Sales returns and allowances
- Bad-debts expense
- Allowance for uncollectible accounts

Three of these accounts, cost of sales, inventory, and cash, are also affected by transaction classes in other cycles. Accordingly, coverage of the audit of these accounts is deferred to later chapters. Of the remaining accounts, attention is focused in this chapter on meeting the audit objectives for accounts receivable, including the related allowance for uncollectible accounts.

AUDIT OBJECTIVES

OBJECTIVE 2

Identify transaction class and account balance audit objectives for the revenue cycle.

The audit objectives for the revenue cycle relate to obtaining sufficient competent evidence about each significant financial statement assertion that pertains to revenue cycle transactions and balances. It will be recalled from Chapter 5 that specific audit objectives are derived from the five categories of management's assertions. Several specific audit objectives derived in this manner for the transaction classes and account balances pertaining to the revenue cycle are shown in Figure 14-1. The objectives shown are not intended to be all-inclusive for all client situations. Rather, they represent the primary objectives that would apply to most merchandising clients selling on credit, and they are the objectives that are addressed in detail in this chapter. Consistent with the scope of coverage described in the preceding paragraph, the account balance objectives selected for illustration are limited primarily to accounts receivable.

To achieve each of these specific audit objectives, the auditor employs various parts of the audit planning and audit testing methodology described in Parts 2 and 3 of this text (Chapters 5 through 13). Page references to key topics and figures in those chapters are provided at appropriate points in this chapter to facilitate your review should you find it necessary. In addition, the application of this methodology to the revenue cycle is keyed to the numbered specific audit objectives (**EO1, EO2 . . . C1 . . . VA4,** . . . and so on) in Figure 14-1. *As is*

FIGURE 14-1 • SELECTED SPECIFIC AUDIT OBJECTIVES FOR THE REVENUE CYCLE

Assertion Category	Transaction Class Audit Objectives	Account Balance Audit Objectives
Existence or occurrence	Recorded sales transactions represent goods shipped during the period **(EO1).** Recorded cash receipts transactions represent cash received during the period **(EO2).** Recorded sales adjustment transactions during the period represent authorized discounts, returns and allowances, and uncollectible accounts **(EO3).**	Accounts receivable representing amounts owed by customers exists at the balance sheet date **(EO4).**
Completeness	All sales **(C1),** cash receipts **(C2),** and sales adjustment **(C3)** transactions that occurred during the period have been recorded.	Accounts receivable includes all claims on customers at the balance sheet date **(C4).**
Rights and obligations	The entity has rights to the receivables **(RO1)** and cash **(RO2)** resulting from recorded revenue cycle transactions.	Accounts receivable at the balance sheet date represents legal claims of the entity on customers for payment **(RO3).**
Valuation or allocation	All sales **(VA1),** cash receipts **(VA2),** and sales adjustment **(VA3)** transactions are correctly journalized, summarized, and posted.	Accounts receivable represents gross claims on customers at the balance sheet date and agrees with the sum of the accounts receivable subsidiary ledger **(VA4).** The allowance for uncollectible accounts represents a reasonable estimate of the difference between gross receivables and their net realizable value **(VA5).**
Presentation and disclosure	The details of sales **(PD1),** cash receipts **(PD2),** and sales adjustment **(PD3)** transactions support their presentation in the financial statements including their classification and related disclosures.	Accounts receivable are properly identified and classified in the balance sheet **(PD4).** Appropriate disclosures have been made concerning accounts receivable that have been assigned or pledged **(PD5).**

explained further later, achieving the transaction class audit objectives also contributes to achieving the account balance audit objectives.

MATERIALITY, RISK, AND AUDIT STRATEGY

We begin the process of applying the audit planning and testing methodologies to the revenue cycle by considering the applicability of the concepts of materiality, risk, and audit strategy that were explained in Chapter 7.

Materiality

OBJECTIVE 3

Apply the concepts of materiality, risk, and audit strategy to the revenue cycle.

Sales transactions are the principal source of operating revenue for many business enterprises, and they are a major component in determining net income. They also give rise to accounts receivable and cash. The accounts receivable produced by credit sales transactions are nearly always material to the balance sheet. As indicated in Chapter 7, because of the high risk of misstatements in accounts receivable and the high costs of certain procedures used in auditing receivables (such as sending confirmation requests to customers), it is often appropriate to allocate a proportionately larger share of financial statement materiality to this account.

Thus, tolerable misstatement (or account balance materiality) for accounts receivable may be relatively higher than for certain other asset accounts such as plant assets where the risks and/or audit costs may be lower. This will help to reduce the overall cost of evidence accumulation.

Cash balances at a particular balance sheet date may not be material. But the flow of cash through the entity from cash receipts transactions during an accounting period can have a material effect on sales and accounts receivable as well as the cash balance. Regarding sales adjustment transactions, the significance of sales discounts and sales returns and allowances varies considerably from one entity to another. However, the provision for uncollectible accounts (bad debts expense) and related allowance are often material, respectively, to the income statements and balance sheets of entities that sell to customers on credit.

In summary, the transaction classes and account balances comprising the revenue cycle generally have material effects on the financial statements. To enhance the auditor's effectiveness and efficiency in meeting specific audit objectives in this cycle, careful attention should be given to considering inherent and control risks and to choosing the audit strategy appropriate to each objective.

Inherent and Control Risks

In assessing inherent risk for revenue cycle assertions, the auditor should consider pervasive factors that may affect assertions in several cycles, including the revenue cycle, as well as factors that may pertain only to specific assertions in the revenue cycle. These include factors that might motivate management to misstate revenue cycle assertions such as

- Pressures to overstate revenues in order to report achieving announced revenue or profitability targets or industry norms that were not achieved in reality owing to such factors as global, national, or regional economic conditions, the impact of technological developments on the entity's competitiveness, or poor management. Devices employed to overstate revenues include recording fictitious sales, holding the books open to record subsequent period sales in the current period (improper cutoff), and shipping unordered goods to customers near year-end and recording them as sales of the current period only to have them returned in the subsequent period.
- Pressures to overstate cash and gross receivables or understate the allowance for doubtful accounts in order to report a higher level of working capital in the face of liquidity problems or going concern doubts.

Other factors that might contribute to misstatements in revenue cycle assertions include:

- The volume of sales, cash receipts, and sales adjustments transactions is often high, resulting in numerous opportunities for errors to occur.
- The timing and amount of revenue to be recognized may be contentious owing to factors such as ambiguous accounting standards, the need to make estimates, the complexity of the calculations involved, and purchasers' rights of return.
- When receivables are factored with recourse, the correct classification of the transaction as a sale or a borrowing may be contentious.

- Receivables may be misclassified as current or noncurrent owing to difficulties in estimating the likelihood of collection within the next year or the outcome of events on which collection is contingent.
- Cash receipts transactions generate liquid assets that are particularly susceptible to misappropriation.
- Sales adjustments transactions may be used to conceal thefts of cash received from customers by overstating discounts, recording fictitious sales returns, or writing off customers' balances as uncollectible.

Because of the variety and potential magnitude of the misstatements enumerated above that can occur in the absence of effective controls, the auditor must always give careful consideration to inherent risks in the revenue cycle. Recognizing these risks through their own risk assessment procedures, management frequently adopts extensive internal control structure policies and procedures to address many of the risks. Thus, the auditor also needs to consider control risk in deciding on the appropriate audit strategy for revenue cycle assertions. Internal control considerations are discussed at length in later sections of this chapter.

Audit Strategy

Two major preliminary audit strategies for accumulating audit evidence about individual financial statement assertions or groups of assertions were introduced in Chapter 7—the primarily substantive approach and the lower assessed level of control risk approach. To refresh your memory of the differences between the two strategies, it is suggested that you once again review Figure 7-5 on page 241. Note that the first of the four components of each audit strategy is the *planned assessed level of control risk.* This component in turn determines the specification of the other three components that relate to the proportions of audit effort for particular assertions that are allocated to obtaining an understanding of the internal control structure, testing controls, and performing substantive tests. Furthermore, recall that the lower assessed level of control risk approach is generally more cost efficient for assertions affected by a high volume of transactions and for which there are effective controls. This will often be the case for some or all assertions pertaining to credit sales and cash receipts transactions, and may be the case for sales adjustments transactions. Conversely, when there is a low volume of these transactions, or relevant controls do not exist or are believed to be ineffective for particular assertions, the primarily substantive approach should be used.

CONSIDERATION OF INTERNAL CONTROL STRUCTURE COMPONENTS

OBJECTIVE 4

Explain the applicability of relevant aspects of the internal control structure components to the revenue cycle.

Before proceeding, it is further suggested that you review Figure 9-2 on page 307 which shows the steps and decision paths for considering the internal control structure and designing substantive tests under each audit strategy. As Figure 9-2 reminds us, under either strategy the process begins with obtaining an understanding of relevant internal control structure policies and procedures.

In this section, we consider the applicability of four of the five ICS components to the revenue cycle—the control environment, risk assessment, information and communication (which includes the accounting system), and monitoring. An understanding of these components is required under either strategy. Based on the methodology explained in Chapter 8, the understanding of applicable aspects of the ICS components is obtained through reviewing previous experience with the entity, inquiring of management and other personnel, inspecting relevant portions of manuals, records, and other documents, and observing revenue cycle activities and operations. As Chapter 8 also explains and illustrates, the understanding is documented in the form of completed questionnaires, flowcharts, and/or narrative memoranda. This documentation should address the points raised in the sections that follow on the four components identified at the beginning of this paragraph.

The applicability of the fifth ICS component, control activities, is discussed later in the chapter in separate sections for each of the three major transaction classes in the revenue cycle.

Control Environment

The control enviroment consists of several factors. These factors may mitigate several of the inherent risks related to the revenue cycle that were discussed earlier in this chapter. In addition, they may enhance or negate the effectiveness of other ICS components in controlling the risk of misstatements in revenue cycle assertions.

A key control environment factor in reducing the risk of fraudulent financial reporting through the overstatement of revenues and receivables, for example, is managements's adoption of and adherence to high standards of *integrity and ethical values.* Related aspects include eliminating incentives to dishonest reporting such as undue emphasis on meeting unrealistic sales or profit targets, and eliminating temptations such as an indifferent or ineffective board of directors and audit committee.

Several of the identified inherent risks related to contentious accounting issues, complex calculations, and accounting estimates that may pertain to revenue cycle assertions may be controlled if management has made the appropriate *commitment to competence* on the part of chief financial officers and accounting personnel. In obtaining an understanding of this factor, in addition to current inquiries and observations of personnel, the auditor may consider prior experience with the client and review personnel files.

Also relevant to mitigating several of the inherent risks discussed earlier is a characteristic of *management's philosophy and operating style* which may be described as its attitudes and actions toward financial reporting. This characteristic includes management's conservative or aggressive selection from alternative accounting principles, and its conscientiousness and conservatism in developing accounting estimates such as the allowances for uncollectible accounts and sales returns.

The control environment is enhanced when the *assignment of authority and responsibility* for all activities in the revenue cycle is clearly communicated through, among other means, written job descriptions. The multiple functions performed in processing each of the three types of revenue cycle transactions are described in later sections of this chapter.

A number of special *human resource policies and practices* are often adopted for employees who handle cash receipts because of the susceptibility of cash to misappropriation. For example, many entities bond employees who handle cash.

Bonding involves the purchase of a fidelity insurance policy against losses from the theft of cash and similar defalcations perpetrated by dishonest employees. Before the insurer issues a policy or adds an employee to an existing policy, it generally investigates the individual's honesty and integrity in previous positions. Bonding contributes to the control environment over cash receipts in two ways: (1) it may prevent the hiring or continued employment of dishonest individuals, and (2) it serves as a deterrent to dishonesty because employees know that the insurance company may vigorously investigate and prosecute any dishonest act. Additional practices include having employees who handle cash take mandatory vacations, and rotating employees' duties periodically. The thrust of these controls is to deter dishonesty by making employees aware that they may not be able to permanently conceal their misdeeds. Some embezzlements from banks and other entities, for example, have been traced to the seemingly dedicated employee who held the same job without taking a vacation for ten, twenty, or more years in order not to disrupt his or her routine of concealment.

Risk Assessment

As noted in Chapter 8, management's risk assessment for financial reporting purposes is similar to the external auditor's assessment of inherent risk. A conscientious effort on management's part to identify the kinds of risks related to revenue cycle transactions and balances described earlier in the chapter, together with a conmmitment to initiate control activities to address those risks, should reduce the risk of misstatements. Of particular interest to the auditor is evidence of management's assessment of the risks that arise from changed circumstances such as new types of revenue transactions, new accounting standards for revenue cycle transactions, and the impact on accounting and reporting of rapid growth in revenue cycle activities or changes in personnel.

Information and Communication (Accounting System)

Our primary concern with this component in this chapter pertains to the portion of the accounting system used in processing revenue cycle transactions and balances. An understanding of the accounting system requires knowledge of the *audit (or transaction) trail* for each transaction class, including the methods of data processing and the key documents and records used.

Figure 14-2 presents an *overview* flowchart that highlights key features of manual and computerized systems for processing the following specific types of revenue cycle transactions: credit sales, collections from customers, sales returns, and write-offs of uncollectible accounts. The flowchart is not intended to show every document, record, process, or account involved. More detailed flowcharts are presented later in the chapter.

The overview of the manual system shows the familiar accounting cycle sequence of preparing source documents, journalizing, and posting. It also shows the primary effects of the transactions on the general ledger accounts. Formal definitions of the key documents and records shown in Figure 14-2, as well as of additional supporting documents and records, are given later in the chapter.

The overview of the computerized system emphasizes the input, processing, and output dimensions of computerized accounting operations. As noted in Chapter 13, input may occur in user departments or in a data entry section of the

FIGURE 14-2 • OVERVIEW OF TRANSACTION PROCESSING IN THE REVENUE CYCLE

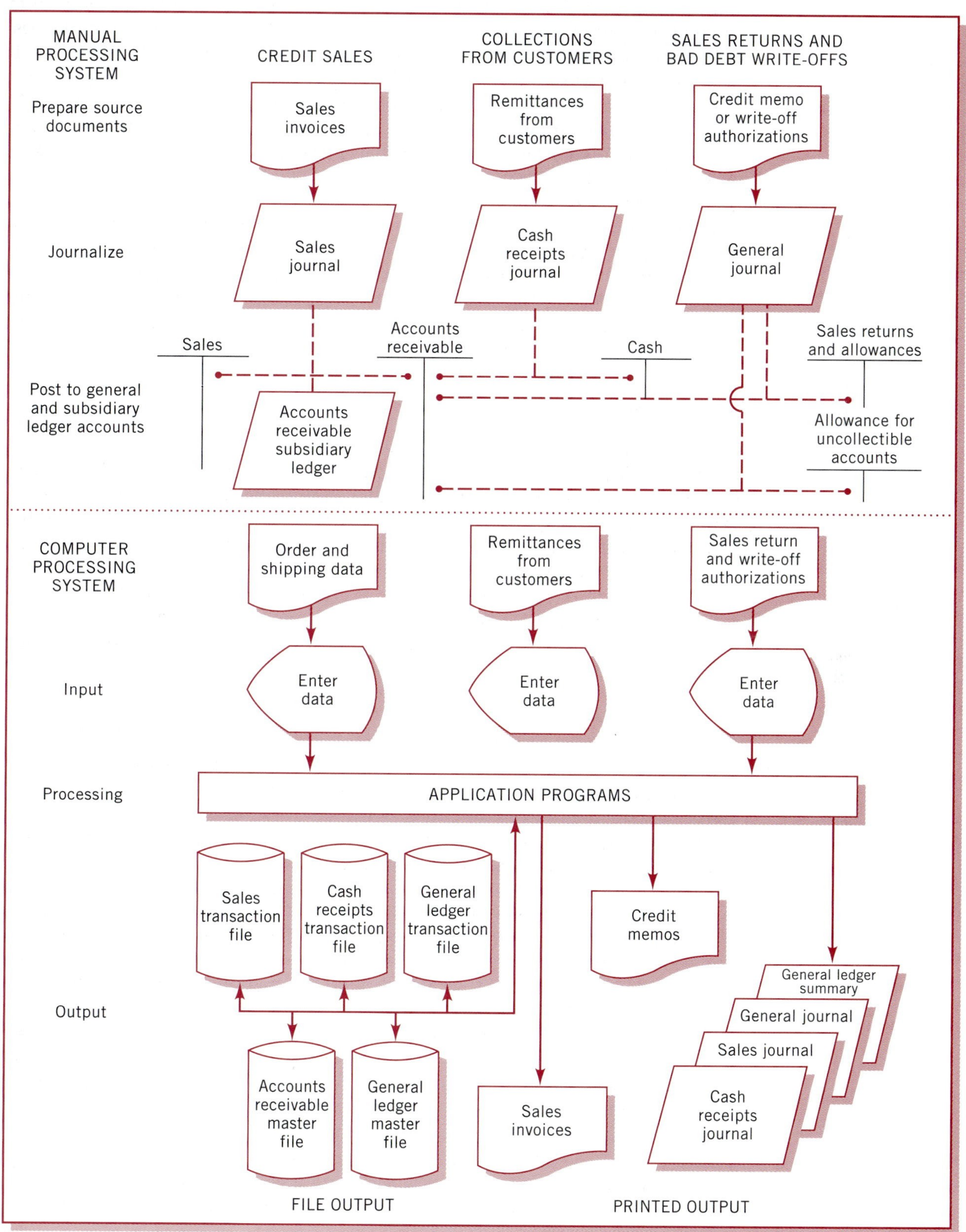

EDP department. In either case, the auditor must acquire an understanding of the relevant general and application controls as explained in Chapter 13, and will need to be familiar with the key transaction files and master files shown in the figure. Formal definitions of these files are also provided later in the chapter.

Appropriate provisions for processing and reporting on revenue cycle transactions and balances should be included in the chart of accounts, policy manuals, accounting and financial reporting manuals, and system flowcharts, all of which constitute an important part of this ICS component.

Monitoring

This component should provide management with feedback as to whether control policies and procedures pertaining to revenue cycle transactions and balances are operating as intended. The auditor should obtain an understanding of this feedback and whether management has initiated any corrective actions based on the information received from the monitoring activities. Possibilities include information received from (1) customers concerning billing errors, (2) regulatory agencies concerning disagreements on revenue recognition policies or related internal control matters, and (3) external auditors concerning reportable conditions or material weaknesses in relevant internal controls found in prior audits. Potentially of particular significance to the external auditor is information provided by internal auditors based on their assessments of internal controls pertaining to the revenue cycle. To review the possible effects of the internal auditor's findings on the external auditor's work, see the related discussions on pages 276 and 315 of this text.

Initial Assessment of Control Risk

Recall that the auditor's procedures to obtain an understanding of the four ICS components just discussed extend to the design of policies and procedures and whether they have been placed in operation. It may also be noted that in the process of obtaining the understanding of these four components, the auditor may become aware of additional policies and procedures pertaining to an assertion that are part of the control activities component of the ICS. However, the procedures to obtain an understanding do not extend to determining the effectiveness of the controls in any of the components unless *tests of controls* are performed concurrently. In the absence of such tests, the auditor's initial assessment of control risk must be at the maximum.

When concurrent tests of controls are performed as described in Chapter 9, they usually provide limited assurance about the effectiveness of the controls based on limited application of the procedures of inquiring, inspecting, and observing. Evidence from such concurrent tests may support a reduction in the initial assessment of control risk for related assertions to slightly below the maximum or high. In either case, with the knowledge obtained from the understanding of these components together with the results of concurrent tests of controls, if any, the auditor can identify types of potential misstatements that could occur in the entity's accounting for the revenue cycle. He or she may then proceed with the design of substantive tests to detect the misstatements under the primarily substantive approach.

When the auditor initially selects the lower assessed level of control risk approach, or decides to switch to that strategy after learning about additional controls or obtaining favorable results from concurrent tests of controls under the primarily substantive approach, he or she must obtain additional evidence to support a final assessment of control risk of moderate or low. This ordinarily involves obtaining an understanding of additional control activities in the fifth component of the ICS and performing additional tests of controls. These control activities and related tests of controls are discussed next for each of the three major transaction classes in the revenue cycle.

LEARNING CHECK:

14-1 a. Describe the nature of the revenue cycle.
 b. Identify the major classes of transactions in this cycle for a merchandising company and the primary accounts that are affected by these transactions.

14-2 a. How are specific audit objectives derived for the revenue cycle?
 b. State the specific audit objectives for credit sales transactions.

14-3 a. Why might the auditor specify a tolerable misstatement for accounts receivable that is relatively higher than for some other asset accounts?
 b. State two inherent risk factors that might motivate management to deliberately misstate revenues and receivables and two factors that might cause unintentional misstatements.
 c. Which preliminary audit strategy does the auditor ordinarily prefer to use for most revenue cycle assertions for a merchandising company and why?

14-4 a. State the applicability of several control environment factors to revenue cycle assertions.
 b. What is the primary source document for each of the three major transaction classes in the manual processing of revenue cycle transactions?
 c. What are the major files and printed outputs in an EDP system for processing revenue cycle transactions?

KEY TERMS:

Revenue cycle, p. 494

Bonding, p. 500

CONTROL ACTIVITIES—CREDIT SALES TRANSACTIONS

Sales orders may be taken over-the-counter, via telephone, mail order, traveling sales representatives, fax, or electronic data interchange. The goods may be picked up by the customer or shipped by the seller. The accounting for sales transactions may be done manually or with a computer, in real-time or batch processing mode. Control activities over sales transactions should be tailored to these varying circumstances.

OBJECTIVE 5

Discuss considerations applicable to assessing control risk for credit sales transactions.

For simplicity, in this section we consider the control activities of an entity that are relevant to the specific audit objectives for credit sales transactions and related account balances only. We begin by identifying the numerous documents and records that are commonly used in processing these transactions. We then explain each of the functions involved in processing the transactions, and how control activities are interwoven into each to reduce the risk of misstatements in the financial statement assertions that are affected by sales transactions. As explained in Chapter 8, control activities include information processing controls, segregation of duties, physical controls, and performance reviews. Information processing controls specific to credit sales transactions include, in addition to documents and records, proper authorization and independent checks.

COMMON DOCUMENTS AND RECORDS

The numerous documents and records used by large companies in processing credit sales transactions often include the following:

- **Customer order.** Request for merchandise by a customer received directly from the customer or through a salesperson. May be a form furnished by the seller or the buyer's *purchase order* form.
- **Sales order.** Form showing the description, quantity, and other data pertaining to a customer order. It serves as the basis for internal processing of the customer order by the seller.
- **Shipping document.** Form used to show the details and date of each shipment. It may be in the form of a **bill of lading,** which serves as a formal acknowledgment of the receipt of goods for delivery by a freight carrier.
- **Sales invoice.** Form stating the particulars of a sale, including the amount owed, terms, and date of sale. It is used to bill customers and provides the basis for recording the sale.
- **Authorized price list.** Listing or computer master file containing authorized prices for goods offered for sale.
- **Accounts receivable subsidiary ledger** or **accounts receivable master file.** Contains information on transactions with, and the balance due from, each customer. May also contain the customer's credit limit.
- **Sales transactions file.** Computer file of completed sales transactions. Used to print the sales invoices and sales journal, and update the accounts receivable, inventory, and general ledger master files.
- **Sales journal.** Journal listing completed sales transactions.
- **Customer monthly statement.** Report sent to each customer showing the beginning balance, transactions during the month, and the ending balance.

FUNCTIONS

The processing of credit sales transactions involves a sequence of steps or **credit sales functions** as follows:

- Accepting customer orders.
- Approving credit.
- Filling sales orders.

- Shipping sales orders.
- Billing customers.
- Recording the sales.

The functions, applicable control activities, and relevant assertions and specific audit objectives are explained in the following sections.

Accepting Customer Orders

Sales orders from customers should be accepted only in accordance with management's authorized criteria. The criteria generally provide for specific approval of the order in the sales order department by (1) tracing the customer to an approved customer list, or (2) using a computer terminal to determine that the customer exists in an approved customer file such as the accounts receivable master file. If the customer is not listed, approval by a sales order department supervisor is usually required.

In many companies, the next step is preparing a multicopy sales order form. This represents the start of the transaction trail of documentary evidence in support of management's assertion as to the existence or occurrence of sales transactions and thus relates to the specific audit objective coded **EO1** in Figure 14-1 on page 496. Information on open (unfilled) and filled sales orders is usually maintained in hard copy files in the sales order department and/or in computer files.

Approving Credit

Credit approval is given by the credit department in accordance with management's credit policies and authorized credit limits for each customer. On receipt of a sales order form from the sales order department, a credit department employee compares the order with the customer's authorized credit limit and the current balance owed by the customer. Alternatively, in an EDP system, the computer can be programmed to make this comparison at the same time the sales order clerk determines whether a customer exists in the approved customer master file. Segregating responsibility for performing a manual credit check, or having the computer reject orders from customers without adequate credit, prevents sales personnel from subjecting the company to undue credit risks to boost sales.

For a new customer, a credit check is made, which may include obtaining a credit report from a rating agency such as Dun & Bradstreet. Approval or nonapproval of credit is indicated by an authorized credit employee by signing or initialing the sales order form and returning it to the sales order department. In an EDP system, authorized personnel must follow prescribed procedures in having the new customer and credit information added to the accounts receivable master file.

Controls over approving credit are designed to reduce the risk of initially recording an individual revenue transaction at an amount in excess of the amount of cash expected to be realized from the transaction. Thus, they relate to the valuation or allocation assertion for sales transactions (**VA1**). Of course, the expectations of realizability for some of these amounts will change over time, resulting in the need for an allowance for uncollectible accounts. Controls over approving credit will enable management to make a more reliable estimate of the size of the allowance needed. Thus, these controls also relate to the valuation or allocation assertion for the allowance for uncollectible accounts (**VA5**).

Filling Sales Orders

Company policy generally prohibits the release of any goods from the warehouse without an approved sales order. This control procedure is designed to prevent the unauthorized removal of items from inventory. Thus, a copy of the approved sales order form is normally sent to the warehouse as authorization to fill the order and release the goods to the shipping department. It provides further evidence that the sale occurred (**EO1**).

Shipping Sales Orders

Segregating the responsibility for shipping from approving and filling orders helps to prevent shipping clerks from making unauthorized shipments. In addition, before making shipments, shipping clerks are normally required to make independent checks to determine (1) that goods received from the warehouse are accompanied by an approved sales order form, and (2) that the order was properly filled (goods received agree with the details of the sales order).

The shipping function also involves preparing multicopy shipping documents or bills of lading. Shipping documents can be prepared manually on prenumbered forms. Alternatively, the documents can be produced with the computer by using order information already in the computer and adding appropriate shipping data such as quantities shipped, carrier, freight charges, and so on.

Shipping documents provide evidence that goods were actually shipped. Thus, they represent another form of documentary evidence in support of the existence or occurrence assertion for sales transactions (**EO1**). A numerical file of shipping documents is normally maintained in the shipping department. Periodic manual or computerized checks to account for all shipping documents and determine that a sales invoice was subsequently prepared for each document contributes to the completeness assertion for sales transactions (**C1**).

Billing Customers

The billing function involves preparing and sending prenumbered sales invoices to customers. Major concerns in this function are that customers are billed (1) for all shipments, (2) only for actual shipments (no duplicate billings or fictitious transactions), and (3) at authorized prices. Controls designed to reduce the risk of omissions, duplications, incorrect pricing, and other types of errors in the billing process *(and related specific audit objectives)* include the following:

- An independent check by billing department personnel of the existence of a shipping document and matching approved sales order before each invoice is prepared (**EO1**).[1]
- Use of an authorized price list or computerized master price file in preparing the sales invoices (**VA1**).

---

[1] Note that the alphabetic characters in the specific audit objective codes from Figure 14-1 denote the assertion category—that is , EO = existence or occurrence and so on.

- Manual independent checks or computer programmed checks on the pricing and mathematical accuracy of sales invoices (**VA1**).
- Comparison of control totals for shipping documents with corresponding totals for sales invoices (**EO1** and **C1**).

File copies of the sales invoices are usually maintained in the billing department. A computer record of the billings is maintained in a sales transactions file.

Recording the Sales

The auditor's primary concerns pertaining to this function are that the sales invoices are recorded accurately and in the proper period. The latter pertains to when the revenue is earned, which is usually when the goods are shipped.

In a manual system, the recording process involves entering the sales invoices in a sales journal, posting the invoices to the accounts receivable subsidiary ledger, and posting the sales journal to the general ledger accounts. In a computerized system, the sales transactions file created in the billing process is used to (1) update the accounts receivable, inventory, and general ledger master files, and (2) produce the sales journal and a general ledger transactions summary showing the postings to each general ledger account.

Controls over recording *(and related specific audit objectives)* include the following:

- Recording sales only on the basis of a sales invoice with a matching shipping document and sales order evidencing the sale and transaction date **(EO1, R1, VA1)**.
- Accounting for all prenumbered sales invoices (**C1**).
- Manual or computer programmed checks on agreement of control totals for invoices processed and the total of amounts recorded (**EO1,C1,VA1**).
- Using a chart of accounts for invoice coding (account classification) and independent check of coding by supervisor **(PD1)**.
- Segregating the responsibility for recording from the previous functions in processing sales transactions (**EO1, C1**).
- Restricting access to records and computer programs involved in the recording process to reduce the risk of unauthorized entries (**EO1**).
- Performing periodic independent checks on the agreement of the accounts receivable subsidiary ledger or master file with the general ledger control account (**VA4**).
- Mailing monthly statements to customers with instructions to report any exceptions to a designated accounting supervisor not otherwise involved in the execution or recording of revenue cycle transactions (*all revenue cycle objectives*).
- Periodic performance reviews by sales executives of sales analyses by product, division, salesperson, or region, and comparisons with budgets (*all sales transaction objectives*).

As an exercise, it is suggested that the student consider the rationale for the linkage of the above controls to the specific audit objectives indicated for each.

Illustrative System for Processing Credit Sales

In practice, there are many variations in the systems used to perform the functions involved in processing credit sales transactions. Figure 14-3 shows a flowchart of an on-line / batch entry processing system that incorporates most of the controls discussed in the preceding sections.

In the illustrated system, as orders are received sales order clerks use on-line terminals and an order program to determine that the customer has been approved, and that the order will not cause the customer's balance to exceed the customer's authorized credit limit. The program also checks the inventory master file to determine that goods are on hand to fill the order. If the order is accepted, the computer enters it into an open order file and a multicopy sales order form is produced on a printer in the sales order department. When an order is not accepted, a message is displayed on the terminal indicating the reason for rejection.

Copies of the approved sales order are forwarded to the warehouse as authorization to release goods to shipping. In shipping, personnel first make an independent check on agreement of the goods received with the accompanying sales order form. They then use their on-line terminals and a shipping program to retrieve the corresponding sales order from the open order file and add appropriate shipping data. Next the computer transfers the transaction from the open order file to a shipping file and produces a shipping document on the printer in the shipping department.

As matching shipping documents and sales order forms are received in the billing department, they are batched and batch totals are manually prepared. Using their on-line terminals and a billing program, billing department personnel first enter the manually prepared batch totals. Next the previously entered order and shipping data for each transaction are retrieved from the shipping file and a sales invoice is generated using prices from the master price file. As each billing is completed, the computer enters it into a sales transaction file. After all the transactions in a batch have been processed in this manner, the billing program compares a computer-generated batch total with the manual batch total previously entered by the billing clerk. Discrepancies are displayed on the terminal and corrected by the billing clerks before processing continues. Finally, sales invoices for the batch are printed in the EDP department and distributed as shown in the flowchart.

The recording of sales transactions is completed at the end of each day when the EDP department runs the master file update program. As shown, this program updates three master files and produces a sales journal and general ledger transaction summary which are sent to accounting. The use of separate programs to produce monthly customer statements and periodic sales analyses for use in performance reviews is not shown in the flowchart.

OBTAINING THE UNDERSTANDING AND ASSESSING CONTROL RISK

The methodology for obtaining and documenting the understanding of control activities is the same as described previously for the other four ICS components. However, the process of identifying and testing controls in this component is ordinarily more involved owing to the potential variety of applicable control activities and the fact that when they are being considered the auditor is usually

FIGURE 14-3 • SYSTEM FLOWCHART—CREDIT SALES TRANSACTIONS

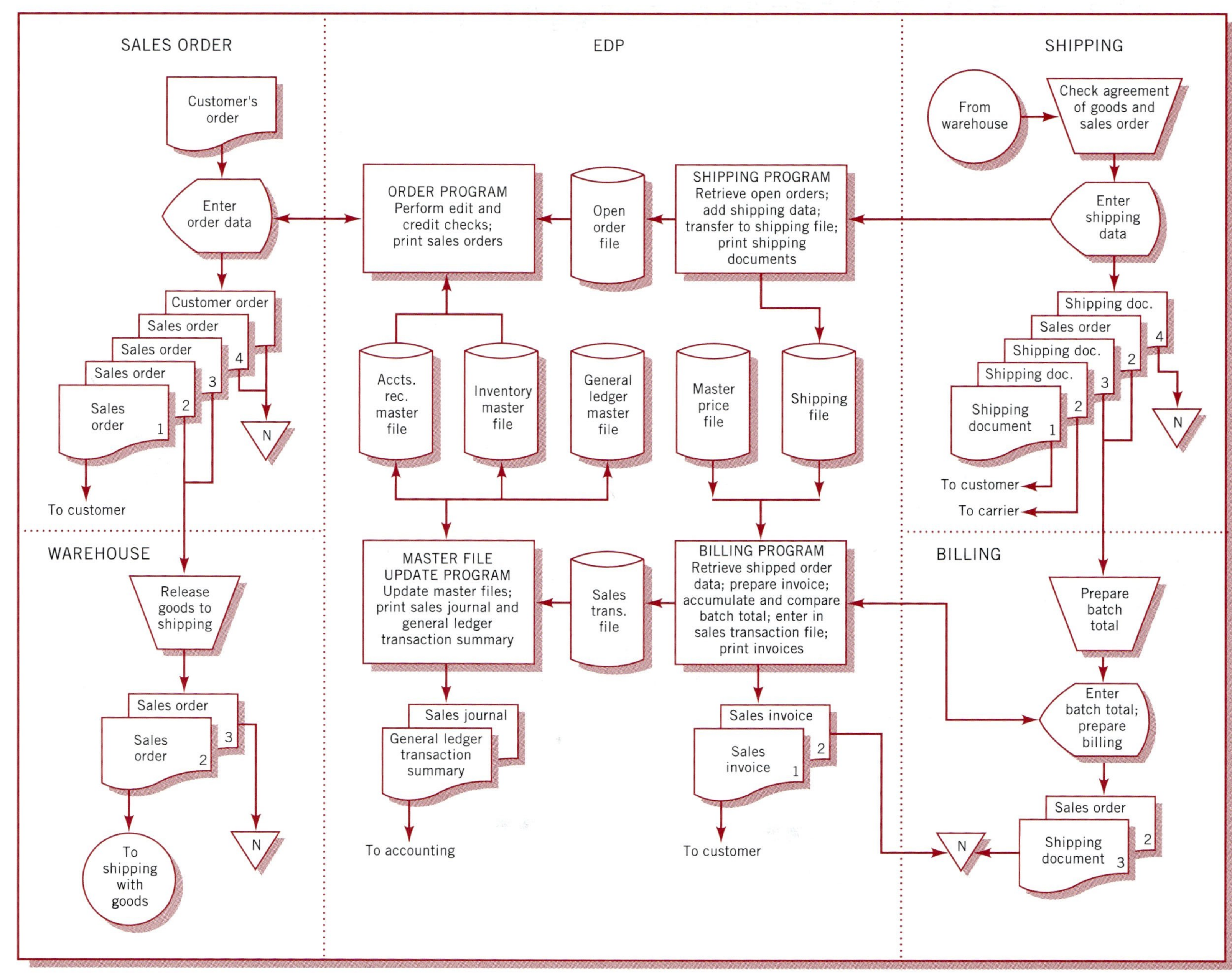

seeking support for a moderate or low control risk assessment rather than an assessment of high or maximum. Furthermore, whereas the concurrent tests of controls performed in the other four components often involve only inquiries, inspections, or observations at a single point in time, several of the tests in this component are based on samples drawn from the entire audit period.

Figure 14-4 contains a partial listing of potential misstatements, necessary controls, potential tests of controls, and the specific transaction class audit objectives for credit sales to which each relates. The potential misstatements and necessary controls are identified based on the auditor's knowledge of the client's internal control structure as documented in the questionnaires, flowcharts, and narrative memoranda, as well as firm checklists and possibly computerized aids. Note that the tests of controls involve a variety of audit procedures including reperformance of certain control activities by the auditor. Statistical or nonstatistical sampling procedures as discussed in Chapter 11 may be applied in performing some of the tests. For example, an attribute sampling plan may be used to design, select, and evaluate a sample of sales journal entries for vouching to matching supporting invoices, shipping documents, and approved sales orders. Recall that the *direction of testing* involved in the foregoing test (backward along the audit trail) is appropriate when the objective is to assess control risk for the existence or occurrence assertion. Conversely, if the objective were to test controls pertaining to the completeness assertion, a sample of sales orders or shipping documents would be selected and traced forward along the audit trail to the sales journal to determine that all the transactions were recorded.

Also, recall that some of the tests can be performed as dual purpose tests, that is, simultaneously serve as substantive tests of details of credit sales transactions. In particular, in addition to providing evidence about the effectiveness of controls, several of the tests related to the billing and recording functions can provide evidence about the dollar effects of the transactions on the fairness of the account balances affected by those transactions. These tests are marked with an asterisk in Figure 14-4.

The tests of controls performed, the evidence obtained, and the conclusions reached must be documented. A formal audit program incorporating several of the tests from Figure 14-4 is presented in Figure 14-5. Examples of documenting specific tests and results when an attribute sampling plan is used can be seen in Figures 11-9, 10, and 11 beginning on page 384.

Based on the evidence obtained from the procedures to obtain an understanding of relevant portions of *all five* components of the ICS and related tests of controls, a final assessment of control risk is made and documented for each significant assertion related to credit sales transactions. For an example of documentation in the form of a memorandum, review Figure 9-5 on page 320.

Computer-Assisted Tests of Controls

When credit sales transactions are processed on the computer, the auditor may use the computer in performing tests of controls. The auditor should first consider the effectiveness of general controls pertaining to program changes and file security. For example, the auditor should make inquiries and inspect documentation concerning changes made to the programs and master files used in the sales order, shipping, billing, and recording (updating) functions. When the general controls are adequate, the auditor has greater assurance that the information obtained from

FIGURE 14-4 • CONTROL RISK ASSESSMENT CONSIDERATIONS—CREDIT SALES TRANSACTIONS

Function	Potential Misstatement	Necessary Control	Potential Test of Control*	Relevant Transaction Class Audit Objective (from p. 496)				
				EOI	CI	ROI	VAI	PDI
Accepting customer orders	Sales may be made to unauthorized customers.	Determination that customer is on approved customer list.	Observe procedure; reperform.	✓				
		Approved sales order form for each sale.	Examine approved sales order forms.	✓				
Approving credit	Sales may be made without credit approval.	Credit department credit check on all new customers.	Inquire about procedures for checking credit on new customers.				✓	
		Check on customer's credit limit prior to each sale.	Examine evidence of credit limit check prior to each sale.				✓	
Filling sales orders	Goods may be released from warehouse for unauthorized orders.	Approved sales order for all goods released to shipping.	Observe warehouse personnel filling orders.	✓				
Shipping sales orders	Goods shipped may not agree with goods ordered.	Independent check by shipping clerks of agreement of goods received from warehouse with approved sales order.	Examine evidence of performance of independent check.	✓	✓			
	Unauthorized shipments may be made.	Segregation of duties for filling and shipping orders.	Observe segregation of duties.	✓				
		Preparation of shipping document for each shipment.	Inspect shipping documents.	✓				
Billing customers	Billings may be made for fictitious transactions or duplicate billings may be made.	Matching shipping document and approved sales order for each invoice.	Vouch invoices to shipping documents and approved sales orders.*	✓				
	Some shipments may not be billed.	Matching sales invoice for each shipping document.	Trace shipping documents to sales invoices.*		✓			
		Periodic accounting for all shipping documents.	Observe procedure; reperform.		✓			
	Sales invoices may have incorrect prices.	Independent check on pricing of invoices.	Reperform check on accuracy of pricing.*				✓	

FIGURE 14-4 *(Continued)*

Function	Potential Misstatement	Necessary Control	Potential Test of Control*	Relevant Transaction Class Audit Objective (from p. 496) EOI	CI	ROI	VAI	PDI
Recording the sales	Fictitious sales transactions may be recorded.	Sales invoice and matching documents required for all entries.	Vouch recorded sales to supporting documents.*	✓		✓	✓	
	Invoices may not be journalized or posted to customer accounts.	Independent check of agreement of sales journal entries and amounts posted to customer accounts with control totals of invoices.	Review evidence of independent check; reperform check; trace sales invoices to sales journal and customer accounts.*		✓		✓	
		Perodic accounting for all sales invoices.	Observe procedure; reperform		✓			
	Invoices may be posted to wrong customer account.	Chart of accounts and supervisory review of account coding.	Observe procedures; reperform.*					✓
		Mailing of monthly statements to customers with independent followup on customer complaints.	Observe mailing and followup procedures.*	✓	✓	✓	✓	✓

* Tests marked with an asterisk are sometimes performed as a part of dual-purpose tests.

his or her computer-assisted tests pertains to the programs and master files used throughout the period under audit.

In addition to examining exception reports produced during the client's regular processing, the auditor may use test data to determine whether the programs are functioning properly. For example, when the client's order program includes an edit routine to detect incorrect or missing data on sales orders, the auditor can enter test data to determine whether expected results are produced by the program in circumstances such as the following:

- A missing or invalid customer number.
- An invalid product code.
- Missing or unreasonable order quantities.
- Alphabetical characters entered in numeric fields.
- An order that exceeds a customer's credit limit.
- An order for a product that is out of stock.

Examples of other possible computer-assisted audit tests are:

- Using generalized audit software or a utility program to perform sequence checks to detect missing or duplicate sales order, shipping document, and sales invoice numbers in computer files.

FIGURE 14-5 • PARTIAL AUDIT PROGRAM FOR TESTS OF CONTROLS—CREDIT SALES TRANSACTIONS

Prepared by:________ Date:________
Reviewed by:________ Date:________

Amalgamated Products, Inc.
Planned Tests of Controls—Credit Sales Transactions
Year Ending December 31, 19X1

Working Paper Reference	Assertion/Test of Control	Auditor	Date
	Existence or occurrence: 1. Observe procedures, including segregation of duties, for: a. Approving sales orders. b. Filling sales orders. c. Shipping sales orders. d. Billing customers. e. Mailing monthly statements to customers and following up on customer complaints. 2. Select a sample of sales transactions from the sales journal and verify transaction dates, customer names, and amounts by vouching entries to following matching supporting documents: a. Sales invoices. b. Shipping documents. c. Approved sales orders. *Completeness:* 3. Examine evidence of use of and accounting for prenumbered sales orders, shipping documents, and sales invoices. Scan sequence of sales invoice numbers in sales journal. 4. Select a sample of approved sales orders and trace to matching a. Shipping documents. b. Sales invoices. c. Entries in the sales journal. *Valuation or allocation:* 5. For the sample in Step 2 above, examine evidence of a. Proper credit approval for each transaction. b. Independent check on proper pricing of invoices. c. Independent check on mathematical accuracy of invoices. 6. For sales invoices processed in batches, examine evidence of independent check on agreement of totals for sales journal entries and amounts posted to customer accounts with batch totals.		

- Designing, selecting, and evaluating an attribute sample of shipping documents.
- Selecting and printing a sample of sales prices from the sales price master file for manual comparison with authorized prices established by management.

LEARNING CHECK:

14-5 a. What functions are involved in the processing of credit sales transactions?
b. Identify important controls related to the first three functions.

14-6 Indicate several potential misstatements and related necessary controls in
a. The shipping function.
b. The billing function.

14-7 For the billing function, identify:
a. Several potential misstatements.
b. Necessary controls to prevent or detect the misstatements identified in a.
c. Potential tests of the controls identified in b.

14-8 Identify three controls that may help to reduce control risk pertaining to each of the following assertions for credit sales transactions:
a. Existence or occurrence.
b. Completeness.
c. Valuation or allocation.

14-9 Vouching recorded sales to supporting documents is a test often performed by auditors as a dual purpose test. Explain.

KEY TERMS:

Accounts receivable master file, p. 504
Accounts receivable subsidiary ledger, p. 504
Authorized price list, p. 504
Bill of lading, p. 504
Credit sales functions, p. 504
Customer monthly statement, p. 504
Customer order, p. 504
Sales invoice, p. 504
Sales journal, p. 504
Sales order, p. 504
Sales transactions file, p. 504
Shipping document, p. 504

CONTROL ACTIVITIES—CASH RECEIPTS TRANSACTIONS

OBJECTIVE 6

Discuss considerations applicable to assessing control risk for cash receipts and sales adjustments transactions.

Cash receipts result from a variety of activities. For example, cash is received from revenue transactions, short- and long-term borrowings, the issuance of capital stock, and the sale of marketable securities, long-term investments, and other assets. The scope of this section is limited to cash receipts from cash sales and collections from customers on credit sales. Other sources of cash receipts are discussed in the investing and financing cycles in Chapter 17.

COMMON DOCUMENTS AND RECORDS

Important documents and records used in processing cash receipts include the following:

- **Remittance advice.** Document mailed to the customer with the sales invoice to be returned with the payment showing the customer's name and account number, invoice number, and amount owed (e.g., the portion of a telephone bill returned with payment). If not returned by the customer, one is usually prepared by the person opening the mail.
- **Prelist.** Listing of cash receipts received through the mail.
- **Cash count sheet.** Listing of cash and checks in a cash register. Used in reconciling total receipts with the total printed by the cash register.
- **Daily cash summary.** Report showing total over-the-counter and mail receipts received by the cashier for deposit.
- **Validated deposit slip.** Listing prepared by the depositor and stamped by the bank showing the date and total of a deposit accepted by the bank and the detail of receipts comprising the deposit.
- **Cash receipts transactions file.** Computer file of validated cash receipts transactions accepted for processing; used to update the accounts receivable master file.
- **Cash receipts journal.** Journal listing cash receipts from cash sales and collections on accounts receivable.

Reference is made to each of the above in the following sections.

FUNCTIONS

The processing of receipts from cash and credit sales involves the following **cash receipts functions:**

- Receiving cash receipts.
- Depositing cash in bank.
- Recording the receipts.

As in the case of credit sales transactions, segregation of duties in performing these functions is an important internal control activity. The functions, applicable control activities, and relevant assertions and specific audit objectives are explained in the following sections.

Receiving Cash Receipts

A major risk in processing cash receipts transactions is the possible theft of cash before or after a record of the receipt is made. Thus, control procedures should provide reasonable assurance that documentation establishing accountability is created at the moment cash is received and that the cash is subsequently safeguarded. A second risk is the possibility of errors occurring in the subsequent processing of the receipts.

OVER-THE-COUNTER RECEIPTS. For over-the-counter receipts, the use of a cash register or point-of-sale terminal is indispensable. These devices provide

- Immediate visual display for the customer of the amount of the cash sale and the cash tendered.

- A printed receipt for the customer and an internal record of the transaction on a computer file or a tape locked inside the register.
- Printed control totals of the day's receipts processed on the device.

The customer's expectation of a printed receipt and supervisory surveillance of over-the-counter sales transactions helps to ensure that all cash sales are processed through the cash registers or terminals (**C2**). In addition, supervisors may be assigned responsibility for performing independent checks on the accuracy of cash count sheets, and verifying agreement of cash on hand with the totals printed by the register or terminal (**EO2, VA2**). The cash, count sheets, and register or terminal-printed totals are then forwarded to the cashier's department for further processing and inclusion in the bank deposit (**EO2, C2, VA2**).

MAIL RECEIPTS. To minimize the likelihood of diversion of mail receipts, most companies request customers to pay by check. Some companies with a large volume of mail receipts use a **lockbox system.** A lockbox is a post office box that is controlled by the company's bank. The bank picks up the mail daily, credits the company for the cash, and sends the remittance advices to the company for use in updating accounts receivable. This system expedites the depositing of checks, permits the company to receive credit for the receipts sooner, and provides external evidence of the existence of the transactions (**EO2**). It also eliminates the risk of diversion of the receipts by company employees and failure to record the receipts (**C2**).

In companies that process their own mail receipts, mailroom clerks should (1) immediately restrictively endorse checks *for deposit only* (**C2**-increases likelihood receipts will be deposited and recorded) and (2) list the checks on a multicopy prelist. The latter may be done manually or on a computer terminal. Immediate preparation of the prelist establishes accountability for the receipts (**EO2**) and provides a batch or control total for use in independent checks on the completeness (**C2**) and accuracy (**VA2**) of processing. Remittance advices received with the checks are forwarded to accounts receivable accounting for use in updating customer accounts.

Depositing Cash in Bank

Proper physical controls over cash require that all cash receipts be **deposited intact daily.** Intact means *all* receipts should be deposited; that is, cash disbursements should not be made out of undeposited receipts. This control reduces the risk that receipts will not be recorded (**C2**), and the resulting bank deposit record establishes the existence or occurrence of the transactions (**EO2**).

When the over-the-counter and mail receipts are received by the cashier, an independent check should be made to determine their agreement with the accompanying cash count sheets and prelist, respectively (**EO2, C2, VA2**). The totals for each are then entered on a daily cash summary, and the deposit is prepared. After making the deposit, the daily cash summary and validated deposit slip should be forwarded to general accounting.

Recording the Receipts

This function involves journalizing over-the-counter and mail receipts and posting mail receipts to customer accounts. Controls should ensure that only valid receipts are entered (**EO2**) and that all actual receipts are entered (**C2**), at the correct amounts (**VA2**).

To ensure that only valid transactions are entered, physical access to the accounting records or computer terminals used in recording should be restricted to authorized personnel. Over-the-counter receipts are generally recorded in general accounting based on the daily cash summary received from the cashier.

For mail receipts, in manual systems the duties of journalizing and posting to customer accounts should be segregated. The receipts may be journalized in general accounting from the prelist or daily cash summary. Posting the receipts to the accounts receivable subsidiary ledger may be done in accounts receivable accounting based on the remittance advices received from the mailroom. In EDP systems, it is common for accounts receivable clerks to use a terminal to enter mail receipts into a cash receipts transactions file, which is subsequently used in updating both the accounts receivable and general ledger master files.

To ensure the completeness (**C2**) and accuracy (**VA2**) of recording mail receipts, independent checks are made of the agreement of (1) the amounts journalized and posted with the amounts shown on the prelists received from the mailroom and (2) the total amounts journalized and posted for over-the-counter and mail receipts with the daily cash summary and validated deposit slip received from the cashier. In addition, periodic bank reconciliations should be performed by an employee not otherwise involved in executing or recording cash transactions.

Illustrative System for Processing Cash Receipts

As noted previously for credit sales systems, there are also many variations in systems for processing receipts. A flowchart for an illustrative system for processing mail receipts is presented in Figure 8-7 on page 287. It is suggested that the flowchart and the accompanying narrative on page 286 be reviewed at this time.

OBTAINING THE UNDERSTANDING AND ASSESSING CONTROL RISK

The auditor's responsibilities and methodology for meeting these requirements of the second standard of field work for cash receipts transactions are the same as described earlier for credit sales transactions. Accordingly, a detailed discussion is not repeated here. Figure 14-6 illustrates a partial listing of potential misstatements, necessary controls, potential tests of controls, and related transaction class audit objectives for cash receipts transactions. In practice, the particulars of the items listed in this figure would vary based on such factors as the method of data processing used. Though not illustrated here, an audit program for tests of controls for cash receipts transactions similar to the one for sales transactions in Figure 14-5 can be prepared based on the potential tests of controls in Figure 14-6.

CONTROL ACTIVITIES—SALES ADJUSTMENTS TRANSACTIONS

Sales adjustments transactions involve the following **sales adjustments functions:**

FIGURE 14-6 • CONTROL RISK ASSESSMENT CONSIDERATIONS—CASH RECEIPTS TRANSACTIONS

Function	Potential Misstatement	Necessary Control	Potential Test of Control*	Relevant Transaction Class Audit Objective (from p. 496)				
				EO2	C2	RO2	VA2	PD2
Receiving cash receipts	Cash sales may not be registered.	Use of cash registers or point-of-sale devices.	Observe cash sales procedures.		✓			
		Periodic surveillance of cash sales procedures.	Inquire of supervisors about results of surveillance.		✓			
	Mail receipts may be lost or misappropriated after receipt.	Restrictive endorsement of checks immediately on receipt.	Examine checks for restrictive endorsement.		✓			
		Immediate preparation of prelist of mail receipts.	Observe preparation of prelists.	✓	✓		✓	
Depositing cash in bank	Cash and checks received for deposit may not agree with cash count sheets and prelist.	Independent check of agreement of cash and checks with cash count sheets and prelist.	Examine evidence of independent check.*	✓	✓		✓	
	Cash may not be deposited intact daily.	Independent check of agreement of validated deposit slip with daily cash summary.	Reperform independent check.*	✓	✓			
Recording the receipts	Remittance advices may not agree with prelist.	Independent check of agreement of remittance advices with prelist.	Examine evidence of independent check.*				✓	
	Some receipts may not be recorded.	Independent check of agreement of amounts journalized and posted with daily cash summary.	Reperform independent check.*		✓			
	Errors may be made in journalizing receipts.	Preparation of periodic independent bank reconciliations.	Examine bank reconciliations.*	✓	✓	✓	✓	
	Receipts may be posted to the wrong customer account.	Mailing of monthly statements to customers.	Observe mailing of monthly statements.*	✓	✓		✓	✓

* Tests marked with an asterisk are sometimes performed as a part of dual-purpose tests.

- Granting cash discounts.
- Granting sales returns and allowances.
- Determining uncollectible accounts.

In many companies, the number and dollar value of these transactions is immaterial. However, in some companies, the potential for misstatements resulting from errors and irregularities in the processing of these transactions is considerable. Of primary concern is the possibility of fictitious sales adjustments transactions being recorded to conceal irregularities in processing cash receipts. For example, an employee might misappropriate cash received from a customer and cover up the irregularity by writing the customer's account off against the allowance for uncollectible accounts. Alternatively, the misappropriations of cash could be covered by overstating cash discounts or sales returns and allowances. Accordingly, control activities useful in reducing the risk of such irregularities focus on establishing the validity, or existence or occurrence, of such transactions (**EO3**) and include the following:

- Proper authorization of all sales adjustments transactions. For example, all write-offs of uncollectible accounts should be authorized by the treasurer's office (**EO3**).
- The use of appropriate documents and records, particularly the use of an approved **credit memo** for granting credit for returned or damaged goods, and an approved **write-off authorization memo** for writing off uncollectible customer accounts.
- Segregation of duties for authorizing sales adjustments transactions and handling and recording cash receipts.

When there is the potential for material misstatements from sales adjustments transactions, the auditor should obtain an understanding of all relevant aspects of the internal control structure components and consider the factors that affect the risk of such misstatements. When applicable, tests of controls such as the following can be performed:

- Recalculating cash discounts and determining that the payments were received within the discount period.
- Inspecting credit memoranda for sales returns for (1) indication of proper approval and (2) accompanying receiving reports evidencing the actual return of goods.
- Inspecting written authorizations and supporting documentation, such as correspondence with the customer or collection agencies, for the write-off of uncollectible accounts.

LEARNING CHECK:

14-10 What functions are involved in the processing of cash receipts transactions?

14-11 a. Describe two important controls pertaining to cash sales and indicate the transaction class audit objective(s) to which they relate.

b. Describe two important controls pertaining to the initial handling of mail receipts for companies that process their own receipts.

14-12 a. What is a lockbox system, and how can it affect control risk for cash receipts transactions?

b. What is the meaning of *deposited intact daily*, and how does this control affect control risk for cash receipts assertions?

14-13 Identify four controls that can aid in preventing or detecting errors or irregularities in recording cash receipts.

14-14 a. Identify the functions pertaining to sales adjustments transactions.
b. State three types of controls pertaining to sales adjustments transactions and identify their common focus.

KEY TERMS:

Cash count sheet, p. 515
Cash receipts functions, p. 515
Cash receipts journal, p. 515
Cash receipts transactions file, p. 515
Credit memo, p. 519
Daily cash summary, p. 515
Deposited intact daily, p. 516
Lockbox system, p. 516
Prelist, p. 515
Remittance advice, p. 515
Sales adjustments functions, p. 517
Validated deposit slip, p. 515
Write-off authorization memo, p. 519

SUBSTANTIVE TESTS OF ACCOUNTS RECEIVABLE

Receivables include amounts due from customers, employees, and affiliates on open accounts, notes, and loans, and accrued interest on such balances. Our consideration here is directed at gross receivables due from customers on credit sales transactions and the related contra account, the allowance for uncollectible accounts. To design substantive tests for these accounts, the auditor must first determine the acceptable level of detection risk for each significant related assertion.

DETERMINING DETECTION RISK

It will be recalled that for a specified level of audit risk, detection risk is inversely related to the assessed levels of inherent risk and control risk. Thus, factors pertaining to these assessments must be considered in determining the acceptable level of detection risk for each accounts receivable assertion.

Several pervasive inherent risk factors that affect gross and net receivables as well as factors specific to revenue cycle transactions are discussed earlier in the chapter on pages 497 and 498. The combined effects of these factors, especially those contributing to the risk of credit sales being overstated and the allowance for uncollectible accounts being understated, may result, respectively, in high assessments of inherent risk for the existence or occurrence and valuation or allocation assertions for gross accounts receivable, and the valuation or allocation assertion for the related allowance account. Even when this is the case, lower inherent risk assessments may be appropriate for the other assertions.

OBJECTIVE 7

Indicate the factors involved in determining the acceptable level of detection risk for accounts receivable assertions.

Control risk assessments for accounts receivable assertions are dependent on the related control risk assessments for the transaction classes (credit sales, cash receipts, and sales adjustments) that affect the accounts receivable balance. Recall that the assessments for transaction class assertions affect the same account balance assertions for accounts affected by the transactions with the following exception: control risk assessments for the existence or occurrence and completeness assertions for a transaction class that decreases an account balance affect the assessments for the opposite account balance assertions. Thus, because both cash receipts and sales adjustments transactions decrease the accounts receivable balance, the assessments for existence or occurrence for these transaction classes affect the combined assessment for the completeness assertion for the accounts receivable balance. Similarly, the assessments for completeness for these transaction classes affect the combined assessment for the existence or occurrence assertion for the accounts receivable balance. (To review the initial presentation of linking control risk assessments for transaction class assertions to arrive at combined control risk assessments for account balance assertions, see pages 317–319 in Chapter 9.)

The appropriate inherent risk assessments and *planned assessed levels of control risk* for account balance assertions are used in the audit risk model in the planning phase to arrive at the appropriate *planned detection risk* and associated *planned level of substantive tests* embodied in the preliminary audit strategy for each assertion. If the *actual* or *final control risk assessments* differ from the planned control risk assessments, the audit risk model is used again with the actual data to determine a *revised acceptable level of detection risk* and associated *revised level of substantive tests* for each assertion. Either the planned levels, if supported, or the revised levels are used in completing the design of appropriate substantive tests.

Some auditors use a matrix similar to the one illustrated in Figure 14-7 to document and correlate the various risk components that must be considered in designing substantive tests for each account balance assertion. The risk levels specified in this matrix are illustrative only and would, of course, vary based on the client's circumstances. Alternatively, when the risk components are quantified, the audit risk model can be solved mathematically for the acceptable levels of detection risk.

FIGURE 14-7 • CORRELATION OF RISK COMPONENTS—ACCOUNTS RECEIVABLE ASSERTIONS

Risk Component	Existence or Occurrence	Completeness	Rights and Obligations	Valuation or Allocation	Presentation and Disclosure
Audit risk	Low	Low	Low	Low	Low
Inherent risk	High	Moderate	Low	High	Moderate
Control risk—sales transactions	Low[1]	Low[2]	Moderate[3]	Moderate[4]	Moderate[5]
Control risk—cash receipts	Low[2]	Low[1]	Low[3]	Low[4]	Low[5]
Control risk—sales adjustments	Moderate[2]	Low[1]	Moderate[3]	High[4]	Moderate[5]
Combined control risk[n]	Low[1]	Moderate[2]	Moderate[3]	High[4]	Moderate[5]
Acceptable detection risk[6]	Moderate	Moderate	High	Low	Moderate

[n,1,2,3,4,5] Most conservative (highest) of transaction class control risk assessments with a common superscript used as the combined control risk assessment with the same superscript per the methodology discussed in Chapter 9 on pages 317 to 319.

[6] Determined from risk components matrix in Figure 7-3 on page 236, based on levels of audit risk, inherent risk, and combined control risk indicated above for each assertion category.

DESIGNING SUBSTANTIVE TESTS

OBJECTIVE 8

Design and execute an audit program for substantive tests to achieve specific audit objectives for accounts receivable.

The next step is to finalize the audit program to achieve the specific audit objectives for each category of account balance assertions. The specific audit objectives addressed here are the ones listed in the *Account Balance Audit Objectives* column of Figure 14-1 on page 496.

In Chapter 10, we introduced a general framework for developing audit programs for substantive tests (see Figure 10-4 on page 346). Of the steps listed under the heading *Complete Preliminary Planning* in Figure 10-4, the application of items 1 through 4 to accounts receivable has already been considered in this chapter. In this section, we consider the options regarding the design of substantive tests identified in step 5, and proceed with the specification of substantive tests for accounts receivable following the sequence suggested in the lower portion of Figure 10-4.

A listing of possible substantive tests that might be included in an audit program developed on this basis appears in Figure 14-8. Note that this figure does not represent a formal audit program because there is no working paper heading and there are no columns for supporting working paper references, initials, and dates. Instead, for instructional purposes there are columns to indicate the categories of substantive tests referred to in Figure 10-4 and the specific account balance audit objectives from Figure 14-1 to which each test applies. Note that several of the tests apply to more than one audit objective and that each objective is addressed by multiple possible tests. Each of the tests is explained in a following section, including comments on how some tests can be tailored based on the applicable acceptable level of detection risk to be achieved.

INITIAL PROCEDURES

The starting point for verifying accounts receivable and the related allowance account is tracing the current period's beginning balances to the ending audited balances in the prior year's working papers (when applicable). Next, the current period's activity in the general ledger control account and related allowance account should be reviewed for any significant entries that are unusual in nature or amount that require special investigation. In addition, a listing of all customer balances, called an **accounts receivable trial balance,** is obtained. This listing should be footed and the total compared with (1) the total of the subsidiary ledger or master file from which it was prepared and (2) the general ledger control account balance. When the client furnishes the trial balance, a sample of the customers and balances shown on the trial balance should be compared with those in the subsidiary ledger or master file and vice versa to determine that the trial balance is an accurate and complete representation of the underlying accounting records. It can then serve as the physical representation of the population of accounts receivable to be subjected to further substantive testing. Alternatively, the auditor can produce the accounts receivable trial balance directly from the client's master file using audit software.

An example of an aged trial balance of receivables working paper is presented in Figure 14-9. This working paper not only provides evidence of performance of the initial procedures just described, but several of the other substantive tests as discussed in subsequent sections. The initial procedures in verifying the accuracy of the trial balance and determining its agreement with the general ledger balance

FIGURE 14-8 • POSSIBLE SUBSTANTIVE TESTS OF ACCOUNTS RECEIVABLE ASSERTIONS

Category	Substantive Test	Account Balance Audit Objective (from p. 496)				
		EO4	C4	RO3	VA#	PD#
Initial procedures	1. Perform initial procedures on accounts receivable balances and records that will be subjected to further testing. a. Trace beginning balances for accounts receivable and related allowance to prior year's working papers. b. Review activity in general ledger accounts for accounts receivable and related allowance and investigate entries that appear unusual in amount or source. c. Obtain accounts receivable trial balance and determine that it accurately represents the underlying accounting records by: • Footing trial balance and determining agreement with (1) the total of the subsidiary ledger or accounts receivable master file and (2) the general ledger balance. • Testing agreement of customers and balances listed on trial balance with those included in subsidiary ledger or master file.				✓4,5	
Analytical procedures	2. Perform analytical procedures. a. Calculate ratios: • Accounts receivable turnover • Accounts receivable to total current assets • Rate of return on net sales • Uncollectible accounts expense to net credit sales • Uncollectible accounts expense to actual uncollectibles b. Analyze results relative to expectations based on prior years, industry data, budgeted amounts, or other data.	✓	✓		✓4,5	
Tests of details of transactions	3. Vouch a sample of recorded receivables transactions to supporting documentation (see also step 6c below). a. Vouch debits to supporting sales invoices, shipping documents, and sales orders. b. Vouch credits to remittance advices or sales adjustment authorizations for sales returns and allowances or uncollectible account write-offs.	✓	✓	✓	✓4	
	4. Perform cutoff tests for sales and sales returns. a. Select a sample of recorded sales transactions from several days before and after year-end and examine supporting sales invoices and shipping documents to determine sales were recorded in proper period. b. Select sample of credit memos issued after year-end, examine supporting documentation such as dated receiving reports, and determine that returns were recorded in proper period. Also, consider whether volume of sales returns after year-end suggests possibility of unauthorized shipments before year-end.	✓	✓			
	5. Perform cash receipts cutoff test. a. Observe that all cash received through the close of business on the last day of the fiscal year is included in cash on hand or deposits in transit and that no receipts of the subsequent period are included, or b. Review documentation such as daily cash summaries, duplicate desposit slips, and bank statements covering several days before and after the year-end date to determine proper cutoff.	✓	✓			

FIGURE 14-8 • *(Continued)*

Category	Substantive Test	Account Balance Audit Objective (from p. 496)				
		EO4	C4	RO3	VA#	PD#
Tests of details of balances	6. Confirm accounts receivable. a. Determine the form, timing, and extent of confirmation requests. b. Select and execute sample and investigate exceptions. c. For positive confirmation requests for which no reply was received, perform alternative followup procedures: • Vouch subsequent payments identifiable with items comprising account balance at confirmation date to supporting documentation as in step 3b above. • Vouch items comprising balance at confirmation date to documentary support as in step 3a above. d. Summarize results of confirmation and alternative followup procedures.	✓	✓	✓	✓4	
	7. Evaluate adequacy of allowance for uncollectible accounts. a. Foot and crossfoot aged trial balance of receivables and agree total to general ledger. b. Test aging by vouching amounts in aging categories for sample of accounts to supporting documentation. c. For past-due accounts: • Examine evidence of collectibility such as correspondence with customers and outside collection agencies, credit reports, and customers' financial statements. • Discuss collectibility of accounts with appropriate management personnel. d. Evaluate adequacy of allowance component for each aging category and in the aggregate.				✓5	
Required procedures	Confirmation of receivables included as step 6 above.					
Presentation and disclosure	8. Compare statement presentation with GAAP. a. Determine that receivables are properly identified and classified as to type and expected period of realization. b Determine whether there are credit balances that are significant in the aggregate and that should be reclassified as liabilities. c. Determine the appropriateness of disclosures and accounting for related party, pledged, assigned, or factored receivables.				✓4	✓4,5

relate primarily to the clerical and mathematical accuracy component of the valuation or allocation assertion.

ANALYTICAL PROCEDURES

The following financial ratios are often used in applying analytical procedures to accounts receivable:

FIGURE 14-9 • AGED TRIAL BALANCE WORKING PAPER

Bates Company
Aged Trial Balance - Accounts Receivable - Trade
December 31, 19X1
(PBC)

Acct. 120

W/P Ref: B-1
Prepared By: A.C.E. Date: 1/15/X2
Reviewed By: P.A.R. Date: 1/20/X2

	Account Name	Past Due Over 90 Days	Past Due Over 60 Days	Past Due Over 30 Days	Current	Balance Per Books 12/31/X1	Adjustments	Balance Per Audit 12/31/X1	
	Ace Engineering		2,529.04	2,016.14	11,875.90	16,421.08 √		16,421.08	
ø	Applied Devices			15,938.89 Ч	27,901.11 Ч	43,840.00 √		43,840.00	C1
ø	Barry Manufacturing	1,088.92 Ч	743.12 Ч	3,176.22 Ч	8,993.01 Ч	14,001.27 √		14,001.27	C2
ø	Brandt Electronics	501.10 Ч	7,309.50 Ч	30,948.01 Ч	24,441.25 Ч	63,199.86 √		63,199.86	C3
	Cermetrics, Inc.			3,813.76	8,617.30	12,431.06 √		12,431.06	
ø	Columbia Components				4,321.18 Ч	4,321.18 √		4,321.18	
	Drake Manufacturing			739.57	2,953.88	3,693.45 √		3,693.45	
	EMC		1,261.01	1,048.23	16,194.76	18,504.00 √		18,504.00	
ø	Groton Electric		7,799.36 Ч	20,006.63 Ч	89,017.15 Ч	116,823.14 √		116,823.14	C4
	Harvey Industries		1,709.16	6,111.25	18,247.31	26,067.72 √		26,067.72	
ø	Jed Inc.	2,615.87 Ч	12,098.00 Ч	15,434.46 Ч	56,536.88 Ч	86,685.21 √	(9,416.96)	77,268.25	C5
	Jericho Electric		1,198.72	13,123.14		14,321.86 √		14,321.86	
	⋮	⋮	⋮	⋮	⋮	⋮	⋮	⋮	
ø	W & M Manufacturing Corp.		1,904.65 Ч	2,166.78 Ч	28,389.69 Ч	32,461.12 √		32,461.12	C60
	Yancey Corp.	814.98	2,861.05	9,874.13	13,561.80	27,111.96 √		27,111.96	
		10,157.46	56,705.59	160,537.28	392,136.41	619,536.74 √	(9,416.96)	610,119.78	
		√	√	√	√	√ B	√ B	√ B	

√ Footed or crossfooted.
ø Customer name and balance per books agreed to subsidiary ledger
Ч Aging verified by examining transaction/dates of related unpaid sales invoices in subsidiary ledger
C# Account selected for confirmation - see W/P B-2

Ratio	Formula
Accounts receivable turnover	Net sales ÷ Accounts receivable (average or yearend as explained on page 215)
Accounts receivable to total current assets	Accounts receivable ÷ Total current assets
Rate of return on net sales	Net income ÷ Net sales
Uncollectible accounts expense to net credit sales	Uncollectible accounts expense ÷ Net sales
Uncollectible accounts expense to actual uncollectibles	Uncollectible accounts expense ÷ Actual uncollectibles

Note that several of the ratios are based on the direct relationship between accounts receivable and sales. The absence of unexpected significant fluctuations in comparing each ratio with prior year, expected results, and industry data provides evidence that supports the reasonableness of the account balance and other components used in the calculations. In contrast, an unexpected significant fluctuation requires further investigation by the auditor to determine whether one or more of the components used in the calculation is misstated. For example, an unexpected increase in the accounts receivable turnover ratio could result from overstated net sales, understated accounts receivable, or both. In addition to the annual aggregates referred to in the ratios, the auditor might utilize month-to-month comparisons of sales and/or accounts receivable data for the current and prior years.

As noted in Chapter 10, analytical procedures may be particularly effective and efficient as a substantive test when independent variables can be used to predict revenue and the related receivables as would be the case for a regulated utility or a university. For accounts receivable and sales, analytical procedures can provide evidence pertaining to the existence or occurrence, completeness, and valuation or allocation assertions.

TESTS OF DETAILS OF TRANSACTIONS

As discussed previously, certain tests of details of transactions may be performed during interim work along with tests of controls in the form of dual-purpose tests. This includes the tests described in the next section. The cutoff tests described in subsequent sections are always performed as part of year-end work.

Vouch Recorded Receivables to Supporting Transactions

The customer account file maintained by the client should contain such documents as customer orders, sales orders, shipping documents, sales invoices, credit memoranda, and correspondence. In performing this test, a sample of debits to customers' accounts can be vouched to supporting sales invoices and matching documents to provide evidence pertaining to the existence or occurrence, rights and obligations, and valuation or allocation assertions. Credits can be vouched to remittance advices and sales adjustment authorizations. Evidence that these reductions in customer balances are legitimate pertains to the completeness assertion for accounts receivable.

These tests may be performed more extensively when the acceptable level of detection risk to be achieved is low, when confirmation procedures are not practicable, or to supplement confirmation procedures when certain circumstances arise, as discussed in a later section.

Perform Cutoff Tests for Sales and Sales Returns

The **sales cutoff test** is designed to obtain reasonable assurance that (1) sales and accounts receivable are recorded in the accounting period in which the transactions occurred and (2) the corresponding entries for inventories and cost of goods sold are made in the same period.

Sales should be recorded in the period in which legal title to the goods passes to the buyer. When goods are shipped from inventory F.O.B. (free on board) shipping point, title passes on the date of shipment. When the terms of sale are F.O.B. destination, title does not pass until the buyer receives the goods. In such a case, as a practical matter the seller may add one to a few days to the shipping date to estimate the date the goods will arrive at their destination as a basis for determining the date on which to record the sale. In the case of goods custom-manufactured for the buyer, title may pass and the sale may be recorded as soon as the goods are ready for delivery, even though shipment does not occur until a later date.

The sales cutoff test is made as of the balance sheet date. For sales of goods from inventory, the test involves comparison of a sample of recorded sales from the last few days of the current period and the first few days of the next period with shipping documents to determine whether the transactions were recorded in the proper period. When prenumbered shipping documents are issued in sequence and the auditor is on hand to observe the number of the last shipping document used in the current period, he or she can then determine that each sales transaction recorded prior to year-end is supported by a shipping document with a number issued in the current period and that each sales transaction recorded after year-end is supported by a shipping document with a number issued in the subsequent period. For custom-manufactured goods, the auditor may need to examine related sales agreements. It may also be necessary to determine the accuracy of the cutoff for any *drop-shipments* made by the client's suppliers directly to the client's customers.

The sales cutoff test provides evidence concerning the existence or occurrence and completeness assertions for accounts receivable and sales. For a calendar-year client, if January sales are recorded in December, there is a misstatement of the existence or occurrence assertion. Conversely, if December sales are not recorded until January, there is a misstatement of the completeness assertion.

The **sales return cutoff test** is similar and is particularly directed toward the possibility that returns made prior to year-end are not recorded until after year-end, resulting in the overstatement of receivables and sales. The correct timing can be determined by examining dated receiving reports for returned merchandise and correspondence with customers. The auditor should also be alert to the possibility that an unusually heavy volume of sales returns shortly after year-end could signal unauthorized shipments before year-end to inflate recorded sales and receivables.

Perform Cash Receipts Cutoff Test

The **cash receipts cutoff test** is designed to obtain reasonable assurance that cash receipts are recorded in the accounting period in which received. A proper cutoff at the balance sheet date is essential to the correct presentation of both cash and accounts receivable. For example, if December collections from customers are not recorded until January, accounts receivable will be overstated and cash will be understated at the balance sheet date. Conversely, if January collections from customers are recorded in December, cash will be overstated and accounts receivable will be understated. Thus, this test relates to the existence or occurrence and completeness assertions for both cash and accounts receivable.

Evidence concerning the promptness of the cutoff can be obtained by personal observation or a review of documentation. If the auditor can be present at the year-end date, he or she can observe that all collections received prior to the close of business are included in cash on hand or in deposits in transit and are credited to accounts receivable. An alternative to personal observation is to review supporting documentation such as the daily cash summary and validated deposit slip for the last day of the year. The objective of the review is to determine that the deposit slip total agrees with the receipts shown on the daily cash summary. In addition, the auditor should determine that the receipts were recorded on the closing date.

TESTS OF DETAILS OF BALANCES

Two primary sets of procedures in this category of substantive tests for accounts receivable are discussed in the following sections: (1) the confirmation of receivables and related followup procedures and (2) procedures for evaluating the adequacy of the allowance for uncollectible accounts.

Confirm Accounts Receivable

Confirmation of accounts receivable involves direct written communication between individual customers and the auditor. As indicated earlier, this substantive test is used extensively by the auditor. Relevant considerations in performing this substantive test are as follows.

OBJECTIVE 9

Explain the use of confirmation procedures in auditing accounts receivable.

GENERALLY ACCEPTED AUDITING PROCEDURE. The confirmation of receivables is a generally accepted auditing procedure. SAS 67, *The Confirmation Process* (AU330) states that there is a presumption that the auditor will request the confirmation of accounts receivable during an audit unless

- Accounts receivable are immaterial to the financial statements,
- The use of confirmations would be ineffective as an audit procedure, or
- The auditor's combined assessment of inherent risk and control risk is low, and that assessment, in conjunction with the evidence expected to be provided by analytical procedures or other substantive tests of details, is sufficient to reduce audit risk to an acceptably low level for the applicable financial statement assertions. In many situations, both confirmation of accounts receivable and other substantive tests of details are necessary to reduce audit risk to an acceptably low level for the applicable financial statement assertions.

An auditor who does not request confirmation of receivables should document in the working papers how he or she overcame the presumption that confirmations should be requested. For example, the auditor might state the conclusion that based on the prior year's audit experience on that engagement, it is expected that the responses would be unreliable or the response rates would be inadequate in the current year. Also, in some cases, debtors may be unable to confirm balances if they use voucher systems that show the amount owed on individual transactions, but not the total amount owed to one creditor. This is generally true of governmental agencies. The auditor may be able to overcome this problem by confirming individual transactions rather than balances.

Occasionally, clients have prohibited auditors from confirming any or certain accounts receivable. Complete prohibition represents a serious limitation on the scope of the audit that generally results in a disclaimer of opinion on the financial statements. The effect of partial prohibition should be evaluated on the basis of management's reasons therefor, and whether the auditor can obtain sufficient evidence from other auditing procedures.

FORM OF CONFIRMATION. There are two forms of confirmation request: (1) the *positive* form, which requires the debtor to respond whether or not the balance shown is correct and (2) the *negative* form, which requires the debtor to respond only when the amount shown is incorrect. The two forms are illustrated in Figure 14-10. The positive confirmation request is usually made in the form of a separate letter, but it may be in the form of a stamp on the customer's monthly statement. In contrast, the negative request is usually in the form of a stamp. The positive form generally produces the better evidence, because under the negative form, the failure to receive a response can only lead to a presumption that the balance is correct, whereas the customer may have overlooked the request or neglected to return an exception.

A variation of the positive form is "the blank form," so named because the customer's balance is not stated. Instead, the customer is asked to fill in the balance. The use of this form provides a high degree of assurance about the information confirmed. However, the extra work required of the respondent may significantly reduce the response rate.

The selection of the form of the confirmation request rests with the auditor. In making the decision, the auditor considers the acceptable level of detection risk and the composition of the customer balances. The positive form is used when detection risk is low or individual customer balances are relatively large. AU 330.20 indicates that the negative form should be used only when all three of the following conditions apply:

- The acceptable level of detection risk for the related assertions is moderate or high.
- A large number of small balances is involved.
- The auditor has no reason to believe that the recipients of the requests are unlikely to give them consideration.

Frequently, a combination of the two forms is used in a single engagement. For example, in the audit of a public utility, the auditor may elect to use the negative form for residential customers and the positive form for commercial customers. When the positive form is used, the auditor should generally follow up with a second and sometimes an additional request to those debtors that fail to reply.

FIGURE 14-10 • CONFIRMATION REQUEST FORMS

Positive request—letter form:

Bates Company
P.O. Box 1922
Sandusky, Ohio 44870

Ace Engineering Service
Box 131
Indiana, Pennsylvania 15701

This request is being sent to you to enable our independent auditors to confirm the correctness of our records. It is not a request for payment.

Our records on December 31, 19X1 showed an amount of $16,421.08 receivable from you. Please confirm whether this agrees with your records on that date by signing and returning this form direct to our auditors. An addressed envelope is enclosed for this purpose. If you find any difference please report details direct to our auditors in the space provided below.

____
Controller

The above amount is correct ☐. The above amount is incorrect for the following reasons: _____
____
____

____
(Individual or Company Name)

By: ____________________________

Conf. No. 1.

Negative request—stamp form:

Please examine this monthly statement carefully and advise our auditors

Reddy & Abel
Certified Public Accountants
465 City Center Bldg.
Marian, New York 11748

____

as to any exceptions.

A self-addressed stamped envelope is enclosed for your convenience.

THIS IS NOT A REQUEST FOR PAYMENT

TIMING AND EXTENT OF REQUESTS. When the acceptable level of detection risk is low, the auditor ordinarily requests confirmation of receivables as of the balance sheet date. Otherwise, the confirmation date may be one or two months earlier. In such case, the auditor is expected to vouch material changes between the confirmation date and the balance sheet date and may elect to reconfirm accounts with unusual changes.

The extent of requests, or sample size, is inversely related to each of the following factors: (1) the acceptable level of detection risk for the assertions to which the confirmation evidence will apply, (2) the extent to which other substantive tests contribute to achieving that detection risk, and (3) tolerable misstatement for accounts receivable. Negative confirmation requests require larger sample sizes than positive requests. Stratification may also affect sample size. For example, auditors frequently seek confirmation of all accounts in excess of a certain dollar balance or in excess of a certain age, and select a random sample of all other accounts. Sample size may be determined judgmentally or with the aid of a statistical sampling plan as explained in Chapter 12.

CONTROLLING THE REQUESTS. The auditor must control every step in the confirmation process. This means

- Ascertaining that the amount, name, and address on the confirmation agree with the corresponding data in the customer's account.
- Maintaining custody of the confirmations until they are mailed.
- Using the firm's own return address envelopes for the confirmations.
- Personally depositing the requests in the mail.
- Insisting that the returns be sent directly to the auditor.

Client assistance can be used in the preparation of the requests, provided the foregoing controls are observed.

A working paper should indicate each account selected for confirmation, the results obtained from each request, and cross references to the actual confirmation responses. A confirmation control working paper is illustrated in Figure 14-11. The actual confirmation responses should also be retained in the working papers.

DISPOSITION OF EXCEPTIONS. Confirmation responses will inevitably contain some exceptions. Exceptions may be attributed to goods in transit from the client to the customer, returned goods or payments in transit from the customer to the client, items in dispute, errors, and irregularities. All exceptions should be investigated by the auditor and their resolution indicated in the working papers, as illustrated in Figure 14-11.

ALTERNATIVE PROCEDURES FOR DEALING WITH NONRESPONSES. When no response has been received after the second or third positive confirmation request to a customer, alternative procedures should ordinarily be performed. AU330.31 acknowledges that the omission of such procedures may be acceptable when both of the following conditions apply:

FIGURE 14-11 • CONFIRMATION CONTROL WORKING PAPER

Bates Company
Accounts Receivable Confirmation Control—Acct. 120
December 31, 19X1

W/P Ref: B-2
Prepared By: A.C.E. Date: 1/28/X2
Reviewed By: P.A.R. Date: 1/31/X2

Conf. No.	Customer	Book Value	Confirmed Value ø	Audited Value	(Over) Under Statement	Subsequent Collections Examined Thru 1-28-X2
1	Applied Devices	43,840.00	43,480.00	43,480.00		
2	Barry Mfg.	14,001.27	NR	14,001.27		14,001.27 ✓
3	Brandt Electronics	63,199.96	63,199.96	63,199.96		
4	Groton Electric	116,823.14	116,823.14	116,823.14		
5	Jed Inc.	86,685.21	77,268.25	77,268.25	(9,416.96) (X1)	
60	W & M Mfg. Corp.	32,461.12	NR	32,461.12 ᛋ		4,071.43 ✓
	Totals	470,847.92	414,968.57	461,430.96	(9,416.96)	

Response Recap:	# Items	$ Value
Confirmations mailed	60	470,847.92
Confirmations received	58	414,968.57
Response %	97	88

Summary of Results:	# Items	$ Value
Account total	300	619,536.74
Book value of confirmation sample	60	470,847.92
% Coverage of book value		76
Audited value of sample	60	461,430.96
Ratio of audited to book value of sample		98

ø Signed confirmation response attached for confirmed values.
NR Nonresponse—alternative procedures performed.
✓ Examined entries in cash receipts journal and related remittance advices for total collections indicated.
ᛋ Examined supporting documentation for portion of book value remaining uncollected as of 1/28/X2.
(X1) Credit memo issued 1/12/X2 for merchandise returned 12/28/X1. Adjusting entry:

	Dr.	Cr.	
Dr. Sales Returns	9,416.96		See W/P B-1 and AE-1
Cr. Accounts Receivable		9,416.96	

- There are no unusual qualitative factors or systematic characteristics related to the nonresponses, such as that all nonresponses pertain to year-end transactions.
- The nonresponses, projected as 100% misstatements to the population and added to the sum of all other unadjusted differences, would not affect the auditor's decision about whether the financial statements are materially misstated.

The two main alternative procedures are examining subsequent collections and vouching open invoices comprising customer balances.

EXAMINE SUBSEQUENT COLLECTIONS. The best evidence of existence and collectibility is the receipt of payment from the customer. Before the conclusion of the audit field work, the client will receive payments from many customers on amounts owed at the confirmation date. The matching of such collections back to open (unpaid) invoices comprising the customers' balances at the confirmation date establishes the collectibility of the accounts.

In performing this test, the auditor should recognize the possible adverse implications of collections that cannot be matched to specific transactions or balances. For example, a round sum amount may, on investigation, reveal items in dispute, and token payments on large balances may indicate financial instability on the part of the customer.

VOUCH OPEN INVOICES COMPRISING BALANCES. This is a variation of step 3a in Figure 14-8. The only difference is that the procedure is limited to items comprising the balances of accounts as of the confirmation date for which confirmation responses were not received rather than the entire population of accounts receivable.

SUMMARIZING AND EVALUATING RESULTS. The auditor's working papers should contain a summary of the results from confirming accounts receivable. The summary should provide, as a minimum, statistical data on

- The number and dollar value of confirmations sent and responses received.
- The proportion of the population total covered by the sample.
- The relationship between the audited and book values of items included in the sample.

The lower portion of Figure 14-11 illustrates how such data might be presented. Statistical or nonstatistical procedures may be used to project misstatements found in the sample to the population as explained in Chapter 12.

The combined evidence from the confirmations, alternative procedures performed on nonresponses, and other tests of details and analytical procedures is evaluated to determine whether sufficient evidence has been obtained to support management's assertions about gross accounts receivable. When numerous exceptions are found, or insufficient responses are received from confirmation requests and the auditor is unable to obtain sufficient competent evidence from other substantive tests, he or she will be unable to issue a standard auditor's report.

APPLICABILITY TO ASSERTIONS. The confirmation of accounts receivable is the primary source of evidence in meeting the existence or occurrence assertion. Acknowledgment of the debt by the customer in the response confirms that the client has a legal claim on the customer. Thus, this test also provides evidence concerning the rights and obligations assertion. The confirmation of accounts receivable is not a request for payment. Thus, it does not provide evidence as to the collectibility of the balance due. However, the responses may reveal previously paid items or disputed items that affect the proper valuation of the amount due. In this sense, confirming accounts receivable relates to the valuation or allocation assertion for gross accounts receivable.

When a customer's response indicates agreement with the book balance, there is evidence that the balance is complete. However, the evidence about the completeness assertion is limited because (1) unrecorded receivables cannot be confirmed and (2) customers are more likely to report errors of overstatement than errors of understatement.

Evaluate Adequacy of Allowance for Uncollectible Accounts

This test of balances involves

- Footing and crossfooting the **aged trial balance** of accounts receivable and agreeing the total to the general ledger balance (if different than the one used in step 1c in Figure 14-8).
- Testing the aging of the amounts shown in the aging categories on the aged trial balance.
- Considering evidence concerning the collectibility of past due amounts.
- Assessing the reasonableness of the percentages used to compute the allowance component required for each aging category and the adequacy of the overall allowance.

An example of an aged trial balance is presented in Figure 14-9 on page 525. The aging of a customer's balance can be tested by vouching the amounts shown in each aging category to the subsidiary ledger or master file and determining the length of time between the dates the unpaid sales invoices comprising each aged amount were recorded and the trial balance date. Alternatively, the auditor can use generalized audit software to reperform the entire aging of the client's master file.

In considering the collectibility of past due amounts, the auditor may examine correspondence with customers and outside collection agencies, review customers' credit reports and financial statements, and discuss the collectibility of specific accounts with appropriate management personnel. The allowance for uncollectible accounts is an accounting estimate made by management that involves both objective and subjective considerations. The auditor's responsibility is to judge the reasonableness of the allowance and related provision for uncollectible accounts expense. From the aging data, information about collectibility, and analysis of the client's prior experience with uncollectible accounts, the auditor can assess the reasonableness of the percentages used to compute the allowance component required for each aging category and the adequacy of the overall allowance. When the client's controls over (1) granting credit and (2) writing off uncollectible accounts are strong, less evidence will be required in making this assessment than when controls are weak.

COMPARISON OF STATEMENT PRESENTATION WITH GAAP

The auditor must be knowledgeable about the statement presentation and disclosure requirements for accounts receivable and sales under GAAP. The requirements include proper identification and classification. A review of the accounts receivable trial balance may indicate receivables from employees, officers, affiliated companies, and other related parties that should be reclassified or separately disclosed, if material. The same source may reveal receivables with credit balances that if significant in the aggregate should be reclassified as current liabilities. GAAP also requires proper classification of receivables as current or noncurrent, and disclosures concerning the pledging, assigning, or factoring of receivables. Evidence relevant to these matters should be obtainable by inquiring of management and reviewing the minutes of board of directors' meetings and loan agreements. Management's representations on these matters should be obtained in writing in a *client representation letter* as one of the final steps in the audit as explained in Chapter 19.

LEARNING CHECK:

14-15 a. Identify the transaction classes that should be considered in assessing control risk for accounts receivable assertions.
b. Which transaction class control risk assessments should be considered in assessing control risk for the existence or occurrence account balance assertion for accounts receivable?
c. When is it necessary to determine a *revised acceptable level of detection risk* and a *revised level of substantive tests?*

14-16 State several financial ratios and their formulas that can be used by the auditor in applying analytical procedures to accounts receivable.

14-17 What is involved in vouching recorded receivables transactions to supporting documentation and to what specific account balance audit objectives does the evidence pertain?

14-18 What cutoff tests are performed for accounts receivable, how are they performed, and to what account balance audit objectives does the evidence pertain?

14-19 a. Under what circumstances may it not be necessary to confirm accounts receivable?
b. What factors should be considered in determining the form of the confirmation request?
c. When positive confirmation requests are used, how does the auditor deal with nonresponses?

14-20 a. What roles does an *aged trial balance* play in an audit?
b. What procedures should be applied to the aged trial balance?

KEY TERMS:

Accounts receivable trial balance, p. 522
Aged trial balance, p. 534
Cash receipts cutoff test, p. 527
Sales cutoff test, p. 527
Sales return cutoff test, p. 527

SUMMARY

An entity's revenue cycle includes the activities pertaining to sales, cash receipts, and sales adjustments transactions. These transactions affect several significant accounts in the financial statements, including cash, accounts receivable, inventories, and sales. The nature of many of the activities in this cycle results in high inherent risk for several significant financial statement assertions such as the existence or occurrence of accounts receivable. Because of this, many companies have adopted extensive provisions within their internal control structures to prevent or detect misstatements. When the auditor expects these controls to be effective, he or she adopts the lower assessed level of control risk approach in auditing the related revenue cycle assertions. In planning substantive tests of accounts receivable, the auditor is particularly concerned with the risk of overstatement of net receivables due to the inclusion of fictitious receivables or an inadequate allowance for uncollectible accounts. There is a presumption that the auditor will request the confirmation of accounts receivable during an audit unless certain specified conditions apply.

BIBLIOGRAPHY

AICPA Professional Standards:

SAS 67 (AU 330), The Confirmation Process.

IAU 8 (AU 8008A), Additional Guidance on—Observation of Inventory, Confirmation of Accounts Receivable and Inquiry Regarding Litigation and Claims.

AICPA, *Confirmation of Accounts Receivable.* Auditing Procedures Study. New York, 1984.

Bailey, Charles D., and Ballard, Gene. "Improving Response Rates to Accounts Receivable Confirmations: An Experiment Using Four Techniques," *Auditing: A Journal of Practice & Theory* (Spring 1986), pp. 77–85.

Beran, Denny, and Evans, Richard. "Auditing for Sales Adjustment Fraud," *Internal Auditor* (February 1990), pp. 51–56.

Caster, Paul. "The Role of Confirmations as Audit Evidence," *Journal of Accountancy* (February 1992), pp. 73–76.

Guerico, John P., Rice, E. Barry, and Sherman, Martin F. "Old Fashioned Fraud by Employees Is Alive and Well: Results of a Survey of Practicing CPAs," *The CPA Journal* (September 1988), pp. 74–77.

Levine, M., and Fitzsimmons, A. "SAS No. 67 Fine Tunes the Confirmation Process," *The CPA Journal* (October 1992), pp. 26–30.

Swearingen, James G., Wilkes, James A., and Swearingen, Sandra L. "Confirmation Response Differences Between Businesses, Clerks, and Consumers," *The CPA Journal* (May 1991), pp. 58–60.

Williams, David D., and Ziegler, Teresa J. "Positive-Out Negative-In Confirmations—An Innovative Approach," *The CPA Journal* (July 1987), pp. 78–80.

OBJECTIVE QUESTIONS

Indicate the best answer for each of the following multiple choice questions.

14-21 This question applies to internal control over credit sales and sales adjustment transactions.

1. Which of the following controls most likely would be effective in offsetting the tendency of sales personnel to maximize sales volume at the expense of high bad debt write-offs?
   a. Employees responsible for authorizing sales and bad debt write-offs are denied access to cash.
   b. Shipping documents and sales invoices are matched by an employee who does *not* have authority to write off bad debts.
   c. Employees involved in the credit-granting function are separated from the sales function.

d. Subsidiary accounts receivable records are reconciled to the control account by an employee independent of the authorization of credit.

2. Which of the following controls most likely would help ensure that all credit sales transactions of an entity are recorded?
   a. The billing department supervisor sends copies of approved sales orders to the credit department for comparison to authorized credit limits and current customer account balances.
   b. The accounting department supervisor independently reconciles the accounts receivable subsidiary ledger to the accounts receivable control account monthly.
   c. The accounting department supervisor controls the mailing of monthly statements to customers and investigates any differences reported by customers.
   d. The billing department supervisor matches prenumbered shipping documents with entries in the sales journal.

3. Which of the following internal control procedures most likely would assure that all billed sales are correctly posted to the accounts receivable ledger?
   a. Daily sales summaries are compared to daily postings to the accounts receivable ledger.
   b. Each sales invoice is supported by a prenumbered shipping document.
   c. The accounts receivable ledger is reconciled daily to the control account in the general ledger.
   d. Each shipment on credit is supported by a prenumbered sales invoice.

4. An auditor most likely would review an entity's periodic accounting for the numerical sequence of shipping documents and invoices to support management's financial statement assertion of
   a. Existence or occurrence.
   b. Rights and obligations.
   c. Valuation or allocation.
   d. Completeness.

5. Sound internal control procedures dictate that defective merchandise returned by customers should be presented initially to the
   a. Accounts receivable supervisor.
   b. Receiving clerk.
   c. Shipping department supervisor.
   d. Sales clerk.

14-22 This question pertains to internal control over cash receipts transactions.

1. An auditor would consider a cashier's job description to contain compatible duties if the cashier receives remittances from the mailroom and also prepares the
   a. Prelist of individual checks.
   b. Monthly bank reconciliation.
   c. Daily deposit slip.
   d. Remittance advices.

2. The questions below appear on an Internal Control Questionnaire. Which question, if answered NO, would have disclosed that the cashier diverted cash received over the counter from a customer to his or her own use and wrote off the receivable as a bad debt?
   a. Are aging schedules of accounts receivable prepared periodically and reviewed by a responsible official?
   b. Are journal entries approved by a responsible official?
   c. Are receipts given directly to the cashier by the person who opens the mail?
   d. Are remittance advices, letters, or envelopes that accompany receipts separated and given directly to the accounting department?

3. In updating a computerized accounts receivable file, which one of the following would be used as a batch control to verify the accuracy of posting cash remittances?
   a. The sum of net sales.
   b. The sum of cash deposits less discounts taken by customers.
   c. The sum of cash deposits plus discounts taken by customers.
   d. The sum of net sales plus discounts taken by customers.

4. An entity with a large volume of customer remittances by mail could most likely reduce the risk of employee misappropriation of cash by using
   a. Employee fidelity bonds.
   b. Independently prepared mailroom prelists.
   c. Daily check summaries.
   d. A bank lockbox system.

5. Immediately upon receipt of cash, a responsible employee should
   a. Record the amount in the cash receipts journal.
   b. Prepare a remittance listing.
   c. Update the subsidiary accounts receivable records.
   d. Prepare a deposit slip in triplicate.

14-23 This question relates to substantive tests of accounts receivable.

1. An auditor's purpose in reviewing credit ratings of customers with delinquent accounts receivable most likely to obtain evidence concerning management's assertions about
   a. Presentation and disclosure.
   b. Existence or occurrence.
   c. Rights and obligations.
   d. Valuation or allocation.

2. The negative request form of accounts receivable confirmation is useful particularly when the

	Assessed Level of Control Risk Relating to Receivables is	**Number of Small Balances is**	**Consideration by the Recipient is**
a.	Low	Many	Likely
b.	Low	Few	Unlikely
c.	High	Few	Likely
d.	High	Many	Likely

3. Which of the following most likely would be detected by an auditor's review of a client's sales cutoff?
   a. Unrecorded sales for the year.
   b. Lapping of year-end accounts receivable.
   c. Excessive sales discounts.
   d. Unauthorized goods returned for credit.

4. Which of the following most likely would give the most assurance concerning the valuation assertion of accounts receivable?
   a. Tracing amounts in the subsidiary ledger to details on shipping documents.
   b. Comparing receivable turnover ratios to industry statistics for reasonableness.
   c. Inquiring about receivables pledged under loan agreements.
   d. Assessing the allowance for uncollectible accounts for reasonableness.

5. Cutoff tests designed to detect credit sales made before the end of the year that have been recorded in the subsequent year provide assurance about management's assertion of

a. Presentation.
b. Completeness.
c. Rights.
d. Existence.

Comprehensive Questions

14-24 **(Controls over sales and cash receipts processing)** The flowchart on page 540 depicts the activities relating to the shipping, billing, and collecting processes used by Smallco Lumber Company.

Required

Identify weaknesses in the internal control structure relating to the activities of (a) warehouse clerk, (b) bookkeeper #1, (c) bookkeeper #2, and (d) collection clerk.

AICPA

14-25 **(Internal control questionnaire—cash receipts)** Harris, CPA, has been engaged to audit the financial statements of the Spartan Drug Store, Inc. Spartan is a medium-sized retail outlet that sells a wide variety of consumer goods. All sales are for cash or check. Cashiers utilize cash registers to process these transactions. There are no receipts by mail, and there are no credit card or charge sales.

Required

Construct the "Processing Cash Collections" segment of the internal control questionnaire on "Cash Receipts" to be used in the evaluation of the internal control structure for the Spartan Drug Store, Inc. Each question should elicit either a YES or NO response.

AICPA (adapted)

14-26 **(Controls over cash receipts processing at a church)** You have been asked by the board of trustees of a local church to review its accounting procedures. As a part of this review, you have prepared the following comments relating to the collections made at weekly services and recordkeeping for members' contributions:

1. The church's board of trustees has delegated responsibility for financial management and audit of the financial records to the finance committee. This group prepares the annual budget and approves major disbursements but is not involved in collections or recordkeeping. No audit has been considered necessary in recent years because the same trusted employee has kept church records and served as financial secretary for 15 years.
2. The collection at the weekly service is taken by a team of ushers. The head usher counts the collection in the church following each service. He then places the collection and a notation of the amount counted in the church safe. Next morning the financial secretary opens the safe and counts the collection again. She withholds about $100 to meet cash expenditures during the coming week and deposits the remainder of the collection intact. To facilitate the deposit, members who contribute by check are asked to draw their checks to "cash."

Required

Describe the weaknesses and recommend improvements in procedures for collections made at weekly services. Organize your answer using the following format:

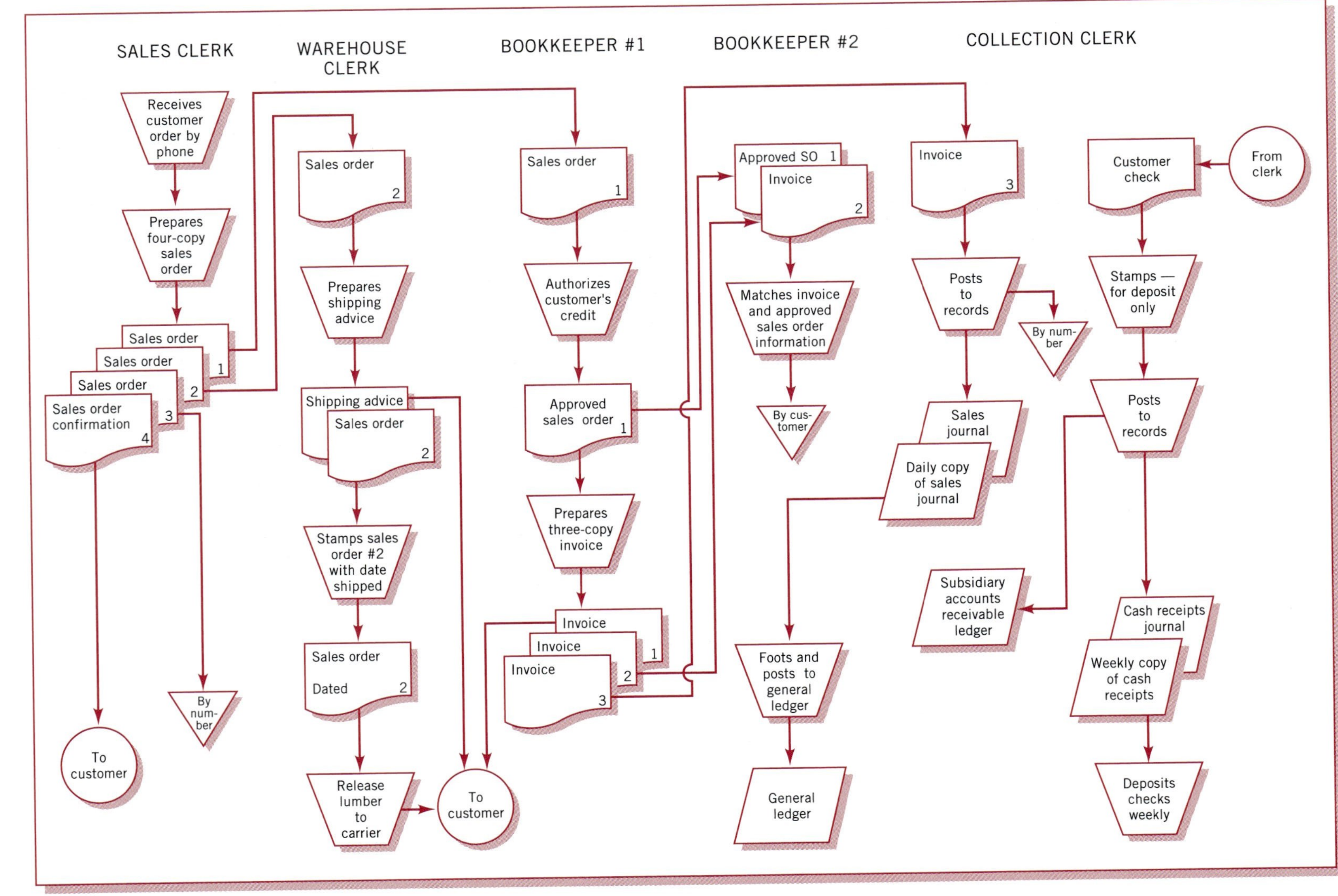

SALES CLERK
WAREHOUSE CLERK
BOOKKEEPER #1
BOOKKEEPER #2
COLLECTION CLERK
Receives customer order by phone
Prepares four-copy sales order
Sales order 1
Sales order 2
Sales order 3
Sales order confirmation 4
To customer
By num-ber
Sales order 2
Prepares shipping advice
Shipping advice
Sales order 2
Stamps sales order #2 with date shipped
Sales order Dated 2
Release lumber to carrier
To customer
Sales order 1
Authorizes customer's credit
Approved sales order 1
Prepares three-copy invoice
Invoice 1
Invoice 2
Invoice 3
Approved SO 1
Invoice 2
Matches invoice and approved sales order information
By cus-tomer
Foots and posts to general ledger
General ledger
Invoice 3
Posts to records
By num-ber
Sales journal
Daily copy of sales journal
Subsidiary accounts receivable ledger
From clerk
Customer check
Stamps — for deposit only
Posts to records
Cash receipts journal
Weekly copy of cash receipts
Deposits checks weekly

Weakness	Recommended Improvement(s)

AICPA (adapted)

14-27 **(Controls over processing cash admission fees at a museum)** The Art Appreciation Society operates a museum for the benefit and enjoyment of the community. During hours when the museum is open to the public, two clerks who are positioned at the entrance collect a five-dollar admission fee from each nonmember patron. Members of the Art Appreciation Society are permitted to enter free of charge on presentation of their membership cards.

At the end of the day, one of the clerks delivers the proceeds to the treasurer. The treasurer counts the cash in the presence of the clerk and places it in a safe. Each Friday afternoon, the treasurer and one of the clerks deliver all cash held in the safe to the bank and receive an authenticated deposit slip that provides the basis for the weekly entry in the cash receipts journal.

The board of directors of the Art Appreciation Society has identified a need to improve its internal control over cash admission fees. The board has determined that the cost of installing turnstiles or sales booths or otherwise altering the physical layout of the museum will greatly exceed any benefits that may be derived. However, the board has agreed that the sale of admission tickets must be an integral part of its improvement efforts.

Smith has been asked by the board of directors of the Art Appreciation Society to review the internal control over cash admission fees and provide suggestions for improvement.

REQUIRED

Indicate weaknesses in the existing internal control over cash admission fees that Smith should identify and recommend one improvement for each of the weaknesses identified.

Organize the answer as indicated in the following illustrative example:

Weakness	Recommendation
1. There is no basis for establishing the documentation of the number of paying patrons.	1. Prenumbered admission tickets should be issued on payment of the admission fee.

AICPA

14-28 **(Flowcharting and evaluating on-line computer processing of cash receipts)** Until recently, Consolidated Electricity Company employed a batch processing system for recording the receipt of customer payments. The following narrative describes the procedures involved in this system.

The customer's payment and the remittance advice (a punch card) are received in the treasurer's office. An accounts receivable clerk in the treasurer's office keypunches the cash receipt into the remittance advice and forwards the card to the EDP department. The cash receipt is added to a control tape listing and then filed for deposit later in the day. When the deposit slips are received from EDP later in the day (approximately 2:30 P.M. each day), the cash receipts are removed from the file and deposited with the original deposit slip. The second copy of the deposit slip and the control tape are compared for accuracy before the deposit is made and then filed together.

In the EDP department, the remittance advices received from the treasurer's office are held until 2:00 P.M. daily. At that time, the customer payments are processed to update the records on magnetic tape and prepare a deposit slip in triplicate. During the update process, data are read, nondestructively, from the master accounts receivable tape, processed, and then recorded on a new master tape. The original and second copy of the deposit slip are forwarded to the treasurer's office. The old master tape (former accounts receivable file), the remittance advices (in customer number order), and the third copy of the deposit slip are stored and filed in a secure place. The updated accounts receivable master tape is maintained in the system for processing the next day.

Consolidated Electricity Company has revised and redesigned its computer system so that it has on-line capabilities. The new cash receipts procedures, described below, are designed to take advantage of the new system.

The customer's payment and remittance advice are received in the treasurer's office as before. A cathode ray tube terminal is located in the treasurer's office to enter the cash receipts. An operator keys in the customer's number and payment from the remittance advice and checks. The cash receipt is entered into the system once the operator has confirmed that the proper account and amount are displayed on the screen. The payment is then processed on-line against the accounts receivable file maintained on magnetic disk. The cash receipts are filed for deposit later in the day. The remittance advices are filed in the order they are processed; these cards will be kept until the next working day and then destroyed. The computer prints out a deposit slip in duplicate at 2:00 P.M. for all cash receipts since the last deposit. The deposit slips are forwarded to the treasurer's office. The cash receipts are removed from the file and deposited with the original deposit slip; the duplicate deposit slip is filed for further reference. At the close of business hours (5:00 P.M.) each day, the EDP department prepares a record of the current day's cash receipts activity on a magnetic tape. This tape is then stored in a secure place in the event of a systems malfunction; after 10 working days, the tape is released for further use.

REQUIRED

a. Prepare a systems flowchart for the company's new on-line cash receipts procedures.

b. Have the new cash receipts procedures as designed and implemented by Consolidated Electricity Company created any internal control structure problems for the company? Explain your answer.

ICMA (adapted)

14-29 **(Substantive tests of accounts receivable)** The following situations were not discovered by an inexperienced staff auditor in the audit of the Parson Company.

1. Several accounts were incorrectly aged in the client's aging schedule.
2. The accounts receivable turnover ratio was far below expected results.
3. Goods billed were not shipped.
4. Some year-end sales were recorded in the wrong accounting period.
5. Several sales were posted for the correct amount but to the wrong customers in the accounts receivable ledger.
6. The allowance for uncollectible accounts was understated.
7. Several sales were entered and posted at incorrect amounts.
8. Mathematical errors were made in totaling the accounts receivable ledger.
9. An unrecorded sale at the balance sheet date was collected in the next month.
10. Several fictitious sales were recorded.

11. The pledging of some customer accounts as security for a loan was not reported in the balance sheet.

12. Some year-end cash receipts were recorded in the wrong accounting period.

REQUIRED

a. Identify the substantive test that should have detected each error.

b. For each substantive test identified in (a), indicate the account balance audit objective to which it pertains.

c. Indicate the type of evidence obtained (i.e., physical, confirmations, documentary, written representations, mathematical, oral, or analytical) from each substantive test.

(Use a tabular format for your answers with one column for each part.)

14-30 **(Sales cutoff test)** You are engaged to perform an audit for the Wilcox Corporation for the year ended December 31, 19X0.

Only merchandise shipped by the Wilcox Corporation to customers up to and including December 30, 19X0, has been eliminated from inventory. The inventory, as determined by physical inventory count, has been recorded on the books by the company's controller. No perpetual inventory records are maintained. All sales are made on an F.O.B. shipping point basis. You are to assume that all purchase invoices have been correctly recorded.

The following lists of sales invoices are entered in the sales journal for the months of December 19X0 and January 19X1, respectively.

	Sales Invoice Amount	Sales Invoice Date	Cost of Merchandise Sold	Date Shipped
			December	
a.	$ 3,000	Dec. 21	$2,000	Dec. 31
b.	2,000	Dec. 31	800	Nov. 3
c.	1,000	Dec. 29	600	Dec. 30
d.	4,000	Dec. 31	2,400	Jan. 3
e.	10,000	Dec. 30	5,600	Dec. 29 (shipped to consignee)
			January	
f.	$ 6,000	Dec. 31	$4,000	Dec. 30
g.	4,000	Jan. 2	2,300	Jan. 2
h.	8,000	Jan. 3	5,500	Dec. 31

REQUIRED

Based on a sales cutoff analysis, record necessary adjusting journal entries at December 31, in connection with the foregoing data.

AICPA

14-31 **(Confirmation procedures)** King, CPA, is auditing the financial statements of Cycle Co., an entity that has receivables from customers, which have arisen from the sale of goods in the normal course of business. King is aware that the confirmation of accounts receivable is a generally accepted auditing procedure.

REQUIRED

a. Under what circumstances could King justify omitting the confirmation of Cycle's accounts receivable?

b. In designing confirmation requests, what factors are likely to affect King's assessment of the reliability of confirmations that King sends?

c. What alternative procedures would King consider performing when replies to positive confirmation requests are **not** received?

14-32 **(Confirmation forms; collectibility of receivables)** Dodge, CPA, is auditing the financial statements of a manufacturing company with a significant amount of trade accounts receivable. Dodge is satisfied that the accounts are properly summarized and classified and that allocation, reclassifications, and valuations are made in accordance with GAAP. Dodge is planning to use accounts receivable confirmation requests to satisfy the third standard of field work as to trade accounts receivable.

REQUIRED

a. Identify and describe the two forms of accounts receivable confirmation requests and indicate what factors Dodge will consider in determining when to use each.

b. Assume Dodge has received a satisfactory response to the confirmation requests. Describe how Dodge could evaluate collectibility of the trade accounts receivable.

AICPA

14-33 **(Computer-assisted substantive tests for accounts receivable)** An auditor is conducting an audit of the financial statements of a wholesale appliance distributor. The distributor supplies appliances to hundreds of individual customers in the metropolitan area. The distributor maintains detailed accounts receivable records on a computer disk. At the end of each business day, the customer account file is updated. Each customer record in the computer file contains the following data:

1. Customer account number.
2. Address.
3. Open (unpaid) invoices at the beginning of the month, by invoice number and date.
4. Sales during the current month, by invoice number and date.
5. Individual cash receipts during the current month.
6. Date of last sale.
7. Date of last cash receipt.
8. Total sales during the year.

The auditor is planning to confirm selected accounts receivable as of the end of the current month. The auditor will have available a computer tape of the data on the accounts receivable master file on the date that the company regularly sends monthly statements to its customers. The auditor also has a general-purpose software package.

REQUIRED

The auditor is planning to perform the customary audit tests involved in the verification of accounts receivable. Identify the basic tests to be performed and describe how the use of the general-purpose software package and the tape of the accounts receivable file data might be helpful to the auditor in performing such tests. Organize your answer as follows:

Basic Receivable Audit Test	How General-Purpose Computer Software Package and Tape of Accounts Receivable Data Might Be Helpful

(Note: You may wish to refer to Chapter 13 as well as this chapter in answering this question.)

AICPA (adapted)

CASES

14-34 **(Confirming receivables; evaluating allowance)** The Ohio River Authority is an instrumentality of the state created to control, store, and preserve the waters of the Ohio River within its reservoirs and to regulate the flow therefrom to develop hydroelectric energy, to provide water for irrigation, and to conserve and protect the soil along its watershed.

The board of directors of the authority has selected us as auditors for the year ended June 30, 19X1. The interim work is completed in March, and the review of operating procedures and tests of internal controls have enabled us to determine the following:

1. The Authority has three branch offices, all located within a 300-mile radius of the home office, to conduct operations in their respective districts. The functions of these branches include the installation and servicing of power facilities, meter reading, billing, maintaining detail customers' ledgers, receiving collections on accounts receivable, and the preparation of various daily reports that are forwarded to the home office accounting department for entry to the general ledger accounts.

2. The Authority maintains separate departments under the supervision of responsible employees for each of the following functions: (a) meter installation, (b) meter reading, (c) billing and posting receivable ledgers, (d) cash collections, (e) credit approval and follow-up, (f) accounting.

3. The employees of the home office accounting department function as internal auditors and perform an audit of each branch office at least once every two years. The internal audits are comprehensive but do not include circularization (i.e., confirmation) of accounts receivable, bank balances, or outstanding liabilities.

4. Sales of primary power at wholesale rates and power sales to most of the larger commercial and industrial customers are billed at rates established under contracts with the customers. All sales of irrigation water are charged to customers at contract rates.

5. The number of customers served, classified according to major income statement captions, are wholesale 50, retail-residential 9,000, retail-commercial 1,600, and water 150.

6. Revenues from irrigation water contracts are based on a standard rate per acre as stated in the contract, regardless of the amount of water used for irrigation during the growing season from April to September. The Authority accrues this income monthly and bills the farmer at the end of the growing season.

7. The Authority requires all power customers to put up a deposit prior to installation of the power meters. Residential consumers must deposit $5; deposits of other customers range from $5 to $100. Bad debts are infrequent and, after deducting deposits, have been minor in the past.

8. Total kilowatt-hours of electricity energy sales are accounted for in the same classifications used for revenue in the income statement.
9. Accounts receivable substantially turn over every month.
10. Our internal control work did not disclose any significant exceptions in recording transactions or safeguarding assets.
11. Excerpts from financial statements audited by another CPA firm one year ago are as follows:

Balance Sheet		Income Statement	
Cash	$277,710	Sales of primary power:	
Accounts Receivable:		Wholesale	
Customer electrical	401,823	Municipalities	$1,802,516
Accrued irrigation contracts	141,825	Rural co-ops	954,919
Notes receivable	484	Other utilities	759,160
Allowance for uncollectible accounts	(584)	Retail	
Total assets	37,306,309	Commercial	771,565
Customer deposits	(57,226)	Residential	345,045
		Other operating revenues	
		Sales of water	280,460
		Fees—operating co-ops	131,699
		Other	32,209
		Net income	1,263,700

These data are comparable with the current year's statements prepared by the Authority.

REQUIRED

a. What procedures will be used in confirming accounts receivable? Indicate when confirmations will be mailed, what type of confirmations will be used, how many accounts will be circularized, and how control of detail accounts balances will be established.

b. What methods should be utilized to determine the adequacy of the allowance for uncollectible accounts?

c. What audit steps should be performed to determine that the revenue reported on the income statement is reasonable?

14-35 **(Controls and substantive tests for accounts receivable)** You have completed a study of internal controls over the accounts receivable function of a plumbing wholesale company. The plumbing wholesaler's financial statements shows sales of $4,000,000 and accounts receivable of $650,000. Sixty percent of sales are to plumbing contractors and 40% are to small independent hardware stores. A four-tiered pricing system is used, with customer price determined by previous purchases volume. Results of your study of the internal controls over accounts receivable are presented below.

1. After determining product availability, sales personnel write up the customer order using prenumbered sales invoices. Prices to be charged are determined by reference to an approved price list and to an annual customer sales volume report. Credit is automatically granted to previous customers, whereas first-time customers must receive credit approval from the sales manager. Ninety percent of sales are credit sales.
2. A four-part sales invoice is used for all sales. One copy authorizes shipment or customer pickup, and a second copy goes to the customer. A third copy is used to compile sales data. The fourth copy goes to accounts receivable for credit sales and is destroyed at the time of the sale for cash sales.

3. Accounts receivable, including all subsidiary accounts receivable ledgers, are maintained on a microcomputer using an off-the-shelf software package. There is an automatic interface between the general ledger and accounts receivable. The fourth copy of sales invoices for credit sales is sent directly to the computer operator at the same time as the sales manager collects cash register receipts and prepares the daily bank deposit.

4. Customer statements are prepared each month, immediately following the last posting of the month. A receptionist picks up customer statements from the computer operator, prepares the mailing, and sends them to the post office by courier. Prior to the mailing, the sales manager reviews each statement to ensure that unusually large balances are investigated.

5. Payments on accounts receivable are separated from remittance advices in the mailroom, with remittance advices sent to the computer operator for posting and payments forwarded to the cashier for preparation of a bank deposit. Credits to accounts receivable arising from merchandise returned originate with the sales manager, who authorizes and prepares a two-part credit memorandum. One copy goes to the customer and one goes to accounts receivable. No other means of reducing accounts receivable are authorized.

REQUIRED

a. Identify and list at least four control strengths in the internal control structure.

b. Identify and list at least seven control weaknesses present in the internal control structure.

c. List at least seven substantive tests suggested by the study results that are needed to complete the audit of account balances.

IIA (adapted)

14-36 **(Analysis of confirmation responses)** The Accounts Receivable—Confirmation Statistics working paper (indexed B-3) that appears on pages 548 and 549 was prepared by an audit assistant during the calendar year 1991 audit of Lewis County Water Co., Inc., a continuing audit client. The engagement supervisor is reviewing the working papers.

REQUIRED

Describe the deficiencies in the working paper that the engagement supervisor should discover. Assume that the accounts were selected for confirmation on the basis of a sample that was properly planned and documented on working paper B-2.

AICPA

RESEARCH QUESTIONS

14-37 **(Confirmation reliability)** A number of studies have been conducted to gather evidence about the reliability of confirmations. The article by Paul Caster listed in the bibliography to this chapter reports the results of one such study involving a field experiment. Read and prepare a review of Caster's article, including a description of the field experiment performed and the results obtained.

14-38 **(AAERs dealing with the audit of receivables)** Several SEC enforcement actions have focused on issues pertaining to the audit of receivables. For any *AAER* of your choice dealing with receivables, determine what the issues were, what position the SEC took, and what the outcome was for the auditors involved. If reference is made to any auditing standard then in effect, determine whether the standard is still in effect and, if not, how the facts of the case would relate to any relevant standard subsequently issued.

Index	B-3

LEWIS COUNTY WATER CO., INC.
ACCOUNTS RECEIVABLE—CONFIRMATION STATISTICS
12/31/91

	Accounts		Dollars	
	Number	**Percent**	**Amount**	**Percent**
Confirmation Requests Positives	54	2.7%	$ 260,000	13.0%
Negatives	140	7.0%	20,000	10.0%
Total sent	194	9.7%	280,000	23.0%
Accounts selected/client asked us not to confirm	6	0.3%		
Total selected for testing	200	10.0%		
Total accounts receivable at 12/31/91, confirm date	2,000	100.0%	$2,000,000 ✓★	100.0%
RESULTS				
Replies received through 2/25/92				
Positives—no exception	44 C	2.2%	180,000	9.0%
Negatives—did not reply or replied "no exception"	120 C	6.0%	16,000	.8%
Total confirmed without exception	164	8.2%	196,000	9.8%
Differences reported and resolved, no adjustment				
Positives	6 Ⓒ	.3%	30,000	1.5%
Negatives	12	.6%	2,000	.1%
Total	18 ‡	.9%	32,000	1.6%
Differences found to be potential adjustments				
Positives	2 CX	.1%	10,000	.5%
Negatives	8 CX	.4%	2,000	.1%
Total—.6% adjustment, immaterial	10	.5%	12,000	.6%
Accounts selected/client asked us not to confirm	6	.3%		

Tickmark Legend

✓	Agreed to accounts receivable subsidiary ledger
★	Agreed to general ledger and lead schedule
⦶	Includes one related party transaction
C	Confirmed without exception, W/P B-4
CX	Confirmed with exception, W/P B-5

Overall conclusion—The potential adjustment of $12,000 or .6% is below materiality threshold; therefore, the accounts receivable balance is fairly stated.

CHAPTER 15

AUDITING THE EXPENDITURE CYCLE

LEARNING OBJECTIVES

After studying this chapter, you should be able to

1. Describe the nature of the expenditure cycle and the transaction classes and accounts involved.
2. Identify transaction class and account balance audit objectives for the expenditure cycle.
3. Apply the concepts of materiality, risk, and audit strategy to the expenditure cycle.
4. Explain the applicability of relevant aspects of the internal control structure components to the expenditure cycle.
5. Discuss considerations applicable to assessing control risk for purchases transactions.
6. Discuss considerations applicable to assessing control risk for cash disbursements transactions.
7. Indicate the factors involved in determining the acceptable level of detection risk for accounts payable assertions.

NATURE OF THE EXPENDITURE CYCLE
- AUDIT OBJECTIVES
- MATERIALITY, RISK, AND AUDIT STRATEGY
- CONSIDERATION OF INTERNAL CONTROL STRUCTURE COMPONENTS

CONTROL ACTIVITIES—PURCHASES TRANSACTIONS
- COMMON DOCUMENTS AND RECORDS
- FUNCTIONS
- OBTAINING THE UNDERSTANDING AND ASSESSING CONTROL RISK

CONTROL ACTIVITIES—CASH DISBURSEMENTS TRANSACTIONS
- COMMON DOCUMENTS AND RECORDS
- FUNCTIONS
- OBTAINING THE UNDERSTANDING AND ASSESSING CONTROL RISK

SUBSTANTIVE TESTS OF ACCOUNTS PAYABLE BALANCES
- DETERMINING DETECTION RISK
- DESIGNING SUBSTANTIVE TESTS
- INITIAL PROCEDURES
- ANALYTICAL PROCEDURES
- TESTS OF DETAILS OF TRANSACTIONS
- TESTS OF DETAILS OF BALANCES
- COMPARISON OF STATEMENT PRESENTATION WITH GAAP

SUBSTANTIVE TESTS OF PLANT ASSET BALANCES
- DETERMINING DETECTION RISK
- DESIGNING SUBSTANTIVE TESTS
- INITIAL PROCEDURES
- ANALYTICAL PROCEDURES
- TESTS OF DETAILS OF TRANSACTIONS
- TESTS OF DETAILS OF BALANCES
- COMPARISON OF STATEMENT PRESENTATION WITH GAAP

SUMMARY
BIBLIOGRAPHY
OBJECTIVE QUESTIONS
COMPREHENSIVE QUESTIONS
CASE
RESEARCH QUESTIONS

This chapter begins with an explanation of the nature and importance of the expenditure cycle. Audit objectives relevant to the cycle are identified, and considerations pertaining to materiality, risk, and audit strategy are discussed. Attention is then given to internal control considerations for the major classes of transactions within the cycle. The chapter concludes with a discussion of substantive tests for accounts payable and plant asset balances.

NATURE OF THE EXPENDITURE CYCLE

The **expenditure cycle** consists of the activities related to the acquisition of and payment for plant assets and goods and services. The following are the two major transaction classes in this cycle: (1) **purchases transactions** and (2) **cash disbursements transactions.**

8. Design and execute an audit program for substantive tests to achieve specific audit objectives for accounts payable.
9. Indicate the factors involved in determining the acceptable level of detection risk for plant asset assertions.
10. Design and execute an audit program for substantive tests to achieve specific audit objectives for plant assets.

This cycle does not include payroll transactions, which are covered in the personnel services cycle in Chapter 16. Also not included in this cycle are transactions involving the purchase or sale of another entity's securities, or transactions involving an entity's own securities. These transactions are considered part of the investing and financing cycles, respectively, and are explained in Chapter 17.

Purchases and cash disbursements transactions affect numerous accounts including

- Merchandise inventory
- Raw materials inventory
- Prepaid expenses
- Plant assets
- Other assets
- Accounts payable
- Purchase returns
- Purchase discounts
- Various expenses
- Cash

OBJECTIVE 1

Describe the nature of the expenditure cycle and the transaction classes and accounts involved.

The inherent and control risk considerations discussed in this chapter touch on all these accounts. Substantive tests of inventory and cash balances are covered in Chapters 16 and 18, respectively. Of the remaining accounts, attention is focused in this chapter on substantive tests for meeting the audit objectives for accounts payable and plant assets.

AUDIT OBJECTIVES

OBJECTIVE 2

Identify transaction class and account balance audit objectives for the expenditure cycle.

The specific audit objectives for the expenditure cycle that are addressed in this chapter are presented in Figure 15-1. Each of the objectives is derived from management's implicit or explicit assertions about expenditure cycle transactions and balances. These objectives are the primary ones for this cycle in most audits. They are not intended to be all-inclusive for all client situations.

To achieve each of these specific audit objectives, the auditor employs various parts of the audit planning and testing methodologies described in Parts 2 and 3 of this textbook in much the same manner as illustrated for the revenue cycle in Chapter 14. This includes applying the concepts of materiality, risk, and audit strategies, considering relevant aspects of the entity's internal control structure components and assessing control risk, and designing and performing substantive tests. The application of this methodology to the expenditure cycle as discussed in subsequent sections of this chapter is keyed, where appropriate, to the numbered specific audit objectives in Figure 15-1.

OBJECTIVE 3

Apply the concepts of materiality, risk, and audit strategy to the expenditure cycle.

MATERIALITY, RISK, AND AUDIT STRATEGY

We begin the process of applying the audit planning and testing methodologies to the expenditure cycle by considering the applicability of the concepts of materiality, risk, and audit strategy that were explained in Chapter 7.

FIGURE 552 • SELECTED SPECIFIC AUDIT OBJECTIVES FOR THE EXPENDITURE CYCLE

Assertion Category	Transaction Class Audit Objectives	Account Balance Audit Objectives
Existence or occurrence	Recorded purchases transactions represent goods, productive assets, and services received during the period under audit **(EO1).** Recorded cash disbursements transactions represent payments made during the period to suppliers and creditors **(EO2).**	Recorded accounts payable represent amounts owed by the entity at the balance sheet date **(EO3).** Recorded plant assets represent productive assets that are in use at the balance sheet date **(EO4).**
Completeness	All purchases **(C1)** and cash disbursements **(C2)** transactions that occurred during the period have been recorded.	Accounts payable includes all amounts owed by the entity to suppliers of goods and services at the balance sheet date **(C3).** Plant asset balances include the effects of all applicable transactions for the period **(C4).**
Rights and obligations	The entity is obligated for the payables resulting from recorded purchases transactions **(R1).** The entity has rights to the plant assets resulting from recorded purchases transactions **(R2).**	Accounts payable are obligations of the entity at the balance sheet date **(R3).** The entity owns or has rights to all recorded plant assets at the balance sheet date **(R4).**
Valuation or allocation	Purchase transactions **(VA1)** and cash disbursements transactions **(VA2)** are correctly journalized, summarized, and posted.	Accounts payable are stated at the correct amount owed **(VA3).** Plant assets are stated at cost less accumulated depreciation **(VA4).** Related expense balances are in conformity with GAAP **(VA5).**
Presentation and disclosure	The details of purchases **(PD1)** and cash disbursements **(PD2)** transactions support their presentation in the financial statements including their classification and disclosure.	Accounts payable **(PD3),** plant assets **(PD4),** and related expenses **(PD5)** are properly identified and classified in the financial statements. Disclosures pertaining to commitments, contingent liabilities, and collateralized and related party payables are adequate **(PD6).** Disclosures pertaining to the cost, book value, depreciation methods, and useful lives of major classes of plant assets, the pledging of plant assets as collateral, and the major terms of capital lease contracts are adequate **(PD7).**

Materiality

Numerous accounts affected by expenditure cycle transactions are identified earlier in this chapter. In fact, transactions in this cycle often affect more financial statement accounts than the other cycles combined. Several of these accounts, such as inventories, property, plant, and equipment, and major expense types may be individually material to the statements. Thus, the auditor seeks to achieve a low level of risk that expenditure cycle transactions are the source of material misstatements in the financial statements.

The allocation of materiality to accounts affected by transactions in this cycle will vary according to considerations explained earlier in this text. For example, the materiality threshhold for accounts payable might be specified as a relatively small amount because of the potential effects of even small errors in this account on key ratios such as the quick and current ratios. The allocation of materiality to plant assets might be specified as relatively small amounts for a different reason —namely, the desire to allocate proportionately greater amounts of financial statement materiality to accounts like accounts receivable and inventories that may be more susceptible to errors and for which the audit costs of detection per dollar of error may be greater.

Inherent and Control Risks

In assessing inherent risk for expenditure cycle assertions, the auditor should consider pervasive factors that may affect assertions in several cycles as well as factors that may pertain only to specific assertions in the expenditure cycle. Pervasive factors that might motivate management to misstate expenditure cycle assertions could include:

- Pressures to understate expenses in order to report achieving announced profitability targets or industry norms which were not achieved in reality owing to such factors as global, national, or regional economic conditions that affect operating costs, the impact of technological developments on the entity's productivity, or poor management.
- Pressures to understate payables in order to report a higher level of working capital in the face of liquidity problems or going concern doubts.

Other factors that might contribute to misstatements in expenditure cycle assertions include:

- There is usually a high volume of transactions.
- Unauthorized purchases and cash disbursements may be made.
- Purchased assets may be misappropriated.
- Contentious accounting issues may arise concerning such matters as whether a cost should be capitalized or expensed (e.g., the treatment of repairs and maintenance costs or the classification of a lease as an operating or capital lease).

In most well-established companies, management's own risk assessment procedures will have led it to adopt numerous internal control structure policies and procedures to reduce the risk of misstatements occurring in the processing and reporting of expenditure cycle transactions. However, the existence and effectiveness of controls pertaining to different transaction class assertions for purchases and cash disbursements can vary considerably among clients and even among assertions for the same client. Moreover, the auditor must remain mindful of the inherent limitations of internal control, including the possibility of management override, collusion, errors due to fatigue or misunderstandings, and failure to adapt the control structure for changed circumstances. The auditor's consideration of the effects of the entity's internal control structure on expenditure cycle assertions is discussed at length in subsequent sections of this chapter.

Audit Strategy

Because of varying expectations about control risk assessments, use of either the lower assessed level of control risk or primarily substantive strategies, or a combination of the two, may be appropriate in auditing the expenditure cycle for a particular client. The lower assessed level of control risk approach will generally be more efficient for assertions affected by voluminous routine transactions and for which appropriate control policies and procedures have been placed in operation and are expected to be operating effectively.

CONSIDERATION OF INTERNAL CONTROL STRUCTURE COMPONENTS

OBJECTIVE 4

Explain the applicability of relevant aspects of the internal control structure components to the expenditure cycle.

As in other parts of the audit, the auditor's required understanding of the internal control structure (ICS) applicable to the expenditure cycle extends to all five components. Four of the components are discussed in the following subsections. The fifth component, control activities, is discussed later in the chapter in separate sections for each of the two major transaction classes in the expenditure cycle. Recall that the auditor's understanding of the ICS components is obtained by reviewing prior experience with the client, when applicable, and by inquiring of management and other entity personnel, observing activities and conditions, and inspecting documents, records, manuals, and so on. In addition, recall that the understanding should be documented in the form of completed questionnaires, flowcharts, or narrative memoranda.

Control Environment

Following are several examples of the relevance of control environment factors to the expenditure cycle that should be included in the auditor's understanding:

- Numerous opportunities for employee fraud in processing purchase and cash disbursements transactions, and for fraudulent financial reporting by management of expenditure cycle account balances, make the control environment factor of *integrity and ethical values* no less important in the expenditure cycle than in the revenue cycle. For example, purchasing agents may be subjected to pressures from solicitous vendors, including offers of "kickbacks" for transacting more business with those vendors.
- Management's *commitment to competence* should be reflected in the assignment and training of personnel involved in processing purchase and cash disbursement transactions, maintaining custody of purchased assets, and reporting on expenditure cycle activities.
- The client's *organizational structure* and management's *assignment of authority and responsibility* over expenditure cycle activities should be clearly communicated and provide for clear lines of authority, responsibility, and reporting relationships. For example, purchasing, receiving, and stores or warehousing activities may fall under the vice president for operations, accounting under the controller, and cash disbursements under the treasurer or vice president for finance.
- *Human resource policies and practices* might include the bonding of employees involved in processing cash disbursements or maintaining custody of purchased assets.

Risk Assessment

Management risk assessments related to expenditure cycle activities that would be of interest to the auditor include consideration of such matters as (1) the entity's ability to meet cash flow requirements for purchase transactions, (2) loss contingencies associated with purchase commitments, (3) the continued availability of important supplies and the stability of important suppliers, (4) the effect of cost increases on the entity, and (5) the realizability of plant asset carrying values. Appropriate consideration of these risks by management together with a commitment to initiate control activities to address the risks should reduce the likelihood of misstatements associated with these circumstances.

Information and Communication (Accounting System)

An understanding of the accounting system requires knowledge of the methods of data processing and key documents and records used in processing expenditure cycle transactions. Figure 15-2 presents an *overview* flowchart that shows the basic features of manual and computerized systems for processing purchases and cash disbursements transactions. The flowchart is not intended to show every document, record, process, or account involved. More detailed flowcharts are presented later in the chapter.

Variations in accounting systems include the use of either a purchases journal or a voucher register for recording purchases. A voucher system is assumed in this chapter. Thus, the key accounting records shown in the flowchart are the voucher register for recording purchases and the cash disbursements journal or a check register for recording payments to suppliers. Key functions and documents involved in processing purchases and cash disbursements are explained further in later sections. In computerized systems, the auditor must acquire an understanding of the relevant general and application controls, and be familiar with the key transaction and master files shown in the figure.

Monitoring

Several types of ongoing and periodic monitoring activities in this component may provide management with information concerning the effectiveness of the other ICS components in reducing the risk of misstatements related to expenditure cycle transactions and balances. Monitoring activities about which the auditor should obtain knowledge, when applicable, include (1) ongoing feedback from the entity's suppliers concerning any payment problems or future delivery problems, (2) communications from external auditors regarding reportable conditions or material weaknesses in relevant internal controls found in prior audits, and (3) periodic assessments by internal auditors of control policies and procedures related to the expenditure cycle.

Initial Assessment of Control Risk

Recall that the auditor's procedures to obtain an understanding of the four ICS components just discussed extend to the design of policies and procedures and whether they have been placed in operation, but not to determining the effectiveness of such controls. Thus, based on the information from the understanding only, the auditor's initial assessment of control risk must be at the maximum.

FIGURE 15-2 • OVERVIEW OF TRANSACTION PROCESSING IN THE EXPENDITURE CYCLE

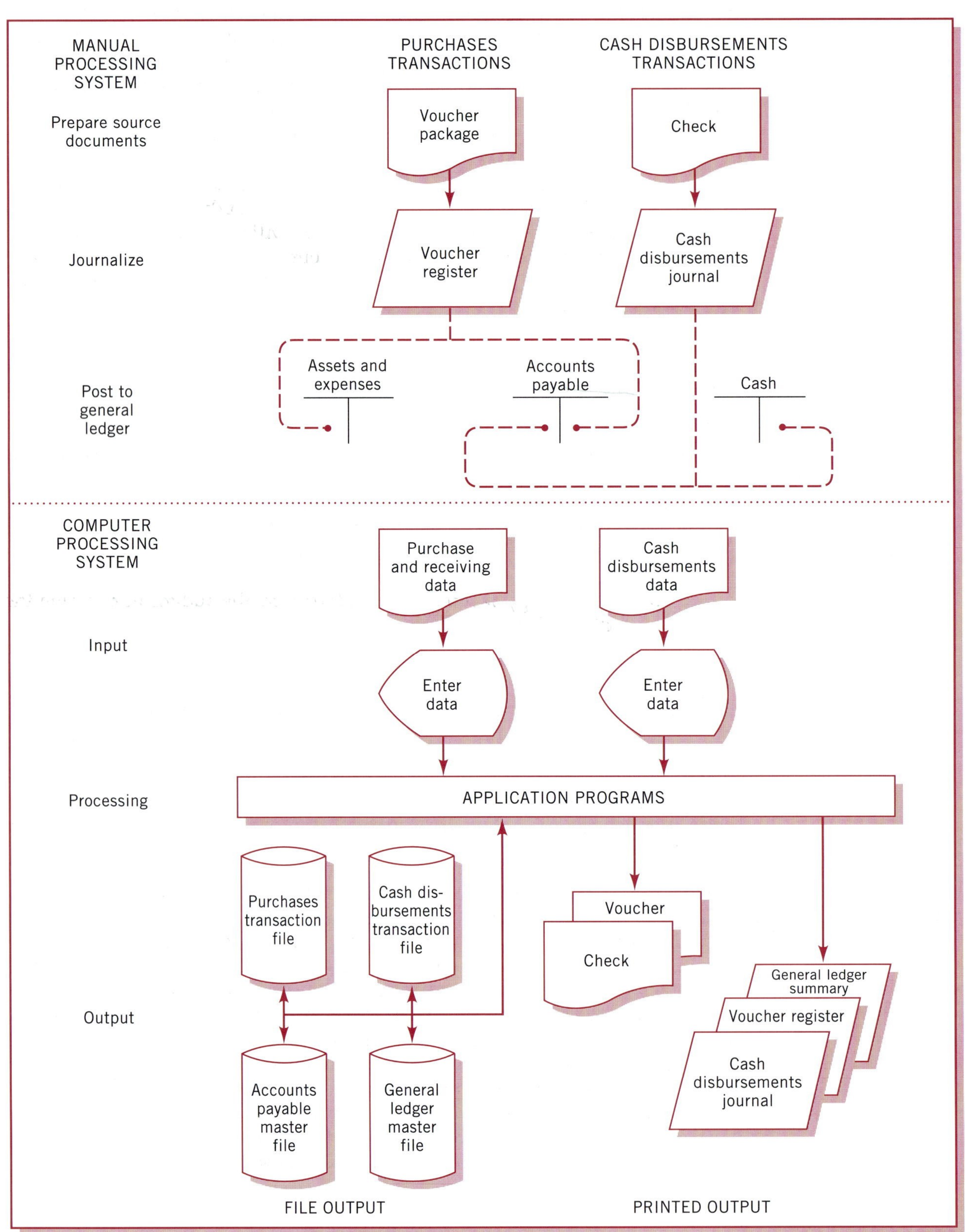

Occasionally, tests of some controls are performed *concurrently* with the procedures to obtain the understanding. In such cases, limited assurance may be obtained about the effectiveness of those controls. The evidence from such concurrent tests of controls may support a reduction in the initial assessment of control risk for certain related assertions to slightly below the maximum or high. In either case, for expenditure cycle assertions for which the auditor plans to use the primarily substantive approach, he or she should have the knowledge needed to identify types of potential misstatements that could occur and to proceed with the design of substantive tests.

For those expenditure cycle assertions for which the auditor intends to use the lower assessed level of control risk approach, it will ordinarily be necessary to obtain an understanding of additional control activities in the fifth component of the ICS and perform additional tests of those controls. Those control activities and the related tests of controls are discussed next for each of the two major transaction classes in the expenditure cycle.

LEARNING CHECK:

15-1 Describe the nature of the expenditure cycle and identify the major classes of transactions in the cycle.

15-2 State the audit objectives for expenditure cycle transactions and balances that relate to each financial statement assertion category.

15-3 a. Is materiality likely to be a factor in auditing expenditure cycle transactions? Why?

b. What strategy will usually be adopted by the auditor in planning the audit for this cycle? Why?

KEY TERMS:

Cash disbursements transactions, p. 550

Expenditure cycle, p. 550

Purchases transactions, p. 550

CONTROL ACTIVITIES—PURCHASES TRANSACTIONS

OBJECTIVE 5

Discuss considerations applicable to assessing control risk for purchases transactions.

In this section, we consider control activities of an entity that are relevant to the specific audit objectives for purchases transactions. We begin by identifying some of the key documents and records used in processing transactions for purchases on account. Next, the major functions involved in executing and recording purchases of goods and services are identified and explained. The discussion of the functions includes how control activities are interwoven into each to reduce the risk of misstatements in the financial statement assertions that are affected by purchases transactions. Among the control activities considered are information processing controls, segregation of duties, physical controls, and performance reviews. Finally, consideration is given to procedures used by the auditor to (1) obtain and document an understanding of the internal control structure and (2) make a final assessment of control risk for purchases transactions.

COMMON DOCUMENTS AND RECORDS

Proper control over purchases transactions involves the use of several common documents and records including the following:

- **Purchase requisition.** Written request made by an employee to the purchasing department to buy goods and services.
- **Purchase order.** Written offer by purchasing to another entity to purchase goods and services specified in the order.
- **Receiving report.** Report prepared on the receipt of goods showing the kinds and quantities of goods received from vendors.
- **Vendor's invoice.** Form stating the items shipped or services rendered, the amount due, and the payment terms.
- **Voucher.** Form indicating the vendor, amount due, and payment date for purchases received. It is used internally as the authorization for recording and paying the liability.
- **Voucher summary.** Report of total vouchers processed in a batch or during a day.
- **Voucher register.** Formal accounting record of vouchers recorded for payment.
- **Open purchase order file.** Hard copy and/or computer file of purchase orders submitted to vendors for which the goods or services have not been received.
- **Purchases transactions file.** Computer file containing data for approved vouchers for purchases that have been received. Used to print the voucher register and update the accounts payable, inventory, and general ledger master files.
- **Unpaid vouchers file.** Hard copy file of approved vouchers with supporting documents for goods and services received and recorded. Unpaid vouchers should sum to the balance in the accounts payable control account.
- **Paid vouchers file.** Holds vouchers and supporting documents for vouchers that have been paid.
- **Accounts payable master file.** Computer file containing data on approved unpaid vouchers. May or may not be organized by vendor. Should sum to the balance in the accounts payable control account.

FUNCTIONS

The processing of purchases transactions involves the following **purchasing functions:**

- Requisitioning goods and services.
- Preparing purchase orders.
- Receiving the goods.
- Storing goods received for inventory.
- Preparing the payment voucher.
- Recording the liability.

When practicable, each of these functions should be assigned to a different individual or department. In such cases, the work of one employee or department can provide an independent check on the accuracy of the work of another. The functions, applicable control activities, and relevant assertions and related specific audit objectives are explained in the following sections.

Requisitioning Goods and Services

Purchase requisitions may originate from stores (the warehouse) for inventoried items or any department for items not inventoried. Most companies permit general authorizations for regular operating needs. Such authorizations usually extend to purchases of inventory and raw materials when reorder points are reached, to normal repair and maintenance work, and to similar items. In contrast, company policy frequently requires specific authorizations for capital expenditures and lease contracts. Operating within these policies, designated individuals are permitted to initiate purchase requests.

Purchase requisition forms may be prepared manually or electronically. Each request should be signed by a supervisor who has budgetary responsibility for the category of expenditure. Because purchase requisitions may originate in any department, they are rarely prenumbered. When applicable and prepared properly, the purchase requisition represents the start of the transaction trail of documentary evidence in support of management's assertion as to the existence or occurrence of purchase transactions. Thus, it provides evidence that relates to the specific audit objective coded **EO1** in Figure 15-1.

Preparing Purchase Orders

The purchasing department should have the authority to issue purchase orders only on the receipt of properly approved purchase requisitions. Before placing an order, purchasing should ascertain the best source of supply, and for major items it should obtain competitive bids.

Purchase orders should contain a precise description of the goods and services desired, quantities, price, and vendor name and address. Purchase orders should be prenumbered and signed by an authorized purchasing agent. The original is sent to the vendor and copies are distributed internally to the receiving department, the vouchers payable department, and the department that submitted the requisition. The quantity ordered is generally obliterated on the receiving department copy, so that receiving clerks will make careful counts when the goods are received.

The purchase orders also become part of the transaction trail of documentary evidence that supports the existence or occurrence assertion for purchase transactions **(EO1).** In addition to hard copies of the purchase orders, an open purchase order file is generally maintained on the computer. A subsequent independent check on the disposition of purchase orders to determine that the goods and services were received and recorded relates to the completeness assertion for purchases transactions **(C1).**

Receiving the Goods

A valid purchase order represents the authorization for the receiving department to accept goods delivered by vendors. Receiving department personnel should compare the goods received with the description of the goods on the purchase order, count the goods, and inspect the goods for damage.

A prenumbered receiving report should be prepared for each order received. In computerized systems, the receiving report may be prepared by using information already in the computer and adding the appropriate receiving data such as quantities received.

The receiving report is an important document in supporting the existence or occurrence assertion for purchase transactions **(EO1).** A copy of the report is forwarded to vouchers payable. A subsequent periodic independent check on the sequence of prenumbered receiving reports to determine that a voucher was prepared for each relates to the completeness assertion **(C1).**

Storing Goods Received for Inventory

Upon delivery of goods to stores or other requisitioning departments, receiving clerks should obtain a signed receipt. Obtaining initials on a copy of the receiving report serves this purpose and provides further evidence for the existence or occurrence assertion for the purchase transaction **(EO1).** The signed receipt also establishes subsequent accountability for the purchased goods. Separating custody of goods received for inventory from other functions involved in purchasing reduces the risk of unauthorized purchases and the misappropriation of goods. The goods should be kept in locked storage areas with limited access and proper surveillance by security personnel.

Preparing the Payment Voucher

Prior to recording purchases, vouchers are prepared in the vouchers payable department. Controls over this function and the assertions/specific audit objectives to which they relate include

- Establishing the agreement of the details of vendors' invoices with the related receiving reports and purchase orders **(EO1, C1, VA1).**
- Determining the mathematical accuracy of the vendors' invoices **(VA1).**
- Preparing prenumbered vouchers and attaching the supporting documents (purchase orders, receiving reports, and vendors' invoices) **(EO1).**
- Performing an independent check on the mathematical accuracy of the vouchers **(VA1).**
- Coding the account distributions on the vouchers (i.e., indicating the asset and expense accounts to be debited) **(PD1).**
- Approving the vouchers for payment by having an authorized person sign the vouchers **(EO1, RO1).**

Other kinds of supporting documentation such as copies of contracts may be required when the voucher relates to certain types of services or to leased assets. In other cases, such as monthly utility bills, the vendor's invoice alone may suffice (i.e., there is no monthly purchase order and receiving report).

In computerized systems, personnel in the vouchers payable department either send data for preparation of the vouchers to EDP or enter the data via terminals. Programmed edit checks are made for such matters as valid vendor numbers and the reasonableness of amounts. When the data for a voucher are accepted by the computer, a computer record of the voucher is created and added to the purchases transactions file. Additional controls over the accuracy of the data entry process include the use of batch totals and exception reports. The vouchers and a voucher summary are then printed. The vouchers are collated with the supporting documents, and the voucher summary is forwarded to accounting.

Copies of all unpaid vouchers are maintained in an unpaid vouchers file in the vouchers payable department pending their subsequent payment. Properly approved, prenumbered vouchers provide the basis for recording purchase transactions.

Recording the Liability

In manual systems, copies of the approved unpaid vouchers are sent with the daily voucher summary to the accounting department for recording in the voucher register and general ledger. An accounting supervisor should perform an independent check of the agreement of the total of the vouchers recorded by accounting personnel with the daily voucher summary received from vouchers payable **(EO1, C1, VA1).**

In computerized systems, the purchases transactions file is used to update the accounts payable, inventory, and general ledger master files. Printouts of the voucher register and a general ledger summary showing the amounts posted to general ledger accounts are produced by the update program and sent to accounting. An accounting supervisor determines the agreement of the printouts with the voucher summary received from vouchers payable **(EO1, C1, VA1).**

In both manual and computerized systems, an accounting supervisor should monitor (1) the appropriateness of account classifications shown in the voucher register **(PD1),** and (2) the timeliness of recording by periodically comparing the dates of voucher register entries with dates on copies of the vouchers **(EO1, C1).** A periodic independent check should also be made of the agreement of the balance of the accounts payable control account with the sum of the vouchers in the unpaid voucher file in the vouchers payable department **(VA1).** In computerized systems, this independent check should extend to determining that the accounts payable master file has the same total. In addition, when the accounts payable master file is organized by vendor, monthly statements received from vendors can be reconciled with the recorded vendor balances **(EO1, C1, VA1).** Finally, periodic performance reviews by management in the form of comparisons of asset, payable, and expense balances with budgeted amounts can provide a means for not only controlling expenditures, but for also detecting misstatements related to each of the specific audit objectives for purchase transactions.

Illustrative System for Purchases Transactions

A flowchart of a representative system for processing purchases transactions is shown in Figure 15-3. In this system, purchase orders are prepared in the purchasing department using on-line terminals. Multicopy purchase orders are printed and distributed as shown in the figure. In addition, an open purchase order file is maintained on the computer.

When goods arrive in the receiving department, a copy of the matching purchase order is pulled from the file. The goods are then counted, inspected, and compared against the copy of the purchase order. Next, receiving clerks use their computer terminals to retrieve the computer record of the purchase order from the open purchase order file. After a clerk keys in the quantities received on an order,

FIGURE 15-3 • SYSTEM FLOWCHART—PURCHASES TRANSACTIONS

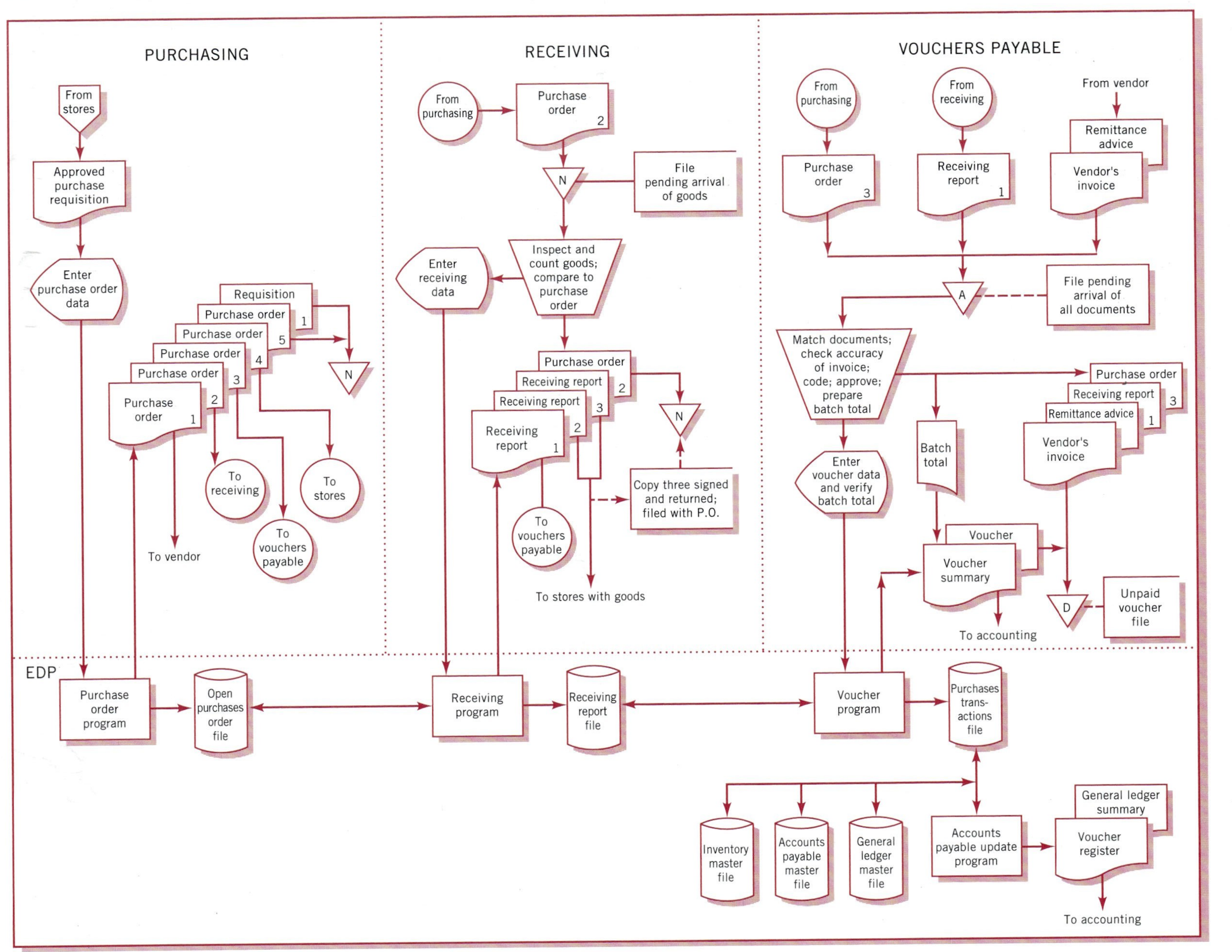

the computer produces a multicopy receiving report and transfers the record from the open purchase order file to the receiving report file. The copies of the receiving report are distributed as shown in the flowchart.

Copies of the purchase order and receiving report for each transaction are placed in a holding file in the vouchers payable department pending arrival of the matching vendor's invoice. Once the vendor's invoice arrives, a vouchers payable clerk checks its mathematical accuracy and compares it with the purchase order and receiving report. Batches of approved matched documents are assembled, and a batch total is calculated manually. Data keyed in from the vendors' invoices, together with matching data extracted by the computer from the receiving report file, are then used to create a record for each voucher in the purchases transactions file. The vouchers and a voucher summary are then printed. The voucher summary is compared with the manual batch total in vouchers payable, and any differences are resolved. The summary is then forwarded to accounting. The vouchers are collated with the supporting documents and placed in a file by due date in the vouchers payable department.

The purchases transactions file is subsequently used to update the accounts payable, inventory, and general ledger master files. Outputs of that run include a voucher register listing the newly processed vouchers, and a general ledger summary showing the totals posted to the general ledger accounts. These printouts are fowarded to accounting where they are reviewed on a daily basis and reconciled with the voucher summaries received from vouchers payable.

OBTAINING THE UNDERSTANDING AND ASSESSING CONTROL RISK

As with the other four components of the ICS, an understanding of the control activities component pertaining to purchase transactions is obtained primarily through prior experience with the client, inquiry, observation, and inspection of documents. For example, the auditor may inquire about procedures followed in processing purchase orders, observe receiving procedures, and inspect vouchers and supporting documents in the vouchers payable department. The use of questionnaires and flowcharts is helpful in obtaining and documenting the understanding. The process of assessing control risk for purchase transactions is the same as that described in Chapter 9 and previously illustrated for transaction classes in the revenue cycle in Chapter 14.

Figure 15-4 contains a partial listing of potential misstatements, necessary controls, potential tests of controls, and the specific transaction class audit objectives for purchases to which each relates. The auditor's determination as to whether the necessary controls have been designed and placed in operation is based on the information documented in the questionnaires, flowcharts, and narrative memoranda. The tests of controls provide the means for determining the effectiveness of such controls.

The extent of the auditor's consideration of factors related to assessing control risk for any given assertion depends on whether the lower assessed level of control risk or primarily substantive audit strategy is being used for that assertion. Some of the tests of controls may be performed concurrently with obtaining the understanding in the planning phase of the audit. Others will be performed during interim field work. The extent of tests of controls will vary inversely with the auditor's planned level of control risk. Statistical or nonstatistical attribute sam-

FIGURE 15-4 • CONTROL RISK ASSESSMENT CONSIDERATIONS—PURCHASES TRANSACTIONS

Function	Potential Misstatement	Necessary Control	Potential Test of Control*	Relevant Transaction Class Audit Objective (from p. 552)				
				EOI	CI	ROI	VAI	PDI
Requisitioning goods and services	Goods may be requisitioned for unauthorized purposes or quantities.	General and specific authorization procedures.	Inquire about procedures.	✓				
Preparing purchase orders	Purchases may be made for unauthorized purposes.	Approved purchase requisition for each order.	Examine purchase orders for approved requisitions.	✓				
Receiving goods	Goods received may not have been ordered.	Approved purchase order for each shipment.	Examine receiving report for matching purchase order.	✓				
	Incorrect quantities, damaged goods, or incorrect items may be received.	Receiving clerks count, inspect, and compare goods received to purchase order.	Observe performance by receiving clerks.	✓				
Storing goods received for inventory	Stores clerks may deny taking custody of purchased goods.	Obtain signed receipt upon delivery of goods from receiving to stores.	Inspect signed receipts.	✓				
Preparing the payment voucher	Vouchers may be prepared for goods not ordered or received or be prepared incorrectly.	Matching purchase order, receiving report, and vendor's invoice for each voucher.	Examine supporting documentation for vouchers.*	✓	✓	✓	✓	✓
Recording the liability	Vouchers may be recorded incorrectly or not be recorded.	Independent check of agreement of daily voucher summary to amounts recorded in voucher register.	Examine evidence of independent check; reperform independent check.*	✓	✓		✓	✓
		Periodic accounting for prenumbered receiving reports, purchase orders, and vouchers.	Observe procedure; reperform.		✓			
		Periodic performance reviews by management of reports comparing actual asset, payable, and expense balances with budgeted amounts.	Inquire of management about results of performance reviews; inspect reports.*	✓	✓	✓	✓	✓

* Tests marked with an asterisk are sometimes performed as a part of dual-purpose tests.

pling procedures as illustrated in Chapter 11 may be applicable to certain tests. Recall that the direction of testing must be compatible with the specific audit objective to which the test relates—vouching for existence or occurrence and tracing for completeness. Evidence applicable to the other assertion categories can be obtained from testing in either direction. Also, recall that certain of the tests, particularly those pertaining to preparing the payment voucher and recording the liability, may be performed as dual purpose tests. In these tests, evidence is obtained about the effects measured in dollars of processing errors on account balances as well as the frequency of deviations from controls. These tests are marked with an asterisk in Figure 15-4.

Based on assimilating the evidence obtained from procedures to obtain an understanding of relevant portions of *all five* components of the ICS and related tests of controls, a final assessment of control risk is made and documented for each significant assertion related to purchase transactions.

Computer-Assisted Tests of Controls

When some of the functions pertaining to purchases transactions are computerized, the auditor may use the computer in performing tests of controls. The general methodology for obtaining an understanding of the EDP control structure and testing the effectiveness of EDP controls is explained in Chapter 13. In particular, tests of effectiveness must be performed for any controls that serve as the basis for a control risk assessment below the maximum. This includes making inquiries and inspecting documentation concerning general controls over changes to programs and master files used in processing purchases transactions.

Tests of application controls may include the use of test data to determine whether expected results are produced by the client's program for accepting and recording data for unpaid vouchers in circumstances such as the following:

- Missing or invalid vendor number.
- Missing or invalid account classification code number.
- Missing or unreasonable dollar amount.
- Missing due date or payment terms.
- Alphabetical characters in a numeric field.

Examples of other possible computer-assisted audit tests are

- Using generalized audit software or a utility program to perform sequence checks and print lists of purchase orders, receiving reports, or vouchers whose numbers are missing in designated computer files.
- Designing, selecting, and evaluating an attribute sample of receiving reports or unpaid vouchers.

LEARNING CHECK:

15-4 a. State the functions that apply to purchases transactions.
b. For each purchasing function, indicate (1) the department that performs the function and (2) the principal document or record, if any, produced in performing the function.

c. Indicate one question for each purchasing function that may be included in an internal control questionnaire.

15-5 For each of the following potential misstatements for purchases transactions, indicate a necessary control procedure and a possible test of controls:
a. Vouchers may be prepared for goods not ordered or received.
b. Goods may be taken from storage areas.
c. Vouchers may not be recorded.
d. Goods received may not have been ordered.

15-6 a. What is the direction of testing controls for purchases transactions that pertains to the existence or occurrence assertion?
b. What is the direction of testing controls for purchases transactions that pertains to the completeness assertion?
c. How can the auditor use the computer in performing tests of controls of purchases transactions?

KEY TERMS:

Accounts payable master file, p. 558
Open purchase order file, p. 558
Paid vouchers file, p. 558
Purchase order, p. 558
Purchase requisition, p. 558
Purchases transactions file, p. 558
Purchasing functions, p. 558
Receiving report, p. 558
Unpaid vouchers file, p. 558
Vendor's invoice, p. 558
Voucher, p. 558
Voucher register, p. 558
Voucher summary, p. 558

CONTROL ACTIVITIES—CASH DISBURSEMENTS TRANSACTIONS

OBJECTIVE 6

Discuss considerations applicable to assessing control risk for cash disbursements transactions.

In this section, we consider the common documents and records, functions, and control activities for cash disbursements transactions.

COMMON DOCUMENTS AND RECORDS

Important documents and records used in processing cash disbursements transactions include the following:

- **Check.** Formal order to a bank to pay the payee the amount indicated on demand.
- **Check summary.** Report of total checks issued in a batch or during a day.
- **Cash disbursements transactions file.** Information on payments by check to vendors and others. Used for posting to the accounts payable and general ledger master files.
- **Cash disbursements journal** or **check register.** Formal accounting record of checks issued to vendors and others.

FUNCTIONS

There are two **cash disbursements functions** as follows:

- Paying the liability.
- Recording the cash disbursements.

These functions should not be performed by the same department or individual. The functions, applicable control activities, and relevant assertions/specific audit objectives are explained in the following sections.

Paying the Liability

The vouchers payable department is generally responsible for determining that unpaid vouchers are processed for payment on their due dates. All payments should be by check. In a manual system, the vouchers are forwarded to the treasurer's department for preparation of the checks, or the checks are prepared in vouchers payable and forwarded with the vouchers to the treasurer's department for signing.

In a computerized system, the vouchers payable department submits batches of vouchers due for payment to EDP, or enters the data on vouchers due via terminals. Alternatively, the computer can be programmed to extract the vouchers due on each day from the accounts payable master file. In either case, typically the checks and a check summary are produced, and the computer enters the payment data in a cash disbursements transactions file. The checks are then forwarded to vouchers payable where they are physically matched with the supporting voucher before being forwarded to the treasurer's office for signing.

Controls over the preparation and signing of the checks and related specific audit objectives include the following:

- An independent check should be made of the agreement of the total of the checks issued (usually reported on a check summary) with a batch total of the vouchers processed for payment **(EO2, C2, VA2).**
- Authorized personnel in the treasurer's department should be responsible for signing the checks **(EO2)** (note segregation of duties).
- Authorized check signers should determine that each check is accompanied by a properly approved unpaid voucher and that the name of the payee and amount on the check agree with the voucher **(VA2).**
- The voucher and supporting documents should be stamped, perforated, or otherwise canceled when the check is signed **(EO2)** (to prevent resubmission for duplicate payment).
- The check signer should control the mailing of the checks **(EO2)** (to reduce the risk of theft or alterations).
- No checks should be made payable to "cash" or "bearer," and no blank checks should be issued **(EO2, VA2, PD2).**
- Prenumbered checks should be used **(C2).**
- Access to blank checks and to signature plates should be limited to authorized personnel **(C2).**

Disbursement checks generally include a stub, similar to a payroll check stub, which identifies by vendor invoice number the invoice(s) being paid. Alternatively, copies of the vendor invoices or vendor remittance advices can be enclosed with the checks mailed to vendors. A copy of each check should be filed with the supporting voucher in the paid voucher file.

U.S. FIRMS PAYING $3.5 BILLION IN DUPLICATE PAYMENTS

Can you imagine paying twice for a $40,000 item? That's what an unnamed Silicon Valley maker of integrated circuits did when buying chemicals, according to Fields & Associates, a consulting firm in Burlingame, California. Fields checked the books of 300 clients, including 20 Fortune 500 industrials, and found overpayments common. President Robert Fields' conclusion: an estimated $3.5 billion a year can be wasted on duplicate payments. (*SOURCE:* "How Companies Waste $3.5 Billion," *FORTUNE* (News/Trends), January 11, 1993, p. 16.)

The incidence of duplicate payments across all companies in the United States may not be as high as that found in companies that retained this consulting firm. However, these data do indicate the importance of controls requiring vendors' bills to be matched with supporting documentation before payment, and stamping, perforating, or otherwise canceling those documents when the related invoice is initially paid so as to prevent their being resubmitted as support for duplicate invoices and payments.

Recording the Cash Disbursements

In manual systems, accounting personnel journalize the cash disbursements from the checks issued. These personnel should not participate in the execution of purchase transactions or the preparation of the vouchers or checks. In computerized systems, the cash disbursements transactions file created when the checks were prepared is used to update the accounts payable master file and general ledger accounts. The update program also produces the cash disbursements journal and a general ledger summary that are forwarded to accounting.

Controls over the recording of cash disbursements include:

- An independent check by an accounting supervisor of the agreement of the amounts journalized and posted to accounts payable with the check summary received from the treasurer **(EO2, C2, VA2).**
- An independent check on the timeliness of recording by periodic comparisons of the dates of cash disbursements entries with the dates on copies of the checks **(EO2, C2).**
- Independently prepared bank reconciliations **(EO2, C2, VA2).**

Illustrative System for Cash Disbursements Transactions

A representative system for processing cash disbursements transactions is shown in Figure 15-5. The batch system shown is a continuation of the system for purchases shown in Figure 15-3. On their due dates, approved vouchers are manually pulled from the unpaid voucher file in the vouchers payable department and a batch total is prepared. In the system shown, as clerks key in each voucher number, the cash disbursements program is used to prepare a check based on information in the accounts payable master file. In addition, the program enters the pay-

FIGURE 15-5 • SYSTEM FLOWCHART—CASH DISBURSEMENTS TRANSACTIONS

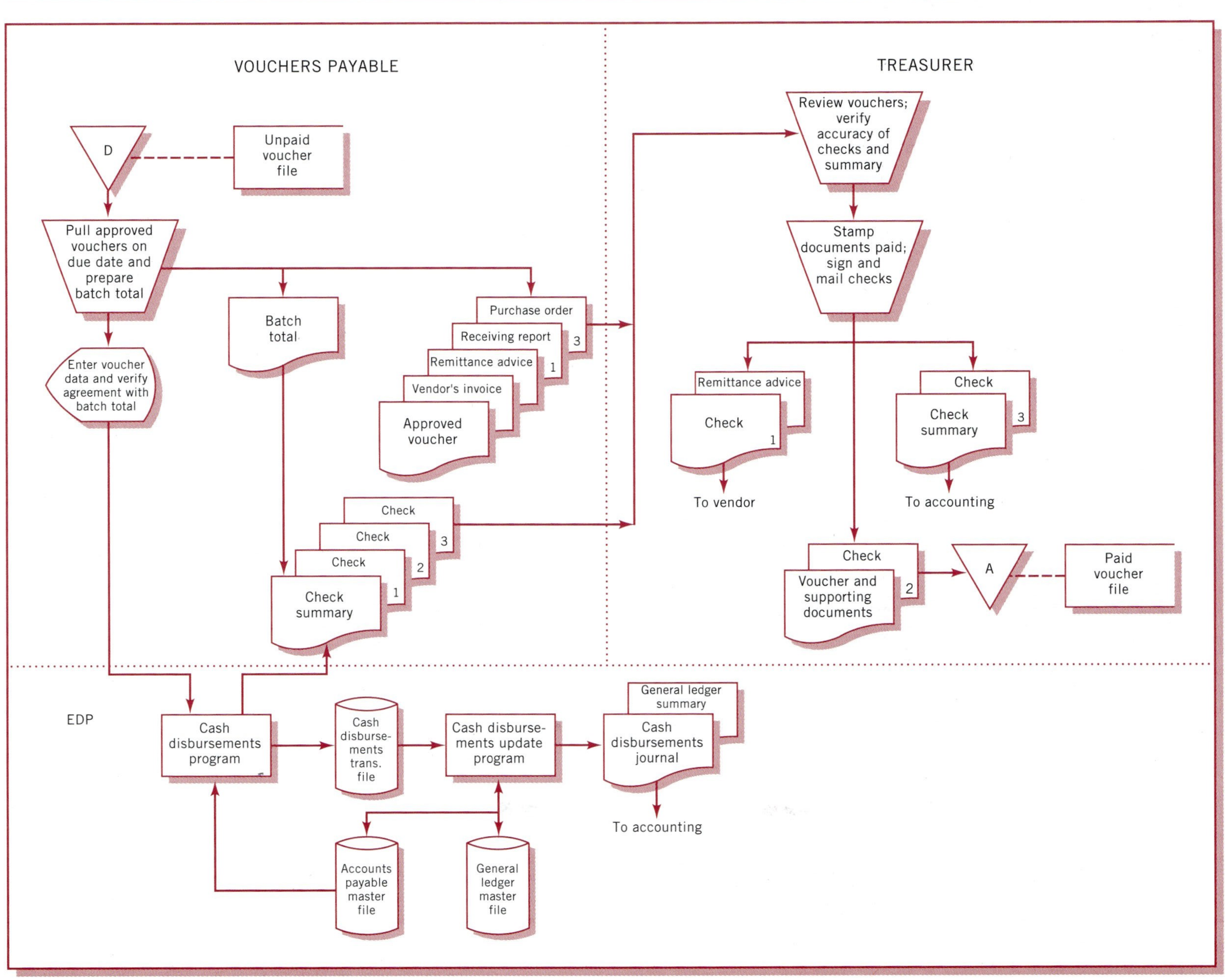

ment data in a cash disbursements transaction file and produces a check summary which is compared with the batch total prepared in vouchers payable. The checks, check summary, and vouchers are then forwarded to the treasurer's department.

In the treasurer's department, an independent check is made to determine the existence of an approved voucher for each check, and agreement of the payee's name and the check amount with the voucher. The supporting documents for each voucher are then stamped paid, and the check is signed and mailed with the remittance advice. A copy of the check is attached to the voucher and filed in the paid voucher file. The check summary and copies of all the checks are sent to accounting.

The cash disbursements update program is then used to update the accounts payable and general ledger master files based on data in the cash disbursements transaction file. This program also produces the cash disbursements journal and a general ledger summary showing the totals posted to general ledger accounts. These are forwarded from EDP to the accounting department where they are compared with the check summary received from the treasurer.

OBTAINING THE UNDERSTANDING AND ASSESSING CONTROL RISK

The procedures used in performing these steps for cash disbursements transactions are the same as those described previously for purchases transactions. Figure 15-6 contains a partial listing of potential misstatements, necessary controls, potential tests of controls, and the specific transaction class audit objectives for cash disbursements transactions to which each relates.

Possibilities for computer-assisted tests of controls are also similar to those for purchases transactions. Thus, for example, test data can be used to test edit checks and other programmed controls pertaining to the preparation and recording of checks. Computer assistance can also be used to design, select, and evaluate an attribute sample for cash disbursements.

Based on assimilating the evidence acquired from procedures to obtain an understanding of relevant portions of *all five* components of the ICS and related tests of controls, a final assessment of control risk is made and documented for each significant assertion related to cash disbursements transactions.

LEARNING CHECK:

15-7 a. State the functions that apply to cash disbursements transactions.
b. For each cash disbursements function, indicate (1) the department that performs the function and (2) the principal document or record, if any, produced in performing the function.
c. Indicate two questions for each cash disbursements function that may be included in the internal control questionnaire.

15-8 For each function pertaining to cash disbursements transactions, indicate the applicability, if any, of (a) proper authorization and (b) independent checks.

FIGURE 15-6 • CONTROL RISK ASSESSMENT CONSIDERATIONS—CASH DISBURSEMENTS TRANSACTIONS

Function	Potential Misstatement	Necessary Control	Potential Test of Control*	Relevant Transaction Class Audit Objective (from p. 552) EO2	C2	RO2	VA2	PD2
Paying the liability	Checks may be issued for unauthorized purchases.	Check signers review supporting voucher for completeness and approval.	Observe check signers performing independent check of supporting documentation.	✓		✓		
	A voucher may be paid twice.	Stamp voucher and supporting documents paid when check issued.	Examine paid vouchers for paid stamp.	✓				
	A check may be issued for the wrong amount.	Independent check of agreement of amount on check and voucher.	Reperform independent check.*				✓	
	A check may be altered after being signed.	Check signers mail checks.	Inquire about mailing procedures; observe mailing.				✓	
Recording the cash disbursement	A check may not be recorded.	Use and account for prenumbered checks.	Examine evidence of use of and accounting for prenumbered checks.		✓			
	Errors may be made in recording checks.	Independent check of agreement of amounts journalized and posted with check summary.	Observe procedure; reperform.*	✓	✓		✓	
		Periodic independent bank reconciliations.	Examine bank reconciliations.*	✓	✓		✓	✓
	Checks may not be recorded promptly.	Independent check of dates on checks with dates recorded.	Reperform independent check.	✓	✓			

* Tests marked with an asterisk are sometimes performed as a part of dual-purpose tests.

15-9 For each of the following necessary controls pertaining to cash disbursements transactions, indicate the related potential misstatement and possible test of controls.

a. Use and account for prenumbered checks.
b. Independent check of agreement of amount on check and voucher.
c. Stamp voucher and supporting documentation PAID when check issued.
d. Check signers mail checks.

KEY TERMS:

Check, p. 566
Cash disbursements functions, p. 567
Cash disbursements transactions file, p. 566
Check register, p. 566
Check summary, p. 566

SUBSTANTIVE TESTS OF ACCOUNTS PAYABLE BALANCES

Accounts payable is usually the largest current liability in a balance sheet and a significant factor in evaluating an entity's short-term solvency. Like accounts receivable, it is typically affected by a high volume of transactions and thus is susceptible to misstatements. However, as compared with the audit of asset balances, the audit of payables places greater emphasis on gathering evidence about the completeness assertion relative to the existence or occurrence assertion. The reason for this is that if management were motivated to misrepresent payables, it would likely be to understate them in order to report a more favorable financial position.

Our attention here is focused on trade payables arising from expenditure cycle transactions. Other payables, such as wages and payroll taxes and various noncurrent liabilities, are covered in other cycle chapters.

DETERMINING DETECTION RISK

OBJECTIVE 7

Indicate the factors involved in determining the acceptable level of detection risk for accounts payable assertions.

Accounts payable is affected both by purchases transactions that increase the balance and by cash disbursements transactions that decrease the balance. Thus, detection risk for accounts payable assertions is affected by inherent and control risk factors related to both of these transaction classes. The auditor uses the methodology explained in Chapter 9 for combining the appropriate control risk assessments for transaction class assertions to arrive at control risk assessments for accounts payable account balance assertions. The methodology explained in Chapter 10 involving the audit risk model or a risk matrix is then used to determine either the planned acceptable levels of detection risk in the planning phase of the audit, or revised acceptable detection risk levels in the testing phase. The application of this process for accounts payable is summarized in Figure 15-7. The risk levels specified in this matrix are illustrative only and would, of course, vary based on the client's circumstances. Furthermore, note that the acceptable detection risk levels shown in Figure 15-7 indicate the need for more persuasive evidence for the completeness and valuation or allocation assertions than for the other assertions.

OBJECTIVE 8

Design and execute an audit program for substantive tests to achieve specific audit objectives for accounts payable.

DESIGNING SUBSTANTIVE TESTS

Recall that the acceptable level of detection risk for each significant financial statement assertion is achieved by gathering evidence through appropriately designed substantive tests. The general framework for developing audit programs for substantive tests that was explained in Chapter 10 and illustrated in Chapter 14 for

FIGURE 15-7 • CORRELATION OF RISK COMPONENTS—ACCOUNTS PAYABLE ASSERTIONS

Risk Component	Existence or Occurrence	Completeness	Rights and Obligations	Valuation or Allocation	Presentation and Disclosure
Audit risk	Low	Low	Low	Low	Low
Inherent risk	Moderate	High	Moderate	High	Low
Control risk-purchases transactions	Low[1]	High[2]	Moderate[3]	High[4]	Moderate[5]
Control risk-cash disbursements	Moderate[2]	Low[1]	Low[3]	Low[4]	Low[5]
Combined control risk[n]	Low[1]	High[2]	Moderate[3]	High[4]	Moderate[5]
Acceptable detection risk[6]	High	Low	Moderate	Low	High

[n,1,2,3,4,5] Most conservative (highest) of transaction class control risk assessments with a common superscript used as the combined control risk assessment with the same superscript per the methodology discussed in Chapter 9 on pages 317–319.

[6] Determined from risk components matrix in Figure 7-3 on page 236, based on levels of audit risk, inherent risk, and combined control risk indicated above for each assertion category.

accounts receivable can also be used in designing substantive tests for accounts payable. A listing of possible substantive tests that might be included in an audit program developed on this basis appears in Figure 15-8. Note that each of the tests in the figure is keyed to one or more of the specific account balance audit objectives for accounts payable from Figure 15-1. Also note that multiple tests are keyed to each account balance audit objective. Each of the tests is explained in a following section, including comments on how some tests can be tailored based on the applicable acceptable level of detection risk to be achieved.

INITIAL PROCEDURES

The starting point for substantive tests of accounts payable is tracing the beginning balance to the prior year's working papers, when applicable, reviewing activity in the general ledger account for any unusual entries, and obtaining a listing of amounts owed at the balance sheet date. Ordinarily, the listing is prepared by the client from the unpaid voucher file or the accounts payable subsidiary ledger or master file. The auditor must determine the mathematical accuracy of the listing by refooting the total and verifying that it agrees with the underlying accounting records and the general ledger control account balance. In addition, the auditor selectively compares vendors and amounts on the listing with the underlying records to determine that it is an accurate representation of the records from which it was prepared.

ANALYTICAL PROCEDURES

Several analytical procedures that can be performed to provide evidence about accounts payable are shown in Figure 15-8. An abnormal increase in the accounts payable turnover ratio, or unexpected decreases in the percentage of accounts payable to total current liabilities or in one or more expense account balances, could indicate the possibility of unrecorded accounts payable. Comparison of amounts due individual creditors with prior year amounts might also be helpful.

FIGURE 15-8 • POSSIBLE SUBSTANTIVE TESTS OF ACCOUNTS PAYABLE ASSERTIONS

Category	Substantive Test	Account Balance Audit Objective (from p. 552)				
		EO3	C3	RO3	VA3	PD#
Initial procedures	1. Perform initial procedures on accounts payable balances and records that will be subjected to further testing. a. Trace beginning balance for accounts payable to prior year's working papers. b. Review activity in general ledger account for accounts payable and investigate entries that appear unusual in amount or source. c. Obtain listing of accounts payable at balance sheet date and determine that it accurately represents the underlying accounting records by: • Footing the listing and determining agreement with (1) the total of the unpaid voucher file, subsidiary ledger, or accounts payable master file and (2) the general ledger control account balance. • Testing agreement of vendors and balances on listing with those included in the underlying accounting records.				✓	
Analytical procedures	2. Perform analytical procedures. a. Calculate ratios: • Accounts payable turnover (purchases ÷ accounts payable) • Accounts payable to total current liabilites b. Analyze ratio results relative to expectations based on prior years, industry data, budgeted amounts, or other data. c. Compare expense balances to prior year or budgeted amounts for indications of possible understatement related to unrecorded payables.	✓	✓		✓	
Tests of details of transactions	3. Vouch a sample of recorded accounts payable transactions to supporting documentation. a. Vouch credits to supporting vouchers, vendor invoices, receiving reports, and purchase orders or other supporting documents. b. Vouch debits to cash disbursements or purchase return memoranda.	✓	✓	✓	✓	✓
	4. Perform purchases cutoff test. a. Select a sample of recorded purchase transactions from several days before and after year-end and examine supporting vouchers, vendor invoices, and receiving reports to determine that purchases were recorded in proper period, or b. Observe the number of the last receiving report issued on the last business day of the audit period and trace sample of lower and higher numbered receiving reports to related purchase documents and determine transactions were recorded in proper period.	✓	✓			
	5. Perform cash disbursements cutoff test. a. Observe the number of the last check issued and mailed on the last day of audit period and trace to accounting records to verify accuracy of cutoff, or b. Trace dates on "paid" checks returned with year-end and cutoff bank statements to dates recorded.	✓	✓			

FIGURE 15-8 • *(Continued)*

Category	Substantive Test	Account Balance Audit Objective (from p. 552)				
		EO3	C3	RO3	VA3	PD#
Tests of details of transactions (continued)	6. Perform search for unrecorded liabilities. a. Examine subsequent payments between balance sheet date and end of field work, and when related documentation indicates payment was for obligation in existence at balance sheet date, trace to accounts payable listing. b. Examine documentation for payables recorded after year-end that are still unpaid at end of field work. c. Investigate unmatched purchase orders, receiving reports, and vendor invoices at year-end. d. Inquire of accounting and purchasing personnel about unrecorded payables. e. Review capital budgets, work orders, and construction contracts for evidence of unrecorded payables.		✓			
Tests of details of balances	7. Confirm accounts payable. a. Identify major vendors by reviewing voucher register or accounts payable subsidiary ledger or master file and send confirmation requests to vendors with large balances, unusual activity, small or zero balances, and debit balances. b. Investigate and reconcile differences.	✓	✓	✓	✓	✓ 3,5,6
	8. Reconcile unconfirmed payables to monthly statements received by client from vendors.	✓	✓	✓	✓	✓ 3,5,6
Presentation and disclosure	9. Compare statement presentation with GAAP. a. Determine that payables are properly identified and classified as to type and expected period of payment. b. Determine whether there are debit balances that are significant in the aggregate and that should be reclassified. c. Determine the appropriateness of disclosures pertaining to related party or collateralized payables. d. Inquire of management about existence of undisclosed commitments or contingent liabilities.				✓	✓ 3,5,6

TESTS OF DETAILS OF TRANSACTIONS

There are four major substantive tests of details of accounts payable transactions as shown in Figure 15-8 and as discussed in the following subsections. Recall that in performing these tests, the auditor is usually primarily concerned with detecting understatements of recorded payables as well as unrecorded payables. The extent to which each test is performed varies based on the acceptable levels of detection risk specified for the related assertions.

Vouch Recorded Payables to Supporting Documentation

In this test, credit entries to accounts payable are vouched to supporting documentation in the client's files such as vouchers, vendor invoices, receiving reports, and purchase orders. Debits are vouched to documentation of cash disbursements transactions, such as paid checks, or memoranda from vendors pertaining to purchase returns and allowances. Some vouching may have been performed during interim work as part of dual-purpose tests along with tracing from source documents to the accounting records. This test can provide evidence for the specific audit objectives related to all five assertion categories. However, its applicability to the completeness assertion is limited because, whereas the improper reduction of recorded payables through invalid debits may be detected, the test will not detect payables that have never been recorded.

Perform Purchases Cutoff Test

The **purchases cutoff test** involves determining that purchases transactions occurring near the balance sheet date are recorded in the proper period. This may be done by tracing dated receiving reports to voucher register entries and vouching recorded entries to supporting documentation. The test usually covers a period of five to ten business days before and after the balance sheet date. Evidence from the test pertains to the existence or occurrence and completeness assertions for accounts payable.

In examining documentation as part of this test, special consideration must be given to goods in transit at the balance sheet date. Goods shipped F.O.B. (free on board) shipping point should be included in the inventory and accounts payable of the buyer. In contrast, goods in transit shipped F.O.B. destination should remain in the inventory of the seller and be excluded from the buyer's inventory and accounts payable until arrival at the buyer's receiving department. In performing this test, the auditor should determine that a proper cutoff is achieved in the taking of the physical inventory, as explained further in Chapter 16, as well as in the recording of the purchases transactions.

Perform Cash Disbursements Cutoff Test

A proper cutoff of cash disbursements transactions at the end of the year is essential to the correct presentation of cash and accounts payable at the balance sheet date. As in the case of the cash receipts cutoff test described in the preceding chapter, evidence for the **cash disbursements cutoff test** may be obtained by personal observation and review of internal documentation. When the auditor can be present at the balance sheet date, he or she can personally determine the last check written and mailed by the client. Subsequent tracing of this evidence to the accounting records will verify the accuracy of the cutoff. Alternatively, the auditor can trace "paid" checks dated within a period of several days before and after the balance sheet date to the dates the checks were recorded. Evidence from this test also pertains to the existence or occurrence and completeness assertions for accounts payable.

Perform Search for Unrecorded Payables

The **search for unrecorded accounts payable** consists of procedures designed specifically to detect significant unrecorded obligations at the balance sheet date. Thus, it relates to the completeness assertion for accounts payable.

SUBSEQUENT PAYMENTS. Examining **subsequent payments** consists of examining the documentation for checks issued or vouchers paid after the balance sheet date. When the documentation indicates the payment is for an obligation that existed at the balance sheet date, it is traced to the accounts payable listing to determine whether it was included. This test is performed toward the end of field work to enhance the opportunity of obtaining evidence concerning payables that were intentionally or inadvertently excluded from the listing of payables at the statement date. Thus, the test extends beyond the periods used in the cutoff tests described earlier.

OTHER PROCEDURES. Documentation supporting payables recorded but remaining unpaid through the end of field work should also be examined on a test basis. This may also reveal obligations that existed but that were unrecorded as of the balance sheet date. Other procedures that may reveal unrecorded payables include (1) investigating unmatched purchase orders, receiving reports, and vendor invoices at year-end, (2) inquiring of accounting and purchasing personnel about unrecorded payables, and (3) reviewing capital budgets, work orders, and construction contracts for evidence of unrecorded payables.

TESTS OF DETAILS OF BALANCES

Two tests included in this category are (1) confirming accounts payable and (2) reconciling unconfirmed payables to monthly statements received by the client from vendors.

Confirm Accounts Payable

Unlike the confirmation of accounts receivable, there is no presumption made about the confirmation of accounts payable. This procedure is optional because (1) confirmation offers no assurance that unrecorded payables will be discovered and (2) external evidence in the form of invoices and vendor monthly statements should be available to substantiate the balances. Confirmation of accounts payable is recommended when detection risk is low, there are individual creditors with relatively large balances, or a company is experiencing difficulties in meeting its obligations. As in the case of confirming accounts receivable, the auditor must control the preparation and mailing of the requests and should receive the responses directly from the respondent.

When confirmation is to be undertaken, accounts with zero or small balances should be among those selected for confirmation because they may be more understated than accounts with large balances. In addition, confirmations should be sent to major vendors who (1) were used in the prior year but not in the current year and (2) do not send monthly statements. The positive form should be used in making the confirmation request as illustrated in Figure 15-9. It may be observed that the confirmation does not specify the amount due. In confirming a payable, the auditor prefers to have the creditor indicate the amount due because that is the amount to be reconciled to the client's records. Note that information is also requested regarding purchase commitments of the client and any collateral for the payable.

This test produces evidence for all accounts payable assertions. However, the evidence provided for the completeness assertion is limited because of the possible failure to identify and send confirmation requests to vendors with whom the client has unrecorded obligations.

FIGURE 15-9 • ACCOUNTS PAYABLE CONFIRMATION

HIGHLIFT COMPANY
P.O. Box 1777
Cleveland, Ohio 39087

January 4, 19X1

Supplier, Inc.
2001 Lakeview Drive
Cleveland, Ohio 39089

Dear Sir or Madam:

Will you please send directly to our auditors, Reddy & Abel, Certified Public Accountants, an itemized statement of the amount owed to you by us at the close of business December 31, 19X0? Will you please also supply the following information:

Amount not yet due $ __________
Amount past due $ __________
Amount of purchase commitments $ __________
Description of any collateral held __________

A business reply envelope addressed to our auditors is enclosed. A prompt reply will be very much appreciated.

Very truly yours,

D.R. Owens

Controller
Highlift Company

Reconcile Unconfirmed Payables to Vendor Statements

In many cases, vendors provide monthly statements that are available in client files. In such cases, amounts owed to vendors per the client's listing of payables can be reconciled to those statements. The evidence from this procedure applies to the same assertions as confirmations, but is less reliable because the vendors' statements were sent to the client rather than directly to the auditor. In addition, statements may not be available from certain vendors.

COMPARISON OF STATEMENT PRESENTATION WITH GAAP

Accounts payable should be properly identified and classified as a current liability. If the accounts payable balance includes material advance payments to some vendors for future delivery of goods and services, such amounts should be reclassified as *advances to suppliers* and included as assets. In addition, disclosures may be required for collateralized and related party payables, purchase commitments, and contingent liabilities. Thus, management's presentation and disclosures must be compared with these GAAP requirements.

LEARNING CHECK:

15-10 a. Which assertion is of primary importance to the auditor in auditing accounts payable? Why?
b. Indicate the relationship of control risk assessments for expenditure cycle transactions to the completeness assertion for accounts payable.

15-11 a. Identify the substantive tests that apply to the completeness assertion for accounts payable.
b. For each of the foregoing tests, indicate the other assertions to which they may relate.

15-12 Chris Cole believes the auditor's responsibilities for confirming accounts payable are the same as for accounts receivable. Do you agree with Chris? Explain.

15-13 a. How does the auditor perform (1) a purchases cutoff test and (2) a cash disbursements cutoff test?
b. What assertions are affected by these tests?

15-14 Distinguish among the following tests and indicate the assertions to which each test pertains:
a. Vouch recorded payables to supporting documentation.
b. Examine subsequent payments.
c. Determine that payables are properly identified and classified.

KEY TERMS:

Cash disbursements cutoff test, p. 576
Purchases cutoff test, p. 576
Search for unrecorded accounts payable, p. 576
Subsequent payments, p. 576

SUBSTANTIVE TESTS OF PLANT ASSET BALANCES

Plant assets consist of tangible resources that are used in operations. This category on the balance sheet includes (1) land, buildings, equipment, furniture, and fixtures; (2) leaseholds; and (3) accumulated depreciation. The principal related income accounts are depreciation expense, repairs expense, and rent on operating leases.

Plant assets often represent the largest component of total assets on the balance sheet, and expenses associated with plant assets are material factors in the determination of net income. Yet the verification of plant assets typically involves significantly less time and cost than the verification of current assets. This relates to the risk and substantive test considerations discussed next.

OBJECTIVE 9

Indicate the factors involved in determining the acceptable level of detection risk for plant asset assertions.

DETERMINING DETECTION RISK

There may be significant variations in the inherent and control risk assessments for assertions pertaining to different plant asset accounts. These differences must be considered in determining appropriate detection risk levels for plant asset assertions.

In a merchandising company, for example, the assessment of inherent risk for the existence or occurrence assertion may be low because the fixed assets are not normally vulnerable to theft. However, in a manufacturing company, inherent risk may be moderate or high for this assertion because of the possibility that scrapped or retired equipment may not be written off the books, or that small tools and equipment used in production may be stolen. A similar situation pertains to the valuation assertion. Inherent risk may be low when equipment items are purchased for cash or on short-term credit. However, the assessment for the valuation or allocation assertion is likely to be high for accounts that include the cost of major construction projects such as plant additions. Similarly, the complexity of accounting for leases may contribute to high inherent risk for the valuation or allocation, rights and obligations, and presentation and disclosure assertions for plant assets acquired under capital leases.

Unlike accounts receivable or cash balances, control risk assessments for plant asset balances are usually less dependent on control over major transaction classes. This is because expenditures for land, buildings, and major capital improvements occur infrequently and often are not subject to the routine purchasing controls. These transactions may be subject to separate controls including capital budgeting and specific authorization by the board of directors. However, because such transactions are frequently individually material, a primarily substantive approach is often adopted for the related plant assets, resulting in the specification of low detection risk levels.

When expenditures for furniture, fixtures, and equipment are processed as routine purchases transactions, the auditor may elect to use a lower assessed level of control risk approach. In such cases, the auditor's tests of controls should include some purchases of these assets, and the control risk assessments for purchases transactions assertions are relevant in assessing control risk and detection risk for the affected plant asset assertions.

In determining detection risk for the valuation or allocation assertion for depreciation expense and accumulated depreciation, it should be recognized that inherent risk is affected by the degree of difficulty in estimating useful lives and salvage values and the complexity of the depreciation methods used. Control risk is affected by the effectiveness of any controls related to these estimates and calculations.

DESIGNING SUBSTANTIVE TESTS

OBJECTIVE 10

Design and execute an audit program for substantive tests to achieve specific audit objectives for plant assets.

The auditor's substantive tests will be much more extensive in an initial audit of a client than in a repeat engagement. In the first audit, evidence must be obtained on the propriety of the beginning balances in the accounts and the ownership of the assets comprising the balances. When the client has previously been audited by another independent auditor, the acquisition of such evidence is facilitated when the successor auditor is able to review the predecessor auditor's working papers. However, if the client has not been previously audited, the auditor must undertake the investigation of the balances and the ownership of major units of plant currently in service. Information concerning beginning balances in an initial audit is usually summarized and kept in the auditor's permanent working papers.

In a recurring engagement, the auditor concentrates on the current year's transactions because the balances at the beginning of the year have been verified through the preceding year's audit. Heavy reliance is placed on documentary evidence in verifying the details of the current year's additions and retirements, and on mathematical evidence in verifying accumulated depreciation. The auditor has considerable flexibility in scheduling tests of plant asset balances as they do not need to be performed at or near the balance sheet date.

Possible substantive tests for plant asset balances in a recurring engagement, and the specific account balance audit objectives to which the tests relate, are shown in Figure 15-10. Risk considerations usually result in greater emphasis being placed on the existence or occurrence and valuation or allocation assertions. Each substantive test is explained in a following section.

INITIAL PROCEDURES

Before performing any of the other tests in the audit program, the auditor determines that the beginning general ledger balances for plant asset accounts agree with the prior period's working papers. Among other things, this comparison will confirm that any adjustments determined to be necessary at the conclusion of the prior audit and reflected in the prior period's published financial statements were also properly booked and carried forward. Next, the auditor should test the mathematical accuracy of client-prepared schedules of additions and disposals and reconcile the totals with changes in the related general ledger balances for plant assets during the period. In addition, the auditor should test the schedules by vouching items on the schedules to entries in the ledger accounts and tracing ledger entries to the schedules to determine they are an accurate representation of the accounting records from which they were prepared. The schedules may then be used as the basis for several of the other audit procedures. Figure 15-11 illustrates an auditor's lead schedule for plant assets and accumulated depreciation.

ANALYTICAL PROCEDURES

The following financial relationships are often used in applying analytical procedures to plant assets:

Ratio	Formula
Plant asset turnover	Net sales ÷ Average plant assets
Rate of return on plant assets	Net income ÷ Average plant assets
Plant assets to stockholders' equity	Plant assets ÷ Stockholders' equity
Repairs expense to net sales	Repairs expense ÷ Net sales

When comparisons of these relationships with other data reveal normal or expected results, the auditor obtains corroborating evidence on the existence or occurrence, completeness, and valuation or allocation assertions of the account balance. However, an abnormal result should be investigated. For example, an extreme decrease in the ratio of repairs expense to net sales may indicate that some maintenance expenditures have not been recorded or that they have been capitalized in error.

FIGURE 15-10 • POSSIBLE SUBSTANTIVE TESTS OF PLANT ASSET ASSERTIONS

Category	Substantive Test	Account Balance Audit Objective (from p. 552)				
		EO4	**C4**	**RO4**	**VA#**	**PD#**
Initial procedures	1. Perform initial procedures on plant asset balances and records that will be subjected to further testing. a. Trace beginning balances for plant assets and related accumulated depreciation accounts to prior year's working papers. b. Review activity in general ledger plant asset, accumulated depreciation, and depreciation expense accounts and investigate entries that appear unusual in amount or source. c. Obtain client-prepared schedules of plant asset additions and retirements and determine that they accurately represent the underlying accounting records from which prepared by: • Footing and crossfooting the schedules and reconciling the totals with increases or decreases in the related general ledger balances during period. • Testing agreement of items on schedules with entries in related general ledger accounts.				✓4,5	
Analytical procedures	2. Perform analytical procedures. a. Calculate ratios: • Plant asset turnover. • Rate of return on plant assets. • Plant assets to stockholders' equity. • Repairs expense to net sales. b. Analyze ratio results relative to expectations based on prior years, industry data, budgeted amounts, or other data.	✓	✓		✓4,5	✓4,5
Tests of details of transactions	3. Vouch plant asset additions to supporting documentation.	✓		✓	✓4	
	4. Vouch plant asset disposals to supporting documentation.	✓	✓	✓	✓4	
	5. Review entries to repairs and maintenance expense.		✓		✓4,5	✓4,5
Tests of details of balances	6. Inspect plant assets. a. Inspect plant asset additions. b. Tour other plant assets and be alert to evidence of additions and disposals not included on client's schedules and to conditions that bear on the proper valuation and classification of the plant assets.	✓	✓		✓4	✓4,5
	7. Examine title documents and contracts.	✓		✓	✓4	✓ 4,5,7
	8. Review provisions for depreciation.	✓	✓		✓4,5	✓ 4,5,7
Presentation and disclosure	9. Compare statement presentation with GAAP. a. Determine that plant assets and related expenses, gains, and losses are properly identified and classified in the financial statements.					✓4,5
	b. Determine the appropriateness of disclosures pertaining to the cost, book value, depreciation methods, and useful lives of major classes of plant assets, the pledging of plant assets as collateral, and the terms of lease contracts.					✓7

FIGURE 15-11 • PLANT ASSET AND ACCUMULATED DEPRECIATION LEAD SCHEDULE

Highlift Company
Property, Plant, and Equipment and Accumulated Depreciation
Lead Schedule
December 31, 19X1

W/P Ref: G
Prepared by: C.J.G. Date: 2/4/x2
Reviewed by: R.C.P. Date: 2/12/x2

W/P Ref.	Acct. No.	Account Title	Asset Cost: Balance 12/31/X0	Asset Cost: Additions	Asset Cost: Disposals	Asset Cost: Adjustments DR/(CR)	Asset Cost: Balance 12/31/X1	Accumulated Depreciation: Balance 12/31/X0	Accumulated Depreciation: Provisions	Accumulated Depreciation: Disposals	Accumulated Depreciation: Adjustments (DR)/CR	Accumulated Depreciation: Balance 12/31/X1
G-1	301	Land	450,000✓				450,000					
G-1	302	Buildings	2,108,000✓	125,000		(21) (25,000)	2,208,000	379,440✓	84,320		(21) (1,000)	462,760
G-3	303	Mach. and equip.	3,757,250✓	980,000	370,000	(21) 25,000	4,392,250	1,074,210✓	352,910	172,500	(21) 1,000	1,255,620
G-4	304	Furn. and fixtures	853,400✓	144,000	110,000		887,400	217,450✓	43,250	21,000		239,700
			7,168,650	1,249,000	480,000	0	7,937,650	1,671,100	480,480	193,500	0	1,958,080
			F	F	F	F	FF	F	F	F	F	FF

✓ Traced to general ledger and 12/31/x0 working papers

F Footed

FF Crossfooted and footed

(21) To reclassify cost and related accumulated depreciation for purchased addition recorded in Buildings account that should have been recorded in Machinery and Equipment account. See adjusting entry #21 on W/P AE-4

TESTS OF DETAILS OF TRANSACTIONS

These substantive tests cover three types of transactions related to plant assets: (1) additions, (2) disposals, and (3) repairs and maintenance.

Vouch Plant Asset Additions

All major additions should be supported by documentation in the form of authorizations in the minutes, vouchers, invoices, contracts, and canceled checks. The recorded amounts should be vouched to supporting documentation. If there are numerous transactions, the vouching may be done on a test basis. In performing this test, the auditor ascertains that appropriate accounting recognition has been given to installation, freight, and similar costs. For construction in progress, the auditor may review the contract and documentation in support of construction costs.

When plant assets are acquired under a capital lease, the cost of the property and the related liability should be recorded at the present value of the future minimum lease payments. The accuracy of the client's determination of the present value of the lease liability should also be verified by recomputation.

The vouching of additions provides evidence about the existence or occurrence, rights and obligations, and valuation or allocation assertions.

Vouch Plant Asset Disposals

Evidence of sales, retirements, and trade-ins should be available to the auditor in the form of cash remittance advices, written authorizations, and sales agreements. Such documentation should be carefully examined to determine the accuracy and propriety of the accounting records, including the recognition of gain or loss, if any.

The following procedures may also be useful to the auditor in determining whether all retirements have been recorded:

- Analyze the miscellaneous revenue account for proceeds from sales of plant assets.
- Investigate the disposition of facilities associated with discontinued product lines and operations.
- Trace retirement work orders and authorizations for retirements to the accounting records.
- Review insurance policies for termination or reductions of coverage.
- Make inquiry of management as to retirements.

Evidence that all retirements or disposals have been properly recorded relates to the existence or occurrence, rights and obligations, and valuation or allocation assertions. Evidence supporting the validity of transactions that reduce plant asset balances relates to the completeness assertion.

Review Entries to Repairs and Maintenance Expense

The auditor's objectives in performing this test are to determine the propriety and consistency of the charges to repairs expense. Propriety involves a consideration of whether the client has made appropriate distinctions between capital and revenue expenditures. Accordingly, the auditor should scan the individual charges to identify those that are sufficiently material to be capitalized. For these items, the auditor should examine supporting documentation, such as the vendor's invoice, company work order, and management authorization to determine the propriety of the charge or the need for an adjusting entry.

Consistency involves a determination of whether the company's criteria for distinguishing between capital and revenue expenditures are the same as in the preceding year.

This substantive test provides important evidence concerning the completeness assertion for plant assets because it should reveal expenditures that should be capitalized. Analyzing the entries to repairs expense also results in evidence about the valuation of the plant assets. In addition, the analysis may reveal misclassifications in the accounts that related to the presentation and disclosure assertion.

TESTS OF DETAILS OF BALANCES

Three procedures in this category of substantive tests are: (1) inspect plant assets, (2) examine title documents and contracts, and (3) review provisions for depreciation.

Inspect Plant Assets

The inspection of plant assets enables the auditor to obtain direct personal knowledge of their existence. In a recurring engagement, detailed inspections may be limited to items listed on the schedule of plant asset additions. However, the auditor should take a tour of other plant assets during which he or she should be alert to other evidence relevant to plant assets. For example, the astute auditor will look for indications of additions or retirements not listed on the schedules, which relates to the completeness and existence assertions, respectively, and to evidence regarding the general condition of other plant assets and whether they are currently being used, which relates to the valuation or allocation and presentation and disclosure assertions.

Examine Title Documents and Contracts

The ownership of vehicles may be established by examining certificates of title, registration certificates, and insurance policies. For equipment, furniture, and fixtures, the "paid" invoice may be the best evidence of ownership. Evidence of ownership in real property is found in deeds, title insurance policies, property tax bills, mortgage payment receipts, and fire insurance policies. Verification of ownership in real property can also be substantiated by a review of public records. When this form of additional evidence is desired, the auditor may seek the help of an attorney. The examination of ownership documents contributes to the existence or occurrence and rights and obligations assertions for plant assets.

Lease agreements convey to a lessee the right to use property, plant, or equipment, usually for a specified period of time. For accounting purposes, leases may be classified as either capital leases or as operating leases. The auditor should read the lease agreement to determine the proper accounting classification of the lease in accordance with Financial Accounting Standards Board pronouncements. When a capital lease exists, both an asset and a liability should be recognized in the accounts and statements. In addition to the existence or occurrence and rights and obligations assertions, the examination of lease contracts pertains to the presentation and disclosure assertion owing to the disclosures that are required under GAAP. The auditor should also examine contracts governing construction in progress, when applicable, to obtain evidence relevant to evaluating the client's accounting and reporting for the related assets.

Review Provisions for Depreciation

In this test, the auditor seeks evidence on the reasonableness, consistency, and accuracy of depreciation charges. An essential starting point for the auditor in making this test is to ascertain the depreciation methods used by the client during the year under audit. The identity of the methods can be obtained from a review of depreciation schedules prepared by the client and inquiry of the client. The auditor must then determine whether the methods currently in use are consistent with the preceding year. On a recurring audit, this can be established by a review of last year's working papers.

Determination of the reasonableness of depreciation provisions involves a consideration of such factors as (1) the client's past history in estimating useful lives and (2) the remaining useful lives of existing assets.

The auditor's verification of accuracy is achieved through recalculation. Ordinarily, this is done on a selective basis by recomputing the depreciation on major assets and testing depreciation taken on additions and retirements during the year. This substantive test provides evidence about all the financial statement assertions except the rights and obligations assertion.

COMPARISON OF STATEMENT PRESENTATION WITH GAAP

The financial statement presentation requirements for plant assets are extensive. For example, the financial statements should show depreciation expense for the year, the cost and book value for major classes of plant assets, and the depreciation method(s) used. Evidence concerning these matters is acquired through the substantive tests described in the preceding sections.

Property pledged as security for loans should be disclosed. Information on pledging may be obtained from reviewing the minutes and long-term contractual agreements, by confirming debt agreements, and through inquiries of management. The appropriateness of the client's disclosures related to assets under lease can be determined by recourse to the authoritative accounting pronouncements and the related lease agreements.

LEARNING CHECK:

15-15 What circumstances pertaining to property, plant, and equipment may warrant the following assessments of inherent risk (IR)?

a. Low for the existence or occurrence assertion.
b. Moderate or high for the existence or occurrence assertion.
c. High for the valuation or allocation assertion.

15-16 What considerations are important in determining control risk for plant assets?

15-17 a. Contrast the auditor's responsibilities in verifying beginning plant asset balances between a first time and a repeat audit engagement.
b. Identify the substantive tests of plant assets that apply to three or more assertions.

15-18 Distinguish among the following substantive tests of plant assets and indicate the assertion(s) to which each test pertains:
a. Apply analytical procedures.
b. Inspect plant assets.
c. Examine title documents and lease contracts.
d. Vouch plant asset additions.

15-19 What procedures may be helpful in determining whether all retirements of plant assets have been recorded?

15-20 What factors should be considered by the auditor in reviewing depreciation entries and computations?

SUMMARY

Expenditure cycle transactions and balances offer myriad challenges for the auditor. In meeting the second standard of field work, the auditor ordinarily adopts a lower planned level of control risk approach for some assertions and a primarily substantive approach for other assertions. In performing substantive tests, the auditor places special emphasis on the completeness assertion for accounts payable, and the existence or occurrence and valuation or allocation assertions for plant assets.

BIBLIOGRAPHY

Bodner, Stanley, and Kiss, Martin. "Impairment of Long-Lived Assets: An Emerging Controversial Issue," *The CPA Journal* (July 1988), pp. 70–72.

Saunders, George D., and Munter, Paul. "The Search for Unrecorded Liabilities—The Implications of Maislin," *The CPA Journal* (February 1991), pp. 48–51.

Schwersenz, Jack. "Accounts Payable Confirmations: Why and How Used," *The CPA Journal* (May 1987), pp. 101–193.

OBJECTIVE QUESTIONS

Indicate the *best* answer for each of the following multiple choice questions.

15-21 These questions pertain to internal control over purchases transactions.

1. When goods are received, the receiving clerk should match the goods with the
   a. Purchase order and the requisition form.
   b. Vendor's invoice and the receiving report.
   c. Vendor's shipping document and the purchase order.
   d. Receiving report and the vendor's shipping document.

2. An auditor performs a test to determine whether all merchandise for which the client was billed was received. The population for this test consists of all
   a. Merchandise received.
   b. Vendors' invoices.
   c. Canceled checks.
   d. Receiving reports.

3. Internal control is strengthened when the quantity of merchandise ordered is omitted from the copy of the purchase order sent to the
   a. Department that initiated the requisition.
   b. Receiving department.
   c. Purchasing agent.
   d. Accounts payable department.

4. Which of the following controls would be most effective in assuring that recorded purchases are free of material misstatements?
   a. The receiving department compares the quantity ordered on purchase orders with the quantity received on receiving reports.
   b. Vendors' invoices are compared with purchase orders by an employee who is independent of the receiving department.
   c. Receiving reports require the signature of the individual who authorized the purchase.
   d. Purchase orders, receiving reports, and vendors' invoices are independently matched in preparing vouchers.

15-22 These questions relate to internal controls and tests of controls for cash disbursements transactions.

1. Which of the following control procedures is not usually performed in the vouchers payable department?
   a. Determining the mathematical accuracy of the vendor's invoice.
   b. Having an authorized person approve the voucher.
   c. Controlling the mailing of the check and remittance advice.
   d. Matching the receiving report with the purchase order.

2. In performing tests of controls over authorization of cash disbursements, which of the following sampling methods would be most appropriate?
   a. Ratio.
   b. Attributes.
   c. Variables.
   d. Stratified.

3. An auditor wishes to perform tests of controls on a client's cash disbursements procedures. If the control procedures leave no audit trail of documentary evidence, the auditor most likely will test the procedures by
   a. Inquiry and analytical procedures.
   b. Confirmation and observation.
   c. Observation and inquiry.
   d. Analytical procedures and confirmation.

15-23 These questions apply to substantive tests of expenditure cycle balances.

1. Which of the following auditing procedures is best for identifying unrecorded trade accounts payable?
   a. Examining unusual relationships between monthly accounts payable balances and recorded cash payments.

b. Reconciling vendors' statements to the file of receiving reports to identify items received just prior to the balance sheet date.
c. Reviewing cash disbursements recorded subsequent to the balance sheet date to determine whether the related payables apply to the prior period.
d. Investigating payables recorded just prior to and just subsequent to the balance sheet date to determine whether they are supported by receiving reports.

2. An auditor analyzes repairs and maintenance accounts primarily to obtain evidence in support of the assertion that all
   a. Noncapitalizable expenditures for repairs and maintenance have been properly charged to expense.
   b. Expenditures for property and equipment have not been charged to expense.
   c. Noncapitalizable expenditures for repairs and maintenance have been recorded in the proper period.
   d. Expenditures for property and equipment have been recorded in the proper period.

3. Which of the following procedures is least likely to be performed before the balance sheet date?
   a. Testing of internal control over cash.
   b. Confirmation of receivables.
   c. Search for unrecorded liabilities.
   d. Observation of inventory.

Comprehensive Questions

15-24 **(Internal control questionnaire—purchasing functions)** Green, CPA, has been engaged to audit the financial statements of Star Manufacturing, Inc. Star is a medium-sized entity that produces a wide variety of household goods. All acquisitions of materials are processed through the purchasing, receiving, accounts payable, and treasury functions.

Required

Prepare the purchase order and receiving segments of the internal control questionnaire to be used in the evaluation of Star's internal control structure. Each question should elicit either a YES or NO response.

Do *not* prepare segments of the internal control questionnaire for other functions.

Do *not* discuss the internal controls over purchases.

AICPA (adapted)

15-25 **(Control functions served by purchase order forms)** Properly designed and utilized forms facilitate adherence to prescribed internal control policies and procedures. One such form might be a multicopy purchase order with one copy intended to be mailed to the vendor. The remaining copies would ordinarily be distributed to the stores, purchasing, receiving, and vouchers payable departments.

The following purchase order is currently being used by National Industrial Corporation:

PURCHASE ORDER

SEND INVOICE ONLY TO:
297 Hardingten Dr., Bronx, NY 10461

TO ______________________ SHIP TO ______________________

DATE TO BE SHIPPED	SHIP VIA	DISC. TERMS	FREIGHT TERMS	ADV. ALLOWANCE	SPECIAL ALLOWANCE

QUANTITY	DESCRIPTION

PURCHASE CONDITIONS

1. Supplier will be responsible for extra freight cost on partial shipment, unless prior permission is obtained.
2. Please acknowledge this order.
3. Please notify us immediately if you are unable to complete order.
4. All items must be individually packed.

REQUIRED

a. In addition to the name of the company, what other necessary information would an auditor recommend be included in the illustrative purchase order?
b. What primary internal control functions are served by the purchase order copies that are distributed to the stores, purchasing, receiving, and vouchers payable departments?

AICPA (adapted)

15-26 **(Internal control evaluation—receiving function)** Dunbar Camera Manufacturing, Inc., is a manufacturer of high-priced precision motion picture cameras in which the specifications of component parts are vital to the manufacturing process. Dunbar buys valuable camera lenses and large quantities of sheetmetal and screws. Screws and lenses are ordered by Dunbar and are billed by the vendors on a unit basis. Sheetmetal is ordered by Dunbar and is billed by the vendors on the basis of weight. The receiving clerk is responsible for documenting the quality and quantity of merchandise received.

Your understanding of the internal control structure indicates that the following procedures are being followed:

1. *Receiving Report.* Properly approved purchase orders, which are prenumbered, are filed numerically. The copy sent to the receiving clerk is an exact duplicate of the copy sent to the vendor. Receipts of merchandise are recorded on the duplicate copy by the receiving clerk.
2. *Sheetmetal.* The company receives sheetmetal by railroad. The railroad independently weighs the sheetmetal and reports the weight and date of receipt on a bill of lading (waybill), which accompanies all deliveries. The receiving clerk only checks the weight on the waybill to the purchase order.

3. *Screws.* The receiving clerk opens cartons containing screws, then inspects and weighs the contents. The weight is converted to number of units by means of conversion charts. The receiving clerk then checks the computed quantity to the purchase order.
4. *Camera Lenses.* Each camera lens is delivered in a separate corrugated carton. Cartons are counted as they are received by the receiving clerk, and the number of cartons are checked to purchase orders.

REQUIRED

a. Explain why the internal control procedures as they apply individually to receiving reports and the receipt of sheetmetal, screws, and camera lenses are adequate or inadequate. Do not discuss recommendations for improvements.
b. What financial statement misstatements may arise because of the inadequacies in Dunbar's internal control structure, and how may they occur?

AICPA

15-27 **(Internal control evaluation—purchases and accounts payable)** The flowchart on the following page depicts the activities relating to the purchasing, receiving, and accounts payable departments of Model Company, Inc.

REQUIRED

Based on only the flowchart, describe the internal control procedures (strengths) that most likely would provide reasonable assurance that management's financial statement assertions regarding purchases and accounts payable will be achieved. Do **not** describe weaknesses in the internal control structure.

AICPA (adapted)

15-28 **(Internal control evaluation—purchasing and cash disbursements)** In 19X4, XY Company purchased over $10 million of office equipment under its "special" ordering system, with individual orders ranging from $5,000 to $30,000. "Special" orders entail low-volume items that have been included in an authorized user's budget. Department heads include in their annual budget requests the types of equipment and their estimated cost. The budget, which limits the types and dollar amounts of office equipment a department head can requisition, is approved at the beginning of the year by the board of directors. Department heads prepare a purchase requisition form for equipment and forward the requisition to the purchasing department. XY's "special" ordering system functions as follows:

Purchasing: Upon receiving a purchase requisition, one of five buyers verifies that the person requesting the equipment is a department head. The buyer then selects the appropriate vendor by searching the various vendor catalogs on file. The buyer then phones the vendor, requesting a price quotation, and gives the vendor a verbal order. A prenumbered purchase order is then processed with the original sent to the vendor, a copy to the department head, a copy to receiving, a copy to accounts payable, and a copy filed in the open requisition file. When the buyer is orally informed by the receiving department that the item has been received, the buyer transfers the purchase order from the unfilled file to the filled file. Once a month the buyer reviews the unfilled file to follow up and expedite open orders.

Receiving. The receiving department receives a copy of the purchase order. When equipment is received, the receiving clerk stamps the purchase order with the date received, and if applicable, in red pen, prints any differences between quantity on the purchase order and quantity received. The receiving clerk forwards the stamped purchase order and equipment to the requisitioning department head and orally notifies the purchasing department.

Accounts payable. On receipt of a purchase order, the accounts payable clerk files the purchase order in the open purchase order file. When a vendor invoice is received, the invoice is matched with the applicable purchase order, and a payable is set up by debiting the equipment account of the department requesting the items. Unpaid invoices are filed by due date and, at due date, a check is prepared. The invoice and purchase order are filed by purchase order number in a paid invoice file, and then the check is forwarded to the treasurer for signature.

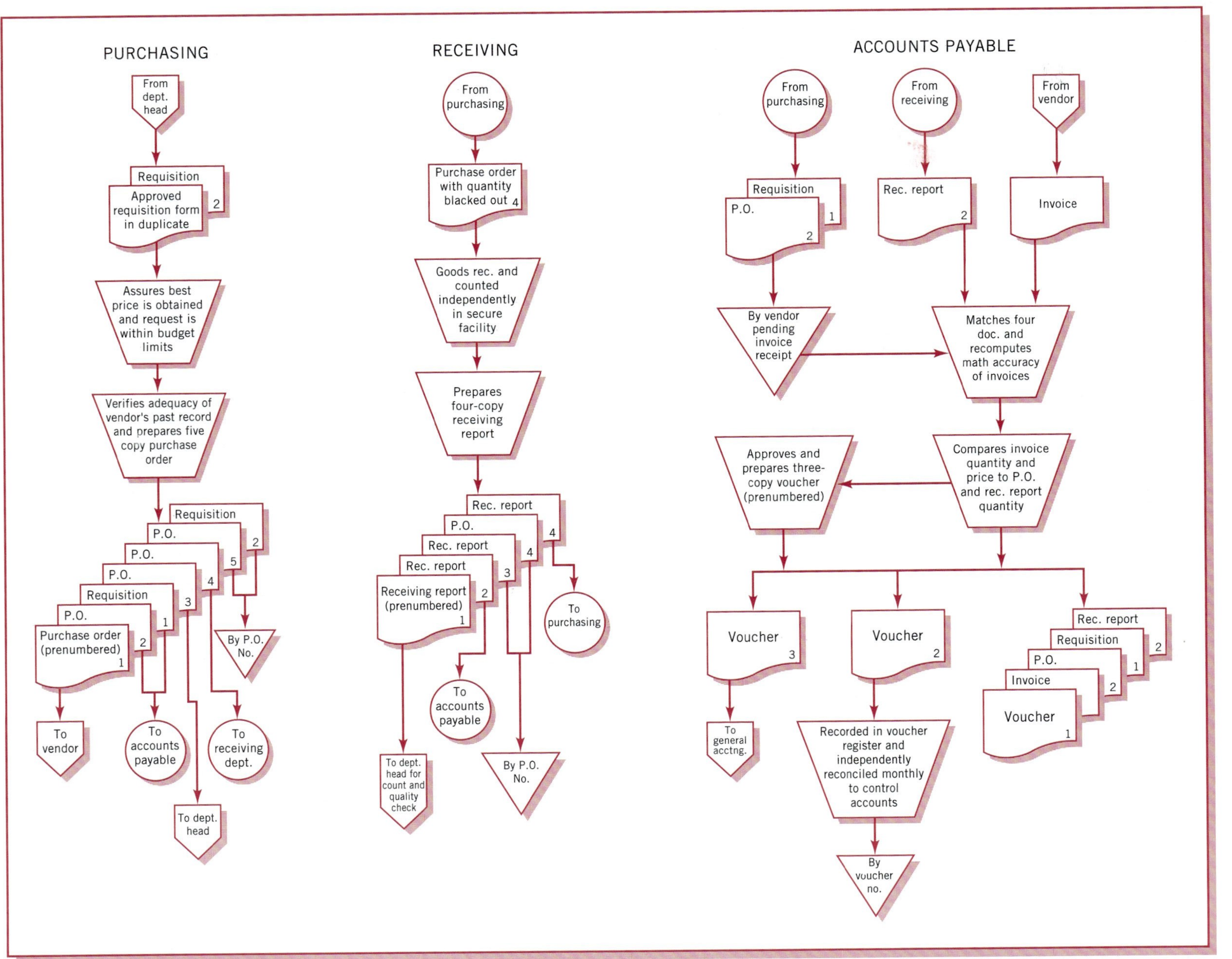

PURCHASING
From dept. head
Requisition
Approved requisition form in duplicate
2
Assures best price is obtained and request is within budget limits
Verifies adequacy of vendor's past record and prepares five copy purchase order
Requisition
P.O.
P.O.
P.O.
Requisition
P.O.
Purchase order (prenumbered)
1
2
1
3
4
5
2
By P.O. No.
To vendor
To accounts payable
To receiving dept.
To dept. head
RECEIVING
From purchasing
Purchase order with quantity blacked out
4
Goods rec. and counted independently in secure facility
Prepares four-copy receiving report
Rec. report
P.O.
Rec. report
Rec. report
Receiving report (prenumbered)
1
2
3
4
4
To purchasing
To accounts payable
To dept. head for count and quality check
By P.O. No.
ACCOUNTS PAYABLE
From purchasing
From receiving
From vendor
Requisition
P.O.
1
2
Rec. report
2
Invoice
By vendor pending invoice receipt
Matches four doc. and recomputes math accuracy of invoices
Approves and prepares three-copy voucher (prenumbered)
Compares invoice quantity and price to P.O. and rec. report quantity
Voucher
3
Voucher
2
Rec. report
Requisition
P.O.
Invoice
Voucher
1
2
1
2
To general acctng.
Recorded in voucher register and independently reconciled monthly to control accounts
By voucher no.

Treasurer. Checks received daily from the accounts payable department are sorted into two groups, those greater than $10,000 and those $10,000 and less. Checks for $10,000 and less are machine signed. The cashier maintains the key and signature plate to the check-signing machine, and maintains a record of usage of the check-signing machine. All checks over $10,000 are signed by the treasurer or the controller.

REQUIRED

Describe the internal control weaknesses relating to purchases and payments of "special" orders of XY Company for each of the following functions:

a. Purchasing.
b. Receiving.
c. Accounts payable.
d. Treasurer.

AICPA

15-29 **(Internal control evaluation—cash disbursements)** Management has requested a review of internal control over cash disbursements for parts and supplies purchased at manufacturing plants. Cash disbursements are centrally processed at corporate headquarters based on disbursement vouchers prepared and approved at manufacturing plants. Each manufacturing plant purchases parts and supplies for its own production needs.

In response to management's request, a thorough evaluation of internal control over disbursements for manufacturing plant purchases of parts and supplies is being planned. As a preliminary step in planning the engagement, each plant manager has been requested to provide a written description of their plant's procedures for processing disbursement vouchers for parts and supplies. Presented below are some excerpts from one of the written descriptions.

1. The purchasing department acts on purchase requisitions issued by the stores department.
2. Orders are placed on prenumbered purchase order forms.
3. A complete purchase order copy is sent to the receiving department.
4. When goods are received, the receiving department logs the shipment in by stamping "order received" on its purchase order copy and forwards the annotated order to accounts payable.
5. Purchase orders, receiving department annotated purchase order copies, and vendor invoices are matched by accounts payable.
6. Clerical accuracy of vendor invoices is checked by accounts payable.
7. A prenumbered disbursement voucher is prepared and forwarded along with supporting documentation to the plant controller who reviews and approves the voucher.
8. Supporting documents are returned to accounts payable for filing, and approved disbursement vouchers are forwarded to corporate headquarters for payment.
9. A report listing checks issued by corporate headquarters is received and promptly filed by accounts payable.

REQUIRED

For each of the disbursement system procedures listed above, state whether the procedure is consistent with good internal control and describe how each procedure strengthens or weakens internal control.

Consistent/ Inconsistent	Strengthen or Weaken
1. (Example) Consistent.	Purchase requisitions provide the authorization for purchasing to order.

IIA

15-30 **(Internal control evaluation—cash disbursements)** ConSport Corporation is a regional wholesaler of sporting goods. The systems flowchart on page 595 and the following description present ConSport's cash distribution system.

1. The accounts payable department approves for payment all invoices (I) for the purchase of inventory. Invoices are matched with the purchase requisitions (PR), purchase orders (PO), and receiving reports (RR). The accounts payable clerks focus on vendor name and skim the documents when they are combined.
2. When all the documents for an invoice are assembled, a two-copy disbursement voucher (DV) is prepared and the transaction is recorded in the voucher register (VR). The disbursement voucher and supporting documents are then filed alphabetically by vendor.
3. A two-copy journal voucher (JV) that summarizes each day's entries in the voucher register is prepared daily. The first copy is sent to the general ledger department, and the second copy is filed in the accounts payable department by date.
4. The vendor file is searched daily for the disbursement vouchers of invoices that are due to be paid. Both copies of disbursement vouchers that are due to be paid are sent to the treasury department along with the supporting documents. The cashier prepares a check for each vendor, signs the check, and records it in the check register (CR). Copy 1 of the disbursement voucher is attached to the check copy and filed in check number order in the treasury department. Copy 2 and the supporting documents are returned to the accounts payable department and filed alphabetically by vendor.
5. A two-copy journal voucher that summarizes each day's checks is prepared. Copy 1 is sent to the general ledger department, and Copy 2 is filed in the treasury department by date.
6. The cashier receives the monthly bank statement with canceled checks and prepares the bank reconciliation (BR). If an adjustment is required as a consequence of the bank reconciliation, a two-copy journal voucher is prepared. Copy 1 is sent to the general ledger department. Copy 2 is attached to Copy 1 of the bank reconciliation and filed by month in the treasury department. Copy 2 of the bank reconciliation is sent to the internal audit department.

REQUIRED

ConSport Corporation's cash disbursement system has some weaknesses. Review the cash disbursement system and for each weakness in the system

a. Identify where the weakness exists by using the reference number that appears to the left of each symbol.
b. Describe the nature of the weakness.
c. Make a recommendation on how to correct the weakness.

Use the following format in preparing your answer:

Reference Number	Nature of Weakness	Recommendation to Correct Weakness

ICMA

15-31 **(Accounts payable assertions/confirmations)** Mincin, CPA, is the auditor of the Raleigh Corporation. Mincin is considering the audit work to be performed in the accounts payable area for the current year's engagement.

The prior year's papers show that confirmation requests were mailed to 100 of Raleigh's 1,000 suppliers. The selected suppliers were based on Mincin's sample that was designed to select accounts with large dollar balances. A substantial number of hours were spent by Raleigh and Mincin resolving relatively minor differences between the confirmation replies

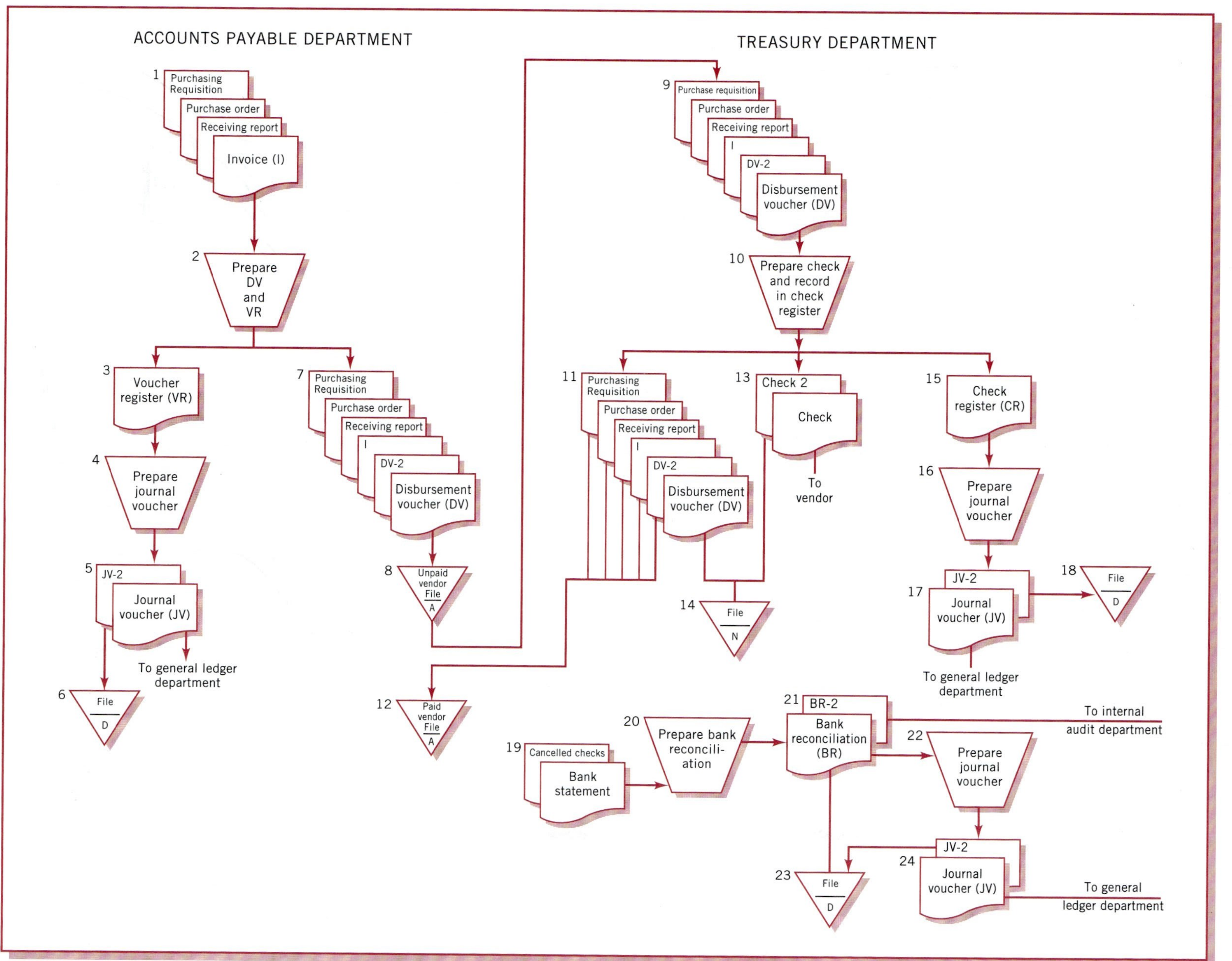

ACCOUNTS PAYABLE DEPARTMENT
TREASURY DEPARTMENT
1
Purchasing Requisition
Purchase order
Receiving report
Invoice (I)
2
Prepare DV and VR
3
Voucher register (VR)
4
Prepare journal voucher
5
JV-2
Journal voucher (JV)
To general ledger department
6
File D
7
Purchasing Requisition
Purchase order
Receiving report
I
DV-2
Disbursement voucher (DV)
8
Unpaid vendor File A
12
Paid vendor File A
9
Purchase requisition
Purchase order
Receiving report
I
DV-2
Disbursement voucher (DV)
10
Prepare check and record in check register
11
Purchasing Requisition
Purchase order
Receiving report
I
DV-2
Disbursement voucher (DV)
13
Check 2
Check
To vendor
14
File N
15
Check register (CR)
16
Prepare journal voucher
17
JV-2
Journal voucher (JV)
To general ledger department
18
File D
19
Cancelled checks
Bank statement
20
Prepare bank reconcili-ation
21
BR-2
Bank reconciliation (BR)
To internal audit department
22
Prepare journal voucher
23
File D
24
JV-2
Journal voucher (JV)
To general ledger department

and Raleigh's accounting records. Alternative auditing procedures were used for those suppliers who did not respond to the confirmation requests.

REQUIRED

a. Identify the accounts payable assertions that Mincin must consider in determining the substantive tests to be followed.
b. Identify situations when Mincin should use accounts payable confirmations and discuss whether Mincin is required to use them.
c. Discuss why the use of large dollar balances as the basis for selecting accounts payable for confirmation might not be the most efficient approach and indicate what more efficient procedures could be followed when selecting accounts payable for confirmation.

AICPA (adapted)

15-32 **(Search for unrecorded liabilities)** You were in the final stages of your audit of the financial statements of Ozine Corporation for the year ended December 31, 19X0, when you were consulted by the Corporation's president, who believes there is no point in your examining the 19X1 voucher register and testing data in support of 19X1 entries. He stated that (a) bills pertaining to 19X0 that were received too late to be included in the December voucher register were recorded as of the year-end by the Corporation by journal entry, (b) the internal auditor made tests after the year-end, and (c) he would furnish you with a letter certifying that there were no unrecorded liabilities.

REQUIRED

a. Should a CPA's test for unrecorded liabilities be affected by the fact that the client made a journal entry to record 19X0 bills that were received late? Explain.
b. Should a CPA's test for unrecorded liabilities be affected by the fact that a letter is obtained in which a responsible management official certifies that to the best of his knowledge all liabilities have been recorded? Explain.
c. Should a CPA's test for unrecorded liabilities be eliminated or reduced because of the internal audit tests? Explain.
d. Assume that the Corporation, which handled some government contracts, had no internal auditor but that an auditor for a federal agency spent three weeks auditing the records and was just completing his work at this time. How would the CPA's unrecorded liability test be affected by the work of the auditor for a federal agency?
e. What sources in addition to the 19X1 voucher register should the CPA consider to locate possible unrecorded liabilities?

AICPA

15-33 **(Substantive tests for accounts payable)** Taylor, CPA, is engaged in the audit of Rex Wholesaling for the year ended December 31, 19X2. Taylor performed a proper study of the internal control structure relating to the purchasing, receiving, trade accounts payable, and cash disbursement cycles, and has decided not to proceed with tests of controls. Based on analytical review procedures, Taylor believes that the trade accounts payable balance on the balance sheet as of December 31, 19X2, may be understated.

Taylor requested and obtained a client-prepared trade accounts payable schedule listing the total amount owed to each vendor.

REQUIRED

What additional substantive auditing procedures should Taylor apply in auditing the trade accounts payable?

AICPA

15-34 **(Internal controls for plant assets)** Harris, CPA, has accepted an engagement to audit the financial statements of Grant Manufacturing Co., a new client. Grant has an adequate control environment and a reasonable segregation of duties. Harris is about to assess control risk for the assertions related to Grant's property and equipment.

REQUIRED

Describe the key internal control structure policies and procedures related to Grant's property, equipment, and related transactions (additions, transfers, major maintenance and repairs, retirements, and dispositions) that Harris may consider in assessing control risk.

AICPA

15-35 **(Audit objectives for plant assets)** Rivers, CPA, is the auditor for a manufacturing company with a balance sheet that includes the caption "Property, Plant & Equipment." Rivers has been asked by the company's management if audit adjustments or reclassifications are required for the following material items that have been included in or excluded from "Property, Plant & Equipment":

1. A tract of land was acquired during the year. The land is the future site of the client's new headquarters, which will be constructed in the following year. Commissions were paid to the real estate agent used to acquire the land, and expenditures were made to relocate the previous owner's equipment. These commissions and expenditures were expensed and are excluded from "Property, Plant & Equipment."
2. Clearing costs were incurred to make the land ready for construction. These costs were included in "Property, Plant & Equipment."
3. During the land clearing process, timber and gravel were recovered and sold. The proceeds from the sale were recorded as other income and are excluded from "Property, Plant & Equipment."
4. A group of machines was purchased under a royalty agreement that provides royalty payments based on units of production from the machines. The cost of the machines, freight costs, unloading charges, and royalty payments were capitalized and are included in "Property, Plant & Equipment."

REQUIRED

a. Identify the audit objectives (assertions) for "Property, Plant & Equipment" and indicate the principal substantive tests pertaining to each.
b. Indicate whether each of the items numbered 1 to 4 above requires one or more audit adjustments or reclassifications, and explain why such adjustments or reclassifications are required or not required. Organize your answers as follows:

Item Number	Is Audit Adjustment or Reclassification Required? Yes or No	Reasons Why Audit Adjustment or Reclassification Is Required or Not Required

AICPA (adapted)

15-36 **(Substantive tests for plant assets)** Pierce, an independent auditor, was engaged to audit the financial statements of Mayfair Construction Incorporated for the year ended December 31, 19X3. Mayfair's financial statements reflect a substantial amount of mobile construction equipment used in the firm's operations. The equipment is accounted for in a subsidiary ledger. Pierce performed a study and evaluation of the internal control structure and found it satisfactory.

REQUIRED

Identify the substantive tests that Pierce should utilize in examining mobile construction equipment and related depreciation in Mayfair's financial statements.

AICPA

CASE

15-37 **(Trade accounts payable)** Your firm has been engaged to audit the financial statements of Brown Appliances, Inc., for the year ended December 31. The company manufactures major appliances sold to the general public through dealers and distributors.

You are to audit the trade accounts payable of a division of Brown Appliances, Inc. The trade accounts payable of this division aggregate $2.5 million, which is 60% of total accounts payable. Accounts payable total 40% of total liabilities and 30% of total liabilities and stockholders' equity. Net income for the year is $3 million.

Excerpts from the internal control memorandum follow:

"Invoices from suppliers are received in the purchasing department, where they are matched with receiving reports and checked to the applicable purchase order for quantities and pricing. Invoices and receiving reports are then forwarded to the accounting department for clerical checking and final approval for payment.

"On the payment date (the seventh working day of the month), invoices with attached receiving reports are separated into two groups: one group of invoices with receiving reports dated in the prior month, the other group with receiving reports dated in the current month. The check register is then prepared, with each group having a separate total and check number sequence. The accounts payable for monthly financial statement purposes is the total of the check register for invoices with receiving reports dated in the prior month. A voucher register is not maintained.

"The purchasing department holds unmatched receiving reports and unmatched invoices.

"Cutoff procedures as established by the company appear adequate; however, the company makes it a practice not to record inventory in transit.

"Vendors' statements received by the company are forwarded to a clerk in the accounting department. The clerk does not check all charges appearing on the vendors' statements, but does reconcile all old outstanding charges appearing thereon."

An accounts payable listing has been prepared by the company for the auditors. As explained above, this listing was prepared from the check register of December charges paid in January, and shows vendor, check number, invoice date, date paid, and amount. A quick review of the listing reveals the following:

1. January-dated invoices amounting to $200,000 appear on the listing payable to Talley and Park Advertising Agency, for advertising to appear in *Better Homes and Gardens* magazine in February and March. This was included in the year-end accounts payable listing at the request of the vice president of advertising because he said he wanted to more closely match advertising department budgeted expenses with actual expenditures for the year. The distribution was made to advertising expense.
2. Amounts appear on the listing as payments for payrolls, payroll taxes, other taxes, and profit-sharing plans.
3. No amounts appear on the listing for legal or accounting services.

REQUIRED

Discuss the problems and substantive tests involved in auditing this company's accounts payable. Specifically discuss (a) the tests you would use in your examination and (b) the adjustments you would recommend be made to the accounts payable listing.

RESEARCH QUESTIONS

15-38 **(Selected readings)** Three articles dealing with topics covered in this chapter are cited in the chapter bibliography. For any one of these readings of your choice, or one specifically assigned to you by your instructor, prepare a brief written summary of the article.

15-39 **(AAERs dealing with payables)** Several SEC enforcement actions have focused on issues pertaining to unrecorded or understated payables. For any *AAER* of your choice dealing with payables, identify the parties involved, what the issues were, what position the SEC took, and what the outcome was for the auditors involved.

15-40 **(AAERs dealing with plant assets)** Several SEC enforcement actions have focused on issues pertaining to plant, or fixed, assets. One of these, *AAER 312,* describes certain deficiencies in the reporting and audit of certain fixed assets of ZZZZ Best Corporation. After reviewing this *AAER,* (a) summarize the SEC's findings with respect to the reporting and audit of ZZZZ Best's fixed assets, (b) briefly identify other deficiencies found in ZZZZ Best's reporting and audit, and (c) indicate the nature of the enforcement action taken against the auditor.

CHAPTER

16

AUDITING THE PRODUCTION AND PERSONNEL SERVICES CYCLES

LEARNING OBJECTIVES

After studying this chapter, you should be able to

1. Explain the nature of the production cycle and identify the transaction class and accounts involved.
2. Identify transaction class and account balance audit objectives for the production cycle.
3. Explain the applicability of relevant aspects of the internal control structure components to the production cycle.
4. Describe the functions and related control activities pertaining to manufacturing transactions.
5. Design an audit program of substantive tests for inventory balances.
6. Explain the nature of the personnel services cycle and identify the transaction class and accounts involved.
7. Identify specific audit objectives for the personnel services cycle.

THE PRODUCTION CYCLE
- AUDIT OBJECTIVES
- MATERIALITY, RISK, AND AUDIT STRATEGY
- CONSIDERATION OF INTERNAL CONTROL STRUCTURE COMPONENTS

CONTROL ACTIVITIES—MANUFACTURING TRANSACTIONS
- COMMON DOCUMENTS AND RECORDS
- FUNCTIONS AND RELATED CONTROLS
- OBTAINING THE UNDERSTANDING AND ASSESSING CONTROL RISK

SUBSTANTIVE TESTS OF INVENTORY BALANCES
- DETERMINING DETECTION RISK
- DESIGNING SUBSTANTIVE TESTS
- INITIAL PROCEDURES
- ANALYTICAL PROCEDURES
- TESTS OF DETAILS OF TRANSACTIONS
- TESTS OF DETAILS OF BALANCES
- COMPARISON OF STATEMENT PRESENTATION WITH GAAP

THE PERSONNEL SERVICES CYCLE
- AUDIT OBJECTIVES
- MATERIALITY, RISK, AND AUDIT STRATEGY
- CONSIDERATION OF INTERNAL CONTROL STRUCTURE COMPONENTS

CONTROL ACTIVITIES—PAYROLL TRANSACTIONS
- COMMON DOCUMENTS AND RECORDS
- FUNCTIONS AND RELATED CONTROLS
- OBTAINING THE UNDERSTANDING AND ASSESSING CONTROL RISK

SUBSTANTIVE TESTS OF PAYROLL BALANCES
- DETERMINING DETECTION RISK
- DESIGNING SUBSTANTIVE TESTS

SUMMARY

BIBLIOGRAPHY

OBJECTIVE QUESTIONS

COMPREHENSIVE QUESTIONS

CASE

RESEARCH QUESTION

The first half of this chapter deals with auditing the production cycle. This part includes consideration of the internal control structure components that pertain to manufacturing transactions, and gives particular attention to substantive tests of inventory balances for both manufactured and purchased inventories. The second half of the chapter deals with auditing the personnel services cycle. This part focuses on internal control structure considerations for payroll transactions and substantive tests of related account balances.

8. Explain the applicability of relevant aspects of the internal control structure components to the personnel services cycle.
9. Describe the functions and related control activities pertaining to payroll transactions.
10. Discuss the application of selected substantive tests to payroll balances.

THE PRODUCTION CYCLE

The **production cycle** relates to the conversion of raw materials into finished goods. This cycle includes production planning and control of the types and quantities of goods to be manufactured, the inventory levels to be maintained, and the transactions and events pertaining to the manufacturing process. Transactions in this cycle begin at the point where raw materials are requisitioned for production, and end with the transfer of the manufactured product to finished goods. The transactions in this cycle are called **manufacturing transactions.**

OBJECTIVE 1

Explain the nature of the production cycle and identify the transaction class and accounts involved.

The production cycle interfaces with the following three other cycles: (1) the expenditure cycle in purchasing raw materials and incurring various overhead costs, (2) the personnel services cycle in incurring factory labor costs, and (3) the revenue cycle in selling finished goods. The interaction of these cycles and the major accounts affected by manufacturing transactions are shown in Figure 16-1. It should be noted that the credits to raw materials, direct labor, and manufacturing overhead, the debits to work in process inventory, and the subsequent entries to record the transfer of the cost of completed production from work in process to finished goods, result from manufacturing transactions in the production cycle. Finally, although usually considered a revenue cycle transaction, the transfer of costs from manufactured finished goods to cost of goods sold is based on cost data accumulated in the production cycle.

AUDIT OBJECTIVES

OBJECTIVE 2

Identify transaction class and account balance audit objectives for the production cycle.

Two groups of audit objectives are addressed in this section: (1) transaction class audit objectives pertaining to manufacturing transactions and (2) account balance audit objectives pertaining to inventory balances and cost of goods sold. Selected audit objectives in each group are listed in Figure 16-2.

To avoid redundancy, discussion of account balance audit objectives and related audit procedures for purchased inventories was deferred in the expenditure cycle in favor of joint coverage in this chapter with manufactured inventories. Similarly, discussion of audit objectives and related audit procedures for cost of goods sold was deferred in the revenue cycle chapter pending coverage of the origin of such costs through purchases transactions in the expenditure cycle chapter and manufacturing transactions in this chapter. Thus, some of the evidence obtained in connection with objectives related to purchases and sales transactions in Chapters 15 and 14, respectively, is relevant to meeting the account balance audit objectives identified in Figure 16-2. Some specific instances are noted in the following sections that address the audit methodology for meeting these objectives.

MATERIALITY, RISK, AND AUDIT STRATEGY

In a manufacturing company, inventories and cost of goods sold are usually significant to both the company's financial position and results of operations. Moreover, there are numerous factors that contribute to the risk of misstatements in the assertions for these accounts, including the following:

FIGURE 16-1 • INTERFACE OF PRODUCTION CYCLE WITH OTHER CYCLES

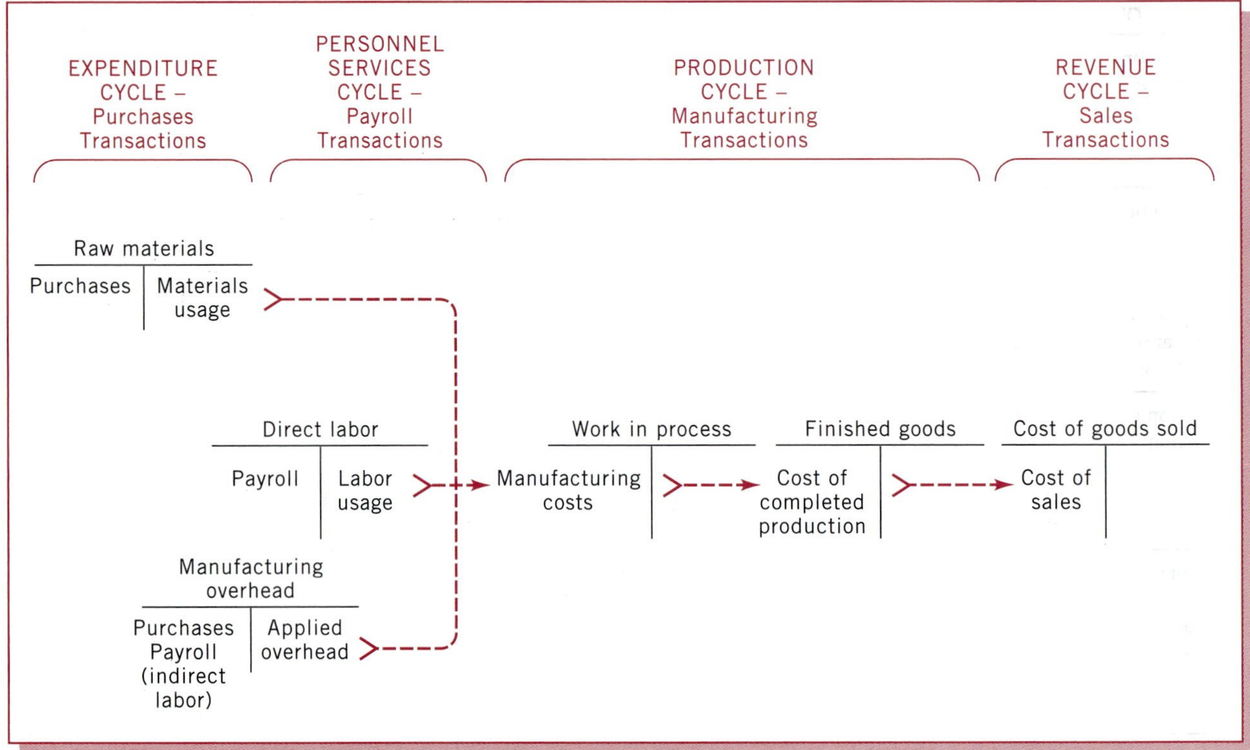

- The volume of purchases, manufacturing, and sales transactions that affects these accounts is generally high, increasing the opportunities for misstatements to occur.
- There are often contentious issues surrounding the identification, measurement, and allocation of inventoriable costs such as indirect materials, labor, and manufacturing overhead, joint product costs, the disposition of cost variances, accounting for scrap, and other cost accounting issues.
- The wide diversity of inventory items sometimes requires the use of special procedures to determine inventory quantities, such as geometric volume measurements of stockpiles, aerial photography, and estimation of quantities by experts.
- Inventories are often stored at multiple sites, adding to the difficulties associated with maintaining physical controls over theft and damage, and properly accounting for goods in transit between sites.
- The wide diversity of inventory items may present special problems in determining their quality and market value.
- Inventories are vulnerable to spoilage, obsolescence, and other factors such as general economic conditions that may affect demand and salability, and thus the proper valuation of the inventories.
- Inventories may be sold subject to right of return and repurchase agreements.

FIGURE 16-2 • SELECTED SPECIFIC AUDIT OBJECTIVES FOR THE PRODUCTION CYCLE

Assertion Category	Transaction Class Audit Objectives	Account Balance Audit Objectives
Existence or occurrence	Recorded manufacturing transactions represent materials, labor, and overhead transferred to production and the movement of completed production to finished goods during the current period **(EO1).**	Inventories included in the balance sheet physically exist **(EO2).** Cost of goods sold represents the cost of goods shipped (sold) during the period **(EO3).**
Completeness	All manufacturing transactions that occurred during the period have been recorded **(C1).**	Inventories include all materials, products, and supplies on hand at the balance sheet date. **(C2).** Cost of goods sold includes the effects of all sales transactions during the period **(C3).**
Rights and obligations	The entity has rights to the inventories resulting from recorded manufacturing transactions **(RO1).**	The reporting entity has legal title to the inventories at the balance sheet date.**(RO2).**
Valuation or allocation	Manufacturing transactions are correctly journalized, summarized, and posted **(VA1).**	Inventories are properly stated at the lower of cost or market **(VA2).** Cost of goods sold is based on the consistent application of an acceptable cost flow method or methods **(VA3).**
Presentation and disclosure	The details of manufacturing transactions support their presentation in the financial statements including their classification and disclosure **(PD1).**	Inventories **(PD2)** and cost of goods sold **(PD3)** are properly identified and classified in the financial statements. Disclosures pertaining to basis of valuation and the pledging or assignment of inventories are adequate **(PD4).**

To properly plan the audit of manufacturing transactions and related inventory and cost of goods sold balances, the auditor must obtain an understanding of the extent to which an entity's internal control structure addresses the inherent risks enumerated above. Within a single entity, the extent to which each of these risks is addressed can vary for a particular type of inventory, as well as vary across types of inventories. Thus, for a single client the auditor may use the primarily substantive strategy in auditing certain transaction class and account balance assertions in the production cycle, and the lower assessed level of control risk strategy for other assertions in the same cycle.

CONSIDERATION OF INTERNAL CONTROL STRUCTURE COMPONENTS

OBJECTIVE 3

Explain the applicability of relevant aspects of the internal control structure components to the production cycle.

As in the case of the revenue and expenditure cycles, aspects of all five components of an entity's internal control structure (ICS) are applicable to manufacturing transactions in the production cycle. For example, within the control environment component, the organizational structure should include an officer who has overall responsibility for production. With a title such as vice president of operations, manufacturing, or production, this individual usually has line authority over the production planning and control department and each manufacturing department. Management's philosophy and operating style includes its approach to taking and monitoring business risks related to production decisions and inventory levels. And the entity's human resource policies and practices pertaining to production department employees can significantly impact the use of, and accountability for, the factors of production.

Accounting systems for inventories include the use of control accounts and supporting records such as product or master files. For manufacturing companies, separate records exist for raw materials, work in process, and finished goods inventories. An entity's systems may include job order and process cost systems, and both actual and standard costs may be recorded. In a job order system, manufacturing costs are accumulated by jobs and the work in process account is supported by individual job cost records. In a process cost system, costs are accumulated by departments or processes.

The numerous control activities pertaining to manufacturing transactions, including the use of budgets and performance reviews, are discussed in the next section of this chapter. Management's monitoring of controls in the production cycle includes feedback from customers about product quality and timely delivery, and the use of internal auditors to assess the effectiveness of cost controls, the accuracy of cost data, and physical controls over inventories.

LEARNING CHECK:

16-1 a. Describe the nature of the production cycle.
  b. Identify the major transaction class within this cycle.
  c. Name three other cycles that interface with the production cycle.

16-2 a. Identify several transaction class audit objectives for the production cycle.
  b. Identify several account balance audit objectives for the production cycle.

16-3 a. Discuss materiality from the perspective of the production cycle.
  b. Discuss inherent risk from the perspective of the production cycle.
  c. Why might the auditor use different audit strategies for different assertions in the production cycle?

16-4 a. Explain several control environment factors that impact the production cycle.
  b. Identify several unique elements of an entity's accounting information system that pertain to the production cycle.

KEY TERMS:

Manufacturing transactions, p. 601 — Production cycle, p. 601

OBJECTIVE 4

Describe the functions and related control activities pertaining to manufacturing transactions.

CONTROL ACTIVITIES—MANUFACTURING TRANSACTIONS

Recall that the control activities component of the ICS consists of four categories of activities: (1) information processing controls that include proper authorization, documents and records, and independent checks, (2) segregation of duties,

(3) physical controls, and (4) performance reviews. The next section identifies the common documents and records used in processing manufacturing transactions. The following section explains how all four categories of control activities relate to the functions that are performed in the production cycle.

COMMON DOCUMENTS AND RECORDS

Following are some of the common documents and records used in processing manufacturing transactions:

- **Production order.** Form indicating the quantity and kind of goods to be manufactured. An order may pertain to a job order or a continuous process.
- **Material requirements report.** Listing of raw materials and parts needed to fill a production order.
- **Materials issue slip.** Written authorization from a production department for stores to release materials for use on an approved production order.
- **Time ticket.** Record of time worked by an employee on a specific job.
- **Move ticket.** Notice authorizing the physical movement of work in process between production departments and between work in process and finished goods.
- **Daily production activity report.** Report showing raw materials and labor used during the day.
- **Completed production report.** Report showing that work has been completed on a production order.
- **Inventory subsidiary ledgers or master files (perpetual inventory records).** Records maintained separately for raw materials, work in process, and finished goods. Contain information on units and costs added to and deducted from the respective inventory accounts, and units on hand and associated costs comprising the inventory balances at a point in time.

The use of each of these documents and records is explained in the following sections.

FUNCTIONS AND RELATED CONTROLS

Executing and recording manufacturing transactions and safeguarding inventories involve the following **manufacturing functions:**

- Planning and controlling production.
- Issuing raw materials.
- Processing goods in production.
- Transferring completed work to finished goods.
- Protecting inventories.
- Determining and recording manufacturing costs.
- Maintaining the correctness of inventory balances.

The performance of these functions involves several departments such as production planning and control, stores (raw materials), the production departments, timekeeping, finished goods, EDP, cost accounting, and general accounting. As with each of the other major transaction classes, there should be segregation of duties for executing and recording manufacturing transactions and maintaining custody of the manufacturing inventories. Controls pertaining to the first five foregoing functions are relevant in assessing control risk for the existence or occurrence and completeness assertions for manufacturing transactions and related inventories. Controls pertaining to the last two functions are important in assessing control risk for the rights and obligations, valuation or allocation, and presentation and disclosure assertions for manufacturing transactions and inventories

Planning and Controlling Production

The authorization of production occurs in the production planning and control department based on orders received from customers or analysis of sales forecasts and inventory requirements. Documentation of the authorizations is provided by issuing prenumbered production orders. There should be a subsequent accounting for all production order numbers issued. A material requirements report is also prepared showing materials and parts needed and on hand. When orders must be placed with suppliers, a copy of this report is sent to purchasing.

Production planning and control is also responsible for monitoring materials and labor usage, and tracking the progress on production orders until they are completed and transferred to finished goods. The review of daily production activity reports and completed production reports is essential in meeting these responsibilities.

Issuing Raw Materials

Stores release raw materials to production on receipt of materials issue slips (or requisitions) from the production departments. The slips show the quantity and type of material requested and the production order number to be charged. Each slip should be signed by a supervisor or an authorized production worker. A daily summary of materials usage is typically prepared as a component of the daily production activity report used in production planning and control.

Processing Goods in Production

Labor incurred on specific production orders is recorded on time tickets, the timekeeping function may be accomplished by having employees insert their badges in a computer terminal and key in the production order number whenever they start or stop work on a job. In either case, a daily summary of labor usage is typically prepared from the timekeeping data as a component of the daily production activity report.

When work on a production order is completed in one department and the goods have passed inspection, transfer to the next department is authorized by a move ticket that should be signed by the department receiving the goods.

Transferring Completed Work to Finished Goods

When production of an order is complete and the goods have passed a final inspection, a completed production report is prepared. The goods are then forwarded to the finished goods warehouse, which accepts accountability for the goods by signing the final move ticket.

Protecting Inventories

Manufacturing inventories are vulnerable to theft and damage. The storage of raw materials and finished goods inventories in locked storerooms with access restricted to authorized individuals is important in safeguarding these assets. The protection of work in process is facilitated through surveillance of production areas by supervisory and plant security employees, the tagging of goods, and the use of prenumbered move tickets to control the transfer of work in process through the plant.

Determining and Recording Manufacturing Costs

This function involves the following:

- Charging direct materials and direct labor to work in process.
- Assigning manufacturing overhead to work in process.
- Transferring costs between production departments (in a process cost system).
- Transferring the cost of completed production to finished goods.

To ensure that manufacturing costs are properly recorded, the chart of accounts should provide for the many accounts needed to properly classify and track such costs. In addition, the timely reporting of cost data for use in management performance reviews of production activity and cost control provides a useful means of detecting misclassifications in recording manufacturing costs. Such reports normally include comparisons of actual and budgeted data by various cost classifications.

Manufacturing costs may be assigned to work in process based on actual costs or standard costs. When the latter are used, they should be approved by management, and there should be timely reporting of variances from actual or budgeted amounts for investigation and follow-up as a part of the periodic performance reviews by management. Additional controls over the recording of manufacturing costs include

- Independent checks on the agreement of entries for the allocation of manufacturing costs to work in process with data on materials and labor usage in *daily production activity reports.*
- Independent checks on the agreement of entries for the transfer of work in process to finished goods with data in *completed production reports.*

Maintaining Correctness of Inventory Balances

This function involves three activities. First, there should be periodic independent counts of inventory on hand and comparison with recorded quantities per the perpetual inventory records. These comparisons may reveal recorded quantities that no longer exist, incomplete records of quantities on hand, or inventory items that are misclassified in the records. This activity may occur just once a year in connection with the annual audit, or it may occur on a more frequent cyclical basis throughout the year. Second, there should be periodic independent checks on the agreement of the dollar carrying amounts for the raw materials, work in process, and finished goods inventory master files with their respective general ledger control accounts. Third, through periodic inspections of inventory condition and management review of inventory activity reports, adjustments to reduce inventory carrying values to market should be made when required.

FIGURE 16-3 • OVERVIEW FLOWCHART—MANUFACTURING TRANSACTIONS

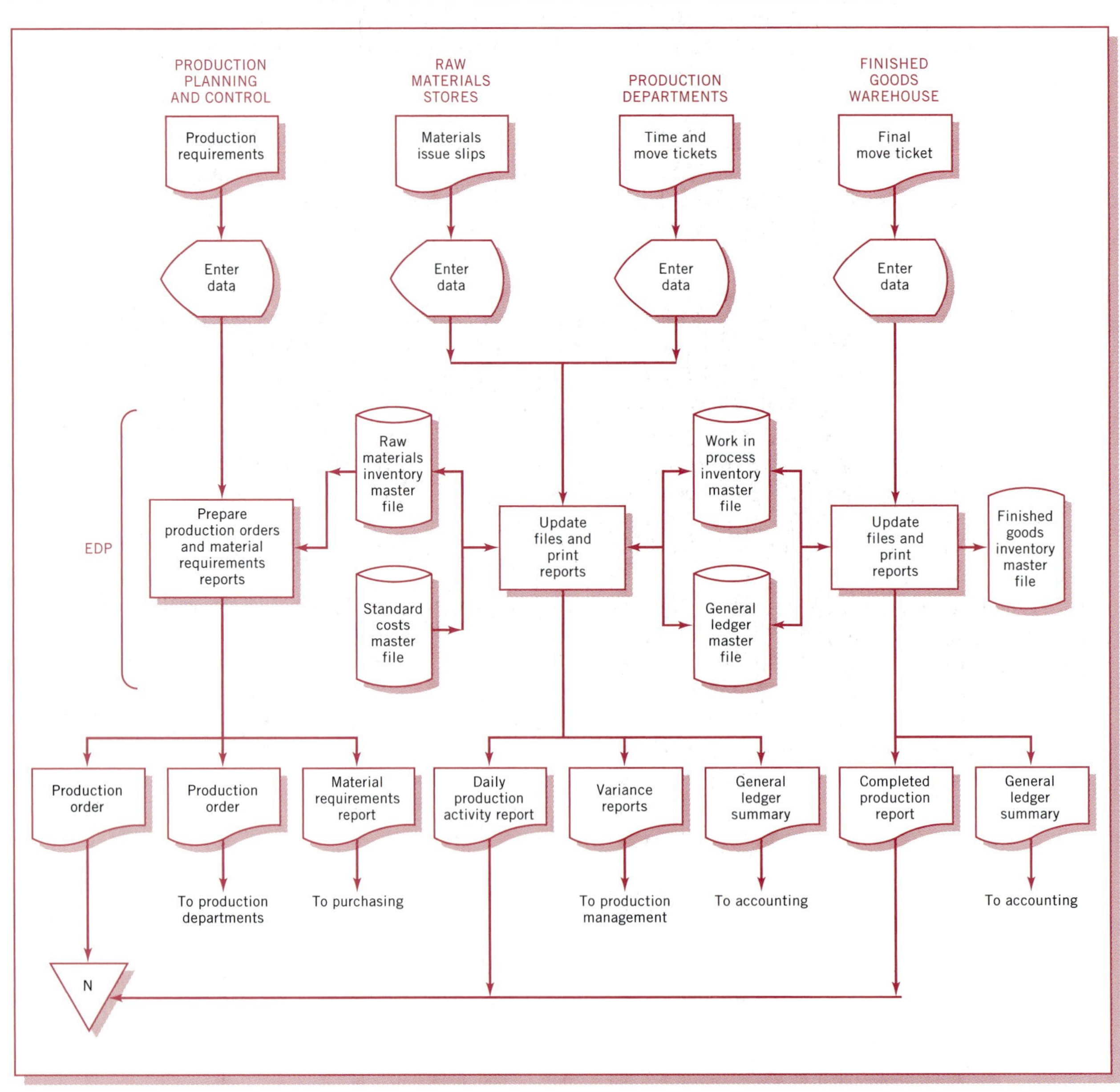

Illustrative System for Processing Manufacturing Transactions

Figure 16-3 presents an *overview* flowchart of an on-line computer system for processing manufacturing transactions. This system illustrates many of the processing controls discussed in the preceding sections, such as the segregation of duties among departments and the key production documents, records, files, and reports used.

OBTAINING THE UNDERSTANDING AND ASSESSING CONTROL RISK

In obtaining and documenting the understanding of portions of the internal control structure components relevant to manufacturing transactions, the auditor uses the same procedures as for other transaction classes. Thus, this includes reviewing prior experience with the client, if any, making inquiries of management and other production personnel, inspecting production documents and records, and observing production activities and conditions. It may also include the use of internal control questionnaires, flowcharts, and narrative memoranda.

Similarly, the familiar three-step process of identifying potential misstatements, necessary controls, and tests of controls pertains to assessing control risk for transactions in the production cycle. Examples of these factors extracted from the foregoing discussions of functions performed in the production cycle are presented in Figure 16-4, which also includes cross references to the related specific audit objectives for each of the five categories of assertions. From the list of necessary controls, the auditor selects those for which he or she seeks further evidence to support a lower assessment of control risk and performs the related tests of controls indicated in the figure. As indicated in the figure, these tests may involve additional inquiries, inspections of documents and reports, and observations of client personnel performing control activities, as well as reperformance of some control activities by the auditor. The results of any such tests should be documented to establish the basis for the auditor's final control risk assessments for significant assertions pertaining to manufacturing transactions.

LEARNING CHECK:

16-5 Identify the documents and records that provide a basis of authorization and control in the four functions that culminate in transferring completed production to finished goods.

16-6 What controls are important in determining and recording manufacturing costs?

16-7 What controls are important in protecting inventories and maintaining the correctness of inventory balances?

FIGURE 16-4 • CONTROL RISK ASSESSMENT CONSIDERATIONS FOR MANUFACTURING TRANSACTIONS

Function	Potential Misstatement	Necessary Control	Possible Test of Control*	Relevant Transaction Class Audit Objective (from p. 603) EOI	CI	ROI	VAI	PDI
Planning and controlling production	Excessive production may be ordered.	Approval of production orders in production planning and control.	Inquire about procedures for approving production orders.	✓	✓			
Issuing raw materials	Unauthorized use of raw materials.	Signed materials issue slips for approved production orders required for all material released to production.	Examine materials issue slips and compare with production orders.	✓	✓			
Processing goods in production	Direct labor hours may not be charged to production orders.	Use of time tickets to record direct labor hours on production orders.	Observe use of time tickets and timekeeping procedures.	✓	✓			
Transferring completed work to finished goods inventory	Finished goods personnel may claim goods were not received from production.	Signature of finished goods warehouse personnel on final move ticket on receipt of goods.	Examine final move tickets for authorized signatures.	✓	✓			
Protecting inventories	Inventories may be stolen from warehouses.	Use of locked warehouses with access restricted to authorized personnel.	Observe security procedures.	✓				
	Work in process may be stolen or misrouted during production.	Use of plant surveillance personnel and signed move tickets to control movement of goods through production departments.	Observe procedures; examine move tickets.	✓	✓			
Determining and recording manufacturing costs.	Manufacturing costs may be recorded in incorrect accounts.	Use chart of accounts; timely reporting of manufacturing cost data for management performance reviews including budget comparisons.	Examine chart of accounts and observe use; examine cost reports; inquire about management performance reviews.*				✓	✓
	Direct manufacturing costs allocated to work in process may not be recorded or be recorded at incorrect amounts.	Independent check of agreement of entries with daily production activity report data.	Examine evidence of independent check; reperform.*		✓		✓	

FIGURE 16-4 • *(Continued)*

				Relevant Transaction Class Audit Objective (from p. 603)				
Function	**Potential Misstatement**	**Necessary Control**	**Possible Test of Control***	**EOI**	**CI**	**ROI**	**VAI**	**PDI**
Determining and recording manufacturing costs (continued)	Inappropriate overhead rates or standard costs may be used.	Management approval of overhead rates and standard costs; timely reporting for management performance reviews and investigation of variances.	Inquire about procedures for developing and approving rates and standards; review performance reports and management follow-up.*				✓	✓
	Costs of completed production may not be transferred to completed goods or be transferred at incorrect amounts	Independent check of agreement of entries with completed production report data.	Examine evidence of independent check; reperform.*				✓	✓
Maintaining the correctness of inventory balances	Recorded inventory quantities may not agree with owned quantities on hand.	Periodic independent counts of inventories; comparison with records of amounts and ownership.	Observe periodic inventory counts and comparisons; examine adjusting entries.*	✓	✓	✓		✓
	Inventory carrying values in subsidiary ledgers or master files may not agree with control accounts.	Periodic independent check on agreement of subsidiary records and control accounts.	Examine evidence of independent check; reperform.*				✓	
	Inventories may be carried at amounts in excess of market values.	Periodic inspection of inventory condition; periodic inventory activity reports for management performance reviews.	Observe inspections; review activity reports; examine adjusting entries.*				✓	

* Tests marked with an asterisk are sometimes performed as a part of dual-purpose tests.

KEY TERMS:

Completed production report, p. 605
Daily production activity report, p. 605
Inventory subsidiary ledgers or master files (perpetual inventory records), p. 605
Manufacturing functions, p. 605
Materials issue slip, p. 605
Material requirements report, p. 605
Move ticket, p. 605
Production order, p. 605
Time ticket, p. 605

SUBSTANTIVE TESTS OF INVENTORY BALANCES

OBJECTIVE 5

Design an audit program of substantive tests for inventory balances.

This section pertains to substantive tests of purchased merchandise inventories held by wholesalers and retailers as well as raw materials, work in process, and finished goods inventories held by manufacturers. The audit of inventory balances requires careful planning and a very substantial investment in audit time, cost, and effort. To ensure that the examination is both efficient and effective in obtaining sufficient competent evidence, careful consideration must be given to determining the acceptable levels of detection risk and designing appropriate substantive tests for inventory assertions.

DETERMINING DETECTION RISK

In keeping with the audit risk model described and applied in previous chapters, the auditor's specification of acceptable levels of detection risk for inventory assertions will reflect an inverse relationship with relevant inherent and control risk assessments pertaining to those assertions. Several inherent risk factors pertaining to inventories are enumerated earlier in this chapter on page 602. Although some of those factors pertain only to manufactured inventories, others apply to all types of inventories.

Relevant control risk assessments vary based on the transaction classes that affect the particular inventory account as shown in the following tabulation:

	Transaction Class that	
Inventory Account	**Increases Account**	**Decreases Account**
Merchandise inventory	Purchases	Sales
Raw materials	Purchases	Manufacturing transactions that transfer materials costs to production
Work in process	Manufacturing transactions that transfer in the costs of materials, labor, and overhead	Manufacturing transactions that transfer costs out to other work in process accounts or finished goods
Finished goods	Manufacturing transactions that transfer the costs of completed production to finished goods	Sales

Thus, for example, in assessing control risk for the existence or occurrence assertion for merchandise inventory, the auditor would consider her or his control risk assessments for the existence or occurrence assertion for purchases transactions that increase the inventory balance, and the completeness assertion for sales transactions that decrease the inventory balance. Recall that the reason for the latter is that if some sales transactions are not recorded, some of the recorded inventory will no longer exist. As another example, the control risk assessment for the valuation or allocation assertion for raw materials inventory requires consideration of the combined control risk assessments for the valuation or allocation assertions for both purchases transactions and manufacturing transactions that transfer costs to production.[1]

Because the combined inherent and control risk assessments are often highest for the existence or occurrence and valuation or allocation assertions for inventory balances, the acceptable levels of detection risk may need to be lower for these assertions than for the others. This in turn affects decisions about the design of substantive tests.

DESIGNING SUBSTANTIVE TESTS

Possible substantive tests of inventory balance assertions and the specific account balance audit objectives to which they relate are shown in Figure 16-5. Evidence from some of the tests applicable to merchandise inventory and to manufactured finished goods inventories also relates to objectives for the corresponding cost of goods sold accounts because of the reciprocal relationship of these accounts. Note that there are numerous tests that apply to the specific audit objectives related to the existence or occurrence, completeness, and valuation or allocation assertions. Each of the substantive tests is discussed in a following section together with selected comments about how the tests can be tailored based on the acceptable level of detection risk to be achieved.

INITIAL PROCEDURES

In tracing beginning inventory balances to prior year working papers, the auditor should make certain that any audit adjustments agreed upon in the prior year did in fact get recorded. In addition, current period entries in the general ledger inventory accounts should be scanned to identify any postings that are unusual in amount or nature that require special investigation. Initial procedures also involve determining that the detailed perpetual or other inventory schedules tie in with the general ledger balances. Additional work on inventory listings prepared on the basis of the physical inventory is discussed in a later section dealing with tests of details of balances.

ANALYTICAL PROCEDURES

The application of analytical procedures to inventories is often extensive as suggested by the steps shown in Figure 16-5. A review of industry experience and trends may be essential in developing expectations to be used in evaluating analytical data for the client. For example, knowing that a sharp drop in the client's inventory turnover ratio mirrors what is happening in the industry may help the auditor in concluding that the drop is not indicative of errors pertaining to existence or occurrence or completeness of the client data used in calculating the inventory turnover ratio, but may instead be indicative of a valuation problem related to a drop in demand that is likely to be followed by falling market prices. A review of relationships of inventory balances to recent purchasing, production,

[1] The student needing to refresh his or her memory regarding the relationships among control risk assessments for transaction class and account balance assertions can once again review Figure 9-4 on page 319.

FIGURE 16-5 • POSSIBLE SUBSTANTIVE TESTS OF INVENTORY BALANCE ASSERTIONS

Category	Substantive Test	Account Balance Audit Objective (from p. 603)				
		EO#	C#	RO2	VA#	PD#
Initial procedures	1. Perform initial procedures on inventory balances and records that will be subjected to further testing. a. Trace beginning inventory balances to prior year's working papers. b. Review activity in inventory accounts and investigate entries that appear unusual in amount or source. c. Verify totals of perpetual records and other inventory schedules and their agreement with ending general ledger balances.				✓2	
Analytical procedures	2. Perform analytical procedures. a. Review industry experience and trends. b. Examine an analysis of inventory turnover. c. Review relationships of inventory balances to recent purchasing, production, and sales activities. d. Compare inventory balances to anticipated sales volume.	✓2,3	✓2,3		✓2,3	
Tests of details of transactions	3. On a test basis, vouch entries in inventory accounts to supporting documentation (e.g., vendors' invoices, manufacturing cost records, completed production reports, and sales and sales returns records).	✓2,3	✓2,3	✓	✓2,3	
	4. On a test basis, trace data from purchases, manufacturing, completed production, and sales records to inventory accounts.	✓2,3	✓2,3	✓	✓2,3	
	5. Test cutoff of purchases and sales returns (receiving), movement of goods through manufacturing departments (routing), and sales (shipping).	✓2,3	✓2,3	✓		
Tests of details of balances	6. Observe client's physical inventory count. a. Decide on timing and extent of test. b. Evaluate adequacy of client's inventory-taking plans. c. Observe care taken in client's counts and make test counts. d. Look for indications of slow-moving, damaged, or obsolete inventory. e. Account for all inventory tags and count sheets used in physical count.	✓2	✓2		✓2	
	7. Test clerical accuracy of inventory listings. a. Recalculate totals and extensions of quantities times unit prices. b. Trace test counts (from item 6c) to listings. c. Vouch items on listings to inventory tags and count sheets. d. Reconcile physical counts to perpetual records and general ledger balances and review adjusting entries.	✓2	✓2		✓2	
	8. Test inventory pricing. a. Examine vendors' paid invoices for purchased inventories. b. Examine propriety of direct labor and overhead rates, standard costs, and disposition of variances pertaining to manufactured inventories. c. Obtain market quotations and perform lower-of-cost or market test. d. Compare inventories with entity's current sales catalog and sales reports. e. Inquire about slow-moving, excess, or obsolete inventories and determine need for write-down.				✓2	
	9. Confirm inventories at locations outside the entity.	✓2	✓2	✓		
	10. Examine consignment agreements and contracts.			✓		✓2

FIGURE 16-5 • *(Continued)*

Category	Substantive Test	Account Balance Audit Objective (from p. 603)				
		EO#	C#	RO2	VA#	PD#
Required procedure	Observation of physical inventory count included as Step 6 above.					
Presentation and disclosure	11. Compare statement presentation with GAAP. a. Confirm agreements for assignment and pledging of inventories. b. Review presentation and disclosures for inventories in drafts of financial statements and determine conformity with GAAP.					✓ 2,3,4

and sales activities should also aid the auditor in understanding changes in inventory levels. For example, an increase in the reported level of finished goods inventory when purchasing, production, and sales levels have remained steady might be indicative of misstatements related to the existence or valuation of the finished goods inventory.

In addition to the calculation of an overall inventory turnover ratio for each inventory account, it may be appropriate to calculate the ratio for disaggregated data, such as by product line. The number of days sales in inventory (365 divided by inventory turnover) may also be analyzed in assessing the implications of inventory levels. Several other ratios involving inventories are also commonly calculated, such as the rate of gross profit (gross profit divided by net sales) and the percentage of inventories to total current assets.

Because of the reciprocal relationship between inventories and cost of goods sold, these procedures may provide evidence useful in determining the fairness of management's assertions pertaining to both accounts. For example, an unexpectedly high inventory turnover ratio or an unexpectedly low gross profit rate might be caused by an overstatement of cost of goods sold and corresponding understatement of inventories. Conversely, conformity of these ratios with expectations may provide some limited assurance of the fairness of the historical data used in the calculations unless evidence from other sources is contradictory. Finally, analysis of inventory levels and ratios based on anticipated sales volume in the subsequent period may be useful in conjunction with the market valuation tests discussed in a later section.

TESTS OF DETAILS OF TRANSACTIONS

These tests involve the procedures of vouching and tracing to obtain evidence about the processing of individual transactions that affect inventory balances. Special consideration is given to determining the propriety of the cutoff of inventory transactions at the end of the accounting period.

Test Entries to Inventory Accounts

Some or all of this type of testing may be done as part of dual-purpose tests during interim work. Examples of vouching recorded entries in inventory accounts include the vouching of

- Debits in merchandise or raw materials inventories to vendors' invoices, receiving reports, and purchase orders.
- Debits in work in process or finished goods inventories to manufacturing cost records and production reports.
- Credits to merchandise and finished goods inventories to sales documents and records.
- Credits to raw materials and work in process inventories to manufacturing cost records and production reports.

Recall that vouching entries that increase inventory balances provides evidence about the existence and valuation of the inventory at the time of the transaction. Vouching entries that decrease inventory balances to determine the propriety of the inventory reductions provides further evidence about the valuation assertion and could indicate a problem with the completeness assertion if support for the credits does not exist. Tracing documentation for purchases and the cost of factors added to production to entries in the inventory accounts provides evidence for the completeness and valuation inventory assertions. Tracing documentation of transactions that decrease inventory balances, such as sales, to determine that entries were recorded and at the right amounts provides further evidence for the existence and valuation assertions for inventory. (If the transactions were not recorded, part of the recorded inventories would not exist. If entries were made for incorrect amounts, the reported valuation of the inventory on hand would be misstated.) Tracing and vouching also contributes evidence for the rights and obligations (ownership) assertion for inventories.

Test Cutoff of Purchases, Manufacturing, and Sales Transactions

The purpose and nature of sales and purchases cutoff tests are explained in Chapters 14 and 15, respectively, in connection with the audit of accounts receivable and accounts payable balances. Both tests are important in establishing that transactions occurring near the end of the year are recorded in the correct accounting period. For example, purchases in transit at year-end with terms F.O.B. shipping point should be included in inventory and accounts payable, but purchases in transit with terms F.O.B. destination should not be included in either. Similarly, inventory in transit to customers at year-end with terms F.O.B. shipping point should be included in sales and excluded from inventory. Inventory in transit to customers with terms F.O.B. destination should be included in inventory and excluded from sales. In a manufacturing company, it must also be determined that entries are recorded in the proper period for the transfer of costs for goods moved between (1) stores and production departments, (2) one production department and another, or (3) production departments and finished goods.

In each case, the auditor must ascertain through inspection of documents and physical observation that the paperwork cutoff and the physical cutoff for inventory taking are coordinated. For example, if the auditor determines that an entry transferring the cost of the period's last lot of completed production to finished goods has been recorded, he or she should determine that the goods, even if in transit, were included in the physical inventory of finished goods only—that is, that they were neither counted as part of work in process, nor double counted, nor missed altogether. Evidence from these cutoff tests relates to both the existence or occurrence and completeness assertions for inventory balances.

TESTS OF DETAILS OF BALANCES

As Figure 16-5 shows, these tests are extensive for inventories, primarily because of the required procedure of observing the client's physical inventory and related tests.

Observe Client's Physical Inventory Count

The observation of inventories has been a generally accepted auditing procedure for more than 50 years. This procedure is required whenever inventories are material to a company's financial statements and it is practicable and reasonable. The observation of inventories may prove to be inconvenient, time consuming, and difficult for the auditor, but it is seldom impracticable and unreasonable.

In performing this auditing procedure, the auditor has no responsibility to take or supervise the taking of the inventory. SAS 1 (AU 331.09), *Receivables and Inventories,* states that from this substantive test, the auditor obtains direct knowledge of the effectiveness of the client's inventory taking and the measure of reliance that may be placed on management's assertions as to the quantities and physical condition of the inventories. In some cases, outside inventory specialists may be hired by the client to take the inventory. When this occurs, the auditor must also be present to observe their counts because from an auditing standpoint, the specialists are basically the same as company employees. The primary audit considerations applicable to this required procedure are explained in the following subsections.

SEEING IS BELIEVING

During the 1930s, audit evidence for inventories was usually restricted to obtaining a certification from management as to the correctness of the stated amount. In 1938, the discovery of a major fraud in the McKesson & Robbins Company, a major pharmaceutical firm, caused a reappraisal of the auditor's responsibilities for inventories. The company's December 1937 financial statements "certified" by a national public accounting firm reported \$87 million of total assets. Of this amount, \$19 million was subsequently determined to be fictitious: \$10 million in inventory and \$9 million in receivables. The auditors were exonerated of blame because they had complied with existing auditing standards. However, promptly thereafter, in Statement on Auditing Procedure No. 1, auditing standards were changed to include physical observation of inventories.

SOURCE: SEC Financial Reporting Release No. 1.

TIMING AND EXTENT OF THE TEST. The timing of an inventory observation depends on the client's inventory system and the effectiveness of internal controls. In a periodic inventory system, quantities are determined by a physical count, and all counts are made as of a specific date. The date should be at or near the balance sheet date, and the auditor should ordinarily be present on the specific date.

In a perpetual inventory system with effective internal controls, physical counts may be taken and compared with inventory records at interim dates. When the perpetual records are well kept and comparisons with physical counts are made periodically by the client, the auditor should be present to observe a representative sample of such counts. In such case, this procedure may occur either during or after the end of the period under audit. In companies where inventories are at multiple locations, the auditor's observations ordinarily should encompass all significant inventory locations.

Inventory-Taking Plans. The taking of a physical inventory by a client is usually done according to a plan or a list of instructions. The client's instructions should include such matters as the

- Names of employees responsible for supervising the inventory taking.
- Date of the counts.
- Locations to be counted.
- Detailed instructions on how the counts are to be made.
- Use and control of prenumbered inventory tags and summary (compilation) sheets.
- Provisions for handling the receipt, shipment, and movement of goods during the counts if such activity is unavoidable.
- Segregation or identification of goods not owned.

The auditor should review and evaluate the client's inventory-taking plans well in advance of the counting date. With ample lead time, the client should be able to respond favorably to suggested modifications in the plans before the count is begun. It is common for the auditor to assist the client in designing an inventory-taking plan that will facilitate both the taking and the observing of the inventory.

Advance planning must be done by the auditor if an inventory observation is to be done efficiently and effectively. An experienced auditor usually has the responsibility for (1) planning the procedure, (2) determining the manpower needs, and (3) assigning members of the audit team to specific locations. Each observer should be provided with a copy of the client's inventory plans and written instructions of his or her duties.

Performing the Test. In observing inventories, the auditor should

- Scrutinize the care with which client employees are following the inventory plan.
- See that all merchandise is tagged and no items are double tagged.
- Determine that prenumbered inventory tags and compilation sheets are properly controlled.
- Make some test counts and trace quantities to compilation sheets.
- Be alert for empty containers and hollow squares (empty spaces) that may exist when goods are stacked in solid formations.
- Watch for damaged and obsolete inventory items.
- Appraise the general condition of the inventory.
- Identify the last receiving and shipping documents used and determine that goods received during the count are properly segregated.
- Inquire about the existence of slow-moving inventory items.

The extent of the auditor's test counts depends, in part, on the care exercised by client employees in taking the inventory, the nature and composition of the inventory, and the effectiveness of controls pertaining to the physical safeguarding of the inventory and the maintenance of perpetual records. Ordinarily, the auditor will stratify the inventory items to include the items of highest dollar value in the count and take a representative sample of other items. Recourse to perpetual inventory records is helpful in identifying the high-value items and selecting the sample items.

In making test counts, the auditor should record the count and give a complete and accurate description of the item (identification number, unit of measurement, location, etc.) in the working papers as shown in Figure 16-6. Such data are essen-

FIGURE 16-6 • INVENTORY TEST COUNTS WORKING PAPER

Prepared by: L.R.S. Date: 12/31/x1

Reviewed by: B.E.M. Date: 1/7/x2

Highlift Company

Raw Materials Test Counts F-2

12/31/x1

Tag no.	Inventory sheet no.	Inventory Number	Inventory Description	Count Client	Count Audit	Count Difference
6531	15	1-42-003	Back plate	125 √	125	
8340	18	1-83-012	1/4" Copper plate	93 √	93	
1483	24	2-11-004	Single end wire	1321 yds. √	1325 yds.	4 yds.
4486	26	2-28-811	Copper tubing	220 ft. √	220 ft.	
3334	48	4-26-204	Side plate	424 √	424	
8502	64	7-44-310	1/2" Copper wire	276 ft. √	276 ft.	
8844	68	7-72-460	3/8" Copper wire	419 ft. √	419 ft.	
6295	92	3-48-260	Front plate	96 √	69	27 units

Each difference was corrected by the client. The net effect of the corrections was to increase inventory by $840. Total inventory values for which test counts were made and traced to inventory summaries without exception = $26,460 or 22% of the total. In my opinion, errors were immaterial.

√ = Traced to clients inventory summary sheets (F-4) noting corrections for all differences.

tial for the auditor's comparison of the test counts with the client's counts, and the subsequent tracing of the counts to inventory summary sheets and perpetual inventory records.

On conclusion of the observation procedure, a designated member of the audit team should prepare an overall summary. The summary should include a description of such matters as (1) departures from the client's inventory-taking plan, (2) the extent of test counts and any material discrepancies resulting therefrom, and (3) conclusions on the accuracy of the counts and the general condition of the inventory.

When inventories are material and the auditor does not observe the inventory at or near the year-end, AU 331.12 states that

- Tests of the accounting records alone will not be sufficient as to quantities.
- It will always be necessary for the auditor to make, or observe, some physical counts of the inventory and to apply appropriate tests of intervening transactions.

This language is unequivocal; the observation (or counting) of the inventory can be postponed, but it cannot be eliminated. The auditor must obtain some physical evidence pertaining to ending inventories to comply with generally accepted auditing standards. In addition, the auditor should review the records of any counts made by the client.

INVENTORIES DETERMINED BY STATISTICAL SAMPLING. A company may have inventory controls or use methods of determining inventories, such as statistical sampling, that do not require an annual physical count of every item of inventory. Such methods do not relieve the auditor of the responsibility to observe the taking of inventories. It is still necessary to observe such counts as deemed necessary in the circumstances. In addition, the auditor must obtain evidence on the appropriateness of the method used to determine inventory quantities. When statistical sampling methods are used by the client, AU 331.11 indicates the auditor must ascertain that (1) the sampling plan has statistical validity, (2) it has been properly applied, and (3) the results in terms of precision and reliability are reasonable in the circumstances.

OBSERVATION OF BEGINNING INVENTORIES. To express an unqualified opinion on the income statement, the auditor must observe the taking of both the beginning and ending inventories. On a recurring audit engagement, this requirement is met by observing the ending inventory of each year. However, in the initial audit of an established company, the auditor may either be appointed after the beginning inventory has been taken or be asked to report on the financial statements of one or more prior periods. In such circumstances, it is clearly impracticable and unreasonable for the auditor to have observed the inventory taking, and generally accepted auditing standards permit the auditor to verify the inventories by other auditing procedures.

When the client has been audited by another firm of independent auditors in the prior period(s), the other procedures may include a review of the predecessor auditor's report and/or working papers and a review of the client's inventory summaries for the prior period(s). If the client has not been audited previously, the auditor may be able to obtain audit satisfaction by reviewing the summaries of any client counts, testing prior inventory transactions, and applying gross profit tests to the inventories. Such procedures are appropriate only when the auditor is able to verify the validity and propriety of the ending inventory for the period under audit.

EFFECTS ON AUDITOR'S REPORT. When inventories have been observed, the auditor may be able to issue a standard audit report. This is also permissible when the auditor has used alternative substantive tests to verify the beginning inventory. However, when sufficient evidence has not been obtained as to the beginning inventories or the auditor is unable to observe the taking of ending inventories, the auditor is precluded from issuing a standard audit report. The specific effects on the auditor's report are considered in Chapter 20.

APPLICABILITY TO ASSERTIONS. Like the confirmation of accounts receivable, the observation of the client's inventory taking applies to many assertions. This test is the *primary* source of evidence that the inventory exists. In addition, this test relates to the following assertions:

Assertion	Explanation
Completeness	Quantities in excess of perpetual records indicate that the records were incomplete.
Valuation or allocation	Quantities observed provide the basis for compiling the total dollar amounts on inventory summaries.
	Damaged and obsolete goods observed can be valued at net realizable value.

Observation does not provide evidence for the rights and obligations assertion because goods on hand may be held under consignment contracts or for the convenience of a customer who has taken title to the goods.

Test Clerical Accuracy of Inventory Listings

After the physical inventory has been taken, the client uses the inventory tags or count sheets to prepare or compile a listing or listings of all items counted. The inventory items are then priced to arrive at the total dollar valuation of the inventory on hand. Because this listing serves as the client's basis for any entries required to adjust recorded inventories to agree with those on hand, the auditor must perform certain tests to determine that the listing is clerically accurate and that it accurately represents the results of the physical counts.

Tests of clerical accuracy include recalculating the totals shown on the inventory listings and verifying the accuracy of the extensions of quantities times unit prices on a test basis. To determine that the list accurately represents the results of the count, the auditor traces his or her own test counts to the inventory listings, and vouches items on the listings to the inventory tags and count sheets used in the physical inventory. The physical counts are then compared, on a test basis with amounts per perpetual records, when applicable, and any differences are noted and investigated and traced to adjusting entries when required. This test provides evidence for the existence or occurrence, completeness, and valuation or allocation assertions.

Test Inventory Pricing

This test involves examining supporting documentation for both the cost and market value of inventories. Thus, it relates primarily to the valuation or allocation assertion. It also involves determining that the costing procedures used are consistent with those used in prior years.

A review of perpetual inventory records and inquiry of the client should enable the auditor to determine both the basis and costing methods used in pricing inventory quantities. The consistency of the pricing, in turn, can be established by recourse to last year's working papers on a recurring audit and/or to the prior year's financial statements. This step in the verification of pricing includes a review of the pricing of obsolete and damaged goods to ascertain that they are not valued in excess of net realizable value at the statement date. Evidence in support of unit costs varies with the nature of the inventory.

TEST COST OF PURCHASED INVENTORIES. For items purchased for resale, use, or consumption (merchandise inventory, raw materials, and supplies), costs should be vouched to representative vendor invoices. When the lower of cost or market method is used, the auditor must verify both cost and market. The current replacement cost of an item may be obtained (1) from purchases made at or near the balance sheet date or (2) by inquiries of suppliers.

TEST COST OF MANUFACTURED INVENTORIES. The nature and extent of the auditor's pricing tests of work in process and finished goods depend on the reliability of the client's cost accounting records and the methods used by the client in accumulating such costs. The methods should be reviewed by the auditor for propriety and the accuracy and consistency of application. For example, when standard costs are used, the auditor should test the calculation of the standards, compare the calculations with engineering specifications, determine that the standards are current, and evaluate whether the standards approximate actual costs by examining the variance accounts. When variance accounts have large balances, the auditor must consider whether fair presentation requires a pro rata allocation to inventories and costs of goods sold, rather than simply charging the variances to cost of goods sold.

REVIEW OTHER DATA PERTAINING TO INVENTORY QUALITY AND SALABILITY. The auditor's responsibility for quality is limited to that of a reasonably informed observer. This means that the auditor is expected to determine whether the inventory appears to be in condition for sale, use, or consumption, and whether there are any obsolete, slow-moving, or damaged goods. The auditor obtains evidence of general condition or obsolescence by

- Observing the client's inventory taking.
- Scanning perpetual inventory records for slow-moving items.
- Reviewing quality control production reports.
- Comparing inventory items with the entity's current sales catalog and sales reports.
- Making inquiries of client.

When the evidence suggests a decline in the utility of the goods, appropriate write-down below cost is required by GAAP.

When client assertions about the nature of the inventory pertain to highly technical matters, the auditor may require the assistance of an outside expert. This might occur, for example, in an oil company with different grades of gasoline and motor oil, or in a jewelry store with different carat diamonds and different jeweled watches. As explained in Chapter 6, the auditor may use the work of a specialist as an auditing procedure to obtain competent evidential matter, when he or she is satisfied about the qualifications and independence of the expert.

Confirm Inventories at Locations Outside the Entity

When client inventories are stored in public warehouses or with other outside custodians, the auditor should obtain evidence as to the existence of the inventory by direct communication with the custodian. This type of evidence is deemed sufficient except when the amounts involved represent a significant proportion of current or total assets. When this is the case, AU 331.14 states the auditor should apply one or more of the following procedures:

- Test the owner's procedures for investigating the warehouseman and evaluating the warehouseman's performance.
- Obtain an independent accountant's report on the warehouseman's control procedures relevant to custody of goods and, if applicable, pledging of receipts, or apply alternative procedures at the warehouse to gain reasonable assurance that information received from the warehouseman is reliable.
- Observe physical counts of the goods, if practicable and reasonable.
- If warehouse receipts have been pledged as collateral, confirm with lenders pertinent details of the pledged receipts (on a test basis, if appropriate).

This test also provides evidence about the rights and obligations assertion. In addition, it will result in evidence as to the completeness assertion if the custodian confirms more goods on hand than stated in the confirmation request. Confirming inventories does not provide any evidence about the value of the inventory because the custodian is not asked to report on the cost, condition, or market value of the goods stored in the warehouse.

Examine Consignment Agreements and Contracts

Goods on hand may be held for customers, at their request, after a sale has occurred, and goods may be held on consignment. Thus, management is requested to segregate goods not owned during the inventory taking. In addition, the auditor usually requests a written assertion on ownership of inventories in the client representation letter. This letter is illustrated in Chapter 19.

The auditor should also inquire of management as to any goods held on consignment. When consignments exist, the agreement should be examined for terms and conditions. If the client has shipped goods on consignment, the auditor should review the documentation to determine that goods held by the consignee are included in the consignor's inventory at the balance sheet date.

As to be expected, the evidence obtained from this test relates to the rights and obligations assertion. For goods held on consignment, the test also provides evidence concerning the presentation and disclosure assertion.

COMPARISON OF STATEMENT PRESENTATION WITH GAAP

It is customary to identify the major inventory categories in the balance sheet and the cost of goods sold in the income statement. In addition, there should be disclosure of the inventory costing method(s) used, the assignment or pledging of inventories, and the existence of major purchase commitments.

Evidence pertaining to statement presentation and disclosure is provided by the substantive tests described above. Further evidence may be obtained, as needed, from a review of the minutes of board of directors' meetings and from inquiries of management. Based on the evidence and a comparison of the client's financial statements with applicable accounting pronouncements, the auditor determines the propriety of the presentation and disclosures.

Inquiry of management is also used to determine the existence of binding contracts for future purchases of goods. When such commitments exist, the auditor should examine the terms of the contracts and evaluate the propriety of the company's accounting and reporting. When material losses exist on purchase commitments, they should be recognized in the statements, together with a disclosure of the attendant circumstances as noted in the discussion of accounts payable in the previous chapter.

Based on the evidence obtained from some combination of the foregoing substantive tests, the auditor should be able to satisfy each of the account balance audit objectives for inventories.

LEARNING CHECK:

16-8 What factors should be considered by an auditor in specifying the acceptable level of detection risk for assertions pertaining to (a) merchandise inventory and (b) manufactured finished goods inventory?

16-9 Indicate several ratios and their formulas that may be used in applying analytical procedures to inventory balances.

16-10 a. Identify five tests of details of balances that may be applied to inventories.

b. For the test of observing the client's physical inventory count, indicate (1) when this test is required, (2) factors that affect the timing and extent of the test, (3) what should be considered in evaluating the client's inventory-taking plans, and (4) what the auditor should do during the actual taking of the physical inventory.

16-11 a. What documents and other information are used by the auditor in performing an inventory pricing test?

b. How are confirmations used in the audit of inventory balances?

THE PERSONNEL SERVICES CYCLE

An entity's **personnel services cycle** involves the events and activities that pertain to executive and employee compensation. The types of compensation include salaries, hourly and incentive (piecework) wages, commissions, bonuses, and employee benefits (e.g., health insurance and paid vacations). The major class of transactions in this cycle is **payroll transactions.** Accounts affected by these transactions include the following:

OBJECTIVE 6

Explain the nature of the personnel services cycle and identify the transaction class and accounts involved.

- Compensation expense (including salaries and wages, commissions, bonuses, and employee benefits)
- Payroll tax expenses
- Direct labor
- Manufacturing overhead (indirect labor)
- Accrued compensation payable
- Liabilities for amounts withheld from employees
- Accrued payroll taxes payable
- Imprest payroll bank account

The personnel services cycle interfaces with two other cycles. The paying of the payroll and the payment of payroll taxes relates to cash disbursements transactions in the expenditure cycle. The audit of the imprest payroll bank account used for payroll disbursements is covered in Chapter 18. The distribution of factory labor costs to work in process pertains to the production cycle. Attention in the remainder of this section is focused primarily on hourly compensation to employees and related payroll taxes.

OBJECTIVE 7

Identify specific audit objectives for the personnel services cycle.

AUDIT OBJECTIVES

Selected specific audit objectives for the personnel services cycle are shown in Figure 16-7. The procedures used by the auditor to meet these objectives are described in the remainder of this chapter.

FIGURE 16-7 • SELECTED SPECIFIC AUDIT OBJECTIVES FOR THE PERSONNEL SERVICES CYCLE

Assertion Category	Account Balance Audit Objectives
Existence or occurrence	Recorded payroll expenses and payroll tax expenses relate to compensation for services rendered during the period **(EO1).** Accrued payroll and payroll tax liability balances represent amounts owed at the balance sheet date **(EO2).**
Completeness	Recorded payroll expenses and payroll tax expenses include all such expenses incurred for personnel services during the year **(C1).** Accrued payroll and payroll tax liabilities include all amounts owed to personnel and governmental agencies at the balance sheet date **(C2).**
Rights and obligations	Accrued payroll and payroll tax liabilities are obligations of the reporting entity **(RO1).**
Valuation or allocation	Payroll expenses and payroll tax expenses are accurately computed and recorded **(VA1).** Accrued payroll and payroll tax liabilities are accurately computed and recorded **(VA2).** Factory labor distributions are correctly computed and recorded **(VA3).**
Presentation and disclosure	Payroll expenses and payroll tax expenses are properly identified and classified in the income statement **(PD1).** Accrued payroll and payroll tax liability accounts are properly identified and classified in the balance sheet **(PD2).**

MATERIALITY, RISK, AND AUDIT STRATEGY

For merchandising companies, the gross earnings of personnel is generally the largest operating expense. The same is true for service enterprises such as banks and firms in professional fields such as public accounting and law.

Payroll fraud is a major concern for the auditor. Fraud may occur at two levels. Employees involved in preparing and paying the payroll may process data for fictitious employees and then divert the paychecks to their own use. Alternatively, management may overtly misclassify or "pad" labor costs in government contract work to defraud the agency.

Pay periods may be weekly, bimonthly, or monthly. In each case, the volume of payroll transactions may be high. For factory workers, gross earnings may be based on time and/or productivity. Thus, the computations may be complex, and inherent risk for the valuation or allocation assertion may be high. When there is frequent turnover of personnel in a company, there is the risk that a terminated employee is continued on the payroll.

Several circumstances affect audit strategy.

- The audit risk is primarily in the processing of payroll transactions.
- Most companies have extensive internal controls for payroll transactions.
- Year-end payroll liability balances are often immaterial.

Accordingly, the lower assessed level of control risk approach is generally adopted for most payroll transaction assertions. Recall that this approach involves planned tests of controls during interim work.

CONSIDERATION OF INTERNAL CONTROL STRUCTURE COMPONENTS

OBJECTIVE 8

Explain the applicability of relevant aspects of the internal control structure components to the personnel services cycle.

As for other major transaction classes, the auditor must obtain an understanding of how the entity's internal control structure components pertain to payroll transactions. Several control environment factors have direct relevance. Overall responsibility for personnel matters is often assigned to a vice president of industrial or labor relations, or a manager of human or personnel resources. Departments that may be significantly involved in processing payroll transactions include personnel, timekeeping, payroll, and the treasurer's office. Officers' salaries and other forms of compensation are usually set by the board of directors. Personnel policies and practices should ensure that individuals involved in payroll functions are knowledgeable about state and federal payroll laws and regulations and applicable provisions of labor contracts. Management should also assess the risks and consequences associated with errors or irregularities in processing payrolls, including improper or excessive payments, improper handling of payroll tax returns, and improper distribution of manufacturing labor costs.

An understanding of the information and communication component, which includes the accounting system for payroll, requires the auditor to be familiar with the methods of data organization and data processing pertaining to payroll transactions. Although some functions such as the maintenance of personnel records are frequently performed on-line, the preparation of the payroll generally involves batch processing.

All of the categories of control activities are important in establishing adequate controls over payroll. These are discussed in the next section. Monitoring activities applicable to payroll include feedback from employees regarding pay problems, feedback from governmental agencies regarding problems with the reporting and payment of payroll taxes, assessment of the effectiveness of payroll controls by internal auditors, and audit committee oversight of executive compensation.

LEARNING CHECK:

16-12 a. Describe the nature of the personnel services cycle.
b. What cycles interface with this cycle.

16-13 a. Explain the materiality and audit risk associated with the personnel services cycle.
b. What is the auditor's usual audit strategy for this cycle? Why?

16-14 State the audit objectives that pertain to management's assertions about personnel services transactions and balances.

KEY TERMS:

Payroll transactions, p. 625 | Personnel services cycle, p. 624

CONTROL ACTIVITIES—PAYROLL TRANSACTIONS

OBJECTIVE 9

Describe the functions and related control activities pertaining to payroll transactions.

The next section identifies and explains several common documents and records used in processing payroll transactions. The following section describes the functions involved in processing payroll and indicates how the common documents and records, as well as the other categories of control activities (proper authorization and so on), contribute to controlling the risk of misstatements in payroll assertions.

COMMON DOCUMENTS AND RECORDS

The following documents and records are important in executing and recording payroll transactions:

- **Personnel authorization.** Memo issued by personnel department indicating the hiring of an employee and each subsequent change in the employee's status for payroll purposes.
- **Clock card.** Form used by each employee to record hours worked daily during a pay period. It is used with time clocks that record the time on the card. This and the following form may be replaced in modern systems with an employee badge that is inserted into a terminal to cause an electronic record of the time to be made.
- **Time ticket.** Form used to record time worked by an employee on specific jobs. Time worked is often machine imprinted.

- **Payroll register.** Report showing each employee's name, gross earnings, payroll deductions, and net pay for a pay period. It provides the basis for paying employees and recording the payroll.
- **Imprest payroll bank account.** Account to which a deposit equal to the total net payroll is made each pay period, and on which checks for salaries and wages for employees are drawn.
- **Payroll check.** Order drawn on a bank to pay an employee. It is accompanied by a detachable memo indicating gross earnings and payroll deductions.
- **Labor cost distribution summary.** Report showing the account classifications for gross factory earnings for each pay period.
- **Payroll tax returns.** Forms prescribed by tax authorities for filing with payments of taxes withheld from employees and employer's payroll taxes for social security and federal and state unemployment.
- **Employee personnel file.** Holds pertinent employment data for each employee and contains all personnel authorizations issued for the employee, job evaluations, and disciplinary actions, if any.
- **Personnel data master file.** Computer file containing current data on employees needed for calculating payroll such as job classification, wage rate, and deductions.
- **Employee earnings master file.** Computer file containing each employee's gross earnings, payroll deductions, and net pay for the year to date by pay periods.

FUNCTIONS AND RELATED CONTROLS

The processing of payroll transactions involves the following **payroll functions:**

- Hiring employees.
- Authorizing payroll changes.
- Preparing attendance and timekeeping data.
- Preparing the payroll.
- Recording the payroll.
- Paying the payroll and protecting unclaimed wages.
- Filing payroll tax returns.

Each function is explained below. Where applicable, reference is made to the flowchart in Figure 16-8, which shows a representative system for processing payroll transactions. In this case, the company is using on-line entry/on-line processing for payroll authorization changes, and batch entry/batch processing for preparing the payroll.

In the flowchart, it should be observed that responsibility for executing and recording payroll is spread over several departments. This segregation of duties contributes significantly to reducing the risk of payments to fictitious employees or excessive payments to actual employees due to inflated rates or hours.

Hiring Employees

The hiring of employees is done in the personnel department. All hirings should be documented on a personnel authorization form. The form should indicate the

FIGURE 16-8 • SYSTEM FLOWCHART—PAYROLL TRANSACTIONS

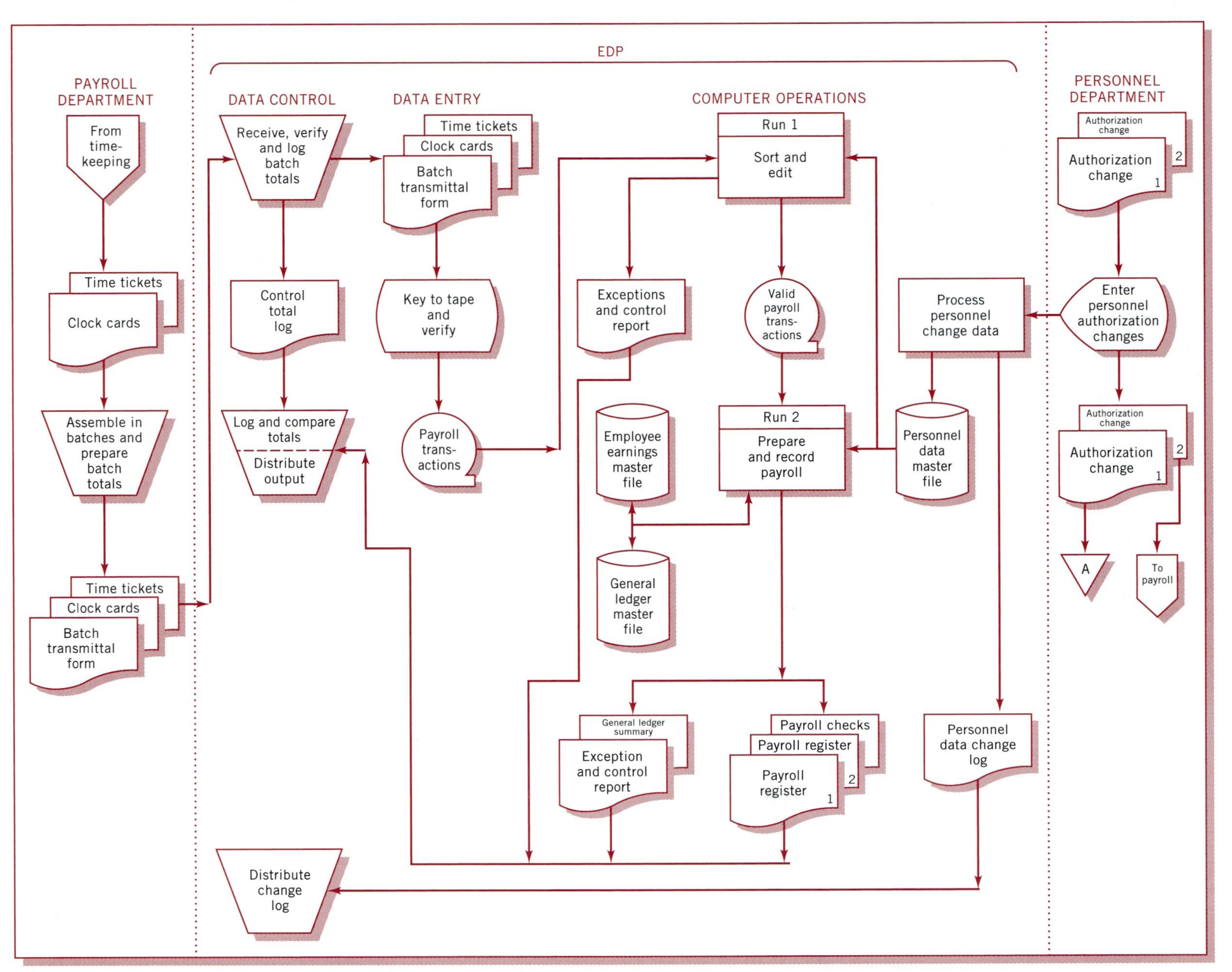

job classification, starting wage rate, and authorized payroll deductions. In the system shown in Figure 16-8, authorized individuals in the personnel department gain access to the personnel data master file by entering a password on an on-line terminal before entering data on new hires. Periodically, a computer-generated log of all changes to the master file is printed and independently checked by a personnel manager not involved in entering the data into the computer. One copy of the personnel authorization form is placed in the employee's personnel file in the personnel department. Another copy is sent to the payroll department.

Controls over adding new hires to the personnel data master file reduce the risk of payroll payments to fictitious employees. Thus, they relate to existence or occurrence and rights and obligations assertions for payroll transactions.

Authorizing Payroll Changes

The request for a change in job classification or a wage rate increase may be initiated by the employee's supervisor. However, all changes should be authorized in writing by the personnel department before being entered in the personnel data master file. Other controls over entering the changes in the computer and distributing the change forms are the same as discussed above for new hires. These controls over payroll changes help to ensure the accuracy of the payroll and relate to the valuation or allocation assertion as well as rights and obligations.

The personnel department should also issue a termination notice on completion of an individual's employment. Prompt notification of the payroll department is vital in preventing terminated employees from continuing on the payroll. Thus, this control relates to existence or occurrence assertions.

Preparing Attendance and Timekeeping Data

In many companies, a timekeeping department is responsible for this function. Time clocks are frequently used to record time worked by an employee when a clock cards or employee badge is inserted in the clock. To prevent one employee from "punching in" for another employee, security personnel should supervise the clock card procedures.

For factory employees, clock card hours must be supported by time tickets showing the type of work done (direct or indirect labor) and the jobs to which direct labor hours are to be charged. All time worked should be approved in writing by a supervisor. Timekeeping then reconciles the approved time tickets and clock cards and forwards them to payroll for use in preparing the payroll.

By ensuring that accurate data are accumulated on time worked, controls over the timekeeping function relate to the existence or occurrence, completeness, and valuation or allocation assertions for payroll transactions. Supervisory approval of the labor classification relates to the presentation and disclosure assertion. The timekeeping function is not shown in Figure 16-8.

Preparing the Payroll

Figure 16-8 illustrates typical controls in a basic system for preparing the payroll in the payroll and EDP departments. On receipt of the clock cards and time tickets in the payroll department, the documents are batched and a batch total is prepared of hours worked. The documents and a batch transmittal form are then sent to data control in the EDP department. Data control verifies the information on the batch transmittal form, enters the batch totals in a control log, and forwards the data to data entry where it is keyed to tape and verified. The resulting payroll transactions tape is then used in preparing the payroll.

In run 1, the payroll transactions are sorted by employee number and the data are subjected to an edit check routine. This includes a check for valid employee number and a limit or reasonableness check on the hours worked. The output of this run consists of a valid payroll transactions tape and an exceptions and control report that is sent to data control. Data control compares the control totals with the batch control log, informs the payroll department of exceptions discovered by the edit routine, and follows up to see that payroll submits corrected data. These controls over the data entry process preceding the calculation of the payroll contribute to the existence or occurrence, completeness, and valuation or allocation assertions for payroll transactions.

In the system shown in Figure 16-8, the calculation of the payroll and the preparation of the payroll register and payroll checks occur in run 2. The program uses data from the valid payroll transactions tape and the personnel data and employee earnings master files. This run also records the payroll as described in the next section.

Recording the Payroll

As the gross pay, deductions, and net pay are calculated in run 2 for each employee, the program updates the employee earnings master file, and accumulates totals for the payroll journal entry that is generated and entered in the general ledger master file at the conclusion of the run. The following printed outputs of this run are sent to data control:

- An exceptions and control report that is reviewed by data control before distributing the other printed output.
- A copy of the payroll register that is returned along with the clock cards and time tickets to the payroll department for comparison with the original batch transmittal data.
- A second copy of the payroll register and prenumbered payroll checks that are sent to the treasurer's office.
- A general ledger summary that is sent to accounting showing the payroll entry generated by the payroll program.

Proper review of each of these outputs by the appropriate personnel contributes to control over misstatements in all five assertion categories.

Paying the Payroll and Protecting Unclaimed Wages

These functions are not shown in Figure 16-8. However, the preceding section indicates a copy of the payroll register, and the payroll checks are sent to the treasurer's office where these functions are commonly performed. Applicable controls include the following:

- An independent check by treasurer's office personnel should be made of the agreement of names and amounts on checks with payroll register entries.

- Payroll checks should be signed and distributed by authorized treasurer's office personnel not involved in preparing or recording the payroll.
- Access to check signing machines and signature plates should be restricted to authorized individuals.
- Payroll checks should be distributed only on proper identification of employees.
- Unclaimed payroll checks should be stored in a safe or vault in the treasurer's office.

Again, collectively these controls pertain to all five categories of assertions.

Another important control over paying the payroll in most large companies is the use of an imprest payroll bank account on which all payroll checks are drawn. Control procedures and substantive tests pertaining to this account are explained in Chapter 18.

Filing Payroll Tax Returns

Payroll tax returns must be filed for amounts withheld from employees for federal income taxes and social security, and for the social security and federal and state unemployment taxes levied on the employer. Returns must be filed on a timely basis to avoid penalties and interest payments, and possibly even criminal charges. Thus, responsibility should be clearly assigned for performing this function according to a schedule that conforms to federal and state filing and payment deadlines.

OBTAINING THE UNDERSTANDING AND ASSESSING CONTROL RISK

The procedures used to obtain and document the understanding of the internal control structure components for payroll transactions are the same as for the other major classes of transactions. It will be recalled that these procedures include inquiry, review of documentation, observation, and consideration of prior experience with the client.

The process of assessing control risk for payroll transactions begins with identifying potential misstatements and necessary controls. These steps are shown in the second and third columns of Figure 16-9. Controls for which the auditor seeks an assessment of control risk below the maximum should then be tested. Sample tests of controls and the audit objectives for which they are relevant are also shown in Figure 16-9.

In assessing control risk, the auditor realizes that misstatements in payroll may result from unintentional errors or fraud. Of particular concern is the risk of overstatement of payroll through the following:

- Payments to fictitious employees.
- Payments to actual employees for hours not worked.
- Payments to actual employees at higher than authorized rates.

The first two risks relate to the existence or occurrence assertion. The third risk relates to the valuation or allocation assertion. The risk of understatement (com-

FIGURE 16-9 • CONTROL RISK ASSESSMENT CONSIDERATIONS FOR PAYROLL TRANSACTIONS

Function	Potential Misstatement	Necessary Control	Possible Test of Control*	Account Balance Audit Objectives (from p. 625)				
				EO#	C#	RO I	VA#	PD#
Hiring employees	Fictitious employees may be added to payroll.	Personnel department authorization for all new hires.	Examine authorization forms for new hires.	✓1,2		✓		
Authorizing payroll changes	Employees may receive unauthorized rate increases.	Personnel department authorization for all rate changes.	Inquire about procedures for authorizing rate changes.			✓	✓1,2	
	Terminated employees may remain on payroll.	Personnel department notification to payroll of all terminations.	Examine termination notices in payroll department.	✓1,2				
Preparing attendance and timekeeping data	Employees may be paid for hours not worked.	Use of time clock procedures and supervisory approval of time tickets.	Observe time clock procedures; examine time tickets for supervisory approval.	✓1,2	✓1,2		✓1, 2,3	✓1
Preparing the payroll	Payroll data may be lost during submission to EDP.	Batch totals of hours worked prepared by payroll department and verified by data control.	Examine evidence of preparation and use of batch totals.		✓1,2			
	Payroll transactions tape may include incorrectly keyed or invalid data.	Key verification in data entry and edit checks of data on payroll transactions tape.	Observe data entry procedures; examine exceptions and control report.*	✓1,2	✓1,2		✓1,2 3	
Recording the payroll	Processing errors may occur in recording the payroll.	Exceptions and control report reviewed by data control.	Inquire about preparation and use of exceptions and control report.*	✓1,2	✓1,2	✓	✓1, 2,3	✓1,2
	Unauthorized changes may be made to payroll data in EDP.	Payroll department comparison of payroll register with original batch transmittal data.	Reperform comparison.*	✓1,2	✓1,2	✓	✓1, 2,3	✓1,2
Paying the payroll and protecting unclaimed wages	Payroll checks may be distributed to unauthorized recipients.	Employee identification on distribution.	Witness distribution of payroll.	✓1,2	✓1,2	✓	✓1,2	✓1,2
Filing payroll tax returns	Payroll tax returns may not be filed on a timely basis.	Assignment of responsibility for timely filing of returns.	Inquire about procedures; examine returns.		✓2	✓	✓2	

* Tests marked with an asterisk are sometimes performed as a part of dual purpose tests.

pleteness assertion) is of minimal concern because employees will promptly complain when they are underpaid.

Accordingly, many tests of payroll controls are directed at controls that prevent or detect overstatements. The direction of testing for these controls is from the recorded payroll data to source documents. For example, the auditor may vouch data for a sample of employees in a payroll register to approved clock card data and authorized pay rates and deductions.

Two tests of controls pertaining to control risk for the existence or occurrence assertion are (1) the test for terminated employees and (2) witnessing a payroll distribution. The former represents an exception to the normal direction of testing for payroll in that the auditor selects a sample of termination notices and scans subsequent payroll registers to determine that the terminated employees did not continue to receive pay checks. In witnessing the distribution of payroll checks, the auditor observes that

- Segregation of duties exists between the preparation and payment of the payroll.
- Each employee receives only one check.
- Each employee is identified by a badge or employee ID card.
- There is proper control and disposition of unclaimed checks.

LEARNING CHECK:

16-15 Identify the functions in processing payroll transactions.

16-16 a. Indicate the responsibilities of the personnel department in the processing of payroll transactions.

b. Describe the control procedures in preparing attendance and timekeeping data.

16-17 Explain the tests of control that involve (a) terminated employees and (b) witnessing a payroll distribution.

KEY TERMS:

Clock card, p. 627
Employee earnings master file, p. 628
Employee personnel file, p. 628
Imprest payroll bank account, p. 628
Labor cost distribution summary, p. 628
Payroll check, p. 628
Payroll functions, p. 628
Payroll register, p. 628
Payroll tax returns, p. 628
Personnel authorization, p. 627
Personnel data master file, p. 628
Time ticket, p. 627

OBJECTIVE 10

Discuss the application of selected substantive tests to payroll balances.

SUBSTANTIVE TESTS OF PAYROLL BALANCES

Substantive tests of payroll balances are normally performed at or near the balance sheet date. The balances include accrued liabilities for salaries, wages, commission, bonuses, employee benefits, and payroll taxes, and the related expense accounts. The imprest payroll account balance is considered in Chapter 18.

DETERMINING DETECTION RISK

Factors contributing to high inherent risk for existence or occurrence and valuation or allocation assertions related to payroll transactions have been noted earlier in this chapter. However, evidence of effective controls over these risks in many cases permits low assessments of control risk, resulting in moderate or high acceptable levels of detection risk for most or all payroll assertions. Consequently, substantive tests of payroll balances are often limited to applying analytical procedures to the expense accounts and related accruals, and limited tests of details. If the analytical procedures reveal unexpected fluctuations, more extensive tests of details will be required.

DESIGNING SUBSTANTIVE TESTS

Audit program considerations for accrued payroll liability balances are similar to those for accounts payable on page 572 of Chapter 15. However, the auditor does not confirm payroll liabilities. Our explanations of specific substantive tests for payroll balances are limited to the following three procedures: (1) applying analytical procedures. (2) recalculating the accruals, and (3) verifying officers' compensation.

Apply Analytical Procedures

The application of analytical procedures to payroll balances may involve the following:

- Compare payroll expenses (salaries and wages, commissions, bonuses, employee benefits, etc.) with prior year balances (adjusted for known differences in wage rates or contractual terms) and with budgeted amounts.
- Compare accrued payroll liability balances with prior year (adjusted for differences in lengths of accrual periods).
- Compute ratio of total payroll expense to net sales and compare with prior year.
- Compute ratio of payroll tax expense to total payroll and compare with prior year (adjusted for changes in tax rates).
- Reconcile total payroll expense with amounts reported on payroll tax returns.

When no unexpected fluctuations are revealed by these procedures, the auditor has obtained evidence in support of audit objectives related to the existence or occurrence, completeness, and valuation or allocation assertions.

Recalculate Accrued Payroll Liabilities

It is necessary for many companies to make a variety of accruals at the balance sheet date for amounts owed to officers and employees for salaries and wages, commissions, bonuses, vacation pay, etc., and for amounts owed to government agencies for payroll taxes. Although the auditor's primary concern for payroll expenses for the year is with overstatement, for the year-end accruals the primary concern is with understatement. Also of concern is consistency in the methods of calculating the accruals from period to period.

In obtaining evidence concerning the reasonableness of management's accruals, the auditor should review management's calculations or make independent calculations. Accruals for payroll taxes should be compared with amounts shown on payroll tax returns. Additional evidence can be obtained by examining subsequent payments made on the accruals prior to the completion of field work. Evidence obtained from these tests pertains primarily to objectives related to the valuation or allocation assertion.

Verify Officers' Compensation

Officers' compensation is audit sensitive for the following two reasons: (1) separate disclosure of officers' compensation is required in 10-K reports that public companies file with the SEC, and (2) officers may be able to override controls and receive salaries, bonuses, stock options, and other forms of compensation in excess of authorized amounts. For these reasons, board of directors' authorizations for officers' salaries and other forms of compensation should be compared with recorded amounts. This test pertains to objectives related to each category of assertions.

LEARNING CHECK:

16-18 a. What is the likely acceptable level of detection risk for payroll expense account assertions? Why?
b. What effect does this have on the design of substantive tests for payroll assertions?

16-19 Identify several analytical procedures that may be applied to payroll balances and indicate the assertions to which the evidence pertains.

16-20 a. What procedures should be performed to obtain evidence about the reasonableness of management's accrued payroll liabilities?
b. Why is officers' compensation audit sensitive and what tests should be performed on such compensation?

SUMMARY

In the production cycle, the auditor focuses on manufacturing transactions involving the allocation of manufacturing costs to work in process and transferring the cost of completed production to finished goods. In auditing this cycle, the auditor is concerned with both the cost and financial accounting systems of the client. The audit of inventories requires careful planning and a very substantial investment in audit time, cost, and effort. Observation of the client's inventory taking is a generally accepted auditing procedure when inventories are material. In the personnel services cycle, the auditor's attention is directed primarily toward payroll transactions and related account balance assertions. Unless circumstances indicate it will not be cost efficient, tests of controls over payroll will be quite extensive to support a lower assessed level of control risk. Substantive tests of payroll expense and liability balances can then be restricted primarily to analytical procedures and limited tests of details.

BIBLIOGRAPHY

AICPA Professional Standards:

SAS 1 (AU 331), Receivables and Inventories.

SAS 1 (AU 901), Public Warehouses: Internal Control Structure Policies and Procedures and Auditing Procedures for Goods Held.

IAU 8 (AU 8008A), Additional Guidance on—Observation of Inventory, Confirmation of Accounts Receivable and Inquiry Regarding Litigation and Claims.

AICPA. *Audit of Inventories.* Auditing Procedures Study. New York: 1986.

Peress, Michael. ''Be Skeptical of Barter Transactions,'' *The CPA Journal* (January 1990), p. 56.

Schwartz, Richard, and Gillmore, Michael J. ''Auditing Pension Costs and Disclosures,'' *The CPA Journal* (June 1988), pp. 16–25.

Windsor, Sean, ''The Use of Audit Sampling Techniques to Test Inventory,'' *Journal of Accountancy* (January 1991), pp. 107–111.

OBJECTIVE QUESTIONS

Indicate the *best* answer for each of the following multiple choice questions.

16-21 These questions involve internal controls in the production cycle.

1. The objectives of the internal control structure for a production cycle are to provide assurance that transactions are properly executed and recorded, and that
   a. Independent internal verification of activity reports is established.
   b. Transfers to finished goods are documented by a completed production report and a quality control report.
   c. Production orders are prenumbered and signed by a supervisor.
   d. Custody of work in process and of finished goods is properly maintained.

2. An auditor's test of controls over the issuance of raw materials to production would most likely include
   a. Reconciling raw materials and work in process perpetual inventory records to general ledger balances.
   b. Inquiring of the custodian about the procedures followed when defective materials are received from vendors.
   c. Observing that raw materials are stored in secure areas and that storeroom security is supervised by a responsible individual.
   d. Examining material requisitions and reperforming client controls designed to process and record issuances.

3. Independent internal verification of inventory occurs when employees who
   a. Issue raw materials obtain material requisitions for each issue and prepare daily totals of materials issued.
   b. Compare records of goods on hand with physical quantities do **not** maintain the records or have custody of the inventory.
   c. Obtain receipts for the transfer of completed work to finished goods prepare a completed production report.
   d. Are independent of issuing production orders update records from completed job cost sheets and production cost reports on a timely basis.

4. Which of the following most likely would be an internal control procedure designed to detect misstatements concerning the custody of inventory?
   a. Periodic reconciliation of work in process with job cost sheets.
   b. Segregation of functions between general accounting and cost accounting.
   c. Independent comparisons of finished goods records with counts of goods on hand.
   d. Approval of inventory journal entries by the storekeeper.

16-22 These questions pertain to substantive tests of inventory balances.

1. In an audit of inventories, an auditor would **least** likely verify that
   a. All inventory owned by the client is on hand at the time of the count.
   b. The client has used proper inventory pricing.
   c. The financial statement presentation of inventories is appropriate.
   d. Damaged goods and obsolete items have been properly accounted for.

2. A client maintains perpetual inventory records in both quantities and dollars. If the assessed level of control risk is high, an auditor would probably
   a. Insist that the client perform physical counts of inventory items several times during the year.
   b. Apply gross profit tests to ascertain the reasonableness of the physical counts.
   c. Increase the extent of tests of controls of the inventory cycle.
   d. Request the client to schedule the physical inventory count at the end of the year.

3. The primary objective of a CPA's observation of a client's physical inventory count is to
   a. Discover whether a client has counted a particular inventory item or group of items.
   b. Obtain direct knowledge that the inventory exists and has been properly counted.
   c. Provide an appraisal of the quality of the merchandise on hand on the day of the physical count.
   d. Allow the auditor to supervise the conduct of the count to obtain assurance that inventory quantities are reasonably accurate.

4. Which one of the following procedures would **not be** appropriate for an auditor in discharging his or her responsibilities concerning the client's physical inventories?
   a. Confirmation of goods in the hands of public warehouses.
   b. Supervising the taking of the annual physical inventory.
   c. Carrying out physical inventory procedures at an interim date.
   d. Obtaining written representation from the client as to the existence, quality, and dollar amount of the inventory.

16-23 These questions relate to internal controls in the personnel services cycle.

1. Effective internal control procedures over the payroll function may include
   a. Reconciliation of totals on job time tickets with job reports by employees responsible for those specific jobs.
   b. Verification of agreement of job time tickets with employee clock card hours by a payroll department employee.
   c. Preparation of payroll transaction journal entries by an employee who reports to the supervisor of the personnel department.
   d. Custody of rate authorization records by the supervisor of the payroll department.

2. In a computerized payroll system environment, an auditor would be **least** likely to use test data to test controls related to
   a. Missing employee numbers.
   b. Proper approval of overtime by supervisors.
   c. Time tickets with invalid job numbers.
   d. Agreement of hours per clock cards with hours on time tickets.

3. The sampling unit in a test of controls pertaining to the existence of payroll transactions ordinarily is a(an)
   a. Clock card or time ticket.
   b. Employee Form W-2.
   c. Employee personnel record.
   d. Payroll register entry.

4. An auditor who is testing EDP controls in a payroll system would most likely use test data that contain conditions such as
   a. Deductions **not** authorized by employees.
   b. Overtime **not** approved by supervisors.
   c. Time tickets with invalid job numbers.
   d. Payroll checks with unauthorized signatures.

COMPREHENSIVE QUESTIONS

16-24 **(Evaluation of internal controls—raw materials and supplies inventory)** The Jameson Company produces a variety of chemical products for use by plastics manufacturers. The plant operates on two shifts, five days per week with maintenance work performed on the third shift and on Saturdays as required.

An audit conducted by the staff of the new corporate internal audit department has recently been completed, and the comments on inventory control were not favorable. Audit comments were particularly directed to the control of raw material ingredients and maintenance materials.

Raw material ingredients are received at the back of the plant, signed for by one of the employees of the batching department, and stored near the location of the initial batching process. Receiving tallies are given to the supervisor during the day and he forwards the tallies to the inventory control department at the end of the day. The inventory control department calculates ingredient use using weekly reports of actual production and standard formulas. Physical inventories are taken quarterly. Purchase requisitions are prepared by the inventory control department and rush orders are frequent. In spite of the need for rush orders, the production superintendent regularly gets memos from the controller stating that there must be excessive inventory because the ingredient inventory dollar value is too high.

Maintenance parts and supplies are received and stored in a storeroom. There is a storeroom clerk on each of the operating shifts. Storeroom requisitions are to be filled out for everything taken from the storeroom; however, this practice is not always followed. The storeroom is not locked when the clerk is out because of the need to obtain parts quickly. The storeroom is also open during the third shift for the maintenance crews to get parts as needed. Purchase requisitions are prepared by the storeroom clerk, and physical inventory is taken on a cycle count basis. Rush orders are frequent.

REQUIRED

a. Identify the weaknesses in Jameson Company's internal control procedures used for (1) ingredients inventory and (2) maintenance material and supplies inventory.
b. Recommend improvements that should be instituted for each of these areas.

ICMA

16-25 **(Evaluation of internal controls—raw materials inventory)** You have been engaged by the management of Alden, Inc., to review its internal controls over the purchase, receipt, storage, and issue of raw materials. You have prepared the following comments that describe Alden's procedures:

1. Raw materials, which consist mainly of high-cost electronic components, are kept in a locked storeroom. Storeroom personnel include a supervisor and four clerks. All are well trained, competent, and adequately bonded. Raw materials are removed from the storeroom only on written or oral authorization of one of the production foremen.
2. There are no perpetual-inventory records; hence, the storeroom clerks do not keep records of goods received or issued. To compensate for the lack of perpetual records, a physical inventory count is taken monthly by the storeroom clerks, who are well supervised. Appropriate procedures are followed in making the inventory count.
3. After the physical count, the storeroom supervisor matches quantities counted against a predetermined reorder level. If the count for a given part is below the reorder level, the supervisor enters the part number on a materials requisition list and sends this list to the accounts payable clerk. The accounts payable clerk prepares a purchase order for a predetermined reorder quantity for each part and mails the purchase order to the vendor from whom the part was last purchased.
4. When ordered materials arrive at Alden, they are received by the storeroom clerks. The clerks count the merchandise and agree the counts to the shipper's bill of lading. All vendors' bills of lading are initialed, dated, and filed in the storeroom to serve as receiving reports.

REQUIRED

Describe the weaknesses in internal control and recommend improvements in Alden's procedures for the purchase, receipt, storage, and issue of raw materials. Organize your answer sheet as follows:

Weakness	Recommended Improvements

AICPA (adapted)

16-26 **(Substantive tests and related assertions—inventory balances)** In performing substantive tests of inventory balances in the audit of the Henning Company, Karlene Kerr, CPA, recognizes that the following potential misstatements may occur or exist:

1. All inventory items are not counted or tagged.
2. Extension errors are made on the client's inventory summaries.
3. Purchases received near the balance sheet date may be included in the physical count but may not be booked.
4. Obsolete and damaged goods are not noticed in warehouse.
5. Inventory stored in a public warehouse may not exist.
6. Client personnel may incorrectly count the inventory.
7. The lower-of-cost-or-market method may be incorrectly applied.
8. Empty containers or hollow squares may be included in the inventory.
9. Goods held on consignment may be included as inventory.
10. Losses on purchase commitments may not be recognized.

REQUIRED

a. Identify the substantive test that should detect each error.
b. For each test, indicate the financial statement assertion(s) to which it pertains.

c. Indicate the type of evidence (i.e., physical, confirmations, documentary, written representations, mathematical, oral, or analytical) obtained from each substantive test. (Use a tabular format for your answers with one column for each part.)

16-27 **(Audit procedures for cost/standard cost system)** The client's cost system is often the focal point in the CPA's audit of the financial statements of a manufacturing company.

REQUIRED

a. For what purpose does the CPA review the cost system?
b. The Summerfield Manufacturing Company employs standard costs in its cost accounting system. List the auditing procedures that you would apply to satisfy yourself that Summerfield's cost standards and related variance amounts are acceptable and have not distorted the financial statements. (Confine your auditing procedures to those applicable to *materials*.)

AICPA

16-28 **(Substantive tests for beginning inventory balances)** Decker, CPA, is performing an audit of the financial statements of Allright Wholesale Sales, Inc., for the year ended December 31, 19X0. Allright has been in business for many years and has never had its financial statements audited. Decker has gained satisfaction with respect to the ending inventory and is considering alternative auditing procedures to gain satisfaction with respect to management's representations concerning the beginning inventory, which was not observed.

Allright sells only one product (bottled brand X beer) and maintains perpetual inventory records. In addition, Allright takes physical inventory counts monthly. Decker has already confirmed purchases with the manufacturer and decided to concentrate on evaluating the reliability of perpetual inventory records and performing analytical procedures to the extent that prior years' unaudited records will enable such procedures to be performed.

REQUIRED

What are the substantive tests, including analytical procedures, that Decker should apply in evaluating the reliability of perpetual inventory records and gaining satisfaction with respect to the January 1, 19X0, inventory?

AICPA

16-29 **(Computer assisted substantive tests for inventory)** An auditor is conducting an audit of the financial statements of a wholesale cosmetics distributor with an inventory consisting of thousands of individual items. The distributor keeps its inventory in its own distribution center and two public warehouses. An inventory computer file is maintained on a computer disk and at the end of each day the file is updated. Each record of the inventory file contains the following data:

1. Item number.
2. Location of item.
3. Description of item.
4. Quantity on hand.
5. Cost per item.
6. Date of last purchase.
7. Date of last sale.
8. Quantity sold during year.

The auditor is planning to observe the distributor's physical count of inventories as of a given date. The auditor will have available a computer tape of the data on the inventory file on the date of the physical count and a general-purpose computer software package.

REQUIRED

The auditor is planning to perform inventory substantive tests. Identify the inventory tests and describe how the use of the general-purpose software package and the tape of the inventory file data might be helpful to the auditor in performing such tests. (Hint: You may wish to refer to Chapter 13 as well as this chapter in answering this question.) Organize your answer as follows:

Inventory Substantive Tests	How General-Purpose Computer Software Package and Tape of the Inventory File Data Might Be Helpful
1. Observe the physical count, making and recording test counts when applicable.	Determining which items are to be test counted by selecting a random sample of a representative number of items from the inventory file as of the date of the physical count.

AICPA

16-30 **(Computer-assisted substantive tests for inventory)** Brown, CPA, is auditing the financial statements of Big Z Wholesaling, Inc., a continuing audit client, for the year ended January 31, 19X2. On January 5, 19X2, Brown observed the tagging and counting of Big Z's physical inventory and made appropriate test counts. These test counts have been recorded on a computer file. As in prior years, Big Z gave Brown two computer files. One file represents the perpetual inventory (FIFO) records for the year ended January 31, 19X2. The other file represents the January 5 physical inventory count.

Assume:

- Brown issued an unqualified opinion on the prior year's financial statements.
- All inventory is purchased for resale and located in a single warehouse.
- Brown has appropriate computerized audit software.
- The perpetual inventory file contains the following information in item number sequence:
  - Beginning balances at February 1, 19X1: Item number, item description, total quantity, and prices.
  - For each item purchased during the year: Date received, receiving report number, vendor, item number, item description, quantity, and total dollar amount.
  - For each item sold during the year: Date shipped, invoice number, item number, item description, quantity shipped, and dollar amount of the cost removed from inventory.
  - For each item adjusted for physical inventory count differences: Date, item number, item description, quantity, and dollar amount.
- The physical inventory file contains the following information in item number sequence: Tag number, item number, item description, and count quantity.

REQUIRED

Describe the substantive auditing procedures Brown may consider performing with computerized audit software using Big Z's two computer files and Brown's computer file of test counts. The substantive auditing procedures described may indicate the reports to be printed out for Brown's follow-up by subsequent application of manual procedures. Do **not** describe subsequent manual auditing procedures.

Group the procedures by those using a) the perpetual inventory file and b) the physical inventory and test count files. (Hint: You may wish to refer to Chapter 13 as well as this chapter in answering this question.)

AICPA

16-31 **(MPU statistical sampling for inventory balance)** As auditor for the Court Company, you decide to use variables sampling to estimate the total cost of an inventory of 1,250 items that has a net book value of $280,400 at December 31, 19X1. The auditor decides to use a sampling plan that will provide a risk of 5% that a fairly stated book value is not rejected as being materially misstated. Based on past experience, it is believed that the standard deviation of the population is $120. The audit estimate is to be made with a tolerable misstatement of $30,000 and a risk of incorrect acceptance of 10%.

REQUIRED

a. Calculate the required sample size using MPU sampling.
b. Assume the sample from part (a) has a mean audit value of $225 and a standard deviation of $110. Is the book value fairly stated? Explain.

16-32 **(PPS statistical sampling for inventory balance)** In auditing the December 31, 19X1, physical inventory being taken by employees in the Sutter Company, you decide to use PPS sampling for variables to determine that the inventory is not materially misstated. Thus far, the following information has been compiled:

Book value of inventory	$2,960,000
Tolerable misstatement	$200,000
Population size	6,511
Estimated standard deviation	$100
Desired risk of incorrect acceptance	5%
Anticipated misstatement	$50,000

REQUIRED

a. Calculate sample size and the sampling interval.
b. Assume that three items in the sample contained errors as follows:

Part Number	Book Value	Audit Value
40965	$15,700	$12,560
41139	56,000	50,400
47622	23,200	22,040

Calculate the projected error and the allowance for sampling risk.

c. What conclusion is supported by the sample results? Explain.

16-33 **(Internal control questionnaire—payroll)** Butler, CPA, has been engaged to audit the financial statements of Young Computer Outlets, Inc., a new client. Young is a privately owned chain of retail stores that sells a variety of computer software and video products. Young uses an in-house payroll department at its corporate headquarters to compute payroll data, and to prepare and distribute payroll checks to its 300 salaried employees.

Butler is preparing an internal control questionnaire to assist in obtaining an understanding of Young's internal control structure and in assessing control risk.

REQUIRED

Prepare a "Payroll" segment of Butler's internal control questionnaire that would assist in obtaining an understanding of Young's internal control structure and in assessing control risk.

Do **not** prepare questions relating to cash payrolls, EDP applications, payments based on hourly rates, piecework, commissions, employee benefits (pensions, health care, vacations, etc.), or payroll tax accruals other than withholdings.

Use the format in the following example:

Question	*Yes*	*No*
Are paychecks prenumbered and accounted for?		

16-34 **(Control activities in payroll processing)** As part of the audit of Manor Company, you are assigned to review and test the payroll transactions of the Galena plant. Your tests show that all numerical items were accurate. The proper hourly rates were used and the wages and deductions were calculated correctly. The payroll register was properly footed, totaled, and posted.

Various plant personnel were interviewed to ascertain the payroll procedures being used in the department. You determine that

1. The payroll clerk receives the time cards from the various department supervisors at the end of each pay period, checks the employee's hourly rate against information provided by the personnel department, and records the regular and overtime hours for each employee.
2. The payroll clerk sends the time cards to the plant's data processing department for compilation and processing.
3. The data processing department returns the time cards with the printed checks and payroll register to the payroll clerk on completion of the processing.
4. The payroll clerk verifies the hourly rate and hours worked for each employee by comparing the detail in the payroll register to the time cards.
5. If errors are found, the payroll clerk voids the computer-generated check, prepares another check for the correct amount, and adjusts the payroll register accordingly.
6. The payroll clerk obtains the plant signature plate from the accounting department and signs the payroll checks.
7. An employee of the personnel department picks up the checks and holds them until they are delivered to the department supervisors for distribution to the employees.

REQUIRED

a. Identify the shortcomings in the payroll procedures used in the payroll department of the Galena plant and suggest corrective action.

b. Identify the weaknesses, if any, that you believe are material and the reasons why.

ICMA (adapted)

16-35 **(Potential misstatements/control activities for payroll)** The Kowal Manufacturing Company employs about 50 production workers and has the following payroll procedures.

The factory foreman interviews applicants and on the basis of the interview either hires or rejects the applicants. When the applicant is hired, a W-4 form (Employee's Withholding Exemption Certificate) is prepared and given to the foreman. The foreman writes the hourly rate of pay for the new employee in the corner of the W-4 form and then gives the form to a payroll clerk as notice that the worker has been employed. The foreman verbally advises the payroll department of rate adjustments.

A supply of blank time cards is kept in a box near the entrance to the factory. Each worker takes a time card on Monday morning, fills in his or her name, and notes in pencil on the time card the daily arrival and departure times. At the end of the week, the workers drop the time cards in a box near the door to the factory.

The completed time cards are taken from the box on Monday morning by a payroll clerk. Two payroll clerks divide the cards alphabetically between them, one taking the A to L section of the payroll and the other taking the M to Z section. Each clerk is fully responsible for her section of the payroll. She computes the gross pay, deductions, and net pay, posts the details to the employee's earnings records, and prepares and numbers the payroll checks. Employees are automatically removed from the payroll when they fail to turn in a time card.

The payroll checks are manually signed by the chief accountant and given to the foreman. The foreman distributes the checks to the workers in the factory and arranges for the delivery of the checks to the workers who are absent. The payroll bank account is reconciled by the chief accountant, who also prepares the various quarterly and annual payroll tax reports.

REQUIRED

a. Identify the misstatements that may occur in the Kowal Company's procedures.
b. For each misstatement in (a) above, give your recommended improvements.

AICPA (adapted)

16-36 **(Evaluation of internal controls—payroll)** A CPA's audit working papers contain a narrative description of a segment of the Croyden Factory, Inc., payroll system and the flowchart on page 646.

NARRATIVE

The internal control structure with respect to the personnel department is well functioning and is not included in the accompanying flowchart.

At the beginning of each work week, payroll clerk No. 1 reviews the payroll department files to determine the employment status of factory employees and then prepares time cards and distributes them as each individual arrives at work. This payroll clerk, who is also responsible for custody of the signature stamp machine, verifies the identity of each payee before delivering signed checks to the foreman.

At the end of each work week, the foreman distributes payroll checks for the preceding work week. Concurrent with this activity, the foreman reviews the current week's employee time cards, notes the regular and overtime hours worked on a summary form, and initials the aforementioned time cards. The foreman then delivers all time cards and unclaimed payroll checks to payroll clerk No. 2.

REQUIRED

a. Based on the narrative and accompanying flowchart, what are the weaknesses in the internal control structure?
b. Based on the narrative and accompanying flowchart, what inquiries should be made with respect to clarifying the existence of possible additional weaknesses in the internal control structure?

   Note: Do not discuss the internal control structure of the personnel department.

AICPA

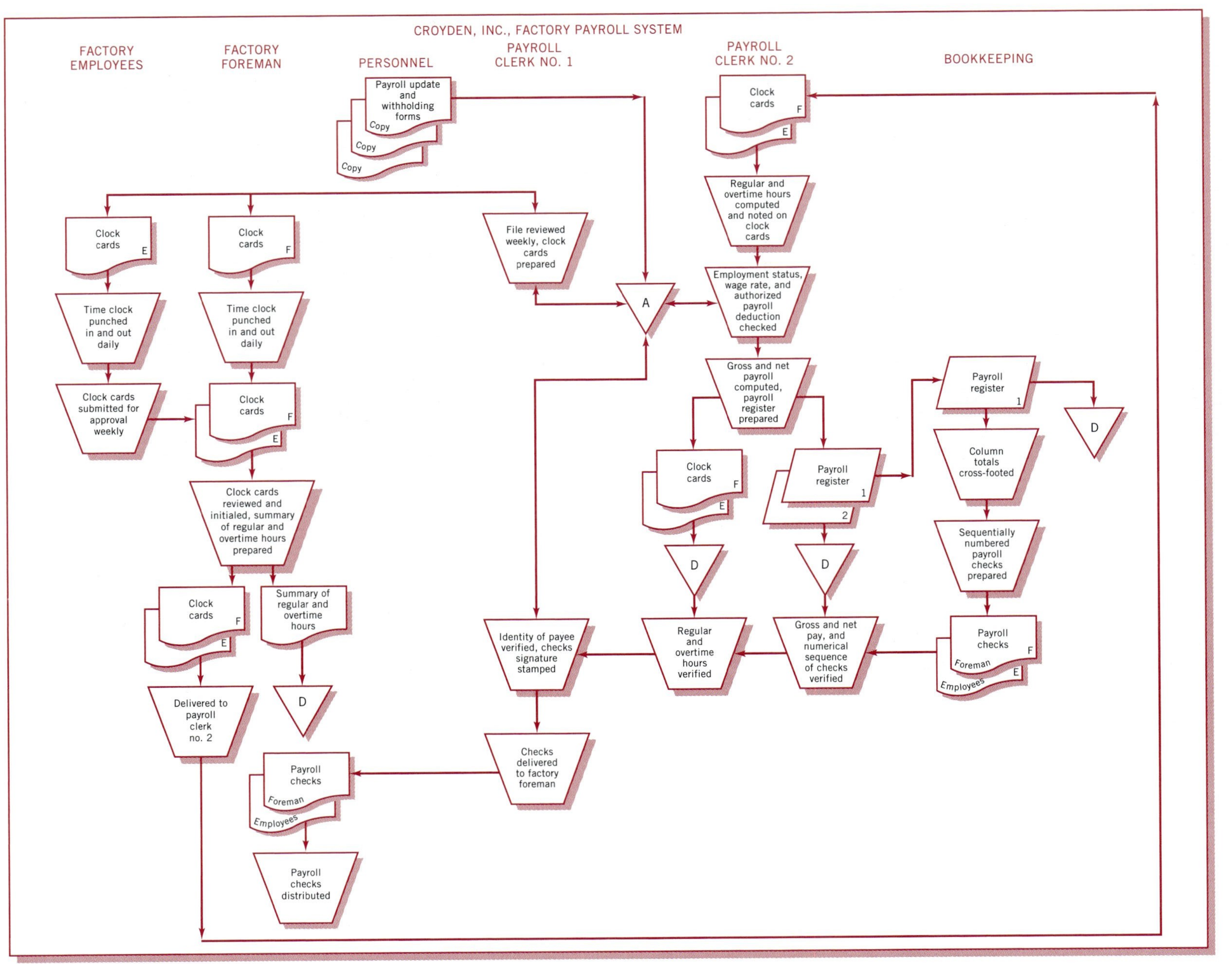
CROYDEN, INC., FACTORY PAYROLL SYSTEM
FACTORY EMPLOYEES
FACTORY FOREMAN
PERSONNEL
PAYROLL CLERK NO. 1
PAYROLL CLERK NO. 2
BOOKKEEPING
Payroll update and withholding forms
Copy
Copy
Copy
Clock cards
E
Time clock punched in and out daily
Clock cards submitted for approval weekly
Clock cards
F
Time clock punched in and out daily
Clock cards
F
E
Clock cards reviewed and initialed, summary of regular and overtime hours prepared
Clock cards
F
E
Summary of regular and overtime hours
D
Delivered to payroll clerk no. 2
Payroll checks
Foreman
Employees
Payroll checks distributed
File reviewed weekly, clock cards prepared
A
Identity of payee verified, checks signature stamped
Checks delivered to factory foreman
Clock cards
F
E
Regular and overtime hours computed and noted on clock cards
Employment status, wage rate, and authorized payroll deduction checked
Gross and net payroll computed, payroll register prepared
Clock cards
F
E
D
Payroll register
1
2
D
Regular and overtime hours verified
Gross and net pay, and numerical sequence of checks verified
Payroll register
1
D
Column totals cross-footed
Sequentially numbered payroll checks prepared
Payroll checks
F
E
Foreman
Employees

16-37 **(Potential misstatements/tests of controls—payroll)** The following questions are included in the internal control questionnaire on control procedures for payroll transactions in the Pena Company:

1. Are pay rates, payroll deductions, and terminations authorized by the personnel department?
2. Are time clocks and clock cards used?
3. Is there supervisory approval of time worked by each employee?
4. Are payroll checks signed and distributed by treasurer office personnel?
5. Is there internal verification of payroll checks with payroll register data?
6. Are unclaimed wages controlled by a treasurer's office employee?
7. Is access restricted to personnel and employee earnings master files?
8. Are hirings authorized by personnel department?
9. Is time clock punching supervised?
10. Is responsibility assigned for the timely filing of payroll tax returns and payment of payroll taxes?

REQUIRED

a. Identify a misstatement that may occur if a NO answer is given to each question.
b. Identify a possible test of controls assuming a YES answer is given to each question. (Present your answers in tabular form using separate columns for each part.)

CASE

16-38 **(Internal control evaluation—payroll)** The Vane Corporation is a manufacturing concern that has been in business for the past 18 years. During this period, the company has grown from a very small family-owned operation to a medium-sized manufacturing concern with several departments. Despite this growth, a substantial number of the procedures employed by Vane Corp. have been in effect since the business was started. Just recently, Vane Corp. has computerized its payroll function.

The payroll function operates in the following manner. Each worker picks up a weekly time card on Monday morning and writes in his name and identification number. These blank cards are kept near the factory entrance. The workers write on the time card the time of their daily arrival and departure. On the following Monday, the factory foremen collect the completed cards for the previous week and send them to data processing.

In data processing, the time cards are used to prepare the weekly time file. This file is processed with the master payroll file, which is maintained on magnetic tape according to worker identification number. The checks are written by the computer on the regular checking account and imprinted with the treasurer's signature. After the payroll file is updated and the checks are prepared, the checks are sent to the factory foremen, who distribute them to the workers or hold them for the workers to pick up later if they are absent.

The foremen notify data processing of new employees and terminations. Any changes in hourly pay rate or any other changes affecting payroll are usually communicated to data processing by the foremen.

The workers also complete a job time ticket for each individual job they work on each day. The job time tickets are collected daily and sent to cost accounting, where they are used to prepare a cost distribution analysis.

Further analysis of the payroll function reveals the following:

1. A worker's gross wages never exceed $300 per week.
2. Raises never exceed $0.55 per hour for the factory workers.
3. No more than 20 hours of overtime are allowed each week.
4. The factory employs 150 workers in ten departments.

The payroll function has not been operating smoothly for some time, but even more problems have surfaced since the payroll was computerized. The foremen have indicated that they would like a weekly report including worker tardiness, absenteeism, and idle time, so they can determine the amount of productive time lost and the reason for the lost time. The following errors and inconsistencies have been encountered in the past few pay periods:

1. A workers's paycheck was not processed properly because he had transposed two numbers in his identification number when he filled out his time card.
2. A worker was issued a check for $1,531.80 when it should have been $153.81.
3. One worker's paycheck was not written, and this error was not detected until the paychecks for that department were distributed by the foreman.
4. Part of the master payroll file was destroyed when the tape reel was inadvertently mounted on the wrong tape drive and used as a scratch tape. Data processing attempted to reestablish the destroyed portion from original source documents and other records.
5. One worker received a paycheck for an amount considerably larger than he should have. Further investigation revealed that 84 had been punched instead of 48 for hours worked.
6. Several records on the master payroll file were skipped and not included on the updated master payroll file. This was not detected for several pay periods.
7. In processing nonroutine changes, a computer operator included a pay rate increase for one of his friends in the factory. This was discovered by chance by another employee.

REQUIRED

Identify the control weakness in the payroll procedure and in the computer processing as it is now conducted by Vane Corp. Recommend the changes necessary to correct the control structure. Arrange your answer in the following columnar format:

Control Weaknesses	Recommendations

ICMA

RESEARCH QUESTION

16-39 **(AAERs dealing with inventory)** Several SEC *Accounting and Auditing Enforcement Releases* have dealt with inventory audit problems, including Nos. 2, 127, 242, 251, and 264. Review one of these, or any other AAER that you may identify as dealing with issues related to inventory, and prepare a brief summary stating the parties involved, the nature of the reporting and auditing deficiencies found, and any remedies imposed by the SEC.

CHAPTER 17

AUDITING THE INVESTING AND FINANCING CYCLES

LEARNING OBJECTIVES

After studying this chapter, you should be able to

1. Describe the nature of the investing cycle.
2. State the major audit objectives in the investing cycle.
3. Explain the rationale for the audit strategy generally used in auditing the investing cycle.
4. Discuss key considerations in determining detection risk and designing substantive tests for investment balance assertions.
5. Describe the nature of the financing cycle.
6. State the major audit objectives in the financing cycle.
7. Explain the rationale for the audit strategy generally used in auditing the financing cycle.
8. Discuss key considerations in determining detection risk and designing substantive tests for long-term debt assertions.

THE INVESTING CYCLE
- AUDIT OBJECTIVES
- MATERIALITY, RISK, AND AUDIT STRATEGY
- CONSIDERATION OF INTERNAL CONTROL STRUCTURE COMPONENTS

SUBSTANTIVE TESTS OF INVESTMENT BALANCES
- DETERMINING DETECTION RISK
- DESIGNING SUBSTANTIVE TESTS
- INITIAL PROCEDURES
- ANALYTICAL PROCEDURES
- TESTS OF DETAILS OF TRANSACTIONS
- TESTS OF DETAILS OF BALANCES
- COMPARISON OF STATEMENT PRESENTATION WITH GAAP

THE FINANCING CYCLE
- AUDIT OBJECTIVES
- MATERIALITY, RISK, AND AUDIT STRATEGY
- CONSIDERATION OF INTERNAL CONTROL STRUCTURE COMPONENTS

SUBSTANTIVE TESTS OF LONG-TERM DEBT BALANCES
- DETERMINING DETECTION RISK
- DESIGNING SUBSTANTIVE TESTS
- INITIAL PROCEDURES
- ANALYTICAL PROCEDURES
- TESTS OF DETAILS OF TRANSACTIONS
- TESTS OF DETAILS OF BALANCES
- COMPARISON OF STATEMENT PRESENTATION WITH GAAP

SUBSTANTIVE TESTS OF STOCKHOLDERS' EQUITY BALANCES
- DETERMINING DETECTION RISK
- DESIGNING SUBSTANTIVE TESTS
- INITIAL PROCEDURES
- ANALYTICAL PROCEDURES
- TESTS OF DETAILS OF TRANSACTIONS
- TESTS OF DETAILS OF BALANCES
- COMPARISON OF STATEMENT PRESENTATION WITH GAAP

SUMMARY
BIBLIOGRAPHY
OBJECTIVE QUESTIONS
COMPREHENSIVE QUESTIONS
CASE
RESEARCH QUESTION

The following four cycles have been discussed in this text: revenue, expenditure, personnel services, and production. This chapter covers the remaining two cycles, the investing cycle and the financing cycle. The coverage here is from the perspective of entities other than those in the financial services industry. For such entities, these cycles embrace the major nonoperating activities.[1]

[1] The AICPA has issued several *Audit and Accounting Guides* to provide specialized guidance pertaining to the audits of several types of entities within the financial services industry. These entities include banks, brokers and dealers in securities, credit unions, employee benefit plans, finance companies, investment companies, property and liability insurance companies, savings institutions, and stock life insurance companies. Coverage of the investing and financing activities of these types of entities is beyond the scope of this text.

9. Discuss key considerations in determining detection risk and designing substantive tests for stockholders' equity assertions.

THE INVESTING CYCLE

OBJECTIVE 1

Describe the nature of the investing cycle.

An entity's **investing cycle** pertains to activities relating to the ownership of securities issued by other entities. These securities include certificates of deposit (CDs), preferred and common stocks, and corporate and government bonds. Consideration is given here to investments in common stock and corporate bonds only.

The investing cycle interfaces with two other cycles. Dividends and interest received on investments involve cash receipts transactions discussed in this text as part of the revenue cycle. Purchases of securities with cash involves cash disbursements transactions discussed in this text as part of the expenditure cycle. These transactions may be subjected to the same controls as other cash receipts and disbursements transactions as discussed in Chapters 14 and 15, as well as additional controls applicable only to **investing transactions** as discussed in later sections.

The following accounts are used in recording short-term and long-term investing transactions and the resulting income statement effects of those investments:

Balance Sheet Accounts	Income Statement Accounts
Investments in equity and debt securities classified as trading or available for sale securities	Dividend revenue (from equity investments not accounted for by the equity method)
Market adjustment accounts (asset accounts) for above (when above are carried in accounts at cost and there is an accumulated difference between cost and fair value of those securities)	Interest revenue (on investments in debt securities)
Cumulative unrealized holding gains and losses on equity and debt securities classified as available-for-sale securities (equity account)	Realized gains and losses (on equity and debt securities transactions)
Investments in equity securities accounted for by the equity method (investor exercises significant influence over investee)	Unrealized holding gains and losses on equity and debt securities classified as trading (from changes in fair value during current period)
Investments in equity securities accounted for at cost (fair value not determinable)	Equity in investee's earnings (for investments accounted for by the equity method)
Investments in debt securities classified as held-to-maturity (carried at amortized cost)	

The variety of accounts listed above indicates that the auditor must be familiar with the many dimensions of valuation, classification, and disclosures pertaining to investments in equity and debt securities.

AUDIT OBJECTIVES

OBJECTIVE 2

State the major audit objectives in the investing cycle.

For each of the five categories of financial statement assertions, Figure 17-1 lists a number of specific account balance audit objectives pertaining to accounts affected by investing transactions. Considerations and procedures relevant to meeting these objectives are explained in the following sections.

MATERIALITY, RISK, AND AUDIT STRATEGY

OBJECTIVE 3

Explain the rationale for the audit strategy generally used in auditing the investing cycle.

Securities held as short-term investments may be material to an entity's short-term solvency, but income from such securities is seldom significant to the results of operations of entities outside of the financial services sector. Securities held as long-term investments may be material to both the balance sheet and income statement.

Inherent risk for investments is affected by many factors. The volume of investing transactions is generally quite low. However, securities are susceptible to theft, and the accounting for investments can become complex. Examples of the latter include certain equity method investments for which the acquisition costs exceed book values, and the accounting required when certain investments are reclassified from one category to another. In addition, certain inherent risks are more challenging to address with controls, and afford management an opportunity for manipulating the reporting for investments. Specifically, the proper classification of an investment may be contentious, which in turn affects the valuation method,

FIGURE 17-1 • SELECTED SPECIFIC AUDIT OBJECTIVES FOR THE INVESTING CYCLE

Assertion Category	Account Balance Audit Objectives
Existence or occurrence	Recorded investment asset and equity balances represent investments that exist at the balance sheet date **(EO1)**. Investment revenues, realized gains and losses, and unrealized holding gains and losses included in income resulted from transactions and events that occurred during the period **(EO2)**.
Completeness	All investments are included in the balance sheet investment accounts **(C1)**. The income statement effects of all investment transactions and events during the period are included in the income statement accounts **(C2)**.
Rights and obligations	All recorded investments are owned by the reporting entity **(RO1)**.
Valuation or allocation	Investments are reported on the balance sheet at fair value, cost, amortized cost, or the amount determined by the equity method, as appropriate for particular investments **(VA1)**. Investment revenues, and realized and unrealized gains and losses are reported at proper amounts **(VA2)**.
Presentation and disclosure	Investment balances are properly identified and classified in the financial statements **(PD1)**. Appropriate disclosures are made concerning (1) related party investments, (2) the bases for valuing investments, and (3) the pledging of investments as collateral **(PD2)**.

income effects, and disclosure requirements applicable to the investment. For example, the accounting treatment of debt securities classified as *held-to-maturity* versus *available-for-sale* is quite different, as is the treatment of equity securities classified as *available-for-sale* versus *trading*. By misrepresenting the appropriate classification of an investment, management can defer or accelerate the recognition of unrealized gains and losses in income. Moreover, fair values, when required, may be difficult to determine or they may be volatile. Thus, these factors, when applicable, may contribute to high levels of inherent risk for the valuation or allocation and presentation and disclosure assertions.

Because of the typically low volume of investing transactions noted above, it is generally most cost efficient to use the primarily substantive approach in auditing investment balances. This approach is assumed in this chapter. Recall, however, that even under the primarily substantive approach, the auditor must obtain a sufficient understanding of relevant components of the internal control structure as a basis for identifying potential misstatements before designing substantive tests.

CONSIDERATION OF INTERNAL CONTROL STRUCTURE COMPONENTS

The understanding of several control environment factors is relevant to the audit of the investing cycle. For example, the authority and responsibility for investing transactions should be assigned to a company officer such as the treasurer. This individual should be a person who (1) is of unquestioned integrity, (2) possesses the knowledge and skills required of a person charged with executing such transactions, (3) realizes the importance of observing all prescribed control procedures, and (4) can assist other participating members of management in making initial and ongoing assessments of risks associated with individual investments.

The accounting system must include provision for capturing and retaining all the necessary cost, fair value, and other data required for each method of accounting for the various categories of investments in equity and debt securities, both at acquisition and at subsequent reporting dates. Thus, accounting personnel must be familiar with these requirements and capable of implementing them. Separate subsidiary investment ledgers may be maintained for the various categories of investments.

Each of the categories of control activities applies to investments. Several common documents and records used in investing activities are explained in the next section, followed by descriptions of important investing functions and selected control activities pertaining to each. In addition, the effectiveness of controls over investing activities should be closely monitored by internal auditors and the audit committee of the board of directors.

Common Documents and Records

The documents and records applicable to this cycle are

- **Stock certificate.** An engraved form showing the number of shares of stock owned by a shareholder in a corporation. This document provides evidence for the existence or occurrence assertion.

- **Bond certificate.** An engraved form showing the number of bonds owned by a bondholder.
- **Bond indenture.** A contract stating the terms of bonds issued by a corporation.
- **Broker's advice.** A document issued by a broker specifying the exchange price of investing transactions; it is the primary source document for recording investing transactions. The advice provides evidence for the valuation or allocation assertion.
- **Books of original entry.** The general journal is used to record such items as the accrual of bond interest revenue, market adjustments under the fair value method, and income earned under the equity method of accounting. The cash receipts journal is used to record the proceeds from sales transactions and the receipt of interest and dividends. The voucher and check registers are used in purchasing and paying for the cost of securities.
- **Investment subsidiary ledger.** Separate subsidiary ledgers may be used for each different class of investments when the company has a portfolio consisting of many different investments.

Functions and Related Controls

Activities in the investing cycle include the following **investing functions** and related controls:

- **Purchasing securities.** Purchases are made in accordance with management's authorizations.
- **Receiving periodic income.** Dividend and interest checks are promptly deposited intact.
- **Selling securities.** Sales are made in accordance with management's authorizations, and the receipts are deposited intact.
- **Recording transactions.** Transactions are recorded based on appropriate supporting documentation; the duties of recording transactions and maintaining custody of the securities are segregated.
- **Safeguarding securities.** Securities are stored in safes or vaults, and access is restricted to authorized personnel; securities are periodically inspected and counted and compared with recorded balances.
- **Recording market adjustments and reclassifications.** Changes in fair values and in circumstances pertaining to the proper classification of investments are periodically analyzed and recorded.
- **Assessing investment performance and reporting.** Performance reviews are made by management to detect poor investment performance and/or erroneous reporting, including comparisons of investment balances and rates of return for various classes of investments with budgeted amounts, and reviews of the propriety of the classification of individual investments.

Careful consideration of the foregoing descriptions of investing functions should suggest a variety of potential misstatements that could occur in investment balances.

LEARNING CHECK:

17-1 a. Describe the nature of the investment cycle.
b. Does the investing cycle interface with any other cycles? Explain.

17-2 State the audit objectives for each of the management assertions that pertain to the investing cycle.

17-3 a. Shad Sloan contends that investments are seldom material to the financial statements. Is Shad correct? Explain.
b. Keri Kline states that the auditor should generally use a primarily substantive approach strategy in auditing the investing cycle. Is Keri right? Explain.

17-4 Describe the applicability of internal control structure components to the investing cycle.

17-5 Identify and describe the functions that pertain to investing cycle transactions.

KEY TERMS:

Bond certificate, p. 654
Bond indenture, p. 654
Books of original entry, p. 654
Broker's advice, p. 654
Investing cycle, p. 651
Investing functions, p. 654
Investing transactions, p. 651
Investment subsidiary ledger, p. 654
Stock certificate, p. 653

SUBSTANTIVE TESTS OF INVESTMENT BALANCES

OBJECTIVE 4

Discuss key considerations in determining detection risk and designing substantive tests for investment balance assertions.

It is common in substantive testing in the investing cycle to test related balance sheet and income statement investment balances at the same time. As in the case of each of the cycles covered in previous chapters, appropriate acceptable levels of detection risk must be specified for each category of financial statement assertions for investing cycle balances before substantive tests can be designed.

DETERMINING DETECTION RISK

In applying the audit risk model to determine detection risk for investing cycle assertions, it may be necessary for the auditor to combine her or his inherent and control risk assessments for cash receipts and cash disbursements transactions with the additional considerations unique to investing transactions discussed earlier in this chapter. Because the relevant inherent and control risk assessments can vary widely owing to the variety of types of investments and circumstances across entities, acceptable detection risk levels will also vary significantly both across entities and across assertion categories for the same entity. Again, difficulties in designing controls to adequately address risks associated with (1) the use of fair values, when required, and (2) the proper classification of investments often means that low acceptable levels of detection risk must be specified for the valuation or allocation and presentation and disclosure assertions.

FIGURE 17-2 • POSSIBLE SUBSTANTIVE TESTS OF INVESTMENT BALANCE ASSERTIONS

Category	Substantive Test	Account Balance Audit Objective (from p. 652)				
		EO#	C#	RO I	VA#	PD#
Initial procedures	1. Perform initial procedures on investment balances and records that will be subjected to further testing. a. Trace beginning balances for investment asset and equity accounts to prior year's working papers. b. Review activity in all investment-related balance sheet and income statement accounts and investigate entries that appear unusual in amount or source. c. Obtain client-prepared schedules of investments and determine that they accurately represent the underlying accounting records from which prepared by: • Footing and crossfooting the schedules and reconciling the totals with the related subsidiary and general ledger balances. • Testing agreement of items on schedules with entries in related subsidiary and general ledger accounts.				✓1,2	
Analytical procedures	2. Perform analytical procedures. a. Calculate ratios: • Short-term investments to total current assets. • Long-term investments to total assets. • Rates of return by investment classifications. b. Analyze ratio results relative to expectations based on prior year, budgeted, or other data.	✓1,2	✓1,2		✓1,2	✓1,2
Tests of details of transactions	3. Vouch entries in investment and related income and equity accounts.	✓1,2	✓1,2	✓	✓1,2	✓1
Tests of details of balances	4. Inspect and count securities on hand.	✓1	✓1		✓1	✓1
	5. Confirm securities held by others.	✓1	✓1	✓		
	6. Recalculate investment revenue earned.				✓2	
	7. Review documentation concerning fair values.				✓1,2	
Presentation and disclosure	8. Compare statement presentation with GAAP. a. Determine that investment balances are properly identified and classified in the financial statements. b. Determine the appropriateness of disclosures concerning the valuation bases for investments, realized and unrealized gain or loss components, related party investments, and pledged investments.					✓1 ✓2

DESIGNING SUBSTANTIVE TESTS

A list of possible substantive tests of investment balances and the specific audit objectives to which they relate is presented in Figure 17-2. Note that the tests of details of balances category contains the largest number of possible tests, and that a variety of tests can contribute to achieving the low acceptable levels of detection risk that may be needed for the valuation or allocation and presentation and disclosure assertions. Each of the tests is explained in a following section.

INITIAL PROCEDURES

The series of procedures in this category as shown in Figure 17-2 follows the pattern established for major accounts in the other cycle chapters. That is, first, agreement of beginning investment balances with audited amounts in the prior year's working papers is verified. Next, the activity in investment-related accounts is reviewed to determine the presence of any entries that are unusual in nature or amount that should be investigated. Then, client-prepared schedules of all investments, or additions and disposals in the current period, are checked for mathematical accuracy and agreement with the underlying accounting records. The latter procedure includes determining that schedules and subsidiary investment ledgers agree with related general ledger control account balances. The schedules can then serve as the basis for additional substantive tests.

ANALYTICAL PROCEDURES

Analytical procedures for investment balances involve the interrelationship of specific accounts within the current period and comparisons with prior year data, budgeted amounts, or other expectations. For example, the percentage of short- and long-term investment balances to current and total assets, respectively, and rates of return on various classes of investments can be compared with expectations. Unexpected differences might indicate misstatements pertaining to the existence or occurrence, completeness, valuation or allocation, and presentation and disclosure assertions. For example, upon investigation a higher than expected rate of return on trading securities might be found to have been caused by erroneously recording the unrealized gain from an increase in the fair value of available-for-sale securities in the income account for trading securities rather than in the equity account for unrealized gains on available-for-sale securities. Similarly, investigation of a lower than expected rate of return on an equity method investment might be found to have been caused by an error in recording (1) the investor's share of the investee's earnings or (2) amortization of the excess of the investor's cost over the underlying book value of the investment. On the other hand, for example, declines in the percentages of investment balances to current and total assets might be due to unexpected declines in the fair values of investments rather than to any errors in the accounts.

TESTS OF DETAILS OF TRANSACTIONS

These substantive tests consist of vouching the individual debits and credits in the various investment accounts. For example, debits to asset accounts for acquisition transactions can be vouched to brokers' advices and canceled checks. Other debits to the investment accounts or related market adjustment accounts can be vouched to documentation verifying increases in fair values to be recognized in the accounts. Credits posted to asset accounts can be vouched to bank or broker's advices evidencing the sale of investments, or to documentation of decreases in fair values to be recognized in the accounts. Similarly, entries to income statement and equity accounts for realized and unrealized gains and losses can be vouched to documentation of sales transactions or changes in fair values to be recognized in these accounts. Entries for major purchases and sales of investments can often be vouched to authorizations in the minutes of the board of directors.

For investments accounted for by the equity method, post-acquisition debits can be vouched to documentation showing the investor's share of the investee's earnings. Credits can be vouched to documentation of dividends received from investees or to worksheets showing the calculation of the periodic amortization of the excess of cost over underlying book value. Audited financial statements of the investee generally constitute sufficient evidence regarding the underlying net assets and the results of operations of the investee.

Knowledge of the proper accounting for investing activities affecting other investment balances will inform the auditor as to the sources to which the debits and credits can be vouched. Depending on the particular debits or credits being vouched, careful examination of the supporting documentation can provide evidence bearing on any of the five categories of assertions. For example, brokers' advices provide evidence about the existence or occurrence of transactions, the transfer of ownership of securities, and the valuation of the securities at the transaction date. Documentation may also be helpful in determining that the debits and credits have been made to the proper accounts (proper classification).

TESTS OF DETAILS OF BALANCES

Four substantive tests in this category are explained in the following subsections.

Inspect and Count Securities on Hand

This test ordinarily is performed simultaneously with the auditor's count of cash and other negotiable instruments. In performing the test, (1) the custodian of the securities should be present throughout the count, (2) a receipt should be obtained from the custodian when the securities are returned, and (3) all securities should be controlled by the auditor until the count is completed.

In inspecting securities, the auditor should observe such matters as the certificate number on the document, name of owner (which should be the client, either directly or through endorsement), description of the security, number of shares (or bonds), and name of issuer. These data should be recorded as part of the auditor's analysis of the investment account. Figure 17-3 illustrates an audit working paper for one class of equity securities. For securities purchased in prior years, the data should be compared with those shown on last year's working papers. A lack of agreement between the certificate numbers may be indicative of unauthorized transactions for those securities.

Figure 17-3 • AVAILABLE-FOR-SALE SECURITIES WORKING PAPER

WILLIAMS COMPANY
AVAILABLE-FOR-SALE SECURITIES
DECEMBER 31, 19X1

W/P REF: H-2
PREPARED BY: A.E.R DATE: 1/3/X2
REVIEWED BY: R.E.G DATE: 1/10/X2

ACCTS. 115, 116, AND 425

DESCRIPTION	CTF. NO.	DATE ACQUIRED	NO. OF SHARES	COST PER SHARE	BALANCE 1/1/X1	PURCHASES	SALES	BALANCE 12/31/X1	MARKET PRICE AT 12/31/X1 PER SHARE	MARKET PRICE AT 12/31/X1 TOTAL	DIVIDEND INCOME
GENERAL MANUFACTURING CO.	C2779	4/21/X0	900	22.00	19,800 ✓			19,800 ✓X ^	24.50 ∀	22,050 ^	675 ⊗
METROPOLITAN EDISON CO.	M82931	9/21/X0	500	33.20	16,600 ✓		16,600 ø	^			127 ⊗
PACIFIC PAPERS, INC.	54942	2/14/X1	200	18.50		3,700 ø		3,700 ✓X ^	17.00 ∀	3,400 ^	
WARRENTON CORP.	7336	7/19/X0	400	27.25	10,900 ✓			10,900 ✓X ^	29.25 ∀	11,700 ^	120 ⊗
					47,300 ✓	3,700	16,600	34,400 ✓		37,150	922
					F	F	F	FF To H-1		F	F To R-1
FAIR VALUE OVER (UNDER) COST AT 12/31/X1										2,750	To H-1
BALANCE IN MARKET ADJUSTMENT - AVAILABLE-FOR-SALE SECURITIES (ACCT. 116) BEFORE CURRENT ADJUSTMENT										1,250	
CURRENT ADJUSTMENT REQUIRED - INCREASE (DECREASE)										1,500 (AE)	

M Examined stock ctf. at Federal Trust Co.
✓ Traced to prior years working papers
X Traced to general ledger balance
F Footed
FF Footed and crossfooted
^ Extension checked
ø Vouched to brokers advices and board of directors' authorization
∀ Per market quotation in 1/2/X2 Wall Street Journal
⊗ Dividend rates checked to Standard and Poors;
dividends received traced to cash receipts journal.

(AE) Adjusting entry-posted to W/P AE-2:
Dr. Market Adjustment--Available-for-Sale Securities (Acct. 116) 1,500
Cr. Unrealized Gain (Loss) in Available-for-Sale Secs. (Acct 376) 1,500

Securities on hand may be stored for safekeeping in several different locations. In such a case, either simultaneous counts should be made at the locations or the securities should be kept under seal until all locations have been counted. For example, banks will generally seal a safety deposit box at the client's request and will confirm to the auditor that there was no access to the box during the counting period. When the count is not made on the balance sheet date, the auditor should prepare a reconciliation from the date of count to the statement date by reviewing any intervening security transactions.

This substantive test provides evidence about the existence or occurrence, completeness, rights and obligations, and presentation and disclosure assertions.

Confirm Securities Held by Others

Securities held by outsiders for safekeeping must be confirmed. Confirmations should be requested as of the date securities held by the client are counted. The confirmation process for securities is identical with the steps required in confirming receivables. Thus, the auditor must control the mailings and receive the responses directly from the custodian. The data confirmed are the same as the data that should be noted when the auditor is able to inspect the securities.

Securities may also be held by creditors as collateral against loans or be placed in escrow by court order. In such cases, the confirmation should be sent to the indicated custodian. The confirmation of securities held by third parties provides evidence as to the existence or occurrence and rights and obligations assertions. It will also furnish evidence about the completeness assertion if the confirmation response indicates more securities on hand than recorded.

Recalculate Investment Revenue Earned

Income from investments is verified by documentary evidence and recalculation. Dividends on all stocks listed on stock exchanges and many others are included in dividend record books published by investment services. The auditor can independently verify the dividend revenue by reference to the declaration date, amount, and payment date shown in the record book. The verification of dividend income is usually incorporated into the schedule of investments, as illustrated in Figure 17-3.

Interest earned and interest collected on investments in bonds can be verified by examining the interest rates and payment dates indicated on the bond certificate. In addition, the auditor reviews the client's amortization schedule for bond premium and discount and recalculates the amount amortized, if any.

Verification of the investor's share of investee earnings for equity method investments was discussed as part of vouching entries in the earlier section on tests of details of transactions. Recalculation of investment revenue balances pertains primarily to the valuation or allocation assertion.

Review Documentation Concerning Fair Values

Subsequent to the issuance of *Statement of Financial Accounting Standards 115: Accounting for Certain Investments in Debt and Equity Securities,* most investments are reported at fair value. Exceptions are debt securities qualifying as held-to-maturity securities which are reported at amortized cost, investments for which a fair value cannot be determined which are carried at cost, and equity method investments. The auditor can verify fair values for most securities required to be reported at fair value by referring to market quotations for stock exchanges available in printed or electronic format from a variety of sources. The change in the fair value of such an investment between the acquisition date or beginning of the year, whichever is later, and the reporting date should also be verified and traced to entries in the appropriate unrealized gain or loss account (income account for trading securities or equity account for available-for-sale securities). This substantive test relates primarily to the valuation or allocation assertion for investment balances.

COMPARISON OF STATEMENT PRESENTATION WITH GAAP

The foregoing substantive tests should provide much of the evidence needed by the auditor to determine whether investment balances are properly identified and classified in the financial statements. However, regarding classification as to current or noncurrent, or trading versus available-for-sale, the auditor must also make inquiries of management concerning its intentions regarding holding periods, and so on. In the case of debt securities classified as held-to-maturity, the auditor must also assess the entity's ability to hold the investment until maturity. Most auditors use checklists as an aid in determining that all required disclosures are made concerning valuation bases for investments, the various components of realized and unrealized gains and losses, related party investments, and securities that have been pledged as collateral.

LEARNING CHECK:

17-6 What factors are relevant in determining the acceptable level of detection risk for investment balances?

17-7 a. What precautions should be taken in counting and inspecting securities?
b. Identify the financial statement assertions affected by this test?

17-8 What data should be shown in the working papers concerning securities that have been examined by the auditor?

17-9 a. Indicate the form and timing of confirming securities held by outside custodians.
b. State the financial statement assertions affected by this test.

THE FINANCING CYCLE

OBJECTIVE 5

Describe the nature of the financing cycle.

An entity's **financing cycle** consists of transactions pertaining to the acquisition and payback of capital funds. This cycle includes two major transaction classes as follows:

- **Long-term debt transactions** include borrowings from bonds, mortgages, notes, and loans, and the related principal and interest payments.
- **Stockholders' equity transactions** include the issuance and redemption of preferred and common stock, treasury stock transactions, and dividend payments.

Bond and common stock issues typically represent the primary sources of capital funds. Accordingly, attention is focused primarily on these two sources of financing.

The financing cycle interfaces with the expenditure cycle when cash is disbursed for bond interest, the redemption of bonds, cash dividends, and the purchase of treasury stock. The accounts used in recording financing cycle transactions include:

Long-term Debt Transactions	Stockholder's Equity Transactions
Bonds, Mortgages, Notes, and Loans Payable	Preferred Stock
Bond Premium (Discount)	Common Stock
Interest Payable	Treasury Stock
Interest Expense	Pain-in Capital
Gain (Loss) on Retirement of Bonds	Retained Earnings
	Dividends
	Dividends Payable

OBJECTIVE 6

State the major audit objectives in the financing cycle.

AUDIT OBJECTIVES

For each of the five categories of financial statement assertions, Figure 17-4 lists a number of specific account balance audit objectives pertaining to accounts affected by financing transactions. Considerations and procedures relevant to meeting these objectives are explained in the following sections.

MATERIALITY, RISK, AND AUDIT STRATEGY

OBJECTIVE 7

Explain the rationale for the audit strategy generally used in auditing the financing cycle.

There is considerable variation in the importance of long-term debt to the fair presentation of financial position. In some major corporations, long-term debt is immaterial to total liabilities and stockholders' equity, whereas in many public utilities such liabilities represent more than 50% of the total claims on corporate assets. Stockholder's equity clearly is a material component of a balance sheet. The income statement effects of financing cycle transactions also vary widely in significance as does the effect of dividends on the retained earnings statement. The disclosure requirements for long-term debt and stockholders' equity are usually significant.

The risk of misstatements in executing and recording financing cycle transactions is usually low. In many companies, these transactions occur infrequently, except for the payment of dividends and interest, which are often handled by outside agents. In addition, board of director authorizations are required for most transactions, and company officers participate in their execution.

As in the case of the investing cycle, audit strategy for the financing cycle is based primarily on the frequency of transactions. Because these transactions

FIGURE 17-4 • SELECTED SPECIFIC AUDIT OBJECTIVES FOR THE FINANCING CYCLE

Assertion Category	Account Balance Audit Objectives
Existence or occurrence	Recorded long-term debt balances represent debt that exists at the balance sheet date **(EO1)**, and related income statement balances represent the effects of long-term debt transactions and events that occurred during the period **(EO2)**. Stockholders' equity balances represent the owners' interests that exist at the balance sheet date **(EO3)**.
Completeness	Long-term debt balances represent all payables to long-term creditors at the balance sheet date **(C1)**, and related income statement balances represent the effects of all long-term debt transactions and events that occurred during the period **(C2)**. Stockholders' equity balances include the effects of all transactions pertaining to paid-in capital and retained earnings through the balance sheet date **(C3)**.
Rights and obligations	All recorded long-term debt balances are obligations of the reporting entity **(RO1)**. Stockholders' equity balances represent owners' claims on the reporting entity's assets **(RO2)**.
Valuation or allocation	Long-term debt and related income statement balances **(VA1)** and stockholders' equity balances **(VA2)** are properly valued in accordance with GAAP.
Presentation and disclosure	Long-term debt and related income statement balances **(PD1)** and stockholders' equity balances **(PD2)** are properly identified and classified in the financial statements. All terms, covenants, commitments, and retirement provisions pertaining to long-term debt are adequately disclosed **(PD3)**. All facts concerning stock issues such as the par or stated value of the shares, shares authorized and issued, and the number of shares held as treasury stock or subject to options are disclosed **(PD4)**.

generally occur infrequently, it usually is more cost efficient to adopt a primarily substantive approach in the audit. This is especially true when the company uses outside independent agents for the payment of bond interest and dividends.

CONSIDERATION OF INTERNAL CONTROL STRUCTURE COMPONENTS

The applicability of the internal control structure components to financing cycle transactions and balances is similar in many respects to that described earlier for the investing cycle. In the control environment, for instance, responsibility for the transactions is usually assigned to the treasurer or chief financial officer who must possess the integrity and competence to perform these duties. Major transactions will require authorization by the board of directors, and the board's audit committee may closely monitor activities and controls in this cycle.

The accounting system element of the information and communication component will generally provide for subsidiary ledgers for both bonds payable and capital stock. These may be maintained by entity personnel or outside agents. Applications of each of the categories of control activities can be found in the financing cycle and are commented upon in the next two sections.

Common Documents and Records

Several of the documents described in the investing cycle, such as stock and bond certificates and a bond indenture, are also important in the financing cycle except the perspective is changed from that of the investor to the issuer. As noted above, separate bondholder and stockholder subsidiary ledgers may be maintained. In addition, financing cycle transactions may involve entries in the general journal and cash receipts and disbursements journals for the issuance and retirement of debt and equity securities, the accrual and payment of interest, and the declaration and payment of dividends.

Functions and Related Controls

The following **financing functions** and related control activities are associated with the financing cycle:

- **Issuing bonds and capital stock.** Issues are made in accordance with board of directors authorizations and legal requirements, and proceeds are promptly deposited intact; unissued bond and stock certificates are physically safeguarded.
- **Paying bond interest and cash dividends.** Payments are made to proper payees in accordance with board of directors or management authorizations.
- **Redeeming and reacquiring bonds and capital stock.** Transactions are executed in accordance with board of directors authorizations; treasury stock certificates are physically safeguarded.
- **Recording financing transactions.** Transactions are correctly recorded as to amount, classification, and accounting period based on supporting authorizations and documentation; the duties of executing and recording financing transactions are segregated; periodic independent checks are made of agreement of subsidiary ledgers and control accounts, including confirmation with the **bond trustee** or **transfer agent**, if applicable.

Recall that even when the primarily substantive approach is adopted, it is necessary to obtain a sufficient understanding of the internal control structure components to plan the audit under that strategy. Accordingly, the auditor should obtain and document his or her understanding of each of the control structure components that affect the financing cycle as discussed in the preceding sections. With this knowledge, the auditor should be able to identify potential misstatements in financing cycle assertions, determine appropriate acceptable levels of detection risk, and design appropriate substantive tests.

LEARNING CHECK:

17-10 a. Describe the nature of the financing cycle.
b. Identify other cycles that interface with the financing cycle.

17-11 State the specific audit objectives that apply to the financing cycle.

17-12 Indicate the materiality, audit risk, and audit strategy matters that relate to the financing cycle.

17-13 Discuss the applicability of the internal control structure components to financing cycle transactions.
17-14 State and describe the functions that relate to financing cycle transactions.

KEY TERMS:

Bond trustee, p. 664
Financing cycle, p. 661
Financing functions, p. 664
Long-term debt transactions, p.662
Stockholders' equity transactions, p. 662
Transfer agent, p. 664

SUBSTANTIVE TESTS OF LONG-TERM DEBT BALANCES

OBJECTIVE 8

Discuss key considerations in determining detection risk and designing substantive tests for long-term debt assertions.

From an auditing standpoint, notes payable, mortgages payable, and bonds payable have similar characteristics. Generally, these forms of debt (1) involve interest-bearing contractual agreements, (2) require approval by the board of directors, and (3) may be secured by the pledging of collateral. For these accounts, there are relatively few problems in meeting audit objectives.

Ordinarily, a company will have infrequent transactions pertaining to long-term debt, but the amount per transaction is often very significant. Long-term debt transactions rarely present year-end cutoff problems. Thus, substantive tests of long-term debt balances may be performed either before or after the balance sheet date. It is customary for the auditor to test related expense accounts when liability balances are tested.

DETERMINING DETECTION RISK

Because of the nature and infrequency of most types of long-term debt transactions, inherent risk is often low for all related account balance assertions except valuation or allocation. Inherent risk for this assertion may be moderate or high due to complexities involved in computing amortization of bond discount or premium. Based on consideration of these factors and any relevant control risk assessments, an appropriate level of detection risk is determined for each significant assertion related to long-term debt balances.

DESIGNING SUBSTANTIVE TESTS

Figure 17-5 shows a list of possible substantive tests of long-term debt balances together with the specific audit objectives to which each test relates. From the possible tests, the auditor designs an audit program to meet the acceptable level of detection risk for each significant assertion. As in the case of accounts payable in Chapter 15, the auditor is primarily concerned about the understatement (completeness assertion) of long-term debt.

The auditor relies primarily on (1) direct communication with outside independent sources, (2) review of documentation, and (3) recomputations in obtaining sufficient competent evidential matter about the assertions pertaining to long-term debt balances. Audit working papers, such as the analysis of long-term notes

FIGURE 17-5 • POSSIBLE SUBSTANTIVE TESTS OF LONG-TERM DEBT ASSERTIONS

Category	Substantive Test	Account Balance Audit Objective (from p. 663)				
		EO#	C#	RO#	VA#	PD#
Initial procedures	1. Perform initial procedures on long-term debt balances and records that will be subjected to further testing. a. Trace beginning balances for long-term debt accounts to prior year's working papers. b. Review activity in all long-term debt and related income statement accounts and investigate entries that appear unusual in amount or source. c. Obtain client-prepared schedules of long-term debt and determine that they accurately represent the underlying accounting records from which prepared by: • Footing and crossfooting the schedules and reconciling the totals with the related subsidiary and general ledger balances. • Testing agreement of items on schedules with entries in related subsidiary and general ledger accounts.				✓1	
Analytical procedures	2. Perform analytical procedures. a. Calculate ratios: • Debt to total assets • Debt to equity • Times interest earned • Interest expense to debt b. Analyze ratio results relative to expectations based on prior year, budgeted, industry, or other data.	✓1,2	✓1,2		✓1	
Tests of details of transactions	3. Vouch entries in long-term debt and related income statement accounts.	✓1,2	✓1,2	✓1	✓1	
Tests of details of balances	4. Review authorizations and contracts for long-term debt.	✓1,2	✓1,2	✓1	✓1	✓1,3
	5. Confirm debt with lenders and bond trustees.	✓1	✓1	✓1	✓1	
	6. Recalculate interest expense.				✓1	
Presentation and disclosure	7. Compare statement presentation with GAAP. a. Determine that long-term debt balances are properly identified and classified in the financial statements.					✓1
	b. Determine the appropriateness of disclosures concerning all terms, covenants, commitments, and retirement provisions pertaining to long-term debt.					✓3

payable and interest in Figure 17-6, are used to document the auditor's tests. Each of the substantive tests is explained in a following section.

INITIAL PROCEDURES

As shown in Figure 17-5, the familiar initial procedures are applicable to long-term debt balances. The schedules involved may include separate schedules of long-term notes payable to banks, obligations under capital leases, and listings of registered bondholders prepared by bond trustees. As in each of the previous listings of possible substantive tests, these procedures pertain to the mathematical and clerical accuracy component of the valuation or allocation assertion, and are performed preparatory to using the long-term debt schedules as a basis for additional substantive tests.

ANALYTICAL PROCEDURES

Four ratios often used in applying analytical procedures to long-term debt balances, and the formulas for the ratios are as follows.

Ratio	Formula
Debt to total assets	Total liabilities ÷ Total assets
Debt to equity	Total liabilities ÷ Total equity
Times interest earned	Operating income (income before income taxes and interest expense) ÷ Bond interest expense
Interest expense to debt	Interest expense ÷ Average debt

Each ratio can be compared internally with prior period results and budget expectations. In addition, they can be used for external comparisons with industry data. Any unusual fluctuations should be investigated. These analytical procedures provide evidence about the existence or occurrence, completeness, and valuation or allocation assertions.

TESTS OF DETAILS OF TRANSACTIONS

For bonds, the auditor should obtain evidence on both the face value and net proceeds of the obligation at the date of issue. Issuances of debt instruments should be traced to cash receipts as evidenced by brokers' advices. Payments on principal of long-term debt can be verified by an examination of vouchers and canceled checks; payments in full can be validated by an inspection of the canceled notes or bond certificates. When installment payments are involved, their propriety can be traced to repayment schedules. Bonds may also be converted into stock. Evidence of such transactions is available in the form of canceled bond certificates and the issuance of related stock certificates.

When bond interest is paid by an independent agent, the auditor should examine the agent's reports on payments. The vouching of entries to long-term debt accounts provides evidence about the following four assertions: existence or occurrence, completeness, rights and obligations, and valuation or allocation. Again, the completeness assertion is addressed only in the sense that vouching debits to long-term debt provides evidence that entries made to reduce debt balances are not invalid. Vouching recorded entries will not reveal unrecorded long-term debt.

FIGURE 17-6 • NOTES AND INTEREST PAYABLE WORKING PAPER

WILLIAMS COMPANY
LONG-TERM PAYABLE AND ACCRUED INTEREST
DECEMBER 31, 19X1

W/P REF: N-3
PREPARED BY: C.J.G. DATE: 1/24/X2
REVIEWED BY: R.C.P. DATE: 1/30/X2

ACCTS. 220, 225, 475

	NOTES PAYABLE				INTEREST PAYABLE			
DESCRIPTION	BALANCE 1/1/X1	ADDITIONS	PAYMENTS	BALANCE 12/31/X1	BALANCE 1/1/X1	EXPENSE	PAYMENTS	BALANCE 12/31/X1
10% NOTE PAYABLE TO CULVER NATIONAL BANK, DUE \$100,000 PER YEAR TO 7/1/X3 (1)	300,000 ✓		100,000 ø	200,000 (CI) ⌿	15,000 ⋎	25,000 (R)	30,000 ⊖	10,000
9% NOTE PAYABLE TO FIRST TRUST COMPANY, DUE 9/1/X3 (2)		250,000 ✓ ø		250,000 (CI) ⌿		7,500 (R)		7,500
	300,000	250,000	100,000	450,000	15,000	32,500	30,000	17,500 ⌿
	F	F	F	FF To N-1	F	F To S-5	F	FF To N-1

(1) Long-term investments in stock of Afton Co. and Boley Inc pledged as security-see confirmation received from bank-A-4
(2) Land and building pledged as security-see bank confirmation-A-5
⋎ Traced to prior years working papers
⌿ Traced to ledger at 12/31/X1
(CI) Confirmed by bank-see A-4 and A-5
✓ Examined copy of note
⊖ Traced to cash journal and supporting documentation
(R) Recomputed interest expense-no exception
F Footed
FF Footed and crossfooted

TESTS OF DETAILS OF BALANCES

There are three substantive tests in this category: (1) review authorizations and contracts for long-term debt, (2) confirm debt with lenders and bond trustees, and (3) recalculate interest expense.

Review Authorizations and Contracts

The authority of a corporation to enter into a contractual agreement to borrow money through the issuance or incurrence of long-term debt rests with the board of directors. Accordingly, evidence of authorizations should be found in the minutes of board meetings. Normally, the auditor reviews only the authorizations that have occurred during the year under audit because evidence of the authorizations for debt outstanding at the beginning of the year should be in the permanent working paper file.

Authorization for the debt issue should include reference to the applicable sections of the bylaws that pertain to such financing. It may also include the opinion of the company's legal counsel on the legality of the debt. The review of contracts should also include the details of covenants and the entity's compliance therewith, and the details of obligations under capital leases. Evidence obtained from this test may pertain to all five assertion categories.

Confirm Debt

The auditor is expected to confirm the existence and terms of long-term debt by direct communication with lenders and bond trustees. Notes payable to banks in which the client has an account are confirmed as part of the confirmation of bank balances as explained in Chapter 18. Other notes are confirmed with the holders by separate letter. Such requests should be made by the client and mailed by the auditor. The existence of mortgages and bonds payable normally can be confirmed directly with the trustee. Each confirmation should include a request for the current status of the debt and current year's transactions. All confirmation responses should be compared with the records and any differences should be investigated.

Confirming long-term debt relates to the same assertions as confirming accounts payable; that is, existence or occurrence, completeness, rights and obligations, and valuation or allocation.

Recalculate Interest Expense

Evidence of interest expense and accrued interest payable is easily obtainable by the auditor. The auditor reperforms the client's interest calculations and traces interest payments to supporting vouchers, canceled checks, and confirmation responses. Accrued interest, in turn, is verified by identifying the last interest payment date and recalculating the amount booked by the client.

When bond interest coupons are involved, the auditor can examine the canceled coupons and reconcile them to the amount paid. When bonds were originally sold at a premium or discount, the auditor should review the client's amortization schedule and verify the recorded amount of amortization by recalculation.

This test is directed primarily at the existence or occurrence, valuation or allocation, and completeness assertions for interest expense and interest payable. It also provides evidence about the rights and obligations assertion for interest payable.

COMPARISON OF STATEMENT PRESENTATION WITH GAAP

In evaluating the appropriateness of the client's classification and disclosure of long-term debt, the auditor should be aware of applicable FASB Statements on Financial Accounting Standards (SFASs). The foregoing tests of inspecting debt contracts and confirming debt provide the client data for use in the comparison. This test relates to the presentation and disclosure assertion.

LEARNING CHECK:

17-15 What factors pertain to determining the acceptable level of detection risk for long-term debt transactions?

17-16 What substantive tests apply to the existence and valuation assertions for long-term debt balances?

17-17 Describe the nature of each of the following substantive tests and indicate the assertions to which each relates:

a. Vouch entries to long-term debt accounts.

b. Confirm debt.

c. Recalculate interest expense.

SUBSTANTIVE TESTS OF STOCKHOLDERS' EQUITY BALANCES

OBJECTIVE 9

Discuss key considerations in determining detection risk and designing substantive tests for stockholders' equity assertions.

As in the case of long-term debt, tests of stockholders' equity balances may be made prior to or after the balance sheet date. For these balances, the valuation or allocation and presentation and disclosure assertions involve maintaining the distinction between paid-in capital and retained earnings.

DETERMINING DETECTION RISK

Inherent risk assessments for assertions pertaining to stockholders' equity balances depend on the nature and frequency of transactions affecting the accounts. Routine stock transactions for publicly held companies are often handled by a **registrar** and **transfer agent.** In such cases, both inherent and control risk assessments for account balance assertions affected by these transactions may be low. Inherent and control risk assessments may be higher when there are nonroutine transactions involving stock issued in acquisitions, convertible securities, or stock options. Such factors must be considered in using the audit risk model to determine the acceptable level of detection risk for each significant assertion pertaining to stockholders' equity balances.

DESIGNING SUBSTANTIVE TESTS

A list of possible substantive tests of stockholders' equity balances and the specific audit objectives to which each test relates is illustrated in Figure 17-7. Each of the possible substantive tests is explained in a following section.

INITIAL PROCEDURES

The schedules referred to in Figure 17-7 for this group of procedures might include a trial balance of the stockholders' ledger or listings of stockholders supplied by the registrar and transfer agent. The auditor should test the agreement of the data in the schedules with any underlying accounting records and verify that the schedules or subsidiary ledgers agree with general ledger control accounts. This evidence pertains to the mathematical and clerical accuracy component of the valuation or allocation assertion.

ANALYTICAL PROCEDURES

Formulas for the ratios listed in Figure 17-7 are given below:

Ratio	Formula
Book value per share of common stock	Stockholders' equity ÷ Average shares of common stock outstanding
Return on common stockholders' equity	Net income ÷ Average common stockholders' equity
Equity to total liabilities and equity	Stockholders' equity ÷ Total liabilities and stockholders' equity
Dividend payout	Cash dividends ÷ Net income
Earnings per share	Net income ÷ Weighted average common shares outstanding

The financial relationships expressed in these ratios may be helpful in evaluating the reasonableness of stockholders' equity balances. The evidence obtained from these analytical procedures pertains to the existence or occurrence, completeness, and valuation or allocation assertions.

TESTS OF DETAILS OF TRANSACTIONS

This category of tests includes vouching entries in the paid-in capital and retained earnings accounts as explained in the following sections.

Vouch Entries to Pain-in Capital Accounts

Each change in a capital stock account should be vouched to supporting documentation. For a new issue of stock, the auditor can examine remittance advices of

FIGURE 17-7 • POSSIBLE SUBSTANTIVE TESTS OF STOCKHOLDERS' EQUITY ASSERTIONS

Category	Substantive Test	Account Balance Audit Objective (from p. 663)				
		EO3	C3	RO2	VA2	PD#
Initial procedures	1. Perform initial procedures on stockholder equity balances and records that will be subjected to further testing. a. Trace beginning balances for stockholder equity accounts to prior year's working papers. b. Review activity in stockholder equity accounts and investigate entries that appear unusual in amount or source. c. Obtain client-prepared schedules of changes in stockholder equity balances and determine that they accurately represent the underlying accounting records from which prepared by: • Footing and crossfooting the schedules and reconciling the totals with the related subsidiary and general ledger balances. • Testing agreement of items on schedules with entries in related subsidiary and general ledger accounts.				✓	
Analytical procedures	2. Perform analytical procedures. a. Calculate ratios: • Book value per share of common stock • Return on common stockholders' equity • Equity to total liabilities and equity • Dividend payout • Earnings per share b. Analyze ratio results relative to expectations based on prior year, budgeted, industry, or other data.	✓	✓		✓	
Tests of details of transactions	3. Vouch entries in paid-in capital accounts.	✓		✓	✓	
	4. Vouch entries in retained earnings.	✓		✓	✓	
Tests of details of balances	5. Review articles of incorporation and bylaws.	✓		✓		
	6. Review authorizations and terms of stock issues.	✓		✓		
	7. Confirm shares outstanding with registrar and transfer agent.	✓	✓	✓		
	8. Inspect stock certificate book.	✓	✓	✓		
	9. Inspect certificates of shares held in treasury.	✓	✓	✓		
Presentation and disclosure	10. Compare statement presentation with GAAP. a. Determine that stockholder equity balances are properly identified and classified in the financial statements. b. Determine the appropriateness of disclosures concerning all changes in stockholders' equity account balances during the period, par or stated values, dividend and liquidation preferences, dividends in arrears, stock option plans, conversion features, and treasury shares.					✓2 ✓4

FIGURE 17-8 • CAPITAL STOCK WORKING PAPER

Prepared by: A.E.R. Date: 1/12/x2

Reviewed by: R.C.P. Date: 1/12/x2

Willens Company
Capital Stock $100 par
12/31/x1

P-2

Acc. #600

	Authorized	Shares Issued and outstanding	Amount	
Balances, 1/1/x1	10000 ✓	5000 ✓	500000 ✓	
Shares issued at par for cash on 4/1/x1		1000 ɣ	100000 ɣϕ	
Balances, 12/31/x1	10000	6000 C	600000	To P-1

✓ Traced to prior years working papers
ɣ Traced to approval per minutes of Board of Directors meeting on 3/20/x1
ϕ Traced proceeds to cash receipts
C Confirmed by First Trust Company, transfer agent for the company - See P-3

Reviewed minutes of all Board of Directors meetings for evidence of capital stock transactions. Only reference was to transaction of 4/1/x1 as per above.

the cash proceeds from the issue. If the consideration for the shares was other than cash, the auditor should carefully examine the basis for the valuation, such as the market value of the consideration received or given. For the shares issued, market quotations may be useful in determining the propriety of the valuation; when the value of the property received is used, an appraisal may be necessary.

An analysis of a capital stock account is illustrated in Figure 17-8. Similar analyses are prepared for treasury stock and other stockholders' equity accounts.

The auditor should exercise care in determining the propriety of the accounting treatment for shares issued as part of stock option, stock warrant, or stock conversion plans or in connection with a stock split. Documentation of the cost of treasury stock should be available to the auditor in the form of authorizations in the minutes, disbursement vouchers, and canceled checks.

Evidence from vouching of entries to capital stock accounts relates most closely to the existence or occurrence, rights and obligations, and valuation or allocation assertions.

Vouch Entries to Retained Earnings

Each entry to retained earnings except the posting of net income (or net loss) should be vouched to supporting documentation. Entries for dividend declarations and retained earnings appropriations are traced to the minutes book. In determining the propriety of the distribution, the auditor should

- Establish that preferential or other rights of stockholders and any restrictions on dividend distributions have been recognized.
- Establish the number of shares outstanding on the date of record and verify the accuracy of the total dividend declaration by recalculation.
- Ascertain the propriety of the entry to record the declaration.
- Trace dividend payments to canceled checks and other documentation.

The client is also expected to furnish support for any prior-period adjustments. Vouching enables the auditor to ascertain whether (1) a proper distinction has been made between paid-in capital and retained earnings and (2) applicable legal and contractual requirements have been met. In addition to the valuation or allocation assertion, this test also relates to the existence or occurrence and rights and obligations assertions.

TESTS OF DETAILS OF BALANCES

Substantive tests in this category are explained in the next five sections.

Review Articles of Incorporation and Bylaws

Copies of the articles of incorporation and the bylaws should be in the auditor's permanent working paper file in the audit of a continuing client. The auditor should inquire of management and the client's legal counsel about changes in either or both of the documents. Preferably, the responses from both parties should be in writing.

In the initial audit of a corporation, the auditor will make an extensive review of the articles and bylaws and note key matters in his working papers.

This substantive test is designed to determine that capital stock has been legally issued and that the board of directors has been acting within the scope of its authority. Thus, this test provides important evidence about the existence or occurrence and rights and obligations assertions.

Review Authorizations and Terms of Stock Issues

All stock issues, stock reacquisitions, and dividend declarations should be authorized by the board of directors. Accordingly, a review of the minutes should provide evidence of stockholders' equity transactions authorized during the year.

Different classes of stock may contain restriction provisions or convey preferences in dividend declarations and liquidation. The auditor should examine each issue for such terms and make appropriate notation in the working papers.

This substantive test relates to the existence or occurrence and rights and obligations assertions.

Confirm Shares Outstanding with Registrar and Transfer Agent

When the client uses a registrar, the auditor should confirm total shares authorized, issued, and outstanding at the balance sheet date with the registrar. Confirmation with the transfer agent, in turn, provides evidence of shares held by each stockholder. The confirmation responses are then compared with the capital stock accounts and the stockholders' ledger.

The confirming of shares outstanding relates to the following three assertions: existence or occurrence, completeness, and rights and obligations.

Inspect Stock Certificate Book

This test is required when the client serves as its own transfer agent. Several steps are involved in the test. First, the auditor should examine the stock certificate book to determine that (1) stubs for shares issued and outstanding have been properly filled out, (2) canceled certificates are attached to original stubs, and (3) all unissued certificates are intact.

Second, the auditor should ascertain that the changes during the year have been correctly recorded in the individual stockholders' accounts in the subsidiary ledger. When there are numerous issuances and cancellations, this comparison may be done on a test basis.

Third, the auditor should reconcile the total shares issued and outstanding as shown in the stock certificate book with total shares reported in the stockholders' ledger and capital stock accounts.

This test relates to the same assertions as confirming shares with registrar and transfer agent.

Inspect Certificates of Shares Held in Treasury

If capital stock is held in the treasury, the auditor should count the certificates at the same time other securities are counted. Ideally, the count should be made at the balance sheet date. If this is not possible, there must be a reconciliation from the date of the count to the balance sheet date. The number of shares held should also be agreed to the shares shown in the treasury stock account. In inspecting the certificates, the auditor should note in the working papers the number of shares acquired during the year for subsequent tracing to the cash records.

This test pertains to the following three assertions: existence or occurrence, completeness, and rights and obligations.

COMPARISON OF STATEMENT PRESENTATION WITH GAAP

APB Opinion No. 12 provides that disclosure of changes in the separate accounts comprising stockholders' equity is required to make the financial statements sufficiently informative. Such disclosure may be made in the basic statements and notes thereto or be presented in a separate statement.

Disclosures related to the equity section include details of stock option plans, dividends in arrears, par or stated value, and dividend and liquidation preferences. The auditor obtains evidence about the presentation and disclosure assertion from the foregoing tests and from a review of the corporate minutes for provisions and agreements affecting the stockholders' equity accounts. In reviewing the minutes, the auditor should note whether any shares of stock have been reserved for stock option or similar plans, commitments for future issuance of stock in the purchase of or merger with another company, and restrictions limiting dividend payments or requiring minimum working capital requirements. Relevant evidence may also be obtained from discussions and communications with legal counsel.

LEARNING CHECK:

17-18 What considerations apply to determining the acceptable level of detection risk for stockholders' equity balances?

17-19 What substantive tests apply to the existence or occurrence and completeness assertions for stockholders' equity balances?

17-20 Identify the ratios that may be used in applying analytical procedures to stockholders' equity balances.

KEY TERMS:

Registrar, p. 670

Transfer agent, p. 670

SUMMARY

The investing and financing cycles have a number of similar characteristics. Transactions within each cycle occur infrequently, and internal controls over the processing of the transactions is generally good. From an auditing standpoint, it is common for the auditor to use a primarily substantive approach in meeting the second standard of field work and to perform extensive substantive tests of investing and financing cycle balances. Substantive tests for these balances normally provide very reliable evidence concerning management's financial statement assertions.

BIBLIOGRAPHY

AICPA Professional Standards:

SAS 1 (AU332), Long-Term Investments.

IAU 8 (AU8008B), Additional Guidance on Long-Term Investments and Segment Information.

Apostolou, Barbara, and Apostolou, Nicholas G. "Auditing Financial Futures," *The CPA Journal* (November 1987), pp. 110–113.

Byington, J. Ralph, and Munter, Paul. "Disclosures About Financial Instruments," *The CPA Journal* (September 1990), pp. 42–48.

Lamb, David. "Auditing Investments Accounted for by the Equity Method," *The CPA Journal* (March 1987), pp. 70–71.

Morris, David M., and Fisher, Donna J. "Investment vs. Trading—A Misnomer," *The CPA Journal* (May 1990), pp. 28–37.

Pomeroy, Harlan. "Restrictive Covenants: What the CPA Should Know," *Journal of Accountancy* (February 1981), pp. 61–68.

Stewart, John E., and Nuehousen, Benjamin S. "Financial Instruments and Transactions: The CPA's Newest Challenge," *Journal of Accountancy* (August 1986), pp. 102–112.

OBJECTIVE QUESTIONS

Indicate the best answer choice for each of the following multiple choice questions.

17-21 These questions relate to auditing the investing cycle.

1. An auditor testing long-term investments would ordinarily use analytical procedures to ascertain the reasonableness of the
   a. Existence of unrealized gains or losses in the portfolio.
   b. Completeness of recorded investment income.
   c. Classification between current and noncurrent portfolios.
   d. Valuation of marketable equity securities.
2. An auditor would most likely verify the interest earned on bond investments by
   a. Vouching the receipt and deposit of interest checks.
   b. Confirming the bond interest rate with the issuer of the bonds.
   c. Recomputing the interest earned on the basis of face amount, interest rate, and period held.
   d. Testing the internal controls over cash receipts.
3. Which of the following controls would be most effective in assuring that the proper custody of assets in the investing cycle is maintained?
   a. Direct access to securities in the safety deposit box is limited to only one corporate officer.
   b. Personnel who post investment transactions to the general ledger are **not** permitted to update the investment subsidiary ledger.
   c. The purchase and sale of investments are executed on the specific authorization of the board of directors.
   d. The recorded balances in the investment subsidiary ledger are periodically compared with the contents of the safety deposit box by independent personnel.
4. To establish the existence and ownership of a long-term investment in the common stock of a publicly traded company, an auditor ordinarily performs a security count or
   a. Relies on the client's internal controls if the auditor has reasonable assurance that the control procedures are being applied as prescribed.
   b. Confirms the number of shares owned that are held by an independent custodian.

c. Determines the market price per share at the balance sheet date from published quotations.
d. Confirms the number of shares owned with the issuing company.

17-22 This question applies to auditing the financing cycle.

1. An auditor's program to examine long-term debt most likely would include steps that require
   a. Comparing the carrying amount of the debt to its year-end market value.
   b. Correlating interest expense recorded for the period with outstanding debt.
   c. Verifying the existence of the holders of the debt by direct confirmation.
   d. Inspecting the accounts payable subsidiary ledger for unrecorded long-term debt.
2. An auditor's program to examine long-term debt should include steps that require
   a. Examining bond trust indentures.
   b. Inspecting the accounts payable subsidiary ledger.
   c. Investigating credits to the bond interest income account.
   d. Verifying the existence of the bondholders.
3. An auditor should trace corporate stock issuances and treasury stock transactions to the
   a. Numbered stock certificates.
   b. Articles of incorporation.
   c. Transfer agent's records.
   d. Minutes of the board of directors.
4. When a client company does **not** maintain its own stock records, the auditor should obtain written confirmation from the transfer agent and registrar concerning
   a. Restrictions on the payment of dividends.
   b. The number of shares issued and outstanding.
   c. Guarantees of preferred stock liquidation value.
   d. The number of shares subject to agreements to repurchase.

COMPREHENSIVE QUESTIONS

17-23 **(Controls and substantive tests for investment transaction)** You have been assigned to audit the "investments" account of one of your firm's older clients, the *D* Co. During the prior year, your client received more than $1 million from the sale of all its stock in a subsidiary. The proceeds from this sale were promptly invested in time certificates of deposit (CDs) having various maturities. More than one year has elapsed since the sale of the stock, and your client continues to invest the funds in CDs. Investment decisions are made by the company treasurer, who also is responsible for custody of the CDs.

During the current year, *D*'s treasurer obtained $100,000 from the surrender of a CD at maturity and invested the proceeds in another six-month certificate having an interest rate of 10%. This transaction was recorded on the books of the company as being for a CD bearing an interest rate of 8%. At the end of the six months, the treasurer redeemed this CD for its $105,000 maturity value. On the books of the company, the transaction was recorded as having been for $104,000, and the treasurer deposited that amount in the company's bank account prior to reinvesting the proceeds in another security.

REQUIRED

a. What internal controls could have prevented or permitted detection of the treasurer's action?
b. What substantive tests could you perform to discover this irregularity?

17-24 **(Substantive tests of investment balances)** In verifying investing cycle balances in the Travis Company, C.J. Kupec, CPA, recognizes that the following misstatements may occur or exist:

1. A mathematical error is made in accruing interest earned.
2. A 25% common stock investment in an affiliated company is accounted for on the cost basis.
3. Securities held by an outside custodian are in the treasurer's name.
4. Securities on hand at the beginning of the year are diverted to personal use in July and are replaced in December.
5. An authorized purchase is recorded at cost and the broker's fee is expensed.
6. Ten shares of stock reported to be on hand are missing.
7. Marketable equity securities are reported at cost, which is above market.
8. The schedule of marketable securities does not reconcile to the general ledger accounts.
9. Gain on a sale of securities is reported net of taxes.
10. Securities pledged as collateral on a bank loan are not disclosed.

REQUIRED

a. Identify the substantive test that should detect each misstatement.
b. For each test, indicate the financial statement assertion(s) to which it pertains.
c. Indicate the type of evidence obtained from the substantive test (i.e., physical, confirmation, documentary, written representation, mathematical, oral, or analytical). (Use a tabular format for your answers with one column for each part.)

17-25 **(Investments—audit objectives, confirmations, disclosures)** As a result of highly profitable operations over a number of years, Eastern Manufacturing Corporation accumulated a substantial investment portfolio. In the audit of the financial statements for the year ended December 31, 19X0, the following information came to the attention of the corporation's independent auditor (CPA):

1. The manufacturing operations of the corporation resulted in an operating loss for the year.
2. In 19X0, the corporation placed the securities making up the investment portfolio with a financial institution that will serve as custodian of the securities. Formerly, the securities were kept in the corporation's safe deposit box in the local bank.
3. On December 22, 19X0, the corporation sold and then repurchased on the same day a number of securities that had appreciated greatly in value. Management stated that the purpose of the sale and repurchase was to establish a higher cost and book value for the securities and to avoid the reporting of a loss for the year.

REQUIRED

a. List the audit objectives of the CPA's examination of the investment account.
b. Under what conditions would the CPA accept a confirmation of the securities on hand from the custodian in lieu of inspecting and counting the securities?
c. What disclosure, if any, of the sale and repurchase of the securities would the CPA recommend for the financial statements?

AICPA

17-26 **(Inspection of investment securities)** In connection with the audit of the financial statements of Belasco Chemicals, Inc., Kenneth Mack, CPA, is considering the necessity of inspecting marketable securities on the balance sheet date, May 31, 19X1, or at some other date. The marketable securities held by Belasco include negotiable bearer bonds, which are kept in a safe in the treasurer's office, and miscellaneous stocks and bonds kept in a safe

World Manufacturing Inc. Marketable Securities Year Ended December 31, 19X1

Description of Security			Serial No.	Face Value of Bonds	Gen. Ledger 1/1	Purch. in 19X1	Sold in 19X1	Cost	Gen. Ledger 12/31	12/31 Market	Dividend and Interest: Pay Date(s)	Dividend and Interest: Amt. Rec.	Dividend and Interest: Accruals 12/31
CORP.		YR.											
BONDS	%	DUE											
											1/15	300*b*, *d*	
A	6	91	21–7	10,000	9,400*a*				9,400	9,400	7/15	300*b*, *d*	275
D	4	83	73–0	30,000	27,500*a*				27,500	26,220	12/1	1,200*b*, *d*	100
G	9	98	16–4	5,000	4,000*a*				4,000	5,080	8/1	450*b*, *d*	188
Rc	5	85	08–2	70,000	66,000*a*		57,000*b*	66,000					
Sc	10	99	07–4	100,000		100,000*e*			100,000	101,250	7/1	5,000*b*, *d*	5,000
					106,900	100,000	57,000	66,000	140,900	141,650		7,250	5,563
					a, *f*	*f*	*f*	*f*	*f*, *g*	*f*		*f*	*f*
STOCKS											3/1	750*b*, *d*	
P 1,000 shs.			1,044		7,500*a*				7,500	7,600	6/1	750*b*, *d*	
Common											9/1	750*b*, *d*	
											12/1	750*b*, *d*	250
U 50 shs.			8,530		9,700*a*				9,700	9,800	2/1	800*b*, *d*	
Common											8/1	800*b*, *d*	667
					17,200				17,200	17,400		4,600	917
					a, *f*				*f*	*f*, *g*		*f*	*f*

Legends and comments relative to above:

a = Beginning balances agreed to 19X0 working papers.
b = Traced to cash receipts.
c = Minutes examined (purchase and sales approved by the board of directors).
d = Agreed to 1099 (tax form).

e = Confirmed by tracing to broker's advice.
f = Totals footed.
g = Agreed to general ledger.

deposit box at The Merchants Bank. Both the negotiable bearer bonds and the miscellaneous stocks and bonds are material to proper presentation of Belasco's financial position.

REQUIRED

a. What are the factors that Mr. Mack should consider in determining the necessity for inspecting these securities on May 31, 19X1, as opposed to other dates?
b. Assume that Mr. Mack plans to send a member of the staff to Belasco's offices and The Merchants Bank on May 31, 19X1, to make the securities inspection. What instructions should be given to the staff member as to the conduct of the inspection and the evidence to be included in the audit working papers? (*Note:* Do not discuss the valuation of securities, the income from securities, or the examination of information contained in the books and records of the company.)
c. Assume that Mack finds it impracticable to send a staff member to Belasco's offices and The Merchants Bank on May 31, 19X1. What alternative procedures may be employed to obtain assurance that the company had physical possession of its marketable securities on May 31, 19X1, if the securities are inspected (1) May 28, 19X1? (2) June 5, 19X1?

AICPA (adapted)

17-27 **(Evaluation of working paper for investments)** The schedule on page 680 was prepared by the controller of World Manufacturing Inc. for use by the independent auditors during their audit of World's year-end financial statements. All procedures performed by the audit assistant were noted in the "Legend" section at the bottom. The schedule was properly initialed, dated, and indexed, and then submitted to a senior member of the audit staff for review. Internal control was reviewed and is considered satisfactory.

REQUIRED

a. What information that is essential to the audit of marketable securities is missing from this schedule?
b. What are the essential substantive tests that were noted as having been performed by the audit assistant?

AICPA

17-28 **(Audit objectives and substantive tests for long-term debt and investments)** You were engaged to audit the financial statements of Ronlyn Corporation for the year ended June 30.

On May 1, the Corporation borrowed $500,000 from Second National Bank to finance plant expansion. The long-term note agreement provided for the annual payment of principal and interest over five years. The existing plant was pledged as security for the loan.

Due to unexpected difficulties in acquiring the building site, the plant expansion had not begun at June 30. To make use of the borrowed funds, management decided to invest in stocks and bonds, and on May 16, the $500,000 was invested in securities.

REQUIRED

a. What are the audit objectives in the examination of long-term debt?
b. Prepare an audit program for the examination of the long-term note agreement between Ronlyn and Second National Bank.
c. How could you verify the security position of Ronlyn at June 30?
d. In your audit of investments, how would you
   1. Verify the dividend or interest income recorded?
   2. Determine market value?
   3. Establish the authority for security purchases?

AICPA

17-29 **(Substantive tests, assertions, and types of evidence for financing cycle transactions)** The following transactions and events relate to financing cycle transactions in Weber Inc.

1. Declare cash dividend on common stock.
2. Issue bonds.
3. Pay bond interest.
4. Purchase 500 shares of treasury stock.
5. Pay cash dividend declared in 1 above.
6. Issue additional common stock for cash.
7. Accrue bond interest payable at year end.
8. Redeem outstanding bonds.
9. Establish appropriation for bond retirement.
10. Announce a two-for-one stock split.

REQUIRED

a. Identify the substantive test that should verify each transaction or event.
b. For each test, indicate the financial statement assertion(s) to which it pertains.
c. Indicate the type of evidence obtained from the substantive test (i.e., physical, confirmation, documentary, written representation, mathematical, oral, or analytical). (Use a tabular format for your answers with one column for each part.)

17-30 **(Substantive tests and disclosures for long-term debt)** Andrews, CPA, has been engaged to audit the financial statements of Broadwall Corporation for the year ended December 31, 19X1. During the year, Broadwall obtained a long-term loan from a local bank pursuant to a financing agreement that provided that the

1. Loan was to be secured by the company's inventory and accounts receivable.
2. Company was to maintain a debt-to-equity ratio not to exceed two to one.
3. Company was not to pay dividends without permission from the bank.
4. Monthly installment payments were to commence July 1, 19X1.

In addition, during the year the company also borrowed, on a short-term basis, from the president of the company, including substantial amounts just prior to the year end.

REQUIRED

a. For purposes of Andrews' audit of the financial statements of Broadwall Corporation, what substantive tests should Andrews employ in examining the described loans? *Do not discuss internal control.*
b. What are the financial statement disclosures that Andrews should expect to find with respect to the loans from the president?

AICPA

17-31 **(Substantive tests for stockholders' equity balances)** Jones, CPA, the continuing auditor of Sussex, Inc., is beginning the audit of the common stock and treasury stock accounts. Jones has decided to design substantive tests with control risk at the maximum level.

Sussex has no par, no stated value common stock, and acts as its own registrar and transfer agent. During the past year, Sussex both issued and reacquired shares of its own common stock, some of which the company still owned at year end. Additional common stock transactions occurred among the shareholders during the year.

Common stock transactions can be traced to individual shareholders' accounts in a subsidiary ledger and to a stock certificate book. The company has not paid any cash or stock dividends. There are no other classes of stock, stock rights, warrants, or option plans.

REQUIRED

What substantive tests should Jones apply in examining the common stock and treasury stock accounts?

AICPA

17-32 **(Confirmation of stock outstanding)** You are engaged in doing the audit of a corporation whose records have not previously been audited by you. The corporation has both an independent transfer agent and a registrar for its capital stock. The transfer agent maintains the record of stockholders, and the registrar checks that there is no overissue of stock. Signatures of both are required to validate certificates.

It has been proposed that confirmations be obtained from both the transfer agent and the registrar as to the stock outstanding at balance sheet date. If such confirmations agree with the books, no additional work is to be performed as to capital stock.

REQUIRED

If you agree that obtaining the confirmations as suggested would be sufficient in this case, give the justification for your position. If you do not agree, state specifically all additional steps you would take and explain your reason for taking them.

AICPA

CASE

17-33 **(Substantive tests of investment balances)** The Jones Company, located in Chicago, has been your client for many years. The company manufactures light machinery and has a calendar year closing. At December 31, 19X1, and 19X0, the following items appeared in the accounts applicable to investment securities. Investments in securities represent approximately 8% of total assets. Income from securities represents approximately 3% of income before federal income tax.

Balance Sheet Accounts	*19X0*	*19X1*
U.S. government certificates of indebtedness, 3% series D dated May 15, 19X0, due May 15, 19X2 (at cost)	$300,000	$300,000
Available-for-sale equity securities (at fair value):		
50 shares of AP Company	5,800	5,000
100 shares of UC Corporation	—	8,000
75 shares of IC Corporation	12,000	—
Investment in a 60% owned subsidiary —SUB, Inc.	50,000	50,000
Unrealized gain (loss) on available-for-sale securities (equity account)	1,450	(1,075)
Accrued interest receivable	1,125	1,125
Income Statement Accounts		
Interest income	9,000	9,000
Gain (loss) on sale of securities	(2,000)	3,000
Dividend income	13,000	14,000

The U.S. Government securities shown above are held at the Utah Banking Company. The AP Company securities are held in the Jones Company's safe and the UC Corporation securities are in a safety deposit box at the Chicago Bank Company, which is the company's bank. Access to the company's safe is limited to the treasurer or his assistant. Access to the safety deposit box is limited to any two of the treasurer, the assistant treasurer, or the controller. The securities of SUB, Inc., are also held by the Chicago Bank Company as collateral for a loan that the Jones Company has outstanding. SUB, Inc., has a June 30 closing and is audited by your firm.

Your tests of internal control indicate unusual strengths in the areas of cash receipts and cash disbursements. The treasurer is responsible for the physical control of securities, whereas the controller is responsible for the recording of all transactions affecting securities. An assistant to the assistant controller maintains an investment ledger that shows the name of each investment, the number of shares held or the face value of bonds, the date of purchase and sale, if applicable, the cost, the physical location of the securities and the income thereon. This person prepares monthly statements of securities on hand showing their description and cost. All purchases and sales of securities are authorized by the company's finance committee. The following audit program has been prepared for the examination of securities at December 31, 19X1.

1. *U.S. Government Securities:*
   a. Prepare a schedule of the securities at December 31, 19X1.
   b. Obtain direct confirmation from the Utah Banking Company as to description and amount of securities held.
   c. Trace the confirmation to the schedule and so indicate.
   d. Verify the interest earned for the year and accrued interest receivable at December 31, 19X1.
   e. Trace the appropriate totals to the general ledger accounts.
2. *Available-for-Sale Equity Securities:*
   a. Prepare an analysis of the securities account for the year under audit, including the market value of the securities at December 31, 19X1.
   b. Count AP Company securities at the company's office at the close of business on December 31, 19X1. Inspection of the securities should be in the presence of client's representative. Note the time of count, name of client's representative, and name of the auditor on the count sheet. Accompanied by the client's representative, inspect the UC Corporation securities at the Chicago Bank Company. Inspection should be completed at the close of business on December 31, 19X1. The same information should be shown on this count sheet as is indicated to be appropriate for the count sheet mentioned above. The count sheets should show the number of shares, the full name of security, and the type of security (preferred or common shares).
   c. Vouch purchases and sales by reference to brokers' advices. Compare authorizations of the finance committee to the schedule.
   d. Compare dividends received for the year with a published dividend record.
   e. Verify the recorded gain or loss on sale of securities.
   f. Trace the appropriate totals on the schedule to the general ledger accounts.
3. *Investment in 60% Owned Subsidiary–SUB, Inc.:*
   a. Request the Chicago Bank Company to confirm that it holds the securities for SUB, Inc., as collateral for a loan. The amount payable to the bank may be confirmed concurrently.
   b. Review the monthly statements of SUB, Inc., since your latest examination and compare them with the audited statements at June 30. Obtain an explanation of all unusual transactions and fluctuations.
   c. Discuss the December 31, 19X1, financial statements with the management of the company. Inquire as to material amounts not recorded.
   d. Establish that the intercompany accounts are in agreement at December 31.
   e. Record the company's equity in the net assets and net income of SUB, Inc. at December 31, 19X1.

REQUIRED

a. List the substantive tests that you believe are appropriate and identify the assertions to which each test relates.
b. List the substantive tests that you believe are inappropriate and give the reasons for your conclusion.
c. List additional substantive tests, if any, that you believe are appropriate and state why.

RESEARCH QUESTION

17-34 **(Fair value disclosures)** The FASB has issued *Statement of Financial Accounting Standards 107: Disclosures about Fair Value of Financial Instruments.* Subsequently, the Auditing Standards Division of the AICPA issued an interpretation of SAS 57, *Auditing Accounting Estimates,* titled "Performance and Reporting Guidance Related to Fair Value Disclosures." The interpretation provides guidance for auditors whose clients are disclosing the fair value of certain financial instruments in accordance with FASB Statement 107. It also provides guidance for auditors whose clients are disclosing voluntarily the fair value of assets and liabilities not encompassed by FASB Statement 107. Review both the FASB statement and the Auditing Standards Division interpretation referred to above and prepare brief summaries of each.

CHAPTER 18

AUDITING CASH BALANCES

LEARNING OBJECTIVES

After studying this chapter, you should be able to

1. Indicate the relationship of the transaction cycles to cash balances.
2. State the account balance audit objectives for cash.
3. Design and execute an audit program to achieve the audit objectives for cash balances.
4. Describe the irregularity known as *kiting* and how the auditor can detect it.
5. State the role of confirmations in the audit of cash balances.
6. Explain the use of a bank cutoff statement.
7. Describe the irregularity known as *lapping* and how the auditor can detect it.
8. Explain the unique features and audit procedures applicable to *imprest accounts* for petty cash and payroll bank balances.

GENERAL CONSIDERATIONS
- Relationship of Cash Balances to Transaction Cycles
- Audit Objectives
- Materiality, Risk, and Audit Strategy

SUBSTANTIVE TESTS OF CASH BALANCES
- Determining Detection Risk
- Designing Substantive Tests
- Initial Procedures
- Analytical Procedures
- Tests of Details of Transactions
- Tests of Details of Balances
- Comparison of Statement Presentation with GAAP

OTHER CONSIDERATIONS
- Tests to Detect Lapping
- Auditing Imprest Petty Cash Funds
- Auditing Imprest Payroll Bank Accounts

SUMMARY

BIBLIOGRAPHY

OBJECTIVE QUESTIONS

COMPREHENSIVE QUESTIONS

CASE

RESEARCH QUESTION

The previous four chapters focus on six defined transaction cycles that form a basis for organizing both (1) an entity's activities and (2) the audit of the effects of those activities on the financial statements. This chapter differs in that it focuses on auditing the cash balances that result from the cumulative effects of transactions in several of those cycles. We begin the chapter by considering the nature of cash balances and how they relate to the transaction cycles. Following the pattern of prior chapters, next we identify the appropriate specific audit objectives for cash and consider the applicability of the general concepts of materiality, risk, and audit strategy. Then, attention is given to procedures for auditing various types of cash balances, including procedures for detecting two special types of irregularities involving cash—*kiting* which involves interbank transfers and *lapping* which involves misappropriating cash receipts.

GENERAL CONSIDERATIONS

Cash balances include undeposited receipts on hand, cash in bank in general checking and savings accounts, and imprest accounts such as petty cash and payroll bank accounts. Certain balances, such as certificates of deposit, bond sinking fund cash, certain foreign currency balances, and other accounts that have restrictions on their use, should ordinarily be classified as investments rather than as part of cash balances.

RELATIONSHIP OF CASH BALANCES TO TRANSACTION CYCLES

OBJECTIVE 1

Indicate the relationship of the transaction cycles to cash balances.

Five transaction cycles relate directly to general cash balances, as shown in Figure 18-1. The cycles are revenue, expenditure, financing, investing, and personnel services. The production cycle does not have transactions that relate directly to cash. Note that the financing and investing cycles both increase and decrease cash, while the revenue cycle increases, and the expenditure and personnel services cycles decrease, cash. For many entities, the volume of revenue and expenditure cycle transactions is large and can also be large for the personnel services cycle. The volume and size of individual cash transactions in the financing and investing cycles vary greatly from one entity to another and can also vary greatly from year to year for a single entity.

AUDIT OBJECTIVES

OBJECTIVE 2

State the account balance audit objectives for cash.

Because (1) internal control considerations pertaining to the various transaction classes that affect cash and (2) the related transaction class audit objectives for those transactions are addressed in the previous four chapters, this chapter focuses primarily on substantive tests for cash balances. Accordingly, Figure 18-2 only includes account balance audit objectives for cash. Note that specific objectives are included for each of the five categories of financial statement assertions. The substantive tests used to meet these objectives are explained later in the chapter.

MATERIALITY, RISK, AND AUDIT STRATEGY

For many entities, the portion of current or total assets at any point in time represented by cash balances is a very small percentage. However, with transactions in five of the six transaction cycles affecting cash, the amount of cash flowing through the accounts over a period of time can be very large indeed. In fact, the volume of transactions that affects cash is usually greater than for any other account in the financial statements.

The high volume of transactions alone contributes to a significant level of inherent risk for certain cash balance assertions, particularly existence or occurrence and completeness. In addition, the nature of cash balances makes them susceptible to theft as numerous kinds of fraudulent schemes involving cash have borne out. In contrast to receivables or inventories, however, the risks pertaining to the rights and obligations, valuation or allocation, and presentation and disclosure assertions for cash are minimal due to the absence of complexities involving rights, accounting measurements, estimates, and disclosures.

Because of the unique aspects of cash, auditors tend to plan their procedures to detect much smaller levels of misstatements than for other accounts. Thus, even when the lower assessed level of control risk approach is applied in auditing the transaction cycles, auditors tend to perform a significant level of work on cash balances in the form of substantive tests as discussed in the following sections.

FIGURE 18-1 • RELATIONSHIP OF TRANSACTION CYCLES TO CASH

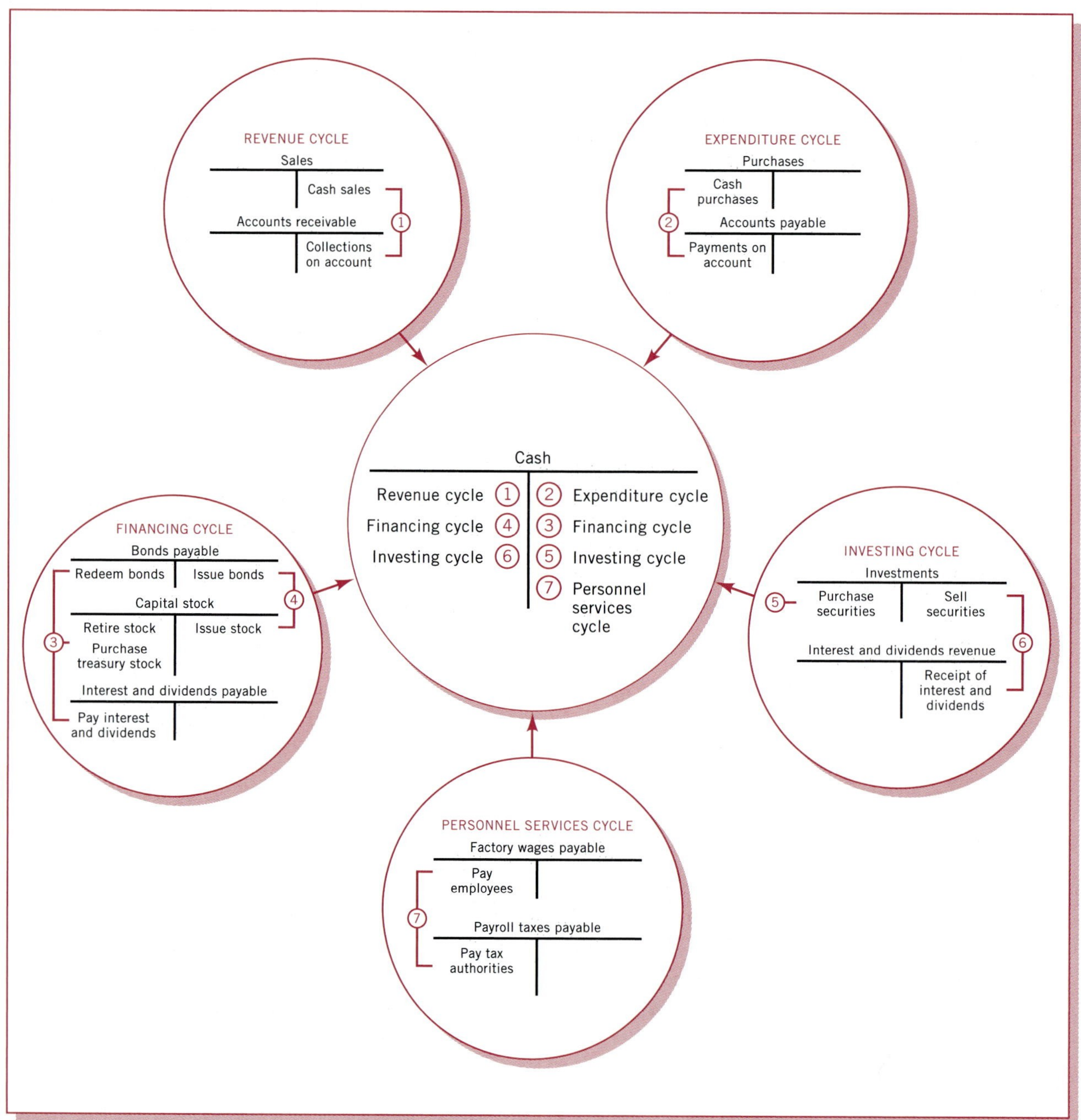

FIGURE 18-2 • SELECTED SPECIFIC AUDIT OBJECTIVES FOR CASH BALANCES

Assertion Category	Account Balance Audit Objectives
Existence or occurrence	Recorded cash balances exist at the balance sheet date **(EO1)**.
Completeness	Recorded cash balances include the effects of all cash transactions that have occurred **(C1)**. Year-end transfers of cash between banks are recorded in the proper period **(C2)**.
Rights and obligations	The entity has legal title to all cash balances shown at the balance sheet date **(RO1)**.
Valuation or allocation	Recorded cash balances are realizable at the amounts stated on the balance sheet and agree with supporting schedules **(VA1)**.
Presentation and disclosure	Cash balances are properly identified and classified in the balance sheet **(PD1)**. Lines of credit, loan guarantees, compensating balance agreements, and other restrictions on cash balances are appropriately disclosed **(PD2)**.

LEARNING CHECK:

18-1 Identify several types of cash accounts that should be included as cash balances on the balance sheet and several others that should not.

18-2 Which transaction cycles relate directly to cash and how?

18-3 a. State the account balance audit objectives for cash that are associated with each category of financial statement assertions.
b. Indicate the relative degree of inherent risk associated with each assertion category for cash balances.

18-4 Cash balances often constitute a very small percentage of an entity's current or total assets. Why then isn't less effort allocated to auditing cash balances?

18-5 What special considerations relate to applying the concepts of materiality and preliminary audit strategies to the audit of cash balances?

SUBSTANTIVE TESTS OF CASH BALANCES

In this section and the following subsections, the term *cash balances* refers only to *cash on hand and in bank,* excluding petty cash and other imprest funds. Because of their unique features, the latter are considered separately at the end of the chapter.

DETERMINING DETECTION RISK

Although the previous section noted that auditors typically perform a significant level of substantive tests on cash balances in nearly all audits, the nature, timing, and extent of those procedures can nonetheless be varied substantially to accommodate varying risk levels. In addition to the inherent risk factors discussed earlier in this chapter, the auditor should consider the relevant control risk assessments pertaining to cash receipts and disbursements transactions in each of the cycles affecting the cash balances. The methodology for combining control risk assessments for transaction class assertions that is explained in Chapter 9 on pages 316 to 319 is used in determining control risk assessments for the cash balance assertions. The audit risk model or a risk matrix is then used as illustrated in previous chapters to determine the acceptable level of detection risk for each cash balance assertion.

DESIGNING SUBSTANTIVE TESTS

OBJECTIVE 3

Design and execute an audit program to achieve the audit objectives for cash balances.

A listing of possible substantive tests to achieve the specific audit objectives for cash balances is presented in Figure 18-3. The listing is organized following the general framework for developing audit programs for substantive tests that is explained in Chapter 10 and that is used in each of the cycle chapters. Note that several of the tests apply to more than one audit objective, and that each objective is addressed by multiple possible tests. Not all of the tests are performed in every audit. Each of the tests is explained in a following section, including comments on when certain of the tests might be omitted and how some of the tests can be tailored based on applicable risk factors.

INITIAL PROCEDURES

The starting point for verifying cash balances is tracing the current period's beginning balances to the ending audited balances in the prior year's working papers (when applicable). Next, the current period's activity in the general ledger cash accounts should be reviewed for any significant entries that are unusual in nature or amount that require special investigation. In addition, any schedules prepared by the client showing summaries of undeposited cash receipts at different locations and/or summaries of bank balances are obtained. The mathematical accuracy of any such schedules should be determined and their agreement with related cash balances in the general ledger checked. This test provides evidence about the valuation or allocation assertion.

ANALYTICAL PROCEDURES

Cash balances are affected significantly by management's financing decisions and strategies. Consequently, in some audits these balances may not be expected to show a stable or predictable relationship with other current or historical financial or operating data. In other cases, however, the application of analytical procedures to cash balances may be useful. For example, cash balances and the percentage of cash to current assets can be compared to budgeted amounts, prior year balances, or other expected amounts. When reasonable expectations can be formulated and the data conform to those expectations, the analytical evidence may be viewed as providing some assurance as to the existence or occurrence, completeness, and valuation or allocation assertions for cash balances. This may reduce the amount of evidence required from other substantive tests relative to that required when the data do not conform to reasonable expectations.

FIGURE 18-3 • POSSIBLE SUBSTANTIVE TESTS OF CASH BALANCE ASSERTIONS

Category	Substantive Test	Cash Balance Audit Objective (from p. 689)				
		EO1	C#	RO1	VA1	PD#
Initial procedures	1. Perform initial procedures on cash balances and records that will be subjected to further testing. a. Trace beginning balances for cash on hand and in bank to prior year's working papers. b. Review activity in general ledger accounts for cash and investigate entries that appear unusual in amount or source. c. Obtain client prepared summaries of cash on hand and in bank, verify mathematical accuracy, and determine agreement with general ledger.				✓	
Analytical procedures	2. Perform analytical procedures: a. Compare cash balances with budgeted amounts, prior year balances, or other expected amounts. b. Calculate cash as percent of current assets and compare to expectations.	✓	✓1		✓	
Tests of details of transactions	3. Perform cash cutoff tests (note—these tests may have been performed as part of the audit programs for accounts receivable and accounts payable): a. Observe that all cash received through the close of business on the last day of the fiscal year is included in cash on hand or deposits in transit and that no receipts of the subsequent period are included, or b. Review documentation such as daily cash summaries, duplicate deposit slips, and bank statements covering several days before and after the year-end date to determine proper cutoff. c. Observe the last check issued and mailed on the last business day of the fiscal year and trace to the accounting records to determine the accuracy of the cash disbursements cutoff, or d. Compare dates on checks issued for several days before and after the year-end date to the dates the checks were recorded to determine proper cutoff.	✓	✓1			
	4. Trace bank transfers for several days before and after the year-end date to determine that each transfer is properly recorded as a disbursement and a receipt in the same accounting period and is properly reflected in bank reconciliations when applicable.	✓	✓2			
	5. Prepare proof of cash for any bank accounts the entity has been unable to reconcile or for which there is a high risk that fraudulent transactions have occurred.	✓	✓1,2	✓	✓	
Tests of details of balances	6. Count undeposited cash on hand and determine that such amounts are included in cash balances.	✓	✓1	✓	✓	
	7. Confirm bank deposit and loan balances with banks.	✓	✓1	✓	✓	
	8. Confirm other arrangements with banks such as lines of credit, compensating balance agreements, and loan guarantees or other parties.	✓	✓1	✓	✓	✓2
	9. Scan, review, or prepare bank reconciliations as appropriate.	✓	✓1,2	✓	✓	
	10. Obtain and use bank cutoff statements to verify bank reconciliation items, detect any unrecorded checks that have cleared the bank, and look for evidence of window dressing.	✓	✓1,2	✓	✓	

FIGURE 18-3 • (Continued)

Category	Substantive Test	Cash Balance Audit Objective (from p. 689)				
		EO1	C#	RO1	VA1	PD#
Presentation and disclosure	11. Compare statement presentation with GAAP: a. Determine that cash balances are properly identified and classified. b. Determine that bank overdrafts are reclassified as current liabilities. c. Make inquiries of management, review correspondence with banks, and review minutes of board of directors meetings to determine matters requiring disclosure such as lines of credit, loan guarantees, compensating balance agreements, or other restrictions on cash balances.					 ✔1 ✔1 ✔2

TESTS OF DETAILS OF TRANSACTIONS

As discussed previously in Chapters 14 and 15, some substantive tests of details involving the tracing and vouching of cash receipts and cash disbursements transactions are ordinarily performed concurrently with tests of controls as dual-purpose tests. The evidence from such tests should be combined with the evidence from the procedures discussed here in reaching a conclusion as to the fair presentation of cash balances. In the next three subsections, consideration is given to three tests of transactions that are generally performed at or near the balance sheet date.

Perform Cash Cutoff Tests

A proper cutoff of cash receipts and cash disbursements at the end of the year is essential to the proper statement of cash at the balance sheet date. Two **cash cutoff tests** are performed: (1) a cash receipts cutoff test, which is explained in Chapter 14, and (2) a cash disbursements cutoff test, as explained in Chapter 15. The use of a bank cutoff statement, described below, is also helpful in determining whether a proper cash cutoff has been made.

Cash cutoff tests are directed primarily at the financial statement assertions of existence or occurrence and completeness.

Trace Bank Transfers

OBJECTIVE 4

Describe the irregularity known as kiting and how the auditor can detect it.

Many entities maintain accounts with more than one bank. A company with multiple bank accounts may make authorized transfers of money between bank accounts. For example, money may be transferred from a general bank account to a payroll bank account for payroll checks that are to be distributed on payday. When a bank transfer occurs, several days (called the *float period*) generally will elapse before the check clears the bank on which it is drawn. Thus, cash on deposit per bank records will be overstated during this period because the check will be included in the balance of the bank in which it is deposited and will not be deducted from the bank on which it is drawn. Bank transfers may also result in a misstatement of the bank balance per books if the disbursement and receipt are not recorded in the same accounting period.

Intentionally recording a bank transfer as a deposit in the receiving bank while failing to show a deduction from the bank account on which the transfer check is drawn is an irregularity known as **kiting.** Kiting may be used to conceal a cash shortage or overstate cash in bank at the statement date.

An auditor requires evidence on the validity of bank transfers or, conversely, of misstatements therein. This is obtained by preparing a **bank transfer schedule.** Data for the schedule are obtained from an analysis of the cash entries per books and applicable bank and cutoff bank statements. The schedule lists all transfer checks issued at or near the end of the client's fiscal year, and shows the dates that the checks were recorded by the client and the bank, as illustrated in Figure 18-4.

If we assume all checks are dated and issued on December 31, check 4100 in Figure 18-4 has been handled properly because both book entries were made in December and both bank entries occurred in January. This check would be listed as an outstanding check in reconciling the general bank account at December 31 and as a deposit in transit in reconciling the payroll bank account. Check 4275 illustrates a transfer check in transit at the closing date. Cash per books is understated $10,000 because the check has been deducted from the balance per books by the issuer in December, but has not been added to the Branch #1 account per books by the depositor until January. Thus, an adjusting entry is required at December 31 to increase the branch balance per books.

Checks 4280 and B403 illustrate the likelihood of kiting because these December checks were not recorded as disbursements per books until January, even though they were deposited in the receiving banks in December. Check 4280 results in a $20,000 overstatement of cash in bank because the receipt per books occurred in December, but the corresponding book deduction was not made until January. Check B403 may illustrate an attempt to conceal a cash shortage because the bank deposit occurred in December presumably to permit reconcilement of bank and book balances, and all other entries were made in January.

Kiting is possible when weaknesses in internal controls allow one individual to issue and record checks (i.e., improper segregation of duties), or there is collusion between the individuals who are responsible for the two functions. In addition to tracing bank transfers, kiting may be detected by (1) obtaining and using a bank cutoff statement (as discussed in a later section) because the kited check clearing in January will not appear on the list of outstanding checks for December and (2) performing a cash cutoff test because the last check issued in December will not be recorded in the check register.

FIGURE 18-4 • BANK TRANSFER SCHEDULE

Check Number	Bank Accounts		Amount of Check	Disbursement Date		Receipt Date	
	From	To		Per Books	Per Bank	Per Books	Per Bank
4100	General	Payroll	$50,000	12/31	1/3	12/31	1/2
4275	General	Branch #1	$10,000	12/31	1/4	1/2	1/2
4280	General	Branch #2	$20,000	1/2	1/2	12/31	12/31
B403	Branch #4	General	$5,000	1/2	1/3	1/3	12/31

The tracing of bank transfers provides reliable evidence concerning the existence or occurrence and completeness assertions.

Prepare Proof of Cash

A **proof of cash** is a simultaneous reconciliation of bank transactions and balances with corresponding data per books for a specified period of time. The time period may be for one or more interim months or for the last month of the fiscal year. This test is generally made only when the auditor has concluded that a low level of detection risk for bank balances must be achieved. As illustrated in Figure 18-5, a proof of cash permits a reconciliation of four bank and book items: beginning balances, cash receipts transactions, cash disbursements transactions, and ending balances. The illustrated format may be extended to show the "true cash" balance by adding (or subtracting) book adjustments from the ending balance per books.

The following steps are helpful in preparing a proof of cash:

- Obtain the bank and book totals from the bank statement and cash in bank account, respectively.
- Obtain the beginning and ending balance reconciling items from the bank reconciliations at the designated dates.
- Determine the reconciling items for the two middle columns by analysis.

Because of expected weaknesses in controls, all book data should be verified for mathematical accuracy, and total receipts and disbursements should be vouched to corresponding cash journals.

All reconciling items in the schedule are attributable to either negating (for purposes of reconciliation only) items recorded by the bank that have not been recorded on the books, or recognizing items recorded on the books that have not been recorded by the bank. In Figure 18-5, for instance, the deposit in transit on November 30 is subtracted from December bank receipts because that deposit is not included in the December receipts per books. In contrast, deposits in transit on December 31 are added to receipts per bank and to the ending bank balance because this amount has been recorded on the books but not by the bank.

The occurrence of a dishonored customer check sometimes proves to be troublesome in preparing a proof of cash. When the bank receives notice of "not sufficient funds" (NSF) from the customer's bank, it issues a debit memorandum (often referred to as an *NSF charge*) that is posted as a debit on the depositor's bank statement to cancel the credit that was made when the check was originally deposited. The action taken by the depositor on notification of dishonor determines the effect on the proof of cash. The disposition of the NSF check in Figure 18-5 is based on the fact that the depositor made no entry on notification and that the check was not redeposited prior to December 31. Alternatively, if the client had reduced cash receipts for the NSF check on notification, both cash receipts and cash disbursements per bank would be $200 greater than book amounts. Thus, the effect in the proof of cash would be a $200 deduction in both the receipts and disbursements columns.

The failure of any of the four columns of a proof of cash to reconcile is indicative of an unexplained error or irregularity that should be investigated by the auditor. A proof of cash provides evidence about each financial statement assertion except presentation and disclosure.

FIGURE 18-5 • PROOF OF CASH WORKING PAPER

Prepared by: W.E.R. Date: 1/12/x2

Reviewed by: W.K.S. Date: 1/12/x2

Bates Company
Proof of Cash for December
12/31/x1

Acc. #10 City Bank - General — A-3

	Balance 11/30/x1	Receipts	Disbursements	Balance 12/31/x1
Per bank statement	115,261.40	912,274.60	907,273.53	120,262.47 C
Deposit in transit:				
Beginning (11/30)	21,320.81 ✓	(21,320.81)		
Ending (12/31)		26,269.94		26,269.94 ⊖
Outstanding checks:				
Beginning (11/30)	(27,264.45) ⌀		(27,264.45)	
Ending (12/31)			25,174.49 ⌀	(25,174.49)
Other items:				
NSF check			(200.00) Ɣ	200.00
Per books	109,317.76 ✗	917,223.73 ✗	904,983.57 ✗	121,557.92 ✗
	F	F	F	FF

C Traced to bank confirmation

✓ Traced to December bank statement

✗ Traced to cash in bank account

Ɣ Examined debit memo (See adjusting entry on WP AE-1)

⌀ Agrees with list of outstanding checks

F Footed

FF Footed and crossfooted

⊖ Traced to January cutoff bank statement

TESTS OF DETAILS OF BALANCES

There are five commonly used substantive tests of cash balances in this category. Each test is described in a following section.

Count Cash on Hand

Undeposited cash receipts and change funds are ordinarily considered cash on hand. To properly perform **cash counts,** the auditor should

- Control all cash and negotiable instruments held by the client until all funds have been counted.
- Insist that the custodian of the cash be present throughout the count.
- Obtain a signed receipt from the custodian on return of the funds to the client.
- Ascertain that all undeposited checks are payable to the order of the client, either directly or through endorsement.

VAULT TELLER LACKED CENTS

A long-term bank employee worked as a vault teller in a large commercial bank vault that contained large quantities of bagged coins. In previous audits, he had observed that the auditors selected bags positioned in the front rows of the bins for test counting because moving the front bags and counting the bags in the back of the bins was physically difficult. The vault teller devised a scheme to put pennies in the quarter bags in the back rows. A newly hired staff auditor misunderstood the audit instructions and attempted to physically count all bagged coins. On opening all the quarter bags, much to the dismay of the vault teller, the auditor discovered the irregularity which amounted to a $3,800 vault shortage. The vault teller confessed to the scheme and was prosecuted. New procedures were implemented to include periodic test counts and to open bags to verify correct denominations.

SOURCE: Hilliard T. Steele, ed. "Fraud Findings," *The Internal Auditor* (April 1990), p. 67.

The control of all funds is designed to prevent transfers by the client of counted funds to uncounted funds. The sealing of funds and the use of additional auditors are often required when cash is held in many locations. The safeguards pertaining to the custodian serve to minimize the possibility, in the event of a shortage, of the client claiming that all cash was intact when released to the auditor for counting.

This test provides evidence about each of the financial statement assertions except presentation and disclosure. It should be noted that the evidence about rights is weak because the custodian of the fund, such as a petty cash fund, may have substituted personal cash to cover a shortage.

Confirm Bank Deposit and Loan Balances

OBJECTIVE 5

State the role of confirmations in the audit of cash balances.

It is customary for the auditor to obtain a **bank confirmation** for cash on deposit and loan balances as of the balance sheet date. Figure 18-6 illustrates a *Standard Form to Confirm Account Balance Information with Financial Institutions.* This form was jointly developed and approved by the American Bankers Association, the AICPA, and the Bank Administration Institute. Notice that the form requests information about the following three items: (1) deposit balances, (2) loan balances,

FIGURE 18-6 • STANDARD CONFIRMATION FORM FOR BANK BALANCES

STANDARD FORM TO CONFIRM ACCOUNT BALANCE INFORMATION WITH FINANCIAL INSTITUTIONS

ORIGINAL
To be mailed to accountant

CUSTOMER NAME

Financial Institution's Name and Address [ ]

[ ]

We have provided to our accountants the following information as of the close of business on ______, 19___, regarding our deposit and loan balances. Please confirm the accuracy of the information, noting any exceptions to the information provided. If the balances have been left blank, please complete this form by furnishing the balance in the appropriate space below.* Although we do not request nor expect you to conduct a comprehensive, detailed search of your records, if during the process of completing this confirmation additional information about other deposit and loan accounts we may have with you comes to your attention, please include such information below. Please use the enclosed envelope to return the form directly to our accountants.

1. At the close of business on the date listed above, our records indicated the following deposit balance(s):

ACCOUNT NAME	ACCOUNT NO.	INTEREST RATE	BALANCE*

2. We were directly liable to the financial institution for loans at the close of business on the date listed above as follows:

ACCOUNT NO./ DESCRIPTION	BALANCE*	DATE DUE	INTEREST RATE	DATE THROUGH WHICH INTEREST IS PAID	DESCRIPTION OF COLLATERAL

also interest income

(Customer's Authorized Signature) (Date)

The information presented above by the customer is in agreement with our records. Although we have not conducted a comprehensive, detailed search of our records, no other deposit or loan accounts have come to our attention except as noted below.

(Financial Institution Authorized Signature) (Date)

(Title)

EXCEPTIONS AND/OR COMMENTS

Please return this form directly to our accountants: [ ]

[ ]

*Ordinarily, balances are intentionally left blank if they are not available at the time the form is prepared.

Approved 1990 by American Bankers Association, American Institute of Certified Public Accountants, and Bank Administration Institute. Additional forms available from: AICPA – Order Department, P.O. Box 1003, NY, NY 10108-1003

D451 5951

and (3) other deposit or loan accounts that may have come to the attention of the authorized bank official.

The confirmation request is prepared in duplicate and signed by an authorized check signer of the client. Both copies are sent to the bank, and the original is returned to the auditor. To assure the competency of the evidence from this procedure, the auditor should personally mail the request in his or her own return address envelope and the response should be returned directly to the auditor by the bank. Bank confirmation requests should be sent to all banks in which the client has an account, including those that may have a zero balance at the end of the year.

The confirming of cash on deposit provides evidence primarily for the following two assertions pertaining to cash in bank: (1) existence or occurrence because there is written acknowledgment that the balance exists, and (2) rights and obligations because the balances are in the name of the client. The response from the bank also provides some evidence for two other assertions. It contributes to the valuation or allocation assertion for cash in bank in that the confirmed balance is used in arriving at the correct cash balance at the balance sheet date. Furthermore, it contributes to the completeness assertion, but it cannot be relied on entirely because the respondent is not required to search bank records for deposit and loan balances not listed on the confirmation request form.

The confirming of loan balances provides evidence primarily for the following three assertions: (1) existence or occurrence because there is written acknowledgment that the loan balance exists, (2) rights and obligations because the loan is a debt of the client, and (3) valuation or allocation because the response indicates the amount of the loan balance. This test contributes to the completeness assertion in the same manner as confirming deposit balances.

Confirm Other Arrangements with Banks

Other arrangements with banks include such matters as lines of credit, compensating balances, and contingent liabilities. The arrangements for establishing a line of credit with a bank may require the borrower to maintain a cash balance with the bank. The amount may be an agreed-on-percentage of the amount borrowed, or it may be a specified dollar amount. The required minimum amount is referred to as a **compensating balance.** A contingent liability may exist when the client is the guarantor of a loan made by the bank to a third party.

If, after assessing inherent and control risk, the auditor believes such arrangements may exist, he or she should send a confirmation letter to the bank. The letter should specifically identify the information requested and be signed by the client. The AICPA has developed standard confirmation letters for the three arrangements identified above. Preferably, the letter should be sent to the bank official who is in charge of the client's relationship with the bank. Directing the letter to such an individual will expedite the confirmation process and enhance the quality of the evidence the auditor obtains. The auditor's request for information on line of credit and contingent liabilities does not require the respondent to make a detailed search of the bank's records. The confirming of other arrangements with banks is especially helpful in meeting the presentation and disclosure assertion. It also provides evidence for each of the other assertions. However, the evidence for the completeness assertion is limited to information known by the respondent.

Scan, Review, or Prepare Bank Reconciliations

When the acceptable level of detection risk is high, the auditor may scan the client-prepared **bank reconciliation** and verify the mathematical accuracy of the reconciliation. If detection risk is moderate, the auditor may review the client's bank reconciliation. The review will normally include

- Comparing the ending bank balance with the balance confirmed on the bank confirmation form.
- Verifying the validity of deposits in transit and outstanding checks.
- Establishing the mathematical accuracy of the reconciliation.
- Vouching reconciling items such as bank charges and credits and errors to supporting documentation.
- Investigating old items such as checks outstanding for a long period of time and unusual items.

The working paper for an auditor review of a client-prepared bank reconciliation is illustrated in Figure 18-7.

When detection risk is low, the auditor may prepare the bank reconciliation using bank data in the client's possession. When detection risk is very low or the auditor suspects possible material misstatements, the auditor may obtain the year-end bank statement directly from the bank and prepare the bank reconciliation. To do so, the auditor must request the client to instruct the bank to send the bank statement and accompanying data (paid checks, debit memos, etc.) directly to the auditor. This procedure will prevent the client from making alterations of the data to cover any misstatements.

The evidence provided by a bank reconciliation alone is generally not considered sufficient to verify the balance of cash in bank because of uncertainties concerning the following two most important reconciling items: (1) deposits in transit and (2) outstanding checks. Such evidence is obtainable only by tracing these items to the bank statement in the next accounting period. The procedure of obtaining a bank cutoff statement is designed, in part, for this purpose. When the cutoff statement validates these and other reconciling items, the reliance that an auditor can place on a bank reconciliation is significantly enhanced.

Scanning, testing, or preparing a bank reconciliation establishes the correct cash in bank balance at the balance sheet date. Thus, it is a primary source of evidence for the valuation or allocation assertion. This test also provides evidence for the existence or occurrence, completeness, and rights and obligations assertions.

Obtain and Use Bank Cutoff Statements

OBJECTIVE 6

Explain the use of a bank cutoff statement.

A **bank cutoff statement** is a bank statement as of a date subsequent to the date of the balance sheet. The date should be at a point in time that will permit most of the year-end outstanding checks to clear the bank. Usually, the date is seven to ten business days following the end of the client's fiscal year.

The client must request the cutoff statement from the bank and instruct that it be sent directly to the auditor. On receipt of the cutoff statement, with enclosed canceled checks and bank memoranda, the auditor should

- Trace all prior-year dated checks to the outstanding checks listed on the bank reconciliation.

FIGURE 18-7 • REVIEW OF CLIENT-PREPARED BANK RECONCILIATION

Prepared by: C.J.G. Date: 1/15/x2

Reviewed by: A.C.E. Date: 1/18/x2

Bates Company

(PBC) Bank Reconciliation - City Bank - General

Acc. #110 12/31/x1 A-1

Bank Acc. No. 12345-642				
Balance per bank				120262.47 ᛘ
Deposits in transit	Per books	Per bank		
	12-30	1-2	8425.15 √	
	12-31	1-7	17844.79 √	
				26269.94 ✗
Outstanding checks:				
		1047	225.94 √	
		1429	21600.00 √	
		1435	47.25 √	
		1436	1428.14 √	
		1437	1000.00 √	
		1440	832.08 √	
		1441	41.08 √	(25174.49) ✗
Add NSF check - R. Zim-12/29				200.00 ϕ
Balance per books				121557.92 ✗̸
Adjusting entry - see below				200.00
Balance as adjusted				121357.92
				To A
Adjusting entry				
Dr. accounts receivable R. Zim			200	
Cr. cash in bank				200
NSF check charged by bank 12/29 - See W/P AE-1				

ᛘ Agreed to bank statement and bank confirmation
√ Traced to cut off bank statement
✗ Footed
ϕ Traced to statement and debit memoranda
✗̸ Traced to general ledger

- Trace deposits in transit on the bank reconciliation to deposits on the cutoff statement.
- Scan the cutoff statement and enclosed data for unusual items

The tracing of checks is designed to verify the list of outstanding checks. In this step, the auditor may also find that a prior-period check not on the list of outstanding checks has cleared the bank and that some of the checks listed as outstanding have not cleared the bank. The former may be indicative of an irregularity known as kiting, which is explained on page 693; the latter may be due to delays in (1) mailing the checks by the client, (2) depositing the checks by the payees, and (3) processing the checks by the bank. The auditor should investigate any unusual circumstances.

When the aggregate effect of uncleared checks is material, it may be indicative of an irregularity known as **window dressing,** which is a deliberate attempt to overstate a company's short-term solvency.[1] In such a case, the auditor should trace the uncleared checks to the check register and supporting documentation and, if necessary, make inquiries of the treasurer.

The tracing of deposits in transit to the cutoff statement is normally a relatively simple matter because the first deposit on the cutoff statement should be the deposit in transit shown on the reconciliation. When this is not the case, the auditor should determine the underlying circumstances for the time lag from the treasurer and corroborate his or her explanations.

In scanning the cutoff statement for unusual items, the auditor should be alert for such items as unrecorded bank debits and credits and bank errors and corrections.

Inasmuch as the cutoff statement is obtained directly by the auditor from an independent source outside the client's organization, it provides a high degree of competent corroborating information about the validity of the year-end bank reconciliation and the existence or occurrence, completeness, rights and obligations, and valuation or allocation assertions for cash in bank.

COMPARISON OF STATEMENT PRESENTATION WITH GAAP

Cash should be correctly identified and classified in the balance sheet. For example, cash on deposit is a current asset. However, bond sinking fund cash is a long-term investment. In addition, there should be appropriate disclosure of arrangements with banks such as lines of credit, compensating balances, and contingent liabilities. A bank overdraft is normally reported as a current liability.

The auditor determines the appropriateness of the statement presentation from a review of the draft of the client's statements and the evidence obtained from the foregoing substantive tests. In addition, the auditor should review the minutes of board of director meetings and make inquiry of management for evidence of restrictions on the use of cash balances.

LEARNING CHECK:

18-6 a. Identify three different tests of details of transactions that can be performed in auditing cash balances.

---

[1] Assume at the balance sheet date, the client's balances show current assets of $800,000 and current liabilities of $400,000. If $100,000 of checks to short-term creditors have been prematurely entered, the correct totals are current assets of $900,000 and current liabilities of $500,000, which results in a 1.8:1 current ratio instead of the reported 2:1.

b. Which of these tests need not be performed when control risk pertaining to cash transactions and balances is low and the entity's bank accounts have been reconciled?

18-7 How does a *proof of cash* differ from an ordinary bank reconciliation?

18-8 a. What is meant by the term *kiting?*
b. What procedures can be used by the auditor to detect kiting?

18-9 What precautions should be taken by the auditor in counting cash on hand?

18-10 a. What types of information does the auditor seek to have confirmed on the standard form to confirm account balance information with financial institutions?
b. What assertions are addressed by the confirmation data?

18-11 a. What is a *compensating balance?*
b. What is the auditor's primary source of evidence about this item, and to what assertion does it pertain?

18-12 How may the auditor vary his or her work on bank reconciliations based on the applicable acceptable level of detection risk?

18-13 a. What safeguards should be taken by the auditor in obtaining a bank cutoff statement?
b. For what purposes does the auditor use a bank cutoff statement?

18-14 Identify several considerations the auditor should make regarding management's presentation and disclosure of cash balances.

KEY TERMS:

Bank confirmation, p. 696
Bank cutoff statement, p. 699
Bank reconciliation, p. 699
Bank transfer schedule, p. 693
Cash counts, p. 696
Cash cutoff tests, p. 692
Compensating balance, p. 698
Kiting, p. 693
Proof of cash, p. 694
Window dressing, p. 701

OTHER CONSIDERATIONS

This concluding section covers three topics: (1) tests to detect an irregularity known as lapping, (2) auditing imprest petty cash funds, and (3) auditing imprest payroll bank accounts.

TESTS TO DETECT LAPPING

OBJECTIVE 7

Describe the irregularity known as lapping and how the auditor can detect it.

Lapping is an irregularity that results in the deliberate misappropriation of cash receipts. It may involve either a temporary or a permanent abstraction of cash receipts for the personal use of the individual perpetrating the unauthorized act. Lapping is usually associated with collections from customers, but it may also involve other types of cash receipts. Conditions conducive to lapping exist when an individual who handles cash receipts also maintains the accounts receivable ledger. The auditor should assess the likelihood of lapping in obtaining an understanding about the segregation of duties in the receiving and recording of collections from customers.

Lapping Illustrated

To illustrate lapping, assume on a given day that cash register tapes totaled $600 and mail receipts opened by the lapper consisted of one payment on account by check for $200 from customer *A*. The lapper would proceed to abstract $200 in cash and destroy all evidence pertaining to the mail receipt except for the customer's check. The cash receipts journal entry would agree with the register tape ($600), and the deposit slip would show cash $400 and *A*'s check for $200. These facts can be tabulated as follows:

Actual Receipts		Documentation		Cash Receipts Journal Entry		Bank Deposit Slip	
Cash	$600	Cash tape	$600	Cash sales	$600	Cash	$400
A check	200		—		—	*A* check	$200
	$800		$600		$600		$600

In an effort to conceal the shortage, the defrauder usually attempts to (1) keep bank and book amounts in daily agreement so that a bank reconciliation will not detect the irregularity and (2) correct the customer's account within three to four days of actual collection so that any discovered discrepancy in the customer's account can be explained as a delay in receiving the money or posting. To accomplish the latter, the abstraction is shifted to another customer's account several days later as follows:

Actual Receipts		Documentation		Cash Receipts Journal Entry		Bank Deposit Slip	
Cash	$500	Cash tape	$500	Cash sales	$500	Cash	$400
B check	300	*A* check	200	*A* check	200	*B* check	$300
	$800		$700		$700		$700

The total shortage is now $300, $200 from the first example plus $100 from the second example.

Auditing Procedures

Tests to detect lapping are only performed when control risk for cash receipts transactions is moderate or high. There are three procedures that should detect lapping.

- *Confirm Accounts Receivable.* This test will be more effective if it is performed on a surprise basis at an interim date. Confirming at this time will prevent the individual engaged in lapping from bringing the "lapped" accounts up to date. Confirmation at the balance sheet date may be ineffective because the "lapper" may anticipate this procedure and adjust the "lapped" accounts to their correct balances at this date.
- *Make a Surprise Cash Count.* The cash count will include coin, currency, and customer checks on hand. The auditor should oversee the deposit of these funds. Subsequently, the details of the deposit shown on the duplicate de-

posit slip should be compared with cash receipts journal entries and postings to the customers' accounts.

- *Compare Details of Cash Receipts Journal Entries with the Details of Corresponding Daily Deposit Slips.* This procedure should uncover discrepancies in the details such as those shown in the two examples above. When there is appropriate segregation of duties in the handling of mail receipts, some auditors prefer to use prelists in this procedure. In such a case, the dates of the actual collections are compared with the dates of the postings of the collections to the accounts receivable ledger.

AUDITING IMPREST PETTY CASH FUNDS

The petty cash account is unusual in that it is audited even though its balance is almost always immaterial in amount. The reason is that material irregularities may occur in disbursing petty cash and in replenishing the fund throughout the year.

Internal Control Considerations

OBJECTIVE 8

Explain the unique features and audit procedures applicable to imprest accounts for petty cash and payroll bank balances.

A petty cash fund is established by transferring a specified amount of cash, such as $200 or $500 to an **imprest petty cash fund.** The following internal control features pertain to a petty cash fund:

- The fund should be maintained at the imprest level. That is, cash in the fund plus receipts for payments should always equal the imprest amount.
- The fund should be in the custody of one individual.
- The fund should be locked and stored in the safe when not in use.
- Disbursements from the fund should be for small amounts, and prenumbered receipts and documentation should support each payment.
- The fund should not be mingled with other receipts or other activities.
- Replenishment of the fund should be based on prenumbered receipts and a review of supporting documentation.
- Upon payment, supporting documents should be stamped PAID to prevent their reuse.

Substantive Tests

In auditing petty cash, the auditor performs tests of details of transactions and tests of balances. The extent of tests of transactions will vary with the auditor's specification of detection risk. When detection risk is high, the auditor may only test a very small number of replenishing transactions. The test will include reviewing supporting documentation, accounting for all prenumbered receipts, and determining that the reimbursement check was for the correct amount.

The test of balances involves the counting of cash in the fund. When the acceptable level of detection risk is high, the count is often made at an interim date rather than at the balance sheet date. When detection risk is low, one or more surprise counts may be made and the fund will also be counted at the balance sheet date.

AUDITING IMPREST PAYROLL BANK ACCOUNTS

As explained in the personnel services cycle, a company may use an **imprest payroll bank account** to pay its employees. In such a case, the bank account is typically handled on an imprest basis and is kept separate from the company's other bank accounts.

Internal Control Considerations

A payroll bank account is established by the deposit of the ongoing imprest balance such as $1,000. Internal controls over a payroll bank account include the following:

- An individual such as a paymaster or assistant treasurer should be authorized to sign checks drawn on the account.
- Only payroll checks should be written against the account.
- Each pay period a check for the total net amount payable to employees should be deposited in the payroll bank account.
- The payroll bank account should be independently reconciled monthly.

Substantive Tests

Both inherent and control risk should be low for the payroll bank account. Thus, the acceptable level of detection risk will often be high. Few, if any, problems should be encountered in applying substantive tests to the payroll bank account. The tests should include confirming the balance with the bank, reviewing the client's reconciliation, and using a bank cutoff statement. The adjusted or true cash balance at the balance sheet date should be the imprest amount. The only reconciling items on the bank statement should be outstanding checks made out to employees. Because employees usually cash their paychecks promptly, most or all of the outstanding checks should clear the bank in time to appear on the cutoff statement.

LEARNING CHECK:

18-15 a. What is *lapping?*
b. What circumstance is conducive to lapping?

18-16 a. What precautions are taken by the embezzler to prevent detection of lapping?
b. What tests can the auditor use to detect lapping?

18-17 What internal control features are applicable to petty cash?

18-18 Identify the tests of details that an auditor may use in auditing petty cash.

18-19 What internal controls are applicable to a payroll bank account?

18-20 Identify the tests of details that an auditor may use in auditing a payroll bank account.

KEY TERMS:

Imprest payroll bank account, p. 705
Imprest petty cash fund, p. 704
Lapping, p. 702

SUMMARY

The verification of cash balances is an important part of a financial statement audit because even though the balances as of the balance sheet date may appear immaterial relative to other assets, the amount of cash flowing through the accounts during the audit period can be very material. In addition, cash is susceptible to misappropriation and is involved in many fraudulent schemes including kiting and lapping. Thus, several types of substantive tests of cash balances are performed on most audits including, among others, cash cutoff tests, tracing bank transfers, counting cash on hand, confirming certain balances and other arrangements with banks, scanning, reviewing or preparing bank reconciliations, obtaining and using bank cutoff statements, and determining the adequacy of management's presentation and disclosures pertaining to cash balances.

BIBLIOGRAPHY

Braid, Michael. "Counting the Cash," *The CPA Journal* (September 1979), pp. 82–84.

Carleton, Camryn O., and Compton, John C. "Bank Confirmations: A New Look," *The CPA Journal* (January 1988), pp. 93–96.

Carmichael, Douglas R. "Audit Reporting Considerations for the New Statement of Cash Flows," *The CPA Journal* (June 1988), pp. 72–73.

Compton, John C. and Van Son, W. Peter. "Check Truncation: The Auditor's Dilemma," *Journal of Accountancy* (January 1983), pp. 36–38.

Doppelt, Andrew B. "The Telltale Signs of Money Laundering," *Journal of Accountancy* (March 1990), pp. 31–33.

Sauls, Walter S. "Developing a Kite-Detection System," *The Internal Auditor* (December 1984), pp. 39–42.

OBJECTIVE QUESTIONS

Indicate the best answer for each of the following multiple choice questions.

18-21 These questions relate to substantive tests of cash on hand and in bank.

1. The primary evidence regarding year-end bank balances is documented in the
   a. Standard bank confirmations.
   b. Bank reconciliations.
   c. Interbank transfer schedule.
   d. Bank deposit lead schedule.

2. Which of the following cash transfers results in a misstatement of cash at December 31, 1987?

Bank Transfer Schedule

	Disbursement		Receipt	
Transfer	Recorded in books	Paid by bank	Recorded in books	Received by bank
a.	12/31/87	1/4/88	12/31/87	12/31/87
b.	1/4/88	1/5/88	12/31/87	1/4/88
c.	12/31/87	1/5/88	12/31/87	1/4/88
d.	1/4/88	1/11/88	1/4/88	1/4/88

3. The auditor's count of the client's cash should be coordinated to coincide with
   a. Study of the internal control structure with respect to cash.
   b. Close of business on the balance sheet date.
   c. Count of marketable securities.
   d. Count of inventories.

4. Which of the following is one of the better auditing techniques that might be used by an auditor to detect kiting?
   a. Review composition of authenticated deposit slips.
   b. Review subsequent bank statements and canceled checks received directly from the banks.
   c. Prepare a schedule of bank transfers from the client's books.
   d. Prepare year-end bank reconciliations.

5. A cash shortage may be concealed by transporting funds from one location to another or by converting negotiable assets to cash. Because of this, which of the following is vital?
   a. Simultaneous confirmations.
   b. Simultaneous bank reconciliations.
   c. Simultaneous verification.
   d. Simultaneous surprise cash count.

18-22 This question pertains to substantive tests for petty cash and lapping.

1. Under which of the following circumstances would an auditor be most likely to intensify an examination of a $500 imprest petty cash fund?
   a. Reimbursement vouchers are not prenumbered.
   b. Reimbursement occurs twice each week.
   c. The custodian occasionally uses the cash fund to cash employee checks.
   d. The custodian endorses reimbursement checks.

2. An auditor confirms a representative number of open accounts receivable as of December 31, 19X2, and investigates respondents' exceptions and comments. By this procedure, the auditor would be most likely to learn of which of the following?
   a. One of the cashiers has been covering a personal embezzlement by lapping.
   b. One of the sales clerks has not been preparing charge slips for credit sales to family and friends.
   c. One of the EDP control clerks has been removing all sales invoices applicable to his account from the data file.
   d. The credit manager has misappropriated remittances from customers whose accounts have been written off.

3. Which of the following would be the best protection for a company that wishes to prevent the "lapping" of trade accounts receivable?
   a. Segregate duties so that the bookkeeper in charge of the general ledger has no access to incoming mail.
   b. Segregate duties so that no employee has access to both checks from customers and currency from daily cash receipts.
   c. Have customers send payments directly to the company's depository bank.
   d. Request that customers' payment checks to be made payable to the company and addressed to the treasurer.

COMPREHENSIVE QUESTIONS

18-23 **(Audit program for cash balances)** MLG Company's auditor received directly from the banks, confirmations and cutoff statements with related checks and deposit tickets for

MLG's three general-purpose bank accounts. The auditor determined that control risk for cash balance assertions was low. The proper cutoff of external cash receipts and disbursements was established. No bank accounts were opened or closed during the year.

REQUIRED

Prepare the audit program of substantive procedures to verify MLG's bank balances. Ignore any other cash accounts.

AICPA (adapted)

18-24 **(Selected substantive tests for cash balances)** Lingham Company's fiscal year ends on April 30, and the company's certified public accountant, Sanders & Stein, conducts the annual audit during May and June. Sanders & Stein has prepared auditing procedures for the different phases of the audit engagement with Lingham Company. Included among the audit program steps for cash on deposit with the Union State Bank are the following:

1. Obtain a bank confirmation as of April 30, 19X0, directly from Union State Bank.
2. Prepare a proof of cash for the month of April 19X0.
3. Obtain a cutoff bank statement directly from Union State Bank for a fifteen-day period (May 15) subsequent to the close of operations on April 30, 19X0.

REQUIRED

a. Why should Sanders & Stein obtain a bank confirmation directly from the Union State Bank?
b. What is a "proof of cash," and why is it important in the audit of the cash in the bank account?
c. What is the purpose of obtaining a cutoff bank statement for a fifteen-day period after the end of Lingham Company's fiscal year?

ICMA

18-25 **(Cash irregularities)** The Patricia Company had poor internal control over its cash transactions. Facts about its cash position at November 30, 19X0, were as follows:

The cashbook showed a balance of $18,901.62, which included undeposited receipts. A credit of $100 on the bank's records did not appear on the books of the company. The balance per bank statement was $15,550. Outstanding checks were: #62 for $116.25, #183 for $150, #284 for $253.25, #8621 for $190.71, #8623 for $206.80, and #8632 for $145.28.

The cashier abstracted all undeposited receipts in excess of $3,794.41 and prepared the following reconciliation:

Balance per books, November 30, 19X0		$18,901.62
Add: Outstanding checks:		
8621	$190.71	
8623	206.80	
8632	145.28	442.79
		$19,344.41
Less: undeposited receipts		3,794.41
Balance per bank, November 30, 19X0		$15,550.00
Deduct: unrecorded credit		100.00
True cash, November 30, 19X0		$15,450.00

REQUIRED

a. Prepare a working paper showing how much the cashier abstracted.
b. How did he attempt to conceal his theft?
c. Using only the information given, name two specific features of internal control that were apparently lacking.

AICPA

18-26 **(Substantive tests for cash balances)** You are the in-charge accountant examining the financial statements of the Gutzler Company for the year ended December 31, 19X0. During late October 19X0, you, with the help of Gutzler's controller, completed an internal control questionnaire and prepared the appropriate memoranda describing Gutzler's accounting procedures. Your comments relative to cash receipts are as follows:

All cash receipts are sent directly to the accounts receivable clerk with no processing by the mail department. The accounts receivable clerk keeps the cash receipts journal, prepares the bank deposit slip in duplicate, posts from the deposit slip to the subsidiary accounts receivable ledger, and mails the deposit to the bank.

The controller receives the validated deposit slips directly (unopened) from the bank. He also receives the monthly bank statement directly (unopened) from the bank and promptly reconciles it.

At the end of each month, the accounts receivable clerk notifies the general ledger clerk by journal voucher of the monthly totals of the cash receipts journal for posting to the general ledger.

Each month, with regard to the general ledger cash account, the general ledger clerk makes an entry to record the total debits to cash from the cash receipts journal. In addition, the general ledger clerk on occasion makes debit entries in the general ledger cash account from sources other than the cash receipts journal (e.g., funds borrowed from the bank).

Certain standard auditing procedures that are listed below have already been performed by you in the audit of cash receipts. The extent to which these procedures were performed is not relevant to the question.

1. Total and cross-total all columns in the cash receipts journal.
2. Trace postings from the cash receipts journal to the general ledger.
3. Examine remittance advices and related correspondence to support entries in the cash receipts journal.

REQUIRED

Considering Gutzler's internal control over cash receipts and standard auditing procedures already performed, list all other auditing procedures and reasons therefor which should be performed to obtain sufficient audit evidence regarding cash receipts. Do not discuss the procedures for cash disbursements and cash balances. Also do not discuss the extent to which any of the procedures are to be performed. Assume adequate controls exist to assure that all sales transactions are recorded. Organize your answer sheet as follows:

Other Audit Procedures	Reasons for Other Audit Procedures

AICPA

18-27 **(Review of client-prepared bank reconciliation)** The following client-prepared bank reconciliation is being examined by Kautz, CPA, during an examination of the financial statements of Cynthia Company:

Cynthia Company
BANK RECONCILIATION
VILLAGE BANK ACCOUNT 2
December 31, 19X2

Balance per bank (a)		$18,375.91
Deposits in Transit (b)		
12/30	1,471.10	
12/31	2,840.69	4,311.79
Subtotal		22,687.70
Outstanding checks (c)		
837	6,000.00	
1941	671.80	
1966	320.00	
1984	1,855.42	
1985	3,621.22	
1987	2,576.89	
1991	4,420.88	(19,466.21)
Subtotal		3,221.49
NSF check returned 12/29 (d)		200.00
Bank charges		5.50
Error Check No. 1932		148.10
Customer note collected by the bank ($2,750 plus $275 interest) (e)		(3,025.00)
Balance per books (f)		$ 550.09

REQUIRED

Indicate one or more auditing procedures that should be performed by Kautz in gathering evidence in support of each of the items (a) through (f) above.

AICPA

18-28 **(Bank transfer schedule; kiting)** The LMN Company maintains three bank accounts: City Bank–Regular, City Bank–Payroll, and Metro Bank–Special. Your analysis of cash disbursements records for the period June 23 to July 6 reveals the following bank transfers:

Check No.	Date of Check	Bank Drawn On	Payee	Amount
2476	June 23	Regular	Payroll	$100,000
2890	June 25	Regular	Payroll	200,000
3140	June 28	Regular	Special	100,000
A1006	June 29	Special	Payroll	50,000
A1245	June 30	Special	Regular	25,000
3402	June 30	Regular	Special	125,000

You determine the following facts about each of the first five checks: (1) the date of the cash disbursements journal entry is the same as the date of the check, (2) the payee receives the check two days later, (3) the payee records and deposits the check on the day it is received, and (4) it takes five days for a deposited check to clear banking channels and be paid by the bank on which it is drawn. Check 3402 was not recorded as a disbursement until July 1. This check was picked up by the payee on the date it was issued, and it was included in the payee's after-hours bank deposit on June 30.

REQUIRED

a. What are the purposes of the audit of bank transfers?
b. Prepare a bank transfer schedule as of June 30 using the format illustrated in Figure 18-4.
c. Prepare separate adjusting entries for any checks that require adjustment.
d. In the reconciliation for the three bank accounts, indicate the check numbers that should appear as (1) an outstanding check or (2) a deposit in transit.
e. Which check(s) may be indicative of kiting?

18-29 **(Proof of cash)** Data pertaining to the bank account of the Damon Company are as follows:

1. Balance in cash in bank, per books: November 30, $38,500; December 31, $47,030.
2. Balance per bank: November 30, $39,580; December 31, $44,500.
3. Deposits in transit: November 30, $5,200; December 31, $6,500.
4. Outstanding checks: November 30, $6,300; December 31, $4,300.
5. Bank service charge: November 30, $20; December 31, $30. Damon records service charges in the following month.
6. NSF charge in December: $300. Damon made no entry on notification. The check was redeposited in January.
7. Total deposits for December per the bank statement: $247,700.
8. December cash receipts per books (including deposits in transit): $250,000.
9. December cash disbursements per books: $241,470.

REQUIRED

a. Prepare a proof of cash for the month of December.
b. Did any irregularities occur? Explain.
c. What is the true cash balance at December 31?

18-30 **(Substantive tests, related assertions, and types of evidence)** As the senior auditor on the audit of the Elles Company for the year ending December 31, you discover the following errors in cash working papers prepared by your assistants:

1. Compensating bank balances were overlooked.
2. Kiting was missed.
3. Several December 31 checks were not recorded as disbursements until January. These checks are not listed as outstanding on the December 31 bank reconciliation.
4. The petty cash on hand was $25 short of the imprest fund balance.
5. The December cash disbursements journal included the checks issued January 2 and 3.
6. The December 31 bank balance per the bank on the bank reconciliation was incorrect.
7. Several mathematical errors were made in preparing cash schedules.
8. Year-end bank transfers were incorrectly accounted for.
9. A contingent liability to the bank as an endorser was missed.
10. Aggregated cash balances at December 31 were substantially below budget expectations.
11. Contingent liabilities to a bank noted in the working papers were not reported in the balance sheet.

REQUIRED

a. Identify the substantive test of balances that should have detected each error.
b. For each test of balances indicate the financial statement assertions to which it pertains.
c. Indicate the type of evidential matter (i.e., physical, confirmations, documentary, written representations, mathematical, oral, or analytical) obtained from each substantive test. (Use a tabular format for your answers with one column for each part.)

18-31 **(Procedures to detect lapping)** During the year, Strang Corporation began to encounter cash flow difficulties, and a cursory review by management revealed receivable collection problems. Strang's management engaged Stanley, CPA, to perform a special investigation. Stanley studied the billing and collection cycle and noted the following:

The accounting department employs one bookkeeper who receives and opens all incoming mail. This bookkeeper is also responsible for depositing receipts, filing remittance advices on a daily basis, recording receipts in the cash receipts journal, and posting receipts in the individual customer accounts and the general ledger accounts. There are no cash sales. The bookkeeper prepares and controls the mailing of monthly statements to customers.

The concentration of functions and the receivable collection problems caused Stanley to suspect that a systematic defalcation of customers' payments through a delayed posting of remittances (lapping of accounts receivable) is present. Stanley was surprised to find that no customers complained about receiving erroneous monthly statements.

REQUIRED

Identify the procedures that Stanley should perform to determine whether lapping exists. Do not discuss deficiencies in the internal control structure.

AICPA

18-32 **(Impress petty cash fund controls)** Mr. William Green recently acquired the financial controlling interest of Importers and Wholesalers, Inc., importers and distributors of cutlery. In his review of the duties of employees, Mr. Green became aware of loose practices in the operation of the petty cash fund, which has a working balance of about $200 and about $500 is expended by the fund each month.

You have been engaged as the company's CPA and Mr. Green's first request is that you suggest a system of sound practices for the operation of the petty cash fund.

REQUIRED

Prepare a letter to Mr. Green containing your recommendations for good internal control procedures for the operation of the petty cash fund. (Where the effect of the control procedure is not evident, give the reason for the procedure.)

AICPA (adapted)

18-33 **(Imprest petty cash fund audit procedures)** A surprise count of the *Y* Company's imprest petty cash fund, carried on the books at $5,000, was made on November 10, 19X0.

The company acts as agent for an Express Company in the issuance and sale of money orders. Blank money orders are held by the cashier for issuance upon payments of the designated amounts by employees. Settlement with the Express Company is made weekly with its representative who calls at the *Y* Company office. At that time he collects for orders issued, accounts for unissued orders, and leaves additional blank money orders serially numbered.

The items presented by the cashier as composing the fund were:

Currency (bills and coin)		$2,200
Cashed checks		500
Vouchers (made out in pencil and signed by recipient)		740
N.S.F. checks (dated June 10 and 15, 19X0)		260
Copy of petty cash receipt vouchers:		
Return of expense advance	$200	
Sale of money orders (#C1015-1021)	100	300
Blank money orders—claimed to have been purchased for $100 each from the Express Company (#C1022 to 1027)		600

At the time of the count, there was also on hand the following:

Unissued money orders #C1028-1037.
Unclaimed wage envelopes (sealed and amounts not shown).

The following day the custodian of the fund produced vouchers aggregating $400 and explained that these vouchers had been temporarily misplaced the previous day. They were for wage advances to employees.

REQUIRED

a. Show the proper composition of the fund at November 10, 19X0.
b. State the auditing procedures necessary for the verification of the items in the fund.

AICPA

CASE

18-34 **(Proof of cash)** The following information was obtained in an audit of the cash account of Tuck Company as of December 31, 19X0. Assume that the CPA is satisfied as to the validity of the cash book, the bank statements, and the returned checks, except as noted.

1. The bookkeeper's bank reconciliation at November 30, 19X0.

Balance per bank statement		$ 19,400
Add deposit in transit		1,100
Total		$ 20,500
Less: Outstanding checks		
#2540	$140	
1501	750	
1503	480	
1504	800	
1505	30	2,300
Balance per books		$ 18,200

2. A summary of the bank statement for December 19X0.

Balance brought forward	$ 19,400
Deposits	148,700
	$168,100
Charges	132,500
Balance, December 31, 19X0	$ 35,600

3. A summary of the cash book for December 19X0, before adjustments.

Balance brought forward	$ 18,200
Receipts	149,690
	$167,890
Disbursements	124,885
Balance, December 31, 19X0	$ 43,005

4. Included with the canceled checks returned with the December bank statement were the following:

Number	Date of Check	Amount of Check	Comment
1501	November 28, 19X0	$75	This check was in payment of an invoice for $750 and was recorded in the cash book as $750.
1503	November 28, 19X0	$580	This check was in payment of an invoice for $580 and was recorded in the cash book as $580.
1523	December 5, 19X0	$150	Examination of this check revealed that it was unsigned. A discussion with the client disclosed that it had been mailed inadvertently before it was signed. The check was endorsed and deposited by the payee and processed by the bank even though it was a legal nullity. The check was recorded in the cash disbursements.
1528	December 12, 19X0	$800	This check replaced 1504 that was returned by the payee because it was mutilated. Check 1504 was not canceled on the books.
—	December 19, 19X0	$200	This was a counter check drawn at the bank by the president of the company as a cash advance for travel expense. The president overlooked informing the bookkeeper about the check.
—	December 20, 19X0	$300	The drawer of this check was the Tucker Company.
1535	December 20, 19X0	$350	This check had been labeled NSF and returned to the payee because the bank had erroneously believed that the check was drawn by the Tuck Company. Subsequently, the payee was advised to redeposit the check.

Number	Date of Check	Amount of Check	Comment
1575	January 5, 19X1	$10,000	This check was given to the payee on December 30, 19X0, as a postdated check with the understanding that it would not be deposited until January 5. The check was not recorded on the books in December.

5. The Tuck Company discounted its own 60-day note for $9,000 with the bank on December 1, 19X0. The discount rate was 6%. The bookkeeper recorded the proceeds as a cash receipt at the face value of the note.

6. The bookkeeper records customers' dishonored checks as a reduction of cash receipts. When the dishonored checks are redeposited, they are recorded as a regular cash receipt. Two NSF checks for $180 and $220 were returned by the bank during December. The $180 check was redeposited, but the $220 check was still on hand at December 31. Cancellations of Tuck Company checks are recorded by a reduction of cash disbursements.

7. December bank charges were $20. In addition, a $10 service charge was made in December for the collection of a foreign draft in November. These charges were not recorded on the books.

8. Check 2540 listed in the November outstanding checks was drawn three years ago. Because the payee cannot be located, the president of Tuck Company agreed to the CPA's suggestion that the check be written back into the accounts by a journal entry.

9. Outstanding checks at December 31, 19X0, totaled $4,000 excluding checks 2540 and 1504.

10. The bank had recorded a deposit of $2,400 on January 2, 19X1. The bookkeeper had recorded this deposit on the books on December 31, 19X0, and then mailed the deposit to the bank.

REQUIRED

Prepare a four-column reconciliation ("proof of cash") of the cash receipts and cash disbursements recorded on the bank statement and on the company's books for the month of December 19X0. Use the format illustrated in this chapter.

AICPA (adapted)

RESEARCH QUESTION

18-35 **(AAERs dealing with cash)** Two SEC *Accounting and Auditing Enforcement Releases* that refer to cash audit deficiencies are Nos. 2 and 251. Review one of these, or any other AAER that you may identify as dealing with issues related to cash, and prepare a brief summary stating the parties involved, the nature of the reporting and auditing deficiencies found, and any remedies imposed by the SEC.

PART

5

Completing the Audit, Reporting, and Other Services

CHAPTER

19

COMPLETING THE AUDIT/POSTAUDIT RESPONSIBILITIES

LEARNING OBJECTIVES

When you have concluded your study of this chapter, you should be able to

1. Describe the auditor's responsibilities in completing the audit.
2. Enumerate the procedures in completing the field work.
3. Understand the auditor's responsibilities with respect to subsequent events.
4. Describe and state the purpose of a letter of audit inquiry.
5. Describe and state the purpose of a client representation letter.
6. Identify the steps in evaluating audit findings.
7. Indicate the communications with the client at the conclusion of the audit.
8. State the auditor's postaudit responsibilities.

COMPLETING THE FIELD WORK
- MAKING SUBSEQUENT EVENTS REVIEW
- READING MINUTES OF MEETINGS
- OBTAINING EVIDENCE CONCERNING LITIGATION, CLAIMS, AND ASSESSMENTS
- OBTAINING CLIENT REPRESENTATION LETTER
- PERFORMING ANALYTICAL PROCEDURES

EVALUATING THE FINDINGS
- MAKING FINAL ASSESSMENT OF MATERIALITY AND AUDIT RISK
- MAKING TECHNICAL REVIEW OF FINANCIAL STATEMENTS
- FORMULATING OPINION AND DRAFTING AUDIT REPORT
- MAKING FINAL REVIEW(S) OF WORKING PAPERS

COMMUNICATING WITH THE CLIENT
- COMMUNICATING INTERNAL CONTROL STRUCTURE MATTERS
- COMMUNICATING MATTERS PERTAINING TO CONDUCT OF AUDIT
- PREPARING MANAGEMENT LETTER

POSTAUDIT RESPONSIBILITIES
- SUBSEQUENT EVENTS BETWEEN DATE AND ISSUANCE OF REPORT
- DISCOVERY OF FACTS EXISTING AT REPORT DATE
- DISCOVERY OF OMITTED PROCEDURES

SUMMARY

APPENDIX 19A: EXAMPLES OF REPORTABLE CONDITIONS

BIBLIOGRAPHY

OBJECTIVE QUESTIONS

COMPREHENSIVE QUESTIONS

CASES

RESEARCH QUESTIONS

Many aspects of interim and year-end audit testing have been discussed in previous chapters. This chapter is concerned with two important additional areas of activity in a financial statement audit.

Consideration is first given to completing the audit. The procedures performed in this activity have the following several distinctive characteristics: (1) they do not pertain to specific transaction cycles or accounts, (2) they are performed after the balance sheet date, (3) they involve many subjective judgments by the auditor, and (4) they are usually performed by audit managers or other senior members of the audit team who have extensive audit experience with the client.

The adage, "last but not least," applies to completing the audit. Indeed, the decisions made by the auditor in this part of the audit are usually crucial to the ultimate outcome of the audit. For example, in determining the procedures to be used and in evaluating the evidence obtained, the auditor must be fully aware of the audit risks associated with the engagement. Moreover, the conclusions

OBJECTIVE 1

Describe the auditor's responsibilities in completing the audit.

reached by the auditor in completing the audit often have a direct impact on the opinion to be expressed on the client's financial statements.

In completing the audit, the auditor frequently works under tight time constraints, particularly as clients seek the earliest possible date for the issuance of the audit report. Although time may not be the ally of the auditor, the auditor must take the time to make sound professional judgments and to express the opinion appropriate in the circumstances. For purposes of discussion, the auditor's responsibilities in completing the audit are divided into the following three categories: (1) completing field work, (2) evaluating the findings, and (3) communicating with the client.

After explaining the activities involved in completing the audit, consideration is then given to the auditor's postaudit responsibilities. These responsibilities pertain to events occurring after the date of the auditor's report.

COMPLETING THE FIELD WORK

OBJECTIVE 2

Enumerate the procedures in completing the field work.

In completing the field work, the auditor performs specific auditing procedures to obtain additional audit evidence. The procedures are

- Making subsequent events review.
- Reading minutes of meetings.
- Obtaining evidence concerning litigation, claims, and assessments.
- Obtaining client representation letter.
- Performing analytical procedures.

The procedures do not have to be performed in the foregoing sequence. Each procedure is explained in a following section.

MAKING SUBSEQUENT EVENTS REVIEW

OBJECTIVE 3

Understand the auditor's responsibilities with respect to subsequent events.

The auditor's responsibility for assessing the fairness of a client's financial statements is not limited to an examination of events and transactions that occur up to the balance sheet date. SAS 1, *Codification of Statements on Auditing Standards* (AU 560, *Subsequent Events*), states that the auditor also has specified responsibilities for events and transactions that (1) have a material effect on the financial statements and (2) occur after the balance sheet date but prior to the issuance of the financial statements and the auditor's report. These occurrences are referred to as **subsequent events.**

As shown in Figure 19-1, the time frame for a subsequent event extends from the balance sheet date to the issuance of the auditor's report. Figure 19-1 also identifies a **subsequent events period,** which extends from the balance sheet date to the end of field work. During this period, the auditor is required under GAAS to discover the occurrence of subsequent events. As explained later in the chapter, the auditor has no responsibility to discover subsequent events that occur between the end of field work and the issuance of the audit report.

FIGURE 19-1 • SUBSEQUENT EVENTS TIME DIMENSIONS

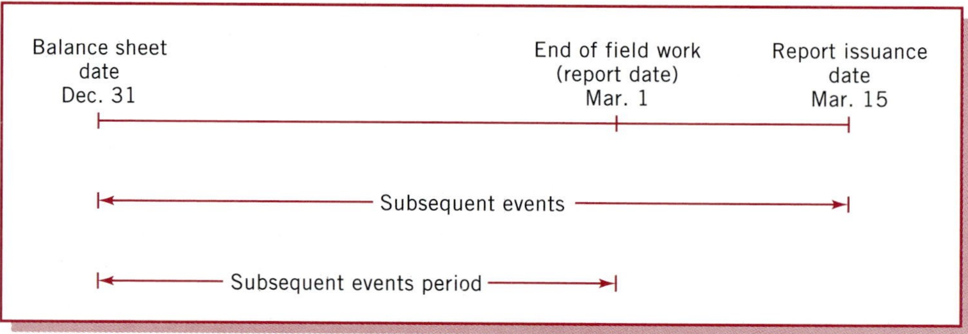

Types of Events

AU 560.03 and .05 indicate that there are two types of subsequent events.

- **Type 1 subsequent events** provide additional evidence with respect to conditions that existed at the date of the balance sheet and affect the estimates inherent in the process of preparing financial statements.
- **Type 2 subsequent events** provide evidence with respect to conditions that did not exist at the date of the balance sheet but arose subsequent to that date.

Type 1 events require *adjustment* of the financial statements; type 2 events require *disclosure* in the statements, or in very material cases, attaching pro-forma (as if) data to the financial statements. The following examples are illustrative of the two types of events:

Type 1	Type 2
Realization of recorded year-end assets, such as receivables and inventories, at a different amount than recorded. Settlement of recorded year-end estimated liabilities, such as litigation and product warranties, at a different amount than recorded.	Issuance of long-term bonds or preferred or common stock. Purchase of a business. Casualty losses resulting from fire or flood.

An example may help in distinguishing between the two types of events. Assume that a major customer becomes bankrupt on February 1, 19X1, and that the client considered the customer's balance to be totally collectible in making its estimate of potentially uncollectible accounts in its December 31, 19X0, statements. If, on review of the subsequent event, the auditor determines that the bankruptcy was attributable to the customer's deteriorating financial position that existed (but was unknown to the client) at the balance sheet date, the client should be requested to adjust the December 31, 19X0, statements for the loss. If, on the other hand, the auditor determines that the customer was financially sound at December 31 and the bankruptcy resulted from a fire or similar catastrophe that occurred after the balance sheet date, only disclosure in the notes to the December 31 statements is needed. Ordinarily, type 1 events require adjustment because they typically represent conditions that have accumulated over an extended period of time.

Auditing Procedures in the Subsequent Period

The auditor should identify and evaluate subsequent events up to the date of the auditor's report, which should be as of the end of field work. This responsibility is discharged in the following two ways: (1) by being alert for subsequent events in performing year-end substantive tests such as cutoff tests and the search for unrecorded liabilities and (2) by performing the following auditing procedures specified in AU 560.12 at or near the completion of field work:

- Read the latest available interim financial statements and compare them with the statements being reported on and make other comparisons appropriate in the circumstances.
- Inquire of management having responsibility for financial and accounting matters as to
  - Any substantial contingent liabilities or commitments existing at the balance sheet date or date of inquiry.
  - Any significant changes in capital stock, long-term debt, or working capital to the date of inquiry.
  - The current status of items previously accounted for on the basis of tentative, preliminary, or inconclusive data.
  - Whether any unusual adjustments have been made since the balance sheet date.
- Read minutes of meetings of directors, stockholders, and other appropriate committees.
- Inquire of client's legal counsel concerning litigation, claims, and assessments.
- Obtain letter of representation from client about subsequent events that would, in its opinion, require adjustment or disclosure.
- Make additional inquiries or perform additional procedures considered necessary in the circumstances.

The procedures pertaining to legal counsel and the representation letter are explained later in the chapter.

Effects on Auditor's Report

The failure to record or properly disclose subsequent events in the financial statements will result in a departure from the auditor's standard report. Depending on materiality, the auditor should express either a qualified opinion or an adverse opinion because the financial statements are not presented fairly in conformity with GAAP.

READING MINUTES OF MEETINGS

The minutes of meetings of stockholders, the board of directors, and its subcommittees, such as the finance committee and the audit committee, may contain matters that have audit significance. For example, the board of directors may authorize a new bond issue, the purchase of treasury stock, payment of a cash dividend, or the discontinuance of a product line. Each of these circumstances affects management's assertions in the financial statements. The auditor should determine that all minutes of board meetings held during the period under audit and during the period from the balance sheet date to the end of field work have been provided for his or her review. The reading of minutes is ordinarily done as soon as they become available, to give the auditor the maximum opportunity to assess their significance to the audit. For example, information learned from the minutes might cause the auditor to modify planned substantive tests, or to request the client to include the disclosure of a subsequent event in the financial statements. The auditor's reading of the minutes should be documented in the working papers.

OBTAINING EVIDENCE CONCERNING LITIGATION, CLAIMS, AND ASSESSMENTS

The FASB in SFAS 5, *Accounting for Contingencies,* defines a contingency as an existing condition, situation, or set of circumstances involving uncertainty as to possible gain (gain contingency) or loss (loss contingency) that will be resolved when one or more future events occur or fail to occur. Gain contingencies, such as a client's claim against others for patent infringement, present only a relatively small problem for the auditor because under GAAP they normally are not recorded until they are realized. Loss contingencies, on the other hand, often represent a significant problem for the auditor. Depending on subjective evaluations of the likelihood of future payment, GAAP requires that loss contingencies either be (1) recorded as contingent liabilities, (2) disclosed in the notes to the financial statements, or (3) ignored. These contingencies include potential liabilities from income tax disputes; product warranties; guarantees of obligations of others; and litigation, claims, and assessments.

The auditor's concerns about contingent liabilities are not limited to completing the audit. During audit testing and particularly in searching for unrecorded liabilities (see Chapter 15), the auditor should be alert for the possibility of contingent liabilities. Moreover, in reading the minutes of board of directors' meetings and in reviewing contracts, the auditor should look for circumstances that may indicate contingencies that should be investigated. GAAS does not specify auditing requirements for all contingencies. However, GAAS does contain requirements for auditing litigation, claims, and assessments. These requirements are usually met at the time of completing the audit because the auditor desires that the evidential matter be obtained as close to the end of field work as is feasible.

Audit Considerations

SAS 12, *Inquiry of a Client's Lawyer Concerning Litigation, Claims, and Assessments* (AU 337.04), states that the auditor should obtain evidential matter on

- The existence of a condition, situation, or set of circumstances indicating an uncertainty as to the possible loss to an entity arising from **litigation, claims, and assessments (LCA).**
- The period in which the underlying cause for legal action occurred.
- The degree of probability of an unfavorable outcome.
- The amount or range of potential loss.

Because LCAs usually are within the direct knowledge of management, management is the primary source of information about such matters. Accordingly, the auditor should (1) inquire of and discuss with management its means of identifying LCA, (2) obtain from management a description and evaluation of LCA that existed at the balance sheet date, and (3) obtain assurance from management, preferably in writing, of the existence of any unasserted claims. In addition, the auditor should examine documents in the client's possession concerning LCA. The auditor may also obtain information about LCA through reading minutes of board of directors' meetings, contracts and loan agreements, and bank confirmation responses concerning loan guarantees.

Letter of Audit Inquiry

OBJECTIVE 4

Describe and state the purpose of a letter of audit inquiry.

It should be recognized that an auditor normally does not possess sufficient legal skills to make an informed judgment about all LCA. Thus, AU 337.08 indicates that a **letter of audit inquiry** to the client's lawyer(s) is the auditor's primary means of obtaining corroboration of the information about LCA furnished by management. A letter of audit inquiry is illustrated in Figure 19-2. It should be sent by management to each lawyer who has been engaged by the client and has given substantive attention during the year to LCA or significant unasserted claims that may be material. As shown in Figure 19-2, the letter should ask the lawyer to respond directly to the auditor.

Effects of Responses on Auditor's Report

Lawyer's responses may have no effect on the auditor's report. That is, the auditor may issue a standard report with an unqualified opinion. This can occur when the responses indicate that, based on a reasonable investigation of the matters at issue, there is (1) a high probability of a favorable outcome or (2) the matters at issue are immaterial.

In some cases, the lawyer's response may indicate significant uncertainty about the likelihood of an unfavorable outcome of LCA or the amount or range of potential loss. For example, the matter may be only in the initial stage of litigation and there may be no historical experience of the entity in similar litigation. In this situation, the auditor may conclude that the financial statements are affected by an uncertainty that is not susceptible to reasonable estimation at the balance sheet date. If the uncertainty is adequately disclosed in the financial statements, the auditor's report should contain an unqualified opinion with explanatory language concerning the uncertainty.

A lawyer's refusal to respond to a letter of audit inquiry is a limitation on the scope of the audit. Depending on the materiality of the items, the auditor should express a qualified opinion or disclaim an opinion on the financial statements. The

FIGURE 19-2 • LETTER OF AUDIT INQUIRY

XYZ Corporation
Midtown, Texas 48100

[Name and Address of Legal Counsel]

Dear Sirs:

In connection with an audit of our financial statements at [balance sheet date] and for the [period] then ended, management of the Company has prepared, and furnished to our auditors [name and address of auditors], a description and evaluation of certain contingencies, including those set forth below involving matters with respect to which you have been engaged and to which you have devoted substantive attention on behalf of the Company in the form of legal consultation or representation. These contingencies are regarded by management of the Company as material for this purpose. Your response should include matters that existed at [balance sheet date] and during the period from that date to the date of your response.

Pending or Threatened Litigation
[Description Provided]

Unasserted Claims and Assessments
[Description Provided]

Please furnish to our auditors such explanation, if any, that you consider necessary to supplement the foregoing information, including an explanation of those matters as to which your views may differ from those stated and an identification of the omission of any contingencies or a statement that the list of such matters is complete.

We understand that whenever, in the course of performing legal services for us with respect to a matter recognized to involve an unasserted possible claim or assessment that may call for financial statement disclosure, if you have formed a professional conclusion that we should disclose or consider disclosure concerning such possible claim or assessment, as a matter of professional responsibility to us, you will so advise us and will consult with us concerning the question of such disclosure and the applicable requirements of *Statement of Financial Accounting Standards No. 5.* Please specifically confirm to our auditors that our understanding is correct.

Please specifically identify the nature of and reasons for any limitation on your response. A return envelope is enclosed for your reply.

Very truly yours,

____

Signature of Client

SOURCE: AU 337A.01.

auditor may obtain assistance about LCA from the client's legal department. However, because of possible management bias, such help is not a substitute for corroborating information that an outside lawyer refuses to furnish.

Further consideration is given to the effects of contingencies and uncertainties on the auditor's report in the next chapter.

OBTAINING CLIENT REPRESENTATION LETTER

The auditor is required to obtain certain written representations from management in meeting the third standard of field work. This is accomplished through a **client representation letter,** commonly referred to as a **rep letter.** SAS 19, *Client Representations* (AU 333.02), explains that the auditor relies on a rep letter to

OBJECTIVE 5

Describe and state the purpose of a client representation letter.

- Confirm oral representations given to the auditor.
- Document the continuing appropriateness of such representations.
- Reduce the possibility of misunderstandings concerning management's representations.

A rep letter may complement other auditing procedures. For example, as indicated in the preceding section, a letter of audit inquiry is the auditor's primary means of obtaining evidence about LCA. Nevertheless, the rep letter may also contain management's statements that LCAs are properly accounted for and that there are no unasserted claims or assessments that require disclosure in the financial statements. In some cases, however, a rep letter may be the primary source of audit evidence. For instance, when a client plans to discontinue a line of business, the auditor may not be able to corroborate this event through other auditing procedures. Accordingly, the auditor should request management to indicate its intent in the rep letter.

Content of Representation Letter

AU 333.04 identifies 20 matters that may be included in a rep letter. When the representations pertain directly to financial statement amounts, they may be limited to matters that are either individually or collectively material to the financial statements. Rep letters should be prepared on the client's stationery, addressed to the auditor, and dated as of the date of the auditor's report. Normally, the letter is signed by the chief executive officer and the chief financial officer. In many audits, the auditor will draft the representations that subsequently become the responsibility of the officers who sign the letter. A rep letter is illustrated in Figure 19-3.

Effects on the Auditor's Report

When the auditor obtains a rep letter and he or she is able to corroborate management's representations, a standard audit report can be issued. However, there is a limitation on the scope of the audit when the auditor is unable to (1) obtain a rep letter or (2) support a management representation that is material to the financial statements by other auditing procedures. A scope limitation will result in a departure from the auditor's standard report with either a qualified opinion or a disclaimer of opinion.

PERFORMING ANALYTICAL PROCEDURES

Earlier chapters have explained and illustrated the application of analytical procedures in audit planning and in performing year-end substantive tests. It will be recalled that analytical procedures involve the use of ratios and other comparative techniques. Analytical procedures are also used in completing the audit as an **overall (or final) review** of the financial statements. SAS 56, *Analytical Procedures* (AU 329.22), states that the objective of the overall review is to assist the auditor in assessing conclusions reached in the audit and in evaluating the financial statement presentation taken as a whole.

FIGURE 19-3 • CLIENT REPRESENTATION LETTER

(Date of Auditor's Report)

(To the Independent Auditor)

In connection with your audit of the (identification of financial statements) of (name of client) as of (date) and for the (period of examination) for the purpose of expressing an opinion as to whether the (consolidated) financial statements present fairly the financial position, results of operations, and cash flows of (name of client) in conformity with generally accepted accounting principles (other comprehensive basis of accounting), we confirm, to the best of our knowledge and belief, the following representations made to you during your audit.

1. We are responsible for the fair presentation in the (consolidated) financial statements of financial position, results of operations, and cash flows in conformity with generally accepted accounting principles (other comprehensive basis of accounting).
2. We have made available to you all
   a. Financial records and related data.
   b. Minutes of the meetings of stockholders, directors, and committees of directors, or summaries of actions of recent meetings for which minutes have not yet been prepared.
3. There have been no
   a. Irregularities involving management or employees who have significant roles in the internal control structure.
   b. Irregularities involving other employees that could have a material effect on the financial statements.
   c. Communications from regulatory agencies concerning noncompliance with, or deficiencies in, financial reporting practices that could have a material effect on the financial statements.
4. We have no plans or intentions that may materially affect the carrying value or classification of assets and liabilities.
5. The following have been properly recorded or disclosed in the financial statements:
   a. Related party transactions and related amounts receivable or payable, including sales, purchases, loans, transfers, leasing arrangements, and guarantees.
   b. Capital stock repurchase options or agreements or capital stock reserved for options, warrants, conversions, or other requirements.
   c. Arrangements with banks involving compensating balances or other arrangements involving restrictions on cash balances and line-of-credit or similar arrangements.
   d. Agreements to repurchase assets previously sold.
6. There are no
   a. Violations or possible violations of laws or regulations whose effects should be considered for disclosure in the financial statements or as a basis for recording a loss contingency.
   b. Other material liabilities or gain or loss contingencies that are required to be accrued or disclosed by *Statement of Financial Accounting Standards No. 5.*
7. There are no unasserted claims or assessments that our lawyer has advised us are probable of assertion and must be disclosed in accordance with *SFAS No. 5.*
8. There are no material transactions that have not been properly recorded in the accounting records underlying the financial statements.
9. Provision, when material, has been made to reduce excess or obsolete inventories to their estimated net realizable value.
10. The company has satisfactory title to all owned assets, and there are no liens or encumbrances on such assets nor has any asset been pledged.
11. Provision has been made for any material loss to be sustained in the fulfillment of, or from inability to fulfill, any sales commitments.
12. Provision has been made for any material loss to be sustained as a result of purchase commitments for inventory quantities in excess of normal requirements or at prices in excess of the prevailing market prices.
13. We have complied with all aspects of contractual agreements that would have a material effect on the financial statements on the event of noncompliance.
14. No events have occurred subsequent to the balance sheet date that would require adjustment to, or disclosure in, the financial statements.

______________________________	______________________________
(Signature of Chief Executive Officer and Title)	(Signature of Chief Financial Officer and Title)

SOURCE: AU 333A.05.

DO THE FINANCIAL STATEMENTS MAKE SENSE?

An important additional objective of the overall review in one Big Six firm is: Do the financial statements make sense from the point of view of users of the statements? The focus is not on unusual relationships but on whether the impression a user is likely to obtain, based solely on the financial statements, is consistent with the auditor's accumulated knowledge of the entity. In meeting this objective, the firm requires the auditor to consider business ratios and other rules of thumb commonly used in the particular industry because these are the measures that users ordinarily use to evaluate the entity. As in other types of overall reviews, the findings may result in recommendations for changes in presentation and disclosures in the financial statements, additional auditing procedures, or changes in the audit opinion.

SOURCE: KPMG Peat Marwick, Audit Manual—U.S. (May 1988), pp. II–146–147.

In making an overall review, the auditor reads the financial statements and accompanying notes and considers the adequacy of the evidence gathered in response to unusual or unexpected balances and relationships (1) anticipated in planning the audit or (2) identified during the audit in substantive testing. Analytical procedures are then applied to the financial statements to determine if any additional unusual or unexpected relationships exist. If such relationships exist, additional auditing procedures should be performed in completing the audit.

Analytical procedures in the overall review should be performed by an individual having comprehensive knowledge of the client's business and industry such as a partner or manager on the audit. A variety of analytical procedures may be used. The procedures should be

- Applied to critical audit areas identified during the audit.
- Based on the financial statement data after all audit adjustments and reclassifications have been recognized.

As in earlier applications of analytical procedures, company data may be compared with (1) expected company results, (2) available industry data, and (3) relevant nonfinancial data such as units produced or sold and the number of employees.

LEARNING CHECK:

19-1 Identify the three categories of activities that pertain to completing the audit.

19-2 List the activities involved in completing field work.

19-3 a. Distinguish between the terms *subsequent events* and *subsequent events period*.
  b. Define the two types of subsequent events and indicate the accounting treatment of each type.
  c. What is the auditor's responsibility for subsequent events?

19-4 a. What evidence is required in an audit of litigation, claims, and assessments?
  b. What is a *letter of audit inquiry*?
  c. What effects may failure of a lawyer to respond to a letter of audit inquiry have on the audit report?

19-5 a. What objectives are met in obtaining a client representation letter?
b. What is the impact of a client's refusal to provide a *rep letter*.

19-6 a. What are the objectives of making an overall review?
b. Who should make this review?
c. How should analytical procedures be used in this review?

KEY TERMS:

Client representation letter, p. 724
Letter of audit inquiry, p. 723
Litigation, claims, and assessments (LCA), p. 723
Overall (or final) review, p. 725
Rep letter, p. 724
Subsequent events, p. 719
Subsequent events period, p. 719
Type 1 subsequent events, p. 720
Type 2 subsequent events, p. 720

EVALUATING THE FINDINGS

OBJECTIVE 6

Identify the steps in evaluating audit findings.

The auditor has the following two objectives in evaluating the findings: (1) determining the type of opinion to be expressed and (2) determining whether GAAS has been met in the audit. To meet these objectives, the auditor completes the following steps:

- Making final assessment of materiality and audit risk.
- Making technical review of financial statements.
- Formulating opinion and drafting audit report.
- Making final review(s) of working papers.

These steps are performed in the order in which they are listed.

MAKING FINAL ASSESSMENT OF MATERIALITY AND AUDIT RISK

In formulating an opinion on the financial statements, the auditor should assimilate all the evidence gathered during the audit. An essential prerequisite in deciding on the opinion to express is a final assessment of materiality and audit risk. The starting point in this process is to total the misstatements found in examining all accounts that were not corrected by the client. In some cases, the uncorrected misstatements may have been individually immaterial so that no correction was requested by the auditor. In other cases, the client may have been unwilling to make the corrections that were requested. The next step in the process is to determine the effects of the total misstatements on net income and other financial statement totals to which the misstatements pertain, such as current assets or current liabilities.

The auditor's determination of misstatements in an account should include the following components:

- Uncorrected misstatements specifically identified through substantive tests of details of transactions and balances (referred to as **known misstatement**).
- Projected uncorrected misstatements estimated through audit sampling techniques.

- Estimated misstatements detected through analytical procedures and quantified by other auditing procedures.

The total of these components for an account is called **likely misstatement.** The sum of the likely misstatement in all accounts is called **aggregate likely misstatement.** The auditor's assessment of aggregate likely misstatement may also include the effect on the current period's financial statements of any uncorrected likely misstatements from a prior period. This is done when including them may lead to the conclusion that there is an unacceptably high risk that the current period's financial statements are materially misstated. A working paper illustrating one approach to analyzing aggregate likely misstatement is shown in Figure 19-4.

The data that have been accumulated are then compared with the auditor's preliminary judgments concerning materiality that were made in planning the audit. As explained in Chapter 7, planning materiality extends to both the individual account and financial statement levels. If any adjustments in planning materiality have been made during the course of the audit, they should, of course, be included in this assessment.

In planning the audit, the auditor specified an acceptable level of audit risk. As aggregate likely misstatement increases, the risk that the financial statements may be materially misstated also increases. When the auditor concludes that audit risk is at an acceptable level, he or she can proceed to formulate the opinion supported by the findings. However, if the auditor believes audit risk is not acceptable, he or she should either (1) perform additional substantive tests or (2) convince the client to make the corrections necessary to reduce the risk of material misstatement to an acceptable level.

MAKING TECHNICAL REVIEW OF FINANCIAL STATEMENTS

Many public accounting firms have detailed financial statement checklists that are completed by the auditor who performs the initial review of the financial statements. The completed checklist is then reviewed by the manager and partner in charge of the engagement. Prior to the release of the audit report on a publicly held client, there should also be a technical review of the statements by a partner who was not a member of the audit team.

The checklists include matters pertaining to the form and content of each of the basic financial statements as well as to required disclosures. Most firms now have separate checklists for SEC and non-SEC clients. The completed checklist and the findings of the reviewers should be included in the working papers.

FORMULATING OPINION AND DRAFTING AUDIT REPORT

During the course of an audit engagement, a variety of audit tests are performed. These tests often are performed by staff personnel whose participation in the audit may be limited to a few areas or accounts. As the tests for each functional area or statement item are completed, the staff auditor is expected to summarize his or her findings.

It is necessary in completing the audit for the separate findings to be summarized and evaluated for the purpose of expressing an opinion on the financial

FIGURE 19-4 • ANALYSIS OF AGGREGATE LIKELY MISSTATEMENT WORKING PAPER

W/P REF: S-1

AMBIENT CORPORATION
ANALYSIS OF AGGREGATE LIKELY MISSTATEMENT
DECEMBER 31, 19X1

PREPARED BY: C.J.G DATE: 2/12/X2
REVIEWED BY: R.C.P DATE: 2/16/X2

DEBIT (CREDIT)

W/P REF.	ACCT. NO.	DESCRIPTION	ASSETS CURRENT	ASSETS NON-CURRENT	LIABILITIES CURRENT	LIABILITIES NON-CURRENT	STOCKHOLDERS' EQUITY	PRE-TAX EARNINGS	INCOME TAX EXPENSE
UNCORRECTED KNOWN MISSTATEMENTS:									
D-1	1590	ACCUMULATED DEPRECIATION		3,500.00					
	4590	DEPRECIATION EXPENSE					(3,500.00)	(3,500.00)	
	2295	INCOME TAXES PAYABLE			(1,750.00)		1,750.00		1,750.00
		OVERSTATEMENT OF DEPRECIATION EXPENSE							
UNCORRECTED PROJECTED MISSTATEMENTS:									
C-1	4200	COST OF GOODS SOLD					8,000.00	8,000.00	
	1200	INVENTORY	(8,000.00)						
	2295	INCOME TAXES PAYABLE			4,000.00		(4,000.00)		(4,000.00)
		OVERSTATEMENT OF ENDING INVENTORY PROJECTED FROM STATISTICAL SAMPLE							
OTHER ESTIMATED MISSTATEMENTS:									
		NONE							
AGGREGATE LIKELY MISSTATEMENT			(8,000.00)	3,500.00	2,250.00	0.00	2,250.00	4,500.00	(2,250.0)
FINAL BALANCE FROM TRIAL BALANCE			400,000.00	735,000.00	225,000.00	375,000.00	535,000.00	150,000.00	75,000.00
AGGREGATE LIKELY MISSTATEMENT %			2%	.5%	1%	0%	.4%	3%	3%

CONCLUSION: *The likely misstatements listed above are deemed not to be material, either individually or in their aggregate effects on the individual accounts, the financial statement categories, or the financial statement totals to which they relate.*

statements taken as a whole. The ultimate responsibility for these steps rests with the partner in charge of the engagement. In some cases, the audit manager makes the initial determinations that are then carefully reviewed by the partner.

Before reaching a final decision on the opinion, a conference generally is held with the client. At this meeting, the auditor reports the findings orally and attempts to provide a rationale for proposed adjustments and/or additional disclosures. Management, in turn, may attempt to defend its position. In the end, some agreement is generally reached on the changes to be made and the auditor can proceed to issue an unqualified opinion. When such an agreement is not obtained, the auditor may have to issue another type of opinion. Communication of the auditor's opinion is made through an audit report. The various types of auditors' reports are discussed in Chapter 20.

MAKING FINAL REVIEW(S) OF WORKING PAPERS

In Chapter 5, the first-level review of working papers by a supervisor was explained. This review is made to evaluate the work done, the evidence obtained, and the conclusions reached by the preparer of the working paper. Additional reviews of the working papers are made at the end of field work by members of the audit team. The levels of review that may be made in completing the audit are shown in the following table:

REVIEWER	NATURE OF REVIEW
Manager	Reviews working papers prepared by seniors and reviews some or all of the working papers reviewed by seniors.
Partner in charge of engagement	Reviews working papers prepared by managers and reviews other working papers on a selective basis.

The partner's review of the working papers is designed to obtain assurance that

- The work done by subordinates has been accurate and thorough.
- The judgments exercised by subordinates were reasonable and appropriate in the circumstances.
- The audit engagement has been completed in accordance with the conditions and terms specified in the engagement letter.
- All significant accounting, auditing, and reporting questions raised during the audit have been properly resolved.
- The working papers support the auditor's opinion.
- GAAS and the firm's quality control policies and procedures have been met.

Detailed checklists covering the above matters are commonly used in performing the review of working papers.

Some firms require an independent **"cold" (or second) review** of the working papers by a partner who did not participate in the audit. Such reviews are mandatory in audits of SEC registrants. The rationale for a second partner review is based on the objectivity of the reviewer who may challenge matters approved by earlier reviewers. Thus, the review provides additional assurance that all GAAS have been met in the engagement.

LEARNING CHECK:

19-7 a. What are the two objectives to be achieved in *evaluating the findings*?
b. List four steps in meeting these objectives.

19-8 a. What are the purposes of the auditor's final assessment of materiality and audit risk?
b. Distinguish between the terms *known misstatement, likely misstatement,* and *aggregate likely misstatement.*

19-9 What is included in the technical review of the financial statements, what aids are used in the review, and who makes the review?

19-10 a. How and by whom is the opinion on the financial statements formulated, and how is it communicated?
b. How are proposed adjustments and disclosures generally resolved?

19-11 a. Identify the primary reviewers of working papers and the nature of their reviews.
b. What are the objectives of the engagement partner's review?
c. Why may a second partner review be desirable?

KEY TERMS:

Aggregate likely misstatement, p. 729
"Cold" (or second) review, p. 731
Known misstatement, p. 728
Likely misstatement, p. 729

COMMUNICATING WITH THE CLIENT

OBJECTIVE 7

Indicate the communications with the client at the conclusion of the audit.

The auditor's communications with the client at the conclusion of the audit involve the audit committee and management. The communications to the audit committee involve matters pertaining to (1) the client's internal control structure and (2) the conduct of the audit. The communication to management is made in a management letter.

COMMUNICATING INTERNAL CONTROL STRUCTURE MATTERS

During an audit, the auditor may become aware of matters relating to the internal control structure that should be of interest to the client's audit committee or to individuals with equivalent authority and responsibility. SAS 60, *Communication of Internal Control Structure Related Matters Noted in an Audit* (AU 325.02), requires the auditor to communicate **reportable conditions,** which are defined as matters that

represent significant deficiencies in the design or operation of the internal control structure, which could adversely affect the organization's ability to record, process, summarize, and report financial data consistent with the assertions of management in the financial statements.

A reportable condition may pertain to any control structure element. The designation of a deficiency as a reportable condition is influenced by such matters as the size of the entity, the complexity of its operations, its organizational structure, and its ownership characteristics. Examples of reportable conditions are presented in Appendix 18A. AU 325.04 indicates that the auditor is not required to search for reportable conditions. He or she may become aware of a reportable condition in obtaining an understanding of internal control structure elements, performing tests of controls, performing substantive tests, or otherwise during the audit.

The communication preferably should be in writing. The distribution of the report should ordinarily be restricted to the audit committee, management, and others within the organization. However, when such a report is required by governmental authorities, specific reference should be made in the report. AU 325.11 states that any report issued on reportable conditions should

- Indicate that the purpose of the audit is to report on the financial statements and not to provide assurance on the internal control structure.
- Include the definition of reportable conditions.
- Include the restriction on distribution.

AU 325.12 illustrates the sections of the report that include these requirements:

> In planning and performing our audit of the financial statements of the ABC Corporation for the year ended December 31, 19XX, we considered its internal control structure to determine our auditing procedures for the purpose of expressing our opinion on the financial statements and not to provide assurance on the internal control structure. However, we noted certain matters involving the internal control structure and its operation that we consider to be reportable conditions under standards established by the American Institute of Certified Public Accountants. Reportable conditions involve matters coming to our attention relating to significant deficiencies in the design or operation of the internal control structure that, in our judgment, could adversely affect the organization's ability to record, process, summarize, and report financial data consistent with the assertions of management in the financial statements.
>
> *(Include paragraphs to describe the reportable conditions noted.)*
>
> This report is intended solely for the information and use of the audit committee (board of directors, board of trustees, or owners in owner-managed enterprises), management, and others within the organization (or specified regulatory agency or other specified third party).

The communication should be made in a timely manner either during the audit or after its conclusion.

The following additional factors may affect the content of the report:

- Because of the potential for misinterpretation of the highly limited degree of assurance provided by the report, the auditor should not state in the report that *no* reportable conditions were noted.
- By agreement with the client, the report may (1) exclude reportable conditions already known to the audit committee and (2) include matters that do not qualify as reportable conditions.

A reportable condition may be of such magnitude as to be a material weakness. AU 325.15 defines a **material weakness** as

> a reportable condition in which the design or operation of the specific internal control structure elements do not reduce to a relatively low level the risk that misstatements in amounts that would be material in relation to the financial statements being audited may occur and not be detected within a timely period by employees in the normal course of performing their assigned functions.

The auditor is not required by GAAS to separately identify and communicate material weaknesses in the report to the audit committee. However, when either by client request or by auditor choice material weaknesses are identified and described in the report, two additional paragraphs are required. The first paragraph should contain a definition of the term "material weakness" and a description of the reportable conditions that are material weaknesses. As indicated in AU 325.16, the second additional paragraph should describe the limitations of the auditor's work as follows:

> Our consideration of the internal control structure would not necessarily disclose all matters in the internal control structure that might be reportable conditions and, accordingly, would not necessarily disclose all reportable conditions that are also considered to be material weaknesses as defined above.

When the preceding paragraph is included in the report and none of the reportable conditions are considered to be material weaknesses, a statement to this effect is added to the paragraph.

COMMUNICATING MATTERS PERTAINING TO CONDUCT OF AUDIT

SAS 61, *Communication With Audit Committees* (AU 380), requires the auditor to communicate certain matters pertaining to the conduct of the audit to those who have responsibility for overseeing the financial reporting process. Normally this responsibility is assigned to an audit committee of the board of directors or to a group with equivalent authority such as a finance committee. The communication may be oral or written, and it may occur during or shortly after the audit. When the communication is in writing, the report should indicate that it is intended for the audit committee or the board of directors and, if appropriate, management.

AU 380.06–.14 state that the communication with the audit committee may include the following matters:

- *Auditor's responsibility under GAAS* including the assurance provided by an audit that the financial statements are free of material misstatements, concepts of materiality used in the audit, and types of audit tests performed.
- *Significant accounting policies* such as management's initial selection and changes in policies, accounting methods used for significant unusual transactions, and effects of policies in areas that lack authoritative guidance or consensus.
- *Management judgments and accounting estimates* including the basis for judgments and the process for making accounting estimates.
- *Significant audit adjustments* that individually, or in the aggregate, have an important effect on the entity's financial reporting process.
- *Disagreements with management* that are significant to the financial statements or the auditor's report, and disagreements that pertain to the application of accounting principles and the basis for management's judgments about accounting estimates.
- *Consultation with other accountants* on auditing and accounting matters.

- *Major issues discussed with management prior to retention* including those pertaining to accounting principles and auditing standards.
- *Difficulties encountered in performing the audit* such as unreasonable delays by management in permitting the commencement of the audit and in providing needed information, unavailability of client personnel, and failure of the client to complete client-prepared schedules in a timely manner.

In addition, as explained previously, the auditor must communicate reportable conditions in a company's internal control structure to the audit committee.

PREPARING MANAGEMENT LETTER

During the course of an audit engagement, auditors observe many facets of the client's business organization and operations. At the conclusion of an audit, many auditors believe it is desirable to write a letter to management, known as a **management letter,** that contains recommendations not included in the required communication with the audit committee. These recommendations usually relate to improving the efficiency and effectiveness of the company's operations. The issuance of such letters has become an integral part of the services rendered by auditors to their clients. A management letter tangibly demonstrates the auditor's continuing interest in the welfare and future of the client. Preparation of a management letter is not required by GAAS.

Matters that are relevant to management letters should be noted in the audit working papers as the audit progresses to ensure that they are not overlooked. Subsequently, the working papers should provide adequate documentation of the management letter comments. Such support will also be useful in any discussions with management about the comments.

Management letters should be carefully prepared, well organized, and written in a constructive tone. Prompt issuance of the letters creates a favorable impression and may encourage both an early and a positive response by management.

Management letters may include comments on

- Internal control structure matters that are not considered to be reportable conditions.
- Management of resources such as cash, inventories, and investments.
- Tax-related matters.

A summary of the auditor's responsibilities in completing the audit is presented in Figure 19-5.

LEARNING CHECK:

19-12 What parties are involved in the auditor's communications with the client at the conclusion of the audit?

19-13 a. Distinguish between reportable conditions and material weaknesses.
b. What are the essential requirements for a report issued on reportable conditions?

FIGURE 19-5 • SUMMARY OF AUDITOR'S RESPONSIBILITIES IN COMPLETING THE AUDIT

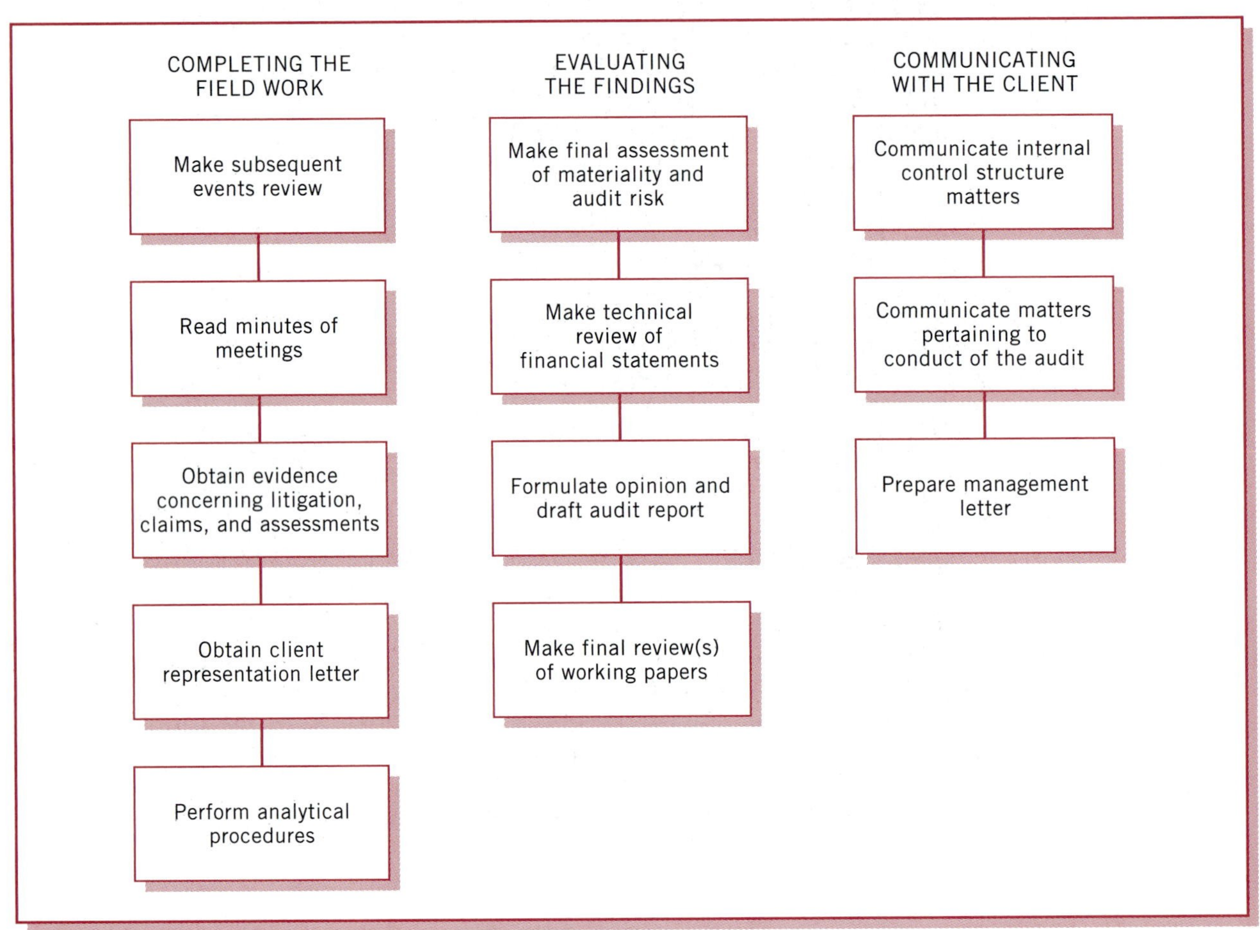

19-14 What are the effects on a report on reportable conditions when the auditor separately identifies and describes material weaknesses?

19-15 a. Indicate the form and timing of the auditor's communication with the audit committee on the conduct of the audit.

b. What matters should be included in the communication?

19-16 a. What purpose is served by a management letter?

b. List the types of data that may be included in a management letter.

KEY TERMS:

Management letter, p. 735
Material weakness, p. 733
Reportable conditions, p. 732

POSTAUDIT RESPONSIBILITIES

OBJECTIVE 8

State the auditor's postaudit responsibilities.

This section pertains to the auditor's responsibilities following the completion of field work. **Postaudit responsibilities** include consideration of

- Subsequent events occurring between the date and issuance of the auditor's report.
- The discovery of existing facts.
- The discovery of omitted procedures.

SUBSEQUENT EVENTS BETWEEN DATE AND ISSUANCE OF REPORT

As shown in Figure 19-1, a time interval of one to three weeks typically elapses between the end of field work and the issuance of the audit report. SAS 1, *Dating of the Independent Auditor's Report* (AU 530), states that the auditor has no responsibility to make any inquiries or to perform any auditing procedures during this time period to discover any material subsequent events. However, if knowledge of such an event comes to the auditor's attention, he or she should consider whether there should be disclosure in or adjustment of the financial statements for the event. When adjustment is required and management appropriately modifies the statements, the auditor may issue a standard audit report. When required disclosure is made by management, the auditor may also issue a standard report providing the report is *redated* to coincide with the date of the subsequent event.

Alternatively, the auditor may use **dual dating** in the audit report. Under this course of action, the original date is retained except for the dating of the subsequent event. The dual date is indicated in the audit report immediately below the signature of the firm in a manner similar to a postscript (P.S.) in a letter. Assuming the original date of the auditor's report was February 28 and the date of the subsequent event is March 7, the dual dating would appear as follows:

February 28, 19X1, except for the information in Note A for which the date is March 7.

Dual dating is the most common practice because redating of the entire report extends the auditor's overall responsibility beyond the completion of field work. Under redating, the auditor should extend the subsequent events review procedures to the later date.

DISCOVERY OF FACTS EXISTING AT REPORT DATE

The auditor has no responsibility for the postaudit discovery of facts existing (but unknown) at the date of the audit report. However, SAS 1, *Subsequent Discovery of Facts Existing at the Date of the Auditor's Report* (AU 561), indicates in AU 561.04 that if (1) the auditor becomes aware of such facts and (2) the facts may have affected the report that was issued, the auditor is required to ascertain the reliability of the information. When the investigation confirms the existence of the fact and the auditor believes the information is important to those relying or likely to rely on the financial statements, the auditor should take steps to prevent future reliance on the audit report.

The preferred result is the preparation of revised statements by the client and the issuance of a revised audit report as soon as practicable. If the client refuses to disclose the newly discovered facts, the auditor should notify each member of the board of directors of such refusal. In addition, AU 561.08 states that the auditor should take the following steps to prevent further reliance on the report:

- Notify the client that the audit report must no longer be associated with the financial statements.
- Notify the regulatory agencies having jurisdiction over the client that the report should no longer be relied on.
- Notify (generally via the regulatory agency) each individual known to be relying on the statements that the report should no longer be relied on.

AU 561.09 provides guidelines for the auditor in notifying parties other than the client. When the auditor has been able to make a satisfactory investigation and has determined that the information is reliable, he or she should describe the effects the subsequently acquired information would have had on the financial statements and the auditor's report. When the client has not cooperated and the auditor has been unable to make a satisfactory investigation, without disclosing the specific information, the auditor should (1) indicate the lack of cooperation and (2) state that if the information is true, the audit report should no longer be relied on.

DISCOVERY OF OMITTED PROCEDURES

After the date of the audit report, the auditor may conclude that one or more auditing procedures considered necessary in the circumstances was omitted from the audit. Auditing standards do not require the auditor to conduct any postaudit reviews of his or her work. However, discovery of an omitted procedure may result from a post-engagement review performed during a firm's quality control inspection program or during an outside peer review.

On discovery of an omitted procedure, the auditor should assess its importance to his or her ability to currently support the opinion expressed on the financial statements. A review of the working papers and a reevaluation of the overall scope of the audit may enable the auditor to conclude that he or she can still support the previously expressed opinion. Alternatively, SAS 46, *Consideration of Omitted Procedures After the Report Date* (AU 390.05), indicates that if the auditor decides that the opinion cannot be supported and he or she believes persons are currently relying on the report, the auditor should promptly perform the omitted procedures or alternative procedures that would provide a satisfactory basis for the opinion.

When a satisfactory basis for an opinion is obtained and the evidence supports the opinion expressed, the auditor has no further responsibility. However, if the performance of the omitted procedures reveals facts existing at the report date that would have changed the previously expressed opinion, the auditor should follow the notification procedures described in the last paragraph of the preceding section to prevent further reliance on the report. If the auditor is unable to perform the omitted or alternative procedures, he or she should consult an attorney to determine an appropriate course of action.

LEARNING CHECK:

19-17 a. Explain the auditor's responsibility for discovery of subsequent events occurring after completion of field work but before issuance of the audit report.

b. When such an event occurs and is appropriately reflected in the financial statements, what are the auditor's alternatives with respect to dating the audit report and the conditions applicable to each alternative?

19-18 a. What responsibility does the auditor have for the postaudit discovery of facts existing at the date of the auditor's report?

b. Identify the steps the auditor should take when the client refuses to make disclosure of the newly discovered facts.

19-19 What information should the auditor include in a notification of parties other than the client about the postaudit discovery of facts when he or she has been (a) able and (b) unable to make a satisfactory investigation of the facts?

19-20 a. What responsibility does the auditor have upon discovery of omitted procedures after the report date?

b. Indicate the possible consequences of the auditor's investigation of omitted procedures.

KEY TERMS:

Dual dating, p. 737

Postaudit responsibilities, p. 737

SUMMARY

This chapter describes several key responsibilities of the auditor in completing an audit of financial statements. Steps performed in completing the field work include making the subsequent events review, reading minutes of meetings, obtaining evidence concerning litigation, claims, and assessments, obtaining the client representation letter, and performing analytical procedures. Steps involved in evaluating the auditor's findings include making a final assessment of materiality and audit risk, making a technical review of the financial statements, formulating an opinion and drafting the audit report, and making a final review of the working papers.

The auditor is required to communicate with the client concerning reportable conditions related to the internal control structure and other matters pertaining to the conduct of the audit. In addition, the auditor typically communicates recommendations regarding the efficiency and effectiveness of the client's operations in a management letter. Finally, auditors have certain postaudit responsibilities relating to subsequent events that occur between the date of the auditor's report and its issuance, the subsequent discovery of facts existing at the report date, and the subsequent discovery of omitted procedures.

APPENDIX 19A EXAMPLES OF POSSIBLE REPORTABLE CONDITIONS[1]

The following are examples of matters that may be reportable conditions. They are grouped by categories of conditions and within categories by specific examples of conditions. Certain of the matters may also require communications under the provisions of other SASs.

Deficiencies in Control Structure Design

- Inadequate overall control structure design.
- Absence of appropriate segregation of duties consistent with appropriate control objectives.
- Absence of appropriate reviews and approvals of transactions, accounting entries, or systems output.
- Inadequate procedures for appropriately assessing and applying accounting principles.
- Absence of other control techniques considered appropriate for the type and level of transaction activity.
- Inadequate provisions for the safeguarding of assets.
- Evidence that a system fails to provide complete and accurate output consistent with objectives and current needs because of design flaws.

Failures in the Operation of the Control Structure

- Evidence of failure of identified controls in preventing or detecting misstatements of accounting information.
- Evidence that a system fails to provide complete and accurate output consistent with the entity's control objectives because of the misapplication of control procedures.
- Evidence of failure to safeguard assets from loss, damage, or misappropriation.
- Evidence of intentional override of the internal control structure by those in authority to the detriment of the overall objectives of the system.
- Evidence of failure to perform tasks that are part of the internal control structure, such as reconciliations not prepared or not timely prepared.
- Evidence of willful wrongdoing by employees or management.
- Evidence of manipulation, falsification, or alteration of accounting records or supporting documents.
- Evidence of intentional misapplication of accounting principles.
- Evidence of misrepresentation by client personnel to the auditor.
- Evidence that employees or management lack the qualifications and training to fulfill their assigned functions.

---

[1] *Source:* AU 325, Appendix A.

Others

- Absence of a sufficient level of control consciousness within the organization.
- Failure to follow up and correct previously identified control structure deficiencies.
- Evidence of significant or extensive undisclosed related party transactions.
- Evidence of undue bias or lack of objectivity by those responsible for accounting decisions.

BIBLIOGRAPHY

AICPA Professional Standards:
SAS 1 Codification of Statements on Auditing Standards:
(AU 530), Dating of the Independent Auditor's Report
(AU 560), Subsequent Events
(AU 561), Subsequent Discovery of Facts Existing at Date of Report
SAS 12 (AU 337), Inquiry of a Client's Lawyer Concerning Litigation, Claims, and Assessments
SAS 19 (AU 333), Client Representations
SAS 46 (AU 390), Consideration of Omitted Procedures After the Report Date
SAS 47 (AU 312), Audit Risk and Materiality in Conducting an Audit
SAS 56 (AU 329), Analytical Procedures
SAS 60 (AU 325), Communication of Internal Control Structure Related Matters Noted in an Audit
SAS 61 (AU 380), Communication with Audit Committees
IAU 8 (AU 8008A), Additional Guidance on—Observation of Inventory, Confirmation of Accounts Receivable and Inquiry Regarding Litigation and Claims.
IAU 21 (AU 8021), Date of the Auditor's Report; Events After the Balance Sheet Date; Discovery of Facts After the Financial Statements Have Been Issued.
IAU 22 (AU 8022), Representations by Management.

Benis, Martin. "The Small Client and Representation Letters," *Journal of Accountancy* (September 1978), pp. 78–84.

Hall, Thomas W., and Butler, A. A. "Assuring Adequate Attorneys' Replies to Audit Inquiries," *Journal of Accountancy* (September 1981), pp. 83–91.

Jiambalvo, James, and Wilner, Neil. "Auditor Evaluation of Contingent Claims," *Auditing: A Journal of Practice and Theory* (Fall 1985), pp. 1–11.

Mautz, Robert K., and Matusiak, Louis W. "Concurrent Partner Review Revisited," *Journal of Accountancy* (March 1988), pp. 56–63.

Roberts, Ray. "Client Representation Letters and the Discovery of Irregularities," *California CPA Quarterly* (June 1980), pp. 19–23.

OBJECTIVE QUESTIONS

Indicate the *best* answer for each of the following multiple choice questions:

19-21 These questions pertain to subsequent events.

1. Which of the following procedures would an auditor ordinarily perform during the review of subsequent events?
   a. Review the cutoff bank statements for the period after the year-end.
   b. Inquire of the client's legal counsel concerning litigation.
   c. Investigate reportable conditions previously communicated to the client.
   d. Analyze related party transactions to discover possible irregularities.

2. An auditor is concerned with completing various phases of the examination after the balance sheet date. This "subsequent period" extends to the date of the
   a. Auditor's report.
   b. Final review of the audit working papers.
   c. Public issuance of the financial statements.
   d. Delivery of the auditor's report to the client.

3. A client acquired 25% of its outstanding capital stock after year-end and prior to completion of the auditor's field work. The auditor should
   a. Advise management to adjust the balance sheet to reflect the acquisition.
   b. Issue pro-forma financial statements giving effect to the acquisition as if it had occurred at year-end.
   c. Advise management to disclose the acquisition in the notes to the financial statements.
   d. Disclose the acquisition in the opinion paragraph of the auditor's report.

19-22 These questions relate to inquiries of client's lawyers and client "rep letters."

1. The scope of an audit is **not** restricted when an attorney's response to an auditor as a result of a client's letter of audit inquiry limits the response to
   a. Matters to which the attorney has given substantive attention in the form of legal representation.
   b. An evaluation of the likelihood of an unfavorable outcome of the matters disclosed by the entity.
   c. The attorney's opinion of the entity's historical experience in recent similar litigation.
   d. The probable outcome of asserted claims and pending or threatened litigation.

2. Auditors should request that an audit client send a letter of inquiry to those attorneys who have been consulted concerning litigation, claims, or assessments. The primary reason for this request is to provide
   a. Information concerning the progress of cases to date.
   b. Corroborative evidential matter.
   c. An estimate of the dollar amount of the probable loss.
   d. An expert opinion as to whether a loss is possible, probable, or remote.

3. Which of the following statements ordinarily is included among the written client representations obtained by the auditor?
   a. Sufficient evidential matter has been made available to permit the issuance of an unqualified opinion.
   b. Compensating balances and other arrangements involving restrictions on cash balances have been disclosed.
   c. Management acknowledges responsibility for illegal actions committed by employees.
   d. Management acknowledges that there are *no* material weaknesses in internal control.

4. Hall accepted an engagement to audit the 19X5 financial statements of XYZ Company. XYZ completed the preparation of the 19X5 financial statements on February 13, 19X6, and Hall began the field work on February 17, 19X6. Hall completed the field work on March 24, 19X6, and completed the report on March 28, 19X6. The client's representation letter normally would be dated
   a. February 13, 19X6.
   b. February 17, 19X6.
   c. March 24, 19X6.
   d. March 28, 19X6.

19-23 These questions pertain to the auditor's postaudit responsibilities.

1. An auditor issued an audit report that was dual dated for a subsequent event occurring after the completion of field work but before issuance of the auditor's report. The auditor's responsibility for events occurring subsequent to the completion of field work was
   a. Limited to the specific event referenced.
   b. Limited to include only events occurring before the date of the last subsequent event referenced.
   c. Extended to subsequent events occurring through the date of issuance of the report.
   d. Extended to include all events occurring since the completion of field work.
2. Six months after issuing an unqualified opinion on audited financial statements, an auditor discovered that the engagement personnel failed to confirm several of the client's material accounts receivable balances. The auditor should first
   a. Request the permission of the client to undertake the confirmation of accounts receivable.
   b. Perform alternative procedures to provide a satisfactory basis for the unqualified opinion.
   c. Assess the importance of the omitted procedures to the auditor's ability to support the previously expressed opinion.
   d. Inquire whether there are persons currently relying, or likely to rely, on the unqualified opinion.
3. Subsequent to the issuance of the auditor's report, the auditor became aware of facts existing at the report date that would have affected the report had the auditor then been aware of such facts. After determining that the information is reliable, the auditor should next
   a. Notify the board of directors that the auditor's report must no longer be associated with the financial statements.
   b. Determine whether there are persons relying or likely to rely on the financial statements who would attach importance to the information.
   c. Request that management disclose the effects of the newly discovered information by adding a footnote to subsequently issued financial statements.
   d. Issue revised pro-forma financial statements taking into consideration the newly discovered information.

Comprehensive Questions

19-24 **(Subsequent events)** Green, CPA, is auditing the financial statements of Taylor Corporation for the year ended December 31, 19X1. Green plans to complete the field work and sign the auditor's report about May 10, 19X2. Green is concerned about events and transactions occurring after December 31, 19X1, that may affect the 19X1, financial statements.

Required

a. What are the general types of subsequent events that require Green's consideration and evaluation?
b. What are the auditing procedures Green should consider performing to gather evidence concerning subsequent events?

AICPA

19-25 **(Subsequent events/client representation letter/management letter)** Charles Jones is the controller of Precision Tool & Die Corporation, a closely held firm. The principal owners of the company are seeking to retire soon and to sell their share interests. As audited financial statements will be needed during the process, the firm of Higgins & Clark has been hired to audit the financial statements for the fiscal year ended November 30, 19X8.

At a recent meeting with the owners, Jones presented a status report on the audit. Most of the field work has been completed, and the preliminary financial statements will be prepared within the next ten days. Higgins & Clark has targeted a report issue date of January 15, 19X9. In response to a query regarding work remaining to be done, Jones identified the following three major tasks that must be accomplished:

- A subsequent events review.
- The client representation letter.
- The management letter.

REQUIRED

a. 1. Describe the purpose of a subsequent events review.
   2. Describe the two actions that might be taken on discovery of a material subsequent event and the potential effect of each action on the firm's financial statements.

b. 1. Describe the purpose of the client representation letter.
   2. Identify four items that may appear in a client representation letter.

c. 1. Define the purpose served by the management letter.
   2. Identify three major subjects that may be addressed in the management letter.

ICMA

19-26 **(Subsequent events)** In connection with the audit of Flowmeter, Inc., for the year ended December 31, 19X0, Hirsch, CPA, is aware that certain events and transactions that took place after December 31, 19X0, but before he issues his report dated February 8, 19X1, may affect the company's financial statements.

The following material events or transactions have come to his attention.

1. On January 3, 19X1, Flowmeter, Inc., received a shipment of raw materials from Canada. The materials had been ordered in October 19X0 and shipped FOB shipping point in November 19X0.
2. On January 15, 19X1, the company settled and paid a personal injury claim of a former employee as the result of an accident that occurred in March 19X0. The company had not previously recorded a liability for the claim.
3. On January 25, 19X1, the company agreed to purchase for cash the outstanding stock of Porter Electrical Co. The acquisition is likely to double the sales volume of Flowmeter, Inc.
4. On February 1, 19X1, a plant owned by Flowmeter, Inc., was damaged by a flood resulting in an uninsured loss of inventory.
5. On February 5, 19X1, Flowmeter, Inc., issued and sold to the general public \$2,000,000 in convertible bonds.

REQUIRED

For each of the above events or transactions, indicate the audit procedures that should have brought the item to the attention of the auditor and the form of disclosure in the financial statements including the reasons for such disclosure. Organize your answers in the following format:

Item No.	Audit Procedures	Required Disclosures or Entry and Reasons

AICPA

19-27 **(Litigation, claims, and assessments)** Young, CPA, is considering the procedures to be applied concerning a client's loss contingencies relating to litigation, claims, and assessments.

REQUIRED

What substantive audit procedures should Young apply when testing for loss contingencies relating to litigation, claims, and assessments?

AICPA

19-28 **(Litigation, claims, and assessments)** During an audit engagement, an auditor is expected to communicate with lawyers concerning litigation, claims, and assessments. Listed below are five situations regarding LCA. The last clause or sentence of each case states a conclusion.

1. If the client's lawyer is silent on certain aspects of an attorney's letter request, the auditor may infer the response is complete.
2. Letters of audit inquiry ask for the lawyer's evaluation of the probable outcome of matters reported in the response. If the lawyer's response does not contain this evaluation, the auditor should conclude the scope of the audit has been restricted.
3. The Top Dollar Corporation is involved in litigation for which the potential liability is so great that an unfavorable judgment at or near the claimed amount would seriously impair its operations. This is how the company's attorneys answered the legal confirmation request:

   Although no assurance can be given as to the outcome of this action, based on the facts known by us to date, in the confidence of the attorney/client relationship and otherwise, and our understanding of the present law, we believe the company has good and meritorious defense to the claims asserted against it and should prevail.

   On this basis, the independent auditor may issue an unqualified opinion.
4. In situations where the auditor has orally discussed matters involving litigation with the client's legal counsel and obtained his oral opinion on the outcome of disputed matters, it is not necessary to obtain written confirmation of these oral opinions if the auditor has summarized the attorney's opinion in a memo to the working papers.
5. For the past ten years, XYZ Company has used the services of JJH&I for its primary legal advice and in many significant matters of litigation. Ninety-five percent of JJH&I's legal fees originate from services performed for XYZ Company. At December 31, JJH&I was handling litigation involving great potential liability to the company and has now responded to the auditor's letter of inquiry. If we assume full disclosure, complete reliance can be placed on this response.

REQUIRED

For each case, indicate whether you agree or disagree with the conclusion and the reason(s) therefor.

19-29 **(Client representation letter)** During the audit of the annual financial statements of Amis Manufacturing, Inc., the company's president, R. Alderman, and Luddy, the auditor, reviewed matters that were supposed to be included in a written representation letter. On receipt of the following client representation letter, Luddy contacted Alderman to state that it was incomplete:

To E. K. Luddy, CPA

In connection with your audit of the balance sheet of Amis Manufacturing, Inc., as of December 31, 19X5, and the related statements of income, retained earnings, and changes in cash flows for the year then ended, for the purpose of expressing an opinion as to whether the financial statements present fairly the financial position, results of operations, and changes in cash flows of Amis Manufacturing, Inc., in conformity with generally accepted accounting principles, we confirm, to the best of our knowledge and belief, the following representations made to you during your audit. There were no

- Plans or intentions that may materially affect the carrying value or classification of assets and liabilities.
- Communications from regulatory agencies concerning noncompliance with, or deficiencies in, financial reporting practices.
- Agreements to repurchase assets previously sold.
- Violations or possible violations of laws or regulations whose effects should be considered for disclosure in the financial statements or as a basis for recording a loss contingency.
- Unasserted claims or assessments that our lawyer has advised are probable of assertion and must be disclosed in accordance with *Statement of Financial Accounting Standards No. 5.*
- Capital stock repurchase options or agreements or capital stock reserved for options, warrants, conversions, or other requirements.
- Compensating balance or other arrangements involving restrictions on cash balances.

R. Alderman, President
Amis Manufacturing, Inc.

March 14, 19X6

REQUIRED

Identify the other matters that Alderman's representation letter should specifically confirm.

AICPA

19-30 **(Analytical procedures in overall review)** In auditing the financial statements of a manufacturing company that were prepared from data processed by electronic data processing equipment, the CPA has found that his traditional "audit trail" has been obscured. As a result, the CPA may place increased emphasis on overall checks of the data under audit. These overall checks, which are also applied in auditing visibly posted accounting records, include the computation of ratios, which are compared with prior year ratios or industry-wide norms. Examples of such overall checks or ratios are the computation of the rate of inventory turnover and the computation of the number of days' sales in receivables.

REQUIRED

a. Discuss the advantages to the CPA of the use of ratios as overall checks in an audit.
b. In addition to the computations given above, list the ratios that a CPA may compute during an audit as overall checks on balance sheet accounts and related nominal accounts. For each ratio listed, name the two (or more) accounts used in its computation.
c. When a CPA discovers that there has been a significant change in a ratio when compared with the prior year's ratio, he considers the possible reasons for the change. Give the possible reasons for the following significant changes in ratios:
    1. The rate of inventory turnover (ratio of cost of sales and average inventory) has decreased from the prior year's rate.
    2. The number of days' sales in receivables (ratio of average daily accounts receivable and sales) has increased over the prior year.

AICPA

19-31 **(Reportable conditions/material weaknesses)** During the course of an audit made in accordance with generally accepted auditing standards, an auditor may become aware of matters relating to the client's internal control structure that may be of interest to the client's audit committee or to individuals with an equivalent level of authority and responsibility, such as the board of directors, the board of trustees, or the owner in an owner-managed enterprise.

REQUIRED

a. What are meant by the terms "reportable conditions" and "material weaknesses"?
b. What are an auditor's responsibilities in identifying and reporting these matters?

AICPA

19-32 **(Reportable conditions/material weaknesses)** On completing the work on the internal control structure of the Klima Corporation in the 19X4 audit, an inexperienced staff member was asked to prepare the communication for the audit committee. The audit team concluded that there were several reportable conditions but no material weaknesses. The first and last paragraphs of the staff member's draft were as follows:

To the Audit Committee:

In completing our audit of the financial statements of the Klima Corporation for the year ended December 31, 19X4, we considered its internal control environment in order to determine our auditing procedures for the purpose of expressing our opinion on the financial statements and not to express an opinion on the internal control structure. However, we noted certain matters involving the design and effectiveness of the system of internal control that we consider to be reportable conditions under GAAS established by the American Institute of Certified Public Accountants. Reportable conditions involve matters coming to our attention relating to potential weaknesses in the design or operation of the internal control structure that, in our judgment, could adversely affect the organization's ability to prepare financial statements in conformity with GAAP.

. . . .

This report is intended solely for the audit committee and others within the organization.

REQUIRED

a. List the deficiencies in the report. For each deficiency, indicate the proper wording. Use the following format for your answers: (*Note:* Do not write a proper report.)

Deficiency	Proper Wording

b. Distinguish between a reportable condition and a material weakness.
c. Indicate the effects on the report when the auditor wishes to inform the audit committee that identified reportable conditions are not material weaknesses.

19-33 **(Management letter)** The major result of a financial audit conducted by an independent accountant is the expression of an opinion by the auditor on the fairness of the financial statements. Although the auditor's report containing the opinion is the best known report issued by the independent auditor, other reports are often prepared during the course of a normal audit. One such report is the management letter (informal report).

REQUIRED

a. What is the purpose of a management letter?
b. Identify the major types of information that are likely to be covered in a management letter. Support your answer with a detailed example of one of the types identified above.

ICMA

19-34 **(Subsequent events/postaudit discovery of facts)** The fiscal year of the Edie Company ends on December 31. Your audit report, dated February 26, is to be delivered to the client on March 9. Listed below are events that occur or are discovered from the date of the balance sheet to June 30 of the following year. Assume each event has a material effect on the financial statements.

1. Jan 15 Inventory is sold at a price below December 31 net realizable value.
2. Jan 20 A major customer becomes bankrupt from ongoing net losses.
3. Jan 31 The board of directors authorizes the acquisition of a company as a subsidiary.
4. Feb 10 A fire destroys a major company warehouse.
5. Feb 25 A lawsuit is decided against the company for an accident that occurred on October 10. The damages are three times higher than estimated on December 31.
6. Feb 28 The board of directors authorizes a two-for-one stock split.
7. Mar 7 A foreign government expropriates a major foreign subsidiary following the unexpected overthrow of the government.
8. March 31 A court rules that a minority group is the rightful legal owner of land on which an operating division is located.

REQUIRED

a. Identify each event as a (1) type 1 subsequent event during the subsequent events period, (2) type 2 subsequent event during the subsequent events period, (3) type 1 subsequent event occurring after field work but before issuance of report, (4) type 2 subsequent event occurring after field work but before issuance of report, or (5) postaudit discovery of facts existing at date of report.
b. Explain your audit responsibilities for each of the categories in (a).
c. Indicate how you would obtain knowledge of each of the eight items.
d. What additional responsibilities does an auditor have for the postaudit discovery of facts if the client refuses to make required disclosures?

CASES

19-35 **(Subsequent events)** In connection with your audit of the financial statements of Olars Manufacturing Corporation for the year ended December 31, 19X0, your post-balance-sheet-date review disclosed the following items:

1. January 3, 19X1: The state government approved a plan for the construction of an express highway. The plan will result in the appropriation of a portion of the land area owned by Olars Manufacturing Corporation. Construction will begin in late 19X1. No estimate of the condemnation award is available.
2. January 4, 19X1: The funds for a $25,000 loan to the corporation made by Mr. Olars on July 15, 19X0, were obtained by him by a loan on his personal life insurance policy. The loan was recorded in the account Loan from Officers. Mr. Olars's source of the funds was not disclosed in the company records. The corporation pays the premiums on the life insurance policy and Mrs. Olars, wife of the president, is the beneficiary of the policy.

3. January 7, 19X1: The mineral content of a shipment of ore en route on December 31, 19X0, was determined to be 72%. The shipment was recorded at year-end at an estimated content of 50% by a debit to Raw Material Inventory and a credit to Accounts Payable in the amount of $20,600. The final liability to the vendor is based on the actual mineral content of the shipment.
4. January 15, 19X1: Culminating a series of personal disagreements between Mr. Olars, the president, and his brother-in-law, the treasurer, the latter resigned, effective immediately, under an agreement whereby the corporation would purchase his 10% stock ownership at book value as of December 31, 19X0. Payment is to be made in two equal amounts in cash on April 1 and October 1, 19X1. In December, the treasurer had obtained a divorce from his wife, who was Mr. Olars's sister.
5. January 31, 19X1: As a result of reduced sales, production was curtailed in mid-January and some workers were laid off. On February 5, 19X1, all the remaining workers went on strike. To date, the strike is unsettled.
6. February 10, 19X1: A contract was signed whereby Mammoth Enterprises purchased from Olars Manufacturing Corporation all the latter's fixed assets (including rights to receive the proceeds of any property condemnation), inventories, and the right to conduct business under the name "Olars Manufacturing Division." The effective date of the transfer will be March 1, 19X1. The sale price was $500,000 subject to adjustment following the taking of a physical inventory. Important factors contributing to the decision to enter into the contract were the policy of the board of directors of Mammoth Industries to diversify the firm's activities and the report of a survey conducted by an independent market appraisal firm that revealed a declining market for Olars products.

REQUIRED

Assume that the above items came to your attention prior to completion of your audit field work on February 15, 19X1, and that you will render an audit report. For *each* of the above items:

a. Give the audit procedures, if any, that would have brought the item to your attention. Indicate other sources of information that may have revealed the item.
b. Discuss the disclosure that you would recommend for the item, listing all details that you would suggest should be disclosed. Indicate those items or details, if any, that should not be disclosed. Give your reasons for recommending or not recommending disclosure of the items or details.

AICPA

19-36 **(Letter of audit inquiry)** Cole & Cole, CPAs are auditing the financial statements of Consolidated Industries Co. for the year ended December 31, 19X2. On April 2, 19X3, an inquiry letter to J. J. Young, Consolidated's outside attorney, was drafted to corroborate the information furnished to Cole by management concerning pending and threatened litigation, claims, and assessments, and unasserted claims and assessments. On May 6, 19X3, C. R. Brown, Consolidated's Chief Financial Officer, gave Cole a draft of the inquiry letter below for Cole's review before mailing it to Young.

May 6, 19X3

J. J. Young, Attorney at Law
123 Main Street
Anytown, USA

Dear J. J. Young:

In connection with an audit of our financial statements at December 31, 19X2, and for the year then ended, management of the Company has prepared, and furnished to our auditors, Cole & Cole, CPAs, 456 Broadway, Anytown, USA, a description and evaluation of certain contingencies, including those set forth below involving matters with respect to which you have been engaged and to which you have devoted substantive attention on behalf of the Company in the form of legal consultation or representation. Your response should include matters that existed at December 31, 19X2. Because of the confidentiality of all these matters, your response may be limited.

In November 19X2, an action was brought against the Company by an outside salesman alleging breach of contract for sales commissions and pleading a second cause of action for an accounting with respect to claims for fees and commissions. The causes of action claim damages of $300,000, but the Company believes it has meritorious defenses to the claims. The possible exposure of the Company to a successful judgment on behalf of the plaintiff is slight.

In July 19X0, an action was brought against the Company by Industrial Manufacturing Co. (Industrial) alleging patent infringement and seeking damages of $20,000,000. The action in U.S. District Court resulted in a decision on October 16, 19X2, holding that the Company infringed seven Industrial patents and awarded damages of $14,000,000. The Company vigorously denies these allegations and has filed an appeal with the U.S. Court of Appeals for the Federal Circuit. The appeal process is expected to take approximately two years, but there is some chance that Industrial may ultimately prevail.

Please furnish to our auditors such explanation, if any, that you consider necessary to supplement the foregoing information, including an explanation of those matters as to which your views may differ from those stated and an identification of the omission of any pending or threatened litigation, claims, and assessments or a statement that the list of such matters is complete. Your response may be quoted or referred to in the financial statements without further correspondence with you.

You also consulted on various other matters considered pending or threatened litigation. However, you may not comment on these matters because publicizing them may alert potential plaintiffs to the strengths of their cases. In addition, various other matters probable of assertion that have some chance of an unfavorable outcome, as of December 31, 19X2, are unasserted claims and assessments.

C. R. Brown
Chief Financial Officer

REQUIRED

Describe the omissions, ambiguities, and inappropriate statements and terminology in Brown's letter.

(AICPA)

19-37 **(Communication of internal control structure related matters)** Land & Hale, CPAs, are auditing the financial statements of Stone Co., a nonpublic entity, for the year ended December 31, 19X3. Land, the engagement supervisor, anticipates expressing an unqualified opinion on May 20, 19X4.

Wood, an assistant on the engagement, drafted the auditor's communication of internal control structure-related matters that Land plans to send to Stone's board of directors with the May 20th auditor's report.

Land reviewed Wood's draft and indicated in the *Supervisor's Review Notes* that there were deficiencies in Wood's draft.

Independent Auditor's Report

To the Board of Directors of Stone Company:

In planning and performing our audit of the financial statements of Stone Co. for the year ended December 31, 19X3, we considered its internal control structure in order to determine our auditing procedures for the purpose of expressing our opinion on the financial statements and to provide assurance on the internal control structure. However, we noted certain matters involving the internal control structure and its operations that we consider to be reportable conditions under standards established by the American Institute of Certified Public Accountants. Reportable conditions involve matters coming to our attention relating to significant deficiencies in the design or operation of the internal control structure that, in our judgment, could adversely affect the organization's ability to record, process, summarize, and report financial data consistent with our assessment of control risk.

We noted that deficiencies in the internal control structure design included inadequate provisions for the safeguarding of assets, especially concerning cash receipts and inventory stored at remote locations. Additionally, we noted failures in the operation of the internal control structure. Reconciliations of subsidiary ledgers to control accounts were not timely prepared and senior employees in authority intentionally overrode the internal control structure concerning cash payments to the detriment of the overall objectives of the structure.

A material weakness is not necessarily a reportable condition, but is a design defect in which the internal control structure elements do not reduce to a relatively low level the risk that errors or irregularities in amounts that would be material in relation to the financial statements being audited may occur and not be detected by the auditor during the audit.

Our consideration of the internal control structure would not necessarily disclose all matters in the internal control structure that might be reportable conditions and, accordingly, would not necessarily disclose all reportable conditions that are also considered to be material weaknesses as defined above. However, none of the reportable conditions described above is believed to be a material weakness.

This report is intended solely for the information and use of the Board of Directors of Stone Co. Accordingly, it is not intended to be distributed to stockholders, management, or those who are not responsible for these matters.

Land & Hale, CPAs
May 4, 19X4

REQUIRED

Indicate the deficiencies in Wood's draft of the auditor's communication of internal control structure related matters that are likely included in the *Supervisor's Review Notes* prepared by Land.

(AICPA adapted)

RESEARCH QUESTIONS

19-38 **(AAER on completing field work)** The SEC's *Accounting and Auditing Enforcement Release Nos. 111* and *150* address several issues related to completing the field work on an audit. Summarize the facts and conclusions of the SEC pertaining to these issues as set forth in the AAERs.

19-39 **(AAER on evaluating audit findings)** The SEC's *Accounting and Auditing Enforcement Release No. 27* deals with the partner's review of audit working papers. Summarize the facts and conclusions of the SEC on this issue as set forth in the AAER.

19-40 **(AAER on postaudit responsibilities)** The SEC's *Accounting and Auditing Enforcement Release No. 114* deals with a situation involving a postaudit discovery of facts that would have affected the auditor's report. Summarize the facts and conclusions of the SEC on this issue as set forth in the AAER.

CHAPTER

20

REPORTING ON AUDITED FINANCIAL STATEMENTS

LEARNING OBJECTIVES

When you have completed your study of this chapter, you should be able to

1. Explain each of the four reporting standards.
2. Prepare the auditor's standard report.
3. Describe the types of departures from the standard report and enumerate the circumstances when each is appropriate.
4. Describe the effects of various circumstances on the form and content of the auditor's report.
5. Discuss selected other reporting considerations.

STANDARDS OF REPORTING
- FIRST STANDARD OF REPORTING
- SECOND STANDARD OF REPORTING
- THIRD STANDARD OF REPORTING
- FOURTH STANDARD OF REPORTING

THE AUDITOR'S REPORT
- STANDARD REPORT
- DEPARTURES FROM STANDARD REPORT

EFFECTS OF CIRCUMSTANCES CAUSING DEPARTURES FROM THE STANDARD REPORT
- SCOPE LIMITATION
- NONCONFORMITY WITH GAAP
- INCONSISTENCY IN ACCOUNTING PRINCIPLES
- INADEQUATE DISCLOSURE
- UNCERTAINTY
- SUBSTANTIAL DOUBT ABOUT GOING CONCERN STATUS
- EMPHASIS OF A MATTER
- OPINION BASED IN PART ON REPORT OF ANOTHER AUDITOR
- SUMMARY OF EFFECTS OF CIRCUMSTANCES ON AUDITORS' REPORTS

OTHER REPORTING CONSIDERATIONS
- REPORTING WHEN THE CPA IS NOT INDEPENDENT
- CIRCUMSTANCES CONCERNING COMPARATIVE FINANCIAL STATEMENTS
- INFORMATION ACCOMPANYING AUDITED FINANCIAL STATEMENTS
- FINANCIAL STATEMENTS PREPARED FOR USE IN OTHER COUNTRIES

SUMMARY

BIBLIOGRAPHY

OBJECTIVE QUESTIONS

COMPREHENSIVE QUESTIONS

CASES

RESEARCH QUESTIONS

The final phase of an audit engagement is reporting the findings. This chapter expands on the explanation of auditors' reports provided in Chapter 2.

To meet his or her reporting responsibilities, the auditor must (1) have a thorough understanding of the four reporting standards, (2) know the exact wording of the auditor's standard report and the conditions that must be met for it to be issued, (3) understand the types of departures from the standard report and the circumstances when each is appropriate, and (4) be knowledgeable of certain other special reporting considerations. Each of these topics is explained in this chapter.

Throughout the chapter, unless stated otherwise it should be assumed that the auditor is reporting on an engagement to perform an audit in accordance with GAAS for the purpose of rendering an opinion as to whether management's financial statements conform to GAAP.

STANDARDS OF REPORTING

OBJECTIVE 1

Explain each of the four reporting standards.

As explained in Chapter 2, GAAS includes four generally accepted **reporting standards.** These standards relate to GAAP, consistency, adequate disclosure, and expressing an opinion. Each standard is discussed in a following section.

FIRST STANDARD OF REPORTING

The first standard of reporting states:

> The report shall state whether the financial statements are presented in accordance with generally accepted accounting principles.

The first standard of reporting requires the auditor to explicitly state whether the financial statements are **presented fairly in conformity with GAAP.** This standard requires the expression of an opinion rather than a statement of fact. For purposes of this standard, GAAP include not only accounting principles, such as the cost principle, but also the methods of applying them, such as the first-in, first-out (FIFO) and last-in, first-out (LIFO) methods for inventories, and the straight-line and sum-of-the-years'-digits methods of depreciation.

SAS 69, *The Meaning of Present Fairly in Conformity With Generally Accepted Accounting Principles in the Independent Auditor's Report* (AU 411.04), states that the auditor's opinion as to conformity with GAAP should be based on his or her judgment as to whether

- The accounting principles selected and applied have general acceptance.
- The accounting principles are appropriate in the circumstances.
- The financial statements, including the related notes, are informative of matters that may affect their use, understanding, and interpretation.
- The information presented in the financial statements is classified and summarized in a reasonable manner (i.e., neither too detailed nor too condensed).
- The statements reflect the underlying events and transactions in a manner that presents the financial position, results of operations, and cash flows within reasonable and practicable limits.

The third and fourth items relate directly to the adequacy of informative disclosures, which is dealt with separately in the third standard of reporting as explained below.

Sources of GAAP

The phrase **generally accepted accounting principles** includes broad guidelines as well as specific conventions, rules, and procedures. There is no single compilation of all established accounting principles. However, the Auditing Standards Board has established a **GAAP hierarchy** as shown in Figure 20-1. The hierarchy

FIGURE 20-1 • SUMMARY OF GAAP HIERARCHY

GAAP Category		Nongovernmental Entities	State and Local Governments
Established Accounting Principles	A (*Rule 203)*	FASB Statements and Interpretations, APB Opinions, and AICPA Accounting Research Bulletins	GASB Statements and Interpretations, plus AICPA and FASB pronouncements if made applicable to state and local governments by a GASB Statement or Interpretation
	B	FASB Technical Bulletins, AICPA Industry Audit and Accounting Guides, and AICPA Statements of Position	GASB Technical Bulletins, and the following pronouncements if specifically made applicable to state and local governments by the AICPA: AICPA Industry Audit and Accounting Guides and AICPA Statements of Position
	C	Consensus positions of the FASB Emerging Issues Task Force and AICPA Practice Bulletins	Consensus positions of the GASB Emerging Issues Task Force and AICPA Practice Bulletins if specifically made applicable to state and local governments by the AICPA
	D	AICPA accounting interpretations, "Qs and As" published by the FASB staff, as well as industry practices widely recognized and prevalent	"Qs and As" published by the GASB staff, as well as industry practices widely recognized and prevalent
Other Accounting Literature	E	Other accounting literature, including FASB Concepts Statements; AICPA Issues Papers; International Accounting Standards Committee Statements; GASB Statements, Interpretations, and Technical Bulletins; pronouncements of other professional associations or regulatory agencies; AICPA *Technical Practice Aids;* and accounting textbooks, handbooks, and articles	Other accounting literature, including GASB Concepts Statements, pronouncements in categories (a) through (d) of the hierarchy for nongovernmental entities when not specifically made applicable to state and local governments; FASB Concepts Statements; AICPA Issues Papers; International Accounting Standards Committee Statements; pronouncements of other professional associations or regulatory agencies; AICPA *Technical Practice Aids;* and accounting textbooks, handbooks, and articles

SOURCE: AU 411.16.

categorizes the sources of accounting principles for two types of entities: (1) nongovernmental and (2) state and local governments. The sources of principles are further classified into four subcategories (A–D) of *established accounting principles* and one category (E) representing all other accounting literature. When principles from more than one of subcategories B, C, and D appear to be relevant in a particular circumstance, the principle from the higher category should be applied unless the auditor can justify a conclusion that application of a principle from a lower category better presents the substance of the transaction in the circumstances.

Rules and interpretive releases of the SEC have an authority similar to category A pronouncements for SEC registrants. Accounting requirements adopted by certain other regulatory agencies for reports filed with them may differ from GAAP in certain respects. Guidance for auditors reporting on financial statements prepared in conformity with a comprehensive basis of accounting other than GAAP is discussed in the next chapter.

Promulgated GAAP

You may recall that the AICPA has given special recognition to the principles referred to in category A of Figure 20-1. Principles from these sources are referred to in Rule 203 of the AICPA's *Code of Professional Conduct* as **promulgated accounting principles.** In effect, the AICPA says that whenever promulgated principles apply to an entity's financial statements, they must be followed in meeting the first standard of reporting.

Rule 203 does provide for an exception. If due to unusual circumstances compliance with a promulgated principle would cause the financial statement to be misleading, a principle from one of the other categories may be used. The unusual circumstances contemplated in Rule 203 consist primarily of new legislation or the evolution of a new form of business transaction.

SECOND STANDARD OF REPORTING

The second standard of reporting is

> The report shall identify those circumstances in which such principles have not been consistently observed in the current period in relation to the preceding period.

Accordingly, unless the report contains specific language to the contrary, the reader can conclude that accounting principles have been consistently applied. The objectives of this standard are (1) to give assurance that the comparability of financial statements between accounting periods has not been materially affected by changes in accounting principles and (2) to require appropriate reporting by the auditor when comparability has been materially affected by such changes.

The consistency standard does not apply in the first-year audit of a new company. However, it does apply in the first audit of an established company.

Accounting Changes Affecting Consistency

A change in an accounting principle results from the adoption of a GAAP different from the one previously used in the preparation of financial statements.

Accounting changes affecting consistency include

- A change in the principle itself, such as a change from a sales basis to a production basis in recording farm revenue.
- A change in the method of applying a principle, such as a change from the straight-line method of depreciation to the sum-of-the-years'-digits method.
- A change in the reporting entity, such as presenting consolidated statements in place of individual company statements or changes in specific subsidiaries constituting the consolidated group.
- The correction of an error in principle, as, for example, a change from a principle not generally accepted to one that is generally accepted.
- A change in principle inseparable from a change in estimate, such as a change from capitalizing and amortizing a cost to recording it as an expense when incurred because future benefits are now doubtful.

Changes Not Affecting Consistency

The consistency standard does not extend to the effects on comparability of the following:

- Changed business conditions, such as the acquisition (or disposal) of a subsidiary company.
- The introduction of a new product line.
- Acts of God (e.g., fires, floods, and similar occurrences).
- Accounting changes involving accounting estimates.
- Corrections of errors not involving a principle.
- Classifications and reclassifications.
- Variations in the format of the statement of cash flows.
- Substantially different transactions or events.

These matters, however, may require disclosure under the third standard of reporting.

THIRD STANDARD OF REPORTING

The third standard of reporting states:

> Informative disclosures in the financial statements are to be regarded as reasonably adequate unless otherwise stated in the report.

Thus, in the absence of explicit wording in the auditor's report to the contrary, the reader can conclude that the disclosure reporting standard has been met.

As noted earlier, under AU 411.04, the meaning of the phrase "present fairly in conformity with generally accepted accounting principles" extends to the adequacy of disclosures. If the financial statements and accompanying notes fail to disclose information required by GAAP, the statements are not fairly presented.

Informative disclosures involve material matters relating to the form, arrangement, and content of the financial statements and the accompanying notes. Authoritative bodies, such as the FASB and the SEC, frequently include disclosure requirements in their pronouncements. Informative disclosure extends to subsequent events and reporting segment information. In previous chapters of this book, many specific disclosure requirements have been enumerated, such as the basis and methods of inventory costing, market values of securities, liens on assets, and contingencies.

FOURTH STANDARD OF REPORTING

The fourth standard of reporting is:

> The report shall either contain an expression of opinion regarding the financial statements, taken as a whole, or an assertion to the effect that an opinion cannot be expressed. When an overall opinion cannot be expressed, the reasons therefor should be stated. In all cases where an auditor's name is associated with financial statements, the report should contain a clear-cut indication of the character of the auditor's work, if any, and the degree of responsibility the auditor is taking.

The objective of the fourth standard is to prevent misinterpretation of the degree of responsibility the auditor is assuming when his or her name is associated with financial statements. This standard directly influences the form, content, and language of the auditor's report.

Expressing an Opinion

This standard requires the auditor to express an opinion or assert that an opinion cannot be expressed. In the latter case, the reasons therefor should be stated in the auditor's report.

Financial Statements

The financial statements referred to in this standard apply to a single statement, such as a balance sheet, as well as to a complete set of basic statements (balance sheet, income statement, retained earnings statement, and cash flow statement). In some cases, the basic statements may be accompanied by a statement of changes in stockholders' equity accounts. The financial statements may be individual company statements, consolidated statements, and statements of one or more prior periods that are presented on a comparative basis with those of the current period. The auditor's opinion must be expressed (or disclaimed) in terms of the financial statement(s) identified in the introductory paragraph of the auditor's report.

Reference in the fourth standard of reporting to the words "taken as a whole" is important to the auditor in several ways. First, it means that the auditor's opinion should pertain to what the individual statement, in its entirety, purports to present. For example, this is financial position for the balance sheet and results of operations for the income statement. The auditor is not expected to express an opinion on individual components of an individual statement in the ordinary audit engagement. Second, "taken as a whole" does not mean that the auditor is prohibited from expressing different opinions on the statements included in a complete set of financial statements. It is possible, for example, for the auditor to express an unqualified opinion on the balance sheet and another type of opinion on the income, retained earnings, and cash flow statements. Different opinions within a given set of basic financial statements are rare.

Character of the Audit

Along with the expression (or disclaimer) of an opinion regarding the financial statements, the auditor is required to include in the report a clear-cut indication of the character of the audit. This is described in the first sentence of the scope paragraph of the auditor's report through the phrase "in accordance with generally accepted auditing standards." In lay terms, this phrase can be interpreted to mean that the audit was made according to established professional standards.

The scope paragraph also indicates that an audit includes (1) examining evidence on a test basis and (2) assessing the accounting principles used, significant estimates made by management, and the overall financial statement presentation.

Association with Financial Statements

A certified public accountant may be associated with audited or unaudited financial statements. The concern in this chapter is with audited financial statements. A

CPA is associated with audited financial statements when he or she has been engaged to audit the statements in accordance with GAAS and has applied auditing procedures to such statements. Association also exists when a CPA consents to the use of his or her name in a report, document, or written communication containing audited financial statements.

Degree of Responsibility

The final requirement of the fourth reporting standard is that the auditor must indicate the degree of responsibility that is being taken for the audit and the opinion. This is done through such wording as "we have audited," "our audit," and "in our opinion." The use of these words without qualification means that the auditor is assuming full or complete responsibility for the work done and the opinion rendered. When more than one auditor is involved in the audit and each auditor assumes responsibility only for his or her own work and opinion, the audit report must indicate the divided responsibility that exists, as explained later in this chapter.

LEARNING CHECK:

20-1 State the four generally accepted standards of reporting.

20-2 a. What factors should an auditor consider in deciding whether financial statements are in conformity with GAAP?
b. What is the *GAAP hierarchy* and how is it organized?

20-3 a. What pronouncements are recognized as promulgated accounting principles?
b. Must a company always comply with promulgated accounting principles under Ethics Rule 203?

20-4 a. When is a change in an accounting principle made in conformity with GAAP?
b. What circumstances result in a change in an accounting principle under the consistency standard?

20-5 a. Is there explicit or implicit recognition of adequate informative disclosures in the auditor's report?
b. What is the objective of the fourth reporting standard?

KEY TERMS:

Accounting changes affecting consistency, p. 755
GAAP hierarchy, p. 753
Generally accepted accounting principles, p. 753
Informative disclosures, p. 756
Presented fairly in conformity with GAAP, p. 753
Promulgated accounting principles, p. 755
Reporting Standards, p. 753

THE AUDITOR'S REPORT

The four generally accepted auditing standards of reporting are met by issuing an auditor's report in the appropriate form. Although a *standard report* is issued in a majority of audits, a limited number of variations or *departures from the standard report* are required to be used in specific circumstances.

STANDARD REPORT

OBJECTIVE 2

Prepare the auditor's standard report.

The auditor's **standard report** was introduced in Chapter 2. Recall that it consists of an introductory (or beginning) paragraph, a scope (or middle) paragraph, an opinion (or concluding) paragraph, and standard language. The report language varies slightly depending on whether the auditor is reporting on financial statements for a single year or on comparative financial statements. The standard report for a single year is illustrated in SAS 58, *Reports on Audited Financial Statements* (AU 508.08). The standard report on comparative financial statements is shown in Figure 20-2. The standard report has a heading that includes the word "independent" and contains an **unqualified opinion.**

The report is normally addressed to the individuals or groups that appointed the auditors. For a corporate client, this is the board of directors and/or stockholders; for unincorporated clients, the addressee is the partners or proprietor. The auditor's standard report should be dated as of the completion of field work. The signature on the report is generally the CPA firm's name because the firm assumes responsibility for the work and the findings of its professional staff. (Note: While the standard report on comparative financial statements is reproduced in Figure 20-2 for convenience, it is suggested that you review the annotated illustration presented in Figure 2-3 on page 46, which identifies each of the report's basic elements and key phrases.)

FIGURE 20-2 • AUDITOR'S STANDARD REPORT ON COMPARATIVE FINANCIAL STATEMENTS

INDEPENDENT AUDITOR'S REPORT

We have audited the accompanying balance sheets of X Company as of December 31, 19X2, and 19X1, and the related statements of income, retained earnings, and cash flows for the years then ended. These financial statements are the responsibility of the Company's management. Our responsibility is to express an opinion on these financial statements based on our audits.

We conducted our audits in accordance with generally accepted auditing standards. Those standards require that we plan and perform the audit to obtain reasonable assurance about whether the financial statements are free of material misstatement. An audit includes examining, on a test basis, evidence supporting the amounts and disclosures in the financial statements. An audit also includes assessing the accounting principles used and significant estimates made by management, as well as evaluating the overall financial statement presentation. We believe that our audits provide a reasonable basis for our opinion.

In our opinion, the financial statements referred to above present fairly, in all material respects, the financial position of X Company as of [at] December 31, 19X2 and 19X1, and the results of its operations and its cash flows for the years then ended in conformity with generally accepted accounting principles.

[Signature]

[Date]

SOURCE: AU 508.08.

DEPARTURES FROM STANDARD REPORT

OBJECTIVE 3

Describe the types of departures from the standard report and enumerate the circumstances when each is appropriate.

Departures from the standard report occur when the auditor concludes that (1) explanatory language should be added to the report while still expressing an unqualified opinion or (2) a different type of opinion should be expressed on the financial statements.

Explanatory Language with Unqualified Opinion

Circumstances may occur when **explanatory language** is added to the report but the auditor still expresses an unqualified opinion on the financial statements. The purpose of the explanatory information is to inform users of the report about one or more material facts pertaining to the audit or to the audited financial statements.

Following is a list of circumstances that may result in adding explanatory information to a standard report with an unqualified opinion:

- Noncomformity with a promulgated accounting principle necessary for fair presentation in unusual circumstances.
- Inconsistency in accounting principles accounted for in conformity with GAAP.
- Uncertainty accounted for in conformity with GAAP.
- Substantial doubt about an entity's going concern status accounted for in conformity with GAAP.
- Emphasis of a matter by the auditor.
- Opinion based in part on report of another auditor where there is no scope limitation or nonconformity with GAAP.

As illustrated later in the chapter, the explanatory information may be presented in an explanatory paragraph or the information can be added to one or more of the standard paragraphs. Generally, there should be no reference to the explanatory information in the opinion paragraph.

Other Types of Opinions

The auditor may conclude that an unqualified opinion cannot be expressed. In such case, AU 508.10 indicates that the auditor may express one of the following **other types of opinions:**

- A **qualified opinion** which states that except for the effects of the matter(s) to which the qualification relates, the financial statements present fairly . . . in conformity with GAAP.
- An **adverse opinion** which states that the financial statements do not present fairly . . . in conformity with GAAP.
- A **disclaimer of opinion** which states that the auditor does not express an opinion on the financial statements.

In addition to containing one of the foregoing opinions, the auditor's report should contain one or more explanatory paragraphs before the opinion paragraph that gives the substantive reason(s) for the opinion expressed. Moreover, in the opinion paragraph, reference should be made to the explanatory paragraph(s).

The auditor's judgment concerning the fairness of the financial statements taken as a whole is made within the framework of generally accepted auditing standards and generally accepted accounting principles. In deciding on the appropriate opinion, the auditor must answer the following questions:

- Was sufficient evidence obtained in the audit(s) to have a reasonable basis for an opinion on the financial statements?
- Do the financial statements present fairly, in all material respects, the financial position, results of operations, and cash flows in conformity with GAAP?

Materiality is important in answering the two questions. When the effects of a matter on which insufficient evidence is obtained are immaterial, or when a nonconformity with GAAP has an immaterial effect on the financial statements, affirmative answers can be given to each question resulting in the issuance of an unqualified opinion. A negative answer to the first question means that there was a **scope limitation** in conducting the audit. Similarly, a negative answer to the second question means that there is a material **nonconformity with GAAP.**

The reporting options for these two types of departures are as follows:

- Scope limitation: Qualified opinion or disclaimer of opinion.
- Nonconformity with GAAP: Qualified opinion or adverse opinion.

The choice between the two audit opinions for each type of departure is a matter of audit judgment. When the effect on the financial statements of the scope limitation or nonconformity with GAAP is extremely material, the auditor is likely to issue a disclaimer of opinion or adverse opinion, respectively. When the effect is not extremely material, a qualified opinion may be appropriate.

Corollary to the concept of materiality is *pervasiveness,* which relates to the number of financial statement items affected by a circumstance. When a small number of items is affected, the auditor will usually render a qualified opinion because the effects can adequately be explained in an explanatory paragraph, and the overall financial statements will still be useful. Conversely, when a large number of items is affected, it may be impractical to attempt to explain all the effects in explanatory paragraphs, and a disclaimer of opinion or adverse opinion will be issued.

Following is a list of circumstances that may result in issuing a qualified opinion, adverse opinion, or disclaimer of opinion:

- Scope limitation.
- Nonconformity with GAAP (other than required nonconformity with promulgated GAAP in unusual circumstances).
- Inconsistency in accounting principles not accounted for in conformity with GAAP.
- Inadequate disclosure.
- Uncertainty not accounted for in conformity with GAAP.
- Substantial doubt about an entity's going concern status not accounted for in conformity with GAAP.
- Circumstances pertaining to opinion based in part on report of another auditor involving a scope limitation or nonconformity with GAAP.

Fortunately, these circumstances occur infrequently in practice. Nonetheless, the auditor must be able to recognize them and know how they affect the audit report.

LEARNING CHECK:

20-6 a. Describe the form of the auditor's standard report and identify each of its paragraphs.
b. How should the report be addressed, signed, and dated?

20-7 a. Describe the two types of departures from the auditor's standard report.
b. Indicate the circumstances that may result in each of the two types of departures.

20-8 a. Distinguish among a qualified opinion, an adverse opinion, and a disclaimer of opinion.
b. What effects will these opinions have on the form and content of the auditor's standard report?

20-9 What questions should be asked by an auditor in determining the appropriate opinion to express?

KEY TERMS:

Adverse opinion, p. 760
Departures from the standard report, p. 760
Disclaimer of opinion, p. 760
Explanatory language, p. 760
Nonconformity with GAAP, p. 761
Other types of opinions, p. 760
Qualified opinion, p. 760
Scope limitation, p. 761
Standard report, p. 759
Unqualified opinion, p. 759

OBJECTIVE 4

Describe the effects of various circumstances on the form and content of the auditor's report.

EFFECTS OF CIRCUMSTANCES CAUSING DEPARTURES FROM THE STANDARD REPORT

In the following sections, consideration is given to the effects on the auditor's report of the circumstances that require a departure from the standard report. Illustrative reports are presented for many of the circumstances.

SCOPE LIMITATION

In an audit made in accordance with GAAS, the auditor is able to perform all auditing procedures considered necessary in the circumstances. From these procedures, it is expected that the auditor will obtain sufficient competent evidential matter to have a reasonable basis for expressing an opinion on the financial statements. When the auditor cannot perform the necessary procedures or the procedures do not provide sufficient evidence, the auditor is said to have a **scope limitation.**

A scope limitation may be imposed by the client or result from circumstances. Examples of client restrictions are refusal to (1) permit confirmation of receivables, (2) sign a client representation letter, or (3) give the auditor access to the minutes of board of directors' meetings. Examples of restrictions attributable to circumstances are the timing of procedures, such as appointment too late to perform procedures considered necessary in the circumstances, and inadequate client records.

Limited Reporting Engagements

The auditor may be asked to audit one basic financial statement, such as the balance sheet, but not the others. Such an engagement does not involve a scope limitation as long as the auditor can apply all the procedures considered necessary in the circumstances. Rather, this type of an engagement involves a limited reporting objective. For example, in the first year a company is audited, the auditor may be asked to audit the balance sheet only. In such case, a three-paragraph report is issued with an unqualified opinion. The language in each paragraph is modified to refer only to the balance sheet. For example, the first sentence of the introductory paragraph is:

> We have audited the accompanying balance sheet of X Company as of December 31, 19XX.

Other Types of Opinions

As indicated above, a scope limitation will require the auditor to express either a qualified opinion or a disclaimer of opinion on the financial statements. The appropriate opinion depends on the nature and magnitude of the potential effects of the matters in question and their significance to the financial statements. If the potential effects relate to many financial statement items, their significance is likely to be greater than if only a limited number of items is involved. The effects on the auditor's report depend on the type of opinion expressed.

QUALIFIED OPINION. When a qualified opinion is expressed the auditor should

- Indicate the scope limitation in the scope paragraph.
- Give the substantive reasons for the limitation in an explanatory paragraph.
- Express a qualified opinion in the opinion paragraph with reference to the explanatory paragraph.

The wording of the opinion paragraph should refer to the potential effects on the financial statements of the items for which the auditor has not obtained audit satisfaction, rather than to the scope limitation itself, because the auditor's opinion relates to the financial statements. The effects on the auditor's report of issuing a qualified opinion because of a scope limitation and the appropriate wording of the opinion paragraph are illustrated in Figure 20-3. Note that (1) the scope paragraph begins with an except clause and (2) the "except for" wording in the opinion paragraph refers to the effects of possible adjustments.

FIGURE 20-3 • AUDITOR'S REPORT WITH QUALIFIED OPINION BECAUSE OF A SCOPE LIMITATION

INDEPENDENT AUDITOR'S REPORT

(Same first paragraph as the standard report.)

Except as discussed in the following paragraph, we conducted our audits in accordance with generally accepted auditing standards. Those standards require that we plan and perform the audits to obtain reasonable assurance about whether the financial statements are free of material misstatement. An audit includes examining, on a test basis, evidence supporting the amounts and disclosures in the financial statements. An audit also includes assessing the accounting principles used and significant estimates made by management, as well as evaluating the overall financial statement presentation. We believe that our audits provide a reasonable basis for our opinion.

We were unable to obtain audited financial statements supporting the Company's investment in a foreign affiliate stated at $________ and $________ at December 31, 19X2, and 19X1, respectively, or its equity in earnings of that affiliate of $________ and $________, which is included in net income for the years then ended as described in Note X to the financial statements; nor were we able to satisfy ourselves as to the carrying value of the investment in the foreign affiliate or the equity in its earnings by other auditing procedures.

In our opinion, except for the effects of such adjustments, if any, as might have been determined to be necessary had we been able to examine evidence regarding the foreign affiliate investment and earnings, the financial statements referred to above present fairly, in all material respects, the financial position of X Company as of December 31, 19X2 and 19X1, and the results of its operations and its cash flows for the years then ended in conformity with generally accepted accounting principles.

SOURCE: AU 508.44.

DISCLAIMER OF OPINION. When a disclaimer of opinion is expressed

- The introductory paragraph is modified.
- The scope paragraph is omitted.
- An explanatory paragraph is included after the introductory paragraph.
- The third and concluding paragraph contains a denial of an opinion.

An example of an audit report with a disclaimer of opinion because of a scope limitation is shown in Figure 20-4 on page 766.

Note that the first sentence of the report says, "We were engaged to audit" rather than "We have audited," and the last sentence of the standard introductory paragraph is omitted. In addition, the concluding paragraph does not begin with "In our opinion" because an opinion is not being expressed. Whenever a disclaimer of opinion is issued, the auditor should also disclose other reservations he or she has concerning fair presentation in conformity with GAAP.

NONCONFORMITY WITH GAAP

When the client's financial statements contain a **nonconformity with GAAP,** the effects on the auditor's report differ based on whether it is a necessary nonconformity with promulgated GAAP or other nonconformity with GAAP.

Explanatory Language with Unqualified Opinion

When the auditor concurs that due to unusual circumstances nonconformity with a promulgated accounting principle is necessary to keep the client's financial statements from being misleading, a standard report with explanatory language is issued. Specifically, the report contains

- Standard introductory and scope paragraphs.
- An explanatory paragraph preceding the opinion paragraph that explains the circumstances and states that the use of the alternative principle is justified.
- An unqualified opinion in a standard opinion paragraph.

Because, as mentioned previously, Rule 203 requires unusual circumstances to justify such a nonconformity, this type of report is rarely found in practice.

NECESSARY DEPARTURE FROM PROMULGATED GAAP

The auditor's report on the 1987 consolidated financial statements of Oak Industries, Inc. and Subsidiaries included the following explanatory paragraph in an otherwise standard report:

> As described in Note 3, in May 1987, the Company exchanged shares of its common stock for $5,060,000 of its outstanding public debt. The fair value of the common stock issued exceeded the carrying amount of the debt by $466,000, which has been shown as an extraordinary loss in the 1987 statement of operations. Because a portion of the debt exchanged was convertible debt, a literal application of Statement of Financial Accounting Standards No. 84, "Induced Conversions of Convertible Debt," would have resulted in a further reduction in net income of $3,611,000, which would have been offset by a corresponding $3,611,000 credit to additional paid-in capital; accordingly, there would have been no net effect on stockholders' investment. In the opinion of Company management, with which we agree, a literal application of accounting literature would have resulted in misleading financial statements that do not properly portray the economic consequences of the exchange.

SOURCE: AICPA, *Accounting Trends and Techniques*, 43rd ed. (1989), p. 429.

Other Types of Opinions

Most nonconformities with promulgated and other generally accepted accounting principles that have a material effect on the financial statements result in expressing either a qualified opinion or an adverse opinion. AU 508.50 states that in deciding on the appropriate opinion, the auditor should consider such factors as (1) dollar magnitude of the effects, (2) significance of the item to the client, (3) the pervasiveness of the misstatement (number of statement items affected), and (4) the effect of the misstatement on the statements taken as a whole. The issuance of an adverse opinion normally occurs only when the nonconformity with GAAP has an extremely material effect on the financial statements.

QUALIFIED OPINION. When a qualified opinion is issued, the auditor should

FIGURE 20-4 • AUDITOR'S REPORT WITH A DISCLAIMER OF OPINION BECAUSE OF A SCOPE LIMITATION

INDEPENDENT AUDITOR'S REPORT

We were engaged to audit the accompanying balance sheets of X Company as of December 31, 19X2 and 19X1, and the related statements of income, retained earnings, and cash flows for the years then ended. These financial statements are the responsibility of the Company's management.

(Second paragraph of standard report should be omitted.)

The Company did not make a count of its physical inventory in 19X2 or 19X1, stated in the accompanying financial statements at $______ as of December 31, 19X2, and at $______ as of December 31, 19X1. Further, evidence supporting the cost of property and equipment acquired prior to December 31, 19X1, is no longer available. The Company's records do not permit the application of other auditing procedures to inventories or property and equipment.

Since the Company did not take physical inventories and we were not able to apply other auditing procedures to satisfy ourselves as to inventory quantities and the cost of property and equipment, the scope of our work was not sufficient to enable us to express, and we do not express, an opinion on these financial statements.

SOURCE: AU 508.72.

- Disclose in an explanatory paragraph(s) preceding the opinion paragraph all of the substantive reasons for the opinion.
- Disclose in the explanatory paragraph(s) the principal effects of the subject matter of the qualification on financial position, results of operations, and cash flows, if practicable. If not practicable, the report should so state.
- Express a qualified opinion in the opinion paragraph with reference to the explanatory paragraph(s).

An example of a report where the opinion is qualified because of nonconformity with GAAP is illustrated in Figure 20-5.

ADVERSE OPINION. The effects on the auditor's report of issuing an adverse opinion are similar but not identical to the effects of a qualified opinion. In this case, (1) the explanatory paragraph(s) should indicate the substantive reasons for the adverse opinion and the principal effects of the subject matter of the adverse opinion, if practicable, and (2) the opinion paragraph should state that because of the effects of the matter(s) described in the explanatory paragraph(s), the financial statements do not present fairly. AU 508.69 contains the following illustrative wording for the opinion paragraph:

In our opinion, because of the effects of the matters discussed in the preceding paragraphs, the financial statements referred to above do not present fairly, in conformity with generally accepted accounting principles, the financial position of X Company as of December 31, 19X2 and 19X1, or the results of its operations or its cash flows for the years then ended.

FIGURE 20-5 • AUDITOR'S REPORT WITH QUALIFIED OPINION BECAUSE OF NONCONFORMITY WITH GAAP

INDEPENDENT AUDITOR'S REPORT

(Same first and second paragraphs as the standard report.)

The Company has excluded, from property and debt in the accompanying balance sheets, certain lease obligations that, in our opinion, should be capitalized in order to conform with generally accepted accounting principles. If these lease obligations were capitalized, property would be increased by $______ and $______, long-term debt by $______ and $______, and retained earnings by $______ and $______ as of December 31, 19X2 and 19X1, respectively. Additionally, net income would be increased (decreased) by $______ and $______ and earnings per share would be increased (decreased) by $______ and $______, respectively, for the years then ended.

In our opinion, except for the effects of not capitalizing certain lease obligations as discussed in the preceding paragraph, the financial statements referred to above present fairly, in all material respects, the financial position of X Company as of December 31, 19X2 and 19X1, and the results of its operations and its cash flows for the years then ended in conformity with generally accepted accounting principles.

SOURCE: AU 508.53.

If in addition to the circumstance directly causing the adverse opinion there are other scope limitations or nonconformities with GAAP, these matters must also be explained in separate explanatory paragraphs.

INCONSISTENCY IN ACCOUNTING PRINCIPLES

The effect on the audit report of a change in accounting principles depends on whether the change has been accounted for in conformity with GAAP. A change in principle is made in conformity with GAAP when (1) the new principle is a generally accepted accounting principle, (2) the change is properly accounted for and disclosed in the financial statements, and (3) management can justify that the new principle is preferable.

Explanatory Language with Unqualified Opinion

When the change is made in conformity with GAAP, the auditor should express an unqualified opinion on the financial statements and explain the change in an additional paragraph following the opinion paragraph. The effects on the standard report, and an example of the wording of the explanatory paragraph, are shown in Figure 20-6.

Note that the explanatory paragraph identifies the lack of consistency and refers the reader to the note in the financial statements that describes the change in principle. The auditor's concurrence with the change is implicit in the issuance of an unqualified opinion. The explanatory paragraph in the auditor's report satisfies the second standard of reporting that reference to consistency is needed only when accounting principles have not been consistently applied in the current period in relation to the preceding period.

FIGURE 20-6 • STANDARD AUDIT REPORT WITH EXPLANATORY PARAGRAPH BECAUSE OF INCONSISTENCY IN ACCOUNTING PRINCIPLES IN CONFORMITY WITH GAAP

INDEPENDENT AUDITOR'S REPORT

(Same first three paragraphs as the standard report.)

As discussed in Note X to the financial statements, the Company changed its method of computing depreciation in 19X2.

SOURCE: 508.35.

Other Types of Opinions

When the change in accounting principles is not made in conformity with GAAP, the auditor should express either a qualified opinion or an adverse opinion, depending on the materiality of the change. In addition, the auditor should add an explanatory paragraph immediately before the opinion paragraph to describe the nonconformity with GAAP. The effects on the standard report and an example of the wording of the explanatory paragraph when management did not justify the change in accounting principle are illustrated in Figure 20-7.

INADEQUATE DISCLOSURE

If the financial statements and accompanying notes fail to disclose information required by GAAP, the statements are not fairly presented. In such case, the auditor should express a qualified opinion or an adverse opinion because of noncon-

FIGURE 20-7 • AUDITOR'S REPORT WITH QUALIFIED OPINION BECAUSE OF INCONSISTENCY IN ACCOUNTING PRINCIPLES NOT IN CONFORMITY WITH GAAP

INDEPENDENT AUDITOR'S REPORT

(Same first and second paragraphs as the standard report.)

As disclosed in Note X to the financial statements, the Company adopted, in 19X2, the first-in, first-out method of accounting for its inventories, whereas it previously used the last-in, first-out method. Although use of the first-in, first-out method is in conformity with generally accepted accounting principles, in our opinion, the Company has not provided reasonable justification as required by generally accepted accounting principles.

In our opinion, except for the effects of the change in accounting principle discussed in the preceding paragraph, the financial statements referred to in the first paragraph present fairly, in all material respects, the financial position of X Company as of December 31, 19X2 and 19X1, and the results of its operations and its cash flows for the years then ended in conformity with generally accepted accounting principles.

SOURCE: AU 508.61.

formity with GAAP, and there is a departure from the standard report. If a company issues financial statements that purport to present financial position and results of operations but omits the related statement of cash flows, the auditor will normally conclude that the omission requires qualification of the opinion.

If it is practicable, the essential information should be provided in one or more explanatory paragraphs of the auditor's report, unless its omission from the report is recognized in an SAS. Two omissions have been recognized: the auditor is not required to present (1) a statement of cash flows when that statement is omitted by a client or (2) omitted segment information. In both instances, however, the auditor should identify the omitted data in an explanatory paragraph and express either a qualified or an adverse opinion on the financial statements.

The effects on the auditor's report in expressing a qualified opinion because of inadequate disclosure are illustrated in Figure 20-8. This report satisfies the third standard of reporting, which requires comment in the auditor's report when management's disclosures in the financial statements are not adequate for fair presentation.

Departures from the auditor's standard report because of inadequate disclosure occur infrequently. Because the necessary data, in most cases, are going to be disclosed in the auditor's report, management ordinarily prefers to make the disclosures that will permit a standard report.

UNCERTAINTY

The term **uncertainty** applies to the outcome of a financial statement item that is not susceptible to reasonable estimation prior to the issuance of the statements. Uncertainties include, but are not limited to, contingencies included in FASB Statement No. 5, *Accounting for Contingencies.* Uncertainties differ from accounting estimates in that the latter are capable of reasonable estimation by management. An uncertainty may pertain to the unknown outcome of such events as a lawsuit, an IRS audit of the client's tax return, a serious deficiency in working capital, or failure to comply with the terms of a loan agreement.

FIGURE 20-8 • AUDITOR'S REPORT WITH QUALIFIED OPINION BECAUSE OF INADEQUATE DISCLOSURE

INDEPENDENT AUDITOR'S REPORT

(Same first and second paragraphs as the standard report.)

The Company's financial statements do not disclose [describe the nature of the omitted disclosures]. In our opinion, disclosure of this information is required by generally accepted accounting principles.

In our opinion, except for the omission of the information discussed in the preceding paragraph. . . .

SOURCE: AU 508.56.

FASB Statement No. 5 specifies the following accounting treatments of loss contingencies (uncertainties) in financial statements:

- Accrual when the loss is (a) probable (likely to occur) *and* (b) reasonably estimable.
- Disclosure when the loss is (a) probable but the amount is not reasonably estimable *or* (b) the loss is only reasonably possible (could occur).
- Neither accrual nor disclosure when the possibility of loss is remote.

On determining whether management's treatment of an uncertainty conforms to FASB Statement No. 5, the auditor must determine whether the uncertainty requires the use of explanatory language with an unqualified opinion or another type of opinion because of either (1) a nonconformity with GAAP or (2) a scope limitation.

In determining whether the financial statements are presented fairly, the auditor should evaluate the materiality of reasonably possible losses, both individually and in the aggregate, on the resolution of the uncertainties. The auditor's consideration of materiality is a matter of professional judgment. Such judgment is made in the light of the surrounding circumstances. In some cases, uncertainties relate primarily to financial position, whereas others more closely pertain to results of operations.

Explanatory Language with Unqualified Opinion

It may be necessary to add an explanatory paragraph to the standard report even when management's treatment of an uncertainty is in conformity with GAAP. AU 508.24–.26 provides the following guidance relating to the need for an explanatory paragraph and the likelihood of a material loss resulting from the resolution of an uncertainty:

- *Probable chance of a material loss.* When management properly discloses a probable loss for which an accrual has not been made because a reasonable estimate could not be obtained, an explanatory paragraph *should* be added to the auditor's report. This is to alert the users of the report to the likelihood of a future accrual. (Note, however, that when a loss is probable and a reasonable estimate of the full amount of the loss has been accrued by management, no explanatory paragraph is necessary.)
- *Reasonable possibility of a material loss.* When the chance of a material loss from a properly disclosed uncertainty is more than remote but less than probable, the auditor *may or may not* add an explanatory paragraph after considering the following:
  - The magnitude by which the amount of a reasonably possible loss exceeds the auditor's judgment about materiality.
  - The likelihood of occurrence of a material loss.

  The auditor is more likely to add an explanatory paragraph as the magnitude of the loss becomes larger or the likelihood of occurrence becomes closer to probable than to remote.
- *Remote likelihood of a material loss.* The auditor should *not* add an explanatory paragraph in this situation.

When an explanatory paragraph is added, it should describe the uncertainty and indicate that its outcome cannot be determined because it depends on future events. As shown in Figure 20-9, the explanatory paragraph should follow the opinion paragraph. In this example, the explanatory paragraph is shortened by reference to the note in the financial statements. There is no mention of the uncertainty in the other paragraphs of the report.

Other Types of Opinions

Uncertainties will result in expressing other than an unqualified opinion when there is either (1) nonconformity with GAAP or (2) a scope limitation.

According to AU 508.19, uncertainties that result in nonconformity with GAAP generally are attributable to either (1) inadequate disclosure, (2) use of inappropriate accounting principles, or (3) unreasonable accounting estimates. When there is nonconformity with GAAP, the auditor should express either a qualified opinion or an adverse opinion. The effects of this departure from the standard report are the same as described earlier for other circumstances involving nonconformity with GAAP.

A scope limitation occurs when sufficient evidential matter does (or did) exist during the audit to support management's assertions about the uncertainties. However, such evidence was not available to the auditor because of management's record retention policies or a client-imposed restriction. For a scope limitation, the auditor should express a qualified opinion or a disclaimer of opinion. The departures from the standard report are the same as described earlier for other scope limitations.

SUBSTANTIAL DOUBT ABOUT GOING CONCERN STATUS

In an audit, the entity is normally assumed to be a **going concern** that will continue in existence. However, the auditor has a responsibility to evaluate whether in fact the entity has the ability to continue as a going concern for a reasonable period of time, not to exceed one year beyond the date of the financial statements

FIGURE 20-9 • STANDARD AUDIT REPORT WITH EXPLANATORY PARAGRAPH BECAUSE OF AN UNCERTAINTY

INDEPENDENT AUDITOR'S REPORT

(Same first three paragraphs as the standard report.)

As discussed in Note X to the financial statements, the Company is a defendant in a lawsuit alleging infringement of certain patent rights and claiming royalties and punitive damages. The Company has filed a counteraction, and preliminary hearings and discovery proceedings on both actions are in progress. The ultimate outcome of the litigation cannot presently be determined. Accordingly, no provision for any liability that may result upon adjudication has been made in the accompanying financial statements.

SOURCE: AU 508.32.

being audited. It is not necessary for the auditor to design audit procedures specifically for this purpose. Ordinarily, auditing procedures performed to achieve other audit objectives should be sufficient to identify conditions and events that, when considered in the aggregate, indicate that there is substantial doubt about the entity's ability to continue as a going concern. For example, conditions and events may be revealed by (1) review of compliance with the terms of debt and loan agreements, (2) reading of minutes of board of director's meetings, and (3) inquiry of an entity's legal counsel about litigation, claims, and assessments. SAS 59, *The Auditor's Consideration of an Entity's Ability to Continue as a Going Concern* (AU 341.06), indicates that information contrary to the going concern assumption includes

- *Negative trends* such as recurring operating losses, working capital deficiencies, negative cash flows from operations, and adverse key financial ratios.
- *Other indications of possible financial difficulties* such as defaulting on loan agreements, arrearages in dividends, restructuring of debt, and noncompliance with statutory capital requirements.
- *Internal matters* such as work stoppages, substantial dependence on the success of a particular project, and uneconomic long-term commitments.
- *External matters* such as loss of a key franchise, and uninsured losses from earthquake or flood.

The auditor is required to consider management's plans for dealing with the adverse effects of the foregoing conditions and events. Management may plan to (1) dispose of assets, (2) borrow money or restructure debt, (3) reduce or delay expenditures, or (4) increase ownership equity.

Explanatory Language with Unqualified Opinion

When the circumstances about the entity's ability to continue as a going concern are adequately disclosed in the notes to the financial statements, the auditor

FIGURE 20-10 • STANDARD AUDIT REPORT WITH EXPLANATORY LANGUAGE BECAUSE OF DOUBT ABOUT THE ENTITY'S ABILITY TO CONTINUE AS A GOING CONCERN

INDEPENDENT AUDITOR'S REPORT

(Same first three paragraphs as the standard report.)

The accompanying financial statements have been prepared assuming that the Company will continue as a going concern. As discussed in Note X to the financial statements, the Company has suffered recurring losses from operations and has a net capital deficiency that raise substantial doubt about its ability to continue as a going concern. Management's plans in regard to these matters are also described in Note X. The financial statements do not include any adjustments that might result from the outcome of this uncertainty.

SOURCE: AU 341.13.

should (1) express an unqualified opinion and (2) add an explanatory paragraph after the opinion paragraph that refers to the notes. The effects on the standard report are illustrated in Figure 20-10. If there is doubt about the recoverability of assets or the amounts of liabilities, such information should be included in the explanatory paragraph.

The Auditing Standards Board believes that the foregoing report should adequately inform users of the financial statements about the circumstances. However, the auditor is not prohibited from issuing an audit report that contains a disclaimer of opinion.

Other Types of Opinions

If the auditor concludes that the entity's disclosures in the financial statements are inadequate, the statements do not present fairly. Accordingly, the auditor should express either a qualified opinion or an adverse opinion due to nonconformity with GAAP, which includes informative disclosures. In addition, the auditor's report should contain an explanatory paragraph describing the circumstances, and, if practicable, the disclosures needed for fair presentation should be made.

EMPHASIS OF A MATTER

In some situations, the auditor may wish to emphasize in the audit report a matter that is properly accounted for and adequately disclosed while still expressing an unqualified opinion. Emphasis of a matter results in adding an explanatory paragraph to the standard report. In the report, the auditor should (1) use standard wording in the introductory, scope, and opinion paragraphs, (2) describe the matter being emphasized in an explanatory paragraph, and (3) make no reference to the explanatory material in the opinion paragraph. Reference in the opinion paragraph to the matter being emphasized is prohibited by AU 508.37 because a phrase "with the foregoing explanation" could be misconstrued as a qualification of the auditor's opinion. Items that may merit emphasis in a given case include related party transactions, a change in an accounting estimate, and changes in operating conditions.

OPINION BASED IN PART ON REPORT OF ANOTHER AUDITOR

When a client has one or more subsidiaries, divisions, or branches, it may be necessary for more than one auditing firm to participate in the audit. Assume, for example, that a client with its major operations located in the Midwest has a foreign subsidiary that is audited by a foreign firm. When two or more auditing firms are involved in an audit, one firm should be the principal auditor. This decision should be based on such factors as the relative amount and significance of the work done and the extent of the firm's knowledge of the overall statements. In this example, the firm auditing the Midwest operations would be the principal auditor.

The principal auditor must then decide whether or not he or she is willing to assume responsibility for the work of the other auditors insofar as it relates to the client's statements taken as a whole. If the principal auditor accepts this responsibility, no reference should be made in the audit report to the other auditors' examination. However, if the principal auditor is not willing to assume this responsibility, the fourth standard of reporting requires that reference be made to the other auditors in the auditor's report. Such action is necessary to indicate the shared responsibility that exists among the auditors for both the audit and the expression of an opinion on the financial statements.

Decision Not to Make Reference

If the principal auditor is able to obtain satisfaction as to the (1) independence and professional reputation of the other auditors and (2) scope and quality of the other auditors' examination, reference to the other auditors ordinarily is not made. The principal auditor would be able to reach this decision when

- The other auditors are associated or correspondent firms whose work is well known to the principal auditor.
- The work is performed under the principal auditor's guidance and control.
- The principal auditor reviews the audit programs and working papers of the other auditors.

The principal auditor may also elect not to make reference to another auditor if the portion of the financial statements audited by the other auditor is not material to the financial statements taken as a whole.

A standard audit report is issued when the principal auditor decides not to make reference to the other auditors. Mention of the other auditors in such case is inappropriate because the principal auditor is assuming full responsibility for the audit and the opinion.

Decision to Make Reference

The principal auditor may decide to make reference to another auditor when one or more of the foregoing factors are not present. The principal auditor may also decide to make reference whenever the portion of the financial statements examined by another auditor is material to the financial statements taken as a whole.

The principal auditor is required under this decision to make inquiries concerning the professional reputation of the other auditor and to obtain a representation from the other auditor that he is independent of the client. In cases where the other firm's primary practice is in a foreign country, the principal auditor should also communicate with the other auditor to ascertain the auditor's familiarity with GAAS and GAAP in the United States.

Explanatory Language with Unqualified Opinion

When the auditor decides to make reference to another auditor, the report should indicate clearly the division of responsibility that exists between the auditors. This is accomplished by the following changes in the report:

- In the introductory paragraph, the magnitude of the portion of the financial statements audited by the other auditors should be indicated.

- In the scope paragraph, the reports of other auditors should be included in the sources of the auditor's reasonable basis for an opinion.
- In the opinion paragraph, reference should be made to the other auditor's report.

These changes do not result in a four-paragraph report or a qualified opinion. Reference to the other auditor in the opinion paragraph indicates only the divided responsibility among the auditors. This form of reporting should not be regarded as being inferior to a report in which no reference is made to another auditor. An example of a report in which reference is made to another auditor is shown in Figure 20-11.

Other Types of Opinions

If the principal auditor concludes that reliance cannot be placed on the other auditor's work and the work done by the other auditor is material to the financial statements taken as a whole, a scope limitation exists. In such case, a qualified opinion or a disclaimer of opinion should be expressed. A qualified opinion may also be expressed by the principal auditor when the other auditor's report on a significant portion of the financial statements contains other than an unqualified opinion.

FIGURE 20-11 • STANDARD AUDIT REPORT WITH EXPLANATORY LANGUAGE BECAUSE OF REFERENCE TO ANOTHER AUDITOR

INDEPENDENT AUDITOR'S REPORT

We have audited the consolidated balance sheets of ABC Company as of December 31, 19X2 and 19X1, and the related consolidated statements of income, retained earnings, and cash flows for the years then ended. These financial statements are the responsibility of the Company's management. Our responsibility is to express an opinion on these financial statements based on our audits. We did not audit the financial statements of B Company, a wholly owned subsidiary, which statements reflect total assets of $________ and $________ as of December 31, 19X2 and 19X1, respectively, and total revenues of $________ and $________ for the years then ended. These statements were audited by other auditors whose report has been furnished to us and our opinion, insofar as it relates to the amounts included for B Company, is based solely on the report of the other auditors.

We conducted our audits in accordance with generally accepted auditing standards. Those standards required that we plan and perform the audit to obtain reasonable assurance about whether the financial statements are free of material misstatement. An audit includes examining, on a test basis, evidence supporting the amounts and disclosures in the financial statements. An audit also includes assessing the accounting principles used and significant estimates made by management, as well as evaluating the overall financial statement presentation. We believe that our audits and the report of other auditors provide a reasonable basis for our opinion.

In our opinion, based on our audits and the report of other auditors, the consolidated financial statements referred to above present fairly, in all material respects, the financial position of ABC Company as of December 31, 19X2 and 19X1, and the results of its operations and its cash flows for the years then ended in conformity with generally accepted accounting principles.

SOURCE: AU 508.13.

SUMMARY OF EFFECTS OF CIRCUMSTANCES ON AUDITORS' REPORTS

A summary of the effects of the circumstances discussed above that result in departures from the auditor's standard report is provided in Figure 20-12. For each circumstance, the type of departure is indicated together with the location of any explanatory information and a description of any other major effects on the report. After studying Figure 20-12, it is recommended that the less detailed summary of types of auditors' reports and circumstances in Figure 2-4 on page 51 also be reviewed.

LEARNING CHECK:

20-10 Indicate the opinions that may be expressed for (a) a scope limitation and (b) nonconformity with GAAP.

20-11 a. Explain the circumstance and the effects on the auditor's report when nonconformity with a promulgated principle results in an unqualified opinion.

b. Contrast the effects on the auditor's report when nonconformity with GAAP results in (1) a qualified opinion and (2) an adverse opinion.

20-12 a. Explain the effects on the auditor's report when the auditor is only asked to audit one basic financial statement.

b. Contrast the effects on the auditor's report when a scope limitation results in (1) a qualified opinion and (2) a disclaimer of opinion.

20-13 Indicate the effects on the auditor's report when a change in an accounting principle is (a) made in conformity with GAAP and (b) not made in conformity with GAAP.

20-14 a. What is an uncertainty?

b. What circumstances may result in only adding explanatory language to the auditor's report for an uncertainty?

c. Explain the circumstances when there may be (1) a scope limitation or (2) nonconformity with GAAP for an uncertainty.

20-15 a. Identify the factors that may provide information contrary to the going concern assumption.

b. What are the effects on the auditor's report when there is adequate disclosure in the financial statements about the entity's ability to continue as a going concern?

20-16 a. Contrast the conditions that may enable the principal auditor to (1) not make or (2) make reference to another auditor in the auditor's report.

b. Explain the effects on the auditor's report when the auditor decides to make reference to another auditor.

KEY TERMS:

Going concern, p. 771
Nonconformity with GAAP, p. 764
Scope limitation, p. 762
Uncertainty, p. 769

FIGURE 20-12 • SUMMARY OF EFFECTS OF CIRCUMSTANCES ON AUDITOR'S REPORTS

Circumstance	Type of Departure: Standard Report with Explanatory Language	Other Types of Opinions: Qualified	Adverse	Disclaimer	Presentation of Explanatory Information and Other Report Effects
Scope limitation (including an uncertainty involving a scope limitation) (pp. 762-764)		√			Begin scope paragraph with "Except..." clause. In explanatory paragraph before opinion paragraph, describe limitation. In opinion paragraph, use "except for effects of adjustments..." language.
				√	Begin introductory paragraph with "We were engaged to audit ..." and omit last sentence, Omit scope paragraph. Describe limitation in explanatory paragraph. Disclaim opinion in third paragraph.
Nonconformity with GAAP (pp. 764-767): Departure from promulgated GAAP necessary for fair presentation	√				In explanatory paragraph before opinion paragraph, explain circumstance and justify nonconformity.
Other nonconformity with GAAP		√	√		In explanatory paragraph before opinion paragraph, state reasons for opinion and principal effects of the nonconformity.
Inconsistency (pp. 767-768): In conformity with GAAP	√				In explanatory paragraph following opinion paragraph, explain change.
Not in conformity with GAAP		√	√		Same as "Other nonconformity with GAAP."
Inadequate disclosure (pp. 768-769)		√	√		In one or more explanatory paragraphs before opinion paragraph, state reasons for opinion and, except for omitted statement of cash flows or segment information, provide essential information if practicable.

FIGURE 20-12 • *(Continued)*

	Type of Departure				
		Other Types of Opinions			
Circumstance	**Standard Report with Explanatory Language**	**Qualified**	**Adverse**	**Disclaimer**	**Presentation of Explanatory Information and Other Report Effects**
Uncertainty (pp. 769-771): In conformity with GAAP	√				In explanatory paragraph after opinion paragraph, describe uncertainty and state outcome depends on future events.
Not in conformity with GAAP		√	√		Same as "Other nonconformity with GAAP."
Going concern doubt (pp. 771-773): In conformity with GAAP	√				In explanatory paragraph after opinion paragraph, refer to applicable note to financial statements, and include information about recoverability of assets and amounts of liabilities, if applicable.
Not in conformity with GAAP		√	√		In explanatory paragraph before opinion paragraph, state reasons for opinion and, if practical, provide the disclosures needed for fair presentation.
Emphasis of a matter (p. 773)	√				In separate explanatory paragraph, describe matter being emphasized.
Opinion based in part on report of another auditor (pp. 773-775): Decision to make reference—no scope limitation or nonconformity	√				Explanatory language added in introductory, scope, and opinion paragraphs.
Scope limitation or nonconformity		√	√	√	In separate explanatory paragraph, describe limitation or nonconformity. Modify other paragraphs as appropriate based on type of opinion.

OTHER REPORTING CONSIDERATIONS

OBJECTIVE 5

Discuss selected other reporting considerations.

This section discusses reporting responsibilities relating to four additional situations: (1) reporting when the CPA is not independent, (2) circumstances concerning comparative financial statements, (3) information accompanying audited financial statements, and (4) financial statements prepared for use in other countries.

REPORTING WHEN THE CPA IS NOT INDEPENDENT

A CPA may audit financial statements when he or she is not independent of the client. For example, the CPA may be an officer or director of the client, or he or she may have a direct financial interest in the client as a creditor or stockholder. When the CPA lacks independence as required by GAAS (General Standard No. 2), the CPA is precluded from using the auditor's standard report and is required to issue a disclaimer of opinion.

SAS 26, *Association with Financial Statements* (AU 504.10), indicates that a one-paragraph report should be issued as illustrated in Figure 20-13. The report should not state why the CPA is not independent. In addition, the report does not include a heading, and any auditing procedures that were performed should not be described. These disclosures might confuse the reader concerning the importance of the impairment of independence.

A CPA who is aware of material departures from GAAP should either (1) insist on revision of the financial statements, (2) describe the departures in the disclaimer, or (3) refuse to be associated with the financial statements.

CIRCUMSTANCES CONCERNING COMPARATIVE FINANCIAL STATEMENTS

As indicated earlier in this chapter, the fourth standard of reporting applies not only to the financial statements of the current period, but also to statements of any prior periods presented on a comparative basis with those of the current period. During the audit for the current year, the auditor should be alert to circumstances and events relating to prior-period financial statements. The circumstances may include (1) different audit opinions, (2) updating an opinion, and (3) a change in auditors.

FIGURE 20-13 • REPORT WHEN A CPA IS NOT INDEPENDENT

> We are not independent with respect to XYZ Company, and the accompanying balance sheet as of December 31, 19X1, and the related statements of income, retained earnings, and cash flows for the year then ended were not audited by us and, accordingly, we do not express an opinion on them.

SOURCE: AU 504.10.

Different Opinions

For a given year, an auditor may express an unqualified opinion on one statement while expressing a different type of opinion on the other statements. Similarly, in comparative statements, another type of opinion may be expressed on one or more statements for a prior year while an unqualified opinion is expressed on the same statement(s) for the current year. A report containing an unqualified opinion on the current year statements and a disclaimer of opinion on all but the balance sheet of the prior year is illustrated in Figure 20-14.

Notice that the scope paragraph begins with the words "Except as explained in the following paragraph. . . ." The remainder of the scope paragraph contains standard wording. The next paragraph contains a disclaimer on the results of operations and cash flows for the prior year. The final paragraph contains an unqualified opinion on the identified financial statements of each year.

Updating an Opinion

The auditor's current audit may produce evidence that the opinion on the prior year's statements should be different from the opinion originally expressed. This

FIGURE 20-14 • REPORT ON COMPARATIVE FINANCIAL STATEMENTS WITH DIFFERENT OPINIONS

INDEPENDENT AUDITOR'S REPORT

(Same first paragraph as the standard report.)

Except as explained in the following paragraph, we conducted our audits in accordance with generally accepted auditing standards. Those standards require that we plan and perform our audit to obtain reasonable assurance about whether the financial statements are free of material misstatement. An audit includes examining, on a test basis, evidence supporting the amounts and disclosures in the financial statements. An audit also includes assessing the accounting principles used and significant estimates made by management, as well as evaluating the overall financial statement presentation. We believe that our audits provide a reasonable basis for our opinion.

We did not observe the taking of the physical inventory as of December 31, 19X0, since that date was prior to our appointment as auditors for the Company, and we were unable to satisfy ourselves regarding inventory quantities by means of other auditing procedures. Inventory amounts as of December 31, 19X0, enter into the determination of net income and cash flows for the year ended December 31, 19X1.

Because of the matter discussed in the preceding paragraph, the scope of our work was not sufficient to enable us to express, and we do not express, an opinion on the results of operations and cash flows for the year ended December 31, 19X1.

In our opinion, the balance sheets of ABC Company as of December 31, 19X2 and 19X1, and the related statements of income, retained earnings, and cash flows for the year ended December 31, 19X2, present fairly, in all material respects, the financial position of ABC Company as of December 31, 19X2 and 19X1, and the results of its operations and its cash flows for the year ended December 31, 19X2, in conformity with generally accepted accounting principles.

SOURCE: AU 508.76.

could result from such events as (1) subsequent resolution of an uncertainty that existed in the prior year, (2) discovery of an uncertainty applicable to the prior year that was not known when the opinion on the prior year's statements was rendered, or (3) restatement of prior-period statements to bring them into conformity with GAAP. The updating of a prior year's opinion results in a standard report except for the addition of an explanatory paragraph that details the different opinion and all substantive reasons for the change in opinion. AU 508.78 indicates that the following explanatory paragraph may be appropriate for the updating.

In our report dated March 1, 19X2, we expressed an opinion that the 19X1 financial statements did not fairly present financial position, results of operations, and cash flows in conformity with generally accepted accounting principles because of two departures from such principles: (1) the Company carried its property, plant, and equipment at appraisal values, and provided for depreciation on the basis of such values, and (2) the Company did not provide for deferred income taxes with respect to differences between income for financial reporting purposes and taxable income. As described in Note X, the Company has restated its 19X1 financial statements to conform with generally accepted accounting principles. Accordingly, our present opinion on the 19X1 financial statements, as presented herein, is different from that expressed in our previous report.

The explanatory paragraph is positioned just before the opinion paragraph in the report.

Change of Auditors

Additional reporting requirements must be met when there has been a change in auditors during the periods covered by the comparative statements. If the predecessor auditor's report of a prior year is not presented, which is the usual case, it is necessary for the successor auditor to modify the standard report to explain the circumstances. Because the circumstances pertain to the auditing firm that did the audit, the explanatory information is added in the introductory paragraph rather than as a separate paragraph. The successor auditor should indicate in the report on the current year

- That the financial statements of the prior period were audited by another auditor.
- The date of the predecessor auditor's report.
- The type of report issued by the predecessor.
- If the report was other than a standard report, the substantive reasons therefor.

The introductory paragraph shown below illustrates the wording recommended by AU 508.83 when the predecessor auditor issued a standard report.

> We have audited the balance sheet of ABC Company as of December 31, 19X2, and the related statements of income, retained earnings, and cash flows for the year then ended. These financial statements are the responsibility of the Company's management. Our responsibility is to express an opinion on these financial statements based on our audit. The financial statements of ABC Company as of December 31, 19X1, were audited by other auditors whose report dated March 31, 19X2, expressed an unqualified opinion on those statements.

No additional changes are required in the scope and opinion paragraphs of the report. The predecessor auditor should not be named in the report unless the predecessor's practice was acquired by, or merged with, the successor auditor. A predecessor auditor who agrees to reissue a report or consents to the reuse of a report should perform procedures to determine whether the previous opinion on the financial statements is still appropriate. AU 508.83 specifies additional requirements when the prior year's statements have been restated.

INFORMATION ACCOMPANYING AUDITED FINANCIAL STATEMENTS

Information accompanying financial statements consists of (1) supplementary information required by the FASB and the GASB, (2) voluntary information provided by management, and (3) additional information provided by the auditor. The auditor is not required by GAAS to examine any of the information because the data are outside the basic financial statements. However, the auditor has some responsibilities concerning the information, as explained below.

Required Supplementary Information

The FASB and the Governmental Accounting Standards Board (GASB) have concluded that certain supplementary information is an essential part of an entity's financial reporting. For example, the FASB requires information on oil, gas, and mineral reserves.

The auditor is required to apply certain limited procedures to the information and report any deficiencies in or omissions of such information. The limited procedures involve inquiry of management regarding the methods of preparing the information, and comparison of the information for consistency with other available data. Because the information is neither audited nor a required part of the basic financial statements, SAS 52, *Omnibus Statement on Auditing Standards–1987* (AU 558.08), states that a standard report should be issued except in the following circumstances:

- The required supplementary information is omitted.
- The measurement or presentation of the information departs materially from prescribed guidelines.
- The auditor is unable to complete the prescribed procedures.
- The auditor is unable to remove substantial doubts about whether the information conforms to prescribed guidelines.

These circumstances do not affect the auditor's opinion on the fairness of the financial statements. However, the auditor should add an explanatory paragraph to the report that describes the circumstance(s). There is no change in any of the other paragraphs of the standard report. The auditor is not required to supply the supplementary information when it is omitted by the entity.

Voluntary Information Provided by Management

The audited financial statements of a client are usually presented in a document called an annual report. This document includes such information as financial highlights, a letter from the president and/or chairman of the board, comparative financial statistics, schedules, and graphic presentations of financial data that are voluntarily provided by management. The auditor is required to read this information to determine whether the data, or the manner of presentation, are materially inconsistent with the financial statements on which an opinion is being expressed.

For example, in referring to per-share earnings in the president's letter, a client may state earnings per share only before an extraordinary loss when the income statement shows earnings per share data in accordance with APB Opinion 15, *Earnings per Share.* When a material inconsistency appears to exist, the auditor should determine whether the statements, the audit report, or the other information should be revised. If the latter case holds and the client refuses to make the necessary changes, SAS 8, *Other Information in Documents Containing Audited Financial Statements* (AU 550.04), states that the auditor may elect to (1) include an explanatory paragraph in the audit report on the matter, (2) withhold the audit report, or (3) withdraw from the engagement. When an explanatory paragraph is added, there are no other changes in the standard report.

Additional Information Provided by the Auditor

At the conclusion of an audit engagement, the auditor gives the client a document that contains the client's basic financial statements and the auditor's report thereon. The auditor may include additional information that pertains to the basic statements. The information, such as details and historical summaries of selected statement items, is intended to facilitate the analysis and interpretation of the basic financial statements. It is important to recognize that the additional information in the *auditor-submitted document* is presented outside the basic statements and is not necessary for a fair presentation of the statements. Like the basic financial statements, the data in the additional information are representations of management because they are derived from the basic statements.

The auditor is required by the fourth standard of reporting to report on all the information included in an auditor-submitted document. Thus, he or she must describe the character of the examination of the information, if any, and either express or disclaim an opinion. SAS 29, *Reporting on Information Accompanying the Basic Financial Statements in an Auditor-Submitted Document* (AU 551.06), indicates that in expressing an opinion, the auditor should indicate whether the additional information is fairly stated *in all material respects in relation to the basic financial* statements taken as a whole. The report may be added to the auditor's standard report or appear separately in the document.

FINANCIAL STATEMENTS PREPARED FOR USE IN OTHER COUNTRIES

The auditor's report on financial statements prepared in conformity with generally accepted accounting principles of another country depends on the intended use of the financial statements. SAS 51, *Reporting on Financial Statements Prepared for Use in Other Countries* (AU 534.07), indicates that

- If the use is only outside the United States, the report may either be (1) the U.S.-style auditor's report modified for the accounting principles of another country or (2) the standard report of the other country.
- If the use will also be within the United States, the U.S.-style report should be used with a qualified or adverse opinion, depending on the materiality of departures from U.S. GAAP.

The following modifications are necessary when the U.S.-style report is used:

- The introductory paragraph should state that the financial statements are prepared on the basis of accounting principles generally accepted in (name of country).
- The scope paragraph should indicate that the audit was made in accordance with generally accepted auditing standards in the United States and, if appropriate, the auditing standards of (name of country).
- The opinion paragraph should state in conformity with generally accepted accounting principles in (name of country).

An auditor who elects to use the standard report of another country should (1) ascertain that the report would be used by auditors in the other country in similar circumstances and (2) understand, and be in a position to make, the attestations contained in such a report. The attestations may include explicit or implicit assurance of statutory compliance with the local laws.

LEARNING CHECK:

20-17 Indicate the effects on the auditor's report when the accountant is not independent.

20-18 In reporting on comparative financial statements, what are the effects on the auditor's report of (a) different opinions, (b) updating a prior year's opinion, and (c) changing auditors?

20-19 a. Distinguish three situations involving information accompanying audited financial statements.
b. Describe the auditor's responsibilities for each type of information.

20-20 a. What reporting options does a U.S. auditor have in reporting on financial statements prepared for use in other countries?
b. Explain the effects on the standard U.S. report when the financial statements are also to be used within the United States.

INTERNATIONAL AUDITOR'S STANDARD UNQUALIFIED REPORT

The auditor's standard unqualified report varies considerably from one country to another. The following is an unqualified report incorporating the principles set forth in *International Standard on Auditing No. 13* as illustrated in Appendix I to the standard:

AUDITOR'S REPORT TO . . . .

We have audited the financial statements[1] in accordance with International Standards on Auditing.[2]

In our opinion, the financial statements give a true and fair view of (or "present fairly") the financial position of . . . . at . . . . and the results of its operations for the year then ended in accordance with . . . .[3] (and comply with . . . .[4]).

AUDITOR (name of firm or person)

Date
Auditor's address

[1] Provide suitable identification such as by referring to page numbers or by identifying the individual statements.

[2] Or refer to relevant national standards or practices.

[3] Indicate the relevant national standards or refer to International Accounting Standards.

[4] Refer to relevant statutes or law.

SOURCE: AU 8013.27.

SUMMARY

After evaluating the audit findings and formulating an opinion on the overall financial statements, the auditor communicates his or her opinion through an auditor's report prepared in accordance with the four reporting standards of GAAS. Depending on the circumstances, the auditor's report may take one of the following forms: (1) a standard report that contains an *unqualified opinion,* (2) a report that contains an *unqualified opinion with added explanatory language,* or (3) a report that expresses one of three *other types of opinions—qualified, adverse, or disclaimer.* Special reporting considerations pertain to circumstances involving a CPA who is not independent, comparative financial statements, information accompanying audited financial statements, and financial statements prepared for use in other countries.

BIBLIOGRAPHY

AICPA Professional Standards:

SAS 1 (AU 420), Consistency of Application of Generally Accepted Accounting Principles

(AU 543), Part of Audit Performed by Other Independent Auditors

(AU 544), Lack of Conformity with Generally Accepted Accounting Principles

SAS 8 (AU 550), Other Information in Documents Containing Audited Financial Statements

SAS 21 (AU 435), Segment Information

SAS 26 (AU 504), Association with Financial Statements
SAS 29 (AU 551), Reporting on Information Accompanying the Basic Financial Statements in Auditor-Submitted Documents
SAS 32 (AU 431), Adequacy of Disclosure in Financial Statements
SAS 42 (AU 552), Reporting on Condensed Financial Statements and Selected Financial Data
SAS 51 (AU 534), Reporting on Financial Statements Prepared for Use in Other Countries
SAS 52 (AU 411, 551, 558), Omnibus Statement on Auditing Standards—1987
SAS 58 (AU 508), Reports on Audited Financial Statements
SAS 59 (AU 341), The Auditor's Consideration of an Entity's Ability to Continue as a Going Concern
SAS 64 (AU 341, 508, 543), Omnibus Statement on Auditing Standards—1990
SAS 69 (AU 411, The Meaning of "Present Fairly in Conformity with Generally Accepted Accounting Principles" in the Independent Auditor's Report
IAU 5 (AU 8005), Using the Work of an Other Auditor
IAU 13 (AU 8013), The Auditor's Report on Financial Statements

Ellingsen, John E., Pany, Kurt, and Fagan, Peg. "SAS No. 59: How to Evaluate Going Concern," *Journal of Accountancy* (January 1989), pp. 24–31.

Geiger, Marshall A. "SAS No. 58: Did the ASB Really Listen?" *Journal of Accountancy* (December 1988), pp. 55–57.

Hopwood, William, McKeown, James, and Mutchler, Jane. "A Test of the Incremental Explanatory Power of Opinions Qualified for Consistency and Uncertainty," *The Accounting Review* (January 1989), pp. 28–48.

Robertson, Jack C. "Analysts' Reactions to Auditors' Messages in Qualified Reports," *Accounting Horizons* (June 1988), pp. 82–89.

Roussey, Robert S., Ten Eyck, Ernest L., and Blanco-Best, Mimi. "Three New SASs: Closing the Communications Gap," *Journal of Accountancy* (December 1988), pp. 44–52.

OBJECTIVE QUESTIONS

Indicate the *best* answer choice for each of the following multiple choice questions.

20-21 These questions relate to the four reporting standards.

1. The fourth standard of reporting requires the auditor's report to contain either an expression of opinion regarding the financial statements taken as a whole or an assertion to the effect that an opinion cannot be expressed. The objective of the fourth standard is to prevent
   a. Misinterpretations regarding the degree of responsibility the auditor is assuming.
   b. An auditor from reporting on one basic financial statement and not the others.
   c. An auditor from expressing different opinions on each of the basic financial statements.
   d. Restrictions on the scope of the examination, whether imposed by the client or by the inability to obtain evidence.

2. Which of the following requires recognition in the auditor's opinion as to consistency?
   a. The correction of an error in the prior year's financial statements resulting from a mathematical mistake in capitalizing interest.
   b. The change from the cost method to the equity method of accounting for investments in common stock.
   c. A change in the estimate of provisions for warranty costs.
   d. A change in depreciation method that has no effect on the current year's financial statements but is certain to affect future years.

3. The first standard of reporting requires that "the report shall state whether the financial statements are presented in accordance with generally accepted accounting principles." This should be construed to require
   a. A statement of fact by the auditor.
   b. An opinion by the auditor.
   c. An implied measure of fairness.
   d. An objective measure of compliance.

20-22 These questions relate to the type of opinion that an auditor should express.

1. Restrictions imposed by a client prohibit the observation of physical inventories, which account for 35% of all assets. Alternative auditing procedures cannot be applied, although the auditor was able to examine satisfactory evidence for all other items in the financial statements. The auditor should issue a(an)
   a. "Except for" qualified opinion.
   b. Disclaimer of opinion.
   c. Unqualified opinion with a separate explanatory paragraph.
   d. Unqualified opinion with an explanation in the scope paragraph.

2. Management of Hill Company has decided not to account for a material transaction in accordance with the provisions of an FASB standard. In setting forth its reasons in a note to the financial statements, management has clearly demonstrated that due to unusual circumstances the financial statements presented in accordance with the FASB standard would be misleading. The auditor's report should include a separate explanatory paragraph and contain a(an)
   a. "Except for" qualified opinion.
   b. "Subject to" qualified opinion.
   c. Adverse opinion.
   d. Unqualified opinion.

3. If a publicly held company issues financial statements that purport to present its financial position and results of operations but omits the statement of cash flows, the auditor ordinarily will express a(an)
   a. Unqualified opinion with a separate explanatory paragraph.
   b. Disclaimer of opinion.
   c. Adverse opinion.
   d. Qualified opinion.

20-23 These questions pertain to the form and content of the auditor's report.

1. When a qualified opinion results from a limitation on the scope of the audit, the situation should be described in an explanatory paragraph
   a. Preceding the opinion paragraph and referred to only in the scope paragraph of the auditor's report.
   b. Following the opinion paragraph and referred to in both the scope and opinion paragraphs of the auditor's report.
   c. Following the opinion paragraph and referred to only in the scope paragraph of the auditor's report.
   d. Preceding the opinion paragraph and referred to in both the scope and opinion paragraphs of the auditor's report.

2. An auditor's report that refers to the use of an accounting principle at variance with generally accepted accounting principles contains the words, "In our opinion, with the foregoing explanation, the financial statements referred to above present fairly. . . ." This is considered an
   a. Adverse opinion.
   b. "Except for" qualified opinion.

c. Unqualified opinion with an explanatory paragraph.
d. Example of inappropriate reporting.

3. When a principal auditor decides to make reference to another auditor's examination, the principal auditor's report should always indicate clearly, in the introductory, scope, and opinion paragraphs, the
a. Magnitude of the portion of the financial statements examined by the other auditor.
b. Disclaimer of responsibility concerning the portion of the financial statements examined by the other auditor.
c. Name of the other auditor.
d. Division of responsibility.

20-24 These questions are based on other reporting considerations.

1. When reporting on comparative financial statements, an auditor ordinarily should change the previously issued opinions on the prior year's financial statements if
a. The prior year's opinion was unqualified and the opinion on the current year's financial statements is modified due to a lack of consistency.
b. The prior year's financial statements are restated following a pooling of interests in the current year.
c. The prior year's financial statements are restated to conform with generally accepted accounting principles.
d. The auditor is a predecessor auditor who has been requested by a former client to reissue the previously issued report.

2. The predecessor auditor, who is satisfied after properly communicating with the successor auditor, has reissued a report because the audit client desires comparative financial statements. The predecessor auditor's report should make
a. Reference to the report of the successor auditor only in the scope paragraph.
b. Reference to the work of the successor auditor in the scope and opinion paragraphs.
c. Reference to both the work and the report of the successor auditor only in the opinion paragraph.
d. No reference to the report or the work of the successor auditor.

3. An auditor concludes that there is a material inconsistency in the other information in an annual report to shareholders containing audited financial statements. If the auditor concludes that the financial statements do **not** require revision, but the client refuses to revise or eliminate the material inconsistency, the auditor may
a. Issue an "except for" qualified opinion after discussing the matter with the client's board of directors.
b. Consider the matter closed because the other information is **not** in the audited financial statements.
c. Disclaim an opinion on the financial statements after explaining the material inconsistency in a separate explanatory paragraph.
d. Revise the auditor's report to include a separate explanatory paragraph describing the material inconsistency.

COMPREHENSIVE QUESTIONS

20-25 **(Circumstances requiring addition of explanatory language to an unqualified opinion)** Circumstances may occur in the audit of an entity's financial statements when the auditor concludes that it is necessary to add explanatory language to the report while still expressing an unqualified opinion.

REQUIRED

Identify the circumstances that cause a departure from the standard audit report while still expressing an unqualified opinion. For each circumstance indicate how the explanatory language is presented. Organize your answer according to the following example:

Circumstances	Presentation of Explanatory Information
1. Inconsistency in accounting principles in conformity with GAAP.	1. In explanatory paragraph following opinion paragraph, explain change.

20-26 **(Consistency standard)** The CPA must comply with the GAAS of reporting when preparing an opinion on the client's financial statements. One of the reporting standards relates to consistency.

REQUIRED

a. When must an auditor's report include a statement regarding consistency? What is the objective of requiring the CPA to make this statement about consistency?
b. Discuss what mention of consistency, if any, the CPA must make in a report relating to a first audit of the financial statements of the following companies:
   1. A newly organized company ending its first accounting period.
   2. A company established for a number of years.
c. Discuss whether the changes described in each of the cases below pertain to the consistency standard. (Assume the amounts are material.)
   1. The company disposed of one of its subsidiaries that had been included in its consolidated statements for prior years.
   2. After two years of computing depreciation under the declining balance method for income tax purposes and under the straight-line method for reporting purposes, the declining balance method was adopted for reporting purposes.
   3. The estimated remaining useful life of plant property was reduced because of obsolescence.
d. Explain the effects on the auditor's standard report when a change in the application of an accounting principle occurs and
   1. The change is made in conformity with GAAP.
   2. The change is not made in conformity with GAAP.

AICPA (adapted)

20-27 **(Preparation of audit report—various circumstances)** Roscoe, CPA, has completed the audit of the financial statements of Excelsior Corporation as of and for the year ended December 31, 19X1. Roscoe also audited and reported on the Excelsior financial statements for the prior year. Roscoe drafted the following report for 19X1:

We have audited the balance sheet and statements of income, retained earnings, and cash flows of Excelsior Corporation as of December 31, 19X1. Our audit was made in accordance with generally accepted accounting standards and accordingly included such tests of the accounting records as we considered necessary in the circumstances.

In our opinion, the above-mentioned financial statements are accurately and fairly presented in accordance with generally accepted accounting principles in effect at December 31, 19X1.

Roscoe, CPA
(Signed)
March 15, 19X2

Other information:

1. Excelsior is presenting comparative financial statements for 19X1 and 19X0.
2. During 19X1, Excelsior changed its method of accounting for long-term construction contracts and properly reflected the effects of the change in the current year's financial statements and restated the prior-year's statements. Roscoe is satisfied with Excelsior's justification for making the change. The change is discussed in footnote number 12.
3. Roscoe was unable to perform normal accounts receivable confirmation procedures but alternative procedures were used to satisfy Roscoe as to the validity of the receivables.
4. Excelsior Corporation is the defendant in a litigation, the outcome of which is highly uncertain. If the case is settled in favor of the plaintiff, Excelsior will be required to pay a substantial amount of cash that might require the sale of certain fixed assets. The litigation and the possible effects have been properly disclosed in footnote number 11.
5. Excelsior issued debentures on January 31, 19X0, in the amount of $10 million. The funds obtained from the issuance were used to finance the expansion of plant facilities. The debenture agreement restricts the payment of future cash dividends to earnings after December 31, 19X6. Excelsior declined to disclose this essential data in the footnotes to the financial statements.

Required

Consider all facts given and rewrite the auditor's report in acceptable and complete format incorporating any necessary departures from the standard report.

Do not discuss the draft of Roscoe's report but identify and explain any items included in *"Other Information"* that need not be part of the auditors report.

AICPA (adapted)

20-28 **(Preparation of audit report—comparative statements, predecessor auditors, different opinions)** Ross, Sandler & Co., CPAs, completed an audit of the 19X2 financial statements of Fairfax Corporation on March 17, 19X3, and concluded that an unqualified opinion was warranted. Because of a scope limitation arising from the inability to observe the January 1, 19X1, inventory, the predecessor auditors, Smith, Ellis & Co., issued a report that contained an unqualified opinion on the December 31, 19X1, balance sheet and a qualified opinion with respect to the statements of income, retained earnings, and cash flows for the year then ended.

The management of Fairfax Corporation has decided to present a complete set of comparative (19X2 and 19X1) financial statements in their annual report.

Required

Prepare an auditor's report, assuming the March 1, 19X2, auditor's report of Smith, Ellis & Co. is not presented.

AICPA

20-29 **(Determining type of opinion—various circumstances)** An independent auditing firm, Meyers and Richardson (M&R), recently encountered the following situations on four engagements:

1. Parker Corporation has decided to value fixed assets using replacement costs and to record inventory at the selling price rather than the original cost (both practices produce a higher cost and were significant in nature). Parker assumed that this would better suit the information needs of the shareholders. After M&R informed Parker that these practices were departures from generally accepted accounting prin-

ciples, Parker insisted that if the information is allowed in supplemental reporting, it should also be permitted in the body of the statements.

2. Eaton Industries has been an audit client for three years. Eaton's operations are profitable, and business is accelerating. Because it is 85 days after the end of Eaton's fiscal year, management is urging M&R to prepare the auditor's report. Eaton's net inventory balance is 20% of total assets, but Eaton's management has not authorized the taking of a physical inventory because it would disrupt company activities to the extent where sales would be lost. M&R has been unable to verify the inventory balance using alternative methods and believes there is not sufficient evidence to form an opinion.
3. Carter Corporation has recently sold common stock to the public market and has hired M&R as the auditor. After completion of the field work, M&R was told that the company does not wish to issue a Statement of Cash Flows, as Carter's management believes it is misleading and not necessary to evaluate company activities. No other problems were noted during the audit.
4. Markay Corporation has been a client for several years and has received "a clean opinion" on every engagement. During the current year, Markay changed the estimates used in the depreciation of its major assets because of new engineering information. This change increased Markay's net income and is disclosed in a footnote to the financial statements.

REQUIRED

Identify the type of opinion Meyers and Richardson (M&R), the independent audit firm, would render for each engagement. Be sure to explain the rationale for the type of opinion selected.

ICMA (adapted)

20-30 **Report deficiencies—going concern uncertainty)** The auditors' report below was drafted by a staff accountant of Turner & Turner, CPAs, at the completion of the audit of the financial statements of Lyon Computers, Inc., for the year ended March 31, 19X9. It was submitted to the engagement partner who reviewed matters thoroughly and properly concluded that Lyon's disclosures concerning its ability to continue as a going concern for a reasonable period of time were adequate.

To the Board of Directors of Lyon Computers, Inc.:

We have audited the accompanying balance sheet of Lyon Computers, Inc. as of March 31, 19X9, and the other related financial statements for the year then ended. Our responsibility is to express an opinion on these financial statements based on our audit.

We conducted our audit in accordance with standards that require that we plan and perform the audit to obtain reasonable assurance about whether the financial statements are in conformity with generally accepted accounting principles. An audit includes examining, on a test basis, evidence supporting the amounts and disclosures in the financial statements. An audit also includes assessing the accounting principles used and significant estimates made by management.

The accompanying financial statements have been prepared assuming that the Company will continue as a going concern. As discussed in Note X to the financial statements, the Company has suffered recurring losses from operations and has a net capital deficiency that raises substantial doubt about its ability to continue as a going concern. We believe that management's plans in regard to these matters, which are also described in Note X, will permit the Company to continue as a going concern beyond a reasonable period of time. The financial statements do not include any adjustments that might result from the outcome of this uncertainty.

In our opinion, subject to the effects on the financial statements of such adjustments, if any, as might have been required had the outcome of the uncertainty referred to in the preceding paragraph been known, the financial statements referred to above present fairly, in all material respects, the financial position of Lyon Computers, Inc., and the results of its operations and its cash flows in conformity with generally accepted accounting principles applied on a basis consistent with that of the preceding year.

Turner & Turner, CPAs
April 28, 19X9

REQUIRED

Identify the deficiencies contained in the auditor's report as drafted by the staff accountant. Group the deficiencies by paragraph. Do **not** redraft the report.

20-31 **(Report deficiencies—adverse opinion, subsequent event, predecessor auditors)** Brown & Brown, CPAs, was engaged by the board of directors of Cook Industries, Inc. to audit Cook's calendar year 19X5 financial statements. The following report was drafted by an audit assistant at the completion of the engagement. It was submitted to Brown, the partner with client responsibility for review on March 7, 19X6, the date of the completion of field work. Brown has reviewed matters thoroughly and properly concluded that an adverse opinion was appropriate.

Brown also became aware of a March 14, 19X6, subsequent event that the client has properly disclosed in the notes to the financial statements. Brown wants responsibility for subsequent events to be limited to the specific event referred to in the applicable note to the client's financial statements.

The financial statements of Cook Industries, Inc. for the calendar year 19X4 were audited by predecessor auditors who also expressed an adverse opinion and have not reissued their report. The financial statements for 19X4 and 19X5 are presented in comparative form.

Report of Independent Accountants

To the President of Cook Industries, Inc.:

We have audited the financial statements of Cook Industries, Inc., which are the responsibility of management, for the year ended December 31, 19X5. Our responsibility is to express an opinion on these financial statements.

Our audit was made in accordance with generally accepted auditing standards and, accordingly, included such tests of the accounting records as we considered necessary in the circumstances. We believe that our audit provides a reasonable basis for our opinion. As discussed in Note K to the financial statements, the Company has properly disclosed a subsequent event dated March 14, 19X6.

As discussed in Note G to the financial statements, the Company carries its property and equipment at appraisal values, and provides depreciation on the basis of such values. Further, the Company does not provide for income taxes with respect to differences between financial income and taxable income arising because of the use, for income tax purposes, of the installment method of reporting gross profit from certain types of sales.

In our opinion, the financial statements referred to above do not present fairly the financial position of Cook Industries, Inc. as of December 31, 19X5, or the results of its operations and cash flows for the year then ended in conformity with generally accepted accounting principles.

Brown & Brown, CPAs
March 7, 19X6

REQUIRED

Identify the deficiencies in the draft of the proposed report. Do **not** redraft the report or discuss corrections.

AICPA (adapted)

20-32 **(Report deficiencies—change in principle, comparative statements, other auditors)** George & Searls, CPAs, have audited the financial statements of the Dunham Corporation for the past several years with the help of the CPA firm of Lacy & Tracy that audits the corporation's wholly owned West Coast subsidiary, Western Inc. The subsidiary's operations normally account for 20% and 18% of consolidated assets and revenues, respectively. The audit report of Lacy & Tracy for the current year contains an unqualified opinion. In 19X8, the corporation changed its method of accounting for depreciation from the straight-line method to the declining balance method. The change was made in conformity with GAAP. On completing this year's engagement on February 26, 19X9, George & Searls issued the following audit report:

CPA's REPORT

To Ronald Beach, Controller:

We have audited the consolidated balance sheets of Dunham Corporation as of December 31, 19X8 and 19X7, and the related consolidated statements of income, retained earnings, and cash flows for the years then ended. These statements are the responsibility of the company's audit committee. Our responsibility is to express an opinion on these financial statements, and we believe that our audit provided us with a reasonable basis for the opinion expressed below.

We conducted our audits in accordance with generally accepted auditing standards except that the audit of Western Inc., a wholly owned subsidiary, was audited by Lacy & Tracy, a West Coast CPA firm. These standards require that we plan and perform the audit to obtain reasonable assurance that the financial statements are true and correct. An audit includes examining on a test basis, sufficient competent evidential matter that supports the assertions made by management in the financial statements. An audit also includes assessing the accounting principles used and judgments exercised by management, as well as evaluating the fairness of the financial statements. The report of other auditors was used in part as a basis for our opinion.

In our opinion, based on our audits, the consolidated financial statements referred to above present fairly the financial position of Dunham Inc. as of December 31, 19X8 and 19X7, and the results of its operations and cash flows for the years then ended in conformity with generally accepted accounting principles except for the change in depreciation methods as explained in note 4 in the financial statements.

R. A. George, CPA
December 31, 19X8

REQUIRED

Identify the deficiencies in the above audit report. Organize your answer by (a) introductory paragraph, (b) scope paragraph, (c) explanatory paragraph, (d) opinion paragraph, and (e) other.

CASES

20-33 **(Preparation of audit report—various circumstances)** Devon Incorporated engaged Smith to examine its financial statements for the year ended December 31, 19X3. The financial statements of Devon Incorporated for the year ended December 31, 19X2, were examined by Jones whose March 31, 19X3 auditor's report expressed an unqualified opinion. This report of Jones is not presented with the 19X3–19X2 comparative financial statements.

Smith's working papers contain the following information that does not appear in footnotes to the 19X3 financial statements as prepared by Devon Incorporated:

- One director appointed in 19X3 was formerly a partner in Jones's accounting firm. Jones's firm provided financial consulting services to Devon during 19X2 and 19X1, for which Devon paid approximately $1,600 and $9,000, respectively.

- The company refused to capitalize certain lease obligations for equipment acquired in 19X3. Capitalization of the leases in conformity with generally accepted accounting principles would have increased assets and liabilities by $312,000 and $387,000, respectively, and decreased retained earnings as of December 31, 19X3, by $75,000, and would have decreased net income and earnings per share by $75,000 and $.75, respectively, for the year then ended. Smith has concluded that the leases should have been capitalized.
- During the year, Devon changed its method of valuing inventory from the first-in, first-out method to the last-in, first-out method. This change was made because management believes LIFO more clearly reflects net income by providing a closer matching of current costs and current revenues. The change had the effect of reducing inventory at December 31, 19X3, by $65,000 and net income and earnings per share by $38,000 and $.38, respectively, for the year then ended. The effect of the change on prior years was immaterial; accordingly, there was no cumulative effect of the change. Smith firmly supports the company's position.

After completion of the field work on February 29, 19X4, Smith concludes that the expression of an adverse opinion is not warranted.

REQUIRED

Prepare the body of Smith's report dated February 29, 19X4, and addressed to the Board of Directors to accompany the 19X3–19X2 comparative financial statements.

AICPA

20-34 **(Report deficiencies—various circumstances)** The auditors' report below was drafted by Moore, a staff accountant of Tyler & Tyler, CPAs, at the completion of the audit of the financial statements of Park Publishing Co., Inc., for the year ended September 30, 19X2. The report was submitted to the engagement partner who reviewed the audit working papers and properly concluded that an unqualified opinion should be issued. In drafting the report, Moore considered the following:

- During fiscal year 19X2, Park changed its depreciation method. The engagement partner concurred with this change in accounting principle and its justification, and Moore included an explanatory paragraph in the auditors' report.
- The 19X2 financial statements are affected by an uncertainty concerning a lawsuit, the outcome of which cannot presently be estimated. Moore has included an explanatory paragraph in the auditors' report.
- The financial statements for the year ended September 30, 19X1, are to be presented for comparative purposes. Tyler & Tyler previously audited these statements and expressed an unqualified opinion.

Independent Auditors' Report

To the Board of Directors of Park Publishing Co., Inc.:

We have audited the accompanying balance sheets of Park Publishing Co., Inc. as of September 30, 19X2, and 19X1, and the related statements of income and cash flows for the years then ended. These financial statements are the responsibility of the company's management.

We conducted our audits in accordance with generally accepted auditing standards. Those standards require that we plan and perform the audit to obtain reasonable assurance about whether the financial statements are fairly presented. An audit includes examining, on a test basis, evidence supporting the amounts and disclosures in the financial statements. An audit also includes assessing significant estimates made by management, as well as evaluating the overall financial statement presentation. We believe that our audits provide a basis for determining whether any material modifications should be made to the accompanying financial statements.

As discussed in Note X to the financial statements, the company changed its method of computing depreciation in fiscal 19X2.

In our opinion, except for the accounting change, with which we concur, the financial statements referred to above present fairly, in all material respects, the financial position of Park Publishing Co., Inc. as of September 30, 19X2, and the results of its operations and its cash flows for the year then ended in conformity with generally accepted accounting principles.

As discussed in Note Y to the financial statements, the company is a defendant in a lawsuit alleging infringement of certain copyrights. The company has filed a counteraction, and preliminary hearings on both actions are in progress. Accordingly, any provision for liability is subject to adjudication of this matter.

Tyler & Tyler, CPAs
November 5, 19X2

REQUIRED

Identify the deficiencies in the auditors' report as drafted by Moore. Group the deficiencies by paragraph and in the order in which the deficiencies appear. Do **not** redraft the report. *(AICPA)*

RESEARCH QUESTIONS

20-35 **(Frequency of types of auditors' reports)** The chapter noted that the majority of audits culminate in the issuance of a standard report containing an unqualified opinion. Several sources are available from which information can be obtained as to the frequency of issuance of reports involving departures from the standard report. These include the printed and electronic versions of the AICPA's annual survey published under the title *Accounting Trends and Techniques* and several other electronic databases. Consult one or more of these sources and prepare a report of your findings as to the frequency of different types of reports issued. Include information as to the size of the database examined (number of companies) and the period (years) covered. (Note: Although *Accounting Trends and Techniques* includes some tabular data, if using one of the other databases, you may need to construct tabular data by keeping track of the number of hits found via carefully specified search terms designed to identify reports of each type on which you wish frequency data.)

20-36 **(Revision of the auditor's standard report)** At the time this text went to press, the Auditing Standards Board was considering several possible revisions to the auditor's standard report including the following: (1) amending the report to clearly communicate that the purpose of the consideration of the internal control structure in a financial statement audit is solely to determine the auditing procedures to be performed and not to provide assurance on the internal control structure itself, (2) revising the reference in the report to accounting estimates to clarify their prospective nature and to include a caveat that the estimates may not be achieved, (3) amending the report to better communicate the auditors' responsibilities for detecting fraud, and (4) eliminating the need for a consistency explanatory paragraph in years subsequent to the first year of change in an accounting principle. Discuss the pros and cons of these possible revisions. Also, include any information available on sources of support for the revisions and the status of the Auditing Standards Board's consideration of the revisions.

20-37 **(Foreign auditors' reports)** An international box in the chapter described the auditor's standard unqualified report recommended in *International Standard on Auditing No. 13.* Locate and make a copy of an actual auditor's report issued in each of two foreign countries. First, compare each of the reports with the basic elements of the international report shown in the box on page 785, noting areas of compliance and, if any, noncompliance. Next, compare each of the reports with the U.S. report that would be issued for the entity under similar circumstances if it were operating as a domestic U.S. company, noting similarities and differences.

CHAPTER

21

Other Services and Reports

Learning Objectives

After studying this chapter, you should be able to

1. State the standards applicable to attest engagements.
2. Indicate the types of attest engagements and the assurance, risk, and report distribution characteristics of each.
3. Identify the types of "special reports" that may be issued.
4. Describe the effects on the auditor's report when financial statements are prepared on a comprehensive basis of accounting other than GAAP.
5. Explain the nature of review services and the type of assurance associated with them.
6. Differentiate between a SAS 71 review and a SSARS review.
7. Discuss reporting on internal control based on a management assertion and the processing of transactions by service organizations.

Accepting and Performing Attest Engagements
- Attestation Standards
- Types of Attest Engagements
- Levels of Assurance and Attestation Risk
- Report Distribution

Special Reports
- Other Comprehensive Bases of Accounting
- Specified Elements, Accounts, or Items of a Financial Statement
- Compliance Reports Related to Audited Financial Statements

Review Services
- SAS 71 Review of Interim Financial Information
- SSARS Review of Financial Statements

Other Attest Services
- Reporting on Internal Control
- Reporting on Prospective Financial Information
- Compliance Attestation
- Summary of Attest Services

Nonattest Accounting Services
- Unaudited Financial Statements of a Public Entity
- Compilation of Financial Statements of a Nonpublic Entity
- Compilation of Prospective Financial Statements
- Reporting on the Application of Accounting Principles
- Change of Engagement

Summary

Bibliography

Objective Questions

Comprehensive Questions

Case

Research Questions

The audit of financial statements prepared in conformity with GAAP is just one of several types of attest services that a CPA may render. Based largely on the skills, experience, and reputation CPAs have acquired as auditors, their clients, regulatory agencies, and others have increasingly turned to the public accounting profession for a widening range of other types of attest and nonattest services. The AICPA has responded by developing standards for these services to promote uniformity in quality of practice and to enhance users' understanding of the differences in the types of services rendered and the levels of assurance associated with them.

In this chapter, first we consider the attestation standards that apply to all attest services and compare those standards with GAAS. Next, we review the four broad types of attest engagements that were introduced in Chapter 1 and identify the levels of assurance, the levels of attestation risk, and the reporting options associated with each. We then explain several specific types of attest engagements that are frequently performed by CPAs. Finally, we consider several types of nonattest

8. State the purpose of compliance attestations and the conditions under which they may be performed.
9. State the accountant's responsibilities when associated with unaudited statements of a public entity.
10. Differentiate a compilation service from an audit or review.

services performed by CPAs and the standards and reporting options applicable to those services.

ACCEPTING AND PERFORMING ATTEST ENGAGEMENTS

In 1986, the AICPA issued the first in a new series of authoritative statements entitled *Statements on Standards for Attestation Engagements (SSAEs).* Intended to provide guidance and establish a broad framework for performing and reporting on attest services, SSAE 1, *Attestation Standards* (AT 100.01) defines an attest engagement as follows:

> An **attest engagement** is one in which a practitioner (CPA) is engaged to issue or does issue a written communication that expresses a conclusion about the reliability of a written assertion that is the responsibility of another party.

A CPA should accept only those attest engagements that can be completed in accordance with the attestation standards described in the next section. In performing an attest engagement, a CPA (1) gathers evidence to support the assertion, (2) objectively assesses the measurements and communications of the individual making the assertion, and (3) reports the findings. Thus, primarily concerned with the basis and support for written assertions, attest services are analytical, critical, and investigative in nature.

ATTESTATION STANDARDS

OBJECTIVE 1

State the standards applicable to attest engagements.

In an attest engagement, the CPA must meet the eleven general **attestation standards** presented in SSAE 1. These standards are shown in Figure 21-1 where they are compared with the ten generally accepted auditing standards (GAAS) with which we are already familiar.

As the figure shows, the attestation standards, like GAAS, are classified into three categories: general, field work, and reporting. Comparison of the standards in each category reveals that the attestation standards are a natural extension of GAAS to accommodate the broader array of attest services. However, several significant conceptual differences between the two sets of standards may be observed. Specifically, the attestation standards

- Extend the attest function beyond historical financial statements. Thus, the standards omit references to financial statements and to GAAP.
- Allow the CPA to give assurances on the assertions below the level of the "positive expression of opinion" associated with the traditional financial statement audit.
- Provide for attest services tailored to the needs of specific users based on "agreed-upon procedures" and "limited-use" reports.

The two new general standards (numbers 2 and 3) establish the boundaries for attest services. This type of service is limited to engagements in which (1) the CPA

FIGURE 21-1 • ATTESTATION STANDARDS COMPARED WITH GAAS

Attestation Standards	Generally Accepted Auditing Standards
General Standards	
1. The engagement shall be performed by a practitioner or practitioners having adequate technical training and proficiency in the attest function.	1. The audit is to be performed by a person or persons having adequate technical training and proficiency as an auditor.
2. The engagement shall be performed by a practitioner or practitioners having adequate knowledge in the subject matter of the assertion.	
3. The practitioner shall perform an engagement only if he or she has reason to believe that the following two conditions exist: • The assertion is capable of evaluation against reasonable criteria that either have been established by a recognized body or are stated in the presentation of the assertion in a sufficiently clear and comprehensive manner for a knowledgeable reader to be able to understand them. • The assertion is capable of reasonably consistent estimation or measurement using such criteria.	
4. In all matters relating to the engagement, an independence in mental attitude shall be maintained by the practitioner or practitioners.	2. In all matters relating to the assignment, an independence in mental attitude is to be maintained by the auditor or auditors.
5. Due professional care shall be exercised in the performance of the engagement.	3. Due professional care is to be exercised in the performance of the audit and the preparation of the report.
Standards of Field Work	
1. The work shall be adequately planned, and assistants, if any, shall be properly supervised.	1. The work is to be adequately planned, and assistants, if any, are to be properly supervised.
	2. A sufficient understanding of the internal control structure is to be obtained to plan the audit and to determine the nature, timing, and extent of tests to be performed.
2. Sufficient evidence shall be obtained to provide a reasonable basis for the conclusion that is expressed in the report.	3. Sufficient competent evidential matter is to be obtained through inspection, observation, inquiries, and confirmations to afford a reasonable basis for an opinion regarding the financial statements under audit.
Standards of Reporting	
1. The report shall identify the assertion being reported on and state the character of the engagement.	
2. The report shall state the practitioner's conclusion about whether the assertion is presented in conformity with the established or stated criteria against which it was measured.	1. The report shall state whether the financial statements are presented in accordance with generally accepted accounting principles.
	2. The report shall identify the circumstances in which such principles have not been consistently observed in the current period in relation to the preceding period.
	3. Informative disclosures in the financial statements are to be regarded as reasonably adequate unless otherwise stated in the report.
3. The report shall state all of the practitioner's significant reservations about the engagement and the presentation of the assertion. 4. The report on an engagement to evaluate an assertion that has been prepared in conformity with agreed-upon criteria or on an engagement to apply agreed-upon procedures should contain a statement limiting its use to the parties who have agreed on such criteria or procedures.	4. The report shall either contain an expression of opinion regarding the financial statements, taken as a whole, or an assertion to the effect that an opinion cannot be expressed. When an overall opinion cannot be expressed, the reasons therefor should be stated. In all cases where an auditor's name is associated with financial statements, the report should contain a clear-cut indication of the character of the auditor's work, if any, and the degree of responsibility the auditor is taking.

SOURCE: AT 100.77.

has adequate knowledge of the subject matter of the assertion and (2) the assertion is capable of reasonably consistent measurement using established or stated criteria. Though not explicity stated in the general standards, the definition of an attest engagement given in SSAE 1 requires that the assertion be in writing as stated in the preceding section.

The second standard of field work under GAAS requires the auditor to obtain an understanding of the internal control structure. This standard is omitted from the attestation field work standards for two reasons:

- When obtaining an understanding of internal control is applicable, it is an activity that pertains to accumulating sufficient evidence as required by the second attestation standard of field work.
- Obtaining an understanding of internal control is not applicable in all attest engagements.

The separate GAAS reporting standards pertaining to consistency and informative disclosures are encompassed, when applicable, in the second attestation standard of reporting which requires a conclusion as to whether the assertions are presented in conformity with established criteria. The fourth attestation standard of reporting explicitly acknowledges the "limited-use" attribute of many attestation reports which imposes restrictions on their distribution.

TYPES OF ATTEST ENGAGEMENTS

OBJECTIVE 2

Indicate the types of attest engagements and the assurance, risk, and report distribution characteristics of each.

Four types of attest engagements have been recognized in the professional standards as follows:

- Audit
- Examination
- Review
- Agreed-upon procedures

Brief explanations and examples of each of these types of engagements and the levels of assurance associated with them are presented on page 11 in Chapter 1 of this text which should be reviewed at this time.

LEVELS OF ASSURANCE AND ATTESTATION RISK

The levels of assurance that CPAs may express in attest engagements may be recapped as follows:

- *Positive expression of opinion* based on an audit or examination of an assertion.
- *Negative assurance* based on a review of an assertion.
- *Summary of findings with varying levels of assurance* based on agreed-upon procedures applied to an assertion.[1]

---

[1] As originally issued, SSAE 1 authorized the issuance of either a summary of findings or a negative assurance, or both, for certain agreed-upon procedures engagements. At the time this text went to press, it was reported that the Auditing Standards Board had decided to prohibit the issuance of a negative assurance in agreed-upon procedures engagements.

FIGURE 21-2 • SUMMARY OF ATTEST ENGAGEMENTS

Type of Attest Engagement	Level of Assurance	Level of Attestation Risk	Report Distribution
Audit	Positive expression of opinion	Low	Unrestricted
Examination	Positive expression of opinion	Low	Unrestricted with some exceptions
Review	Negative assurance	Moderate	Unrestricted
Agreed-upon procedures	Summary of findings with varying levels of assurance	Low to moderate	Restricted

In planning an attest engagement, the CPA should consider the level of attestation risk appropriate to the engagement. In concept, **attestation risk** is similar to audit risk. It is the risk that a CPA will unknowingly fail to appropriately modify a report when an assertion is materially misstated. Generally, attestation risk should be kept low when issuing a positive expression of opinion in an audit or examination, moderate when issuing a negative assurance in a review engagement, and in the range of low to moderate when issuing a summary of findings in an agreed-upon procedures engagement.

REPORT DISTRIBUTION

When a positive expression of opinion is issued based on an audit or examination or a negative assurance is issued based on a review, there is generally no restriction on the distribution of the report. There are a few exceptions involving restrictions in the case of examinations. When a summary of findings is issued based on the performance of agreed-upon procedures, the distribution of the report should always be restricted to the party or parties who specified the procedures.

Figure 21-2 presents a summary of the types of attest engagements and the level of assurance, level of attestation risk, and report distribution requirements applicable to each type. Specific applications of each type of attest engagement are explained in the following three sections of this chapter: (1) special reports, (2) review services, and (3) other attest services. It is emphasized that, pursuant to the fourth general standard of the attestation standards, independence is required in performing each of the engagements described in these three sections.

LEARNING CHECK:

21-1 a. Define an attest engagement.
 b. State the three major activities involved in performing an attest engagement.

21-2 a. How are the attestation standards classified?
 b. Indicate the principal differences between the attestation standards and GAAS.

21-3 a. Identify the four types of attest engagements that have been recognized in professional standards.
 b. Indicate the levels of assurance and attestation risk associated with each type.

KEY TERMS:

Attest engagement, p. 797
Attestation risk, p. 800
Attestation standards, p. 797

SPECIAL REPORTS

Special reports are reports resulting from the audit of, or application of agreed-upon procedures to, historical financial data other than financial statements prepared in conformity with GAAP. SAS 62, *Special Reports* (Au 623.01), indicates that the term *special reports* applies to auditors' reports on

OBJECTIVE 3

Identify the types of "special reports" that may be issued.

- Financial statements that are prepared in conformity with a comprehensive basis of accounting other than generally accepted accounting principles.
- Specified elements, accounts, or items of a financial statement.
- Compliance with aspects of contractual agreements or regulatory requirements related to audited financial statements.
- Financial presentations to comply with contractual agreements or regulatory provisions.
- Financial information presented in prescribed forms or schedules that require a prescribed form of auditors' report.

Special reports based on an audit are similar to the auditor's standard report in that they usually contain an introductory paragraph, a scope paragraph, and an opinion paragraph. However, as explained and illustrated below, special reports have wording that differs from the language in the auditor's standard report. In addition, the "standard" special report may have four or even five paragraphs depending on the circumstances.

The explanation of special reports in this chapter is limited to the first three items in the foregoing list. Specific guidance to CPAs in issuing these special reports is currently provided in SASs because the reports are either based on an audit or pertain to services for which standards were initially issued in the form of an SAS prior to establishment of the SSAEs.

OTHER COMPREHENSIVE BASES OF ACCOUNTING

Four comprehensive bases of accounting other than GAAP are recognized in AU 623.04:

- A basis used to comply with the requirements or financial reporting provisions of a governmental regulatory agency.
- A basis used to file the entity's income tax return.
- The cash receipts and disbursements basis of accounting and modifications of the cash basis having substantial support.
- A basis that uses a definite set of criteria that has substantial support such as the price-level basis of accounting.

The use of an **other comprehensive basis of accounting (OCBOA)** is common. Many companies subject to regulatory bodies keep their accounts solely on the basis prescribed by the agency. For example, railroads conform with the requirements of the Interstate Commerce Commission (ICC), public utilities use the basis set forth by the Federal Energy Regulatory Commission, and insurance companies follow state insurance commission accounting requirements. In addition, many small companies and individual practitioners, such as doctors, lawyers, and CPAs, use the income tax, cash, or modified cash basis of accounting. When an entity uses a basis other than GAAP, the notes to the financial statements should indicate the basis.

OBJECTIVE 4

Describe the effects on the auditor's report when financial statements are prepared on a comprehensive basis of accounting other than GAAP.

All of the ten GAAS are applicable whenever the auditor audits and reports on any financial statement, regardless of the basis of accounting used in preparing the statement. The major difference in this case is that the statements are not intended to present fairly financial position, and so forth, in conformity with GAAP. However, the first standard of reporting is satisfied by indicating whether the statements are presented fairly in conformity with the basis of accounting used.

The auditor's special report on financial statements prepared on an OCBOA should contain four paragraphs:

- An *introductory paragraph* that is the same as in the auditor's standard report except that more distinctive titles should be used for the financial statements, such as statement of assets and liabilities arising from cash transactions.
- A *scope paragraph* that is the same as in the auditor's standard report.
- An *explanatory paragraph* following the scope paragraph that states the basis of presentation and refers to the note to the financial statements that describes the comprehensive basis of accounting other than GAAP.
- An *opinion paragraph* that expresses the auditor's opinion (or disclaims an opinion) on whether the financial statements are presented fairly, in all material respects, in conformity with the basis of accounting described.

As in the case of financial statements prepared in conformity with GAAP, the auditor's special report on statements prepared on an OCBOA may contain additional explanatory language when (1) the auditor cannot express an unqualified opinion or (2) circumstances require explanatory language with an unqualified opinion. An example of a special report on financial statements prepared on a cash basis of accounting is illustrated in Figure 21-3.

Notice that distinctive language is used in describing the financial statements in the introductory paragraph and in the wording of the opinion paragraph. A special report on financial statements prepared on an OCBOA will have five paragraphs when distribution of the report is restricted. Such a restriction may occur for the first type of OCBOA mentioned in the list at the beginning of this section. The restrictive language should be in the final paragraph of the report.

SPECIFIED ELEMENTS, ACCOUNTS, OR ITEMS OF A FINANCIAL STATEMENT

These data may include rentals, royalties, profit participation plans, or the provision for income taxes. A special report may be issued on these data as a result of an audit or the application of agreed-upon procedures.

FIGURE 21-3 • SPECIAL REPORT—CASH BASIS OF ACCOUNTING

INDEPENDENT AUDITOR'S REPORT

We have audited the accompanying statements of assets and liabilities arising from cash transactions of XYZ Company as of December 31, 19X2 and 19X1, and the related statements of revenue collected and expenses paid for the years then ended. These financial statements are the responsibility of the Company's management. Our responsibility is to express an opinion on these financial statements based on our audits.

We conducted our audits in accordance with generally accepted auditing standards. Those standards require that we plan and perform the audit to obtain reasonable assurance about whether the financial statements are free of material misstatement. An audit includes examining, on a test basis, evidence supporting the amounts and disclosures in the financial statements. An audit also includes assessing the accounting principles used and significant estimates made by management, as well as evaluating the overall financial statement presentation. We believe that our audits provide a reasonable basis for our opinion.

As described in Note X, these financial statements were prepared on the basis of cash receipts and disbursements, which is a comprehensive basis of accounting other than generally accepted accounting principles.

In our opinion, the financial statements referred to above present fairly, in all material respects, the assets and liabilities arising from cash transactions of XYZ Company as of December 31, 19X2 and 19X1, and its revenue collected and expenses paid during the years then ended, on the basis of accounting described in Note X.

SOURCE: AU 623.08.

Audit

An audit culminates in the expression of an opinion on the fairness of the presentation of the specified elements, accounts, or items. The specified data may be presented in conformity with GAAP, an OCBOA, or on the basis of an agreement such as a lease contract. All ten GAAS are applicable when the specified data are presented in conformity with GAAP or an OCBOA. Otherwise, the first reporting standard is inapplicable. An engagement to express an opinion on specified elements, accounts, or items may be made in conjunction with the audit of the financial statements or in a separate engagement.

Distinctive wording is required in the introductory, scope, and opinion paragraphs of the special report because the auditor is not reporting on financial statements taken as a whole. A special report on a royalty contract is illustrated in Figure 21-4. This report contains an optional feature. In describing the basis of presentation (paragraph 3), if considered necessary, the auditor may include any significant interpretations of the contract made by the company's management. In expressing an opinion, AU 623.13 indicates the auditor should recognize that the concept of materiality must be related to each individual element, account, or item being reported on rather than to the financial statements taken as a whole. Furthermore, the auditor should not express an opinion on the specified data when he or she has expressed an adverse opinion or disclaimed an opinion on the financial statements unless the specified data constitute only an insignificant portion of the financial statements.

Agreed-upon Procedures

The application of **agreed-upon procedures** does not constitute an audit. This type of service might occur, for example, in a proposed acquisition when the prospective purchaser asks the accountant only to reconcile bank balances and confirm the

FIGURE 21-4 • SPECIAL REPORT ON ROYALTIES: SEPARATE AUDIT ENGAGEMENT; AUDITED DATA PRESENTED PER AGREEMENT

INDEPENDENT AUDITOR'S REPORT

We have audited the accompanying schedule of royalties applicable to engine production of the Q Division of XYZ Corporation for the year ended December 31, 19X2, under the terms of a license agreement dated May 14, 19XX, between ABC Company and XYZ Corporation. This schedule is the responsibility of XYZ Corporation's management. Our responsibility is to express an opinion on this schedule based on our audit.

We conducted our audit in accordance with generally accepted auditing standards. Those standards require that we plan and perform the audit to obtain reasonable assurance about whether the schedule of royalties is free of material misstatement. An audit includes examining, on a test basis, evidence supporting the amounts and disclosures in the schedule. An audit also includes assessing the accounting principles used and significant estimates made by management, as well as evaluating the overall schedule presentation. We believe that our audit provides a reasonable basis for our opinion.

We have been informed that, under XYZ Corporation's interpretation of the agreement referred to in the first paragraph, royalties were based on the number of engines produced after giving effect to a reduction for production retirements that were scrapped, but without a reduction for field returns that were scrapped, even though the field returns were replaced with new engines without charge to customers.

In our opinion, the schedule of royalties referred to above presents fairly, in all material respects, the number of engines produced by the Q Division of XYZ Corporation during the year ended December 31, 19X2, and the amount of royalties applicable thereto, under the license agreement referred to above.

This report is intended solely for the information and use of the boards of directors and managements of XYZ Corporation and ABC Company and should not be used for any other purpose.

SOURCE: AU 623.18.

accounts receivable. An independent accountant may accept an engagement to apply agreed-upon procedures to specified elements, accounts, or items of a financial statement under two conditions: (1) the accountant and the party requesting the service must have a clear understanding of the procedures to be performed and (2) distribution of the report must be restricted to the named parties involved.

SAS 35, *Special Reports—Applying Agreed-upon Procedures to Specified Elements, Accounts, or Items of a Financial Statement* (AU 622.04), states that the CPA's report on the results of agreed-upon procedures should

- Indicate the elements, accounts, or items to which the procedures were applied.
- State the limited distribution of the report.
- Enumerate the procedures performed.
- Express a summary of the findings or negative assurance or both.[2]
- Disclaim an opinion with respect to the elements, accounts, or items.
- State that the report relates only to the specified items and does not extend to the entity's financial statements taken as a whole.

[2] At the time this text went to press, the Auditing Standards Board was planning a revision of SAS 35 which would eliminate the negative assurance reporting option for this type of engagement, as well as provide additional guidance for performing and reporting on such engagements.

COMPLIANCE REPORTS RELATED TO AUDITED FINANCIAL STATEMENTS

Companies may be required by contractual agreements or regulatory agencies to furnish compliance reports by independent auditors. For example, bond indentures often impose a variety of obligations on borrowers such as payments to sinking funds, maintenance of a minimum current ratio, and restrictions on dividend payments. In addition to requiring audited financial statements, lenders or their trustees often request assurance from the independent auditor that the borrower has complied with the accounting and auditing covenants of the agreement. The auditor satisfies this request by giving negative assurance on compliance by stating that "nothing came to our attention which would indicate that the company is not in compliance." AU 623.19 states that this assurance should not be given unless the auditor has audited the financial statements to which the agreements or regulatory requirements relate. Furthermore, such assurance should not extend to covenants that relate to matters that have not been subjected to the audit procedures performed in the financial statement audit, and should not be given when the audit resulted in an adverse opinion or a disclaimer of opinion.

The auditor's assurance on compliance may be given in a separate report or in one or more explanatory paragraphs following the opinion paragraph of the report on the audited financial statements. The report language should restrict the distribution of the information on negative assurance to parties within the entity (such as the board of directors), parties to the loan agreement, or the regulatory agency. A separate report on debt compliance is illustrated in Figure 21-5.

In addition to the compliance reports related to audited financial statements described here as part of "special reports," the AICPA has issued an SAS dealing with compliance auditing applicable to governmental entities and recipients of governmental financial assistance (discussed in Chapter 22 of this text) and an SSAE pertaining to other types of compliance attestations (discussed later in this chapter).

FIGURE 21-5 • SPECIAL REPORT ON DEBT COMPLIANCE GIVEN AS A SEPARATE REPORT

INDEPENDENT AUDITOR'S REPORT

We have audited, in accordance with generally accepted auditing standards, the balance sheet of XYZ Company as of December 31, 19X2, and the related statements of income, retained earnings, and cash flows for the year then ended, and have issued our report thereon dated February 16, 19X3.

In connection with our audit, nothing came to our attention that caused us to believe that the Company failed to comply with the terms, covenants, provisions, or conditions of sections XX to XX, inclusive, of the Indenture dated July 21, 19X0, with ABC Bank insofar as they relate to accounting matters. However, our audit was not directed primarily toward obtaining knowledge of such noncompliance.

This report is intended solely for the information and use of the boards of directors and management of XYZ Company and ABC Bank and should not be used for any other purpose.

SOURCE: AU 623.21.

LEARNING CHECK:

21-4 a. What types of reports are encompassed by the term *special reports* as described in SAS 62?
b. State a common characteristic of the types of data covered by special reports.

21-5 a. When is a basis of accounting considered to be an *other comprehensive basis of accounting (OCBOA)*?
b. Explain the effects on the auditor's standard report when reporting on financial statements prepared on an OCBOA.

21-6 Distinguish between the levels of assurance that may be given when (a) auditing and (b) applying agreed-upon procedures to specified elements, accounts, or items of a financial statement.

21-7 a. Under what circumstances may an auditor issue a negative assurance in a compliance report related to audited financial statements?
b. What are the reporting options for conveying the negative assurance in these circumstances?

KEY TERMS:

Agreed-upon procedures, p. 803
Other comprehensive basis of accounting (OCBOA), p. 802
Special reports, p. 801

REVIEW SERVICES

A **review service** involves the application of limited procedures to financial information or financial statements to provide an independent accountant with limited assurance that there are no material modifications that should be made to the information in order for it to be in conformity with generally accepted accounting principles or another comprehensive basis of accounting. Thus, review services culminate in the issuance of a negative assurance. Note that the term *independent accountant* rather than *independent auditor* is used in connection with a review service to reduce the risk of confusion about the type of service performed.

Separate standards apply to the following two types of review services:

OBJECTIVE 5

Explain the nature of review services and the type of assurance associated with them.

- Reviews of the interim financial information (a) of a public entity that is either presented alone or that accompanies the entity's audited financial statements, or (b) that is included in a note to the audited financial statements of either a public or nonpublic entity. The standards for these reviews, hereafter called **SAS 71 reviews,** are provided in SAS 71, *Interim Financial Information* (AU 722).
- Reviews of the financial statements of nonpublic entities, as well as the annual and interim statements of public entities whose annual statements are not audited as explained later. The standards for these reviews (hereafter called **SSARS reviews,** are provided in SSARS 1 (as amended), *Compilation and Review of Financial Statements* (AR 100).

A review service is substantially less in scope than an audit. However, the accountant must possess (1) an adequate knowledge of the accounting principles and practices of the industry in which the entity operates and (2) an understanding of the entity's business, including its organization, its operating characteristics, and the nature of its assets, liabilities, revenues, and expenses. The limited procedures common to both types of reviews include

- Making certain prescribed inquiries of management and others with financial and accounting responsibilities concerning the entity's accounting principles and practices and any changes therein.
- Performing analytical procedures designed to identify relationships and individual items in the financial information that appear to be unusual.
- Obtaining information about actions taken at meetings of stockholders and the board of directors and its committees that may affect the financial information.
- Reading the financial information to consider whether on the basis of information coming to the accountant's attention, the information appears to conform with GAAP.
- Obtaining written representations from management concerning the reviewed financial information and management's responsibility for it.

A review may enable the independent accountant to discover a misstatement or the omission of a material disclosure required by GAAP. However, a review cannot be relied on to reveal all significant matters that would be discovered in an audit. The evidence obtained from the foregoing procedures, though significantly less than that required in an audit, should be sufficient to reduce the level of attestation risk to a moderate level.

Unique features and reporting requirements applicable to each of the two types of reviews are explained in the following sections.

SAS 71 REVIEW OF INTERIM FINANCIAL INFORMATION

SAS 71 pertains to reviews of **interim financial information (IFI)** for less than a full year or for a twelve-month period ending on a date other than the entity's fiscal year end. IFI includes data on financial position, results of operations, and cash flows in the form of complete or summarized financial statements or summarized financial data. Such information may be issued on a monthly or quarterly basis or at other intervals.

A major impetus for these reviews is the SEC's reporting requirement related to IFI. The information that public entities must file in quarterly 10-Q reports within 45 days of the end of each of the first three quarters of the fiscal year is not required to be audited or reviewed prior to filing. However, certain IFI for each quarter of the last two years must be included in a footnote to the annual audited financial statements filed with the SEC. The footnote is usually labeled "unaudited," but the interim information in the footnote must, at a minimum, be subjected to an SAS 71 review. The review of this information can be performed concurrently with the annual audit. But many entities elect to have the interim information reviewed before each quarterly filing. In this way they can reduce the risk of having to adjust the data already filed in the 10-Q reports based on any misstatements or omissions found in the required review of the quarterly information included in the footnote to the annual statements.

TIMELY QUARTERLY REVIEWS

In spite of the lack of an SEC requirement, Deloitte & Touche became the first Big Six firm to require its public clients to have quarterly information reviewed by the firm on a timely basis—that is, before the quarterly information is filed. The firm based its mandate on a recognition that quarterly information is having more of an impact, that most of its public clients already received timely reviews, and that those who didn't would incur little if any additional cost because of greater efficiencies during the annual audit. Regarding the latter point, the firm's director of auditing services noted that "the staff get a tremendous amount of additional information about the client and end up more knowledgeable."

It has also been reported that Price Waterhouse encourages its clients to request the timely review service, and that Arthur Andersen has formulated a policy that requires quarterly involvement for clients that meet certain criteria.

SOURCE: "D&T Requires Timely Quarterly Reviews," *Public Accounting Report*, June 30, 1994, p. 5.

Additional Requirements in SAS 71 Reviews

SAS 71 reviews of IFI are performed only for entities whose annual financial statements are audited. As a result, the reviewing independent accountant is expected to have an understanding of relevant internal control structure policies and procedures that relate to the preparation of *both* annual and interim financial information. Furthermore, the accountant is expected to use this knowledge to (1) identify types of potential material misstatements in the IFI and consider the likelihood of their occurrence and (2) select the inquiries and analytical procedures that will provide a basis for reporting whether material modifications should be made to the IFI to conform with GAAP. Consideration should also be given to whether the review procedures should be modified in any way to take into account the results of auditing procedures performed in the annual audit. In addition, in this type of review, the accountant should read the minutes of meetings of stockholders and the board of directors and its committees to obtain information about actions that may affect the IFI rather than relying on other means such as inquiry.

OBJECTIVE 6

Differentiate between an SAS 71 review and an SSARS review.

As a result of the procedures performed in an SAS 71 review, the accountant may conclude that the IFI filed or to be filed with a regulatory agency is probably materially misstated because of a departure from GAAP. In such a case, the accountant should discuss the matter with management. If management does not respond appropriately, the accountant should communicate, either orally or in writing, with the audit committee as soon as practicable. If the audit committee does not respond appropriately or within a reasonable time, the accountant should evaluate whether to resign (1) from the engagement related to IFI and (2) as the entity's auditor for its annual financial statements. A reviewing accountant should also assure herself or himself that the audit committee is adequately informed about any of the following matters about which she or he becomes aware as a result of performing the review procedures: (1) irregularities or illegal acts that are not clearly inconsequential and (2) reportable conditions pertaining to the internal control structure.

FIGURE 21-6 • ACCOUNTANT'S REPORT ON SAS 71 REVIEW OF INTERIM FINANCIAL INFORMATION

Independent Accountant's Report

We have reviewed the accompanying *[describe the statements or information reviewed]* of ABC Company and consolidated subsidiaries as of September 30, 19X1, and for the three-month and nine-month periods then ended. These financial statements (information) are (is) the responsibility of the company's management.

We conducted our review in accordance with standards established by the American Institute of Certified Public Accountants. A review of interim financial information consists principally of applying analytical procedures to financial data and making inquiries of persons responsible for financial and accounting matters. It is substantially less in scope than an audit conducted in accordance with generally accepted auditing standards, the objective of which is the expression of an opinion regarding the financial statements taken as a whole. Accordingly, we do not express such an opinion.

Based on our review, we are not aware of any material modifications that should be made to the accompanying financial statements (information) for them (it) to be in conformity with generally accepted accounting principles.

SOURCE: AU 722.28.

Accountant's Report on SAS 71 Review of IFI

The sample standard report recommended in SAS 71 for a review of IFI presented separately from the audited financial statements is shown in Figure 21-6. Notice that it starts with a title that includes the words *independent accountant's.* The introductory paragraph identifies the type of service performed ("We have reviewed . . ."), the information reviewed, the name of the entity, and management's responsibility for the information. The second, or scope, paragraph asserts that the review was conducted in accordance with the AICPA's standards, briefly describes a review, differentiates a review from an audit, and disclaims an opinion on the information reviewed. The third paragraph contains the negative assurance that is based on the review. The report should be addressed and dated in the same manner as an auditor's standard report. In addition, each page of the IFI should be clearly marked "unaudited." SAS 71 also provides guidance for situations involving modifications to the report for departures from GAAP, inadequate disclosures, and reference to the report of another accountant who reviewed the IFI of a significant component of the reporting entity.

When IFI accompanies audited financial statements as supplementary information or in a footnote, the auditor is not required to modify the auditor's report to refer to the IFI or the review unless (1) IFI required by the SEC in an annual 10-K filing has been omitted or has not been reviewed, (2) the IFI is not clearly labeled unaudited, or (3) the IFI does not conform to GAAP.

SSARS REVIEW OF FINANCIAL STATEMENTS

The SSARS review service was originally developed as a lower cost and lower assurance alternative to an audit of the financial statements for nonpublic entities. However, in recent years a number of states have passed securities laws that permit public companies to raise limited amounts of capital without submitting audited financial statements. Some of those states require reviewed statements instead. In addition, entities making certain limited interstate securities offerings that are exempt from audit requirements related to the federal Securities Act of 1933 may elect to have a SSARS review. SSARS reviews pertain only to complete annual or interim financial statements, not summarized or selected information. A review report may be issued on a single statement, such as the balance sheet, and not on the related statements, provided no restriction has been placed on the scope of the accountant's inquiries and analytical procedures.

Procedurally, the major difference between a SAS 71 and a SSARS review is that the latter does not require the auditor to obtain an understanding of the entity's internal control structure as a basis for identifying potential misstatements and selecting the inquiries and analytical procedures to be performed. However, inquiries should be made concerning the entity's procedures for recording, classifying, and summarizing transactions, and accumulating information for disclosure in the financial statements. In a SSARS review, the accountant may obtain information about the actions taken at meetings of stockholders and the board of directors and its committees by inquiry or other means rather than reading the minutes.

Accountant's Report on SSARS Review of Financial Statements

The sample standard review report recommended in SSARS 1 is shown in Figure 21-7. Note that the report contains three paragraphs and is similar to the one shown in Figure 21-6 for a SAS 71 review except that reference to the standards followed by the accountant is given in the first paragraph instead of the second, and the reference makes explicit mention of the *Statements on Standards for Accounting and Review Services.* In addition, each page of the reviewed financial statements should include a reference such as "See Accountant's Review Report."

FIGURE 21-7 • ACCOUNTANT'S REPORT ON SSARS REVIEW OF FINANCIAL STATEMENTS

I [we] have reviewed the accompanying balance sheet of XYZ Company as of December 31, 19XX, and the related statements of income, retained earnings, and cash flows for the year then ended, in accordance with Statements on Standards for Accounting and Review Services issued by the American Institute of Certified Public Accountants. All information included in these financial statements is the representation of the management [owners] of XYZ Company.

A review consists principally of inquiries of company personnel and analytical procedures applied to financial data. It is substantially less in scope than an audit in accordance with generally accepted auditing standards, the objective of which is the expression of an opinion regarding the financial statements taken as a whole. Accordingly, I [we] do not express such an opinion.

Based on my [our] review, I am [we are] not aware of any material modifications that should be made to the accompanying financial statements in order for them to be in conformity with generally accepted accounting principles.

SOURCE: AR 100.35.

LEARNING CHECK:

21-8 a. How do the objectives of a review service differ from those of an audit?
b. Identify two types of review services and the professional standards that apply to each.
c. What is the principal source of demand for each of the two types of reviews?

21-9 a. What limited procedures are common to both types of reviews?
b. What additional procedures are required in SAS 71 reviews?

21-10 a. Under what circumstances might a nonpublic entity have a SAS 71 review?
b. Under what circumstances might a public entity have a SSARS review?

KEY TERMS:

Interim financial information (IFI), p. 807
Review service, p. 806
SAS 71 reviews, p. 806
SSARS reviews, p. 806

OTHER ATTEST SERVICES

This section provides an overview of the following types of services: (1) reporting on internal control, (2) reporting on prospective financial information, and (3) compliance attestation. An additional attest service, letters for underwriters and certain other requesting parties issued in connection with securities offerings, is explained in Chapter 23.

REPORTING ON INTERNAL CONTROL

This section deals with the following two types of engagements:

OBJECTIVE 7

Discuss reporting on internal control based on a management assertion and the processing of transactions by service organizations.

- *Reporting on management's written assertion about the effectiveness of an entity's internal control structure (ICS) over financial reporting.* This type of attest service is governed by SSAE 2, *Reporting on an Entity's Internal Control Structure Over Financial Reporting* (AT 400).
- *Reporting on the ICS over the processing of transactions by service organizations.* This type of reporting is governed by SAS 70, *Reports on the Processing of Transactions by Service Organizations* (AU 324).

Care must be taken in distinguishing these types of reporting on internal control from the following types of reporting to which different standards apply as indicated:

- *Communication of ICS-related matters noted in an audit* (reportable conditions and material weaknesses). This involves a communication from the auditor to management and the board of directors only, as part of an audit, and does not constitute a separate attest engagement. The applicable standard is SAS 60 (AU 325), which is discussed in Chapters 9 and 19 of this text.

- *Reporting on the ICS in audits conducted in accordance with Government Auditing Standards.* Guidance on this type of reporting is presented in SAS 68, *Compliance Auditing Applicable to Governmental Entities and Other Recipients of Governmental Financial Assistance* (AU 801) as discussed in Chapter 22 of this text.
- *Reporting on management's written assertion about the effectiveness of an entity's ICS over compliance with specified requirements.* This type of reporting is governed by SSAE 3, *Compliance Attestation* (AT 500) as discussed later in this chapter.

Reporting on Management's Written Assertion About the Effectiveness of an Entity's ICS Over Financial Reporting

As noted in Chapter 8, a variety of factors has contributed to a growing recognition of the importance of an entity's ICS. Concurrent with this recognition has been an increasing interest on the part of investors, regulators, the U.S. Congress, and others in having management issue a written assertion about an entity's ICS, and having an independent accountant attest to management's assertion. The AICPA has recommended that public companies be required to issue such reports, including an independent accountant's attestation.

SSAE 2 provides guidance concerning engagements to examine and report on a management assertion about any of the following aspects of an entity's ICS over financial reporting:

- Design and operating effectiveness of the overall ICS.
- Design and operating effectiveness of a segment of the ICS.
- Suitability of the design of the ICS only.
- Design and operating effectiveness of the ICS based on criteria established by a regulatory agency.

In addition to performing *examination* services on the foregoing types of assertions, independent accountants may perform more limited *agreed-upon procedures* engagements in certain situations. However, SSAE 2 prohibits performing review services or issuing negative assurances on management assertions about the effectiveness of internal control.

CONDITIONS FOR ENGAGEMENT PERFORMANCE. An independent accountant should perform the foregoing types of engagements only when management (1) accepts responsibility for the effectiveness of the entity's ICS, (2) evaluates the effectiveness of its ICS using reasonable criteria established by a recognized body, and (3) refers to those criteria in a report containing its written assertion. In addition, sufficient evidential matter must exist or be capable of development to support management's evaluation. Reasonable criteria include those developed by the Committee of Sponsoring Organizations (COSO) as presented in its report entitled *Internal Control—Integrated Framework*.[3] SSAE 2 notes that some criteria, such as those established by certain regulatory agencies, are reasonable only for the parties who have participated in establishing them. In such cases, the accountant's report should be modified to include a restriction on the report's distribution to those parties only. An example of a management assertion that meets the conditions enumerated above, and that includes reference to the COSO criteria, is shown on the left side of Figure 21-8. The illustration is an actual assertion issued by the management of the AICPA on that organization's own internal structure and included in its own 1992–93 Annual Report, showing that the Institute took its own recommendations to heart!

PLANNING AND PERFORMING THE ENGAGEMENT. Although there are many similarities in the methodologies for considering the ICS in a financial statement audit and in performing an engagement to examine management's written assertion about the effectiveness of the ICS, the latter is more extensive. For example, in an audit tests of controls need only be performed on those control policies and procedures for which the auditor assesses control risk at below the maximum as part of a strategy to reduce substantive tests. In an engagement to examine a management assertion about the ICS, the tests of controls depend on the nature of the assertion and the criteria cited by management in the report containing the assertion. The time period to be covered by tests of controls, which is the entire audit period in a financial statement audit, may also vary based on the nature of the assertion in an examination under SSAE 2. In both an audit and an examination, however, an understanding of the ICS must be obtained, and any reportable conditions and material weaknesses gleaned from the understanding or tests of controls must be communicated to the audit committee. SSAE 2 contains extensive guidance on dealing with various situations that can arise in an examination of any of the several types of management assertions about an entity's ICS listed earlier.

ACCOUNTANT'S REPORT. The right half of Figure 21-8 shows the actual report issued by the independent accountant who attested to the written assertion of AICPA management that is shown in the left half of the figure.[4] The report of J. H. Cohn & Company conforms in all respects with the form of report recommended in SSAE 2 (AT 400.51) when the accountant has examined a management assertion that is presented in a separate report about the effectiveness of an entity's ICS as of a particular date. Note that the first paragraph includes the date to which management's assertion applies, the second paragraph describes the scope and character of the accountant's examination, the third paragraph states caveats re-

---

[3] In 1994, COSO issued an addendum to its report. In the addendum, COSO encourages managements that report to external parties on controls over financial reporting to also cover controls over the safeguarding of assets against unauthorized acquisition, use, or disposition.

[4] The Institute has reported that the first year cost of the independent accountant's examination of its assertion added 20% to its audit fee of $100,000, but that the cost in subsequent years would likely add less than 2% to audit fees.

FIGURE 21-8 • MANAGEMENT ASSERTION ABOUT INTERNAL CONTROL AND ACCOMPANYING ACCOUNTANT'S REPORT

MANAGEMENT'S RESPONSIBILITY FOR INTERNAL CONTROL SYSTEM

The Institute maintains an internal control system over financial reporting, which is designed to provide reasonable assurance to the Institute's management and Board of Directors regarding the preparation of reliable financial statements. The system includes a documented organizational structure, the division of responsibility and established policies and procedures, including a code of conduct to foster a strong ethical climate.

Established policies are communicated throughout the Institute and enhanced through the careful selection, training, and development of its staff. Internal auditors monitor the operation of the internal control system and report findings and recommendations to management and the Board of Directors. Corrective actions are taken, as required, to address control deficiencies and implement improvements in the system.

There are inherent limitations in the effectiveness of any system of internal control, including the possibility of human error and the circumvention or overriding of controls. Accordingly, even the most effective internal control system can provide only reasonable assurance with respect to financial statement preparation. Furthermore, the effectiveness of an internal control system can change with circumstances.

The Institute has assessed its internal control system over financial reporting in relation to criteria for effective internal control over financial reporting described in *Internal Control—Integrated Framework* issued by the Committee of Sponsoring Organizations of the Treadway Commission. Based on this assessment, the Institute believes that, as of July 31, 1993, its system of internal control over financial reporting met those objectives.

J. H. Cohn & Company was also engaged to report separately on the Institute's assessment of its internal control system over financial reporting. The report of the independent public accountant follows this statement.

/Signature
Donald L. Adams
Vice President
Financial and Administration (CFO)

REPORT OF INDEPENDENT PUBLIC ACCOUNTANTS

To The Members of the American
Institute of Certified Public Accountants

We have examined management's assertion that the American Institute of Certified Public Accountants maintained an effective internal control system over financial reporting as of July 31, 1993 included in the accompanying statement of management's responsibilities for financial statements and internal control system.

Our examination was made in accordance with standards established by the American Institute of Certified Public Accountants and, accordingly, included obtaining an understanding of the internal control system over financial reporting, testing and evaluating the design and operating effectiveness of the internal control system, and such other procedures as we considered necessary in the circumstances. We believe that our examination provides a reasonable basis for our opinion.

Because of inherent limitations in an internal control system, errors or irregularities may occur and not be detected. Also, projections of any evaluation of the internal control system over financial reporting to future periods are subject to the risk that the internal control system may become inadequate because of changes in conditions, or that the degree of compliance with the policies or procedures may deteriorate.

In our opinion, management's assertion that the American Institute of Certified Public Accountants maintained an effective internal control system over financial reporting as of July 31, 1993 is fairly stated, in all material respects, based on criteria established in "Internal Control—Integrated Framework" issued by the Committee of Sponsoring Organizations of the Treadway Commission ("COSO").

/Signature
J. H. Cohn & Company

New York, New York
September 2, 1993

SOURCE: American Institute of Certified Public Accountants, *Annual Report 1992–1993*, pp. 17 and 19.

garding the inherent limitations of any ICS, and the fourth paragraph contains a positive expression of opinion. SSAE 2 provides guidance on numerous situations requiring modifications to the standard report.[5]

Reporting on the ICS over the Processing of Transactions by Service Organizations

Note that this service does not involve reporting on a management assertion about internal control. Rather, as explained in Chapter 13, this type of reporting arises when an organization that provides data processing services asks its auditor (the service auditor) to issue a report on the service organization's ICS over the processing of transactions. The report is then provided to the service organization's customers and their independent auditors (user auditors) who use the report in considering the customers' internal control structures as part of the customers' annual audits. This is appropriate because parts of the customers' internal control structures typically encompass some of the controls at the service organization.

SAS 70 provides guidance for engagements leading to two types of reports on a service organization's ICS:

- A report on policies and procedures placed in operation.
- A report on policies and procedures placed in operation and tests of operating effectiveness.

In the first type of report, the service auditor expresses an opinion as to whether an accompanying description of applicable control policies and procedures at the service organization is fairly presented in all material respects, and whether those policies and procedures are suitably designed to provide reasonable assurance that specified control objectives would be achieved *if the described controls were complied with satisfactorily.* The first type of report may assist user auditors in obtaining an understanding of their clients' internal control structures.

The second type of report includes the same information as the first type, as well as reference to an accompanying description of the specific controls tested by the service auditor, the nature, timing, and extent of those tests, and the resultant auditor's opinion as to the effectiveness of those controls in meeting the specified control objectives during a specified period of time. This type of report may assist user auditors both in obtaining an understanding and in providing a basis for assessing control risk at below the maximum for assertions affected by the controls.

Both types of reports include a statement that the report is intended solely for use by the management of the service organization, its customers, and the independent auditors of its customers. Although the service auditor's report is used in the audit of the user organization's financial statements, the user auditor should not make reference to the service auditor's report in his or her audit report on those financial statements.

---

[5] When management's assertion pertains to the effectiveness of the ICS over financial reporting *and additional control policies and procedures over the safeguarding of assets* pursuant to the COSO addendum described in footnote 3, additional wording to that effect in the first, third, and fourth paragraphs of the accountant's report would be appropriate.

REPORTING ON PROSPECTIVE FINANCIAL INFORMATION

Prospective financial information is generally provided in public offerings of bonds and other securities. In addition, banks and other lending institutions often insist on projections of future earnings in extending credit to individuals and companies, and governmental agencies sometimes require forecasts in applications for grants and government contracts. To enhance the reliability of the prospective financial information, CPAs may be asked to become associated with such data.

The AICPA has issued the following two documents pertaining to a CPA's association with prospective financial information:

- A Statement on Standards for Accountants' Services on Prospective Financial Information entitled *Financial Forecasts and Projections.*
- *Guide for Prospective Financial Statements.*

The Statement on Financial Forecasts and Projections (AT 200) is similar in authority to an SAS. The Guide is an interpretation of the Statement.

Types of Prospective Financial Information

AT 200.06 recognizes two types of **prospective financial information** as follows:

- **Financial forecast.** Prospective financial statements that present, to the best of the responsible party's knowledge and belief, an entity's expected financial position, results of operations, and cash flows.
- **Financial projection.** Prospective financial statements that present, to the best of the responsible party's knowledge and belief, given one or more hypothetical assumptions, an entity's expected financial position, results of operations, and cash flows.

A financial forecast and a financial projection differ in terms of assumptions and the expected course of action. A forecast is based on conditions expected to exist and the course of action expected to be taken. In contrast, a projection involves one or more hypothetical courses of action. Both a forecast and a projection may be stated either as a single-point estimate or as a range. The two types of prospective financial information also differ as to use; a forecast is appropriate for general use, whereas a projection is for limited use by the entity alone or by the entity and third parties with whom the entity is negotiating directly.

A CPA may accept an engagement to perform one of three types of services pertaining to prospective financial statements when third-party use is anticipated: (1) compilation (preparation), (2) examination, and (3) application of agreed-upon procedures. An engagement to compile prospective information is an accounting service to a client and is discussed later in this chapter. This type of service does not result in the expression of any assurance (positive or negative) on the prospective statements. The other types of service constitute attestation engagements in which the CPA must satisfy the eleven attestation standards.

Examination of Prospective Financial Statements

AT 200.27 indicates that an **examination** of prospective financial statements involves (1) evaluating the preparation and the support underlying the assumptions of the prospective financial statements, (2) determining whether the presentation of the statements is in conformity with the presentation guidelines set forth in the AICPA *Guide for Prospective Financial Statements,* and (3) issuing an examination report.

STANDARD REPORT ON PROSPECTIVE FINANCIAL STATEMENTS. AT 200.31 provides that the CPA's standard report on an examination of prospective financial statements should include

- An identification of the prospective financial statements presented.
- A statement that the examination of the prospective financial statements was made in accordance with AICPA standards and a brief description of the nature of such an examination.
- The accountant's opinion that the prospective financial statements are presented in conformity with AICPA presentation guidelines and that the underlying assumptions provide a reasonable basis for the forecast or a reasonable basis for the projection given the hypothetical assumptions.
- A caveat that the prospective results may not be achieved.
- A statement that the accountant assumes no responsibility to update the report for events and circumstances occurring after the date of the report.

The suggested wording of a standard report on the examination of a financial forecast is illustrated in Figure 21-9.

In reporting on a financial projection, the CPA should express an opinion as to whether the assumptions provide a reasonable basis for the projection given the hypothetical assumptions. In addition, AT 200.33 indicates that the standard re-

FIGURE 21-9 • ACCOUNTANT'S STANDARD REPORT ON EXAMINATION OF A FINANCIAL FORECAST

We have examined the accompanying forecasted balance sheet, statements of income, retained earnings, and cash flows of *XYZ* Company as of December 31, 19XX, and for the year then ending. Our examination was made in accordance with standards for an examination of a forecast established by the American Institute of Certified Public Accountants and, accordingly, included such procedures as we considered necessary to evaluate both the assumptions used by management and the preparation and presentation of the forecast.

In our opinion, the accompanying forecast is presented in conformity with guidelines for presentation of a forecast established by the American Institute of Certified Public Accountants, and the underlying assumptions provide a reasonable basis for management's forecast. However, there will usually be differences between the forecasted and actual results, because events and circumstances frequently do not occur as expected, and those differences may be material. We have no responsibility to update this report for events and circumstances occurring after the date of this report.

SOURCE: AT 200.32.

port should contain an explanatory paragraph stating the purpose and restricted use of the data and report, as follows:

> The accompanying projection and this report were prepared for [state special purpose, for example, "the DEF National Bank for the purpose of negotiating a loan to expand XYZ Company's plant"] and should not be used for any other purpose.

The accountant's report should be dated as of the completion of the examination.

DEPARTURES FROM STANDARD REPORT. As in the case of reports on historical financial statements, other types of opinions may be expressed on prospective financial statements. The circumstances and their effects on the CPA's opinion are as follows:

- If the prospective financial statements depart from AICPA presentation guidelines, a qualified or adverse opinion should be expressed.
- If the departure from AICPA guidelines is due to the failure to disclose significant assumptions, an adverse opinion should be issued.
- If one or more significant assumptions do not provide a reasonable basis for the forecast, or for the projection, given the hypothetical assumptions, an adverse opinion should be expressed.
- If the accountant's examination did not include all procedures considered necessary in the circumstances, a disclaimer of opinion should be issued.

In each case, the report should contain an explanatory paragraph that describes the circumstances.

Applying Agreed-upon Procedures

AT 200.49 states that a CPA may accept an engagement to apply **agreed-upon procedures** to prospective financial statements when (1) the specified users involved have participated in establishing the nature and scope of the engagement and take responsibility for the adequacy of the procedures to be performed, (2) distribution of the report is to be restricted to the specified users involved, and (3) the prospective financial statements include a summary of significant assumptions. The accountant's report on the results of applying agreed-upon procedures should

- Enumerate the procedures performed and refer to conformity with the arrangements made with the specified users.
- If the procedures are less than those performed in an examination, (1) state this fact and (2) disclaim an opinion on the prospective financial statements and on whether the underlying assumptions provide a reasonable basis for the forecast or a reasonable basis for the projection given the hypothetical assumptions.
- State the accountant's findings.

In addition, the report should include the identification of the prospective financial statements, a caveat that the results may not be achieved, wording that restricts the distribution of the report, and a statement that the accountant has no responsibility to update the report.

COMPLIANCE ATTESTATION

OBJECTIVE 8

State the purpose of compliance attestations and the conditions under which they may be performed.

Another area in which CPAs are increasingly being asked by regulatory bodies and others to perform additional services is in regard to an entity's **compliance with specified requirements** such as laws, regulations, contracts, rules, or grants. These requirements may be financial or nonfinancial in nature. For example, the Federal Depository Insurance Corporation Improvement Act of 1991 (FDICIA) requires certain insured depository institutions to engage independent accountants to perform agreed-upon procedures to test an institution's compliance with certain FDIC-designated "safety and soundness" laws and regulations. A nonfinancial example is the Environmental Protection Agency's (EPA) requirement that certain entities engage independent accountants to perform agreed-upon procedures regarding compliance with an EPA regulation that gasoline contain at least 2% oxygen.

Agreed-upon Procedures Engagements

In 1993, the AICPA issued SSAE 3, *Compliance Attestation* (AT 500), to provide guidance to CPAs engaged to perform agreed-upon procedures on management's *written assertions* about (1) an entity's compliance with specified requirements, (2) the effectiveness of an entity's internal control structure over compliance (i.e., the process by which management obtains reasonable assurance of compliance with specified requirements), or (3) both. To reduce the risk of misunderstandings between users and independent accountants, such engagements should only be performed when the following conditions are met: management must accept responsibility for compliance and its assertion, in addition to being written, must (1) be capable of evaluation against reasonable criteria, (2) be capable of reasonably consistent estimation or measurement using the criteria, and (3) contain management's own evaluation.

In agreed-upon procedures engagements, the client and users of the report specify the procedures to be performed. The CPA issues a report on the specified procedures and findings, but neither evaluates the adequacy of the procedures for the users needs nor expresses an opinion on compliance. Rather, the CPA's report is intended to *assist users* in evaluating an entity's compliance which is often a legal determination. Distribution of the report is restricted to the audit committee, management, and identified parties who participated in determining the procedures.

Examination Engagements

SSAE 3 permits examination engagements that result in an independent accountant's expression of opinion on compliance when certain additional specified conditions are met, but agreed-upon procedures engagements are encouraged because they may be better tailored to the users' needs. Because in an examination the independent accountant determines the procedures to be performed and the evidence needed to provide a reasonable basis for the expression of an opinion, these engagements may involve greater complexities in setting materiality levels and in assessing and achieving the inherent, control, and detection risk components of attestation risk.

SSAE 3 does not apply to situations in which an auditor reports on compliance with specified requirements based solely on an audit of financial statements as discussed in a previous subsection under the heading "Special Reports."

SUMMARY OF ATTEST SERVICES

Figure 21-10 provides a summary of the attestation subjects that are covered in this chapter, the types of attest services applicable to each, the associated types of assurance, and whether there are restrictions on report distribution.

FIGURE 21-10 • SUMMARY OF ATTEST SERVICES AND REPORTS

Subject of Engagement	Type of Service	Type of Assurance	Restriction on Use of Report
Special reports:			
Other comprehensive basis of accounting (OCBOA)	Audit	Positive expression of opinion	No
Specified elements, accounts, or items of a financial statement	Audit	Positive expression of opinion	No
	Agreed-upon procedures	Summary of findings	Yes
Compliance reports	By-product of audit	Negative assurance	Yes
Review services:			
SAS 71 review of interim financial information (IFI)	Review	Negative assurance	No
SSARS review of financial statements	Review	Negative assurance	No
Reporting on internal control:			
Written management assertion	Examination	Positive expression of opinion	No
	Agreed-upon procedures	Summary of findings	Yes
Processing of transactions by service organizations	Examination	Positive expression of opinion	Yes
Reporting on prospective financial information:			
Forecast	Examination	Positive expression of opinion	No
	Agreed-upon procedures	Summary of findings	Yes
Projection	Examination	Positive expression of opinion	No
	Agreed-upon procedures	Summary of findings	Yes
Compliance attestation:			
Compliance with specified requirements	Agreed-upon procedures	Summary of findings	Yes
	Examination	Positive expression of opinion	No
Internal control structure over compliance	Agreed-upon procedures	Summary of findings	Yes
	Examination	Positive expression of opinion	No

LEARNING CHECK:

21-11 a. What conditions must be met for an independent accountant to perform an examination of a management assertion about the effectiveness of an entity's internal control structure?

b. Briefly describe the content of each of the four paragraphs of a standard report issued on such an engagement.

21-12 Identify two types of reports that may be issued on the internal control structure over the processing of transactions by service organizations and indicate by whom and for what purposes the reports are used.

21-13 a. Identify and distinguish between two types of prospective financial information.

b. What types of service may a CPA perform on such information?

21-14 a. What matters should be covered in an accountant's examination report on prospective financial statements?

b. How does an examination report on a financial projection differ from one on a financial forecast?

c. How does a report on applying agreed-upon procedures to prospective financial statements differ from an examination report?

21-15 a. What conditions must be met for an independent accountant to perform an agreed-upon procedures compliance attestation?

b. Who determines the procedures in such an engagement?

c. What is the character and purpose of the accountant's report in such an engagement?

KEY TERMS:

Agreed-upon procedures, p. 818
Compliance with specified requirements, p. 819
Examination, p. 817
Financial forecast, p. 816
Financial projection, p. 816
Prospective financial information, p. 816

NONATTEST ACCOUNTING SERVICES

AR 100.02 indicates that **accounting services** include engagements to (1) prepare a working trial balance, (2) assist in adjusting the books of account, (3) prepare tax returns, and (4) provide manual or automated bookkeeping or data processing services. An accounting service does not result in expressing any kind of assurance. Thus, the accountant does not have to be independent of the client in performing this type of service. The accountant's responsibilities in four types of accounting services are explained in following sections.

Our explanations of accounting services will be in the following sequence: (1) reporting on unaudited financial statements, (2) compilation of financial statements, (3) compilation of prospective financial statements, and (4) reporting on the application of accounting principles. A final section deals with a change in an engagement from one type of service to another.

UNAUDITED FINANCIAL STATEMENTS OF A PUBLIC ENTITY

OBJECTIVE 9

State the accountant's responsibilities when associated with unaudited statements of a public entity.

A CPA may be associated with the financial statements of a public company even though he or she has not audited them. For example, the CPA may assist the company in preparing its unaudited and (unreviewed) interim financial statements for inclusion in certain SEC filings. In performing this type of an accounting service, the accountant must follow guidelines prescribed by the Auditing Standards Board. This type of service is rare.

SAS 26, *Association with Financial Statements* (AU 504.03), states that a CPA is associated with financial statements when the CPA (1) has consented to the use of his or her name in a report, document, or written communication containing the statements, or (2) submits to clients or others financial statements that the CPA has prepared or assisted in preparing even though his or her name is not appended to the statements.

When accountants are associated with **unaudited financial statements** of public entities, they are required to state in their report that an audit was not made and include a disclaimer of opinion. In addition, each page of the financial statements should be marked "unaudited." A report on unaudited financial statements is illustrated in Figure 21-11.

When this type of disclaimer is issued, the accountant is not required to perform any auditing procedures beyond reading the financial statements for obvious material misstatements. If any procedures are performed, they should not be described in the accountant's report. When a CPA knows, from knowledge about the client or the work done, that the unaudited statements are not in conformity with generally accepted accounting principles, the client should be requested to make the necessary revisions in the statements. If the client refuses, the accountant should clearly state his reservations on the statements along with a disclaimer of opinion. If the client will not accept the accountant's report, the CPA should refuse to be associated with the statements and, if necessary, withdraw from the engagement.

COMPILATION OF FINANCIAL STATEMENTS OF A NONPUBLIC ENTITY

OBJECTIVE 10

Differentiate a compilation service from an audit or review.

Many nonpublic entities desire only accounting services from a CPA. This frequently occurs when the owners are able to personally supervise business operations, and audited or reviewed financial statements are not required to obtain a loan from the local bank. The rendering of accounting services is a major part of the practice of some small CPA firms.

FIGURE 21-11 • ACCOUNTANT'S REPORT ON UNAUDITED STATEMENTS

The accompanying balance sheet of X Company as of December 31, 19XX, and the related statements of income, retained earnings, and cash flows for the year then ended were not audited by us, and accordingly, we do not express an opinion on them.

(Signature and Date)

SOURCE: AU 504.05.

Small enterprises may ask a CPA to prepare or assist in preparing their financial statements. This type of accounting service for a nonpublic entity is referred to as a **compilation engagement.** In this type of engagement, the accountant must follow the guidelines prescribed by the AICPA's Accounting and Review Services Committee. As in other engagements, the CPA should establish a clear understanding with the client as to the service to be performed. The understanding should be set forth in an engagement letter describing (1) the nature of the service, (2) the limitations of the service (i.e., cannot be relied on to disclose misstatements), and (3) the nature of the compilation report.

Objective and Nature

The objective of this type of accounting service is to present, in the form of financial statements, information supplied by an entity without giving any assurance about the conformity of the statements with generally accepted accounting principles or another comprehensive basis of accounting. In completing a compilation engagement, the CPA is expected to be knowledgeable of the client and the accounting principles and practices of the industry in which the client operates. The CPA should also have a general understanding of its accounting records, the qualifications of its accounting personnel, and the form and content of its financial statements. Such knowledge is ordinarily obtained from experience with the client and inquiry of client personnel.

The CPA is not required to verify the information furnished by the client. However, he or she may deem it necessary to perform other accounting services during the compilation engagement. Before issuing the report, the accountant should read the compiled statements to determine that they are appropriate in form and free from obvious material misstatements.

Accountant's Report on Compilation

AR 100.14 indicates that the CPA's standard report should state that

- A compilation has been performed in accordance with standards established by the AICPA.
- A compilation is limited to presenting in the form of financial statements information that is the representation of management (owners).
- The statements have not been audited or reviewed and, accordingly, the accountant does not express an opinion or any other form of assurance on them.

In addition, each page of the financial statements should include a reference such as "See Accountant's Compilation Report." The standard report for this type of service is illustrated in Figure 21-12.

Departures from the standard report are required in the following circumstances:

- *The financial statements are not in conformity with generally accepted accounting principles.* When the accountant becomes aware of this fact and the client is unwilling to change the statements, the CPA should indicate the departure by

FIGURE 21-12 • ACCOUNTANT'S REPORT ON COMPILATION OF FINANCIAL STATEMENTS

I [we] have compiled the accompanying balance sheet of *XYZ* Company as of December 31, 19XX, and the related statements of income, retained earnings, and cash flows for the year then ended, in accordance with statements on Standards for Accounting and Review Services issued by the American Institute of Certified Public Accountants.

A compilation is limited to presenting in the form of financial statements information that is the representation of management [owners]. I [we] have not audited or reviewed the accompanying financial statements and, accordingly, do not express an opinion or any other form of assurance on them.

SOURCE: AR 100.17.

adding the following sentence to the second paragraph of the report followed by a separate explanatory paragraph:

> However, I (we) did become aware of a departure (certain departures) from generally accepted accounting principles that is (are) described in the following paragraph(s). (AR 100.40)

- *The financial statements omit substantially all disclosures.* When the accountant concludes that the omissions were not intended to mislead users, the only change from the standard report is the addition of the following paragraph:

> Management has elected to omit substantially all of the disclosures (and the statement of cash flows) required by generally accepted accounting principles. If the omitted disclosures were included in the financial statements, they might influence the user's conclusions about the company's financial position, results of operations, and cash flows. Accordingly, these financial statements are not designed for those who are not informed about such matters. (AR 100.21)

- *The CPA is not independent of the client.* The only change from the standard report is the addition of a final paragraph with the following wording:

> I am (we are) not independent with respect to XYZ Company. (AR 100.22)

COMPILATION OF PROSPECTIVE FINANCIAL STATEMENTS

Financial Forecasts and Projections (AT 200.10) states that a **compilation of prospective financial statements** involves

- Assembling, to the extent necessary, the prospective financial statements based on the responsible party's assumptions.
- Performing the required compilation procedures, including reading the prospective financial statements with their summaries of significant assumptions and accounting policies, and considering whether they appear (1) presented in conformity with AICPA presentation guidelines and (2) not obviously inappropriate.
- Issuing a compilation report.

In performing this service, the CPA is expected to meet the compilation procedures set forth in the AICPA *Guide for Prospective Financial Statements.*

AT 200.16 indicates that the accountant's standard report on a compilation of prospective financial statements should include

- An identification of the prospective financial statements presented by the responsible party.
- A statement that the accountant has compiled the prospective financial statements in accordance with standards established by the AICPA.
- A statement that a compilation is limited in scope and does not enable the accountant to express an opinion or any other form of assurance on the prospective financial statements or the assumptions.
- A caveat that the prospective results may not be achieved.
- A statement that the accountant assumes no responsibility to update the report for events and circumstances occurring after the date of the report.

Based on the foregoing, the suggested wording of the report when a forecast does not contain a range is shown in Figure 21-13.

When the forecast contains a range, the report should contain an explanatory middle paragraph stating that the preparer of the forecast has elected to portray the expected results as a range. When the presentation is a financial projection, the standard report should contain an explanatory middle paragraph that describes the limitations on the usefulness of the data. When the CPA is not independent, the standard report may be issued, but a sentence saying "We are not independent with respect to XYZ Company" should be added following the last paragraph.

REPORTING ON THE APPLICATION OF ACCOUNTING PRINCIPLES

Management, other accountants, and intermediaries often consult with CPAs on the proper application of accounting principles to both specified transactions, completed or proposed, and hypothetical transactions. A CPA may also be asked to indicate the type of opinion that may be rendered on an entity's financial state-

FIGURE 21-13 • ACCOUNTANT'S STANDARD REPORT ON COMPILATION OF A FORECAST

We have compiled the accompanying forecasted balance sheet and statements of income, retained earnings, and cash flows of *XYZ* Company as of December 31, 19XX, and for the year then ending, in accordance with standards established by the American Institute of Certified Public Accounts.

A compilation is limited to presenting in the form of a forecast information that is the representation of management and does not include evaluation of the support for the assumptions underlying the forecast. We have not examined the forecast and, accordingly, do not express an opinion or any other form of assurance on the accompanying statements or assumptions. Furthermore, there will usually be differences between the forecasted and actual results, because events and circumstances frequently do not occur as expected, and those differences may be material. We have no responsibility to update this report for events and circumstances occurring after the date of this report.

SOURCE: AT 200.17.

ments in connection with the application of accounting principles. The CPA may express the conclusions either orally or in writing.

SAS 50, *Reports on the Application of Accounting Principles* (AU 625.08), indicates that the accountant's written report should include the following:

- A brief description of the nature of the engagement and a statement that the engagement was performed in accordance with applicable AICPA standards.
- A description of the transaction(s), a statement of the relevant facts, circumstances, and assumptions, and a statement about the source of the information. Principals to specific transactions should be identified, and hypothetical transactions should be described as involving nonspecific principals (e.g., Company A, Company B).
- A statement describing the appropriate accounting principle(s) to be applied or type of opinion that may be rendered on the entity's financial statements, and, if appropriate, a description of the reasons for the reporting accountant's conclusion.
- A statement that the responsibility for the proper accounting treatment rests with the preparers of the financial statements, who should consult with their continuing accountants.
- A statement that any difference in the facts, circumstances, or assumptions presented may change the report.

CHANGE OF ENGAGEMENT

In the course of rendering professional services, a CPA may be asked to change from one type of service to another. A change is a **step up** when it results in a higher level of assurance than originally agreed to (e.g., change from a compilation to a review or from a review to an audit). The CPA can agree to this type of change when (1) there appears to be sufficient evidence to support the higher level of assurance and (2) it seems likely that the revised engagement can be completed in accordance with professional standards. Constraining factors for the CPA may be the availability of personnel and practical considerations relating to the timing of the work.

In contrast, a change in engagement is a **step down** when a lower level of assurance is requested by the client. This change may be accepted by the CPA if there has been a misunderstanding concerning the original engagement or client circumstances have changed. For example, the client's potential loan grantors may conclude that reviewed financial statements will suffice instead of audited statements as initially requested. However, a CPA is precluded from agreeing to a step-down change when the client has imposed restrictions on the CPA's work at the higher level of assurance. The restrictions may include refusing to furnish a client representation letter or prohibiting the CPA from making inquiry with the client's outside legal counsel.

LEARNING CHECK:

21-16 a. How may a CPA be associated with unaudited financial statements?
b. Describe the reporting and additional disclosure requirements when a CPA is associated with unaudited financial statements.

21-17 a. What is the objective and nature of a compilation service on historical financial statements?
b. Indicate the content of the accountant's standard report on a compilation of historical financial statements.

21-18 a. What is involved when a CPA compiles prospective financial statements?
b. Indicate the content of the report on the compilation of prospective financial statements.

21-19 Explain the content of the accountant's report on the application of accounting principles.

21-20 Distinguish between a "step up" and a "step down" change of engagement and explain when a change is acceptable.

KEY TERMS:

Accounting services, p. 821
Compilation engagement, p. 823
Compilation of prospective financial statements, p. 824
Step down, p. 826
Step up, p. 826
Unaudited financial statements, p. 822

SUMMARY

In the practice of public accounting, a CPA may be called on to perform attest services that extend beyond the audit of financial statements prepared in conformity with GAAP. In rendering these services, the accountant must meet attestation standards that are similar but not identical to GAAS, including a requirement that the accountant be independent. Depending on the scope of the work, on completing an engagement a CPA may issue a positive expression of opinion, negative assurance, or summary of findings. The extent of procedures performed and evidence obtained should be appropriate for the level of attestation risk associated with the engagement. A CPA may also perform accounting services for a client. No assurance is provided in accounting services, and the accountant is not required to be independent. In issuing reports on other services, it is imperative that the CPA clearly indicate the nature of the service performed, express the assurance, if any, appropriate to the service, and specify any restrictions on the distribution of the report.

BIBLIOGRAPHY

AICPA Professional Standards:

SAS 35 (AU 622), Special Reports—Applying Agreed Upon Procedures to Specified Elements, Accounts, or Items of a Financial Statement.

SAS 50 (AU 625), Reports on Application of Accounting Principles.

SAS 62 (AU 623), Special Reports.

SAS 70 (AU 324), Reports on the Processing of Transactions by Service Organizations.

SAS 71 (AU 722), Interim Financial Information

SSAE 1 (AT 100, 200, 300), Attestation Standards, Financial Forecasts and Projections, Reporting on Pro Forma Financial Information.

SSAE 2 (AT 400), Reporting on an Entity's Internal Control Structure Over Financial Reporting.
SSAE 3 (AT 500), Compliance Attestation.
SSARS 1 (AR 100), Compilation and Review of Financial Statements.
SSARS 2 (AR 200), Reporting on Comparative Financial Statements.
SSARS 3 (AR 300), Compilation Reports on Financial Statements Included in Prescribed Forms.
SSARS 4 (AR 400), Communications Between Predecessor and Successor Accountants.
SSARS 6 (AR 600), Reporting on Personal Financial Statements Included in Written Personal Financial Plans.
Statement on Standards for Accountants' Services on Prospective Financial Information (AT 200), *Financial Forecasts and Projections.*
IAU 24 (AU 8024), Special Purpose Auditor's Reports.
IAU 27 (AU 8027), The Examination of Prospective Financial Information
IAU/RS 1 (AU 8501), Basic Principles Governing Review Engagements.
IAU/RS 2 (AU 8502), Review of Financial Statements.
IAU/RS 3 (AU 8503), Engagements to Perform Agreed-Upon Procedures.
IAU/RS 4 (AU 8504), Engagements to Compile Financial Information.

AICPA. *Audit and Accounting Guide: Guide for Prospective Financial Statements,* New York: AICPA, 1993.

Committee of Sponsoring Organizations of the Treadway Commission. *Internal Control—Integrated Framework: Reporting to External Parties,* Jersey City, NJ: American Institute of Certified Public Accountants, 1992.

——— *Internal Control—Integrated Framework: Addendum to "Reporting to External Parties,"* Jersey City, NJ: American Institute of Certified Public Accountants, 1994.

Mancino, Jane M., and Guy, Dan M. "Review of Financial Statements—SAS 71 vs. SSARS," *Journal of Accountancy* (March 1993), pp. 61–67.

Stilwell, Martin C., and Elliott, Robert K. "A Model for Expanding the Attest Function," *Journal of Accountancy* (May 1985), pp. 66–78.

OBJECTIVE QUESTIONS

Indicate the best answer choice for each of the following multiple choice questions.

21-21 These questions relate to special reports.

1. An auditor's special report on financial statements prepared in conformity with the cash basis of accounting should include a separate explanatory paragraph before the opinion paragraph that
   a. Justifies the reasons for departing from generally accepted accounting principles.
   b. States whether the financial statements are fairly presented in conformity with another comprehensive basis of accounting.
   c. Refers to the note to the financial statements that describes the basis of accounting.
   d. Explains how the results of operations differ from financial statements prepared in conformity with generally accepted accounting principles.

2. An auditor's report on financial statements prepared in accordance with an other comprehensive basis of accounting should include all of the following **except**
   a. An opinion as to whether the basis of accounting used is appropriate under the circumstances.
   b. An opinion as to whether the financial statements are presented fairly in conformity with the other comprehensive basis of accounting.
   c. Reference to the note to the financial statements that describes the basis of presentation.

d. A statement that the basis of presentation is a comprehensive basis of accounting other than generally accepted accounting principles.

3. When reporting on financial statements prepared on the same basis of accounting used for income tax purposes, the auditor should include in the report a paragraph that
   a. Emphasizes that the financial statements are **not** intended to have been examined in accordance with generally accepted auditing standards.
   b. Refers to the authoritative pronouncements that explain the income tax basis of accounting being used.
   c. States that the income tax basis of accounting is a comprehensive basis of accounting other than generally accepted accounting principles.
   d. Justifies the use of the income tax basis of accounting.

4. An auditor's report would be designated a special report when it is issued in connection with
   a. Interim financial information of a publicly held company that is subject to a limited review.
   b. Compliance with aspects of regulatory requirements related to audited financial statements.
   c. Application of accounting principles to specified transactions.
   d. Limited use prospective financial statements such as a financial projection.

21-22 These questions pertain to attestation standards and review services.

1. Which of the following is a conceptual difference between the attestation standards and generally accepted auditing standards?
   a. The attestation standards provide a framework for the attest function beyond historical financial statements.
   b. The requirement that the practitioner be independent in mental attitude is omitted from the attestation standards.
   c. The attestation standards do **not** permit an attest engagement to be part of a business acquisition study or a feasibility study.
   d. **None** of the standards of field work in generally accepted auditing standards are included in the attestation standards.

2. The objective of a review of interim financial information of a public entity is to provide the accountant with a basis for
   a. Determining whether the prospective financial information is based on reasonable assumptions.
   b. Expressing a limited opinion that the financial information is presented in conformity with generally accepted accounting principles.
   c. Deciding whether to perform substantive audit procedures prior to the balance sheet date.
   d. Reporting whether material modifications should be made for such information to conform with generally accepted accounting principles.

3. Which of the following procedures is more likely to be performed in a review engagement of a nonpublic entity than in a compilation engagement?
   a. Gaining an understanding of the entity's business transactions.
   b. Making a preliminary assessment of control risk.
   c. Obtaining a representation letter from the chief executive officer.
   d. Assisting the entity in adjusting the accounting records.

4. Which of the following procedures ordinarily should be applied when an independent accountant conducts a review of interim financial information of a publicly held entity?
   a. Verify changes in key account balances.
   b. Read the minutes of the board of directors' meetings.
   c. Inspect the open purchase order file.
   d. Perform cutoff tests for cash receipts and disbursements.

21-23 These questions involve reporting on internal control and prospective financial statements.

1. Which of the following best describes a CPA's engagement to report on an entity's internal control structure over financial reporting?
   a. An attestation engagement to examine and report on management's written assertions about the effectiveness of its internal control structure.
   b. An audit engagement to render an opinion on the entity's internal control structure.
   c. A prospective engagement to project, for a period of time **not** to exceed one year, and report on the expected benefits of the entity's internal control structure.
   d. A consulting engagement to provide constructive advice to the entity on its internal control structure.

2. How do the scope, procedures, and purpose of an engagement to express an opinion on an entity's internal control structure compare with those for obtaining an understanding of the internal control structure and assessing control risk as part of an audit?

Scope	Procedures	Purpose
a. Similar	Different	Similar
b. Different	Similar	Similar
c. Different	Different	Different
d. Different	Similar	Different

3. Accepting an engagement to *examine* an entity's financial *projection* most likely would be appropriate if the projection were to be distributed to
   a. All employees who work for the entity.
   b. Potential stockholders who request a prospectus or a registration statement.
   c. A bank with which the entity is negotiating for a loan.
   d. All stockholders of record as of the report date.

4. An accountant may accept an engagement to apply agreed-upon procedures to prospective financial statements provided that
   a. The prospective financial statements are also examined.
   b. Responsibility for the adequacy of the procedures performed is taken by the accountant.
   c. Negative assurance is expressed on the prospective financial statements taken as a whole.
   d. Distribution of the report is restricted to the specified users.

21-24 These questions pertain to nonattest services.

1. When an independent CPA assists in preparing the financial statements of a publicly held entity, but has **not** audited or reviewed them, the CPA should issue a disclaimer of opinion. In such situations, the CPA has **no** responsibility to apply any procedures beyond
   a. Ascertaining whether the financial statements are in conformity with generally accepted accounting principles.
   b. Determining whether management has elected to omit substantially all required disclosures.
   c. Documenting that the internal control structure is **not** being relied on.
   d. Reading the financial statements for obvious material misstatements.

2. Compiled financial statements should be accompanied by a report stating that
   a. A compilation is substantially smaller in scope than a review or an audit in accordance with generally accepted auditing standards.

b. The accountant does **not** express an opinion but expresses only limited assurance on the compiled financial statements.
c. A compilation is limited to presenting in the form of financial statements information that is the representation of management.
d. The accountant has compiled the financial statements in accordance with standards established by the Auditing Standards Board.

3. In connection with a proposal to obtain a new client, an accountant in public practice is asked to prepare a written report on the application of accounting principles to a specific transaction. The accountant's report should include a statement that
   a. Any difference in the facts, circumstances, or assumptions presented may change the report.
   b. The engagement was performed in accordance with Statements on Standards for Consulting Services.
   c. The guidance provided is for management use only and may **not** be communicated to the prior or continuing auditors.
   d. Nothing came to the accountant's attention that caused the accountant to believe that the accounting principles violated GAAP.

4. An accountant who had begun an audit of the financial statements of a nonpublic entity was asked to change the engagement to a review because of a restriction on the scope of the audit. If there is reasonable justification for the change, the accountant's review report should include reference to the

	Original engagement that was agreed to	Scope limitation that caused the changed engagement
a.	Yes	Yes
b.	Yes	No
c.	No	Yes
d.	No	No

5. When compiling the financial statements of a nonpublic entity, an accountant should
   a. Review agreements with financial institutions for restrictions on cash balances.
   b. Understand the accounting principles and practices of the entity's industry.
   c. Inquire of key personnel concerning related parties and subsequent events.
   d. Perform ratio analyses of the financial data of comparable prior periods.

COMPREHENSIVE QUESTIONS

21-25 **(Special reports)** Jiffy Clerical Services is a corporation that furnishes temporary office help to its customers. Billings are rendered monthly based on predetermined hourly rates. You have examined the company's financial statements for several years. Following is an abbreviated statement of assets and liabilities on the modified cash basis as of December 31, 19X0:

Assets:	
Cash	$20,000
Advances to employees	1,000
Equipment and autos, less accumulated depreciation	25,000
Total assets	$46,000

Liabilities	
Employees' payroll taxes withheld	$ 8,000
Bank loan payable	10,000
Estimated income taxes on cash basis profits	10,000
Total liabilities	$28,000
Net assets	$18,000
Represented by:	
Common stock	$ 3,000
Cash profits retained in the business	15,000
	$18,000

Unrecorded receivables were $55,000 and payables were $30,000.

REQUIRED

a. Prepare the report you would issue covering the statement of assets and liabilities as of December 31, 19X0, as summarized above, and the related statements of cash revenue and expenses for the year ended that date.
b. Briefly discuss and justify your modifications of the conventional report on accrual basis statements.

21-26 **(Special reports)** Young and Young, CPAs, completed an audit of the financial statements of XYZ Company, Inc., for the year ended June 30, 19X3, and issued a standard unqualified auditor's report dated August 15, 19X3. At the time of the engagement, the Board of Directors of XYZ requested a special report attesting to the adequacy of the provision for federal and state income taxes and the related accruals and deferred income taxes as presented in the June 30, 19X3, financial statements.

Young and Young submitted the appropriate special report on August 22, 19X3.

REQUIRED

Prepare the special report that Young and Young should have submitted to XYZ Company, Inc.

AICPA

21-27 (**Compliance report based on audit**) In addition to examining the financial statements of the ABC Company at December 31, 19X0, the auditor agrees to review the loan agreement dated July 1, 19X0, with the Main Street Bank to determine whether the borrower is complying with the terms, provisions, and requirements of sections 14 to 30 inclusive. The auditor finds that the ABC Company is in full compliance with the loan agreement.

REQUIRED

a. Prepare a report on compliance with contractual provisions, assuming it is to be a separate report.
b. Indicate how the report on compliance would differ if it were included as part of the auditor's report on the financial statements.

21-28 (**Reporting on management assertion on internal control**) Martin, CPA, has been engaged to express an opinion or management's assertion about the effectiveness of Beta Manufacturing Company's internal control structure in effect as of June 1, 19X7.

REQUIRED

a. Compare Martin's examination of the internal control structure for the purpose of expressing an opinion on it with the study and evaluation of internal accounting control made as part of an audit of the financial statements in accordance with generally accepted auditing standards. The comparison should be made as to the (1) scope, (2) purpose, and (3) procedures.

b. Identify the major contents of Martin's report expressing an opinion on Beta's internal control structure. Do ***not*** draft the report.

AICPA (adapted)

21-29 **(Reporting on prospective financial statements)** An accountant is sometimes called on by clients to report on or assemble prospective financial statements for use by third parties.

REQUIRED

a. 1. Identify the types of engagements that an accountant may perform under these circumstances.
   2. Explain the difference between "general use" and "limited use" of prospective financial statements.
   3. Explain what types of prospective financial statements are appropriate for "general use" and what types are appropriate for "limited use."

b. Describe the contents of the accountant's standard report on a compilation of a financial projection.

AICPA

21-30 **(Situations involving unaudited, compiled, or reviewed financial statements)** The limitations of the CPA's professional responsibilities when he or she is associated with unaudited financial statements are often misunderstood. These misunderstandings can be substantially reduced by carefully following professional pronouncements in the course of the work and taking other appropriate measures.

REQUIRED

The following list describes seven situations the CPA may encounter or contentions he or she may have to deal with in the association with and preparation of unaudited financial statements. Briefly discuss the extent of the CPA's responsibilities and, if appropriate, the actions that should be taken to minimize any misunderstandings. Number your answers to correspond with the numbering in the following list:

1. The CPA was engaged by telephone to perform write-up work including the preparation of financial statements. The client believes that the CPA has been engaged to audit the financial statements and examine the records accordingly.
2. A group of businessmen who own a farm that is managed by an independent agent engage a CPA to prepare quarterly unaudited financial statements for them. The CPA prepares the financial statements from information given by the independent agent. Subsequently, the businessmen find the statements were inaccurate because their independent agent was embezzling funds. The businessmen refuse to pay the CPA's fee and blame the CPA for allowing the situation to go undetected, contending that the CPA should not have relied on representations from the independent agent.
3. In comparing the trial balance with the general ledger, the CPA finds an account labeled "audit fees" in which the client has accumulated the CPA's quarterly billings for accounting services including the preparation of quarterly unaudited financial statements.
4. Unaudited financial statements were accompanied by the following letter of transmittal from the CPA:

We are enclosing your company's balance sheet as of June 30, 19X0, and the related statements of income and retained earnings and cash flows for the six months then ended that we have reviewed.

5. To determine appropriate account classification, the CPA reviewed a number of the client's invoices. The CPA noted in the working papers that some invoices were missing but did nothing further because the CPA felt they did not affect the unaudited financial statements he or she was preparing. When the client subsequently discovered that invoices were missing, the client contended that the CPA should not have ignored the missing invoices when preparing the financial statements and had a responsibility to at least inform the client that they were missing.
6. The CPA has prepared a draft of unaudited financial statements from the client's records. While reviewing this draft with the client, the CPA learns that the land and building were recorded at appraisal value.
7. The CPA is engaged to review without audit the financial statements prepared by the client's controller. During this review, the CPA learns of several items that by generally accepted accounting principles would require adjustment of the statements and footnote disclosure. The controller agrees to make the recommended adjustments to the statements but says that he or she is not going to add the footnotes because the statements are unaudited.

AICPA

21-31 (**Compilation and review engagements**) Ann Martin, CPA, has been asked by Harry Adams, owner of Adams Cleaners, to prepare the company's annual financial statements from the company's records. Adams, who is unfamiliar with the services of a CPA, also requests Ms. Martin to add as much prestige to the statements as possible in the form of an opinion or some type of assurance.

REQUIRED

a. Explain the nature and limitations of an engagement to compile financial statements.
b. Write the accountant's report on a compilation of financial statements.
c. Explain the type of assurance that may be given if Martin is engaged to review Adams's financial statements.
d. Explain why an opinion cannot be expressed.

21-32 (**Evaluate compilation report**) The following report was drafted on October 25, 19X0, by Major, CPA, at the completion of the engagement to compile the financial statements of Ajax Company for the year ended September 30, 19X0. Ajax is a nonpublic entity in which Major's child has a material direct financial interest. Ajax decided to omit substantially all of the disclosures required by generally accepted accounting principles because the financial statements will be for management's use only. The statement of cash flows was also omitted because management does not believe it to be a useful financial statement.

To the Board of Directors of Ajax Company:

I have compiled the accompanying financial statements of Ajax Company as of September 30, 19X0, and for the year then ended. I planned and performed the compilation to obtain limited assurance about whether the financial statements are free of material misstatements.

A compilation is limited to presenting information in the form of financial statements. It is substantially less in scope than an audit in accordance with generally accepted auditing standards, the objective of which is the expression of an opinion regarding the financial statements taken as a whole. I have not audited the accompanying financial statements and, accordingly, do not express any opinion on them.

Management has elected to omit substantially all of the disclosures required by generally accepted accounting principles. If the omitted disclosures were included in the financial statements, they might influence the user's conclusions about the Company's financial position, results of operations, and changes in financial position.

I am not independent with respect to Ajax Company. This lack of independence is due to my child's ownership of a material direct financial interest in Ajax Company.

This report is intended solely for the information and use of the Board of Directors and management of Ajax Company and should not be used for any other purpose.

Major, CPA

REQUIRED

Identify the deficiencies contained in Major's report on the compiled financial statements. Group the deficiencies by paragraph where applicable. Do **not** redraft the report.

CASE

21-33 (**Evaluate compilation engagement performance**) Brown, CPA, received a telephone call from Calhoun, the sole owner and manager of a small corporation. Calhoun asked Brown to prepare the financial statements for the corporation and told Brown that the statements were needed in two weeks for external financing purposes. Calhoun was vague when Brown inquired about the intended use of the statements. Brown was convinced that Calhoun thought Brown's work would constitute an audit. To avoid confusion, Brown decided not to explain to Calhoun that the engagement would only be to prepare the financial statements. Brown, with the understanding that a substantial fee would be paid if the work were completed in two weeks, accepted the engagement and started the work at once.

During the course of the work, Brown discovered an accrued expense account labeled "professional fees" and learned that the balance in the account represented an accrual for the cost of Brown's services. Brown suggested to Calhoun's bookkeeper that the account name be changed to "fees for limited audit engagement." Brown also reviewed several invoices to determine whether accounts were being properly classified. Some of the invoices were missing. Brown listed the missing invoice numbers in the working papers with a note indicating that there should be a follow-up on the next engagement. Brown also discovered that the available records included the fixed asset values at estimated current replacement costs. Based on the records available, Brown prepared a balance sheet, income statement, and statements of stockholders' equity. In addition, Brown drafted the footnotes but decided that any mention of the replacement costs would only mislead the readers. Brown suggested to Calhoun that readers of the financial statements would be better informed if they received a separate letter from Calhoun explaining the meaning and effect of the estimated replacement costs of the fixed assets. Brown mailed the financial statements and footnotes to Calhoun with the following note included on each page:

> The accompanying financial statements are submitted to you without complete audit verification.

REQUIRED

Identify the inappropriate actions of Brown and indicate what Brown should have done to avoid each inappropriate action. Organize your answer sheet as follows:

Inappropriate Action	What Brown Should Have Done to Avoid Inappropriate Action

AICPA

RESEARCH QUESTIONS

21-34 **(Reporting on interim financial information)** The chapter contains limited information about the SEC's quarterly reporting requirements for public companies and the independent accountant's involvement with those filings. Using printed or electronic media, cite and summarize the pertinent SEC regulations governing the form, content, and filing deadlines for quarterly filings, and the SEC's current position on timely reviews of those filings. Then, locate an actual quarterly filing that is accompanied by a timely review report and be prepared to share the results of your research with your classmates, including demonstrating the conformity of the independent accountant's review report with the applicable professional standards cited in the chapter.

21-35 **(Reporting on comparative statements under SSARS)** Assume that the report presented below was drafted by a staff assistant upon completion of the calendar year 19X6 review engagement of RLG Company, a continuing client. The 19X5 financial statements were compiled. On March 6, the date of the completion of the review, the report was submitted to the partner with client responsibility. The financial statements for 19X5 and 19X6 were presented in comparative form. The report as drafted contains a number of deficiencies that you should identify and list.

The chapter provides basic coverage of reporting on compilation and review engagements under SSARS and is sufficient to permit you to identify most of the deficiencies in the report. However, you may need to consult the AICPA's *Professional Standards* to determine how certain matters should be handled. If so, record the appropriate citation for the section or sections of the *Professional Standards* consulted. After listing the deficiencies, prepare a revised draft in good form.

To the Board of Directors of RLG Company

We have reviewed the accompanying financial statements of RLG Company for the year ended December 31, 19X6, in accordance with standards established by Statements on Standards for Auditing and Review Services.

A review consists principally of analytical procedures applied to financial data. It is substantially more in scope than a compilation, but less in scope than an examination in accordance with generally accepted auditing standards, the objective of which is the expression of an opinion regarding the financial statements taken as a whole.

Based on our compilation and review, we are not aware of any material modifications that should be made to the 19X5 and 19X6 financial statements.

December 31, 19X6

AICPA (adapted)

CHAPTER

22

INTERNAL, OPERATIONAL, AND GOVERNMENTAL AUDITING

LEARNING OBJECTIVES

After studying this chapter, you should be able to

1. Define internal auditing and describe its objectives and scope.
2. State the source and nature of standards for the professional practice of internal auditing.
3. Define operational auditing and describe the phases of an operational audit.
4. Identify the standards that independent public accountants should follow in performing operational audits.
5. Explain the types of government audits identified in government auditing standards.
6. State the differences between GAAS and generally accepted government auditing standards (GAGAS).
7. Explain the objectives and applicability of the Single Audit Act.
8. Distinguish the components of a single audit and the procedures and reports associated with each.

INTERNAL AUDITING
- INTERNAL AUDITING DEFINED
- EVOLUTION OF INTERNAL AUDITING
- OBJECTIVES AND SCOPE
- PRACTICE STANDARDS
- RELATIONSHIP WITH EXTERNAL AUDITORS

OPERATIONAL AUDITING
- OPERATIONAL AUDITING DEFINED
- PHASES OF AN OPERATIONAL AUDIT
- INDEPENDENT PUBLIC ACCOUNTANT INVOLVEMENT AND STANDARDS

GOVERNMENTAL AUDITING
- TYPES OF GOVERNMENT AUDITS
- GENERALLY ACCEPTED GOVERNMENT AUDITING STANDARDS (GAGAS)
- REPORTING ON COMPLIANCE WITH LAWS AND REGULATIONS
- REPORTING ON INTERNAL CONTROL

THE SINGLE AUDIT ACT
- OBJECTIVES OF THE ACT
- APPLICABILITY AND ADMINISTRATION
- AUDITORS' RESPONSIBILITIES UNDER THE ACT

SUMMARY

APPENDIX 22A: INTERNAL AUDITOR CODE OF ETHICS

BIBLIOGRAPHY

OBJECTIVE QUESTIONS

COMPREHENSIVE QUESTIONS

CASE

RESEARCH QUESTION

Thus far in this textbook, the focus has been primarily on financial statement audits for nongovernmental entities made by independent auditors. In this chapter, attention is directed at other types of auditing. For each type of auditing, consideration is given to its objectives, scope, and applicable standards. Coverage of governmental auditing includes the auditing and reporting requirements of the Single Audit Act.

INTERNAL AUDITING

As explained in Chapter 8, internal auditing is an important part of the monitoring component of an entity's internal control structure. As explained in the following sections, internal auditing also provides other valuable services to an entity.

INTERNAL AUDITING DEFINED

The *Statement of Responsibilities of Internal Auditing* (the *Statement*) issued by the Institute of Internal Auditors (IIA) defines **internal auditing** as

> an independent appraisal function established within an organization to examine and evaluate its activities as a service to the organization.

OBJECTIVE 1

Define internal auditing and describe its objectives and scope.

Several parts of this definition merit comment.

- *Internal* indicates that the auditing is carried on within an organization by employees of the organization.
- *Independent appraisal function* makes it clear that there are no limitations or restrictions on the auditor's judgment.
- *Established* states that the entity has specifically authorized the creation of an internal audit function.
- *Examine and evaluate* describe the nature of internal auditing as first, a search for facts, and second, a subjective process of evaluating the results.
- *Activities* implies that all of an organization's activities fall within the scope of internal auditing.
- *Service to the organization* indicates that internal auditing exists to aid or benefit the entire organization. The term *service* also suggests that internal auditing is a staff rather than a line activity within the entity.

Internal auditing is a control function that exists by examining and evaluating the adequacy and effectiveness of other controls.

EVOLUTION OF INTERNAL AUDITING

Internal auditing began as a one-person clerical function that consisted primarily of performing independent verification of bills before payment. Over the years, internal auditing has evolved into a highly professional activity that extends to the appraisal of the efficiency and effectiveness of all phases of a company's operations, both financial and nonfinancial. These changes have led to the formation of internal auditing departments, senior management status for the director/manager of the internal audit function, and a reporting responsibility directly to the board of directors or its audit committee.

Passage of the Foreign Corrupt Practices Act in 1977 added further emphasis on internal auditing. This Act requires companies to maintain effective internal control systems (structures). Companies subject to this Act quickly realized that an expanded internal auditing function provided the best assurance of compliance. Accordingly, budgets for internal auditing were dramatically enlarged, and the size and quality of internal auditing departments were significantly increased.

The growth and importance of internal auditing to a company has been accompanied by increased professional recognition for the internal auditor. The Institute of Internal Auditors (IIA) was formed in 1941, and its current membership is 50,000. In 1972, the IIA administered its first Certificate of Internal Auditor's Examination. The examination takes two days and consists of four parts:

- Theory and practice of internal auditing (two parts).
- Management, quantitative methods, and information systems (one part).
- Accounting, finance, and economics (one part).

To become a certified internal auditor (CIA), an individual must pass the examination and have a minimum of two years of experience as an internal auditor or the equivalent. The criteria for internal auditing experience include auditing experience in public accounting. To retain the CIA certificate, the individual must comply with the IIA's practice standards and code of ethics (shown in Appendix 22A) and meet continuing professional education requirements. Certified internal auditors are not licensed by any governmental agency.

OBJECTIVES AND SCOPE

The *Statement* indicates that the objective of internal auditing is to assist members of an organization in the effective discharge of their responsibilities. In meeting this objective, internal auditing provides analyses, appraisals, recommendations, counsel, and information concerning the activities that have been audited. The objective of internal auditing includes promoting effective control throughout the organization at reasonable cost.

The *Statement* indicates that the scope of internal auditing includes:

- Reviewing the reliability and integrity of financial and operating information and the means used to identify, measure, classify, and report such information.
- Reviewing the systems established to ensure compliance with those policies, plans, procedures, laws, and regulations that could have a significant impact on operations and reports, and determining whether the organization is in compliance.
- Reviewing the means of safeguarding assets and, as appropriate, verifying the existence of such assets.
- Appraising the economy and efficiency with which resources are employed.
- Reviewing operations or programs to ascertain whether results are consistent with established objectives and goals and whether the operations or programs are being carried out as planned.

The last two activities relate to operational auditing. Internal auditing carries out its activities under the policies established by management and the board of directors of the organization.

PRACTICE STANDARDS

OBJECTIVE 2

State the source and nature of standards for the professional practice of internal auditing.

The IIA has established practice standards (the *Standards*) that are binding on its members. There are five general standards that pertain to the following matters:

- Independence.
- Professional proficiency.
- Scope of work.
- Performance of audit work.
- Management of the internal auditing department.

Each general standard is supported by specific standards. Figure 22-1 shows a summary of the general and specific standards for the professional practice of internal auditing. It can be seen that there are similarities between the IIA general standards and the AICPA generally accepted auditing standards (GAAS). The IIA standards of independence and professional proficiency pertain to the general category of GAAS, and the IIA standards for the performance of audit work relate to the AICPA field work and reporting standards. There are also similarities in specific standards between the two organizations such as the standards for due professional care, planning the audit, and examining and evaluating information (evidence). Each specific standard, in turn, is accompanied by guidelines describing suitable ways of meeting the standard. For example, the guidelines for two of the standards are as follows:

410 Planning the Audit

Internal auditors should plan each audit.

.01 Planning should be documented and should include:

- *.1* Establishing audit objectives and scope of work.
- *.2* Obtaining background information about the activities to be audited.
- *.3* Determining the resources necessary to perform the audit.
- *.4* Communicating with all who need to know about the audit.
- *.5* Performing, as appropriate, an on-site survey to become familiar with the activities and controls to be audited, to identify areas for audit emphasis, and to invite auditee comments and suggestions.
- *.6* Writing the audit program.
- *.7* Determining how, when, and to whom audit results will be communicated.
- *.8* Obtaining approval of the audit work plan.

430 Communicating Results

Internal auditors should report the results of their audit work.

- *.1* A signed, written report should be issued after the audit examination is completed. Interim reports may be written or oral and may be transmitted formally or informally.
- *.2* The internal auditor should discuss conclusions and recommendations at appropriate levels of management before issuing final written reports.
- *.3* Reports should be objective, clear, concise, constructive, and timely.
- *.4* Reports should present the purpose, scope, and results of the audit; and, where appropriate, reports should contain an expression of the auditor's opinion.
- *.5* Reports may include recommendations for potential improvements and acknowledge satisfactory performance and corrective action.
- *.6* The auditee's views about audit conclusions or recommendations may be included in the audit report.
- *.7* The director of internal auditing or designee should review and approve the final audit report before issuance and should decide to whom the report will be distributed.

FIGURE 22-1 • IIA PRACTICE STANDARDS

SUMMARY OF GENERAL AND SPECIFIC STANDARDS FOR THE PROFESSIONAL PRACTICE OF INTERNAL AUDITING

100 INDEPENDENCE. Internal auditors should be independent of the activities they audit.

- 110 *Organizational Status.* The organizational status of the internal auditing department should be sufficient to permit the accomplishment of its audit responsibilities.
- 120 *Objectivity.* Internal auditors should be objective in performing audits.

200 PROFESSIONAL PROFICIENCY. Internal audits should be performed with proficiency and due professional care.

The Internal Auditing Department

- 210 *Staffing.* The internal auditing department should provide assurance that the technical proficiency and educational background of internal auditors are appropriate for the audits to be performed.
- 220 *Knowledge, Skills, and Disciplines.* The internal auditing department should possess or should obtain the knowledge, skills, and disciplines needed to carry out its audit responsibilities.
- 230 *Supervision.* The internal auditing department should provide assurance that internal audits are properly supervised.

The Internal Auditor

- 240 *Compliance with Standards of Conduct.* Internal auditors should comply with professional standards of conduct.
- 250 *Knowledge, Skills, and Disciplines.* Internal auditors should possess the knowledge, skills, and disciplines essential to the performance of internal audits.
- 260 *Human Relations and Communications.* Internal auditors should be skilled in dealing with people and communicating effectively.
- 270 *Continuing Education.* Internal auditors should maintain their technical competence through continuing education.
- 280 *Due Professional Care.* Internal auditors should exercise due professional care in performing internal audits.

300 SCOPE OF WORK. The scope of internal auditing should encompass the examination and evaluation of the adequacy and effectiveness of the organization's system of internal control and the quality of performance in carrying out assigned responsibilities.

- 310 *Reliability and Integrity of Information.* Internal auditors should review the reliability and integrity of financial and operating information and the means used to identify, measure, classify, and report such information.
- 320 *Compliance with Policies, Plans, Procedures, Laws, and Regulations.* Internal auditors should review the systems established to ensure compliance with those policies, plans, procedures, laws, and regulations which could have a significant impact on operations and reports and should determine whether the organization is in compliance.
- 330 *Safeguarding of Assets.* Internal auditors should review the means of safeguarding assets and, as appropriate, verify the existence of such assets.
- 340 *Economical and Efficient Use of Resources.* Internal auditors should appraise the economy and efficiency with which resources are employed.
- 350 *Accomplishment of Established Objectives and Goals for Operations or Programs.* Internal auditors should review operations or programs to ascertain whether results are consistent with established objectives and goals and whether the operations or programs are being carried out as planned.

400 PERFORMANCE OF AUDIT WORK. Audit work should include planning the audit, examining and evaluating information, communicating results, and following up.

- 410 *Planning the Audit.* Internal auditors should plan each audit.
- 420 *Examining and Evaluating Information.* Internal auditors should collect, analyze, interpret, and document information to support audit results.
- 430 *Communicating Results.* Internal auditors should report the results of their audit work.
- 440 *Following Up.* Internal auditors should follow up to ascertain that appropriate action is taken on reported audit findings.

500 MANAGEMENT OF THE INTERNAL AUDITING DEPARTMENT. The director of internal auditing should properly manage the internal auditing department.

- 510 *Purpose, Authority, and Responsibility.* The director of internal auditing should have a statement of purpose, authority, and responsibility for the internal auditing department.
- 520 *Planning.* The director of internal auditing should establish plans to carry out the responsibilities of the internal auditing department.
- 530 *Policies and Procedures.* The director of internal auditing should provide written policies and procedures to guide the audit staff.
- 540 *Personnel Management and Development.* The director of internal auditing should establish a program for selecting and developing the human resources of the internal auditing department.
- 550 *External Auditors.* The director of internal auditing should coordinate internal and external audit efforts.
- 560 *Quality Assurance.* The director of internal auditing should establish and maintain a quality assurance program to evaluate the operations of the internal auditing department.

SOURCE: CODIFICATION OF *STANDARDS FOR THE PROFESSIONAL PRACTICE OF INTERNAL AUDITING* (ALTAMONTE SPRINGS, FLA.: THE INSTITUTE OF INTERNAL AUDITORS, 1993), PP. 5–8.

The IIA has a Professional Standards Committee (PSC) that issues *Statements on Internal Auditing Standards (SIASs)* as authoritative interpretations of the practice standards. The complete standards framework for internal auditors is shown in Figure 22-2. A brief explanation of each of the five general standards is given in the following sections.

Independence

The IIA's concept of **independence** is different from the AICPA's concept of independence. Internal auditors are employees of the companies they audit. As indicated in Standard 100, they should be independent of the activities they audit.

FIGURE 22-2 • COMPLETE INTERNAL AUDITING STANDARDS FRAMEWORK

Document Name	Final Approval Authority	Definition
Statement of Responsibilities of Internal Auditing	IIA Board of Directors	Discusses the role and responsibilities of internal auditing.
Code of Ethics	IIA Board of Directors	Defines the standards of professional behavior for IIA members and/or certified internal auditors.
Standards for the Professional Practice of Internal Auditing (Standards)		
General Standards	IIA Board of Directors	States the five general internal auditing standards that must be followed to comply with the *Standards.*
Specific Standards	Professional Standards Committee (PSC)	States the 25 specific standards that must be followed to comply with the general standards.
Guidelines	PSC	States the most generally accepted guidelines to meet the general and specific standards.
Statements on Internal Auditing Standards (SIASs)	PSC	Provides authoritative interpretations of the general standards, specific standards, and guidelines contained in the *Standards.* Additionally, *SIASs* are used to add or change existing guidelines.
Practice Directives (PDs)	PSC	Specifies policies and procedures The Institute follows in administering professional standards.
Professional Standards Bulletins (PSBs)	PSC Chairperson	Addresses questions resulting from the application of the Institute's standards pronouncements. *PSBs* are not official pronouncements of the IIA. For official guidance, auditors are referred to The Institute's standards pronouncements listed above.

SOURCE: MILLER, MARJO, N., "THE IIA'S INTERNAL AUDITING STANDARDS: MEETING THE PROFESSION'S NEEDS," *THE INTERNAL AUDITOR* (JUNE, 1988), P. 21.

Independence is achieved through organizational status and objectivity. Independence is enhanced, for example, when the director of the internal auditing department (1) is responsible to an individual in the organization with sufficient authority to ensure broad audit coverage and adequate consideration of, and effective action on, audit recommendations, and (2) has direct communication with the board of directors or its audit committee.

Objectivity requires internal auditors to have an independent mental attitude in performing their audits. Objectivity is impaired when the internal auditor assumes operating responsibilities or makes management decisions.

Professional Proficiency

This category of practice standards recognizes the need for proficiency, competence, and due care in performing internal audits. Specific standards are established for the internal auditing department and for the internal auditor. The standards recognize that both the department and the individual auditor should possess the knowledge, skills, and disciplines to carry out audit responsibilities. The standards for the internal auditor include (1) compliance with standards of conduct, (2) human relations and communications skills, and (3) continuing professional education.

Scope of Work

These standards recognize that the work of internal auditors may extend beyond financial audit considerations of internal control (reliability and integrity of financial information and safeguarding of assets). Standard 320 pertains to compliance audits, and Standards 340 and 350 relate to operational audits. The scope of work standards provide guidance in performing each type of audit.

Performance of Audit Work

The performance standards recognize each of the indispensable parts of any audit: planning, examining and evaluating evidence, and communicating the results. They establish performance goals rather than specific guidelines. Standard 440, Following Up, is unique to internal auditing. This standard requires the internal auditor to be involved in assessing the action taken on reported audit findings and any recommendations included in the report.

Management of the Internal Auditing Department

These standards provide directives for the manager of the internal auditing department. The directives range from having a statement of the purpose, authority, and responsibility of the department to establishing and maintaining a quality control program for the department. The standards include establishing a program for hiring and promoting the development of members of the department, and coordinating the internal audits with the work of the external auditor.

RELATIONSHIP WITH EXTERNAL AUDITORS

There is usually a close relationship between internal auditors and an entity's outside independent auditors. As indicated in an earlier chapter, the work of internal auditors may be a supplement to, but not a substitute for, the work of independent auditors in a financial statement audit. As noted above, one of the responsibilities of the director of internal auditing is to coordinate the work of internal auditors with the work of the external auditor. It is not uncommon in practice for the external auditor to review the internal auditing department's planned work program for the year to minimize duplication of effort.

Although they often have a close working relationship, the following important differences exist between the two types of auditors:

	Internal Auditors	**External Auditors**
Employer	Companies and governmental units	CPA firms
National organization	Institute of Internal Auditors (IIA)	American Institute of Certified Public Accountants (AICPA)
Certifying designation	Certified Internal Auditor (CIA)	Certified Public Accountant (CPA)
License to practice	No	Yes
Primary responsibility	To board of directors	To third parties
Scope of audits	All activities of an organization	Primarily financial statements

LEARNING CHECK:

22-1 a. Is internal auditing a management or an accounting function? Explain.
b. Jill Jensen is confused as to the scope and primary beneficiary of internal auditing. Clarify these points for Jill.

22-2 a. State the requirements for becoming a Certified Internal Auditor.
b. What must a CIA do to retain the certificate?

22-3 a. What is the objective of internal auditing?
b. The scope of internal auditing is limited to financial statement audits. Do you agree? Explain.

22-4 a. Identify the five categories of general practice standards for internal auditors.
b. Indicate the components of the standards framework for internal auditing and the purpose of each component.

22-5 How does the independence of an internal auditor differ from that of an external auditor?

KEY TERMS:

Independence, p. 843

Internal auditing, p. 839

OPERATIONAL AUDITING

Operational auditing has been used in the past to identify a variety of activities that include evaluating management's performance, management's planning and quality control systems, and specific operating activities and departments. As suggested by its name, this type of auditing pertains to an entity's nonfinancial operations. Operational audits of nongovernmental units are generally made by internal auditors. However, in some cases, external auditors may be engaged to perform the audit.

OPERATIONAL AUDITING DEFINED

A IIA publication defines **operational auditing** as follows:

> Operational auditing is a systematic process of evaluating an organization's effectiveness, efficiency, and economy of operations under management's control and reporting to appropriate persons the results of the evaluation along with recommendations for improvement.[1]

OBJECTIVE 3

Define operational auditing and describe the phases of an operational audit.

The essential parts of this definition are as follows:

- *Systematic process.* As in the case of a financial statement audit, an operational audit involves a logical, structured, and organized series of steps or procedures. This aspect includes proper planning, as well as obtaining and objectively evaluating evidence pertaining to the activity being audited.
- *Evaluating an organization's operations.* The evaluation of operations should be based on some established or agreed-upon criteria. In operational auditing, the criteria are often expressed in terms of performance standards established by management. However, in some cases, the standards may be set by a governmental agency or by industry. These criteria frequently are less clearly defined than the criteria used in financial statement audits. Operational auditing measures the degree of correspondence between actual performance and the criteria.
- *Effectiveness, efficiency, and economy of operations.* The primary purpose of operational auditing is to help management of the audited organization to improve the effectiveness, efficiency, and economy of operations. Thus, operational auditing focuses on the future. This is in direct contrast to a financial statement audit, which has a historical focus.
- *Reporting to appropriate persons.* The appropriate recipient of an operational audit report is management or the individual or agency that requested the audit. Except when the audit is requested by a third party, the distribution of the report remains within the entity. In most cases, the board of directors or its audit committee receives copies of operational audit reports.

---

[1] Darwin J. Casler, and James R. Crockett, *Operational Auditing: An Introduction* (Altamonte Springs, FL: The Institute of Internal Auditors, Inc., 1982), p. 14.

- *Recommendations for improvement.* Unlike financial statement audits, an operational audit does not end with a report on the findings. It extends to making recommendations for improvement. Developing recommendations is, in fact, one of the most challenging aspects of this type of auditing.

PHASES OF AN OPERATIONAL AUDIT

There are more phases in an operational audit than in a financial statement audit. The similarities and differences in the phases between these two types of audits are shown in Figure 22-3. Each of the phases of an operational audit is explained in the following sections.

Select Auditee

Like many other activities within an entity, operational auditing is usually subject to budgetary or economic constraints. It is important, therefore, that the resources for operational auditing be put to the best use. Selecting the auditee begins with a preliminary study (or survey) of potential auditees within an entity to identify the activities that have the highest audit potential in terms of improving the effectiveness, efficiency, and economy of operations. In essence, the preliminary study is a screening process that results in a ranking of potential auditees.

The starting point of the preliminary study is to obtain a comprehensive understanding of the entity's organizational structure and operating characteristics. In addition, the auditor should be knowledgeable of the industry in which the entity operates and the nature and extent of applicable government regulations. Attention is next focused on the activity, unit, or function that could be audited. An understanding of the potential auditees is obtained by

- Reviewing background file data on each auditee.
- Touring the auditee's facilities to ascertain how it accomplishes its objectives.

FIGURE 22-3 • FINANCIAL STATEMENT VS. OPERATIONAL AUDITS

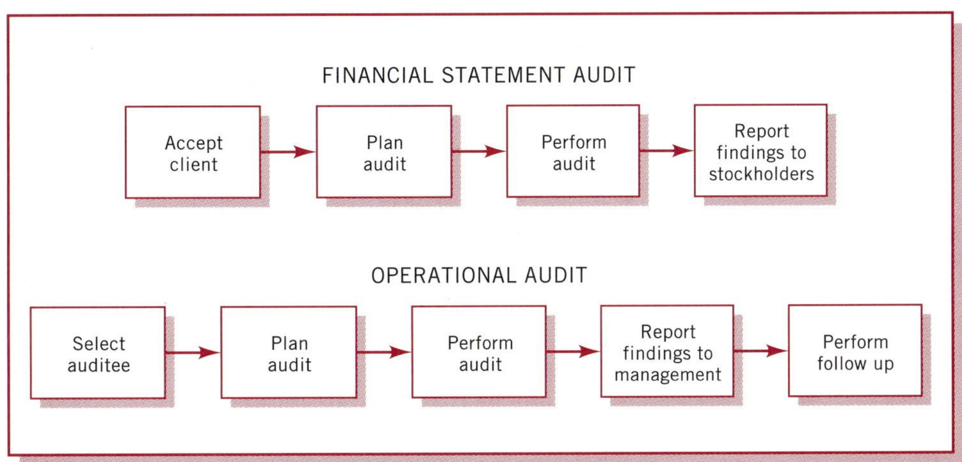

- Studying relevant documentation about the auditee's operations such as policies and procedures manuals, flowcharts, performance and quality control standards, and job descriptions.
- Interviewing the manager of the activity about specific problem areas (often called the entry interview).
- Applying analytical procedures to identify trends and unusual relationships.
- Conducting mini audit probes (or tests) to confirm or clarify the auditor's understanding of potential problems.

The auditor's understanding of each auditee should be documented through completed questionnaires, flowcharts, and narrative memoranda. Based on this understanding, the auditor prepares a preliminary study report or memorandum, which summarizes the findings and includes a recommendation as to the auditee(s) that should be audited. The report is for the exclusive use of the internal auditing department. It is not a report for management.

Plan Audit

Careful audit planning is essential to both the effectiveness and efficiency of an operational audit. Planning is especially critical in this type of an audit because of the diversity of operational audits. The cornerstone of audit planning is the development of an audit program. The program must be tailor-made to the circumstances found in the auditee in the preliminary study phase of the audit. As in the case of a financial statement audit, the audit program contains a set of procedures designed to obtain evidence pertaining to one or more objectives. The evidence examined is usually based on samples of data. Thus, consideration should be given in audit planning to the use of statistical sampling techniques. In addition, the auditor should recognize when computer-assisted techniques will be cost efficient.

Audit planning also includes selecting the audit team and scheduling the work. The audit team must include auditors who have the technical expertise needed to meet the audit objective(s). The work should be scheduled in consultation with the auditee to obtain the maximum cooperation from the auditee's personnel during the audit.

Perform Audit

During the audit, the auditor makes an extensive search for facts pertaining to the problems identified in the auditee during the preliminary study. Making the audit is the most time-consuming phase of an operational audit. This phase is often referred to as making the in-depth audit.

In an operational audit, the auditor relies primarily on inquiry and observation. A common approach is to develop a questionnaire for the auditee and to use it as a basis for interviewing the auditee's personnel. From the inquiries, the auditor expects to obtain opinions, comments, and suggested solutions to the problems. Effective interviewing is indispensable in an operational audit. Through observation of the auditee's personnel, the auditor may be able to detect inefficiencies and other conditions that are contributing to the problem(s).

The auditor must also use analysis in an operational audit. For this purpose, analysis involves the study and measurement of actual performance in relation to some criteria. The criteria may be internally developed by the entity such as stated productivity goals and budgets. Alternatively, the criteria may be externally generated in the form of industry standards or be derived by the auditor from previous audits of similar activities. Analysis provides a basis for determining the degree to which the auditee is meeting specified objectives.

The work done, the findings, and the recommendations should be documented in working papers. As in a financial statement audit, the working papers represent the primary support for the auditor's report. The in-charge auditor normally has the responsibility for reviewing the working papers both during and at the completion of the examination. Reviews during the audit are helpful in monitoring progress, whereas the review at the end of the audit ensures the overall quality of the work.

Report Findings

Operational auditing is similar to other types of auditing in that the final product of the audit is an audit report. There are, however, many unique circumstances pertaining to reporting in an operational audit. For example, in contrast to the standard language contained in the auditor's report in a financial statement audit, the language of the report in an operational audit varies for each auditee. The report should contain

- A statement of the objectives and scope of the audit.
- A general description of the work done in the audit.
- A summary of the findings.
- Recommendations for improvement.
- Comments of the auditee.

The report is generally drafted by the in-charge auditor. The draft is then discussed with the manager of the audited unit. This discussion serves several important purposes: (1) it gives the auditor an opportunity to test the accuracy of the findings and the appropriateness of the recommendations, and (2) it enables the auditor to obtain the auditee's comments for inclusion in the report. The initial draft is then revised as necessary, and the final draft is prepared.

In some cases, the recommendations may just suggest the need for further study of the problems. The inclusion of the auditee's comments is optional. Ordinarily, they are included only when the auditee disagrees with the findings and recommendations.

The auditor's findings basically result in constructive criticism. In writing the report, the auditor should be sensitive to the recipient's reactions. When the language is less threatening, the response of the recipient to the report is likely to be more positive. Ordinarily, copies of operational auditing reports are sent to senior management and to the audit committee. The introductory language for an operational audit report is illustrated in Figure 22-4. If the report is long and detailed, the report may begin with an executive summary of the findings and recommendations.

Perform Follow-Up

The final or **follow-up phase** of an operational audit is for the auditor to follow up on the auditee's response to the audit report. Ideally, the policies of the entity

FIGURE 22-4 • PARTIAL OPERATIONAL AUDIT REPORT

ILLUSTRATION OF INTRODUCTORY LANGUAGE FOR AN OPERATIONAL AUDIT REPORT

To the Report Recipient
The Engaging Party
New York, New York 12345

In December 19_____ we concluded an operational audit of XYZ (company, department, and so forth).

Objectives, Scope, and Approach

The general objectives of this engagement, which were more specifically outlined in our letter dated September _____, 19_____, were as follows:

- To document, analyze, and report on the status of current operations
- To identify areas that require attention
- To make recommendations for corrective action or improvements

Our operational audit encompassed the following units: Branch A, Branch B, and Branch C, and the entire home office operation. Our evaluations included both the financial and operational conditions of the units. Financial data consulted in the course of our analyses were not audited or reviewed by us, and, accordingly, we do not express an opinion or any other form of assurance on them.

The operational audit involved interviews with management personnel and selected operations personnel in each of the units studied. We also evaluated selected documents, files, reports, systems, procedures, and policies as we considered appropriate. After analyzing the data, we developed recommendations for improvements. We then discussed our findings and recommendations with appropriate unit management personnel, and with you, prior to submitting this written report.

All significant findings are included in this report for your consideration. The recommendations in this report represent, in our judgment, those most likely to bring about beneficial improvements to the operations of the organization. The recommendations differ in such aspects as difficulty of implementation, urgency, visibility of benefits, required investment in facilities, and equipment or additional personnel. The varying nature of the recommendations, their implementation costs, and their potential impact on operations should be considered in reaching your decisions on courses of action.

SOURCE: REPORT OF THE SPECIAL COMMITTEE ON OPERATIONAL AND MANAGEMENT AUDITING. *OPERATIONAL AUDIT ENGAGEMENTS* (NEW YORK: AMERICAN INSTITUTE OF CERTIFIED PUBLIC ACCOUNTANTS, 1982), P. 16.

should require the manager of the audited unit to respond to the report in writing within a specified time period. However, the follow-up should extend to determining the adequacy of the measures taken by the auditee in implementing the recommendations. Practice Standard 440 of the IIA states that internal auditors should follow up to ascertain that appropriate action has been taken on the report findings. The failure of the auditor to receive an appropriate response should be communicated to senior management.

INDEPENDENT PUBLIC ACCOUNTANT INVOLVEMENT AND STANDARDS

OBJECTIVE 4

Identify the standards that independent public accountants should follow in performing operational audits.

Based on their expertise and experience, independent public accountants are qualified to perform operational audits. In 1982, the AICPA appointed the Special Committee on Operational and Management Auditing to study the involvement of independent accountants in operational auditing. The Committee concluded in its report entitled *Operational Audit Engagements* that an operational audit engagement is a distinct form of management consulting services (MCS). It also made the following observations (p. 1):

- Independent accountants will increasingly be asked to provide this service for both private-sector and governmental clients.
- This type of service provides independent evaluation and advice to boards of directors, senior management, and elected officials who are being held to high standards of responsibility and stewardship.
- The experience gained in public accounting in the diagnostic and fact-finding aspects of financial auditing and management consulting services provides an excellent background for performing operational audits.

Management consulting services have become an important part of the services performed today by many CPA firms.

In performing operational audits, independent CPAs should follow the practice standards for MCS engagements established by the Management Consulting Services Executive Committee of the AICPA. The independent accountant must also comply with Rule 201, General Standards, of the AICPA's *Code of Professional Conduct*, which is explained in Chapter 3. When the audit is conducted for governmental entities, the independent auditor must also follow applicable government *performance audit standards* described later in the chapter.

LEARNING CHECK:

22-6 a. Like internal auditing, operational auditing involves independent appraisal. Do you agree? Explain.
b. The scope of operational auditing is similar to the scope of internal auditing. Is this true? Explain.

22-7 a. Identify the phases of an operational audit.
b. How do these phases differ from a financial statement audit?

22-8 Explain the auditor's responsibilities in (a) selecting the auditee and (b) reporting the findings.

22-9 Identify the applicable standards when a CPA performs an operational audit.

KEY TERMS:

Follow-up phase, p. 849

Operational auditing, p. 846

GOVERNMENTAL AUDITING

Governmental auditing includes all audits made by government audit agencies and all audits of governmental organizations. Government audit agencies include the U.S. General Accounting Office, the Defense Contract Audit Agency, and state audit agencies. Audits of governmental organizations include audits of state and local government units made by federal government auditors and independent public accountants. In some cases, these audits may include specific programs, activities, functions, and funds. Audits of governmental organizations are premised largely on the concept that the officials and employees who manage public funds are accountable to the public. Our interest here is in the audits of governmental organizations.

TYPES OF GOVERNMENT AUDITS

OBJECTIVE 5

Explain the types of government audits identified in government auditing standards.

Two types of government audits are identified in *Government Auditing Standards*[2]:

- **Financial audits** include financial statement audits and financial related audits.
  - **Financial statement audits** provide reasonable assurance about whether the financial statements of an audited entity present fairly the financial position, results of operations, and cash flows in conformity with GAAP or any of several other bases of accounting discussed in auditing standards issued by the AICPA.
  - **Financial related audits** include determining whether (1) financial information is presented in accordance with established or stated criteria, (2) the entity has adhered to specific financial compliance requirements, or (3) the entity's internal control structure over financial reporting and/or safeguarding assets is suitably designed and implemented to achieve the control objectives. Specific examples include segments of financial statements, internal controls over compliance with laws and regulations, such as those governing the bidding, accounting, and reporting related to grants and contracts, as well as internal controls over financial reporting and safeguarding assets, budget requests, and variances between estimated and actual financial performance.
- **Performance audits** include economy and efficiency and program audits.
  - **Economy and efficiency audits** include determining (1) whether the entity is acquiring, protecting and using its resources (such as personnel, property, and space) economically and efficiently, (2) the causes of inefficiencies or uneconomical practices, and (3) whether the entity has complied with laws and regulations concerning matters of economy and efficiency.
  - **Program audits** include determining (1) the extent to which the desired results or benefits established by the legislature or other authorizing body are being achieved, (2) the effectiveness of organizations, programs, activities, or functions, and (3) whether the entity has complied with significant laws and regulations applicable to the program.

From the foregoing descriptions, it may be observed that (1) government financial statement audits are similar to those described throughout this text for nongovernment entities, (2) the subject matter of government financial related audits includes, but is not limited to, the subject matter of several of the attest services described in Chapter 21, and (3) the two types of government performance audits include, but are not limited to, the types of operational audit activities described in the previous section of this chapter. A formal definition of performance audits is provided in *Government Auditing Standards* as follows:

---

[2] Comptroller General of the United States, *Government Auditing Standards* (Washington, D.C.: U.S. General Accounting Office, 1994), paragraphs 2.4 and 2.7.

A **performance audit** is an objective and systematic examination of evidence for the purpose of providing an independent assessment of the performance of a government organization, program, activity, or function in order to provide information to improve public accountability and facilitate decision-making by parties with responsibility to oversee or initiate corrective action.[3]

Government audit engagements may include either financial or performance audit objectives, or both. Auditors performing such engagements, whether employed by government auditing agencies or by CPA firms, must be careful to observe all applicable AICPA and government auditing standards as discussed in the remaining sections of this chapter.

GENERALLY ACCEPTED GOVERNMENT AUDITING STANDARDS (GAGAS)

The U.S. General Accounting Office (GAO) establishes audit standards for audits of government organizations, programs, activities, functions, and of government funds received by nongovernment organizations. The standards pertain to the auditor's professional qualifications, the quality of audit effort, and the characteristics of professional and meaningful audit reports. The GAO audit standards must be followed by auditors and audit organizations when required by law, regulation, agreement or contract, or policy. Audit organizations consist of government audit agencies and nongovernment entities such as public accounting firms and consulting firms.

OBJECTIVE 6

State the differences between GAAS and generally accepted government auditing standards (GAGAS).

The GAO audit standards are recognized as **generally accepted government auditing standards (GAGAS).** They were revised and updated in 1994. The GAO standards are commonly referred to as the **Yellow Book standards** because of the color of the pamphlet in which they are published. GAGAS include the AICPA generally accepted auditing standards for field work and reporting. As they are issued, any relevant new AICPA auditing and attestation standards will be adopted and incorporated into GAGAS unless the GAO excludes them by formal announcement. Independent auditors who are members of the AICPA must follow GAGAS in government audits or be in violation of the AICPA *Code of Professional Conduct.*

GAGAS are classified into the following five categories: general, field work standards for financial audits, reporting standards for financial audits, field work standards for performance audits, and reporting standards for performance audits. The performance audit standards in the last two categories are presented in Figure 22-5 for information purposes only and are not discussed further here. The standards in the first three categories are identified and discussed in the following sections. The citation following each standard refers to the paragraph number in *Government Auditing Standards.*

General Standards

The general category of GAGAS pertains primarily to the qualifications of the auditor and audit organizations. These standards apply to both types of govern-

[3] *Ibid.*, paragraph 2.6.

FIGURE 22-5 • FIELD WORK AND REPORTING STANDARDS FOR PERFORMANCE AUDITS

Field Work Standards

1. **Planning:**
   Work is to be adequately planned.

2. **Supervision:**
   Staff are to be properly supervised.

3. **Compliance with laws and regulations:**
   When laws, regulations, and other compliance requirements are significant to audit objectives, auditors should design the audit to provide reasonable assurance about compliance with them. In all performance audits, auditors should be alert to situations or transactions that could be indicative of illegal acts or abuse.

4. **Management controls:**
   Auditors should obtain an understanding of management controls that are relevant to the audit. When management controls are significant to audit objectives, auditors should obtain sufficient evidence to support their judgments about those controls.

5. **Evidence:**
   Sufficient, competent, and relevant evidence is to be obtained to afford a reasonable basis for the auditors' findings and conclusions. A record of the auditors' work should be retained in the form of working papers. Working papers should contain sufficient information to enable an experienced auditor having no previous connection with the audit to ascertain from them the evidence that supports the auditors' significant conclusions and judgments.

Reporting Standards

1. **Form:**
   Auditors should prepare written audit reports communicating the results of each audit.

2. **Timeliness:**
   Auditors should appropriately issue the reports to make the information available for timely use by management, legislative officials, and other interested parties.

3. **Report contents:**
   Auditors should report the audit objectives and the audit scope and methodology.

4. **Report presentation:**
   The report should be complete, accurate, objective, convincing, and as clear and concise as the subject permits.

5. **Report distribution:**
   Written audit reports are to be submitted by the audit organization to the appropriate officials of the auditee and to the appropriate officials of the organizations requiring or arranging for the audits, including external funding organizations, unless legal restrictions prevent it. Copies of the reports should also be sent to other officials who have legal oversight authority or who may be responsible for acting on audit findings and recommendations and to others authorized to receive such reports. Unless restricted by law or regulation, copies should be made available for public inspection.

SOURCE: *GOVERNMENT AUDITING STANDARDS,* CHAPTERS 6 AND 7.

ment audits. There are four standards in this category:

- **Qualifications.** The staff assigned to conduct the audit should collectively possess adequate professional proficiency for the tasks required. (Par. 3.3)
- **Independence.** In all matters relating to the audit work, the audit organization and the individual auditors, whether government or public, should be free from personal and external impairments to independence, should be organizationally independent, and should maintain an independent attitude and appearance. (Par. 3.11)
- **Due Professional Care.** Due professional care should be used in conducting the audit and in preparing related reports. (Par. 3.26)
- **Quality Control.** Each audit organization conducting audits in accordance with this standard should have an appropriate internal quality control system in place and undergo an external quality control review. (Par. 3.31)

The first three general standards are similar to the AICPA's general category of GAAS. However, the *qualifications* standard incorporates continuing education and training requirements for each auditor who has a significant role in government audits, including a minimum of 24 hours within each two-year period in subjects directly related to the government environment or government auditing. The fourth GAGAS general standard does not have an equivalent in GAAS, but you should recall that the AICPA has established separate quality control standards and requires its members in public practice to be associated with firms that participate in a qualifying quality review or practice monitoring program.

Field Work Standards for Financial Audits

The GAGAS field work standards incorporate the three AICPA field work standards without modification. Also incorporated, by reference, are all of the related SASs issued by the AICPA that may be viewed as interpretations of the field work standards. Complementing these standards, GAGAS include three additional field work standards as follows:

- **Planning—Follow up.** Auditors should follow up on known material findings and recommendations from previous audits. (Par. 4.7)
- **Compliance—Contracts and Grant Agreements.** Auditors should design the audit to provide reasonable assurance of detecting material misstatements resulting from noncompliance with provisions of contracts or grant agreements that have a direct material effect on the determination of financial statement amounts. If specific information comes to the auditors' attention that provides evidence concerning the existence of possible noncompliance that could have a material indirect effect on the financial statements, auditors should apply audit procedures specifically directed to ascertaining whether that noncompliance has occurred. (Par. 4.13)
- **Evidence—Working Papers.** Working papers should contain sufficient information to enable an experienced auditor having no previous connection with the audit to ascertain from them the evidence that supports the auditors' significant conclusions and judgments. (Par. 4.35)

The first additional standard recognizes the GAO's conclusion that much of the benefit from audit work is not in the findings reported or recommendations made, but in their effective resolution which is a responsibility of auditee management. This additional standard establishes part of a process to track the status of previous findings and resolutions and is intended to help auditors assure that the benefits of their work are realized. The second additional standard recognizes that governmental organizations are often subject to more specific rules and regulations than entities in the private sector and that noncompliance can have material effects on the financial statements. This standard represents an elaboration on, and is patterned after, the GAAS requirements regarding auditors' responsibilities for detecting irregularities and illegal acts. In meeting this standard, auditors should request management to state in its rep letter that it has identified and disclosed to the auditor all laws and regulations that have a direct and material effect on the financial statements. The third additional standard codifies a requirement that, although not explicitly stated in GAAS, should certainly apply to all types of financial statement audits.

GAGAS do not prescribe additional internal control standards for financial statement audits. However, the *Yellow Book* does include guidance on applying the second standard of field work of GAAS when considering the control environment, safeguarding controls, controls over compliance with laws and regulations, and control risk assessments in government audits. The *Yellow Book* also provides additional guidance on setting materiality. Specifically, it states that in an audit of a government entity or an entity that receives government assistance, it may be appropriate to set materiality levels lower than in audits of other entities because of the public accountability of the auditee, the various legal and regulatory requirements, and the visibility and sensitivity of government programs, activities, and functions.

All AICPA standards (SASs and SSAEs) that apply to financial related audits are also incorporated by reference into GAGAS.

Reporting Standards for Financial Audits

Complementing the AICPA's four generally accepted reporting standards and related SASs, all of which are incorporated into GAGAS by reference, the *Yellow Book* includes the following five additional reporting standards:

- **Communication with Audit Committees.** Auditors should communicate certain information related to the conduct and reporting of the audit to the audit committee or to the individuals with whom they have contracted for the audit. (Par. 5.5)
- **Compliance with GAGAS.** Audit reports should state that the audit was made in accordance with generally accepted government auditing standards. (Par. 5.11)
- **Compliance with Laws and Regulations and Internal Controls.** The report on financial statements should either (1) describe the scope of the auditors' testing of compliance with laws and regulations and internal controls and present the results of those tests or (2) refer to separate reports containing that information. In presenting the results of those tests, auditors should report irregularities, illegal acts, and other material noncompliance, and reportable conditions in internal controls. In some circumstances, auditors should report irregularities and illegal acts directly to parties external to the audited entity. (Par. 5.15)
- **Privileged and Confidential Information.** If certain information is prohibited from general disclosure, the audit report should state the nature of the information omitted and the requirement that makes the omission necessary. (Par. 5.29)
- **Report Distribution.** Written audit reports are to be submitted by the audit organization to the appropriate officials of the auditee and to the appropriate officials of the organizations requiring or arranging for the audits, including external funding organizations, unless legal restrictions prevent it. Copies of the reports should also be sent to other officials who have legal oversight authority or who may be responsible for acting on audit findings and recommendations and to others authorized to receive such reports. Unless restricted by law or regulation, copies should be made available for public inspection. (Par. 5.32)

The first additional reporting standard expands on the guidance provided in SAS 61, *Communication with Audit Committees,* and formalizes the guidance as a reporting standard. Among matters to be included in the communication beyond those required by SAS 61 is the nature of any additional testing of internal controls and compliance required by laws and regulations. The second additional standard requires that the audit report on financial statements explicitly state that the audit was conducted in accordance with GAGAS whenever the report is submitted to comply with a legal, regulatory, or contractual requirement for a GAGAS audit. This standard does not prohibit issuing a report that does not refer to GAGAS when the auditee needs an audit report for purposes other than complying with requirements calling for a GAGAS audit.

The third additional standard involves the most extensive differences between reporting on financial statement audits under GAAS and GAGAS. These differences are explained in the next two sections. The fourth additional reporting standard recognizes that certain information may be prohibited from general disclosure by federal, state, or local laws or regulations. The report distribution requirements detailed in the fifth additional standard make it important for the engaging organization and the auditor to have a clear understanding as to what officials or organizations will receive the report and who will make the distribution.

In reporting on financial related audits, auditors should follow all applicable portions of the GAAS and GAGAS reporting standards for financial audits as well as applicable portions of the AICPA's SASs, and SSAEs such as those discussed in Chapter 21. For financial related audits not covered by the above, the GAGAS reporting standards for performance audits (see Figure 22-5) should be followed.

REPORTING ON COMPLIANCE WITH LAWS AND REGULATIONS

The third additional reporting standard requires that either the auditors' reports on financial statements or a separate report referred to therein include the same information on irregularities and illegal acts that is reported to audit committees under AICPA standards. Other instances of noncompliance that are material to the financial statements such as violations of contract provisions or grant agreements must also be reported. Examples of the latter include failure of grantees to contribute their own resources pursuant to matching requirements, violations of restrictions on the purposes for which funds can be expended, and improper allocations of indirect costs. When noncompliance is found, the manner of reporting should provide the reader with a basis for judging the prevalence and consequences of such conditions by referring to such variables as the number of cases examined, frequency of noncompliance, dollar value, and so on.

This standard also requires auditors to report irregularities or illegal acts directly to external parties in two circumstances when the auditee fails to do so as soon as practicable after the auditor has communicated the matter to the auditee's governing body: (1) when the auditee is required by law or regulation to report such events to external parties and (2) when an auditee that receives assistance from a government agency fails to report to the agency an irregularity or illegal act involving that assistance. When laws, regulations, or policies require auditors to report indications of certain types of irregularities or illegal acts to law enforcement or investigatory authorities, they should consult with those authorities

FIGURE 22-6 • REPORT ON COMPLIANCE: NO MATERIAL INSTANCE OF NONCOMPLIANCE

We have audited the financial statement of [*name of entity*] as of and for the year ended June 30, 19X1, and have issued our report thereon dated August 15, 19X1.

We conducted our audit in accordance with generally accepted auditing standards and *Government Auditing Standards,* issued by the Comptroller General of the United States. Those standards require that we plan and perform the audit to obtain reasonable assurance about whether the financial statements are free of material misstatement.

Compliance with laws, regulations, contracts, and grants applicable to [*name of entity*] is the responsibility of [*name of entity*]'s management. As part of obtaining reasonable assurance about whether the financial statements are free of material misstatement, we performed tests of [*name of entity*]'s compliance with certain provisions of laws, regulations, contracts, and grants. However, our objective was not to provide an opinion on overall compliance with such provisions.

The result of our tests indicate that, with respect to the items tested, [*name of entity*] complied, in all material respects, with the provisions referred to in the preceding paragraph. With respect to items not tested, nothing came to our attention that caused us to believe that [*name of entity*] had not complied, in all material respects, with those provisions.

This report is intended for the information of the audit committee, management, and [*specify legislative or regulatory body*]. This restriction is not intended to limit the distribution of this report, which is a matter of public record.

[*Signature*]

[*Date*]

SOURCE: AU 801.25

and/or legal counsel to determine whether broader reporting would compromise investigative or legal proceedings already underway. In such cases, auditors may limit their reporting to information that is already part of the public record.

Extensive guidance on **compliance auditing** and reporting thereon is provided in SAS 68, *Compliance Auditing Applicable to Governmental Entities and Other Recipients of Governmental Financial Assistance* (AU 801). A sample separate report on compliance when no material instances of noncompliance are found is presented in Figure 22-6.[4] Note that the report does not provide an opinion on overall compliance. Rather, the fourth paragraph provides positive assurance of compliance for specific items tested and negative assurance as to items not tested. Furthermore, note that the third paragraph indicates that the basis for the auditors' conclusions about compliance is limited to the procedures performed in the financial statement audit as part of obtaining reasonable assurance about whether the statements are free of material misstatements, rather than a separate service or engagement.

[4] The reader is cautioned that as of mid-1994, the Auditing Standards Board was considering revisions to SAS 68. Upon completion, the revised SAS is expected to refer practitioners to applicable AICPA audit and accounting guides and statements of position referred to later in this chapter for specific performance and reporting guidance.

REPORTING ON INTERNAL CONTROL

As indicated in the third additional reporting standard, GAGAS requires auditors' reports on financial statements to either include a report on internal controls or refer to a separate report thereon. In the report, the auditor

- Identifies the categories into which the controls are classified for purposes of the report (e.g., by transaction cycle or financial statement caption).
- Describes the scope of the work in obtaining an understanding of the internal control structure and assessing control risk (i.e., limited to the consideration of the ICS made as part of the audit of the financial statements).
- Reports internal control deficiencies that under AICPA standards are communicated separately to management and the audit committee as *reportable conditions* (as discussed in Chapters 9 and 19 of this text).

Furthermore, GAGAS requires that reportable conditions that constitute material weaknesses be so identified which is optional under GAAS. When there are deficiencies that do not qualify as reportable conditions, they should be communicated to the auditee, preferably in writing such as in a management letter. When this occurs, reference should be made to the communication in the auditor's report on controls.

The report on controls does not express any form of assurance on the effectiveness of the internal control structure. Additional guidance on reporting on the internal control structure of a governmental entity, including the suggested content and format of separate reports suitable for a variety of circumstances, can be found in SAS 68.

LEARNING CHECK:

22-10 a. Explain the scope of governmental auditing.
b. Identify the types of government audits.

22-11 a. What agency establishes audit standards for government audits?
b. What is the relationship between GAGAS and GAAS?

22-12 a. Identify the categories of GAGAS.
b. State the general standards that apply to all government audits.

22-13 a. Identify the supplemental field work standards that apply in a financial statement audit.
b. What reports are required by the supplemental reporting standards in a financial statement audit?

22-14 a. Indicate the nature of each paragraph of the auditor's unqualified report on compliance with applicable laws and regulations when no material instance of noncompliance is found.
b. Identify the requirements for reporting on internal control under GAGAS that differ or are in addition to GAAS.

KEY TERMS:

Compliance auditing, p. 858
Economy and efficiency audits, p. 852
Financial audits, p. 852
Financial related audits, p. 852
Financial statement audits, p. 852
Generally accepted government auditing standards (GAGAS), p. 853
Governmental auditing, p. 851
Performance audit, p. 853
Performance audits, p. 852
Program audits, p. 852
Yellow Book standards, p. 853

THE SINGLE AUDIT ACT

The **Single Audit Act** (the Act), passed by Congress in 1984, established the concept of a single organization-wide government audit (the **single audit**) encompassing both financial and compliance audits. The Act reduces the need for federal agencies to conduct, and for recipients of federal financial assistance to undergo, multiple separate financial and compliance audits.

OBJECTIVES OF THE ACT

OBJECTIVE 7

Explain the objectives and applicability of the Single Audit Act.

Section 1(a) of the Act states that the Act's objectives are to

- Improve the financial management of state and local governments with respect to federal financial assistance programs.
- Establish uniform requirements for audits of federal financial assistance provided to state and local governments.
- Promote the efficient and effective use of audit resources.
- Ensure that federal departments and agencies, to the maximum extent practicable, rely on and use audit work done pursuant to the requirements of the Single Audit Act.

As implemented, the Act also has become an instrument for ensuring that the recipients of federal financial assistance comply with several significant national policies pertaining to such matters as wages, work conditions, and civil rights as explained further in a subsequent section.

APPLICABILITY AND ADMINISTRATION

Under the Act, state and local governments that receive $100,000 or more in federal financial assistance in any fiscal year, either directly from a federal agency or indirectly through another state or local government entity, are required to have an annual single audit pursuant to the Act. Entities receiving $25,000 or more but less than $100,000 in any fiscal year have the option to have a single audit or to have separate audits according to other federal statutes and regulations. The Act adds to the requirements contained in the *Yellow Book* standards, with special emphasis on defined major federal financial assistance programs.

Federal financial assistance is broadly defined in the Act as assistance provided by a federal government agency in the form of grants, contracts, loans, loan guarantees, property, cooperative agreements, interest subsidies, insurance, or direct appropriations, but not direct federal cash assistance to individuals. A **major program** of federal financial assistance is defined as any program for which total expenditures of such assistance by an entity during a program year exceed a specified amount relative to the total expenditures for all programs. For example, for local government entities whose total expenditures for all programs exceed $100,000 but are less than or equal to $100 million, a major program is one for which total expenditures of that assistance exceed the larger of $300,000 or 3% of the total expenditures for all programs. Programs not qualifying as major programs are designated **nonmajor programs.**

The Director of the Office of Management and Budget (OMB) has prescribed policies, procedures, and guidelines to implement the Act in *OMB Circular A-128 —Audits of State and Local Governments.*[5] The director also designates cognizant agencies to monitor compliance with the Act. A **cognizant agency** is a federal agency that has the responsibility for implementing the requirements for single audits for a particular state or local government. The cognizant agency represents the collective interests of all federal government agencies in the results of the audit. The responsibilities of the agency include providing technical advice and liaison to state and local governments and independent auditors. Thus, the governmental unit can work directly with one agency rather than with several.

AUDITORS' RESPONSIBILITIES UNDER THE ACT

OBJECTIVE 8

Distinguish the components of a single audit and the procedures and reports associated with each.

A single audit conducted as specified in the Act and *OMB Circular A-128* has two main components, each of which involves a variety of procedures and reports as shown in Figure 22-7. Note that the first component, the financial statement audit, and its related procedures and reports, are based on the standards contained in GAAS as discussed in previous chapters of this text and GAGAS as discussed in previous sections of this chapter. The second component, the audit of federal financial assistance, and its related procedures and reports, involve additional federal audit requirements as specified in the Act and *OMB Circular A-128.* In addition to the guidance provided in the Act itself and the *OMB Circular,* auditors can look to the following primary sources for guidance in completing this component of a single audit.[6]

- *OMB Compliance Supplement for Single Audits of State and Local Governments.*
- AICPA Audit and Accounting Guide, *Audits of State and Local Governmental Units.*

[5] A companion document, *OMB Circular A-133—Audits of Institutions of Higher Education and Other Nonprofit Institutions,* prescribes audit requirements for institutions of higher education and other nonprofit institutions that receive *federal awards* of $100,000 or more per year. (The definition of federal award is slightly broader than the definition of federal financial assistance.) To assist auditors in complying with *OMB Circular A-133,* the AICPA has issued Statement of Position 92-9, *Audits of Not-for-Profit Organizations Receiving Federal Awards.* These materials are beyond the scope of this chapter.

[6] The AICPA was in the process of revising the second, third, and fourth items at the time this text went to press.

- AICPA Statement of Position (SOP) 92-7, *Audits of State and Local Governmental Entities Receiving Federal Financial Assistance.*
- SAS 68, *Compliance Auditing Applicable to Governmental Entities and Other Recipients of Governmental Financial Assistance* (AU 801).

Certain aspects of the additional federal audit requirements pertaining to the federal financial assistance component of a single audit are explained in the following sections.

FIGURE 22-7 • SUMMARY OF AUDITORS' RESPONSIBILITIES UNDER THE SINGLE AUDIT ACT

Component	Procedures Performed	Report Issued
Financial statement audit	1. Audit of the financial statements in accordance with GAAS and the general standards of GAGAS.	1a. Opinion on the financial statements. 1b. Report on supplementary schedule of federal financial assistance.
	2. Audit of the financial statements in accordance with the additional GAGAS standards of field work and reporting.	2a. Report on internal control based on the audit. 2b. Report on compliance with laws and regulations that may have a material effect on the financial statements.
Audit of federal financial assistance	3. Procedures to obtain understanding of the internal control structure over federal financial assistance, tests of controls, and assessment of control risk.	3a. Report on internal controls over federal financial assistance.
	4. Tests of compliance with *general requirements* applicable to *all* federal financial assistance programs and *specific requirements* applicable to *major* federal financial assistance programs.	4a. Report on compliance with general requirements applicable to federal financial assistance programs. 4b. Opinion on compliance with specific requirements applicable to *each major* federal financial assistance program. 4c. Schedule of findings and questioned costs.
	5. Tests of compliance with laws and regulations applicable to *nonmajor* federal financial assistance program transactions selected for testing in connection with procedure 1 or 3.	5a. Report on compliance with laws and regulations applicable to nonmajor federal financial assistance program transactions tested. 5b. Schedule of findings and questioned costs.

SOURCE: AU 801.102 (ADAPTED).

Consideration of the Internal Control Structure Over Federal Financial Assistance

Under the Act, the internal control structure over federal financial assistance is defined as the plan of organization and methods and procedures adopted by management to ensure that (1) resource use is consistent with laws, regulations, and policies, (2) resources are safeguarded against waste, loss, and misuse, and (3) reliable data are obtained, maintained, and fairly disclosed in reports. Based on this definition, the auditor is required to (1) obtain an understanding of the ICS used in administering all federal financial assistance programs of an entity and (2) perform tests of controls to evaluate the effectiveness of the design and operation of the policies and procedures in preventing or detecting material noncompliance for each major program and such additional nonmajor programs as required to cover at least 50% of the total federal financial assistance program expenditures. The control risk assessments obtained are then used in determining the nature, timing, and extent of the tests of compliance with the specific requirements referred to in procedure four in Figure 22-7 and discussed further in a later section.

Testing Compliance with General Requirements

There are nine general requirements with which all recipients of federal financial assistance are expected to comply. As noted previously, they involve significant national policies and include prohibitions against using federal funds for partisan political activity, violating anyone's civil rights, violating work conditions and wage requirements including failing to maintain a drug-free workplace, charging costs to federal programs that violate federal cost principles, and failing to file prescribed federal financial reports. Other general requirements pertain to cash management, real property acquisition and relocation assistance for displaced persons, and certain administrative requirements. Failure to comply with these requirements could have a material impact on an organization's financial statements.

Guidance for testing compliance with these general requirements and reporting thereon is provided in the *OMB Compliance Supplement* referred to previously. The report is in the form of "procedures and findings" rather than an opinion, and should be issued regardless of whether the auditee has any *major* programs.

Testing Compliance with Specific Requirements

Specific requirements of federal financial assistance programs pertain to the following matters:

- *Types of services allowed or not allowed,* which specifies the types of goods or services entities may purchase with financial assistance.
- *Eligibility,* which specifies the characteristics of individuals or groups to which entities may give financial assistance.

- *Matching,* which specifies amounts entities should contribute from their own resources toward projects for which financial assistance is provided.
- *Reporting,* which specifies other reports entities must file.
- *Special tests and provisions,* which might include such requirements as holding hearings regarding the proposed use of funds and deadlines for expending funds.

In determining the scope of the tests of compliance for each major federal financial assistance program, the auditor uses the audit risk concepts discussed earlier in this text (inherent, control, and detection risk), except that here the risk components relate to noncompliance with specific requirements rather than misstatements in financial statement assertions. The materiality of any findings of noncompliance is evaluated in the context of the program to which the findings relate rather than to the auditee's overall financial statements.

Based on the evidence obtained from the tests of compliance, as shown in Figure 22-7, the auditor expresses an opinion on compliance with specific requirements for each major program. Regardless of the type of opinion expressed (unqualified, qualified, adverse, or disclaimer), any instances of noncompliance or questioned costs should be reported in a *schedule of findings and questioned costs.* **Questioned costs** include any costs charged to a program that are unallowable, undocumented, unapproved, or unreasonable.

Testing Compliance for Nonmajor Programs

Compliance testing of nonmajor programs is limited to transactions selected by the auditor either as part of the audit of financial statements or in meeting the 50% rule pertaining to consideration of the internal control structure over federal financial assistance as explained in a previous section. Each selected transaction is tested for compliance with the specific requirements applicable to the transaction. To illustrate, assume that a payroll transaction charged to a nonmajor program is selected for testing. Among the determinations to be made are whether (1) the individual's job classification could reasonably be linked to the program and (2) the recipient's salary was correctly charged to the program.

The auditor's report on compliance for nonmajor programs may be issued separately or be combined with the report on major programs. It should be accompanied by a schedule of findings of any instances of noncompliance and questioned costs.

LEARNING CHECK:

22-15 What are the objectives of the Single Audit Act?

22-16 a. Who is required to have a single audit under the Single Audit Act?

b. Who prescribes policies, procedures, and guidelines to implement the Act?

c. What is a *cognizant agency,* and what are its responsibilities?

22-17 a. Identify the two main components of a single audit.

b. What is the source of the standards that govern performance of each component?

22-18 a. What is the purpose of the auditor's consideration of the internal control structure used in administering federal financial assistance programs?

b. To which federal financial assistance programs should the auditor's understanding of the internal control structure and tests of controls extend?

22-19 a. State the nature of the general requirements with which all recipients of federal financial assistance are expected to comply, and give several examples.

b. State the types of specific requirements with which major programs are expected to comply.

c. How is the application of the concept of materiality in evaluating findings of noncompliance with specific requirements different from its application under GAAS?

22-20 Identify the reports required under the Single Audit Act that are not required by GAAS or GAGAS.

KEY TERMS:

Cognizant agency, p. 861
Federal financial assistance, p. 861
Major program, p. 861
Nonmajor programs, p. 861
Questioned costs, p. 864
Single audit, p. 860
Single Audit Act, p. 860

SUMMARY

Internal, operational, and governmental auditing represent a significant part of the professional practice of auditing. These audits involve independent auditors, internal auditors, and government auditors. As in the case of financial statement audits, certain standards must be met in performing and reporting on each type of audit. Government auditing standards include specific continuing education and training requirements pertaining to the governmental environment and governmental auditing. The Single Audit Act imposes additional federal audit requirements pertaining to federal financial assistance programs that expand on the requirements for financial statement audits imposed by GAAS and GAGAS. An understanding of all applicable standards is essential to achieve the quality of results expected by the primary recipients of reports on these audits.

APPENDIX 22A INTERNAL AUDITOR CODE OF ETHICS

The Institute of Internal Auditors adopted the following Code of Ethics for its members in July 1988:

THE INSTITUTE OF INTERNAL AUDITORS
CODE OF ETHICS

PURPOSE: A distinguishing mark of a profession is acceptance by its members of responsibility to the interests of those it serves. Members of The Institute of Internal Auditors (Members) and Certified Internal Auditors (CIAs) must maintain high standards of conduct in order to effectively discharge this responsibility. The Institute of Internal Auditors (Institute) adopts this *Code of Ethics* for Members and CIAs.

APPLICABILITY: This *Code of Ethics* is applicable to all Members and CIAs. Membership in The Institute and acceptance of the "Certified Internal Auditor" designation are voluntary actions. By acceptance, Members and CIAs assume an obligation of self-discipline above and beyond the requirements of laws and regulations.

The standards of conduct set forth in this *Code of Ethics* provide basic principles in the practice of internal auditing. Members and CIAs should realize that their individual judgment is required in the application of these principles.

CIAs shall use the "Certified Internal Auditor" designation with discretion and in a dignified manner, fully aware of what the designation denotes. The designation shall also be used in a manner consistent with all statutory requirements.

Members who are judged by the Board of Directors of The Institute to be in violation of the standards of conduct of the *Code of Ethics* shall be subject to forfeiture of their membership in The Institute. CIAs who are similarly judged also shall be subject to forfeiture of the "Certified Internal Auditor" designation.

STANDARDS OF CONDUCT

I. Members and CIAs shall exercise honesty, objectivity, and diligence in the performance of their duties and responsibilities.

II. Members and CIAs shall exhibit loyalty in all matters pertaining to the affairs of their organization or to whomever they may be rendering a service. However, Members and CIAs shall not knowingly be a party to any illegal or improper activity.

III. Members and CIAs shall not knowingly engage in acts or activities which are discreditable to the profession of internal auditing or to their organization.

IV. Members and CIAs shall refrain from entering into any activity which may be in conflict with the interest of their organization or which would prejudice their ability to carry out objectively their duties and responsibilities.

V. Members and CIAs shall not accept anything of value from an employee, client, customer, supplier, or business associate of their organization which would impair or be presumed to impair their professional judgment.

VI. Members and CIAs shall undertake only those services which they can reasonably expect to complete with professional competence.

VII. Members and CIAs shall adopt suitable means to comply with the *Standards for the Professional Practice of Internal Auditing.*

VIII. Members and CIAs shall be prudent in the use of information acquired in the course of their duties. They shall not use confidential information for any personal gain nor in any manner which would be contrary to law or detrimental to the welfare of their organization.

IX. Members and CIAs, when reporting on the results of their work, shall reveal all material facts known to them which, if not revealed, could either distort reports of operations under review or conceal unlawful practices.

X. Members and CIAs shall continually strive for improvement in their proficiency, and in the effectiveness and quality of their service.

XI. Members and CIAs, in the practice of their profession, shall be ever mindful of the obligation to maintain the high standards of competence, morality, and dignity promulgated by The Institute. Members shall abide by the *Bylaws* and uphold the objectives of The Institute.

BIBLIOGRAPHY

AICPA *Professional Standards:*

AU 801, Compliance Auditing Applicable to Governmental Entities and Other Recipients of Governmental Financial Assistance.

AICPA Audit and Accounting Guide, *Audits of State and Local Governments.* New York: American Institute of Certified Public Accountants, 1986 (as amended by subsequently issued AICPA Statements of Position).

AICPA Statement of Position 92-7, *Audits of State and Local Governmental Entities Receiving Federal Financial Assistance,* September 1992.

AICPA Statement of Position 92-9, *Audits of Not-for-Profit Organizations Receiving Federal Awards,* December 1992.

Broadus, W. A., Jr., and Comtois, J. D. "The Single Audit Act: A Needed Reform," *Journal of Accountancy* (April 1985), pp. 62–71.

Brown, Clifford D., and Bumaby, Priscilla. "The Evolution of the Single Audit: A 20-Year Process," *Accounting Horizons* (June 1988), pp. 58–64.

Casler, Darwin J., and Crockett, James R. *Operational Auditing: An Introduction.* Altamonte Springs, FL: The Institute of Internal Auditors, Inc., 1982.

Codification of Standards for the Professional Practice of Internal Auditing. Altamonte Springs, FL: The Institute of Internal Auditors, Inc., 1993.

Comptroller General of the United States, *Government Auditing Standards.* Washington, D.C.: U.S. General Accounting Office, 1994 Revision.

Granof, Michael H. "Privatization: The Road to Federal Regulation of Auditing," *Accounting Horizons* (December 1992), pp. 76–85.

Hardman, D. "Towards a Conceptual Framework for Government Auditing," *Accounting and Finance* (May 1991), pp. 22–37.

Office of Management and Budget, *OMB Circular A-128—Audits of State and Local Governments,* 1985.

———, *OMB Circular A-133—Audits of Institutions of Higher Education and Other Not-for-Profit Organizations,* 1990.

Raman, K. K., and Van Daniker, Relmond P. "Materiality in Government Auditing," *Journal of Accountancy* (February 1994), pp. 71–76.

Special Committee on Operational and Management Auditing, *Operational Auditing Engagements.* New York: AICPA, 1983.

OBJECTIVE QUESTIONS[1]

Indicate the best answer choice for each of the following multiple choice questions.

22-21 These questions pertain to internal auditing.

[1] All questions marked by an asterisk are from the Certified Internal Auditor Examination.

*1. Internal auditing is an independent appraisal function established within an organization to examine and evaluate its activities. To that end, internal auditing provides assistance to:
   a. External auditors.
   b. Management and the board of directors.
   c. Shareholders.
   d. Statutory authorities.

*2. According to the *Standards,* who is responsible for coordinating internal and external audit efforts?
   a. Director of internal auditing.
   b. External auditors.
   c. Audit committee of the board of directors.
   d. Chief financial officer.

*3. According to the *Statement of Responsibilities,* the authority of the internal auditing department is limited to that granted by:
   a. The board of directors and the controller.
   b. Senior management and the *Standards.*
   c. Management and the board of directors.
   d. The audit committee and the chief financial officer.

*4. According to the *Statement of Responsibilities,* an internal auditing department's scope should include:
   a. Only financial auditing.
   b. Both financial and operational auditing.
   c. Only audits dealing with safeguarding of assets.
   d. Only financial and compliance auditing.

22-22 These questions relate to operational auditing.

*1. Auditing to determine whether an entity is managing and utilizing its resources economically and efficiently would most appropriately be classified as:
   a. Compliance auditing.
   b. Financial auditing.
   c. Operational auditing.
   d. Program results auditing.

2. A typical objective of an operational audit is to determine whether an entity's
   a. Internal control structure is adequately operating as designed.
   b. Operational information is in accordance with generally accepted governmental auditing standards.
   c. Financial statements present fairly the results of operations.
   d. Specific operating units are functioning efficiently and effectively.

3. Operational auditing is primarily oriented toward
   a. Future improvements to accomplish the goals of management.
   b. The accuracy of data reflected in management's financial records.
   c. The verification that a company's financial statements are fairly presented.
   d. Past protection provided by existing internal control.

22-23 These questions apply to governmental auditing.

1. Which of the following bodies promulgates standards for audits of federal financial assistance recipients?
   a. Governmental Accounting Standards Board.
   b. Financial Accounting Standards Board.

c. General Accounting Office.
d. Governmental Auditing Standards Board.

2. Because of the pervasive effects of laws and regulations on the financial statements of governmental units, an auditor should obtain written management representations acknowledging that management has
   a. Implemented internal control policies and procedures designed to detect all illegal acts.
   b. Documented the procedures performed to evaluate the governmental unit's compliance with laws and regulations.
   c. Identified and disclosed all laws and regulations that have a direct and material effect on its financial statements.
   d. Reported all known illegal acts and material weaknesses in internal control structure to the funding agency or regulatory body.

3. Reporting on the internal control structure under *Government Auditing Standards* differs from reporting under generally accepted auditing standards in that *Government Auditing Standards* requires a
   a. Written report describing the entity's internal control structure procedures specifically designed to prevent fraud, abuse, and illegal acts.
   b. Written report describing each reportable condition observed including identification of those considered material weaknesses.
   c. Statement of negative assurance that the internal control structure procedures **not** tested have an immaterial effect on the entity's financial statements.
   d. Statement of positive assurance that internal control structure procedures designed to detect material errors and irregularities were tested.

4. In an audit in accordance with *Government Auditing Standards* an auditor is required to report on the auditor's tests of the entity's compliance with applicable laws and regulations. This requirement is satisfied by designing the audit to provide
   a. Positive assurance that the internal control policies and procedures tested by the auditor are operating as prescribed.
   b. Reasonable assurance of detecting misstatements that are material to the financial statements.
   c. Negative assurance that reportable conditions communicated during the audit do **not** prevent the auditor from expressing an opinion.
   d. Limited assurance that the internal control structure designed by management will prevent or detect errors, irregularities, and illegal acts.

5. The concept of materiality for financial statements audited under the Single Audit Act of 1984 differs from materiality in an audit in accordance with generally accepted auditing standards. Under the Act, materiality is
   a. Determined by the federal agency requiring the audit.
   b. Ignored, because all account balances, regardless of size, are fully tested.
   c. Determined separately for each major federal financial assistance program.
   d. Calculated without consideration of the auditor's risk assessment.

COMPREHENSIVE QUESTIONS

22-24 **(Internal auditing)** The Institute of Internal Auditors is the national organization for internal auditors. Two authoritative pronouncements of the Institute of Internal Auditors are the

Statement of Responsibilities of Internal Auditing (the *Statement*) and *Standards for the Professional Practice of Internal Auditing* (the *Standards*).

REQUIRED

1. State the definition of internal auditing as given in the *Statement.*
2. Explain the essential parts of the definition.
3. What are the objectives and scope of internal auditing as indicated in the *Statement?*
4. Distinguish between the terms *general standards, specific standards,* and *guidelines* as they are used in the *Standards.*
5. Identify and state the general standards.
6. State the specific standards that pertain to the professional proficiency of an internal auditor.
7. Indicate the specific standards that pertain to the internal auditing department.
8. Identify the specific scope of work standards that relate to (a) compliance auditing and (b) operational auditing.
9. State the specific performance of audit work standards.
10. Explain the similarities between the practice standards of the IIA and generally accepted auditing standards (GAAS) of the AICPA.

ICMA

22-25 **(Internal auditing practice standards)** Standards for the Professional Practice of Internal Auditing have been established by the Institute of Internal Auditors. Listed below are specific policies adopted by the Marco Corporation for its internal auditors:

1. Internal auditors must comply with the Institute of Internal Auditor Code of Ethics.
2. Internal auditors should periodically inspect the safeguards over inventories and cash.
3. Internal auditors should have valid evidence for audit findings.
4. Inexperienced internal auditors must be supervised by certified internal auditors.
5. Internal auditors should attend professional seminars on EDP.
6. Internal auditors should be unbiased in performing audits.
7. Internal auditors should make a study of the efficiency of personnel in the receiving department.
8. Internal auditors should make postaudit reviews of actions taken by a department following an audit.
9. Internal auditors should periodically review the company's compliance with federal governmental regulations.
10. Internal auditors' reports of audit findings should be communicated to appropriate levels of management.
11. The director of internal auditing should plan the activities for the year.
12. Internal auditors should exercise due care in doing each audit.
13. A quality assurance program should be established and maintained.
14. All new internal auditors must be college graduates.
15. There should be a statement of purpose, authority, and responsibility for the internal audit department.

REQUIRED

a. Identify and state the specific IIA practice standard that pertains to each policy.
b. For each specific standard identified in (a) above, identify the related category of general standard (independence, professional proficiency, scope of work, performance of audit work, and management of the internal auditing department). Use the following format for your answers:

Policy No.	Specific Standard (a)	General Standard (b)

22-26 **(Internal auditing standards)**The Standards for the Professional Practice of Internal Auditing contain general standards for independence and performance of audit work

REQUIRED

a. State the general and specific standards that pertain to independence.
b. How, if at all, does the standard of independence for internal auditors differ from the standard of independence for independent auditors?
c. State the general and specific standards that relate to the performance of audit work.
d. Identify four guidelines that apply to the specific standard pertaining to planning.
e. Identify four guidelines that apply to the specific standard of communicating results.

22-27 **(Internal auditing scope-of-work standards)** You are a senior internal auditor for a savings and loan association. You are discussing the preliminary findings of your audit with the branch manager. Some of the findings you feel need to be investigated further are

1. The branch seems to have too many tellers.
2. No security officer has been appointed, and camera surveillance seems to be insufficient.
3. Although the association does not have a specific dress code, the attire of the branch personnel appears to be too casual, even after considering a recent directive to conserve energy during the summer months.
4. Some of the branch loan officers appear to lack adequate qualifications.
5. Some customers are not charged penalties for late payments on loans.
6. Granting new home mortgages seems to be encouraged in spite of an association policy to discourage expanded activity in this area.

REQUIRED

On your answer sheet, list the title of each of the specific scope-of-work standards as set forth in the Standards for the Professional Practice of Internal Auditing and, to the right of each specific standard, list the number(s) of the finding above that apply.

IIA

22-28 **(Operational auditing)** Enclosure Products, a large, nationwide organization, manufactures and markets several lines of equipment used in packaging. Product reliability and customer service are considered critical to the company's success. The Customer Service Department is charged with the following responsibilities:

- Providing prospective customers with product information.
- Monitoring the adequacy of spare parts availability.
- Providing information to customers about equipment operation and maintenance.
- Preparing and providing customer training courses.
- Providing backup service and support in the event of critical breakdowns.
- Handling warranty claims.
- Maintaining general liaison with customers.

The company recently computerized its Customer Service Department to improve operational efficiency and customer satisfaction. This change represented a sizable investment by Enclosure Products. The new system includes management information to monitor performance in the areas listed above. The Audit Committee of Enclosure Products' Board of Directors has requested that the Internal Audit Department perform an operational audit of the Customer Service Department. The Audit Committee has asked that the audit objectives include evaluation of the following:

- Security of assets, including computer information.
- Compliance with applicable laws and company policies.
- Reliability of financial records.
- Effectiveness of performing assigned responsibilities.
- Determination of the value of the spare parts inventory.

REQUIRED

a. Explain why each of the five audit objectives suggested by the Audit Committee is, or is not, appropriate for an operational audit of Enclosure Products' Customer Service Department.
b. Outline the basic procedures for performing an operational audit.

ICMA (adapted)

22-29 **(Operational auditing)** Janet Joebert is an internal auditor for the Beamer Company. Janet is assigned to conduct an operational audit on the company's receiving department. This is to be Janet's first operational audit. In preparing for the audit, she asks the following questions:

1. What are the similarities and differences between the phases of an operational audit and the phases of a financial statement audit?
2. What is involved in making a preliminary study?
3. What are the key factors in making the examination?
4. What are the essential elements of the report on audit findings?
5. What is the nature and extent of performing a follow-up on the audit?

REQUIRED

a. Answer Janet's questions.
b. If Janet were a CPA in public practice, what standards would she have to follow in conducting the operational audit?

22-30 **(Government auditing standards)** Generally accepted government auditing standards (GAGAS) for a financial statement audit are classified into three categories: general, field work, and reporting. The following statements relate to the specific GAGAS:

1. Due professional care should be used in conducting the audit and in preparing related reports.
2. Working papers should contain sufficient information to ascertain that the evidence supports the auditor's significant conclusions and judgments.
3. The auditor's report on financial statements should either describe the scope of the auditor's testing of compliance with internal controls and present the results of those tests or refer to separate reports containing that information.
4. Planning should include following up on known and material findings and recommendations from previous audits.
5. Auditors should communicate certain information to the audit committee or individuals with whom they have contracted for the audit.
6. The staff assigned to conduct the audit should collectively possess adequate professional proficiency for the tasks required.
7. The auditors should prepare a written report on their tests of compliance with applicable laws and regulations.

8. The auditor should also be aware of the possibility of illegal acts that could have an indirect and material effect on the financial statements.
9. Audit organizations conducting government audits should have an appropriate internal quality control system in place.
10. A record of the auditors' work should be retained in the form of working papers.
11. A statement should be included in the auditors' report that the audit was made in accordance with generally accepted government auditing standards.
12. In all matters relating to the audit work, the audit organization and the individual auditors should be free from personal and external impairments to independence.
13. The auditor should design audit steps and procedures to provide reasonable assurance of detecting errors, irregularities, and illegal acts.
14. Written audit reports are to be submitted by the audit organization to the appropriate officials of the organization audited.
15. If certain information is prohibited from general disclosure, the report should state the nature of the information omitted.

REQUIRED

a. Indicate the category and specific standard to which each of the statements pertains.
b. Explain the relationship of GAAS to the above standards.
c. Identify the reports that should be issued in a financial audit.

22-31 **(Single Audit Act)** Laura Level, CPA, is assigned to the single audit of the city of Plainville. This is Laura's first single audit. As the manager on the audit, you decide to test Laura on her understanding of the Single Audit Act and the auditing requirements of that Act. Your questions to Laura are:

1. What criteria determine whether the city of Plainville must have a single audit?
2. What are the objectives of the Single Audit Act?
3. What is the role of the Director of the Office of Management and Budget in the audit?
4. What is a cognizant agency? What are the responsibilities of this agency in the audit?
5. What are the audit objectives of the Act?
6. What audit reports are required on the city's federal financial assistance programs?
7. How may the required reports be issued?

REQUIRED

Supply the answers that Laura should give.

22-32 **(Single Audit Act)** Jones and Baker, a CPA firm, has a number of governmental audit clients. Some of the clients have federal government financial assistance programs.

REQUIRED

a. What responsibility does the auditor have for reporting on compliance under the Single Audit Act?
b. What responsibility does the auditor have for testing compliance in (1) major and (2) nonmajor federal financial assistance programs?

CASE

22-33 **(Objectivity in internal auditing)** Lajod Company has an Internal Audit Department consisting of a manager and three staff auditors. The Manager of Internal Audits, in turn, reports to the Corporate Controller. Copies of audit reports are routinely sent to the Board of Directors as well as the Corporate Controller and the individual responsible for the area or activity being audited.

The Manager of Internal Audits is aware that the external auditors have relied on the internal audit function to a substantial degree in the past. However, in recent months, the external auditors have suggested there may be a problem related to the objectivity of the internal audit function. This objectivity problem may result in more extensive testing and analysis by the external auditors.

The external auditors are concerned about the amount of nonaudit work performed by the Internal Audit Department. The percentage of nonaudit work performed by the internal auditors in recent years has increased to about 25% of their total hours worked. A sample of five recent nonaudit activities is as follows:

1. One of the internal auditors assisted in the preparation of policy statements on internal control. These statements included such items as policies regarding sensitive payments and standards of control for systems.
2. The bank statements of the corporation are reconciled each month as a regular assignment for one of the internal auditors. The Corporate Controller believes this strengthens the internal control function because the internal auditor is not involved in the receipt and disbursement of cash.
3. The internal auditors are asked to review the budget data in every area each year for relevance and reasonableness before the budget is approved. In addition, an internal auditor examines the variances each month, along with the associated explanations. These variance analyses are prepared by the Corporate Controller's staff after consultation with the individuals involved.
4. One of the internal auditors has recently been involved in the design, installation, and initial operation of a new computer system. The auditor was primarily concerned with the design and implementation of internal accounting controls and the computer application controls for the new system. The auditor also conducted the testing of the controls during the test runs.
5. The internal auditors are frequently asked to make accounting entries for complex transactions before the transactions are recorded. The employees in the accounting department are not adequately trained to handle such transactions. In addition, this serves as a means of maintaining internal control over complex transactions.

The Manager of Internal Audits has always made an effort to remain independent of the Corporate Controller's office and believes the internal auditors are objective and independent in their audit and nonaudit activities.

REQUIRED

a. Define objectivity as it relates to the internal audit function.
b. For each of the five situations outlined above, explain whether the objectivity of Lajod Company's Internal Audit Department has been materially impaired. Consider each situation independently.
c. The Manager of Audits reports to the Corporate Controller.
   1. Does this reporting relationship result in a problem of objectivity? Explain your answer.
   2. Would your answer to any of the five situations in requirement (b) above have changed if the Manager of Internal Audits reported to the Board of Directors? Explain your answer.

ICMA (adapted)

RESEARCH QUESTION

22-34 **(Reporting on compliance with laws and regulations)** Toxic Waste Disposal Co., Inc. (TWD) is a not-for-profit organization that receives grants and fees from various state and municipal governments as well as grants from several federal government agencies.

TWD engaged Hall & Hall, CPAs, to audit its financial statements for the year ended July 31, 19X1, in accordance with *Government Auditing Standards.* Accordingly, the auditors' reports are to be submitted by TWD to the granting government agencies, which make the reports available for public inspection.

The auditors' separate report on compliance with laws and regulations that was drafted by a staff accountant of Hall & Hall at the completion of the engagement contained the statements below. It was submitted to the engagement partner who reviewed matters thoroughly and properly concluded that no material instances of noncompliance were identified.

Locate the official standards governing this type of reporting. For each of the following statements indicate whether it is an appropriate or inappropriate element within the report on compliance with laws and regulations. If a statement is not appropriate, explain why.

1. A statement that the audit was conducted in accordance with generally accepted auditing standards and with *Government Auditing Standards* issued by the Comptroller General of the United States.
2. A statement that the auditors' procedures included tests of compliance.
3. A statement that the standards require the auditors to plan and to perform the audit to detect all instances of noncompliance with applicable laws and regulations.
4. A statement that management is responsible for compliance with laws, regulations, contracts, and grants.
5. A statement that the auditors' objective was to provide an opinion on compliance with the provisions of laws and regulations equivalent to that to be expressed on the financial statements.
6. A statement of positive assurance that the results of the tests indicate that, with respect to the items tested, the entity complied, in all material respects, with the provisions of laws, regulations, contracts, and grants.
7. A statement of negative assurance that, with respect to items tested, nothing came to the auditors' attention that caused the auditors to believe that the entity had not complied, in all material respects, with the provisions of laws, regulations, contracts, and grants.
8. A statement that the report is intended only for the information of the specific legislative or regulatory bodies, and that this restriction is intended to limit the distribution of the report.

AICPA (adapted)

CHAPTER

23

THE INDEPENDENT ACCOUNTANT AND THE SECURITIES AND EXCHANGE COMMISSION

LEARNING OBJECTIVES

After studying this chapter, you should be able to

1. Describe the origins of the SEC and its areas of jurisdiction.
2. Describe the organizational structure of the SEC and the principal division and office that relate to the independent accountant.
3. List the components of the standard package of information required under the SEC's integrated disclosure system.
4. Indicate the nature and purpose of EDGAR.
5. Identify and describe the major types of SEC accounting-related pronouncements.
6. State the SEC's qualifications for independent accountants and requirements for accountant's reports.
7. Understand the purpose and process of registering securities.
8. Explain the independent accountant's primary responsibilities in filings under the Securities Act of 1933.

SECURITIES AND EXCHANGE COMMISSION
- AUTHORITY OF THE SEC
- ORGANIZATION OF THE SEC

REPORTING AND REGISTRATION REQUIREMENTS
- INTEGRATED DISCLOSURE SYSTEM
- ELECTRONIC DATA GATHERING, ANALYSIS, AND RETRIEVAL SYSTEM
- TYPES OF ACCOUNTING PRONOUNCEMENTS
- QUALIFICATIONS OF INDEPENDENT ACCOUNTANTS
- REQUIREMENTS FOR ACCOUNTANTS' REPORTS
- REGISTRATION OF SECURITIES

SECURITIES ACT OF 1933
- REGISTRATION UNDER THE 1933 ACT
- INDEPENDENT ACCOUNTANT'S INVOLVEMENT IN REGISTRATIONS
- ACCOUNTANT'S REPORT

SECURITIES EXCHANGE ACT OF 1934
- REGISTRATION UNDER THE 1934 ACT
- ANNUAL REPORTING
- QUARTERLY REPORTING
- SPECIAL REPORTING

ENFORCEMENT OF THE SECURITIES ACTS
- INJUNCTIVE PROCEEDINGS
- ADMINISTRATIVE PROCEEDINGS
- THE SECURITIES LAW ENFORCEMENT REMEDIES ACT OF 1990

SUMMARY

BIBLIOGRAPHY

OBJECTIVE QUESTIONS

COMPREHENSIVE QUESTIONS

CASE

RESEARCH QUESTIONS

In Chapter 4, the liability of the certified public accountant (CPA) under the securities acts was explained. It is the purpose of this chapter to describe the organization of the Securities and Exchange Commission (SEC), the impact it has on the day-to-day activities of independent CPAs who have clients that are subject to SEC regulations, and the principal financial reporting requirements of the Securities Act of 1933 (the 1933 Act) and the Securities Exchange Act of 1934 (the 1934 Act).

The discussion of the responsibilities of the CPA concerning filings under the federal securities acts is limited to accounting and auditing matters and is not intended to offer legal interpretations of the acts.

In the acts, the term *independent public accountant* is used to describe the individual who is required to perform the audit function. Technically, the individual

9. Explain the independent accountant's primary responsibilities in filings under the Securities Exchange Act of 1934.
10. Distinguish among the types of enforcement actions the SEC may take against independent accountants.

need not be certified (he may be either a CPA or a public accountant), but, in practically all cases, the individual is a CPA. Throughout this chapter, the terms *independent public accountant* and *independent accountant* are considered synonymous with the term *auditor* used in previous chapters of this book.

SECURITIES AND EXCHANGE COMMISSION

OBJECTIVE 1

Describe the origins of the SEC and its areas of jurisdiction.

The SEC was established by the 1934 Act as an independent bipartisan, quasi-judicial federal regulatory agency to administer the federal securities acts. Both the SEC and the 1933 and 1934 Acts, which it administers, resulted from efforts by Congress to restore investor confidence in the securities markets that had been severely shaken during the depression. In the words of the SEC,

> Congress, in enacting the Federal Securities laws, created a continuous disclosure system designed to protect investors and to assure the maintenance of fair and honest securities markets. The Commission, in administering and implementing these laws, has sought to coordinate and integrate this disclosure system. . . . The legislative history of the Securities Act of 1933 indicates that the main concern of Congress was to provide full and fair disclosure in connection with the offer and sale of securities.[1]

AUTHORITY OF THE SEC

The authority of the SEC extends to the offer and initial sale of the securities to the public and to the subsequent trading of such securities on national stock exchanges and over-the-counter markets. Thus, virtually all companies offering securities for sale to the public and all companies that have securities publicly traded are subject to the jurisdiction of the SEC. Currently, approximately 14,000 companies are registered with the SEC.

To aid in assuring the fair and orderly operation of the nation's securities markets, the SEC has regulations affecting brokers, stock exchanges, and publicly held companies. These regulations encompass the monitoring of trading practices, the financial condition of brokers, and the activities and trading rules of securities exchanges. The Commission also requires the registration of publicly traded securities and continuing disclosure of financial and other information about companies that have issued the securities.

In addition, the SEC encourages shareholder participation in the governance of corporations by requiring corporations to hold annual shareholder meetings and provide proxy ballots to shareholders so that they may vote on certain decisions.

In administering the securities acts, the SEC does not pass on the merit of a security, and federal laws do not prohibit the sale or trading of highly speculative securities if their speculative characteristics or risks are disclosed in the filing with the Commission. Information filed with the SEC generally is a matter of public

[1] Securities and Exchange Commission, *SEC Docket* (Vol 4, No. 5, May 7, 1974), p. 155.

record. Information previously considered confidential is now available to the general public under the Freedom of Information Act, commonly referred to as the Sunshine Act.

ORGANIZATION OF THE SEC

OBJECTIVE 2

Describe the organizational structure of the SEC and the principal division and office that relate to the independent accountant.

The SEC is headed by a five-person commission appointed by the President of the United States with the approval of the U.S. Senate. Each commissioner serves for a five-year term, with one member's term expiring each year. No more than three commissioners may be from the same political party. Traditionally, most appointees have been from the legal profession. One member of the Commission is designated by the President as chairman. The Commission directs a staff of about 2,500 that includes accountants, lawyers, securities analysts, engineers, examiners, and administrative and clerical personnel. The professional staff is organized into five divisions and numerous offices as illustrated in Figure 23-1. The independent accountant's involvement with the SEC is primarily through the Division of Corporation Finance and the Office of the Chief Accountant.

Division of Corporation Finance

The principal responsibility of this Division is to prevent (1) fraudulent offerings of securities to the public and (2) the distribution of incomplete, false, or misleading information pertaining to security offerings. In discharging its responsibility, the **Division of Corporation Finance**

- Assists the Commission in the establishment of standards of economic and financial information to be included in documents filed with the SEC.
- Enforces adherence to such standards by issuers, underwriters, and others with respect to securities offered for sale to the public or listed for trading on securities exchanges or in over-the-counter markets by reviewing and processing registration statements and periodic reports under the applicable securities acts.
- Prescribes and enforces the information to be included in proxy solicitations.
- Administers the disclosure requirements of the federal securities laws.
- Prepares Staff Accounting Bulletins (SABs) in conjunction with the Office of the Chief Accountant.

The Division also (1) drafts the rules, regulations, and forms to be used in filings with the SEC and (2) gives advice and answers inquiries pertaining to the application and interpretation of the statutes and registration and reporting procedures.

Office of the Chief Accountant

The **chief accountant** is the SEC's principal expert adviser on all matters relating to accounting and auditing. The chief accountant

- Carries out SEC policy on accounting principles and the form and content of financial statements filed with it.
- Consults and rules on accounting questions from registrants and independent accountants.

FIGURE 23-1 • ORGANIZATION OF THE SECURITIES AND EXCHANGE COMMISSION

SECURITIES AND EXCHANGE COMMISSION
The Commissioner
The Commissioner
The Chairman
The Commissioner
The Commissioner
The Executive Director
Office of Administrative Law Judges
Office of EDGAR Management
Office of Inspector General
Office of the Secretary
Office of the Chief Accountant
Office of Economic Analysis
Office of the General Counsel
Division of Investment Management
Division of Corporation Finance
Division of Enforcement
Division of International Affairs
Division of Market Regulation
Office of Public Affairs
Office of Filings, Information, and Consumer Services
Office of the Comptroller
Office of Information Systems Management
Office of Administrative Services
Office of Personnel
Atlanta Regional Office
Boston Regional Office
Chicago Regional Office
Denver Regional Office
Fort Worth Regional Office
Los Angeles Regional Office
New York Regional Office
Seattle Regional Office
Philadelphia Regional Office
—— Lines of budget and management authority
- - - Lines of policy and judicial authority

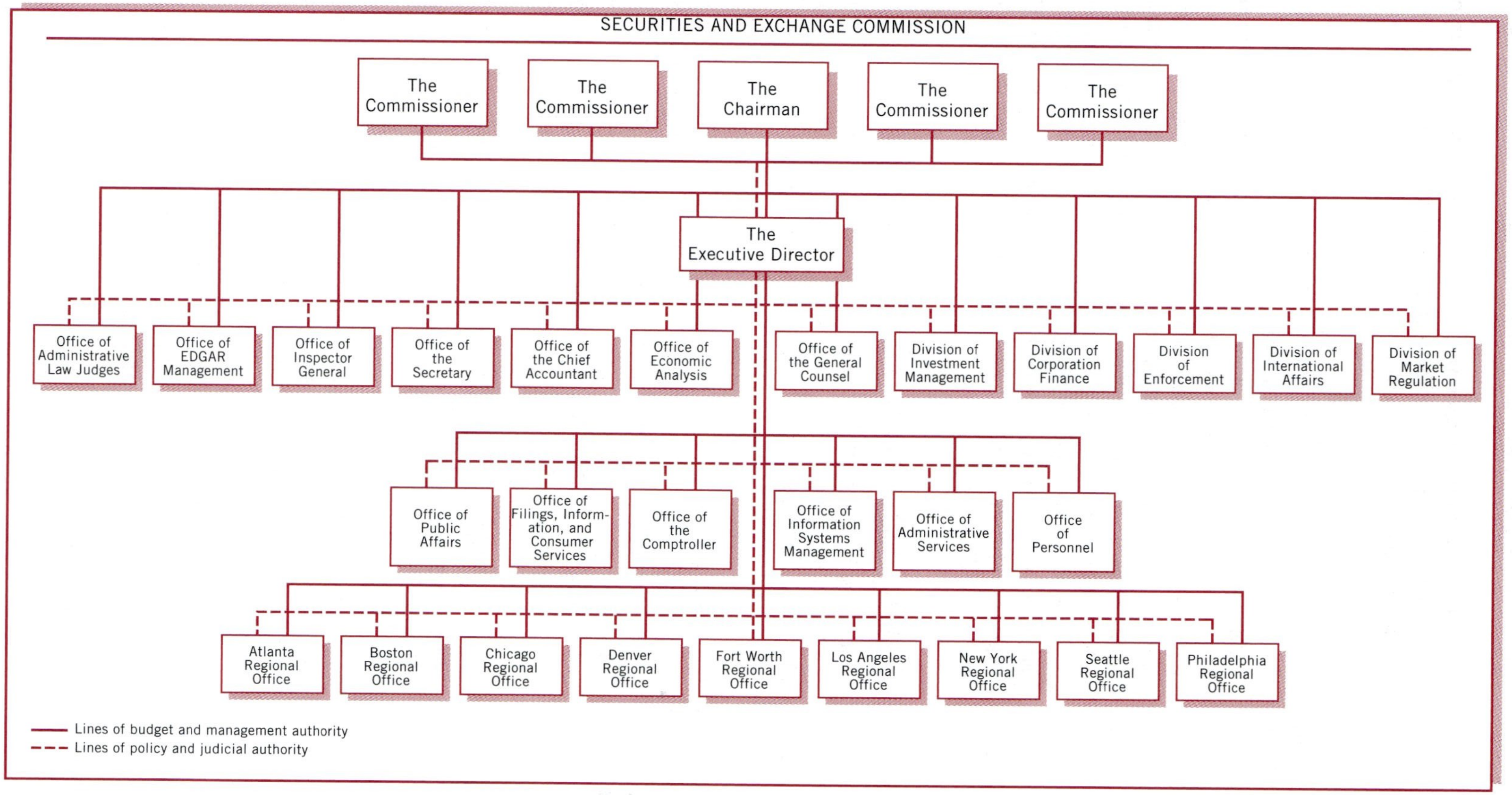

- Directs administrative policy pertaining to accounting and auditing matters.
- Maintains liaison with accounting authorities, professional organizations, independent public accountants, and government officials.
- Participates in administrative and court proceedings involving accounting and auditing matters.
- Recommends to the Commission the taking of disciplinary action against accountants under the SEC's Rules of Practice.
- Considers cases on the independence and qualifications of independent accountants who practice before the SEC.
- Prepares Financial Reporting Releases (FRRs).
- Issues Accounting and Auditing Enforcement Releases (AAERs).
- Issues SABs in conjunction with the Division of Corporation Finance.

The chief accountant is in a position to exert substantial influence on the development of generally accepted accounting principles (GAAP) and generally accepted auditing standards (GAAS). There is no fixed term of office for the chief accountant.

LEARNING CHECK:

23-1 What is the nature and extent of the SEC's authority over the public sale of securities?

23-2 a. Explain the composition of the Commission that heads the SEC.
b. Describe the principal responsibility and primary functions of the Division of Corporation Finance.

23-3 Enumerate the principal duties of the chief accountant.

KEY TERMS:

Chief accountant, p. 878

Division of Corporation Finance, p. 878

REPORTING AND REGISTRATION REQUIREMENTS

The SEC has the authority to prescribe the accounting and reporting requirements for companies under its jurisdiction. Throughout its history, however, the SEC has cooperated with the private sector in the development of GAAP, and it has indicated that it

> Intends to continue its policy of looking to the private sector for leadership in establishing and improving accounting principles and standards through the [Financial Accounting Standards Board] with the expectation that the body's conclusions will promote the interests of investors.[2]

[2] SEC Financial Reporting Release No. 1, Section 1 (1982).

While delegating some of its responsibility for standards setting, the SEC exercises an ongoing oversight role in establishing accounting standards.

SEC OVER-SIGHT OF FASB

In a speech, former SEC Chairman David S. Ruder indicated that:

The Commission engages in active oversight of the FASB. It interacts daily with the FASB. It monitors the development of new standards and then deals with subsequent implementation and interpretation of the standards through ongoing advisory, examination, and enforcement programs.

The SEC's oversight is extensive and covers all aspects of the FASB's activities. The Commission staff discusses issues with the FASB staff, and the two staffs meet regularly to discuss the FASB's agenda, current problems, and other matters of mutual interest. The Commission's staff also actively monitors the structure, activities, and decisions of the FASB. In addition, the FASB meets periodically with the Commission members in open meetings to discuss topical issues.

SOURCE: Remarks before the AICPA Sixteenth National Conference on Current SEC Developments, Washington, D.C., January 10, 1989.

Only infrequently has the SEC deemed it necessary to establish standards or to supplement or amend existing standards.

The SEC's authority also extends to annual reports to shareholders that are issued by corporations, as well as to the periodic reports required under the 1934 Act and registration statements filed under the 1933 Act.

INTEGRATED DISCLOSURE SYSTEM

OBJECTIVE 3

List the components of the standard package of information required under the SEC's integrated disclosure system.

In 1980, the SEC adopted new requirements for reporting financial and other business information by publicly held companies. Known as the **integrated disclosure system,** the requirements provide for a standard package of information consisting of

- Audited consolidated financial statements consisting of balance sheets for the latest two years, and statements of income, retained earnings, and cash flows for the most recent three years.
- A five-year summary of selected financial data.
- A management discussion and analysis of the company's financial condition and results of operations.
- Market price and dividend information on the company's common stock and related security holder matters.

The requirements for this information are basically the same in all SEC forms. To avoid duplication, a company is permitted to **incorporate by reference** information required in one filing that is already contained in another filing. In addition, information required in the SEC's annual report form, Form 10-K, can be incorporated by reference to the company's annual report to shareholders when the latter is enclosed with Form 10-K. The integrated disclosure system has significantly reduced the effort and cost of complying with the SEC's reporting requirements.

The system also requires **continuing reporting** through periodic and special reports that update the company's information included in its original registration statement. The integrated disclosure system is illustrated in Figure 23-2.

In addition to the standard information package, the SEC requires *supplementary financial information* in many filings. This information includes exhibits, schedules, and specialized financial and business data.

The SEC's reporting system is intended to serve both the average and the sophisticated investor. Certain of the disclosures required are intended to meet the needs of the average investor. In addition to being filed with the SEC, these disclosures must also be furnished to all present security holders or to any potential purchasers of the securities, as appropriate. Other disclosures are intended primarily for institutional investors, security analysts, or the sophisticated individual investor. The information is contained in the filing made by a company with the SEC. Generally, all information in filings made with the SEC is considered public information. Copies of any reported data may be obtained from the SEC at nominal cost. The SEC's disclosures are not intended to guarantee the worth or value of any security; rather, it is to provide investors with material financial and other information concerning securities offered for public sale.

For companies required to report to the SEC, the first step is to select the proper form for filing. Although the instructions for each form contain the rule or

FIGURE 23-2 • SEC INTEGRATED DISCLOSURE SYSTEM

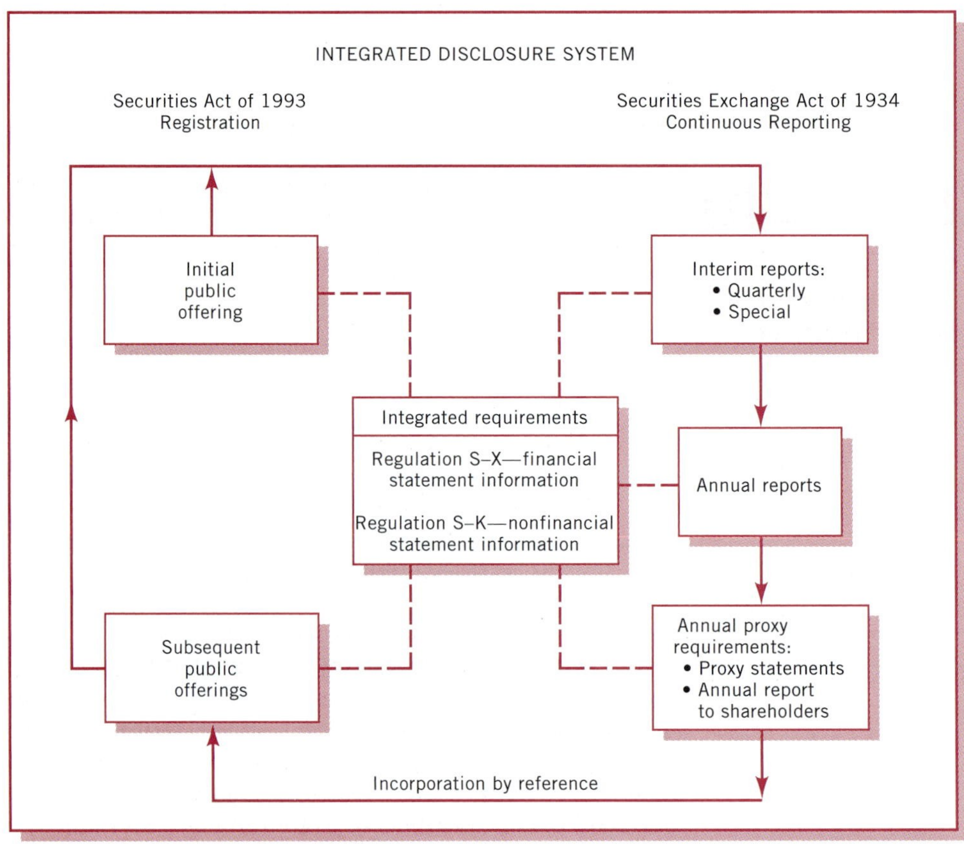

eligibility requirements for its use, it often is necessary for legal counsel to be consulted in making this determination. Once the form has been selected, additional instructions on the form identify the number in the pronouncements of the SEC that specify the business disclosures and financial reporting requirements that are to accompany the filing.

ELECTRONIC DATA GATHERING, ANALYSIS, AND RETRIEVAL SYSTEM

OBJECTIVE 4

Indicate the nature and purpose of EDGAR.

Under this system, commonly known by the acronym **EDGAR,** approximately 2,500 companies began filing documents with the SEC electronically in 1993. Virtually all SEC registrants are scheduled to be phased in to the electronic filing format by 1996, replacing most of the nearly 12 million pages of filings currently submitted to the Commission annually. Electronic filings may be transmitted via modem or submitted on disk or magnetic tape.

Besides facilitating the filing of SEC documents, EDGAR is intended to increase the accessibility of the data to users. In addition to making the electronic data available to the public via terminals in SEC offices in thirteen major U.S. cities, new filings will be published monthly by the U.S. Government Printing office on CD-ROM disks and distributed to the 1,400 libraries that serve as repositories for federal documents including many major university libraries. The Commission is also arranging for the electronic filings to be available from a number of commercial data services, and, on an experimental basis under a National Science Foundation Grant, over the Internet.

TYPES OF ACCOUNTING PRONOUNCEMENTS

OBJECTIVE 5

Identify and describe the major types of SEC accounting-related pronouncements.

Five major types of SEC accounting-related pronouncements to be used by companies and their independent accountants in filings with the agency are explained in the following sections. These are Regulation S–X, Regulation S-K, Regulation S–T, FRRs, and SABs. Nearly all the disclosure requirements under the 1933 and 1934 Acts are contained in these pronouncements.

Regulation S–X

Regulation S–X is the principal accounting regulation of the SEC. It covers the requirements for auditor's independence, audit reports, and financial statements to be filed with the SEC. The instructions specify the required time periods and the form and content of financial statements, including the classification, presentation, and disclosure of material financial statement items. Regulation S–X is subject to amendments in response to changing conditions and the need for additional or less information by investors. Amendments are made by issuing FRRs.

In accordance with the SEC's policy of cooperating with the private sector, Regulation S–X contains an explicit requirement that the financial statements are to be prepared in accordance with generally accepted accounting principles (GAAP). In a few instances, the financial statement disclosure requirements of the Regulation exceed the disclosure requirements under GAAP. These additional regulatory requirements are referred to as **compliance notes.**

Regulation S–K

Regulation S–K is referred to as the uniform disclosure regulation. It covers the disclosure requirements for nonfinancial statement or text information required under the Acts in the same manner that Regulation S–X prescribes the requirements for financial statements.

The Regulation has nine major sections. Some of the sections include instructions regarding disclosures about the company's business, securities, management, and financial information other than the financial statements. Another section covers the information to be provided about the securities being sold. The final section lists the SEC-prepared industry guides to be used by companies operating in specialized areas, such as those with oil and gas operations, bank holding companies, real estate limited partnerships, and insurance companies.

The particular items of Regulation S–K that are to be included in filings are indicated by the instructions accompanying the form to be filed. Inclusion of an item of information as prescribed under Regulation S–K is required only to the extent that the form governing a particular document specifically directs the inclusion of such information.

Regulation S–T

Adopted in February 1993, **Regulation S–T** governs the phased-in mandated electronic filing of documents under **EDGAR.** It addresses issues such as gaining access to the system, timing the transmissions, electronic filing of exhibits and financial data schedules, handling graphical and image materials, handling annual reports to stockholders, paying and filing registration fees, handling signature requirements, and exemptions.

To assist filers, the Commission also provides an *EDGAR Filing Manual*, *EDGARlink* software, a technical assistance hotline, and an EDGAR electronic mail and bulletin board service.

Financial Reporting Releases (FRRs)

To amend the existing rules or regulations or to issue new ones, the Commission issues **Financial Reporting Releases (FRRs).** Prior to 1982, changes in accounting-related matters were issued as Accounting Series Releases (ASRs). In 1982, the ASRs that were considered relevant were recompiled as a *Codification of Financial Reporting Policies* and issued as FRR No. 1. FRRs contain the Commission's current positions on accounting and auditing matters related to financial reporting and are the means by which the *Codification* and Regulation S–X are updated. These releases include

- New disclosure requirements or specified accounting treatment for certain types of transactions.
- Opinions of the Commission on major accounting issues.
- Amendments to the financial statement requirements.
- Clarification of existing rules and regulations, such as the rule on independence.

Releases on accounting and auditing matters are usually issued initially as proposals, and copies are available to various professional and other interested groups for their criticism and suggestions. Individuals and firms may also submit their views on proposals. Experience demonstrates that the SEC carefully considers comments on the proposals before adopting any changes.

Staff Accounting Bulletins (SABs)

The Division of Corporation Finance and the Office of the Chief Accountant have the authority to issue **Staff Accounting Bulletins (SABs)**.[3] They are issued to provide guidance for handling events and transactions with similar accounting implications.

SABs are not rules or interpretations of the Commission, and they are not published as bearing the Commission's official approval. However, they are generally regarded as "interpretations" of Regulation S–X and GAAP. When a registrant and its independent accountant believe that due to its peculiar circumstances, the appropriate accounting should be different than would result from following the practice expressed in an SAB, the registrant is encouraged to discuss the specifics with the staff.

QUALIFICATIONS OF INDEPENDENT ACCOUNTANTS

Regulation S–X, Rule 2-01, prescribes the qualifications of accountants as follows:

OBJECTIVE 6

State the SEC's qualifications for independent accountants and requirements for accountant's reports.

(a) The Commission will not recognize any person as a certified public accountant who is not duly registered and in good standing as such under the laws of the place of his residence or principal office. The Commission will not recognize any person as a public accountant who is not in good standing and entitled to practice as such under the laws of the place of his residence or principal office.

(b) The Commission will not recognize any certified public accountant or public accountant as independent who is not in fact independent.

(c) In determining whether an accountant may in fact be not independent with respect to a particular person, the Commission will give appropriate consideration to all relevant circumstances, including evidence bearing on all relationships between the accountant and that person or any affiliate thereof, and will not confine itself to the relationships existing in connection with the filing of reports with the Commission.

The SEC rules on independence closely parallel the AICPA's Rules of Conduct on independence (Rule 101), but there are exceptions. For example, the SEC will not consider an accountant independent if he or she provides any bookkeeping services to an audit client. The SEC believes that such services automatically impair the accountant's independence, whereas the American Institute of Certified Public Accountants (AICPA) permits the rendering of bookkeeping services to an audit client.

[3] In 1981, the SEC codified all relevant SABs in *Staff Accounting Bulletin No. 40.*

The Commission offers informal guidance relating to matters concerning the independence of accountants. This is accomplished by publishing the text of letters of inquiry received by the Office of the Chief Accountant, together with the response provided by the chief accountant's staff. As with other unofficial guidance, the staff's responses are not necessarily binding on the Commission.

REQUIREMENTS FOR ACCOUNTANTS' REPORTS

Regulation S–X, Rule 2-02, sets forth the standards of reporting for accountants' reports. The requirements are as follows:

(a) **Technical requirements.** The accountant's report (1) shall be dated; (2) shall be signed manually; (3) shall indicate the city and state where issued; and (4) shall identify without detailed enumeration the financial statements covered by the report.

(b) **Representations as to the audit.** The accountant's report (1) shall state whether the audit was made in accordance with generally accepted auditing standards; and (2) shall designate any auditing procedures deemed necessary by the accountant under the circumstances of the particular case, which have been omitted, and the reasons for their omission.

Nothing in this rule shall be construed to imply authority for the omission of any procedure which independent accountants would ordinarily employ in the course of an audit made for the purpose of expressing the opinions required by paragraph (c) of this rule.

(c) **Opinion to be expressed.** The accountant's report shall state clearly: (1) the opinion of the accountant in respect of the financial statements covered by the report and the accounting principles and practices reflected therein; and (2) the opinion of the accountant as to the consistency of the application of the accounting principles, or as to any changes in such principles which have a material effect on the financial statements.

(d) **Exceptions.** Any matters to which the accountant takes exception shall be clearly identified, the exception thereto specifically and clearly stated, and, to the extent practicable, the effect of each such exception on the related financial statements given. (See Section 101 of Codification of Financial Reporting Policies.)

From the foregoing, it can be seen that the responsibility of the independent accountant resulting from the inclusion of the report on financial statements in a filing under the securities acts is, in substance, essentially the same as that involved in reporting on audited financial statements as explained in Chapter 20 of this text.

Pursuant to Rule 2-02, the SEC will not accept (1) an adverse opinion or (2) a qualified opinion on audited financial statements when there is nonconformity with GAAP. When there is doubt about the entity's ability to continue as a going concern, there should be full and fair disclosure of the registrant's financial difficulties and plans to overcome them. However, if the financial statements are prepared on a going concern basis but a liquidation basis would be more appropriate, FRR No. 16 states that the financials will be considered false and misleading.

As in the case of financial statements used for other purposes, management is responsible for the assertions made in financial statements filed under the federal securities statutes.

REGISTRATION OF SECURITIES

OBJECTIVE 7

Understand the purpose and process of registering securities.

Registration is a major part of all the acts administered by the SEC. The primary purpose of registration is to provide prospective investors with financial and other information concerning the company and its securities being offered for public sale. The reporting standard in a registration statement is disclosure of all material facts needed by investors to appraise the merits of the securities.

Registration does not insure investors against loss in their purchases nor does it guarantee the accuracy of all the information presented. As stated earlier, the SEC does not pass on the merits of the securities. Moreover, it has no authority to disapprove a registration because securities lack merit. The Commission has the power to deny registration when disclosures are incomplete, inaccurate, or misleading. In addition, the federal securities acts prohibit false and misleading information under penalty of fine, or imprisonment, or both.

All data contained in a registration are kept by the SEC and are available to the general public. Securities cannot be sold until the registration is accepted by the SEC and the registration becomes effective.

Registration is a time-consuming, complex, and expensive undertaking. This is especially true the first time a privately owned company decides to "go public" with its equity securities. In a recent year, expenses for large offerings averaged $617,000, with $300,000 earmarked for legal and accounting fees.[4] To reduce the cost of raising capital for small businesses, in 1992 the SEC eliminated audit requirements for initial public offerings of less than $5 million and loosened its accounting rules for smaller registrants whose revenues and equity on the market are each less than $25 million. The special regulations and forms pertaining to these registrations are beyond the scope of this chapter.

Review of Registration Statements

The SEC's review process is designed to ascertain compliance with the securities laws or, conversely, to detect materially untrue, incomplete, or misleading information in the filing of registration statements. Reviews are made by the Division of Corporation Finance.

A review may be complete or limited, based on an initial evaluation of the registration by the staff. The SEC's practice is to do a complete review of only certain filings, including

- Initial public offerings under the Securities Act of 1933.
- Initial registration statements under the Securities Exchange Act of 1934.

Other filings may be reviewed only on a sample basis. In some instances, registration statements of established companies may be allowed to become effective with no staff review.

In the case of a complete review, the examination of the registration statement is made by a team consisting of a financial analyst, an attorney, and an accountant. Memoranda are submitted by each reviewer, which culminate in a **letter of comments** (generally known as a **deficiency letter**) that is sent to the registrant for required amendments to the registration statement and other appropriate action.

---

[4] "SEC Loosens Audit Rules for Small Businesses," *Public Accounting Report* (August 15, 1992), p. 3.

If the prospective registrant is unwilling or unable to eliminate the deficiencies in its original filing, the SEC has three courses of action.

- *Allow the deficient financial statements to become effective.* This is rarely done because it is contrary to the SEC's objective of protecting the investor and it exposes the issuing company to possible lawsuits.
- *Issue a refusal order.* This action has been used sparingly because the order must be issued within ten days of the filing and a hearing must be held during the next ten days to allow for correction.
- *Issue a stop order.* This action halts further consideration of the registration statement if issued before the effective date. Alternatively, it halts further trading of the security if it is issued after the effective date.

These actions ordinarily are not needed because most companies act promptly to correct any deficiencies in the filing.

Registration Process

The registration process involves a number of participants, including the board of directors, representatives of management (usually the president and/or vice president of finance), legal counsel, a lead underwriter (i.e., an investment brokerage firm that assumes responsibility for selling the securities), the independent accountant, and company accountants.

Once a decision to raise capital by issuing securities has been made, management has the responsibility of providing the necessary information to complete the registration statement. Management also is responsible for selecting the underwriter, outside legal counsel, and independent accountant. An illustrative timetable and specific steps in the registration process are presented in Figure 23-3. The example assumes an issue of common stock by a company that has a fiscal year ending December 31. The foregoing are specifically applicable to the 1933 Act but also have general applicability to registrations under other acts.

LEARNING CHECK:

23-4 a. Identify the components of the standard package of information required in the integrated disclosure system.
b. What is meant by (1) incorporate by reference and (2) continuing reporting?
c. What is EDGAR?

23-5 Identify and briefly describe the types of authoritative pronouncements issued by the SEC and the specific types of information included in each.

23-6 Briefly describe the SEC's rules concerning (a) qualifications of independent accountants and (b) accountant's reports.

23-7 The registration of securities is designed to insure investors against loss. Do you agree or disagree? Why?

23-8 a. Describe the complete review that is made of a registration statement.
b. Indicate the courses of action the SEC may take when an original filing is deficient.

FIGURE 23-3 • REGISTRATION PROCESS TIMETABLE

June 1	Board of directors authorizes filing of registration statement and notifies independent auditors, lawyers, and underwriter(s) of the pending filing.
June 5	Management meets with underwriters, and tentative agreement is reached concerning sale of securities.
June 15	Management, independent accountant, and legal counsel have prefiling conference with SEC staff in Washington, D.C.
June 20	Management and legal counsel select appropriate registration form.
June 25–July 25	Data for registration are collected by company accountants, reviewed by lawyers, and reviewed and/or audited by independent accountants.
July 28	Management prepares draft of registration statement and obtains board of directors' approval.
August 1	Management finalizes registration statement, which is filed with SEC by legal counsel.
August 25	Management receives letter of comment from SEC concerning deficiencies and necessary adjustments.
September 5	Management prepares amendments that are responsive to SEC's comments—these are filed with SEC by legal counsel.
September 7	Due diligence meeting is held to review registration statement and other matters affecting sale of issue—this meeting is primarily for the benefit of the underwriter(s) and is attended by management, legal counsel, the independent accountant, and underwriter(s).
September 10	SEC notifies management by phone of acceptance of registration statement.
September 11	Management approves offering price of securities and the agreement with underwriter(s) for sale of the stock is finalized.
September 12	Legal counsel files amendment to registration statement for offering price—registration statement becomes effective 5:00 P.M.
September 17	Underwriter transfers net proceeds of issue to issuer.

23-9 Identify the steps in the registration process that occur after the registration statement is filed with the Commission.

KEY TERMS:

Compliance notes, p. 883
Continuing reporting, p. 882
Deficiency letter, p. 887
EDGAR, p. 883
Financial Reporting Releases, p. 884
Incorporate by reference, p. 881
Integrated disclosure system, p. 881
Letter of comments, p. 887
Regulation S–K, p. 884
Regulation S–X, p. 883
Regulation S–T, p. 884
Staff Accounting Bulletins (SABs), p. 885

OBJECTIVE 8

Explain the independent accountant's primary responsibilities in filings under the Securities Act of 1933.

SECURITIES ACT OF 1933

The **Securities Act of 1933** pertains to the initial offer and distribution of securities to the public. Often referred to as the *truth in securities* law, the Act has two basic objectives:

- To provide investors with material financial and other information concerning the company whose securities are offered for public sale.

- To prohibit misrepresentation, deceit, and other fraudulent acts and practices in the sale of securities generally (whether or not required to be registered).[5]

The 1933 Act does not require that all securities for public sale be registered. The exceptions are divided into two main categories: (1) exempt securities and (2) exempt transactions. The former include securities offered by banks and savings and loan companies, charitable institutions, governmental instrumentalities, and common carriers. The latter include public offerings of less than $5 million, qualified private offerings, and offerings restricted to residents of the state in which the issuing company is organized and doing business. Such offerings, though exempt from registration, may nonetheless be subject to certain SEC disclosure requirements and other regulations.

REGISTRATION UNDER THE 1933 ACT

Registration under the 1933 Act consists of preparing and filing a **registration statement** with the SEC. The registration statement consists of two parts: a prospectus and other detailed information.

A **prospectus** is a separate booklet, given to prospective purchasers of the security, that describes the company and the securities offered. The prospectus includes or incorporates by reference all information to be presented to prospective investors. Part II of the registration statement contains ancillary information, including expenses of issuance and distribution, indemnification of directors and officers, and certain exhibits and financial statement schedules. Part II is required to be filed only with the SEC, although the information is available to interested investors on request.

There are three primary forms used by most companies in filings under the 1933 Act. The choice of form depends on the size of the company and the period of time it has been subject to the SEC's periodic reporting requirements.

- *Form S–3* is an abbreviated filing that incorporates by reference information that is available in previous reports filed with the SEC. It is intended for use by large companies that are widely followed by financial analysts.
- *Form S–2* is designed for use by companies that have been subject to the periodic reporting requirements of the SEC for at least three years, but are not as widely followed by analysts. An S–2 filing may include only the information required for an S–3 filing if the company delivers its latest annual report to all potential investors. If the annual report is not included, then this information must be in the filing. Financial information for the most recent quarter and for interim periods also must be provided.
- *Form S–1* is used by companies that do not fit other categories.

Form S–1 is the most widely used under this Act. The principal financial information requirements under this form are explained below.

---

[5] Securities and Exchange Commission, *The Work of the Securities and Exchange Commission* (Washington, D.C.: U.S. Government Printing Office, 1974), p. 1.

Business Disclosures

Form S–1 requires disclosure of a considerable amount of information about the company and its business. These disclosures, which are described in Regulation S–K, include items such as the following:

- History and description of the business (including industry segments and foreign operations).
- Description of properties.
- Background information about directors and executive officers, including their security holdings, compensation, and material pending legal proceedings to which management is a party.
- Description of the securities being registered, including details of any underwriting arrangements, an estimate of the net proceeds, and the uses to which such proceeds will be put.

Financial Statements

Financial statements must be presented for the issuing company in one of the following forms:

- Financial statements for the company itself, if it has no subsidiaries that must be consolidated.
- Consolidated financial statements only, unless it is necessary to include "separate parent company" statements on a supplemental schedule.

In addition, under some circumstances, the issuer may have to present financial statements for (1) unconsolidated subsidiaries and 50% or less owned companies accounted for under the equity method, (2) affiliated companies whose securities are pledged as collateral for debt securities that are being registered, and (3) companies acquired or to be acquired.

BALANCE SHEETS. Audited balance sheets must be filed as of the end of each of the two preceding fiscal years. In addition, the general rule is that the filing must include a balance sheet as of an interim date within 135 days of the date of the filing if the most recent audited balance sheet does not fall within this period. The interim balance sheet may be in condensed form and need not be audited.

OTHER STATEMENTS. An income statement must be filed for each of the three fiscal years preceding the date of the latest fiscal year-end balance sheet filed, and for the period, if any, between the close of the latest fiscal year and the date of the latest balance sheet filed. The statements of cash flows and changes in stockholders' equity must be filed for the same periods as the income statement. All statements relating to the three fiscal years must be audited; comparative statements covering the period from the latest fiscal year to the date of the latest balance sheet may be in condensed form and need not be audited.

Selected Financial Data

Form S–1 requires a five-year summary of selected financial data. This requirement is intended to present significant trend data relating both to an enterprise's financial condition and its results of operations. The selected financial data are not required to be audited and usually are not encompassed within the auditor's report.

Elements from the company's balance sheet and income statement that must be presented include the following:

- Net sales or operating revenues.
- Income (loss) from continuing operations.
- Income (loss) from continuing operations per common share.
- Total assets.
- Long-term obligations (including capital leases) and redeemable preferred stock.
- Cash dividends declared per common share.

Figure 23-4 shows a five-year summary of selected financial data. A discussion of the factors that materially affect the comparability of the selected financial data also should be included.

Management's Discussion and Analysis (MD & A)

Management's discussion and analysis (MD & A) is intended to provide a meaningful analysis of significant changes in financial condition and results of

FIGURE 23-4 • FIVE-YEAR SUMMARY OF SELECTED FINANCIAL DATA

County Lake Foods, Inc.
Excerpts from Five-Year Summary of Selected Financial Data

	Years Ended December 31				
	Historical				
	19X3	**19X4**	**19X5**	**19X6**	**19X7**
Statement of Earnings Data					
	(In thousands, except per share data)				
Net sales	$138,587	$134,447	$137,223	$140,781	$147,513
Cost of sales	117,472	111,177	110,931	112,575	117,586
Selling, general and administrative	23,242	19,983	22,184	22,634	23,525
Income (loss) from operations	(2,127)	3,287	4,108	5,572	6,402
Interest expense	1,857	2,142	1,850	1,438	1,167
Interest income	127	239	327	231	174
Earnings (loss) before income taxes and extraordinary item	(3,857)	1,384	2,585	4,365	5,409
Provision (benefit) for income taxes	(378)	266	178	1,306	1,886
Extraordinary item	—	374	—	—	—
Net earnings (loss)	(3,479)	1,492	2,407	3,059	3,523
Balance Sheet Data (End of Period)					
Current assets	$ 14,822	$ 15,072	$ 14,158	$ 15,172	$ 15,679
Total assets	28,687	28,288	27,548	28,623	32,156
Notes payable	—	—	—	—	8,900
Total liabilities	27,682	26,698	25,053	24,676	22,995
Stockholders' equity	1,005	1,590	2,495	3,947	9,161

operations. The discussion must cover the three years presented in the audited financial statements and the statements for any interim period. When trends are discussed, reference may be made to the five years of selected financial data or to more extensive detail in the income statements, as appropriate. The discussion must include at least the following aspects of the business.

- The company's liquidity, capital resources, and results of operations.
- Favorable or unfavorable trends, significant uncertainties, and unusual or infrequent events and their possible effects.
- Causes of material changes in the financial statements.
- Narrative discussion of the effects of inflation, if material.

The discussion of liquidity and capital resources should deal with available sources of funds and the company's expected short- and long-term requirements. Trend information on cash flows from operations may be included, together with plans to deal with any insufficiency of funds from internal sources or changed circumstances. In 1989, the SEC issued FRR 36, *Management's Discussion and Analysis of Financial Condition and Results of Operations,* to provide guidance for registrants in meeting MD & A regulations.

DEFICIENCIES IN MD & A DISCLOSURES

In its formal enforcement actions, the SEC has been quick to cite deficiencies in MD & A disclosures. For example, the SEC concluded that the Burroughs Corporation omitted material information about the increase in work-in-process inventory in excess of 30 months' demand and the increase in amount of unreserved finished goods inventory more than two years old. The SEC argued that in the computer industry, where change is rapid, this information was important to shareholders and investors.

SOURCE: Richard Dieter and Keith Sandefur, "Spotlight on Management's Discussion and Analysis," *Journal of Accountancy* (December 1989), p. 66.

At its option, the company also may include forward-looking information. This may be the form of formal financial forecasts or simply commentary on known future events (e.g., a new union contract) that may be useful to those who wish to work out a forecast of future operating results.

INDEPENDENT ACCOUNTANT'S INVOLVEMENT IN REGISTRATIONS

The independent accountant is an active participant in the registration process. The accountant's major responsibilities are to

- Audit the financial statements in accordance with GAAS.
- Read any unaudited condensed financial statements included therein for matters that might require disclosure in the audited financial statements.

- Read the entire registration statement for data that may be materially inconsistent with the financial statements or be a material misstatement of fact.
- Perform a subsequent events review up to the effective date of the registration statement.
- Issue a comfort letter to underwriters.

The accountant advises the company on the SEC's reporting and disclosure requirements that are in addition to those required by generally accepted accounting principles; arranges for a prefiling conference with the SEC, if necessary, to resolve accounting or reporting problems; and advises the company's legal counsel on the financial portions of the registration statement. The accountant may also draft responses to deficiency letters, if any, received from the SEC staff.

Audited Financial Statements

The audit of the financial statements included in a registration is the same as the audit of any financial statements prepared in conformity with GAAP. Accordingly, the ten GAAS and the audit procedures described in previous chapters of this book are applicable.

Unaudited Financial Statements

When unaudited financial statements for an interim period are included with audited financial statements, the independent accountant who performed the audit is associated with the unaudited statements. The independent accountant's responsibilities for the interim statements are basically the same as described in Chapter 21 for other unaudited financial statements. However, in an SEC registration, SAS 37, *Filings Under Federal Securities Statutes* (AU 711.13), states that the accountant should consider withholding consent to the use of a report on audited financial statements if the client is unwilling to make any revisions known to be necessary to make the unaudited statements conform with GAAP.

Other Data

The independent accountant is required to read the nonfinancial statement data in the prospectus and the other detailed information in the registration statement. The independent accountant is not expected to perform any auditing procedures on the data. The primary objective is to determine whether there are any material inconsistencies or statements in the text that contradict data relied on in preparing the financial statements included in the registration. When such instances are found, the independent accountant should see that appropriate revision is made.

Subsequent Events Review

The independent accountant's statutory liability under the 1933 Act extends to the circumstances existing as of the effective date of the registration statement. Specifically, the accountant is required by Section 11(b) to make a "reasonable investigation" and have "reasonable grounds" as to the fairness of the financial statements included in a registration up to the effective date of the filing. To provide proof of a "reasonable investigation," the accountant should extend the subsequent events procedures described in Chapter 19 up to the effective date or as close thereto as possible.

In addition, the accountant should

- Read the entire prospectus and other pertinent parts of the registration statement.
- Inquire of and obtain written confirmation from officers and other executives having responsibility for financial and accounting matters (limited when appropriate to major locations) as to whether there have occurred any events other than those reflected or disclosed in the registration statement that, in the officers' or other executives' opinion, have a material effect on the audited financial statements included therein or that should be disclosed to keep those statements from being misleading.

The performance of these procedures is facilitated when the client keeps the accountant informed during the progress of the registration proceedings. The subsequent events review described above is referred to as an **S–1 review.** This is not an accurate description, as the same review applies to other registration forms under the 1933 Act. This review was one of the key issues in the *BarChris* case discussed in Chapter 4. In the registration schedule shown in Figure 23-3, the S–1 review, would extend from the date of the audit report through September 12, the effective date of the registration statement.

Letters for Underwriters and Certain Others

As indicated earlier in the chapter, an underwriting agreement is common in the issuance of securities under the securities acts. This agreement is a contract between the underwriters and the issuer of the securities. Typically, the provisions of an underwriting agreement provide for a **comfort letter** from an independent accountant. The letter is so named because it is designed to give comfort (assurance) to the underwriters on the financial and accounting data included in a prospectus that are not covered by the independent accountant's opinion on the audited financial statements. Underwriters seek this comfort in the form of negative assurance as a due diligence (or reasonable investigation) defense against possible legal claims under the Act. Accountants may also provide comfort letters to broker–dealers or other financial intermediaries who act as principals or agents in offerings or placements of securities, and in connection with acquisition or merger transactions in which there is an exchange of stock and such letters are requested by the buyer or seller.

Comfort letters are not required under the 1933 Act, and copies of such letters are not filed with the SEC. The rendering of this type of letter should be based on an agreement between the underwriter or other party and the independent accountant. A comfort letter involves a limited review by the independent accountant based on procedures specified by the underwriter or other party and agreed upon by the accountant. The underwriter or other party takes responsibility for the adequacy of the procedures performed for its purposes.

SAS 72, *Letters for Underwriters and Certain Other Requesting Parties* (AU 634.21), identifies the following subjects that may be addressed in a comfort letter:

- The independence of the accountants.
- Whether the audited financial statements and schedules included in a registration statement comply as to form in all material respects with the applicable accounting requirements of the Act and the related published rules and regulations.
- Unaudited financial statements, condensed interim financial information, capsule financial information, pro forma financial information, financial forecasts, and changes in selected financial statement items during a period subsequent to the date and period of the latest financial statements included in the registration statement.
- Tables, statistics, and other financial information included in the registration statement.
- Negative assurance as to whether certain nonfinancial statement information included in the registration statement complies as to form in all material respects with Regulation S–K.

The accountant should be able to express an opinion on compliance of the data referred to in the second subject listed above based on the audit of that data. However, the CPA's comments on the other items should generally be in the form of negative assurance. Except for the procedures performed in an SAS 71 review of interim financial statements, the agreed-upon procedures performed on these items should be enumerated in the comfort letter. In addition, the letter should state that the procedures do not constitute an audit made in accordance with GAAS, that they would not necessarily reveal matters of significance regarding items on which negative assurance is given, and that the accountant makes no representations regarding the sufficiency of the procedures for the addressees' purposes.

The comfort letter should conclude with the caveat that it is solely for the use of the addressees and to assist the underwriter in connection with a specified security offering under the Act, and that it is not to be used, circulated, quoted, or otherwise referred to, for any other purpose. Illustrative comfort letters are shown in AU 634.63.

ACCOUNTANT'S REPORT

The 1933 Act imposes a variety of reporting requirements on the independent accountant when he or she is associated with a registration statement. The major circumstances are explained below.

Report on Financial Statements

The accountant's report on the audited financial statements included in a registration statement is, for all practical purposes, identical with the auditor's standard report described in Chapter 20. The report must cover the two years of balance sheets and the three years of statements of income and cash flows that are included. In addition, the accountant reports on certain supporting schedules.

Accountant's Consent

Section 7 of the 1933 Act provides that "if any accountant is named as having prepared or certified any part of the registration . . . the written consent of such

FIGURE 23-5 • ACCOUNTANT'S CONSENT

To the Board of Directors of Illustrative Company:

We consent to the reference to our firm under the captions "Selected Financial Data" and "Experts" and to the use of our reports dated ______________ in the Registration Statement (Form S-1) and related Prospectus of the Illustrative Company in the registration of 1,000,000 shares of its common stock.

____

CPA's Signature

person shall be filed with the registration." In addition, Section 11 of the Act requires consent to the use of the accountant's name as an expert. These requirements are met by issuing an **accountant's consent,** as illustrated in Figure 23-5.

If the accountant has reported on unaudited financial information included in a registration statement, a *letter of acknowledgment* must be included. Although the accountant does not have responsibility for a report on unaudited information within the meaning of Section 11 of the 1933 Act, the SEC nevertheless requests that the accountant acknowledge awareness of the use of such a report in a separate letter included in the filing.

LEARNING CHECK:

23-10 a. What are the two basic objectives of the Securities Act of 1933?
b. Distinguish between a registration statement and a prospectus.

23-11 Enumerate the basic information that is common to registrations under the 1933 Act.

23-12 Describe the basic types of financial data required under the 1933 Act, including the time period covered and whether the data must be audited.

23-13 Identify the major responsibilities of the accountant in a 1933 Act registration.

23-14 a. What is an S–1 Review?
b. List the specific steps required in making an S–1 Review.

23-15 a. What procedures are generally required in a comfort letter engagement?
b. Indicate the items included in a comfort letter.

KEY TERMS:

Accountant's consent, p. 897
Comfort letter, p. 895
Form S–1, p. 890
Management's discussion and analysis (MD&A), p. 892
Prospectus, p. 890
Registration statement, p. 890
S–1 review, p. 895
Securities Act of 1933, p. 889

SECURITIES EXCHANGE ACT OF 1934

The **Securities Exchange Act of 1934** is known as the **continuous disclosure act.** It provides for both the registration of securities and the filing of annual and other periodic reports to keep current the data in the original filing. This Act originally

OBJECTIVE 9

Explain the independent accountant's primary responsibilities in filings under the Securities Exchange Act of 1934.

applied to the public trading of securities on national securities exchanges. Through the enactment of a subsequent amendment to the securities acts, the provisions of the 1934 Act also apply to equity securities of companies traded over-the-counter when company assets exceed $5 million and shareholders number 500 or more. In general, transactions in securities that are consummated other than on a national exchange are said to be traded over-the-counter.

The scope of the 1934 Act extends to other matters as well. One example is a **proxy statement,** which contains information about all matters to be voted on at the next meeting of stockholders. A *proxy* is the authorization given by a shareholder to another person allowing that person to vote the stockholder's shares of stock in a corporate meeting. The proxy rules require that certain information be furnished to shareholders before shareholders may authorize another individual to vote on their behalf. Other matters covered by the 1934 Act include tender-offer solicitations, insider trading, margin trading, and other matters that are beyond the scope of this chapter.

REGISTRATION UNDER THE 1934 ACT

Before trading can occur on a national securities exchange, companies must file a registration application with both the exchange and the SEC. A similar registration form must be filed with the SEC for over-the-counter trading when the foregoing size test is met. The financial and other data prescribed under a 1934 Act registration generally are identical with that required in a 1933 Act registration. However, there is no provision for the dissemination of the registration statement to investors through a prospectus or similar medium. Instead, the information is available for public inspection at the offices of the SEC and the exchanges and from various data services.

Under the 1934 Act, an either class of securities can be registered for trading at one time with no amount specified. Thus, the number of registrations is significantly fewer under this Act than under the 1933 Act. A variety of registration forms are prescribed under the Act. Form 10 (not to be confused with annual reporting Form 10–K, which is discussed later) is the most commonly used form. It is required when no other form applies.

Information to be filed in a listing application with an exchange may differ from SEC requirements. The New York Stock Exchange (NYSE), for example, requires a ten-year earnings summary. The requirements of an exchange are not a substitute for the SEC requirements or vice versa. The involvement of the independent accountant in the registration process under the 1934 Act is similar to the involvement in 1933 Act registrations.

ANNUAL REPORTING

Rule 12b–23 of the 1934 Act provides for continuous reporting by the registrant of "adequate and accurate disclosure of material facts" to investors because the securities may be actively traded for many years. The foregoing disclosure requirement is met through annual, quarterly, and special reports.

Form 10–K is the general report form to be used by companies when no other report form is authorized or prescribed. The purpose of a Form 10–K filing is to provide an annual update of the data included in the registration statement. The information in Form 10–K is organized in four parts:

Part I. Description of the business, properties, legal proceedings, and matters voted on by security holders during the fourth quarter.
Part II. Financial statements and supplementary data, selected financial data, management's discussion and analysis, certain information about the market for the company's stock and related stockholder matters, and disagreements on accounting and financial disclosures.
Part III. Information about the directors and executive officers of the company, executive compensation, certain relationships and related transactions, and security ownership of certain beneficial owners and management.
Part IV. Exhibits, financial statement schedules, and other data.

The requirements for audited financial statements, selected financial data, and management's discussion and analysis are the same as those described under 1933 Act filings.

The SEC's regulations further prescribe that certain of the information in Form 10–K must be included in the annual report issued by the corporation to its shareholders. By requiring that only certain information on Form 10–K be provided directly to stockholders, the SEC is recognizing that not all financial statement users are interested in the detailed information that is provided.

Examples of information that might be included in the Form 10–K annual report but not in the annual report to stockholders include

- Remuneration of directors and officers.
- Indemnification arrangements for directors and officers.
- Principal holders of equity securities and holdings by directors and officers.
- Interest of management in certain transactions.

Some corporations voluntarily include all Form 10–K information in their annual reports. When this is not done, there must be a statement in the annual report that a copy of Form 10–K is available, without charge, to any shareholder on request.

Conversely, all information in an annual report to shareholders may not be required in a Form 10–K report. Examples of information that may voluntarily be included in the annual report provided by the company to its shareholders include

- Financial charts (bar graphs, pie charts, etc.).
- Ratio analysis of operations and financial position.
- Ten-year summary of financial data.
- Analysis of operations and future prospects in president's letter.

The time constraints on the filing of Form 10–K often are demanding on both the company and the independent accountant. Parts of Form 10–K must be filed with the SEC within 90 days of the company's year-end. The remaining information may be filed separately and is due within 120 days.

QUARTERLY REPORTING

A registrant under the 1934 Act is required to keep investors and other interested parties informed of interim changes in its operations and financial position by submitting quarterly reports to the SEC. **Form 10–Q** serves to update the most recent 10–K information for events during the current year. A company must file the 10–Q within 45 days after the end of each of the first three quarters of the fiscal year. Form 10–Q contains two major accounting requirements: (1) interim financial information (IFI) and (2) an accountant's letter on the preferability of changes in accounting principles.

Interim Financial Information

Form 10–Q requires condensed financial statements, management's discussion and analysis of financial condition and results of operations, and certain other information. The IFI is to be prepared in accordance with GAAP applied on a consistent basis.

The financial statement requirements for the Form 10–Q include (1) condensed balance sheets at the end of the most recent quarter and preceding fiscal year and (2) condensed statements of income and cash flows for specified interim periods. Disclosures for condensed interim statements must be adequate, within the context of the most recent audited financial statements, to prevent them from being misleading. Management's discussion and analysis should include material changes and give special attention to liquidity, capital resources, and operating results.

The SEC does not require that IFI be either audited or reviewed by an independent accountant. However, companies that meet certain trading and size tests must show quarterly revenues, gross profit, net income, and earnings per share data as supplemental information in the annual financial statements. The supplemental information must be reviewed by the independent accountant. For these companies, the question is whether to have quarterly reviews or to have only an annual review of interim financial information. Many companies elect the former to avoid year-end embarrassment or potentially more serious consequences if changes in quarterly data are needed. When a review has been made of IFI, the accountant's report may be included as an exhibit to the filing.

Changes in Accounting Principles

Registrants must report any change in accounting principles or practices or changes in the method of applying them that will materially affect the financial statements filed or to be filed in the current year. This requirement must be met in the first Form 10–Q filed subsequent to the date of the accounting change.

Regardless of whether the independent accountant has reviewed interim financial information in a Form 10–Q filing, Regulation S–X requires

> [I]n the first Form 10–Q filed subsequent to the date of an accounting change, a letter from the registrant's independent accountants indicating whether any change . . . is to an alternative principle that in his judgment is preferable in the circumstances. Except that no letter from the accountant needs to be filed when the change is made in response to a standard adopted by the Financial Accounting Standards Board . . .

Thus, a preferability letter must be sent to the client to file as an exhibit to Form 10–Q. The wording of the accountant's letter should state

> In our opinion, the change in accounting principle described in Note X is preferable in your circumstances.

SAB 40 contains guidance to assist the independent accountant in meeting this requirement.

SPECIAL REPORTING

The SEC requires companies under the jurisdiction of this statute to file special reports when certain material corporate events have occurred. The reporting is done on **Form 8–K.** The following are illustrative of events that must be considered for inclusion in a Form 8–K filing:

- Changes in control of the company.
- Major acquisitions and disposals of assets.
- Bankruptcy or receivership.
- Changes in the company's independent accountant.
- Resignation of the company directors.

A company is also expected to report any other significant events, such as losses from fire, flood, and so on, within a reasonable time after their occurrence. Form 8–K does not have a specific format but is a narrative report that gives the registrant considerable flexibility in reporting. This form must be filed within 15 calendar days after the occurrence of the event except for changes in the registrant's independent auditors when the time period for filing is 5 business days.

Form 8–K requires the registrant to submit written statements on any auditor changes. Auditor changes must be reported when the principal accountant resigns, declines to stand for reelection, or is dismissed, as well as when a new auditor is engaged. In addition, any changes in other auditors of significant subsidiaries or divisions relied on by the principal auditor must be reported. The report must state whether there were any disagreements with the former auditor during the audits of the last two fiscal years and subsequent interim period on any matter of (1) accounting principles, (2) financial statement disclosure, or (3) auditing scope or procedure, which if not resolved to the former auditor's satisfaction would have caused the auditor to refer to the subject matter of the disagreement in the audit report. When disagreements with former accountants are reported, the report must state whether the audit committee of the client had discussed the subject matter of the disagreement with the former auditor and whether the client authorized the former auditor to respond fully to inquiries of a successor auditor related to such disagreements.

In addition to disagreements, the SEC also requires that certain reportable events involving a company and its former auditor be reported. Examples include events in which the former auditor has advised the client that (1) the internal controls necessary to develop reliable financial statements do not exist and (2) information has come to the former auditing firm's attention that has caused it to conclude that it may no longer rely on the representations of management.

Disclosures relating to a change in auditors may extend to a successor auditor. If a successor auditor is consulted by a company before being selected as its new auditor, the nature of the consultation must be disclosed if it pertained to an important accounting, auditing, or other financial reporting issue.

The SEC has also concurred in the requirement that the SEC Practice Section of the AICPA's Division for CPA Firms has imposed on its members to notify the SEC of changes in auditors for SEC registrants. Each CPA firm that has been the auditor for an SEC registrant and has resigned, declined to stand for reelection, or been dismissed is required to confirm that fact directly in writing to the former SEC client, with a simultaneous copy sent directly by the firm to the chief accountant of the SEC. This letter must be sent by the end of the fifth business day following the CPA firm's determination that the client-auditor relationship has ended.

LEARNING CHECK:

23-16 Identify the four categories of data required in a Form 10–K filing and what data, if any, must be audited.

23-17 Briefly explain the two major accounting requirements in filing quarterly reports under the 1934 Act.

21-18 a. What data are required in a Form 8–K filing?
b. Indicate the information that must be submitted in regard to auditor changes.

KEY TERMS:

Continuous disclosure act, p. 897
Form 8–K, p. 901
Form 10–K, p. 898
Form 10–Q, p. 900
Proxy statement, p. 898
Securities Exchange Act of 1934, p. 897

ENFORCEMENT OF THE SECURITIES ACT

OBJECTIVE 10

Distinguish among the types of enforcement actions the SEC may take against independent accountants.

As indicated in Chapter 4, the SEC has the authority to initiate legal actions against independent accountants for violations of the securities acts. Through its Division of Enforcement, the SEC also has the authority to impose sanctions against independent accountants through administrative proceedings. Actions taken by the SEC against accountants are published in **Accounting and Auditing Enforcement Releases (AAERs).**

INJUNCTIVE PROCEEDINGS

The SEC has the authority under both the 1933 and the 1934 Acts to initiate **injunctive proceedings** in the courts to restrain future violations of the provisions of these Acts. In addition to stopping the unacceptable practice, an injunction seeks assurances that future actions will be in compliance with the securities acts. The effect of an injunction may be damaging to a defendant in subsequent civil suits for damages, and it may expose the person(s) enjoined to criminal action.

The conditions under which the SEC will bring injunctive proceedings were generalized by an SEC chairman as follows:

> Put very simply, when the Commission discerns that the auditor has not been alert to his duty, that he has gone through an exercise by rote, or that he has not been true to the duty of fair presentation, then in my estimation, the Commission should properly authorize an action to enjoin the accountant from a repetition of those faults.[6]

An injunction must be issued by a court of law. The SEC has consistently maintained that ordinary negligence is sufficient to support an injunctive action except when antifraud provisions are involved.

ADMINISTRATIVE PROCEEDINGS

Sanctions against auditors in **administrative proceedings** may be brought under the SEC's Administrative Rule 2(e), which states that

> *The Commission may disqualify and deny, temporarily or permanently, the privilege of appearing or practicing before it* to any accountant who is found by the Commission . . . (1) not to possess the requisite qualifications to represent others, (2) to be lacking in character or integrity, (3) to have engaged in unethical or improper professional conduct, (4) to have willfully violated, or willfully aided and abetted the violation of any provision of the federal securities laws.

In addition, the Commission may suspend from appearing or practicing before it an auditor who has been (1) "convicted of a felony, or a misdemeanor involving moral turpitude," (2) the subject of a revocation or suspension of his license to practice, (3) "permanently enjoined . . . from violation . . . of any provision of the federal securities laws," or (4) "found by any court . . . or found by this Commission in any administrative proceeding . . . to have violated . . . any provision of the federal securities laws . . . (unless the violation was found not to have been willful)."

The SEC has imposed the following innovative sanctions against independent accountants under Rule 2(e):

- Peer reviews and inspections of accounting firms to determine the extent of compliance with professional and firm auditing standards and procedures.
- Restrictions for specified periods against mergers with other firms.
- Prohibitions for specified periods against undertaking new engagements likely to result in filings with the SEC.
- Requirements to develop and implement auditing procedures for certain types of transactions.
- Imposition of continuing education programs.

[6] A. A. Sommer, Jr., "Accountants: A Flexible Standard," *Litigation* (Winter 1975), pp. 35–39.

These sanctions are viewed by one commissioner as being neither punitive nor retributive but rather as providing assurance that the possibility of recurrence of specific problems caused by pervasive control deficiencies will be reduced.[7]

BIG SIX FIRM BARRED

In an administrative proceeding, the SEC barred a Big Six public accounting firm from accepting any new SEC engagements in the New York area for a 45-day period. The action was triggered by the finding of an SEC law judge that the firm engaged in "unethical and improper professional conduct" in two audits of U.S. Surgical Corp. because it failed to (1) exercise due care, (2) maintain the proper level of professional skepticism, and (3) resolve the serious question of client integrity before certifying the financial statements. The alleged misconduct resulted in the issuance of unqualified audit reports on statements that were incorrect for significantly overstating income. The firm denied the charges but indicated that there would be no appeal.

SOURCE: *Accounting Today*, July 23, 1990.

Rule 2(e) proceedings are public unless the SEC, on its own motion or at the request of a party, should direct otherwise. All known Rule 2(e) proceedings have involved consent decrees. Consent decrees are negotiated settlements in which the SEC publishes only the settlement and the CPA firm neither denies nor admits guilt.

THE SECURITIES LAW ENFORCEMENT REMEDIES ACT OF 1990

This Act provides additional remedies for violations of the federal securities laws. Specifically, it grants to courts discretionary power to impose civil penalties on violators, and it also authorizes the SEC to impose civil penalties in administrative proceedings. The maximum fine for a *natural person* is \$100,000 for each violation and \$500,000 for any *other person*. Courts have the option to increase the maximum fine otherwise applicable to the amount of a violator's gross pecuniary gain from any wrongdoing. The Act also authorizes the Commission to enter orders in any administrative proceedings requiring a violator to account for and surrender any profits from a wrongdoing. Finally, the Act empowers the Commission to enter temporary and permanent cease and desist orders for any violations of the federal securities laws.

LEARNING CHECK:

23-19 Distinguish between injunctive and administrative proceedings in enforcement of the securities acts and indicate how the SEC publicizes its enforcement actions.

23-20 Identify the sanctions that may be imposed by the SEC under Rule 2(e) and the Securities Law Enforcement Remedies Act of 1990.

[7] Sommer, *ibid.*, p. 37.

KEY TERMS:

Accounting and Auditing Enforcement Releases (AAERs), p. 902

Administrative proceedings, p. 903

Injunctive proceedings, p. 902

SUMMARY

The SEC has had a profound influence on the public accounting profession, accounting firms, and individual CPAs. In the exercise of its regulatory powers, the SEC has maintained direct interaction with such groups as the Financial Accounting Standards Board and the AICPA's Auditing Standards Board in the development of GAAP and GAAS. A number of the *Statements on Auditing Standards*, for example, were initiated by new requirements of the SEC.

The provisions of the federal securities acts administered by the SEC have significantly affected the day-to-day practice of accounting firms and independent public accountants. Moreover, these statutes establish the basis for both civil and criminal actions against independent accountants.

Based on its record to date and its ongoing responsibility to see that investors are provided with reliable financial data, it is certain that the SEC will continue to have a significant influence on the accounting profession and independent accountants.

BIBLIOGRAPHY

AICPA Professional Standards:

SAS 37 (AU 711), Filings Under Federal Securities Statutes

SAS 72 (AU 634), Letters for Underwriters and Certain Other Requesting Parties

Arnold, Jerry L., Greende, Edward F., and Keller, Earl C. *The Impact of Electronic Technology at the SEC: An Analysis of Policies Concerning the Content and Dissemination of Corporate Disclosures.* University of Southern California, Los Angeles: Financial Executives Institute and SEC and Financial Reporting Institute, 1987.

Benston, George J. "The Value of the SEC's Accounting Disclosure Requirements," *The Accounting Review* (July 1969), pp. 515–532.

Collins, Stephen H. "The SEC on Full and Fair Disclosure," *Journal of Accountancy* (January 1989), pp. 79–84.

Dieter, Richard, and Sandefur, Keith. "Spotlight on Management's Discussion and Analysis," *Journal of Accountancy* (December 1989), pp. 64–70.

Pava, Moses L., and Epstein, Marc J. "How Good Is MD&A As an Investment Tool?" *Journal of Accountancy* (March 1993), pp. 51–53.

SEC, Compliance. Englewood Cliffs, NJ: Prentice-Hall, Inc.

Skousen, K. Fred. *An Introduction to the SEC,* 5th ed. Cincinnati: South-Western Publishing Co., 1991.

U.S. Securities and Exchange Commission. *The Work of the SEC.* Washington, D.C.: The Office of Public Affairs, U.S. Securities and Exchange Commission, 1988.

OBJECTIVE QUESTIONS[1]

Indicate the *best* answer choice for each of the following multiple choice questions.

23-21 These questions pertain to the purpose of the SEC and its accounting pronouncements.

[1] All five-part questions are from ICMA examinations.

1. A primary purpose of the registration requirements of the Securities Act of 1933 is to
   a. Ensure investors receive fair value for their investments.
   b. Provide investors with information concerning a public offering of securities so that they can make informed investment decisions.
   c. Detect and prevent a public offering of securities where management fraud and unethical conduct are suspected present.
   d. Prevent the offering of securities considered to be unsound.

2. Regulation S–X
   a. Specifies the information that can be incorporated by reference from the annual report into the registration statement filed with the SEC.
   b. Specifies the regulations and reporting requirements of proxy solicitations.
   c. Provides the basis for generally accepted accounting principles.
   d. Specifies the general form and content requirements of financial statements filed with the SEC.
   e. Provides explanations and clarifications of changes in accounting or auditing procedures used in reports filed with the SEC.

3. Financial Reporting Releases (FRRs), called Accounting Series Releases (ASRs) prior to 1982, issued by the SEC
   a. Provide the basis for generally accepted accounting principles.
   b. Specify the regulations and reporting requirements of proxy solicitations.
   c. Provide explanations, interpretations, and procedures used by the SEC in administering the federal securities laws.
   d. Specify the general form and content requirements of financial statements filed with the SEC.
   e. Provide explanations and clarifications of changes in accounting or auditing procedures used in reports filed with the SEC.

4. Staff Accounting Bulletins issued by the SEC
   a. Specify the information that can be incorporated by reference from the annual report into the registration statement filed with the SEC.
   b. Specify the regulations and reporting requirements of proxy solicitations.
   c. Provide explanations, interpretations, and procedures used by the SEC in administering the federal securities laws.
   d. Specify the general form and content requirements of financial statements filed with the SEC.
   e. Provide explanations and clarifications of changes in accounting or auditing procedures used in reports filed with the SEC.

23-22 These questions relate to filing requirements and comfort letters.

1. Form 8–K generally must be submitted to the SEC after the occurrence of a significant event. All of the following events would be reported by Form 8–K except
   a. A change in the registrant's certifying accountant.
   b. Filing for bankruptcy.
   c. The acquisition of a major company.
   d. A change from the percentage-of-completion method of accounting to the completed contract method for a company in the construction business.
   e. The resignation of several directors.

2. Which of the following statements is correct concerning corporations subject to the reporting requirements of the Securities Exchange Act of 1934?
   a. The annual report (Form 10–K) need **not** include audited financial statements.
   b. The annual report (Form 10–K) must be filed with the SEC within 90 days of the end of the corporation's fiscal year.

c. A quarterly report (Form 10–Q) need only be filed with the SEC by those corporations that are also subject to the registration requirements of the Securities Act of 1933.
d. A monthly report (Form 8–K) must be filed with the SEC after the end of any month in which a materially important event occurs.

3. The management discussion and analysis section of Form 10–K has been revised by the SEC's integrated disclosure system. The revised management discussion and analysis section does **not** require a description of
   a. Factors affecting financial condition as well as the results of operations.
   b. Factors affecting international markets and currency exchange.
   c. Factors that are likely to increase or decrease liquidity materially.
   d. Material commitments for capital expenditures including the purpose of and source of financing for such commitments.
   e. The impact of inflation and changing prices on net sales and revenues and on income from continuing operations.

4. When an independent accountant issues a comfort letter to an underwriter containing comments on data that have **not** been audited, the underwriter most likely will receive
   a. A disclaimer on prospective financial statements.
   b. A limited opinion on "pro-forma" financial statements.
   c. Positive assurance on supplementary disclosures.
   d. Negative assurance on capsule information.

Comprehensive Questions

23-23 **(SEC's authority and organization)** The U.S. Securities and Exchange Commission (SEC) was created in 1934 and consists of five commissioners and a staff of approximately 2500. The SEC professional staff is organized into five divisions and several principal offices. The primary objectives of the SEC are to support fair securities markets and foster enlightened shareholder participation in major corporate decisions. The SEC has a significant presence in financial markets and corporation–shareholder relations and has the authority to exert significant influence on entities whose actions lie within the scope of its authority. The SEC chairman has identified enforcement cases and full disclosure filings as major activities of the SEC.

Required

a. The SEC must have some "license" to exercise power. Explain where the SEC receives its authority.
b. Discuss, in general terms, the major ways in which the SEC
   1. Supports fair securities markets.
   2. Fosters enlightened shareholder participation in major corporate decisions.
c. The major responsibilities of the SEC's Division of Corporation Finance include full disclosure filings. Describe the means by which the SEC attempts to assure the material accuracy and completeness of registrants' financial disclosure filings.
d. The Division of Enforcement of the SEC is responsible for the review and direction of all enforcement activities.
   1. Give an example of a violation the SEC might identify.
   2. For the violation, indicate the sanction or penalty, other than fine or imprisonment, that the SEC could impose.

ICMA

23-24 **(Integrated disclosure system/continuous reporting)** The Securities and Exchange Commission (SEC) has encouraged managements of public companies to disclose more information in the shareholders' annual report. As a consequence, a significant amount of the information required in the SEC's Form 10–K now appears in published annual reports.

At the same time, the SEC has attempted to make the annual financial reporting process simpler and more efficient. During 1980, the SEC approved a new integrated disclosure system.

REQUIRED

a. Identify the major classes of information that must be included in both the annual report to shareholders and Form 10–K filed with the SEC.
b. The integrated disclosure system is intended to simplify the annual reporting process with the SEC by expanding the ability to incorporate by reference.
    1. Define what is meant by *incorporating by reference* and identify the documents that are involved when incorporating by reference.
    2. Explain how the integrated disclosure system should reduce management's efforts in filing annual reports with the SEC.
    3. Explain the SEC's principal reasons for making the changes in the annual reporting process.
    4. Identify and explain potential problems the integrated disclosure system could have on the annual reporting process from the aspect of users of financial information.

ICMA

23-25 **(SEC pronouncements)** The accounting-related pronouncements issued by the SEC include Regulation S–X, Regulation S–K, Regulation S–T, Financial Reporting Releases (FRRs), and Staff Accounting Bulletins (SABs). The SEC also issues Accounting and Auditing Enforcement Releases (AAERs). Listed below are statements that relate to these pronouncements:

1. Contains accounting provisions that closely parallel GAAP.
2. Includes opinions of the Commission on major accounting issues.
3. Contains guidance for handling events and transactions with similar accounting interpretations.
4. Pertains to disclosure of management remuneration.
5. Contains disclosure requirements that may exceed GAAP.
6. Sets forth the results of disciplinary proceedings against accountants.
7. Requires disclosure of material pending legal proceedings to which management is a party.
8. Provides clarification of existing rules and regulations.
9. Requires disclosure of securities holdings of management.
10. Includes amendments to financial statement requirements of various forms.
11. Contains regulations pertaining to electronic filings.

REQUIRED

a. Describe briefly the nature of each of the three regulations and three other types of pronouncements and identify who is authorized to issue each.
b. List the numbers of the foregoing statements and indicate the regulation or other type of pronouncements to which each statement pertains.

23-26 **(Registration process)** Bandex Inc. has been in business for 15 years. The company has compiled a record of steady, but not spectacular, growth. Bandex's engineers have recently perfected a product that has an application in the small-computer market. Initial orders have exceeded the company's capacity, and the decision has been made to expand.

Bandex has financed past growth from internally generated funds and, since the initial stock offering in 19X0, no further shares have been sold. Bandex's Finance Committee has been discussing methods of financing the proposed expansion. Both short-term and long-term notes were ruled out because of high interest rates. Mel Greene, the Chief Financial Officer said, "It boils down to either bonds, preferred stock, or additional common stock." Alice Dexter, a consultant employed to help in the financing decision, stated, "Regardless of your choice, you will have to file a Registration Statement with the SEC."

Bob Schultz, Bandex's Chief Accountant for the past five years, stated, "I've coordinated the filing of all periodic reports required by the SEC—10–Ks, 10–Qs, and 8–Ks. I see no reason why I can't prepare a Registration Statement also."

REQUIRED

a. Identify the circumstances under which a firm must file a Registration Statement with the Securities and Exchange Commission (SEC).
b. Explain the objectives of the registration process required by the Securities Act of 1933.
c. Identify and explain the SEC publications Bob Schultz would use for guidance in preparing the Registration Statement.

23-27 **(Registration process under 1933 Act)** A number of steps are involved in the registration process under the 1933 Securities Act. Ten of these steps are listed below in randon order:

1. Data for registration are collected by company accountants, reviewed by lawyers, and reviewed and audited by independent accountants.
2. Management and legal counsel select appropriate registration form.
3. Management prepares amendments that are responsive to SEC's comments. These are filed with SEC by legal counsel.
4. Management prepares draft of registration statement and obtains board of director's approval.
5. Management receives letter of comment from SEC concerning deficiencies and necessary adjustments.
6. SEC notifies management by phone of acceptance of registration statement.
7. Due diligence meeting is held to review registration statement and other matters affecting sale of issue.
8. Management finalizes registration statement, which is filed with the SEC by legal counsel.
9. Legal counsel files amendment to registration statement for offering price. Registration statement becomes effective 5:00 P.M.
10. Management, independent accountant, and legal counsel have prefiling conference with SEC staff in Washington, D.C.

REQUIRED

Arrange the steps in proper sequence.

23-28 **("Selected financial data")** The most common annual report required by the SEC is Form 10–K. Form 10, another SEC report, is often used to register under the Securities Exchange Act of 1934. Both Form 10–K and Form 10 call for "Selected Financial Data." Form S–1, used in the registration of securities for public sale under the Securities Act of 1933, also requires this information. Thus, this summary is an important disclosure requirement in meeting annual reporting and initial filing requirements with the SEC.

REQUIRED

a. Identify the basic information that must be disclosed in the "Selected Financial Data," including the period covered and any explanatory notes needed.
b. Is the "Selected Financial Data" required to be audited?

ICMA (adapted)

23-29 **(SEC reporting forms/accountants' responsibilities)** Below are events pertaining to a public client subject to SEC jurisdiction:

1. There is a change in independent accountants not related to a disagreement over accounting principles.
2. There is a change in an accounting principle that the auditor believes is preferable.
3. Interim financial information is filed following review by the independent accountant.
4. A comfort letter is issued by the accountant to an underwriter.
5. Selected financial data for five years is filed.
6. There was a major acquisition during the year.
7. Unaudited financial statements for a "stub" period are included.

REQUIRED

a. Indicate the SEC reporting form(s), if any, on which each of the foregoing would appear.
b. Explain the independent accountant's responsibilities related to items 1 to 4 above.

23-30 **(Form 10–K and Form 8–K filings)** The Jerford Company is a well-known manufacturing company with several wholly owned subsidiaries. The company's stock is traded on the New York Stock Exchange, and the company files all appropriate reports with the Securities and Exchange Commission. Jerford Company's financial statements are audited by a public accounting firm.
Part I: Jerford Company's Annual Report to Stockholders for the year ended December 31, 19X1, contained the following phrase in boldface type: The company's 10–K is available on written request.

REQUIRED

a. What is Form 10–K, who requires that the form be completed, and why is the phrase "The company's 10–K is available on written request" shown in the annual report?
b. What information not normally included in the company's annual report could be ascertained from the 10–K?
c. Indicate three items of financial information that are often included in annual reports that are not required for the 10–K.

Part II: Jerford Company changed independent auditors during 19X1. Consequently, the financial statements were certified in 19X1 by a different public accounting firm than in 19X0.

REQUIRED

What information is Jerford Company responsible for filing with the SEC with respect to this change in auditors? Explain your answer completely.

ICMA

23-31 **(Quarterly reports)** To aid in integrating quarterly reports to shareholders with Form 10–Q, the Securities and Exchange Commission issued Accounting Series Release (ASR) 286 in February 1981. The ASR modifies and expands the financial information content of the previous Form 10–Q disclosures. Specific guidelines are set forth in the ASR as to what information must be included on Form 10–Q.

REQUIRED

a. Corporations are required by the SEC to file a Form 10–Q.
   1. What is Form 10–Q and how often is it filed with the SEC?
   2. Explain why the SEC requires corporations to file Form 10–Q.
b. Discuss the disclosure requirement now pertaining to Form 10–Q with specific regard to the

1. Condensed balance sheet.
2. Condensed income statement.
3. Condensed statement of cash flows.
4. Management's discussion and analysis of the interim period(s).
5. Footnote disclosures.

ICMA

CASE

23-32 **(Registration process)** Ensign Corporation is a manufacturing firm with ten domestic plants. Increased demand for the company's products and a near full-capacity production have caused management to decide to build a new plant. The plant expansion is to be financed by a public issue of $10,000,000 of long-term bonds. Before the issue can be sold to the public, a registration statement will have to be filed with the Securities and Exchange Commission using a Form S–1. Ensign Corporation's financial statements have been certified by the corporation's independent accountants for many years.

REQUIRED

a. Several parties are involved in the preparation, filing, and approval of the registration statement. Briefly indicate the responsibility of (1) Ensign Corporation management, (2) Ensign's independent accountants, and (3) the Securities and Exchange Commission in this procedure.
b. Indicate the general types of financial information and statistical data that would be disclosed in the schedules and reports included in the registration statement and the time period(s) to which this information and data must refer.

ICMA

RESEARCH QUESTIONS

23-33 **(SEC Annual Report)** Each year, the SEC presents a report on its own activities to the U.S. Congress. The reports are available in the documents section of most university libraries. Obtain a copy of the report for a recent year and prepare a brief summary of highlights from the report.

23-34 **(SEC Docket)** The *SEC Docket* is a publication that is not described in the chapter. If available from your library, obtain a recent issue of this publication. Who issues it? How often? What types of items are included? Prepare a brief summary of several items of interest from the recent issue.

23-35 **(EDGAR)** Determine whether you can access electronic filings of SEC registrants through your university library. They may be available on CD-ROM in the documents section, via a commercial data service to which the library subscribes, or via the Internet. Peruse one or more filings for a company of your choice. You may not be able to find filings for a particular company, because not all registrants are scheduled to be phased in to mandatory electronic filing until 1996. If you are able to gain access, prepare a brief report on your experience, describing how you obtained access and what filings you perused. If you are not able to access EDGAR filings, perform the same requirements specified above using a source of nonelectronic SEC filings, such as microfiche copies of paper filings.

APPENDIX X: AUDITING RESEARCH

This appendix has two purposes: (1) to briefly describe the types and roles of auditing research and (2) to acquaint the student with some references and tools used in performing applied auditing and accounting research.

THE ROLE OF AUDITING RESEARCH

As in other disciplines, auditing research can be classified into two primary types —*pure* or *basic research* and *practical* or *applied research.* The purpose of basic auditing research is to increase the level of knowledge or understanding of auditing as an intellectual discipline and a profession. Two examples of outcomes of this type of research are:

- *The Philosophy of Auditing.* Cited at several points in this text, this monograph completed in 1961 by R. K. Mautz and Hussein A. Sharaf reports the results of their efforts to develop an outline of the theory of auditing. Among other topics, their report includes a scholarly comparison of the scientific method with audit methodology, the identification of a set of tentative postulates or assumptions about auditing that serve as the foundation for their theoretical framework, and the development of a small number of primary operational concepts of auditing dealing with evidence, due audit care, fair presentation, independence, and ethical conduct.
- *A Statement of Basic Auditing Concepts.* Published in 1973, this report presents the results of research undertaken by the Committee on Basic Auditing Concepts of the American Accounting Association. Among other contributions, this report is the source of the comprehensive definition of auditing given on page 4 of this text.

Other examples of basic auditing research include investigations into the interrelationships among different fields of knowledge and how knowledge can be borrowed from other fields to further develop auditing theory and methods. This body of research includes inquiries into the theories of evidence, statistics, and judgment and decision-making processes including expert systems. Other examples of auditing research include investigations into the efficacy of procedures such as confirmation and analytical procedures. Such research is aimed at developing improvements in audit methodology. In addition to conceptual analyses, the research methods for such investigations include empirical analysis, field experiments, and surveys.

In contrast, auditors must often engage in practical or applied auditing research with the more limited objective of finding solutions to problems that arise in specific audit engagements. In servicing a variety of audit clients, individual auditors frequently encounter new auditing or accounting matters that they have not confronted previously. Moreover, even in areas which an auditor has developed considerable experience and expertise, new or revised standards may be issued that require changes in professional practice. To deal with these situations, the auditor must be prepared to perform applied research. Examples include determining the effect of (1) a specific scope limitation on the auditor's report, (2) a particular auditor-client relationship on the auditor's compliance with Rule 101 —Independence of the *Code of Professional Conduct,* or (3) a new accounting standard on a client's financial reporting for a particular matter. The next section explores approaches the auditor can take in research such issues.

TOOLS FOR APPLIED AUDITING AND ACCOUNTING RESEARCH

Fortunately, a wide variety of research tools is readily available to the auditor who must perform applied research. These include indexes to accounting literature, professional standards, technical practice aids, financial reports surveys and data bases, and professional journals. Many of these are available in both printed and electronic media. An introduction to these resources is provided in the following sections.

Indexes to Accounting Literature

Two indexes that are particularly helpful in conducting applied auditing and accounting research are

- *Index to Accounting and Auditing Technical Pronouncements (IAATP).* Published annually by the AICPA, this reference provides a cumulative index of authoritative accounting and auditing pronouncements issued by such bodies as the AICPA; the Financial, Governmental, and Cost Accounting Standards Boards; the International Accounting Standards Committee and International Federation of Accountants; the National Council on Governmental Accounting; and the Securities and Exchange Commission. The index is organized based upon *main terms* or *keywords* taken from a comprehensive listing of accounting and auditing terms. Cross-references between main terms and broader, narrower, and related terms facilitate broadening, narrowing, or otherwise modifying a search strategy as needed. An electronic version of the index known as the *Electronic Index to Technical Pronouncements (EITP)* is also available.

- *Accounting and Tax Index.* Available in quarterly and annual supplements from University Microfilms, this subject / author index provides full citations to materials in a wide variety of professional publications covering accounting, auditing, taxation, and related topics. This source is particularly useful in locating articles, books, documents, and speeches.

Of course, in researching a topic, an auditor may also find it useful to consult other indexes such as the *Business Periodicals Index* or *The Wall Street Journal Index.*

Professional Standards

Three of the most widely used reference works containing accounting and auditing professional standards are the following:

- *AICPA Professional Standards Volume 1.* This volume contains the contents of:
  - *Statements on Auditing Standards* and related *Auditing Interpretations.*
  - *Statements on Standards for Attestation Engagements* and related *Attestation Engagements Interpretations.*
- *AICPA Professional Standards Volume II.* This volume contains the contents of:
  - *Statements on Standards for Accounting and Review Services* and related *Accounting and Review Services Interpretaions.*
  - *Code of Professional Conduct* and related *Interpretations* and *Ethics Rulings.*
  - AICPA Bylaws.
  - *International Accounting Standards.*
  - *International Standards on Auditing.*
  - *International Statements on Auditing.*
  - *Statements on Standards for Management Consulting Services.*
  - *Statements on Quality Review Standards*
  - *Standards for Performing and Reporting on Quality Reviews.*
  - *Statements on Responsibilities in Personal Financial Planning Practice.*
  - *Statements on Responsibilities in Tax Practice.*
- *FASB Accounting Standards—Current Text.* This volume contains the contents of:
  - *FASB Statements of Financial Accounting Standards.*
  - *FASB Technical Bulletins.*
  - *FASB Interpretations of Financial Accounting Standards.*
  - *Opinions of the Accounting Principles Board.*
  - *Interpretations of the Accounting Principles Board.*
  - *Accounting Research Bulletins.*

Each of the above volumes is available as a loose-leaf service, in an annual paperback edition, and in electronic format. Each is organized by subject, contains only material currently in effect, and is fully indexed for easy reference. In addition to the above, separate *Codifications* of statements on standards for (1) auditing, (2) accounting and review services, and (3) attestation engagements are published annually by the AICPA.

Two additional popular reference works are *Auditing Standards—Original Pronouncements* and *FASB Accounting Standards—Original Pronouncements.* The former contains all of the *Statements on Auditing Standards* in chronological sequence and related interpretations. The latter contains all of the *Accounting Standards, Interpretations, APB Opinions,* and *Accounting Research Bulletins* arranged chronologically. Both publications include annotations as to how a given standard was impacted by subsequently issued standards and how a given standard impacted previously issued standards.

Chronological listings of the *Statements on Auditing Standards, Statements on Standards for Accounting and Review Services,* and *Statements on Standards for Attestation Engagements* are provided on the inside of the front cover of this text.

Technical Practice Aids

A variety of materials is available to assist the auditor in researching technical issues. Among these are two volumes of nonauthoritative guidance issued by the AICPA under the title *Technical Practice Aids.* Volume I is a compendium of responses to hundreds of selected questions on a wide range of accounting and auditing issues directed to the AICPA's Technical Information Service by AICPA members. The questions and responses are thoroughly indexed and include citations to relevant standards and other authoritative sources. Volume 2 contains *Statements of Position* issued by the AICPA Accounting Standards Division and Auditing Standards Division, plus AICPA *Practice Bulletins* and a list of outstanding AICPA *Issues Papers.*

Another resource for addressing general and industry-specific problems is the AICPA series of *Audit and Accounting Guides.* There are currently six general and twenty-one industry specific guides as listed in the box on page 206 of this text. Many CPA firms also identify industry experts available for consultation within the firm, or join an association of CPA firms to gain access to industry experts throughout the association member firms.

Of particular relevance in planning audits are the AICPA's *Audit Risk Alerts.* As explained further in Chapter 7, an annual *general* audit risk alert and a number of *industry-specific* audit risk alerts, are published. These alerts are designed to focus auditors' attentions on current economic, regulatory, and professional developments that can have a significant impact on audits.

To assist small and medium-sized CPA firms, the AICPA has developed an *Audit and Accounting Manual* which provides a wide variety of practical samples and illustrations of audit programs, working papers, internal control questionnaires, and other tools useful in performing professional services. Another practice aid prepared by the AICPA's Technical Information Division is its series of checklists and illustrative financial statements prepared for more than fifteen different types of businesses.

Financial Reporting Surveys and Databases

Auditors frequently find it helpful to see how other companies and their auditors have dealt with particular accounting or auditing issues. A number of resources are available to the auditor for this type of research. One such source is the AICPA's annual edition of *Accounting Trends & Techniques.* Based on a survey of the annual reports of 600 industrial and merchandising corporations, this study .includes sample footnotes and auditors' reports taken from the annual reports, and tabulations summarizing such matters as the frequency of use of alternative accounting methods, different forms of auditors' reports, and the early or voluntary implementation of new accounting standards.

Access to a larger database containing the full text of the annual reports for 4,000 companies is available on CD-ROM or on-line via the AICPA's *National*

Automated Accounting Research System (NAARS). The latter is available as one of the libraries accessible via Mead Data Central, Inc.'s electronic service—*LEXIS/NEXIS.* This service also includes the full text of all authoritative accounting and auditing pronouncements, including the SEC's rules and regulations. Another source of information on SEC filings made by more than 12,000 public companies is the compact disk database available from *Disclosure, Inc.* Occasionally, the AICPA publishes special surveys of current reporting practices. For example, in 1993, it published *Illustrations of Accounting for Income Taxes: Survey of the Application of FASB 109,* and *Illustrations of Accounting for Environmental Costs.*

PROFESSIONAL ACCOUNTING IN FOREIGN COUNTRIES

A series of studies published by the AICPA under this title provides information on the business environment, professional accounting principles and practices, and auditing procedures as they currently exist in various foreign countries. Supplementing the international accounting and auditing standards contained in the AICPA's *Professional Standards, Volume II,* as noted above, studies in this series are currently available for the following countries:

Argentina	Nigeria
Australia	Norway
Belgium	The Philippines
Canada	Singapore
France	South Africa
Hong Kong	South Korea
Italy	Sweden
Japan	Taiwan
Mexico	United Kingdom
The Netherlands	

Professional Journals

To maintain currency, in addition to reading current official pronouncements, all practicing professionals should read a variety of professional journals. Among those most widely read are the following.

- *Accounting Review,* Sarasota, FL: American Accounting Association (quarterly).
- *Auditing: A Journal of Practice and Theory,* Sarasota, FL: American Accounting Association (quarterly).
- *The Internal Auditor,* Altamonte Springs, FL: The Institute of Internal Auditors (monthly).
- *Journal of Accountancy,* New York: American Institute of Certified Public Accountants (monthly).
- *The CPA Journal,* New York: The New York State Society of Certified Public Accountants (monthly).

Among other topics, these journals frequently include interpretative and illustrative articles dealing with recent official pronouncements and how they have been implemented in practice. As noted earlier, articles in these and other professional accounting and auditing journals are indexed in the *Accounting and Tax Index.*

INDEX

Absolute data comparisons, *207, 209–13*
Access controls, *461*
Accountant
  independent, *876–77*
  independent public, *876–77*
  SEC chief, *878–80*
Accountant's consent, *896–97*
Accountant's report
  on compilation of financial statements, *823–24*
  on financial forecast examination, *817–18*
  on unaudited financial statement, *822–23*
Accounting
  other comprehensive bases of, *801–2*
  relationship to auditing, *33–34*
Accounting and Auditing Enforcement Releases (AAERs), 902
Accounting changes
  affecting consistency, *755*
  not affecting consistency, *756*
Accounting estimates, *350–51*
Accounting principles
  AICPA Rule 203, 87
  generally accepted, *753*
  inconsistency, *767*
  promulgated, *755*
Accounting services
  attest service standards, *12–13*
  compilation engagement, *823*
  nonattest service, *12, 821*
Accounting standards, *880–81*
  See also American Institute of Certified Public Accountants (AICPA); Financial Accounting Standards Board (FASB); Generally accepted auditing standards (GAAS); Governmental Accounting Standards Board (GASB)
Accounting system
  audit or transaction trail, *264*
  function of internal, *263–64*
Accounts payable
  detection risk, *572*
  master file, *558*
  search for unrecorded, *576*
  substantive tests, *572*
Accounts receivable
  analytical procedures, *524, 526*
  confirmation procedure, *528–35*
  master file, *504*
  subsidiary ledger, *504*
  trial balance, *522–24*
Achieved allowance for sampling risk (A′), 426, 431, 433
Acts discreditable, *89*
Actual assessed level of control risk, *233*
Additional tests of controls, *311*
Adjusted achieved allowance for sampling risk (A″), 427
Adjusting entries, *174*
Administrative proceedings, *903–4*
Adverse opinion (auditor's report), *50–51, 760, 766, 777–78*
Advertising, AICPA Rule 502, *89–90*
Aged trial balance, *534*
Aggregate likely misstatement, *729*
Agreed-upon procedures
  applied to prospective financial statements, *818–19*
  engagements with, *819*
  scope, *11–12*
  uses for, *803–4*
Aiding-and-abetting, *126*
Allowance for sampling risk, *381–83, 411,436*
American Institute of Certified Public Accountants (AICPA)
  Accounting and Review Services committee, *12*
  attestation engagements and standards, *797–99*
  attest service standards, *12–13*
  audit and accounting guides, *205–6*
  Auditing Standards Division, *40*
  Code of Professional Conduct, *72–73*
  Division for CPA firms, *21–22*
  Federal Taxation Executive Committee, *12*
  Joint Ethics Enforcement Program (JEEP), 93
  Management Consulting Services Executive Committee, *13*
  Professional Ethics Division, *14, 19, 72–73, 93*
  Quality Review Division, *23*
  role, mission, and organization, *9, 14–15*
  standards and standard setting, *19, 41–42*
  standards for accounting services, *12–13*
American rule, *107*
Analytical procedures
  See also Absolute data comparisons; Common-size financial statements; Ratio analysis; Trend analysis
  accounts payable, *573*
  for accounts receivable, *524, 526*
  in audit, *206–13*
  in audit testing phase, *334–38*
  detection risk, *353–54*
  financial ratios used in, *214–16*
  inventories, *613, 615*
  long-term debt balances, *667*
  plant assets, *581–86*
Anticipated misstatement, *408–9*
Application controls, *265, 464–66*
Application programs, *450–51*
Assertions, financial statement. *See* Financial statement assertions
Assessing control risk
  See also Control risk assessment
  for account balance assertions, *317–18*
  cash disbursements, *570–71*
  cash receipt transactions, *517–18*
  in control activities, *508, 510–11*
  documentation, *319–20*
  expenditure cycle, *555, 557*
  final or actual assessment, *308–9*
  initial, *306–8*
  lower assessed level of control risk approach, *308–9*
  manufacturing transactions, *609–11*
  payroll transactions, *632–34*
  primarily substantive approach, *306–8*
  process, *301–6*
  purchases transactions control activities, *563–64*

Assessing control risk *(Continued)*
  using computer service organization, *481*
Assignment of authority and responsibility, *262, 499*
Attestation risk, *800*
Attestation standards
  of attest engagement, *797*
  comparison of AICPA and GAAS, *797–99*
Attest engagement
  defined, *797*
  types of, *799–80*
Attest services
  See also Nonattest services
  defined, *10–11*
  summary, *820*
Attribute
  for controls, *372*
  sample size, *373*
Attribute sampling
  See also Discovery sampling
  design for tests of controls, *370*
  factors affecting sample size, *377*
  reliability or confidence level, *375n1*
  sample deviation rate, *381*
  statistical, *380–85*
  in tests of controls, *369, 370–73*
  upper deviation limit, *381*
Audit
  auditor's responsibilities in completing, *736*
  compliance audit, *5*
  internal controls relevant to, *255–56*
  operational audit, *5*
  phases of, *189–90*
  postaudit responsibilities, *737–39*
  single, *860*
  through the computer, *472–75*
  time budget, *197–98*
Audit, financial statement, *4–5*
  economic benefits, *36–37*
  limitations, *37*
  overall and specific audit objectives, *144*
  specific audit objectives, *144, 148–49*
Audit committee
  auditor's communication with, *734–35*
  auditor's relationship with, *38–39*
  impact on control environment, *261*
  information from, *204*
  responsibility for internal control, *257*
Audit engagement
  acceptance, *189, 191–201*
  engagement letter, *198–200*
  initial and recurring, *347*
Audit evidence. *See* Evidence; Evidential matter
Audit hook, *475*
Auditing
  around the computer, *471–72*
  compliance (government), *858*
  defined, *4*
  operational, *846–50*
  relationship to accounting, *33–34*
  uncertainties in, *365*
Auditing procedures
  discovery of omitted, *738–39*
  relationship of auditing standards to, *44*
  subsequent period, *721*
  tests of controls, *309–16*
Auditing standards
  See also Generally accepted auditing standards (GAAS)
  field work, *42–43, 151*
  general, *42*
  international, *44*
  relationship to procedures to, *44*
  reporting, *43, 46–49*
Auditing Standards Board (ASB), AICPA
  financial statement assertions, *145–49*
  role of, *40*
Audit log, *475*
  See also Systems control audit review file (SCARF)
Audit memoranda, *171–72*
Audit objectives
  cash balances, *687–89*
  expenditure cycle, *551–52*
  financial statement assertions, *652–54*
  financing cycle, *662–64*
  overall, *144*
  personnel services cycle, *625–26*
  production cycle, *601–3*
  for the revenue cycle, *495–96*
  specific, *144, 148–49, 495–96*
Auditors
  external, *4*
  government, *7*
  independent, *5–6*
  internal, *7, 39*
  postaudit responsibilities, *737–39*
  predecessor and successor, *192*
  professional relationships, *38–39*
  responsibilities in audit completion, *736*
Auditor's report
  with adverse opinion, *50–51, 760, 766*
  departures from standard, *49–51, 760*
  with disclaimer of opinion, *50–51, 760, 764*
  effects of circumstances on, *777–78*
  explanatory language, *760, 765*
  introductory, scope, and opinion paragraphs, *46–49, 51*
  with qualified opinion, *763–64, 765–67, 769–70*
  standard, *45, 759*
Auditor's responsibility, *54–55*
Audit planning, *202–13*
Audit procedures
  See also Audit programs; Audit sampling
  analytical procedures, *162, 167, 206–7*
  computer-assisted audit techniques, *164–65*
  confirming, *162*
  counting, *163*
  defined, *161*
  dual-purpose test, *167*
  imprest accounts, *704–5*
  inquiring, *163*
  inspecting, *162*
  observing, *163–64*
  to obtain understanding, *165*
  to obtain understanding of internal control structure, *276–77*
  relation to assertions and evidence, *165–66*
  reperforming, *164*
  under Single Audit Act, *861–62*
  substantive tests, *165, 167*
  tests of controls, *165, 167*
  tests of details of balances, *167–68*
  tests of details of transactions, *167–68*
  tracing, *163*
  vouching, *163*
Audit programs
  for credit sales tests of controls, *513*
  for substantive tests, *341, 343–47, 522–23*
  for tests of controls, *313–14*
Audit risk
  See also Control risk; Detection risk; Planned acceptable level of detection risk; Risk components matrix
  components, *231–35*
  defined, *231, 365*
  reduction, *240*
  relationship to audit evidence, *237–38*
Audit risk alerts, *238*
Audit risk model, *235–36*

Audits
  costs of, *198*
  government, *852–53*
  of government organizations, *851–53*
Audit sampling
  See also Attribute sampling; Audit risk; Random number sampling
  attribute and variables sampling, *369*
  computer selection and printing, *477*
  defined, *364*
  nonsampling risk, *366–67*
  statistical or nonstatistical, *367–69*
  statistical sampling, *370–73*
  systmatic sampling, *379*
  for tests of controls and substantive tests, *367*
  uses of, *365*
  with and without replacement, *378*
Audit-sensitive position, *82*
Audit service, *11*
Audit strategy *See also* Lower assessed level of control risk; Primarily substantive approach
  alternatives, *240–42*
  components of preliminary, *240*
  effect of preliminary, *273–74, 306*
  expenditure cycle, *553–54*
  relation to transaction cycles, *242–44*
Audit team, *195*
Audit trail, *264, 500*
Authorized price list, *504*
Automatic disciplinary provisions, *94*

Balances
  See also Tests of details of balances
  account balance assertions, *317–18*
  aged trial, *534*
  cash, *689–92*
  compensating, *698*
  investment, *655–57*
  long-term debt, *655–70*
  payroll, *634–36*
  tests of details of, *335–36*
  trial, *522–24, 534*
  working trial, *169–71*
Bank
  confirmation, *696–98*
  cutoff statement, *699–701*
  reconciliation, *699–700*
  transfer schedule, *693*
BarChris case. *See Escott* v. *BarChris Construction Corp.* (1968)
Basic precision, *411*
Batch entry/batch processing, *452–53*

Beneficiaries
  other, *111*
  primary, *111*
Robert R. Bily v. *Arthur Young & Co.* (1992), *115, 132*
Blue sky laws, *118*
Board of directors
  auditor's relationship with, *38–39*
  impact on control environment, *261*
  responsibility for internal control, *257*
Boards of accountancy, state-level, *16–17, 94*
Bond certificate, *654*
Bond indenture, *654*
Bonding, *500*
Bond trustee, *664*
Books of original entry, *654*
Breach of contract, *109, 116*
Broker's advice, *654*

Cash
  balances, *689–92*
  counts, *696*
  count sheet, *515*
  imprest petty cash fund, *704*
  proof of, *694–95*
Cash disbursements
  cutoff test, *576*
  functions, *567*
  journal or check register, *566*
Cash disbursements transactions
  control activities, *566–70*
  file, *566*
  identified, *550–51*
Cash receipts
  See also Deposited intact daily; Lockbox system
  cutoff test, *527–28*
  functions, *515*
  journal, *515*
  lapping, *702–4*
  processing, *286–87, 517*
  sources, *514*
  transactions file, *515*
Cenco Inc. v. *Seidman & Seidman* (1982), *133–34*
Central Bank of Denver N. A. v. *First Interstate Bank of Denver N. A.* (1994), *126*
Certified public accountant (CPA)
  national and state societies, *14–15*
Certified public accountant (CPA) firms
  services, *10–13*
Check
  defined, *566*
  payroll, *628*
  summary, *566*

Chief accountant (SEC), *878–80*
Classical variables sampling
  advantages and disadvantages, *433–34*
  difference estimation sampling, *428–31*
  MPU (mean-per-unit) estimation sampling, *420–28*
  ratio estimation sampling, *431–33*
  statistical sampling using, *403*
  techniques, *419*
Client, *73*
Client representation letter, *724–26*
Clock card, *627*
Coalition to Eliminate Abusive Securities Suits (CEASS), *107*
Code definitions, AICPA, *73–74*
Code of Professional Conduct, AICPA, *72–73*
Cognizant agency, *861*
"Cold" (or second) review, *731*
Comfort letter, *895–96*
Commissions, *90–91*
Commitment to competence, *260–61*
Committee of Sponsoring Organizations (COSO) (Treadway Commission)
  criteria, *813–14*
  report, *254–58, 260*
Common law, *108, 111, 115–16, 131–32*
Common-size financial statements, *207*
Communication
  accounting system, *555–56*
  with audit committe, *734–35*
  internal, *263–64, 500–501*
  of internal control structure matters, *320–21*
  reportable conditions, *732–34*
  understanding of internal, *275*
Compensating balance, *698*
Compensating control, *304*
Compilation
  engagement, *823–24*
  of financial statements, *823–24*
  of prospective financial statements, *824–26*
Compilation service, *12*
Completed production report, *605*
Completeness, *146*
Complexity, *35–36*
Compliance
  auditing (government), 858
  audits, *5*
  notes, *883*
  with specified requirements, *819*
  testing, *863–64*

Computer processing
cash disbursements, *567–69*
differences from manual processing, *457–58*
for expenditure cycle, *555–56*
manufacturing transactions, *608–9*
for revenue cycle transactions, *500–502*
Computer service organization, *480–81*
Concurrent tests of controls, *310–11*
Confidential client information, *87–88*
See also Privileged communication
Conflict of interest, *35*
Consequence, *35*
Constructive fraud, *109n7*
Consulting services, *12–13*
Continental Vending case. *See United States* v. *Simon* (1969)
Contingent fees, *88–89*
Continuing reporting, *882*
Continuous disclosure act, *897*
Continuous monitoring, *475*
Contracts
breach of, *109, 116*
privity of, *108–9*
Contributory negligence, *116–17*
Control activities
cash disbursements tranactions, *566–70*
cash receipts transactions, *514–17*
documents and records, *266*
independent checks, *266–67*
information processing, *264–65*
manufacturing transactions, *604–9*
over sales transactions, *503–14*
payroll transactions, *627–34*
performance reviews, *269*
physical controls, *268*
proper authorization, *265*
purchases transactions, *557–65*
segregation of duties, *267–68*
understanding, *275*
Control environment
assignment of authority and responsibility, *262*
commitment to competence, *260–61*
defined, *259*
factors in, *499–503*
human resource policy, *262*
integrity and ethical values, *260*
management philosophy, *261*
narrative memorandum documenting, *283*
organizational structure, *261–62*
relevance to expenditure cycle, *554*
understanding of, *274*
Control risk
See also Assessing control risk; Initial assessment of control risk; Internal control; Planned assessed level of control risk; Risk components matrix
actual assessed level, *233*
as component of audit risk, *231, 233–35*
expenditure cycle, *553*
Control risk assessment, *301–6, 354*
for account balance assertions, *317–18*
combining assessments, *318–19*
of credit sales transactions, *510–12*
documenting assessed level, *319–20*
lower assessed level, *240*
of manufacturing transactions, *609–11*
payroll transactions, *632–34*
planned assessed level, *233*
in revenue cycle assertions, *497–98*
Controls
See also Application controls; Compensating control; Input controls; Internal control; Necessary controls; Output controls; Processing controls; Quality control; Tests of controls
attributes, *372–73*
compensating, *304*
deviations, occurrences, or exceptions, *310*
expected population deviation rate, *376*
necessary, *302–3*
tests of, *303, 304–5, 309–16*
Corroborating information
analytical evidence, *156*
confirmations, *158*
documentary evidence, *156–58*
documentation, *171–74*
electronic evidence, *160–61*
mathematical evidence, *159–60*
oral evidence, *160*
physical evidence, *160*
types of, *150*
written representations, *159*
COSO. *See* Committee of Sponsoring Organizations (COSO) (Treadway Commission)
Cost-efficient, *308*
Council, AICPA, *73, 91*
CPA firms
Division for CPA firms in AICPA, *21–22*
practice units, *15–16*
regulation by, *20*
Credit Alliance Corp. v. *Arthur Andersen & Co.* (1985), *115, 131–32*
Credit memo, *519*
Credit sales
audit program for tests of controls, *513*
control risk assessment of transactions, *510–12*
functions, *504–5*
processing transactions, *508*
Current file (working papers), *175*
Customer monthly statement, *504*
Customer order
defined, *504*
specific audit objective EO1, *505*
Cycles. *See* Expenditure cycle; Financing cycle; Investing cycle; Personnel services cycle; Production cycle; Revenue cycle

Daily cash summary, *515*
Daily production activity report, *605*
Data
absolute data comparisons, *207*
analysis of, *208–13*
verifiable, *34–35*
See also Ratio analysis; Trend analysis
Data and procedural controls, *462–63*
Database method, *452*
Data organization methods
data base method, *452*
traditional file method, *451*
Data processing methods
batch entry/batch processing, *452*
on-line entry/batch processing, *452–53; 452–54*
on-line entry/on-line processing, *453, 455*
Deep pockets, *105*
Deficiency letter, *887*
Departures from GAAP, *50*
Departures from the standard report, *760*
Deposited intact daily, *516*
Detection risk
See also Risk components matrix
accounts payable, *572*
for accounts receivable assertions, *520–21*
as component of audit risk, *231, 233–35*
for inventory assertions, *612*
investing cycle, *655*
long-term debt balances, *665*
planned acceptable level, *235, 331*
for plant asset assertions, *579–80*
revised or final acceptable level, *332*

specification for substantive tests, *332–33*
Deviations
from control policy, *310*
expected population deviation rate, *376*
qualitative aspects, *383, 385*
sample deviation rate, *381*
standard deviation, *421*
tolerable deviation rate, *375–76*
upper deviation limit, *381–82*
working paper list, *386*
Difference estimation sampling, *428, 430–32*
Disciplinary actions, *94*
Disclaimer of opinion (auditor's report), *50–51, 760, 764, 766, 777–78*
Discovery sampling, *389*
Division of Corporate Finance (SEC), *878*
Documentation of the control risk assessment, *319–20*
Documenting the understanding, *277–83, 301–2*
Documents
cash disbursements, *566*
defined, *266*
financing cycle, *664*
investing cycle, *653–54*
manufacturing transactions, *605*
payroll transactions, *627–28*
in processing cash receipts, *514–15*
Dual dating, *737*
Dual-purpose testing, *316*
Due care defense, *116*
Due diligence defense, *119*

Economy and efficiency audits (government), *852*
EDGAR, *883, 884*
EDP department
application controls, *464–66*
general controls, *458–63*
EDP system, *467–72*
Efficiency ratios, *215*
1136 Tenants' Corp. v. Max Rothenberg & Co. (1971), *110*
Employee
earnings master file, *628*
personnel file, *628*
Employee fraud, *55*
Engagement
with agreed-upon procedures, *819*
compilation, *823*
examination, *819–20*
step up or down, *826*
Engagement letter, *198–200*
English rule, *107*
Enterprise, *74*
Ernst & Ernst v. *Hochfelder* (1976), *124*
Errors (auditor's responsibility), *54–56*
Escott v. *BarChris Construction Corp.* (1968), *120*
ESM Government Securities Litigation v. *Alexander Grant & Co.* (1986), *134*
Estimated total population value (X), *426, 431*
See also Range for the estimated total population value
Estimated total projected difference (D), *431*
Ethical dilemma, *71*
Ethics
See also Joint Ethics Enforcement Program (JEEP); Joint trial board, AICPA; Morality
derivation and meaning, *70–71*
general, *71*
professional, *71*
Ethics rulings, AICPA, *73, 85*
Evidence
See also Evidential matter
analytical, *156*
in assessment of control risk, *305–6*
documentary, *156–58*
electronic, *160*
mathematical, *159–60*
oral, *160*
physical, *160*
Evidential matter
See also Corroborating information; Evidence
categories and types, *150–51*
competency of, *153–55*
relationship to audit risk, *237–38*
relation to audit procedures and assertions, *165–66*
sufficiency, *151–52*
use of specialists to obtain, *195–96*
Examinations
as attest service, *11*
of prospective financial statements, *817*
Exceptions (control policy), *310*
Existence, *145–46*
Expansion factor, *408–9*
Expectation gap, *53–55*
Expected population deviation rate, *376*
Expenditure cycle
audit objectives, *551–52*
interface with production cycle, *601–2*
materiality in, *552–53*
transaction classes in, *550–51*
Expert system, *478–79*
Explanatory language, *760, 765, 767, 770–75*
Explanatory paragraph (auditor's report), *49, 51*
Extent of substantive tests, *339*
Extent of tests of controls, *313*

Federal financial assistance
audit of, *861–64*
defined, *861*
Fees
contingent, *88–89*
referral, *90–91*
Field work
GAAS standards, *42–43, 151, 201–2, 252, 855*
GAGAS standards, *855*
interim and year-end work, *197*
performing audit tests, *189*
Final or actual assessment of control risk, *308–9*
Financial Accounting Standards Board (FASB)
relevance and reliability of information, *35*
SEC oversight, *880–81*
standard setting, *19*
Statements of Financial Accounting Standards (SFAS), *16*
Financial audits (government), *852–53*
Financial forecast, *816*
Financial projection, *816*
Financial related audits (government), *852*
Financial reporting
fraudulent, *55*
relationship between accounting and auditing, *33–34*
Financial Reporting Releases (FRRs), *884*
Financial statement assertions
completeness, *146*
existence or occurrence, *145*
presentation and disclosure, *148–49*
relation to audit objectives and substantive tests, 342–43
relation to audit procedures and evidence, *165–66*
rights and obligations, *146–47*
valuation or allocation, *147–48*
Financial statement audits
as audit service, *4–5, 11*
government, *852*
Financial statement materiality, *226–30*

Financial statements
common-size, *207*
compilation, *823–26*
nonconformity with GAAP, *761, 764, 767*
special report prepared on OCBOA, *802–4*
SSARS review, *809–10*
unaudited, *822*
Financing cycle
auditing objectives, *662–64*
identified, *661*
Financing functions, *664*
Finite correction factor, *424*
Firm (defined), *74*
Firm regulation, *20, 24*
Fischer v. *Kletz* (1967), *133*
Flowchart
comprehensive flowcharting, *284–88*
definition and components, *280–82*
on-line/batch entry processing system, *508–9*
payroll transactions, *628–30*
processing purchases transactions, *561–63*
Follow-up phase (operational audit), *849–50*
Foreign Corrupt Practices Act (1977), *253, 839*
Foreseeable parties concept, *113–14*
Foreseen class concept, *112–14*
Form 8-K, *901*
Form 10-K, *898–99*
Form of organization and name, *91–92*
Form 10-Q, *900*
Form S-1, 890–92
Fraud
constructive, *109n7*
defined, *109*
employee, *55*
liability under common law, *116*
management, *55*
Fraudulent financial reporting, *55*
Freedom of Information Act, *878*
Fundamental concepts (of internal control), *255*
Fund of Funds, Ltd. v. *Arthur Andersen & Co.* (1982), *110–11, 125*

GAAP hierarchy, *753*
GAGAS. *See* Generally accepted government auditing standards (GAGAS)
General controls, *265, 458–63*
General ethics, *71*
Generalized audit software, *476–77*
Generally accepted accounting principles, *753*
Generally accepted auditing principles (GAAP)
confirmation of receivables, *528–35*
departures from, *50*
presented fairly in conformity with, *753*
SEC role in, *17*
Generally accepted auditing standards (GAAS)
attestation standards, *797–99*
defined, *41–42*
field work standards, *201–2*
pre-acceptance of engagement standards, *194–96*
Generally accepted government auditing standards (GAGAS), *853–59*
Going concern, *771*
Governmental Accounting Standards Board (GASB)
standard setting, *19*
Statements of Governmental Accounting Standards (SGAS), 16
Governmental auditing, *851–52*
Government auditors, *7*
Government regulation, *23–24*
Grandfather-father-son concept, *463*
Gross negligence, *116*
Group schedule, *171*

Hardware and systems software controls, *461*
Holding out, *74*
Human resource policies and practices, *262, 499*

ICS. *See* Internal control structure (ICS)
IIA. *See* Institute of Internal Auditors (IIA)
Illegal acts, client, *56–57*
Imprest payroll bank account, *628, 705*
Imprest petty cash funds, *704*
Incorporate by reference, *881*
Incremental allowance for sampling risk, *413*
Independence
AICPA Rule 101, *78–84*
IIA concept, *843–44*
Independent accountant
defined, *876–77*
involvement in registrations, *893–94*
qualifications, *885–86*
Independent auditors, *5–6*
Independent checks, *266–67*
Independent public accountant, *876–77*
Information
See also Confidential client information; Corroborating information; Incorporate by reference; Integrated disclosure system; Interim financial information (IFI); Prospective financial information
in data analysis, *208–13*
FASB, *35*
prospective financial, *816–19*
understanding of internal, *275*
Information processing controls, *264–65*
Information risk, *35–36*
Information system
accounting system in, *263, 500, 555–56*
communication, *263–64*
Informative disclosures, *756*
Inherent limitations (internal control structure), *256–57*
Inherent risk, *231–35, 354*
affecting gross and net receivables, *520–21*
assessment in revenue cycle assertions, *497–98*
expenditure cycle, *553*
See also Risk components matrix
Initial assessment of control risk, *306–8, 502–3*
Initial engagement, *347*
Injunctive proceedings, *902–3*
Input controls, *464*
Institute, *74*
Institute of Internal Auditors (IIA)
code of ethics, *865–67*
examination, *839–40*
independence concept, *843–44*
practice standards, *840–43*
Integrated disclosure system, *881–82*
Integrated test facility (ITF) approach, *474*
Integrity and objectivity, *84–85*
Interim financial information (IFI), *807–9*
Interim work (field work), *197*
Internal auditing
as control function, *839*
defined, *839*
objective and scope, *840*
practice standards, *840–44*
Internal auditors, *7*
auditor's relationship with, *39*
certified (CIA), *840*
responsibility for internal control, *257–58*
in tests of controls, *315*

Internal control
components, *255*
defined, *254*
fundamental concepts, *255*
GAGAS standards for reporting, *859*
importance, *252–54*
reporting on, *811–19*
Internal control questionnaire
control activities, *279–80*
control environment, *278*
EDP application controls, *469–70*
EDP general controls, *468–69*
Internal control structure (ICS)
See also Control environment
communicating matters related to, *732–34*
communication of related matters, *320–21*
components, *259–71*
control activities, *264–69*
documenting understanding, *277–83*
EDP system understanding of, *467–72*
expenditure cycle, *554–57*
financing cycle, *663–64*
information system, *263–64*
inherent limitations in, *256–57*
investing cycle, *653*
management assertions, *812–15*
monitoring, *269*
obtaining understanding, *272–77*
over federal financial assistance, *863*
personnel services cycle, *626–27*
procedures to obtain understanding, *276–77, 301–2*
production cycle, *603–4*
revenue cycle, *498–503*
risk assessment, *262–63*
roles and responsibilities for, *257–58*
with small computer systems, *479–80*
Internal Revenue Service (IRS), 17
International Federation of Accountants (IFAC), *44*
Interpretations of Rules of Conduct
defined, *73*
independence: Rule 101, *79–84, 85*
Introductory paragraph (auditor's report), *46–47*
Inventory subsidiary ledgers or master files (perpetual inventory records), *605*
Investing cycle
audit objectives, *652–54*
identified, *651*
interface with revenue cycle, *651*
Investing functions, *654*
Investing transactions, *651*
Investment subsidiary ledger, *654*
Irregularities (auditor's responsibility), *55–56*

Joint and several liability, *107*
Joint Ethics Enforcement Program (JEEP), AICPA, *93*
Joint trial board, AICPA, *93–94*

Kiting, *692–93*
Known misstatements, *728*

Labor cost distribution summary, *628*
Lapping, *702*
Laws
blue sky, *118*
common law, *108, 111, 115–16, 131–32*
statutory, *118*
LCAs. *See* Litigation, claims, and assessments (LCAs)
Lead schedule, *171*
Letter of audit inquiry, *723–24*
Letter of comments, *887*
Letters
client representation, *724–26*
comfort, *895–96*
deficiency, *887*
engagement, *198–200*
management, *735*
peer review, *22*
rep, *724–26*
for underwriters and certain others, *895–96*
Liability
of auditor to clients, *110–11*
under common law, *108, 111, 115–16, 131–32*
under contract and tort law, *109–10*
to foreseeable parties, *113–14*
to foreseen parties, *112–14*
joint and several, *107*
for negligence, *111–12*
proportionate, *107*
under Securities Act (1933), *118–21*
under Securities Exchange Act (1934), *122–26*
to third parties, *111–12*
Licensing, *9*
See also Boards of accountancy, state-level
Likely misstatements, *729*
Litigation
minimizing risk of, *129–30*
proportionate, and joint and several liability, *107*
proposed legal reforms, *107*
Litigation, claims, and assessments (LCAs), *723*
Lockbox system, *516*
Logical sampling unit, *406–7, 410*
Long-term debt
tests of balances, *665–70*
transactions, *662*
Lower assessed level of control risk, *240–41, 308–9*

In re McKesson & Robbins (1940) [Securities and Exchange Commission], *132*
Major programs, *861–64*
Management
auditor's relationship with, *38*
information from, *204*
responsibility for internal control, *257*
Management fraud, *55*
Management letter, *735*
Management responsibility report, *52*
Management's discussion and analysis (MD& A), *892–93*
Management's philosophy and operating style, *261, 499*
Manual processing
cash disbursements, *567–68*
differences from computer processing, *457–58*
for expenditure cycle, *555–56*
for revenue cycle transactions, *500–502*
Manufacturing functions, *605–9*
Manufacturing transactions
control activities, *604–9*
in production cycle, *601*
Material fact, *118–19*
Materiality
account balance, *228–29*
applicability to revenue cycle, *496–97*
assessment, *225–28*
concept, *225, 228*
in expenditure cycle, *552–53*
financial statement, *226*
planning, *225*
relationship to audit risk and audit evidence, *238–39*
Material requirements report, *605*
Materials issue slip, *605*
Material weakness, *320–21, 733*
Member, *74*
Member or member's firm, *81–82*
Microcomputer-based audit software, *478*

Misleading financial statement, *118–19*
Misstatements
- anticipated, *408–9*
- detecting, *334–35*
- expenditure cycle, *553*
- known, *728*
- likely and aggregate likely, *729*
- potential, *302–3*
- projected, *411, 436*
- tolerable, *228–30, 422*
- upper misstatement limit, *411*

Monitoring, *269*
- continuous, *475*
- related to expenditure cycle, *555*
- relevant to revenue cycle, *502*
- understanding, *276*

Morality, *70*
Move ticket, *605*
MPU (mean-per-unit) estimation sampling, *420*

Narrative memorandum, *282–83*
National Commission on Fraudulent Financial Reporting (Treadway Commission), *253–54*
National Student Marketing Corporation case. *See United States* v. *Natelli* (1975)
National Surety Corp. v. *Lybrand* (1939), *117n15*
Nature of substantive tests, *333, 336–38*
Nature of tests of controls, *311–12*
Necessary controls
- for EDP general and application controls, *470–71*
- identified, *302–4*

Negligence
- contributory, *116–17*
- gross and ordinary, *109, 116*
- liability for, *111–12*

Nonattest services, *12–13*
Nonconformity with GAAP, *761, 764, 767*
Nonmajor programs, *861–64*
Nonsampling risk, *366–67*
Nonstatistical sampling, *367–69, 389–90, 435–37*

Obtaining an understanding
- cash disbursements, *570*
- of cash receipt transactions, *517–18*
- of control risk in control activities, *508, 510–11*
- internal control structure components, *272–77*
- manufacturing transactions, *609*
- payroll transactions, *632–34*
- procedures for, *276–77, 301–2*
- purchase transactions control activities, *563–65*
- using computer service organization, *481*

OCBOA. *See* Other comprehensive basis of accounting (OCBOA)
Occurrences
- control policy, *310*
- financial statement assertions about, *145–46*

On-line entry/batch processing, *452–54*
On-line entry/on-line processing, *453, 455, 475*
Open purchase order file, *558*
Operational audit
- defined, *5*
- phases, *847–50*

Operational auditing, *846–47*
Opinion paragraph (auditor's report), *48–49*
Opinions, auditor's
- adverse, *50–51, 760, 766*
- disclaimer of, *50, 760, 764*
- other types, *760–61, 763, 765–67*
- qualified, *50–51, 760–61, 763–64, 765–6, 769–70, 777–78*
- unqualified, *4, 51, 759, 765, 767–68, 770–72, 774–75*

Ordinary negligence, *116*
Organization and operation controls, *458–59*
Organized Crime Control Act (1970), *127*
Other beneficiaries, *111*
Other comprehensive basis of accounting (OCBOA), *802*
Other types of opinions, *760–61, 763, 765–68, 771, 775*
Output controls, *466*
Overall objective, *144*
Overall (or final) review, *725, 727*

Paid vouchers file, *558*
Parallel simulation, *472–74*
Payroll
- functions, *628–32*
- imprest bank account, *628, 705*
- register, *628*
- tax returns, *628*

Payroll check, *628*
Payroll transactions
- control activities, *627–34*
- functions and controls, *628–32*
- in personnel services cycle, *625*

Peer review
- defined, *21–22*
- letter, *22*

Performance audits (government), *852–53*
Performance reviews, *269*
Permanent file (working papers), *175*
Personnel authorization, *627*
Personnel data master file, *628*
Personnel services cycle
- audit objectives, *625–26*
- defined, *624–25*
- interface with production cycle, *601–2*

Pervasiveness, *761*
Phases of an audit, *189–90*
Physical controls, *268*
Planned acceptable level of detection risk, *235, 331*
Planned allowance for sampling risk (A), *423*
Planned assessed level of control risk, *233, 498*
Planned level of substantive tests, *331–32*
Planning materiality, *225*
Plant assets
- analytical procedures, *581–86*
- balances, *579–86*
- detection risk, *579–80*
- tests of details, *584–86*

Population
- estimated total population value, *426*
- expected population deviation rate, *376*
- in MPU estimation sampling, *420*
- for PPS sampling plan, *406*
- range for the estimated total population value, *426*
- size, *377*
- with stratified sampling, *421–22*
- in test of controls, *371*

Postaudit responsibilities, *737–39*
Potential misstatements
- for EDP general and application controls, *470–71*
- identification, *302–3*

PPS (probability-proportional-to-size) sampling
- advantages and disadvantages, *416–17*
- expansion factors, *408–9*
- plan, *405–18*
- reliability factors in sample size, *407–8, 414*
- selection method, *409–10*
- statistical sampling approach, *403*

Practice of public accounting, *74*
Practice units (CPA firms), *15–16*
Predecessor auditor, *192*

Preliminary audit strategy
alternative, *240–42*
effects, *273–74, 306*
Prelist, *515*
Presentation and disclosure, *148–49*
Presented fairly in conformity with GAAP, *753*
Primarily substantive approach
in assessing control risk, *306–8*
preliminary audit strategy, *240–42*
Primary beneficiary, *111*
Privileged communication, *88*
Privity of contract, *108–9, 114*
Probability-proportional-to-size (PPS) sampling. *See* PPS (probability-proportional-to-size) sampling
Procedures to obtain an understanding, *276–77, 301–2*
Processing controls, *465*
Production cycle, *601–2*
Production order, *605*
Production report
completed, *605*
daily activity, *605*
Professional ethics, *71*
Professional services, *74*
Professional skepticism, *38*
Profitability ratios, *216*
Program audits (government), *852*
Programs. *See* Application programs; Audit programs; Joint Ethics Enforcement Program (JEEP), AICPA; Major programs; Nonmajor programs; Systems programs
Projected misstatement, *411, 436*
Promulgated accounting principles, *755*
Proof of cash, *694–95*
Proper authorization, *265*
Proportionate liability, *107*
Propriety, *35*
Prospective financial information, *816–19, 824–26*
Prospectus, *890*
Proxy statement, *898*
Public accounting profession, *8*
Public Oversight Board, SEC, *23*
Purchase order
identified, *558*
open file, *558*
preparing, *559*
Purchase requisition, *558, 559*
Purchases cutoff test, *576*
Purchases transactions
control activities, *557–65*
file, *558, 561–63*
identified, *550–51*
See also Purchasing functions
Purchasing functions, *558–59*
Purchasing securities, *654*

Qualified opinion (auditor's report), *50–51, 760–61, 763–64, 765–66, 769–70, 777–78*
Quality control
elements, *19–20*
standards, *19–20*
Quality Control Inquiry Committee (QCIC), SEC, *23*
Quality Review Division, AICPA, *23*
Questioned costs, *864*
Questionnaire, *279*
See also Internal control questionnaire

Racketeer Influenced and Corrupt Organization Act (1970), *127*
Random number sampling, *378–79*
Range for the estimated total population value, *426, 431, 433*
Ratio analysis, *207, 209–12*
Ratio estimation sampling, *431, 433–34*
Ratios, financial
efficiency, *25*
profitability, *216*
solvency, *215*
Receiving periodic income, *654*
Receiving report, *558*
Reclassifying entries (working papers), *174*
Recording
market adjustments and reclassifications, *654*
transactions, *654*
Records
cash disbursements, *566*
defined, *266*
financing cycle, *664*
investing cycle, *653–54*
manufacturing transactions, *605*
payroll transactions, *627–28*
in processing cash receipts, *514–15*
Recurring engagement, *347*
Referral fees, *90–91*
Registrar, *670*
Registration statement, *890*
Regulation
See also Firm regulation; Government regulation; Peer review
framework to ensure quality service, *18–25*
Securities and Exchange Commission, *17*
self-regulation, *21, 24*
Regulation S-K, *884*
Regulation S-T, *884, 891*
Regulation S-X, *883, 900*
Related parties, *205*
Related party transactions, *351*
Reliability factor, *407–8, 414*
Remittance advice, *515*
Remoteness, *36*
Rep letter, *724–26*
Reportable conditions, *320, 732–34*
Reporting, *57–58*
See also Whistle blowing
Reporting standards
GAGAS financial audit, *856–57*
generally accepted first, *753–55*
generally accepted second, *755–56*
generally accepted third, *756*
generally accepted fourth, *756–58*
Resolutions of Council, AICPA, *91*
Revenue Act (1913), *9*
Revenue cycle
assessing inherent risk for assertions of, *497*
audit objectives, *495–98*
interface with investing cycle, *651*
interface with production cycle, *601–2*
nature of, *494–95*
Reves v. *Ernst & Young* (1993), *128*
Reviews
"cold" (or second) working paper, *731*
of interim financial information, *807–9*
overall (or final), *725, 727*
peer, *21–22*
performance, *269*
S-1, *895*
SAS 71, *806, 807–9*
SSARS, *806, 808–10*
transaction walk-through, *277, 306*
working papers final, *731*
Review service, *11, 806–7*
Revised or final acceptable level of detection risk, *332*
Rhode Island Hospital Trust National Bank v. *Swartz, Bresenhoff, Yavner & Jacobs* (1972), *131, 148*
RICO (Racketeer Influenced and Corrupt Organization Act), *127–28, 134*
Rights and obligations, *146–47*
Risk
See also Attestation risk; Control risk; Detection risk; Inherent risk; Uncertainty
of assessing control risk too high, *366, 374–75, 382*
of assessing control risk too low, *366*
audit risk components, *231–35*
audit risk model, *235–36*

of incorrect acceptance, *366, 403, 407–8, 422–23, 437–38*
of incorrect rejection, *366, 403, 422–23*
inherent, *231–35, 354, 497–98*
of overreliance, *366*
in processing cash receipts, *515–16*
sampling risk, *365*
of underreliance, *366*
Risk assessment
See also Assessing control risk
in audit strategy, *500*
control risk, *366*
cost-efficient, *308*
expenditure cycle, *555*
for financial reporting, *262–63*
understanding of, *274*
Risk components matrix, *236, 353–54*
accounts payable, *573*
accounts receivable assertions, *521*
Risk matrix, *353–54*
H.Rosenblum, Inc. v. *Adler* (1983), *114*
Rules of Conduct
AICPA Code of Professional Conduct, *73, 77–92*
enforcement, *93–94*
See also Interpretations of Rules of Conduct
Rusch Factors, Inc. v. *Levin* (1968), *113–14*

Safeguarding securities, *654*
Sales
See also Credit sales
adjustment functions, *517–19*
cutoff test, *527*
invoice, *504*
invoices to customers, *506–7*
journal, *504*
recording, *507*
Sales orders
defined, *504*
filling, *506*
shipping, *506*
Sales return cutoff test, *527*
Sales transactions
file, *504*
specific audit objective VA1, *505*
Sample deviations
rate, *381*
working paper, *388*
Sample size, *423–25*
Sample unit, *406*
Sampling
See also Audit sampling; Attribute sampling; Discovery sampling; MPU (mean-per-unit) estimation sampling; PPS (probability-proportional-to size) sampling; Ratio estimation sampling; Statistical sampling; Variables sampling
discovery, *389*
statistical and nonstatistical, *367–69, 389–90, 435–37*
stratified, *421*
with and without replacement, *378*
Sampling interval, *409*
Sampling risk, *365–67*
See also Nonsampling risk
achieved allowance for (A′), *426, 433*
adjusted achieved allowance for (A″), *427*
allowance for, *381–83, 411, 436*
incremental allowance for, *413*
planned allowance for (A), *423*
Sampling unit
defined, *371–72*
logical, *406*
in MPU estimation ssampling, *420*
SAS. *See Statements on Auditing Standards (SAS)*
SAS 71 reviews, *806–9*
Schacht v. *Brown* (1983), *134*
Scienter, *125*
Scope limitations, *50, 761, 762–64*
Scope paragraph (auditor's report), *47–48*
Search for unrecorded accounts payable, *576*
Securities
available-for-sale working paper of, *658–59*
purchasing, selling, and safeguarding, *654*
Securities Act (1933), *9, 118–21, 123–24, 877*
objectives, *889–90*
provisions, *890–97*
Securities and Exchange Commission (SEC)
authority, *877–78, 880–81*
chief accountant, *878–79*
Division of Corporate Finance, *878*
establishment and organization, *877–79*
influence on auditing and public accounting, *17*
laws administered by, *118–19*
Practice Section Public Oversight Board, *23*
Practice Section Quality Control Inquiry Committee, *23*
reporting requirements, *881–83*
Securities Exchange Act (1934), *9, 17, 118, 122–26, 877, 897–902*
Securities Law Enforcement Remedies Act (1990), *904*
Sedima v. *Imrex* (1985), *127*
Segregation of duties, *267–68*
Selection method
MPU estimation sample, *425*
PPS (probability-proportional-to-size) sampling, *409–10*
Self-regulation, *21, 24*
Selling securities, *654*
Services
accounting, *12–13, 821, 823*
attest and nonattest, *10–13, 820–21*
audit, *11*
compilation, *12*
computer service organization, *480–81*
personnel services cycle, *601–2, 624–27*
professional, *74*
review, *11, 806–7*
specialist, *195–96*
Shipping document, *504*
Significant influence, *82*
Single audit
components, *861*
defined, *860–61*
Single Audit Act (1984), *860–64*
Skip interval, *379*
Small computer systems, *479*
Software
generalized audit, *476–77*
microcomputer-based audit, *478*
Solvency ratios, *215*
Specialist services, *195–96*
Special reports
financial statements prepared on OCBOA, *802–4*
types of, *801–2*
Specific audit objectives, *144, 148–49*
S-1 review, *895*
SSARS reviews, *806, 808–10*
Staff Accounting bulletins (SABs), *885*
Standard deviation
formula
in MPU estimation sampling, *421*
Standard report
auditor's, *759*
departures from, *760, 762–63*
on financial forecast examination, *817–18*
with uncertainty, *771–72*
Standards
See also Attestation standards; Auditing standards; Reporting standards; Standard setting; Yellow book standards
AICPA Rule 201 and 202, *86*
for attest services, *12–13*

quality control, *19–20*
Standard setting
AICPA, *19, 41–42*
auditing, *40–45*
as regulation, *19, 24*
Statements on Auditing Standards (SASs), *40–41, 54–55*
Statistical sampling
See also Sample deviations; Upper deviation limit
attribute and variables sampling, *369*
attribute samples, *380–85*
classical variables sampling, *403, 419–34*
differences from nonstatistical sampling, *389–90*
inventories, *620*
PPS (probability-proportional-to-size [PPS]) sampling, *403*
uses of, *367–69*
Statutory law, *118*
Step down, *826*
Step up, *826*
Stock certificate, *653*
Stockholders' equity
tests of balances, *670–76*
transactions, *662*
Stratified sampling, *421*
Subrogee, *109*
Subsequent events
defined, *719*
period, *719*
Type 1 and Type 2, *720–21*
Subsequent payments, *576–77*
Substantive tests, *165, 167*
See also Audit programs; Audit sampling
of accounts receivable, *520*
audit programs for, *343–47*
cash balances, *689–92*
compared to tests of controls, *351–52*
design for accounts payable audit programs, *572–75*
designing, *333, 348–51*
designs for accounts receivable assertions, *522–25*
of details of transactions and balances, *335–36*
extent, *339*
inventory balance assertions, *613–15*
investment balances, *655–57*
level of detection risk in design, *353*
long-term debt balances, *665–70*
nature of, *333*
nonstatistical sampling, *435–37*
payroll balances, *634–36*
performance using computer service organization, 481–82
planned level of, *331*
plant asset balances, *579–86*
relation to assertions and specific audit objectives, *342–43*
relation to audit risk components, *340*
risk of incorrect acceptance or rejection, *366*
specifying detection risk, *332–33*
timing, *338–39*
Successor auditor, *192*
Sunshine Act. *See* Freedom of Information Act
Systems control audit review file (SCARF), *475*
Systems development and documentation controls, *460*
Systems programs, *449–50*

Tagging transactions, *475*
Tainting perspective, *412*
Tax services, *12*
Test data approach, *473–74*
Tests for inventory balances, *612*
Tests of controls
See also Audit sampling; Dual-purpose testing; Substantive tests
additional, *311*
audit program for credit sales, *513*
audit programs for, *313–14*
compared to substantive tests, *351–52*
computer-assisted, *510, 512–13, 565*
concurrent, *310–11*
designing, *311*
dual-purpose testing, *316*
extent of, *313*
function of and policy for, *309–10*
internal control structure, *303, 304–5, 309*
nature of, *311–12*
in on-line entry/on-line processing, *475*
planned, *311*
risk of control risk assessment, *366*
role of internal auditors, *315*
statistical and nonstatistical sampling, *389–90*
timing, *312–13*
without and with computer, *471–75*
Tests of details of balances, *335–38*
accounts payable, *577–78*
for accounts receivable, *528*
inventories, *617–23*
investing cycle, *658–61*
long-term debt balances, *669–70*
plant assets, *585–86*
Tests of details of transactions, *335, 337*
accounts payable, *575–77*
accounts receivable, *526–28*
inventories, *615–16*
investing cycle, *657–58*
long-term debt balances, *667*
plant assets, *584–85*
Third party, *111–12*
Time budget (for audit), *197–98*
Time ticket, *605, 627*
Timing
of substantive tests, *338*
of tests of controls, *312–13*
Tolerable deviation rate, *375–76*
Tolerable misstatement, *228–30, 408, 422*
Tort, *109*
Traditional file method, *451*
Transaction class
defined, *242–43*
population, *371*
Transaction cycle, *242–43*
Transactions
See also Manufacturing transactions; Payroll transactions
in accounting system, *263–64*
cash disbursement, *550–51, 566–70*
cash receipt, *514–18*
credit sales, *510–12*
investing, *651*
long-term debt, *662*
manufacturing, *601, 604–12*
payroll, *627–34*
purchases, *557–65*
recording, *654*
related party, *351*
revenue cycle, *500–502*
sales, *503–14*
stockholders' equity, *662*
tagging, *475*
tests of details, *167–68, 335, 337, 526–28, 575–77, 584–85, 615–16, 657–58, 667*
Transaction trail, *264*
Transaction walk-through review, *277, 306*
Transfer agent, *664, 670*
Treadway Commission (Committee of Sponsoring Organizations [COSO]), *254*
See also National Commission on Fraudulent Financial Reporting (Treadway Commission)
Trend analysis, *207*
Trial balance
accounts receivable, *522–24*
accounts receivable aged, *534*

Trial balance *(Continued)*
  working, *169–71*
Type 1 subsequent events, *720–21*
Type 2 subsequent events, *720–21*

Ultramares Corp. v. *Touche* (1931), *111–12, 114, 123*
Unaudited financial statements, *822–23*
Uncertainty, *769–71*
Underlying accounting data, *150*
Understanding
  See also Obtaining an understanding
  control environment, *274*
  documenting, *277–83*
  of internal communication, *275*
  monitoring, *276*
  of risk assessment, *274*
U. S. General Accounting Office (GAO)
  generally accepted government auditing standards, *853–59*
  standards, *17*
United States v. *Arthur Young & Co.* (1984), *176*
United States v. *Benjamin* (1964), *133*
United States v. *Natelli* (1975), *126*
United States v. *Simon* (1969), *120–21*
United States v. *Weiner*, *133*
United States v. *White* (1941), *132–33*
Unpaid vouchers file, *558*
Unqualified opinion (auditor's report), *45, 51, 759–60, 765, 767–68, 770–72, 774–75*
Upper deviation limit, *381–82*
Upper misstatement limit, *411*
U_R factor, *422–23*

Validated deposit slip, *515*
Validity, *35*
Valuation or allocation, *147–48*
Variables sampling
  classical, *403, 419–34*
  defined, *369*
Vendor's invoice, *558*
Verifiable data, *34–35*
Voucher
  identified, *558*
  paid and unpaid file, *558, 560–61*
  payment, *560–61*
  register, *558*
  summary, *558*

Whistle blowing, *57*
Window dressing, *701*
Working papers
  aggregate likely misstatement, *729–30*
  analysis, *171*
  attribute sampling plan, *384*
  capital stock, *673–74*
  "cold" (or second) review, *731*
  confidentiality, *176*
  confirmation control, *531–32*
  difference estimation sampling plan, *432*
  final review, *731*
  inventory test counts, *619–20*
  MPU estimation sampling plan, *428–29*
  ownership and custody, *175–76*
  partial working trial balance, *169–71*
  permanent and current files, *175*
  PPS sampling plan, *417*
  preparation, *174*
  proof of cash, *694–95*
  schedules, *171*
  for statistical attribute sampling plan, *385–88*
  types, *169–71*
Working trial balance, *169–71*
Write-off authorization, *519*

Year-end work (field work), *197*
Yellow Book standards, *853, 856, 860*